CHICAGO MUNICIPAL CODE HANDBOOK

2005 EDITION

(Includes enactments of the City Council of the City of Chi, 2004)

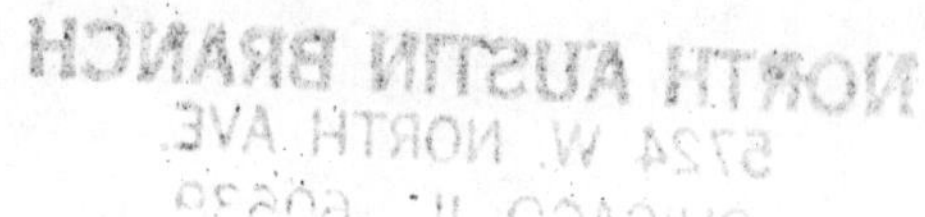

QUESTIONS ABOUT THIS PUBLICATION?

For CUSTOMER SERVICE ASSISTANCE concerning replacement pages, shipments, billing, reprint permission, or other matters,

please call Customer Service Department at 800-833-9844
email *customer.support@lexisnexis.com*
or visit our interactive customer service website at *www.lexisnexis.com/printcdsc*

For EDITORIAL **content questions** concerning this publication,

please call 800-446-3410 ext. 7447
or email: *LLP.CLP@lexisnexis.com*

For **information on other LEXISNEXIS MATTHEW BENDER publications,**

please call us at 800-223-1940
or visit our online bookstore at *www.lexisnexis.com/bookstore*

ISBN: 1-422-40223-1

Matthew Bender & Company, Inc.
Editorial Offices
P.O. Box 7587
Charlottesville, VA 22906-7587
800-446-3410
www.lexisnexis.com

Product Number 2175711 (Pub. 21757)

Foreword

As publishers of the Municipal Code of Chicago, we are pleased to offer to the legal and law enforcement community the 2005 edition of *Chicago Municipal Code Handbook*, relating to police operations. This compilation of selected sections is fully up to date through the ordinance passed by the city council on December 15, 2004 found at page 40508 of the Journal of the Proceedings of the City Council.

We are committed to providing attorneys and law enforcement professionals with the most comprehensive, current and useful manuals possible. We actively solicit your comments and suggestions. If you believe that there are ordinances which should be included (or excluded), or if you have suggestions regarding index improvements, please write to us or call us toll-free at 1-800-833-9844; fax us toll-free at 1-800-643-1280; visit our website at http://www.lexisnexis.com; or E-mail us at llp.clp@lexisnexis.com. By providing us with your informed comments, you will be assured of having available a working tool which increases in value each year.

March 2005

This page intentionally left blank

2004-2005 Legislative Changes to the
CHICAGO MUNICIPAL CODE HANDBOOK

Chap./Sec.	*Change*	*Coun. J. Date*	*Page*
1-4-125	New	1/14/04	17349
1-16-030	Repeal	3/31/04	20916
1-21	New	12/15/04	39915
1-22	New	12/15/04	39918
2-8-070	Amend	3/31/04	20916
2-14-030	Amend	3/31/04	20968
2-14-132	Amend	11/3/04	34974
2-24-060	Amend	3/31/04	20916
2-24-080	Amend	3/31/04	20916
2-84-010	Amend	3/31/04	20916
2-84-090	Amend	3/31/04	20916
2-84-480	Amend	3/31/04	20916
3-8-010	Amend	3/31/04	20916
3-8-190	Amend	3/31/04	20916
3-56-021	Amend	12/8/04	38063
3-56-030	Amend	12/8/04	38063
3-56-050	Amend	12/15/04	39840
3-56-050	Amend	3/31/04	20916
4-4-060	Amend	12/15/04	39840
4-5-010	Amend	12/15/04	39840
4-4-313	New	5/5/04	22740
4-5-010	Amend	5/5/04	22743
4-5-010	Amend	9/29/04	32144
4-60-010	Amend	9/29/04	32144
4-60-024	Amend	9/29/04	32144
4-60-030	Amend	9/29/04	32144
4-60-040	Amend	9/29/04	32144
4-60-042	Amend	9/29/04	32144
4-60-050	Amend	9/29/04	32144
4-60-060	Amend	9/29/04	32144
4-60-080	Amend	9/29/04	32141
4-60-081	Amend	9/29/04	32141
4-60-110	Amend	9/29/04	32144
4-60-130	Amend	12/1/04	36203
4-60-205	New	9/29/04	32144
4-156-020	Amend	12/15/04	39840
4-156-033	Amend	12/15/04	39840
4-156-100	Amend	12/8/04	38063
4-156-430	Amend	2/11/04	18722
4-233-050	Amend	1/14/04	17355
4-233-060	Amend	1/14/04	17355
4-233-070	Amend	7/21/04	28633
4-400-010	Amend	12/15/04	39840
4-400-020	Amend	12/15/04	39840
4-400-030	Amend	12/15/04	39840

2004-2005 Legislative Changes to the
CHICAGO MUNICIPAL CODE HANDBOOK
(Continued)

Chap./Sec.	*Change*	*Coun. J. Date*	*Page*
4-400-060	Amend	12/15/04	39840
5-4	Repeal	3/31/04	20916
5-12-010	Amend	3/31/04	20916
5-12-080	Amend	3/31/04	20916
7-12-030	Amend	3/31/04	20916
7-12-090	Amend	3/31/04	20916
7-20-100	Amend	3/31/04	20916
7-16-070	Repeal	3/31/04	20916
7-16-080	Repeal	3/31/04	20916
7-16-090	Repeal	3/31/04	20916
7-24-225	Amend	12/15/04	39840
7-24-226	Amend	12/15/04	39840
7-28-390	Amend	11/3/04	34974
7-28-410	Repeal	11/3/04	34974
7-28-440	Amend	11/3/04	34974
7-28-450	Amend	11/3/04	34974
7-28-610	Amend	12/15/04	40435
7-28-800	Amend	12/15/04	40435
7-38-540	Repeal	3/31/04	20916
8-4-025	New	9/24/04	32193
8-4-125	New	3/10/04	19865
8-4-125	Amend	3/31/04	21244
8-4-145	Amend	12/15/04	40218
8-4-160	Repeal	3/31/04	20916
8-8-060	Amend	12/15/04	39840
8-16-020	New	3/10/04	19860
8-20-015	Amend	12/15/04	39840
9-40-120	Amend	5/26/04	24880
9-52-070	Amend	7/21/04	28659
9-52-071	New	7/21/04	28659
9-64-110	Amend	5/26/04	24880
9-64-125	Amend	12/8/04	38063
9-64-170	Amend	12/8/04	38063
9-68-020	Amend	12/15/04	39840
9-68-050	Amend	5/26/04	24882
9-76-200	Amend	5/26/04	24938
9-80-200	Amend	5/26/04	24884
9-92-035	Amend	12/15/04	39840
9-92-100	Amend	12/15/04	40508
9-100-020	Amend	5/26/04	24880
9-100-020	Amend	12/15/04	39840
9-100-101	Amend	1/14/04	16857
9-100-101	Amend	12/15/04	40508
9-100-120	Amend	12/15/04	40508

2004-2005 Legislative Changes to the
CHICAGO MUNICIPAL CODE HANDBOOK
(Continued)

Chap./Sec.	*Change*	*Coun. J. Date*	*Page*
10-8-260	Repeal	3/31/04	20916
10-8-335	Amend	12/15/04	39840
10-8-400	Amend	2/11/04	18364
10-8-335	Amend	2/11/04	18380
10-28-281.5	Amend	12/15/04	39840
10-28-899	Amend	12/15/04	40435
10-36-358	Amend	3/31/04	20916
10-40-131	Amend	12/15/04	39840
11-4-020	Amend	12/15/04	40435
11-4-26810	Amend	3/31/04	20916
13-12-080	Amend	12/15/04	39840
13-20-010	Amend	9/29/04	32144
13-32-230	Corrects	12/8/04	38063
13-32-315	Amend	12/15/04	39840
16-8	Amend	5/26/04	25277
16-8	Amend	5/26/04	25287
16-8	Amend	5/26/04	25299
16-8-030	Amend	3/31/04	21667
16-8-060	Amend	2/11/04	18592
16-19	New	12/15/04	39840

This page intentionally left blank

TABLE OF CONTENTS

Chapter			Page

TITLE 1—GENERAL PROVISIONS

1-4	Code Adoption Organization		1
1-12	Official City Time		2
1-16	Nuclear Weapon Free Zone		3
1-21	False Statements		5
1-22	False Claims		6

TITLE 2—CITY GOVERNMENT AND ADMINISTRATION

DIVISION I—OFFICERS AND DEPARTMENTS

2-4	Mayor		17
2-14	Department of Administrative Hearings		17
	Art. I.	General Provisions	18
	Art. II.	Vehicle Hearings Division	28
	Art. III.	Buildings Hearings Division	28
	Art. VI.	Municipal Hearings Division	29
2-24	Department of Consumer Services		31
2-36	Fire Department		39
	Art. I.	Organization	39
	Art. IV.	Bureau of Fire Prevention	39
	Art. V.	Bureau of Fire Control and Extinguishment	40
2-56	Office of Inspector General		43
2-74	Department of Personnel		48
2-84	Department of Police		49
	Art. I.	Organization and Functions	50
	Art. II.	Powers and Duties of Police Force	58
	Art. III.	Temporary Questioning	60
	Art. IV.	Sworn member Bill of Rights	60
	Art. V.	Regulation of Police Force	62

DIVISION II—BOARDS, COMMISSIONS AND COMMITTEES

2-112	Board of Health		65
2-120	Commissioners and Commissions		68

DIVISION III—ETHICS AND EMPLOYMENT POLICIES

2-152	Officers and Employees		70
	Art. I.	General Provisions	70
	Art. IV.	Career Service Regulations	70
2-160	Human Rights		71

TABLE OF CONTENTS
(Continued)

Chapter *Page*

TITLE 3—REVENUE AND FINANCE

DIVISION I—FUNDS

3-8 Policemen's and Firemen's Death Benefit Fund 77
Art. I. Administration of Death Awards 78
Art. II. Determination of Death Awards 81
Art. III. Medical and Hospital Care 84

DIVISION II—TAXES

3-56 Wheel Tax Licenses 87

TITLE 4—BUSINESSES, OCCUPATIONS AND CONSUMER PROTECTION

DIVISION I—GENERAL REGULATIONS AND FEES

4-4 General Licensing Provisions 99
4-5 License Fees for Title 4 Licenses 120

DIVISION II—BUSINESSES INVOLVING FOOD PRODUCTS

4-8 Food Establishments 125
Art. II. General Provisions 125
4-11 New Maxwell Street Market 127
4-48 *Reserved* 131

DIVISION III—BUSINESSES INVOLVING LIQUOR AND TOBACCO PRODUCTS

4-60 Liquor Dealers 131
4-64 Tobacco Dealers 163
Art. I. Wholesale Tobacco Dealers 164
Art. II. Retail Tobacco Dealers and Tobacco Product Samplers 165
Art. III. Cigarette-Vending Machines 170
Art. IV. Violation of Chapter Penalties Enforcement 172

DIVISION IV—HEALTH SERVICES

4-68 Ambulances 174
4-72 Day Care Centers 183
4-80 Funeral Business 187
4-84 Hospitals 189

TABLE OF CONTENTS
(Continued)

Chapter			*Page*
4-92	Massage Establishments and Massage Services		193
4-93	Body Piercing		199
4-96	Long-Term Care Facilities		201

DIVISION V—HAZARDOUS AND RELATED ACTIVITIES

4-100	Dry Cleaners		204
	Art. II.	Self-Service Coin-Operated Dry-Cleaning Establishments	204
4-108	Filling Stations		205
	Art. I.	Filling Stations	205
4-115	Hazardous Materials License		206
4-128	Motion Pictures		208
	Art. I.	Motion Picture Projecting Machine Operators	208
	Art. IV.	Violation of Chapter Provisions	210
4-144	Weapons		210
	Art. I.	Deadly Weapons	211
	Art. II.	Gunsmiths	214
	Art. III.	Air Rifles and Toy Weapons	214
	Art. IV.	Violation of Chapter Provisions	217

DIVISION VI—WHOLESALE, RETAIL AND SERVICE ACTIVITIES

4-156	Amusements		218
	Art. I.	Amusements	219
	Art. II.	Automatic Amusement Devices	228
	Art. III.	Public Places of Amusement	231
4-168	Bicycle Messenger Services		239
4-208	Hotels		241
4-209	Single Room Occupancy Buildings		244
4-212	Itinerant Merchants		245
4-216	Junk Peddlers		247
4-220	Laundries and Laundry Vehicles		250
	Art. I.	Laundries	250
	Art. II.	Self-Service Coin-Operated Laundry Establishments	251
	Art. IV.	Violation of Chapter Provisions	252
4-224	Manufacturing Establishments		252
4-228	Motor Vehicle Repair Shops		255
4-229	Tire Facilities		263
4-232	Motor Vehicle Storage and Sales		266
	Art. I.	General Provisions	266
	Art. II.	Valet Parking	266
	Art. III.	Motor Vehicle Salesrooms	269
	Art. IV.	Public Garages	269

TABLE OF CONTENTS
(Continued)

Chapter			*Page*
	Art. V.	Violation of Chapter Provisions	271
4-233	Motor Vehicle Booting License		271
4-240	Pawnbrokers		274
4-244	Peddlers		278
4-253	Retail Computing Centers		286
4-256	Roofers		288
4-260	Scavengers		288
	Art. II.	Private Scavengers	289
	Art. VI.	Violation of Chapter Provisions	291
4-264	Secondhand Dealers		291
	Art. I.	Secondhand Dealers Generally	291
	Art. II.	*Reserved*	297
	Art. III.	*Reserved*	297
	Art. IV.	Violation of Chapter Provisions	297
4-268	Chicago Street Performers Ordinance		297

DIVISION VII—OTHER OCCUPATIONS AND SERVICES

4-276	Regulation of Weights and Measures	300
4-328	News Media Credentials	301
4-340	Special Policemen and Security Guards	303
4-360	Vendor Licensing and Regulation at Navy Pier	305
4-380	Home Occupations	308
4-388	Rooftops in Wrigley Field Adjacent Area	311
4-400	Burglar Alarms	315

TITLE 5—HOUSING AND ECONOMIC DEVELOPMENT

5-4	*Reserved*	321
5-12	Residential Landlords and Tenants	321

TITLE 7—HEALTH AND SAFETY

7-12	Animal Care and Control		323
7-16	Births and Deaths		341
	Art. I.	Report of Births and Deaths	341
	Art. II.	Care and Disposition of Dead Human Bodies	341
	Art. III.	Violation of Chapter Provisions	343
7-20	Contagious and Epidemic Diseases		343
7-24	Drugs and Narcotics		345
	Art. I.	Distribution of Drugs and Medicines	346
	Art. II.	Drug Paraphernalia	347
	Art. II-A.	Controlled Substances	349
	Art. III.	Carbolic Acid	349
	Art. IV.	Wood Alcohol	350

TABLE OF CONTENTS
(Continued)

Chapter			Page
	Art. V.	Tobacco	351
	Art. V-A.	Office of Local Drug Control Policy	352
	Art. VI.	Use of Motor Vehicle	353
	Art. VII.	Violation of Chapter Provisions	354
7-28	Health Nuisances		354
	Art. I.	Nuisances in General	356
	Art. II.	Refuse	362
	Art. III.	Privies, Catch Basins, and Similar Vaults	376
	Art. IV.	Offensive Chemicals and Substances	379
	Art. V.	Rat Control	380
	Art. VI.	Lot Maintenance	383
	Art. VII.	Violation of Chapter Provisions	384
7-32	No-Smoking Regulations		385
	Art. I.	Generally	385
	Art. II.	Clean Indoor Air Ordinance	386
7-38	Food Establishments Sanitary Operating Requirements		389
	Art. I.	All Food Establishments	390
	Art. II.	Mobile Food Dispensers	396
	Art. III.	Automatic Food-Vending Machines	397
	Art. IV.	Coffee Cart Vendors	398
	Art. V.	Cold Storage Establishments	399
	Art. VI.	Slaughtering, Rendering and Packing Establishments	400
	Art. VII.	Penalty for Violation of Chapter Provisions	402
7-40	Food Establishments—Care of Foods		403
	Art. I.	General Provisions	403
	Art. II.	Meat	404
	Art. III.	Vegetables, Fruits and Berries	405
	Art. IV.	Water	405
	Art. V.	Candy	406
	Art. VI.	Poultry	406
	Art. VII.	Bottled-Water and Nonalcoholic Beverages	407
	Art. VIII.	Frozen Desserts and Mixes	407
	Art. IX.	Milk and Milk Products	408
	Art. X.	Violation of Chapter Provisions	409
7-42	Food Establishments—Inspections, Violations and Hearing Procedures		409
7-44	Extermination by Fumigation		412

TITLE 8—OFFENSES AFFECTING PUBLIC PEACE, MORALS AND WELFARE

8-4	Public Peace and Welfare	421
8-8	Public Morals	448
8-12	Gambling	455

TABLE OF CONTENTS
(Continued)

Chapter		Page
8-16	Offenses By or Against Minors	459
8-20	Weapons	466
	Art. I. Possession of Firearms	466
	Art. II. Registration of Firearms	468
8-24	Firearms and Other Weapons	480
8-28	*Reserved*	485
8-30	Evictions for Unlawful Use of Premises	485

TITLE 9—VEHICLES, TRAFFIC AND RAIL TRANSPORTATION

9-4	Traffic Definitions and General Provisions	487
9-8	Traffic Control Devices and Signals	494
9-12	Traffic and Speed Restrictions	497
9-16	Turning Movements	500
9-20	Movement of Traffic	502
9-24	Right-of-Way	503
9-28	Railroad and Bridge Crossings	505
9-32	Funeral Processions	507
9-36	Overtaking Vehicles	508
9-40	Driving Rules	510
9-44	Towing Disabled Vehicles	515
9-48	Types of Vehicles Regulations	517
9-52	Bicycles Operation	521
9-56	Reporting of Accidents	523
9-60	Pedestrians Rights and Duties	524
9-64	Parking Regulations	526
9-68	Restricted Parking Permits and Regulations	546
9-72	Size and Weight Limits	553
9-76	Vehicle Equipment	559
9-80	Miscellaneous Rules	567
9-84	Towing Unauthorized Vehicles	576
9-88	Duties of Police Department	579
9-92	Impounding and Relocation of Vehicles	581
9-96	*Reserved*	587
9-100	Administrative Adjudication of Parking or Compliance Violations	587
9-102	Automated Red Light Camera Program	602
9-103	Automated Bus Lane and Bus Stop Camera Enforcement Program	605
9-104	Public Chauffeurs	608
9-108	Horse-Drawn Carriages	615
9-112	Public Passenger Vehicles	626
9-116	Registration of School Vehicles	671
9-120	Bicycles	674

TABLE OF CONTENTS
(Continued)

Chapter			*Page*
9-124	Transportation Services and Rail Transportation		675
	Art. I.	General Requirements	676
	Art. II.	Street Railroads	680
	Art. III.	Elevated Railroads	687
	Art. IV.	Other Railroads	691

TITLE 10—STREETS, PUBLIC WAYS, PARKS, AIRPORTS AND HARBORS

10-8	Use of Public Ways and Places		695
	Art. I.	Zones of Quiet	696
	Art. II.	Charitable Solicitation	698
	Art. III.	Requirements and Restrictions	700
	Art. IV.	Occasional Sales	721
	Art. V.	Prohibited Uses	722
	Art. VI.	Violation of Chapter Provisions	726
10-20	Work On and Under Public Ways		727
	Art. I.	Openings, Construction and Repair in Public Ways	728
	Art. II.	Underground Transmitting Devices	733
	Art. III.	Private Paving	733
	Art. IV.	Driveways	733
	Art. V.	Streets, Curbs and Sidewalks	736
	Art. VI.	Barricades	737
	Art. VII.	Viaducts	739
	Art. VIII.	Miscellaneous	739
10-28	Structures On and Under Public Ways		740
	Art. I.	General Requirements	741
	Art. II.	Carts Belonging to Retail Stores	743
	Art. III.	Newspaper Stands	743
	Art. IV.	Canopies and Marquees	745
	Art. IV-A.	Placement of Pay Telephones in Public Way	745
	Art. V.	Awnings	748
	Art. V-A.	Obstruction of Streets, Sidewalks and Public Places	748
	Art. V-B.	Protection of the Public Way and Public Places	751
	Art. V-C.	Construction Canopies	752
	Art. IX.	Use of Sub-sidewalk Space	753
	Art. XI-A.	Newsracks	754
	Art. XI-B.	Refuse Compactors/Grease Containers	759
	Art. XI-C.	Dumpsters/Roll-Off Boxes on the Public Way	761
	Art. XII.	Sidewalk Cafes	765
	Art. XIII.	Violation of Chapter Provisions	768

TABLE OF CONTENTS
(Continued)

Chapter			Page
10-32	Trees, Plants and Shrubs		768
10-36	Parks, Playgrounds and Airports		774
	Art. I.	General Regulations	774
	Art. II.	Airports	777
	Art. III.	Heliports	778
10-40	Chicago Harbor		778
	Art. I.	Harbor Jurisdiction	779
	Art. II.	Navigation of the Harbor	783
	Art. III.	Wharves and Docks	791
	Art. IV.	Bridges	795
	Art. V.	Violations of Chapter Provisions	798

TITLE 11—UTILITIES AND ENVIRONMENTAL PROTECTION

Chapter			Page
11-4	Environmental Protection and Control		799
	Art. I.	General Provisions	800
	Art. II.	Air Pollution Control	801
	Art. VII.	Noise and Vibration Control	804
	Art. VIII.	Pollution of Waters	807
	Art. IX.	Solid and Liquid Waste Control	810
	Art. XVI.	Storage Tanks	813
	Art. XVI-A	Asbestos, Sandblasting and Grinding Standards	816
	Art. XVII.	Junk Facility Permits	816
	Art. XVIII.	Recycling Facility Permits	821
11-12	Water Supply and Service		822

TITLE 13—BUILDINGS AND CONSTRUCTION

Chapter			Page
13-12	Enforcement of Building, Electrical and Fire Regulations		825
	Art. I.	General	825
	Art. II.	Electrical Provisions	833
13-20	Building Inspection		834
	Art. I.	General	835
	Art. II.	Buildings	835
	Art. XIII.	Signs, Billboards, Signboards and Related Structures	836
	Part A.	General	836
	Part C.	Permits	839
	Part E.	Other Requirements	840
13-32	Building Permits		841
	Art. I.	Permit Requirements	841
	Art. II.	Permit Fees	852

TABLE OF CONTENTS
(Continued)

Chapter			*Page*
13-40	Building Plans		854
13-64	Residential Units		858
13-84	Assembly Units		859
13-88	Open Air Assembly Units		860
13-96	Miscellaneous Buildings and Structures		860
	Art. XVII.	Private Residential Swimming Pools	862
13-128	Use of Public Property		

TITLE 15—FIRE PREVENTION

15-4	Bureau of Fire Prevention		867
	Art. I.	Bureau of Fire Prevention	868
	Art. II.	General Provisions	868
	Art. III.	Licenses	871
	Art. VI.	Liquefied Petroleum Gas Tanks	876
	Art. VII.	Fire Extinguisher Servicemen	877
	Art. VIII.	Other License Requirements	878
	Art. IX.	Permits	879
15-20	Explosives and Fireworks		880
	Art. I.	Explosives	880
	Art. II.	Fireworks	883
15-24	Flammable Liquids		886
	Art. I.	General Regulations	886
	Art. II.	Tank Storage	886
	Art. X.	Carriers for Transportation of Flammable Liquids	887
	Art. XI.	Underground Storage Tank Violations	890
15-26	Fume and Flammable Compressed Gases		890
	Art. I.	General	890
	Art. II.	Buildings and Rooms	891
	Art. III.	Transportation	891
	Art. IV.	Generation of Acetylene Gas	891
	Art. VI.	Miscellaneous	892

TITLE 16—LAND USE

16-16	Adult Uses		893

This page intentionally left blank

TITLE 1
GENERAL PROVISIONS
(Selected Chapters)

Chapters:

1-4.	Code Adoption—Organization. (Selected Sections)
1-12.	Official City Time. (Complete Chapter)
1-16.	Nuclear Weapon Free Zone. (Complete Chapter)
1-21	False Statements. (Complete Chapter)
1-22	False Claims. (Complete Chapter)

CHAPTER 1-4
CODE ADOPTION—ORGANIZATION
(Selected Sections)

Sections:

1-4-120	Penalty for violation of code.
1-4-125	Restitution—License or permit violations.
1-4-130	Maximum fine or penalty.
1-4-140	Offenses having two penalties.

§1-4-120 Penalty for violation of code.

Whenever in any section of this code the doing of any act or the omission to do any act or duty is declared to be a violation thereof, and there shall be no fine or penalty declared for such violation, any person who shall be convicted or found liable of any such violation shall be fined not less than $25.00 nor more than $500.00 for each such violation.

In any case that this code specifies a mandatory fine, mandatory period of incarceration or other mandatory penalty for a code violation, any requirement of community service or assessment of costs imposed for the code violation pursuant to this section shall be in addition to the mandatory penalty.

Whenever this code refers to an offense, violation, or conviction for purposes of establishing a penalty for a violation of this code, the offense, violation, or conviction may either be the result of an administrative hearing or a court proceeding.

(Added. Coun. J. 6-27-90, p. 17764; Amend. 6-10-96, p. 23795; 7-10-96, p. 24982; 4-29-98, p. 66564; 6-9-99, p. 5102)

§1-4-125 Restitution—License or permit violations.

(a) Any person who violates any provision of this code by failing to obtain a license or permit when required by the code, or by failing to obtain any insurance required under any permit or license issued to such person, shall in addition to any fine or penalty specified by this code, be required to make restitution to the city in the full amount of all liabilities, judgments, settlements, costs, damages and expenses which may in any way come against the city, in whole or in part as a result of any act, omission or thing done by said person, for which the license or permit was required.

(b) The restitution requirement of this section shall apply whether or not any negligence on the part of the city or its officers or employees also contributed in part to any such liabilities, judgments, settlements, costs, damages and expenses.
(Added. Coun. J. 1-14-04, p. 17349)

§1-4-130 Maximum fine or penalty.

Whenever in this code a minimum but no maximum fine or penalty is imposed, the court may in its discretion fine the offender any sum of money exceeding the minimum fine or penalty so fixed, but not exceeding the sum of $500.00.
(Added. Coun. J. 6-27-90, p. 17764)

§1-4-140 Offenses having two penalties.

In all cases where the same offense is made punishable or is created by different clauses or sections of this code, the corporation counsel may elect under which to proceed; but not more than one recovery shall be had against the same person for the same offense.
(Added. Coun. J. 6-27-90, p. 17764)

CHAPTER 1-12
OFFICIAL CITY TIME
(Complete Chapter)

Sections:

1-12-010 Official city time designated.
1-12-020 City clocks to show official time.
1-12-030 Violation—Penalty.

§1-12-010 Official city time designated.

Central standard time shall be the official time within the city of Chicago for the transaction of all city business, except that from 2:00 a.m. on the last Sunday in April to 2:00 a.m. on the last Sunday in October in each year the official time for the city of Chicago shall be one hour in advance of central standard time.

When reference is made to any time without qualification in any ordinance, resolution or order heretofore passed or which may be passed hereafter by the city council or any official notice, advertisement or document of the city or in any contract to which the city is party, it shall be understood to refer to the official time of the city as herein prescribed. When the words "daylight saving time" are used, the reference shall be to the advanced time herein prescribed as the official time from the last Sunday in April until the last Sunday in October.

In all ordinances, resolutions or orders of the city council and in all official notices, advertisements or documents of the city and in all contracts to which the city is a party relating to the time of performance of any act by any officer or department of the city or relating to the time within which any rights shall accrue or determine or within which any act shall or shall not be performed by any person it shall be understood and intended that the time shall be the official time of the city as herein prescribed.
(Prior code § 193-33)

§1-12-020 City clocks to show official time.

All clocks or other timepieces in or upon public buildings or other premises maintained at the expense of the city shall be set and run according to the official time as provided in Section 1-12-010. It is hereby made the duty of the officer or other person having control and charge of such building or buildings and premises to see that said clocks or other timepieces are set and run in accordance with official time.

(Prior code § 193-34)

§1-12-030 Violation—Penalty.

Any person violating any of the provisions of this chapter, where no other penalty is specifically provided, shall be fined not more than $200.00 for each offense.

(Prior code § 193-35 (part))

CHAPTER 1-16
NUCLEAR WEAPON FREE ZONE
(Complete Chapter)

Sections:

1-16-010 Definitions.
1-16-020 Nuclear weapons work— Unlawful activities—Exceptions.
1-16-030 Reserved.
1-16-040 Civil defense participation limitations.
1-16-050 Annual commemoration day.
1-16-060 Sign requirements.
1-16-070 Violation—Penalty.
1-16-080 Severability.

§1-16-010 Definitions.

For the purposes of this ordinance, the following definitions shall apply:

(a) "Person" means a natural person, as well as a corporation, institution or other entity, but shall not include the federal government or any agency thereof.

(b) "Nuclear weapon" means any device, the purpose of which is use as a weapon, a weapon prototype or a weapon test device, the intended detonation of which results from the energy released by fission and/or fusion reactions involving atomic nuclei. For the purpose of this ordinance, "nuclear weapon" includes the weapon 's guidance and propulsion system and triggering mechanism, i.e., the means of transporting, guiding, propelling, triggering or detonating the weapon, provided that such means is destroyed or rendered useless in the normal transporting, guiding, propelling, triggering or detonation of the weapon.

(c) "Component of a nuclear weapon" means any device, radioactive or nonradioactive, specifically designed to be installed in and contribute to the operation of a nuclear weapon.

(d) "Direct activities of the federal government" means actions of the federal government or any agency thereof created by statute, but shall exclude actions of independent contractors.

(Prior code § 202-1; Added. Coun. J. 3-12-86, p. 28521; Corrected. 2-3-87, p. 39355)

§1-16-020 Nuclear weapons work—Unlawful activities—Exceptions.

(a) Phase-out of Present Activities. No person shall knowingly, within the city of Chicago, design, produce, deploy, launch, maintain, or store nuclear weapons or components of nuclear weapons. This prohibition shall take effect two years after the adoption and publication of this ordinance.

(b) Prohibition of Commencement of Nuclear Weapons Work. No person who is not, as of the effective date of this ordinance, engaged in the design, production, deployment, launching, maintenance or storage of nuclear weapons or components of nuclear weapons, shall, within the city of Chicago, commence any such activities after the effective date of this ordinance.

(c) Exclusion. Nothing in this section shall be construed to prohibit:

(i) Any activity not specifically described in this section;

(ii) Basic research;

(iii) Any writing or speech devoted to public commentary or debate or other speech protected by the First Amendment of the United States Constitution;

(iv) The research and application of nuclear medicine;

(v) Uses of fissionable materials for smoke detectors, light-emitting watches and clocks and other consumer products; or

(vi) Direct activities of the federal government.

(Prior code § 202-2; Added. Coun. J. 3-12-86, p. 28521; Corrected. 2-3-87, p. 39355)

§1-16-030 Reserved.

(Deleted. 3-31-04, p. 20916)

§1-16-040 Civil defense participation limitations.

Recognizing the futility of civil defense against nuclear war and its ensuing radioactive contamination, the city declares that planning for or participating in civil defense programs purporting to prepare for nuclear attack is futile and dangerous. Therefore, the city will not participate in any civil defense or population evacuation program exclusively intended to be implemented upon the outbreak or threatened outbreak of nuclear hostilities.

Nothing in this section shall be construed to prohibit or limit any other type of civil defense or emergency preparedness program.

(Prior code § 202-4; Added. Coun. J. 3-12-86, p. 28521; Corrected. 2-3-87, p. 39355)

§1-16-050 Annual commemoration day.

In recognition of the first use of nuclear weapons against the Japanese city of Hiroshima in 1945, August 6th shall be declared "Nuclear Weapon Free Zone Commemoration Day" within the city of Chicago. The city shall sponsor an appropriate observation annually on this date. This annual observation shall include a report by the mayor on the city's activities to enforce this ordinance.

(Prior code § 202-5; Added. Coun. J. 3-12-86, p. 28521; Corrected. 2-3-87, p. 39355)

§1-16-060 Sign requirements.

The city shall post and maintain appropriate signs at recognized entrances to the city and in City Hall proclaiming the city of Chicago ‘s status as a nuclear weapon free zone. When posted on city streets or on state or federally supported roads entering the city of Chicago, such signs shall conform with the standards set forth in Section 28-44 of the Federal Highway Administration's "Manual on Uniform Traffic Control Devices for Streets and Highways."

(Prior code § 202-6; Added. Coun. J. 3-12-86, p. 28521; Corrected. 2-3-87, p. 39355)

§1-16-070 Violation—Penalty.

Each violation of this ordinance shall be punishable by up to 30 days' imprisonment and a $1,000.00 fine. Each day of violation shall be deemed a separate violation.

(Prior code § 202-7; Added. Coun. J. 3-12-86, p. 28521; Corrected. 2-3-87, p. 39355)

§1-16-080 Severability.

If any section, subsection, paragraph, sentence or word of this ordinance shall be held to be invalid, either on its face or as applied, the invalidity of such provision shall not affect the other sections, subsections, paragraphs, sentences or words of this ordinance, and the applications thereof; and to that end the sections, subsections, paragraphs, sentences or words of this ordinance shall be deemed to be severable.

(Prior code § 202-8; Added. Coun. J. 3-12-86, p. 28521; Corrected. 2-3-87, p. 39355)

CHAPTER 1-21
FALSE STATEMENTS
(Complete Chapter)

Sections:

1-21-010 False statements.
1-21-020 Aiding and abetting.
1-21-030 Enforcement.

§1-21-010 False statements.

Any person who knowingly makes a false statement of material fact to the city in violation of any statute, ordinance or regulation, or who knowingly falsifies any statement of material fact made in connection with an application, report affidavit, oath, or attestation, including a statement of material fact made in connection with a bid, proposal, contract or economic disclosure statement or affidavit, is liable to the city for civil penalty of not less than $500.00 and not more than $1,000.00, plus up to three times the amount of damages which the city sustains because of the person's violation of this section. A person who violates this section shall also be liable for the city's litigation and collection costs and attorney's fees.

The penalties imposed by this section shall be in addition to any other penalty provided for in the municipal code.
(Added. Coun. J. 12-15-04, p. 39915)

§1-21-020 Aiding and abetting.
Any person who aids, abets, incites, compels or coerces the doing of any act prohibited by this chapter shall be liable to the city for the same penalties for the violation.
(Added. Coun. J. 12-15-04, p. 39915)

§1-21-030 Enforcement.
In addition to any other means authorized by law, the corporation counsel may enforce this chapter by instituting and action with the department of administrative hearings.
(Added. Coun. J. 12-15-04, p. 39915)

CHAPTER 1-22
FALSE CLAIMS
(Complete Chapter)

Sections:

1-22-010 Definitions.
1-22-020 False claims.
1-22-030 Civil actions for false claims.
1-22-040 False claims procedure.
1-22-050 Subpoenas.
1-22-060 Procedure.

§1-22-010 Definitions.
As used in this chapter:

"Claim" includes any request or demand, whether under a contract or otherwise, for money or property which is made by a city contractor, grantee, or other recipient if the city is the source of any portion of the money or property which is requested or demanded, or if the city will reimburse such contractor, grantee, or other recipient for any portion of the money or property which is requested or demanded.

"Contract" means any agreement or transaction pursuant to which a person: (i) receives or may be entitled to receive city funds or other property, including grant funds, in consideration for services, work or goods provided or rendered, including contracts for legal or other professional services; (ii) purchases the city's real or personal property or is granted the right to use it by virtue of a lease, license or otherwise; or (iii) collects monies (other than taxes) on behalf of the city.

"City contractor" means a person who enters into a contract or who has taken any action to obtain a contract, or any owner, officer, director, employee or agent of such a person, or any subcontractor, or any person acting in concert or conspiring with such person, but shall not include any person who is a city official or employee or was a city official or employee at the time of the alleged conduct.

"Investigation" means any inquiry conducted by any investigator for the purpose of ascertaining whether any person is or has been engaged in any violation of this chapter.

"Knowing" and "knowingly" means that a person, with respect to information:

(1) Has actual knowledge of the information:

(2) Acts in deliberate ignorance of the truth or falsity of the information; or

(3) Acts in reckless disregard of the truth or falsity of the information, regardless of whether there is specific proof of intent to defraud.

(Added. Coun. J. 12-15-04, p. 39918)

§1-22-020 False claims.

Any person who:

(1) Knowingly presents, or causes to be presented, to an official or employee of the city a false or fraudulent claim for payment or approval;

(2) Knowingly makes, uses, or causes to be made or used, a false record or statement to get a false or fraudulent claim paid or approved by the city;

(3) Conspires to defraud the city by getting a false or fraudulent claim allowed or paid;

(4) Has possession, custody, or control of property or money used, or to be used, by the city and, intending to defraud the city or to conceal the property, delivers, or causes to be delivered, less property than the amount for which the person receives a certificate or receipt;

(5) Authorized to make or deliver a document certifying receipt of property used, or to be used, by the city and, intending to defraud the city, makes or delivers the receipt without complete knowledge that the information on the receipt is true;

(6) Knowingly buys, or receives as a pledge of an obligation or debt, public property from an officer or employee of the city who lawfully may not sell or pledge the property; or

(7) Knowingly makes, uses, or causes to be made or used, a false record or statement to conceal, avoid or decrease an obligation to pay or transmit money or property to the city, is liable to the city for a civil penalty of not less than $5,000.00 and not more than $10,000.00, plus three times the amount of damages which the city sustains because of the act of that person. A person violating this section shall also be liable to the city for the attorneys' fees and costs of a civil action brought to recover any such penalty or damages.

(Added. Coun. J. 12-15-04, p. 39918)

§1-22-030 Civil actions for false claims.

(a) The corporation counsel may bring a civil action under this section against any person who has violated or is violating Section 1-22-020.

(b) Actions by Private Persons.

(1) A person may bring a civil action against a city contractor for a violation of Section 1-22-020 for the person and for the city. The action shall be brought in the name of the city. The action may be dismissed only if the court and the corporation counsel give written consent to the dismissal and their reasons for consenting.

(2) A copy of the complaint and written disclosure of substantially all material evidence and information the person possess shall be served on the city. In all such actions, service upon the city shall be made by leaving a copy with the city clerk. The complaint shall be filed in camera, shall remain under seal for at least 60 days, and shall not be served on the defendant until the court so orders. The city may elect to intervene and proceed with the action 60 days after it receives both the complaint and the material evidence and information.

(3) The city may, for good cause shown, move the court of the time during which the complaint remains under seal under paragraph (2) of this subsection. Any such motions may be supported by affidavits or other submissions in camera. The defendant shall not be required to respond to any complaint filed under this section until 20 days after the complaint is unsealed and served upon the defendant.

(4) Before the expiration of the 60-day period or any extensions obtained under paragraph (3) of this subsection, the city shall:

(A) Proceed with the action, in which case the action shall be conducted by the city; or

(B) Notify the court that it declines to take over the action, in which case the person bringing the action shall have the right to conduct the action.

(5) When a person brings an action under this subsection (b), no person other than the city may intervene or bring a related action based on the facts underlying the pending action.

(c) Rights of the Parties to Qui Tam Actions.

(1) If the city proceeds with the action, it shall have the primary responsibility for prosecuting the action, and shall not be bound by an act of the person bringing the action. Such person shall have the right to continue as a party to the action, subject to the limitations set forth in paragraph (2) of this subsection.

(2) (A) The city may dismiss the action notwithstanding the objections of the person initiating the action if the person has been notified by the city of the filing of the motion to dismiss and the court has provided the person with an opportunity for a hearing on the motion.

(B) The city may settle the action with the defendant notwithstanding the objections of the person initiating the action if the court determines, after a hearing, that the proposed settlement is fair, adequate, and reasonable under all the circumstances. Upon a showing of good cause, such hearing may be held in camera.

(C) Upon a showing by the city that unrestricted participation during the course of the litigation by the person initiating the action would interfere with or unduly delay the city's prosecution of the case, would repetitious, irrelevant, or for purposes of harassment, the court may, in its discretion, impose limitations on the person's participation, such as:

(i) Limiting the number of witnesses the person may call;

(ii) Limiting the length of the testimony of such witnesses;

(iii) Limiting the person's cross-examination of the witnesses; or

(iv) Otherwise limiting the participation by the person in the litigation.

(D) Upon a showing by the defendant that unrestricted participation during the course of the litigation by the person initiating the action would be for purposes of harassment or would cause the defendant undue burden or unnecessary expense, the court may limit the participation by the person in the litigation.

(3) If the city elects not to proceed with the action, the person who initiated the action shall have the right to conduct the action. If the city so requests, it shall be served with copies of all pleadings filed in the action and shall be supplied with copies of all discovery and deposition transcripts at the city's expense. When a person proceeds with the action, the court, without limiting the status and rights of the person initiating the action, may nevertheless permit the city to intervene at a later date upon a showing of good cause.

(4) Whether or not the city proceeds with the action, upon a showing by the city that certain actions of discovery by the person initiating the action would interfere with the city's investigation of prosecution of a criminal or civil matter arising out of the same facts, the court may stay such discovery for a period of not more than 60 days. Such a showing shall be conducted in camera. The court may extend the 60-day period upon a further showing in camera that the city has pursued the criminal or civil investigation or proceedings with reasonable diligence and any proposed discovery in the civil action will interfere with the ongoing criminal or civil investigation or proceeding.

(5) Notwithstanding any other provision in subsection (b) of this section, the city may elect to pursue its claim through any alternate remedy available to the city, including an administrative proceeding in the department of administrative hearings. If any such alternate remedy is pursued in another proceeding, the person initiating the action shall have the same rights in such proceeding as such person would have had if the action had continued under this section. Any finding of fact or conclusion of law made in such other proceeding that has become final shall be conclusive on all parties to an action under this section. For purposes of the preceding sentence, a finding or conclusion is final if it has been finally determined on appeal to the appropriate court, if all time for filing such an appeal with respect to the finding or conclusion has expired, or if the finding or conclusion is not subject to judicial review.

(d) Award to Qui Tam Plaintiff.

(1) If the city proceeds with an action brought by a person under this section, such person shall, subject to the second sentence of this paragraph, receive at least 15 percent but not more 20 percent of the proceeds of the action or settlement of the claim, depending upon the extent to which the person substantially contributed to the prosecution of the action. Where the action is one which the court finds to be based primarily on disclosures of specific information (other than information provided by the person bringing the action) relating to allegations or transactions in a criminal, civil, or administrative hearing, in a legislative, administrative, or inspector general's report, hearing, audit, or investigation, or from the news media, the court may award such sums as it considers appropriate, but in no case more than 10 percent of the proceeds, taking into account the significance of the information and the role of the person bringing the action in advancing the case to litigation.

(2) If the city does not proceed with an action under this section and the action is successfully brought or the claim is settled by another person, that person shall, subject to the exception set forth in this paragraph, receive an amount which the court decides is reasonable for collecting the civil penalty and damages. The amount shall be not less than 25 percent and not more than

30 percent of the proceeds of the action or settlement and shall be paid out of such proceeds.

(3) Any person entitled to an award under paragraphs (1) and (2) of this subsection, shall also receive an amount for reasonable expenses which the court finds to have been necessarily incurred, plus reasonable attorney's fees and costs. The city shall also receive an amount for reasonable expenses which the court finds to have been necessarily incurred by the corporation counsel, including the reasonable attorney's fees and costs. All such expenses, fees and costs awarded pursuant to this subsection shall be awarded against the defendant.

(4) Whether or not the city proceeds with the action, if the court finds that the action was brought by a person who planned, initiated or participated in the violation of Section 1-22-020 upon which the action was brought, then the court may, to the extent the court considers appropriate, reduce the share of the proceeds of the action which the person would otherwise receive under paragraph (1) or (2) of this subsection, taking into account the role of that person in advancing the case to litigation and any relevant circumstances pertaining to this violation. If the person bringing the action is convicted of criminal conduct arising from his or her role in the violation of Section 1-22-020, that person shall dismissed from the civil action and shall not receive any share of the proceeds of the action. Such dismissal shall not prejudice the right of the city to continue the action.

(5) If the city does not proceed with the action and the person bringing the action conducts the action, the court may award to the defendant it reasonable attorney's fees and expenses if the defendant prevails in the action and the court finds that the claim of the person bringing the action was clearly frivolous, clearly vexations, or brought primarily for the purposes or harassment.

(e) In no event may a person bring an action under subsection (b) of this section, which is based upon allegations or transactions which are the subject of a civil suit or an administrative proceeding in which the city is already a party.

(f) No court shall have jurisdiction over an action under this section based upon the public disclosure of allegations or transactions in a criminal, civil, or administrative hearing, in a legislative, administrative, or inspector general's report, hearing, audit, or investigation, or from the news media, unless the action is brought by the corporation counsel or the person bringing the action is an original source of the information. For purposes of this subsection, "original source" means an individual who has direct and independent knowledge of the information on which the allegations are based and has voluntarily provided the information to the city before filing an action under this section which is based on the information.

(g) The city is not liable for expenses, including attorney's fees, which a person incurs in bringing an action under this section.

(Added. Coun. J. 12-15-04, p. 39918)

§1-22-040 False claims procedure.

(a) A subpoena requiring the attendance of a witness at a trial or hearing conducted under Section 1-22-030 may be served at any place in the state.

(b) A civil action under Section 1-22-030 may not be brought:

(1) More than six years after the date on which the violation of Section 1-22-020 is committed; or

(2) More than three years after the date when facts material to the right of action or known or reasonably should have been known by the official of the city charged with the responsibility to act in the circumstances, but in no event more than 10 years after the date on which the violation is committed, whichever occurs last.

(c) In any action brought under Section 1-22-030, the city shall be required to prove all essential elements of the cause of action, including damages, by preponderance of the evidence.

(d) Notwithstanding any other provision of law, a final judgement rendered in favor of the city in any criminal proceeding charging fraud or false statements, whether upon a verdict after trial or upon a plea of guilty, shall stop the defendant from denying the essential elements of the offense in any action which involves the same transaction as in the criminal proceeding and which brought under subsection (a) or (b) of Section 1-22-030.

(Added. Coun. J. 12-15-04, p. 39918)

§1-22-050 Subpoenas.

(a) In general.

(1) Issuance and Service. Whenever the corporation counsel has reason to believe that any person may be in possession custody, or control of any documentary material or information relevant to an investigation, the corporation counsel may, before commencing a civil proceeding under this chapter, issue in writing and cause to be served upon such person, a subpoena requiring such person:

(A) To produce such documentary material for inspection and copying;

(B) To answer, in writing, written interrogatories with respect to such documentary material or information;

(C) To give oral testimony concerning such documentary material or information; or

(D) To furnish any combination of such material answers, or testimony. Whenever a subpoena is an express demand for any product of discovery, the corporation counsel shall cause to be served, in any manner authorized by this section, a copy of such demand upon the person from whom the discovery was obtained and shall notify the person to whom such demand is issued of the date on which such copy was served.

(2) Contents and Deadlines. Each subpoena issued under paragraph (1) of this subsection:

(A) Shall state the nature of the conduct constituting an alleged violation that is under investigation and the applicable provision of law alleged to be violated.

(B) Shall identify the individual causing the subpoena to be served and to whom communications regarding the subpoena should be directed.

(C) Shall state the date, place, and time at which the person is required to appear, produce written answers to interrogatories produce documentary material or give oral testimony. The date shall not be less than 10 days from the date of service of the subpoena. Compliance with the subpoena shall be at the office of the corporation counsel.

(D) If the subpoena is for documentary material or interrogatories, shall describe the documents or information requested with specificity.

(E) Shall notify the person of the right to be assisted by counsel.

(F) Shall advise that the person has 20 days from the date of service or up until the return date specified in the demand, whichever date is earlier to move, modify, or set aside the subpoena pursuant to subsection (j)(2)(A) of this section.

(b) Protected Material or Information.

(1) In General. A subpoena issued under subsection (a) may not require the production of any documentary material the submission of any answers to written interrogatories, or the giving of any oral testimony if such material, answers, or testimony would be protected from disclosure under:

(A) The standards applicable to subpoenas or subpoenas duces tecum issued by a court of this state to aid in a grand jury investigation; or

(B) The standards applicable to discovery requests under the code of civil procedure, to the extent that the application of such standards to any such subpoena is appropriate and consistent with the provisions and purposes of this section.

(2) Effect on other Orders, Rules and Laws. Any such subpoena which is an express demand for any product of discovery supersedes any inconsistent order, rule, or provision of law (other than this section) preventing or restraining disclosure of such product of discovery to any person. Disclosure of any product of discovery pursuant to any such subpoena does not constitute a waiver of any right or privilege which the person making such disclosure may be entitled to invoke to resist discovery of trial preparation materials.

(c) Service in General. Any subpoena issued under subsection (a) of this section may be served by any person so authorized by the corporation counsel or by any person authorized to serve process on individuals within Illinois, through any method prescribed in the code of civil procedure or as otherwise set forth in this chapter.

(d) Service upon Legal Entities and Natural Persons.

(1) Legal Entities. Service of any subpoena issued under subsection (a) of this section or of any petition filed under subsection (j) of this section, may be made upon a partnership, corporations association, or other legal entity by:

(A) Delivering an executed copy of such subpoena or petition to any partner, executive officer, managing agent, general agent, or registered agent of the partnerships corporation, association or entity;

(B) Delivering an executed copy of such subpoena or petition to the principal office or place of business of the partnership, corporation, association, or entity; or

(C) Depositing an executed copy of such subpoena or petition in the United States mails by registered or certified mail, with a return receipt requested, addressed to such partnership, corporation, association, or entity as its principal office or place of business.

(2) Natural Person. Service of any such subpoena or petition may be made upon any natural person by:

(A) Delivering an executed copy of such subpoena or petition to the person; or

(B) Depositing an executed copy of such subpoena or petition in the United States mail by registered or certified mail, with a return receipt requested, addressed to the person at the person's residence or principal office or place of business.

(e) Proof of Service. A verified return by the individual serving any subpoena issued under subsection (a) of this section or any petition filed under subsection (j) of this section setting forth the manner of such service shall be proof of such service. In the case of service by registered or certified mail, such return shall be accompanied by the return post office receipt of delivery of such subpoena.

(f) Documentary Material.

(1) Sworn Certificates. The production of documentary material in response to a subpoena served under this section shall be made under a sworn certificate, in such form as the subpoena designates by:

(A) In the case of a natural persons the person to whom the subpoena is directed;

(B) In the case of a person other than a natural person, a person having knowledge of the facts and circumstances relating to such production and authorized to act on behalf of such person.

The certificate shall state that all of the documentary material required by the demand and in the possession, custody, or control of the person to whom the subpoena is directed has been produced and made available to the corporation counsel.

(2) Production of Materials. Any person upon whom any subpoena for the production of documentary material has been served under this section shall make such material available for inspection and copying to the corporation counsel at the place designated in the subpoena, or at such other place as the corporation counsel and the person thereafter may agree and prescribe in writing, or as the court may direct under subsection (j)(1). Such material shall be made so available on the return date specified in such subpoena, or on such later date as the corporation counsel may prescribe in writing. Such person may upon written agreement between the person and the corporation counsel, substitute copies for originals of all or any part of such material.

(g) Interrogatories. Each interrogatory in a subpoena served under this section shall be answered separately and fully in writing under oath and shall be submitted under a sworn certificate, in such form as the subpoena designates by:

(1) In the case of a natural person, the person to whom the subpoena is directed; or

(2) In the case of a person other than a natural person, the person or persons responsible for answering each interrogatory.

If any interrogatory is objected to, the reasons for the objection shall be stated in the certificate instead of an answer. The certificate shall state that all information required by the subpoena and in the possession, custody, control, or knowledge of the person to whom the demand is directed has been submitted. To the extent that any information is not furnished, the information shall be identified and reasons set forth with particularity regarding the reasons why the information was not furnished.

(h) Oral Examinations.

(1) Procedures. The examination of any person pursuant to a subpoena for oral testimony served under this section shall be taken before an officer authorized to administer oaths and affirmations by the laws of this state or of the place where the examination is held. The officer before whom the testimony is to be taken shall put the witness on oath or affirmation and shall, personally or by someone acting under the direction of the officer and in the officer's presence, record the testimony of the witness. The testimony shall be taken stenographically and shall be transcribed. When the testimony is fully transcribed, the officer before whom the testimony is taken shall promptly transmit a certified copy of the transcript of the testimony in accordance with the instructions of the corporation counsel. This subsection shall not preclude the taking of testimony by any means authorized by, and in a manner consistent with, the code of civil procedure.

(2) Persons Present. The investigator conducting the examination shall exclude from the place where the examination is held all persons except the person giving the testimony, the attorney for and any other representative of the person giving the testimony, the attorney for the city, any person who may be agreed upon by the attorney for the city and the person giving the testimony, the officer before whom the testimony is to be taken, and any stenographer taking such testimony.

(3) Where Testimony Taken. The oral testimony of any person taken pursuant to a subpoena served under this section shall be taken in the county within which such person resides, is found, or transacts business, or in such other place as may be agreed upon by the corporation counsel and such person.

(4) Transcript of Testimony. When the testimony is fully transcribed, the corporation counsel or the officer before whom the testimony is taken shall afford the witness, who may be accompanied by counsel, a reasonable opportunity to review and correct the transcript, in accordance with the rules applicable to deposition witnesses in civil cases. Upon payment of reasonable charges, the corporation counsel shall furnish a copy of the transcript to the witness, except that the corporation counsel may, for good cause, limit the witness to inspection of the official transcript of the witness' testimony

(5) Conduct of Oral Testimony.

(A) Any person compelled to appear for oral testimony under a subpoena issued under subsection (a) of this section may be accompanied, represented, and advised by counsel, who may raise objections based on matters of privilege in accordance with the rules applicable to depositions in civil cases. If such person refuses to answer any question, a petition may be filed in circuit court under subsection (j)(1) of this section for an order compelling such person to answer such question.

(B) If such person refuses any question on the grounds of the privilege against self-incrimination, the testimony of such person may be compelled in accordance with Article 106 of the Code of Criminal Procedure of 1963.

(6) Witness Fees and Allowances. Any person appearing for oral testimony under a subpoena issued under subsection (a) of this section shall be entitled to the same fees and allowances which are paid to witnesses in the circuit court.

(i) Custodians of Documents, Answers, and Transcripts.

(1) Designation. The corporation counsel shall serve as custodian of documentary material, answers to interrogatories, and transcripts of oral testimony received under this section.

(2) Except as otherwise provided in this section. no documentary material answers to interrogatories, or transcripts of oral testimony, or copies thereof, while in the possession of the custodian, shall be available for examination by any individual except as determined necessary by the corporation counsel and subject to the conditions imposed by him or her for effective enforcement of the laws of this city, or as otherwise provided by court order.

(3) Conditions for Return of Material. If any documentary material has been produced by any person in the course of any investigation pursuant to a subpoena under this section and:

(A) Any case or proceeding before the court or grand jury arising out of such investigations, or any proceeding before any city agency involving such material has been completed; or

(B) No case or proceeding in which such material may be used has been commenced within a reasonable time after completion of the examination and analysis of all documentary material and other information assembled in the course of such investigation, the custodian shall, upon written request of the person who produced such material, return to such person any such material which has not passed into the control of any court, grand jury, or agency through introduction into the record of such case or proceeding.

(j) Judicial Proceedings.

(1) Petition for Enforcement. Whenever any person fails to comply with any subpoena issued under subsection (a) of this section, or whenever satisfactory copying or reproduction of any material requested in such demand cannot be done and such person refuses to surrender such material, the corporation counsel may file, in the circuit court of any county in which such person resides, is found, or transacts business, or the circuit court of the county in which an action filed pursuant to Section 1-22-030 is pending if the action relates to the subject matter of the subpoena and serve upon such person a petition for an order of such court for the enforcement of the subpoena.

(2) Petition to Modify or Set Aside Subpoena.

(A) Any person who has received a subpoena issued under subsection (a) of this section may file, in the circuit court of any county within which such person resides, is found, or transacts business, and serve upon the corporation counsel a petition for an order of the court to modify or set aside such subpoena. In the case of a petition addressed to an express demand for any product of discovery, a petition to modify or set aside such demand may be brought only in the circuit court of the county in which the proceeding in which such discovery was obtained is or was last pending. Any petition under this subparagraph must be filed:

(i) Within 20 days after the date of service of the subpoena, or at any time before the return date specified in the subpoena, whichever date is earlier; or

(ii) Within such longer period as may be prescribed in writing by the corporation counsel.

(B) The petition shall specify each ground upon which the petitioner relies in seeking relief under subsection (j)(2)(A) of this section, and may be based upon any failure pf the subpoena to comply with the provisions of this section or upon any constitutional or other legal right or privilege of such person. During the pendency of the petition in the court, the court may stay, as it deems proper, the running of the time allowed for compliance with the subpoena, in whole or parts except that the person filing the petition shall comply with any portion of the subpoena not sought to be modified or set aside.

(3) Petition to Modify or Set Aside Demand for Product of Discovery. In the case of any subpoena issued under subsection (a) of this section which is an express demand for any product of discovery, the person from whom such discovery was obtained may file, in the circuit court of the county in which the proceeding in which such discovery was obtained is or was last pending, a petition for an order of such court to modify or set aside those portions of the subpoena requiring production of any such product of discovery, subject to the same terms, conditions and limitations set forth in subsection (j)(2) of this section.

(4) Jurisdiction. Whenever any petition is filed in any circuit court under this subsection, such court shall have jurisdiction to hear and determine the matter so presented, and to enter such orders as may be required to carry out the provisions of this section. Any final order so entered shall be subject to appeal in the same manner as appeals of other final orders in civil matters. Any disobedience of any final order entered under this section by any court shall be punished as a contempt of the court.

(k) Disclosure Exemption. Any documentary material, answers to written interrogatories, or oral testimony provided under any subpoena issued under subsection (a) of this section shall be exempt from disclosure under the Illinois Administrative Procedure Act.

(Added. Coun. J. 12-15-04, p. 39918)

§1-22-060 Procedure.

The Illinois Code of Civil Procedure shall apply to all proceedings under this chapter, except when that code is inconsistent with this chapter.

(Added. Coun. J. 12-15-04, p. 39918)

TITLE 2
CITY GOVERNMENT AND ADMINISTRATION
(Selected Chapters)

Divisions:

I.	Officers and Departments. (Selected Chapters)
II.	Division II. Boards, Commissions and Committees. (Selected Chapters)
III.	Ethics and Employment Policies. (Selected Chapters)

DIVISION I
OFFICERS AND DEPARTMENTS
(Selected Chapters)

Chapters:

2-4	Mayor. (Selected Section)
2-14	Department of Administrative Hearings. (Selected Sections)
2-24	Department of Consumer Services. (Complete Chapter)
2-36	Fire Department. (Selected Sections)
2-56	Office of Inspector General. (Complete Chapter)
2-74	Department of Personnel. (Selected Sections)
2-84	Department of Police. (Complete Chapter)

CHAPTER 2-4
MAYOR
(Selected Section)

Sections:

2-4-110	Coordinator of emergency activities.

§2-4-110 Coordinator of emergency activities.

The mayor shall be ex officio coordinator of activities in cases of emergency resulting from any explosion, fire, flood, riot, storm or other cause requiring concerted measures for the maintenance of public peace and order, the preservation of life and property and the relief of suffering, or for any of these purposes. He shall formulate, and, as occasion therefor arises, he shall execute plans for the prevention of such emergencies so far as possible and for meeting them effectively when they arise. Obedience to his orders in executing such plans and meeting such emergencies is obligatory upon all departments and heads of departments and upon all other officers and employees of the city of Chicago.

(Prior code § 3-11; Amend. Coun. J. 12-4-02, p. 99026)

CHAPTER 2-14
DEPARTMENT OF ADMINISTRATIVE HEARINGS
(Selected Sections)

Sections:

Article I. General Provisions

2-14-010	Department of administrative hearings—Establishment and composition.
2-14-030	Powers and duties of the director.
2-14-040	Administrative law officers—Powers and duties.

2-14-065 General provisions.
2-14-070 Instituting administrative adjudication proceedings.
2-14-074 Notice.
2-14-076 Administrative hearings.
2-14-078 Default.
2-14-080 Subpoenas.
2-14-090 Compliance bond.
2-14-100 Violations of orders.
2-14-101 Seized/unclaimed property.
2-14-102 Review under the administrative review law.
2-14-103 Enforcement of administrative law officer's order.
2-14-110 Election of remedies.
2-14-130 Other provisions not limiting.
2-14-132 Impoundment.

Article II. Vehicle Hearings Division
2-14-140 Vehicle hearings division.

Article III. Buildings Hearings Division
2-14-154 Rights of occupants.
2-14-155 Defenses to building code violations.

Article VI. Municipal Hearings Division
2-14-190 Municipal hearings division—Jurisdiction.
2-14-195 Fine of $10,000.00 or more—Petition for review to the director.
2-14-200 Eviction proceedings.

Article I. General Provisions

§2-14-010 Department of administrative hearings—Establishment and composition.

There is hereby established an office of the municipal government to be known as the department of administrative hearings which shall be authorized to conduct administrative adjudication proceedings for departments and agencies of the city.

The department shall be administered by a director, who shall be appointed by the mayor, subject to approval by the city council, and staffed by administrative law officers and other employees as may be provided for in the annual appropriation ordinance.

The provisions of Division 2.1 of Article 1 of the Illinois Municipal Code are hereby adopted and incorporated into this chapter as if fully set forth herein. *(Added. Coun. J. 7-10-96, p. 24982; Amend. 11-12-97, p. 56813; 4-29-98, p. 66564)*

§2-14-030 Powers and duties of the director.

The powers and duties of the director of the department of administrative hearings shall include:

(1) Directing the department with respect to its management and structure, including the creation or reorganization of hearing divisions within the department;

(2) Appointing and removing administrative law officers, as necessary;

(3) Promulgating rules and regulations for the conduct of administrative adjudication proceedings;

(4) Monitoring and supervising the work of administrative law officers and, upon receipt of a timely petition for review authorized by the code, reviewing, modifying or reversing their decisions;

(5) Establishing a system for hearing of grievances brought by tenants of the Chicago Housing Authority against the authority and/or its property managers, all in accordance with an intergovernmental agreement between the city of Chicago and the Chicago Housing Authority; and

(6) Establishing any other necessary rules and regulations as may be required to carry out the provisions of this chapter.

(Added. Coun. J. 7-10-96, p. 24982; Amend. 11-12-97, p. 56813; 4-29-98, p. 66564; 3-31-04, p. 20968)

§2-14-040 Administrative law officers—Powers and duties.

Each administrative law officer appointed by the director shall be an attorney admitted to the practice of law in the state of Illinois for at least three years. Administrative law officers shall have all powers necessary to conduct fair and impartial hearings including, but not limited to, the power to:

(1) Hold conferences for the settlement or simplification of the issues;

(2) Administer oaths and affirmations;

(3) Hear testimony;

(4) Rule upon motions, objections, and the admissibility of evidence;

(5) Subject to the restrictions contained in Section 2-14-080, at the request of any party or on the administrative law officer's own motion, subpoena the attendance of relevant witnesses and the production of relevant books, records, or other information;

(6) Preserve and authenticate the record of the hearing and all exhibits and evidence introduced at the hearing;

(7) Regulate the course of the hearing in accordance with this chapter, the rules adopted by the department for the conduct of administrative hearings, or other applicable law;

(8) Discuss administrative adjudication proceedings with their supervisors;

(9) Issue a final order which includes findings of fact and conclusions of law;

(10) Impose penalties and fines and issue orders that are consistent with applicable code provisions and assess costs upon finding a party liable for the charged violation; provided, however, that in no event shall an administrative law officer have the authority to: (i) impose a penalty of imprisonment; or (ii) except in cases to enforce the collection of any tax imposed and collected by the city, in which this limitation shall not apply, impose a fine in excess of $50,000 exclusive of costs of enforcement or costs imposed to secure compliance with this code; and

(11) In any case in which a party has sought review by the department of administrative hearings of an order or determination of another city department or agency, when such review is authorized by this code, assess costs upon affirming the order or determination.

(Added. Coun. J. 7-10-96, p. 24982; Amend. 11-12-97, p. 56813; 4-29-98, p. 66564)

§2-14-065 General provisions.

The provisions of this article shall apply to administrative adjudication proceedings conducted by the department of administrative hearings to the extent that they are not inconsistent with the provisions of this code which set forth specific procedures for the administrative adjudication of particular code provisions.
(Added. Coun. J. 4-29-98, p. 66564)

§2-14-070 Instituting administrative adjudication proceedings.

Any authorized department or agency of the city may institute an administration adjudication proceeding with the department of administrative hearings by forwarding a copy of a notice of violation or a notice of hearing, which has been properly served, to the department of administrative hearings.
(Added. Coun. J. 7-10-96, p. 24982; Amend. 11-12-97, p. 56813; 4-29-98, p. 66564)

§2-14-074 Notice.

(a) Before any administrative adjudication proceeding may be conducted, the parties shall be afforded notice in compliance with this section.

(b) Unless otherwise provided by law or rule, the issuer of a notice of violation or notice of hearing shall specify on the notice his or her name and department; where known, the name and address of the person or entity charged with the violation; the date, time and place of the violation; and the section of the code or departmental rule or regulation which was allegedly violated; and shall certify the correctness of the specified information by signing his or her name to the notice. A notice of hearing shall also include the date, time and location of the hearing and the penalties for failure to appear at the hearing.

(c) Unless otherwise provided by law or rule, a notice of violation or notice of hearing shall be served upon the alleged violator no less than seven calendar days prior to the date of the hearing: (i) by first class or express mail or by overnight carrier at the violator's residence address or, if the violator is a business entity, at any address identified for its registered agent or at its principal place of business; or (ii) by personal service, including personal service upon an employee or agent of the alleged violator at a place of business of the alleged violator or otherwise if such service is reasonably calculated to give the alleged violator actual notice; or (iii) if service cannot be made by either of subsection (c)(i) or (ii) above, when the alleged violator is the owner or manager of the property by posting a copy of the violation notice on the front entrance of the building or other structure where the violation is found, or if the property is unimproved or fenced off, by posting a copy of the violation notice in a prominent place upon the property where the violation is found.

(d) In all non-emergency situations, if requested by the defendant, the defendant shall have at least 15 days after the date of mailing or other service of a notice of violation or notice of hearing to prepare for a hearing. For purposes of this section, "non-emergency situation" means any situation that does not reasonably constitute a threat to the public interest, safety or welfare.
(Added. Coun. J. 7-10-96, p. 24982; Amend. 4-29-98, p. 66564)

§2-14-076 Administrative hearings.

(a) Any administrative adjudication proceeding conducted by the department of administrative hearings shall afford the parties an opportunity for a hearing before an administrative law officer.

(b) An attorney who appears on behalf of any person shall file with the administrative law officer a written appearance on a form provided by the department of administrative hearings for such purpose.

(c) In no event shall the case for the city be presented by an employee of the department of administrative hearings; provided, however, that documentary evidence, including the notice of violation, which has been prepared by another department or agency of the city, may be presented at the hearing by the administrative law officer.

(d) The administrative law officer may grant continuances only upon a finding of good cause.

(e) All testimony shall be given under oath or affirmation.

(f) The administrative law officer may issue subpoenas to secure the attendance and testimony of relevant witnesses and the production of relevant documents. Issuance of subpoenas shall be subject to the restrictions contained in Section 2-14-080.

(g) Subject to subsection (j) of this section, the administrative law officer may permit witnesses to submit their testimony by affidavit or by telephone.

(h) The formal and technical rules of evidence shall not apply in the conduct of the hearing. Evidence, including hearsay, may be admitted only if it is of a type commonly relied upon by reasonably prudent persons in the conduct of their affairs.

(i) No violation may be established except upon proof by a preponderance of the evidence; provided, however, that a violation notice, or a copy thereof issued and signed in accordance with Section 2-14-074, shall be prima facie evidence of the correctness of the facts specified therein.

(j) Upon the timely request of any party to the proceeding, any person who the administrative law officer determines may reasonably be expected to provide testimony which is material and which does not constitute a needless presentation of cumulative evidence, shall be made available for cross-examination prior to a final determination of liability.

(k) The record of all hearings before an administrative law officer shall include: (i) a record of the testimony presented at the hearing, which may be made by tape recording or other appropriate means; (ii) all documents presented at the hearing; (iii) a copy of the notice of violation or notice of hearing; and (iv) a copy of the findings and decision of the administrative law officer.

(l) Upon conclusion of a hearing, the administrative law officer shall issue a final determination of liability or no liability. Upon issuing a final determination of liability the administrative law officer may: (i) impose penalties and/or fines that are consistent with applicable provisions of the Municipal Code; (ii) issue orders that are consistent with applicable provisions of the Municipal Code; and/or (iii) assess costs reasonably related to instituting the administrative adjudication proceeding; provided, however, that in no event shall the administrative law officer have the authority to impose a penalty of imprisonment; or, except in cases to enforce the collection of any tax imposed and collected by the city, where this limitation shall not apply, impose a fine in excess of $50,000.00 exclusive of costs of enforcement or costs imposed to secure compliance with this code.

(m) In the issuance of a final determination of liability, an administrative law officer shall inform the respondent of his or her right to seek judicial review of the final determination.

(Added. Coun. J. 7-10-96, p. 24982; Amend. 11-12-97, p. 56813; 4-29-98, p. 66564)

§2-14-078 Default.

(a) If at the time set for a hearing the recipient of a notice of violation or a notice of hearing, or his or her attorney of record, fails to appear, the administrative law officer may find the recipient in default and proceed with the hearing and accept evidence relevant to the existence of a code violation and conclude with a finding, decision and order. A copy of the order or default shall be served in any manner permitted by Section 2-14-074(c).

(b) The recipient of a notice of violation or a notice of hearing who is found to be in default may petition the administrative law officer to set aside the order of default and set a new hearing date in accordance with Section 2-14-108.

(Added. Coun. J. 7-10-96, p. 24982; Amend. 4-29-98, p. 66564)

§2-14-080 Subpoenas.

(a) An administrative law officer may issue a subpoena only if he or she determines that the testimony of the witnesses or the documents or items sought by the subpoena are necessary to present evidence that is:

(i) Relevant to the case; and

(ii) Relates to a contested issue in the case.

(b) A subpoena issued under this chapter shall identify:

(i) The person to whom it is directed;

(ii) The documents or other items sought by the subpoena, if any;

(iii) The date for the appearance of the witnesses and the production of the documents or other items described in the subpoena;

(iv) The time for the appearance of the witnesses and the production of the documents or other items described in the subpoena; and

(v) The place for the appearance of the witnesses and the production of the documents or other items described in the subpoena.

(c) In no event shall the date identified for the appearance of the witnesses or the production of the documents or other items be less than seven days after service of the subpoena.

(d) Within three business days of being served with a subpoena issued in accordance with this chapter, the recipient of the subpoena may appeal the order authorizing the issuance of the subpoena to an administrative law officer, who shall not be the same administrative law officer who ordered the issuance of the subpoena.

(Added. Coun. J. 7-10-96, p. 24982; Amend 4-29-98, p. 66564)

§2-14-090 Compliance bond.

In order to ensure that code violations are remedied or fines are paid in a timely manner, an administrative law officer, upon issuing a final determination of liability, may require a code violator to post with the city a compliance bond

or, as appropriate, to consent to the granting and recording of a lien against titled property. Bonds and liens shall be approved by the city comptroller and the corporation counsel as to form and amount. Whenever it is necessary for the city to make repairs or otherwise expend funds relating to a code violation for which a bond was posted, or whenever fines or costs remain unpaid after a code violator has exhausted or failed to exhaust judicial review procedures, the administrative law officer may, after giving the parties notice and opportunity to be heard, issue an order permitting the city to draw against the bond in an appropriate amount, or to foreclose on the lien. The administrative law officer shall order the bond or the titled property or proceeds from the titled property, less the costs incurred by the city, returned to the code violator upon proof of compliance with the applicable code provisions and the payment of applicable fines or costs.
(Added. Coun. J. 7-10-96, p. 24982; Amend 4-29-98, p. 66564)

§2-14-100 Violations of orders.

(a) Elements of the Offense. A person violates this section if he or she:

(1) Receives notice and an opportunity to be heard under this code; and

(2) Knowingly fails to comply with an order issued by an administrative law officer under this chapter, including any requirement of a subpoena.

Each day that the violation occurs shall be considered a separate and distinct offense.

(b) Defenses. It shall be an affirmative defense to this section that a court of competent jurisdiction stayed the order issued by the administrative law officer prior to the effective date of the order.

(c) Prohibited Defenses. It is not a defense to this section that a person:

(1) Came into compliance or attempted to come into compliance with the order after the date the order by its terms required compliance; or

(2) Sought judicial review of the order but failed to obtain a stay of the order prior to the date the order by its terms required compliance.

(d) Sentence. A person convicted under this section shall be punished by:

(1) A fine of not less than $200.00 and not more than $500.00 for each offense;

(2) Incarceration for not more than 180 days for each offense; and/or

(3) An order to perform community service for a period not to exceed 200 hours for each offense.

However, whenever the order giving rise to the offense is an order of abatement pursuant to Chapter 7-4, Section 8-4-090 or Section 1 3-12-145 of this code, the sentence shall include a mandatory minimum sentence of no less than four days incarceration.

(e) Venue. The corporation counsel shall institute actions under this section in a court of competent jurisdiction.
(Added. Coun. J. 7-10-96, p. 24982; Amend 4-29-98, p. 66564; Amend. 8-30-00, p. 40306)

§2-14-101 Seized/unclaimed property.

After an administrative law officer has issued a final determination of liability or no liability, any property seized by the city in relation to the subject matter of the final determination of liability or no liability that is not forfeited by operation of law may be reclaimed by the lawful owner provided

that all penalties and fees have been paid. The procedures for the reclamation shall be within the discretion of the department head of the city department or agency charged with maintaining custody of the property. After the expiration of time during which judicial review of the final determination of liability may be sought or 35 days after the final determination of no liability, unless stayed by a court of competent jurisdiction, any property not so reclaimed may be disposed of by the city department or agency charged with maintaining custody of the property as provided by law.
(Added. Coun. J. 4-29-98, p. 66564)

§2-14-102 Review under the administrative review law.

Any final decision by the department of administrative hearings that a code violation does or does not exist shall constitute a final determination for purposes of judicial review and shall be subject to review under the Illinois Administrative Review Law, except as otherwise may be provided by law for decisions issued prior to the effective date of this ordinance.
(Added. Coun. J. 4-29-98, p. 66564)

§2-14-103 Enforcement of administrative law officer's order.

(a) Any fine, other sanction or costs imposed by an administrative law officer's order that remain unpaid after the exhaustion of, or the failure to exhaust, judicial review procedures shall be a debt due and owing the city and, as such, may be collected in accordance with applicable law.

(b) After the expiration of the period in which judicial review may be sought, unless stayed by a court of competent jurisdiction, the findings, decision and order of an administrative law officer may be enforced in the same manner as a judgment entered by a court of competent jurisdiction.

(c) In any case in which a respondent fails to comply with an administrative law officer's order to correct a code violation or imposing a fine or other sanction as a result of a code violation, any expenses incurred by the city to enforce the administrative law officer's order, including but not limited to attorney's fees, court costs and costs related to property demolition or foreclosure, after they are fixed by a court of competent jurisdiction or an administrative law officer, shall be a debt due and owing the city. Prior to any expenses being fixed by an administrative law officer, the respondent shall be provided with notice that states that the respondent shall appear at a hearing before an administrative law officer to determine whether the respondent has failed to comply with the administrative law officer's order. The notice shall set the time for the hearing, which shall not be less than seven days from the date that notice is served. Notice shall be served by first class mail and the seven-day period shall begin to run on the date that the notice was deposited in the mail.

(d) Upon being recorded in the manner required by Article XII of the Code of Civil Procedure or by the Uniform Commercial Code, a lien shall be imposed on the real estate or personal estate, or both, of the respondent in the amount of a debt due and owing the city. The lien may be enforced in the same manner as a judgment lien pursuant to a judgment of a court of competent jurisdiction.

(e) Nothing in this section shall prevent the city from enforcing or seeking to enforce any order of an administrative law officer in any manner which is in accordance with applicable law.
(Added. Coun. J. 4-29-98, p. 66564)

§2-14-110 Election of remedies.

In no case may the department of administrative hearings conduct an administrative adjudication proceeding for an alleged violation of the Municipal Code where the requested remedy is a punishment of imprisonment; provided, however, where a violation of the code is punishable by fines and other penalties in addition to imprisonment, the city may elect to institute an action with the department of administrative hearings and thereby waive any imprisonment for the code violation. Nothing in this chapter, however, shall preclude the city from seeking the remedy of imprisonment in a court of law, including imprisonment for failure to comply with the order of an administrative law officer, pursuant to Section 2-14-100.
(Added. Coun. J. 7-10-96, p. 24982; Amend. 11-12-97, p. 56813; 4-29-98, p. 66564)

§2-14-130 Other provisions not limiting.

(a) Notwithstanding any other provision of the Municipal Code, all provisions of the code, except for those specified in Section 2-14-190(a), may be enforced by instituting an administrative adjudication proceeding with the department of administrative hearings as provided in this chapter.

(b) Notwithstanding any other provision of the Municipal Code, any enforcement action, including but not limited to license suspension or revocation, which may be exercised by another department or agency of the city may also be exercised by the department of administrative hearings.

(c) Nothing in this chapter shall affect the jurisdiction of the mayor's license commission, the Chicago commission on human relations, the zoning board of appeals, the personnel board, the board of ethics, the police board, or the commission on Chicago landmarks.
(Added. Coun. J. 7-10-96, p. 24982; Amend. 11-12-97, p. 56813; 4-29-98, p. 66564)

§2-14-132 Impoundment.

(1) Whenever the owner of a vehicle seized and impounded pursuant to Section 3-46-076, 4-68-195, 7-24-225, 7-24-226, 7-28-390, 7-28-440, 8-4-130, 8-8-060, 8-16-020, 8-20-015, 9-12-090, 9-80-220, 9-92-035, 9-112-555, 11-4-1115, 11-4-1410, 11-4-1500 or 15-20-270 of this code requests a preliminary hearing in person and in writing at the department of administrative hearings, within 15 days after the vehicle is seized and impounded an administrative law officer of the department of administrative hearings shall conduct such preliminary hearing within 48 hours of the request, excluding Saturdays, Sundays and legal holidays, unless the vehicle was seized and impounded pursuant to Section 7-24-225 and the department of police determines that it must retain custody of the vehicle under applicable state or federal forfeiture law. If, after the preliminary hearing, the administrative law officer determines that there is probable cause to believe that the vehicle was

used in a violation of this code for which seizure and impoundment applies, or, if the impoundment is pursuant to Section 9-92-035, that the subject vehicle is eligible for impoundment under that section, the administrative law officer shall order the continued impoundment of the vehicle as provided in this section unless the owner of the vehicle pays to the city the amount of the administrative penalty prescribed for the code violation plus fees for towing and storing the vehicle. If the vehicle is also subject to immobilization for unpaid final determinations of parking and/or compliance violations, the owner of the vehicle must also pay the amounts due for all such outstanding violations prior to the release of the vehicle. If the administrative law officer determines that there is no such probable cause, or, if the impoundment is pursuant to Section 9-92-035, that the subject vehicle has previously been determined not to be eligible for impoundment under that section, the vehicle will be returned without penalty or other fees.

(2) Within 10 days after a vehicle is seized and impounded, the department of streets and sanitation or other appropriate department shall notify by certified mail the owner of record, any lien holder of record of the owner's right to request a hearing before the department of administrative hearings to challenge whether a violation of this code for which seizure and impoundment applies has occurred or, if the impoundment is pursuant to Section 9-92-035, whether the subject vehicle is eligible for impoundment under that section. However, no such notice need be sent to the owner of record if the owner is personally served with the notice within 10 days after the vehicle is seized and impounded, and the owner acknowledges receipt of the notice in writing. A copy of the notice shall be forwarded to the department of administrative hearings. The notice shall state the penalties that may be imposed if no hearing is requested, including that a vehicle not released by payment of the penalty and fees and remaining in the city pound may be sold or disposed of by the city in accordance with applicable law. The owner of record seeking a hearing must file a written request for a hearing with the department of administrative hearings no later than 15 days after notice was mailed or otherwise given under this subsection. The hearing date must be no more than 30 days after a request for a hearing has been filed. If, after the hearing, the administrative law officer determines by a preponderance of the evidence that the vehicle was used in the violation, or, if the impoundment is pursuant to Section 9-92-035, that the subject vehicle was properly impounded under that section, the administrative law officer shall enter an order finding the owner of record liable to the city for the amount of the administrative penalty prescribed for the violation, plus towing and storage fees. If, after a hearing, the administrative law officer does not determine by a preponderance of the evidence that the vehicle was used in such a violation, the administrative law officer shall enter an order finding for the owner and for the return of the vehicle or previously paid penalty and fees; provided that if the vehicle was seized and impounded pursuant to Section 7-24-225, the vehicle shall not be returned unless and until the city receives notice from the appropriate state, or where applicable, federal officials that (i) forfeiture proceedings will not be instituted; or (ii) forfeiture proceedings have concluded and there is a settlement or a court order providing that the vehicle shall be returned to the owner of record. If the owner of record requests a full hearing but fails to appear at the hearing or fails to request a hearing in a timely

manner, the owner of record shall be deemed to have waived his or her right to a hearing and an administrative law officer of the department of administrative hearings shall enter a default order in favor of the city in the amount of the administrative penalty prescribed for the violation, plus towing and storage fees. However, if the owner of record pays such penalty and fees and the vehicle is returned to the owner, no default order need be entered if the owner is informed of his or her right to a hearing and signs a written waiver, in which case an order of liability shall be deemed to have been made when the city receives the written waiver.

(3) An administrative penalty, plus towing and storage fees, imposed pursuant to this section shall constitute a debt due and owing to the city which may be enforced pursuant to Section 2-14-103 or in any other manner provided by law. Any amounts paid pursuant to this section shall be applied to the penalty. Except as provided otherwise in this section, a vehicle shall continue to be impounded until (1) the administrative penalty, plus any applicable towing and storage fees, plus all amounts due for outstanding final determinations of parking and/or compliance violations (if the vehicle is also subject to immobilization for unpaid final determinations of parking and/or compliance violations), is paid to the city, in which case possession of the vehicle shall be given to the person who is legally entitled to possess the vehicle; or (2) the vehicle is sold or otherwise disposed of to satisfy a judgment or enforce a lien as provided by law. Notwithstanding any other provision of this section, whenever a person with a lien of record against a vehicle impounded under this section has commenced foreclosure proceedings, possession of the vehicle shall be given to that person if he or she pays the applicable towing and storage fees and agrees in writing to refund to the city the net proceeds of any foreclosure sale, less any amounts necessary to pay all lien holders of record, up to the total amount of penalties imposed under this section. Notwithstanding any other provision of this section, no vehicle that was seized and impounded pursuant to Section 7-24-225 shall be returned to the record owner unless and until the city has received notice from the appropriate state, or where applicable, federal officials that (i) forfeiture proceedings will not be instituted; or (ii) forfeiture proceedings have concluded and there is a settlement or a court order providing that the vehicle shall be returned to the owner of record.

(4) Any motor vehicle that is not reclaimed within 10 days after the expiration of the time during which the owner of record may seek judicial review of the city's action under this section, or, if judicial review is sought, the time at which a final judgment is rendered in favor of the city, or the time a final administrative decision is rendered against an owner of record who is in default may be disposed of as an unclaimed vehicle as provided by law; provided that, if the vehicle was seized and impounded pursuant to Section 7-24-225 and proceedings have been instituted under state or federal drug asset forfeiture laws, the vehicle may not be disposed of by the city except as consistent with those proceedings.

(5) As used in this section, "owner of record" of a vehicle means the record titleholder and includes, for purposes of enforcing Section 3-46-076, the "license holder of a ground transportation vehicle" as that term is defined in Chapter 3-46.

(6) Fees for towing and storage of a vehicle under this section shall be the same as those charged pursuant to Chapter 9-92 of this code.

(7) In a hearing on the property of impoundment under Section 7-24-226, any sworn or affirmed report, including a report prepared in compliance with Section 11-501.1 of the Illinois Vehicle Code, that (a) is prepared in the performance of a law enforcement officer's duties and (b) sufficiently describes the circumstances leading to the impoundment, shall be admissible evidence of the vehicle owner's liability under Section 7-24-226 of this code, and shall support a finding of the vehicle owner's liability under Section 7-24-226, unless rebutted by clear and convincing evidence.

(8) For purposes of this section, a vehicle is not considered to have been used in a violation that would render the vehicle eligible for towing if: (1) the vehicle used in the violation was stolen at the time and the theft was reported to the appropriate police authorities within 24 hours after the theft was discovered or reasonably should have been discovered; (2) the vehicle was operating as a common carrier and the violation occurred without the knowledge of the person in control of the vehicle; or (3) the alleged owner provides adequate proof that the vehicle had been sold to another person prior to the violation.

(Added. Coun. J. 4-29-98, p. 66564; Amend. 7-21-99, p. 9095; 12-15-99, p. 21529; 3-15-00, p. 27700; 6-6-01, p. 60138; 12-12-01, p. 76443; 7-31-02, p. 90675; 12-4-02, p. 99026; 5-7-03, p. 564; 9-4-03, p. 7167; 11-3-04, pr 34974)

Article II. Vehicle Hearings Division

§2-14-140 Vehicle hearings division.

(a) The department of administrative hearings shall operate a system of administrative adjudication of violations of ordinances regulating vehicular standing, parking and compliance in accordance with Chapter 9-100 of this code.

(b) The system shall be operated within a vehicle hearings division created within the department of administrative hearings.

(Added. Coun. J. 7-10-96, p. 24982; Amend. 11-12-97, p. 56813; 4-29-98, p. 66564)

Article III. Buildings Hearings Division

§2-14-154 Rights of occupants.

No action for eviction, abatement of a nuisance, forcible entry and detainer or other similar action, including but not limited to increase of rent, decrease of services and refusal to renew a lease, shall be threatened or instituted against an occupant of a building or other structure because such occupant has in good faith agreed to testify or testified at an administrative hearing before the department of administrative hearings or has complained of a building code violation to the landlord, to a government agency, public official or elected representative, or to a community organization or news medium. Nothing in this section shall be construed to limit any rights or defenses available to tenants or other occupants under other city ordinances or applicable law.

(Added. Coun. J. 4-29-98, p. 66564)

§2-14-155 Defenses to building code violations.

It shall be a defense to a building code violation adjudicated under this article, if the owner, manager, person exercising control, his attorney, or any other agent or representative proves to the administrative law officer that:

(a) The building code violation alleged in the notice did not in fact exist or at the time of inspection resulting in the notice;

(b) At the time of the hearing on the issue of whether the building code violation does or does not exist, the violation has been remedied or removed. This subsection (b) shall not create a defense to a person or entity that is an architect, structural engineer, contractor or builder who has been charged with a violation of Section 13-12-050 or Section 3-12-060 of this Code. However, for violations of Sections 13-196-400 through 13-196-440 of this Code, it shall be a defense under this subsection only where the violation has been remedied or removed within seven days of service of notice of the building code violations as provided under Section 2-14-152;

(c) The building code violation has been caused by the current building occupants and that in spite of reasonable attempts by the owner, manager, or person exercising control to maintain the building free of such violations, the current occupants continued to cause the violations;

(d) An occupant or resident of the building has refused entry to the owner or his agent to all or a part of the building for the purpose of correcting the building code violation.

This section does not create a defense to a person who has been charged with encouraging or permitting illegal activity on any premises in violation of Section 8-4-090 of this code, or with a violation of Sections 13-124-140, 13-124-150 or 13-124-170 of this code.

(Added. Coun. J. 4-29-98, p. 66564; Amend. 4-21-99, p. 92160; Amend. 7-25-01, p.64898; 12-4-02, p. 99026, 100455)

Article VI. Municipal Hearings Division

§2-14-190 Municipal hearings division—Jurisdiction.

(a) The department of administrative hearings is authorized to establish a system of administrative adjudication for the enforcement of all provisions of the Municipal Code that are not adjudicated by the vehicle, buildings, environmental safety or consumer affairs hearings divisions, except that it shall not adjudicate violations of the following chapters and sections: Chapter 4-92 (Massage Establishments and Massage Services); Chapter 4-144 (Weapons); Section 7-28-190 (Health nuisances—Throwing objects into roadways); Chapter 8-20 (Weapons), other than Section 8-20-015 (Unlawful firearm in motor vehicle—Impoundment); and Chapter 8-24 (Firearms and Other Weapons).

(b) The system may be operated within a municipal hearings division or such other division or divisions established by the director within the department of administrative hearings.

(c) Notwithstanding any other provision of this code, except Section 2-14-130(c), the jurisdiction granted to the department of administrative hearings by this article shall be exercised exclusively by the department of administrative hearings upon written notification by the director to any affected

department or agency of the city. Subsequent to the issuance of the written notification, no city department or agency, except those specified in Section 2-14-130(c), may adjudicate code provisions identified in the notice other than the department of administrative hearings.
(Added. Coun. J. 7-10-96, p. 24982; Amend. 11-12-97, p. 56813; 4-29-98, p. 66564)

§2-14-195 Fine of $10,000.00 or more—Petition for review to the director.

(a) Except as otherwise provided in Section 3-4-340(H)(5), in any matter adjudicated by the municipal hearings division where an administrative law officer imposes or the city seeks a fine or judgment of $10,000.00 or more, either party may, within 10 business days of said fine or judgment determination, petition the director of the department of administrative hearings or his or her designee to review the determination as well as the underlying final determination of liability. A final decision by the director or his or her designee to reverse or modify any determination shall be based on the record created by the administrative law officer, and the director shall not make any determination of credibility without consulting the administrative law officer.

(b) If the director or his or her designee does not act on a petition within 10 business days after receiving the petition, the petition shall be deemed denied on that date and the determination of the administrative law officer shall be final.

(c) The failure to submit a petition for review shall not waive or affect a party's right to judicial review.
(Added. Coun. J. 7-10-96, p. 24982; Amend. 11-12-97, p. 56813; 4-29-98, p. 66564)

§2-14-200 Eviction proceedings.

(a) The provisions of Article I of this chapter shall apply to eviction proceedings except to the extent that those provisions are inconsistent with this section. At a proceeding under this section, notwithstanding Section 2-14-076 of this code, a violation notice shall not be treated as prima facie evidence.

(b) Whenever an administrative law officer determines that a tenant is subject to eviction based upon a pattern of controlled substance violations under Chapter 8-28, he or she will issue an order of eviction effective on a specified date not less than 30 days after the date the order is issued. On that date and thereafter the landlord shall be entitled to re-enter and take possession of the premises. Any person who violates an order of eviction issued under this section by failing to surrender the premises shall be subject to prosecution under Section 2-14-100.

(c) Whenever an administrative law officer issues an eviction order, he or she may order the landlord to retain the services of a licensed private security contractor to ensure the removal of the tenant from the premises in accordance with the order. In addition, the corporation counsel is hereby authorized to enter into an intergovernmental agreement with the county of Cook under which the city will authorize the sheriff's police of that county to take appropriate action to ensure the removal of a tenant from premises in accordance with an order of eviction issued under this section. Any such agreement shall be subject to the approval of the corporation counsel and executed by the mayor. If the dwelling unit or premises are owned, managed or subsidized by a public housing agency, the public housing authority may be a party to the intergovernmental agreement.

(d) If the tenant does not vacate and remove his or her personal property from the premises as of the effective date of an eviction order specified in subsection (b), the landlord shall dispose of the property as provided in subsection (f) of Section 5-12-130.

(Added. Coun. J. 8-30-00, p. 40306)

CHAPTER 2-24
DEPARTMENT OF CONSUMER SERVICES
(Complete Chapter)

Sections:

2-24-010 Establishment—Composition.
2-24-020 Commissioner—Appointment and authority.
2-24-030 Employees.
2-24-040 Commissioner—Powers and duties designated.
2-24-041 Commercial passenger vessels.
2-24-050 Interfering with or obstructing official duties unlawful.
2-24-060 Prohibited acts—Enforcement.
2-24-070 Failure to secure required license, permit or franchise.
2-24-080 Violation—Penalty.

§2-24-010 Establishment—Composition.

There is hereby created and established an executive department of the municipal government of the city of Chicago which shall be known as the department of consumer services. The department shall embrace a commissioner of consumer services, the city's cable administrator and such other deputies, assistants, and employees as the city council may provide by the annual appropriation ordinance.

(Prior code § 16-1: Amend. Coun. J. 11-19-03, p. 13426)

§2-24-020 Commissioner—Appointment and authority.

There is hereby created the office of commissioner of consumer services. The commissioner shall be the head of the department of consumer services, and shall have supervision over the said department. The commissioner shall be appointed by the mayor, by and with the advice and consent of the city council.

(Prior code § 16-2)

§2-24-030 Employees.

All employees of the department of consumer services shall be under the direction and supervision of the commissioner and shall perform such duties as may be required of them by the commissioner by the provisions of this code.

(Prior code § 16-3)

§2-24-040 Commissioner—Powers and duties designated.

The duties and powers of the commissioner of consumer services shall be as follows:

1. To investigate complaints to ascertain whether any person has engaged in, is engaging in, or is about to engage in, any illegal, fraudulent or other deceptive practices in connection with the sale for cash or on credit or advertisement of any merchandise to any consumer, any practices which violate any law governing or regulating such sales and advertisements, and to report forthwith to the corporation counsel, the state's attorney, the attorney general, and such other governmental agency as may have jurisdiction or an interest in the subject matter, the names and places of business of all persons suspected of having engaged in fraud, false pretense, misrepresentation and other deceptive practices as described herein;

2. To be in control of the administration and enforcement of all ordinances relating to public passenger vehicles and ambulances, and make such investigations as the commissioner deems necessary for the proper performance of his functions;

3. To adopt such orders, rules and regulations as he may deem expedient for the proper administration and enforcement of the provisions of this code and ordinances governing public chauffeurs and public passenger vehicles and their operation. The commissioner shall give public notice of any proposed rule or regulation, prior to its effective date, in one or more newspapers of general circulation, and in no case shall the publication be before 10 days prior to the effective date of the proposed rule or regulation, or an amendment to any rule or regulation. Such public notice shall include information concerning where the rule or regulation can be reviewed and where comments may be directed. Notice of every such order, rule and regulation shall be given to all persons affected, and copies of all such rules and regulations shall be published and kept on file in the department;

4. To keep a register containing the names and Chicago addresses of all cabmen, coachmen and their affiliates, a description of their public passenger vehicle with their license numbers and a complete record of all inspections of such vehicles and their equipment. He shall also keep a register containing the names and Chicago addresses of all public chauffeurs, together with their license numbers;

5. To keep a complete record of all suspensions and revocations of public passenger vehicle licenses and public chauffeur licenses which shall be kept on file with the original applications for such licenses;

6. To do research, conduct educational programs, and disseminate information to the public regarding consumer affairs;

7. To supervise the investigation, execution and enforcement of all laws, ordinances, rules, and regulations contained in the Toy Safety Ordinance, Chapter 7-36 and in the Condominium Ordinance, Chapter 13-72 of this code;

8. To advise, consult and cooperate with other agencies of the county, state, and federal governments in furtherance of the duties prescribed herein;

9. To prepare and maintain all records as required by ordinance or as may be necessary for the efficient and orderly conduct of the business of this department;

10. To investigate and make recommendations, from time to time, to the mayor with respect to additions or revisions of the Municipal Code as may be necessary for the enforcement and regulations of the duties and powers described herein;

11. To enforce the provisions of Chapters 4-32, 4-60, 4-92, 4-204, 4-228 and 4-276 of this code, including all rules and regulations promulgated thereunder, and to oversee the enforcement of the provisions of Chapters 4-280 and 4-284 of this code and of the various cable franchises awared by the city council;

12. To inspect and examine, or cause to be inspected and examined, all standard test meter and meters for electricity, as provided in Chapters 4-296 and 14-4 of this code, and gas meters, as provided in Chapter 11-20 of this code;

13. To inspect and examine or cause to be inspected or examined all truck scales of a capacity of three tons or upwards;

14. To inspect and examine or cause to be inspected or examined once each year all other weights, measures, scales and weighing and measuring devices, automatic or mechanical pumps or liquid measuring devices at the stores and places where they may be used;

15. To stamp with a suitable seal all weights, measures, scales and weighing and measuring devices which the commissioner may find accurate and deliver to the owners thereof certificates of their accuracy. The commissioner shall also provide a table of tolerances and specifications in conformity with those approved by the National Bureau of Standards. Once the commissioner has caused a stamp or seal to be affixed to any weights, measures, scales, weighing or measuring device as provided herein, it shall be unlawful for any person to remove, destroy or erase the said stamp or seal;

16. To investigate and determine, or cause to be investigated and determined, whether all persons required by this code to pay a tax or secure licenses, permits and franchises have complied with such provisions, and in cases of evasion of payment, or failure to obtain the necessary license, permit or franchise, the commissioner shall issue the appropriate notice of violation and shall request the corporation counsel to institute an appropriate legal proceeding to enforce such provisions and collections;

17. To establish a compliance procedure to determine whether violations have been corrected. If such violation or violations have not been corrected within 30 days from date of first inspection showing such violation or violations to have existed, a request for prosecution shall be forwarded to the corporation counsel; provided, however, that if within 30 days the person subject to prosecution shall have presented an executed contract for the completion of the work necessary to correct such violation or violations and shall have obtained all permits required by this code, prosecution may be withheld for a period not to exceed 45 days;

18. (a) To operate and maintain one or more scales for the weighing of vehicles that operate on the public ways of the city in order to determine whether such vehicles are in violation of the weight limitations imposed by Chapter 9-72 of this code, and to enforce those limitations with the assistance of the department of police,

(b) Prior to the exercise of exclusive jurisdiction by the department of administrative hearings in accordance with Section 2-14-190 of this code, the commissioner may by rule establish a system by which the commissioner may impose administrative fines on persons who violate the weight limitations imposed by this code. The rules establishing the system shall provide for:

(1) The imposition of fines only after the person accused of a violation has been given notice and an opportunity to be heard. Fines imposed for violation of weight limitations shall be as provided in the Illinois Motor Vehicle Code,

(2) The appointment of hearing officers to hear the testimony of witnesses under oath, evaluate evidence, and make recommendations to the commissioner. All hearing officers shall be attorneys licensed to practice law in Illinois,

(c) After the exercise of exclusive jurisdiction by the department of administrative hearings in accordance with Section 2-14-190 of this code, the commissioner may institute an action with the department of administrative hearings in order to determine liability and seek administrative fines for violations of weight limitations imposed by this code. Fines imposed for a violation of weight limitations shall be as provided in the Illinois Motor Vehicle Code,

(d) The findings by the commissioner or the department of administrative hearings of a violation of vehicle weight limitations and the imposition of any fine therefor may be appealed to the circuit court as provided by law;

19. To take any and all actions necessary or helpful for carrying out all child support compliance ordinances throughout this code, including but not limited to investigating the child support payment records of all city license applicants, licensees, applicants for employment, employees, bidders, potential contractors, contractors, loan applicants, borrowers and, where applicable, any substantial owner thereof;

20. To review city records regarding property owners who pay city water bills and persons who have worker's compensation claims against the city, in cooperation with the commissioner of water management and the corporation counsel, respectively, to identify those with child support delinquencies and (i) to provide information on such persons to the appropriate Cook County and state of Illinois governmental entities, to the extent allowed by law, to assist those offices in enforcement of child support obligations and, further, (ii) to provide the names of city property owners and worker's compensation claimants, and business addresses, where known, to persons seeking to enforce court-ordered child support arrearages and child support withholding notices, and their legal representatives, to the extent allowed by law, on the condition that such information be used solely for the purpose of assisting in child support enforcement; provided that the names and identifying information of persons seeking to enforce child support orders shall be deemed confidential.

(Prior code § 16-4; Amend. Coun. J. 12-29-87, p. 9169; 12-11-91, p. 10975; 5-19-93, p. 32394; 7-1-96, p. 24982; 11-12-97, p. 56813; 7-29-98, p. 75051; 12-4-02, p. 99026; 11-19-03, p. 13426; 3-31-04, p. 20916)

§2-24-041 Commercial passenger vessels.

(a) The commissioner of consumer services may promulgate and enforce rules or regulations applicable to commercial passenger vessels designed to protect and promote the health, safety and welfare of passengers who embark on and disembark from commercial passenger vessels in the city of Chicago. Such rules and regulations may include, but are not limited to, provisions applicable to the commercial passenger vessel owner's license required by this section, fines and penalties including impoundment for unlicensed operation and limitations on customer solicitation. The commissioner may establish fines, not to exceed $750.00 per offense, for violations of this section or the regulations promulgated pursuant to this section. In addition to such fines, the violation of any provision of this section or of the regulations promulgated hereunder may result in any one or more of the following: (1) suspension or revocation of the commercial passenger vessel owner's license, (2) restitution, and (3) injunctive and other equitable relief. For purposes of this section, "commercial passenger vessel" shall be defined as set forth in Section 4-4-311 of this code.

(b) No person may engage in the business of operating one or more commercial passenger vessels on any public or private property within the city without first obtaining a commercial passenger vessel owner's license from the commissioner of consumer services. The fee for such a license, and for any renewals, shall be $75.00 per license term if every vessel operated pursuant to the license will carry fewer than 20 passengers. The fee for such a license, and for any renewals, shall be $350.00 per license term if any one or more vessels operated pursuant to the license will carry 20 or more passengers. The license term shall be from May 1 of each year through April 30 of the following year. Requirements for issuance and renewals of such a license shall be payment of the required fee and compliance with the department of consumer services rules and regulations pertaining to commercial passenger vessels. The license shall be in addition to any other license required by law; provided, however, that a commercial passenger vessel licensed pursuant to this section shall not be required to obtain a public place of amusement license for the vessel.

(c) Any licensee who cancels a commercial passenger vessel excursion or event without proper cause shall refund to all customers the full amount of any funds advanced for that excursion or event.

(d) In addition to fines and other penalties as set forth herein, any person subject to the commercial passenger vessel owner's license who operates without such a license shall be subject to impoundment, at the commissioner's direction, of any commercial passenger vessel used in unlicensed operation.
(Added. Coun. J. 10-7-93, p. 38999; Amend. 4-21-99, p. 92450)

§2-24-050 Interfering with or obstructing official duties unlawful.

No person shall in any way or manner obstruct the commissioner of consumer services, his deputies, assistants and employees, in the performance of his duties or refuse to permit the examination of any document relating to the sale or advertisement of any commodity or to weigh or measure any article of merchandise or any other commodity whatsoever in order that the said commissioner of consumer services, his deputies, assistants and employees, may ascertain the form and substance of any document or advertisement or the weight or measure of any article of merchandise, or any other commodity whatsoever which may be sold or offered for sale. Further it shall be unlawful for any person to falsely represent that he is the commissioner of consumer services, or any of his deputies, assistants or employees.
(Prior code § 16-5)

§2-24-060 Prohibited acts—Enforcement.

(a) No person shall engage in any act of consumer fraud, unfair method of competition or deceptive practice while conducting any trade or business in the city. Any conduct constituting an unlawful practice under the Consumer Fraud and Deceptive Business Practices Act, Illinois Revised Statutes Chapter 121-1/2, paragraph 261 et seq., as now or hereafter amended, or constituting a violation of Sections 7-4-040, 7-4-050 or 7-4-060 of this code, shall be a violation of this section. In construing this section consideration shall be given to court interpretations relating to the Consumer Fraud and Deceptive Business Practices Act, Illinois Revised Statutes Chapter 121-1/2, paragraph 261 et seq. In construing this section consideration shall also be given to the interpretations of the Federal Trade Commission and the federal courts relating to Section 5(a) of the Federal Trade Commission Act, 15 U.S.C.A. Section 45. Nothing in this section shall be construed as permitting the regulation of any business to the extent that such regulation is not permitted under the statutory or home rule powers of the city.

(b) The commissioner of consumer services shall be charged with the enforcement of this section and shall construe this section in compliance with subsection (a).

(c) Compliance with applicable rules and regulations promulgated pursuant to the Consumer Fraud and Deceptive Business Practices Act and with court interpretations relating to such Act shall be an absolute defense to a finding of a violation of this section. Compliance with applicable Federal Trade Commission rules, regulations and guidelines, and with interpretations by the Federal Trade Commission and the federal courts relating to Section 5(a) of the Federal Trade Commission Act, 15 U.S.C.A. Section 45, shall be an absolute defense to a finding of a violation of this section.

(d) When it appears to the commissioner, after receiving a written complaint or otherwise, that a person has engaged in, is engaging in or is about to engage in a practice that is in violation of this section, the commissioner may, after serving a 30-day notice:

(1) Require that person to file on such terms as the commissioner may prescribe a statement or report in writing as to all relevant and material information;

(2) Examine any person in connection with relevant and material issues concerning the conduct of any trade or business;

(3) Examine any merchandise or sample thereof, any record, book, document, account or paper relevant and material to the inquiry;

(4) Retain copies of any record, book, document, account, paper or sample of merchandise that is produced in accordance with this section, and retain it in his or her possession until the completion of all proceedings in connection with which it is produced; and

(5) (i) Prior to the exercise of exclusive jurisdiction by the department of administrative hearings in accordance with Section 2-14-190(c) of this code, conduct hearings under oath on issues that are relevant and material to the inquiry. Such hearings shall be recorded on audio tape or by other appropriate means. All hearing officers shall be attorneys licensed to practice law in Illinois,

(ii) After the exercise of exclusive jurisdiction by the department of administrative hearings in accordance with Section 2-14-190(c) of this code, institute an action with the department of administrative hearings in order to determine liability and seek remedies authorized by this section.

(e) If, after completing an investigation pursuant to this section, the commissioner determines that a person has engaged in, is engaging in, or is about to engage in a practice prohibited by this section, the commissioner may:

(1) Order the person to discontinue the prohibited practice;

(2) Order the person to pay restitution to persons aggrieved by the practice;

(3) Request that the mayor take action under Section 4-4-280 of this code to revoke or suspend a license of the person; or

(4) Request the city to bring an action in circuit court for injunctive relief or such other equitable relief that the commissioner considers appropriate.

(f) (1) Prior to the exercise of exclusive jurisdiction by the department of administrative hearings in accordance with Section 2-14-190(c) of this code, the commissioner may by rule establish a system by which the commissioner may impose administrative fines on persons who violate this section. Each day that a violation occurs shall be considered a separate and distinct offense. The rules establishing the system shall:

(i) Provide for the imposition of fines only after the person accused of the violations has been given notice and an opportunity to be heard;

(ii) Provide for the appointment of hearing officers to hear the testimony of witnesses under oath, evaluate evidence, and make recommendations to the commissioner. Such hearing shall be recorded on audio tape or by other appropriate means. All hearing officers shall be attorneys licensed to practice law in Illinois;

(iii) Prescribe minimum and maximum fine amounts for specific violations; provided that the maximum fine for a single violation shall not exceed $500.00.

The notice given under this subsection shall be made: (i) by first class or express mail or by overnight carrier; or (ii) by personal service; and shall specify the section of the code which was allegedly violated and the date, time and place of the alleged violation.

(2) After the exercise of exclusive jurisdiction by the department of administrative hearings in accordance with Section 2-14-190(c) of this code, the commissioner may institute an action with the department of administrative hearings in order to determine liability and seek remedies authorized by this section. The commissioner may by rule prescribe minimum and maximum fine amounts for specific violations; provided that the maximum fine for a single violation shall not exceed $500.00. Each day that a violation occurs shall be considered a separate and distinct offense.

(3) The commissioner may take action pursuant to paragraphs (3) and (4) of subsection (e) against any person who fails to pay a fine imposed under this subsection within a reasonable time as specified by the commissioner for such payment. Such action shall be stayed pending the appeal by any person of a fine imposed under this subsection.

(g) The findings of a violation of this section, any order issued by the commissioner, and the imposition of any fine under subsection (f), may be appealed to the mayor's license commission by the person against whom it is imposed and shall be subject to a de novo hearing wherein additional evidence may be adduced. Further appeal may be taken to the circuit court as provided by law. All orders and the imposition of any fine under this subsection shall be stayed pending appeal. The right to appeal to the mayor's license commission shall not apply to findings of a violation, orders, or fines imposed by the department of administrative hearings.

(h) A violation of this section does not preempt the city from prosecution under any other ordinance that the commissioner is authorized to enforce.

(Prior code § 16-6; Added. Coun. J. 4-6-90, p. 13833; Amend. 12-9-92, p. 25465; 11-5-93, p. 40561; 7-10-96, p. 24982; 11-12-97, p. 56813)

§2-24-070 Failure to secure required license, permit or franchise.

If any person conducts any trade or business in the city of Chicago without securing any license, permit or franchise required by the city for such activity, the commissioner of consumer services shall have the authority to order the person to discontinue such activity and to close the establishment in which the activity is conducted after serving a 30-day written notice on the statutory agent or on another person otherwise designated to receive legal documents. Nothing in this subsection shall prevent the commissioner from serving a notice of less than 30 days if a shorter notice period is authorized by an ordinance specifically regulating an activity.

(Prior code § 16-7; Added. Coun. J. 4-6-90, p. 13833)

§2-24-080 Violation—Penalty.

Any person who: (1) unless an appeal is pending, fails to obey an order issued by the commissioner of consumer services pursuant to this chapter; (2) unless an appeal is pending, fails to pay a fine imposed under Section 2-24-060 within a reasonable time specified by the commissioner; (3) makes a deliberately false or deliberately misleading information to the commissioner; or (4) deliberately interferes with an investigation conducted by the commissioner pursuant to this chapter; shall be subject to a fine of not less than $100.00 nor more than $500.00 or imprisonment for a period not to exceed six months, or both. Such violations shall be punishable as a misdemeanor pursuant to Section 1-2-1.1 of the Illinois Municipal Code, as amended. Any person who otherwise violates Section 2-24-060 shall be subject to a fine of not less than $50.00 nor more than $500.00. All sanctions imposed pursuant to this section shall be imposed only after a judicial hearing and only pursuant to an order of the circuit court.

(Prior code § 16-8; Added. Coun. J. 4-6-90, p. 13833; 3-31-04, p. 20916)

CHAPTER 2-36
FIRE DEPARTMENT
(Selected Sections)

Sections:

Article I. Organization

2-36-010 Department established—Composition.

Article IV. Bureau of Fire Prevention

2-36-250 Police department aid authorized—Scope.
2-36-270 Inspection of buildings—Right of entry—Standards.
2-36-280 Investigation of complaints—Notice of violations.

Article V. Bureau of Fire Control and Extinguishment

2-36-380 Fire apparatus—Authority to require aid in conveyance.
2-36-390 Fires—Authority of fire department personnel.
2-36-400 Fires—Cordon of limits.
2-36-410 Fires—Badges for admission within cordoned limits.
2-36-420 Fires—Removal or destruction of property authorized when.
2-36-430 Removal of hydrant obstructions.
2-36-440 Fires or emergencies—Power of arrest.
2-36-450 Recovery of property from fire.
2-36-460 Hindering firefighting activities unlawful.

Article I. Organization

§2-36-010 Department established—Composition.

There is hereby established an executive department of the city which shall be known as the fire department. The department shall include the fire commissioner, the bureau of fire control and extinguishment, the bureau of fire prevention, the bureau of fire instruction, and such employees as shall be provided for in the annual appropriation billed.
(Prior code § 12-1)

Article IV. Bureau of Fire Prevention

§2-36-250 Police department aid authorized—Scope.

The division marshal in charge of the bureau of fire prevention shall have the authority to call upon the department of police for aid in the enforcement of any fire regulations of this code.

It shall be the duty of the commissioner or any member of the police force, when so called upon by said division marshal or his duly authorized agent, to act according to the instructions of and to perform such duties as may be required of him in order to enforce or put into effect the fire regulations of this code.
(Prior code § 12-23)

§2-36-270 Inspection of buildings—Right of entry—Standards.

The division marshal in charge of the bureau of fire prevention and his assistants are hereby empowered to enter any building, structure or premises, whether completed or in the course of construction, for the purpose of determining whether such buildings, structures or premises have been or are being constructed and maintained in accordance with the fire regulations of this code. It shall be unlawful to exclude them from any such building, structure or premises.

The division marshal in charge of the bureau of fire prevention shall make, or cause to be made, regular inspections, with sufficient frequency to secure efficient supervision of all buildings, structures, or places used either for manufacturing or commercial purposes, or occupied or frequented by large numbers of people, and of all school buildings, public halls, churches, institutional buildings, theaters, multiple dwellings and all places of amusement, recreation or employment:

(a) To determine the safety of the occupants of such buildings, structures, or places in the event of fire, panic, or accident;

(b) To examine the working order and repair of all doors, fire escapes, firefighting appliances; the condition and maintenance of exits, corridors, stairways, and fire escapes and their approaches with regard to obstructions; the disposition, the quantity, arrangement and protection of stock, combustible material and rubbish, heating devices and ovens, flammable liquids and explosives with regard to safety from fire; the protection of hazardous machinery, appliances and apparatus; and

(c) To ascertain whether the fire regulations of this code are being efficiently carried out.

(Prior code § 12-25)

§2-36-280 Investigation of complaints—Notice of violations.

It shall be the duty of the division marshal in charge of the bureau of fire prevention to make an examination of any building, structure, or place when any citizen represents that any of the fire regulations of this code are being violated, or that combustible materials are kept in any place in the city in any insecure manner, or that doors, stairways, corridors, exits, or fire escapes in any factory, workshop, or place of employment, amusement, education, or recreation are obstructed or are not in a safe condition, or that any door or exit is kept locked or fastened during the time such places are occupied or frequented by employees or by the public, or that any building, structure, or place is occupied or crowded beyond the capacity of its exits, or that the heating apparatus, appliances, or devices in any building are insecure or dangerous, or that any building, structure, or place is being maintained in such a manner as to be a fire menace or dangerous in case of fire, panic, or accident. If such representation is found to be true, said division marshal shall give notice as provided for in Section 2-36-320 of this code.

(Prior code § 12-26)

Article V. Bureau of Fire Control and Extinguishment

§2-36-380 Fire apparatus—Authority to require aid in conveyance.

It shall be lawful for any member in charge of fire apparatus to require the aid of any motor vehicle or other source of power in drawing or conveying fire apparatus to the scene of a fire or other emergency. In case of refusal or neglect to assist as required in this section, or to comply with a requisition made thereunder, the offender shall be fined not less than $5.00 nor more than $20.00.

(Prior code § 12-36)

§2-36-390 Fires—Authority of fire department personnel.

All persons in the vicinity of a fire or other emergency shall be subject to the orders of the chief fire marshal or other member of the fire department in charge of the control and extinguishment thereof and of removal of property; provided, however, that no person not a member of the fire department shall be bound to obey any member of the fire department in charge at fires or other emergency unless such member shall wear an insignia indicating his status or that such status shall be made known to the person charged with obedience of orders as herein specified. The chief fire marshal or other member of the fire department in charge shall have power to arrest any person refusing to obey lawful orders issued in accordance with this section, and in event any person shall persist in refusing to obey such orders he shall be fined $5.00 for such offense.

(Prior code § 12-37)

§2-36-400 Fires—Cordon of limits.

The chief fire marshal or other member of the fire department in charge at fires or other emergency may prescribe and maintain the limits in the vicinity thereof within which no person may be permitted to enter except by his permission.

(Prior code § 12-38)

§2-36-410 Fires—Badges for admission within cordoned limits.

The chief fire marshal may issue badges to newspaper reporters upon the written request of their city editors, and to employees of gas, telephone, electric light, and high-tension wire companies upon the written request of any such company over the signature of its president and secretary when, in his discretion, the issuance of such badges is necessary to prevent the destruction of property or to serve the general public. The chief fire marshal or any other person acting in that capacity at his discretion may recall any badge so issued.

Any person entitled to a badge who exhibits it shall be admitted within the cordon of fire limits established by the chief fire marshal or other member in charge of any fire or other emergency, but the possession of such a badge shall not authorize the person holding it to enter a burning building except upon the express permission of the chief fire marshal or other member in charge of operations at the scene.

The badges shall be of distinctive character and different in form and appearance from those worn by members of the fire department. A register shall be maintained containing a list of the badges so issued together with their identifying numbers and the names and addresses and such other details as may be necessary to identify holders of them. All expenses incident to the issuance of such badges shall be borne by the applicants therefor, and the badges shall be returned by the persons holding them at the time of leaving the employment of the newspaper or company that obtained the badges for them. Aside from the cost of the badge, the recipient thereof shall deposit $2.00, which shall be refunded upon its return.

Any person who shall wear a badge as provided for in this section without authority, or who shall fail to return it upon leaving the employ of the newspaper or company which obtained it for him or upon recall by the chief

fire marshal, or who shall, after being admitted within the cordon of fire limits established as aforesaid, enter a burning building without express permission as provided herein, shall be fined not less than $10.00 nor more than $50.00 for each offense.
(Prior code § 12-39)

§2-36-420 Fires—Removal or destruction of property authorized when.
The chief fire marshal or other member in charge at a fire or other emergency shall have the power to cause the removal or destruction of any property whenever, in his judgment, it shall become necessary to do so to prevent the destruction of property or the communication of fire.
(Prior code § 12-40)

§2-36-430 Removal of hydrant obstructions.
The fire department may, at the risk, cost and expense of the owner or claimant thereof, remove any obstructions to fire hydrants existing contrary to obstruct the provisions of Section 11-12-080 of this code.
(Prior code § 12-41)

§2-36-440 Fires or emergencies—Power of arrest.
The chief fire marshal or any other member in command at the scene of a fire or other emergency, or while in charge of fire apparatus, companies, or units, shall, at the time the offense is committed or at any time thereafter, have the authority to arrest any person suspected of arson, incendiarism, or malicious mischief, or who conducts himself in a disorderly manner, or who refuses to obey such member while acting in the discharge of duty, or who illegally gives or transmits false alarms, or who wilfully, maliciously, or negligently causes damage to fire apparatus or houses. Said members shall be and they are hereby vested with the power and authority of police officers to command all persons to assist them in making such arrests.
(Prior code § 12-42)

§2-36-450 Recovery of property from fire.
No person shall be entitled to take away any property in the possession of the fire department saved from any fire until he shall make satisfactory proof of ownership thereof.
(Prior code § 12-43)

§2-36-460 Hindering firefighting activities unlawful.
No person shall wilfully hinder any police officer or fireman in the performance of his duty at a fire, or shall wilfully in any manner injure, deface or destroy any engine or fire apparatus belonging to the city. Any person violating any provision of this section shall be fined not less than $50.00 nor more than $200.00.
(Prior code § 12-44)

CHAPTER 2-56
OFFICE OF INSPECTOR GENERAL
(Complete Chapter)

Sections:

2-56-010 Establishment—Composition.
2-56-020 Inspector general—Appointment and authority.
2-56-030 Inspector general—Powers and duties.
2-56-040 Subpoena issuance and contents—Objections.
2-56-050 Conduct of city officers, employees and other entities.
2-56-060 Investigation reports.
2-56-070 Confidentiality of informants—Exceptions.
2-56-080 Investigations not concluded within six months.
2-56-090 Cooperation in investigations.
2-56-100 Retaliation prohibited—Penalty.
2-56-110 Files and reports confidential—Public statements authorized when.
2-56-120 Quarterly reports to city council.
2-56-130 Inspector general—Conditions for removal from office.
2-56-140 Obstructing or interfering with investigations—Penalty.
2-56-150 Political activities prohibited.
2-56-160 Violation—Penalty—Discharge or other discipline.
2-56-170 Severability.

§2-56-010 Establishment—Composition.

There is hereby established an office of the municipal government to be known as the office of inspector general, which shall include an inspector general and such deputies, assistants and other employees as may be provided in the annual appropriation ordinance.
(Prior code § 19-1; Added. Coun. J. 10-4-89, p. 5726)

§2-56-020 Inspector general—Appointment and authority.

The inspector general shall be appointed by the mayor, subject to approval of the city council, and shall have responsibility for the operation and management of the office of inspector general. He shall be appointed for a term of four years.
(Prior code § 19-2; Added. Coun. J. 10-4-89, p. 5726)

§2-56-030 Inspector general—Powers and duties.

In addition to other powers conferred herein, the inspector general shall have the following powers and duties:

(a) To receive and register complaints and information concerning misconduct, inefficiency and waste within the city government;

(b) To investigate the performance of governmental officers, employees, functions and programs, either in response to complaint or on the inspector general's own initiative, in order to detect and prevent misconduct, inefficiency and waste within the programs and operations of the city government;

(c) To promote economy, efficiency, effectiveness and integrity in the administration of the programs and operations of the city government by reviewing programs, identifying any inefficiencies, waste and potential for misconduct therein, and recommending to the mayor and the city council policies and methods for the elimination of inefficiencies and waste, and the prevention of misconduct;

(d) To report to the mayor concerning results of investigations undertaken by the office of inspector general;

(e) To request information related to an investigation from any employee, officer, agent or licensee of the city;

(f) To conduct public hearings, at his discretion, in the court of an investigation hereunder;

(g) To administer oaths and to examine witnesses under oath;

(h) To issue subpoenas to compel the attendance of witnesses for purposes of examination and the production of documents and other items for inspection and/or duplication. Issuance of subpoenas shall be subject to the restrictions contained in Section 2-56-040;

(i) To promulgate rules and regulations for the conduct of investigations and public hearings consistent with the requirements of due process of law and equal protection under the law.

(Prior code § 19-3; Added. Coun. J. 10-4-89, p. 5726)

§2-56-040 Subpoena issuance and contents—Objections.

The inspector general shall issue subpoenas only if (a) he is conducting an investigation authorized by this chapter; and (b) the investigation relates to misconduct within the programs and operation of the city government by any person described in Section 2-56-050; and (c) the inspector general has a reasonable belief that such misconduct has occurred; and the testimony of the witness or the documents or items sought by the subpoena are relevant to the investigation. A subpoena shall be served in the same manner as subpoenas issued under the Rules of the Illinois Supreme Court to compel appearance of a deponent, and subject to the same witness and mileage fees fixed by law for such subpoenas.

A subpoena issued under this chapter shall identify the person to whom it is directed and the documents or other items sought thereby, if any, and the date, time and place for the appearance of the witness and production of the documents or other items described in the subpoena. In no event shall the date for examination or production be less than seven days after service of the subpoena.

No later than the time for appearance or production required by the subpoena, the person to whom the subpoena is directed may object to the subpoena, in whole or in part. The objection shall be in writing, delivered to the inspector general, and shall specify the grounds for the objection. For seven days after receipt of a timely objection to a subpoena, the inspector general shall take no action to enforce the subpoena or to initiate prosecution of the person to whom the subpoena is directed. During this seven-day period, the inspector general shall consider the grounds for the objection and may attempt to resolve the objection through negotiation with the person to whom the subpoena is directed. The seven-day period may be extended by the inspector general in order to allow completion of any negotiations. The extension shall be in writing addressed to the person to whom the subpoena is directed, and shall specify the date on which the negotiation period will end. Negotiations may include such matters as the scope of the subpoena and the time, place and manner of response thereto. The filing of an objection to a subpoena, and negotia-

tions pursuant to an objection, shall not constitute refusal to comply with the subpoena, or interference with or obstruction of an investigation.
(Prior code § 19-4; Added. Coun. J. 10-4-89, p. 5726)

§2-56-050 Conduct of city officers, employees and other entities.

The powers and duties of the inspector general shall extend to the conduct of the following: (a) except as limited in this section all elected and appointed officers of the city government in the performance of their official duties; (b) except as limited in this section, all employees of the city government in the performance of their official duties; (c) all contractors and subcontractors in the providing of goods or services to the city pursuant to a contract; (d) business entities in seeking contracts or certification of eligibility for city contracts; and (e) persons seeking certification of eligibility for participation in any city program. Notwithstanding anything to the contrary contained herein, the office of inspector general shall have no power or authority over any member of the city council, any employee or staff person of any member of the city council or any employee or staff person of any city council committee. If the office of inspector general receives any complaint alleging misconduct, inefficiency or waste against any member of the city council or any employee or staff person of any city council committee, the inspector general shall promptly transmit said complaint to the chairman of the city council committee on committees, rules and ethics, or such successor committee having jurisdiction over said matters. The committee on committees, rules and ethics, or such successor committee, shall conduct an investigation of each complaint referred to it by the office of inspector general. Nothing in this section shall preclude the inspector general from referring a complaint or information concerning a member of the city council or any employee or staff person of any member of the city council or any employee or any staff person of any city council committee to the appropriate federal, state or local law enforcement authorities.
(Prior code § 19-5; Added. Coun. J. 10-4-89, p. 5726)

§2-56-060 Investigation reports.

Upon conclusion of an investigation the inspector general shall issue a summary report thereon. The report shall be filed with the mayor, and may be filed with the head of each department or other agency affected by or involved in the investigation. The report shall include the following:

(a) A description of any complaints or other information received by the inspector general pertinent to the investigation;

(b) A description of any illegal conduct, inefficiencies or waste observed or discovered in the course of the investigation;

(c) Recommendations for correction of any illegal conduct, inefficiencies or waste described in the report;

(d) Such other information as the inspector general may deem relevant to the investigation or resulting recommendations.
(Prior code § 19-6; Added. Coun. J. 10-4-89, p. 5726)

§2-56-070 Confidentiality of informants—Exceptions.

The summary report shall not mention the name of any informant, complainant, witness or person investigated, except in the following instances:

(a) Where the copy of the report given to the head of any department or agency recommends disciplinary action against an employee of that agency;

(b) Where the copy of the report given to the chief procurement officer makes recommendations concerning any contractor, subcontractor, applicant for a contract, or person seeking certification of eligibility for a contract;

(c) Where the copy of the report given to the head of a department or agency makes recommendations concerning a person seeking certification of eligibility for a program administered by the department or agency;

(d) Where the copy given to the mayor recommends disciplinary action against the head or any employee of any executive department or agency.
(Prior code § 19-7; Added. Coun. J. 10-4-89, p. 5726; Amend. 7-19-00, p. 38206)

§2-56-080 Investigations not concluded within six months.

If any investigation is not concluded within six months after its initiation, the inspector general shall notify the mayor of the general nature of the complaint or information giving rise to the investigation and the reasons for failure to complete the investigation within six months.
(Prior code § 19-8; Added. Coun. J. 10-4-89, p. 5726)

§2-56-090 Cooperation in investigations.

It shall be the duty of every officer, employee, department, agency, contractor, subcontractor and licensee of the city, and every applicant for certification of eligibility for a city contract or program, to cooperate with the inspector general in any investigation or hearing undertaken pursuant to this chapter. Every city contract and every bid, proposal, application or solicitation for a city contract, and every application for certification of eligibility for a city contract or program shall contain a statement that the person understands and will abide by all provisions of this chapter.
(Prior code § 19-9; Added. Coun. J. 10-4-89, p. 5726)

§2-56-100 Retaliation prohibited—Penalty.

No person shall retaliate against, punish or penalize any other person for complaining to, cooperating with or assisting the inspector general in the performance of his office. Any person who violates the provisions of this section shall be subject to a fine of not less than $300.00 and not more than $500.00 for each violation.
(Prior code § 19-10; Added. Coun. J. 10-4-89, p. 5726)

§2-56-110 Files and reports confidential—Public statements authorized when.

All investigatory files and reports of the office of inspector general shall be confidential and shall not be divulged to any person or agency, except to the United States Attorney, the Illinois Attorney General or the State's Attorney of Cook County, or as otherwise provided in this chapter. The inspector general is authorized to issue public statements concerning: (a) an investiga-

tion that exonerates an individual who is publicly known to have been under investigation, where the subject requests such a statement; and (b) an investigation that concerns inefficient or wasteful management, as opposed to individual misconduct or illegality.
(Prior code § 19-11; Added. Coun. J. 10-4-89, p. 5726)

§2-56-120 Quarterly reports to city council.

No later than the fifteenth day of January, April, July and October of each year, the inspector general shall file with the city council a report, accurate as of the last day of the preceding month, indicating: the number of investigations initiated since the date of the last report; the number of investigations concluded since the last report; and the number of investigations pending as of the reporting date. The report shall also include the number of investigations of the conduct of employees; the number of investigations of the conduct of appointed officials; the number of investigations of the conduct of elected officials; the number of investigations of the conduct of contractors, subcontractors and persons seeking city contracts; the number of investigations of the conduct of persons seeking certification of eligibility for city contracts or other city programs; the number of investigations involving alleged misconduct; the number of investigations involving alleged waste or inefficiency.
(Prior code § 19-12; Added. Coun. J. 10-4-89, p. 5726)

§2-56-130 Inspector general—Conditions for removal from office.

The inspector general may be removed prior to the expiration of his term only for cause and in accordance with the provisions of this section. The mayor shall give written notice (a) to the city council of his intent to remove the inspector general; and (b) to the inspector general of the cause of his intended removal. Within 10 days after receipt of the notice, the inspector general may file with the city council a request for hearing on the cause for removal. If no such request is made within 10 days, the inspector general shall be deemed to have resigned his office as of the tenth day after receipt of the notice of intended removal. If such a request is made, the city council shall convene a hearing on the cause for removal of the inspector general, at which the inspector general may appear, be represented by counsel and be heard. The hearing shall be convened within 10 days after receipt of the request therefor and conclude within 14 days thereafter. The mayor's notice of intended removal shall constitute the charge against the inspector general. Removal of the inspector general for cause after the hearing shall require the affirmative vote of a majority of the members of the city council then holding office.
(Prior code § 19-13; Added. Coun. J. 10-4-89, p. 5726)

§2-56-140 Obstructing or interfering with investigations—Penalty.

No person shall wilfully refuse to comply with a subpoena issued by the inspector general, or otherwise knowingly interfere with or obstruct an investigation authorized by this chapter and conducted by an announced investigator of the office of inspector general. Any person who wilfully violates the provisions of this section shall be subject to a fine of not less than $300.00 and not more than $500.00 for each such offense, or imprisonment for a period of not less than 30 days and not more than six months, or both a fine and imprison-

ment. Each day that a violation continues shall constitute a separate and distinct offense. Actions seeking the imposition of a fine only shall be filed as quasi-criminal actions subject to the provisions of the Illinois Code of Civil Procedure, as amended. Actions seeking incarceration, or incarceration and a fine, shall be filed and prosecuted as misdemeanor actions under the procedure set forth in Section 1-2-1.1 of the Illinois Municipal Code, as amended.
(Prior code § 19-14; Added. Coun. J. 10-4-89, p. 5726)

§2-56-150 Political activities prohibited.

Neither the inspector general nor any employee of the office of inspector general shall engage in any political activity as defined in Chapter 2-156 of the Municipal Code.
(Prior code § 19-15; Added. Coun. J. 10-4-89, p. 5726)

§2-56-160 Violation—Penalty—Discharge or other discipline.

Any employee or appointed officer of the city who violates any provision of this chapter shall be subject to discharge (or such other discipline as may be specified in an applicable collective bargaining agreement) in addition to any other penalty provided in this chapter.
(Prior code § 19-16; Added. Coun. J. 10-4-89, p. 5726)

§2-56-170 Severability.

If any provision, clause, section, part or application of this chapter to any person or circumstance is declared invalid by any court of competent jurisdiction, such invalidity shall not affect, impair or invalidate the remainder hereof or its application to any other person or circumstance. It is hereby declared to be the legislative intent of the city council that this chapter would have been adopted had such invalid provision, clause, section, part or application not been included herein. Nothing contained in this chapter is intended otherwise to alter or amend the rights or obligations of the city or any person affected by this ordinance.
(Prior code § 19-17; Added. Coun. J. 10-4-89, p. 5726)

CHAPTER 2-74
DEPARTMENT OF PERSONNEL
(Selected Sections)

Sections:

2-74-095 Employment applications—Unlawful practices.
2-74-130 Exemptions to chapter applicability.

§2-74-095 Employment applications—Unlawful practices.

No person shall knowingly make any false statement or material omission on any application for employment with the city. Any person who violates this section shall be fined an amount up to $500.00 for each offense.
(Added Coun. J. 4-16-97, p. 42638)

§2-74-130 Exemptions to chapter applicability.

This ordinance shall not apply nor have any effect upon the police board, its manner of selection, composition, or its powers and duties as set forth in Sections 2-84-020 and 2-84-030 of this code and Section 3-7-3.1, Section 10-1-18.1 and Section 10-1-45 of the Illinois Municipal Code. Nor shall this ordinance have any effect upon the selection, powers or duties of the superintendent of police as set forth in the Municipal Code of the city of Chicago and Section 3-7-3.2 of the Illinois Municipal Code.
(Prior code § 25.1-13)

CHAPTER 2-84
DEPARTMENT OF POLICE
(Complete Chapter)

Sections:

Article I. Organization and Functions

2-84-010 Establishment—Composition and organization.
2-84-020 Police board—Establishment, membership and organization.
2-84-030 Police board—Powers and duties.
2-84-040 Superintendent of police—Appointment as chief administrative authority.
2-84-050 Superintendent of police—Powers and duties.
2-84-051 Notification to news media.
2-84-052 Maintenance and distribution of certain records.
2-84-053 Authority to enter into task force agreements.
2-84-055 Contracts and agreements—Continuation authority.
2-84-060 Superintendent of police—Warrants for expenditures.
2-84-070 Reserved.
2-84-080 Police board—Custody of buildings and property—Enforcement powers.
2-84-090 Medical section—Administrator.
2-84-100 Reserved.
2-84-110 Reserved.
2-84-140 Police dogs—Interference with activities unlawful.
2-84-150 Lost and stolen property—Custody.
2-84-160 Sale of seized or unclaimed property.
2-84-170 Emergency sale of property.
2-84-180 Proceeds of sales—Disposition.
2-84-190 Disposal of weapons.
2-84-200 Special police—Harbor police and bridge tenders.
2-84-210 Special police—For humane societies.

Article II. Powers and Duties of Police Force

2-84-220 General duties.
2-84-230 Power of arrest—Service of warrants.
2-84-240 Process serving.
2-84-250 Aid to fire department.
2-84-260 Street openings and excavations.
2-84-270 Notice of sidewalk defects.
2-84-280 Violation of duties—Discharge from service.
2-84-290 Additional penalty authorized when.
2-84-300 Resisting police officer or aiding escape—Penalty.

Article III. Temporary Questioning

2-84-310 Stopping suspects permitted when.
2-84-320 Searching suspects for weapons—Conditions.

Article IV. Sworn Member Bill of Rights

2-84-330 Conduct of disciplinary investigations.
2-84-340 Rights of officers to bring suit.
2-84-350 Photos of officer under investigation.
2-84-360 No compulsion to testify before nongovernmental agencies.
2-84-370 Auto-Residency Card limitations.
2-84-380 Polygraph test conditions.

Article V. Regulation of Police Force

2-84-390 Badges.
2-84-400 Efficiency rating system.
2-84-410 Merit roll records—Medals and ribbons.
2-84-420 Rewards permitted when.
2-84-430 Complaints against police—Investigation.
2-84-440 Memorial services.
2-84-450 Salary to widow or other dependents.
2-84-460 Furloughs and leaves of absence.
2-84-470 Salary payment—Absence from duty.
2-84-480 Salary payment—Injury in discharge of duty.
2-84-490 Resignation procedure.
2-84-500 Unlawful representation as police officer—Penalty.

Article I. Organization and Functions

§2-84-010 Establishment—Composition and organization.

There is hereby established an executive department of the municipal government of the city which shall be known as the department of police. The said department shall consist of: captains, lieutenants, sergeants, police officers and such other personnel as the police board deems necessary. All of the foregoing is subject to the appropriations for such positions and compensation therefor as is provided in the annual appropriation ordinance.

To supplement the police department, the board may appoint such number of civilian crossing guards to regulate traffic in the vicinity of grade schools during such hours of school days as may be required for that purpose. *(Prior code § 11-1; Amend. Coun. J. 3-31-04, p. 20916)*

§2-84-020 Police board—Establishment, membership and organization.

There is hereby created a police board consisting of nine members to be appointed by the mayor by and with the advice and consent of the city council. They shall be appointed for a term of five years, or until their respective successors are appointed and qualified. Board members shall serve without compensation.

Vacancies shall be filled for the remainder of an unexpired term in the same manner as original appointments.

Members of the board may be removed by the mayor as provided by law.

The mayor shall designate a president and a vice-president from among the members of the board. The board shall hold a regular meeting at least once a month. All regular meetings shall be in a public office of the board with reasonable provision for attendance by the public. The superintendent of police may be present at all meetings of the board and shall have the right to take part in the discussions and deliberations but shall have no vote.

The board shall appoint a secretary not a member of the board. The secretary shall keep a record of the proceedings and transactions of the board specifying therein the names of the members of the board at all meetings and giving the ayes and noes upon all votes. He shall post and publish all orders, resolutions and notices which the board shall order to be posted and published and shall perform such other duties as are herein or may be by order of the board imposed on him.

The powers of the board shall be exercised by order or resolution adopted by a majority of its members and recorded in the minutes with ayes and noes at length. Such action shall be attested by the signatures of the president or vice-president or two members of the board and by the signature of the secretary of the board.

(Prior code § 11-2)

§2-84-030 Police board—Powers and duties.

The board shall exercise the following powers:

1. When a vacancy occurs in the position of superintendent of police, it shall nominate three candidates to fill the position and submit the nominations to the mayor;
2. Adopt rules and regulations for the governance of the police department of the city;
3. Review, approve, and submit to the budget director of the city the annual budget of the police department;
4. Serve as a board to hear disciplinary actions for which a suspension for more than the 30 days expressly reserved to the superintendent is recommended, or removal or discharge involving officers and employees of the police department in the classified civil service of the city.

The board may appoint any member thereof or a hearing officer to hear disciplinary actions.

No officer or employee of the police department in the classified civil service of the city whose appointment has become complete may be removed or discharged, or suspended for more than 30 days except for cause upon written charges and after an opportunity to be heard in his own defense by the police board, or any member or hearing officer designated by it.

Before any such officer or employee may be interrogated or examined by or before the police board, or any member or hearing officer designated by it, or departmental agent or investigator, the results of which hearing, interrogation or examination may be the basis for filing charges seeking his removal or discharge, he must be advised in writing as to what specific improper or illegal act he is alleged to have committed; he must be advised in writing that his admissions made in the course of the hearing, interrogation or examination may be used as the basis for charges seeking his removal or discharge; and he must be advised in writing that he has the right to counsel of his own choosing present to advise him at any hearing, interrogation or examination; and a complete record of any hearing, interrogation or examination shall be made and a complete transcript thereof made available to such officer or employee without charge and without delay.

Upon the filing of charges for which removal or discharge or suspension of more than 30 days is recommended, a hearing before the police board, or any member or hearing officer designated by it shall be held.

The police board shall establish rules of procedure not inconsistent with this section respecting notice of charges and the conduct of the hearings before the police board, or any member or hearing officer designated by it. The police board, or any member or hearing officer designated by it, is not bound by formal or technical rules of evidence, but hearsay evidence is inadmissible. The person against whom charges have been filed may appear before the police board, or any member or hearing officer designated by it, with counsel of his own choice and defend himself; shall have the right to be confronted by his accusers; may cross-examine any witness giving evidence against him; and may by counsel present witnesses and evidence in his own behalf.

The police board, or any member or hearing officer designated by it, may administer oaths and secure by its subpoena both the attendance and testimony of witnesses and the production of relevant books and papers. All proceedings before the police board, or any member or hearing officer designated by it, shall be recorded. No continuance may be granted after a hearing has begun unless all parties to the hearing agree thereto. The findings and decision of the police board, when approved by said board, shall be certified to the superintendent and shall forthwith be enforced by said superintendent.

In the designation of hearing officers, the police board shall select only attorneys licensed to practice in the state of Illinois, with a minimum of five years' experience. Hearing officers shall conduct disciplinary hearings in accordance with the provisions of this chapter and the rules of procedures established by the police board. The hearing officer may take judicial notice, rule on offers of proof, receive relevant evidence during the hearing and certify the record and make findings of fact, conclusions of law and recommendations to the police board following the hearing.

A majority of the members of the police board must concur in the entry of any disciplinary recommendation or action.

No member of the board may participate in any disciplinary recommendation or action without having read the record upon which said recommendation or action is based.

Nothing in this section limits the power of the superintendent to suspend a subordinate for a reasonable period, not exceeding 30 days.

In designating the nominees for the position of superintendent of police, the board shall be governed solely by the professional and executive qualifications required for the position which shall be without reference to the residence of the nominees. If none of the nominees accept appointment, the board shall submit new lists of three nominees until the position is filled.

The board's power to adopt rules and regulations for the governance of the police department does not include authority to administer or direct the operations of the police department or the superintendent of police, except as provided in Section 12.1 of "An Act to regulate the civil service of cities" approved March 20, 1895, as amended.
(Prior code § 11-3)

§2-84-040 Superintendent of police—Appointment as chief administrative authority.

The superintendent of police shall be the chief executive officer of the police department. He shall be appointed by the mayor upon recommendation of the police board and with the advice and consent of the city council and shall serve at the pleasure of the mayor. The superintendent shall be responsible for the general management and control of the police department and shall have full and complete authority to administer the department in a manner consistent with the ordinances of the city, the laws of the state, and the rules and regulations of the police board.
(Prior code § 11-5; Amend. Coun. J. 6-5-87, p. 1164)

§2-84-050 Superintendent of police—Powers and duties.

Subject to the rules of the department and the instruction of the board, said superintendent shall have the power and duty:

(1) To administer the affairs of the department as its chief administrative officer;

(2) To organize the department with the approval of the board;

(3) To make appointments, promotions, transfers of and to take disciplinary action against employees of the department other than the secretary of the board;

(4) To appoint, discharge, suspend or transfer the employees of the department other than the secretary of the board and to issue instructions to said employees other than the secretary in the line of their duties. Subsections (3) and (4) are subject to the civil service provisions;

(5) To expend the funds of the department in accordance with the provisions of the budget appropriations;

(6) To recommend to the board an annual departmental budget covering the anticipated revenues and expenditures of the department conforming as far as practicable to the forms and dates provided for in relation to the general city budget;

(7) To certify all expenditures of the department to the city comptroller; and

(8) To exercise such further powers in the administration of the department as may be conferred upon him by the board.
(Prior code § 11-6)

§2-84-051 Notification to news media.

The superintendent of police shall make available to local newspapers, radio and television stations the names and addresses of persons, other than juveniles, arrested on charges of soliciting for a prostitute or patronizing a prostitute, as those offenses are defined in the Illinois Criminal Code of 1961; or attempt possession of a controlled substance, as defined in the Illinois Controlled Substance Act.
(Added. Coun. J. 6-10-96, p. 23795)

§2-84-052 Maintenance and distribution of certain records.

The superintendent of police shall distribute information received under the Child Sex Offender and Murderer Community Notification Act to the various police districts. This information shall be kept available at the district headquarters for inspection and copying by any member of the public.
(Added. Coun. J. 6-10-96, p. 23798)

§2-84-053 Authority to enter into task force agreements.

In addition to any other authority provided in this code, the superintendent of police shall have the authority to enter into agreements to form law enforcement task forces, and other cooperative agreements, with the following law enforcement agencies: United States Drug Enforcement Administration; Federal Bureau of Investigation; Illinois Department of State Police; Illinois Attorney General; United States Department of Justice; United States Department of Justice, Bureau of Alcohol, Tobacco and Firearms; State's Attorney of Cook County; and other law enforcement agencies determined by the superintendent of police to be necessary for the fulfillment of law enforcement functions. Such agreements shall be subject to approval by the corporation counsel as to form and legality. Such agreements may contain provisions to indemnify or hold harmless participating agencies and their personnel in connection with, or resulting from, the use of vehicles and other equipment used for investigatory and surveillance purposes, for training provided by participating agencies, and for other purposes in connection with the purposes of the task force. The agreements may not authorize the deployment of city personnel or use of city equipment unless the city council has duly appropriated funds for such personnel and equipment. The superintendent of police shall notify the chairman of the city council committee on police and fire with respect to multi-jurisdictional agreements entered into in accordance with this section.
(Added. Coun. J. 1-14-98, p. 60005)

§2-84-055 Contracts and agreements—Continuation authority.

In addition to any other authority provided in this code, the superintendent of police shall have the authority, pursuant to Section 14 of the Emergency Telephone System Act, to enter into and certify the continuation of agreements on behalf of the police department and the city, with other units of local government, special purpose districts and public safety agencies, for the provision of emergency services outside jurisdictional boundaries. Such agreements and certifications shall be subject to approval by the corporation counsel as to form and legality. Copies of such agreements and certifications shall be filed with the Illinois Attorney General and the Illinois Commerce Commission pursuant to Section 15 of the Emergency Telephone System Act.
(Added. Coun. J. 4-12-91, p. 32209)

§2-84-060 Superintendent of police—Warrants for expenditures.

No money shall be drawn from any fund under the control of the department except upon warrants authenticated by the signature of the superintendent. The board, by resolution, may authorize a temporary substitution in the case of the absence or inability to act of the person whose signature is

herein required. A copy of any such resolution of substitution shall be filed with the comptroller.
(Prior code § 11-7)

§2-84-070 Reserved.
(Deleted. Coun. J. 3-31-04, p. 20916)

§2-84-080 Police board—Custody of buildings and property—Enforcement powers.

The board shall have the custody and control of the offices, stations and other public buildings occupied by the police department or any division thereof, equipment, books, records and other property belonging to said department.

It shall, through the superintendent of police, preserve the peace and secure good order and cleanliness within the city, and to that end, it shall enforce all laws, ordinances of the city and orders of the city council and of the mayor.
(Prior code § 11-9)

§2-84-090 Medical section—Administrator.

The administrator of the medical services section, under the direction of the superintendent of police, shall have charge and direction of the medical services section, and shall be responsible for all medical activities of the department, all property and equipment used therein and all supplies issued thereto, and shall exercise general supervision over the duties and conduct of all personnel assigned to or retained by that section.

When so directed by the superintendent of police, a physician designated by the administrator of the medical services section shall examine, or cause to be examined, sick and injured members of the department of police who are absent from duty on account of such sickness or injury, and shall make a report of the findings and conclusions thereon to the superintendent or his designee.
(Prior code § 11-10; Amend. Coun. J. 3-31-04, p. 20916)

§2-84-100 Reserved.
(Repealed Coun. J. 10-3-2001, p. 68131)

§2-84-110 Reserved.
(Repealed Coun. J. 10-3-2001, p. 68131)

§2-84-140 Police dogs—Interference with activities unlawful.

It shall be unlawful for any person to wilfully or maliciously torture, torment, beat, kick, strike, mutilate, injure, disable or kill any dog used by the police department of the city of Chicago in the performance of the functions of such department, or to interfere with or meddle with any such dog while being used by said department or any officer or member thereof in the performance of any functions or duties of said department or of such officer or member.
(Prior code § 11-15.1)

§2-84-150 Lost and stolen property—Custody.

The custodian of lost and stolen property, under the direction of the superintendent of police, shall act as custodian of all property seized or taken by the police.

All officers and members of the department into whose possession may come any property seized or taken shall deliver the same at once to the said custodian, unless it is wanted for immediate use as evidence in any case, and in that event, a report and inventory of the same shall be forwarded at once to the said custodian.

Nothing contained in this chapter, however, shall be held to require the custodian to take possession of, or to make disposition of, any lost or stolen property the disposition or possession of which is otherwise provided for by this code.
(Prior code § 11-16)

§2-84-160 Sale of seized or unclaimed property.

The custodian shall keep a record of all property which may be seized or otherwise taken possession of by the police department. If such property shall not be claimed by the rightful owner thereof and possession surrendered to such owner within 30 days from the date of the final disposition of the court proceedings or administrative hearing proceedings in connection with which such property was seized or otherwise taken possession of, or, in case there are no court proceedings, then if such property shall not be claimed by the rightful owner thereof and possession surrendered to such owner within 30 days from the date of such seizure or taking by the police, said custodian shall proceed to dispose of said property. If such property be deemed salable, the custodian shall cause to be published in a daily newspaper of the city a notice of sale at public auction of such property describing in general terms and not by individual items and shall give notice that if such property be not claimed by the rightful owner or owners thereof within 10 days from the date of such publication such property will be sold at public auction at such place as the superintendent of police may direct and in such manner as to expose to the inspection of bidders all property so offered for sale. No member of said department, directly or indirectly, shall participate in the bidding for, or purchase of such unclaimed property. Provided, that any of such unclaimed property, if deemed by the superintendent of police to be of use to any city department, may be retained for use of such department. Provided, further, that any of such unclaimed property deemed by the custodian to be unsalable shall be confiscated and destroyed or turned over to the house of correction for disposal.
(Prior code § 11-17; Amend. Coun. J. 4-29-98, p. 66564)

§2-84-170 Emergency sale of property.

If any property seized or taken possession of by the police force, shall be of a perishable nature or so bulky or of such nature as to make it dangerous or inadvisable to retain possession thereof, for the length of time specified in Section 2-84-160, the custodian, upon certifying such fact to the superintendent of police, and setting forth his reasons why such property should not be retained for the period herein above fixed before disposing of same, shall with the approval of the superintendent of police cause such property, if deemed by the custodian to be salable, to be advertised forthwith in a daily

newspaper of the city, and shall sell such property at public auction at any time after three days have elapsed from the seizure or taking possession thereof, except if any such property be deemed to be unsalable or dangerous, it shall be disposed of as refuse or in such other reasonable manner as may be deemed by the custodian.
(Prior code § 11-18)

§2-84-180 Proceeds of sales—Disposition.
The proceeds of any sale or sales so made, after deducting the cost of storage, advertising, selling, and other expenses incident to the handling or selling of such property, shall be paid by such custodian to the board of trustees of the policemen's annuity and benefit fund, to be credited to that fund.
(Prior code § 11-19)

§2-84-190 Disposal of weapons.
None of the provisions of the preceding sections shall apply to pistols, revolvers, bowie knives, dirks, slung-shots, metallic knuckles or other deadly weapons of like character. All such weapons, except those that the superintendent of police shall deem to be of use to the department of police and retain for the use of said department, shall within six months after their receipt, be taken by either said custodian or his duly appointed deputy, and the superintendent of police or his duly appointed deputy, to a steel mill or other suitably equipped facility where they shall be destroyed by being placed in a furnace and melted down to form new metal.
(Prior code §11-20; Amend. Coun. J. 3-31-04, p. 20916)

§2-84-200 Special police—Harbor police and bridge tenders.
The superintendent of police may appoint as special policemen, persons of suitable character, who are in the employment of the city in the capacity of harbor police or bridge tenders, but such persons so appointed shall receive no additional pay for their services as such special policemen. Such policemen shall possess the same powers as the regular police patrolmen only when within the scope of their constituted duties it becomes necessary for them to act as special policemen. They shall be subject to all the rules and regulations governing the police department.
(Prior code § 11-21)

§2-84-210 Special police—For humane societies.
The superintendent of police shall have power, upon the application in writing of any society for the prevention of cruelty to animals and children, incorporated under and by virtue of the laws of the state, to appoint and swear in not to exceed 25 special policemen, whose names and addresses shall be set forth in such application; provided, the persons so to be appointed shall be recommended by the president of any such society. The superintendent of police shall keep a list of all persons so appointed by him, and he may remove or discharge any of the persons so appointed at any time without assigning any cause therefor, and he may appoint other persons upon similar application and recommendation to take the place of the person of persons removed or discharged.

The special policemen so appointed shall be particularly charged with the duty of enforcing the provisions of this code relating to cruelty to children and cruelty to animals. They shall comply with and be subject to all the rules and regulations prescribed by the superintendent of police for the government, control, and duties of such special policemen. They shall also perform other special and temporary police duties as may, in emergency cases, be required by the superintendent of police or other police officer, or as may be required by the rules and regulations so prescribed. They shall, in the performance of such duties, have all the powers and privileges of patrolmen of the police department of the city.

The appointment of such special policemen shall be upon the condition that the city shall not be liable in any way for the compensation of any such special policemen, and on condition that such compensation shall be provided by the society requesting such appointment to be made.

(Prior code § 11-22)

Article II. Powers and Duties of Police Force

§§2-84-220 General duties.

The members of the police force of the city, when on duty, shall devote their time and attention to the discharge of the duties of their stations, according to the laws of the state and ordinances of the city and rules and regulations of the department, to preserve order, peace and quiet and enforce the laws and ordinances throughout the city.

(Prior code § 11-24)

§2-84-230 Power of arrest—Service of warrants.

The members of the police department shall have power:

(1) To arrest or cause to be arrested, with or without process, all persons who break the peace, or are found violating any municipal ordinance or any criminal law of the state;

(2) To commit arrested persons for examination;

(3) If necessary, to detain arrested persons in custody overnight or Sunday in any safe place, or until they can be brought before the proper court; and

(4) To exercise all other powers as conservators of the peace as are provided in this code.

All warrants for the violation of municipal ordinances or the state criminal law to whomsoever directed, may be served and executed within the limits of the city by any policeman.

(Prior code § 11-25)

§2-84-240 Process serving.

The members of the police force shall have power and authority and it shall be their duty to serve and execute warrants and other process in the city for the summoning, apprehension, and commitment of any person charged with violation of any provision of this code, or with any crime or misdemeanor, or offense against the laws of the city or state.

(Prior code § 11-26)

§2-84-250 Aid to fire department.

It shall be the duty of members of the police force to aid the fire department by giving alarms in case of fire and by clearing the streets or grounds in the immediate vicinity of a fire, so that the members of the fire department shall not by hindered or obstructed in the performance of their duties.
(Prior code § 11-28)

§2-84-260 Street openings and excavations.

It shall be the duty of every police officer, on observing or being informed of any opening or excavation in any public way, to require the person making such opening or excavation to exhibit the authority or permission therefor. If none has been given by the proper officer, or if such exhibition thereof be refused, such police officer shall without delay report the same to the commissioner of transportation.
(Prior code § 11-29; Amend. Coun. J. 12-11-91, p. 10925)

§2-84-270 Notice of sidewalk defects.

It shall be the duty of all policemen to report to the commissioner of streets and sanitation all defects in sidewalks, and in case of accident they shall report the same to the corporation counsel together with the names of any witnesses to such accident.
(Prior code § 11-30)

§2-84-280 Violation of duties—Discharge from service.

Any member of the police force who shall refuse or neglect to perform any duty required of him, when such refusal or neglect to perform any such duty shall tend to hinder, obstruct, or impair in any way the proper and strict enforcement of any law or provision of this code or the efficiency of the police force, is hereby declared to be no longer qualified to be a member of the police force, and shall be discharged from said police force and the service of the city in the manner provided by law.
(Prior code § 11-31)

§2-84-290 Additional penalty authorized when.

Any member of the police department who shall neglect or refuse to perform any duty required of him by the provisions of this code or the rules and regulations of the department of police, or who shall in the discharge of his official duties be guilty of any fraud, extortion, oppression, favoritism or wilful wrong or injustice, may, in addition to any other penalty or punishment imposed by law, be fined not more than $100.00 for each offense.
(Prior code § 11-32)

§2-84-300 Resisting police officer or aiding escape—Penalty.

(a) Any person who knowingly shall resist or obstruct the performance by one known to the person to be a peace officer of any authorized act within his official capacity or shall knowingly interfere or prevent a peace officer from discharging his duty as such officer and whoever shall in any manner knowingly assist any person in the custody of any member of the police department to escape or attempt to escape from such custody, shall be fined not less than $25.00 nor more than $500.00.

(b) For the purposes of this section "resist" shall mean passive as well as active resistance.
(Prior code § 11-33)

Article III. Temporary Questioning

§2-84-310 Stopping suspects permitted when.

A police officer having identified himself as a police officer may stop any person in a public place whom the officer reasonably suspects is committing, has committed or is about to commit a criminal offense under the laws of the state of Illinois or a violation of Chapter 8-20 of this code, and may demand the name and address of such person and an explanation of his actions.
(Prior code § 11.3-1)

§2-84-320 Searching suspects for weapons—Conditions.

When a police officer having identified himself as a police officer has stopped a person for temporary questioning and reasonably suspects that he is in danger of attack, he may search such person for dangerous weapons. If the officer discovers such weapons he may take such property until the completion of the questioning, at which time he shall either return such property if lawfully possessed or arrest the person.
(Prior code § 11.3-2)

Article IV. Sworn Member Bill of Rights

§2-84-330 Conduct of disciplinary investigations.

Whenever a sworn member is the subject of disciplinary investigation other than summary punishment, the interrogation will be conducted in the following manner:

A. The interrogation of the officer, other than in the initial stage of the investigation, shall be scheduled at a reasonable time, preferably while the officer is on duty, or if feasible, during daylight hours.

B. The interrogation, depending upon the allegation, will normally take place at either the officer's unit of assignment, the office of professional standards, the internal affairs division, or other appropriate location.

C. Prior to an interrogation, the officer under investigation shall be informed of the identity of the person in charge of the investigation, the interrogation officer, and the identity of all persons present during the interrogation. When a formal statement is being taken, all questions directed to the officer under interrogation shall be asked by and through one interrogator.

D. No anonymous complaint made against an officer shall be made the subject of a complaint register investigation unless the allegation is of a criminal nature.

E. Immediately prior to the interrogation of an officer under investigation, he shall be informed in writing of the nature of the complaint and the names of all complainants.

F. The length of interrogation sessions will be reasonable, with reasonable interruptions permitted for personal necessities, meals, telephone calls and rest.

G. An officer under interrogation shall not be threatened with transfer, dismissal or disciplinary action or promised a reward as an inducement to provide information relating to the incident under investigation or for exercising any rights contained herein.

H. An officer under investigation will be provided without unnecessary delay, with a copy of any written statement he has made.

I. If the allegation under investigation indicates a recommendation for separation is probable against the officer, the officer will be given the statutory administrative proceedings rights, or if the allegation indicates criminal prosecution is probable against the officer, the officer will be given the constitutional rights concerning self-incrimination prior to the commencement of interrogation.

J. An officer under interrogation shall have the right to be represented by counsel of his own choice and to have that counsel present at all times during the interrogation. The interrogation shall be suspended for a reasonable time until representation can be obtained.
(Prior code § 11-34.1)

§2-84-340 Rights of officers to bring suit.

The city of Chicago shall not adopt any ordinance and the Chicago Police Department shall not adopt any regulation which prohibits the right of an officer to bring suit arising out of his duties as an officer.
(Prior code § 11-34.2)

§2-84-350 Photos of officer under investigation.

No photo of an officer under investigation shall be made available to the media prior to a conviction for a criminal offense or prior to a decision being rendered by the police board.
(Prior code § 11-34.3)

§2-84-360 No compulsion to testify before nongovernmental agencies.

The Chicago Police Department shall not compel an officer under investigation to speak or testify before, or to be questioned by any nongovernmental agency relating to any matter or issue under investigation.
(Prior code § 11-34.4)

§2-84-370 Auto-Residency Card limitations.

No officer shall be required to submit the information now required in an Auto-Residency Card as it applies to any other member of his family or household.
(Prior code § 11-34.5)

§2-84-380 Polygraph test conditions.

When a polygraph exam is deemed necessary, the complainant will be requested to take a polygraph exam first.

If the complainant refuses to take a polygraph exam, the accused police officer will not be required to take a polygraph exam. If the complainant takes the polygraph exam and the results indicate deception, the accused officer may be required to take a polygraph exam covering those issues wherein the examiner determines that the complainant is truthful.

When the polygraph is used, the accused member will be advised 24 hours prior to the administering of the test, in writing, of any questions to which the department will require an answer.

If the officer under investigation requests to take a polygraph exam, he may do so.

In cases where the complainant is unknown or anonymous, an officer will not be ordered to take a polygraph exam.
(Prior code § 11-34.6)

Article V. Regulation of Police Force

§2-84-390 Badges.

The board shall have the power and authority to prescribe an appropriate form of badge to be worn by both regular and special members of the department by which, and at all times, the authority and relation of such officers and members of said department may be known. It shall make suitable regulations as to the wearing of such badge.

Every member of the department of police shall wear a suitable badge to be furnished by the city, and any member who shall lose or destroy the same shall be required to pay the cost of replacing it. Whenever any member shall leave the department he shall immediately deliver his badge to the board.
(Prior code § 11-36)

§2-84-400 Efficiency rating system.

It shall be the duty of the board to maintain a system for the ascertaining and recording of individual efficiency of each member of the police department. Such system shall be as nearly automatic as possible and its application shall be uniform throughout the department.

The efficiency reports respecting the appointees in the classified service of the department shall be submitted to the civil service commission not later than two weeks following the thirty-first of December of each year.
(Prior code § 11-37)

§2-84-410 Merit roll records—Medals and ribbons.

The board shall cause to be kept a record, which shall be known as the "Merit Roll," upon which shall be entered the names of all the members of the department of police who shall have performed any distinguished act of bravery in the protection of life or property. Such record shall specify the details and circumstances of such acts, and shall include the names of witnesses, if any, and all facts corroborating the circumstances of the report.

Such record shall annually, on the thirty-first day of December of each year, be laid before the mayor, comptroller and treasurer, ex officio trustees of the "Harrison Medal" fund and the "Tree Medal" fund. Upon awards being made, the members of the department of police who shall be awarded the "Tree Medal" and the "Harrison Medal" shall be notified to appear before the trustees to receive the medals awarded them.

A ribbon type medal cast in the design of the Chicago flag as described in Section 1-8-030 of the Municipal Code shall be awarded to each recipient of the Lambert Tree or Carter Harrison Medals for the use of the recipient when in uniform.

A ribbon will be presented to active duty members of the Chicago Fire and Police Departments who have received the Lambert Tree and Carter Harrison Award Medals. All persons in the future when receiving these medals will be presented with a ribbon and medal.
(Prior code § 11-38)

§2-84-420 Rewards permitted when.

The board, for meritorious service rendered by any member of the police department in the due discharge of his duty, may permit such member to retain, for his own benefit, any reward or present tendered him therefor, upon report being made of the proposed reward or present. It shall be cause for removal of any member of the department to receive any such reward or present without notice thereto to the board and without its permission.
(Prior code § 11-39)

§2-84-430 Complaints against police—Investigation.

All complaints of citizens regarding officers and members of the department of police shall be investigated promptly and thoroughly. The substance of all oral complaints and copies of written complaints received at the police stations, and by the various bureaus, divisions and sections of the service, shall be forwarded promptly to the superintendent of police.
(Prior code § 11-40)

§2-84-440 Memorial services.

Upon loss of life in the line of duty of any police officer, a memorial service shall be held outside the main entrance (LaSalle Street) of City Hall in which participants shall be the mayor, the commissioner of police, and the alderman or aldermen representing the ward(s) in which said officer lived and/or worked. During such memorial, the official city of Chicago flag shall be flown at half-mast, and the name of the police officer shall be read while Taps are played. Immediately thereafter, said flag shall be lowered and given to the local station where said police officer was assigned, and then presented to the survivors of said police officer as a tribute. In the event of inclement weather the ceremony may be held in the lobby of City Hall.
(Prior code § 11-4; Added. Coun. J. 3-25-86, p. 28874)

§2-84-450 Salary to widow or other dependents.

The salary of any police officer killed in the line of duty shall continue for a period of one year commencing from the date of the death of the deceased police officer and shall be paid out of the specified fund appropriated therefor included in the general finance section of the Annual Appropriation Ordinance for the year 1967 and subsequent years to the widow of the deceased police officer, or in the absence of a widow, to the guardian or person standing in loco parentis of dependent minor children, or in the absence of a widow or minor children, to dependent parents who were residents in the

deceased police officer's household at the time of the injury which resulted in his death. This section shall be retroactive to January 1, 1965.
(Prior code § 11-42)

§2-84-460 Furloughs and leaves of absence.

Members of the department of police shall be entitled to a leave of absence from duty with full pay according to their years of service as follows:

Twenty-eight consecutive days each year for any member who has 10 or more years of service;

Twenty-four consecutive days each year for any member who has five to 10 years of service;

Twenty consecutive days each year for any member who has less than five years of service.

In every case the superintendent of police shall designate when such leave of absence shall be taken; provided, however, that in the computation of the total time of service of any member of the police department, furloughs or leave of absence for over one month shall be excluded from such total time of service of such member of the police department; provided, however, further, that all members and employees of the department of police shall, in addition to the furlough above provided for, have a furlough of two days in each week on the average with full pay.
(Prior code § 11-43)

§2-84-470 Salary payment—Absence from duty.

Any policeman absent from duty on account of sickness for a period not exceeding six months, and any policeman absent from duty on account of death in his immediate family, and any policeman temporarily absent from duty on account of sickness in his immediate family, may, in the discretion of the board, receive full pay for such period of absence.
(Prior code § 11-44)

§2-84-480 Salary payment—Injury in discharge of duty.

Any member of the police department receiving injury or becoming disabled while in the discharge of police duties and by reason of, or as a consequence of, the performance of such duties, so as to prevent him from attending to his duties as such member of the police department, shall, for the space of 12 months, provided his disability shall last that time, or for such portion of 12 months as such disability shall continue, receive his usual salary.

The fact of such disability and its duration shall be certified by a physician designated by the administrator of the medical services section, or by the production of such other evidence as shall be satisfactory to the board. Provided, however, that no member of the police department who is on the pension roll, or who is receiving any benefit from the pension fund by reason of any such disability or injury, shall be entitled to receive any part of his salary during such time as he shall remain on such pension roll or receive any benefit from such pension fund. The word "pension" shall be understood as including a benefit or annuity from the annuity and benefit fund.
(Prior code § 11-45; Amend. Coun. J. 3-31-04, p. 20916)

§2-84-490 Resignation procedure.

Any person desiring to resign from his position in the department shall submit two executed copies of such proposed resignation to the board. Such resignation shall not be effective until accepted by the board and a copy of such proposed resignation is forwarded to the civil service commission with the acceptance of the board noted thereon.

(Prior code § 11-46)

§2-84-500 Unlawful representation as police officer—Penalty.

No person shall falsely assume or pretend to be a policeman or a member of the department of police of this city, or, without being a member of the department of police of this city, wear in public the uniform adopted as the police uniform.

No person shall counterfeit or imitate, or cause to be counterfeited or imitated, any badge, sign, signal or device adopted by the department of police. Nor shall any person use or wear any badge, sign, signal or device adopted or used by said department or any similar in appearance, without authority so to do from the board.

Any person violating any of the provisions of this section shall be fined not less than $10.00 nor more than $100.00 for each offense.

(Prior code § 11-47)

DIVISION II
BOARDS, COMMISSIONS AND COMMITTEES
(Selected Chapters)

Chapters:

2-112 Board of Health. (Selected Sections)
2-120 Commissioners and Commissions. (Selected Sections)

CHAPTER 2-112
BOARD OF HEALTH
(Selected Sections)

Sections:

2-112-160 Commissioner—Enforcement powers and duties.
2-112-170 Commissioner—Communicable disease control procedures.
2-112-200 Disinfection of premises.
2-112-210 Power to order vacation of premises.
2-112-220 Health and safety hazards—Investigation authority.
2-112-260 Emergency cardiopulmonary resuscitation—Liability limitations.
2-112-270 Contaminated food or beverage controls.
2-112-275 Swimming Pool and Bathing Beach Act—Administration and enforcement.

§2-112-160 Commissioner—Enforcement powers and duties.

The commissioner of health shall perform the following duties:

(a) Enforce all the laws of the state and provisions of this code in relation to matters pertaining to the public health and sanitary conditions of the city;

(b) Enforce all regulations of the board of health or any other federal, state or local authority with power to make regulations concerning the public health;

(c) Cause all nuisances affecting the health of the public to be abated with all reasonable promptness;

(d) Determine when a disease is communicable or epidemic, and establish quarantine regulations whenever it is deemed necessary.

For the purpose of carrying out the requirements of this code, relating to the public health and the function of the commissioner of health the commissioner of health or anyone authorized to act for him shall be permitted at all times to enter into any structure in order to make a thorough examination to determine the presence or absence of health hazards.
(Prior code § 9-12; Amend. Coun. J. 6-28-00, p. 36752)

§2-112-170 Commissioner—Communicable disease control procedures.

The commissioner of health may cause all persons reported to it as having, or suspected of having a communicable disease, to be examined, and may impose such restrictions upon, and exercise such supervision over such persons as shall be necessary to protect other persons. To aid in securing the isolation of a person having, or suspected of having, a communicable disease, the board of health may cause a notice of the disease to be placed upon or near the house, apartment, or building in which the person is sick. No person shall deface, alter, conceal, mutilate, destroy, or tear down, any such notice without permission from the board of health, and every occupant of the house, apartment, or building upon which, or near which, the notice is placed, shall be responsible for the removal of the notice. The board of health may cause a person having, or suspected of having, a communicable disease to be removed to a hospital or other safe place. The board of health may cause a person having or suspected of having, a communicable disease to be provided with suitable nurses and medical attention, at his own expense if he is able to pay for the same, but if not, then at the expense of the city.
(Prior code § 9-13)

§2-112-200 Disinfection of premises.

The department of health shall have power to cause any building or any premises to be cleansed, disinfected, or closed to visitors and prevent persons from entering thereto while any such building or premises contains any person having communicable disease. The board of health may direct any nuisance to be abated, or unwholesome matter or substance to be removed from any building or premises, and may prescribe the time and mode of doing so, and take any other measures it may deem necessary and proper to prevent the spread of any communicable disease.
(Prior code § 9-16 (a))

§2-112-210 Power to order vacation of premises.

The department of health shall have the power and is hereby authorized to cause the vacation of buildings and/or premises where such buildings or premises, or any portion thereof, are found to be unfit for human habitation from any of the conditions deemed as health, safety or environmental hazards.
(Prior code § 9-16 (b))

§2-112-220 Health and safety hazards—Investigation authority.

The department of health is hereby authorized to investigate all premises where business and/or manufacturing is carried out for the purpose of determining that such premises are free from health and safety hazards which might affect the health and safety of persons employed therein or of the general public who may enter such premises.
(Prior code § 9-16 (c))

§2-112-260 Emergency cardiopulmonary resuscitation—Liability limitations.

Any person who has successfully completed a course of training in cardiopulmonary resuscitation which has been approved by the department of health and who within the city of Chicago, provides emergency cardiopulmonary resuscitation, without fee, to a person who is an apparent victim of acute cardiopulmonary insufficiency, shall not, as a result of his acts or omissions in providing such resuscitation, be liable for civil damages. This section does not apply to acts or omissions amounting to wilful or wanton misconduct in providing such resuscitation.
(Prior code § 9-18.1)

§2-112-270 Contaminated food or beverage controls.

The department of health is authorized to investigate and to take such action as may be necessary to control the sale and/or distribution of any food, beverage or other product which is found to be:

(a) Contaminated with a pathogenic organism;

(b) Any food, beverage or other product which contains chemical substances which are capable of causing acute or chronic disease and which are deemed to be a hazard to the public health; or

(c) To take all steps necessary to protect the city from any hazard resulting from the presence of any radioactive substance in or near the city or of any dangerous or hazardous substances released into the atmosphere in the city of Chicago or within a mile of the corporate geographic boundaries of the city.
(Prior code § 9-19)

§2-112-275 Swimming Pool and Bathing Beach Act—Administration and enforcement.

(a) The city of Chicago hereby elects to administer and enforce the Illinois Swimming Pool and Bathing Beach Act.

(b) The provisions of the Illinois Swimming Pool and Bathing Beach Act, as well as all rules and regulations promulgated and amended from time to time by the Illinois Department of Public Health under authority of that Act, are hereby incorporated into this section and made a part hereof. However, unless the context requires otherwise, any reference in that Act or those rules and regulations to the Illinois Department of Public Health shall instead refer to the city of Chicago department of health, and any reference in that Act to the Illinois Department of Public Health shall instead refer to the commissioner of health of the city of Chicago.

(c) The department of health shall take all actions necessary and proper to administer and enforce the Illinois Swimming Pool and Bathing

Beach Act and all rules and regulations promulgated thereunder. The department shall impose and collect, on behalf of the city, a license application fee, in the amount specified in Section 6 of the Act, for each application for license renewal; provided that an application submitted by a corporation organized under the General Not-For-Profit Corporation Act of 1986, or an application submitted by the United States, the state of Illinois, or any of their agencies or political subdivisions, shall be exempt from the fee.

(d) Nothing in this section shall affect the requirement for a construction permit issued by the Illinois Department of Public Health under Section 5 of the Act, and nothing in this section shall affect the enforcement of violations of the Act by the State's Attorney or the Attorney General under Sections 21 and 22 of the Act.

(e) If any other provision of this code, or any provision of any other law, is inconsistent with any provision of the section, the provision of this section shall prevail.

(f) The city clerk shall furnish to the Illinois Department of Public Health a copy of this ordinance and the names and qualifications of city employees required by the Act.

(Added. Coun. J. 12-11-96, p. 36358)

CHAPTER 2-120
COMMISSIONERS AND COMMISSIONS
(Selected Sections)

Sections:

Article XIV. Commission on Human Relations

2-120-485 Definitions.

2-120-518 Hate crimes.

Article XIV. Commission on Human Relations

§2-120-485 Definitions.

Wherever used in this Article XIV, the terms "age," "religion," "disability," "sexual orientation," "marital status," "parental status," "military discharge status," "gender identity" and "source of income" shall have the same meanings as described in Chapter 2-160 of this code.

(Added. Coun. J. 11-6-02, p. 96031)

§2-120-518 Hate crimes.

(a) As used in this section, "hate crime" means any action in violation of Section 8-4-020 or 8-4-085 of this code.

(b) Whenever any Chicago police officer has identified a victim of a possible hate crime committed within the city, the Chicago Police Department shall, to the extent known, supply the name, address and telephone number of the alleged victim to the chair of the Chicago commission on human relations, together with other relevant information concerning the alleged crime.

The police department shall also, on at least a monthly basis, prepare a statistical summary concerning all criminal acts and ordinance violations committed within the city of Chicago during the previous month that are believed to be hate crimes. A copy of this summary shall be forwarded to the Chicago commission on human relations. This summary shall be in a form approved by the police department and the chair of the Chicago commission on human relations.

(c) Whenever the Chicago Police Department has provided information concerning a victim of a possible hate crime to the chair of the Chicago commission on human relations, either the chair or a person designated by him shall make reasonable efforts to contact the victim for the purpose of offering to help the victim with the police department, prosecutors and any other interested agencies.

(d) The Chicago Police Department shall train both full-time and part-time new recruits and veteran personnel on an ongoing basis on the subject of hate crimes.

(e) The chair of the Chicago commission on human relations shall keep statistics on hate crimes to determine if such crimes are part of a pattern or if, due to hate or hate-based tensions in the area where the crime was committed, further hate crimes or escalations of tensions are likely to occur if remedial action is not taken. The chair shall present the findings of his report to the Chicago Police Department.

(f) Upon recommendation of the chair, the Chicago commission on human relations may call a hearing to address only perceived patterns of hate crimes or hate-based tensions. The commission may employ a hearing examiner and other employees necessary for such purpose. For the purpose of such hearing, the commission on human relations may:

(1) Receive evidence and hear testimony related to patterns of hate crimes and hate-based tensions; provided, however, that the commission will not invite or suggest the attendance of a victim of or a witness to any matter in which there is an ongoing criminal investigation or prosecution, including any appeal or retrial;

(2) Issue and enforce subpoenas pursuant to Section 2-120-510 of this code to compel the attendance of witnesses and the production of evidence relevant to the matter in question; provided, however, that no subpoena shall be issued to compel the attendance of a victim of or witness to any matter in which there is an ongoing criminal investigation or prosecution, including any appeal or retrial;

(3) Issue findings and recommendations concerning ways in which hate crimes and hate-based tensions can be reduced in the affected area.

The commission on human relations shall conduct such a hearing, and issue and enforce any subpoena, in a manner that will avoid interference with any ongoing criminal investigation or prosecution.

(g) The Chicago commission on human relations is hereby authorized to develop and initiate educational and other programs designed to reduce hate-based tensions and the incidence of hate crimes, either in particular areas or on a citywide basis.

(Added. Coun. J. 12-19-90, p. 27888)

DIVISION III
ETHICS AND EMPLOYMENT POLICIES
(Selected Chapters)

Chapters:

2-152 Officers and Employees. (Selected Sections)
2-160 Human Rights. (Complete Chapter)

CHAPTER 2-152
OFFICERS AND EMPLOYEES
(Selected Sections)

Sections:

Article I. General Provisions
2-152-115 Registration with Federal Selective Service System—Required.

Article IV. Career Service Regulations
2-152-340 Residence restrictions.

Article I. General Provisions

§2-152-115 Registration with Federal Selective Service System—Required.

Every male who is at least 18 years old but not yet attained the age of 26 years old, seeking employment with the city of Chicago, shall submit documentation evidencing his registration with the Federal Selective Service System. Those in this age range offered employment with the city of Chicago shall be prohibited from employment with the city of Chicago until such time as he does submit the required documentation.
(Added. Coun. J. 10-3-90, p. 21783)

Article IV. Career Service Regulations

§2-152-340 Residence restrictions.

All officers and employees in the classified career service of the city, including all employees of the Chicago Board of Education, shall be actual residents of the city. Any officer or employee in the classified career service of the city, including all employees of the Chicago Board of Education, who shall fail to comply with the provisions of this section shall be discharged from the service of the city and board of education in the manner provided by law, provided that employees of the Chicago Board of Education shall have a two-year grace period from the effective date of this amendment, to comply with the residency requirements of this section.
(Prior code § 25-30)

CHAPTER 2-160
HUMAN RIGHTS
(Complete Chapter)

Sections:

2-160-010	Declaration of city policy.
2-160-020	Definitions.
2-160-030	Unlawful discriminatory activities designated.
2-160-040	Sexual harassment.
2-160-050	Religious beliefs and practices.
2-160-060	Discriminatory practices—Credit transactions.
2-160-065	Matricula consular identification cards.
2-160-070	Discriminatory practices—Public accommodations.
2-160-080	Exemptions for certain religious organizations.
2-160-090	Violation—Investigation by commission on human relations—Prosecution.
2-160-100	Retaliation prohibited.
2-160-110	Construction of chapter provisions.
2-160-120	Violation—Penalty.

§2-160-010 Declaration of city policy.

It is the policy of the city of Chicago to assure that all persons within its jurisdiction shall have equal access to public services and shall be protected in the enjoyment of civil rights, and to promote mutual understanding and respect among all who live and work within this city.

The city council of the city of Chicago hereby declares and affirms:

That prejudice, intolerance, bigotry and discrimination occasioned thereby threaten the rights and proper privileges of the city's inhabitants and menace the institutions and foundation of a free and democratic society; and

That behavior which denies equal treatment to any individual because of his or her race, color, sex, gender identity, age, religion, disability, national origin, ancestry, sexual orientation, marital status, parental status, military discharge status, or source of income undermines civil order and deprives persons of the benefits of a free and open society.

Nothing in this ordinance shall be construed as supporting or advocating any particular lifestyle or religious view. To the contrary, it is the intention of this ordinance that all persons be treated fairly and equally and it is the express intent of this ordinance to guarantee to all of our citizens fair and equal treatment under law.

(Prior code § 199-1; Added. Coun. J. 12-21-88, p. 23526; 11-6-02, p. 96031)

§2-160-020 Definitions.

Whenever used in this chapter:

(a) "Age" means chronological age of not less than 40 years.

(b) "Credit transaction" means the grant, denial, extension or termination of credit to an individual.

(c) "Disability" means:

(i) A determinable physical or mental characteristic which may result from disease, injury, congenital condition of birth or functional disorder including, but not limited to, a determinable physical characteristic which necessitates a person's use of a guide, hearing or support dog; or

(ii) The history of such a characteristic; or

(iii) The perception of such a characteristic by the person complained against.

(d) "Employee" means an individual who is engaged to work in the city of Chicago for or under the direction and control of another for monetary or other valuable consideration.

(e) "Employment agency" means a person that undertakes to procure employees or opportunities to work for potential employees, either through interviews, referrals, advertising or any combination thereof.

(f) "Gender identity" means the actual or perceived appearance, expression, identity or behavior, of a person as being male or female, whether or not that appearance, expression, identity or behavior is different from that traditionally associated with the person's designated sex at birth.

(g) "Marital status" means the legal status of being single, married, divorced, separated or widowed.

(h) "Military discharge status" means the fact of discharge from military status and the reasons for such discharge.

(i) "Parental status" means the status of living with one or more dependent minor or disabled children.

(j) "Public accommodation" means a place, business establishment or agency that sells, leases, provides or offers any product, facility or service to the general public, regardless of ownership or operation (i) by a public body or agency; (ii) for or without regard to profit; or (iii) for a fee or not for a fee. An institution, club, association or other place of accommodation which has more than 400 members, and provides regular meal service and regularly receives payment for dues, fees, accommodations, facilities or services from or on behalf of nonmembers for the furtherance of trade or business shall be considered a place of public accommodation for purposes of this chapter.

(k) "Religion" means all aspects of religious observance and practice, as well as belief, except that with respect to employers "religion" has the meaning ascribed to it in Section 2-160-050.

(l) "Sexual orientation" means the actual or perceived state of heterosexuality, homosexuality or bisexuality.

(m) "Sexual harassment" means any unwelcome sexual advances or requests for sexual favors or conduct of a sexual nature when (i) submission to such conduct is made either explicitly or implicitly a term or condition of an individual's employment; or (2) submission to or rejection of such conduct by an individual is used as the basis for any employment decision affecting the individual; or (3) such conduct has the purpose or effect of substantially interfering with an individual's work performance or creating an intimidating, hostile or offensive working environment.

(n) "Source of income" means the lawful manner by which an individual supports himself and his or her dependents.

(Prior code § 199-2; Added. Coun. J. 12-21-88, p. 23526; Amend. Coun. J. 11-6-02, p. 96031)

§2-160-030 Unlawful discriminatory activities designated.

No person shall directly or indirectly discriminate against any individual in hiring, classification, grading, discharge, discipline, compensation or other term or condition of employment because of the individual's race, color, sex, gender identity, age, religion, disability, national origin, ancestry, sexual orientation, marital status, parental status, military discharge status or source of income. No employment agency shall directly or indirectly discriminate against any individual in classification, processing, referral or recommendation for employment because of the individual's race, color, sex, gender identity, age, religion, disability, national origin, ancestry, sexual orientation, marital status, parental status, military discharge status, or source of income. The prohibitions contained in this paragraph shall not apply to any of the following:

(a) Use of an individual's unfavorable discharge from military service as a valid employment criterion where (i) authorized by federal law or regulation; or (ii) where the affected position of employment involves the exercise of fiduciary responsibilities and the reasons for the dishonorable discharge related to his or her fiduciary capacity;

(b) Hiring or selecting between individuals for bona fide occupational qualifications;

(c) Giving preferential treatment to veterans and their relatives as required by federal or state law or regulation.

(Prior code § 199-3; Added. Coun. J. 12-21-88, p. 23526; Amend. Coun. J. 11-6-02, p. 96031)

§2-160-040 Sexual harassment.

No employer, employee, agent of an employer, employment agency or labor organization shall engage in sexual harassment. An employer shall be liable for sexual harassment by nonemployees or nonmanagerial and nonsupervisory employees only if the employer becomes aware of the conduct and fails to take reasonable corrective measures.

(Prior code § 199-4; Added. Coun. J. 12-21-88, p. 23526)

§2-160-050 Religious beliefs and practices.

No employer shall refuse to make all reasonable efforts to accommodate the religious beliefs, observances and practices of employees or prospective employees unless the employer demonstrates that he is unable to reasonably accommodate an employee's or prospective employee's religious observance or practice without undue hardship on the conduct of the employer's business.

Reasonable efforts to accommodate include, but are not limited to allowing an employee: (i) to take a day of paid leave or vacation, where applicable under the employee's employment agreement; or (ii) to be excused from work without pay and without discipline or other penalty; or (iii) to elect to take the day off with pay in order to practice the employee's religious beliefs, and to make up the lost work time at a time and date consistent with the operational need of the employer's business. Any employee who elects such deferred work shall be compensated at his or her regular rate of pay, regardless of the time and date at which the work is made up. The employer may require that any employee who plans to exercise option (iii) of this subsection provide the employer with notice of the employee's intention to do so, no less than five days prior to the date of absence.

(Prior code § 199-5; Added. Coun. J. 12-21-88, p. 23526)

§2-160-060 Discriminatory practices—Credit transactions.

No person shall discriminate against any individual in any aspect of a credit transaction, or in any terms and conditions of bonding because of the individual's race, color, sex, gender identity, age, religion, disability, national origin, ancestry, sexual orientation, marital status, parental status, military discharge status, or source of income.

(Prior code § 199-6; Added. Coun. J. 12-21-88, p. 23526; Amend. Coun. J. 11-6-02, p. 96031)

§2-160-065 Matricula consular identification cards.

When requiring members of the public to provide identification, each city department shall accept as valid identification of the person a "matricula consular" identification card issued by the Mexican Consulate. The requirements of this section do not apply under circumstances where (1) a federal or state statute, administrative regulation or directive or court decision requires the city to obtain different identification, (2) a federal or state statute or administrative regulation or directive preempts local regulation of identification requirements, or (3) the city would be unable to comply with a condition imposed by a funding source, which would cause the city to lose funds from that source.

Nothing in this section is intended to prohibit city departments from (1) asking for additional information from individuals in order to verify a current address or other facts that would enable the department to fulfill its responsibilities, except that this section does not permit the department to require additional information solely in order to establish identification of the person, or (2) using fingerprints for identification purposes under circumstances where the department also requires fingerprints from persons who have a driver's license or state identification card.

(Added. Coun. J. 6-19-02, p. 88685)

§2-160-070 Discriminatory practices—Public accommodations.

No person that owns, leases, rents, operates, manages or in any manner controls a public accommodation shall withhold, deny, curtail, limit or discriminate concerning the full use of such public accommodation by any individual because of the individual's race, color, sex, gender identity, age, religion, disability, national origin, ancestry, sexual orientation, marital status, parental status, military discharge status, or source of income. The prohibition contained in this section shall not apply to the following:

(a) A private club or other establishment not in fact open to the public, except to the extent that the products, facilities or services thereof are made available to the general public or to the customers or patrons of another establishment that is a public accommodation;

(b) Any facility, as to discrimination based on sex, which is distinctly private in nature, such as restrooms, shower rooms, bathhouses, dressing rooms, health clubs;

(c) Any facility, as to discrimination based on sex, which restricts rental of residential or sleeping rooms to individuals of one sex;

(d) Any educational institution, as to discrimination based on sex, which restricts enrollment of students to individuals of one sex.

(e) Notwithstanding subsections (a) through (d) above, any person may use a public accommodation or any of its products, facilities or services that are open to persons of the sex or gender reflected on any government issued identification of that individual including a driver's license, a state identification card or passport.
(Prior code § 199-7; Added. Coun. J. 12-21-88, p. 23526; Amend. Coun. J. 11-6-02, p. 96031)

§2-160-080 Exemptions for certain religious organizations.

Nothing in this chapter shall apply to decisions of a religious society, association, organization or institution affecting the definition, promulgating or advancement of the mission, practices or beliefs of the society, association, organization or institution.
(Prior code § 199-8; Added. Coun. J. 12-21-88, p. 23526)

§2-160-090 Violation—Investigation by commission on human relations—Prosecution.

The Chicago commission on human relations shall receive and investigate complaints of violations of this chapter, except where such duty is modified by intergovernmental agreement, and shall prepare and provide necessary forms for such complaints. No person shall refuse or fail to comply with any subpoena, order or decision issued in the course of or as a result of an investigation.
(Prior code § 199-9; Added. Coun. J. 12-21-88, p. 23526; Amend. 3-21-90, p. 13523; 7-8-98, p. 72891)

§2-160-100 Retaliation prohibited.

No person shall retaliate against any individual because that individual in good faith has made a charge, testified, assisted or participated in an investigation, proceeding or hearing under this chapter.
(Prior code § 199-10; Added. Coun. J. 12-21-88, p. 23526)

§2-160-110 Construction of chapter provisions.

The provision of this chapter shall be liberally construed for the accomplishment of the purpose hereof. Nothing in this chapter shall be construed to limit rights granted under the laws of the state of Illinois or the United States.
(Prior code § 199-11; Added. Coun. J. 12-21-88, p. 23526)

§2-160-120 Violation—Penalty.

Any person who violates any provision of this ordinance as determined by this commission shall be fined not less than $100.00 and not more than $500.00 for each offense. Every day that a violation shall continue shall constitute a separate and distinct offense.
(Prior code § 199-12; Added. Coun. J. 12-21-88, p. 23526; Amend. 7-8-98, p. 72891)

This page intentionally left blank

TITLE 3
REVENUE AND FINANCE
(Selected Chapters)

Divisions:

I. Funds. (Selected Chapter)
II. Taxes. (Selected Chapter)

DIVISION I
FUNDS
(Selected Chapter)

Chapter:

3-8 Policemen's and Firemen's Death Benefit Fund. (Complete Chapter)

CHAPTER 3-8
POLICEMEN'S AND FIREMEN'S DEATH BENEFIT FUND
(Complete Chapter)

Sections:

Article I. Administration of Death Awards

3-8-010 Authorization of fund.
3-8-020 Amount of fund.
3-8-030 Board of trustees.
3-8-040 Report of injury.
3-8-050 Required proof.
3-8-060 Issuance of voucher.
3-8-070 Deposit of awards.
3-8-080 Trust agreements.
3-8-090 Successor trustee bank.
3-8-100 Investments by trustee bank.
3-8-110 Payments to minors and incompetents.

Article II. Determination of Death Awards

3-8-120 Amounts.
3-8-130 Reallocation upon death of beneficiary.
3-8-140 Death of sole beneficiary.
3-8-150 Marriage or attainment of majority—By beneficiary.
3-8-160 Marriage or attainment of majority—By sole beneficiary.
3-8-170 War service.
3-8-180 Loss due to depreciation.

Article III. Medical and Hospital Care

3-8-190 Authorization of fund.
3-8-200 Administration of fund.
3-8-210 Duties of department heads.
3-8-220 Duty of corporation counsel.
3-8-230 Required proof.
3-8-240 Payments during city council vacation periods.
3-8-250 City council to be notified of payments made.
3-8-260 Burial expenses.

Article I. Administration of Death Awards

§3-8-010 Authorization of fund.

Whenever the city council shall appropriate a sum or sums of money in accordance with the provisions of Section 22-301, et. seq. of the Illinois Pension Code, as amended, for the payment of allowances of money to the family or dependents of any policeman or fireman of the city of Chicago in case he is killed or fatally injured while in the performance of his duties, the same shall be paid and disbursed in accordance with the following provisions.
(Prior code § 22-1; Amend. Coun. J. 3-31-04, p. 20916)

§3-8-020 Amount of fund.

The policemen's and firemen's death benefit fund shall consist of such amount as shall be appropriated by the city council in accordance with the said act of the general assembly.
(Prior code § 22-2)

§3-8-030 Board of trustees.

A board composed of four members shall constitute a board of trustees authorized to carry out the following provisions dealing with the policemen's and firemen's death benefit fund, and shall be charged with the duty of administering that fund. The said board shall consist of the chairman of the committee on finance, the superintendent of police, the fire commissioner and the president of the board of health, or if there be no such commissioners or president, then the acting head of the police department, the fire department or the board of health, as the case may be. The board shall be known by the name and title of "Board of Trustees of the Policemen's and Firemen's Death Benefit Fund."
(Prior code § 22-3)

§3-8-040 Report of injury.

It shall be the duty of the superintendent of police in the case of a policeman, and of the fire commissioner in the case of a fireman, upon the occurrence of any injury in the performance of duty, to have immediate medical care and hospital treatment given to such injured policeman or fireman, to make or cause to be made a complete and careful investigation of all facts surrounding the occurrence, to obtain the statements of all material witnesses, and to present the said report without delay to the said board of trustees for consideration and action thereon, including the determination as to whether or not such injury arose from violence or other accidental cause and was received by the deceased policeman or fireman while he was in the performance of his duty. Such report shall show the actual date and hour of the injury, the place of occurrence, the names and addresses of witnesses and the apparent nature and extent of the injury.
(Prior code § 22-4)

§3-8-050 Required proof.

No such award or payment shall be made unless satisfactory proof shall have been presented to the board of trustees that death occurred within one year from the date of injury, that such injury arose from violence or other accidental cause, that such injury was received while in the performance of duty, and that such injury was the direct cause of death. The amount of the award shall be determined by order of court, entered by a court of competent jurisdiction, declaring heirship.

(Prior code § 22-5; Amend. Coun. J. 12-7-84, p. 11497; 12-7-88, p. 20549)

§3-8-060 Issuance of voucher.

Said board of trustees shall submit to the comptroller a report of its findings (including a certificate of the president of the board of health), stating that such death was the result of injury received in the performance of duty, in all cases where such is the determination of the board, naming the trustee bank and attaching a copy of the agreement made by it with the trustee bank so named; and the comptroller upon receipt of said report shall act in lieu of the city clerk and issue the proper voucher, as contemplated by law, from appropriations made by the city council.

(Prior code § 22-6)

§3-8-070 Deposit of awards.

It shall be the duty of the board of trustees to see that all allowances of money to the family or dependents of any policeman or fireman killed or fatally injured while in the performance of his duty shall be deposited in a duly accredited national or state bank acting as trustee and having its principal office in the city of Chicago, as trustee of said money for conservation, investment as herein provided, and disbursement for the necessary support of such family or dependents and for the education of the children or dependent minor brothers and sisters of the deceased policeman or fireman. Said disbursement shall be in such amounts and at such times as the said trustee bank may deem to be to the best interests of such beneficiaries. Provided, that the provisions for the naming of any specific trustee bank by said board of trustees shall not be construed as affecting the carrying out of the other provisions of this chapter in case it shall be found desirable for any reason to designate another trustee bank. Any trustee bank named pursuant to this chapter may be removed as trustee at any time.

(Prior code § 22-7)

§3-8-080 Trust agreements.

The board of trustees shall enter into a trust agreement in each individual award with the trustee bank named by said board of trustees, under such terms and conditions as the said board of trustees shall deem to be for the best interest of the beneficiary or beneficiaries. Said board of trustees shall also fix the compensation to be paid such trustee bank for its services, such compensation to be an annual amount not to exceed one and one half percent per annum on the original allowance of money in each individual award during the first year of said trust agreement, and one percent per annum on the original allowance of money in each individual award for each succeeding year

during the existence of said trust agreement. However, in those cases where the total maximum compensation authorized to be paid per annum to the trustee bank or its services with respect to an award or awards established by the board of trustees as the result of the death of any one policeman or fireman amounts to less than $100.00 per annum, the board of trustees may increase the compensation of the trustee bank to $100.00 per annum for administering any and all awards established as a result of the death of any one policeman or fireman. The compensation paid to the trustee bank shall be a charge against the award as distinguished from a disbursement for the benefit of the beneficiary or beneficiaries. The board of trustees may require at any time a report from the trustee bank as to any trust fund created under this chapter in addition to the annual report of such trustee bank to the comptroller.
(Prior code § 22-8)

§3-8-090 Successor trustee bank.

Whenever a trustee bank resigns or a successor trustee bank is appointed by the board of trustees, it shall be the duty of said board to require such trustee bank theretofore named to transfer and deliver to the successor trustee bank, all trust funds and trust property of any kind, character or description in its possession belonging to any trust created under this chapter, together with an accounting as to moneys received, securities purchased, investments made, interest earned, moneys disbursed, and to whom, and such other information as may be required by said successor trustee bank. Any trustee bank theretofore named as trustee shall immediately transfer and deliver to the trustee bank last named all such moneys or the securities in which such moneys were invested or other property of any kind, character or description, the avails of such moneys together with a financial statement of each separate trust fund theretofore received by it.
(Prior code § 22-9)

§3-8-100 Investments by trustee bank.

It shall be the duty of the trustee bank from time to time to invest all moneys entrusted to it and actually paid to said trustee bank in full faith and credit bonds of the United States, the state of Illinois, the county of Cook, the sanitary district of Chicago, the city of Chicago, or the board of education of the city of Chicago or in tax anticipation warrants of the county of Cook, the sanitary district of Chicago, the city of Chicago or board of education of Chicago, savings and time deposit certificates of a state bank or a national bank doing business in Illinois, to the extent that such deposits are insured by the United States Government or any agency thereof, with the usual powers of trustees of such funds, and to report annually in writing to the city comptroller of the city of Chicago as to each separate fund or allowance of money, said report to show the name of the beneficiary, the amount received, interest earned, disbursements made, balance on hand, and securities representing the balance.
(Prior code § 22-10)

§3-8-110 Payments to minors and incompetents.

Whenever any moneys are payable to a minor whose mother is dead or to a person who is incompetent or has been adjudged insane, the board of trustees shall have the power to waive guardianship or conservatorship proceedings whenever in the judgment of the board it may be advisable to do so. The said board of trustees shall ascertain the name of the person caring for such minor and the name of the parent or relative providing for or caring for such incompetent or insane person, and shall notify in writing the trustee bank to pay such moneys to the person designated by said board of trustees as being the person who is caring for and providing for such minor or for such incompetent or insane person.

(Prior code § 22-11)

Article II. Determination of Death Awards

§3-8-120 Amounts.

Awards made under the terms of this chapter shall be in accordance with the said statute, approved June 27, 1921, as amended, for the use and benefit of the beneficiaries as follows:

(1) The widow of the deceased if there be no minor child or children $20,000
(2) The widow and one minor child of the deceased, in equal parts 30,000
(3) The widow and two or more minor children of the deceased, in equal parts 40,000
(4) The widow and father or mother of the deceased, in equal parts 30,000
(5) The widow and father and mother of the deceased, in equal parts 40,000
(6) The widow, one minor child and mother, father, or both, of the deceased, in equal parts 40,000
(7) The widow, two or more minor children and father, mother, or both, of the deceased, in equal parts 40,000
(8) One minor child of the deceased 20,000
(9) Two minor children of the deceased, in equal parts 25,000
(10) Three or more minor children of the deceased, in equal parts 40,000
(11) One minor child and father or mother of the deceased, in equal parts 30,000
(12) One minor child and father and mother of the deceased, in equal parts 40,000
(13) Two or more minor children and father, mother, or both, of the deceased, in equal parts 40,000

The right of the minor child is understood to mean the child's proportionate part in the benefits set out in subparagraphs (2), (3), (9) and (10) of this section.

(14) If there be no widow or children of the deceased and there be a father or mother surviving the deceased, awards shall be made as follows:

For the father or mother 20,000
For the father and mother 30,000

(15) If there be no widow, children, father or mother of the deceased, and if there be minor brothers or sisters, and brothers or sisters having reached the age of 50 years or over, fully dependent upon the deceased for support at the time of his death, awards shall be made as follows:

One adult brother or more—each $15,000
One adult sister or more—each 15,000
One minor brother or sister 15,000
Two minor brothers or sisters 20,000
Three minor brothers or sisters 22,500
Four or more minor brothers or sisters 25,000

(16) A child that is physically or mentally disabled, in case he or she is dependent upon the deceased for support at the time of his death, shall be granted the allowances herein provided for a minor child.

(17) When there are two or more beneficiaries of any allowance of money awarded for the support, maintenance and education of the family or dependents of any policeman or fireman, such allowances shall be for the use and benefit of such beneficiaries in equal parts.

(18) When no beneficiaries would be eligible to receive awards under the provisions of this chapter then the estate shall be awarded the amount of $15,000. *(Prior code § 22-12; Amend. Coun. J. 12-7-84, p. 11497; 12-7-88, p. 20549; 3-21-90, p. 12809; 3-6-96, p. 16199)*

§3-8-130 Reallocation upon death of beneficiary.

In the event of the death of any beneficiary, leaving one or more beneficiaries surviving, the trust fund remaining shall be reallocated for the use and benefit of the surviving beneficiary or beneficiaries in the following manner:

The trustee bank shall first determine the amount of the original award, in accordance with subparagraphs (1) to (27) inclusive of Section 3-8-120, which would have been made to the surviving beneficiary or beneficiaries had the deceased beneficiary not been a beneficiary upon the date of the original award. If the award thus determined is less than the original award made, the trustee bank shall ascertain the amount to be held by it for the benefit of the surviving beneficiary or beneficiaries by adding to the award thus determined the total interest received by the trust fund from the inception and by deducting from the sum of the redetermined award and the interest received, the total amount actually paid to or for the benefit of the surviving beneficiary or beneficiaries.

If the balance actually remaining in the trust (taken at its market value) is in excess of the net balance (taken at face value) found to be due to surviving beneficiary or beneficiaries, such excess, after deducting the expenses of the last illness and the funeral of the deceased beneficiary, shall revert to the city and be credited to the general corporate fund by the comptroller. If the balance actually remaining in the trust (taken at its market value) is less than the amount (taken at face value) found due to the surviving beneficiary or beneficiaries under the reallocated award, as aforesaid, the entire balance remaining in the trust shall be held by the trustee bank for the use and benefit of the surviving beneficiary or beneficiaries in accordance with the terms hereof. *(Prior code § 22-13)*

§3-8-140 Death of sole beneficiary.

In the event of the death of the last surviving beneficiary or of a sole beneficiary, all funeral expenses and medical expenses incident to the last illness of the deceased beneficiary shall be paid by the trustee bank and if, after payment of such medical and funeral expenses, any portion of the award remains unexpended the trust shall terminate and such unexpended portion shall be returned to the city by the trustee bank and shall revert and be credited to the general corporate fund by the comptroller.

(Prior code § 22-14)

§3-8-150 Marriage or attainment of majority—By beneficiary.

In the event of the marriage of any beneficiary or in the event that any minor beneficiary other than the widow of the deceased policeman or fireman shall attain the age of 21 years and shall be under no mental or physical disability preventing self-support and shall not be attending a school or college deemed accredited by the board of trustees of the policemen's and firemen's death benefit fund, and there are other beneficiaries remaining, the funds remaining in the hands of the trustee bank shall be reallocated for the use and benefit of the other beneficiary or beneficiaries in the following manner:

The trustee bank shall first determine the amount of the original award, in accordance with subparagraphs (1) to (27) inclusive of Section 3-8-120 which would have been made to the remaining beneficiary or beneficiaries had such former beneficiary not been a beneficiary upon the date of the original award.

If the award thus determined is less than the original award made, the trustee bank shall ascertain the amount to be held by it for the benefit of the remaining beneficiary or beneficiaries by adding to the award thus determined the total interest received by the trust fund from the inception and by deducting from the sum of the redetermined award and the interest received, the total amount actually paid to or for the benefit of the remaining beneficiary or beneficiaries. If the balance actually remaining in the trust (taken at its market value) is in excess of the net balance (taken at the face value) found to be due to remaining beneficiary or beneficiaries, such excess shall revert to the city and be credited to the general corporate fund by the comptroller.

If the balance actually remaining in the trust (taken at its market value) is less than the amount (taken at face value) found due to the remaining beneficiary or beneficiaries as aforesaid, the entire balance remaining in the trust shall be held by the trustee bank for the use and benefit of the remaining beneficiary or beneficiaries in accordance with the terms hereof.

(Prior code § 22-15)

§3-8-160 Marriage or attainment of majority—By sole beneficiary.

In the event of the marriage of the last beneficiary of any trust fund, or in the event that the last remaining beneficiary is a minor and shall attain the age of 21 years and shall be under no mental or physical disability preventing self-support, the trust funds remaining in the hands of the trustee bank shall revert to the city and be credited to the general corporate fund by the comptroller. The purpose of this provision is to encourage the said minor dependents to seek and secure educational advantages in the several trades, industrial lines or professions.

(Prior code § 22-16)

§3-8-170 War service.

In the event a beneficiary shall have entered or hereafter shall enter the armed forces of the United States of America or its allies, or if in the judgment of the board of trustees any beneficiary shall be engaged in essential war activity requiring full time service which interferes with regular attendance at an accredited school, the right of such beneficiary with respect to attending school subsequent to attaining the age of 21 years (as allowed by Section 3-8-150), shall be preserved to and retained in such beneficiary for a period terminating six months from and after the date of his official separation or right to withdraw from such armed forces or war activity to the same effect as though such beneficiary had not attained age 21 years, but no part of the trust fund shall be segregated specifically for the use and benefit of such beneficiary. At the expiration of said six months' period, the balance remaining in the trust fund, if any, shall be used for the use and benefit of the said beneficiary and other remaining beneficiaries, in accordance with and subject to the other provisions of the code not in conflict with this section.

(Prior code § 22-16.1)

§3-8-180 Loss due to depreciation.

It is the intention of this chapter that upon reallocation of any award, as aforesaid, any loss to the trust arising from the depreciation in value of any assets held thereunder shall fall upon the reversionary interest of the city and not upon the remaining beneficiaries of the trust.

(Prior code § 22-17)

Article III. Medical and Hospital Care

§3-8-190 Authorization of fund.

(a) Whenever the city council shall appropriate a sum or sums of money for the payment of medical care and hospital treatment in case of an accident resulting in an injury to or death of a policeman or fireman employed by the city while in the performance of his duties, in accordance with the provisions of Sections 22-301, et. seq. of the Illinois Pension Code, as amended, the same shall be paid, disbursed and recouped in accordance with the following provisions.

(b) Such appropriated sum or sums may also be used for vocational retraining of sworn police or uniformed fire personnel who are in receipt of a duty or occupational disability benefit and who, by reason of their service related injuries, are unable ever to return to active service, in accordance with the following provisions.

(Prior code § 22-18; Amend. Coun. J. 6-6-01, p. 60141; Amend. 3-31-04, p. 20916)

§3-8-200 Administration of fund.

(a) The committee on finance is authorized, directed and empowered to provide for payment for proper medical care and hospital treatment for accidental injuries sustained by any policeman or fireman, while in the performance of his duties and to that end may recommend to the city council the authorization for payment of any such necessary expenses.

(b) The committee on finance of the city council shall administer a program of vocational restraining assistance for sworn police and uniformed fire personnel who are in receipt of a duty or occupational disability benefit from their respective annuity and benefit fund and who, by reason of their service related injuries, are unable ever to return to active service. This program shall apply to all sworn police and uniformed fire personnel who receive a duty or occupational disability benefit, irrespective of whether they were in active service on the effective date of this amendatory ordinance. Provided, however, that no person who owes a debt, as defined in Section 2-152-150 of the Municipal Code, or who owes any unpaid court-ordered child support obligation, shall be eligible for vocational retraining assistance.

(c) The vocational retraining assistance program shall be administered in accordance with rules promulgated by the chairman of the committee on finance. These rules shall include, but shall not be limited to, individual eligibility for assistance, the types of expenditures covered by the program, evaluation of retraining programs, disbursement procedures and yearly and lifetime expenditure limits.

(d) No person shall be eligible for vocational retraining assistance under this section unless they apply to the committee on finance within two years of the effective date of this ordinance or two years from the date of the award of the duty or occupational disability benefit, whichever is later.
(Prior code § 22-19; Amend. Coun. J. 6-6-01, p. 60141)

§3-8-210 Duties of department heads.

It shall be the duty of the superintendent of police in the case of a policeman, and of the fire commissioner in the case of a fireman, upon the occurrence of any accidental injury in the performance of duty, to have immediate medical care and hospital treatment given to such policeman or fireman; to make or cause to be made a complete and careful investigation of all facts surrounding the occurrence; to obtain the statements of all material witnesses; and to present a report thereof without delay to the said committee on finance for consideration and action thereon, which consideration shall include the determination by said committee as to whether or not such injury was occasioned by the negligence of any other person or by any agent or servant of such other person. Such report shall show the actual date and hour of the injury, the place of occurrence, the names and addresses of witnesses, and the apparent nature and extent of the injury. Such report shall also show all items of expense, with bills attached, together with a certificate by the chief physician of the department concerned as to the reasonableness of charges made for the services rendered, and the recommendation of the head of the department concerned as to payment of such items of expense by the city.
(Prior code § 22-20)

§3-8-220 Duty of corporation counsel.

In the event that the said committee on finance is of the opinion, from all the facts and circumstances presented to it in the said report or otherwise ascertained by it, that such injury was occasioned by the negligence of some other person, or by the negligence of any agent or servant of such other person, the committee on finance shall so notify the corporation counsel; and it

shall be the duty of the corporation counsel forthwith to demand from such other person reimbursement for the amount expended by the city for the necessary medical care and hospital treatment of such policeman or fireman; and in default of payment of such amount so expended, the corporation counsel shall institute proceedings to recoup for the city the amount so expended, as provided in the aforesaid act of the general assembly.
(Prior code § 22-21)

§3-8-230 Required proof.
No payment shall be made under the provisions hereof unless satisfactory proof shall have been presented to said committee on finance that such injury was sustained by such policeman or fireman while in the performance of his duty.
(Prior code § 22-22)

§3-8-240 Payments during city council vacation periods.
Payment of hospital and medical expenses of police officers and firefighters shall be paid according to the provisions of the Municipal Code of Chicago and the annual appropriation ordinance, except that during the annual vacation period or periods of the city council, the chairman of the committee on finance may order the payment of hospital and medical expenses of police officers and firefighters injured in the line of duty.
(Prior code § 22-23)

§3-8-250 City council to be notified of payments made.
As soon as practical thereafter, the chairman of the committee on finance shall notify the city council of each hospital and medical expense of police officers and firefighters paid during the annual vacation period or periods of the city council.
(Prior code § 22-24)

§3-8-260 Burial expenses.
Burial expenses of police officers and firefighters, employed by the city, killed or fatally injured in the performance of their duties shall be paid and dispersed by the chairman of the committee on finance in the amount not to exceed $4,200.00.
(Added. Coun. J. 10-7-98, p. 78109)

DIVISION II
TAXES
(Selected Chapter)

Chapter:
3-56 Wheel Tax Licenses. (Complete Chapter)

CHAPTER 3-56
WHEEL TAX LICENSES
(Complete Chapter)

Sections:

3-56-010 Interpretation of chapter.
3-56-020 License required.
3-56-021 New city residents or new vehicle purchases.
3-56-030 Application.
3-56-040 Issuance.
3-56-050 Fees.
3-56-060 License plates.
3-56-070 License emblems.
3-56-080 Sale of vehicle.
3-56-090 Affixing plates or emblems.
3-56-100 Transfer to new vehicle.
3-56-110 Allocation of revenues.
3-56-120 Vehicle manufacturers and dealers.
3-56-121 Automobile rental fleet—Payment of wheel tax.
3-56-130 Ownership identification on vehicles.
3-56-135 Right to inspect.
3-56-140 Exemptions.
3-56-145 Vehicle tax liability.
3-56-150 Penalty.

§3-56-010 Interpretation of chapter.

For the purpose of this chapter:

"Antique motor vehicle" means a motor vehicle more than 25 years old, or a bona fide replica, which is driven exclusively to and from antique shows, exhibitions, demonstrations, or for servicing, or a fire-fighting vehicle more than 20 years old which is used exclusively for exhibition and shall be licensed by the state of Illinois, as an antique motor vehicle.

"Automobile rental" means any transfer of the possession or right of possession of an automobile to a user for a valuable consideration for a period of less than one year. "Automobile rental" does not include taxicab, jitney or livery service as defined in Chapter 9-112 of this code.

"Bus" means a motor vehicle designed for carrying more than 10 passengers and used for the transportation of persons.

"Chicago rental revenues" means all revenues derived from rental or leasing of automobiles in a rental fleet as computed for purposes of the Chicago Personal Property Lease Transaction Tax under Chapter 3-32 of this code.

"Larger passenger automobile" means a passenger automobile with a curb weight of at least 4,500 pounds, as determined by the vehicles manufacturer.

"Moped" means a vehicle capable of being powered by either the muscular power of man or as a motor vehicle at the discretion of the operator. For the purpose of licensing, a moped shall be licensed as a motor bicycle or motor tricycle.

"Motor vehicle" means any vehicle propelled otherwise than by the muscular power of man or animal, except such as run on rails or tracks.

"National rental revenues" means the gross consideration for renting or leasing of passenger automobiles at all locations in the United States, valued in money, whether received in money or otherwise. For purposes of this chapter, national rental revenues shall be determined without any deduction on account of the cost of the vehicles rented or leased, the cost of materials used or labor or service costs or any other cost or expense whatsoever, except for (1) taxes on rental transactions imposed on renters and separately charged to and collected from customers; (2) fuel charges to customers in connection with the rental of automobiles; and (3) insurance sold to customers in connection with the rental of automobiles.

"Owner" includes a lessee, licensee, or bailee of a motor vehicle having the exclusive use thereof, under a lease or other similar contractual agreement for a period of not less than 30 days.

"Recreational vehicle" means every motor vehicle originally designed or permanently converted and used for living quarters or for human habitation and not used as a commercial motor vehicle.

"Rental fleet" means passenger automobiles under common ownership and used in an automobile rental business.

"Residing within the city" means and includes the owning, leasing, or otherwise controlling of property or a place of business wherein motor vehicles, trailers, or semi-trailers are stored, repaired, serviced, loaded, or unloaded within the city in connection with such business.

"Semi-trailer" means a vehicle designed for carrying persons or property and for being drawn by a motor vehicle and so constructed that some part of its weight and that of its load rests upon or is carried by another vehicle.

"Situs" or "base of vehicle" means the place where a vehicle is principally garaged, or from whence it is principally dispatched, or where the movements of such vehicle usually originate.

"Smaller passenger automobile" means a passenger automobile with a curb weight of less than 4,500 pounds, as determined by the vehicle's manufacturer.

"Tractor" means any motor vehicle designed and used primarily for drawing other vehicles and not so constructed as to carry a load other than a part of the weight of the vehicle and load so drawn.

"Trailer" means a vehicle designed for carrying persons or property and for being drawn by a motor vehicle and so constructed that no part of its weight rests upon the towing vehicle.

Nothing contained in this chapter shall be construed as in any manner repealing or modifying any provision of the ordinances of the city relating to any particular business now being licensed by the city wherein motor vehicles or other vehicles are being used upon the public ways of the city.

(Prior code § 29-1; Amend. Coun. J. 4-6-90, p. 13691; 6-10-96, p. 22856; 7-2-97, p. 48683; 11-19-03, p. 14216)

§3-56-020 License required.

It shall be unlawful for any motor vehicle owner residing within the city to use, or to cause or permit any of the owner's agents, employees, lessees, licensees or bailees to use, any motor vehicle or any other vehicle upon the public ways of the city or upon any city-owned property, unless such vehicle is licensed as provided in this chapter. Commercial motor vehicles, as defined in Paragraph 2 of Section 18b-101 of the Illinois Vehicle Code, as amended, which are registered pursuant to the International Registration Plan shall be exempt from the licensing requirements of this chapter.

The owner of a motor vehicle or any other vehicle who resides in the city but maintains a situs or base of such vehicle located outside of the city shall be entitled to a credit against the appropriate license fee provided for herein in the amount of any wheel tax license fee paid for such vehicle to the municipality where such vehicle is based; provided, however, that in no event shall the license fee be reduced to an amount less than the wheel tax license fee for passenger automobiles.

It shall be unlawful for any person under the age of 16 years to operate on the streets of the city a motorcycle, powercycle, bicycle with motor attached, or power scooter, with a motor which produces not to exceed five brake horsepower.

No person shall operate a motor vehicle as set forth in this chapter without said vehicle being duly licensed as prescribed herein. The operator of any such motor vehicle shall be subject to the same penalties as the owner for the violation of any of the terms of this ordinance.

(Prior code § 29-2; Amend. Coun. J. 4-6-90, p. 13691; 12-15-92, p. 27387; 7-2-97, p. 48683; 11-19-03, p. 14216)

§3-56-021 New city residents or new vehicle purchases.

Any person alleged to have violated either the license requirement set forth in Section 3-56-020 or the license display requirement set forth in Section 9-64-125 may raise as an affirmative defense that: (1) if such person resided in the city for less than 30 days at the time he or she was cited for violation; or (2) the cited vehicle was purchased less than 30 days prior to the issuance of the violation. If the alleged violator can demonstrate, by clear and convincing evidence, that he or she resided in the city for less than 30 days or owned the vehicle for less than 30 days at the time the citation was issued, and that the appropriate fee was paid in accordance with Chapter 3-56 no later than 30 days following the commencement of city residence or purchase of the vehicle no liability shall exist. A showing of recent residency may be made by a lease, utility billing records or other appropriate documents. A showing of recent vehicle purchase may be made by applicable vehicle registration or title documents issued by the Secretary of State or other appropriate documents. Any person who knowingly provides inaccurate information in connection with this section shall be fined in an amount not to exceed $500.00.

(Added. Coun. J. 7-10-96, p. 24532; Amend. 12-8-04, p. 38063)

§3-56-030 Application.

Any person desiring a license for any such motor vehicle or other vehicle shall file an application with the city clerk, upon a form provided therefor, which shall set forth the name and address of the applicant, a description of the vehicle for which the license is desired, and such other information as may be prescribed. Such application shall be transmitted to the mayor.

(Prior code § 29-3; Amend. Coun. J. 12-8-04, p. 38063)

§3-56-040 Issuance.

Upon the payment by the applicant of the license fee hereinafter provided, the mayor shall issue, or cause to be issued, a license which shall be attested by the city clerk authorizing the use of such vehicle within the city.

The annual period for every such license shall begin on July 1st, and end on June 30th of the year following the year of issuance.
(Prior code § 29-4)

§3-56-050 Fees.

(a) Applicable license fees are as follows:

Vehicle	**Fee**
Smaller passenger automobiles, ambulances and hearses	$ 75.00
Larger passenger automobiles	90.00
The city clerk shall maintain a list of makes and models of passenger automobiles classified as "smaller" or "larger" for the purposes of this provision. The list shall be available for public inspection at any time during the clerk's regular business hours.	
Passenger automobiles only, not more than one vehicle, registered to a person 65 years of age or older, upon satisfactory proof of age and vehicle ownership	$ 30.00
Antique motor vehicles	30.00
Motor bicycles, motor tricycles or mopeds	45.00
Municipally owned vehicles	No fee
Vehicles licensed to disabled veterans or to persons who, while serving in the United States Armed Forces, were taken prisoner of war	No fee
School and church buses	No fee
Trailers, recreational use—5,000 lbs. or less (Class "TA")	45.00
Trailers, commercial use—5,000 lbs. or less (Class "TAC")	55.00
Trailers—over 5,000 lbs. (Class "TB")	100.00
All other vehicles, including trucks, tractor-semitrailer units, motor buses and recreational vehicles:	
14,000 lbs. or less	150.00
14,001—36,000 lbs.	200.00
over 36,000 lbs.	300.00

(b) The license fee for each vehicle shall be $40.00 greater than the amount otherwise specified in this section if the license is purchased after July 15th and: (1) the applicant fails to purchase the license within 30 days of residing in the city; or (2) the applicant fails to purchase the license within 30 days of purchasing the vehicle. unless the city clerk determines that the failure to purchase the license in any case was due to reasonable cause.

(c) If application is made for the license after July 15th, the following fees shall apply:

Between July 16th and November 30th — 100 percent of the applicable fee set forth in subsection (a) plus any additional fee mandated by subsection (b);

Between December 1st and March 3 1st — 66 percent of the applicable fee set forth in subsection (a) plus any additional fee mandated by subsection (b); and

After April 1st — 33 percent of the applicable fee set forth in subsection (a) plus any additional fee mandated by subsection (b).

(d) Before any applicant shall be entitled to a prorated license as provided for in this section, the applicant may be required to furnish an affidavit in form satisfactory to the city clerk accompanied by suitable documentary proof, establishing the date of the purchase of the vehicle or the beginning of residency. Suitable documentary proof of the date of commencement of residency shall include a lease, mortgage or title documents, or other appropriate documents. Suitable documentary proof of the date of vehicle purchase shall include vehicle registration or title documents issued by the Secretary of State or other appropriate documents. All applicants that do not comply with the requirements for a prorated license shall be subject to a full annual license fee.

(e) Failure to purchase the required license shall be a violation of this section.

(Prior code § 29-5; Amended. Coun. J. 5-9-84, p. 6279; 12-12-84, p. 11847; 4-18-85, p. 15174; 4-25-85, p. 15889; 3-30-88, p. 11340; 9-11-91, p. 4611; 11-22-91, p. 9188; 12-15-93, p. 43704; 6-10-96, p. 22856; 11-17-99, p. 17487; 11-19-03, p. 14216; 3-31-04, p. 20916; 12-15-04, p. 39840, § 3.3, effective June 1, 2005)

§3-56-060 License plates.

The city clerk shall deliver to the holder of a license for a motor bicycle, motor tricycle, or trailer, a metal plate or other license emblem which shall bear the word "Chicago" and a number identical with the number of the license, the name of the class to which such vehicle belongs and the year for which such license is issued.

When such metal plate or other license emblem is delivered to the holder of a license for a motor bicycle, motor tricycle, or trailer, it shall be the duty of such licensee to affix such plate or other license emblem in a conspicuous position so that the said plate or other license emblem can be easily seen, upon the rear end of such motor bicycle, motor tricycle, or trailer.

(Prior code § 29-6)

§3-56-070 License emblems.

The city clerk shall deliver to the holder of any license for an automobile, recreational vehicle, motor truck, motor ambulance or hearse, motor coach or motor bus, a sticker license emblem, which shall bear the words "Vehicle Tax" and "Chicago," and the numerals designating the year for which such license is issued, a reproduction of the corporate seal of the city, the names of the mayor and the city clerk, the name of the class to which such vehicle belongs, and a number identical with the number of such license. Such sticker license emblem may bear information indicating residential permit parking, if applicable. In addition, sticker license emblems issued either to disabled veterans or to former prisoners of war, pursuant to Section 3-56-050, shall bear the word "Veteran."

Such sticker emblem shall be affixed, in accordance with the instructions printed thereon which are made a part hereof, and without the use of supplemental adhesives, at the lower right-hand corner on the inside of the glass portion of the windshield of such motor vehicle, approximately one inch from the right and lower sections of the frame of such windshield.

The city clerk shall change annually the predominant background colors of such sticker license emblems.

(Prior code § 29-7; Amend. Coun. J. 4-18-85, p. 15174; 4-25-85, p. 15889; 3-11-98, p. 63453)

§3-56-080 Sale of vehicle.

Immediately upon the sale of any vehicle licensed under this chapter, when such sale is made prior to the date of expiration of such license, the vendor shall remove the license tag, plate, transparent sticker, or other license emblem from the vehicle so sold.

Except where a vehicle license has been regularly transferred as hereinafter provided in Section 3-56-100, it shall be the duty of the purchaser of any used automobile or other vehicle to remove and deliver to the vendor or the vendor's agent immediately any license tag, plate, transparent sticker or other license emblem which may be attached to such vehicle at the time of the purchase thereof, which the vendor of such vehicle may have refused, failed or omitted to detach from such vehicle as hereinabove required. It shall be unlawful for any such purchaser to use, sell or offer for sale such used automobile or other vehicle without first having removed all such license tags, plates, transparent stickers or other license emblems.
(Prior code § 29-8)

§3-56-090 Affixing plates or emblems.

It shall be unlawful for any person to affix or cause to be affixed any license tag, plate, transparent sticker or other license emblem to any automobile or other vehicle other than the vehicle to which such license tag, plate, transparent sticker or other license emblem was intended to be affixed at the time of the issuance thereof by the city clerk.
(Prior code § 29-9)

§3-56-100 Transfer to new vehicle.

Whenever the owner of any vehicle licensed under this chapter, before the expiration of such license, sells or otherwise disposes of such vehicle, and thereafter acquires another vehicle and desires to transfer the vehicle license originally issued for the vehicle disposed of, to such newly acquired vehicle, such owner shall immediately make application to the city clerk for a transfer of said vehicle license to the newly purchased vehicle. Said application shall state the name and address of the licensee and the name and address of the purchaser of said vehicle, together with a description of the newly purchased vehicle. Upon surrender of the original license and transparent sticker, or vehicle tag in case a metal tag has been issued, or upon proof that the transparent sticker or plate has been destroyed, the city clerk shall transfer said license to apply to the newly acquired vehicle upon payment of the proper license fee, provided, that the city clerk shall not transfer any license when the transparent sticker emblem issued under said license is defaced or mutilated so as to prevent identification of the emblem. It shall be unlawful for any person to display a transparent sticker emblem on any vehicle other than the vehicle for which the emblem was originally issued, without first transferring the license to such other vehicle, as provided for herein.

The owner of any vehicle licensed under this chapter shall promptly notify the clerk and the department of police whenever the transparent sticker emblem issued under such license is lost, stolen, or destroyed.

The fee for a duplicate vehicle sticker shall be $20.00.

The transfer fee shall be $20.00. If the newly acquired vehicle is of a class requiring the payment of a license fee higher than was paid for the license originally obtained for the vehicle disposed of, the fee required to be paid for such transfer shall be a sum equal to the difference between the fee paid for the original license and the fee fixed for licenses for vehicles of such class, plus the transfer fee of $20.00.
(Prior code § 29-11; Amended Coun. J. 12-15-93, p. 43704; 11-17-99, p. 17487; 11-19-03, p. 14216)

§3-56-110 Allocation of revenues.

All revenues derived from license and transfer fees shall be kept as a separate fund and used for paying the cost of repair, maintenance and improvement of streets and alleys; traffic law enforcement; automobile emission control testing and such other uses as the city council shall authorize in the annual appropriation ordinance, or otherwise direct.
(Prior code § 29-12)

§3-56-120 Vehicle manufacturers and dealers.

If any manufacturer or dealer in any of the motor vehicles mentioned in this chapter shall make application to the city clerk and shall state that he is a manufacturer operating a plant for the construction of motor vehicles within the city or dealer in such motor vehicles with a salesroom located within the city and that he desires a license emblem to be used by him or it, the city clerk shall upon payment by such applicant to the director of revenue of the fee hereinafter set forth issue to such manufacturer or dealer a distinctive license plate or transparent sticker
license emblem with a number thereon. Said emblem must be attached to or borne by any such motor vehicles while being operated on the streets of the city. When any such vehicle is in use and carries such license plate or transparent sticker license emblem, no other license fee shall be collected under the provisions of this chapter.

The annual license fee to be paid for each such license plate or transparent sticker license emblem shall be $55.00, and said fee shall not be prorated.

Every manufacturer or dealer applying for said plates or transparent sticker license emblems must submit to the city clerk satisfactory proof of his status as such manufacturer or dealer and satisfactory proof of the number of sets of dealer's plates issued to the applicant by the state of Illinois. Provided, that no license plates or transparent sticker license emblems shall be issued hereunder unless the applicant is in possession of an Illinois state manufacturer's or dealer's license for the current year. The total number of license plates and transparent sticker license emblems that may be obtained hereunder shall not exceed the number of sets of dealer's license plates issued to the applicant by the state.

No such license plate or emblem shall be used on any motor vehicle rented by such manufacturer or dealer, or on any vehicle used to transport persons or property for hire, or on any vehicle unless such vehicle is operated under a dealer's license issued by the state of Illinois and to which both state license plates are attached.
(Prior code § 29-13; Amend. Coun. J. 5-9-84, p. 6280; 11-22-91, p. 9188; 11-17-99, p. 17487; 11-19-03, p. 14216)

§3-56-121 Automobile rental fleet—Payment of wheel tax.

(a) Notwithstanding any provision of this chapter, the owner of a rental fleet used in the city as well as elsewhere shall purchase wheel tax licenses in accordance with the procedures of this section. No later than July 15th of each year, the owner of a rental fleet shall file with the city clerk a remittance return in a form approved by the department of revenue and indicating the owner's Chicago rental revenues, national revenue rentals, and the number of passenger automobiles in the owner's fleet. Revenue figures shall be for the most recently completed 12-month period from April 1st to March 31st. Fleet size shall be determined as of March 31st. The return filed for every 12-month period beginning on or after April 1, 1997, shall also include the net additions to the fleet (number of passenger automobiles added to the fleet for any purpose less those disposed of and replaced) and the number of passenger automobiles in the fleet disposed of and replaced. All figures shall be certified by an independent auditor. The return shall also include the payment for wheel tax licenses for the owner's rental fleet, calculated as follows:

Step 1: Chicago rental revenue divided by national rental revenue, and the resulting number expressed as a percentage:

Step 2: The number of automobiles in the national fleet multiplied by the Step 1 percentage;

Step 3: The product of Step 2 times the passenger automobile license fee;

Step 4: The number of automobiles added to the fleet since the last annual return times the Step 1 percentage:

Step 5: The product of Step 4 times the passenger automobile license fee;

Step 6: The number of passenger automobiles replaced in the fleet since the last annual return times the Step 1 percentage;

Step 7: The product of Step 6 times the transfer fee described in Section 3-56-100;

Step 8: The sum of the results of Steps 3, 5 and 7 is the annual rental fleet fee.

The city clerk shall issue the appropriate number of wheel tax licenses, based on combining Steps 3 and 5.

(b) If a fleet owner fails or refuses to provide audited revenue and fleet size figures for the specified period, the owner shall purchase a wheel tax license for each and every automobile in its rental fleet that is used in the city of Chicago.

(c) Nothing in this section prevents the director of revenue and the city clerk from disputing any figure provided by a fleet owner. Whenever not inconsistent with the provisions of this section, or when this section is silent, the provisions of the Uniform Revenue Procedures Ordinance, Chapter 3-4 of this code, shall apply to and supplement this section.
(Added. Coun. J. 7-2-97, p. 48683)

§3-56-130 Ownership identification on vehicles.

It shall be unlawful for any person to use or to cause or permit any of his employees to use any motor vehicle, or other vehicle in the transportation of property upon the public ways of the city unless such vehicle shall have the name and address of the owner thereof, and a serial number distinguishing said vehicle from any other vehicle controlled or used by the same person

plainly painted, in letters at least one and one-half inches in length, in a conspicuous place on the outside of such vehicle. Provided, that any such person using and operating in the city more than five such vehicles may cause such name and serial number to be painted on each vehicle as aforesaid in letters not less than three inches in length and omit therefrom the address of such person. Provided, further, that in event such vehicle is used or operated continuously by a lessee or bailee or other person having complete control of such vehicle, instead of the owner thereof, the name, address and serial number or name and serial number, as the case may be, of such lessee, bailee or other person may be painted on said vehicle as if such lessee, bailee, or other person using and operating said vehicle were the owner thereof. Such name, address and serial number, or name and serial number, as the case may be, shall be kept so painted, plainly and distinctly, at all times while such vehicle is in use on the public ways of the city. This section shall not be construed as applying to street cars running on metallic rails, or to any motor vehicle, or other vehicle which is used exclusively for pleasure.
(Prior code § 29-14)

§3-56-135 Right to inspect.

Members of the police department, investigators of the department of revenue and investigators of the city clerk's office shall have the authority to enter the following places for purposes of ascertaining whether vehicles parked therein are in compliance with this chapter:

(1) Any public garage, as defined in Chapter 4-232;
(2) Any parking lot that is open to pedestrian traffic.

Nothing in this section authorizes any police officer or investigator to force, break or remove any lock or door in order to gain entry to any of the foregoing places.
(Added. Coun. J. 11-12-03, p. 11505)

§3-56-140 Exemptions.

All vehicles owned and operated upon the public ways of the city by the United States Government or any agency thereof, or by the state of Illinois or any department thereof, or by any political subdivision, public or municipal corporation of the state of Illinois or any department or other agency of such corporation, or by the American Red Cross, all buses owned and operated by churches in conjunction with the authorized activities of said institutions, and all vehicles exempt from payment of a registration fee under Section 3-608 of the Motor Vehicle Law of the state of Illinois, and all vehicles registered under Section 3-616 of the Motor Vehicle Law of the state of Illinois, shall be exempt from the vehicle tax. Every exempt vehicle, except those vehicles owned by the city of Chicago which are used by said governmental agencies in confidential or undercover investigatory services or by an officer of any of said agencies as his official car, shall have the name of the owner painted in letters at least one and one-half inches in length in a conspicuous place on the outside of each side of the vehicle; provided, that in lieu of such identification every vehicle which is exempt from payment of the state motor vehicle registration fee, shall have a license plate or emblem as provided in Sections 3-56-060 and 3-56-070; and every vehicle owned by the United States gov-

ernment or any agency thereof, which is not identified as herein required, shall have such license plate or emblem. All license plates or emblems for vehicles exempt from payment of the vehicle tax shall be furnished by the city clerk free of charge.
(Prior code § 29-15)

§3-56-145 Vehicle tax liability.

(a) As used in this section:

(1) "Director" means the director of revenue.

(2) "Vehicle tax" means the wheel tax license fee required to be paid under this chapter, including any penalties associated with the fee.

(b) The director shall establish and administer a system whereby the city notifies the Secretary of State of vehicle tax liability and the Secretary of State suspends the registration of vehicles for which the tax has not been paid. The system shall be operated in accordance with Section 3-704.1 of the Illinois Vehicle Code, 625 ILCS 5/3-704.1, as amended. The determination of the director that the vehicle owner has failed to pay the vehicle tax as required by this chapter shall be prima facie correct, and the protesting party shall have the burden of proving with books, records and other documentary evidence (including, but not limited to, affidavits submitted by the city clerk, or other affidavits) that the determination is incorrect.

(c) The system shall provide for the following:

(1) The director shall send by first class mail to the vehicle owner at the owner's address recorded with the Secretary of State a first notice for failure to pay a vehicle tax whenever the director has reasonable cause to believe that the vehicle owner has failed to pay a vehicle tax as required by this chapter. Such reasonable belief may, but need not be, based upon a report from the city clerk stating that the vehicle tax is delinquent. The notice sent to the owner shall include at least the following:

(A) The name and address of the vehicle owner;

(B) The registration plate number of the vehicle;

(C) The period for which the vehicle tax is due;

(D) The amount of vehicle tax that is due;

(E) A statement that the vehicle owner's registration for the vehicle will be subject to suspension proceedings unless the vehicle owner pays the vehicle tax or successfully contests the owner's alleged liability within 30 days of the date of the notice;

(F) An explanation of the vehicle owner's opportunity to be heard under subsection (d).

(2) If a vehicle owner fails to pay the vehicle tax or to contest successfully the owner's alleged liability within the period specified in the first notice, the director shall send by first class mail to the vehicle owner at the owner's address recorded with the Secretary of State a second notice of impending registration suspension. The notice shall contain the same information as the first notice, but shall also state that the failure to pay the amount owing, or to contest successfully the alleged liability within 45 days of the second notice, will result in the city's notification of the Secretary of State that the vehicle owner is eligible for the initiation of suspension proceedings under Section 3-704.1 of the Illinois Vehicle Code.

(d) The vehicle owner may file with the director a request for an opportunity to be heard under this subsection. The owner may contest the alleged liability either through an adjudication by mail or at an administrative hearing, at the option of the vehicle owner. The grounds upon which the liability may be contested shall be limited to the following:

(1) The alleged vehicle owner does not own the vehicle.

(2) The vehicle is not subject to the vehicle tax by law.

(3) The vehicle tax for the period in question has been paid.

At an administrative hearing, the formal or technical rules of evidence shall not apply. Evidence may be admitted if it is a type commonly relied upon by reasonably prudent persons in the conduct of their affairs. The hearing shall be recorded. The person conducting the hearing shall have the power to administer oaths and to secure by subpoena the attendance and testimony of witnesses and the production of relevant documents.

(e) If a vehicle owner who has been sent a first notice of failure to pay a vehicle tax and a second notice of impending registration suspension fails to pay the vehicle tax or to contest successfully the vehicle owner's liability within the periods specified in the notices, the director shall cause a certified report to be sent to the Secretary of State pursuant to this subsection. The report, which shall be certified by the director, shall notify the Secretary of State of the vehicle owner's failure to pay the vehicle tax or related penalties, and shall contain the following:

(1) The name, last known address and registration plate number of the vehicle of the person who failed to pay the vehicle tax;

(2) An indication that the report is made by and on behalf of the city of Chicago;

(3) A statement that the city sent notices as required by subsection (c); the date on which the notices were sent; the address to which the notices were sent; and the date of the hearing, if any.

(f) A person named in a certified report filed with the Secretary of State pursuant to Section 3-704.1 of the Illinois Vehicle Code in accordance with subsection (e) of this section may, within 45 days of the date on the Secretary of State's notice to the person named in the certified report of the possible suspension as required by Section 3-704.1(f) of the Illinois Vehicle Code, file with the director a written statement and provide books, records and other supporting documentation to challenge the certified report. The grounds for challenging the accuracy of the certified report shall be limited to the following:

(1) That the city failed to send notices to the alleged vehicle owner as required by Section 3-704.1(b) of the Illinois Vehicle Code;

(2) That the city failed to indicate the dates on which the notices were sent;

(3) That the city failed to indicate the date of the hearing, if held;

(4) That the alleged vehicle owner did not own the vehicle during the relevant tax period;

(5) That the vehicle is not subject to the vehicle tax by law;

(6) That vehicle tax for the relevant tax period has been paid.

(g) The director shall notify the vehicle owner of the director's decision. The director shall also notify the Secretary of State whenever a person named in a certified report has subsequently paid a vehicle tax or whenever the director determines that the original report was in error. The director shall also give a certified copy of the notification upon request at no additional charge to the person named in the report.

(h) From time to time, the city treasurer and the city comptroller shall reimburse the Secretary of State for the Secretary's expenses in administering the vehicle suspension program as required by Section 3-704.1 of the Illinois Vehicle Code.

(i) Whenever a certified report is sent to the Secretary of State pursuant to this subsection, the director shall assess against the vehicle owner a processing fee to reimburse the city for its expenses. The amount of the processing fee shall be $30.00, plus an amount equal to the amount that the city is required to reimburse the Secretary of State for the Secretary of State's expenses in suspending the vehicle registration of the vehicle owner.

The fee imposed by this subsection shall be imposed only if the vehicle owner's registration is suspended.

(Added Coun. J. 8-4-93, p. 36336; Amend. 6-10-96, p. 22858)

§3-56-150 Penalty.

Any person who shall take, destroy, remove or obliterate any license tag, plate or emblem provided for in this chapter, without the consent of the owner of the vehicle, shall be fined not less than $25.00 nor more than $200.00 for each offense. Every such wrongful destruction, obliteration or removal of such license tag, plate or emblem from any vehicle shall be considered a separate offense. Any person who fails to display the license tag, plate or emblem as required by this chapter shall be fined $120.00.

Any person violating any provision of this chapter where the penalty is not otherwise herein provided for, shall be fined not less than $5.00 nor more than $100.00 for each offense. A separate and distinct offense shall be considered as committed for each and every day any vehicle is used upon the public ways of the city without having procured a license and without having complied with the provisions of this chapter.

Notwithstanding any other provision of this chapter, persons who reside in the city, register their motor vehicle at a location outside the city and fail to pay the license tax fee imposed by this chapter shall be fined not less than $200.00 nor more than $500.00.

(Prior code § 29-17; Amend. Coun. J. 2-4-92, p. 12811; 11-10-94, p. 59125; 7-9-03, p. 3281)

TITLE 4
BUSINESSES, OCCUPATIONS AND CONSUMER PROTECTION
(Selected Chapters)

Divisions:

I.	General Regulations and Fees. (Selected Chapters)
II.	Businesses Involving Food Products. (Selected Chapters)
III.	Businesses Involving Liquor and Tobacco. (Selected Chapters)
IV.	Health Services. (Selected Chapters)
V.	Hazardous and Related Activities. (Selected Chapters)
VI.	Wholesale, Retail and Service Activities. (Selected Chapters)
VII.	Other Occupations and Services. (Selected Chapters)

DIVISION I
GENERAL REGULATIONS AND FEES
(Selected Chapters)

Chapters:

4-4	General Licensing Provisions. (Selected Sections)
4-5	License Fees for Title 4 Licenses. (Complete Chapter)

CHAPTER 4-4
GENERAL LICENSING PROVISIONS
(Selected Sections)

Sections:

4-4-010	License—Required—Violation—Penalty.
4-4-015	Closure order—Violation—Penalty.
4-4-020	License—Required for businesses and occupations not provided for by other code provisions.
4-4-030	License—Grant.
4-4-040	License—Issuance.
4-4-050	License—Application.
4-4-060	License—Application—Inspection or investigation.
4-4-070	License—Application—Affidavits.
4-4-080	Bonds.
4-4-084	License suspension pending payment of fines, costs or other sum to the city.
4-4-090	Prepayment of license fees.
4-4-110	Term—Temporary license.
4-4-130	Rebate or refund of fees.
4-4-140	Foreign representatives—Exempted.
4-4-152	Child support delinquencies.
4-4-155	Predatory lenders.
4-4-160	Mailing of license and related material.
4-4-170	Change of location.
4-4-180	Adjustments.
4-4-190	Nontransferability.
4-4-200	License insignia—Distribution.
4-4-210	License insignia—Display.
4-4-220	License insignia—Loss—Issuance of duplicate.
4-4-230	License certificates and insignia—Alteration or removal prohibited.
4-4-240	License insignia—Unlawful transfer or use.
4-4-250	Notice of expiration.
4-4-260	License renewal.
4-4-265	Remediation conferences.

4-4-270 Renewal of frontage consents.
4-4-280 License revocation.
4-4-281 License rescission.
4-4-282 License suspension or revocation—Illegal activities on premises.
4-4-283 Closure due to dangerous or hazardous conditions—Effect on license or application.
4-4-285 Trademark violations.
4-4-290 Enforcement of license ordinances.
4-4-295 Unlawful interference with enforcement.
4-4-300 Hazardous use units.
4-4-310 Public ways—Maintenance—Littering prohibited.
4-4-311 Commercial passenger vessels—Responsibility for use agreements and code enforcement.
4-4-313 Restriction on hours of operation.
4-4-320 Public ways—Maintenance—Liability.
4-4-335 Spray paint cans and markers.
4-4-336 Improper business signs.
4-4-337 Illegal use of parking facilities.
4-4-340 Violation—Penalty.
4-4-350 Severability.

§4-4-010 License—Required—Violation—Penalty.

It shall be unlawful for any person (which refers to, for purposes of this title, any individual, partnership, corporation or entity which conducts, engages in, maintains, operates, carries on or manages a business or occupation within the city of Chicago) to conduct, engage in, maintain, operate, carry on or manage a business or occupation for which a license is required by any provision of this code, including Section 4-4-020 of this chapter, without a license first having been procured for such business or occupation. A separate license shall be required for each separate place of business. Any person violating this section shall be fined not less than $200.00 nor more than $500.00 for each offense, and every day such violation continues shall constitute a separate and distinct offense. In addition, any person who continues to violate this section after notification of such violation may be punished as committing a misdemeanor by incarceration in the county jail for a term not to exceed six months under the procedures set forth in Section 1-2-1.1 of the Illinois Municipal Code and under the provisions of the Illinois Code of Criminal Procedure.
(Coun. J. 12-9-92, p. 25465; Amend. 4-16-97, p. 42588; 12-15-99, p. 21529)

§4-4-015 Closure order—Violation—Penalty.

Any business or occupation for which a license is required under Section 4-4-020 of this chapter or any other provision of this code, and to which no license to operate for the period in question has been issued, may be closed by the director of revenue until such license is procured. The failure to make any required partial payment or to renew a license shall also constitute grounds for closing by the director of revenue, provided that the director of revenue shall be required to issue a 30-day notice of violation before the closure may take place. Any person who continues to operate a business or occupation which has been closed by the director pursuant to this section shall be subject to fine of not less than $500.00 nor more than $1,000.00 for each offense, and every day that such violation continues shall constitute a separate and distinct offense. In addition, any person who continues to violate this section after notification of such violation may be punished as committing a misdemeanor by incarceration in the

county jail for a term not to exceed six months under the procedures set forth in Section 1-2-1.1 of the Illinois Municipal Code and under the provisions of the Illinois Code of Criminal Procedure.
(Coun. J. 12-9-92, p. 25465; Amend. 4-16-97, p. 42588 12-15-99, p. 21529)

§4-4-020 License—Required for businesses and occupations not provided for by other code provisions.

All persons who conduct, engage in, maintain, operate, carry on or manage a business or occupation for which a license is not required under any other provision of this code, other than those businesses or occupations which are exempt from city licensing pursuant to law, shall be required to register with the department of revenue of the city and obtain a limited business license for such business or occupation. The license fee for said license shall be as set forth in Section 4-5-010. All such businesses or occupations licensed hereunder or under any other provision of this code shall provide the following information to the department of revenue: (1) the names of the owners (excepting stockholders who own less than 25 percent of the voting shares), general partners and officers of the business or occupation, where applicable; (2) the addresses of all offices of such business or occupation located within the city; (3) a detailed and comprehensive description of such business or occupation; (4) notification of any bankruptcy proceedings instituted by the business or occupation; (5) whether or not the business was purchased as a bulk sale; and (6) any other information as may be required by the director of revenue for the protection of the public health, safety or welfare of the patrons of such businesses or occupations, their employees and the general public. Any person who obtains a limited business license shall limit the activities carried on in such business or occupation to those identified in the license application. If the licensee intends to add activities not identified in the application, he or she shall inform the department of revenue license division prior to commencing such activities; said licensee shall also apply for any new license or licenses as may be appropriate.

A limited business license shall not be required for the retail sale of general merchandise that is secondary to a primary business activity for which a license is required and has been obtained under another provision of this code. For purposes of this section, a primary business activity is an activity that constitutes at least 51 percent of the gross receipts of a business.

Notwithstanding the foregoing. the licensing requirements of this chapter shall not apply to the sale or exchange of used merchandise conducted by or controlled by charitable organizations.
(Coun. J. 12-9-92, p. 25465; Amend. 4-16-97, p. 42588; 9-29-04, p. 32140)

§4-4-030 License—Grant.

In all cases where licenses are required to be procured, such licenses shall be granted by the mayor and attested by the city clerk, except where provision is expressly made for the granting of licenses by some other officer of the city.
(Coun. J. 12-9-92, p. 25465)

§4-4-040 License—Issuance.

All licenses, authorized to be issued and required to be procured by any provision of this code, which are granted by the mayor, shall be issued by the city clerk, except where otherwise specifically provided, upon instruction or direction from the mayor so to do.

All such licenses so issued shall bear the seal of the city, the name of the licensee, address, nature or kind of business or occupation licensed, amount of fee paid, and such other material information as the mayor and city clerk shall prescribe. All licenses shall be subject to the provisions of this code which may be in force at the time of the issuance thereof or which may subsequently be passed by the city council.

(Coun. J. 12-9-92, p. 25465)

§4-4-050 License—Application.

All applications for licenses of any character whatsoever, including those issued under Title 9 of this code, but excluding those licenses specifically excepted, shall be made in writing to the director of revenue, or the commissioner of the applicable department, on a form provided for that purpose.

Every application for a license shall contain the name of the person desiring the same and the place of business of such applicant. If the applicant is a sole proprietorship, the application shall contain the name, residence address, date of birth, and social security number of its sole proprietor; if the applicant is a partnership or firm, the application shall contain the names, residence addresses, date of birth, social security number, and percentage of interest therein of the three members who own the highest percentage interests in such partnership and of any other member who holds a 25 percent or more interest therein; if a limited partnership, the names, residence addresses, dates of birth, social security numbers, and percentage of interest therein of the three limited partners who own the highest percentage interests in such limited partnership and of any other member who holds a 25 percent or more interest therein; if a corporation, the application shall contain the names, residence addresses, dates of birth, and social security numbers of its principal officers and of those stockholders who own 25 percent or more of its voting shares; and if a limited liability company, the names, residence addresses, dates of birth, social security numbers, and percentage of interest of the three members who own the highest percentage interests in such limited liability company and of any other member who holds a 25 percent or more interest therein; provided that, with respect to those licenses for which the Municipal Code requires disclosure of additional information, including a lesser percentage of ownership, the specific licensing provision shall govern. The director of revenue, or commissioner of the applicable department, shall promulgate rules and regulations to provide for the eventuality of any of the above-required information being unavailable. In addition to such statements, there shall be set forth in said application the location of the place of business, or proposed location thereof, for which the license is sought, and such other information as may be required by the director of revenue, or commissioner of the applicable department, in conformity with the provisions of this code prescribing the requirements of such license.

Except as otherwise specifically provided, when provision is made for the division of any license year into periods and the issuance of a license for any such period is provided for, a new application for the purpose of renewing such license need not be made in such case by the beginning of each succeeding period unless required by the director of revenue or the head of a department charged with enforcement of a provision of this code under which the license is issued.

The director of revenue, or commissioner of the department charged with the issuance of the license(s), shall be the custodian of all applications for licenses which, under the provisions of this code, are required to be made to him or her.

It shall be grounds for the revocation of any license issued under the provisions of this code whenever the license applicant knowingly includes false or incomplete information in the license application.

(Coun. J. 12-9-92, p. 25465; Amend. 2-7-96, p. 15393; 7-29-98, p. 75051; 3-10-99, p. 91043)

§4-4-060 License—Application—Inspection or investigation.

Upon receipt of an application for a license which requires an investigation or an inspection by any department or board of the city, pursuant to the licensing requirements for the particular license as set forth in the relevant sections of the code governing the particular license, or as to the proper location or condition of the premises in which the business, for which a license is applied, is to be managed, conducted, operated, or carried on, the director of revenue shall transmit to each department or board charged with the investigation and approval of any such application such information as may be necessary in order that the required investigation or inspection may be made. Each department head or president of a board charged with such investigation or inspection shall, immediately upon receipt of such information from the director of revenue, cause an investigation or inspection to be made, and shall, within 10 days after the receipt of said information from the director of revenue, determine that the applicant has complied or has not complied with the relevant requirements for the particular license and shall notify the director of revenue accordingly. After the initial and one follow-up inspection by any one department or board of the city, the following reinspection fees shall be assessed against the license applicant, other than applicants for a license issued pursuant to Chapter 4-60 of the code, for each subsequent inspection, except where the subsequent inspection was necessary due to an error made by the city: for all reinspections conducted by the department of buildings, the fee set forth in Section 13-20-051, and for all other reinspections, a fee of $50.00. Within two business days, the director of revenue shall transmit the application and reports of the investigations and inspections to the mayor with a recommendation that the application be approved or denied.

If any department head or president of a board shall disapprove such application and the applicant for license shall be in business or shall have engaged in the occupation for which a license is sought, it shall be the duty of such department head or president of a board to take such action as shall be necessary to compel compliance with the provisions of this code.

Upon receipt of the report and recommendation of the director of revenue, the mayor shall have the right to examine, or cause to be examined under oath, any applicant for a license or for a renewal thereof, and to examine or cause to be examined the books and records of any applicant. Such examination shall be commenced within 15 days after receipt of the report and recommendation of the director of revenue, and concluded within 30 days thereafter; provided, however, that the mayor may extend the period of such investigation for an additional 15 days to allow completion of the investigation, if necessary. The mayor shall give the applicant written notice of the extension, stating the reasons therefor. If the applicant fails to appear to answer any question or to produce the books and records, said conduct shall be sufficient grounds for denial of the license application. The mayor may authorize a hearing examiner to act on his behalf for the purpose of obtaining any of the desired information.

If the mayor determines that no such examination is necessary, and that the applicant or each of the principal officers, if the applicant is a corporation, has complied with all of the necessary licensing requirements for the particular license, and that all laws and provisions of this code regulating the business or occupation for which such license is applied for have been complied with, the mayor shall immediately authorize the issue of the said license by the city clerk.

If the mayor disapproves the license application, he shall notify the unsuccessful applicant in writing of the reasons for the disapproval. The notice shall be sent to the applicant within five days after the disapproval, by first class mail addressed to the applicant at the address shown in the application. The license applicant may within 10 days after receiving notice of the disapproval make a request in writing to the mayor for a hearing on the disapproved application. Within 10 days after a request for a hearing is made, a public hearing shall be authorized before a hearing examiner appointed by the mayor, who shall report his findings to the mayor within 14 days after completion of the hearing. The public hearing shall be commenced within 10 days after it is authorized.

The mayor shall within 15 days after such hearing has been concluded, if he determines after such hearing that the license application be disapproved, state the reason for such determination in a written finding and shall serve a copy of such finding upon the license applicant.

No license, other than licenses issued pursuant to Chapters 4-60 and 4-156 of the code, shall be approved and the license application fee shall be forfeited if the application review process is not completed within 90 days after the license application is filed, except where the delay in completing the process has been occasioned by the city. A new application and filing fee must be submitted to the department of revenue after the expiration of the 90-day period.
(Coun. J. 12-9-92, p. 25465; Amend. 4-16-97, p. 42588; 6-4-03, p. 2443; 12-15-04, p. 39840)

§4-4-070 License—Application—Affidavits.

All applicants may be required to swear to any statement made in connection with the application for the issuance of any license. When any applicant for a license is required to make any statement contained in the application under oath, or when the sureties on the bond to be executed in connection with the issuance of a license are required to be sworn to any statement made therein, or when any affidavit is required to be made in connection with the issuance of a plate or emblem by the city clerk, such affidavit may be made by the applicant before a notary in the office of the director of revenue, and such affidavit shall be drawn by such notary and the oath administered without cost. The director

of revenue shall designate a sufficient number of notaries public in his office to draw the affidavits and administer the oaths as herein provided for, and all expenses in connection with the commissions and seals for said notaries public shall be borne by the city.
(Added. Coun. J. 12-9-92, p. 25465)

§4-4-080 Bonds.

Any bond given by any person to the city under the license provisions of this code shall, before a license is granted, be approved as to form by the corporation counsel or one of his assistants.

Except as otherwise specifically required, the comptroller shall investigate the sureties on any license bond and, if upon investigation he shall find that the same are good, shall approve such bond.
(Added. Coun. J. 12-9-92, p. 25465)

§4-4-084 License suspension pending payment of fines, costs or other sum to the city.

The license of any person who has failed to pay any fine, assessment of costs or other sum of money owed to the city pursuant to a court order, an order of the department of administrative hearings, or an order of the mayor's license commission within 30 calendar days of becoming a debt due and owing may be suspended by the mayor's license commission, following a hearing conducted in accordance with its rules. The license shall be suspended until such time that the fine, assessment of costs or other sum of money has been fully paid. The licensee shall be given written notice at least five days prior to the hearing.
(Added. Coun. J. 7-29-98, p. 75071)

§4-4-090 Prepayment of license fees.

All applications for a license made to the director of revenue shall, after approval by the zoning administrator as to compliance with the zoning ordinance, be accompanied by the full amount of the fee payable for such license.

Whenever a license cannot be issued at the time the application for the same is made, the director of revenue shall issue a receipt to the applicant for the money paid in advance. All such receipts shall have plainly indicated thereon that the receipt of payment of the license fee is not to be construed as the issuance of a license.

No such receipt, or the payment of any license fee in advance of the issuance of the license in due form, shall entitle or authorize any person to any of the rights or privileges conferred by the issuance of any license or to the opening or maintaining of any business or establishment contrary to any of the provisions of this code.
(Added. Coun. J. 12-9-92, p. 25465)

§4-4-110 Term—Temporary license.

(a) Except where otherwise expressly provided, no license shall be granted for a period longer than one year. No license shall be issued for any period of time less than a year or for a sum less than the full annual license fee, except when otherwise expressly provided. A temporary, nonrenewable license may be issued by the mayor for a period ending on the last day of the license period, where the application in question is approved by all departments except the department of buildings and where violations on the premises to be licensed are not of a serious or dangerous nature.

(b) An initial license, if approved by all appropriate departments and issued within 45 days of the start of a new license period, may be issued for a term ending on the last day of the new license period. This subsection (b) shall not apply to licenses issued to businesses cited for operating without a license in the current or a prior license period, nor to licenses for retail liquor dealers.
(Added. Coun. J. 12-9-92, p. 25465; Amend. 4-16-97, p. 42588; 3-5-03, p. 104990)

§4-4-130 Rebate or refund of fees.

In no event shall any rebate or refund be made of any license fee or part thereof by reason of the death of the licensee or by reason of nonuse of such license, or by reason of a change of location or occupation of such licensee; provided, however, that the provisions of this section shall not be construed to prevent the city council from authorizing a refund of a license fee or a portion thereof, where the license fee was collected through an error, or where the holder of a license has been prevented from enjoying the full license privilege due to induction into the armed services of the United States under the provisions of the Federal Selective Service and Training Act and has been stationed beyond the limits of the city, or where a licensed business is forced to close before the expiration of the license period by reason of the taking over of the licensed premises by the United States Government or an agency thereof. Where any rebate of any such license fee is made because of induction into such federal service, or because of the taking over of the licensed premises by the United States Government or an agency thereof, it shall not be a sum greater than the amount of the license fee divided by the number of months of the license period remaining after such induction and change of station.
(Added. Coun. J. 12-9-92, p. 25465)

§4-4-140 Foreign representatives—Exempted.

The mayor shall in his discretion exempt from the payment of any license fee provided by any provision of this code all foreign consuls or other authorized representatives of any foreign government residing within the city who shall be citizens of such foreign governments.
(Added. Coun. J. 12-9-92, p. 25465)

§4-4-152 Child support delinquencies.

(a) Definitions. For purposes of this section, the following words and phrases shall have the following meanings:

"Court-ordered child support arrearage" means that the circuit court of Cook County has issued an order declaring the respondent in arrearage on his or her child support obligations in a specific amount as of the date of that order or, upon the discretion of the commissioner, may mean that another Illinois court of competent jurisdiction has issued such an order.

"Child support withholding notice" means any income withholding notice which, pursuant to the applicable governing law, directs the payor (i) to withhold a dollar amount equal to the order of child support, and/or (ii) to withhold a dollar amount equal to or towards paying off any unpaid child support obligations, and/or (iii) to enroll a child as a beneficiary of a health insurance plan and withhold or cause to be withheld any required premiums, and also includes any order issued by the circuit court of Cook County (or, upon the discretion of the commissioner, another Illinois court of competent jurisdiction), which similarly directs the payor.

"License" means all licenses of any character whatsoever that are either required by Title 4 of this code or required by Title 9 of this code and issued by the department of consumer services.

"Substantial owner" means any person who holds a 25 percent or more percentage interest in any corporation, partnership or firm, limited partnership, professional corporation or limited liability company.

(b) Obligors—Child Support Arrearages. When public records reflect an outstanding court-ordered child support arrearage, no license shall be issued or renewed to any person, and outstanding licenses may be revoked, unless the applicant or licensee establishes:

(1) The applicant or licensee has paid to the obligee all child support due under the court order, as evidenced by a certified court order or official clerk's records that no support is due and owing; or

(2) The applicant or licensee has entered into a court-approved agreement for the payment of all child support owed and is in compliance with that agreement; or

(3) (A) The applicant or licensee has filed and served a motion requesting a judicial finding of compliance or court approval of an agreement for payment of arrearages; and

(B) In those cases where the motion has not been granted within 60 days of filing, such delay is not due to any failure to exercise reasonable diligence on the part of the applicant or licensee; provided, that the applicant or licensee may not use this subsection (b)(3) on more than one occasion, unless he or she is asserting an error in the public records which postdates the first occasion he or she used this subsection (b)(3); or

(4) The applicant or licensee is not an obligor under a court-ordered child support arrearage.

(c) Employers—Child Support Withholding Notices. Where reliable evidence shows that an applicant or licensee has failed to comply with a properly served child support withholding notice directed to it, no license shall be issued or renewed, and outstanding licenses may be revoked, unless the applicant or licensee establishes:

(1) The applicant or licensee is in compliance with the child support withholding notice at issue, as evidenced by canceled checks paid to obligee or official clerk's records that payments were received on behalf of the obligee; or

(2) The applicant or licensee is not now, and was not at the time of the alleged noncompliance, a payor of income to the obligor named in the child support withholding notice at issue; or

(3) The child support withholding notice at issue was not properly served upon the payor or is otherwise not in compliance with the applicable statute.

(d) Hearings—Procedures. Where the commissioner of consumer services has reason to believe, based on official records reflecting court orders and an accounting of payments, that an applicant or licensee is delinquent on a court-ordered child support arrearage, or has reason to believe, based on reliable evidence and proof of service, that an applicant or licensee has failed to comply with a child support withholding notice, then:

(1) For any proposed action with respect to city liquor dealers' licenses, package goods licenses, and tavern licenses, and for revocations of any other type of license, the commissioner shall refer the matter to the mayor's license commission for actions consistent with this section; and

(2) With respect to all other licenses, the commissioner shall institute an action with the department of administrative hearings and shall send a notice to the applicant or licensee, stating that the application shall be denied or the license shall be ineligible for renewal, as applicable, unless such applicant or licensee provides sufficient evidence, in writing and/or orally at the administrative hearing, or prior to the scheduled hearing date at the department of consumer services, that one of the conditions set forth as (b)(1)—(4) or (c)(1)—(2), whichever is applicable, is satisfied. Such notice shall be mailed to the licensee's last known business address, which shall mean that address provided by the licensee at the last license renewal or by the applicant in the license application, or to the home address where that is the last known address provided.

(A) After the commissioner institutes an action with the department of administrative hearings, that department shall appoint an administrative law officer who shall conduct the administrative hearing. The hearing shall be limited to the defenses set forth in (b)(1)—(4) or (c) (1)—(2) above. Where the applicant elects to present such evidence, no application shall be denied and no license shall be found ineligible for renewal until the administrative law officer issues a written determination of whether the applicant or licensee has presented sufficient evidence to demonstrate any of the above defenses and serves it by certified mail addressed to the last known address that the applicant or licensee has provided. The hearings shall be conducted in accordance with the rules and regulations promulgated by the commissioner pursuant to this section, except that general provisions and rules governing hearings by the department of administrative hearings, including the provision for judicial review under the Illinois Administrative Review Law, shall apply where not inconsistent with the commissioner's rules and regulations and the provisions of this section.

(B) Where the applicant or licensee fails to appear on the scheduled hearing date and fails to request a continuance, an administrative law officer may find the applicant or licensee in default and enter an order that the license application be denied or the license be ineligible for renewal.

(i) The administrative law officer shall serve a copy of the default order on the applicant or licensee by certified mail, addressed to the last known business address of the applicant or licensee.

(ii) Within 21 days after receipt of the default order, an applicant or licensee may petition the administrative law officer to set aside the default order on the basis that the failure to appear was for extraordinary cause, and shall set forth the extenuating circumstances, of which the administrative law officer may require proof. If the petition is granted, the administrative law officer shall send notice by certified mail of a rescheduled time for an administrative hearing.

(C) Where an administrative law officer appointed by the department of administrative hearings determines that a license application should be denied or a license should not be renewed, the commissioner or the department of administrative hearings shall notify the department of revenue and the city clerk of such determination.

(e) Commissioner—Powers. The commissioner of consumer services is hereby authorized to do the following:

(1) Investigate the child support payment records of any applicant or licensee, and any substantial owner thereof, to determine court-ordered child support arrearages and compliance with child support withholding notices;

(2) Provide information on applicants, licensees, and any substantial owners thereof, to the appropriate Cook County and state of Illinois governmental entities, to the extent allowed by law, to assist those offices in enforcement of child support obligations;

(3) Provide the names and business addresses of applicants, licensees, and substantial owners to persons seeking to enforce court-ordered child support arrearages and compliance with child support withholding notices, and their legal representatives, to the extent allowed by law, on the condition that such information be used solely for the purpose of assisting in child support enforcement; provided that the names and identifying information of persons seeking to enforce child support orders shall be deemed confidential;

(4) Subpoena the business records, financial statements, and other relevant records, including those reflecting ownership interests, of any applicant or licensee, where relevant to determining child support compliance;

(5) To take all actions necessary to carry out the provisions of this section;

(6) Work with the bar associations, the court system and other interested groups to facilitate compliance with the requirements of this ordinance; and

(7) To promulgate regulations relating to the operation of this section.

(Added. Coun. J. 2-7-96, p. 15393; Amend. 7-10-96, p. 24982; 11-12-97, p. 56813; 4-29-98, p. 66564; 7-29-98, p. 75051)

§4-4-155 Predatory lenders.

(a) No person licensed under this Title 4 may receive, under a home repair or improvement contract, the payment of proceeds from any loan secured by residential real estate located within this city, unless the payment:

(i) Is in the form of an instrument that is payable to the borrower or jointly to the consumer and the contractor; or

(ii) Is made by a third party escrow agent in accordance with terms established in a written agreement signed by the borrower, the lender and the contractor before the date of payment.

(b) No person licensed under this Title 4 may, in connection with any home repair or improvement contract, act as agent for, or advertise, promote or recommend the services of, a predatory lender or its affiliate, as those terms are defined in Section 2-32-455.

(Added. Coun. J. 8-30-00, p. 39074)

§4-4-160 Mailing of license and related material.

Where all preliminary requirements provided in this code have been complied with, the city clerk shall be permitted to transmit by mail any license certificates and license plates, tags, badges, emblems, and other insignia to qualified applicants therefor.

(Coun. J. 12-9-92, p. 25465)

§4-4-170 Change of location.

If any person licensed to engage in a business or occupation at a particular place shall, before the expiration of the license period, desire to change the location of such place of business, he shall be required to obtain a new license before conducting the business or occupation at the new location. It shall be unlawful to conduct the business or occupation at the new location prior to obtaining the new license. Any new license obtained for a change of location shall remain in effect until the time prescribed for renewal of the license under Section 4-4-021. The fee for the new license shall be the annual fee charged for the license reduced on a prorated basis to reflect the number of days of the license period remaining until the license is required to be renewed under Section 4-4-021.

(Coun. J. 12-9-92, p. 25465; Amend. 12-15-99, p. 21529)

§4-4-180 Adjustments.

When any licensee, by increasing the number of his employees, or the amount of business done by him, or the size of his plant, or the number or size of his vehicles, or by making any change of any kind in his business, places himself in a class where the provisions of this code require him to pay a higher license fee, he shall pay the additional license fee and shall be entitled to receive a supplemental license and such additional license plates, badges, tags, emblems, or insignia as may be required.

(Coun. J. 12-9-92, p. 25465)

§4-4-190 Nontransferability.

No transfer of ownership shall be allowed on any license.

(Coun. J. 12-9-92, p. 25465)

§4-4-200 License insignia—Distribution.

In all cases where any provisions of this code require a license to be obtained and the regulations pertaining thereto also require the licensee to obtain and exhibit a plate, tag, badge, emblem or other insignia, it shall be the duty of the city clerk to deliver such insignia free of charge to the person paying the license fee, and such fee shall be considered as including the cost of such insignia.

Such plate, tag, badge, emblem or other insignia shall be impervious to weather and bear the same serial number as the license. Except in the case of metal tags or badges, such number shall be reproduced in words as well as figures. It shall be the duty of the city clerk to change annually the predominant background color of such insignia.

(Coun. J. 12-9-92, p. 25465)

§4-4-210 License insignia—Display.

It shall be the duty of every person conducting, engaging in, maintaining, operating, carrying on or managing a business or occupation for which a license is required by any provision of this code to post such license in a conspicuous place at the premises where the business or occupation is being conducted.

Where a license emblem or other insignia is delivered to a licensee for use in connection with a business or establishment of a licensee, it shall be the duty of the licensee to affix said insigne on the inside glass part of the window of said establishment licensed which faces upon the public way or to the inside glass part of the door opening upon the public way. Such insigne shall be placed so as to be plainly visible from the public sidewalk, and the view of it shall not be obstructed by merchandise or other obstacles. Where a license is issued for premises which do not have a window or door with glass opening directly upon the public way at a first floor level, such license insigne shall be affixed to the glass in the door, window, showcase or other prominent place in the proximity of the public or principal entrance to such establishment.

Every licensee operating a wagon or other vehicle for which a metal plate is issued under the provisions of this code shall have said plate securely fastened on the outside of the right side of the box of each vehicle used in the conduct of the business or occupation. Every licensee operating a motor vehicle for which a license emblem is issued under the provisions of this code shall affix said emblem on the inside of the windshield of the vehicle.

No license certificate, plate, badge, tag, emblem or other insigne shall be permitted to remain posted or played after the period for which the license was issued has expired.

(Coun. J. 12-9-92, p. 25465; Amend. 12-15-99, p. 21529)

§4-4-220 License insignia—Loss—Issuance of duplicate.

In case any licensee who has been furnished a plate, badge, tag, emblem or other insigne in accordance with the provisions of this code shall lose the same, it shall be within the discretion of the mayor to authorize the issuance of a duplicate insigne upon the making of an affidavit of loss by such person and the payment of a fee of $5.00 to the director of revenue.

(Coun. J. 12-9-92, p. 25465)

§4-4-230 License certificates and insignia—Alteration or removal prohibited.

No person shall add to, alter, deface, forge or counterfeit any license certificate or license plate, tag, badge, emblem or other insigne which has been or is being issued by the city.

No person shall destroy, obliterate, take, remove or carry away without the consent of the owner, any license certificate or license plate, tag, badge, emblem or other insigne which has been issued by the city; except that said certificate, plate tag, badge, emblem or other insigne may be removed after the licensed business has been discontinued or the licensed premises have been abandoned. Nothing herein contained shall prevent the mayor or his duly authorized representatives from removing any license certificate, emblem or in-

signe from the possession of a former licensee, his premises or any vehicle when said license has been revoked under the provisions of this code.
(Coun. J. 12-9-92, p. 25465)

§4-4-240 License insignia—Unlawful transfer or use.

It shall be unlawful for any licensee to loan or give away any license certificate or any license plate, tag, badge, emblem or other insigne issued to such licensee.

It shall be unlawful for any person to use or display any license certificate or license plate, tag, badge, emblem or other insigne which has been unlawfully acquired.
(Coun. J. 12-9-92, p. 25465)

§4-4-250 Notice of expiration.

It shall be the duty of the director of revenue, from 10 to 60 days prior to the expiration of the license period, to cause a written notice to be mailed to each licensee directing the attention of such licensee to the fact that a new license will be required on the day following the expiration of his existing license, and directing his attention also to the amount of the license fee and to the penalty for failure to procure a license in accordance with the provisions of this code governing the issuance of such license; provided, however, that failure on the part of the director of revenue to cause such notice to be mailed to each licensee shall not be deemed a defense to a suit brought by the city to recover the penalty for a violation of the provision of this code under which the licensee is required to obtain a license.
(Coun. J. 12-9-92, p. 25465)

§4-4-260 License renewal.

Except where otherwise specifically provided, the director of revenue, or commissioner of the applicable department, may renew any license at the beginning of a new license period upon proper application and payment of the required fee. Prior to renewal, all licensees and substantial owners shall provide the director of revenue, or commissioner of the applicable department, with the following information: the names, residence addresses, business addresses, social security numbers, dates of birth, and percentages of interest required in the initial license application by Section 4-4-050 or, where such information already has been provided in a license application, any new information necessary to make such information current and accurate. It is the express duty of the licensee to notify the director of revenue, or other city department charged with its license renewal, of any change of business or home address. Upon request in writing by any department or board in control of any regulation affecting the licensees or the licensed premises, the director of revenue shall furnish said department or board lists of licenses renewed in any designated class of licenses.

All license renewal applications filed after the date specified in Section 4-4-021 shall be charged a late license fee in the amount of 25 percent of the amount of the annual license fee, but in no event less than $25.00.
(Coun. J. 12-9-92, p. 25465; Amend. 2-7-97, p. 15393; 7-29-98, p. 75051; 6-4-03, p. 2443)

§4-4-265 Remediation conferences.

(a) Any city department or agency that is responsible for enforcing any of the license requirements of this code or any other provision of the code related to the conduct of a business or occupation that is licensed by the city shall have authority to require a licensee to appear at a remediation conference at which the licensee shall be required to produce books and records or answer questions for the purpose of determining the licensee's compliance with any provision of the code that is within the department or agency's enforcement authority.

(b) When a department or agency requires a licensee to appear at a remediation conference, the licensee shall be given no less than 30 calendar days' notice that they are directed to appear at the offices of the department or agency for a remediation conference, in person or by first class mail prior to the expiration of the license term. The license of any licensee who is directed to appear at a remediation conference scheduled or offered prior to expiration of the license term and who fails or is yet to appear at the remediation conference, notwithstanding any other law to the contrary, shall not be eligible for renewal and shall constitute grounds for closure of the licensed business or occupation, provided that any business authorized by the prior license may be conducted until the 30-day notice period required by this section has expired.

(Added. Coun. J. 7-29-98, p. 75071)

§4-4-270 Renewal of frontage consents.

In any case where frontage consents are required to be procured before a license shall issue, it shall not be necessary to secure the renewal of such frontage consents upon the expiration of such license if such license be renewed or a new license for the same business be procured forthwith.

(Coun. J. 12-9-92, p. 25465)

§4-4-280 License revocation.

The mayor shall have the power to fine a licensee or suspend or revoke any license issued under the provisions of this code for good and sufficient cause or if he determines that the licensee shall have violated any of the provisions of this code or any of the statutes of the state. However, no such license shall be so revoked or suspended except after a public hearing, the licensee first having been given five days' written notice of said hearing, affording the licensee an opportunity to appear and defend. The public hearing shall be held before a license commissioner appointed by the mayor, or such other hearing officer as the mayor may designate in his stead, who shall report his findings to the mayor.

The mayor shall have the right to authorize the examination of the books and records of any licensee upon whom notice of a public hearing has been served.

If the mayor shall determine after such hearing that the license should be revoked or suspended, within 60 days he shall state the reason or reasons for such determination in a written order of revocation or suspension and shall serve a copy of such order upon the licensee. No person shall remove any sign indicating that a business has been closed by official order until such time, if any, that a business reopens in compliance with the provisions of this code.

If the mayor determines that a fine is an appropriate penalty, the amount of the fine shall not exceed the fine imposed in the chapter creating the subject license. If no fine is specified in that chapter, the fines specified in this chapter shall apply.

Whenever it shall appear from the books or records kept by the city clerk, director of revenue or city comptroller that any person holding any license, permit or any kind of privilege granted by the city has failed to pay the amount due thereon, the city clerk, director of revenue or city comptroller, as the case may be, shall report the fact to the mayor, and the mayor may revoke such license, permit or privilege.

(Coun. J. 12-9-92, p. 25465; Amend. 2-7-96, p. 15393)

§4-4-281 License rescission.

The director of the department of revenue shall have the power to rescind any license erroneously issued by the department of revenue. In order for such a rescission to be effective, the director must notify the licensee whose license may be rescinded at least 10 days before the rescission will take effect. The notice shall take place by certified mail. The director must indicate in such notice the basis for the proposed rescission and must also indicate a date and time, prior to the proposed rescission date, upon which the licensee may appear before the director, or his or her designee, to contest the proposed rescission. The licensee shall also be informed that he or she shall be entitled to present to the director or his or her designee any document, including affidavits, relating to the proposed rescission. Following the appearance of the licensee before the director, the director may affirm or reverse his or her rescission decision. The director's decision shall be in writing and shall be mailed to the licensee at least five days before a license rescission is effective. A licensee may appeal the director's decision to any court of competent jurisdiction.

(Coun. J. 12-9-92, p. 25465)

§4-4-282 License suspension or revocation—Illegal activities on premises.

The license of any person may be suspended or revoked pursuant to Section 4-4-280 if the mayor determines that the person or his agent or employee has violated the provisions of Section 8-4-090(b) on any premises for which the license was issued.

(Coun. J. 12-9-92, p. 25465)

§4-4-283 Closure due to dangerous or hazardous conditions—Effect on license or application.

(a) Whenever any authorized officer issues an order pursuant to Section 13-8-100 or Section 13-12-120 of this code to vacate and close any building, structure or portion thereof used to conduct any activity requiring a license under this code, all such activity within any closed portion shall cease immediately. If an application for an initial or renewed license has been filed for any activity at any closed portion of the subject property, the application shall not be processed or considered unless (1) in a proceeding filed by the city for enforcement of the building provisions of this code, the department of administrative hearings or the circuit court, as the case may be, finds that the violation or violations leading to the closure and vacation of the property either did not exist or have been corrected; or (2) the officer who ordered the closure and vacation determines that the violation or violations leading to the close and vacation of the property either did not exist or have been corrected; or (3) the mayor's license commission, in an appeal brought by the applicant, determines that the activity requiring the license can be conducted by the applicant in full compliance with this code, in a portion of the property not subject to the order to vacate and close. The period of delay in considering or processing an application caused by enforcement of this section shall not be counted against any maximum period of time for acting on or rendering a decision on an application.

(b) A determination in favor of an applicant under subsection (a) of this section shall not entitle the applicant to a license, but only consideration of his application for a license. The procedures described in subsection (a) of this section shall be the only methods by which an applicant may obtain consideration of an application for a license to conduct activity requiring a license at a property ordered vacated and closed under either Section 13-8-100 or Section 13-12-120 of this code.

(Added. Coun. J. 10-1-03, p. 9163)

§4-4-285 Trademark violations.

(a) All business licenses of a licensee under this code shall be revoked if the licensee knowingly sells, offers for sale, exposes for sale, or acquires for purpose of sale, any item (1) that bears a false or counterfeit trademark, or (2) that bears a genuine trademark that has been attached to the item without permission of the rightful holder of the trademark.

(b) A licensee whose business licenses are revoked pursuant to subsection (a) of this section shall be ineligible for any license under this code for a period of one year from the effective date of the revocation.

(Added. Coun. J. 8-30-00, p. 39777)

§4-4-290 Enforcement of license ordinances.

It shall be the duty of the director of revenue to examine or cause to be examined all persons and places of business subject to license for the purpose of ascertaining whether or not such licenses have been procured. In case of the neglect or refusal of any person to procure a license as required by this code, the director of revenue shall have the authority, and it shall be his duty, to take such action as he deems necessary to enforce said license requirement.

The director of revenue and all license investigators and employees of this office who may be designated by the director of revenue shall have full police powers to enforce the license provisions of this chapter, and shall have the right to arrest or cause to be arrested any person who violates any of the license provisions of this code, and shall have the right of entry at any time to any place of business for which a license is required by this code, for the purpose of ascertaining whether or not the said license provisions have been complied with.

It shall be the duty of the head of the department or board charged with the enforcement of any regulatory provision of this code, other than the mere procurement of a license, to take such action as shall be necessary to compel compliance with said regulatory provision. Such head of department or board shall have the authority to call upon the department of police for aid in the enforcement of any regulatory provision of this code the enforcement of which is placed upon such head, and it shall be the duty of the superintendent of police,

when called upon by said head of department or board, to act according to the instructions and to perform such duties as may be required of him in order to enforce or put into effect said regulatory provision.
(Coun. J. 12-9-92, p. 25465)

§4-4-295 Unlawful interference with enforcement.
When the director of revenue or a department of revenue investigator is charged with the enforcement of any provision of the code, it shall be unlawful for any person to knowingly interfere with or impede the director of revenue or revenue investigator in the enforcement of his or her duties. Any person who violates this section shall be subject to a fine of not less than $300.00 nor more than $500.00, imprisonment for a term not to exceed six months, or both such fine and imprisonment under the procedures set forth in Section 1-2-1.1 of the Illinois Municipal Code and under the provisions of the Illinois Code of Criminal Procedure.
(Added Coun. J. 12-15-99, p. 21529)

§4-4-300 Hazardous use units.
Every license required to engage in any business or occupy or use any premises, structure or building for any purpose classified as a hazardous use unit in Chapter 13-112 of this code, and every extension or renewal thereof, shall require the approval of the division marshal in charge of the bureau of fire prevention, as a condition precedent to the issuance of every such license and to every extension or renewal thereof. The division marshal in charge of the bureau of fire prevention shall make, or cause to be made, an inspection of every hazardous use unit for which an application for license, or for an extension or renewal thereof, has been made. If such inspection shall prove the entire compliance of such hazardous use unit with the requirements of Chapter 13-112, the division marshal in charge of the bureau of fire prevention shall issue, or cause to be issued, a certificate of compliance and approval. Such certificate shall be subject to revocation for cause by the division marshal in charge of the bureau of fire prevention at any time, and upon notification of the revocation of such certificate, the mayor shall revoke any license conditioned upon said certificate. The provisions of this section shall be construed as remedial and retroactive as well as prospective.
(Coun. J. 12-9-92, p. 25465)

§4-4-310 Public ways—Maintenance— Littering prohibited.
It shall be unlawful for any person licensed to engage in any business or occupation on premises abutting a public way, or for any person using any part of a public way for or in connection with his business or occupation, to litter or to permit the accumulation of any paper, rubbish or refuse upon that portion of the public way abutting said premises or on and about that portion of the public way so used. It shall also be the duty of the licensee to remove the snow and ice from the sidewalk in front of his premises.
(Coun. J. 12-9-92, p. 25465)

§4-4-311 Commercial passenger vessels—Responsibility for use agreements and code enforcement.

The director of the department of revenue, or his or her designee, may take all necessary steps, including the coordination of activities by other city departments and agencies, to ensure that provisions of the Municipal Code applicable to commercial passenger vessels are enforced. The department of revenue may conduct audits to ensure that taxes, fees and other accounts payable by commercial passenger vessel operators to the city are collected in a timely fashion. Notwithstanding any provision of the Municipal Code to the contrary, the department of revenue may, subject to approval of the city council, negotiate one or more agreements for the use and occupancy of the city-owned real estate along any waterway if such real estate is used exclusively for the purpose of conducting a commercial passenger vessel business. Any agreement entered into in accordance with this section shall be pursuant to a competitive bidding scheme established by regulation. Such competitive bidding scheme shall not affect the authority of the city to negotiate with a highest bidder relating to the terms of use and occupancy other than price. The director of revenue may promulgate and enforce rules or regulations to effectuate the purposes of this section.

For the purposes of this section, a "commercial passenger vessel" shall refer to any boat that carries passengers for hire, including but not limited to: charter, cruise, dinner, excursion, ferry, harbor tender, taxi and tour boats.
(Added. Coun. J. 10-7-93, p. 39001; Amend. 4-21-99, p. 92450)

§4-4-313 Restriction on hours of operation.

(a) Except for those businesses listed in subsection (c) of this section, the operation of a business requiring a license under this code between the hours of 12:00 Midnight and 5:00 A.M. shall be considered a severable privilege under the applicable license. That privilege may be suspended or terminated, in the same manner and pursuant to the same procedures applicable to revocation and suspension of licenses, if the licensee's business is or creates a nuisance during the hours between 12:00 Midnight and 5:00 A.M. A licensed business is or creates a nuisance during those hours if within any consecutive 12 months, not less than five separate incidents occur on the licensed premises, on or in the licensed premises' parking facility, or on the public way adjacent to the licensed premises. between the hours of 12:00 Midnight and 5:00 A.M., involving acts that violate any federal or state law defining a felony or any federal or state law or municipal ordinance regulating narcotics, controlled substances or weapons.

(b) In a proceeding to suspend or revoke the privilege of operating between the hours of 12:00 Midnight and 5:00 A.M.:

(1) It shall not be relevant that the licensee or the licensee's employees or agents were not personally involved in the commission of the illegal acts;

(2) Illegal acts occurring on the public way shall be limited to acts of the licensee, its employees, agents or patrons; and

(3) The occurrence of the illegal acts may be proved by preponderance of the evidence only.

(c) The provisions of subsection (a) of this section shall not apply to any of the following businesses:

(1) A retail liquor establishment licensed under Chapter 4-60 of this code;

(2) A coin laundry licensed under Chapter 4-220 of this code;

(3) A hospital licensed under Chapter 4-84 of this code;

(4) Any public passenger vehicle licensed under Chapter 9-112 of this code;

(5) Any ambulance licensed under Chapter 4-68 of this code;

(6) Any business licensed under this code and providing emergency services such as board-up or repairs to buildings;

(7) A veterinary hospital licensed under Chapter 4-384 of this code;

(8) A hotel, motel, bed and breakfast inn, single-room-occupancy building or other lodging properly licensed under this code;

(9) A retail food establishment licensed under Chapter 4-8 of this code, whose indoor merchandise area is more than 12,000 square feet in area;

(10) A home for the aged, sheltered care home or other residential care facility licensed under Chapter 4-96 of this code;

(11) A day care facility licensed under Chapter 4-72 of this code;

(12) A funeral home;

(13) A pharmacy;

(14) A public utility;

(15) A manufacturing establishment licensed under Chapter 4-224 of this code; and

(16) Any other type of business whose operation between 12:00 Midnight and 5:00 A.M. is determined by the director of revenue to be necessary to the public health, safety and welfare.

(d) Nothing in this section authorizes any business to operate between the hours of 12:00 Midnight and 5:00 A.M. to the extent that any provision of this code, or a special zoning use, or a court order restricts or prohibits operation of that business during those hours, or during any portion of those hours.
(Added. Coun. J. 5-5-04, p. 22740)

§4-4-320 Public ways—Maintenance—Liability.

Any licensee, individually or in cooperation with other persons or community groups, who removes snow or ice from the public sidewalk or street shall not as a result of his acts or omissions in such removal be liable for civil damages. This section shall not apply to acts or omissions amounting to wilful or wanton misconduct in such snow or ice removal.
(Coun. J. 12-9-92, p. 25465)

§4-4-335 Spray paint cans and markers.

It shall be unlawful for any person holding a retail business license to sell paint in spray cans to any person or to sell any marker containing a fluid which is not water soluble and has a point, brush, applicator or other writing surface of three-eighths of an inch or greater to any person. "Retail" means sales other than those for the purpose of resale or for use by manufacturers, contractors, trades, railroads, public service corporations and institutions, or for the supplying of branch or general establishments from a central depot or store, and shall not include the sale at retail of secondhand or used goods, wares or commodities.
(Added. Coun. J. 2-7-96, p. 15616)

§4-4-336 Improper business signs.

(a) No sign shall be placed on the exterior of any business in the city of Chicago unless it is securely affixed to the property of the business. Unsecure methods of affixing a sign shall include, but not be limited to, attaching the sign with tape, string or staples.

(b) This section shall not prohibit the use of canopies, awnings and marquees authorized by Chapter 10-24 of this code.

(c) Any sign which is erected, altered or maintained in violation of this section shall be removed by the owner or operator of the business. Any person who erects, alters or maintains a sign in violation of this section shall be fined up to $200.00 for each offense. Each day that the violation continues shall constitute a separate and distinct offense.

(d) If such sign is not removed, the city of Chicago may remove the sign and charge the expense of such removal to the owner or operator of the business.

(e) Following a hearing conducted in accordance with its rules, the mayor's license commission may suspend or revoke any license issued to a business under the provisions of this code, if a sign is erected, altered or maintained on the property of the business in violation of this section.

(Added. Coun. J. 7-2-97, p. 47904)

§4-4-337 Illegal use of parking facilities.

(a) No licensee under this code shall allow the use of the licensee's outdoor parking facilities for any business activity by any other person, except:

(1) An outdoor sale conducted by a business served by the parking facilities; or

(2) An occasional outdoor sale in support of a tax-exempt charitable, educational, religious or philanthropical institution or organization; or

(3) A special event presented by, or pursuant to permits issued by, the city; or

(4) A farmers' market conducted pursuant to Chapter 4-12 of this code.

Exception (2) above requires that the licensee file with the commander of the police district and with the alderman of the ward in which the parking facilities are located a written statement indicating the date(s) and location of the occasional sale; the name of the tax-exempt charitable, educational, religious or philanthropical institution or organization; the name, title and telephone number of a contact person for that institution or organization; and the licensee's consent for the occasional sale.

(b) The provisions of subsection (a) of this section shall not apply to a licensed peddler who sells or offers merchandise for sale on private property as allowed by Section 4-244-130 of this code.

(Added. Coun. J. 2-11-04, p. 18457)

§4-4-340 Violation—Penalty.

Any person violating any of the provisions of this chapter, where no other penalty is specifically provided, shall be fined not less than $250.00 nor more than $500.00 for each offense. Every day such violation continues shall constitute a separate and distinct offense.

(Coun. J. 12-9-92, p. 25465; 12-4-02, p. 99931)

§4-4-350 Severability.

If any provision, clause, sentence, paragraph, section or chapter of this title, or application thereof to any person, firm, corporation, public agency or circumstance, shall for any reason be adjudged by a court of competent jurisdiction to be unconstitutional or invalid, said judgment shall not affect, impair or invalidate the remainder of this title in the application of provisions unaffected by such an adjudgment to other persons, firms, corporations, public agencies or circumstances, but shall be confined in its operation to the provision, clause, sentence, paragraph, section or chapter or part thereof directly involved in the controversy in which such judgment shall have been rendered and to the person, firm, corporation, public agency or circumstance involved. It is hereby declared to be the legislative intent of the city council that the chapters which comprise this title would have been adopted had any unconstitutional or invalid provision, clause, sentence, paragraph, section or part thereof not been included.
(Coun. J. 12-9-92, p. 25465)

CHAPTER 4-5
LICENSE FEES FOR TITLE 4 LICENSES

(Complete Chapter)

Sections:
4-5-010 Establishment of license fees.

§4-5-010 Establishment of license fees.

This chapter shall establish fees for various licenses created by this title unless otherwise provided. The following fees shall apply for the specified licenses. The chapter in which each fee requirement is created is also provided. Unless otherwise stated, fees shall be assessed on an annual basis.

(1) Limited business (4-4) $125.00
(2) Ambulance (4-68) $600.00
(3) Drain layers $125.00
(3a) Public places of amusement (4-156)
Public place of amusement license

The fee for each public place of amusement license shall be graded according to the capacity in accordance with the following schedule:

Maximum Capacity	Fee
1—350	$ 385.00
351—500	550.00
501—750	825.00
751—1,000	1,100.00
1,001—2,000	1,650.00
2,001—3,000	2,200.00
3,001—4,000	3,300.00
Over 4,000	6,600.00

Notwithstanding the foregoing, the annual license fee for a not-for-profit theatrical community center shall be $55.00.

When computing the capacity of a public place of amusement, the total occupancy of all rooms or other occupancy areas of the premises of the business operating the amusement shall be calculated.

(4) Animal care (4-384)
Kennels and catteries....................$165.00
Veterinary hospitals....................192.50
Pet shops....................137.50
Humane society....................No fee
Animal exhibition....................137.50

No fees shall be required of zoos, museums, cultural institutions operated by any government subdivision or incorporated as not-for-profit under the laws of the state of Illinois, or of humane societies.

(5) Auctioneer (4-160)....................$1,000.00
(6) Electronic equipment repair shop (4-164)....................$125.00
(7) Auto-amusement device operator (4-156)....................$440.00
(8) *(Reserved)*
(9) Bed and Breakfast Establishment (4-210)....................$200.00
(10) *(Reserved)*
(11) Broker (4-184).................... $125.00
(12) *(Reserved)*
(13) *(Reserved)*
(14) *(Reserved)*
(15) Day Care (4-72)
Day Care Center/Under-2;
Day Care Center/ 2-to-6;
and Day Care Center/Under 2
and 2-to-6 combined 100 or fewer children....................$82.50
Over 100 children....................137.50
(16) Day labor agency (4-188)....................$1,100.00
(17) Excavator (Chapter 4-196)....................$125.00
(18) General Contractor (4-36)
Class A....................$2,000.00
Class B....................1,000.00
Class C....................750.00
Class D....................500.00
Class E....................300.00
(19) Hospital (4-84)....................$1,100.00
(20) Filling station (4-108)
Operation of self-service filing station....................$110.00
Each portable wheel tank....................55.00
Per gallon of capacity for containers or tanks....................0.06

In determining the total capacity of containers or tanks under this section, any used exclusively for the storage of kerosene but not exceeding a total capacity of 100 gallons shall be excluded.

(21)-(30) *(Reserved)*
(31) Food—Retail food establishment (4-8)
0-4,500 square feet....................$330.00
4,500-10,000 square feet....................$440.00
over 10,000 square feet....................550.00

In computing the square footage of a retail food establishment, the gross area of the entire premises shall be measured, including the food service, storage and preparation areas.

Special retail food establishment (4-8)

Per event $125.00
Food—Wholesale food establishment (4-8) 330.00
Food—Mobile food dispenser (4-8) 137.50

(32) *(Reserved)*
(33) *(Reserved)*
(34) Fume hazard gases, certificate of fitness $30.00
(35) *(Reserved)*
(36) *(Reserved)*
(37) Garage—Public (4-232)
Per 300 square feet $9.90
(38) *(Reserved)*
(39) Hazardous materials (4-115) $275.00
(40) *(Reserved)*
(41) *(Reserved)*
(42) *(Reserved)*
(42a) Home occupation (4-380) $125.00
(43) Home repair (4-204) $125.00
(44) *(Reserved)*
(45) Hotel (4-208)
Per establishment $82.50
Plus, Per unit 1.10
Single-room occupancy (4-209)
Class I 110.00
Class II 220.00
(46) Itinerant merchant (4-212)
Per participating merchant for two weeks of show or exhibition or fraction thereof, payable at the time of application $25.00
(47) *(Reserved)*
(48) *(Reserved)*
(49) Junk peddler (4-216)
Per peddler $75.00
(50) Laboratory (4-88) $150.00
(51) Laundry, self-service coin-operated, supplemental license (4-220) $5.00
(52) *(Reserved)*
(53) *(Reserved)*
(54) Liquor—Retail (4-60)

Fees for the whole or any portion of the license period for which the application is made shall be as set forth below:

Expanded establishment amended liquor license: additional fee for the remaining portion of the license period to be charged during the first year of operation only $1,000.00

Tavern: per year $2,200.00
Special 150.00

Music and dancing: per year 550.00
Package goods: per year 2,200.00
Consumption on premises—
incidental activity: per year 2,200.00
Caterer, without any other liquor license: per year 2,200.00
Caterer, in conjunction with consumption
on premises—incidental activity $1,100.00
Club: per year 550.00
Outdoor patio: per year 880.00
Late hour: per year 3,000.00

In the case of renewals, the above amounts are incurred by 25 percent if the renewal application is not filed, or the license fee not tendered, by the date specified in Section 4-4-021.

(55) Manufacturing establishment (4-224) $137.50
(56) Massage establishment (4-92) $275.00
(57) Massage therapist (4-92) $137.50
(58) *(Reserved)*
(59) *(Reserved)*
(60) Body piercing (4-93) $200.00
(61) Retail computing center (4-253) $250.00
(62) Motion picture (4-128)
Projecting machine operator
Examination fee $100.00
License fee and renewal fee 50.00
(63) Motor vehicle repair shop (4-228)
Other than engine or body repair
Per establishment $110.00
Engine repair only
Per establishment 275.00
Engine and body repair
Per establishment 495.00
(64) Private booting operation (4-233) $1,100.00
(65) Pawnshop (4-240)
Per year $2,640.00
(66) Peddler (4-244)
Food (fruits and vegetables only) $82.50
Nonfood 82.50

Provided, however, that the fee shall be $44.00 if the licensee is: 65 or more years of age at the time of application; or a veteran of the armed forces of the United States, whose discharge from military or naval service was other than dishonorable; or a person with a physical or mental disability, as certified by a medical doctor.

(67) *(Reserved)*
(68) Raffles (4-156) $100.00
(69) Residential real estate developer (4.40) $125.00
(69a) Long-term care facility (4-96) $1,100.00
(70) Scavenger—Private (4-260)
Per vehicle $220.00
(71) Secondhand dealer (4-264) $550.00

(72) *(Reserved)*
(73) *(Reserved)*
(74) Board-up work $500.00
(75) *(Reserved)*
(76) Street performer (4-268) $50.00
(77) Tire facility (4-229)
Class I (100 to 1,000 tires) $165.00
Class II (1,001 to 5,000 tires) 192.50
Class III (more than 5,000 tires) 247.50
(78) Tobacco dealer, wholesale (4-64) $550.00
(79) Tobacco dealer, retail (4-64)
Per establishment $165.00
Plus, per cash register 165.00
Per cigarette vending machine 165.00
Tobacco product sampler 330.00
(80) Cigarette vending machine operator (4-64) $500.00
(81) Weapon dealer (4-144) $550.00
(82) *(Reserved)*
(83) *(Reserved)*
(84) *(Reserved)*
(85) Valet parking (4-232) $300.00
(86) *(Reserved)*
(87) *(Reserved)*
(88) *(Reserved)*
(89) *(Reserved)*
(90) *(Reserved)*

(Prior code § 98-18.1; Added. Coun. J. 12-9-92, p. 25465; Amend. 1-12-93, p. 27813; 2-10-93, p. 28497; 11-17-93, p. 42192; 3-2-94, p. 96537; 4-13-94, p. 48587; 5-4-94, p. 49750; 9-14-94, p. 56835; 11-10-94, p. 59125; Corrected. 11-30-94, p. 63101; Amend. 5-2-95, p. 459; 7-13-95, p. 4596; 2-7-96, p. 15616; 6-10-96, p. 23652; 2-26-97, p. 40141; 4-16-97, p. 42588; 7-2-97, p. 48017; 7-30-97, p. 50612; 10-7-98, p. 78812; 6-9-99, p. 5362; 6-9-99, p. 5366; 12-15-99, p. 21529; 12-13-00, p. 48188; 3-15-00, p. 27687; 6-28-00, p. 36752; 3-28-01, p. 55769; 7-25-01, p. 64897; 12-12-01, p. 76426; 5-1-02, p. 84247; 10-2-02, p. 94559; 12-4-02, p. 99931; 6-4-03, p. 2443; 9-4-03, p. 7118; 10-1-93, p. 9163, § 2.2, effective 4-1-04; 11-19-03, p. 14216; 5-5-04, p. 22743, 9-29-04, p. 32144; 12-15-04, p. 39840)

DIVISION II
BUSINESSES INVOLVING FOOD PRODUCTS
(Selected Chapters)

Chapters:

4-8	Food Establishments. (Selected Sections)
4-11	New Maxwell Street Market.(Complete Chapter)
4-48	Reserved.

CHAPTER 4-8
FOOD ESTABLISHMENTS
(Selected Sections)

Sections:

Article II. General Provisions

4-8-020	Licensing requirements.
4-8-025	License issuance prohibited.
4-8-037	Restrictions on mobile food dispensers.
4-8-045	License—Posting.
4-8-050	Notification of food poisoning.
4-8-064	Rules and regulations.
4-8-066	Prepackaged and nonperishable food—Exemptions.
4-8-068	Violation—Penalty.

Article II. General Provisions

§4-8-020 Licensing requirements.

(a) No person shall engage in the business of a retail food establishment without first having obtained a retail food establishment license.

(b) No person shall engage in the business of a wholesale food establishment without first having obtained a wholesale food establishment license.

(c) No person shall engage in the business of a mobile food dispenser without first having obtained a mobile food dispenser license.

(d) A separate license shall be required for each separate place of business.

(e) If a person engages in both retail and wholesale food sales at the same establishment, only a retail food establishment [license] shall be required.

(f) It shall be unlawful for any person to permit the installation, operation, or maintenance upon his premises of any automatic food-vending machine owned or operated by a person who has not obtained a license in accordance with the provisions of this chapter.

(g) Nothing in this chapter shall be construed to prohibit the sale of fruits and vegetables from a vehicle or otherwise as permitted in accordance with Sections 4-244-010 and 4-244-020 of the Municipal Code pertaining to peddlers.

(Coun. J. 12-9-92, p. 25465; Amend. 4-13-94, p. 48587; 6-10-96, p. 23652)

Editor's note: Material in brackets editorially supplied.

§4-8-025 License issuance prohibited.

No license shall be issued to:

(a) A person whose license issued under this chapter has been revoked for cause within the past three years; or

(b) A corporation, partnership, limited partnership or limited liability company, if any of the officers, substantial owners, members or other individuals required to be identified in the license application pursuant to Section 4-4-050 would not be eligible to receive a license under subsection (a).

(Added. Coun. J. 3-10-99, p. 91043)

§4-8-037 Restrictions on mobile food dispensers.

The city council may from time to time define areas in which no mobile food dispenser may dispense food from a wheeled vehicle. The city clerk shall maintain for public inspection and copying a file of all ordinances defining such areas.

(Added. Coun. J. 9-27-00, p. 41923)

§4-8-045 License—Posting.

Every license shall be posted in a conspicuous place in that part of a licensed establishment to which the public has access, but every mobile food dispenser and coffee cart vendor shall post each license in a conspicuous place in that part of the vehicle to which the public has access by sight, and every automatic food-vending machine operator shall post evidence of its license on the exterior surface of all automatic food-vending machines in a conspicuous location to which the public has access.

(Added. Coun. J. 6-10-96, p. 23652)

§4-8-050 Notification of food poisoning.

It shall be the duty of any owner, licensee or person in charge of any food establishment who has knowledge of, and of any physician who attends or prescribes for, and of every superintendent or person in charge of any hospital caring for, any person suffering from or suspected of suffering from food poisoning or infection or any form of such poisoning or infection, whether bacterial or chemical, at once to report this fact to the department of health and thereafter to submit to the department of health a written report stating the name and address of the person thus afflicted, the nature of the poisoning or infection and the source or probable source of the same.

(Prior code § 130-1.4; Added. Coun. J. 12-29-87, p. 9169; Amend. 6-10-96, p. 23652)

§4-8-064 Rules and regulations.

(a) A licensee shall comply with all of the particular regulatory provisions pertaining to: (i) each activity to be performed under a license issued pursuant to this chapter; and (ii) each food product used in the performance of such activities, including the provisions contained in Chapters 7-38 and 7-40.

(b) Sections 760.10-760.1760 of the Retail Food Store Sanitation Rules and Regulations of 1987; Sections 750.10-750.1700 of the Food Service Sanitation Rules and Regulations of 1987; 77 Ill. Adm. Code 775, the Illinois Grade A Pasteurized Milk and Milk Products Rules and Regulation; and 77 Ill. Adm. Code 785, the Illinois Manufactured Dairy Products Rules and Regulations, of the Illinois Department of Public Health, as promulgated and amended from time to time pursuant to 20 ILCS 2305/2 (1994), 410 ILCS 620/21 (1994) and 410 ILCS 635/15 (1994), as amended, are expressly adopted as the rules and regulations of the city, except insofar as they may be modified or rejected by regulations promulgated by the board. The board shall promulgate such additional rules and regulations as may be necessary for the proper administration and enforcement of this chapter. The board shall keep on file and available for public examination at least three copies of the current applicable state and city rules and regulations.

(c) At the time of license application, the city clerk shall issue to each applicant a copy of that portion of the Municipal Code of Chicago and a copy of the Board of Health Rules and Regulations relating to retail or wholesale food establishments or mobile food dispensers, as appropriate.
(Added. Coun. J. 6-10-96, p. 23652)

§4-8-066 Prepackaged and nonperishable food—Exemption.

(a) No establishment where the only food, drink, confection or condiment that is stored, sold or offered for sale is prepackaged and nonperishable shall be required to obtain a retail food establishment license. A limited business license may, however, be required pursuant to Chapter 4-4.

(b) In no event, however, shall this section exempt persons in the automatic food-vending machine business from the license requirements of this chapter.
(Added. Coun. J. 6-10-96, p. 23652)

§4-8-068 Violation—Penalty.

Any person who violates or who resists the enforcement of any of the provisions of this chapter shall be fined not less than $200.00 nor more than $1,000.00 for each offense, and a separate and distinct offense shall be deemed to have been committed for each and every day on which any person shall be guilty of such violation.
(Added. Coun. J. 6-10-96, p. 23652)

CHAPTER 4-11
NEW MAXWELL STREET MARKET
(Complete Chapter)

Sections:
4-11-010 Establishment of New Maxwell Street Market.
4-11-020 Market schedule.
4-11-030 License requirements.
4-11-040 License classification.
4-11-050 License application.
4-11-060 Permit and license fees.
4-11-070 Permit requirement.
4-11-080 Permitted sales.
4-11-090 Duties of commissioner of consumer services.
4-11-100 Procedures relating to promulgation of rules.
4-11-110 Health regulations.
4-11-120 Violations—Penalties.
4-11-140 Reserved.

§4-11-010 Establishment of New Maxwell Street Market.

The following public ways and no other shall be set apart and used as a public market, to be known as the New Maxwell Street Market: the roadways from curbline to curbline and the sidewalks adjacent to the following streets: South Canal Street between Roosevelt Road and Depot Place and South Canal Street north of Roosevelt Road to the southern boundary of Taylor Street.
(Added. Coun. J. 4-13-94, p. 49201; Amend. 6-14-95, p. 3180)

§4-11-020 Market schedule.

The New Maxwell Street Market shall be open to the general public each Sunday throughout the year from 7:00 a.m. to 3:00 p.m.

(Added. Coun. J. 4-13-94, p. 49201; Amend 6-14-95, p. 3180)

§4-11-030 License requirements.

No person shall occupy a space in the market or sell merchandise or food at the market without first having obtained an appropriate license. Each person may apply for one license only. Only individuals may apply for licenses. No corporate, partnership, limited partnership, or other such application shall be accepted. Licenses may be obtained from the department of consumer services. The commissioner of consumer services may promulgate regulations establishing lottery procedures and requirements for market spaces that may become available; the regulations may grant preference to alternate licensees based on the record of use of the market by such licensees. Licenses shall be issued for annual periods beginning on a date to be set forth by consumer services regulation, and no such license shall be issued except for the full license period and for the full license fee. The commissioner of consumer services may promulgate regulations to restrict the number of licenses issued to individuals who reside in the same household. For purposes of this chapter, a household refers to one or more related individuals who occupy the same residence.

The commissioner shall also promulgate by regulation a specification of the form in which licenses shall be issued. Licenses may be used only by the person to whom issuance is made, and may not be transferred to any other person. License applicants who do not receive a license due to the unavailability of space may obtain an alternate license which shall entitle such persons to obtain a permit, for use on a specific market date, as set forth in Section 4-11-070. The commissioner of consumer services shall issue rules and regulations governing the alternate licensing process. Any person who has, within the five years immediately preceding his or her application, been convicted in a court of any jurisdiction for the commission of any forcible felony, or crime involving moral turpitude, shall not be eligible for a license.

(Added. Coun. J. 4-13-94, p. 49201; Amend. 6-14-95, p. 3180)

§4-11-040 License classification.

The license required by Section 4-11-030 herein shall be divided into classes as determined by regulations promulgated by the commissioner of consumer services.

(Added. Coun. J. 4-13-94, p. 49201; Amend. 6-14-95, p. 3180)

§4-11-050 License application.

Application for a New Maxwell Street Market license as required by Section 4-11-030 shall be made in writing on a form provided by the commissioner of consumer services and signed by the applicant. Each application shall include:

(a) The full name, address and telephone number of the applicant;
(b) The class or classes of license for which application is made;
(c) A brief description of the type of item or items to be sold;

(d) If applicable, the name and address of at least one individual possessing a valid certificate of registration in food handling who will supervise the sale of food by the applicant;

(e) An Illinois business tax number issued to the individual who will be holding the license or proof of application for the same;

(f) Any other information as may be required by the commissioner of consumer services by regulation promulgated hereunder; and

(g) If applicable, the identity of the food supplier.

(Added. Coun. J. 4-13-94, p. 49201; Amend. 6-14-95, p. 3180)

§4-11-060 Permit and license fees.

The annual fee for application for a New Maxwell Street Market vendor's license shall be $25.00. The annual fee for application for an alternate license shall be $15.00. No license application fee shall be payable until the lottery referred to in Section 4-11-030 has been conducted. The fee for a daily permit shall be $20.00 for market dates from December through March and $40.00 for dates from April through November. For any licensee with a license category authorizing the sale of fruit or other food items, an additional daily permit fee of $5.00 shall apply. The annual and daily fees set forth herein shall be maximum fees. The commissioner of consumer services may establish lower fees based on vending space size, but in no case may the daily permit fee be established at a rate less than $15.00 for market dates from December through March and $20.00 for dates from April through November. Such fees shall be established by regulation.

(Added. Coun. J. 4-13-94, p. 49201; Amend. 6-14-95, p. 3180; 12-4-02, p. 99931)

§4-11-070 Permit requirement.

No person shall occupy any New Maxwell Street Market space unless such person shall possess an appropriate permit issued by the city of Chicago. Persons possessing valid licenses issued pursuant to Section 4-11-030 herein shall, subject to fulfillment of any other applicable requirement, be granted a permit for any market date requested. Persons who possess alternate licenses pursuant to Section 4-11-030 may apply at the site of the market for a permit at the New Maxwell Street Market prior to the opening of such market each Sunday. If market space is available, permits shall be issued on a random basis upon payment of the required permit fee. The commissioner of consumer services may promulgate regulations relating to the issuance of permits, including, but not limited to, the timing of issuance of permits.

(Added. Coun. J. 4-13-94, p. 49201; Amend. 6-14-95, p. 3180)

§4-11-080 Permitted sales.

Notwithstanding any provision of this code to the contrary, it shall be lawful to sell food and merchandise at the New Maxwell Street Market as provided in this chapter.

(Added. Coun. J. 4-13-94, p. 49201; Amend. 6-14-95, p. 3180)

§4-11-090 Duties of commissioner of consumer services.

The duties of the commissioner of consumer services with respect to the New Maxwell Street Market shall be as follows:

(a) Determining the total number of vendor spaces and licenses and permits that will be made available;

(b) Promulgating regulations to effectuate the purposes of this chapter, including, but not limited to, regulations pertaining to license, permit and lottery requirements and procedures, vending stand sizes, display restrictions, space allotment, sanitation, security, conduct of vendors, and regulations that otherwise safeguard the public interest;

(c) Ensuring that the New Maxwell Street Market is safe and secure during hours of operation, and that garbage and refuse is removed from the market site at the end of each day of operation;

(d) Promulgating regulations establishing a system of administrative adjudication with respect to alleged violations of this chapter;

(e) Entering into contracts necessary to effectuate the purposes of this chapter;

(f) Promulgating regulations to promote the proper coordination of the New Maxwell Street Market with any market located in an area bounded by Morgan Street on the west, Roosevelt Road on the north, Canal Street on the east, and 16th Street on the south;

(g) With respect to regulations pertaining to lottery requirements and procedures, establishing benchmarks to ensure that each type of license category is represented, at a minimum threshold level to be determined by regulation, among licenses that are granted pursuant to Section 4-11-030.

(Added. Coun. J. 4-13-94, p. 49201; Amend. 6-14-95, p. 3180)

§4-11-100 Procedures relating to promulgation of rules.

The commissioner of consumer services shall cause to be published in a newspaper of general circulation in the city of Chicago any proposed regulation no fewer than 10 and no more than 20 days prior to the effective date thereof. The effective date of the regulations shall be set forth in the publication. Upon request, the commissioner shall also provide written notice, by first class mail, of any proposed regulation or amended regulation, to each person holding a current license. During the time period between the publication and effective dates of proposed regulations, the commissioner shall accept and consider comments, and may hold one or more public hearings, with respect to the proposed regulations. Upon finding that exigent circumstances exist, the commissioner may amend the proposed regulations during such period without further publication. On the published effective date, the proposed rules and regulations, as amended, shall be published in final form and shall take effect. Regulations shall be maintained in the office of the department of consumer services for public inspection during normal business hours of the department.

(Added. Coun. J. 4-13-94, p. 49201; Amend. 6-14-95, p. 3180)

§4-11-110 Health regulations.

The commissioner of health shall promulgate regulations relating to the health and sanitation of food sold at the New Maxwell Street Market. Notwithstanding any other provision of this code to the contrary, the regulations prom-

ulgated hereunder shall constitute the exclusive local health and sanitation regulations applicable to food sold at the New Maxwell Street Market.
(Added. Coun. J. 4-13-94, p. 49201; Amend. 6-14-95, p. 3180)

§4-11-120 Violations—Penalties.

(a) Any person found to have violated any provision of this chapter, or any regulation promulgated hereunder, shall be subject to a fine of not less than $50.00 nor more than $500.00. Each day that a violation continues shall constitute a separate and distinct offense. Prior to the exercise of exclusive jurisdiction by the department of administrative hearings in accordance with Section 2-14-190(c) of this code, the commissioner of the department of consumer services may issue regulations establishing a system of administrative adjudication to determine liability and assess fines in accordance with this section. After the exercise of exclusive jurisdiction by the department of administrative hearings in accordance with Section 2-14-190(c) of this code, the commissioner may institute an action with the department of administrative hearings in order to determine liability and seek fines authorized by this section.

(b) The commissioner of the department of consumer services may revoke the permit or license of a person, or deny the permit or license application of a person, if such person is adjudged to have committed two or more violations of this chapter, or regulations promulgated hereunder, within a 12-month period.
(Added. Coun. J. 4-13-94, p. 49201; Amend. 6-14-95, p. 3180; 7-10-96, p. 24982; 11-12-97, p. 56813; 12-4-02, p. 99931)

§4-11-140 Reserved.
(Deleted Coun. J. 6-14-95, p3180)

CHAPTER 4-48
RESERVED

(Deleted Coun. J. 3-15-2000, p. 27687)

DIVISION III
BUSINESSES INVOLVING LIQUOR AND TOBACCO

(Selected Chapters)

Chapters:

4-60 Liquor Dealers. (Selected Sections)
4-64 Tobacco Dealers. (Selected Sections)

CHAPTER 4-60
LIQUOR DEALERS

(Selected Sections)

Sections:

4-60-010 Definitions.
4-60-020 License required—Restricted areas.
4-60-021 Ordinance prohibiting issuance of additional liquor licenses—Requirements—Procedure.
4-60-024 Lapse of license—Transfer of interest.
4-60-030 License issuance prohibited when.

4-60-040 License—Application and issuance procedures.
4-60-041 Additional renewal procedure.
4-60-042 Conditional approval.
4-60-043 Application for caterer's liquor license—Additional information.
4-60-044 Additional operational requirements for caterers.
4-60-045 Registration of outside caterers.
4-60-050 Notice and license issuance conditions.
4-60-060 Licenses—Fees and other policies.
4-60-070 Issuance authority—Special licenses.
4-60-071 Navy Pier liquor licenses—Special conditions.
4-60-073 Lakefront venue liquor licenses—Special conditions.
4-60-080 Off-premises sales prohibited—Exemptions.
4-60-081 Restrictions on caterers.
4-60-090 Sales from gas stations or drive-in windows or to motor vehicle occupants prohibited.
4-60-100 Health, sanitation and inspection requirements.
4-60-110 Premises—Change of location.
4-60-120 Music and dancing.
4-60-130 Hours of operation.
4-60-140 Prohibited activities.
4-60-141 Illegal conduct on licensed premises—Cooperation with police.
4-60-142 Responsibilities of licensee.
4-60-143 Additional restrictions on hiring of persons under 21 years of age.
4-60-150 Individual serving amounts.
4-60-160 Receiving money or other value for installation of amusement devices.
4-60-170 Temporary liquor licenses.
4-60-180 License revocation—One-year wait for new license.
4-60-181 Revocation order not stayed by appeal.
4-60-190 Complaint procedure.
4-60-200 Violation—Penalty.
4-60-205 Regulations.
4-60-210 Severability.

§4-60-010 Definitions.

Whenever the following words and phrases are used in this chapter, they shall have the meanings respectively ascribed to them in this section:

"Alcoholic liquor" means and includes alcohol, spirits, wine and beer.

"Caterer" includes a person who holds or is required to obtain a caterer's liquor license pursuant to this chapter, as well as an outside caterer.

"Caterer's liquor license" means a city retailer's license for the sale of alcoholic liquor to be dispensed as part of an off-site catering business.

"City retailer's license for the sale of alcoholic liquor" or "city liquor dealer's license" or "city retailer's license" or "liquor license" means each liquor license category or classification described in this chapter unless otherwise expressly provided.

"Club" means a corporation organized under the laws of the state of Illinois, not for pecuniary profit, solely for the promotion of some common object other than the sale or consumption of alcoholic liquors; which has been in active and continuous existence for at least three years and having a membership roll of more than 50 members with dues paid to date; kept, used and maintained by its members through the payment of annual dues, and owning or leasing a building or space in a building for the use of its members and provided with a suitable and adequate kitchen and dining room for cooking, preparing and serving meals for its members and their guests; and operated solely for objects of national or state-wide social, patriotic, recreational, benevolent or like purpose.

"Consumption on premises — incidental activity license" means a city license for the retail sale of alcoholic liquor for consumption on the premises at a place of business where the sale of alcoholic liquor is incidental or secondary to the primary activity of such place of business. Places of business within this license classification include, but are not limited to, restaurants, hotels, theaters providing live stage performances and bowling alleys. The holder of a consumption on premises — incidental activity license may sell package goods in the licensed premises if such sales are incidental or secondary to the primary activity of such business.

"Employee" means any agent, manager, clerk, entertainer, barkeeper, host, hostess, waiter, waitress or other such person employed by the licensed establishment, or any person hired or employed on a contractual basis by such establishment, or receiving any remuneration for services in such an establishment.

"Expanded establishment amended liquor license" means a city license issued pursuant to Section 4-60-110(c).

"Lakefront venue license" means a license issued for the sale at retail of alcoholic liquor at a location approved by the Chicago Park District other than exclusively within an enclosed, permanent structure having a tavern license or consumption on premises — incidental activity license.

"Late-hour license" means an additional privilege to remain open and permit the sale of alcoholic liquor for an extended period until 4:00 a.m. on Mondays through Saturdays and until 5:00 a.m. on Sundays, subject to the provisions governing a late-hour license.

"Legal voter" means a person who has registered to vote and whose name appears on the last available quarterly poll list compiled by the State Board of Elections since the last preceding election regardless of whether primary, general or special.

"Licensed establishment" means any place of business for which a city license for the retail sale of alcoholic liquor has been issued.

"Navy Pier liquor license" means a license for the retail sale of alcoholic liquor for consumption on the former municipal pier extending into Lake Michigan from the foot of East Grand Avenue other than within an enclosed, permanent structure having a tavern license or consumption on premises — incidental activity license. Navy Pier liquor licenses shall be in two classes: (a) mobile/temporary, which shall include all instances where the sale occurs at a stall, kiosk, pushcart or other temporary or mobile structure located on Navy Pier; and (b) outdoor/fixed seating, which shall include all service at outdoor seating areas of restaurants and taverns located on Navy Pier and all service at outdoor patios on Navy Pier.

"Off-site catering" means the preparation of food at one location for service at another location.

"Outdoor patio" means the privately owned outdoor location adjacent to a premises licensed for consumption on the premises — incidental activity or as a tavern or club, where alcoholic liquor may be sold and consumed subject to the provisions governing outdoor patio licenses.

"Outside caterer" means a person who performs off-site catering by preparing food at a location outside the city for service at a location within the city.

"Package goods license" means a city license for the retail sale of alcoholic liquor enclosed in the original bottle, jug, can, keg, cask or other receptacle or container, corked, capped or sealed and labeled by a manufacturer of alcoholic liquor, to contain and convey any alcoholic liquor.

"Patron" means any customer, patron or visitor of a licensed establishment who is not employed by the licensee of such establishment.

"Premises" means the place of business or other completely enclosed location particularly described in a liquor license where alcoholic liquor is stored, displayed, offered for sale or where drinks containing alcoholic liquor are mixed, concocted or poured and served for consumption. Premises does not include sidewalks, streets or other portions of the public way or private parking areas.

"Restaurant" means any other public place kept, used, maintained, advertised and held out to the public as a place where meals are served and where meals are actually and regularly served pursuant to the required licenses and provided with adequate and sanitary kitchen and dining room equipment and capacity, and having employed therein a sufficient number and kind of employees to prepare, cook and serve suitable meals for its guests.

"Tavern license" means a city license for the retail sale of alcoholic liquor in an enclosed place of business kept, used, maintained, advertised and held out to the public as a place that primarily serves alcoholic liquor for consumption on the premises and in which providing entertainment or the serving of food is only incidental or secondary to the sale of alcoholic beverages for immediate consumption. The holder of a tavern license may sell package goods in the licensed premises if such sales are incidental to the sale of alcoholic liquor for consumption on the premises as the principal activity. Places of business within the tavern license classification include, but are not limited to, cocktail lounges, saloons and bars.

All words and phrases used in this chapter which are not defined herein shall have the meaning ascribed to such words and phrases in the act entitled "An Act relating to alcoholic liquors," approved January 31, 1934, as amended. *(Added. Coun. J. 12-9-92, p. 25465; Amend. 7-13-94, p. 53391; 6-14-95, p. 3087; 7-21-99, p. 9076; 7-21-99, p. 9079; 3-28-01, p. 55769; 6-4-03, p. 2443; 11-5-03, p. 10717; 9-29-04, p. 32144)*

§4-60-020 License required—Restricted areas.

(a) No person shall sell at retail any alcoholic liquor without first having obtained a city retailer's license for each premises where the retailer is located to sell the same.

(b) No license shall be issued for the sale of alcoholic liquor, for consumption on the premises, in those areas designated by the Chicago Zoning Ordinance as B4 or B5 Districts, if the premises sought to be licensed are within 400 feet, excluding streets, alleys and public ways, of existing premises licensed for the sale of alcoholic liquor; said measurement shall be from property line to property line, for consumption on the premises; provided, however, that this prohibition shall not apply to hotels offering restaurant service, restaurants or clubs; nor to the renewal for issuance of a license for the sale of alcoholic liquor for consumption on the premises, where said place of business was established and licensed prior to the effective date of the ordinance codified in this chapter and has operated continuously subsequent to the effective date of the ordinance codified in this chapter.

(c) No license shall be issued to any person if the premises described in the license application are contained in a building or structure located in any B2 through B5 Districts that was previously licensed for the sale of alcoholic liquor, but which is vacant or unused and unlicensed for a continuous period of six months where the issuance of such license would constitute a nonconforming use in the district in which the building or structure is located.

(d) In addition to the restrictions cited in Section 6-11 of the Illinois Liquor Control Act of 1934, as amended, no license shall be issued for the sale of retail alcoholic liquor within 100 feet of any library, with the exception of the main libraries, open to the public, excluding streets, alleys and public ways; provided, however, that this limitation shall not apply to a restaurant and theater housed in separate rooms of the same building, if the theater seats not less than 275 persons for a single performance, and if the restaurant has a legal occupancy of not less than 100 persons, and if the building is separated from the library by a public way not less than 66 feet in width. An initial license for sale of alcoholic liquor on the premises of a restaurant as authorized in this subsection may be issued despite the fact that the adjacent theater is not yet complete and licensed, if the local liquor control commissioner determines that substantial progress has been made toward completion of the theater. Substantial progress refers to the issuance of appropriate permits by the department of constructions and permits. No renewal of the license will be allowed unless the theater has been completed prior to commencement of the next liquor license period.

(e) Where two or more premises are under the same roof or at one street address, a separate city retailer's license shall be obtained for each such premises; provided, that nothing herein contained shall be so construed as to prevent any hotel operator licensed under the provisions of this chapter from serving alcoholic liquor to his registered guests in any room or part of his hotel.

(f) The issuance to or possession by any person of a retail liquor dealer tax stamp issued for a then-existing tax period by the United States government or any of its agencies shall be and constitute prima facie evidence that such person is subject to the provisions of this chapter.

(Added. Coun. J. 12-9-92, p. 25465; Amend. 1-12-93, pp. 27820, 27823, 27825, 27827, 27830; 2-10-93, pp. 28493, 28495; 3-8-93, pp. 29475, 29478, 29479, 29480, 29482; 3-26-93, pp. 30318, 30321, 30323; 6-23-93, p. 34400; 6-14-95, p. 3091; 3-5-03, p. 104990)

§4-60-021 Ordinance prohibiting issuance of additional liquor licenses—Requirements—Procedure.

(a) Notwithstanding any other provision of this chapter, the city council may from time to time prohibit the issuance of additional liquor licenses in a specified area of the city, subject only to the conditions and procedures described in this section.

(b) An ordinance to prohibit the issuance of additional liquor licenses in a specified area must:

(1) Identify the area by boundaries; and

(2) Cover an area including no less than two contiguous city blocks; and

(3) Identify the category or categories of licenses affected; and

(4) Contain a description of the conditions requiring the prohibition on the issuance of new licenses. For any such area established by ordinance passed after November 7, 1995, both sides of each street forming the boundary of the area will be considered as within the area unless otherwise specifically stated in the ordinance establishing the area; provided, however, that (a) if an area is described by boundaries, the boundaries shall be drawn down the center of boundary streets unless otherwise specified in the ordinance establishing the area; and (b) if a street that is a boundary of the area is also a boundary of wards of the city, the middle of that street will be the boundary of the area.

(c) No ordinance to prohibit the issuance of additional liquor licenses in a specified area may:

(1) Prohibit additional licenses for sale of liquor on the premises of any of the following: sports stadiums with a seating capacity of more than 3,000 persons; restaurants; hotels; banquet halls licensed for incidental service of liquor only and where the principal activity is the service of food; theaters whose premises are licensed for incidental service of liquor only, that provide live stage performances and are equipped with fixed seating; any ice rink for which a valid public place of amusement license and a valid retail food license have been issued, and where the sale of alcohol liquor is incidental to those activities; or facilities operated by the metropolitan pier and exposition authority;

(2) Prohibit the issuance of a new license to allow continued operation of a licensed business within the specified area by a new licensee whose application is filed within six months after passage of the ordinance; provided, however, that no application for a successor license under this subsection shall be approved if the application review process is not completed within one year after filing the application, unless the delay in completing the process has been occasioned by the city;

(3) Prohibit the issuance of additional licenses within the specified area to applicants whose applications were pending prior to the passage of the ordinance;

(4) Be considered or take effect within one year after the repeal of an ordinance prohibiting the issuance of additional licenses within any portion of the specified area;

(5) Prohibit the issuance of a license necessary to allow the relocation of a licensed business within the same specified area, or the change of officers of a corporate licensee, where the change in officers does not also involve transfer of more than five percent of the shares of the corporation;

(6) Prohibit the issuance of an off-site caterer's liquor license.

(d) After passage of an ordinance to prohibit the issuance of additional liquor licenses within a specified area, no ordinance may alter the area except by addition of territory or by deletion of all territory within the area.

(e) Upon receiving an ordinance to prohibit the issuance of additional liquor licenses in a specified area, the city clerk shall send one copy of the ordinance to each of the following: the director of the mayor's license commission, the director of revenue, the corporation counsel and the alderman of each ward in which any portion of the specified area is located. The director of revenue shall prepare a list identifying by type all current liquor licenses issued for premises within the specified area to the sponsor of the ordinance, and all pending applications for liquor licenses within the specified area. The director shall send a copy of the list to the city council committee having jurisdiction over the ordinance and to the corporation counsel. The sponsor of the ordinance shall notify each listed licensee and applicant of the introduction of the ordinance. Notices shall be sent by first class mail, postage paid, directed to the address of each licensee or applicant, as the case may be. Copies of all notices shall be filed with the department of revenue.

(f) No member of the city council or other municipal officer shall introduce, and no committee of the city council shall consider or recommend, any ordinance that is contrary in any way to any of the requirements of subsections (b) through (d). No member of the city council shall propose, and no committee of the city council shall consider, any amendment to an ordinance which, if passed, would render the ordinance contrary to any of the requirements of subsections (b) through (d). No officer or employee of the city shall enforce any ordinance that is contrary to any of the requirements of subsections (b) through (d). No member of the city council may recommend action on, and no committee of the city council shall consider, any ordinance to prohibit issuance of additional liquor licenses within a specified area until all required notices have been given.
(Added. Coun. J. 5-19-93, p. 32377; Amend. 5-17-95, p. 1241; 11-15-95, p. 12567; 1-10-96, p. 14707; 3-10-99, p. 91057; 7-21-99, p. 9081; 3-28-01, p. 55769)

§4-60-024 Lapse of license—Transfer of interest.

Whenever the liquor license for a premises located within an area described in Section 4-60-022 or 4-60-023 lapses for failure to renew or is revoked for cause, no new license shall be issued for that premises, unless the premises is a sports stadium with a seating capacity greater than 3,000 persons, a restaurant, or a hotel, or is operated by the metropolitan pier and exhibition authority. If the premises is any of the foregoing, any new license shall be limited to sale of alcoholic liquor for consumption on the premises. Nothing in Section 4-60-022 or Section 4-60-023 prevents or prohibits the issuance of an additional license to allow continued operation of an existing business within an area specified in either section by a new licensee, if the license is of the same type and if the successor licensee is any of the following: (a) the legal spouse of the prior licensee at the time of application for the new license; or (b) a parent, natural or adopted child of the prior licensee; or (c) an heir of the prior licensee by in testate succession, or a testamentary devisee of the prior licensee, and, after the death of the prior licensee, has thereby received the prior owner's interest in the licensed business; or (d) any other person who already shares ownership in the licensed business, or is acquiring less than five percent of the shares of a corporate licensee; or (e) any other person who is acquiring the licensed business by purchase.

Issuance of a new license under subsection (a) or (b) of this section shall be subject to the following conditions: the applicant for the successor license shall bear the burden of proof of the relationship allowing the issuance of the new license. Issuance of a new license under subsection (c) of this section shall be subject to the following conditions: the applicant for the successor license shall establish his or her right to the ownership of the licensed business in proceedings before the appropriate tribunal for the validation of the subject will or the establishment of heirship; rights of inheritance or heirship shall not be determined or affected as part of the license application process.

Issuance of a new license under clause (d) of this section shall be subject to the following conditions: no person to whom less than five percent of the shares of a corporation holding a liquor license is transferred, who did not share ownership in the license prior to issuance of the new license, may purchase more than five percent of the shares of the liquor license in any 12-month period.

Issuance of a new license under subsection (e) of this section is subject to the following conditions: if 50 or more legal voters reside within a distance of 500 feet, from the licensed premises, the applicant shall first notify all legal voters registered within the 500 foot area by certified mail, return receipt requested, stating that application is being made for issuance of a license to a new licensee, and stating the name of the applicant and the location of the licensed premises. The applicant shall sign an affidavit verifying that all legal voters registered within the 500 foot area have been notified by certified mail. The applicant shall cause to be posted at the location of the premises, in a place clearly visible from the public way, notice in the form prescribed by the director of revenue, stating that application is being made for a license for operation of the business by a new licensee. Within 60 days before the filing of an application for the new license, the applicant shall obtain and file with the department of revenue the written consent of at least 51 percent of the legal voters registered within the 500 foot area. Such measurement shall be made from the boundaries of the premises as described in the application for which the privilege is sought, to a radius of 500 feet away. The applicant shall simultaneously deliver a copy of the filing to the alderman of the ward in which the subject premises are located. For a period of 30 days after the application is filed, any person who signed a consent may submit a written revocation of consent with the department of revenue. After expiration of the 30-day period, and after the department of revenue or its designee has verified the legitimacy of all signatures supplied with the application and any revocations that may have been filed, the department shall certify whether sufficient valid signatures have been filed to proceed with the application. Issuance of the requested license will be permitted only if (i) the existing license of the subject business has not been revoked at any time from two years prior to the date of application for the new license until processing of the application of the new license is completed; and (ii) the licensed business has not been closed for a total of more than 10 days during the same time period as described in clause (i) of this paragraph due to suspension of the license or voluntary closing in lieu of suspension, in any combination; and (iii) no proceedings for the revocation or suspension of the existing license are pending during the processing of the application for the new license; and (iv) the successor licensee pays to the city the sum of $1,000.00 prior to issuance of the successor license in addition to all license fees due pursuant to Chapter 4-5 of this code. Notwithstanding any provision of this paragraph, the requirements of consent of voters and proof of consent shall not apply to an application for a new package goods license under subsection (e) of this section if the floor area of the licensee's business is at least 12,000 square feet and if retail sale of alcoholic liquor did not account for more than 25 percent of the gross revenue from all retail sales on the licensed premises during each of the past two tax years. The applicant for a new license under subsection (e) of this section shall bear the burden of proof of eligibility for the new license and compliance with all applicable procedures, including proof of

gross sales and percentages of gross sales attributable to retail sale of alcoholic liquor. Any person who knowingly makes any false statement, submits any false information or misrepresents any information required under this paragraph shall be fined not less than $500.00 per offense, or incarcerated for a period not to exceed three months, or both.
(Added. Coun. J. 5-19-93, p. 32377; Amend. 5-17-95, p. 1241; 9-29-04, p. 32144)

§4-60-030 License issuance prohibited when.

No license for the sale of alcoholic liquor shall be issued to:

(a) A person who knowingly files false or incomplete information on a liquor license application pursuant to Section 4-60-040;

(b) A person who knowingly files false or fraudulently obtained signatures on a petition or petitions for the purpose of obtaining a late-hour license pursuant to Section 4-60-130 or any other petition required by this chapter;

(c) A person who is not a resident of the city of Chicago;

(d) A person who is not of good character and reputation in the community in which he resides or in the community in which his premises are located;

(e) A person who has been convicted of a felony under any federal or state law, if the local liquor control commissioner determines, after investigation, that such person has not been sufficiently rehabilitated to warrant the public trust;

(f) A person who has been convicted of being the keeper or is keeping a house of ill fame;

(g) A person who has been convicted of pandering or other crime or misdemeanor opposed to decency and morality;

(h) A person whose license issued under this chapter has been revoked for cause;

(i) A person who at the time of application or renewal of any license issued pursuant to this chapter would not be eligible for such license upon a first application;

(j) A partnership, if any member of the partnership would not be eligible to receive a license hereunder for any reason other than residence within the city;

(k) A limited liability company or any other legal entity, if any manager or managing member of the company or entity would not be eligible to receive a license hereunder for any reason other than residence within the city; a corporation, if any officer, manager or director thereof or any stockholder owning in the aggregate more than five percent of the stock of such corporation would not be eligible to receive a license hereunder for any reason other than residence within the city; provided, however, that nothing contained herein shall prohibit the issuance of a license to a corporation based on the application of Section 4-60-040(c)(2) of this chapter to an officer, director or manager of the corporation unless such person also owns more than five percent of the stock of the corporation;

(l) A corporation unless it is incorporated in Illinois, or unless it is a foreign corporation which is qualified under the "Business Corporation Act of 1983" to transact business in Illinois;

(m) A person whose place of business is conducted by a manager or agent, unless the manager or agent possesses the qualifications required to obtain a license; provided, however, that a manager or agent need not reside within the city;

(n) A person who has been convicted of a violation of any federal or state law concerning the manufacture, possession or sale of alcoholic liquor or who has forfeited his bond to appear in court to answer charges for any such violation;

(o) A person who has been convicted of a violation of any federal or state law concerning the manufacture, possession or sale of cannabis, narcotics or other controlled substances, or who has forfeited bond to appear in court to answer charges for any such violation;

(p) A person who does not beneficially own the premises for which a license is sought, or does not have a lease thereon for a minimum period of one year;

(q) Any elected public official of local government, or any nonelected law enforcing official or employee of the city of Chicago;

(r) A person who is not a beneficial owner of the business to be operated by the licensee;

(s) A person who is ineligible for or fails to receive a license to sell alcoholic liquor at retail from the state of Illinois;

(t) A person who has been convicted of a gambling offense as prescribed by any of subsections (a)(3) through (a)(10) of Section 28-1 of, or as prescribed by Section 28-3 of, the "Criminal Code of 1961," approved July 8, 1961, as heretofore or hereafter amended, or as prescribed by a statute replaced by any of the aforesaid statutory provisions;

(u) A person to whom a federal wagering stamp has been issued by the federal government for the current tax period;

(v) A partnership to which a federal wagering stamp has been issued by the federal government for the current tax period, or if any of the partners have been issued a federal gambling device stamp or federal wagering stamp by the federal government for the current tax period;

(w) A corporation, if any officer, manager or director thereof, or any stockholder owning in the aggregate more than 20 percent of the stock of such corporation has been issued a federal wagering stamp for the current tax period;

(x) Any premises for which a federal wagering stamp has been issued by the federal government for the current tax period;

(y) Any person who is married to or is the registered domestic partner of an individual who is disqualified from obtaining a license under this chapter or under the Liquor Control Act of 1934, as amended, unless the person can establish by clear and convincing proof that the disqualified individual will not have any direct or indirect beneficial interest in any liquor license issued to the person under this chapter; provided, however, that if the disqualified individual was denied a liquor license pursuant to subsections (d), (e), (f), (g), (h), (n), (o) or (t) of this section, the person who is married to or the registered domestic partner of the disqualified individual shall not be required to comply with this subsection if the local liquor control commissioner determines, after investigation, that the disqualified individual has been sufficiently rehabilitated to warrant the public trust. For purposes of this subsection, the term "registered domestic partner" means any person who has filed a fully executed affidavit of domestic partnership with the office of the county clerk or pursuant to Section 2-152-072 of this code.

(Coun. J. 12-9-92, p. 25465; Amend. 9-29-04, p. 32144)

§4-60-040 License—Application and issuance procedures.

(a) An application for a city retailer's license for the sale of alcoholic liquor shall be made in conformity with the provisions of this chapter and the general requirements of Chapter 4-4 relating to applications for licenses. The director of revenue shall forward the application to the mayor's license commission who shall assist the mayor in the exercise of the powers and the performance of the duties of the local liquor control commissioner, for such action as the local liquor control commissioner may see fit to take pursuant to law.

(b) The application shall be in writing, signed by the applicant if an individual. If the applicant is a club, partnership or corporation, the application shall be signed by a duly authorized agent thereof. If the applicant is a limited liability company managed by managers, the application shall be signed by a manager. If the applicant is a limited liability company managed by its members, the application shall be signed by a member. The application shall be verified by oath or affidavit, and shall include the following statements and information:

(1) In the case of an individual: the name, date of birth, residence address, current telephone number and social security number of the applicant; in the case of a club: the date of its incorporation; the objects for which it was organized; a summary of its activities during the past year; and the names, residence addresses, dates of birth and social security numbers of all officers and directors; in the case of a partnership, limited partnership, corporation, limited liability company or other legal entity: the date of its organization or incorporation; the objects for which it was organized or incorporated; a summary of its activities during the past year; the names, residence addresses, dates of birth and social security numbers of any person owning directly or beneficially any percentage of ownership therein, provided, however, that if the partnership, limited partnership, corporation, limited liability company or other legal entity is publicly traded on an exchange within meaning of the Securities Exchange Act of 1934, the names, residence addresses, dates of birth, social security numbers and percentage of interest of the three members who own the percent or greater interest therein; and where applicable, the names residence addresses, dates of birth and social security numbers of all principal officers and directors; if the entity is a manager-managed limited liability company, the names, residence addresses, dates of birth and social security numbers of all managers; and the name and current telephone number of any authorized agent; and in all cases; the name, address, and a brief description of any work performed by any person in connection with the preparation and filing of the application, including but not limited to, any attorney, accountant, consultant, expediter, promoter or lobbyist;

(2) The character of business of the applicant and the length of time the applicant has been in a business of that character, or in the case of a corporation, the date when its charter was issued;

(3) The location and description of the premises or place of business which is to be operated under such license;

(4) The name and address of the owner of the premises. If the premises are leased:

(A) A copy of the lease;

(B) The name, address and telephone number of the owner of the premises, including the name and address of the beneficiary if title to the premises is held by a person as trustee and if known to the applicant;

(C) The name, address and telephone number of the manager of the premises;

(5) A copy of every agreement for the management of the licensed business;

(6) A statement as to whether the applicant has made application for a similar license on premises other than that described in the application, and the disposition of such application;

(7) A statement as to whether the applicant is disqualified to receive a license by reason of any provision of this chapter or other provisions of this code or the laws of the state of Illinois;

(8) A statement as to whether the applicant has ever been convicted of a felony, gambling offense, violation of law concerning the manufacture, possession or sale of cannabis, narcotics or other controlled substances, or violation of law concerning the manufacture, possession or sale of alcoholic liquor;

(9) A statement as to whether any previous license for the sale of alcoholic liquor issued by any state or subdivision thereof has been revoked, and the reasons for revocation; and

(10) A statement that the applicant will not violate any of the laws of the state of Illinois, or of the United States, or any provision of this code in the conduct of business.

(11) Any other information that the director of revenue or local liquor control commissioner may require to implement the requirements of this chapter.

(c) (1) At the time of filing an application is originally filed for a liquor license or for an expanded establishment amended liquor license, the applicant shall pay the license fee as required by Section 4-5-010, and, no later than 30 days after payment of the license fee, shall submit to the department of revenue all required documentation, as prescribed by the rules and regulations of the department, necessary to complete the liquor license application. If the applicant submits all required documentation in a timely manner, the local liquor control commissioner shall review the application materials and any written objections to the granting of the license and shall approve or deny the application within 60 days after all required documentation has been submitted. If the applicant fails to submit all required documentation in a timely manner, the director of revenue shall deem the application to be incomplete and shall suspend all further processing of the application unless the applicant reactivates the application within six months after the a original application is filed by: (i) submitting all required documentation necessary to complete the application process; and (ii) paying a $500.00 license application reactivation fee which the director of revenue is authorized to assess. If the applicant reactivates the license application in accordance with the requirements of this subsection, the local liquor control commissioner shall review the application materials and any a written objections to the granting of the license and shall approve or deny the application within 60 days after all required documentation has been submitted and the license application reactivation fee paid. If the director of revenue deems the liquor license application to be incomplete and the applicant fails to reactivate the application in accordance with the requirements of this subsection, or, if the applicant withdraws the application, the application shall expire and the applicant shall forfeit the license fee and, if applicable, the license application reactivation fee. If the liquor license application expires or is withdrawn, a new application for a liquor license, accompanied by the license fee and all required documentation prescribed by the rules and regulations of the department of revenue, shall be required to obtain a liquor license under this chapter.

(2) At the time an application for a liquor license is originally filed or subsequently renewed the applicant or licensee shall provide proof to the department of revenue that the applicant or licensee has obtained liquor liability (dramshop) insurance for the operation of the premises described in such application or license in the aggregate amount of $300,000.00; the insurance policy shall be for a term at least in coexistence with the duration of the applicable license period and shall not be subject to cancellation except upon 30 days prior notice to the local liquor control commissioner; and the termination or lapse of the licensee's insurance coverage shall be grounds for the revocation of such license.

(3) No original or renewal license or expanded establishment amended liquor license shall be issued to any applicant or license if any person owning, either directly or indirectly, more than five percent of the interest in the applicant or licensee owes a debt within the meaning of Section 4-4-150(a) of this code.

(d) At the time of filing an initial application for a retailer's license for the sale of alcoholic liquor, each new applicant or manager of an applicant that is a corporation, limited liability company, partnership or club shall provide evidence to the local liquor control commissioner that such person has successfully completed a beverage alcohol sellers and servers education and training program (hereinafter "alcohol sellers training program") pursuant to the Illinois Alcoholism and Other Drug Dependency Act, as amended.

A copy of the certificate of completion from an "alcohol sellers training program" shall be posted in a conspicuous place within the licensed establishment of a person newly licensed to sell alcoholic liquor. The certificate of completion from an "alcohol sellers training program" shall be valid for a period of three years from its date of issuance. Each such person required to obtain the certificate provided herein shall renew such certificate every three years.

The department of revenue shall maintain a list indicating the names and addresses of the "alcohol sellers training program" providers located within the city of Chicago and shall make such list available to the public.

(e) When an application is received by the director of revenue for a liquor license or for an expanded establishment amended liquor license, the director of revenue shall, within five days thereafter, cause to be published in a daily newspaper of general circulation in the city four times over a two-week period, a notice: (1) stating that application has been made for a city retailer's license for the sale of alcoholic liquor; (2) specifying the type of license sought by the applicant, the date the application was filed, the applicant's name and residence address and the street number and location of the premises covered by the application. The notice shall also state that any objection to the granting of the license shall be made to the local liquor control commissioner, in writing, signed by the objector, within 40 days from the date the license application was filed and shall set forth the specific grounds of the objection. The publication may contain notice of more than one application for a license by different persons for different premises. The cost of publishing the notice shall be paid by the applicant. In addition to the required license fee, the director of revenue shall require the applicant to pay, at the time the license application is filed, a sum sufficient to cover the cost of the publication.

(f) Within five days after filing an application for a liquor license or for an expanded establishment amended liquor license, the applicant shall cause to be posted at the location of the premises described in the application, in a place clearly visible from the public way, a notice in the form prescribed by the director of revenue providing the information specified in subsection (e). The applicant shall maintain the notice in place until the local liquor control commissioner has made a decision on the application.

(g) Within five days of receipt of an application for a liquor license or for an expanded establishment amended liquor license, the director of revenue shall cause a written notice to be issued to the alderman of the ward in which the premises described in the application is located, providing the information specified in subsection (e) and the applicant's current telephone number.

(h) The local liquor control commissioner shall review the application materials and any written objections to the granting of the license. The review period for every type of license shall be no fewer than 45 days and no longer than 90 days after the date the license fee is paid, except that there shall be no time limit on review of an application for a late-hour license or for issuance of a license within an area described in Section 4-60-022 or Section 4-60-023. The local liquor control commissioner shall deny an application if the applicant fails to satisfy the requirements of this chapter, and may deny an application for a city liquor dealer's license if the issuance of such license would tend to create a law enforcement problem, result in or add to an undue concentration of licenses, or have a deleterious impact on the health, safety or welfare of the community in which the licensed premises is to be located. Notwithstanding the foregoing, there shall be no minimum time for review of an application for a license for a premises located within either O'Hare International Airport or Midway Airport.

(i) No license of any type under this chapter shall be issued prior to the expiration of 45 days after the date the license fee is paid; provided, however, that this requirement shall not apply to a license for a premises located within either O'Hare International Airport or Midway Airport.

(j) Within five days of issuance of a city retailer's license for the sale of alcoholic liquor or an expanded establishment amended liquor license, the director of revenue shall notify the alderman of the ward in which the premises described in such license is located.

(k) If a change in any information required in subsection (b) of this section occurs at any time during a license period, the licensee shall file a statement, executed in the same manner as an application, indicating the nature and effective date of the change. The supplemental statement shall be filed

within 10 days after the change takes effect. The mayor's license commissioner and the director of revenue shall take measures to prevent disclosure of information required under subsection (b) and not subject to disclosure under the Illinois Freedom of Information Act to persons outside the government.
(Coun. J. 12-9-92, p. 25465; Amend. 12-15-93, p. 43968; 4-13-94, p. 48596; 6-10-96, p. 23652; 4-16-97, p. 42588; 7-2-97, p. 48043; 7-29-98, p. 75071; 7-25-01, p. 65046; 4-9-03, p. 106636; 6-4-03, p. 2443; 9-29-04, p. 32144)

* **Editor's Note:** Because the wording of subsection (c)(1) of this section contained significant discrepancies when amended by Coun. J. 4-16-97 p. 42588 and Coun. J. 7-2-97 p. 48043, the former wording has been retained except for those words specifically marked for amendment by the two ordinances.

§4-60-041 Additional renewal procedure.

In addition to the renewal application described in Section 4-60-040, a licensee shall present the following information to the department of revenue every three years in conjunction with its renewal application:

(a) Satisfactory proof that the licensee has a valid certificate of completion of an alcohol sellers training program; and

(b) Photographic identification of applicant or its duly authorized agent whose name and signature appear on the renewal application pursuant to subsection (b) of Section 4-60-040. The photographic identification must be presented to the department of revenue by the applicant, if an individual, or by the duly authorized agent, and must be either a valid driver's license or a state-issued photographic identification card.
(Added. Coun. J. 7-2-97, p. 48043)

§4-60-042 Conditional approval.

A person may seek conditional approval for a consumption on premises — incidental activity license, or for an expanded establishment amended liquor license, at a premises to be constructed, reconstructed or substantially rehabilitated. The application for conditional approval shall be submitted to the department of revenue in accordance with the rules and regulations promulgated by the local liquor control commissioner. The applicant shall also pay all required license fees for the subject license. Upon receipt of the application for conditional approval and the fee, the department of revenue shall forward the information to the local liquor control commissioner and to appropriate departments for review. Upon completion of the review, which shall take place no longer than 90 days after the date the license fee is paid, the local liquor control commissioner shall notify the applicant whether the applicant is conditionally approved to receive the described license for the subject premises, conditioned upon the applicant: (i) completing the structure substantially as presented in the building plans and floor plan submitted with the application for conditional approval; and (ii) upon inspection approval by the fire department, the department of health and the department of buildings. The conditional approval shall be valid for one year from the date of issuance. The director of revenue shall have authority to issue regulations for the administration of this section.
(Added. Coun. J. 7-2-97, p. 48043; Amend. 9-29-04, p. 32144)

§4-60-043 Application for caterer's liquor license—Additional information.

In addition to the information described in Section 4-60-040, an applicant for a caterer's liquor license shall provide proof of a valid retail food establishment license issued pursuant to Chapter 4-8 for the site where the applicant prepares food for off-site catering.
(Added. Coun. J. 3-28-01, p. 55769)

§4-60-044 Additional operational requirements for caterers.

In order to qualify for a caterer's liquor license under this chapter, an applicant must demonstrate the ability to store, handle, prepare, transport and serve food in a safe and sanitary manner, in accordance with standards promulgated pursuant to this code. The department of health shall inspect an applicant's licensed retail food establishment to assure compliance with this section, and shall report its findings to the local liquor control commissioner.
(Added. Coun. J. 3-28-01, p. 55769)

§4-60-045 Registration of outside caterers.

(a) An outside caterer may register with the department of revenue by: (1) presenting proof of a valid license for the preparation of food for service off the licensed premises, issued by the appropriate licensing authority of the jurisdiction in which the applicant's catering business is located; (2) presenting proof of its ability to store, handle, prepare, transport and serve food in a safe and sanitary manner, in accordance with standards no less stringent than those imposed by this code; (3) presenting proof of a valid license for the sale of alcoholic liquor, issued by the appropriate licensing authority of the jurisdiction in which the applicant's catering business is located; (4) presenting proof of dramshop insurance in an amount equal to that required of a licensee under this chapter; and (5) payment of a fee per registration period, in an amount equal to 150 percent of the fee for a caterer's liquor license under this chapter. Notwithstanding the provisions of subsection (a) of Section 4-60-020, a registered outside caterer may engage in the sale and service of alcoholic liquor on the same terms and conditions as a holder of a caterer's liquor license under this chapter.

(b) The registration periods for each outside caterer shall end on May 15th and November 15th of each year. The local liquor control commissioner may revoke an outside caterer's registration for violation of any ordinance or law. Procedures for revocation shall be in accordance with the procedures for revocation of a business license under Chapter 4-4 of this code. Revocation or suspension of an outside caterer's license for the sale of alcoholic liquor or for the preparation and sale of food, issued by another jurisdiction, shall act as revocation of the outside caterer's registration. A registered outside caterer must notify the local liquor control commissioner of each suspension or revocation of any such license by another jurisdiction, no later than the business day following the suspension or revocation. For purposes of this section, Saturday is a business day. Notification must be in writing, delivered by the outside caterer, or by messenger or transmitted by facsimile to a telephone number designated by the local liquor control commissioner.
(Added. Coun. J. 3-28-01, p. 55769)

§4-60-050 Notice and license issuance conditions.

(a) Within five days after receiving an application under this chapter for a license, the department of revenue shall serve written notice by first class mail on all legal voters residing within 250 feet of the location for which the license is sought. The measurement of such area shall be made from the boundaries of the premises described in the application for which the license is sought, to a radius of 250 feet away. The notice shall state the name and residence address of the applicant, the street number and location of the premises for which the license is sought, the type of license sought by the applicant and the date on which the application was filed. The notice shall also state that any objection to the granting of the license sought shall be made to the local liquor control commissioner, in writing, signed by the objector and delivered to the local liquor control commissioner within 40 days after the date of filing the application as indicated on the notice, and shall set forth the specific grounds for the objection. The department of revenue shall also serve such written notice in the manner and within such time limits as herein provided, upon the alderman of the ward in which the premises described in the notice is located.

(b) No outdoor patio liquor license shall be issued to any applicant who does not currently hold a tavern, consumption on the premises—Incidental activity or club liquor license for an indoor premises adjacent to the location for which an outdoor patio liquor license is sought.

(c) At no time may any live or recorded music be played or performed at any outdoor location licensed as an outdoor patio. This prohibition shall not apply to an outdoor patio operated in conjunction with a consumption on the premises — incidental activity license at the Field Museum of Natural History, the Shedd Aquarium, the Adler Planetarium or the Art Institute of Chicago.

(d) This section does not require additional notice in conjunction with an application for a license to allow continuation of an existing license by a new licensee under subsection (e) of Section 4-60-024, or in conjunction with an application for a late-hour privilege under Section 4-60-130.

(Coun. J. 12-9-92, p. 25465; Amend. Coun. J. 5-19-93, p. 32382; 7-2-97, pp. 48017, 48043; 2-10-99, p. 89271; 6-27-01, p. 62917; 6-4-03, p. 2443; 9-29-04, p. 32144)

§4-60-060 Licenses—Fees and other policies.

(a) The fee for city retailer's license for the sale of alcoholic liquor shall be as set forth in Section 4-5-010. Every applicant or licensee shall obtain a separate liquor license for each category of liquor license as defined in Section 4-60-010 that applies to the business to be conducted at the licensed establishment.

Every city retailer's license for the sale of alcoholic liquor shall expire according to the schedule contained in Section 4-4-021. Retail liquor licensees holding valid licenses that expire on November 15, 2003, shall renew their licenses, regardless of when initially obtained, in accordance with Section 4-4-021 of this code. Licensees who renew their licenses effective November 15, 2003, shall pay on a pro rata basis an amount to cover the appropriate period. The director may issue rules or regulations to administer the provisions of this subsection.

(b) Every city liquor dealer's license shall contain the following information:

(1) The name of the licensee as well as the names of each member of a partnership, the officers and directors of a club, the officers, directors and manager of a corporation;

(2) Language that describes with particularity the premises covered by such license; and

(3) The type or category of liquor license issued to the licensee for such premises.

(c) Whenever any changes occur in the officers of the licensee, the licensee shall notify the department of revenue in accordance with the procedures set forth in items (1), (2) and (3) of this subsection. For purposes of this subsection, the term "officer of the licensee" or "officers of the licensee" means the members of a partnership, the officers or directors of a club, the officers, directors, managers or shareholders of a corporation, or the managers or managing members of a limited liability company or other legal entity licensed pursuant to this chapter.

(1) If any officer of the licensee is removed from office in accordance with the bylaws, operating agreement, partnership agreement for the licensee, pursuant to law or court order, by reason of death, or for any other reason, and such officer is not replaced, then the licensee shall notify the department of revenue of the change by notarized letter within 30 days of the effective date of the change; provided, however, that if the person removed from office but not replaced owned five percent or more of the interest in the licensee at the time of his or her removal from office, the licensee shall comply with item (3) of this subsection.

(2) If any officer of the licensee is removed from office in accordance with the bylaws, operating agreement or partnership agreement for the licensee, pursuant to law or court order, by reason of death or for any other reason, and the person removed from office is replaced by a person who has no ownership interest in the licensee or who owns less than five percent of the ownership interest in the licensee, then the licensee shall notify the department of revenue of the change by filing with the department a change of officer form provided by the department within 30 days of the effective date of the change. The person replacing the removed officer shall be fingerprinted as required by Section 4-60-040(b)(11), and the licensee shall submit to the department of revenue, along with the change of officer form, the following: (i) proof that the person replacing the removed officer has been fingerprinted; (ii) a fee of $100.00 which the director of revenue is authorized to assess; and (iii) any other supplementary materials prescribed by the rules and regulations of the department of revenue.

(3) If any officer of the licensee owning directly or beneficially more than five percent of the interest in the licensee is removed from office in accordance with the bylaws, operating agreement or partnership agreement for the licensee, pursuant to law or court order, by reason of death or for any other reason, and such officer is replaced, or if five percent or more of the ownership interest in the licensee changes hands or is transferred to a non-licensee, the licensee shall notify the department of revenue by submitting to the department within 30 days of the effective date of the change: (i) a change of officers/shareholders application in conformity with the requirements of Section 4-60-040; and (ii) a fee of $250.00 which the director of revenue is authorized to assess. All new partners, officers, directors, managers managing members, or

shareholders or any other person owning directly or beneficially more than five percent of the interest in a licensee shall satisfy all of the eligibility requirements for a liquor licensee as provided in this chapter. Failure to comply with the requirements of this subsection shall be grounds for revocation of any liquor license held by such licensee.

(4) If a change in the officers of the licensee of the type described in items (1) or (2) of this subsection takes place at the same time that a change in the officers of the licensee of the type described in item (3) of this subsection occurs, the licensee shall be required to comply with the requirements of item (3) of this subsection only.

(5) If any change occurs in the officers of the licensee, the licensee shall notify the local liquor commissioner of the change by notarized letter within 30 days of the effective date of the change. The letter shall: (i) describe the nature of the change in the officers of the licensee; and (ii) identify which procedure, as set forth in items (1), (2) and (3) of this subsection, the licensee used to notify the department of revenue of the change.

(Coun. J. 12-9-92, p. 25465; Amend. 5-2-95, p. 555; 7-2-97, p. 48043; 6-4-03, p. 2443; 9-29-04, p. 32144)

§4-60-070 Issuance authority—Special licenses.

(a) A city retailer's license for the sale of alcoholic liquor shall be issued by the local liquor control commissioner, subject to the provisions of an act entitled "An Act relating to alcoholic liquor," approved January 31, 1934, as amended, and subject to the provisions of this chapter and Chapter 4-4 relating to licenses in general not inconsistent with the law relating to alcoholic liquor. The local liquor control commissioner shall also have the authority to issue a special event liquor license. A special event liquor license may be issued by the local liquor control commissioner for a period of time not to exceed 11 days. Such license may be issued only after the mayor has designated an event as a special event. Notwithstanding any provision of this chapter, the fee for a special event liquor license shall be as set forth in Section 4-5-010. The alderman of the ward in which the event is located shall be notified five days prior to issuance of the special event license.

(b) Any qualified organization licensed and approved for the operation of charitable games under the Illinois Charitable Games Act, Illinois Revised Statutes Chapter 120, Section 1121, et seq. (1985), as amended, may apply to the local liquor control commissioner for a special term liquor license. The local liquor control commissioner may, upon the approval of the bureau of fire prevention, issue a special term liquor license to such an organization for the location and for a period not to exceed the actual time specified in the applicant's charitable games license issued by the Illinois Department of Revenue. Any licensee under this section shall be subject to Sections 4-60-100, except as it may incorporate and impose any requirements for separate licensing, 4-60-110, 4-60-130, 4-60-140, 4-60-150 and 4-60-190 with respect to violations of application sections, and shall be exempt from all others. Any special term liquor license issued pursuant to this section shall be automatically suspended or revoked whenever the special term liquor license holder's charitable games license is suspended or revoked. The fee for a special term liquor license shall be $50.00.

(Coun. J. 12-9-92, p. 25465; Amend. 4-15-95, p. 67571)

§4-60-071 Navy Pier liquor licenses—Special conditions.

(a) In addition to the other categories of licenses authorized under this chapter, the local liquor control commissioner may issue Navy Pier liquor licenses. A separate license shall be necessary for each outdoor location, structure or pushcart from which sales of alcoholic liquor are made. In addition to the information required under Section 4-60-040, an application for a Navy Pier liquor license shall include: the written consent of the Metropolitan Pier and Exposition Authority; designation of the specific site or site area on Navy Pier from which the applicant intends to sell alcoholic liquor; for mobile/temporary licenses and outdoor licenses for outdoor areas that are not part of a restaurant or tavern, designation of the location at which the licensee will clean glasses and utensils used in the service of alcoholic liquor. The fee for a Navy Pier liquor license shall be the same as the fee for a consumption on the premises — incidental activity license.

(b) A Navy Pier liquor licensee shall be subject to all provisions of this chapter with the following exceptions:

(1) Subsections (e) and (f) of Section 4-60-040.

(2) Toilet facilities available for public use at Navy Pier shall be considered as compliance with the toilet facilities requirement of subsection (a) of Section 4-60-100 by a mobile/temporary licensee or by an outdoor/fixed seating licensee who operates an outdoor patio that is not an extension of a licensed tavern or restaurant.

(3) A mobile/temporary licensee shall not be required to maintain facilities for the cleaning of glasses and utensils at the point of sale as otherwise required under subsection (a) of Section 4-60-100, if the licensee serves alcoholic liquor only in disposable containers.

(c) Only beer and wine may be sold from a pushcart or other mobile point of sale by a Navy Pier mobile/temporary liquor licensee.

(d) No more than six Navy Pier mobile/temporary liquor licenses shall be issued for pushcarts or other mobile points of sale during any license period.

(e) No more than ten Navy Pier outdoor/fixed seating liquor licenses shall be issued during any license period. One such license may be issued for sale and service of alcoholic liquor at an outdoor location on Navy Pier, not adjacent to any premises licensed for consumption on the premises — incidental activity or as a tavern.

(f) No Navy Pier liquor licensee may serve or permit the service of alcoholic liquor outdoors between the hours of 12:00 midnight and 12:00 noon.

(g) A Navy Pier outdoor/fixed seating liquor license shall be the exclusive license for sale of alcoholic liquor at an outdoor location adjacent to a premises on Navy Pier and licensed for consumption on the premises—incidental activity or as a tavern. No outdoor patio license or sidewalk cafe permit shall be issued for any outdoor location on Navy Pier.

(Added. Coun. J. 6-14-95, p. 3087; Amend. Coun. J. 5-9-96, p. 21855; 3-19-97, p. 41390; 3-15-00, p. 27687; 6-6-01, p. 60075; 6-4-03, p. 2443)

§4-60-073 Lakefront venue liquor licenses— Special conditions.

(a) In addition to the other categories of licenses authorized under this chapter, the local liquor control commissioner may issue Lakefront venue liquor licenses. A separate license shall be necessary for each outdoor location from which sales of alcoholic liquor are made on Chicago park district property. In addition to the information required under Section 4-60-040, an application for a Lakefront venue liquor license shall include: the written consent of the Chicago Park District, designation of the specific site at which the applicant intends to sell alcoholic liquor, areas that are not part of a restaurant or tavern, designation of the location at which the licensee will clean glasses and utensils used in the service of alcoholic liquor. The fee for a Lakefront venue liquor license shall be the same as the fee for a consumption on the premises—incidental activity license. A Lakefront Venue license may be issued notwithstanding the underlying zoning of the park property of the location for which a license is sought.

(b) A Lakefront venue liquor licensee shall be subject to all provisions of this chapter with the following exceptions:

(1) Subsections (e) and (f) and the 45-day review period of subsection (h) of Section 4-60-040.

(2) Toilet facilities on Chicago Park District property available for public use within the same park area of the proposed location of the Lakefront venue license shall be considered as compliance with the toilet facilities requirement of subsection (a) of Section 4-60-100.

(3) A Lakefront venue licensee shall not be required to maintain facilities for the cleaning of glasses and utensils at the point of sale as otherwise required under subsection (a) of Section 4-60-100, if the licensee serves food and alcoholic liquor only in disposable containers.

(c) No more than ten Lakefront Venue liquor licenses shall be issued during any license period. Seven Lakefront Venue licenses may be for the sale of beer and wine only, at the locations listed in paragraph (1) of this subsection (c). Three Lakefront Venue licenses may be for the sale of beer, wine and spirits at the locations listed in paragraph (2) of this subsection (c).

(1) Locations eligible for Lakefront Venue licenses for sale of beer and wine only: Oak Street Beach; the Sidney Marovitz Golf Course; Berger Park; the Theater on the Lake Building in Lincoln Park; Southfield House in Lincoln Park; the Jackson Park Golf Course club house; and Grant Park, at the southern portion of the Daley Bicentennial Plaza.

(2) Locations for Lakefront Venue licenses for the sale of beer, wine and spirits: Burnham Harbor, near the harbor master's office; the upper level of the beach house at North Avenue Beach; a restaurant in Millennium Park.

(d) No Lakefront venue licensee may serve or permit the service of alcoholic liquor outdoors between the hours of 11:00 p.m. and 11:00 a.m.; provided, however, that a Lakefront Venue licensee whose license allows sale of alcoholic liquor within Millennium Park may not serve or permit the service of alcoholic liquor between the hours of 12:00 midnight and 11:00 a.m.

(e) No Lakefront venue licensee shall sell or offer for sale any package goods.

(Added Coun. J. 7-21-99, p. 9076; Amend. Coun. J. 7-21-99, p. 9079; 3-28-01, p. 55781; 6-19-02, p. 88690; 11-5-03, p. 10717)

§4-60-080 Off-premises sales prohibited—Exemptions.

(a) No liquor shall be sold, offered for sale, kept for sale, displayed or advertised for sale at retail or delivered to any person purchasing same at retail except at a location, place, or premises described in a retail liquor dealer's license. Provided, however, that solely with respect to a caterer whose licensed place of business is located in an area where no liquor may be sold at retail as the result of a referendum pursuant to the Liquor Control Act, the retail sale of liquor by such a caterer may take place as provided in section 4-60-081(b).

(b) The holder of an outdoor patio license may serve liquor within the open air location adjacent to a premises licensed as a tavern, club or for consumption on premises—incidental activity; provided, that such location as described in the outdoor patio license is enclosed by a fence or other structure that clearly identifies the licensed location.

(c) The holder of a caterer's liquor license or a registered outside caterer may dispense alcoholic liquor at a place other than the caterer's premises if: (1) the dispensing of alcoholic liquor is incidental to the service of food; and (2) the caterer displays proof of a valid caterer's liquor license or outside caterer's registration at the premises where the alcoholic liquor is dispensed; and (3) the caterer or an employee or agent of the caterer actually dispenses the alcoholic liquor.

(Added. Coun. J. 12-9-92, p. 25465; Amend. Coun. J. 3-28-01, p. 55769; 6-4-03, p. 2443; 9-29-04, p. 32141)

§4-60-081 Restrictions on caterers.

(a) Every person engaged in the sale of alcoholic liquor as a caterer shall keep a record of each event catered by that person. The record shall indicate the place and time of the event; the name of the person hiring the caterer; the compensation paid to the caterer; and the types of alcoholic liquor and the quantity of each type sold at the event. All such records shall be kept at the caterer's place of business and available for inspection by any authorized representative of the department of revenue, the police department or the local liquor control commissioner for at least five years after the event.

(b) Solely with respect to a caterer whose licensed place of business (for purposes of this subsection, "premises") is located in an area where no liquor may be sold at retail as the result of a referendum pursuant to the Liquor Control Act (for purposes of this subsection "vote-dry area"), the following shall apply:

(i) The caterer's on-premises storage of alcoholic liquor shall not be considered selling such liquor; and

(ii) The caterer's sale of alcoholic liquor shall be deemed to take place where such liquor is dispensed.

Accordingly, a caterer's license may be issued under this chapter for premises located in a vote-dry area, and a caterer may store alcoholic liquor on-premises pursuant to such a license. Regardless of where a caterer's premises is located, the caterer may sell or dispense alcoholic liquor only within a private residence in a vote-dry area.

(c) A caterer shall sell alcoholic liquor only to the client or sponsor of a catered event, and only by the full, unopened container. No person shall sell or offer for sale individual drinks or servings of alcoholic liquor at a catered event.

No caterer shall charge the client or sponsor of a catered event a price per individual serving or drink of alcoholic liquor.

(d) Either the caterer or an employee of the caterer shall be present at all times during a catered event where alcohol liquor is dispensed. The caterer or caterer's employee shall have on his person a copy of the caterer's liquor license or outside caterer's registration, as well as proof of an alcohol server's training certificate for at least one server at the event.

(e) Unopened containers of alcoholic liquor delivered to a catered event by the caterer, and not consumed at the event, must be removed by the caterer at the conclusion of the event. If the client or sponsor of the event has prepaid for the unconsumed alcoholic liquor, the caterer either shall refund that portion of the bill to the client, or shall adjust the final bill for the event to reflect a rebate for the unconsumed alcoholic liquor. A caterer may donate unconsumed alcoholic liquor to the client or sponsor of the catered event, if the client or sponsor is a not-for-profit organization. It is a violation of this subsection for any person to open a container of alcoholic liquor for the sole purpose of charging the client or sponsor of the event for the cost of that container.

(Added. Coun. J. 3-28-01, p. 55769; Amend. 9-29-04, p. 32141)

§4-60-090 Sales from gas stations or drive-in windows or to motor vehicle occupants prohibited.

(a) No license for the sale of alcoholic liquor shall be issued to any person, partnership, association or corporation for the sale or dispensing at retail of alcoholic liquor on any premises used as a filling station.

It shall be illegal for any person, partnership, association or corporation licensed under this chapter to engage in the business of a filling station at the licensed establishment.

(b) No person licensed pursuant to this chapter shall sell alcoholic liquor to any patron who is occupying a motor vehicle at the time of such sale. It shall be unlawful to sell alcoholic liquor from a drive-in window or other similar opening in the licensed premises to a person occupying a motor vehicle.

(Coun. J. 12-9-92, p. 25465)

§4-60-100 Health, sanitation and inspection requirements.

(a) Every person licensed hereunder who shall sell any alcoholic liquor for consumption on the premises of such licensee shall keep and maintain the licensed premises equipped with running hot and cold water and adequate sanitary washing facilities for the cleansing of glasses and service utensils, shall provide separate and adequate toilet facilities for both males and females pursuant to the requirements of Section 13-168-1600 of this code and shall comply with all the health, sanitary and inspection requirements of Chapter 4-8 of this code.

(b) All persons licensed to sell alcoholic liquor shall have posted, in a conspicuous place, a sign which clearly reads: "Warning: According to the Surgeon General, women should not drink alcoholic beverages during pregnancy because of the risk of birth defects. Consumption of alcoholic beverages impairs your ability to drive a car or operate machinery, and may cause health problems."

(c) The department of buildings shall make such warning signs available to vendors of alcoholic beverages and shall promulgate regulations with respect to the posting of said signs. A fee may be charged by the department to cover printing, postage and handling expenses.

(d) A sign that measures 14 inches by 14 inches shall be posted in a visible location in every tavern, stating: "A person exiting this establishment must depart in a quiet and courteous fashion, and must not cause disturbances to nearby residents, litter or damage private property." Any person who violates the provisions of this subsection shall be subject to a fine of $500.00 plus $100.00 per each day of a continuing violation. Nothing in this subsection applies to a licensed tavern within a hotel, or to any restaurant.

(e) Any person violating the provisions of this section or any of the regulations promulgated hereunder, unless a specific fine is provided, shall be subject to a fine of not less than $50.00 and not more than $200.00 for each offense and every day on which such violation continues shall be regarded as constituting a separate offense.

(Coun. J. 12-9-92, p. 25465; Amend. 4-22-93, p. 31556)

§4-60-110 Premises—Change of location.

(a) A person licensed pursuant to this chapter is authorized to sell alcoholic liquor at the premises, place or location described in the application and license.

(b) If the licensee desires to change the location of the licensed establishment, the licensee shall, prior to occupying or using the changed location to conduct any activity regulated under this chapter, obtain a new liquor license from the local liquor control commissioner in accordance with the requirements of Section 4-4-170. It shall be unlawful for a licensee to conduct any activity regulated under this chapter at a changed location without first having obtained a new liquor license for that location.

(c) If the licensee expands the licensed establishment, the licensee shall, prior to occupying or using the expanded space for any activity regulated under this chapter, file an expanded establishment amended liquor license application with the department of revenue. The application shall include: (i) a copy of the building plans for the expanded establishment; (ii) the proposed floor plan; (iii) an estimate of the occupancy of the premises for which the expanded establishment amended liquor license is sought; (iv) the license fee; and (v) any other information that the director of revenue may require to determine whether the expansion of the licensed establishment complies with the requirements of this code. It shall be unlawful for a licensee to conduct any activity regulated under this chapter in any expanded space at a licensed establishment without first having obtained an expanded establishment amended liquor license.

If the expansion of the establishment: (i) complies in every respect with the requirements of this code including, but not limited to, the Chicago Zoning Ordinance; and (ii) is not accompanied by any change of officers of the type described in Section 4-60-060(c)(3), an expanded establishment amended liquor license shall be issued authorizing the licensee to engage in the business of selling liquor at the expanded establishment; provided, however, that no expansion of any establishment licensed pursuant to this chapter shall be permitted: (A) if the licensee is subject to any restriction on additional licenses identified in Section 4-60-022 or Section 4-60-023; or (B) in violation of the Chicago

Zoning Ordinance; or (C) if the licensee has been issued a special club license under Chapter 4-388 of this code.

For purposes of this subsection, the term "expand" or "expansion" or "expanded establishment" means any increase in the square footage of the area of an establishment where liquor is offered for sale, or sold to, or served to, or consumed by members of the general public. The term "expand" or "expansion" or "expanded establishment" does not include the mere reconfiguration of existing space as described in the original or renewal license application.

(Coun. J. 12-9-92, p. 25465; Amend. 4-16-97, p. 42580; 12-15-00, p. 21529; 9-29-04, p. 32144)

§4-60-120 Music and dancing.

A music and dancing privilege issued prior to August 16, 1997, may be renewed annually upon the payment of the fee set forth in Section 4-5-010. No new music and dancing privileges shall be issued. Persons holding a current music and dancing privilege shall have the privilege of providing music within the licensed premises to which the privilege applies for the primary purpose of permitting dancing by patrons therein; provided, however, that this privilege shall not apply to any outdoor location licensed as a beer patio; and; provided further, that, the establishment shall be subject to the public place of amusement license requirement if any additional amusement is provided. Such privilege shall terminate upon the termination, for any cause, of the city retail license for the sale of alcoholic liquor. Any establishment having a capacity of more than 120 persons must obtain a public place of amusement license. Additionally, any location holding a music and dance license must pay the city amusement tax for any event for which an entrance fee is charged, unless a tax exemption applies. This section shall apply only to establishments licensed under this chapter prior to August 16, 1997.

(Coun. J. 12-9-92, p. 25465; Amend. 7-2-97, p. 48017; 12-15-99, p. 21529; 6-4-03, p. 2443)

§4-60-130 Hours of operation.

(a) (1) Except as provided in subsection (a)(2) of this subsection, no person licensed hereunder as a retailer of alcoholic liquor shall sell, permit to be sold, or give away any alcoholic liquor between the hours of 2:00 a.m. and 7:00 a.m. on Mondays through Saturdays and between the hours of 3:00 a.m. and 11:00 a.m. on Sundays.

(2) A consumption on the premises—incidental activity licensee, who also has a retail food establishment license for the same premises, shall not sell, permit to be sold or give away any liquor between the hours of 2:00 a.m. and 7:00 a.m. on Mondays through Saturdays and between the hours of 3:00 a.m. and 10:00 a.m. on Sundays at the licensed premises provided that there shall be no sale of package goods in the licensed premises between the hours of 10:00 a.m. and 11:00 a.m. on Sundays.

(b) The operator of a theater presenting live stage performances licensed to sell alcoholic liquor for consumption on the premises as an incidental activity may serve alcoholic liquor during a period limited to one hour prior to the start of the performance and during intermission provided that sales are restricted to lobby areas; provided, however, that the operator of a theater located on Navy Pier may also serve alcoholic liquor for up to one hour after conclusion of the performance.

(c) No person licensed to operate an outdoor patio shall sell, serve or allow the sale or service of alcoholic liquor for consumption in the outdoor, privately owned portion of the licensed premises on Saturdays and Sundays between 12:01 a.m. and the legally established hour of opening, or on Sundays through Thursdays between the hours of 11:00 p.m. and the legally established hour of opening on the following day.

(d) During the prohibited hours of sale, every location, place or premises where alcoholic liquor may be sold at retail shall be kept closed, and no person other than the licensee or an employee or a member of the immediate family of the licensee shall be permitted to remain therein. All doors directly opening into or out of the location, place or premises shall be securely locked during the prohibited hours of sale. The provisions of this section relating to the closing of the premises and the locking of the doors shall not apply to restaurants and hotels licensed as food dispensers nor to clubs, drug stores and delicatessen stores.

(e) All persons licensed under this chapter shall have the privilege, upon application and the payment of an additional fee of the amount specified in Section 4-5-010, of remaining open and selling alcoholic liquor on Sundays until 5:00 a.m. and on Mondays through Saturdays until 4:00 a.m.; provided, however, that, if 50 or more legal voters reside within a distance of 500 feet from the licensed premises, the applicant shall first notify all legal voters registered within such area by certified mail, return receipt requested, stating that application is being made for a late-hour license and stating the name of the applicant and the location of the licensed premises for which the late-hour license is sought. The applicant shall sign an affidavit verifying that all legal voters registered within such area have been notified by certified mail. The applicant shall cause to be posted at the location of the premises for which the late-hour license is sought, in a place clearly visible from the public way, notice in the form prescribed by the director of revenue, stating that application is being made for a late-hour license and listing the name of the applicant. Within 60 days before the filing of an application for a late-hour license, the applicant shall obtain and file with the department of revenue the written consent of a majority of the legal voters registered within the affected area. Such measurement shall be made from the boundaries of the premises as described in the application for which the late-hour license is sought, to a radius of 500 feet away. No late-hour license shall be issued for any outdoor location licensed as an outdoor patio.

(f) It shall be the duty of the commissioner of buildings to cause investigation to be made and to endorse on the application for a late-hour license whether or not one-half of the buildings wholly within such area are used for residence or apartment house purposes. The commissioner of buildings shall give to the applicant and to the alderman of the ward wherein the licensed premises is located an outline of the range of the addresses within 500 feet of the licensed premises if consents are required.

(g) It shall be the further duty of the department of revenue to cause a written notice to be issued to the alderman of the ward wherein the licensed premises are located indicating that an application for a late-hour license has been received. The notice shall be issued within five days of receipt of the application by the department of revenue.

(h) A majority of the legal voters residing within 500 feet of the licensed premises may file a petition with the director of revenue, requesting the local liquor control commissioner to suspend or revoke a late-hour privilege. The director of revenue shall deliver the petition to the local liquor control commissioner within five days of filing. Within 10 days after the petition signatures have been validated, the local liquor control commissioner shall set a hearing date and shall send notice of the hearing to the licensee at the address of the licensed premises and to the alderman of the ward in which the licensed premises are located. Notice shall be sent by certified mail, return receipt requested. The director of revenue shall cause to be published, in a daily newspaper of general circulation in the city, a notice stating that a public hearing has been scheduled regarding the late-hour privilege of the licensee setting forth the name, street number and location of the premises covered by such license and the date, time and location of the hearing. The hearing shall be commenced no later than 30 days after validated petitions have been received by the local liquor control commissioner, and shall be conducted in the same manner as other hearings on the revocation or suspension of licenses issued pursuant to this chapter.

(i) Upon a finding there is due and just cause to discontinue the late-hour privilege granted pursuant to this section, the local liquor control commissioner may either revoke the privilege permanently or suspend the privilege for a period of not more than 30 days.

(j) Notwithstanding any other provision of this chapter, no liquor licensee on Navy Pier, regardless of category, shall be eligible for a late-hour privilege.

(k) The late-hour privilege granted under this section shall be limited to the location of the licensed premises at the time the privilege is granted. In the event that a licensee changes the location of his licensed premises pursuant to Section 4-60-110 and desires to operate during the additional hours described in subsection (e) of this section, the licensee must first obtain a new late-hour privilege for the new location.

(Coun. J. 12-9-92, p. 25465; Amend. 5-17-95, p. 1241; 6-14-95, p. 3087; 6-10-96, p. 23652; 4-16-97, p. 42580; 7-2-97, p. 48043; 9-29-99, p. 12256; 6-4-03, p. 2443; 9-29-04, p. 32144; 12-1-04, p. 36203)

§4-60-140 Prohibited activities.

(a) It shall be unlawful for any licensee or any officer, associate, member, representative, agent or employee of such licensee to sell, give or deliver alcoholic liquor to any person under the age of 21 years. It shall be unlawful for any person licensed to operate a tavern to permit any person under 21 years of age to enter or remain within the licensed premises unless such person is accompanied by a parent or guardian. It shall also be unlawful for any such person licensed pursuant to this chapter to engage or employ or permit any person under the age of 21 years to work or to entertain, or to act as host or hostess in or upon the licensed premises where the principal business is the sale of alcoholic liquor, while such premises are open for the sale at retail of alcoholic liquor. Except to the limited extent allowed by Section 4-60-143, a person under the age of 21 years, engaged or employed or permitted to work in or upon the licensed premises where the sale of alcoholic liquor is not the main or principal business may not work as an entertainer, host or hostess or in connection with the handling, selling, serving or delivering of alcoholic liquor.

(b) No licensee or employee of a licensee shall:

(1) Solicit, induce or request any patron of the licensed establishment to purchase any alcoholic or nonalcoholic beverage for himself or any other employee of the licensed establishment; or

(2) Knowingly serve to any employee any alcoholic or nonalcoholic beverage which was purchased by any patron.

(c) No licensee, manager or barkeeper of a licensed establishment shall permit any employee to remain on the premises of the licensed establishment who solicits, induces or requests a patron to purchase an alcoholic or nonalcoholic beverage for any employee.

Nothing in this subsection prohibits the above activities where the patron and employee are related by blood or marriage.

(d) No person licensed under this chapter shall permit any employee, entertainer or patron to engage in any live act, demonstration, dance or exhibition on the licensed premises which exposes to public view:

(1) His or her genitals, pubic hair, buttocks, perineum and anal region or pubic hair region; or

(2) Any device, costume or covering which gives the appearance of or simulates the genitals, pubic hair, buttocks, perineum, anal region or pubic hair region; or

(3) Any portion of the female breast at or below the areola thereof.

For purposes of this section, any of the items described in subsections (d)(1) through (d)(3) shall be considered exposed to public view if it is uncovered or is less than completely and opaquely covered.

(e) No licensee, or employee or agent of a licensee, shall sell, expose or offer for sale alcoholic liquor whose alcohol content determined by volume exceeds 76 percent, or grain alcohol regardless of proof, in any container with a capacity of less than eight ounces.

(f) No holder of a package goods license shall give, sell, offer for sale or expose for sale any alcoholic liquor in a container having a capacity less than four ounces. No holder of a consumption on the premises license shall give or sell any alcoholic liquor in a container having a capacity less than four ounces, except for consumption on the licensed premises.

(g) At no time may any live or recorded music be played or performed at any outdoor location licensed as an outdoor patio. This prohibition shall not apply to an outdoor patio operated in conjunction with a consumption on the premises — incidental activity license at the Field Museum of National History, the Shedd Aquarium, the Adler Planetarium or the Art Institute of Chicago.

(h) It shall be unlawful for any licensee or any officer, associate, member, representative, agent or employee of a licensee to divide a manufacturer's package containing more than one can or bottle of beer, malt liquor or ale, if the capacity of an individual can or bottle is 16 ounces or less, in order to sell an individual can or bottle, except for consumption on the licensed premises.

(i) It shall be unlawful for any licensee or any officer, associate, member, representative, agent or employee of a licensee to sell, give, offer or expose for sale, or deliver an individual can or bottle of beer, malt liquor or ale with a capacity of 16 ounces or less, except for consumption on the licensed premises.

(j) It shall be unlawful for any licensee or any officer, associate, member, representative, agent or employee of a licensee to sell, give, offer or expose for sale, or deliver any novelty-type alcoholic liquor container that, by virtue of the material from which it is composed or by its shape or design, or that by its ordinary and customary use is likely to mislead the consumer as to the alcohol character of the product, except for consumption on the licensed premises. A "novelty-type" container is an alcoholic liquor container which uses the same shape or design as another non-alcoholic food product, but does not include cans or bottles as allowed by this section. The local liquor control commissioner shall have the authority to publish regulations for implementation of this subsection, including identifying specific products and categories of products falling within the prohibition.

(Coun. J. 12-9-92, p. 25465; Amend. 7-13-94, p. 53394; 8-2-95, p. 21855; 6-10-96, p. 23786; 4-16-97, p. 42584; 7-2-97, p. 48043; 4-1-98, p. 65260; 3-28-01, p. 55783; 6-27-01, p. 62917; 6-4-03, p. 2443)

§4-60-141 Illegal conduct on licensed premises—Cooperation with police.

(a) No licensee shall permit or allow any illegal activity on the licensed premises.

(b) It is the affirmative duty of a licensee to report promptly to the police department all illegal activity reported to or observed by the licensee on or within sight of the licensed premises; to answer fully and truthfully all questions of an identified police officer who inquires or investigates concerning persons or events in or around the licensed business; to cooperate with the police in any such inquiry or investigation, including the giving of oral or written statements to the police at reasonable times and locations in the course of investigations; and to sign a complaint against any person whom the licensee observes in any illegal conduct or activity on or within sight of the licensed premises.

(c) For purposes of this section, "licensee" includes an employee or agent of a licensee.

(Added. Coun. J. 5-17-95, p. 1241)

4-60-142 Responsibilities of licensee.

A licensee is responsible to the community surrounding the licensed premises. A city liquor dealer's license issued or renewed after the effective date of this section shall be subject to suspension or revocation if the licensee's business becomes or creates a nuisance. A licensed business is or creates a nuisance if within any consecutive 12 months not less than five separate incidents occur on the licensed premises, involving acts that violate any federal or state law defining a felony, or any federal or state law or municipal ordinance regulating narcotics, controlled substances or weapons. It is not a defense to a charge of violating this section that the licensee or the licensee's employees or agents were not personally involved in the commission of the illegal acts.

(Added. Coun. J. 5-17-95, p. 1241)

§4-60-143 Additional restrictions on hiring of persons under 21 years of age.

(a) Notwithstanding the provisions of subsection (a) of Section 4-60-140, the holder of a valid consumption on premises — incidental activity license may engage, employ or permit a person under 21 years of age to work on the licensed premises, if the person under 21 years of age has no duties relating to the sale, dispensing, service or delivery of alcoholic liquor on the premises, and complies with the conditions of paragraph (1), (2), (3) or (4) of this subsection.

(1) A person under 21 years of age may be engaged, employed or permitted to work as a musician on the premises, but only pursuant to a written contract. A performer so engaged, employed or permitted to work who is 16 to 18 years of age must either be legally emancipated or be accompanied by a parent or legal guardian while on the licensed premises. Any person under 16 years of age so engaged, employed or permitted to work must be accompanied by a parent or legal guardian while on the licensed premises;

(2) If the licensed premises is a sports stadium with a fixed seating capacity of more than 3,000 persons, a person under 21 years of age may be engaged, employed or permitted to work as an usher or as a participant in an exhibition or athletic competition on the premises; or

(3) If the licensed premises is a theater, a person under 21 years of age may be engaged, employed or permitted to work as a performing member of a theatrical company in the theater if no portion of the performance occurs in the lobby area of the theater building.

(4) A person under 21 years of age may be employed or permitted to work as a host or hostess, or a receptionist in a restaurant.

(b) A licensee who engages, employees or permits a person under 21 years of age to work pursuant to subsection (a) of this section shall not assign or permit that person to perform any duties or acts relating to the sale, dispensing, service or delivery of alcoholic liquor on the premises.

(c) A licensee who engages, employs or permits a person under 21 years of age to work as allowed in subsection (a) of this Section 4-60-143 shall be responsible for compliance with the Illinois Child Labor Law in connection with the employment of any person under the age of 16 years. The licensee shall be responsible for assuring that the person so engaged, employed or permitted to work does not consume, obtain or possess alcoholic liquor on the licensed premises.

(Added. Coun. J. 4-16-97, p. 42584; Amend. Coun. J. 9-4-03, p. 7142)

§4-60-150 Individual serving amounts.

(a) It shall be unlawful for any licensee, other than a hotel offering restaurant service or a regularly organized club or a restaurant within the meaning of the term as defined in an act entitled "An Act relating to alcoholic liquors," approved January 31, 1934, as amended, to sell, give away or permit to be sold, served or given away for consumption on the licensed premises any distilled spirits, except by the glass, or any malt or vinous beverage except in individual servings not exceeding 13 fluid ounces.

(b) Nothing in subsection (a) herein shall be construed to prohibit a licensee from selling pitchers, carafes or bottles of alcoholic liquor which are customarily sold in such manner and delivered to two or more persons at one time.
(Coun. J. 12-9-92, p. 25465)

§4-60-160 Receiving money or other value for installation of amusement devices.

No person licensed under this chapter shall accept, receive or borrow money or anything else of value directly or indirectly from any person connected with or in any way representing any manufacturer or distributor of any coin-operated or amusement device who shall install or furnish such device for use on the licensed premises; provided, that the provisions of this section shall not apply to commissions or rental fees arising out of the use of such coin-operated or amusement device on the licensed premises.
(Coun. J. 12-9-92, p. 25465)

§4-60-170 Temporary liquor licenses.

(a) A temporary, nonrenewable retail liquor license may be issued by the local liquor control commissioner, for a period not greater than six months, and ending the last day of the license period, where the application in question is approved by all departments except the department of buildings, and where violations on the premises to be licensed are not of a serious or dangerous nature.

(b) A temporary, nonrenewable license may also be issued by the local liquor control commissioner, for a period not to exceed 90 days, to an applicant for a full-term license if the licensed premises is a hotel containing more than 200 units for which a valid license in the same category has been issued in the name of another person, and the applicant has assumed ownership of the hotel from that person.
(Coun. J. 12-9-92, p. 25465; Amend. 7-2-97, p. 48043)

§4-60-180 License revocation—One-year wait for new license.

When any licensed issued pursuant to this chapter shall have been revoked for any cause, no license shall be granted to any person for the period of one year thereafter for conducting the business of selling alcoholic liquor in the premises described in such revoked license.
(Coun. J. 12-9-92, p. 25465)

§4-60-181 Revocation order not stayed by appeal.

An order of the liquor control commissioner revoking a city license under this chapter shall take immediate effect if the liquor control commissioner finds that any of the following circumstances are present: (a) the revocation is for violation of any federal or state law or city ordinance regulating the sale, use or possession of firearms; or (b) the revocation is for violation of any federal or state law or city ordinance regulating the sale, use or possession of narcotics or other controlled substances as defined in the Illinois Criminal Code; or (c) the revocation is for violation of any federal or state law or city ordinance relating to prostitution; or (d) the revocation is for sale of alcoholic liquor to a minor, and the licensee was disciplined for three or more similar sales, occurring in separate incidents, within the prior three years; or (e) the revocation is for viola-

tions of this code or the rules and regulations of the city of Chicago Board of Health related to health and sanitation in a food establishment. For purposes of subsection (d) of this section, "discipline" means revocation, suspension or a voluntary closing in lieu of suspension. In the event that a revocation order contains a finding described in subsection (a), (b), (c), (d) or (e) of this section, the effect of the revocation shall not be stayed pending an appeal by the licensee to the License Appeal Commission under the Liquor Control Act.
(Added. Coun. J. 12-13-95, p. 14284; Amend. 3-10-99, p. 91043)

§4-60-190 Complaint procedure.

(a) Any resident of the city of Chicago shall have the right to file a complaint with the local liquor control commissioner stating that a liquor licensee has been or is violating the provisions of this chapter. The complaint shall be in writing in the form prescribed by the local liquor control commissioner and shall be signed and sworn to by the person or persons making the complaint. The complaint shall state the provisions believed to have been violated and the facts in detail upon which such belief is based. If the local liquor control commissioner is satisfied that the complaint substantially charges a violation and that from the facts alleged there is reasonable cause for such belief, he shall set the matter for hearing and shall serve notice upon the licensee of the time and place of such hearing and of the particular charge or charges in the complaint.

(b) Any group of five or more residents may file with the local liquor control commissioner a complaint that a licensee's business is a public nuisance or that the patrons of the business create a nuisance in the area surrounding the licensed premises. The local liquor commissioner may notify the licensee to appear before the commissioner, in the presence of the complaining persons, to define, discuss and seek resolution of problems giving rise to the complaint. The commissioner may also order subsequent meetings to review progress toward resolution of the problems. Failure of a licensee to appear in response to a notice, or to attend subsequent meetings as ordered by the commissioner, shall be grounds for suspension of the licensee's license.
(Coun. J. 12-9-92, p. 25465; Amend. 7-2-97, p. 48043)

§4-60-200 Violation—Penalty.

Any person violating any of the provisions of this chapter shall be fined not less than $300.00 nor more than $1,000.00 for each offense, except where otherwise specifically provided. A separate and distinct offense shall be held to have been committed each day any person continues to violate any of the provisions hereof.
(Coun. J. 12-9-92, p. 25465)

§4-60-205 Regulations.

The director of revenue and the local liquor control commissioner shall have the authority to promulgate rules and regulations necessary to implement the requirements of this chapter.
(Added. Coun. J. 9-29-04, p. 32144)

§4-60-210 Severability.

If any provision, clause, sentence, paragraph or section of this chapter, or the application thereof, shall be held invalid by a court of competent jurisdiction, such invalidity shall not affect the other provisions of this chapter which can be given effect without the invalid provision or application, and to this end the provisions of this chapter are declared severable.
(Coun. J. 12-9-92, p. 25465)

CHAPTER 4-64
TOBACCO DEALERS
(Selected Sections)

Sections:

Article I. Wholesale Tobacco Dealers

4-64-010 Wholesale tobacco dealer defined.
4-64-020 License—Required.
4-64-030 License—Application—Investigation.
4-64-040 License—Fee.
4-64-050 Retail sale of cigarettes.
4-64-060 Recordkeeping.

Article II. Retail Tobacco Dealers and Tobacco Product Samplers

4-64-090 Retail tobacco dealer defined.
4-64-091 Tobacco products defined.
4-64-092 Tobacco accessories defined.
4-64-093 Person defined.
4-64-094 Tobacco product sampler defined.
4-64-095 Tobacco product sample defined.
4-64-096 Tobacco product sampling defined.
4-64-100 Licensing requirements for retail tobacco dealers.
4-64-101 Licensing requirements for tobacco product samplers.
4-64-110 License—Application—Investigation.
4-64-120 License—Fee.
4-64-140 License—Transfer prohibited.
4-64-150 Recordkeeping.
4-64-160 Purchases from unlicensed wholesalers—Report required.
4-64-170 Sanitary and health requirements—Inspections.
4-64-180 Prohibited locations.
4-64-181 Distribution of tobacco products samples prohibited.
4-64-190 Furnishing tobacco products or tobacco accessories to minors prohibited.
4-64-191 Certain transactions prohibited.
4-64-194 Sale of bidi cigarettes and other tobacco products.
4-64-200 Purchase or possession of tobacco products or tobacco accessories by minors prohibited.
4-64-210 Posting of warning to minors.
4-64-220 Identification cards—Prohibited acts.
4-64-240 Suspension, revocation and nonrenewal of licenses.

Article III. Cigarette-Vending Machines

4-64-250 Definitions.
4-64-310 Installation requirements.
4-64-320 Location restrictions.

Article IV. Violation of Chapter— Penalties—Enforcement

4-64-330 In general.
4-64-331 Underage tobacco violations—Civil penalty.
4-64-332 Underage tobacco violations—Director of revenue's duties.
4-64-333 Underage tobacco violations—Notices.

4-64-335 Underage tobacco violations—Administrative hearings.
4-64-337 Underage tobacco violations—Resources for enforcement.
4-64-340 Revocation and other enforcement provisions.

Article I. Wholesale Tobacco Dealers

§4-64-010 Wholesale tobacco dealer defined.

As used in this chapter:

"Wholesale tobacco dealer" means any person making, manufacturing or jobbing cigars, or selling, offering for sale, exposing for sale, or keeping with the intention of cigarette-vending machines with an agreement to maintain, service or supply.

"Distribution" means to give, sell, deliver, dispense or issue, or offer to give, sell, deliver, dispense or issue, selling or exchanging or delivering at wholesale, any tobacco, snuff, cigars, cigarettes or cigarette papers, including leaf tobacco, or any preparations containing tobacco.

(Added. Coun. J. 12-9-92, p. 25465)

§4-64-020 License—Required.

No person shall engage in the business of a wholesale tobacco dealer without first having obtained a license therefor.

(Added. Coun. J. 12-9-92, p. 25465)

§4-64-030 License—Application—Investigation.

An application for a wholesale tobacco dealer's license shall be made in conformity with the general requirements of this code relating to applications for licenses, and shall give the location and a description of the premises.

The director of the fire prevention bureau and the commissioner of buildings shall investigate or cause an investigation to be made of the premises named and described in the application for the purpose of determining the fitness and suitability of such premises for such business from a sanitary standpoint, and for determining whether or not the said premises comply with all the provisions of this code and laws of the state regulating health, safety and sanitation, so as properly to safeguard the lives and health of the employees engaged therein.

The superintendent of police shall cause an investigation to be made to determine the character and fitness of the applicant and to determine whether the premises named in the application comply with the police regulations of this code.

(Added. Coun. J. 12-9-92, p. 25465; Amend. Coun. J. 3-5-03, p. 104990)

§4-64-040 License—Fee.

The annual license fee for a wholesale tobacco dealer shall be set forth in Section 4-5-010.

(Added. Coun. J. 12-9-92, p. 25465)

§4-64-050 Retail sale of cigarettes.

No license issued to any wholesale tobacco dealer shall entitle the holder thereof to engage in the sale, offering for sale, or keeping with the intention of selling, at retail, of any cigarettes or cigarette papers unless such dealer shall

have first obtained a license as a retail tobacco dealer. It shall be unlawful for any person licensed as a wholesale tobacco dealer to sell, offer for sale, or deliver cigarettes or cigarette papers to any retail tobacco dealer within the city not duly licensed under the provisions of this chapter.
(Added. Coun. J. 12-9-92, p. 25465)

§4-64-060 Recordkeeping.

Every wholesale tobacco dealer shall keep a book in which there shall be made at the time of the transaction a record in English of all sales of cigarettes and in which shall be set forth the name and residential or business address of the purchaser, the date of the transaction, the invoice number, the city retail tobacco dealer's license number of the purchaser, and a description of the cigarettes sold. Said book shall be open at all reasonable times to the inspection of any member of the police force, or any member of the department of revenue, duly authorized in writing for such purpose by the superintendent of police or the director of revenue.
(Added. Coun. J. 12-9-92, p. 25465)

Article II. Retail Tobacco Dealers and Tobacco Product Samplers

§4-64-090 Retail tobacco dealer defined.

As used in this chapter:

"Retail tobacco dealer" means any person selling, offering for sale, exposing for sale or keeping with the intention of selling or exchanging at retail, tobacco products, or tobacco accessories in the city.
(Added. Coun. J. 12-9-92, p. 25465)

§4-64-091 Tobacco products defined.

As used in this chapter:

"Tobacco products" means any substance containing tobacco leaf, including but not limited to cigarettes, cigars, smoking tobacco, and/or smokeless tobacco.
(Added. Coun. J. 12-9-92, p. 25465)

§4-64-092 Tobacco accessories defined.

As used in this chapter:

"Tobacco accessories" means cigarette papers or wrappers, pipes, holders of smoking materials of all types, cigarette rolling machines, and any other item designed primarily for the smoking or ingestion of tobacco products.
(Added. Coun. J. 12-9-92, p. 25465)

§4-64-093 Person defined.

As used in this chapter:

"Person" means an individual, firm, partnership, joint venture, association, corporation, estate, trust, trustee, or any other group or combination acting as a unit, excepting the United States of America, the state of Illinois, and any political subdivision thereof.
(Added. Coun. J. 12-9-92, p. 25465)

§4-64-094 Tobacco product sampler defined.

As used in this chapter:

"Tobacco product sampler" means any person engaged in the business of tobacco product sampling, other than a retail tobacco dealer.

(Added. Coun. J. 12-9-92, p. 25465)

§4-64-095 Tobacco product sample defined.

As used in this chapter:

"Tobacco product sample" means a tobacco product distributed to members of the general public at no cost or at nominal cost for product promotional purposes.

(Added. Coun. J. 12-9-92, p. 25465)

§4-64-096 Tobacco product sampling defined.

As used in this chapter:

"Tobacco product sampling" means the distribution of tobacco product samples to members of the general public.

(Added. Coun. J. 12-9-92, p. 25465)

§4-64-100 Licensing requirements for retail tobacco dealers.

No person shall engage in the business of a retail tobacco dealer without first having obtained a license therefor. A separate license shall be required for each establishment at which tobacco products or tobacco accessories are sold. The city clerk shall issue an adhesive self-voiding license emblem to be placed on each licensed cigarette-vending machine. Each license emblem shall be coded to identify the vending operator who has control over each cigarette-vending machine. The license emblem shall bear the words City of Chicago, Licensed Cigarette-Vending Machine. The license shall designate the period of time for which the license is valid, shall contain a reproduction of the city seal along with the names of the mayor and city clerk; shall contain a space for a brief description of the name, style and type of vending machine to be licensed; and such other language as may be prescribed by the mayor. A replacement license emblem will not be issued unless the application for such replacement emblem is accompanied by a police report of the incident in which the emblem to be placed was lost, stolen or mutilated, or unless the remnants of the emblem being replaced are submitted with the replacement application. There shall not be a change of location fee assessed when a cigarette-vending machine is moved from one location to another.

(Added. Coun. J. 12-9-92, p. 25465)

§4-64-101 Licensing requirements for tobacco product samplers.

No person shall engage in the business of a tobacco product sampler without first having obtained a license therefor. A license shall entitle the holder to distribute tobacco product samples during the term of the license. The licensee shall notify the department of revenue of the location(s) at which the licensee proposes to conduct tobacco product sampling pursuant to such license not less than 30 days prior to conducting such tobacco product sampling at such location(s). The license or copy thereof must be carried at all times by the licensee, or employees or agents of the licensee, at any location where such licensee,

employees or agents are engaged in tobacco product sampling. Notwithstanding any other provision of law, a tobacco product sampler's license shall not be required as a condition of distributing tobacco product samples at a location for which a retail tobacco dealer's license has been issued.
(Added. Coun. J. 12-9-92, p. 25465)

§4-64-110 License—Application—Investigation.

An application for a retail tobacco dealer's license and a tobacco product sampler's license shall be made in conformity with the general requirements of this code relating to applications for licenses. When any license issued pursuant to this chapter shall have been revoked for any cause, no retail tobacco dealer's license or tobacco product sampler's license shall be granted to such person for a period of one year thereafter.

The superintendent of police shall cause an investigation to be made of the character and the reputation of the applicant, or whether said applicant is a proper person to be entrusted with the sale of cigarettes, and of whether the premises named in said application comply with the police regulations of this code applicable to said business, including the requirement as to location.
(Added. Coun. J. 12-9-92, p. 25465)

§4-64-120 License—Fee.

The license fee for a retail tobacco dealer's license or tobacco product sampler's license shall be as set forth in Section 4-5-010.
(Coun. J. 12-9-92, p. 25465)

§4-64-140 License—Transfer prohibited.

The transfer of any license issued hereunder is hereby expressly prohibited.
(Coun. J. 12-9-92, p. 25465)

§4-64-150 Recordkeeping.

Every retail tobacco dealer shall keep a book in which there shall be made at the time of the transaction a record in English of all purchases of cigarettes and in which shall be set forth the name and address of the place of business of the person from whom purchased, the date of the transaction, the seller's invoice number, the number of the city wholesale tobacco dealer's license of the person from whom purchased, and a description of the cigarettes purchased.

The said book and all cigarettes purchased, received or kept for sale by every retail tobacco dealer shall be open at all reasonable times to the inspection of the mayor, any member of the police force, or any member of the department of revenue duly authorized in writing for such purpose by the superintendent of police or the director of revenue.
(Coun. J. 12-9-92, p. 25465)

§4-64-160 Purchases from unlicensed wholesalers—Report required.

In case any retail tobacco dealer purchases cigarettes from any source other than a wholesale tobacco dealer duly licensed by the city, such retail tobacco dealer shall make out and deliver to the department of revenue within 24 hours after such purchase a report in writing in English setting forth the name

and address of the person from whom the purchase was made, the quantity, and the description of the cigarettes purchased.
(Coun. J. 12-9-92, p. 25465)

§4-64-170 Sanitary and health requirements—Inspections.

It shall be the duty of the board of health, and it is hereby authorized and empowered, from time to time to inspect and examine all places where cigarettes are licensed to be sold at retail within the city, with a view of ascertaining whether the laws of the state and the provisions of this code in relation to the sale of cigarettes are being complied with at such places, and it shall be its duty to cause all such laws and code provisions to be rigorously enforced; and it shall be the duty of all persons licensed to sell cigarettes at retail within the city, upon the demand of the board of health, to furnish to said board for its inspection samples of all cigarettes sold or offered for sale by them, which samples of cigarettes shall be analyzed by or under the direction of said board, and a record of such analysis shall be made and kept in its office for the inspection of the public.

No person shall expose for sale, sell or offer for sale to any person, directly, indirectly, within the city, any cigarette or cigarettes containing opium, morphine, jimsonweed, belladonna, strychnia, cocaine or other deleterious or poisonous drug or drugs.
(Coun. J. 12-9-92, p. 25465)

§4-64-180 Prohibited locations.

No person shall sell, give away, barter, exchange or otherwise deal in tobacco products, tobacco product samples or tobacco accessories at any place located within 100 feet of any building or other location used primarily as a school, child care facility, or for the education or recreation of children under 18 years of age.
(Coun. J. 12-9-92, p. 25465)

§4-64-181 Distribution of tobacco products samples prohibited.

(a) No person shall give away, barter, exchange, distribute or in any way dispense free of charge or at nominal cost any tobacco products, samples, and/or any coupon redeemable for any tobacco products, on any public street, alley, sidewalk, or in any public park, ground or playground, or in areas open to the public in any publicly owned or operated building except as permitted in subsection (b) of this section.

(b) Tobacco product samples, and coupons redeemable for tobacco products, may be distributed in a publicly owned or operated building: (i) at a location for which a retail tobacco dealer's license has been issued; or (ii) in a separately enclosed area to which persons under the age of 18 are denied admission at an event sponsored in whole or in part by a manufacturer of tobacco products and for which notice has been provided pursuant to Section 4-64-101. This section does not prohibit the distribution of coupons included in newspapers, magazines or other publications.
(Coun. J. 12-9-92, p. 25465)

§4-64-190 Furnishing tobacco products or tobacco accessories to minors prohibited.

No person shall sell, give away, barter, exchange or otherwise furnish any tobacco products, tobacco product samples and/or tobacco accessories to any individual who is under 18 years of age.

(Coun. J. 12-9-92, p. 25465; Amend. 3-11-98, p. 63445; 12-15-99, p. 21529)

§4-64-191 Certain transactions prohibited.

No person shall sell, offer for sale, barter or expose for sale any cigarette, cigarette tobacco or smokeless tobacco except in its original factory-wrapped package. No person shall sell, offer for sale, barter or expose for sale any cigarettes in a package containing fewer than twenty cigarettes.

(Added. Coun. J. 3-11-98, p. 63445; Amend. Coun. J. 5-1-02, p. 84262)

§4-64-194 Sale of bidi cigarettes and other tobacco products.

(a) No person shall sell, give away, barter, exchange or otherwise furnish to any other person a bidi cigarette. As used in this section, "bidi cigarette" means a product that (i) contains tobacco that is wrapped in temburni or tendu leaf, or that is wrapped in any other material identified by regulation of the board of health because the material is similar in appearance or other characteristics to the temburni or tendu leaf; and (ii) does not contain a smoke filtering device.

(b) No person shall sell, give away, barter, exchange or otherwise furnish to any other person any cigarette wrapping paper or wrapping leaf that is or is held out to be, impregnated or scented with, or aged or dipped in, alcoholic liquor, chocolate, any fruit flavoring, vanilla or honey in any combination.

(Added. Coun. J. 12-15-99, p. 21569; Amend. Coun. J. 12-12-01, p. 76445; 10-2-02, p. 94572)

§4-64-200 Purchase or possession of tobacco products or tobacco accessories by minors prohibited.

It shall be unlawful:

(a) For any individual under the age of 18 years to purchase tobacco products, tobacco product samples or tobacco accessories, or to misrepresent the individual's identity or age, or to use any false or altered identification for the purpose of purchasing tobacco products, tobacco product samples or tobacco accessories;

(b) For any individual under the age of 18 years to possess or to accept delivery of any tobacco product, tobacco product samples or tobacco accessories, except (i) in the presence of and with the knowledge and consent of the individual's parent or legal guardian, while on private property that is not open to the public, or (ii) at the direction of the individual's employer when required in the performance of the individual's employment duties; or

(c) For any person to give any individual under the age of 18 years any identification card not duly issued to such individual, for the purpose of buying tobacco products, tobacco product samples or tobacco accessories.

Any minor who illegally possesses any tobacco product, tobacco product sample or tobacco accessory shall be subject to a fine of $25.00 for the first offense and a fine of not less than $50.00 for each subsequent offense.

(Coun. J. 12-9-92, p. 25465; Amend. 11-18-98, p. 84355)

§4-64-210 Posting of warning to minors.

Any person who sells, gives away or distributes tobacco products or accessories shall display a printed card which shall state:

Warning
It Is A Violation of the Law For Cigarettes Or Other
Tobacco Products Or Tobacco Accessories To Be Sold
To Any Person Under The Age of 18. Any Person Who Violates
This Law Is Subject To A Fine And Possible Imprisonment.

The printed card shall not be less than eight inches by 11 inches in size. The text of such printed card shall be in red letters on a white background, said letters to be at least one inch high. The word "warning" shall be in a print of 84-point height and Helvetica type and the remainder of the text in a print of 24-point height and in Helvetica medium-face, Futura medium-face or Universe 65 type.

Such card shall be posted at each location at which tobacco products and/or tobacco accessories are sold or displayed at all times in which the establishment is open, so that a card is visible from each location where such sales or displays occur.

(Coun. J. 12-9-92, p. 25465; Amend. 12-15-99, p. 21529)

§4-64-220 Identification cards—Prohibited acts.

It shall be unlawful for any person (a) to transfer, alter, or deface any identification card issued by a public officer or public agency in the performance of official duties, or (b) to possess a false or forged identification card, or (c) to obtain such an identification card by means of false representation.

(Coun. J. 12-9-92, p. 25465)

§4-64-240 Suspension, revocation and nonrenewal of licenses.

Knowing or repeated violation of any provision of Sections 4-64-100, 4-64-101, 4-64-180, 4-64-181, 4-64-190, 4-64-194, 4-64-200, 4-64-210 and 4-64-220 by a licensee shall be grounds for revocation or suspension of such license. For purposes of this section, "license" includes any and all licenses issued by any officer, department or agency of the city of Chicago required for retail or other business operations at the location at which the offense occurred, and includes but is not limited to retail tobacco licenses.

(Coun. J. 12-9-92, p. 25465; Amend. 12-15-99, p. 21569)

Article III. Cigarette-Vending Machines

§4-64-250 Definitions.

As used in this chapter:

"Cigarette-vending machine" means any mechanical, electronic or other similar device that dispenses cigarettes, cigarette papers or wrappers, including but not limited to any machine that dispenses such items through the use of a locking or remote control device.

"Cigarette-vending machine operator" means any person who conducts or transacts the business of distributing, placing, leasing, operating or selling cigarette-vending machines with an agreement to maintain, service or supply.

"Distribution" means to give, sell, deliver, dispense or issue, or offer to give, sell, deliver, dispense or issue,
or cause or hire any person to give, sell, deliver, dispense, issue or offer to give, sell, deliver, dispense or issue.

"Person" shall have the same meaning as set forth in Section 4-64-093 of this chapter.

"Public place" means any area to which the public is invited or permitted.

"Tavern" means an enclosed place of business kept, used, maintained, advertised and held out to the public as a place that primarily serves alcoholic liquor for consumption on the premises and in which providing entertainment or the serving of food is only incidental or secondary to the sale of alcoholic beverages for immediate consumption. Examples of places of business not deemed to be taverns within the definitions of this paragraph include, but are not limited to, restaurants, catering halls, bowling alleys, billiard parlors, discotheques, theaters and arenas.

"Tobacco product" means any substance which contains tobacco leaf, including but not limited to cigarettes, cigars, smoking tobacco and/or smokeless tobacco.

(Coun. J. 12-9-92, p. 25465)

§4-64-310 Installation requirements.

It is unlawful for any person to install or use, or permit the installation or use of, any cigarette-vending machine at any place unless the person in control of such place is licensed as a retail tobacco dealer and unless said location is described in the registration certificate of that cigarette-vending machine. Any person violating the provisions of this section shall be fined $200.00 for each offense and each day of continuing violation shall constitute a separate and distinct offense.

(Coun. J. 12-9-92, p. 25465)

§4-64-320 Location restrictions.

(a) No license shall be issued pursuant to Section 4-64-260 for the location of a cigarette-vending machine in a public place and it shall be unlawful for any person to locate a cigarette-vending machine in a public place except as permitted in subsection (b) of this section.

(b) Tobacco products may be distributed by a cigarette-vending machine in a tavern only in the following ways:

(i) Through a cigarette-vending machine which must be:

(A) Placed at a distance of a minimum of 25 feet from any entrance to the premises; and

(B) Directly visible by the owner of the premises, or his or her employee or agent during the operation of such vending machine; or

(ii) Directly by the owner of the premises, or his or her employee or agent.

(Coun. J. 12-9-92, p. 25465)

Article IV. Violation of Chapter—Penalties—Enforcement

§4-64-330 In general.

(a) Alleged violations of the provisions of Sections 4-64-100, 4-64-101, 4-64-140, 4-64-150, 4-64-160, 4-64-170, 4-64-180, 4-64-181, 4-64-190(c), 4-64-194, 4-64-200, 4-64-220, 4-64-260, 4-64-300, 4-64-310 and 4-64-320 of this chapter and Sections 3-42-050, 3-42-060, 3-42-070 and 3-42-100 shall be adjudicated by the circuit court of Cook County or the department of administrative hearings pursuant to citation. Penalties shall be as prescribed in this section, notwithstanding any other general penalty provision in this code.

(b) Any person convicted of a first offense for violating any of the provisions referenced in subsection (a) of this section shall be punishable by a fine of not less than $100.00 and not more than $500.00. Any person convicted of a second offense within a two-year period under the foregoing sections shall be punished for such offense by a fine of not less than $250.00 and not more than $500.00. Any person convicted of more than two offenses within a two-year period under the foregoing sections shall be punished for such offense by a fine of not less than $500.00 and not more than $1,000.00 for each additional offense.

(Added. Coun. J. 2-9-94, p. 45231; Amend. 9-11-96, p. 28258; 4-29-98, p. 66564; 12-15-99, p. 21569)

§4-64-331 Underage tobacco violations—Civil penalty.

(a) The director of revenue may institute an action with the department of administrative hearings in order to determine liability and seek penalties for violations of the provisions of Sections 4-64-190 and 4-64-210 of this chapter (which shall hereinafter be referred to collectively as "underage tobacco violations").

(b) Every act or omission which constitutes an underage tobacco violation by an officer, director, manager or other agent or employee of any person licensed pursuant to this chapter shall be deemed to be the act of such licensee, and such licensee shall be liable for all penalties and sanctions provided by this section in the same manner as if such act or omission had been done or omitted by the licensee personally.

(c) Any person who commits an underage tobacco violation under Section 4-64-190 shall be liable for a civil penalty of $500.00 for the first violation; $1,000.00 for the second and subsequent violations within two years; and the person's retail tobacco license shall be revoked for the third offense within two years. A person who commits any other underage tobacco violation shall be liable for a civil penalty of $200.00.

(d) Any civil penalty remaining unpaid after the determination of underage tobacco violation liability has become final for purposes of judicial review shall constitute a debt due and owing the city.

(e) If any person commits three or more violations of Section 4-64-210, within a two-year period, the mayor's license commission shall have the discretion to revoke or suspend any license issued to that person pursuant to this chapter.

(Added. Coun. J. 2-9-94, p. 45231; Amend. 7-10-96, p. 24982; 9-11-96, p. 28258; 11-12-97, p. 56813; 4-29-98, p. 66564; 12-15-99, p. 21529)

§4-64-332 Underage tobacco violations—Director of revenue's duties.

(a) The director of revenue is hereby authorized to institute an action with the department of administrative hearings by forwarding a copy of an underage tobacco violations notice, which has been served in accordance with Section 4-64-333, to the department of administrative hearings.

(b) The director of revenue is authorized to establish a program of testing the sales practices of licensed tobacco dealers, to determine whether licensees are selling tobacco products to minors. The program shall include the use of persons under the age of 18 as purchasers of tobacco products, in accordance with procedures established by the director of revenue. No person under the age of 18 who purchases or attempts to purchase tobacco products as part of this program shall be charged with a violation of Section 4-64-200.

(Added. Coun. J. 2-9-94, p. 45231; Amend. 9-11-96, p. 28258; 4-29-98, p. 66564)

§4-64-333 Underage tobacco violations—Notices.

(a) The issuer of the underage tobacco violations notice shall specify on the notice his or her name and department unit, the name and address of the person or entity charged with the violation, the date, time and place of the violation and the section of the code which was allegedly violated and shall certify the correctness of the specified information by signing his or her name to the notice. The underage tobacco violation notice shall include the date, time and location of an administrative hearing at which the alleged violation may be contested on the merits and the penalties for failure to appear at the hearing.

(b) Underage tobacco violation notices shall be served upon the alleged violator, or, if the alleged violator is licensed pursuant to this chapter, upon the licensee or his or her agent or employee. The issuer of the underage tobacco violation notice shall provide a copy to the director of revenue.

(c) The director of revenue shall distribute underage tobacco violation notices to department of revenue employees and to the superintendent of police.

(Added. Coun. J. 2-9-94, p. 45231; Amend. 4-29-98, p. 66564)

§4-64-335 Underage tobacco violations—Administrative hearings.

Administrative hearings for the adjudication of underage tobacco violations shall be conducted in accordance with Chapter 2-14 of this code.

(Added. Coun. J. 2-9-94, p. 45231; Amend. 7-10-96, p. 24982; 11-12-97, p. 56813; 4-29-98, p. 66564)

§4-64-337 Underage tobacco violations—Resources for enforcement.

The director of revenue shall ensure that sufficient resources of the department are devoted to provide for the adequate enforcement of the provisions of this chapter relating to underage tobacco violations. The director shall, no later than the twenty-first day of January, April, July and October of each year, report to the city council committee on license and consumer protection on the progress of the department in the enforcement of this chapter. The report shall include the following information with respect to the previous three calendar months: (1) the number of notices of underage tobacco violations issued by the department; and (2) the number and results of underage tobacco violation adjudications conducted pursuant to this chapter.

(Added. Coun. J. 2-9-94, p. 45231)

§4-64-340 Revocation and other enforcement provisions.

(a) Any retail tobacco dealer's license, tobacco product sampler's license or cigarette-vending machine operator's license shall be revocable by the mayor upon violation by the licensee of any of the provisions of this chapter or the criminal laws of the state of Illinois.

(b) The director of revenue and the superintendent of police shall have the authority to immediately disable the coin slot of any cigarette-vending machine which is dispensing unstamped cigarettes or which does not have a valid license emblem affixed to it upon notarized affidavit of two investigators of the department of revenue or the Chicago Police Department attesting to the particular violation. The director of revenue or the superintendent of police shall also have the authority to confiscate or remove a cigarette-vending machine which does not have a valid license emblem or which is dispensing unstamped cigarettes.

(Coun. J. 12-9-92, p. 25465)

DIVISION IV
HEALTH SERVICES
(Selected Chapters)

Chapters:

4-68 Ambulances.(Complete Chapter)
4-72 Day Care Centers. (Selected Sections)
4-80 Funeral Business.(Complete Chapter)
4-84 Hospitals. (Selected Sections)
4-92 Massage Establishments and Massage Services. (Selected Sections)
4-93 Body Piercing. (Selected Sections)
4-96 Long-Term Care Facilities.(Complete Chapter)

CHAPTER 4-68
AMBULANCES
(Complete Chapter)

Sections:

4-68-010 Definitions.
4-68-020 License requirements.
4-68-030 License—Application and approval requirements.
4-68-040 Maintenance—Change of ownership.
4-68-045 License—Renewal.
4-68-050 License—Fee.
4-68-060 Inspection authority.
4-68-062 Applicability of Illinois Emergency Medical Services Systems Act.
4-68-064 Availability of names of state-licensed emergency medical technicians.
4-68-070 Exemption from certain traffic laws.
4-68-080 Rules and regulations.
4-68-081 Reserved.
4-68-090 Reserved.
4-68-100 Patient destination.
4-68-110 Peace officer assistance during emergencies.
4-68-120 License suspension and revocation.
4-68-130 Fees for ambulance services.
4-68-140 Reserved.
4-68-150 Insurance.
4-68-160 Reserved.
4-68-170 Reserved.

4-68-180 Discrimination.
4-68-190 Violation—Penalty.
4-68-195 Impoundment of vehicle—Notification of owner—Penalty.
4-68-200 Severability.

§4-68-010 Definitions.

For purposes of this chapter, when any of the following words or terms are used herein they shall have the meaning or construction ascribed to them in this section:

"Person" means any individual, firm, partnership, corporation, company, association or joint stock association, or the legal successor thereof.

"Private ambulance" means an ambulance operated by a private person.

"Public ambulance" means an ambulance operated by the city of Chicago, having primary responsibility in emergency situations.

Any other word or term not defined herein but defined in the Emergency Medical Services Systems Act of the state of Illinois, 210 ILCS 50/1 et seq., as amended, shall have the meaning ascribed to the word or term in that act.
(Coun. J. 12-9-92, p. 25465; Amend. 7-30-97, p. 50612)

§4-68-020 License requirements.

(a) Except as provided below, it shall be unlawful for any person to operate or maintain a private ambulance within the city of Chicago without having first obtained a license for the ambulance from the department of consumer services. A separate license shall be required for each private ambulance operated or maintained within the city. The license shall be posted in the ambulance at all times.

(b) An ambulance license issued by the city of Chicago shall authorize the ambulance to operate only at the level of service (basic life support, intermediate life support, or advanced life support) that has been approved for that particular ambulance by the state of Illinois Department of Public Health.

(c) No license shall be required for any ambulance which is rendering assistance in the case of a disaster declared by the mayor, governor or president, or is transporting patients from beyond the city of Chicago to locations within the city, or from within the city of Chicago to a location outside of the city.
(Coun. J. 12-9-92, p. 25465; Amend. 7-30-97, p. 50612)

§4-68-030 License—Application and approval requirements.

(a) A person seeking an ambulance license shall file an application with the department of consumer services.

(b) Along with the application, the applicant shall submit evidence that an appropriate state of Illinois ambulance license has been granted for each ambulance for which a license is sought and documentation that reflects the successful completion of any required state inspection. Failure to submit such evidence shall result in denial of the application.

(c) Each application for an initial ambulance license and all information required to be furnished in connection therewith shall be approved by the department of health. As a condition of approval, the department shall inspect the ambulance for compliance with this chapter and the rules and regulations adopted by the department of health hereunder.

(d) Each application for an initial or a renewal of an ambulance license and all information required to be furnished in connection therewith shall be approved by the department of consumer services. As a condition of approval, the department shall inspect the ambulance for compliance with this chapter and the rules and regulations adopted by the department of consumer services hereunder.

(e) Prior to the issuance of an initial or a renewal of an ambulance license the fire department shall inspect and approve the ambulance's communication system.

(Coun. J. 12-9-92, p. 25465; Amend. 7-30-97, p. 50612)

§4-68-040 Maintenance—Change of ownership.

Each ambulance shall, at all times when in use as such, be suitable for the transportation of patients from the standpoint of health, sanitation and safety, and be maintained in suitable premises and contain equipment conforming with the standards, requirements and regulations provided for herein. Said equipment shall be in proper and good condition for such use and comply with all applicable laws and local ordinances relating to health, sanitation and safety and be equipped with such lights, sirens and special markings to designate it as an ambulance, as may be prescribed in regulations promulgated by the commissioner of the city of Chicago department of consumer services, the city of Chicago board of health, and federal and state of Illinois laws and any other applicable provisions of this code.

It shall be the duty of every company licensed under this chapter to notify the department of consumer services whenever any change in its address is made, either business or residence. Any notice required to be given to a licensee shall be sufficient if addressed to the last address recorded in the office of the department of consumer services.

Any change of ownership of a licensed company shall terminate the ambulance-operating license and shall require a new application and a new license, and conformance with all the requirements of this chapter as upon original licensing.

(Coun. J. 12-9-92, p. 25465; Amend. 7-30-97, p. 50612)

§4-68-045 License—Renewal.*

Ambulance licenses shall expire on October 31st following the date of issue unless an application for renewal is filed with the department of consumer services prior to that date. No ambulance license shall be renewed unless the renewal application is approved by the departments of consumer services and fire. An applicant for a renewal license shall submit with the application evidence that a state of Illinois license has been granted, and is in force and effect, for the ambulance for which the license is sought along with documentation that reflects the completion of any required state inspection.

(Coun. J. 12-9-92, p. 25465; Amend. 7-30-97, p. 50612)

* **Editor's Note:** Section 4-68-045 was originally added as a second Section 4-68-040. The current Section 4-68-045 was editorially renumbered.

§4-68-050 License—Fee.

(a) The annual license fee for an ambulance shall be as set forth in Section 4-5-010.

(b) Ambulance licenses issued by the department of revenue which have not expired by October 31, 1997 shall pay a fee for any renewed license effective November 1, 1997 on a pro rata basis of the unused period for the ambulance license issued by the department of revenue.

(c) Ambulance licenses are not transferable between parties.

(d) An ambulance licensee may change a vehicle currently operating under a valid license upon the inspection and approval of the departments of consumer services, health and fire and upon the payment of a nonrefundable fee of $50.00.

(Coun. J. 12-9-92, p. 25465; Amend. 7-30-97, p. 50612)

§4-68-060 Inspection authority.

Each licensed ambulance, its equipment, the premises designated in the application for its operation and maintenance, and all records relating to its maintenance, personnel and operation shall be made available for inspection by the departments of health, fire and consumer services at all times.

(Coun. J. 12-9-92, p. 25465; Amend. 7-30-97, p. 50612)

§4-68-062 Applicability of Illinois Emergency Medical Services Systems Act.

Every person who operates or maintains an ambulance within the city of Chicago shall observe all requirements imposed by the Illinois Emergency Medical Services Systems Act, 210 ILCS 50/1, et seq., as amended, and any regulations promulgated pursuant thereto.

(Added. Coun. J. 7-30-97, p. 50612)

§4-68-064 Availability of names of state-licensed emergency medical technicians.

Any person who is granted an ambulance license under this chapter shall provide to the department of consumer services, upon its request: (1) a list of names of all emergency medical technicians employed by the licensee who perform duties in the city; and (2) evidence of the state licensure of such technicians.

(Added. Coun. J. 7-30-97, p. 50612)

§4-68-070 Exemption from certain traffic laws.

While transporting a patient in situations where reasonable grounds exist to believe that a life threatening or potentially life threatening situation is present, emergency medical technicians may park irrespective of the otherwise applicable provisions of law, ordinance or regulations, and proceed past a red or stop signal or stop sign, but only after slowing down or stopping as may be necessary for safe operation. No ambulance shall exceed the lawful speed, but the emergency medical technician may disregard laws or ordinances or regulations governing direction of movement or turning in specified directions, when such activity is specifically provided for in state of Illinois guidelines.

The exemptions herein granted shall apply only when the emergency medical technician, while in motion, sounds an audible signal by siren as may be reasonably necessary and when the vehicle is equipped with lights and markings, as required by federal and state specifications for ambulance vehicles.

The foregoing provisions shall not relieve emergency medical technicians from the duty to drive with due regard for the safety of all persons, nor shall such provisions protect the emergency medical technicians from the consequences of reckless disregard for the safety of others.

No private or public ambulance shall operate in the city without at least two attendants who are duly licensed by the state of Illinois as emergency medical technicians, professional nurses, or physicians.
(Coun. J. 12-9-92, p. 25465; Amend. 7-30-97, p. 50612)

§4-68-080 Rules and regulations.

The commissioner of the department of consumer services shall write and adopt appropriate rules and regulations pertaining to the safety of operation and conditions appropriate to the exterior and general usage of private ambulances. Such regulations shall include but shall not be limited to the size of lettering and identifying information displayed on the ambulance, or the volume, frequency ranges, and use of sirens. The department of consumer services may also adopt rules and regulations pertaining to applications for an ambulance license and establishing standards for the professional conduct of ambulance personnel.

The department of health shall write and adopt health-related rules and regulations regarding the operation and maintenance of private ambulances. These rules and regulations shall adopt the rules and regulations pertaining to the operation and maintenance of private ambulances which have been promulgated by the state of Illinois Department of Public Health.
(Coun. J. 12-9-92, p. 25465; Amend. 7-30-97, p. 50612)

§4-68-081 Reserved.
(Renumbered to §4-68-110)

§4-68-090 Reserved.
(Renumbered to §4-68-030)

§4-68-100 Patient destination.

Any public ambulance, when rendering basic life support services to a patient, shall convey the patient from the place where care was initiated to the nearest emergency medical facility approved by the city of Chicago department of health for the provision of emergency medical care services.

Any public ambulance, when offering advanced life support services to a patient, shall convey the patient from the place where care was initiated to that hospital where, as determined by the resource or associate hospital, the most appropriate and needed service can be rendered to the specific patient; provided that, except as provided below, the destination hospital shall be a participant in a state of Illinois Emergency Medical Services System.

Whenever any private ambulance is offering basic life support services, no sick or injured person shall be conveyed against his/her will by the private ambulance from the place where he/she was overcome by sickness or from the scene of the accident in which he/she was injured, nor to a place to which he/she is unwilling to go; provided, that if such sick or injured person is unable to give any direction in his/her own behalf and there is no immediate relative present to direct where he/she shall be taken, such sick or injured person shall be conveyed to the nearest emergency medical facility approved by the city of Chicago department of health for the provision of emergency medical care services.

Whenever advanced life support services are initiated by a private ambulance, the patient must be conveyed to that hospital where, as determined by the resource or associate hospital, the most appropriate and needed service can be rendered to the specific patient; provided that, except as provided below, the destination hospital shall be a participant in a state of Illinois Emergency Medical Services System.

In instances where advanced life support services are indicated, and the patient demands transport to a hospital not participating in the state of Illinois Emergency Medical Services System, the patient or his/her immediate relative shall sign an appropriate release form absolving the company, the emergency medical technicians and the resource or associate hospital from responsibility related to the medical care rendered and the continuity thereof, resulting from the inability to offer fully appropriate services.
(Coun. J. 12-9-92, p. 25465; Amend. 7-30-97, p. 50612)

§4-68-110 Peace officer assistance during emergencies.

A peace officer may assist an emergency medical technician, as defined in the Illinois Emergency Medical Service Systems Act, 210 ILCS 50/1, et seq., in transporting a person to a hospital licensed to provide comprehensive emergency treatment services when the officer is informed by an emergency medical technician that the situation constitutes an emergency as defined in the Emergency Medical Services Systems Act and that person is in need of immediate hospitalization to protect such person or others from physical harm. The provisions of this section shall not apply when the person sought to be transported objects to transportation or medical treatment on religious grounds.
(Coun. J. 12-9-92, p. 25465; Amend. 7-30-97, p. 50612)

§4-68-120 License suspension and revocation.

When the department of consumer services finds or is notified by another department or agency of the city of a violation of any requirements of this chapter or of the rules and regulations adopted by the department of consumer services hereunder, it may make a second inspection after a lapse of whatever time it deems necessary for the correction of the violation. Provided, however, that whenever an inspection indicates that conditions create an imminent hazard to the public, the license for any ambulance may be immediately suspended.

After receipt from the department of consumer services of a notice of violation by the licensee, as evidenced by said inspection report, but before the allotted time has elapsed for compliance, the licensee may request a hearing to file exceptions to the inspection report or may request an extension of the time allowed for compliance. Such appeal must be filed within three days (excluding Saturdays, Sundays and official city holidays) of the receipt of such notice of violation.

If, upon such second inspection, it is found that the licensee is in continued violation of this chapter or the rules and regulations promulgated by the department of consumer services hereunder, the license may be temporarily suspended.

Upon suspension of the license the Chicago Police Department shall be notified of the suspension and shall enforce the cessation of operation of the ambulance.

The holder of a license may, at any time, make application for a restoration of the license. After receipt by the department of consumer services of such application, accompanied by a statement signed by the licensee indicating that the provision or provisions previously violated have been complied with, a reinspection shall be made on the next regular city of Chicago government business day to assure the department of consumer services that the applicant is complying with requirements of this chapter. When the reinspection indicates full compliance, the license shall be restored, and the Chicago Police Department so notified.

Upon a record of repeated violations of this chapter or the rules and regulations adopted by the department of consumer services hereunder, or repeated suspensions of a license, the department of consumer services may recommend the revocation of the license to the mayor's license commission which may revoke such license in the manner prescribed by law.

When the department of health finds or is notified by another department or agency of the city of a violation of any requirement of this chapter, or of the rules and regulations adopted by the department of health hereunder, it may make a second inspection after a lapse of whatever time it deems necessary for the correction of the violation. Provided, however, that whenever an inspection indicates that conditions create an imminent hazard to the public health, the license for any ambulance may be immediately suspended.

After receipt from the department of health of a notice of violation by the licensee, as evidenced by said inspection report, but before the allotted time has elapsed for compliance, the licensee may request a hearing to file exception to the inspection report or may request an extension of the time allowed for compliance. Such appeal must be filed within three days (excluding Saturdays, Sundays and official city holidays) of the receipt of such notice of violation.

If, upon such second inspection, it is found that the licensee is in continued violation of this chapter or the rules and regulations promulgated by the department of health hereunder, the license may be temporarily suspended.

The holder of a license may, at any time, make application for a restoration of the license. After receipt by the department of health of such application, accompanied by a statement signed by the licensee indicating that the provision or provisions previously violated have been complied with, a reinspection shall be made on the next regular city of Chicago government business day to assure the department of health that the applicant is complying with the requirements of this chapter. When the reinspection indicates full compliance, the license shall be restored, and the Chicago Police Department so notified.

Upon a record of repeated violations of this chapter or the rules and regulations adopted by the department of health hereunder, or repeated suspensions of a license, the department of health may recommend the revocation of the to the mayor's license commission which may revoke such license in the manner prescribed by law.

The department of health shall notify the Illinois Department of Public Health of any ambulance license suspension or revocation.

Nothing in this section shall preclude the initiation of any court action based on any violations of this code.
(Coun. J. 12-9-92, p. 25465; Amend. 7-30-97, p. 50612)

§4-68-130 Fees for ambulance services.
The city of Chicago may levy reasonable fees for ambulance services rendered by public ambulances.
(Coun. J. 12-9-92, p. 25465; Amend. 7-30-97, p. 50612)

§4-68-140 Reserved.
(Repealed Coun. J. 7-30-97. p. 50612)

§4-68-150 Insurance.
Every ambulance owner shall carry public liability and property damage insurance and workmen's compensation insurance for employees with insurers approved by the Illinois Department of Insurance, authorized to transact insurance business in the state of Illinois, and qualified to assure the risks for amounts hereinafter set forth under the laws of the state of Illinois, to secure payments of any loss or damage resulting from an occurrence arising out of or caused by the operation or use of any of the ambulances belonging to the licensee.

The public liability insurance policy or contract may cover one or more ambulance vehicles, but each ambulance shall be insured for the sum of at least $350,000.00 combined single limit coverage per occurrence. Every insurance policy or contract for such insurance shall provide for the payment and satisfaction of any final judgment rendered against the owner, or any person driving any insured vehicle, and that suit may be brought in any court of competent jurisdiction upon such policy or contract by any person having claims arising from the operation or use of such ambulances; it shall contain a description of each ambulance vehicle insured, manufacturer's name and serial number, the state license number, and the ambulance-operating license number.

In lieu of an insurance policy or contract, a surety bond or bonds with a corporate surety or sureties authorized to do business under the laws of the state of Illinois may be accepted by the department of consumer services, for all or any part of such insurance, provided that each bond shall be conditioned for the payment and satisfaction of any final judgment, in conformity with the provisions of an insurance policy required by this section.

All insurance policies, contracts or surety bonds required by this section or copies thereof certified by the insurers or sureties shall be filed with the department of consumer services, and no insurance or bond shall be subject to cancellation, except on 30 days' previous notice to the department of consumer services. If any insurance or bond is canceled or permitted to lapse for any reason, the department of consumer services shall suspend the license for the ambulance affected for a period not to exceed 30 days, to permit the insurance or bond to be supplied in compliance with the provisions of this section. If such other insurance or bond is not supplied within the period of suspension of the license, the mayor shall revoke the certificate of inspection* for such ambulance.

Every company licensed pursuant to this chapter shall pay each judgment or award for the loss or damage in the operation for use of an ambulance rendered against such licensee by any court or commission of competent jurisdiction

within 90 days after its judgment or award shall have become final, and not stayed by supersedeas. If any such judgment shall not be so paid, the mayor shall revoke the ambulance-operating license of the ambulance company concerned.
(Coun. J. 12-9-92, p. 25465; Amend. 7-30-97, p. 50612)

* **Editor's Note:** It may have been the city's intention in Coun. J. 7-30-97 p.50612 to change "certificate of inspection" to "license."

§4-68-160 Reserved.
(Renumbered to §4-68-050)

§4-68-170 Reserved.
(Repealed Coun. J. 7-30-97. p. 50612)

§4-68-180 Discrimination.
There shall be no discrimination against any person employed or seeking employment with a company licensed under this chapter on account of race, sex, color, religion, national origin or ancestry; likewise, it shall be unlawful for any individual licensed or authorized to provide services under this chapter to refuse aid or transportation to any patient on account of race, sex, color, religion, national origin or ancestry, or in a life-threatening situation, the inability to pay.
(Coun. J. 12-9-92, p. 25465; Amend. 7-30-97, p. 50612)

§4-68-190 Violation—Penalty.
Any person who violates any of the provisions of this chapter, or any rule or regulation promulgated hereunder, shall be punished by a fine of not less than $300.00 nor more than $500.00 per violation. Each day that such violation exists shall constitute a separate and distinct offense. A second or subsequent offense may also be punishable as a misdemeanor by incarceration in the county jail for a term not to exceed six months under procedures set forth in Section 1-2-1.1 of the Illinois Municipal Code. In addition to the above penalties, the city may seek appropriate equitable relief.
(Coun. J. 12-9-92, p. 25465; Amend. 7-30-97, p. 50612)

§4-68-195 Impoundment of vehicle—Notification of owner—Penalty.
(a) The owner of record of any motor vehicle that is used in violation of Section 4-68-020 shall be liable to the city for an administrative penalty of $500.00 plus any towing and storage fees applicable under Section 9-92-080. Any such vehicle shall be subject to seizure and impoundment pursuant to this section. This subsection shall not apply if the vehicle used in the violation was stolen at that time and the theft was reported to the appropriate police authorities within 24 hours after the theft was discovered or reasonably should have been discovered.

(b) Whenever a police officer has probable cause to believe that a vehicle is subject to seizure and impoundment pursuant to this section, the police officer shall provide for the towing of the vehicle to a facility controlled by the city or its agents. Before or at the time the vehicle is towed, the police officer shall notify any person identifying himself as the owner of the vehicle, or any person who is found to be in control of the vehicle at the time of the alleged violation, of the fact of the seizure and of the vehicle owner's right to request a vehicle impoundment hearing to be conducted under Section 2-14-132 of this code.

(c) The provisions of Section 2-14-132 shall apply whenever a motor vehicle is seized and impounded pursuant to this section.

(Added. Coun. J. 7-30-97, p. 50612; Amend. 4-29-98, p. 66564)

§4-68-200 Severability.

If any provision, clause, sentence, paragraph, section or part of this chapter, or application thereof to any person, firm, corporation, public agency or circumstance, shall, for any reason, be adjudged by a court of competent jurisdiction to be unconstitutional or invalid, said judgment shall not affect, impair or invalidate the remainder of this chapter and the application of such provision to other persons, firms, corporation, public agencies or circumstances, but shall be confined in its operation to the provision, clause, sentence, paragraph, section or part thereof directly involved in the controversy in which such judgment shall have been rendered and to the person, firm, corporation, public agency or circumstances involved. It is hereby declared to be the legislative intent of the city council that this chapter would have been adopted had such unconstitutional or invalid provision, clause, sentence, paragraph, section or part thereof not been included.

(Coun. J. 12-9-92, p. 25465; Amend. 7-30-97, p. 50612)

CHAPTER 4-72
DAY CARE CENTERS
(Selected Sections)

Sections:

4-72-010 Definitions.
4-72-020 License—Required.
4-72-070 License—Denial and revocation.
4-72-130 Recordkeeping.
4-72-140 Reports to board of health.
4-72-150 Inspections authorized.
4-72-160 Night care.
4-72-170 Violation—Penalties.

§4-72-010 Definitions.

For the purposes of this chapter the following terms are defined to mean:

"Applicant" means the "licensee."

"Board of health" means unless otherwise indicated, the Chicago Board of Health.

"Day care center" or "child care center" means any institution or place in which are received three or more children, not of common parentage, apart from their parent or guardian, between the ages of six weeks and six years for care during part or all of a day. The term is further construed to include similar units operating under any other name whatsoever with or without stated educational purpose.

This definition does not include "day care home," "group day care home," "foster family home," all as defined in this section, nor centers for the mentally retarded licensed by the state of Illinois, bona fide kindergartens, nor "day nursery schools" serving children three years or older, established in connection with grade schools supervised or operated by a private or public board of education or approved by the State Board of Education, nor daytime programs for senior citizens.

"Day care center/two-to-six" means any day care center offering care for children two to six years of age.

"Day care center/under two" means a day care center offering care for children under two years of age and located only at ground level.

Day care center shall comply with regulations of the board of health pertaining to care of infants in institutions.

"Day care home" is hereby defined as any family unit which receives more than three and up to a maximum of 12 children for less than 24 hours per day. The number counted includes the family's natural or adopted children and all other persons under the age of 12. The term does not include facilities which receive only children from a single household.

"Director" means the person or persons under whose management or supervision the day care center shall be conducted.

"Foster family home" is hereby defined as a facility for child care in residences of families who receive no more than eight children unrelated to them, unless all the children are of common parentage, for the purpose of providing family care and training for the children on a full-time basis, and as further defined in the Illinois Child Care Act approved May 15, 1969, P.A. 76-63.

"Ground level" is hereby defined as any floor two feet above or below the level of the sidewalk, public way or other open space at least 30 feet wide.

"Group day care home" is hereby defined as a family home which receives more than three and up to a maximum of 16 children for less than 24 hours per day. The number counted includes the family's natural or adopted children and all other persons under the age of 12.

"Licensee" means the corporate body or individual who files an application for a day care center and who shall be responsible for the operation and maintenance of said day care center in accordance with the provisions provided in this chapter and the "Rules, Regulations and Minimum Standards for Day Care Centers in the City of Chicago" as prescribed by the Chicago Board of Health.

"Owner," in the case of a licensee who is an individual, means a licensee and in the case of a partnership means each member thereof, and in the case of a corporation, firm or association, licensee means the officer thereof.

(Prior code § 158-1; Amend. Coun. J. 12-9-92, p. 25465; 4-16-96, p. 20112; 11-5-97, p. 56325; 11-19-97, p. 57848)

§4-72-020 License—Required.

It shall be unlawful for any person other than the regularly constituted authorities of the United States, the state, the county or the city to conduct or operate any day care center within the city without first obtaining a license therefor. Facilities operating a day care center/under-2 shall obtain a "Day Care Center/Under-2" license. Facilities operating a day care center/2-to-6 shall obtain a "Day Care Center/2-to-6" license. Facilities combining day care center/under-2 and day care center/2-to-6 operations shall obtain a "Day Care Center/Under 2 and 2-to-6 Combined" license.

(Prior code § 158-2; Amend. Coun. J. 12-9-92, p. 25465; 4-16-96, p. 20112; 6-10-96, p. 23652)

§4-72-070 License—Denial and revocation.

A license may be denied or revoked for any of the following reasons:

A. Violation of any provisions of this ordinance or of the rules, regulations and minimum standards promulgated thereunder;

B. Personnel insufficient in number or unqualified by training or experience to provide proper and adequate supervision for the number of children to be cared for;

C. Cruelty or indifference to the welfare of a child;

D. Conviction of the licensee, or if the applicant is a partnership or limited liability company, any member, officer or manager thereof, or if a corporation, any officer or director thereof or any stockholder owning in the aggregate more than five percent of the stock of such corporation, or of the person designated as director of the day care center, of:

(1) An offense specified in Section 4.2 of the Child Care Act of 1969, as amended, which makes the licensee, applicant or director ineligible for a state of Illinois child care facility license,

(2) A felony under any federal or state law,

(3) A misdemeanor sex offense as defined in Article 11 of the Illinois Criminal Code, or

(4) A misdemeanor offense involving drugs or narcotics; or

E. Other satisfactory evidence that the moral character of the licensee, applicant or director of the day care center is not reputable.

(Prior code § 158-7; Amend. Coun. J. 12-9-92, p. 25465; 12-15-99, p. 21529)

§4-72-130 Recordkeeping.

Each day care center shall maintain individual records for each child and personnel records for each employee. These records shall include all identifying information and any other information set forth by the board of health Rules, Regulations and Minimum Standards.

All records shall be open at all times to the inspection of the board of health or its duly authorized representative.

(Prior code § 158-13; Amend. Coun. J. 12-9-92, p. 25465)

§4-72-140 Reports to board of health.

It shall be the duty of every person conducting or operating a day care center to make a report to the board of health daily of all cases and suspect cases of contagious and communicable diseases.

It shall be the further duty of all such persons to make written reports to the board of health on or before the fifth day of each calendar month, showing a complete record of the activities of the day care center during the preceding month and such other information as may be required by the board of health. This monthly report shall be made upon forms furnished for that purpose by the board of health, and shall be signed by licensee and/or director.

(Prior code § 158-14; Amend. Coun. J. 12-9-92, p. 25465)

§4-72-150 Inspections authorized.

Every day care center shall be open at all reasonable times to inspection by the board of health, the bureau of fire prevention, the sections of plumbing, ventilation and electrical of the department of buildings and the department of fire, as often as is deemed necessary.

(Prior code § 158-15; Amend. Coun. J. 12-9-92, p. 25465; 3-5-03, p. 104990)

§4-72-160 Night care.

(a) No licensee shall operate a day care center between the hours of 9:00 p.m. and 6:00 a.m. without a night care privilege granted under this section.

(b) An application for a night care privilege may be filed with the department of revenue as part of an initial or renewal application for a day care center license or as a supplemental application during the term of a day care center license.

(c) In addition to the other requirements for a day care center license, every applicant for a night care privilege shall comply with the following:

(1) The day care center shall comply with the state of Illinois "night care" standards for licensed day care centers, 89 Ill. Admin. Code Section 407.25;

(2) The day care center shall provide a cot with at least three inches of dense padding for use by each child who sleeps longer than two hours and who is not required to sleep in a crib;

(3) Any day care center required to provide a fire alarm system under Section 13-196-200 or Section 15-16-110 of this code shall either be directly connected to a city fire alarm box as provided in Section 15-16-1430 or connected to a central station service as provided in Section 15-16-1460 when operating between the hours of 9:00 p.m. and 6:00 a.m. All day care centers located on a floor that is above or below ground level shall comply with the fire resistive separation requirements for institutional occupancies that are day care centers that serve children under two years of age, as set forth in Chapter 13-56 of this code;

(4) The exterior of all entrances and exits of the building in which the day care center is located shall be adequately lighted at all times;

(5) Every window of the day care center which is operable and which is located within 20 feet of ground level or within 10 feet of an adjacent roof or within 10 feet of an exterior stairway, fire escape, ramp, porch or other structure accessible from the ground level shall be equipped with a lock which when in a locked position will prevent the window from being operated and a motion detector or other detection device which sounds when the window is operated while in a locked position; and shall be capable of being opened without a key from the inside of the building;

(6) All doors of the day care center used in connection with exits, as defined in Section 13-160-020, shall comply with the hardware requirements set forth in Section 13-160-260 of this code;

(7) Each door that permits direct access to the day care center shall be equipped with an alarm or other detection device that sounds whenever a locked door is opened;

(8) The emergency system and exit lighting system of the day care center shall comply with Chapter 18-27 of this code;

(9) During the hours of 9:00 p.m. and 6:00 a.m., access to the day care center shall be permitted only from a single door which is equipped with a security system consisting of: (i) an intercom system that permits communication between an employee of the day care center located in a secure reception area and all persons seeking access to the center; and (ii) an electronic lock that is activated by a release button located within a secure reception area but can be opened manually from the inside of the center.

(d) The department of revenue shall notify the departments of police, fire, health, human services and buildings of the name and address of every day care center licensee who has been granted a night care privilege.

(e) A night care privilege granted pursuant to this section shall be subject to suspension or revocation upon a finding that the day care center is not in compliance with the requirements of this section.

(Added. Coun. J. 11-19-97, p. 57848; Amend. Coun. J. 3-5-03, p. 104990)

§4-72-170 Violation—Penalties.

Any person violating any of the provisions of this chapter shall be fined not less than $25.00 and not more than $200.00 for each offense, and a separate and distinct offense shall be considered as having been committed for each and every day on which any person shall be guilty of any such violation.

Whenever an inspection of a day care center discloses that the continued operation of such day care center would be found to be an immediate and serious menace to public health and safety, the commissioner of health is hereby authorized to close such day care center forthwith.

(Prior code § 158-16; Amend. Coun. J. 12-9-92, p. 25465)

CHAPTER 4-80
FUNERAL BUSINESS
(Complete Chapter)

Sections:

4-80-010 Definitions.
4-80-020 License requirements.
4-80-030 Legal requirements.
4-80-050 Prices for service and merchandise.
4-80-060 Funeral establishments—Other occupations restricted.
4-80-080 Rules and regulations.
4-80-090 Changes in ownership.
4-80-100 Enforcement.

§4-80-010 Definitions.

For purposes of this chapter, the following terms are defined to mean:

"Funeral business" shall refer to the practice of the profession of funeral directing and/or embalming, the sheltering and care of deceased human remains and the provision of facilities to render such shelter and care, the directing and supervision of the final disposition of deceased human remains, the practice of being responsible for the administration of and conducting the arrangements for the funeral ritual and/or orderly transportation and disposition of deceased human remains as well as the furnishing of the necessary facilities, equipment and merchandise and the provision of any necessary business in connection with the foregoing such as accounting and secretarial services.

"Funeral director/embalmer" shall refer to a person who is properly licensed in accordance with 225 ILCS 41/10-10, as amended.

"Funeral director assistant" shall refer to a person who, under the immediate personal supervision of a licensed funeral director/embalmer, assists a licensed funeral director/embalmer in the practice of funeral directing and embalming.

(Added. Coun. J. 6-10-96, p. 23652)

§4-80-020 License requirements.

(a) It shall be unlawful for any person to conduct a funeral business within the city without first obtaining a limited business license. License applications shall be made in conformity with the general requirements of Chapter 4-4 of the Municipal Code relating to applications for licenses. A separate license shall be required for each location at which a funeral business is conducted.

(b) A funeral business shall operate under the direction of a state-licensed funeral director. A copy of the funeral director's state license shall be submitted to the department of revenue at the time of the filing of an application for a license to conduct a funeral business within the city.

(Added. Coun. J. 6-10-96, p. 23652)

§4-80-030 Legal requirements.

Every person who operates a funeral business, or who is a funeral director/embalmer, or who is a funeral director assistant, shall observe all requirements imposed by 225 Illinois Compiled Statutes, 41/1-1, et seq., as amended, and other requirements imposed by state law or regulation, and regulations promulgated by the board of health. No person shall perform services as a funeral director assistant who has not satisfied the requirements of 225 ILCS 41/10-15.

(Added. Coun. J. 6-10-96, p. 23652)

§4-80-050 Prices for service and merchandise.

At any time funeral arrangements are made and prior to rendering the same, funeral businesses shall provide the person or persons making the funeral arrangements with a written statement, signed by the funeral director, which shall include the following:

1. The price of the service selected and the services and merchandise included therein;
2. The supplemental items of service and/or merchandise requested, and the price of each such item;
3. Insofar as can be specified at the time, the amount involved for each of the items for which the funeral director will advance monies as an accommodation to the family;
4. The terms or method of payment agreed upon.

Each and every casket displayed for possible selection by the person or persons making the funeral arrangements shall have placed thereon a card setting forth the price of the service involving the use of said casket and listing the services and other merchandise included in the price, if any. In lieu of the foregoing, each casket displayed shall contain a number which shall conform to the numbers included on a card or brochure, to be presented to the person or per-

sons making the funeral arrangements, which card or brochure shall set forth the price of the service involving the use of said numbered casket and listing the service and other merchandise included in the price, if any.
(Added. Coun. J. 6-10-96, p. 23652)

§4-80-060 Funeral establishments—Other occupations restricted.

No funeral business shall be conducted in any establishment where any other occupation is carried on unless such establishment used for the funeral business shall be provided with a compartment or room completely shut off or capable of being completely shut off from the other parts of such establishment. Such compartment or room shall have free outside ventilation and light, and its floor shall be constructed of or covered with a nonabsorbent material, and shall be connected with a sewer by an approved sanitary drain.
(Added. Coun. J. 6-10-96, p. 23652)

§4-80-080 Rules and regulations.

The board of health and the commissioner of consumer services may adopt and enforce rules and regulations relating to the operation of funeral businesses licensed under this chapter. The board of health and the commissioner of consumer services may, but are not limited to, adopt and enforce all existing and future state rules and regulations relating to funeral businesses.
(Added. Coun. J. 6-10-96, p. 23652)

§4-80-090 Changes in ownership.

In the event of a change in ownership in a funeral business, the new owner or owners must notify the department of revenue within 10 days of such change.
(Added. Coun. J. 6-10-96, p. 23652)

§4-80-100 Enforcement.

Any person violating any of the provisions of this chapter, or regulation promulgated hereunder, or any provision of 225 Illinois Compiled Statutes 41/1-1, et seq., as amended, or any regulation promulgated thereunder, shall be fined not less than $200.00 nor more than $500.00 for each offense. A separate and distinct offense shall be considered as having been committed for each and every day on which any person shall be guilty of such violation.

Licenses issued pursuant to this chapter may be suspended or revoked in accordance with Section 4-4-280 of this code.
(Added. Coun. J. 6-10-96, p. 23652)

CHAPTER 4-84
HOSPITALS
(Selected Sections)

Sections:

4-84-010 Hospital defined.
4-84-020 License—Required.
4-84-100 Report to police—Required when.
4-84-110 Enforcement and penalties—Suspension and revocation.
4-84-120 Status of state license.
4-84-130 Discrimination—Denial of equal treatment.

4-84-140 Rape treatment centers—Treatment—Reports.
4-84-230 Reserved.
4-84-280 Reserved.

§4-84-010 Hospital defined.

For the purposes of this chapter:

"Hospital" means any institution or establishment that satisfies the definition of a "hospital" as set forth in the Hospital Licensing Act, 210 ILCS 8513, as amended; provided, however, that hospital shall not refer to any facility operated by any federal, state, county or local government, or any agency thereof.
(Coun. J. 12-9-92, p. 25465; Amend. 6-28-00, p. 36752)

§4-84-020 License—Required.

It shall be unlawful for any person to operate a hospital within the city without first obtaining a city of Chicago license. No license shall be granted or renewed for the operation of any hospital unless such hospital is licensed by the state of Illinois.
(Coun. J. 12-9-92, p. 25465; Amend. 2-7-96, p. 15616; Amend. 6-28-00, p. 36752)

§4-84-100 Report to police—Required when.

A representative of each hospital required to be licensed under this chapter shall report to the department of police immediately upon the application for treatment of a person, who is not accompanied by a Chicago police officer, when it reasonably appears that the person requesting treatment has received:

(a) Any injury resulting from the discharge of a firearm;

(b) Any injury or wound apparently inflicted by any object used as a weapon;

(c) Any injury sustained in the commission of or as a victim of a criminal offense;

(d) An animal or human bite;

(e) Poisoning;

(f) Any injury sustained on public property;

(g) Any injury in which a moving motor vehicle was involved;

(h) Any injury of any cause where it is evident that death will probably ensue as a direct result thereof, or when death has resulted.

The hospital shall not be responsible for an inaccurate report if such report is based on inaccurate information provided by a patient or a person accompanying the patient.
(Coun. J. 12-9-92, p. 25465; Amend. 6-28-00, p. 36752)

§4-84-110 Enforcement and penalties— Suspension and revocation.

(a) If any person violates any of the provisions of this chapter, any rule or regulation promulgated hereunder, the Illinois Hospital Licensing Act, or any rule or regulation promulgated thereunder, the commissioner may seek revocation or suspension of the licensee's license and/or the imposition of a fine of not less than $300.00 nor more than $500.00 per violation. Each day that such violation exists shall constitute a separate and distinct offense.

(b) Before any suspension or fine is imposed the commissioner of health shall notify the licensee of the specific charges against him and of his right to a hearing. Notice shall be served upon an officer or operator of the hospital at least seven days prior to the hearing date by: (i) first class or express mail or by overnight carrier or (ii) personal service.

(i) Prior to the exercise of exclusive jurisdiction by the department of administrative hearings in accordance with Section 2-14-190(c) of this code, the hearing may be conducted by the commissioner or his or her designee. At the hearing, a hospital and its representatives may be represented by counsel, present documentary evidence and/or live testimony, and may cross-examine witnesses called by the department. The department shall present sufficient evidence from witnesses having personal knowledge of the offense to prove, by a preponderance of the evidence, that one or more violations of the aforementioned provisions occurred. The strict rules of evidence applicable to judicial proceedings shall not apply to hearings under this section. The record of each hearing shall include: (i) a record of the testimony presented at the hearing, which may be by tape recording or other appropriate means; (ii) any document presented at the hearing; and (iii) a copy of the written notice of hearing that was served in accordance with this section. If, after the hearing, the hearing officer determines that a violation has occurred, the hearing officer shall enter an order suspending the license and/or imposing a fine.

(ii) After the exercise of exclusive jurisdiction by the department of administrative hearings in accordance with Section 2-14-190(c) of this code, the commissioner shall institute an action with the department of administrative hearings which shall appoint a hearing officer who shall conduct the hearing in accordance with Chapter 2-14.

(c) The commissioner may file charges before the mayor's license commissioner seeking the revocation of a license under this chapter. Following a hearing conducted in accordance with its rules, the commission shall determine whether revocation is warranted or a lesser penalty, if any, should be imposed.
(Added. Coun. J. 6-28-00, p. 36752)

§4-84-120 Status of state license.

The expiration, revocation or suspension of a hospital license issued by the state of Illinois in accordance with the Hospital Licensing Act shall constitute a violation of this chapter and shall be grounds for license suspension or revocation pursuant to Section 4-84-110.
(Added. Coun. J. 6-28-00, p. 36752)

§4-84-130 Discrimination—Denial of equal treatment.

No hospital, nor any person acting as administrator or who is otherwise in charge or control of any hospital, nor any person connected with or rendering service in any hospital in any capacity whatsoever, nor any agent or employee thereof, shall deny to any person admission for care or treatment, equality of care or treatment in a hospital, or the use of any of the hospital facilities and services relating to care or treatment of such person, on account of race, color, creed, national origin or ancestry, provided that a member of the medical staff of said hospital or an authorized physician designated to act for him may examine such person and determine the need of such person for medical care or treatment.
(Coun. J. 12-9-92, p. 25465; Amend. 6-28-00, p. 36752)

§4-84-140 Rape treatment centers—Treatment—Reports.

Upon reporting a rape, an attempted rape or other felonious sex crime to the police, the victim will be taken to the nearest hospital designated for the comprehensive emergency treatment of patients as defined in the Illinois Hospital Licensing Act and approved by the board of health.

The victim will be taken into the hospital through an entrance appropriate to the maintenance of privacy.

The victim will receive an immediate preliminary physical examination by the attending physician to identify and treat any emergencies other than the rape, such as fractures, knife wounds, contusions or lacerations.

The consenting victim will be interviewed by a trained hospital staff member, preferably a female psychiatric social worker, in a private setting. The hospital staff member will evaluate and counsel the victim and advise follow-up care for the victim, either through the receiving hospital or through the appropriate outside agencies.

The hospital staff member, with consent of the victim, will remain with the victim during the preliminary police investigation primarily to provide support to the victim and to also assist the police in obtaining information needed to properly carry out their investigation.

During this period, the name of the victim and the circumstances attendant to the incident will not be publicized by the hospital, the police department or any other agency. The hospital staff member will so inform the victim.

The consenting victim will be examined by a qualified gynecologist who will fill out a prescribed form detailing the time, date, place and findings of the examination, and note the location of any contusions, abrasions, bruises and lacerations.

With the victim's written consent, a copy of this form will be furnished to the appropriate investigating police officer, the State's Attorney, and the venereal disease section of the Chicago Board of Health when appropriate. Within seven days the form will be typewritten, signed by the examining gynecologist and furnished upon request to the aforementioned agencies.

The consenting victim, if not allergic to specific drugs, will be furnished with anticonception and antivenereal disease treatment, unless contraindicated for medical reasons.

The comprehensive hospital will accept any alleged victim who appears without police assistance. Such hospitals will continue to notify the police department according to Section 4-84-100 of the Municipal Code of Chicago. The hospital will then follow the procedure heretofore enumerated.
(Coun. J. 12-9-92, p. 25465; Amend. 6-28-00, p. 36752)

§4-84-230 Reserved.
(Repealed Coun. J. 6-28-2000, p. 36752)

§4-84-280 Reserved.
(Deleted by Coun. J. 6-28-2000, p. 36752)

CHAPTER 4-92
MASSAGE ESTABLISHMENTS AND MASSAGE SERVICES

(Selected Sections)

Sections:

4-92-010 Definitions.
4-92-020 Massage establishment license—Required.
4-92-025 License—Fee.
4-92-030 Massage establishment license—Application procedure.
4-92-040 Massage establishment license—Application—Contents.
4-92-047 Operating requirements.
4-92-050 Massage establishment license—Issuance conditions—Term.
4-92-051 Employment of licensed massage therapists.
4-92-052 Premises.
4-92-053 Advertising restrictions.
4-92-054 Inspections.
4-92-055 Employment of minors.
4-92-057 License—Display.
4-92-060 Massage establishment license—Revocation and suspension.
4-92-070 Massage therapist—License required.
4-92-140 Out call services.
4-92-200 Violation—Penalty.
4-92-210 Severability.

§4-92-010 Definitions.

For the purpose of this chapter, the following words and phrases shall have the meanings respectively ascribed to them:

(A) "Massage" means any method of pressure on, friction against, or stroking, kneading, rubbing, tapping, pounding, bathing, touching, binding, painting, irritating, or stimulating of external soft parts of the body with hands or with the aid of any manual, mechanical or electrical apparatus or appliance, with or without such supplementary aids as rubbing alcohol, liniments, antiseptic oils, powder, cremes, lotions, soaps, ointments or other similar preparations commonly used in this practice.

(B) "Massage establishment" means any establishment having its place of business where any person, firm, association or corporation engages in or carries on permits to be engaged or carried on any of the activities mentioned in subsection (A) hereof.

(C) "Massage services" means the providing of a massage or massages by any person, firm, association or corporation.

(D) "Massage therapist" means any person who, for any consideration whatever, engages in the practice of massage as above defined.

(E) "Employee" means any and all persons other than massage therapists who render any service for the licensee and who receives compensation directly from the licensee but has no physical contact with customers or clients.

(F) "Persons" means any individual, copartnership, firm, association, joint stock company, corporation, or any combination of individuals of whatever form or character.

(G) "Licensee" means the operator of a massage establishment.

(H) "Sexual or genital area" of any person shall include the genitals, pubic area, anus, or perineum of any person, or the vulva or breasts of a female. *(Coun. J. 12-9-92, p. 25465; Amend. 2-10-93, p. 28497; 7-30-97, p. 50612)*

§4-92-020 Massage establishment license—Required.

It shall be unlawful for any person to engage in, conduct or carry on, or to permit to be engaged in, conducted or carried on, upon any premises in the city of Chicago the operation of a massage establishment as herein defined without first having obtained a license from the department of revenue.
(Coun. J. 12-9-92, p. 25465; Amend. 7-30-97, p. 50612)

§4-92-025 License—Fee.

The annual fee for each massage establishment license shall be as set forth in Section 4-5-010 of this code.
(Added. Coun. J. 7-30-97, p. 50612)

§4-92-030 Massage establishment license—Application procedure.

Every applicant for a license to maintain, operate or conduct a massage establishment shall file an application, under oath, with the department of revenue. The department of revenue shall refer copies of such application and all additional information to the police department, plumbing section of the department of buildings, and bureau of fire prevention. The city agencies shall, within 45 days, inspect the premises proposed to be operated as a massage establishment, and make recommendations to the department of revenue concerning compliance with the codes of the city of Chicago. Upon receipt of the recommendations of the respective city agencies, the department of revenue shall notify the applicant as to whether his/her application has been granted, denied or held for further investigation. The period of such additional investigation shall not exceed an additional 30 days. The department of revenue shall advise the applicant in writing as to whether the application has been granted or denied. If the application is denied or held for further investigation, the department of revenue shall advise the applicant in writing of the reason for such refusal.

The failure or refusal of the applicant to promptly give any information relevant to the investigation of the application, or the refusal or failure of applicant to appear at any reasonable time and place for examination under oath regarding said application, or the refusal of applicant to submit to or cooperate with any inspection required by this section, shall be grounds for denial of the application.
(Coun. J. 12-9-92, p. 25465; Amend. 5-4-94, p. 49800; 7-30-97, p. 50612)

§4-92-040 Massage establishment license—Application—Contents.

The application for a license to operate a massage establishment shall set forth the exact nature of the massage to be administered and the proposed place and facilities thereof. An application for such a license shall be made in conformity with the general requirements of this code relating to applications for license. The application shall be signed under oath by the owner of the business for which a license is sought. If the owner is a corporation, the application shall be signed by an authorized officer of the corporation. If the owner is a partnership, the application shall be signed by a partner.

In addition thereto, any applicant for a license, and each partner or limited partner of an applicant, if a partnership applicant, and each officer and director of a corporate applicant and any stockholder of a corporate applicant holding more than five percent of the stock of the corporate applicant, shall furnish the following information:

(1) Written proof that each individual is at least 18 years of age;

(2) All residential addresses for the past three years;

(3) The business, occupation, or employment of each individual for the three years immediately preceding the date of application;

(4) The previous experience of the individual in massage or similar business;

(5) Whether the individual has had any license denied, revoked or suspended in the city of Chicago or any other state or city for a massage establishment, the reason therefor, and the business activity or occupation of the individual subsequent to such suspension, revocation or denial;

(6) Any conviction, forfeiture of bond, or plea of nolo contendere upon any criminal violation or city ordinance violation (except minor traffic violations), within a five-year period;

(7) If the applicant is a corporation, or a partner of any partnership is a corporation, then the name of the corporation shall be set forth exactly as shown in the articles of incorporation, together with the state of incorporation and proof of authority to do business in the state of Illinois;

(8) Each individual's current residential telephone number;

(9) The name and address of the owner of the premises. If the premises are leased: (a) a copy of the lease; (b) the name, address and telephone number of the owner of the premises, including the name and address of the beneficiary if title to the premises is held by a person as trustee and if known to the applicant; (c) the name, address and telephone number of the manager of the premises.

If a change in any information required under this section occurs at any time during a license period, the licensee shall file a statement, executed in the same manner as an application, indicating the nature and effective date of the change. The supplemental statement shall be filed within 10 days after the change takes effect. The mayor's license commissioner and the director of revenue shall take measures to prevent disclosure of information required under this section and not subject to disclosure under the Illinois Freedom of Information Act to persons outside the government.

(Coun. J. 12-9-92, p. 25465; Amend. 4-13-94, p. 48596; 7-30-97, p. 50612)

§4-92-047 Operating requirements.

(a) Every portion of the massage establishment, including appliances and apparatus, shall be kept clean and operated under sanitary conditions.

(b) Price rates for all services shall be prominently posted in the reception area in a location available to all prospective customers.

(c) All employees, including massage therapists, shall wear clean, nontransparent outer garments covering the sexual and genital areas, and such other garments shall be restricted in use to the massage establishment.

(d) All massage establishments shall be provided with clean laundered sheets and towels in sufficient quantity which shall be laundered after each use thereof and stored in a sanitary manner.

(e) The sexual or genital areas of patrons must be covered with towels, cloths or undergarments when in the presence of an employee or massage therapist.

(f) It shall be unlawful for any massage therapist or employee or licensee of a massage establishment to place his or her hand upon or to touch with any part of his or her body, or to fondle in any manner, or to massage, a sexual or genital area of any person.

(g) No massage therapist, employee or licensee shall perform, offer or agree to perform any act which shall require the touching of the patron's genital area.

(h) All walls, ceilings, floors, pools, showers, baths and steam rooms and any other physical facilities shall be in good repair, and maintained in a clean and sanitary condition.

(i) Oils, creams, lotions and other preparations used in administering massages shall be kept in clean, closed containers or cabinets.

(j) No massage therapist shall administer a massage to a patron exhibiting any skin fungus, skin infection, skin inflammation or skin eruption, unless a physician duly licensed by the state of Illinois shall certify in writing that such person may be safely massaged, describing the conditions under which such massage may be performed.

(k) Each massage therapist shall wash his or her hands in hot running water using a proper soap or disinfectant before administering any massage to any patron.

(Coun. J. 12-9-92, p. 25465; Amend. 2-10-93, p. 28497; 5-4-94, p. 49800; 7-30-97, p. 50612)

§4-92-050 Massage establishment license—Issuance conditions—Term.

Upon receipt of the recommendations of the respective agencies and with the information contained in the application, together with all additional information provided therein, the department of revenue shall direct the issuance of the license by the city clerk to the applicant to maintain, operate or conduct a massage establishment, unless the department of revenue shall find:

(1) That the operation of the massage establishment as proposed by the applicant, if permitted, would not comply with the applicable laws of the state of Illinois and the city of Chicago, including but not limited to the building, health planning, housing, fire prevention and zoning codes of the city of Chicago; or

(2) That the applicant or any other person who shall be directly or indirectly engaged in the management and operation of the massage establishment has been convicted of (a) a felony, (b) an offense involving sexual misconduct with children, (c) any provision of Article 11 of Chapter 720 of the Illinois Compiled Statutes; or

(3) That the operation of the massage establishment as proposed by the applicant, if permitted, would violate the provisions of this chapter.

(Coun. J. 12-9-92, p. 25465; Amend. 7-30-97, p. 50612)

§4-92-051 Employment of licensed massage therapists.

Massage establishments may not employ persons as massage therapists who have not obtained the necessary license required by Section 4-92-070.

Each massage establishment shall maintain a current listing of all licensed massage therapists who perform massage services at the site of the establishment.

(Added. Coun. J. 5-4-94, p. 49800; Amend. 7-30-97, p. 50612)

§4-92-052 Premises.

(a) No massage establishment shall receive a license or be operated, established or maintained unless the establishment shall comply with each of the following minimum regulations:

(1) All massage tables, lavatories and floors shall have surfaces which may be readily disinfected.

(2) Separate dressing, locker, toilet and massage room facilities shall be provided for female and male patrons, so that female and male patrons may be served simultaneously in the event that patrons of both sexes are permitted. Doors to the dressing rooms shall open inward and shall be self-closing.

(3) Toilet facilities shall be provided within the massage establishment. When five or more employees or patrons of different sexes are on the premises at the same time, separate toilet facilities shall be provided. Lavatories shall be provided with both hot and cold running water and shall be installed in the toilet room. Lavatories shall be provided with soap and a dispenser with sanitary towels.

(4) Closed cabinets shall be provided for use in the storage of clean linens, towels and other materials used in administering massages. All soiled linens, towels and other materials shall be kept in properly covered containers or cabinets which shall be kept separate from the clean storage areas.

(b) Subsections (a)(2), (a)(3) and (a)(4) of this section shall not apply to a massage establishment where all massages are administrated to patrons who are fully clothed and without the application of oils, creams, lotions or other liquids to the body of any patron.

(Coun. J. 12-9-92, p. 25465; Amend. 5-4-92, p. 49800; 7-30-97, p. 50612)

§4-92-053 Advertising restrictions.

No massage establishment holding a license under this chapter shall depict, place, publish, distribute or cause to be depicted, placed, published or distributed any advertising matter that suggests to prospective patrons that any services are available other than those services permitted by this chapter, or which would suggest that employees or massage therapists are dressed in any manner other than that permitted by this chapter, and all advertisements shall contain the number of the city license held by the massage establishment.

(Coun. J. 12-9-92, p. 25465; Amend. 2-10-93, p. 28497; 7-30-97, p. 50612)

§4-92-054 Inspections.

Any city department or agency may make an inspection of each massage establishment granted a license under the provisions of this chapter for the purposes of determining that the provisions of this chapter are complied with. Such inspection shall be made at reasonable times and in a reasonable manner. It shall be unlawful for any licensee to fail to allow such inspection officer access to the premises or to hinder such inspection officer in any manner.

(Coun. J. 12-9-92, p. 25465; Amend. 5-4-94, p. 49800; 7-30-97, p. 50612)

§4-92-055 Employment of minors.

It shall be unlawful for any owner, operator, proprietor, manager or other person in charge of any massage establishment to employ any person who is not at least 15 years of age.

(Coun. J. 12-9-92, p. 25465; Amend. 7-30-97, p. 50612)

§4-92-057 License—Display.

Each licensee shall display a valid current license in a conspicuous place within the massage establishment so that the same may be readily seen by persons entering the establishment.

(Coun. J. 12-9-92, p. 25465; Amend. 5-4-94, p. 49800; 7-30-97, p. 50612)

§4-92-060 Massage establishment license—Revocation and suspension.

Any license issued for a massage establishment may be revoked or suspended by the mayor's license commission after a hearing, for a good cause. The licensee shall be given at least 15 days' written notice of the charges and an opportunity for a public hearing before the mayor's license commission, at which time the licensee may present evidence bearing upon the question. Cause for revocation or suspension shall include the violation of the provisions of this chapter or of any criminal statute of the state of Illinois by the applicant, or by any employee of the licensee or any massage therapist employed by the licensee; provided that the violation of this chapter or any criminal law of the state of Illinois shall not be a cause for revocation or suspension unless the licensee shall have had actual or constructive knowledge of such violations in the exercise of due diligence. It shall also be cause for revocation or suspension that the applicant has made a false statement on any application for license under this chapter, or in the event that the licensee shall refuse to permit any authorized police officer or authorized member of the police department, mechanical equipment inspection sections — ventilation, plumbing and electrical sections of the department of buildings, bureau of fire prevention, department of health or of the fire department of the city of Chicago to inspect the premises or the operations thereof at reasonable times.

When any license shall have been revoked for any cause, no license shall be granted to any person for the period one year thereafter for the conduct of a massage establishment in the premises described in such revoked license.

(Coun. J. 12-9-92, p. 25465; Amend. 2-10-93, p. 28497; 5-4-94, p. 49800; 7-30-97, p. 50612)

§4-92-070 Massage therapist—License required.

Any person who engages in the practice of massage as herein defined shall file an application for a license as a massage therapist, which application shall be filed with the department of revenue.

(Coun. J. 12-9-92, p. 25465; Amend. 2-10-93, p. 28497; 5-4-94, p. 49800; 7-30-97, p. 50612)

§4-92-140 Out call services.

Any massage therapist who provides any of the services provided in this chapter at any hotel or motel must first register his or her name and license number with the owner, manager or person in charge of such hotel or motel.

(Coun. J. 12-9-92, p. 25465; Amend. 2-10-93, p. 28497; 5-4-94, p. 49800; 7-30-97, p. 50612)

§4-92-200 Violation—Penalty.

Any person who violates any section of this chapter shall upon conviction thereof be punished by a fine of not less than $200.00 nor more than $500.00 for the first offense and not less than $300.00 nor more than $500.00 for the second offense, and shall be punished as a misdemeanor for each subsequent offense by incarceration in the county jail for a term not to exceed six months under procedures set forth in Section 1-2-1.1 of the Illinois Municipal Code, 65 ILCS 5/1-2-1.1, as amended, or by both fine and imprisonment; except, however, that any violation of Section 4-92-047(c), (e), (f) or (g) shall be a misdemeanor punishable by incarceration in the county jail for a term not less than five days and not to exceed six months.

(Coun. J. 12-9-92, p. 25465; Amend. 7-30-97, p. 50612)

§4-92-210 Severability.

If any section, subsection, paragraph or part of this chapter is for any reason held to be unconstitutional or invalid by any final court of competent jurisdiction, such decision shall not affect the validity or effectiveness of the remaining portions of this chapter.

(Coun. J. 12-9-92, p. 25465; Amend. 7-30-97, p. 50612)

CHAPTER 4-93
BODY PIERCING
(Selected Sections)

Sections:

4-93-010 Definitions.
4-93-020 License required.
4-93-040 Display of license.
4-93-050 Parental consent.
4-93-060 Sanitation.
4-93-080 Department of health to enforce.
4-93-090 Violations—Penalties.

§4-93-010 Definitions.

Whenever used in this chapter:

(a) "Aseptic technique" means a practice that prevents and hinders the transmission of disease-producing microorganisms from one person or place to another, and is approved as effective by the Chicago Board of Health.

(b) "Body piercing" means making a hole in any part of the human body in order to affix, insert or install, or in order to enable the affixing, insertion or installation of, any object or device for the purpose of decoration or ornamentation. "Body piercing" does not include any such activity as part of health-related care or treatment by any of the following: a physician licensed to practice medicine in all its branches under the Illinois Medical Practice Act of 1987; by a podiatrist licensed under the Illinois Podiatric Medical Practice Act of 1987; a dentist licensed under the Illinois Dental Practice Act; or an acupuncturist licensed under the Illinois Acupuncture Practice Act.

(Added. Coun. J. 6-9-99, p. 5362)

§4-93-020 License required.

No person shall perform body piercing, or offer to perform body piercing, without first having obtained a license under this chapter. Except as otherwise provided in this chapter, a license to perform body piercing shall be issued in accordance with the provisions of Chapter 4-4 of this code.
(Added. Coun. J. 6-9-99, p. 5362)

§4-93-040 Display of license.

A licensee shall display his or her body piercing license prominently at the location where he or she performs body piercing.
(Added. Coun. J. 6-9-99, p. 5362)

§4-93-050 Parental consent.

No person shall perform body piercing on an unemancipated minor, except with the written permission and in the presence of a parent or legal guardian of the minor.
(Added. Coun. J. 6-9-99, p. 5362)

§4-93-060 Sanitation.

A licensee shall maintain the place where he or she performs body piercing in a clean and sanitary condition and shall perform body piercing only in a manner consistent with aseptic technique. The department may order the closure of any place where a violation of this section is observed, if the violation creates a risk of infection or injury. Closure shall be effective until, in the department's determination, the condition creating the risk has been abated, and shall be in addition to any fine provided in Section 4-93-090.
(Added. Coun. J. 6-9-99, p. 5362)

§4-93-080 Department of health to enforce.

The department of health shall be responsible for the administration and enforcement of this chapter. The board of health shall promulgate rules and regulations, not inconsistent with this chapter, for the administration of this chapter.
(Added. Coun. J. 6-9-99, p. 5362)

§4-93-090 Violations—Penalties.

Any person who violates Section 4-93-050 or Section 4-93-060 shall be subject to a fine of not less than $500.00 and not more than $1,000.00 for each offense. Any person who violates any other provision of this chapter, or any regulation issued hereunder, shall be subject to a fine of not less than $300.00 and not more than $500.00 for each offense.
(Added. Coun. J. 6-9-99, p. 5362)

CHAPTER 4-96
LONG-TERM CARE FACILITIES
(Complete Chapter)

Sections:

4-96-010 Definitions.
4-96-020 License requirement.
4-96-030 License—Application—Inspection.
4-96-040 License renewal.
4-96-050 License fee.
4-96-055 State license requirement.
4-96-060 Rules and regulations.
4-96-065 Maximum hot-weather temperatures.
4-96-070 Inspections.
4-96-080 Enforcement and penalties.
4-96-090 Status of state license.
4-96-100 Reports.

§4-96-010 Definitions.

For purposes of this chapter:

"Long-term care facility" means private home, institution, building, residence, or any other place that satisfies the definition of a "facility" or "long-term care facility" as set forth in the Nursing Home Care Act, 210 ILCS 45/1-113, as amended.

"Person" means any individual, firm, partnership, corporation, company, association or joint stock association, or the legal successor thereof.

(Added. Coun. J. 7-30-97, p. 50612)

§4-96-020 License requirement.

It shall be unlawful for any person to operate a long-term care facility within the city without first obtaining a city of Chicago license.

(Added. Coun. J. 7-30-97, p. 50612)

§4-96-030 License—Application—Inspection.

Any person seeking a long-term care facility license shall file an application with the department of revenue which shall forward the application to the department of health. The application shall include the location or proposed location of the long-term care facility, the number of residents, the level of care proposed to be given at the facility, a statement indicating ownership of the facility, the name and address of the administrator, and other information as may be required by rules and regulations promulgated by the board of health.

Before a license may be issued, the department of health, the bureau of fire prevention and the department of buildings shall inspect the premises for which the license is sought to determine that the premises are in compliance with the provisions of this code and the rules and regulations promulgated thereunder relating to health and sanitation, buildings and fire prevention.

(Added. Coun. J. 7-30-97, p. 50612)

§4-96-040 License renewal.

Long-term care facility licenses shall be renewed annually in accordance with Section 4-4-021 of this code.
(Added. Coun. J. 7-30-97, p. 50612)

§4-96-050 License fee.

The fee for a long-term care facility license shall be as set forth in Section 4-5-010 of this code.
(Added. Coun. J. 7-30-97, p. 50612)

§4-96-055 State license requirement.

Every long-term care facility shall, no later than 60 days after being issued an initial or a renewal license under this chapter, be licensed by the state of Illinois in accordance with the Nursing Home Care Act, 210 ILCS 45/1-101, et seq. No long-term care facility shall operate without a state license. An initial or renewal license under this chapter shall expire 60 days after its issuance unless the licensee provides the department of revenue with proof of a state license, that is in force and effect, prior to the end of the 60-day period.
(Added. Coun. J. 7-30-97, p. 50612)

§4-96-060 Rules and regulations.

The board of health may adopt and enforce rules and regulations relating to the operation and conduct of long-term care facilities licensed under this chapter. Such rules and regulations may concern, but are not limited to, public health and safety. The board of health may adopt and enforce all existing and future state rules and regulations relating to the operation of long-term care facilities.
(Added. Coun. J. 7-30-97, p. 50612)

§4-96-065 Maximum hot-weather temperatures.

Any existing or newly constructed long-term care facility licensed under the chapter shall be equipped with an automatic air-cooling system or equipment capable of maintaining the interior temperature and relative humidity level required by Section 13-192-205 of this code. The licensee or his designee shall monitor the interior temperature and humidity level in all living quarters, dining areas, bathrooms, common rooms and connecting corridors on a regular basis, and shall provide air cooling as needed to maintain the interior temperature and humidity level specified in that section.
(Added. 9-27-00, p. 41657)

§4-96-070 Inspections.

Each long-term care facility required to be licensed under this chapter shall be open at all times for inspection by the department of health, bureau of fire prevention and department of buildings.
(Added. Coun. J. 7-30-97, p. 50612)

§4-96-080 Enforcement and penalties.

(a) Any person who violates any of the provisions of this chapter, any rule or regulation promulgated hereunder, the Nursing Home Care Act, 210 ILCS 45/1, et seq., or any rule or regulation promulgated thereunder, shall be subject to a fine of not less than $300.00 nor more than $500.00 per violation. Each day that such violation exists shall constitute a separate and distinct offense.

(b) The commissioner of the department of health may also suspend, for a period not to exceed 30 days, or seek revocation of a license issued under this chapter, in accordance with the procedures described in this section, upon the determination that one or more violations of this chapter, any rule or regulation promulgated hereunder, the Nursing Home Care Act or any rule or regulation promulgated thereunder, has occurred.

(c) Before any suspension order shall be issued, the commissioner shall notify the licensee of the specific charges against him/her and of his/her right to a hearing. Notice shall be served upon an officer or operator of the long-term care facility at least seven days prior to the hearing date by: (i) first class or express mail or by overnight carrier; or (ii) personal service. The person before whom the hearing is held shall not have been involved in the initial decision to seek suspension. At the hearing, a long-term care facility and its representatives may be represented by counsel, present documentary evidence and/or live testimony, and may cross-examine witnesses called by the department of health. The department of health shall present sufficient evidence from witnesses having personal knowledge of the offense to prove, by a preponderance of the evidence, that one or more violations of the aforementioned provisions occurred. The strict rules of evidence applicable to judicial proceedings shall not apply to hearings under this section. The record of each hearing shall include: (i) a record of the testimony presented at the hearing, which may be by tape recording or other appropriate means; (ii) any document presented at the hearing; and (iii) a copy of the written notice of hearing that was served in accordance with this section. Following the hearing, the hearing officer shall issue in writing a decision stating whether the long-term care facility license shall be suspended or revoked. The licensee may file a complaint in a court of competent jurisdiction seeking to review a decision to suspend a license. After the exercise of exclusive jurisdiction by the department of administrative hearings in accordance with Section 2-14-190(c) of this code, the commissioner shall institute an action with the department of administrative hearings which shall appoint an administrative law officer who shall conduct the hearing.

(d) The commissioner may file charges before the mayor's license commission seeking the revocation of a license under this chapter. Following a hearing conducted in accordance with its rules, the commission shall determine whether revocation is warranted or a lesser penalty, if any, should be imposed.
(Added. Coun. J. 7-30-97, p. 50612; Amend. 4-29-98, p. 66564)

§4-96-090 Status of state license.

The expiration, revocation or suspension of a state of Illinois license required to operate a long-term care facility as set forth in the Nursing Home Act shall constitute a violation of this chapter and shall be grounds for license suspension or revocation pursuant to Section 4-96-080.
(Added. Coun. J. 7-30-97, p. 50612)

§4-96-100 Reports.

Every person conducting or operating any long-term care facility within the city shall make such reports to the department of health as it may from time to time require by rules as promulgated by the commissioner.

All reports shall be furnished on forms prepared and supplied by the department of health for such purpose, and shall be verified by the signature of the chief physician or administrator of such long-term care facility.

(Added. Coun. J. 7-30-97, p. 50612)

DIVISION V
HAZARDOUS AND RELATED ACTIVITIES
(Selected Chapters)

Chapters:

4-100 Dry Cleaners. (Selected Sections)
4-108 Filling Stations. (Selected Sections)
4-115 Hazardous Materials.(Complete Chapter)
4-128 Motion Pictures. (Selected Sections)
4-144 Weapons.(Complete Chapter)

CHAPTER 4-100
DRY CLEANERS
(Selected Sections)

Sections:

Article II. Self-Service Coin-Operated Dry-Cleaning Establishments
4-100-160 Attendant—Required.
4-100-190 Hours of operation.
4-100-220 Violation—Penalty.

Article II. Self-Service Coin-Operated Dry-Cleaning Establishments

§4-100-160 Attendant—Required.

There shall be present in every self-service coin-operated establishment of this type an attendant during all operational hours of the establishment. The attendant shall not permit any person under the age of 15 years to operate any such machine.

(Added. Coun. J. 12-9-92, p. 25465)

§4-100-190 Hours of operation.

No coin-operated self-service dry-cleaning establishment shall be operated between the hours of 11:30 p.m. and 6:30 a.m.

(Added. Coun. J. 12-9-92, p. 25465)

§4-100-220 Violation—Penalty.

Any person violating any of the provisions of this chapter shall be fined not less than $200.00 nor more than $500.00 for each offense except where otherwise specifically provided. A separate and distinct offense shall be held to have been committed each day any person continues to violate any of the provisions hereof.

(Added. Coun. J. 12-9-92, p. 25465)

CHAPTER 4-108
FILLING STATIONS
(Selected Sections)

Sections:

Article I. Filling Stations

4-108-020	License—Required.
4-108-070	Smoking prohibited.
4-108-071	Certain persons permitted to service vehicle—Violation— Penalty.
4-108-090	Flammable liquids for cleaning—Restrictions.
4-108-100	Waste disposal.
4-108-110	Gasoline spills or overflows.
4-108-111	Proper disposal of tires.
4-108-130	Violation—Penalty.

Article I. Filling Stations

§4-108-020 License—Required.

No person shall engage in the business of a filling station without first having obtained a filling station license therefor. A hazardous materials license shall not be required to perform the activities authorized by a license issued under this chapter.

(Coun. J. 12-9-92, p. 25465; Amend. 4-16-97, p. 42588)

§4-108-070 Smoking prohibited.

It shall be unlawful for any person to permit smoking in any filling station.

(Coun. J. 12-9-92, p. 25465)

§4-108-071 Certain persons permitted to service vehicle—Violation—Penalty.

It is unlawful for any person to dispense fuel or to provide any other service to a vehicle, or to offer to dispense fuel or provide any other service to a vehicle at a filling station unless the person is the licensee of the filling station, an employee or agent of the licensee, or the operator or a passenger of the subject vehicle. Any person who violates any provision of this section shall be subject to a fine of $50.00.

(Added. Coun. J. 7-14-93, p. 35528)

§4-108-090 Flammable liquids for cleaning—Restrictions.

Gasoline, benzine, naphtha and similar flammable liquids shall not be used for washing or cleaning purposes within any filling station nor in the open air within a distance of 50 feet of any repair pit or any opening from any basement space.

(Coun. J. 12-9-92, p. 25465)

§4-108-100 Waste disposal.

Waste oil or other flammable liquids shall be stored in metal containers pending removal from the premises. No such waste shall be permitted to drain into any sewers or stormwater drainage system. Rags and soiled waste shall be kept in metal containers.

(Coun. J. 12-9-92, p. 25465)

§4-108-110 Gasoline spills or overflows.

Provisions shall be made in filling stations, by grading driveways, raising door sills or other means, to prevent gasoline spills or overflows from flowing into or under buildings.
(Coun. J. 12-9-92, p. 25465)

§4-108-111 Proper disposal of tires.

No licensee under this chapter shall replace or repair motor vehicle tires unless the licensee maintains in effect a contract for the removal and disposal of motor vehicle tires replaced by the licensee. The contract shall be kept on the licensed premises and be made available for inspection by representatives of the city during the licensee's business hours.
(Added. Coun. J. 6-14-95, p. 3094)

§4-108-130 Violation—Penalty.

Any person violating any of the provisions of this chapter shall be fined not less than $200.00 nor more than $500.00 for each offense. Every day such violation continues shall constitute a separate and distinct offense.
(Coun. J. 12-9-92, p. 25465)

CHAPTER 4-115
HAZARDOUS MATERIALS
(Complete Chapter)

Sections:
4-115-010 Hazardous materials license—Required.
4-115-020 License—Application.
4-115-030 License—Fee.
4-115-040 Violation—Penalty.

§4-115-010 Hazardous materials license—Required.

No person shall engage in any of the following activities without having first obtained a hazardous materials license:

(a) Use or maintenance of hazardous materials for which a license is required under Section 15-4-130;

(b) Use or maintenance of acetylene gas for which a license is required under Section 15-4-160(a);

(c) Use or maintenance of acetylene gas for which a license is required under Section 15-4-160(b);

(d) Use or maintenance of calcium carbide for which a license is required under Section 15-4-160(c);

(e) Use or maintenance of flammable liquids for which a license is required under Section 15-4-210;

(f) Use or maintenance of liquefied fume hazard gases for which a license is required under Section 15-4-230;

(g) Use or maintenance of oxygen or hydrogen for which a license is required under Section 15-4-240;

(h) Use or maintenance of nitrocellulose products for which a license is required under Section 15-4-250;

(i) Use or maintenance of a lumberyard or lumber storehouse for which a license is required under Section 15-4-252;

(j) Use or maintenance of sawdust, shavings, excelsior or other similar flammable materials for which a license is required under Section 15-4-254;

(k) Use or maintenance of solid fuel for which a license is required under Section 15-4-256 or Section 15-4-257;

(l) Use or maintenance of fuel oil for which a license is required under Section 15-4-258 or Section 15-4-259; or

(m) The business of extermination by fumigation as defined in Section 7-40-010.

(Added. Coun. J. 2-7-96, p. 15616)

§4-115-020 License—Application.

An application for a hazardous materials license shall be made in conformity with the general requirements of this code relating to applications for licenses; and with the particular requirements for each activity to be performed under the license as set forth in the relevant sections of the code governing the particular activity.

In addition, the applicant shall state the location of the place at which it is desired or intended to store or use the hazardous materials enumerated for use in the applicant's business, the maximum aggregate quantity to be so stored for use, and shall give a description of the business engaged in, the location and capacity of all containers or tanks used, a description of all vehicles used in connection with the applicant's business, and such other information as may be required by the division marshal in charge of the bureau of fire prevention.

Before a license required under this chapter may be issued, and, thereafter, as often as it deems necessary, the division marshal in charge of the bureau of fire prevention shall investigate or cause to be investigated the place of business described in such application; all containers, tanks and buildings wherein hazardous materials are to be stored; all vehicles to be used in connection with the applicant's business; and the methods and equipment intended to be used by such applicant to determine whether they are or will be in compliance with all of the fire prevention provisions of the code. In addition, before a license required under this chapter may be issued, and, thereafter, as often as it deems necessary, the department of environment shall inspect all underground storage tanks to be used in connection with the applicant's business.

It shall be the duty of each applicant to notify, within seven days, the division marshal in charge of the bureau of fire prevention when the license for the hazardous materials is no longer required. Notice shall include a verified statement that the licensee is no longer using the materials enumerated in Section 15-4-130 in sufficient quantities to require a license.

(Added. Coun. J. 2-7-96, p. 15616)

§4-115-030 License—Fee.

The annual license fee for each hazardous materials license shall be as set forth in Section 4-5-010.

(Added. Coun. J. 2-7-96, p. 15616)

§4-115-040 Violation—Penalty.

Any person violating any of the provisions of this chapter shall be fined not less than $200.00 nor more than $500.00 for each offense. Every day such violation continues shall constitute a separate and distinct offense.
(Added. Coun. J. 2-7-96, p. 15616)

CHAPTER 4-128
MOTION PICTURES
(Selected Sections)

Sections:

Article I. Motion Picture Projecting Machine Operators

4-128-010 Licensing and attendance requirements.
4-128-090 Apprentice's permit—Required.
4-128-110 Apprentice's permit—Change of place of employment.
4-128-120 Exhibition of license or permit.
4-128-130 Operator's identification card.
4-128-170 Persons in projection booth—Restrictions.
4-128-180 Violation—Penalty.

Article IV. Violation of Chapter Provisions

4-128-380 Violation—Penalty.

Article I. Motion Picture Projecting Machine Operators

§4-128-010 Licensing and attendance requirements.

It shall be unlawful for any person to operate a motion picture projecting machine or device for any public or private gathering where a fee or admission charge has been required from any person, without first having obtained a license as a motion picture projecting machine operator; provided, that this section shall not apply to private organizations organized not-for-profit such as charitable, religious, civic and education organizations.

It shall be unlawful under this section for any motion picture projecting machine or device to be unattended during the showing of any film.
(Coun. J. 12-9-92, p. 25465)

§4-128-090 Apprentice's permit—Required.

It shall be unlawful for any person to act as an apprentice to a motion picture projecting machine operator in the handling, repairing or manipulating of a motion picture projecting machine or device without first obtaining a permit from said building commissioner to act as such.
(Coun. J. 12-9-92, p. 25465)

§4-128-110 Apprentice's permit—Change of place of employment.

An apprentice permit shall not admit the holder thereof into the booth of any motion picture projecting machine or device at any other place except the place of employment designated in said permit, and in case of a change of the place of employment as an apprentice, he shall be required to secure the approval for such change from said building commissioner.

Each operator shall notify said building commissioner promptly in writing on transferring from one place of employment to another.
(Coun. J. 12-9-92, p. 25465)

§4-128-120 Exhibition of license or permit.

Every motion picture projecting machine operator who is licensed under the provisions of this chapter shall have his license certificate posted in a conspicuous place in the box office of any place of amusement where he may be engaged, or in case there is no box office, said license certificate shall be posted in some other conspicuous place where the entertainment or exhibition is given.

Every apprentice who holds a permit as herein provided shall, at all times while employed, have the same on his person or on the premises where he is employed, so that it may be exhibited to any officer or employee of the city authorized to inspect it.
(Coun. J. 12-9-92, p. 25465)

§4-128-130 Operator's identification card.

Every motion picture projecting machine operator, while engaged in the operation of a motion picture projecting machine or device, shall have on his person, or on the premises where he is engaged, an identification card issued by said building commissioner, which card shall show the photograph and signature of the person to whom it is issued.
(Coun. J. 12-9-92, p. 25465)

§4-128-170 Persons in projection booth—Restrictions.

It shall be unlawful for anyone other than a person licensed as a motion picture projecting machine operator or holding a permit as an apprentice under this chapter, or an officer or employee of the city while acting in the discharge of his duty, to enter any compartment or booth where a motion picture projecting machine or device is in operation, or to operate or in any way handle or manage such machine or device while the same is being operated during an exhibition; provided, that this section shall not apply to the proprietor, owner or manager in charge of the premises, who may enter same for the purpose of giving necessary orders and directions. In no case shall more than four persons be within such compartment or booth at one time while such exhibition is going on.
(Coun. J. 12-9-92, p. 25465)

§4-128-180 Violation—Penalty.

Any person violating any of the provisions of Sections 4-128-010 to 4-128-180 or failing to comply with the same shall be subject to the penalties provided for in Section 14-12-950 of this code, and in addition thereto the license of a moving picture projecting machine operator and the permit of an apprentice to a moving picture projecting machine operator, may be suspended or revoked as provided for in Section 4-128-150 of this chapter.
(Coun. J. 12-9-92, p. 25465)

Article IV. Violation of Chapter Provisions

§4-128-380 Violation—Penalty.

Except as otherwise specifically provided in this chapter, any person violating any of the provisions of this chapter shall be fined not less than $200.00 nor more than $500.00 for each and every offense. Every day violation continues shall be considered a separate and distinct offense.
(Coun. J. 12-9-92, p. 25465)

CHAPTER 4-144
WEAPONS
(Complete Chapter)

Sections:

Article I. Deadly Weapons

4-144-010 License—Required.
4-144-020 License—Application.
4-144-030 License—Fee.
4-144-040 Daily report required—Sales or gifts.
4-144-050 Register required.
4-144-060 Restrictions on sales or gifts.
4-144-061 Sale of certain handgun ammunition prohibited.
4-144-062 Sale of handguns without childproofing or safety devices prohibited.
4-144-070 Permit required when—Issuance conditions.
4-144-080 Sales display restrictions.
4-144-090 Reserved.

Article II. Gunsmiths

4-144-100 License—Required.
4-144-110 Reserved.
4-144-120 Reserved.
4-144-130 Daily report required—Repairs.

Article III. Air Rifles and Toy Weapons

4-144-140 License required when.
4-144-150 License—Application.
4-144-160 License—Fee.
4-144-170 Daily report required.
4-144-180 Permit—Required.
4-144-190 Replica firearms and pellet guns.
4-144-200 Granting of permit—Conditions.
4-144-210 Sale or transfer to minors prohibited.
4-144-220 Sales display restrictions.
4-144-230 Alteration restricted.
4-144-240 License—Revocation conditions.

Article IV. Violation of Chapter Provisions

4-144-250 Violation—Penalties.
4-144-260 License—Revocation.

Article I. Deadly Weapons

§4-144-010 License—Required.

It shall be unlawful for any person to engage in the business of selling, or to sell or give away, any pistol, revolver or other firearm, dagger, stiletto, billie, derringer, bowie knife, dirk, stun gun or taser, as defined in Section 24-1 of the Illinois Criminal Code, 720 ILCS 5/24-1, or other deadly weapon which can be carried or concealed on the person, without securing a weapons dealer license. The license required by this chapter shall be in addition to any other license required by law.

(Coun. J. 12-9-92, p. 25465; Amend. 4-16-97, p. 42588)

§4-144-020 License—Application.

An application for a weapons dealer license shall be made in conformity with the general requirements of this code relating to applications for licenses. The superintendent of police shall approve said application before a license shall be issued.

(Coun. J. 12-9-92, p. 25465; Amend. 4-16-97, p. 42588)

§4-144-030 License—Fee.

The annual fee for a weapons dealer license shall be as set forth in Section 4-5-010.

(Coun. J. 12-9-92, p. 25465; Amend. 4-16-97, p. 42588)

§4-144-040 Daily report required—Sales or gifts.

Every person dealing in the aforementioned deadly weapons shall make out and deliver to the superintendent of police every day before the hour of twelve noon, a legible and correct report of every sale or gift made under authority of his license during the preceding 24 hours, which report shall contain the date of such sale or gift, the name of the purchaser or donee with his or her address and age, the number, kind, description and price of such weapon, the number of the purchaser's permit, and the purpose given by such person for the purchase of such weapon, which report shall be substantially in the following form:

Number of permit..
Number of weapon..
Name of purchaser ....
Address of purchaser ....
Age of purchaser...
Kind or description of weapon ....
For what purpose purchased..........................
Price..

(Coun. J. 12-9-92, p. 25465; Amend. 4-16-97, p. 42588)

§4-144-050 Register required.

Every person dealing in the aforementioned deadly weapons or ammunition at retail, within the city, shall keep a register of all such weapons and ammunition sold, loaned, rented or given away by him. Such register shall contain the date of the sale, loaning, renting or gift, the number of the permit, the number of the weapon, the name and age of the person to whom the weapon or ammunition is sold, loaned, rented or given, the quantity of ammunition, the price of each item, and the purpose for which it is purchased or obtained. The said register shall be in the following form (see diagram for Section 4-144-050). Such register shall be kept open for the inspection of the police at all reasonable times during business hours.

Date of sale	Number of superintendent of police permit	Number of weapon	To whom sold, loaned, rented, or given	Age of purchaser or person obtaining weapon	Kind and description of weapon or ammunition	Quantity of ammunition	For what purpose purchased or obtained	Price

(Coun. J. 12-9-92, p. 25465; Amend. 9-14-94, p. 56287)

§4-144-060 Restrictions on sales or gifts.

It shall be unlawful for any person to sell, barter or give away to any person within the city, any deadly weapon mentioned in Section 4-144-010, except to licensed dealers and to persons who have secured a permit for the purchase of such articles from the superintendent of police as hereinafter required. This section shall not apply to sales made of such articles which are to be delivered or furnished outside the city.
(Coun. J. 12-9-92, p. 25465)

§4-144-061 Sale of certain handgun ammunition prohibited.

Except as allowed by subsection (e) of Section 8-20-170 of this code, it shall be unlawful for any person to sell, offer for sale, expose for sale, barter or give away to any person within the city, any ammunition of the following calibers and types:

.45 automatic
.380 automatic
.38 special
.357 magnum
.25 caliber
.22 caliber, including .22 long
9 millimeter

Any other ammunition, regardless of the designation by the manufacturer, distributor or seller, that is capable of being used as a substitute for any of the foregoing.
(Added. Coun. J. 9-14-94, p. 56287)

§4-144-062 Sale of handguns without childproofing or safety devices prohibited.

Except as allowed by subsection (e) of Section 8-20-170 of this code, it shall be unlawful for any person to sell, barter or give away to any person any handgun which does not contain:

(1) A safety mechanism to hinder the use of the handgun by unauthorized users. Such devices shall include, but shall not be limited to, trigger locks, combination handle locks, and solenoid use-limitation devices; and

(2) A load indicator device that provides reasonable warning to potential users such that users even unfamiliar with the weapon would be forewarned and would understand the nature of the warning.

"Safety mechanism" means a design adaption or nondetachable accessory that lessons the likelihood of unanticipated use of the handgun by other than the owner of the handgun and those specifically authorized by the owner to use the handgun.

A "trigger lock" means a device that when locked in place by means of a key, prevents a potential user from pulling the trigger of the handgun without first removing the trigger lock by use of the trigger lock's key.

A "combination handle lock" means a device that is part of the handgun which precludes the use of the handgun unless the combination tumblers are properly aligned.

A "solenoid use-limitation device" means a device which precludes, by use of a solenoid, the firing of the handgun unless a magnet of the appropriate strength is placed in proximity to the handle of the weapon.

A "load indicator" means a device which plainly indicates that a bullet is placed in the handgun in a way that pulling the trigger or otherwise handling the handgun may result in detonation.

(Added. Coun. J. 2-7-97, p. 38729)

§4-144-070 Permit required when—Issuance conditions.

It shall be unlawful for any person to purchase any deadly weapon mentioned in Section 4-144-010 which can be concealed on the person, without first securing from the superintendent of police a permit so to do. Before any such permit is granted, an application in writing shall be made therefor, setting forth in such application the name, address, age, height, weight, complexion, nationality and other elements of identification of the person desiring such permit, and the applicant shall present such evidence of good character as the superintendent of police at his discretion may require.

The superintendent of police shall refuse such permit to any person under 18 years of age, any narcotic addict, any person who has been convicted of a felony under the laws of this state or any other jurisdiction within five years from release from penitentiary or within five years of conviction if penitentiary sentence has not been imposed, and any person who has been released from a mental institution or from the custody of the Illinois Youth Commission within the last five years, or is mentally retarded. Otherwise, in case he shall be satisfied that the applicant is of good moral character, it shall be the duty of the superintendent of police to grant such permit.

(Coun. J. 12-9-92, p. 25465)

§4-144-080 Sales display restrictions.

It shall be unlawful for any person to exhibit for sale in show cases or show windows, on counters or in any other public manner, any deadly weapon mentioned in Section 4-144-010, or to display any signs, posters, cartoons, or display cards suggesting the sale of any such deadly weapons, or any ammunition whose sale is prohibited pursuant to Section 4-144-061 of this code.

(Coun. J. 12-9-92, p. 25465; Amend. 9-14-94, p. 56287)

§4-144-090 Reserved.
(Renumbered to §4-144-260)

Article II. Gunsmiths

§4-144-100 License—Required.

It shall be unlawful for any person to engage in the business of repairing any pistol, revolver, derringer or other firearm which can be concealed on the person without securing a weapons dealer license so to do.
(Coun. J. 12-9-92, p. 25465; Amend. 4-16-97, p. 42588)

§4-144-110 Reserved.
(Deleted Coun. J. 4-16-97, p42588)

§4-144-120 Reserved.
(Deleted Coun. J. 4-16-97, p42588)

§4-144-130 Daily report required—Repairs.

Every person licensed under this chapter shall make out and submit to the superintendent of police every day, before twelve noon, a legible and correct report of each firearm received for repair during the preceding 24 hours, which report shall contain the date, name, physical description, age, address and occupation of the owner of such firearm, the type of weapon, its make, and the serial number and bore length of such weapon, which report shall be substantially in the following form:

Date ....
Name of owner..
Physical description of owner.........................
Age of owner..
Address of owner ....
Occupation of owner.......................................
Type of weapon...
Make of weapon..
Serial number ....
Bore and length of weapon.............................

(Coun. J. 12-9-92, p. 25465; Amend. 4-16-97, p. 42588)

Article III. Air Rifles and Toy Weapons

§4-144-140 License required when.

It shall be unlawful for any person to engage in the business of selling or to sell or to give away any air rifle or air gun, or any toy firearms or other toy in the nature of a firearm in which any explosive substance can be used, without securing a weapons dealer license, and no person having secured such license shall sell or give away any such weapon to any person within the city who has not secured a permit from the superintendent of police to purchase such weapon in the manner hereinafter provided.
(Coun. J. 12-9-92, p. 25465; Amend. 4-16-97, p. 42588)

§4-144-150 License—Application.*

An application for said license shall be made in conformity with the general requirements of this code. The superintendent of police shall approve said application before a license shall be issued.

(Coun. J. 12-9-92, p. 25465)

§4-144-160 License—Fee.*

The annual license fee for said license shall be as set forth in Section 4-5-010.

(Coun. J. 12-9-92, p. 25465)

* **Editor's Note:** It may have been the city's intention in Coun. J. 4-16-97 p. 42588 to delete Sections 4-144-150 and 4-144-160 because a bracket indicating deletion was shown at the end of each section, but no bracket indicating the beginning of deleted text was shown.

§4-144-170 Daily report required.

Every person licensed under this chapter shall make out and deliver to the superintendent of police every day, before the hour of twelve noon, a legible and correct report of every sale or gift made under authority of said license to sell the kind of weapons or other articles named in Section 4-144-140 during the preceding 24 hours, which report shall contain the date of such sale or gift, the name of the purchaser or donee with his or her address and age, the number, kind, description and price of such weapon or other article, the number of the purchaser's permit, and the purpose for the purchase of such weapon or other article, which report shall be substantially in the following form:

Number of permit ....
Number of weapon or article ....
Name of purchaser ....
Address of purchaser ....
Age of purchaser ....
Kind or description of weapon or other article
For what purpose purchased ....
Price ....

(Coun. J. 12-9-92, p. 25465)

§4-144-180 Permit—Required.

It shall be unlawful for any person to purchase any air rifle or air gun, or any toy firearms or other toy in the nature of a firearm in which any explosive substance can be used, without first securing from the superintendent of police a permit so to do. Before any such permit is granted, an application in writing shall be made therefor, setting forth in such application, the name, address, age, height, weight, complexion, nationality and other elements of identification of such person desiring such permit. Such application shall also contain a recommendation from two persons who shall appear to be taxpayers residing within the city that the permit shall issue.

(Coun. J. 12-9-92, p. 25465)

§4-144-190 Replica firearms and pellet guns.

(a) It shall be unlawful for any person to purchase, possess, use, sell, give away or otherwise transfer, or to engage in the business of selling or to exhibit for sale, a replica firearm, paint pellet or paint pellet gun in the city of Chicago, except as provided in subsection (c) of this section.

(b) For the purposes of this chapter, the following terms shall have the following meanings:

"Paint pellet" means a pellet or projectile of paint which explodes upon impact.

"Paint pellet gun" means any firearm, toy firearm or toy in the nature of a firearm which is powered by compressed gas and which fires paint pellets.

"Replica firearm" means any device, object or facsimile made of plastic, wood, metal or any other material, that a person could reasonably perceive as an actual firearm but that is incapable of being fired or discharged, except that the term shall not include any replica of an antique firearm, as defined in Section 8-20-030(b) of this code. Each such replica firearm shall have as an integral part, permanently affixed, a blaze orange plug inserted in the barrel of such replica firearm. Such plug shall be recessed no more than six millimeters from the muzzle end of the barrel of such firearm.

(c) The manufacture, marketing, distribution, sale and possession of replica firearms are permitted if the devices are manufactured, marketed, distributed, sold or held (1) solely for subsequent transportation in intrastate, interstate or foreign commerce, or (2) solely for use in theatrical productions, including motion picture, television and stage productions. Such devices shall not be displayed to the general public or sold for other use in the city. The use or possession of a paint pellet or paint pellet gun is permitted if the use or possession is solely within premises licensed as a public place of amusement; or if the use or possession is solely for the purpose of transporting the paint pellet or paint pellet gun to or from those premises by the licensee or agent or employee of the licensee, or by a common carrier, for purposes of initial delivery, repair or disposal of the paint pellet or paint pellet gun.

(d) Any person who violates the provisions of this section, upon conviction thereof, shall be fined not less than $100.00 nor more than $500.00 for each offense. Any such violation may also be punishable as a misdemeanor by incarceration in a penal institution other than a penitentiary for up to six months under the procedures set forth in Section 1-2-1.1 of the Illinois Municipal Code as amended, and in the Illinois Code of Criminal Procedure, Illinois Revised Statutes, Chapter 38, Sections 100-1 et seq. (1985), as amended, in a separate proceeding. All actions seeking the imposition of fines only shall be filed as quasi-criminal actions subject to the provisions of the Illinois Code of Civil Procedure, Illinois Revised Statutes, Chapter 110, Section 1-101, et seq. (1985), as amended. Each purchase, use, sale, gift or transfer of any such replica firearm, paint pellet or paint pellet gun shall be deemed a separate and distinct offense, and each day a person unlawfully engages in the business of selling or exhibits for sale any such replica firearm, paint pellet or paint pellet gun shall be deemed a separate and distinct offense.

(Coun. J. 12-9-92, p. 25465; Amend. 11-2-94, p. 58607)

§4-144-200 Granting of permit—Conditions.

It shall be the duty of the superintendent of police to refuse such permit to any person having been convicted of any crime, and any minor. Otherwise, if the applicant is of good moral character, the superintendent of police shall grant such permit upon the payment of a fee of $1.00.
(Coun. J. 12-9-92, p. 25465)

§4-144-210 Sale or transfer to minors prohibited.

It is unlawful for any dealer to sell, lend, rent, give or otherwise transfer an air rifle to any person under the age of 18 years where the dealer knows the person to be under 18 years of age, or where such dealer has failed to make reasonable inquiry relative to the age of such person and such person is under 18 years of age.

It is unlawful for any person to sell, lend or otherwise transfer any air rifle to any person under 18 years of age.
(Coun. J. 12-9-92, p. 25465)

§4-144-220 Sales display restrictions.

It shall be unlawful for any person to exhibit for sale in show cases, or show windows, on counters, or in any public manner, any air rifle or air gun, or any toy firearm or other toy in the nature of a firearm in which any explosive substance can be used, or to display any signs, posters, cartoons or display cards suggesting the sale of any such weapon or firearm.
(Coun. J. 12-9-92, p. 25465)

§4-144-230 Alteration restricted.

No person shall alter any air rifle, air gun, toy firearm or toy in the nature of a firearm in such a way that it can fire any type of projectile other than that which it was designed by its manufacturer to fire.
(Coun. J. 12-9-92, p. 25465)

§4-144-240 License—Revocation conditions.

When the license of any said licensee shall be revoked, no other such license shall be issued to such licensee for a period of three years thereafter.
(Coun. J. 12-9-92, p. 25465)

Article IV. Violation of Chapter Provisions

§4-144-250 Violation—Penalties.

Any person violating Section 4-144-010 or Section 4-144-060 or Section 4-144-061 of this chapter shall be fined not less than $500.00 nor more than $1,000.00 for a first offense and $1,000.00 for each subsequent offense. Any person violating any other provision of this chapter shall be fined not less than $250.00 nor more than $500.00 for a first offense and not less than $500.00 nor more than $1,000.00 for each subsequent offense. Each purchase, sale or gift of any weapon or article mentioned in this chapter shall be deemed a separate offense.
(Coun. J. 12-9-92, p. 25465; Amend. 9-14-94, p. 56287)

§4-144-260 License—Revocation.

In case the mayor shall determine that a licensee has violated any provision of this chapter, he shall revoke the weapons dealer license issued to such person, and the money paid for such license shall be forfeited to the city. No other such license shall be issued to such licensee for a period of three years thereafter.
(Coun. J. 12-9-92, p. 25465; Amend. 4-16-97, p. 42588)

DIVISION VI
WHOLESALE, RETAIL AND SERVICE ACTIVITIES
(Selected Chapters)

Chapters:

4-156	Amusements. (Selected Sections)
4-168	Bicycle Messenger Services. (Selected Sections)
4-208	Hotels. (Selected Sections)
4-209	Single-Room Occupancy Buildings. (Complete Chapter)
4-212	Itinerant Merchants. (Complete Chapter)
4-216	Junk Dealers and Peddlers. (Selected Sections)
4-220	Laundries and Laundry Vehicles. (Selected Sections)
4-224	Manufacturing Establishments. (Complete Chapter)
4-228	Motor Vehicle Repair Shops. (Selected Sections)
4-229	Tire Facilities. (Complete Chapter)
4-232	Motor Vehicle Storage and Sales. (Selected Sections)
4-233	Motor Vehicle Booting License (Complete Chapter)
4-240	Pawnbrokers. (Selected Sections)
4-244	Peddlers. (Selected Sections)
4-253	Retail Computing Centers. (Selected Sections)
4-256	Roofers. (Selected Sections)
4-260	Scavengers. (Selected Sections)
4-264	Secondhand Dealers. (Complete Chapter)
4-268	Street Performers. (Complete Chapter)

CHAPTER 4-156
AMUSEMENTS
(Selected Sections)

Sections:

Article I. Amusements

4-156-010	Definitions.
4-156-020	Tax imposed.
4-156-030	Collection, payment and accounting.
4-156-033	Additional tax imposed on sellers of tickets.
4-156-034	Rules and regulations.
4-156-035	Application of Uniform Revenue Procedures Ordinance.
4-156-040	Raffles—Terms defined.
4-156-050	Raffles—Licenses—Issuance by city clerk.
4-156-060	Raffles—Licenses—Requirements.
4-156-070	Raffles—Separate licenses—Fee—Term.
4-156-080	Raffle tickets.
4-156-090	Raffles—Prizes—Fees.
4-156-100	Raffles—Publication of rules and regulations.
4-156-110	Raffles—Fee exemption conditions.
4-156-120	Auxiliaries and affiliates of organizations.
4-156-125	Intertrack wagering.
4-156-130	Severability.
4-156-140	Violations—Penalty.

Article II. Automatic Amusement Devices

4-156-150 Definitions.
4-156-160 Tax imposed.
4-156-170 Tax emblem.
4-156-180 Installation prerequisites.
4-156-190 Seizure for unlawful use.
4-156-200 License—Required.
4-156-210 License—Application—Examination of records authorized.
4-156-220 Application—Investigation.
4-156-230 Number of devices limited.
4-156-270 Restrictions on use by minors.
4-156-280 Violation—Penalty.

Article III. Public Places of Amusement

4-156-290 Definition.
4-156-300 License—Required.
4-156-305 License—Exceptions.
4-156-355 License—Issuance prohibited.
4-156-390 Ticket sales.
4-156-410 Motion picture theaters—Billboard contents.
4-156-420 Billiard rooms and poolrooms.
4-156-424 Beer gardens.
4-156-430 Athletic contests at night and on weekday afternoons—Restrictions.
4-156-435 Unregulated exhibition where intent is to harm a contestant—Prohibited—Enforcement.
4-156-450 Gambling.
4-156-460 Drinking water.
4-156-484 Special event allowance.
4-156-485 License restrictions.
4-156-510 Club violation—Penalty.
4-156-520 Construction of chapter.

Article I. Amusements

§4-156-010 Definitions.

For purposes of this chapter:

"Amusement" means: (1) any exhibition, performance, presentation or show for entertainment purposes, whether viewed within or outside the home, including, but not limited to, any theatrical, dramatic, musical or spectacular performance, promotional show, motion picture show, flower, poultry or animal show, animal act, circus, rodeo, athletic contest, sport, game or similar exhibition such as boxing, wrestling, skating, dancing, swimming, racing or riding on animals or vehicles, baseball, basketball, softball, football, tennis, golf, hockey, track and field games, bowling, or billiard and pool games; (2) any entertainment or recreational activity offered for public participation or on a membership or other basis including, but not limited to, carnivals, amusement park rides and games, bowling, billiards and pool games, dancing, tennis, racquetball, swimming, weightlifting, body building or similar activities; or (3) any paid television programming, whether transmitted by wire, cable, fiberoptics, laser, microwave, radio, satellite or similar means.

"Arcade" means a place of amusement that includes four or more automatic amusement devices; provided, however, that when calculating the number of automatic amusement devices, jukeboxes shall not be counted.

"Legal voter" means a person who has registered to vote and whose name appears on a poll sheet from the last preceding election regardless of whether primary, general or special.

"Live theatrical, live musical or other live cultural performance" means a live performance in any of the disciplines which are commonly regarded as part of the fine arts, such as live theater, music, opera, drama, comedy, ballet, modern or traditional dance, and book or poetry readings. The term does not include such amusements as athletic events, races or performances conducted at adult entertainment cabarets (as defined in Chapter 16-16 of this Code).

"Maximum capacity" means the number of persons that an auditorium, theater or other space may accommodate as determined by the building commissioner or the executive director of the department of construction and permits pursuant to Chapter 13-36 of this code or by any other appropriate government official; provided, however, that "maximum capacity" shall not exceed the maximum number of tickets or admissions that may be made available for sale to a performance as stated in any binding written agreement relating to that performance. If the number of tickets or admissions actually sold to a performance exceeds the legally permissible limit, for purposes of determining the applicable tax, "maximum capacity" shall mean such greater number.

"Owner" means: (1) with respect to the owner of a place where an amusement is being held, any person with an ownership or leasehold interest in a building, structure, vehicle, boat, area or other place who presents, conducts or operates an amusement in such place or who allows, by agreement or otherwise, another person to present, conduct or operate an amusement in such place; (2) with respect to the owner of an amusement, any person who has an ownership or leasehold interest in such amusement or any person who has a proprietary interest in the amusement so as to entitle such person to all or a portion of the proceeds, after payment of reasonable expenses, from the operation, conduct or presentation of such amusement, excluding proceeds from nonamusement services and from sales of tangible personal property; (3) with respect to paid television programming, any person operating a community antenna television system or wireless cable television system, or any person receiving consideration from the patron for furnishing, transmitting, or otherwise providing access to paid television programming.

"Paid television" means programming that can be viewed on a television or other screen, and is transmitted by cable, fiber optics, laser, microwave, radio, satellite or similar means to members of the public for consideration.

"Person" means any natural individual, firm, society, foundation, institution, partnership, limited liability company, association, joint stock company, joint venture, public or private corporation, receiver, executor, trustee or other representative appointed by the order of any court, or any other entity recognized by law.

"Special seating area" means an enclosed or substantially enclosed apartment-style room containing or making available amenities for the exclusive use of the patrons thereof, whether denominated as luxury or super suites or skyboxes or by other similar terms. Such amenities may include, but are not necessarily limited to, television (including closed-circuit capacity), bathroom, refrigerator, telephone service, storage sink, living room or lounge furniture, special spectator seating, food, heat, air conditioning and parking.

"Theatrical community center" means a building or a portion thereof used by a not-for-profit organization chartered by the state of Illinois which has as its purposes the promotion, instruction, study and production of the theater as an

art form. Any single room within said theatrical community center used for theatrical purposes shall provide for a capacity of less than 300 persons, and shall meet all requirements of the Municipal Code of Chicago which apply to small assembly units, Class C-2, as provided in Section 13-56-090 of the Municipal Code.
(Added. Coun. J. 12-9-92, p. 25465; Amend. 11-17-93, p. 42192; 11-15-95, p. 11995; 7-2-97, p. 48017; 11-12-98, p. 81835; 4-21-99, p. 91750; 3-5-03, p. 104990)

§4-156-020 Tax imposed.

A. Except as otherwise provided by this article, an amusement tax is imposed upon the patrons of every amusement within the city. The rate of the tax shall be equal to eight percent of the admission fees or other charges paid for the privilege to enter, to witness, to view or to participate in such amusement, unless subsection E of this section provides for a lower rate.

B. The tax imposed by subsection A shall not apply to the following persons or privileges:

(1) Patrons of automatic amusement machines as defined in Article II of this chapter; or

(2) The privilege of witnessing or participating in any stock show or business show that is not open to the general public; or

(3) The privilege of hiring a horse-drawn carriage licensed under Chapter 9-108 of this code; or

(4) The privilege of witnessing or participating in any amateur production or activity, such as amateur musicals, plays and athletic events, conducted by a not-for-profit organization operated exclusively for charitable, educational or religious purposes; or

(5) Subject to satisfying the requirement contained in subsection C of this section, the privilege of witnessing or participating in any amusement sponsored or conducted by and the proceeds of which, after payment of reasonable expenses, inure exclusively to the benefit of:

(a) Religious, educational and charitable institutions, societies or organizations;

(b) Societies or organizations for the prevention of cruelty to children or animals;

(c) Societies or organizations conducted and maintained for the purpose of civic improvement;

(d) Fraternal organizations, legion posts, social and political groups which conduct amusements, sponsored occasionally but not more often than twice yearly; provided, however, that the entities described in paragraphs (a) to (d) are not-for-profit institutions, organizations, groups or societies, where no part of the net earnings inure to the benefit of any private shareholder or person;

(e) Organizations or persons in the armed services of the United States, or National Guard organizations, reserve officers' associations, or organizations or posts of war veterans, or auxiliary units or societies of such posts or organizations, if such posts, organizations, units or societies are organized in the state of Illinois, and if no part of their earnings inure to the benefit of any private shareholder or person;

(f) Organizations or associations created and maintained for the purpose of benefitting the members, or dependents or heirs of members, of the police or fire departments of any political subdivision of the state of Illinois; provided that the exemptions contained in paragraphs (a) through (f) shall apply only to benefits or other fundraising events and shall not apply to more than two events per calendar year which shall not exceed a total of 14 calendar days;

(g) Societies or organizations conducted for the sole purpose of maintaining symphony orchestras, opera performances or artistic presentations, including, but not limited to, musical presentations ("artistic societies or organizations"), if the artistic society or organization (i) receives substantial support from voluntary contributions, (ii) is a not-for-profit institution where no part of the net earnings inure to the benefit of any private shareholder or person, and (iii) either (a) bears all risk of financial loss from its presentation of the amusement and the amusement is limited to an engagement of not more than eight calendar days over the course of a calendar year, or (b) is substantially and materially involved in the production and performance of the amusement. Where an amusement is sponsored or conducted by two or more artistic societies or organizations, the requirements of subsections (i) and (ii) of this subsection 4-156-020(B)(5)(g) must be met by each of such artistic societies or organizations, but the requirements of subsection (iii) may be met by any of such artistic societies or organizations, individually or in combination.

C. (1) None of the exemptions contained in subsection B(5) of this section shall apply to a person or privilege unless a written notice of the amusement is filed with the department of revenue at least 30 calendar days prior to the amusement or 15 calendar days prior to the date that admission tickets to the amusement are first made available for sale, whichever is earlier. The notice shall be on a form prescribed by the director of revenue, and shall contain all information and materials necessary to permit the department to consider whether the exemption claimed by the applicant is applicable.

(2) Upon the request of the person filing the notice, the department shall indicate within 14 calendar days after receiving the notice whether the claimed exemption does or does not apply, or whether additional information is necessary to make a determination.

D. (1) The tax imposed in subsection A of this section shall not apply to or be imposed upon the admission fees to witness in person live theatrical, live musical or other live cultural performances that take place in any auditorium, theater or other space in the city whose maximum capacity, including all balconies and other sections, is not more than 750 persons.

(2) Initiation fees and membership dues paid to a health club, racquetball club, tennis club or a similar club or organization, when such club or organization is organized and operated on a membership basis and for the recreational purposes of its members and its members' guests, shall be exempt from the tax imposed in subsection A of this section. This exemption shall not be construed to apply to any fees paid or based upon, in any way whatsoever, a per-event or a per-admission basis.

E. The rate of the tax imposed in subsection A of this section shall be four percent of the admission fees or other charges to witness in person live theatrical, live musical or other live cultural performances that take place in any auditorium, theater or other space in the city whose maximum capacity, including all balconies and other sections, is more than 750 persons.

F. The tax imposed in subsection A of this section shall apply to and be imposed upon 60 percent of the admission fees or other charges (including, but not limited to, the gross lease or rental amount) paid for the privilege of using special seating areas to witness or to view an amusement.

G. It shall be presumed that all amusements are subject to tax under this article until the contrary is established by books, records or other documentary evidence.

H. For the purpose of determining the amount of the amusement tax due under Section 4-156-020, admission fees or other charges shall be computed exclusive of this tax, any federal, state or county taxes imposed upon the amusement patron and any separately stated charges for nonamusement services or for sales of tangible personal property.

I. It is unlawful for any person to produce, present, conduct or resell tickets to, any amusement without collection of the tax, except as provided in this article.

J. Notwithstanding subsection A of this section, if an owner, manager or operator of an amusement or of a place where an amusement is being held, or if a reseller of tickets to an amusement, is a party to a franchise agreement or any other agreement with the city pursuant to which the owner, manager, operator or reseller compensates the city for the right to use the public way or to do business in the city, liability under the tax imposed by subsection A shall be reduced by the amount paid to the city pursuant to the agreement.

(Coun. J. 12-9-92, p. 25465; Amend. 12-15-92, p. 27387; 11-10-94, p. 59125; 11-15-95, p. 11995; 7-30-97, p. 48760; 11-12-98, p. 81835; 4-21-99, p. 91750; 4-21-99, p. 91750; 12-15-04, p. 39840)

§4-156-030 Collection, payment and accounting.

A. It shall be the joint and several duty of every owner, manager or operator of an amusement or of a place where an amusement is being held, and of every reseller of tickets to an amusement, to secure from each patron the tax imposed by Section 4-156-020 of this article and to remit the tax to the department of revenue not later than the last day of each calendar month for all admission fees or other charges received during the immediately preceding calendar month; provided, however, that a reseller of tickets shall be required to collect and remit tax to the department only on that portion of the ticket price that exceeds the original or face amount of the tickets. A verified statement of admission fees or charges in a form prescribed by the director of revenue shall accompany each remittance. Acceptance by the city of any amount tendered in payment of the tax shall be without prejudice to any claim, demand or right on account of any deficiency. Effective July 1, 2002, each owner, manager, operator or reseller that collects and remits taxes in accordance with this section may retain 1.0 percent of the taxes it collects under this chapter to reimburse itself for expenses incurred in connection with accounting for and remitting the taxes to the department; provided that this service fee shall not be allowed for taxes not timely remitted to the department; and provided further that this service fee shall not apply to any taxes that are collected and remitted pursuant to the terms of a contract between the operator and the city of Chicago.

B. Every person required to collect and remit the tax imposed by Section 4-156-020 of this article, or pay the tax directly to the department, shall keep accurate books and records of its business or activity, including original source documents and books of entry denoting the transaction that gave rise, or may have given rise, to the tax liability or any exemption that may be claimed. All such books, records and accounts shall be available for inspection by the department at all reasonable times during business hours of the day.

C. Every owner, manager, operator, or reseller of tickets, who is required to collect the tax imposed by Section 4-156-020 of this article shall be considered a tax collector for the city. All amusement tax collected shall be held by such tax collector as trustee for and on behalf of the city. The failure of the tax collector to collect the tax shall not excuse or release the patron from the obligation to pay the tax.

D. Notwithstanding any other provision of this code, in order to permit sound fiscal planning and budgeting by the city, no person shall be entitled to a refund of, or credit for, either tax imposed by this article unless the person files a claim for refund or credit within one year after the date on which the tax was paid or remitted to the department. This provision shall apply to any claim for credit or refund for which the director has not issued a final determination as of the effective date of this subsection 4-156-030(D).

E. Notwithstanding subsection A of this Section 4-156-030, a reseller of tickets shall not be required to collect the tax imposed by Section 4-156-020, and remit the tax to the department of revenue, if the purchaser of such tickets will in turn act as a reseller of the same tickets, provided that the purchaser supplies to the reseller (1) a written verification that the purchaser intends to resell the tickets and (2) the tax registration number issued to the purchaser by the department of revenue.

F. Notwithstanding any other provision of this chapter, for all periods beginning on or after January 1, 2000, (1) all tax returns shall be filed with the department on an annual basis on or before August 15th of each year in accordance with Sections 3-4-186 and 3-4-189 of this code, (2) all tax payments and remittances shall be made in accordance with either Section 3-4-187 (payment of actual tax liabilities) or Section 3-4-188 (payment of estimated taxes), and (3) the provisions of Sections 3-4-186, 3-4-187, 3-4-188 and 3-4-189 shall control over any contrary provisions in this chapter regarding the subjects covered by those sections.

(Coun. J. 12-9-92, p. 25465; Amend. 12-15-92, p. 27387; 11-15-95, p. 11995; 11-12-98, p. 81835; 11-17-99, p. 18040; 12-12-01, p. 75777)

§4-156-033 Additional tax imposed on sellers of tickets.

A. In addition to the tax imposed by Section 4-156-020 of this article, a tax is imposed upon persons that sell tickets in the city for theatricals, shows, exhibitions, athletic events and other amusements within the city at a place other than the theater or location where the amusement is given or exhibited. The rate of this tax shall be eight percent of any service fees or similar charges received by the seller in connection with the sale of such tickets in the city, as distinguished from the admission fees or other charges paid for the privilege to enter, to witness, to view or to participate in such amusements. This tax shall not apply if the theatrical, show, exhibition, athletic event or other amusement is exempt or otherwise not subject to the tax imposed by Section 4-156-020.

B. To prevent multiple taxation, upon proof that a taxpayer has paid a similar tax in another state or municipality with respect to the service fee or similar charge received by a seller in connection with the sale of tickets in the city, the taxpayer shall be allowed a credit against the tax authorized by subsection A of this section to the extent of the amount of such tax properly due and paid in such other state or municipality.

C. Sellers of tickets shall pay the tax imposed by this Section 4-156-033 to the department of revenue not later than the last day of the calendar month following the month they receive the service fees or similar charges. A return prescribed by the director of revenue shall accompany each tax payment. Such sellers of tickets shall keep accurate books and records of their business, including original source documents and books of entry, which shall be made available for inspection by the department at all times during business hours of the day.

D. Notwithstanding any other provision of this chapter, for all periods beginning on or after January 1, 2000, (1) all tax returns shall be filed with the department on an annual basis on or before August 15th of each year in accordance with Sections 3-4-186 and 3-4-189 of this code, (2) all tax payments shall be made in accordance with either Section 3-4-187 (payment of actual tax liabilities) or Section 3-4-188 (payment of estimated taxes), and (3) the provisions of Sections 3-4-186, 3-4-187, 3-4-188 and 3-4-189 shall control over any contrary provisions in this chapter regarding the subjects covered by those sections.

(Added. Coun. J. 11-15-95, p. 11995; Amend. 11-17-99, p. 18040; 12-15-04, p. 39840)

§4-156-034 Rules and regulations.

The director of revenue is authorized to adopt, promulgate and enforce rules and regulations pertaining to the interpretation, administration and enforcement of this article, including but not limited to the meaning and scope of the exemptions contained in Section 4-156-020.

(Added. Coun. J. 11-12-98, p. 81835)

§4-156-035 Application of Uniform Revenue Procedures Ordinance.

Whenever not inconsistent with the provisions of this chapter or whenever this chapter is silent, the provisions of the Uniform Revenue Procedures Ordinance, Chapter 3-4 of this code, as amended, shall apply and supplement this chapter.

(Coun. J. 12-9-92, p. 25465; 11-12-98, p. 81835)

§4-156-040 Raffles—Terms defined.

Whenever used in Sections 4-156-040 through 4-156-120 of this code, the word “Act” shall mean “an Act to provide for licensing and regulating certain games of chance.” Public Law 81-1356, as amended. Whenever used in said sections of this code, the words “raffle,” “religious,” “charitable,” “labor,” “fraternal,” “educational” and “veterans” shall have the respective meanings specified in Section 2 of the Act.

(Coun. J. 12-9-92, p. 25465)

§4-156-050 Raffles—Licenses—Issuance by city clerk.

The city clerk shall have the authority to issue licenses for raffles, as defined in the Act, subject to the limitations stated in Section 4-156-020 of this article.

(Coun. J. 12-9-92, p. 25465)

§4-156-060 Raffles—Licenses—Requirements.

Licenses for raffles shall be issued only to bona fide religious, charitable, labor, fraternal, educational or veterans' organizations which are located within the corporate limits of the city of Chicago and which operate without profit to their members, and which have been in existence continuously for a period of five years immediately before applying for such license and have had during said period a bona fide membership engaged in carrying out their objects. Application shall be made in writing, no fewer than 10 days before the intended sale of raffle chances, on forms provided by the city clerk's office. Each application shall contain the name and address of the applicant, the area in which the raffle chances will be sold or issued, the time and manner and location of determining the winning chances, and such other information as the city clerk's office may require. Each application must contain a sworn statement attesting to the not-for-profit character of the applicant, signed by its presiding officer and secretary.

(Coun. J. 12-9-92, p. 25465)

§4-156-070 Raffles—Separate licenses—Fee—Term.

Each raffle must be authorized by a separate license, and must be conducted in accordance with Sections 4, 5 and 6, inclusive, of the Act. The fee for such license shall be as set forth in Section 4-5-010. The license shall be valid for the duration of one year.

(Coun. J. 12-9-92, p. 25465)

§4-156-080 Raffle tickets.

Each raffle ticket, chance or other raffle token shall state on its face the name and address of the licensee, the date or dates of the drawing, and the prize or prizes to be awarded; provided, however, that this requirement shall not apply to any raffle in which prizes in aggregate value under $50.00 are awarded. No such ticket, chance or token shall be sold or issued more than 364 days before the determination of the winning chance or chances.

(Coun. J. 12-9-92, p. 25465)

§4-156-090 Raffles—Prizes—Fees.

The maximum cash prize awarded in any raffle shall be $100,000.00; the maximum retail value of a non-cash prize awarded in any raffle shall be $100,000.00. The aggregate value of all prizes awarded in any raffle shall not exceed $200,000.00. The maximum fee for any chance shall be $200.00; all such fees shall be paid in currency or by check.

(Coun. J. 12-9-92, p. 25465)

§4-156-100 Raffles—Publication of rules and regulations.

The director of revenue, or his designated agent, shall publish rules and regulations not inconsistent with this chapter or the Act governing the conduct of raffles licensed hereunder.

(Coun. J. 12-9-92, p. 25465; Amend. 12-8-04, p. 38063)

§4-156-110 Raffles—Fee exemption conditions.

Notwithstanding any provision of Section 4-156-060 of the Municipal Code, no license fee shall be charged for any other raffle conducted by a qualifying organization in the same calendar year during which such organization has paid a raffle license fee and conducted the licensed raffle.

(Coun. J. 12-9-92, p. 25465)

§4-156-120 Auxiliaries and affiliates of organizations.

Whenever used in this chapter, the word "organization" shall include an auxiliary or affiliate of a licensee.

(Coun. J. 12-9-92, p. 25465)

§4-156-125 Intertrack wagering.

(a) Whenever used in this section, the word "Act" shall mean the "Illinois Horse Racing Act of 1975," as amended. Whenever used in this section, the words "board" and "intertrack wagering location licensee" shall have the meanings specified in Sections 3.01 and 3.073, respectively, of the Act.

(b) A one-dollar admission fee is imposed upon each patron of an intertrack wagering location facility located wholly within the corporate boundaries of the city. It shall be the duty of each such intertrack wagering location licensee to collect such admission fee and, within 48 hours of collection, to remit the fees to the board. As provided in Section 27 of the Act, the board shall cause such fees to be distributed to the city. The director of the department of revenue is authorized and directed to collect such fees as shall be distributed by the board to the city.

(Coun. J. 12-9-92, p. 25465)

§4-156-130 Severability.

If any provision of this chapter, or the application of any provision to any item in this chapter, is held invalid, the invalidity of that provision or application shall not affect any of the other provisions or the application of those provisions to other items in this chapter.

(Coun. J. 12-9-92, p. 25465)

§4-156-140 Violations—Penalty.

Any person violating any of the provisions of this chapter shall be fined not less than $200.00 nor more than $500.00 for each offense. Every day such violation continues shall constitute a separate and distinct offense.

(Coun. J. 12-9-92, p. 25465)

Article II. Automatic Amusement Devices

§4-156-150 Definitions.

As used in this chapter:

"Automatic amusement device" means any machine, which, upon the insertion of a coin, slug, token, card or similar object, or upon any other payment method, may be operated by the public generally for use as a game, entertainment or amusement, whether or not registering a score, and includes but is not limited to such devices as jukeboxes, marble machines, pinball machines, movie and video booths or stands and all games, operations or transactions similar thereto under whatever name by which they may be indicated. Bingo devices are deemed gambling devices and are therefore prohibited for use except as provided by state law. If a machine consists of more than one game monitor which permits individuals to play separate games simultaneously, each separate game monitor shall be deemed an automatic amusement device.

"Illegal amusement device" means an automatic amusement device that: includes a knock-off circuit; or allows more than 10 replays or free games, or maintains a count of payoffs or the number of times a person has won a game played on the device; or maintains a tally of players' scores other than the tally displayed to players; or fails to display in the required manner a tax emblem required by chapter; or has been used for illegal gambling. "Illegal amusement device" does not include a device that properly displays a required tax emblem, that is not used for illegal gambling and that qualifies either as a crane game as defined in the Illinois Criminal Code of 1961 or as a redemption machine as defined in the Illinois Criminal Code. An automatic amusement device shall not be deemed an illegal automatic amusement device because of internal diagnostic devices or capabilities that are able to record and maintain statistical data such as the number of coins or tokens deposited, the number of games played or the number of games won, if such diagnostic devices or capabilities are intended and used exclusively for auditing of game performance.

"Knock-off circuit" means any mechanical or electrical device, circuitry or modification on an automatic amusement device, whereby free games shown on an externally visible indicator are release, while a record of games so released is maintained on a second indicator, meter or counter, either inside or outside the device. A reset button installed by the manufacturer of the automatic amusement device shall not, without more, constitute a knock-off circuit.

The phrase "more than 10 replays or free games" means more than 10 replays or free games at one time. "Free game or replay" does not include an extension of a game awarded as a result of the player's skill, such as an extra ball in a pinball game or extended playing time in a video game.

"Payoff" means the giving of money or other thing of value in exchange for a player's accumulated points or free games or replays.

The phrase "a count of payoffs or the number of times a player has won a game played on the device" means a tally, whether on paper, mechanical or electronic, and regardless of whether maintained inside, on or outside the automatic amusement device. The phrase is not intended to include a record of scores, accessible to players of the device, and linked to previous players' names, nicknames, initials or other identifiers, for purposes of comparison and competition.

The phrase "tally of players' scores other than the tally displayed to players" does not include a record of scores, accessible to players of the device, and linked to previous players' names, nicknames, initials or other identifiers, for purposes of comparison and competition.
(Coun. J. 12-9-92, p. 25465; Amend. 7-2-97, p. 48017; 4-1-98, p. 65262; 12-15-99, p. 21529; 7-25-01, p.65052)

§4-156-160 Tax imposed.

An annual tax in the amount of $150.00 for nongambling-type automatic amusement devices and $225.00 for gambling-type automatic amusement devices for each calendar year is imposed upon all automatic amusement devices operated for gain or profit per device.
(Coun. J. 12-9-92, p. 25465; Amend. 11-17-99, p. 17487)

§4-156-170 Tax emblem.

The automatic amusement device tax shall be paid by the owner of such device to the department of finance. The city clerk shall issue as evidence of the payment of the tax a self-voiding adhesive tax emblem to be placed on each device. Such emblem shall bear the words "City of Chicago Amusement Device Tax," the names of the mayor and the city clerk, and such other wording as may be prescribed by the mayor. It shall be unlawful for any person to mutilate said tax emblem during the year for which it was issued.
(Coun. J. 12-9-92, p. 25465)

§4-156-180 Installation prerequisites.

It shall be unlawful for the owner of lessee of any premises or person in control of such premises to permit the installation or use of an automatic amusement device within the city of Chicago for gain or profit unless the tax has been paid and is evidenced by a tax emblem affixed to the automatic amusement device in a conspicuous location. Each such device shall be plainly labeled with the name, address and telephone number of its owner. No person shall remove, alter or deface the tax emblem or label required by this section, or allow use of an automatic amusement machine if the tax emblem or label has been removed, altered, defaced or become illegible. The owner or lessee of the premises where the device is placed for operation by the public and every person responsible for the premises shall be jointly and severally liable for a violation of this section.
(Coun. J. 12-9-92, p. 25465; Amend. 12-15-99, p. 21529)

§4-156-190 Seizure for unlawful use.

If the mayor, superintendent of police, or the director of revenue or their duly authorized enforcement officer shall have a reasonable basis for believing any amusement device is an illegal amusement device, said device or any part or contents thereof may be seized by any duly authorized enforcement official, followed by an administrative hearing with notice to the owner within seven days of such seizure for the purpose of reviewing the appropriateness of the seizure, and held until such time as the owner of such device pays the delinquent tax, reimburses the department of revenue for actual cartage cost incurred in the seizure and pays to the department of revenue $20.00 for each day or part

of day said device has been in storage. If criminal charges involving the use or condition of the device are pending, the device shall be held until disposition of the criminal charges. If it is determined at the hearing by a preponderance of the evidence that the seized device is not an illegal amusement device, it shall be returned to the owner without charge. If it is determined at the hearing that the automatic amusement device was used for illegal gambling, it shall be destroyed by the city, and all money found within the device at the time of confiscation shall become the property of the city, and shall be used to defray the costs of cartage, notice, storage and hearings. If the owner of the device does not claim the automatic amusement device within 14 days after the mailing of the notice, the device and its contents will be treated as abandoned property and the device will be destroyed.
(Coun. J. 12-9-92, p. 25465; Amend. 4-1-98, p. 65262)

§4-156-200 License—Required.

No one shall engage in the automatic amusement device operators business which is herein defined to mean the conduct or transaction of the business of distributing, placing, leasing or selling automatic amusement devices with an agreement to maintain, service or supply, without first obtaining a license therefor.
(Coun. J. 12-9-92, p. 25465)

§4-156-210 License—Application—Examination of records authorized.

An application for an automatic amusement device operator's license shall be made in conformity with the general requirements of this code relating to application for a license. The department of revenue, upon reasonable notice, shall have the authority to examine all books and records of automatic amusement device operators to insure compliance with this chapter. The license fee for an automatic amusement device operator's license shall be as set forth in Section 4-5-010.
(Coun. J. 12-9-92, p. 25465)

§4-156-220 Application—Investigation.

The original application shall be referred to the superintendent of police for investigation and verification of the facts stated therein and the business methods of the operator. Unless said superintendent shall find the operator has been convicted of a felony or that he has violated any law or ordinance imposing any tax, or if either the owner or operator has employed coercive or illegal measures to promote the use of his automatic amusement device, or that the place where said automatic device is to be used is not qualified under the provisions of this chapter, he shall return said application to the director of revenue with his approval; otherwise he shall return it with a statement of his reasons for refusing approval of the application.
(Coun. J. 12-9-92, p. 25465)

§4-156-230 Number of devices limited.

It is unlawful for any person to operate or permit the operation of an arcade unless the person in control of such place has first obtained a public place of amusement license.
(Coun. J. 12-9-92, p. 25465; Amend. 7-2-97, p. 48017)

§4-156-270 Restrictions on use by minors.

(a) No person, firm, corporation, organization or other legal entity shall permit, and it shall be unlawful for, any person under 17 years of age, who is not accompanied by a parent or guardian, to operate any automatic amusement device, except upon the premises of the city airports, between the hours of 8:00 a.m. and 3:00 p.m. on days in which the city's public schools are in session.

(b) No person, firm, corporation, organization or other legal entity shall permit, and it shall be unlawful for, any person under the age of 21 to play an automatic amusement device located at an establishment which sells alcoholic liquor for consumption on the premises.

The prohibition described in this subsection (b) shall not prohibit any person or legal entity to permit any person under the age of 21 to play an automatic amusement device located at an establishment which sells alcoholic liquor for consumption on the premises, if:

(1) The minor is accompanied by a parent or guardian, and

(2) The establishment is a restaurant holding a valid license issued under Section 4-156-305 or subsection (b) of Section 4-156-330.

(Coun. J. 12-9-92, p. 25465; Amend. 1-12-94, p. 44537; 7-2-97, p. 48017)

§4-156-280 Violation—Penalty.

(a) The owner, manager, licensee or person in control of premises where an automatic amusement device is used for illegal gambling shall be subject to a fine of $5,000.00 for each device so used. Any person violating any other provision of this chapter by possession or use of an illegal amusement device shall be fined not less than $500.00 nor more than $1,000.00 for each offense. Every day such violation continues shall constitute a separate and distinct offense. Fines under this section shall be in addition to suspension or revocation of business licenses issued under this code, and in addition to confiscation and destruction of illegal amusement devices.

(b) Upon a third violation of the provisions of this chapter relating to possession or use of an illegal amusement device occurring on the same premises for a period of five years, all city licenses issued for business activity on those premises shall be revoked, and no automatic amusement device may be placed on the premises for a period of one year from the date of revocation. Nothing in this section limits the authority of the mayor to revoke a license on a licensee's first or second violation during such period. For purposes of this subsection (b), "licensee" includes an employee or agent of a licensee.

(Coun. J. 12-9-92, p. 25465; Amend. 4-1-98, p. 65262)

Article III. Public Places of Amusement

§4-156-290 Definition.

As used in this chapter, a public place of amusement means any building or part of a building, park or other grounds used or intended to be used for any amusement as defined in Article I of this chapter.

(Coun. J. 12-9-92, p. 25465; Amend. 11-15-95, p. 11995; 7-2-97, p. 48017)

§4-156-300 License—Required.

(a) Unless specifically exempted in Section 4-156-305, it shall be unlawful for the owner, lessee or manager of any property, or for any other person, to produce, present or conduct thereon, for gain or profit, any amusement unless the owner, lessee or manager of such property has first obtained a public place of amusement license. If an amusement is produced, presented or conducted for gain or profit on any property without a valid public place of amusement license first having been obtained, and unless Section 4-156-305 applies, all of the following persons shall be in violation of this subsection: (1) the owner of the property, (2) the lessee of the property, (3) the manager of the property, (4) the producer of the amusement, (5) the presenter of the amusement and (6) the person conducting the amusement. Each person found in violation of this subsection (a) shall be subject to a fine of up to $10,000.00.

(b) If any part of the property is used or intended for use for any amusement, a public place of amusement license shall be required, regardless of whether the use is incidental to the property's principal use.

(c) If more than one amusement is produced, presented or conducted at any single place or premises as part of a single business, only one public place of amusement license shall be required.

(d) A special class of public place of amusement license shall be required for any public resort which is designed, used or intended to be used primarily for participation by minors in entertainment or amusement primarily involving music, music videos and dancing. Examples of such resorts include, but are not limited to, a dry dance hall, nonalcohol bar, "dry cabaret," "juice bar" or "teenage cabaret." This class of license shall be known as a "juice bar license." No juice bar licensee may operate between the hours of 2:00 a.m. and 11:00 a.m. No premises requiring a juice bar license shall be eligible for a retail liquor license under Chapter 4-60 of this code.

(e) Any person who owns, operates or manages an establishment requiring a juice bar license without first obtaining such license shall be subject to revocation of all city licenses pertaining to that establishment.

(Coun. J. 12-9-92, p. 25465; Amend. 7-13-94, p. 53392; 7-2-97, p. 48017; 5-17-00, p. 32887)

§4-156-305 License—Exceptions.

No public place of amusement license shall be required, if the only amusement to be produced, presented, or conducted is one or more of the following:

(a) A single pool or billiard table regardless of whether players must pay to use the pool or billiard table;

(b) Less than four automatic amusement devices; provided, however, that when calculating the number of automatic amusement devices, jukeboxes shall not be counted. A pool or billiard table shall be included when calculating the number of automatic amusement devices for purposes of this subsection if players must pay to use the pool or billiard table; provided that, in no case shall this subsection create an exemption for establishments which contain more than one pool or billiard table regardless of whether any payment is required;

(c) Music, dancing or other amusement, if: (i) it is offered in a venue with a capacity of less than 100 persons; and (ii) no admission fee, minimum purchase requirement, membership fee or other fee or charge is imposed for the privilege of entering the premises or the portion of premises where the music, dancing or other amusement is provided or permitted;

(d) Live or recorded music and dancing in a banquet hall, restaurant or similar establishment if: (i) the owner of the establishment possesses the necessary retail food establishment license; and (ii) the music and dancing is being presented in connection with an event which is not open or advertised to the general public, including a wedding, graduation, or religious celebration; and (iii) no admission fee, minimum purchase requirement, membership fee or other fee or charge is imposed for the privilege of entering the premises or the portion of premises where the music and dancing is provided or permitted;

(e) Live or recorded readings from books or other publications available for sale within the premises of a retail seller of books or other publications, and the presentation of live or recorded music within the premises of a retail seller of printed or recorded music, if: (i) the owner of the establishment possesses the necessary retail establishment license; (ii) the retail activity conducted on the premises is not the sale of alcoholic liquor; and (iii) no admission fee, minimum purchase requirement, or other fee or charge is imposed for the privilege of entering the premises or the portion of premises where the reading or musical presentation takes place;

(f) Instrumental music by an orchestra of not more than eight pieces in a hotel, restaurant or retail establishment if: (i) no dancing or other entertainment is permitted; and (ii) no admission fee, minimum purchase requirement, membership fee or other fee or charge is imposed for the privilege of entering the premises or the portion of premises where the music is provided or permitted;

(g) Any amusement produced, presented or conducted on the premises owned or leased, for a minimum lease term of one year, by a private club or lodge that is produced, presented or conducted either (1) solely for its members and their guests, or (2) as part of a program to augment the support of the fine or performing arts by a club that has been in continuous existence for more than fifty years. For purposes of this subsection (g), "private club or lodge" means any not-for-profit association that: (i) has been in active and continuous existence for at least three years; and (ii) has a membership role of more than 50 bona fide members who pay membership dues on an annual or other periodic basis. For purposes of this subsection (g) "bona fide members" do not include members who pay membership dues at the time of an amusement produced, presented or conducted by the club or lodge or in conjunction with contacting for production, presentation or conduct of an amusement by the club, as a condition to entering the premises where the amusement is produced, presented or conducted. For the purposes of clause (2) of this subsection (g), a private club's program of supporting the fine or performing arts must include offering residential facilities to performers or artists; offering a venue for practice and performances; and availability of facilities for the discussion, promotion and development of skills and interests in the fine or performing arts. A private club or lodge, at the request of the department of revenue or the department of police, shall make available for inspection records and documents that provide evidence of its not-for-profit status and membership roles;

(h) Paid television programming; or

(i) A health club, racquetball club, tennis club or a similar club or organization when such club or organization is organized and operated on a membership basis and for the recreational purposes of its members and its members' guests.

For purposes of this section, when determining whether a venue has a capacity of more than 100 persons, the total occupancy of all rooms or other occupancy areas of the premises of the business operating the amusement shall be calculated.

(Added. Coun. J. 7-2-97, p. 48017; Amend. 12-15-99, p. 21529; 6-6-01, p. 60078)

§4-156-355 License—Issuance prohibited.

No public place of amusement license shall be issued to:

(1) A person who has been convicted of a felony, within the past 10 years, under any federal or state law;

(2) A person who knowingly files false or incomplete information on an application for a public place of amusement license or any other document required by this Chapter 4-156;

(3) A person whose license, issued by the city of Chicago under any chapter of the Municipal Code of Chicago, has been revoked for cause within the past five years;

(4) A person who at the time of application for renewal of a public place of amusement license would not be eligible for such license upon a first application;

(5) A corporation, partnership, limited partnership, or limited liability company, if any of the officers, substantial owners, members or other individuals required to be identified in the initial license application by Section 4-156-310(a) would not be eligible to receive a license hereunder;

(6) A corporation unless it is incorporated in Illinois, or unless it is a foreign corporation which is qualified under the "Business Corporation Act of 1983" to transact business in Illinois; provided that the corporation is not dissolved and is in good standing under the laws of the state of Illinois;

(7) A person who is not a beneficial owner of the business for which a license is sought; or

(8) A person whose place of business is conducted by a manager or agent unless the person demonstrates that the manager or agent possesses the qualifications required to obtain a license hereunder.

(9) A person whose public place of amusement license has not undergone and passed a building inspection as required by Section 13-20-020 of this code within 90 days preceding the date of submission of an annual renewal license application.

(Added. Coun. J. 7-2-97, p. 48017; Amend. Coun. J. 10-1-03, p. 9163)

§4-156-390 Ticket sales.

It is unlawful for any licensee to sell, or permit any person to sell, any ticket of admission to the licensed premises unless it has conspicuously printed upon its face the price of admission.

(Coun. J. 12-9-92, p. 25465; Amend. 7-2-97, p. 48017)

§4-156-410 Motion picture theaters—Billboard contents.

It shall be the duty of the licensee of any motion picture theater to exhibit on a billboard, placed in front of the building or other structure in which such show is given and such motion pictures are exhibited, the title to the pictures, which title shall either be full enough to describe in general terms the nature and character of the picture or pictures to be shown, or shall be accompanied by other explanatory wording, pictures or other advertising matter so as to describe the said picture or pictures.

No such licensee shall place, maintain, or allow to be placed or maintained, in front of or in connection with any such place, any sign, picture or other announcement which in any manner misstates or misrepresents the picture or other amusements which are being shown in said place, or which announces a picture or other form of amusement or entertainment which is not, at the time such announcement is displayed, being shown and exhibited in said place.

(Coun. J. 12-9-92, p. 25465; Amend. 7-2-97, p. 48017)

§4-156-420 Billiard rooms and poolrooms.

It is unlawful for any person who has not reached the age of 18 years, unless accompanied by a parent or guardian, to play billiards or to be permitted to remain in a billiard room for any purpose, or to play any coin-operated pool table; and it is unlawful for any person to represent himself to have reached the age of 18 years in order to obtain admission to such billiard room or to be permitted to remain therein, or to play any coin-operated pool table, when such person is in fact under 18 years of age.

No person shall operate any billiard or poolroom between the hours of 2:00 a.m. and 7:00 a.m. or harbor or permit any person to be or remain in any such room between such hours. This section, however, shall not be construed to prevent regular employees from performing necessary work within the premises during such prohibited hours of operation. Nor shall this section prohibit a licensed billiard or poolroom which is also a duly licensed liquor establishment from operating during the hours established by the liquor license; provided, however, that no game of billiards or pool shall be allowed to commence later than 30 minutes before the end of liquor service as allowed by the license. The licensee of the billiard or poolroom shall post a sign, visible in the area of the billiard or pool table, indicating the latest time for commencing a game of pool or billiards.

No person conducting or operating any billiard or poolroom shall allow or permit any screens, curtains, blinds, partitions or other obstructions to be placed between the front windows and back or rear wall of such room, but an unobstructed view of the entire interior must be maintained at all times. This provision, however, shall not be construed to preclude the maintenance of washrooms or toilet rooms, or the maintenance of closets for storing purposes exclusively.

(Coun. J. 12-9-92, p. 25465; Amend. 7-2-97, p. 48017; 9-29-99, p. 12261)

§4-156-424 Beer gardens.

At no time may any live or recorded music be played or performed on the outdoor premises of a public place of amusement licensed as a beer garden. This prohibition shall not apply to a beer garden operated in conjunction with a consumption on the premises—incidental activity license issued under Chapter

4-60, at a museum located at the Field Museum of Natural History, the Shedd Aquarium, the Adler Planetarium or the Art Institute of Chicago.
(Added. Coun. J. 7-2-97, p. 48017; 6-27-01, p. 62917)

§4-156-430 Athletic contests at night and on weekday afternoons—Restrictions.

(A) It shall be unlawful for any licensee or other person, firm, corporation or other legal entity to produce or present, or permit any other person, firm, corporation or other legal entity to produce or present, any athletic contest, sport, game, including any baseball game, or any other amusement as defined in Article I of this chapter, if any part of such athletic contest, sport, game, including any baseball game, or any other amusement as defined in Article I of this chapter (also known in this section and in this ordinance as ("event(s)") takes place between the hours of 8:00 p.m. and 8:00 a.m., or is scheduled to begin between the hours of 2:01 p.m. and 4:09 p.m. on weekdays (except for Memorial Day, Independence Day or Labor Day), and is presented in the open air portion of any stadium or playing field which is not totally enclosed and contains more than 15,000 seats where any such seats are located within 500 feet of 100 or more dwelling units. The 500-foot distance shall be measured from the seat to the nearest point of the buildings in which the dwelling units are contained. For purposes of this section, "dwelling unit" shall mean a room designed or used for sleeping accommodations, including hotel and dormitory rooms.

(B) The provisions of subsection (A) do not apply, in whole or in part, to any of the following:

(1) All-Star, playoff, post-season or playoff determinative, regular season tie-breaker, divisional or conference championship series, league championship series, World Series, or similar baseball games;

(2) Up to 18 regular season home baseball games of any team in each year, as designated by that team, which games are scheduled to begin at or prior to 7:05 p.m., or scheduled to begin no later than 8:00 p.m. if required by a national television contract;

(3) Any baseball game scheduled to begin at or prior to 2:01 p.m. or in the case of a double-header where the second game is scheduled to begin reasonably promptly after the end of the first game;

(4) Up to 13 non-double-header baseball games scheduled to start on a Friday afternoon between 2:01 p.m. and 4:10 p.m. in calendar year 2004 and up to 4 non-double-header baseball games scheduled to start on a Friday afternoon between 2:01 p.m. and 4:10 p.m. in calendar year 2005, provided, however, that after calendar year 2005, no non-double-header baseball game shall be scheduled to begin on a Friday after 2:00 p.m.;

(5) During the duration of any contract between the city and any person, firm, corporation, legal entity, or professional sports team that is authorized by the city council of the city of Chicago, any games, contests, sports, amusements, or any other events that may be held according to the terms of that contract; and

(6) Any non-major league baseball games or any baseball-related events, or any non-profit event expected to have less than approximately 10,000 in attendance;

(C) The provisions of subsection (A) do not apply to the following regular season home baseball games of any team, as designated by that team, which games are scheduled to begin at, or prior to, 7:05 p.m., or scheduled to begin no later than 8:00 p.m. if required by a national television contract:

(1) Up to four regular season home baseball games in 2004 in addition to the regular season home baseball games allowed in subsection (B)(2);

(2) Up to eight regular season home baseball games in 2005 in addition to the regular season home baseball games allowed in subsection (B)(2);

(3) Up to 12 regular season home baseball games in years 2006 through 2015 inclusive in addition to the regular season home baseball games allowed in subsection (B)(2), provided however, that upon notice (which shall be given on or prior to November 1, 2005) up to two games during the 2006 season only may be delayed by up to one year to review compliance with the obligations of any person, firm, corporation, legal entity, or professional sports team that enters into a contract or agreement with the city of Chicago concerning neighborhood protections around a facility covered by this section; and

(4) Up to 12 regular season home games after year 2015 so long as any contract or agreement between the city of Chicago and any person, firm, corporation, team, or legal entity whose stadium or playing field is subject to this section concerning neighborhood protections for an area adjacent or near or around a facility covered by this section is in effect.

(D) Subject to subsections (B)(1), (B)(5), and (B)(6), no regular season game may be scheduled to begin after 4:10 p.m. on a Friday or a Saturday, except up to two regular season games per year may be scheduled on a Saturday after 4:10 p.m. if required by:

(1) Major League Baseball in a manner generally applicable to all major league baseball teams, or

(2) National television contract, or

(3) Other circumstance beyond the control of any person, firm, corporation, team, or legal entity whose stadium or playing field is subject to this section, such as by a collective bargaining agreement.

(E) Games scheduled to begin at or prior to 8:00 p.m. may begin upon the conclusion of weather delays or delays caused by other similar unexpected natural occurrences or by death or serious personal injury to a fan or a player or management employee of any person, firm, corporation, team, or legal entity whose stadium or playing field is subject to this section, all beyond the control any person, firm, corporation, team, or legal entity whose stadium or playing field is subject to this section, without restriction as to time except those dealing with public safety.

(F) Baseball games and other permissible events scheduled to begin at or prior to 8:00 p.m., as permitted by this section, once commenced, may be concluded without restriction as to time except those dealing with public safety.

(G) The terms of this section may be enforced by the corporation counsel of the city of Chicago through injunction or any other suit, action or proceeding at law or in equity.

(Coun. J. 12-9-92, p. 25465 Amend. 7-2-97, p. 48017; 2-11-04, p. 18722)

§4-156-435 Unregulated exhibition where intent is to harm a contestant—Prohibited—Enforcement.

It shall be unlawful for any licensee to conduct or permit any person to conduct any exhibition where the intent or outcome of the exhibition or match is to injure or harm one of the contestants and the exhibition is unregulated by the state of Illinois. The terms of the section may be enforced by the corporation counsel through injunction or any other suit, action or proceeding at law or in equity.
(Added. Coun. J. 3-26-96, p. 19269; Amend. 7-2-97, p. 48017)

§4-156-450 Gambling.

It is unlawful for any licensee to conduct or permit any person to conduct any raffle, lottery or chance distribution of money, or article of value, or any gift enterprise or any form of gambling upon the licensed premises.
(Coun. J. 12-9-92, p. 25465; Amend. 7-2-97, p. 48017)

§4-156-460 Drinking water.

The licensee of every public place of amusement shall provide sufficient drinking water at each fountain required to be installed by this code.
(Coun. J. 12-9-92, p. 25465; Amend. 7-2-97, p. 48017)

§4-156-484 Special event allowance.

An establishment may host up to six special events in a 12-month period before a public place of amusement license is required. The event organizers must be a recognized not-for-profit corporation and must obtain all necessary food, liquor and special event licenses from the department of revenue. The establishment must have passed an inspection from the department of buildings and the bureau of fire prevention. Private events where no admission fee, minimum purchase requirement, membership fee or other fee or charge is imposed for the privilege of entering the premises or the portion of premises where the event is held and that are not advertised to the public shall not constitute a special event for purposes of this section.
(Added. Coun. J. 7-2-97, p. 48017)

§4-156-485 License restrictions.

No public place of amusement license shall be granted to any establishment required to be licensed in accordance with Title 4, Division V of the Municipal Code (excluding Chapter 4-128), or in accordance with Chapter 4-228 of the Municipal Code, or to any establishment at which motor vehicles are washed, if the public place of amusement will be conducted in the same area in which the other activity licensed in accordance with the provisions of Title 4, as provided herein, is conducted.
(Added. Coun. J. 6-14-95, p. 3098)

§4-156-510 Club violation—Penalty.

Any person violating any of the provisions of this chapter for which no other penalty is specified shall be fined not less than $200.00 nor more than $500.00 for each offense. Every day such violation shall continue shall be regarded as a separate and distinct offense.
(Coun. J. 12-9-92, p. 25465; Amend. 7-2-97, p. 48017; 4-1-98, p. 65262)

§4-156-520 Construction of chapter.

Nothing in this chapter shall be construed to impose a tax upon any person, business or activity which, under the constitutions of the United States or the state of Illinois, may not be made the subject of taxation by the city.
(Added. Coun. J. 11-15-95, p. 11995)

CHAPTER 4-168
BICYCLE MESSENGER SERVICES
(Selected Sections)

Sections:

4-168-010 Definitions.
4-168-020 License—Required.
4-168-070 Helmet and visible identification—Required.
4-168-090 License—Suspension or revocation.
4-168-110 Rules and regulations—Enforcement authority.
4-168-120 Violation—Penalty.

§4-168-010 Definitions.

For the purposes of this chapter, unless the context clearly requires otherwise:

"Central business area" means the area bounded by a line as follows: beginning at the easternmost point of Division Street extended to Lake Michigan; then west on Division Street to LaSalle Street; then south on LaSalle Street to Chicago Avenue; then west on Chicago Avenue to Halstead Street; then south on Halsted Street to Roosevelt Road; then east on Roosevelt Road to its easternmost point extended to Lake Michigan.

"Bicycle messenger services" means the delivery by bicycle for hire of packages, parcels, food, papers or any other items on behalf of any commercial, industrial, governmental, charitable or other enterprise.

"Bicycle" includes any vehicle defined in Section 9-120-010 and any other vehicle that would be included within such definition but for the size of the vehicle's wheels.

"Bicycle operator" means a person who makes deliveries by bicycle on behalf of a bicycle messenger service.

"Person" includes any natural person, corporation, firm, partnership, joint venture, association or other entity.

"Commissioner" means the commissioner of consumer services.
(Added. Coun. J. 7-29-92, p. 20042; Amend. 12-9-92, p. 25465)

§4-168-020 License—Required.

(a) No person shall engage in the occupation of providing bicycle messenger services within the central business area without having secured a license issued under this chapter. The license shall be in addition to any other license required by law.

(b) This section shall not apply to a person who provides bicycle messenger services exclusively for himself or herself, or for his or her employer. This section shall, however, apply to a person who provides bicycle messenger services as an independent contractor for any person other than pursuant to a contract with a person with a license issued under this chapter.
(Added. Coun. J. 7-29-92, p. 20042; Amend. 12-9-92, p. 25465)

§4-168-070 Helmet and visible identification— Required.

(a) Every licensee shall supply each bicycle operator operating on the licensee's behalf: (1) a safety helmet meeting nationally recognized safety requirements; and (2) a safety vest or other garment of a bright color, prominently displaying the name of the licensee in letters at least one and one-half inches high, and a number or letters or a combination thereof at least four inches high which, in conjunction with the displayed name of the licensee, will form a unique combination permitting identification of the bicycle operator. All letters and numbers shall be of a color contrasting with the background of the garment. The identification number or letters required by this paragraph shall also appear on the bicycle in accordance with rules and regulations promulgated by the commissioner.

(b) The operation of a bicycle in the central business area on behalf of any licensee without the equipment required by this section is a violation of this section and shall create a rebuttable presumption that the licensee has violated this section.

(Added. Coun. J. 7-29-92, p. 20042; Coun. J. 12-9-92, p. 25465)

§4-168-090 License—Suspension or revocation.

(a) If any licensee violates any provision of this chapter or any rule or regulation promulgated hereunder, the commissioner may seek revocation or suspension of the licensee's license and/or the imposition of a fine up to $500.00 on the licensee, in accordance with the procedures described in this section.

(b) Before any suspension or fine is imposed, the licensee shall be notified by: (i) first class or express mail, or overnight carrier; or (ii) personal service, of the specific charges against him and of his right to a hearing. The licensee may request such a hearing in writing not more than 10 days after receiving notification of the charges.

(i) Prior to the exercise of exclusive jurisdiction by the department of administrative hearings in accordance with Section 2-14-190(c) of this code, the hearing may be conducted by the commissioner of his designee. If, after the hearing, the commissioner determines that a violation has occurred, the commissioner shall enter an order suspending the license and/or imposing a fine. An order by the commissioner imposing a suspension and/or fine may be appealed by the licensee to the mayor's license commission.

(ii) After the exercise of exclusive jurisdiction by the department of administrative hearings in accordance with Section 2-14-190(c) of this code, upon receipt of a request for a hearing, the commissioner shall institute an action with the department of administrative hearings which shall appoint an administrative law officer who shall conduct the hearing. If after the hearing, the administrative law officer determines that a violation has occurred, the administrative law officer shall enter an order suspending the license and/or imposing a fine.

(iii) Notwithstanding the exercise of exclusive jurisdiction by the department of administrative hearings, if no timely request is made for a hearing and the commissioner determines that a violation has occurred, the commissioner may enter an order suspending the license and/or imposing a fine.

(c) Hearings held under this section shall be conducted in substantially the same manner as those which are conducted pursuant to Chapters 9-104 and

9-112 of this code. Any person whose license is revoked under this chapter shall be ineligible to receive another license under this chapter for a one-year period following revocation.

(d) The commissioner may file a petition with the mayor's license commission to seek revocation of a license. Following a hearing conducted in accordance with its rules, the commission shall determine whether revocation is warranted or a lesser penalty, if any, shall be imposed.

(Added. Coun. J. 7-29-92, p. 20042; Amend. 12-9-92, p. 25465; 7-10-96, p. 24982; 11-12-97, p. 56813; 4-29-98, p. 66564)

§4-168-110 Rules and regulations— Enforcement authority.

The commissioner and the director of revenue shall have the authority to administer and enforce this chapter. The department of police shall have the authority to enforce the safety-related provisions of this chapter and all traffic laws, ordinances, rules and regulations as they apply to bicycle messenger operators.

(Added. Coun. J. 7-29-92, p. 20042; Amend. 12-9-92, p. 25465)

§4-168-120 Violation—Penalty.

Any person who is found guilty of violating this chapter shall be subject to a fine of not less than $25.00 and not more than $500.00 for each such violation. However, any person found guilty of violating this chapter by engaging in the occupation of providing bicycle messenger services in the central business area without a license required by this chapter shall be subject to a minimum fine of $100.00. Each day that any violation shall continue shall be deemed a separate and distinct offense. A second or subsequent intentional violation of this chapter committed within 12 months after a previous conviction under this chapter may be punished as a misdemeanor by a fine of up to $500.00, or a period of incarceration not exceeding seven days, or community service, or any combination thereof, pursuant to Section 1-2-1.1 of the Illinois Municipal Code.

(Added. Coun. J. 7-29-92, p. 20042; Amend. 12-9-92, p. 25465)

CHAPTER 4-208
HOTELS
(Selected Sections)

Sections:

4-208-020 License—Required.
4-208-030 License—Application—Investigation.
4-208-040 License—Fee.
4-208-075 Rates for sleeping accommodations.
4-208-080 Public disorder—Maintenance unlawful.
4-208-090 Public disorder—Licensee's responsibility.
4-208-100 Police investigations.
4-208-110 License suspension or revocation conditions.
4-208-120 Additional penalties.

§4-208-020 License—Required.

No person or entity shall operate a hotel as defined in this code without a license.

(Added. Coun. J. 12-9-92, p. 25465; Amend. Coun. J. 4-16-97, p. 42588)

§4-208-030 License—Application—Investigation.

An application for license shall be made in conformity with the general requirements of this code relating to applications for license. The superintendent of police shall cause an investigation to be made to ascertain that the applicant has complied with all laws and ordinances applicable to said business, and whether the applicant is of good character and repute.

(Added. Coun. J. 12-9-92, p. 25465; Amend. Coun. J. 4-16-97, p. 42588)

§4-208-040 License—Fee.

The annual fee for a hotel license shall be as set forth in Section 4-5-010.

(Added. Coun. J. 12-9-92, p. 25465; Amend. Coun. J. 4-16-97, p. 42588)

§4-208-075 Rates for sleeping accommodations.

No hotel licensed under this chapter or required to be licensed under this chapter shall (i) rent any sleeping room by the hour or for any period of fewer than 10 consecutive hours; or (ii) rent any sleeping room more than once within any consecutive 10-hour period measured from the commencement of one rental to the commence of the next; or (iii) advertise an hourly rate or any other rate for a sleeping room based on a rental period of fewer than 10 consecutive hours; provided, however, that subsections (i) and (ii) shall not apply to any hotel that is located within the central area as defined in Section 10-32-220(1) of this code, or that is located within three miles of property used for airport purposes at the Chicago O'Hare International Airport, or that is within the McCormick Place Complex.

A violation of this section shall be punishable by a fine of not less than $250.00, nor more than $500.00, for each offense. Each day that a violation continues shall constitute a separate and distinct offense.

(Added. Coun. J. 10-2-02, p. 94580; Amend. Coun. J. 1-16-03, p. 102117)

§4-208-080 Public disorder—Maintenance unlawful.

A licensee shall be guilty of maintaining a public disorder when the licensee or any of the licensee's employees knowingly permit prostitution, pimping, gambling or the unlawful sale of narcotic or controlled substances to be conducted upon the premises or immediately adjacent to the premises by any person or persons getting a room or rooms from said licensee.

A licensee shall be held to be guilty of maintaining a public disorder when the licensee or any employee of the licensee, through the exercise of ordinary care and diligence under such circumstances that a reasonable man would infer that prostitution, pimping, gambling or unlawful sale of narcotic or controlled substances is being conducted upon the premises or immediately adjacent to the premises by any person or persons letting a room or rooms from said licensee, fails to discover said fact.

However, no licensee shall be punished for maintaining a public disorder if said licensee notifies the police that he suspects that the aforesaid conduct is occurring on his premises and/or terminates the letting of the room or rooms immediately upon learning that the aforesaid conduct is occurring upon or adjacent to his premises by said person or persons. No employee of the licensee shall be punished for maintaining a public disorder if said employee makes the notification required herein or notifies the licensee of the existence of the pro-

hibited conduct for the licensee's action immediately upon the employee learning that said conduct is occurring on or immediately adjacent to the premises.
(Added. Coun. J. 12-9-92, p. 25465)

§4-208-090 Public disorder—Licensee's responsibility.

The licensee, its officers and directors, if it is a corporation, the licensee's partners and the principal manager shall be deemed to be responsible for the maintaining of a public disorder by any employee of the licensee whenever any employee is convicted of a municipal or state violation involving prostitution, pimping, keeper of disorderly house, gambling, or unlawful sale or possession of narcotic or controlled substances, which conviction arises from acts which occurred upon the licensed premises. The presumption of responsibility is a rebuttable presumption that the class of persons described herein knew of and permitted the aforesaid named unlawful activities to occur on the licensed premises.
(Added. Coun. J. 12-9-92, p. 25465)

§4-208-100 Police investigations.

Whenever the police are called or have occasion to be on the licensed premises for the purpose of making a police report relative to criminal conduct or an arrest, the superintendent of police shall cause to be conducted an investigation as to whether the "maintaining of a public disorder" is occurring as defined herein and prepare a written report of the investigation and his findings and recommendation. The report shall be transmitted within 48 hours to the corporation counsel and to the mayor's license commission director for further actions as warranted. Reports made pursuant to this section shall be available for examination by any alderman or city council committee upon written request made upon the corporation counsel.
(Added. Coun. J. 12-9-92, p. 25465)

§4-208-110 License suspension or revocation conditions.

(a) The violation of Sections 4-208-020, 4-208-040, 4-208-080 and 4-208-090 by any licensee shall be grounds for revocation or suspension of that licensee's hotel license pursuant to the procedures under general licensing provisions of this code.

(b) When any license issued pursuant to this chapter is revoked for any cause, no license shall be granted to any person for the operation of a hotel at the premises described in the revoked license for a period of one year from the date of revocation; provided that this subsection (b) shall not apply to a hotel that is located within the central business district as defined in Section 9-4-010 of this code, or that is located within three miles of property used for airport purposes at the Chicago O'Hare International Airport.
(Added. Coun. J. 12-9-92, p. 25465; Amend. Coun. J. 9-15-93, p. 38404; 4-16-97, p. 42588)

§4-208-120 Additional penalties.

Notwithstanding the penalties provided by Section 4-208-060 of this chapter, violation of Sections 4-208-020, 4-208-040, 4-208-080 and 4-208-090 shall be punishable by a fine of not less than $250.00 nor more than $500.00 for each

separate violation. If any person is convicted a third time for violation of Section 4-208-080 or 4-208-090, said person shall be subject to imprisonment of not less than 30 days nor more than six months and a fine of $500.00.
(Added. Coun. J. 12-9-92, p. 25465; Amend. Coun. J. 4-16-97, p. 42588)

CHAPTER 4-209
SINGLE-ROOM OCCUPANCY BUILDINGS
(Complete Chapter)

Sections:

4-209-010 Single-room occupancy buildings—License required.
4-209-020 Single-room occupancy buildings—Inspection—Fees.
4-209-030 Single-room occupancy building—Identification.
4-209-040 Penalties for violations.

§4-209-010 Single-room occupancy buildings—License required.

Any person or entity operating a single-room occupancy building, as defined in Section 13-4-010, must obtain a single-room occupancy building license on an annual basis. If a single-room occupancy building shall maintain 100 percent of the units for permanent residents then it shall apply for a Class I license. If an S.R.O. building shall dedicate one or more of its units for transient occupancy, it shall apply for a Class II license. A Class II license is restricted to maintaining transient units only on the first floor of a two story building; only on the first or second floor of a building containing three or four floors, and only the first two floors of a building containing five or more floors. Transient occupancy shall be defined as an occupancy of a sleeping facility on a daily or nightly basis, or part thereof. Every person operating a single-room occupancy building shall maintain written records identifying the name(s) of the occupant of each unit, and the date(s) of tenancy for each occupant residing within the building. Such records shall be maintained on an annual basis and shall be open at all times for examination by the building commissioner and commissioner of health or their designees.
(Added. Coun. J. 5-4-94, p. 49750)

§4-209-020 Single-room occupancy buildings—Inspection—Fees.

Every building operated and maintained, in whole or in part, as a Class I single-room occupancy building, as defined in Section 13-4-010, shall be inspected annually by the building commissioner or his designee. Every building operated and maintained, in whole or in part, as a Class II single-room occupancy, as defined in Section 13-4-010, shall be inspected annually by both the building commissioner and the commissioner of health or their designees. With regard to inspections of Class II single-room occupancy buildings, it shall be the responsibility of the commissioner of health or his designee to inspect only those units maintained for transient guests. No single-room occupancy license shall be issued unless the building commissioner and commissioner of health or their designees have conducted such annual inspections and determined that the premises comply with all building, fire prevention and sanitary provisions of this code. It shall be the duty of every person or entity operating a single-room occupancy to pay to the department of revenue an annual inspection fee of $100.00 plus $1.00 for each unit used for the accommodation of transient

guests. Such annual inspection fee shall be assessed under the authority of the department of buildings and may be billed prior or subsequent to the actual inspections conducted by the department of buildings and department of health and shall be payable to the department of revenue within 30 days of receipt of the notice of inspection fee from the department of buildings. Except as otherwise provided in Section 13-20-016, the inspection fee for single-room occupancy buildings shall be assessed only once within a 12-month license period.
(Added. Coun. J. 5-4-94, p. 49750)

§4-209-030 Single-room occupancy building—Identification.

Any person or entity operating a single-room occupancy as defined in Section 13-4-010 and licensed pursuant to this chapter may utilize the word "Hotel" as part of its business name or identification. However, such name or identification shall also include the words "Single-Room Occupancy" or the abbreviation "SRO."
(Added. Coun. J. 5-4-94, p. 49750)

§4-209-040 Penalties for violations.

Any person violating, neglecting or failing to comply with any provisions of this chapter shall be fined not less than $25.00 nor more than $200.00 for each offense. Any person or entity who maintains transient units in violation of Section 4-209-010 which require that transient occupancy be maintained only on the lower floors of a single-room occupancy building shall be grounds for revocation and suspension of that licensee's single-room occupancy license pursuant to the procedures under the general licensing provisions of this code.
(Added. Coun. J. 5-4-94, p. 49750)

CHAPTER 4-212
ITINERANT MERCHANTS
(Complete Chapter)

Sections:

4-212-010 Definitions.
4-212-020 License—Required.
4-212-030 License—Application—Investigation.
4-212-040 License—Fee.
4-212-050 Police reports.
4-212-060 Violation—Penalty.

§4-212-010 Definitions.

"Itinerant merchant," as used in this chapter, means a person who conducts a merchandising or service business in the city but who does not own or rent a store, loft, warehouse, yard office space, or showroom by the year or hold a year's lease on the same. If he delivers the merchandise or service he sells through a duly accredited resident agent who complies with the license requirements of this city applying to his line, he shall then not be classed as an itinerant, the yearly license of the resident agent through whom he sells entitling him to this privilege.

"Organized or sponsored trade show or exhibition," as used in this chapter, means an exposition of limited duration of services or of merchandise, including artworks, arranged through an organization or entity which is primarily responsible for obtaining the space and subsidiary services participant vendors or exhibitors may require for the event. The word "sponsor" means any organization or entity which organizes or sponsors a trade show or exhibition and which is primarily responsible for arranging to obtain the space and subsidiary services which participating vendors or exhibitors may require for such events.

Licensed itinerant merchants who conduct their business at an organized or sponsored trade show or exhibition shall be allowed to give away free samples of food provided that the food is of a nonpotentially hazardous nature as defined in Chapter 4-8, and provided that the processor or manufacturer of the food is approved by the city of Chicago department of health or, if applicable, the appropriate state, county or local health department. In addition, food sampling shall be allowed for up to only four hours per day for no more than three consecutive days.
(Coun. J. 12-9-92, p. 25465)

§4-212-020 License—Required.

No person shall act as an itinerant merchant without first obtaining a license so to do. There shall be two classes of itinerant merchant license. A sponsor shall apply for a Class I license on behalf of each itinerant merchant who is a participant in an organized or sponsored trade show or exhibition. All other itinerant merchants shall apply individually for a Class II license. No organized or sponsored trade show or exhibition shall be permitted to take place unless the sponsor shall have obtained a license for the participating itinerant merchants.
(Coun. J. 12-9-92, p. 25465)

§4-212-030 License—Application—Investigation.

An application for any itinerant merchant license shall be made to the director of revenue on forms provided by him, in conformity with the general requirements of this code relating to applications for licenses. Any sponsor that applies for any Class I license on behalf of itinerant merchant participants in the sponsor's show or exhibition shall provide the director of revenue as to each itinerant merchant his full legal name, street address, the city and state of his principal place of business, his Illinois Retailer's Occupation Tax License number, the firm or firms which the merchant represents, the kinds of merchandise or services he desires to sell under the Class I license, the location, times and dates of the show or exhibition, and shall further provide such identifying information as to itself which the director of revenue may require. Any applicant for a Class II license shall provide the street address, city and state whence he came, his Illinois Retailer's Occupation Tax license number, the firm or firms which the applicant represents, the kinds of merchandise or commodities which he desires to sell under the itinerant merchant's license, and the place where the applicant proposes to sell such merchandise or commodities.

The director of revenue shall investigate to ascertain whether any itinerant merchant is a proper representative of a reliable and responsible business house, and whether the proposed sale of merchandise or commodities complies with other provisions of this code. If the director finds that an applicant or licensee shall have misrepresented his affiliation or authority to represent any business house, or that the itinerant merchant or the business house he repre-

sents has admitted committing deceptive business practices or has been convicted of or pled nolo contendere to charges of deceptive business practices in any jurisdiction or has failed to remit taxes or fees owed to the city, or that the itinerant merchant has failed to comply with any other provisions of this code with respect to the sale of merchandise or services, the director shall withhold or revoke the license, and in the case of a revocation, the director may summarily revoke the license so long as he provides the merchant with an opportunity for a hearing within 24 hours after the revocation.
(Coun. J. 12-9-92, p. 25465)

§4-212-040 License—Fee.

The fee for a Class I or Class II license shall be as set forth in Section 4-5-010.
(Coun. J. 12-9-92, p. 25465)

§4-212-050 Police reports.

The owner, proprietor or manager of any hotel, roominghouse, lodginghouse or store shall report to the director of revenue the name of any person who shall rent a room or other space for the sale and display of merchandise of an itinerant merchant, giving the location of the room so rented within six hours after renting.
(Coun. J. 12-9-92, p. 25465)

§4-212-060 Violation—Penalty.

Any person violating any of the provisions of this chapter, where no specific penalty is provided, shall be fined not less than $200.00 nor more than $500.00 for each offense. Every day such violations continues shall constitute a separate and distinct offense.
(Coun. J. 12-9-92, p. 25465)

CHAPTER 4-216
JUNK DEALERS AND PEDDLERS
(Selected Sections)

Sections:

4-216-010 Definitions.
4-216-020 License—Required.
4-216-050 Identification of vehicles and personnel.
4-216-070 Prohibited activities.
4-216-080 Purchases from minors and intoxicated persons restricted.
4-216-090 Fences.
4-216-100 Hours of business.
4-216-110 Exhibiting lost or stolen goods upon demand.
4-216-120 Inspection by police department.
4-216-130 Proper disposal of junk.
4-216-160 Violation—Penalty.

§4-216-010 Definitions.

For purposes of this chapter:

"Fence" means and includes any place for the purchase, reception or keeping of stolen goods.

"Junk" means and includes old iron, chain, brass, copper, tin, lead or other base metals, old rope, old bags, rags, wastepaper, paper clippings, scraps of woolens, clips, bagging, rubber and glass, and empty bottles of different kinds and sizes when the number of each kind or size is less than one gross, and all articles and things discarded or no longer used as a manufactured article composed of, or consisting of, any one or more of the materials or articles herein mentioned.

Junk includes items and materials stored for resale with no more processing than sorting, crushing or separation from other items and materials.

"Junk peddler" means every person who uses a junk vehicle as defined herein and travels from place to place within the city for the purpose of collecting, transporting or disposing of junk, or makes a business of purchasing junk from anyone who desires to sell it and carries it away upon purchasing it.

"Junk vehicle" means every truck, automobile, or other motorized vehicle used in the collection, disposition or transportation of junk from one place to another.

The term "junk peddler" shall not include any person issued a permit to operate a recycling facility under Article XVII of Chapter 11-4 of this code or agent of such person, or any person issued a permit to operate a junk facility under Article XVI of Chapter 11-4 of this code or any agent of such person.
(Coun. J. 12-9-92, p. 25465; Amend. 10-7-98, p. 78812)

§4-216-020 License—Required.

No person shall operate as a junk peddler in the city of Chicago without having obtained a junk peddler's license from the department of revenue. Each license shall be renewed annually in accordance with Chapter 4-4 of this code.
(Coun. J. 12-9-92, p. 25465; Amend. 10-7-98, p. 78812)

§4-216-050 Identification of vehicles and personnel.

(a) The department of revenue shall issue to each licensee an identification card that states the junk peddler's name, address, telephone number, state driver's license number and city of Chicago junk peddler license number, and the vehicle license plate number, city of Chicago wheel tax license number and insurance policy number for every junk vehicle used by the licensee. The identification card shall be carried by the licensee at all times when engaged in the activities of a junk peddler.

(b) Every junk vehicle used for the collection, transportation or disposal of any junk, shall display on each side of the vehicle in letters not less than two inches in height, in contrasting color, the name and city of Chicago junk peddler license number of the junk peddler.

(c) The driver and/or operator(s) of each junk vehicle shall wear a reflective safety vest or other reflective clothing.
(Coun. J. 12-9-92, p. 25465; Amend. 10-7-98, p. 78812)

§4-216-070 Prohibited activities.

(a) No junk peddler shall receive any article or thing by way of pledge or pawn; nor shall such peddler loan or advance any sum of money on the security of any article or thing.

(b) No junk peddler shall receive or hold a license to conduct the business of a pawnbroker, secondhand dealer or itinerant dealer in secondhand clothing.

(c) No junk peddler shall park any junk vehicle on any residential or business street in violation of Section 9-64-170 of this code.

(d) No junk peddler shall use any junk vehicle in violation of the vehicle size, load and weight restrictions as provided for in Chapter 9-72 of this code.
(Coun. J. 12-9-92, p. 25465; Amend. 10-7-98, p. 78812)

§4-216-080 Purchases from minors and intoxicated persons restricted.

No junk peddler shall purchase any article whatsoever from any minor without the written consent of the minor's parent or guardian. No junk peddler shall purchase any article from any person who appears intoxicated or under the influence of any drug.
(Coun. J. 12-9-92, p. 25465; Amend. 10-7-98, p. 78812)

§4-216-090 Fences.

No person shall keep, maintain or conduct a place for the purchase, reception or keeping of stolen goods as a "fence."
(Coun. J. 12-9-92, p. 25465; Amend. 10-7-98, p. 78812)

§4-216-100 Hours of business.

No junk peddler shall receive, in the conduct of his business, any goods, articles or thing whatsoever from any person except between the hours of 7:00 a.m. and 9:00 p.m., nor shall he sell, purchase or collect any junk in any public alley between the hours of 9:00 p.m. and 7:00 a.m. except as permitted in Section 8-4-240 of this code.
(Coun. J. 12-9-92, p. 25465; Amend. 10-7-98, p. 78812)

§4-216-110 Exhibiting lost or stolen goods upon demand.

Every junk peddler who shall receive or be in possession of any goods, articles, things or junk which may have been lost or stolen, or are alleged or supposed to have been lost or stolen, shall forthwith on demand exhibit the same to any member of the department of police or to any alderman.
(Coun. J. 12-9-92, p. 25465; Amend. 10-7-98, p. 78812)

§4-216-120 Inspection by police department.

The places of business, junk vehicles and junk of every junk peddler shall, at all reasonable times, be open to the inspection of any member of the police department.
(Coun. J. 12-9-92, p. 25465; Amend. 10-7-98, p. 78812)

§4-216-130 Proper disposal of junk.

Every junk peddler who disposes of junk in the city shall lawfully do so by hauling or otherwise bringing the junk to a junk facility, recycling facility, transfer station, landfill or other solid waste disposal facility which has been issued a permit by the city in accordance with Chapter 11-4 of this code. Proof of proper disposal, in the form of records and receipts, shall be maintained by the junk peddler.
(Added. Coun. J. 10-7-98, p. 77812)

§4-216-160 Violation—Penalty.

Any person who violates any of the provisions of this chapter, or any rule or regulation promulgated hereunder, or interferes with the performance of the director of revenue in enforcement of this chapter or the rules and regulations, shall upon conviction be guilty of a misdemeanor and shall be fined not less than $100.00 and not more than $500.00 for each offense. Subsequent offenses within a period of 180 days shall be punishable by incarceration for not less than seven days and not more than 180 days. All prosecutions shall be conducted under the procedure set forth in Section 1-2-1.1 of the Illinois Municipal Code, as amended. Every day on which such violation continues shall be regarded as constituting a separate offense.
(Coun. J. 12-9-92, p. 25465; Amend. 10-7-98, p. 78812)

CHAPTER 4-220
LAUNDRIES AND LAUNDRY VEHICLES
(Selected Sections)

Sections:

Article I. Laundries

4-220-010 Laundry defined.
4-220-020 License—Required.
4-220-055 Laundry identification on vehicle.
4-220-130 Operation in residence structures.

Article II. Self-Service Coin-Operated Laundry Establishments

4-220-260 Attendant required when.
4-220-290 Hours of operation.
4-220-295 Supplemental licenses.

Article IV. Violation of Chapter Provisions

4-220-380 Violation—Penalty.

Article I. Laundries

§4-220-010 Laundry defined.

"Laundry," as used in this chapter, means any place, building, structure, room or establishment, or portion thereof, which is used for the purpose of washing, drying, starching or ironing shirts, dresses, underwear, collars, cuffs or other wearing apparel, table, bed or other household linens, towels, curtains, draperies or other washable fabrics, such work being done for the general public.

The word "laundry," as used in this chapter, shall also be held to include any towel or linen supply laundry maintained or operated for the purpose of washing, drying, starching or ironing towels, aprons, napkins, table linens, washable clothing or other similar articles, the property of such laundry, but rented or loaned for a consideration to patrons or customers of said laundry.

The word "laundry," as used in this chapter, shall also be held to include any private laundry maintained or operated in connection with any hotel, restaurant or public institution, except a hospital or charitable institution where no charge is made for laundry services.

The word "laundry," as used in this chapter, shall also be held to include any establishment wherein washing machine units are available for use by the general public upon the deposit of a coin or the payment of a fee to the operator of such establishment or his agent.

"Laundry vehicle" as used in this chapter, means any wagon, automobile or other vehicle used for the purpose of collecting or delivering laundry within the city limits.

(Coun. J. 12-9-92, p. 25465; Amend. 6-10-96, p. 23652)

§4-220-020 License—Required.

No person shall engage in the business of any laundry within the city without first obtaining a limited business license.

(Coun. J. 12-9-92, p. 25465; Amend. 6-10-96, p. 23652)

§4-220-055 Laundry identification on vehicle.

No vehicle of any kind shall be used for the purpose of collecting or delivering laundry work, unless said vehicle shall carry upon two sides of the same, in plain legible letters, at least one and one-half inches high, the name of the laundry where the laundry work is actually done.

(Added. Coun. J. 6-10-96, p. 23652)

§4-220-130 Operation in residence structures.

No existing laundry situated in any building which is partially used for residence purposes shall be operated after the hour of 8:00 p.m. or before the hour of 6:00 a.m. nor shall such a laundry be eligible for a supplemental license under Section 4-220-295).

No laundry in which washing is done other than by means of enclosed washing machines having a capacity of not to exceed 10 pounds of dry goods per machine shall be established in any building any part of which is used for dwelling purposes.

(Coun. J. 12-9-92, p. 25465; Amend. 6-10-96, p. 23652)

Article II. Self-Service Coin-Operated Laundry Establishments

§4-220-260 Attendant required when.

There shall be present in every self-service coin-operated establishment of this type an attendant between the hours of 6:00 p.m. and 11:30 p.m.

(Coun. J. 12-9-92, p. 25465)

§4-220-290 Hours of operation.

No coin-operated self-service laundry now or hereafter established shall be operated between the hours of 11:30 p.m. and 6:30 a.m. unless the operator obtains a supplemental license to allow operation during those hours.

(Coun. J. 12-9-92, p. 25465; Amend. 6-10-96, p. 23652)

§4-220-295 Supplemental licenses.

The owner of a self-service coin-operated laundry, duly licensed according to this chapter, may apply for a supplemental license for operation between the hours of 11:30 p.m. and 6:30 a.m. In addition to all other requirements contained in this article, the holder of a supplemental license must comply with the following:

(a) Two attendants shall be present between the hours of 11:30 p.m. and 6:30 a.m. in every self-service coin-operated establishment operating under a supplemental license.

(b) No automatic amusement device may be placed on the premises of any self-service coin-operated establishment operating under a supplemental license.

(c) Every holder of such a supplemental license shall install and maintain a 24-hour time-lapse video surveillance system capable of monitoring the establishment premises.

(d) Except for employees and necessary maintenance personnel, between the hours of 11:30 p.m. and 6:30 a.m. no person may be allowed on the premises of a self-service coin-operated establishment operating under a supplemental license unless such person intends to use the equipment and services offered by such establishment.

(Added. Coun. J. 4-29-92, p. 15373; Amend. 6-10-96, p. 23652)

Article IV. Violation of Chapter Provisions

§4-220-380 Violation—Penalty.

Any person violating any of the provisions of this chapter shall be fined not less than $200.00 nor more than $500.00 for each offense, and each day such a violation continues shall be deemed a separate and distinct offense.

(Coun. J. 12-9-92, p. 25465; Amend. 6-10-96, p. 23652)

CHAPTER 4-224
MANUFACTURING ESTABLISHMENTS

(Complete Chapter)

Sections:

4-224-002 Definitions.
4-224-004 Manufacturing license—Required.
4-224-006 License—Application.
4-224-008 License—Fee.
4-224-010 Frontage consents.
4-224-011 Location restrictions.
4-224-012 Noise restrictions.
4-224-013 Operation at night restricted.
4-224-020 Sanitary requirements.
4-224-030 Inspections.
4-224-450 Violation—Penalty.

§4-224-002 Definitions.

Whenever used in this chapter:

(a) "Manufacturing establishment" means any place or establishment where a mechanical or chemical process is used to transform or assemble materials or substances into an article of tangible personal property with a different form, use or name, regardless of whether the new product is finished and ready for utilization or consumption; or semifinished and ready to become a raw material for an establishment engaged in further manufacturing. A manufacturing establishment shall include but not be limited to a drug, chemical or paint factory; a foundry; a machine shop; and a roofing or paving materials factory. In no case shall a manufacturing establishment include a place or establishment where the manufacturing process is an accessory use of the business being conducted, nor shall it include a wholesale food establishment.

(b) "Accessory use" means the production, processing, cleaning, servicing, altering, testing, repair, or storage of merchandise normally incidental to a retail service or business use if conducted by the same ownership as the principal use.

(c) "Drug, chemical or paint factory" means any factory, building, place or establishment where soda, soda ash, salt, sal soda, bicarbonate of soda, caustic soda, alcohol, ether, essential oils, carbonic acid, gas, chlorine, aniline, benzine, perfumes, toilet preparations, coal-tar chemicals, inks, dyes, bluing, washing powders, lye boiler compounds, disinfectants, fertilizers, insect powders, condition powders, furniture polish, shoe polish, metal polish, cleaning compounds, photographic chemicals, glycerine, drugs, medicines, ointments, proprietary or patent medicines, paints, pigments, linseed oil, turpentine, drying oils, paint removers, shellac, varnish, enamels, calcimine, wallpaper cleaners, putty or any other chemicals, paints, oils, medicines, drugs or similar materials or preparations are made, manufactured, mixed, compounded, purified or prepared; provided, however, that this shall not apply to wholesale drugstores or other establishments specifically defined and licensed by other provisions of this code.

(d) "Foundry" means any place or establishment where iron, copper, brass, zinc, lead, aluminum, bronze alloys or any other metal or metals are poured, molded or cast for building, agricultural, mechanical or other industrial or commercial purposes.

(e) "Machine shop" means a workshop in which machines are made, or where parts of machines, or tools, implements, gears, dies, screws or other metal articles are cut, filed, shaped, punched, or stamped by means of a lathe or other machinery.

(f) "Roofing or paving materials factory" means any premises, building or structure where the business of boiling, distilling, mixing or otherwise changing the form of crude asphalt, crude tar, coal-gas byproducts, with or without other materials for roofing, paving or similar uses, is carried on. The byproducts of such boiling, distilling or other process in the manufacture of roofing or paving materials shall be considered as incidental to and a part of such manufacture for the purposes of this chapter.

(g) "Wholesale food establishment" means any place used for the preparation, manufacture, canning, baking, bottling, packing, distribution, storage, selling or offering for sale at wholesale any article of food, packaged or unpackaged, drink or ice used or intended for human consumption, or any such article which is an ingredient of, used for, mixed with or which enters into the composition of any such food, confection, baked goods, condiments, drink or ice.

(Added. Coun. J. 2-7-96, p. 15616)

§4-224-004 Manufacturing license—Required.

No person shall conduct or operate a manufacturing establishment within the city without having first obtained a manufacturing license.

(Added. Coun. J. 2-7-96, p. 15616)

§4-224-006 License—Application.

An application for said license shall be made in conformity with the general requirements of this code relating to applications for licenses; and with the particular requirements for each manufacturing establishment to be performed under the license as set forth in the relevant sections of the code governing the particular establishment.

(Added. Coun. J. 2-7-96, p. 15616)

§4-224-008 License—Fee.

The annual fee for each manufacturing license shall be as set forth in Section 4-5-010.

(Added. Coun. J. 2-7-96, p. 15616)

§4-224-010 Frontage consents.

It shall be unlawful for any person to conduct a drug, chemical or paint factory; a foundry; or a machine shop, excepting wearing apparel shops, on any lot fronting on any street in any block in which one-half of the buildings on both sides of the street are used exclusively for residence purposes, or within 50 feet of any such street, without the written consent of a majority of the property owners according to frontage on both sides of such street.

(Coun. J. 12-9-92, p. 25465; Amend. 2-7-96, p. 15616)

§4-224-011 Location restrictions.

No machine shops shall be conducted or operated on any lot or plot of ground of which any portion shall be within 200 feet of any lot occupied by a public or parochial school, hospital or church.

(Added. Coun. J. 2-7-96, p. 15616)

§4-224-012 Noise restrictions.

It shall be unlawful to maintain, within 200 feet of any residence, a machine shop or a foundry wherein pneumatic hammers or other apparatus are used which cause loud or unusual noises.

(Added. Coun. J. 2-7-96, p. 15616)

§4-224-013 Operation at night restricted.

No machine shop shall be operated in the nighttime between the hours of 8:00 p.m. and 6:00 a.m. in any block in which a majority of the buildings on both sides of the street are used exclusively for residential purposes, or within 100 feet of such block, and it shall be within the power of the board of health, after reasonable notice, to treat such night operation as a public nuisance and to abate the same.

(Added. Coun. J. 2-7-96, p. 15616)

§4-224-020 Sanitary requirements.

No owner, proprietor, lessee, manager or superintendent of any manufacturing establishment where workmen and workwomen are employed for wages shall cause, permit or allow the same or any portion or apartment of, or any room in such manufacturing establishment, to be overcrowded or inadequate, faulty or insufficient in respect of light, ventilation, heat or cleanliness.

In every such building or apartment, or room in any such building, where one or more persons are employed as aforesaid, at least 500 feet of air space shall be allowed to each person employed therein, and fresh air shall be supplied by ventilation at the rate of four complete changes of air per hour during the hours of employment. No part of such air supply shall be taken from any cellar or basement.

All such places shall be kept in a clean condition, free from the effluvia of a sewer, drain, privy, stable or other nuisance; also free as far as practicable from all gases, vapors, dust or other impurities generated by manufacturing processes or otherwise which are injurious to health.

Sufficient and separate water closets shall be provided for male and female employees, and such water closet compartments shall be properly ventilated.
(Coun. J. 12-9-92, p. 25465; Amend. 2-7-96, p. 15616)

§4-224-030 Inspections.

The section of mechanical inspection of the department of buildings and the division marshal in charge of the bureau of fire prevention shall visit, or cause to be visited by any officer, all manufacturing establishments within the city before a license required under this chapter may be issued and as often as it shall deem necessary to see that the provisions of this chapter are complied with and to determine whether the building or place within which the manufacturing establishment is conducted or is to be conducted complies with the provisions of this code relating to health and sanitation, buildings and fire prevention and if such premises are found to be in an unsanitary or unsafe condition, the inspecting department shall require such alterations or arrangements to be made as may be necessary for the safety and health of the employees, pursuant to the terms of this chapter and other provisions of this code and such laws as may be in force concerning health and sanitary measures.
(Coun. J. 12-9-92, p. 25465; Amend. 2-7-96, p. 15616)

§4-224-450 Violation—Penalty.

Any person violating any of the provisions of this chapter shall be fined not less than $200.00 nor more than $500.00 for each offense and every day that any such violation shall continue shall constitute a separate and distinct offense.
(Coun. J. 12-9-92, p. 25465; Amend. 2-7-96, p. 15616)

CHAPTER 4-228
MOTOR VEHICLE REPAIR SHOPS
(Selected Sections)

Sections:
4-228-010 Definitions.
4-228-020 Licensing provisions.
4-228-024 Proper disposal of tires.
4-228-025 Proper disposal of unrepairable or unclaimed vehicle and parts.
4-228-040 Unlawful acts and omissions.
4-228-044 Required—Off-street parking.
4-228-045 Prohibited—Public ways.
4-228-046 Prohibited—Residential buildings.
4-228-047 Frontage and driveway requirement.

4-228-050 Misrepresentation of quality of parts.
4-228-070 Maintenance of records—Advertising requirements.
4-228-096 Towing operations.
4-228-100 Inspection—License revocation.
4-228-110 Violation—Penalty.

§4-228-010 Definitions.

The following definitions shall apply to this chapter:

(a) "Motor vehicle repair shop" or "repair shop" means any building, structure, premises, enclosure or other place including automobile service stations, garages and motor vehicle service shops where the business of doing repair work on or for motor vehicles, the replacing of parts thereto, or the diagnosis of malfunctions of a motor vehicle is conducted in any shop, drive-in station or garage which inspects motor vehicles for the purpose of appraising, evaluating or estimating the extent or value of motor vehicle damage or the necessity or cost of motor vehicle repairs. A motor vehicle repair shop shall include any business, establishment or location where tires are changed or repaired. Provided, however, that this definition shall not include any business operated under a certificate of authority issued under Chapter 215 of the Illinois Compiled Statutes.

(b) "Motor vehicle" means any self-propelled device in, upon or by which persons or property are or may be transported upon public ways, except devices moved by human power or used exclusively upon stationary rails.

(c) "Repair" means any diagnosis, removal, reconditioning, maintenance, alteration, adjustment, installation or replacement of any parts, components or systems of a motor vehicle (including but not limited to upholstery and auto glass), but excluding any repair services which the commissioner by regulation determines to be minor. No service shall be designated as minor, for purposes of this chapter, if the commissioner finds that performance of the service requires mechanical expertise, has given rise to a high incidence of fraud or deceptive practices, or involves a part of the vehicle essential to its safe operation.

(d) "Licensee" means a person licensed to engage in the motor vehicle repair business under the provisions of this article.

(e) "Motor vehicle mechanic" means a person who for salary or wage performs diagnosis, maintenance, repair, removal, reconditioning, adjustment, alteration, replacement or installation of any parts, systems or components of a motor vehicle (including but not limited to upholstery and auto glass), but excluding any repair services which the commissioner by regulation determines to be minor.

(f) "Person" means any individual, firm, partnership, association, corporation, company or group of individuals acting together for a common purpose or organization of any kind.

(g) "Estimated price" means a written determination of the price of parts and the price of labor needed to perform offered services, including the price of teardown and assembly, if necessary.

(h) "Invoice" means a written listing of the details of the transaction between the repair shop and the customer.

(i) "Work order" means an authorization, either oral or written, on the part of the customer for the repair shop to perform a service.

(j) "Guarantee" means an obligation undertaken by a repair shop to repair a vehicle at no charge or at a reduced charge for parts or labor or both.

(k) "Warranty" means a promise made by a manufacturer that a vehicle or part will be repaired at no charge or at a reduced charge for parts or labor or both.

(l) "Place of business" means an address where repairs or service are ordinarily performed.

(m) "Commissioner" means the commissioner of the department of consumer services of the city of Chicago.

(n) "False or secret compartment" means any enclosure that is intended and designed to be used to conceal, hide and prevent discovery by law enforcement officers of the false or secret compartment, or its contents, and which is integrated into a vehicle.

(Coun. J. 12-9-92, p. 25465; Amend. 10-7-93, p. 39429; 6-28-00, p. 36845)

§4-228-020 Licensing provisions.

(a) No person shall own, maintain, conduct, operate or engage in the business of motor vehicle repair for compensation within the city of Chicago, or hold himself/herself out as being able to do so, or act as an agent for another who is engaged in the motor vehicle repair business, or take custody of a motor vehicle within the city of Chicago for the purpose of repair without first obtaining a license from the city of Chicago to do so. If a person maintains a motor vehicle repair shop at more than one location, a license is required for each such location. The license issued to a motor vehicle repair shop authorizes the licensee and all its bona fide employees to engage in the business of motor vehicle repair. Said license shall be issued in accordance with the provisions of Chapter 4-4 of the Municipal Code of the city of Chicago upon favorable recommendations from the department of consumer services and upon payment of the fee prescribed in this chapter.

(b) The following persons are excluded from the term motor vehicle repair shop:

(1) An employee of a motor vehicle repair shop who engages in the business of repairing motor vehicles solely by reason of his employment; or

(2) Any person who is solely engaged in the business of repairing the motor vehicles of a single commercial or industrial establishment, or of the federal, state or local government or any agency thereof; or

(3) Any person solely engaged in the business of repairing road building machines, farm machines, lawn machines, garden machines, vehicles registered as special purpose vehicles; or

(4) Any person who does not work on the vehicle but only rebuilds or reconditions parts of the vehicle removed by others (i.e., after market manufacturers); or

(5) Any person who engages in the business of distributing motor vehicle parts.

(c) Every motor vehicle repair shop shall pay the fee required by this chapter for each place of business operated by him/her within the city of Chicago and shall register with the director of revenue on forms prescribed by the director. The applicant for a motor vehicle repair shop license shall, on his/her application, disclose the following information:

(1) The trade name, address, form of ownership of the facility and, if a corporation, the date and place of incorporation;

(2) If a corporation, the name and address of its registered agent and officers; if a partnership, the name and address of each partner; if a sole proprietorship, the name and address of the sole proprietor;

(3) A description of the motor vehicle repair facility to be licensed. Such description shall include:

(A) Number of working area stalls in the facility and square footage of work area,

(B) Type of repair work to be conducted, i.e., motor, transmission, body, brakes, tire changing or repair,

(C) Number of motor vehicle mechanics employed at the time of application,

(D) If tires are to be replaced or repaired on the premises, a copy of the tire disposal contract required by Section 4-228-024;

(E) Number of off-street parking spaces provided for each repair bay or 300 square feet of vehicle service area, whichever is greater, or evidence that off-street parking is not required by Section 4-228-044 of this code.

(4) A diagram of the motor vehicle repair facility to be licensed. Such diagram shall include the:

(A) Dimensions of the building or buildings housing the repair facility,

(B) Driveway and curb cut-out locations,

(C) Location of bordering streets and alleys,

(D) Location and dimensions of working area stalls, and

(E) Location and dimensions of parking spaces;

(5) Proof that the applicant has scheduled a zoning compliance inspection, as provided in Section 11.12-7 of the Chicago Zoning Ordinance, of the premises for which the license is sought;

(6) The application shall be signed by the applicant or his/her local authorized agent, who shall be an individual responsible for the operation of the applicant's local motor vehicle repair business;

(7) A licensee shall not use or permit to be used more than one trade name at a single location;

(8) The commissioner may, at any time, require additional information of a licensee or an applicant to clarify items on the application.

(d) The annual license fee for a motor vehicle repair shop shall be based upon the classification of the repair work performed. Motor vehicle repair shop licenses shall be divided into classes as follows:

Class I — This class shall be required for auto repair other than engine and body, including, but not limited to, radio, glass work, upholstery, striping, car alarms, car phones, stereos, radios, the repair or changing of tires and other repairs.

Class II — This class shall be required if any of the following repair work is performed: engine work; transmission; oil changes; muffler repairs or replacements; battery replacements or battery charges; heating and air conditioning work. A Class II license shall entitle a licensee to conduct activities that may be carried out under a Class I or Class II license.

Class III — This class shall be required if any of the following repair work is performed: body work; painting; spray painting. A Class III license shall entitle a licensee to conduct activities that may be carried out under a Class I, Class II or Class III license.

(e) Each license issued pursuant to this chapter shall be posted and kept in a conspicuous place in the motor vehicle repair shop.

(f) The department of environment upon notice from the director of revenue of the receipt of an application for a Class III license shall inspect the place of business named in the application to determine compliance with the applicable environmental provisions of this code.

(Coun. J. 12-9-92, p. 25465; Amend. 10-7-93, p. 39429; 6-14-95, p. 3094; 4-16-97, p. 42621; 7-19-00, p. 38593; 12-12-01, p. 75777)

§4-228-024 Proper disposal of tires.

No motor vehicle repair shop shall replace or repair motor vehicle tires unless the motor vehicle repair shop maintains in effect a contract for the removal and disposal of motor vehicle tires replaced by such motor vehicle repair shop. The contract shall be kept on the premises of the motor vehicle repair shop and be made available for inspection by the commissioner or the commissioner's designee or by the commissioner of the departments of environment or streets and sanitation or the director of revenue or their designees, each of whom is authorized to enforce this section, during the repair shop's business hours.

The motor vehicle repair shop shall be jointly and severally liable with the repair shop's waste tire transporter and the repair shop's tire disposal contractor for any illegal disposal of the repair shop's tires by such transporter or disposal contractor.

(Added. Coun. J. 6-14-95, p. 3094; Amend. 12-13-00, p. 48186)

§4-228-025 Proper disposal of unrepairable or unclaimed vehicle and parts.

Motor vehicle repair shops shall lawfully dispose of all unrepairable or unclaimed motor vehicles and motor vehicle parts which are within their custody. Proof of proper disposal, in the form of a receipt, shall be maintained by each motor vehicle repair shop on the business premises of the repair shop for a minimum of one year, and shall be made available for inspection by the commissioner or the commissioner's designee, or by the commissioner of the departments of environment or streets and sanitation or the director of revenue or their designees, each of whom is authorized to enforce this section, during the repair shop's business hours. With respect to tires, the receipt shall include or be accompanied by the following information; the name and address of he motor vehicle repair shop, the date of disposal, the name and address of the disposal facility, the number of tires disposed of, and the name of the transporter of the waste tires, including the truck number or license plate number.

(Added. Coun. J. 5-14-97, p. 44283; Amend. 12-13-00, p. 48186)

§4-228-040 Unlawful acts and omissions.

It shall be unlawful for any motor vehicle repair shop to perform any of the following acts or omissions related to the conduct of the business of the motor vehicle shop, whether done by the owner of the facility, the operator of the business or by any mechanic, employee, partner, officer or member of the motor vehicle repair shop:

(a) Making or authorizing in any manner or by any means whatever any statement, written or oral, which is untrue or misleading, and which is known, or which by the exercise of reasonable care should be known, to be untrue or misleading;

(b) Causing or allowing a customer to sign any work order which does not state the repairs requested or authorized by the customer, and does not state the motor vehicle's odometer reading at the time of repair;

(c) Failing or refusing to give a customer a copy of any document requiring his/her signature, as soon as the customer signs such document;

(d) Any other conduct which constitutes fraud;

(e) Conduct which constitutes gross negligence;

(f) Failure to comply with the provisions of this chapter or regulations adopted pursuant to it;

(g) Any wilful departure from or disregard of accepted trade standards for good and workmanlike repair in any material respect, which is prejudicial to a customer, without the prior consent of the customer or his/her duly authorized representative;

(h) Making false promises of a character likely to influence, persuade or induce a customer to authorize the repair, service or maintenance of motor vehicles;

(i) Having repair work done by someone other than the motor vehicle repair shop without the knowledge and prior consent of the customer unless the repair shop owner can demonstrate that the customer could not reasonably have been notified.

(j) Installing, creating, building or fabricating any false or secret compartment in any motor vehicle. In accordance with Section 4-4-280 of this code, any licensee who violates this subsection shall be punished for a first offense by a fine of $500.00 and shall have his license suspended for not less than seven days nor more than fourteen days; a second or subsequent offense shall be punished by a fine of $1,000.00 and shall result in revocation of the license.

The commissioner of consumer services, where the motor vehicle repair shop cannot show there was bona fide error, may recommend to the mayor the suspension or the revocation of a motor vehicle repair shop license for any of the aforementioned acts or omissions.

(Coun. J. 12-9-92, p. 25465; Amend. 4-16-97, p. 42621; 6-28-00, p. 36845)

§4-228-044 Required—Off-street parking.

Any person who is seeking for the first time to obtain a license to own, maintain, conduct, operate or engage in the business of motor vehicle repair for compensation within the city of Chicago at a location where no motor vehicle repair shop is currently licensed to operate shall be required to provide two parking spaces for each repair bay or 300 square feet of vehicle service area, whichever is greater.

(Added. Coun. J. 7-19-00, p. 38593)

§4-228-045 Prohibited—Public ways.

Prohibition Relating to Use of the Public Way. No motor vehicle repair shop shall be operated or maintained in such a way that the shop, or any vehicle being repaired therein, or any materials associated therewith, are located or placed upon the public way. If the director of revenue or the commissioner of consumer services finds or is notified by an alderman or by another department or agency of the city that a licensee has violated this section on three different days within a 12-month period, the director or commissioner shall immediately and without exception seek revocation of the motor vehicle license by the mayor's license commission.

At any revocation hearing conducted pursuant to Section 4-4-280 of this code, the license commissioner appointed by the mayor or any other hearing officer designated by the mayor shall limit their factual findings to determining (1) the number of times, if any, the licensee violated this section; and (2) the dates on which those violations occurred. Neither the seriousness of the offense nor the existence of any mitigating factors shall be considered or reported to the mayor. If the license commissioner or hearing officer finds that the licensee violated this section of the code on three different days within a 12-month period, the mayor shall revoke the motor vehicle repair license.

Each object placed upon the public way in violation of this section shall constitute a separate and distinct offense. Each offense shall be punished by a fine of $200.00. Under no circumstances shall any administrative law officer appointed pursuant to Chapter 2-14 of this code combine, consolidate, cumulate or otherwise reduce any fine authorized by this section.

(Added. Coun. J. 10-7-93, p. 39429; Amend. 5-14-97, p. 44283; 7-19-00, p. 38593)

§4-228-046 Prohibited—Residential buildings.

No motor vehicle repair shop shall be located in any building that is used for residential purposes unless the motor vehicle repair shop portion of the building is separated vertically and horizontally from the residential use by materials providing at least four hours of fire resistance, as required under Section 13-56-280 of this code. Nothing in this section is intended or shall be construed to allow a motor vehicle repair shop to operate in violation of any other applicable provision of this code.

(Added. Coun. J. 10-7-93, p. 39429; Amend. 7-2-97, p. 48056)

§4-228-047 Frontage and driveway requirement.

A motor vehicle repair shop license shall not be issued unless the premises for which a license is sought: (i) has frontage of not less than 25 feet on a dedicated public or private street and direct vehicle access to and from a dedicated public street through a commercial driveway for which a valid permit has been issued in accordance with Chapter 10-20 of this code; or (ii) was duly licensed as a motor vehicle repair shop prior to the effective date of this ordinance.

(Added. Coun. J. 4-16-97, p. 42621)

§4-228-050 Misrepresentation of quality of parts.

It is hereby declared to be a misdemeanor for any motor vehicle repair shop to represent any part as defective and to knowingly charge customers for unnecessary replacement parts.

The owner or operator of a motor vehicle repair shop shall present advance written notice to all customers as to the state of any and all parts which are recommended for replacement.

Any person found in violation of this section shall be subject to a fine of $500.00, or imprisonment for up to six months, or both such fine and imprisonment, for each offense.

The department of consumer services shall monitor the practices of motor vehicle repair shops by submitting city-owned vehicles for service and by submitting the written report of the motor vehicle repair shop to its own officers for determination of accuracy and fairness.

(Coun. J. 12-9-92, p. 25465)

§4-228-070 Maintenance of records—Advertising requirements.

(a) Each motor vehicle repair shop shall maintain copies of estimates, work orders, invoices, parts purchase orders, appraisals and schedules of charges prepared by that repair shop. Such copies shall be kept for two years and shall be available for inspection by the commissioner of consumer services or his/her designee during all business hours.

(b) A licensee shall disclose in any published or broadcasted advertisement relating to motor vehicle repair the following information:

(1) The name of the licensee, as shown on the license;

(2) The street address of the motor vehicle repair shop;

(3) If a repair shop does not perform repairs on motor vehicles but takes custody of motor vehicles and contracts all repairs to another, it must so state this fact.

(c) An advertisement by a licensee of a warranty which provides for adjustment on a pro rata basis shall conspicuously disclose the basis on which the warranty will be prorated.

(d) No motor vehicle repair shop shall publish, utter or make or cause to be published, uttered or made any false or misleading statement or advertisement which is known to be false or misleading, or which by the exercise of reasonable care should be known to be false or misleading. In determining whether any advertisement, statement or representation is false or misleading, it shall be considered in its entirety as it would be read or heard by persons to whom it is designed to appeal. An advertisement, statement or representation shall be considered to be false or misleading if it tends to deceive the public or impose upon credulous or ignorant persons.

(Coun. J. 12-9-92, p. 25465)

§4-228-096 Towing operations.*

All licensees engaged in the towing of disabled motor vehicles shall comply with Chapter 9-44 of this code and the rules and regulations promulgated thereunder. In addition to the vehicle marking requirements set forth in Chapter 9-44, all licensees shall also display their motor vehicle repair shop license number on each side of the cab in letters, in contrasting color, that are not less than two inches in height.

(Added. Coun. J. 5-14-97, p. 44283)

* **Editor's Note:** Section 4-228-096 was originally added as a second Section 4-228-095. This section was editorially renumbered to be Section 4-228-096.

§4-228-100 Inspection—License revocation.

The commissioner of consumer services and the zoning administrator shall inspect motor vehicle repair shops to determine compliance with the provisions of this chapter and for compliance with the Chicago Zoning Ordinance, respectively. Upon evidence of violation by any facility, the commissioner or the zoning administrator may recommend the revocation of the motor vehicle repair shop license to the mayor, who may revoke the license of the licensee concerned in the manner prescribed by law.

(Coun. J. 12-9-92, p. 25465; Amend. 7-19-00, p. 38593; 12-12-01, p. 75777)

§4-228-110 Violation—Penalty.

Any person found guilty of violating, disobeying, omitting, neglecting or refusing to comply with or resisting or opposing the enforcement of any of the provisions of this chapter or regulations promulgated hereunder, except when otherwise specifically provided, upon conviction thereof shall be punished by a fine of not less than $200.00 nor more than $300.00 for the first offense and not less than $200.00 nor more than $500.00 for the second and each subsequent offense in any 180-day period. Repeated offenses in excess of three within any 180-day period may also be punishable as a misdemeanor by incarceration in the County Jail for a term not to exceed six months, in a separate proceedings. A separate and distinct offense shall be regarded as committed each day upon which each person shall continue any such violation, or permit any such violation to exist after notification thereof.

(Coun. J. 12-9-92, p. 25465)

CHAPTER 4-229
TIRE FACILITIES
(Complete Chapter)

Sections:

4-229-010 Definitions.
4-229-020 Licensing requirement.
4-229-030 Tire facility license fee and renewal.
4-229-040 License suspension or revocation.
4-229-050 Applicability of Motor Vehicle Repair Ordinance.
4-229-060 Standards relating to tire facilities.
4-229-065 Proper disposal of tires.
4-229-070 Regulations.
4-229-080 Violation and penalty; enforcement.

§4-229-010 Definitions.

"Commissioner" shall refer to the fire commissioner or his designee.

"Tire facility" shall refer to any business where 100 or more new or used tires are collected, stored, maintained, altered, repaired, changed, refabricated or disposed at any one time.

(Added. Coun. J. 9-14-94, p. 58635; Amend. 12-15-99, p. 21529)

§4-229-020 Licensing requirement.

Every tire facility shall obtain a tire facility license in accordance with this chapter. The license shall be issued by the department of revenue. Before a tire facility license is issued or renewed by the department of revenue, the commis-

sioner shall cause an inspection of the site to be made. Upon determining that the site complies with the applicable requirements of this chapter and any regulation promulgated hereunder, the commissioner shall inform the department of revenue that a license may be issued. No license shall be issued or renewed in accordance with this chapter unless and until all applicable requirements set forth in the Municipal Code, and the regulations promulgated thereunder, have been satisfied. The license shall be prominently displayed at the tire facility.
(Added. Coun. J. 9-14-94, p. 58635)

§4-229-030 Tire facility license fee and renewal.

The annual fee for a tire facility license shall be as set forth in Section 4-5-010. Licenses shall be renewed in accordance with Section 4-4-021.
(Added. Coun. J. 9-14-94, p. 58635)

§4-229-040 License suspension or revocation.

A license issued in accordance with Section 4-229-020 herein may be suspended or revoked in accordance with Section 4-4-280 of the Municipal Code.
(Added. Coun. J. 9-14-94, p. 58635)

§4-229-050 Applicability of Motor Vehicle Repair Ordinance.

Nothing in this chapter shall affect or alter the applicability of Chapter 4-228 of this code with respect to motor vehicle repair shops where tires are changed or repaired; provided, however, that facilities required to be licensed under Chapter 4-228 shall also obtain a tire facility license, in accordance with this chapter, if appropriate.
(Added. Coun. J. 9-14-94, p. 58635)

§4-229-060 Standards relating to tire facilities.

Every tire facility required to be licensed in accordance with Section 4-229-020 herein shall adhere to the following requirements as indicated:

(a) Tire facilities located within a structure shall adhere to the following requirements:

(1) Every building which houses a tire facility is hereby classified as a Class H storage unit pursuant to Section 13-56-170 of the Municipal Code. All structures in which tire facilities are located shall be subject to the height and area limitations of Chapter 13-48 of the Municipal Code;

(2) Facilities where tires are stored below grade shall comply with Section 15-16-030(b) of the Municipal Code;

(3) Smoking shall be prohibited in the room or other enclosure where the tires are stored or disposed of, and appropriate signs indicating the prohibition shall be posted;

(4) The interior of all structures used for tire storage shall be secured against unauthorized access;

(5) All tires shall be stored no less than 10 feet from any heat producing appliance;

(6) Tires shall be stacked on a level surface, with no less than three feet in clearance from the top of stackage to any sprinkler, fixtures, structural support, ceiling or roof. Aisles shall be no less than four feet wide. Except for tire storage on metal racks approved under N.F.P.A. Standard 231D, Storage of

Rubber Tires, tires shall be stacked in piles no longer than 25 feet and no wider than 10 feet.

(b) Tire facilities located on any open site shall adhere to the following requirements:

(1) Tires shall be stacked, in an orderly manner, in piles not to exceed 25 feet in height;

(2) Individual piles shall be separated by a distance of 10 feet. No pile shall be closer than four feet to any building. No pile covering a total ground area greater than 100 square feet shall be located closer than 25 feet to a lot line, unless in the determination of the commissioner or his designee a greater or lesser setback is required or sufficient for fire prevention purposes.

A greater or lesser setback may be imposed in accordance with the Section 4-229-070 herein;

(3) Each such facility shall be enclosed by a noncombustible fence, six feet high with not less than two gates, unless bounded by a cement abutment, river, or other body of water. The area around or within the tire piles shall be kept free of rubbish, weeds, grass, or other growth. No oil or other flammable liquid shall be permitted to accumulate on the area around or within the piles. No flame cutting or welding operation shall be conducted within 25 feet of any pile of tires.

The requirements of subsections (b)(1), (2) and (3) herein shall not apply to the legal disposal of tires at a state or city permitted landfill.

(Added. Coun. J. 9-14-94, p. 58635)

§4-229-065 Proper disposal of tires.

Every tire facility shall maintain in effect a contract for the disposal of tires. The tire facility shall also maintain all disposal invoices related to the disposal contract for a minimum of one year. The invoices shall include the name and address of the tire facility, the date of disposal, the name and address of the disposal facility, the number of tires disposed of, and the name of the transporter of the waste tires, including the truck number or license plate number. The disposal contract and all related invoices shall be kept on the premises of the tire facility and be made available for inspection by personnel of the departments of streets and sanitation, revenue, or environment, all of whom are authorized to enforce this section, during the tire facility's business hours.

(Added. Coun. J. 12-13-00, p. 48186)

§4-229-070 Regulations.

The commissioner and director of revenue may promulgate regulations to effectuate the purposes of this chapter.

(Added. Coun. J. 9-14-94, p. 58635)

§4-229-080 Violation and penalty; enforcement.

Any person who shall be found to have violated any provision of this ordinance, or any regulation promulgated hereunder, shall be subject to a fine of not less than $200.00, and not more than $500.00, for each offense. A separate and distinct offense shall be deemed to have been committed for each and every day on which any such person shall be guilty of such violation. Repeated

violations of the provisions of this chapter, or any regulation promulgated hereunder, shall be grounds for injunctive relief.
(Added. Coun. J. 9-14-94, p. 58635)

CHAPTER 4-232
MOTOR VEHICLE STORAGE AND SALES
(Selected Sections)

Sections:

Article I. General Provisions

4-232-010 Motor vehicle defined.

Article II. Valet Parking

4-232-050 Definitions.
4-232-060 License—Required—Application—Fee.
4-232-080 Operating procedures.
4-232-090 Applicability of provisions—Exceptions.
4-232-100 Violation of Sections 4-232-060 and 4-232-080—Penalty.

Article III. Motor Vehicle Salesrooms

4-232-110 Motor vehicle salesroom defined.

Article IV. Public Garages

4-232-130 Public and accessory garage defined.
4-232-150 License—Required.
4-232-225 Smoking prohibited.
4-232-240 Return of patron's automobile keys.
4-232-250 Garage register—Required.
4-232-260 Alteration of engine number—Police notification.

Article V. Violation of Chapter Provisions

4-232-320 Violation—Penalty.

Article I. General Provisions

§4-232-010 Motor vehicle defined.
"Motor vehicle," unless a contrary intent is expressly shown, means any self-propelled device in, upon or by which persons or property are or may be transported upon public ways, except devices moved by human power or used exclusively upon stationary rails.
(Coun. J. 12-9-92, p. 25465; Amend. 4-16-97, p. 42588)

Article II. Valet Parking

§4-232-050 Definitions.
(a) For the purpose of this chapter, the following terms shall have the following meanings:

"Valet parking operator" means a person who employs one or more attendants for the purpose of providing a valet parking service or who contracts his own services, but not in the capacity of employee, to any business establishment, for the purpose of providing a valet parking service to such establishment.

"Valet parking service" means a parking service provided to accommodate patrons of any business establishment, which service is incidental to the business of the establishment and by which an attendant on behalf of the establishment takes temporary custody of the patrons' motor vehicle and moves, parks, stores or retrieves the vehicle for the patrons' convenience.

(b) For the purposes of Sections 4-232-060 through 4-232-080, "commissioner" means the commissioner of consumer services or his designee.
(Coun. J. 12-9-92, p. 25465)

§4-232-060 License—Required—Application—Fee.

(a) Except as provided in Section 4-232-090, no person shall conduct a valet parking service unless he has a valid valet parking operator license issued in accordance with this chapter. A separate license is required for each loading area served.

(b) Applications for valet parking operator licenses shall be made to the commissioner of consumer services on forms provided by him for that purpose. Each valet parking operator license issued shall be for a one-year period only, commencing on July 1st, and shall have designated thereon the name and address of the licensee and the business establishment to be served by the licensee. The fee for each license shall be as set forth in Section 4-5-010.

(c) Applications for the renewal of a valet parking operator license shall be made to the commissioner on forms provided by him for that purpose not less than 60 days prior to the expiration of the license to be renewed. The fee for a renewal shall be the same as for a new license.

(d) Valet parking operator licenses shall be nontransferable, and any attempt to transfer a license shall result automatically in the immediate expiration of the license.
(Coun. J. 12-9-92, p. 25465)

§4-232-080 Operating procedures.

(a) Every business establishment for which a valet parking license is issued shall, during the hours of service, display an 18-inch by 24-inch valet parking license sign issued by the department of consumer services. The valet parking license sign is to be attached to the existing loading zone pole during the hours of operation. The valet parking license sign shall only be displayed and the zone shall only be in effect during the hours that valet service is provided. A licensee's improper display of or failure to display the valet parking license sign, or use of such sign to restrict or exclude public parking at unauthorized times or locations, shall subject the operator to the penalties set forth in this article and other applicable provisions of this code. Every licensee providing service must post the name of the operator and rate, if any, onto the valet parking license sign in four-inch dark blue lettering. The commissioner of consumer services shall inspect such establishments to determine that the name, and rates, if any, are accurately and properly posted, and shall suspend any valet parking operator's license as to any business establishment being served for so long as the licensee fails to post its rates and name as required herein.

(b) No valet parking operator shall park or suffer its agents to park patrons' vehicles upon the public way except under lawful conditions upon such main thoroughfares of the city as are designated as snow routes pursuant to Title 9 of this code. In accordance with Section 9-100-150 of this code, the fine for any parking or compliance violations incurred by a vehicle while in the custody of a valet parking operator shall be the sole responsibility of the valet parking operator and shall, upon the occurrence of a final determination of liability, constitute a debt due and owing to the city. The valet parking operator's failure to pay any such fine upon notice by the city shall subject the operator to the penalties set forth in this article and other applicable provisions of this code. The commissioner of consumer services is authorized to seek restitution with respect to any fine paid by the patron of the valet parking operator.

(c) Every valet parking operator shall place or cause his agent to place on the dashboard of each patron vehicle a sign or placard of a size no smaller than eight and one-half inches by 11 inches in such a manner so as to be conspicuously visible through the windshield of the patron vehicle. The sign or placard shall contain the following information in red or black letters no less than one inch high: "This Vehicle Parked By (valet parking operator) For Customer Of (business establishment)." In addition, each attendant of valet parking operator shall, while on duty, wear conspicuously placed on his clothing an insignia which identifies the valet parking operator for whom the attendant is working.

(d) All valet parking attendants must, upon taking custody of a patron's vehicle, issue a numbered receipt to each customer containing the name, address and telephone number of the company providing the valet service, a statement that the company has liability insurance as required by Section 4-232-070(b) of the Municipal Code of Chicago, the charge for the valet service, the time and date the valet parking operator took custody of the vehicle, and the license plate number of the vehicle. When a valet parking attendant returns custody of the vehicle to the owner, the attendant must time stamp the receipt with the time and date the valet parking operator surrendered custody of the vehicle, and return it to the patron.

(e) Every valet parking operator or attendant shall carry on his person a valid current driver's license at all times while in control of a patron's vehicle. In addition to the penalties otherwise provided for violation of this section, any person violating this subsection shall be subject to a fine of not less than $100.00 nor more than $500.00 for each offense. Any penalty for violation of this subsection shall be assessed against, and shall be the responsibility of, the holder of the valet parking operator license.

(f) No valet parking operator may use one-day residential parking permits in the conduct of that operator's valet parking business.

(Coun. J. 12-9-92, p. 25465; Amend. 10-7-93, p. 38995; 10-28-97, p. 54834)

§4-232-090 Applicability of provisions—Exceptions.

Sections 4-232-060 through 4-232-080 shall not apply to any business establishment that provides patron parking entirely and solely on its premises or to any hotel that provides parking entirely on its premises for guests or for patrons of business establishments located on the hotel's premises. However, a valet parking operator license shall be required when the vehicle or the keys to the vehicle are given to the valet parking attendant on any part of the public way, even if the actual parking of the vehicle is done entirely and solely on the establishment's premises.

(Added. Coun. J. 12-9-92, p. 25465)

§4-232-100 Violation of Sections §4-232-060 and §4-232-080—Penalty.

Any person convicted of a violation of any provisions of Sections 4-232-060 or 4-232-080 shall be fined not less than $50.00 and not more than $500.00 for each offense, and each day that an offense continues shall constitute a separate and distinct offense. In addition, the license of a valet parking operator who has been convicted of three such offenses within a 180-day period shall be revoked by the commissioner.

(Added. Coun. J. 12-9-92, p. 25465)

Article III. Motor Vehicle Salesrooms

§4-232-110 Motor vehicle salesroom defined.

"Motor vehicle salesroom," as used in this chapter, means any building, structure, premises, enclosure or other place within the city where the business of dealing in new or secondhand motor vehicles, or any of the parts or accessories thereof, is conducted or operated.

(Added. Coun. J. 12-9-92, p. 25465)

Article IV. Public Garages

§4-232-130 Public and accessory garage defined.

"Public garage," as used in this chapter, means any building, structure, premises, enclosure or other place, except a public way, within the city, where four or more motor vehicles are stored, housed or parked for hire, in a condition ready for use, or where rent or compensation is paid to the owner, manager or lessee of the premises for the housing, storing, sheltering or keeping of such motor vehicles. However, the term "public garage" shall not include the following: (i) any parking facility which is defined as an "accessory garage" pursuant to this section; and (ii) those accessory parking facilities which are open only to those persons who reside on the same zoning lot as the accessory parking facility.

"Public garage — enclosed," as used in this chapter, means any public garage enclosed within a building. The capacity of such building shall be figured on the gross interior floor area, exclusive of elevator shafts, ramps, areas designed for the passage of vehicles such as aisles, and space enclosed by partitions which is actually used for offices, toilets, washrooms and waiting areas for the public, and by allowing 200 square feet of such floor area for each motor vehicle.

"Public garage — not enclosed," as used in this chapter, means any public garage not enclosed within a building having four walls and a roof extending from wall to wall and covering the entire space enclosed by such walls.

"Public garage — entertainment" means any public parking facility accommodating four or more vehicles, not enclosed within a building, and devoted to parking purposes only in conjunction with the presentation of a sporting event, concert or other public entertainment.

"Accessory garage," as used in this chapter, means any building, structure, premises, enclosure or other place, which: (i) meets the definition of an "accessory use," as that term is defined in the Zoning Ordinance; (ii) makes four or more parking spaces available, for any fee or charge, to residents, tenants, users, employees and/or guests of the principal use located on the same zoning lot where the garage is located; and (iii) makes such parking only available to such

residents, tenants, users, employees and guests of the principal use located on the same zoning lot where the garage is located, and not to the general public. However, "accessory garage" shall also mean those accessory residential parking facilities which allot a specified percentage of parking spaces to persons other than residents, pursuant to Article 7 (Chapter 17-28) of the Zoning Ordinance. "Accessory garage" does not include those accessory parking facilities which are open exclusively to those persons who reside on the same zoning lot where the garage is located. Notwithstanding any other provision of this chapter, such resident-only facilities are not required to be licensed under this chapter.
(Added. Coun. J. 12-9-92, p. 25465; Amend. Coun. J. 4-16-97, p. 42588; 2-10-99, p. 89860; 3-10-99, p. 91091)

§4-232-150 License—Required.

No person shall engage in the business of a public garage without first having obtained a public garage license therefor. No person shall engage in the business of an accessory garage without first having obtained an accessory garage license therefor.
(Added. Coun. J. 12-9-92, p. 25465; Amend. Coun. J. 2-10-99, p. 89860)

§4-232-225 Smoking prohibited.

It shall be unlawful for any person to permit smoking in any public garage, or places where flammable material is sorted.
(Added. Coun. J. 12-0-92, p. 25465; Amend. Coun. J. 4-16-97, p. 42588)

§4-232-240 Return of patron's automobile keys.

Each person operating a public parking facility shall remain open for a long enough period of time to return a patron's automobile keys or make arrangements for the safe return of such keys.

Any person found in violation of the provisions of this section shall be subject to a fine of not less than $50.00 nor more than $500.00, revocation of license, or to both such fine and revocation.
(Added. Coun. J. 12-9-92, p. 25465)

§4-232-250 Garage register—Required.

It shall be the duty of the owner or operator of any such public garage or accessory garage to provide a register in book form, in which the owner or driver of any transient car to be stored in such public or accessory garage shall enter legibly in writing, in the English language, at the time any such motor vehicle is brought therein for storage, the date so delivered, the owner's name and address, the chauffeur's or driver's name and address, the trade or other name of the motor vehicle, its type, color, engine number, serial number, state license number and city license number, together with such other distinguishing marks as the owner or operator of such garage may deem necessary in order to identify fully such vehicle. When any such transient vehicle is claimed and taken out by its owner or authorized representative, it shall be the duty of said owner or operator of such public or accessory garage to note the date when the same is taken out.

It shall be unnecessary for such owner or operator of a public or accessory garage to require the signing of the garage register for a car regularly stored therein, except upon the initial date of storage.

The garage register of any public or accessory garage shall at all times be open to the inspection and investigation of all members of the police department of the city.
(Added. Coun. J. 12-9-92, p. 25465; Amend. Coun. J. 2-10-99, p. 89860)

§4-232-260 Alteration of engine number—Police notification.

It shall be the duty of the owner or operator of any public or accessory garage to notify at once the nearest police station, immediately upon the discovery by such owner or operator, or any employee thereof, of any alteration or obliteration of any engine number on any motor vehicle stored in such public or accessory garage, and to hold such motor vehicle for a period of at least 24 hours or until complete investigation of all facts surrounding such alteration or obliteration shall have been made by the police department of the city. If resistance is made, notice shall be given at once to the police department or to any police officer within call.
(Added. Coun. J. 12-9-92, p. 25465; Amend. Coun. J. 2-10-99, p. 89860)

Article V. Violation of Chapter Provisions

§4-232-320 Violation—Penalty.

Except as otherwise provided, any person who violates any of the provisions of this chapter shall be fined not less than $200.00 nor more than $500.00 for each offense, and every day that any violation of this chapter shall occur shall constitute a separate and distinct offense.
(Added. Coun. J. 12-9-92, p. 25465)

CHAPTER 4-233*
MOTOR VEHICLE BOOTING LICENSE
(Complete Chapter)

Sections:

4-233-010 Definitions.
4-233-020 Booting of motor vehicle—License required—Exceptions.
4-233-030 Application for license.
4-233-040 Eligibility for license.
4-233-050 Regulation of booting operations.
4-233-060 Geographical restrictions.
4-233-070 Penalties.

§4-233-010 Definitions.

Whenever used in this chapter, the term "boot" has the meaning ascribed to it in Section 9-84-015 of this code; "motor vehicle" has the same meaning ascribed to it in Section 9-4-010 of this code.
(Added. Coun. J. 12-13-00, p. 48188)

---

* Notwithstanding any prior ordinance to the contrary, Chapter 4-233 shall remain in effect until December 31, 2008. Thereafter, Chapter 4-233 shall be repealed without any additional action of the City Council.

§4-233-020 Booting of motor vehicle—License required—Exceptions.

(a) No person shall engage in the booting of any motor vehicle within the city of Chicago, without first having obtained a license pursuant to this chapter.

(b) Subsection (a) of this section does not apply to the booting of a motor vehicle by the city of Chicago, any other governmental entity, or a person acting under the direction of the city of Chicago or such governmental entity, when such booting is authorized by any provision of law or any rule or regulation promulgated pursuant thereto.

(Added. Coun. J. 12-13-00, p. 48188)

§4-233-030 Application for license.

An application for any license under this chapter shall be made in conformance with general requirements of this code relating to application for license. The application shall include: the name, business address and telephone number of the applicant; if the applicant is other than a natural person, the name, residence address and age of each person having at least ten percent beneficial ownership of the business; the name, residence address and age of the manager of each location; proof of liability insurance in an amount not less than $500,000.00 per person and not less than $1,000,000.00 per incident, issued by an insurer authorized to underwrite risks in this state; payment of a license fee as defined in Chapter 4-5; and such other information as the director of revenue may require to assure compliance with this chapter.

(Added. Coun. J. 12-13-00, p. 48188)

§4-233-040 Eligibility for license.

(a) No applicant shall be eligible to receive, and no licensee shall be eligible to retain, a license under this chapter if the applicant, licensee or any employee of either of them has been convicted of a felony within the last three years; provided, however: (1) as to employees and agents, this restriction shall apply only to persons who physically install or remove booting devices or who receive payment for removal of booting devices; (2) the director of revenue may accept as proof of an employee's or agent's lack of disqualifying convictions an affidavit from a private detective licensed in Illinois, certifying that the detective has examined the criminal history and record of the employee or agent, and that the employee or agent has not been convicted of a felony within the past three years. The director may specify a form for the affidavit by rule. The director of revenue shall notify the superintendent of police and district police commanders within the affected service area of all licenses issued under this chapter.

(b) Any person who misrepresents or falsifies his criminal history, or provides a false or misleading affidavit concerning any person's criminal history, in connection with licensing under this chapter, shall be subject to a fine of not less than $500.00 and not more than $1,000.00, and shall be ineligible for a license or employment by a licensee under this chapter.

(Added. Coun. J. 12-13-00, p. 48188; Amend. Coun. J. 1-16-02, p. 77494)

§4-233-050 Regulation of booting operations.

(a) A licensee shall conduct booting operations exclusively on private property, and only pursuant to a written agreement with the owner or manager of the property.

(b) A license may not provide booting service at any property at which any person having a beneficial interest in the licensee also has a beneficial interest in the subject property.

(c) No fewer than 14 days prior to the commencement of a booting operation at each and every location where a booting operation is to be conducted, the licensee shall post, and maintain in a conspicuous location, a minimum of two signs no smaller than 24 inches in height and 36 inches in width, setting forth: the date upon which a booting operation shall commence and terms of use of the subject property; the fee for removal of a boot; the name, address and a 24-hour telephone number for the licensee; the name and telephone number of the property owner or manager; and a statement notifying consumers of their rights under the ordinance codified in this chapter with language provided by the department of consumer services. The signs shall remain in place as long as a booting operation is being conducted.

(d) Upon discontinuation of booting operations at a property, the signs required by the preceding subsection shall be removed. No person shall post or allow the presence of warning signs as described in the previous subsection on any property not covered by a booting operation agreement. The licensee, the property owner and the property manager shall be jointly and severally responsible for compliance with this subsection.

(e) At every location where a licensee conducts booting operations, the licensee shall post at least one employee or agent to install and remove boots and to receive payments. The employee or agent shall wear, in a conspicuous manner, an identification placard clearly displaying the name of the employee and the name, address and telephone number of the licensee, and shall carry on his or her person a copy of the license under this chapter. Prior to leaving the location where booting operations are conducted, the posted employee must remove all boots from vehicles at that location.

(f) The licensee shall place on the windshield of every vehicle it boots a copy of the "Consumer Bill of Rights," the text of which shall be provided by the department of consumer services and shall make and provide copies of this document available upon request. The owner or manager of the property that authorized the booting operations at that location shall make copies of the "Consumer Bill of Rights" available in its premises upon request.

(g) It is illegal to place a boot upon any occupied motor vehicle or upon any motor vehicle parked in accordance with the terms of use for the subject property.

(h) A licensee must immediately remove a boot, for no charge, from any motor vehicle if the owner of the motor vehicle returns prior to the complete attachment of the boot.

(i) The fee for removal of a boot shall be $115.00.

(j) At each and every location where a booting operation is conducted, the licensee shall have available means of collecting any fees via cash and credit card.

(k) A licensee shall notify the Chicago Police Department of any booted vehicle that remains in a lot or garage for over 24 hours.

(l) Each licensee shall maintain sufficient copies of the relevant portions of this chapter and shall provide a copy to any individual requesting the same.

(m) A licensee's place of business shall maintain minimum business hours of 9:00 a.m. to 5:00 p.m., Monday through Friday.

(n) A licensee may not use any boot of a color prohibited by the director of revenue in rules. The director may prohibit any color which may be confused with a boot used by the city as part of its vehicle immobilization program described in Title 9 of this code.

(o) The department of consumer services shall be responsible for the enforcement of subsections (c) and (f) through (j) of this section.

(p) The commissioner of the department of consumer services is hereby authorized to promulgate rules and regulations pertaining to the administration and enforcement of this chapter.

(Added. Coun. J. 12-13-00, p. 48188; Amend. Coun. J. 1-16-02, p. 77494; 1-14-04, p. 17356; 7-21-04, p. 28633)

§4-233-060 Geographical restrictions.

No person requiring a license under this chapter shall engage in booting operations at any location that is outside the 1st Ward, 30th Ward, 32nd Ward, 33rd Ward, 43rd Ward or 44th Ward, as defined on the effective date of this chapter, and as amended during the effective period of this chapter.

(Added. Coun. J. 12-13-00, p. 48188; Amend. 9-5-01, p. 66146; 11-28-01; p. 72960; 1-16-02, p. 77494; 5-1-02, p. 84263; 5-7-03, p. 790; 9-4-03, p. 7145; 1-14-04, p. 17356)

§4-233-070 Penalties.

A licensee who violates any provision of this chapter shall be subject to a fine not less than $500.00 nor more than $1,000.00 for the violation. A licensee who violates any provision of this chapter two times at one location within 180 days shall be prohibited from conducting booting operations at that location for a period of one week. Every day such violation continues shall constitute a separate and distinct offense.

(Added. Coun. J. 7-21-04, p. 28633)

CHAPTER 4-240
PAWNBROKERS
(Selected Sections)

Sections:

4-240-010 Definitions.
4-240-020 License—Required.
4-240-070 Maintenance of records.
4-240-080 Report to police.
4-240-090 Inspection of records.
4-240-100 Memorandum to pledger.
4-240-110 Exhibition of pledged article.
4-240-120 Display of weapons restricted.
4-240-125 Removal of identifying marks prohibited.

4-240-130 Hours of business.
4-240-140 Sales and redemptions regulated.
4-240-150 Prohibited pledges or purchases.
4-240-160 Employees under sixteen.
4-240-170 Violation—Penalty.

§4-240-010 Definitions.

As used in this chapter:

"Pawnbroker" means every person engaged in the business of receiving property in pledge or as security for money or other things advanced to the pawner or pledger.

"Secondhand property" has the meaning ascribed to that term by Section 4-264-005 of this code.

(Coun. J. 12-9-92, p. 25465; Amend. 2-26-97, p. 40141)

§4-240-020 License—Required.

No person shall engage in the business of a pawnbroker within the city without a license. No junk peddler, junk facility or secondhand dealer shall, during the period for which he shall have been licensed or permitted as such, receive or hold any license to engage in the business of a pawnbroker.

(Coun. J. 12-9-92, p. 25465; Amend. Coun. J. 10-7-98, p. 78812)

§4-240-070 Maintenance of records.

(a) Every such licensee shall keep a book in which there shall be typed or printed in ink at the time of each loan a legible and accurate description in the English language of the goods, articles or things pawned or pledged, the amount of money loaned thereon, the time of pledging the same, the rate of interest to be paid on such loan, and the person pawning or pledging the said goods, article or thing. No entry made in such shall be erased, obliterated or defaced. For purposes of this section, the phrase "typed or printed in ink" may include a computer printout.

(b) The description of each musical instrument, camera, appliance or machine of any type shall include: the brand name, the model number, if available, and any serial number or other identification number installed by the manufacturer; and a description of every other identifying marking, such as an inscription, a social security number, a name, nickname or address, appearing on the item. The description of each watch shall include: the brand name, model number, if available; a description of the metal or metals of its composition; a description of the band, if any; a description of the face by number, color, cut, shape and type of stone or stones, if any; and a description of any inscriptions appearing on the watch. The description of each item of jewelry shall include the type; a description of the metal or metals of its composition; the type, shape and cut of each stone; and a description of all inscriptions. Each ring shall also be identified by ring size. In addition, each watch and item of jewelry shall be photographed in color.

(c) The description of each person who pawns or pledges shall consist of the person's name, residence address, birthdate, social security number, weight, height and gender. If the person has no social security number, the licensee shall record this fact.

(d) Every pawnbroker shall require two forms of identification to be shown to him or her by each person pledging or pawning any goods, articles or other things to the pawnbroker. At least one of the two forms of identification must list the person's name and residence address. Except as provided in subsection (e) of this section, at least one of the two forms of identification must be a photographic identification issued by a federal, state or local governmental entity. Forms of identification may include, but are not limited to: a state driver's license, a state identification card, a passport, a military identification card, or a credit card or utility bill.

(e) If the customer does not have a photographic identification card issued by a federal, state or local governmental entity, the licensee shall photograph the customer. The photograph shall be in color. On the reverse side of the photograph the licensee shall record the customer's name, residence address, date of birth, social security number, gender, height and weight. If the customer has no social security number, the licensee shall record this fact. Two forms of identification shall also be required. At least one of the two forms of identification shall list the person's name and residence address.

(f) Whenever any such licensee shall buy any article of secondhand property, the same shall be recorded in the same manner as a pledge and said record shall show all information required for a pawn or pledge.

(Coun. J. 12-9-92, p. 25465; Amend. 2-26-97, p. 40141)

§4-240-080 Report to police.

(a) It shall be the duty of every such licensee to make out and deliver to a location or locations designated by the superintendent of police every day, before the hour of twelve noon, a legible and correct copy from the books required in Section 4-240-070 of all personal property and other valuable things received on deposit, and all articles of secondhand property purchased during the preceding day, setting forth the hour when received and the description of the person by whom left in pledge or sold.

(b) The photographs required under Section 4-240-070 shall not be included in the records delivered to the superintendent of police, but shall remain available for inspection and duplication by the police department.

(Coun. J. 12-9-92, p. 25465; Amend. 2-26-97, p. 40141)

§4-240-090 Inspection of records.

The said book, the photographs required under Section 4-240-070, and every article or other thing of value pawned or pledged, or any article of secondhand property obtained through purchase or exchange, shall at all times during the licensee's business hours be open to the inspection of the mayor or any member of the police force or any investigator of the department of revenue or the department of consumer services.

(Coun. J. 12-9-92, p. 25465; Amend. 2-26-97, p. 40141)

§4-240-100 Memorandum to pledger.

Every such licensee shall at the time of each loan deliver to the person pawning or pledging any goods, article or thing, a memorandum or note signed by him containing the substance of the entry made in his book as required by

this chapter; and no charge shall be made or received by any pawnbroker or loanbroker or keeper of a loan office for any such entry, memorandum or note.
(Coun. J. 12-9-92, p. 25465)

§4-240-110 Exhibition of pledged article.

Every such licensee shall, during business hours, upon the request of any pledger presenting the memorandum herein provided for, or upon the request of any assignee or transferee thereof presenting such memorandum, exhibit to such person the article pledged and described in such memorandum. Each article pledged shall have attached thereto a tag with the pledge number, the time when said pledge was obtained, and the amount of said pledge.
(Coun. J. 12-9-92, p. 25465)

§4-240-120 Display of weapons restricted.

No such licensee shall show, display or exhibit any pistol, revolver, derringer, bowie knife, dirk or other weapon of like character which can be concealed on the person, in any show window or in or on any premises immediately abutting upon any public way in the city in such a way that the same may be seen from such public way.
(Coun. J. 12-9-92, p. 25465)

§4-240-125 Removal of identifying marks prohibited.

No licensee shall remove, alter or obliterate any manufacturer's make, model, or serial number, personal identification number, or identifying marks engraved or etched upon an item of personal property that was purchased or received in pledge until such time that the licensee becomes the legal owner of the property. In addition, an item shall not be accepted for pledge or purchase where the manufacturer's make, model, or serial number, personal identification number or identifying marks engraved or etched upon an item of personal property has been removed, altered or obliterated.
(Added. Coun. J. 2-26-97, p. 40141)

§4-240-130 Hours of business.

No such licensee shall receive on deposit or pledge any personal property or other valuable thing, or shall buy any article of secondhand property, before the hour of 6:00 a.m. or after the hour of 9:00 p.m.
(Coun. J. 12-9-92, p. 25465; Amend. 2-26-97, p. 40141)

§4-240-140 Sales and redemptions regulated.

(a) No personal property received on deposit or pledge by any such licensed pawnbroker shall be sold or permitted to be redeemed or removed from the place of business of such licensed pawnbroker for the period of two business days, excluding Saturdays, Sundays and holidays, after the copy and statement to be delivered to the superintendent of police shall have been delivered as required by this chapter.

(b) No personal property pawned or pledged shall be sold or disposed of by any such pawnbroker within one year from the time when the pawner or pledger shall make default in the payment of the interest on the money so advanced by such pawnbroker, unless by the written consent of such pawner or pledger.

(c) No licensee shall offer or give any inducement or payment for the consent of the pawner or pledger for the early sale or disposition of personal property.

(d) No article of secondhand property purchased by any such licensed pawnbroker shall be sold or removed from the place of business of such licensed pawnbroker for the period of 30 calendar days after the copy and statement to be delivered to the superintendent of police shall have been delivered as required by this chapter.

(Coun. J. 12-9-92, p. 25465; Amend. 2-26-97, p. 40141)

§4-240-150 Prohibited pledges or purchases.

No such licensee shall take or receive in pawn or pledge, for money loaned, or shall buy any property from a minor, or shall so take, receive or buy any such property the ownership of which is in, or which is claimed by, any minor, or which may be in the possession or under the control of any minor.

No such licensee shall take any article in pawn or buy from any person appearing to be intoxicated or under the influence of any drug, nor from any person known to be a thief or to have been convicted of theft or burglary, and when any person is found to be the owner of stolen property which has been pawned or bought, such property shall be returned to the owner thereof without the payment of the amount advanced by the pawnbroker thereon or any costs or charges of any kind which the pawnbroker may have placed upon the same.

(Coun. J. 12-9-92, p. 25465; Amend. 2-26-97, p. 40141)

§4-240-160 Employees under sixteen.

No such licensee shall permit any person under the age of 16 years to take pledges in pawn for him or to purchase secondhand articles for him.

(Coun. J. 12-9-92, p. 25465)

§4-240-170 Violation—Penalty.

Any person violating any of the provisions of this chapter shall be fined not less than $500.00 nor more than $1,000.00 for each offense. Each violation in regard to a separate transaction shall constitute a separate and distinct offense.

(Coun. J. 12-9-92, p. 25465)

CHAPTER 4-244
PEDDLERS
(Selected Sections)

Sections:

4-244-010 Peddler defined.
4-244-020 Classification.
4-244-030 License—Required.
4-244-080 Identification on peddlers' vehicles.
4-244-090 Vehicle emblems.
4-244-100 Badges.
4-244-110 Assistants on vehicles.
4-244-120 Hours of business.

4-244-130 Peddling in vicinity of Wrigley Field.
4-244-140 Prohibited districts.
4-244-141 Speech peddling—Additional areas allowed.
4-244-145 Peddling in vicinity of Comiskey Park.
4-244-146 Peddling in vicinity of New Maxwell Street Market.
4-244-147 Peddling in vicinity of United Center.
4-244-150 Flower peddling prohibited.
2-244-160 Reserved.
4-244-170 Violation—Penalty.

§4-244-010 Peddler defined.

As used in this chapter:

"Peddler" means any individual who, going from place to place, shall sell, offer for sale, sell and deliver, barter or exchange any goods, wares, merchandise, wood, fruits, vegetables or produce from a vehicle or otherwise. The word "peddler" does not include a grower or producer as defined in Section 4-12-010 of this code.

(Prior code § 160-1)

§4-244-020 Classification.

For the purpose of this chapter peddlers are divided into two types as follows:

Food Peddlers. This class shall include peddlers selling fruits and vegetables and no other food item from wagons, pushcarts, handcarts or other vehicles, or from packs, baskets or similar containers. Food peddlers may peddle non-food commodities to the extent that such commodities do not comprise more than 15 percent of annual gross sales.

Non-Food Peddlers. This class shall include peddlers selling and delivering non-food commodities from wagons, pushcarts, handcarts or other vehicles, and from packs, baskets or similar containers.

(Coun. J. 12-9-92, p. 25465)

§4-244-030 License—Required.

It shall be unlawful for any person to engage in the business of a peddler without a license so to do; provided, however, that the classes of peddlers specifically defined and licensed by other chapters of this code shall be exempt from the provisions of this chapter.

Any person violating this section shall be fined not less than $50.00 nor more than $200.00 for each offense.

(Coun. J. 12-9-92, p. 25465)

§4-244-080 Identification on peddlers' vehicles.

Every wagon, cart or other vehicle used by a licensed peddler in or about his business shall have the name of the owner and his address plainly, distinctly and legibly painted in letters and figures at least two inches in height in a conspicuous place on the outside of each side of every such wagon, cart or other vehicle, and such name and address shall be kept so painted plainly and distinctly at all times while such wagon, cart or other vehicle is in use during the continuance of the license covering the use of such wagon, cart or other vehicle.

(Coun. J. 12-9-92, p. 25465)

§4-244-090 Vehicle emblems.

Every peddler whose license entitles him to use a wagon, motor vehicle, handcart, pushcart or other vehicle shall obtain from the city clerk, at the time his license is issued, a metal plate or other suitable emblem for each such vehicle to be used by him in or about his business. Such plate or emblem shall have stamped or imprinted thereon the words "Chicago Food Peddler," or "Chicago Non-Food Peddler," as the case may be. Such plate or emblem shall be of a different color and design for every license period and shall have stamped thereon a number corresponding to the number of such peddler's license.

(Coun. J. 12-9-92, p. 25465)

§4-244-100 Badges.

Every individual having a license as a peddler, while engaged in the business of peddling, shall wear conspicuously on the outside of his outside coat a metal badge or shield indicating that such individual is licensed as a "Chicago Food Peddler—Fruits and Vegetables Only" or "Chicago Non-Food Peddler."

(Coun. J. 12-9-92, p. 25465)

§4-244-110 Assistants on vehicles.

Upon each wagon or other vehicle licensed under the provisions of this chapter, there shall be permitted but one helper or assistant to the driver or operator of such wagon or vehicle.

(Coun. J. 12-9-92, p. 25465)

§4-244-120 Hours of business.

No one shall peddle any article or thing in any public alley on any day in the week between the hours of 5:00 p.m. and 7:00 a.m., under a penalty of not less than $50.00 and not more than $200.00 for each offense. The provisions of this section shall not apply to a person licensed as a peddler operating in accordance with Section 4-244-130.

(Coun. J. 12-9-92, p. 25465)

§4-244-130 Peddling in vicinity of Wrigley Field.

Notwithstanding the limitations of Section 4-244-120, a person licensed as a peddler may peddle merchandise within 1,000 feet of Wrigley Field; provided that only a peddler selling from packs, baskets or similar containers may peddle merchandise on the public way. A peddler operating under this section shall be mobile, and shall not set up tables, stands or other structures, or obstruct or block the public way with his wares or merchandise. However, a peddler operating under this section may peddle merchandise from a cart, table or temporary stand on private property without obstructing the public way, if the peddler possesses written permission from the property owner to do so.

(Coun. J. 12-9-92, p. 25465)

§4-244-140 Prohibited districts.

No one having a peddler's license shall peddle any merchandise or any other article or thing whatsoever, at any time, within districts which have been or shall be hereafter designated by the city council. A description of such districts shall be kept in the office of the city clerk.

No person other than a peddler selling from packs, baskets or similar containers shall peddle any merchandise on any public way within 1,000 feet of Wrigley Field.

Peddling is prohibited on both sides of North Milwaukee Avenue, between North Kedzie Avenue and West Belmont Avenue and on intersecting streets between North Kedzie Avenue and West Belmont Avenue within 100 feet of the closest right-of-way line of Milwaukee Avenue.

Peddling is prohibited on North Cicero Avenue (west side) to West Fullerton Avenue (north) to North Lamon Avenue (east side) to West Clybourn Avenue (south). Peddling is prohibited on West Le Moyne (south side)—North Lawndale Avenue to West North Avenue (south side) to North Central Park Avenue.

Peddling is prohibited on the north side of West Lawrence Avenue, between North Winthrop Avenue and the "L" tracks.

Peddling is prohibited on Chicago Avenue, from North Lake Shore Drive to North LaSalle Boulevard.

Peddling is prohibited at any time within the following designated district:

Beginning at the intersection of West Belmont Avenue and the centerline of the north branch of the Chicago River; thence northerly on the centerline of the north branch of the Chicago River to West Wilson Avenue; thence east on West Wilson Avenue to North Western Avenue; thence north on North Western Avenue to West Gunnison Street; thence west on West Gunnison Street to North Rockwell Street; thence north on North Rockwell Street to West Winnemac Avenue; thence east on West Winnemac Avenue to North Western Avenue; thence north on North Western Avenue to West Foster Avenue; thence east on West Foster Avenue to North Winchester Avenue; thence south on North Winchester Avenue to West Winona Avenue; thence east on West Winona Avenue to North Wolcott Avenue; thence north on North Wolcott Avenue to West Foster Avenue; thence east on West Foster Avenue to North Ashland Avenue; thence south on North Ashland Avenue to West Lawrence Avenue; thence east on West Lawrence Avenue to North Dover Street; thence south on North Dover Street to West Montrose Avenue; thence west on West Montrose Avenue to North Clark Street; thence southerly on North Clark Street to West Byron Street; thence west on West Byron Street to North Greenview Avenue; thence south on North Greenview Avenue to West Grace Street; thence west on West Grace Street to North Ravenswood Avenue; thence south on North Ravenswood Avenue to West Addison Street; thence west on West Addison Street to North Western Avenue; thence south on North Western Avenue to West Belmont Avenue; thence west on West Belmont Avenue to the place of beginning.

Except where otherwise allowed under this chapter, peddling is prohibited at any time within the following designated district, which may be referred to as the "Central District":

Beginning at the intersection of the south bank of the Chicago River and Lake Michigan; thence west to the north side of Lake Street; thence west to the west side of Halsted Street; thence south to the south side of Depot Street; thence east on Depot Street and Depot Street, extended to the centerline of the south branch of the Chicago River; thence north to the south side of Roosevelt Road; thence east to the west side of State Street; thence south to the north side of 13th Street; thence east to the west side of Michigan Avenue; thence south to the north side of Cermak Road; thence west to the centerline of Clark Street; thence north to the north side of Cullerton Street; thence west extended to the centerline of Grove Street; thence southwest to the Pennsylvania Central Railroad; thence south to the south side of Cermak Road; thence east to the west side of Princeton Avenue; thence south to the south side of 24th Place; thence east to the east side of Wentworth Avenue; thence north to the south side of Cermak Road; thence east to the west side of Dr. Martin Luther King, Jr. Drive; thence south to the north side of 24th Street; thence east extended to Lake Michigan; thence north along Lake Michigan to the place of beginning.

Peddling is prohibited at any time within the following designated areas:

South Ewing Avenue (both sides) between south 9400 and 10900;

East 106th Street (both sides) between South Mackinaw Avenue and South State Line Road;

South Baltimore Avenue (both sides) between 13000 and South Brainard Avenue;

South Brandon Avenue (both sides) between 13200 and South Brainard Avenue;

East 132nd Street between South Houston Avenue and South Burley Avenue;

East 133rd Street between South Houston Avenue and South Burley Avenue;

East 134th Street between South Houston Avenue and South Burley Avenue; and

East 135th Street between South Houston Avenue and South Burley Avenue.

South Dr. Martin Luther King, Jr. Drive (both sides) between 7500 and 9500 south.

South Cottage Grove Avenue (both sides) between 7100 and 7900 south.

South Cottage Grove Avenue (west side only) between 7900 south and 9200 south.

East 75th Street, between South Perry Avenue and South Cottage Grove Avenue.

East 79th Street, between South State Street and South Cottage Grove Avenue.

East 87th Street, between South State Street and South Cottage Grove Avenue.

East 95th Street, between South State Street and South Dr. Martin King, Jr. Drive.

Peddling is prohibited at any time within the following designated areas:

The area known as:

Beginning at the intersection of North Western Avenue and West Cornelia Avenue extended; thence north on North Western Avenue to West Addison Street; thence east on West Addison Street extended to the northwest corner of West Addison Street and North Ravenswood Avenue; thence south extended to the northwest corner of North Ravenswood Avenue and West Cornelia Avenue; thence west extended back to the northeast corner of North Cornelia Avenue and North Western Avenue.

and

The area known as:

Beginning at the intersection of the northeast corner of North Ravenswood Avenue and West Addison Street extended north to the southeast corner of North Ravenswood Avenue and West Grace Street; thence east extended to the northwest corner of North Ashland Avenue and West Grace Street; thence south extended to the northwest corner of West Addison Street and North Ashland Avenue; thence west extended to the northwest corner of West Addison Street and North Ravenswood Avenue.

and

Beginning at the intersection of the northwest corner of West Wilson Avenue and North Western Avenue extended to the southwest corner of North Lincoln Avenue and North Western Avenue; thence continuing north to the southwest corner of North Lincoln Avenue and West Gunnison Street; thence west extended along west Gunnison Street to the southeast corner of the intersection of West Gunnison Street and North Rockwell Street; thence west extended to the Chicago River; thence south along the Chicago River extended to West Wilson Avenue; thence east extended to the northwest corner of West Wilson Avenue and North Western Avenue.

Any person who shall be found in violation of this section shall be fined not less than $200.00 nor more than $500.00 for each offense, and each day such violation shall continue shall be deemed a distinct and separate offense.
(Coun. J. 12-9-92, p. 25465; Amend. Coun. J. 6-9-93, pp. 33609, 33610, 33612; 7-13-95, p. 4599; 6-10-96, p. 23875; 9-11-96, p. 28269; 6-4-97, p. 46440; 5-12-99, p. 2313; 7-29-03, p. 5693, 5695; 10-1-03, p. 8863)

§4-244-141 Speech peddling—Additional areas allowed.

(a) Definitions. For purposes of this section, "speech peddling" shall mean where a licensed peddler sells or exchanges for value anything containing words, printing or pictures that predominantly communicates a noncommercial message.

For purposes of this section, a "noncommercial message" may include, without limitation, a message relating to political, religious, artistic, and/or any other noncommercial idea(s). Where the words, printing and/or pictures do nothing more than identify a product, such as a brand name or logo, or identify the peddled item's origin or place of manufacture, or otherwise do nothing more than advertise or promote the product itself, the item shall not be deemed to communicate a "noncommercial message."

For purposes of this section, "predominately communicates" means that the noncommercial message is the primary purpose of the item which is being sold. Factors that should be considered in determining whether an item predominantly communicates a noncommercial message include: (i) the percentage of the item containing non-commercial printing and/or pictures, (ii) the size of the lettering or pictures, and (iii) any other factor otherwise indicating that the primary purpose of the item being sold is to communicate a noncommercial message. In no event may there be any commercial message which occupies more space on the item than does the noncommercial message.

For purposes of this section, items that may, under the relevant criteria, predominantly communicate a noncommercial message may include T-shirts, books, audiotapes, videotapes, compact disks, posters, flags, banners, signs, buttons, toys, balloons or any other item.

(b) Speech Peddling Locations. There shall be at least 10 locations within the Central District, where peddling is otherwise prohibited under Section 4-244-140 above, including at least four locations within Grant Park, where speech peddling by up to five peddlers per location shall be allowed by permit. Such locations shall be selected by the department of revenue with the advice of the department of planning, the department of transportation, and the police department, regarding pedestrian and vehicular traffic flow, use, density and public safety; provided that, for locations in Grant Park near special events sponsored by the city, the mayor's office of special events shall select the sites during the relevant time periods and the number of Grant Park sites may change. In addition, because of anticipated high demand for speech peddling during special events, permits shall be issued for four-hour time slots and may be issued for more than five persons at a time per location. No person shall be allowed to engage in speech peddling within the Central District without a speech peddling permit, and doing so without such a permit shall be a violation of this section.

(c) Speech Peddling Permits.

(1) All licensed peddlers who wish to apply for a speech peddling permit must complete and submit to the department of revenue a written permit application, which shall require the following information:

(A) Name and peddler's license number;

(B) Any preferred location(s);

(C) A description of the item(s) he or she will be selling that "predominantly communicates a noncommercial message," including description of the type of item(s) to be sold, the nature of the communication, and a picture or graphic depicting the item(s).

This information is requested solely for purposes of determining that the item is within the definition of "speech peddling," and it shall not be used for evaluating the message itself.

(2) Speech peddling permit applications shall be accepted by the department of revenue on a monthly basis for speech peddling in the following month. Permits issued shall pertain only to the item(s) described in the permit application. Where the application shows that the "speech peddling" definition has been met, then the permit request shall be granted, unless the demand for permits is greater than availability. Where demands exceed availability, the department shall assign permits on a lottery basis and may not be able to fulfill requests for specific locations. There shall be a preference lottery for applicants who failed to receive permits in prior permit lotteries. Applicants shall be notified of the permit grant or denial within a reasonable time, as further specified by regulation.

(3) Applicants who were denied a speech peddling permit because of heavy demand may make a request, at the time of their next application, that their application be put in a preference lottery. Applicants who were denied a speech peddling permit (i) because their request was outside the scope of the "speech peddling" definition, or (ii) after not receiving a permit after two consecutive applications, may appeal to the director of revenue, or his or her designee, on a form provided by the department. Any such appeal must be filed

within 10 calendar days of such denial. The appeal form, together with the relevant application(s) and denial(s), shall be reviewed by the director, or his or her designee, and he or she shall issue a written determination within one week whether to uphold or reverse the denial or to grant an alternative permit date.

(d) Identification. All speech peddlers must carry identification and permit authorization from the department, in a form to be further described by regulation.

(e) No Pushcarts. A peddler selling in a speech peddling location pursuant to permit may only sell from packs, baskets or similar containers, shall be mobile, shall not set up tables, stands or other structures, and shall not use pushcarts, place items on the sidewalk or street, or otherwise obstruct or block the public way with his wares or merchandise.

(f) Regulations. The department of revenue has the authority to, and shall, promulgate regulations governing speech peddling permits and activities under this section. The mayor's office of special events has the authority to, and shall, promulgate regulations governing the locations, time, and manner of speech peddling during all city-sponsored special events, including during their set-up and cleanup.

(g) Violations. Any person who shall be found in violation of this section, including the implementing regulations, shall be fined not less than $50.00 nor more than $200.00 for each offense, and each day such violation shall continue shall be deemed a distinct and separate offense.

(Added. Coun. J. 5-12-99, p. 2313)

§4-244-145 Peddling in vicinity of Comiskey Park.

No person shall peddle merchandise of any type on any portion of the public way within 1,000 feet of Comiskey Park. A person holding a valid peddler's license may peddle merchandise while on private property within 1,000 feet of Comiskey Park only from a cart, table or temporary stand on private property without obstructing the public way, and pursuant to prior written permission from the property owner to do so. The provisions of this section shall be in addition to any other limitation on or regulation of peddlers. Any person who violates any provision of this section shall be fined not less than $200.00 nor more than $500.00 for each offense, and each day such violation shall continue shall be deemed a distinct and separate offense.

(Added. Coun. J. 3-8-93, p. 29484)

§4-244-146 Peddling in vicinity of New Maxwell Street Market.

No person shall peddle merchandise of any type on any portion of the public way within 1,000 feet of any portion of the New Maxwell Street Market, as set forth in Section 4-11-010.

(Added. Coun. J. 4-13-94, p. 49201)

§4-244-147 Peddling in vicinity of United Center.

No person shall peddle merchandise of any type on any portion of the public way within 1,000 feet of the United Center. A person holding a valid peddler's license may peddle merchandise while on private property within 1,000 feet of the United Center only from a cart, table or temporary stand on private property without obstructing the public way, and pursuant to prior written per-

mission from the property owner to do so. The provisions of this section shall be in addition to any other limitation on or regulation of peddlers. Any person who violates any provision of this section shall be fined not less than $200.00 nor more than $500.00 for each offense, and each day such violation shall continue shall be deemed a distinct and separate offense.
(Added. Coun. J. 10-2-95, p. 8258)

4-244-150 Flower peddling prohibited.

No person licensed hereunder shall have the privilege of peddling flowers, growing plants, or floral bouquets or designs; provided, however, that nothing in this section prohibits the peddling of flowers within a duly licensed tavern or restaurant, with the consent of the licensee of the tavern or a restaurant.
(Coun. J. 12-9-92, p. 25465; Amended. Coun. J. 9-4-02; p. 92885)

§2-244-160 Reserved.
(Repealed Coun. J. 10-3-2001, p. 68133)

4-244-170 Violation—Penalty.

Any peddler who shall be guilty of any fraud or misrepresentation, or who shall violate any of the provisions of this chapter, shall be fined not less than $50.00 nor more than $200.00 for each offense, where no other penalty is provided in this chapter.
(Coun. J. 12-9-92, p. 25465)

CHAPTER 4-253
RETAIL COMPUTING CENTERS
(Selected Sections)

Sections:

4-253-010 Definitions.
4-253-020 License required.
4-253-040 Limits on activities— Construction with other provisions.
4-253-050 Violations.

§4-253-010 Definitions.

Whenever used in this chapter:

"Computing workstation" or "workstation" means a separate unit including seating, work space, a central processing unit, a keyboard, hard drive and connection to a printing device. A computing workstation typically provides access to a range of applications for various purposes, including business, education, personal computing, communications services, on-line services and internet.

"Retail computing center" means any building, structure, premises or portion thereof containing three or more computing workstations held out to the public for a fee for (a) the rental of computer access at a computing workstation for computing usage; (b) computer training addressed to office, personal communications or other computer-based skills.
(Added. Coun. J. 6-9-99, p. 5366)

§4-253-020 License required.

No person shall engage in the business of a retail computing center without first having obtained a license under this chapter. No more than one retail computing center license shall be required for any location under single ownership and control, regardless of the number of computing workstations available within the center.

(Added. Coun. J. 6-9-99, p. 5366)

§4-253-040 Limits on activities—Construction with other provisions.

(a) No licensee under this chapter shall sell, dispense or offer to sell or dispense alcoholic liquor, as defined in Chapter 4-60, on the licensed premises.

(b) The fee for use of a computing workstation shall be based on the duration of customer use, without consideration of the type or number of applications used by the customer. No premium, rebate, prize or additional time of use shall be given to any customer for any result achieved by use of a workstation.

(c) A computing workstation located in a licensed retail computing center shall not require an automatic amusement device licensee under Chapter 4-156 of this code if the licensee does not advertise that games are available on the computing stations, and if the actual use of the computing station for the playing of games is not more than 25% of the use of the station per month.

(d) A retail computing center operating in compliance with a valid license under this chapter shall not require a public place of amusement license under Chapter 4-156 of this code if (1) a majority of the menu selection categories available to customers are dedicated to applications for business, personal computing, education, communications services and internet access; and (2) the licensee does not advertise that games are available on the computing stations; and (3) the actual use of the computing stations within the licensed location for the playing of games is not more than 25% of the use of the stations per month.

(e) A licensee under this chapter shall maintain an electronic record of the use of the computing stations at the licensed premises, in order to determine which applications are employed and the length of time that each application is used. It is a violation of this section to alter, manipulate, delete or tamper with the required electronic record.

(Added. Coun. J. 6-9-99, p. 5366; Amend. Coun. J. 6-19-02, p. 88692; 7-31-02, p. 91447)

§4-253-050 Violations.

Any person who violates any provision of this chapter shall be subject to a fine of not less than $250.00 and not more than $1,000.00 for each offense.

(Added. Coun. J. 6-9-99, p. 5366)

CHAPTER 4-256
ROOFERS
(Selected Sections)

Sections:

4-256-010 Roofer defined.
4-256-020 License—Required.
4-256-140 Violation—Penalty.

§4-256-010 Roofer defined.

As used in this chapter:

"Roofer" means any person engaged in the business of repairing, recoating, altering or changing roofs of buildings or other structures within the city with tile, plate, sheet metal, mastic and gravel roofing, ready roofing over shingles, asphalt and asphalt shingle roofing, and felt composition roofing, or any other kind of prepared roofing, and who shall use a vehicle in and about such business.
(Coun. J. 12-9-92, p. 25465; Amend. 2-7-96, p. 15616)

§4-256-020 License—Required.

It shall be unlawful for any person to engage in the business of a roofer without obtaining a limited business license.

In addition to a limited business license, if required by Chapter 4-204 of this code, a home repair license shall be obtained in conformity with such chapter before a person may engage in the business of roofer.
(Coun. J. 12-9-92, p. 25465; Amend. 2-7-96, p. 15616; 6-10-96, p. 23652)

§4-256-140 Violation—Penalty.

Any person violating any of the provisions of this chapter shall be fined not less than $200.00 nor more than $500.00 for each offense.
(Coun. J. 12-9-92, p. 25465; Amend. 2-7-96, p. 15616)

CHAPTER 4-260
SCAVENGERS
(Selected Sections)

Sections:

Article II. Private Scavengers
4-260-030 Private scavenger defined.
4-260-035 Refuse container defined.
4-260-040 License—Required.
4-260-060 Notice to commissioner of streets and sanitation.
4-260-080 Emblems and other identification required.
4-260-085 Graffiti on refuse container.
4-260-090 Removal of spilled refuse required.

Article VI. Violation of Chapter Provisions
4-260-390 Violation—Penalties.

Article II. Private Scavengers

§4-260-030 Private scavenger defined.

As used in this chapter:

"Private scavenger" means any person engaged in the removal and disposal of table refuse or animal and vegetable matter usually known as garbage, from hotels, restaurants, cafes, boardinghouses and other places not otherwise provided for by the city; or the removal and disposal of ashes and cinders; or the removal and disposal of manure, swill or any animal or vegetable refuse and wastes, including decaying animal matter and fish from commission houses and other places where such decaying animal matter and fish may accumulate.

(Coun. J. 12-9-92, p. 25465)

§4-260-035 Refuse container defined.

For the purposes of this chapter "refuse container" means any commercial refuse container or compactor as defined in Section 7-28-210.

(Added. Coun. J. 3-27-02, p. 82295)

§4-260-040 License—Required.

No person shall engage in the business of private scavenger, or shall be permitted to remove and dispose of swill, offal, table refuse usually known as garbage, or any other matter enumerated in the preceding section, without first having obtained a license so to do; provided, however, that no license shall be required of any person for the removal of manure from his own premises; and provided further, that any person desiring to gather, remove or dispose of garbage, decaying animal matter, and fish, swill or other animal or vegetable refuse and wastes from his own premises without the aid of a licensed private scavenger may do so only upon the written permission of the commissioner of streets and sanitation, and then only in the manner specified in such permit.

Any person violating this section shall be subject to a fine of not less than $200.00 or more than $500.00 for each offense.

(Added. Coun. J. 12-9-92, p. 25465; Amend. Coun. J. 12-4-02, p. 99931)

§4-260-060 Notice to commissioner of streets and sanitation.

Every licensed scavenger shall inform the commissioner of streets and sanitation of the scavenger's suspension of service at any location within the city. The notice shall be in a form specified by the commissioner, and shall identify the licensed scavenger, the address of the location at which service has been suspended, and the name and nature of the business conducted at the location. The notice shall be delivered to the commissioner within three days after suspension of service. Any person who violates the provisions of this section shall be subject to a fine of not less than $200.00 and not more than $500.00.

(Added. Coun. J. 7-13-94, p. 53272)

§4-260-080 Emblems and other identification required.

Each person licensed as a private scavenger shall receive from the city clerk at the time the license is issued, a metal plate or other emblem for each vehicle used in the conduct of the business so licensed. On such plate or emblem shall be stamped or plainly marked the words "Chicago Private Scavenger." Said plate or emblem shall be conspicuously displayed on every vehicle used in said business.

It shall be the duty of every person licensed as a private scavenger that provides refuse containers to his customers to pain or otherwise permanently affix on each refuse container the name and phone number of the licensees. Upon the suspension of any contract for private scavenger service it shall be the duty of the licensee to remove any refuse container provided to his customer within 30 days of suspension. Upon termination of any contract for private scavenger service it shall be the duty of the licensee to remove any refuse container provided to his customer within 3 days.

It shall be unlawful for any licensee to provide any refuse container to anyone to whom he is not rendering service.

(Added. Coun. J. 12-9-92, p. 25465; Amend. Coun. J. 3-27-02, p. 82295; 6-19-02, p. 88694)

§4-260-085 Graffiti on refuse container.

It shall be the responsibility of any person licensed as a private scavenger:

(a) To be responsible for the appearance of any refuse container that he provides to his customers;

(b) To deliver a required refuse container free of graffiti; and

(c) To remove graffiti from any refuse container within 15 business days of receiving written notification from the commissioner sent by certified mail, return receipt requested, or by facsimile transmission; provided that from December 1 to March 1, if weather conditions makes removal of the graffiti impracticable, the commissioner may, by written order, extend the time for removal of the graffiti to such time that the removal would be practicable.

Along with every notice of a violation of this section, the department of streets and sanitation shall provide to the private scavenger a picture of the refuse container referenced in the notice.

Any person who violates any provision of this section shall be subject to a fine of not less than $100.00 and not more than $300.00.

(Added. Coun. J. 3-27-01, p. 82295)

§4-260-090 Removal of spilled refuse required.

Each person licensed as a private scavenger shall carry in his vehicle a rake, broom, shovel or other implement of sufficient strength and durability for the removal of scattered or spilled refuse. Whenever collecting refuse, a private scavenger shall completely remove scattered refuse lying within six feet of the container or container area which the private scavenger is servicing and all refuse dropped or spilled during collection. The commissioner of streets and sanitation may issue regulations specifying the types and conditions of implements complying with the requirements of this section.

Any person found in violation of this section shall be subject to a fine of not less than $200.00 nor more than $500.00 for each offense. In addition, a violation of this section shall constitute grounds for revocation or suspension of a private scavenger license pursuant to the provisions of Section 4-4-280 of this code.

(Added. Coun. J. 12-9-92, p. 25465; Amend. Coun. J. 7-13-94, p. 53272)

Article VI. Violation of Chapter Provisions

§4-260-390 Violation—Penalties.

Any person who violates any of the provisions of this chapter or the rules of the commissioner of buildings or the department of streets and sanitation concerning the business of scavengers shall, where not otherwise provided, be fined not less than $200.00 nor more than $500.00 for each offense, and a separate and distinct offense shall be regarded as committed each day on which such person shall continue any such violation. In addition, a violation of any of the provisions of this chapter shall constitute grounds for revocation or suspension of a private scavenger license pursuant to the provisions of Section 4-4-280 of this code.

(Added. Coun. J. 12-9-92, p. 25465; Amend. Coun. J. 3-5-03, p. 104990)

CHAPTER 4-264
SECONDHAND DEALERS
(Complete Chapter)

Sections:

Article I. Secondhand Dealers Generally

4-264-005 Definitions.
4-264-010 License—Required.
4-264-020 License—Application—Investigation.
4-264-030 License—Fee.
4-264-040 Frontage consents.
4-264-050 Recordkeeping.
4-264-051 Report to police.
4-264-052 Recordkeeping requirements related to digital audio and video discs.
4-264-060 Use of unlicensed premises prohibited.
4-264-070 Disassembling, melting and rebuilding articles.
4-264-075 Removal of identifying marks prohibited.
4-264-080 Public nuisance abatement.
4-264-090 Prohibited purchases.
4-264-100 Prohibited businesses.
4-264-101 Repurchase agreements prohibited.
4-264-110 Hours of business.
4-264-150 Children's products.

Article II. Itinerant Dealers in Secondhand Clothes. (Reserved)

Article III. Secondhand Bottle Dealers or Exchanges. (Reserved)

Article IV. Violation of Chapter Provisions

4-264-220 Enforcement.
4-264-230 Violation—Penalty.

Article I. Secondhand Dealers Generally

§4-264-005 Definitions.

For purposes of this chapter:

"Audio-video equipment" includes, but is not limited to, any stereo, speaker, radio, video recorder, video camera, television, tape or disc player, digital audio disc, digital video disc, telephone, pager or satellite signal device.

"Children's product" means any item of furniture manufactured for use by children under eight years of age, including, but not limited to, any crib, play-pen, stroller or child carrier.

"Currency" means coin or paper money that is bought, sold or otherwise transferred at greater than face value.

"Precious metal" means gold, silver or platinum.

"Precious stone or gem" means any genuine diamond, emerald, ruby, sapphire or pearl of any value and any other genuine stone or gem with a value of more than $100.00.

"Secondhand dealer" means any person who engages in the business of purchasing, selling, receiving, trading, consignment selling or otherwise transferring for value any secondhand property. Notwithstanding the foregoing, nothing in this chapter applies to: (i) pawnbrokers licensed under Chapter 4-240; junk peddlers licensed under Chapter 4-216; or junk facilities permitted under Chapter 11-4 of this code; (ii) sales or exchanges of used articles and materials conducted by or controlled by charitable or religious organizations; (iii) any person who purchases used articles or materials from a charitable or religious organization for the purpose of resale, if the person spends in excess of $1,000,000.00 per annum on purchases of used articles and materials from religious and charitable organizations for purposes of resale, and maintains an indoor facility of not fewer than 10,000 square feet for the sale of such used articles and materials; (iv) the sale of Chicago Transit Authority fare tokens pursuant to permission of the authority; (v) the purchase or sale of precious metals or currency on the Chicago Mercantile Exchange or on a similar exchange, wherever located; or (vi) the exchange of currency by a licensed currency exchange, national bank, federal savings bank or other financial institution as defined in the Illinois Banking Act.

"Secondhand property" means any previously owned audio-video equipment, camera, children's product, computer hardware, jewelry made of precious metal or stone, article made of precious metal, precious stone or gem, sporting or athletic gear or equipment, including a bicycle, watch or currency.
(Added Coun. J. 2-26-97, p. 40141; Amend. Coun. J. 10-7-98, p. 78812; 9-29-99, p. 12263; 11-3-99, p. 14166; 5-29-02, p. 86303)

§4-264-010 License—Required.

It shall be unlawful for any person to engage in the business of a secondhand dealer without first obtaining a license therefor for each separate place, premises or location where such business is to be conducted.
(Added. Coun. J. 12-9-92, p. 25465; Amend. Coun. J. 4-22-93, p. 31558; 2-26-97, p. 40141)

§4-264-020 License—Application—Investigation.

An application for license as a secondhand dealer shall be made in conformity with the general requirements of this code relating to applications for licenses. When

an application for such license is made, the superintendent of police shall cause an investigation to be made to ascertain whether the applicant has complied with the state laws and the provisions of this code applicable to said business, and whether the applicant is of good character and repute. Provided, however,

that such police investigation shall not be required for a secondhand dealer that deals in only children's products.
(Added. Coun. J. 12-9-92, p. 25465; Amend. Coun. J. 9-29-99, p. 12263)

§4-264-030 License—Fee.

The annual fee for a secondhand dealer's license shall be as set forth in Section 4-5-010. Provided, however, that the annual fee for a secondhand dealer that deals in only children's products shall be $125.00 and the annual fee shall be waived for a not-for-profit secondhand dealer that deals in only children's products.
(Added. Coun. J. 12-9-92, p. 25465; Amend. Coun. J. 9-29-99, p. 12263)

§4-264-040 Frontage consents.

It shall be unlawful to engage in the business of a secondhand dealer on any lot fronting on any public way in any block in which one-half of the buildings on both sides of the public way are used exclusively for residence purposes, or within 50 feet of any such public way, without the written consent of a majority of the property owners according to frontage on both sides of such public way. Such frontage consents shall be filed with the commissioner of buildings. Provided, however, that such frontage consents shall not be required for a secondhand dealer that deals in only children's products.
(Added. Coun. J. 12-9-92, p. 25465; Amend. Coun. J. 9-29-99, p. 12263; 3-5-03, p. 104990)

§4-264-050 Recordkeeping.

(a) Every secondhand dealer shall keep a book in which there shall be typed or printed in ink, at the time of the transaction, a legible and accurate description in the English language of every article of secondhand property received, purchased, sold or exchanged by him, the date of the transaction, and the purchaser or seller. No entry made in such book shall be erased, obliterated or defaced. For purposes of this section, the phrase "typed or printed in ink" may include a computer printout, and "book" includes an accessible computer database capable of being printed at the dealer's business location.

(b) The description of each article of secondhand property, other than digital audio discs or digital video discs, shall include: the brand name; the model number, if available; any serial number or other identification number installed by the manufacturer; and a description of every other identifying marking, such as an inscription, a social security number, a name, nickname or address, appearing on the item. The description of each watch shall include: the brand name; model number, if available; a description of the metal or metals of its composition; a description of the band; a description of the face by number, color and cut, shape and type of stone or stones, if any; and a description of any inscriptions appearing on the watch. The description of each item of jewelry shall include the type; a description of the metal or metals of its composition; the type, cut and shape of each stone; and a description of all inscriptions. Each ring shall also be identified by ring size. In addition, each watch and jewelry shall be photographed in color.

(c) The description of each person who sells an item of secondhand property to the licensee shall consist of the person's name, residence address, birth date, social security number, weight, height and gender. If the person has no social security number, the licensee shall record this fact.

(d) Every licensee shall require two forms of identification to be shown to him or her by each person selling an article of secondhand property to the licensee. At least one of the two forms of identification must list the person's name and residence address. Except as provided in subsection (e) of this section, at least one of the two forms of identification must be a photographic identification issued by a federal, state or local governmental entity. Forms of identification may include, but are not limited to: a state driver's license, a state identification card, a passport, a military identification card, a social security card, or a credit card or utility bill.

(e) If the customer does not have a photographic identification card issued by a federal, state or local governmental entity, the licensee shall photograph the customer. The photograph shall be in color. On the reverse side of the photograph the licensee shall record the customer's name, residence address, date of birth, social security number, gender, height and weight. If the customer has no social security number, the licensee shall record this fact. Two forms of identification shall also be required. At least one of the two forms of identification must include the person's name and residence address.

(f) Such records shall at all times during the licensee's business hours be open to the inspection of the mayor or any member of the police force, or any investigator of the department of revenue or the department of consumer services.

(Added, Coun. J. 12-9-92, p. 25465; Amend. Coun. J. 2-26-97, p. 40141)

§4-264-051 Report to police.

(a) Every person requiring a license under this chapter shall prepare and deliver to a location or locations designated by the superintendent of police every day, before the hour of twelve noon, a legible and correct copy of the records required in Section 4-264-050 of all secondhand property purchased during the preceding day, setting forth the hour when received and the description of the person by whom sold.

(b) The photographs required under Section 4-64-050 shall not be included in the records delivered to the superintendent of police, but shall remain available for inspection and duplication by the police department.

(Added Coun. J. 5-2-01, p. 58600)

§4-264-052 Record keeping requirements related to digital audio and video discs.

(a) Every person requiring a license under this chapter shall prepare and maintain records concerning the receipt of digital audio discs and digital video discs in accordance with this section. Records shall be maintained in English, and either typed, written in ink or stored in an accessible computer database capable of being printed in English at the dealer's business location. The records shall be complete within 24 hours of each transaction in which the person requiring the license acquires one or more digital audio discs or digital video discs. The records shall include: date of transaction; the name, address and date of birth of the source of the disc or discs; the form of identification, and its identifying number, relied on in establishing the person's identity; the number of discs acquired in the transaction; and the amount paid. For purposes of this section, only those forms of identification described in subsection (d) of Section 4-264-050 of this chapter shall be accepted.

(b) Records described in subsection (a) of this section shall, during the secondhand dealer's business hours, be open to inspection and copying by the mayor, any member of the police department and any investigator of the department of revenue.

(c) Any person who violates any provision of this section shall be subject to a fine of not less than $200 and not more than $500 for each transaction requiring to be recorded.

(Added. Coun. J. 10-1-03, p. 8867)

§4-264-060 Use of unlicensed premises prohibited.

No secondhand dealer shall make use of any property, private or public, not included within the licensed premises, for the storage, handling or display of any secondhand article.

(Added. Coun. J. 12-9-92, p. 25465)

§4-264-070 Disassembling, melting and rebuilding articles.

No person requiring a license under this chapter shall sell, dispose of, or remove from the place of business any article of secondhand property for 30 calendar days or take apart or melt up any article of secondhand property, or remodel or rebuild the same until he shall have made a record of his intention so to do along with the description of such article and all other data required to be recorded, in the record of purchases, sales and exchanges hereinbefore in this chapter provided for, and until he shall have kept such article intact in his licensed place of business for inspection for 10 calendar days. Notwithstanding anything to the contrary in this section, a license may resell any used digital audio disc or any used digital video disc five days after acquiring it.

(Added. Coun. J. 12-9-92, p. 25465; Amend. Coun. J. 2-26-97, p. 40141; 8-30-00, p. 39783; 10-1-03, p. 8867)

§4-264-075 Removal of identifying marks prohibited.

No licensee shall remove, alter or obliterate any manufacturer's make, model, or serial number, personal identification number, or identifying marks engraved or etched upon an article of secondhand property that was purchased by the licensee until after the 10-day holding period required by Section 4-264-070 has expired. In addition, no licensee shall purchase an article of secondhand property where the manufacturer's make, model, or serial number, personal identification number or identifying marks engraved or etched upon the article of secondhand property has been removed, altered or obliterated.

(Added Coun. J. 2-26-97, p. 40141)

§4-264-080 Public nuisance abatement.

It is hereby declared to be a public nuisance, and it shall be unlawful, for any secondhand dealer to permit any debris, rubbish, dirt or refuse to be accumulated on his licensed premises or to permit any dense smoke, cinders, dust,

gas or odor which shall be offensive or prejudicial to the health or dangerous to the life of any person to escape from his licensed premises, and the bureau of fire prevention or any officer designated by the said bureau shall take necessary action to abate such nuisance.
(Added. Coun. J. 12-9-92, p. 25465)

§4-264-090 Prohibited purchases.

No secondhand dealer shall purchase any article of secondhand property whatsoever from any minor without the written consent of a parent or legal guardian.

The consent must be signed in the presence of the licensee, who must include the consent in the daily record required under Section 4-264-050.

No secondhand dealer shall purchase any article of secondhand property from any person who appears intoxicated or under the influence of any drug.

No secondhand dealer shall purchase any article of secondhand property from any person known to be a thief or to have been convicted of theft or burglary, and when any person is found to be the owner of stolen property which has been bought, such property shall be returned to the owner thereof without the payment of the amount paid by the secondhand dealer for the stolen property.
(Added. Coun. J. 12-9-92, p. 25465; Amend. Coun. J. 2-26-97, p. 40141)

§4-264-100 Prohibited businesses.

No person licensed as a secondhand dealer shall, during the period of his license, receive or hold a license or permit to carry on the business of a pawnbroker or keeper of a junk facility.
(Added. Coun. J. 12-9-92, p. 25465; Amend. Coun. J. 10-7-98, p. 78812)

§4-264-101 Repurchase agreements prohibited.

No secondhand dealer shall enter into any oral or written agreement or understanding with the seller of an item of merchandise, whereby the seller receives or retains a right to repurchase the item that is superior to the right of any other person willing to purchase such item.
(Added. Coun. J. 2-26-97, p. 40141)

§4-264-110 Hours of business.

No such licensee shall buy any secondhand article or thing, before the hour of 6:00 a.m. or after the hour of 9:00 p.m.
(Added. Coun. J. 2-26-97, p. 40141)

§4-264-150 Children's products.

(a) Every licensee engaged in the business of purchasing, selling, receiving, trading, consignment selling or otherwise transferring any children's product shall obtain and maintain on file in paper form in the licensed premises the recall notifications issued over the preceding nine-year period by the United States Consumer Product Safety Commission.

(b) No secondhand dealer shall purchase, sell, receive, trade, place on consignment or otherwise transfer any children's product that does not contain the manufacturer's original label, tag or other identification; provided that this requirement shall not apply if the secondhand dealer has documentation or pho-

tographic evidence which establishes the identity of the product manufacturer. The commissioner of consumer services may promulgate rules and regulations identifying the types of documentation or photographic evidence that may be used to establish a manufacturer's identity under this subsection.
(Added. Coun. J. 9-29-99, p. 12263)

Article II. Itinerant Dealers in Secondhand Clothes. (Reserved)

Article III. Secondhand Bottle Dealers or Exchanges. (Reserved)

Article IV. Violations of Chapter Provisions

§4-264-220 Enforcement.
The department of consumer services shall have the authority to issue citations for violations of this chapter involving children's products.
(Added. Coun. J. 9-29-99, p. 12263)

§4-264-230 Violation—Penalty.
(a) Where no other penalty is specified, any person violating any of the provisions of this chapter shall be fined not less than $200.00 nor more than $500.00 for each offense, and every day that such violation shall continue shall constitute a separate and distinct offense.
(b) Any person who violates any provision of Sections 4-264-050, 4-264-070, 4-264-090 or 4-264-150 shall be fined not less than $500.00 nor more than $1,000.00 for each offense. Each violation in regard to a separate transaction shall constitute a separate and distinct offense.
(Added. Coun. J. 12-9-92, p. 25465; Amend. Coun. J. 2-26-97, p. 40141; 9-29-99, p. 12263)

CHAPTER 4-268
STREET PERFORMERS
(Complete Chapter)

Sections:
4-268-010 Definitions.
4-268-020 Permit—Required.
4-268-030 Permit—Conditions.
4-268-040 Permit—Display.
4-268-050 Rules and regulations.
4-268-060 Acceptance of contributions.
4-268-070 Violation—Penalty.
4-268-080 Special events.
4-268-090 Constitutionality.

§4-268-010 Definitions.
The following terms are defined for the purpose of this chapter as follows:
(a) "Perform" means and includes, but is not limited to, the following activities: acting, singing, playing musical instruments, pantomime, juggling, magic, dancing and reciting.

(b) "Performer" means an individual to whom a permit was issued pursuant to the provisions of this chapter.

(c) "Public area" means and includes sidewalks, parkways, playgrounds and all other public ways located in the city of Chicago, except transit platforms and stations operated by the Chicago Transit Authority or the Metropolitan Transportation Authority.

(d) "Special event" means any special event conducted by the city of Chicago, including events conducted by permission of the Chicago Park District in parks or other facilities operated by the park district.

(Coun. J. 12-9-92, p. 25465; Amend. 4-21-99, p. 92524)

§4-268-020 Permit—Required.

No person may perform in a public area without having obtained a permit issued under Section 4-268-030 of this chapter.

(Coun. J. 12-9-92, p. 25465)

§4-268-030 Permit—Conditions.

(a) A permit shall be issued by the director of revenue to each applicant therefor in exchange for a completed application and a fee as set forth in Section 4-5-010.

(b) A completed application for a permit shall contain the applicant's name, address and telephone number and shall be signed by the applicant.

(c) A permit shall be valid from the date on which it is issued through December 31st of the year in which it is issued.

(d) A permit shall contain the name and permit number of the applicant plus the year in which it is issued.

(e) A permit shall be nontransferable.

(f) Upon issuing a permit, the director of revenue shall also issue to the performer a printed copy of this chapter.

(Coun. J. 12-9-92, p. 25465)

§4-268-040 Permit—Display.

A performer shall carry and display a permit on his or person at all times while performing in a public area.

(Coun. J. 12-9-92, p. 25465)

§4-268-050 Rules and regulations.

(a) A performance may take place in any public area, but only between the hours of 10:00 a.m. and 9:00 p.m. on Sundays through Thursdays and 10:00 a.m. and 10:00 p.m. on Fridays and Saturdays.

(b) A performer may not block the passage of the public through a public area. If a sufficient crowd gathers to see or hear a performer such that the passage of the public through a public area is blocked, a police officer may disperse that portion of the crowd that is blocking the passage of the public.

(c) A performer may not perform on the public way so as to obstruct access to private property, except with the prior consent of the owner or manager of the property.

(d) A performer shall comply in all respects with the noise and vibration control provisions of the Environmental Protection and Control Ordinance, Article VII of Chapter 11-4 of the Municipal Code, and all other applicable code provisions.

Any performer whose performance in the area bounded by Lake Michigan on the east, Oak Street on the north, Congress Parkway on the south and LaSalle Street and Wacker Drive on the west (including both sides of the named boundary streets), has exceeded the noise limitations set forth in Section 11-4-1110, and who is given notice thereof and a request to move by a police officer or department of environment personnel, shall move the location of his or her performance at least one city block from the location where the noise violation occurred. Failure to obey such a request to move shall be deemed a violation of Section 11-4-1110. Anyone found guilty of three offenses of Section 11-4-1110 in the area bounded by Lake Michigan on the east, Oak Street on the north, Congress Parkway on the south and LaSalle Street and Wacker Drive on the west (including both sides of the named boundary streets) within one calendar year may have his or her street performer's permit revoked by the mayor's license commission for a period of one calendar year. Permit revocations shall be conducted in accordance with procedures established by the mayor's license commission.

(e) No performer shall, while performing on the public way along that portion of Jackson Boulevard that lies between Columbus Drive and Lake Shore Drive at any time during which a concert is being performed in the Petrillo Music Shell, emit noise that is audible to a person with normal hearing more than 20 feet away.

(f) The director of revenue or his designee may direct a performer not to block the passage of the public through a public area and may also direct a performer not to perform on the public way so as to obstruct access to private property.

(Coun. J. 12-9-92, p. 25465; Amend. 7-21-99, p. 9473)

§4-268-060 Acceptance of contributions.

A performer who performs and accepts contributions under the provisions of this chapter shall not be committing disorderly conduct under Section 8-4-010 of the Municipal Code of Chicago by virtue of those acts.

(Coun. J. 12-9-92, p. 25465)

§4-268-070 Violation—Penalty.

Any person who violates the provisions of this chapter, or who knowingly furnishes false information on the permit application, shall be subject to a fine of $200.00.

(Coun. J. 12-9-92, p. 25465)

§4-268-080 Special events.

The mayor, by and through the executive director of the mayor's office of special events, shall have the authority to promulgate reasonable rules and regulations governing the time, place, manner and duration of all performances permitted under this chapter which occur during the course of a special event, including during the setup and cleanup.

Such regulations shall include establishing specified areas within the grounds of a special event to which performers shall be limited, and such other restrictions as are necessary to ensure attendees' enjoyment of planned events and public safety and welfare. Copies of such regulations shall be published and made available both in advance of and at the location of the special event.
(Coun. J. 12-9-92, p. 25465; Amend. 4-21-99, p. 92524)

§4-268-090 Constitutionality.

If any provision, clause, sentence, paragraph, section or part of this chapter shall, for any reason, be adjudged by a court of competent jurisdiction to be unconstitutional or invalid, said judgment shall not affect, impair or invalidate the remainder of this chapter. It is hereby declared to be the legislative intent of the council that this chapter would have been adopted had such unconstitutional or invalid provision, clause, sentence, paragraph, section or part thereof not been included.
(Coun. J. 12-9-92, p. 25465)

DIVISION VII
OTHER OCCUPATIONS AND SERVICES
(Selected Chapters)

Chapters:

4-276	Regulation of Weights and Measures. (Selected Section)
4-328	News Media Credentials.(Complete Chapter)
4-340	Special Policemen and Security Guards.(Complete Chapter)
4-360	Vendor Licensing and Regulation at Navy Pier. (Selected Sections)
4-380	Home Occupations.(Complete Chapter)
4-388	Rooftops in Wrigley Field Adjacent Area. (Selected Sections)
4-400	Burglar Alarms.(Complete Chapter)

CHAPTER 4-276
REGULATION OF WEIGHTS AND MEASURES
(Selected Section)

Sections:

4-276-190 Self-service motor fuel dispensing.

§4-276-190 Self-service motor fuel dispensing.

It shall be unlawful for any person owning or operating a filling station to permit any person other than himself or an employee to dispense flammable and combustible liquids used as motor fuels in a filling station except pursuant to regulations issued by the commissioner of consumer services. Such regulations shall provide for safety in the dispensing of such motor fuels and for fairness in price, in the disclosure of price and service; provided, however, that such regulations will not require that full-service dispensing equipment also be maintained on the station premises.

Any person violating any of the provisions of this section shall be fined not less than $100.00 nor more than $300.00 for the first offense and not less than $300.00 nor more than $500.00 for the second and each subsequent offense in any 180-day period. Each violation of this section shall be considered a separate and distinct offense and shall be regarded as being committed on each day

on which such person shall continue or permit any such violation. In addition to any fine provided herein, violation of this section may be grounds for revocation of any license or permit issued by the city of Chicago to any such violator.
(Coun. J. 12-9-92, p. 25465)

CHAPTER 4-328
NEWS MEDIA CREDENTIALS
(Complete Chapter)

Sections:

4-328-010	Credentials—Required.
4-328-020	Issuance authorized.
4-328-030	Application.
4-328-040	Advisory committee.
4-328-050	Credential—Form and contents.
4-328-060	City seal.
4-328-070	Credential—Revocation.
4-328-080	Violation—Penalty.

§4-328-010 Credentials—Required.

No person shall pass police and fire lines for the purpose of gathering and editing spot news or photographing news events unless such person is a legal holder of a news media credential as provided herein.
(Coun. J. 12-9-92, p. 25465)

§4-328-020 Issuance authorized.

The superintendent of police has power to issue news media credentials entitling the holder thereof to pass police and fire lines for the purpose of gathering and editing spot news or photographing news events in Chicago. Such news media credentials shall be issued only to those engaged in gathering, reporting, editing or photographing current news events for newspapers, press associations, newsreels and radio stations.
(Coun. J. 12-9-92, p. 25465)

§4-328-030 Application.

The application for such news media credentials shall be made in writing by the employer on behalf of the employee qualified to hold news media credentials. The employer shall represent that the employee on whose behalf an application for a news media credential is made is a full-time reporter, editor, writer, photographer or broadcaster of spot news and is of good moral character. No such credential shall be issued unless the applicant meets these requirements and unless and until the fingerprints of the prospective holder are filed in the office of the superintendent of police.
(Coun. J. 12-9-92, p. 25465)

§4-328-040 Advisory committee.

The mayor has power to appoint an advisory committee on news media credentials composed of five members, on which there shall be a representative of the mayor, a representative of the superintendent of police, a representative of the newspapers, a representative of the press associations, and a representative of the radio stations referred to in Section 4-328-020, which committee

shall formulate rules of procedure, recommend standards of qualification, examine all applicants for news media credentials and advise with and make recommendations to the superintendent of police, where applicants are qualified, regarding the issuance of the same.
(Coun. J. 12-9-92, p. 25465)

§4-328-050 Credential—Form and contents.

The news media credentials shall be in such form as is designated and prepared by the superintendent of police and shall contain spaces for signature, photograph and physical description of the authorized news media credential holder, and shall also contain space for the signature of the employer and for the signature of the superintendent of police. There shall also be printed on the news media credential an excerpt from Section 4-328-080 of the code to give notice of the penalty provided therein and the conditions under which the credential is issued. Such news media credential shall be valid for a period to be determined by the superintendent of police but not to exceed one year from the date of issuance.
(Coun. J. 12-9-92, p. 25465)

§4-328-060 City seal.

The city clerk is directed to affix the city seal to each such news media credential so issued, without fee, which impression shall partly cover the photograph of the holder attached thereto.
(Coun. J. 12-9-92, p. 25465)

§4-328-070 Credential—Revocation.

The superintendent of police has power to revoke any news media credential for improper use thereof by the holder, and upon notice thereof to the employer it shall be the duty of the holder and the employer to immediately surrender the news media credential so revoked.
(Coun. J. 12-9-92, p. 25465)

§4-328-080 Violation—Penalty.

No person shall counterfeit or imitate, or attempt to counterfeit or imitate, any such news media credential so issued by the superintendent of police; nor shall any person use or exhibit, or attempt to use or exhibit, any such news media credential or any credential similar in appearance thereto for the purpose of obtaining press privileges or of passing police or fire lines without authority of the superintendent of police; nor shall any person represent that he is a holder of such news media credential unless he is the actual authorized holder. Any person violating any of the provisions of this section shall upon conviction be fined not to exceed $200.00.
(Coun. J. 12-9-92, p. 25465)

CHAPTER 4-340
SPECIAL POLICEMEN AND SECURITY GUARDS
(Complete Chapter)

Sections:

4-340-010 Special policeman defined.
4-340-020 License—Required.
4-340-030 Application—Appointment.
4-340-040 Application—Examination—Fingerprinting.
4-340-050 License—Fee.
4-340-060 Certificate of appointment.
4-340-070 Bond required.
4-340-080 Badges and other insignia.
4-340-090 False representation.
4-340-100 Powers and duties.
4-340-110 Revocation of appointment.
4-340-120 Violation—Penalty.

§4-340-010 Special policeman defined.

"Special policeman" means any person who, for hire or reward, shall guard or protect any building, structure, premises, person or property within the city; provided, however, that this shall not apply to regularly appointed police officers of the city or to any sheriff or deputy sheriff of the county.
(Coun. J. 12-9-92, p. 25465)

§4-340-020 License—Required.

It shall be unlawful for any person to engage in the business of a special policeman without first being appointed and licensed therefor; provided, however, that no license shall be required of a special policeman engaged in the business of protecting persons, passengers and property being transported in interstate or intrastate commerce within the city by a common carrier and the protection of the property of said common carrier within the city, but a special policeman engaged in such business shall comply with all the other provisions of this chapter applicable to him.
(Coun. J. 12-9-92, p. 25465)

§4-340-030 Application—Appointment.

An application of any person showing the necessity of appointment as a special policeman shall be made to the superintendent of police. The superintendent of police shall have power to appoint and swear in any number of special policemen to do special duty at any fixed place in the city, or at any of the necessary places for the protection of persons, passengers and property being transported in interstate or intrastate commerce within the city, at the expense and charge of the applicant.
(Coun. J. 12-9-92, p. 25465)

§4-340-040 Application—Examination—Fingerprinting.

Any person who is an applicant for appointment as a special policeman shall appear in person for examination as to his qualifications for such position, at such place and at such time as may be designated by the superintendent of police. The superintendent of police shall cause an investigation to be made of the character of the applicant and he shall refuse to appoint anyone a special policeman unless, as a result of said investigation, the character of the applicant is found to be satisfactory and above reproach.

Every applicant shall appear at the bureau of identification for the purpose of having fingerprints taken.

(Coun. J. 12-9-92, p. 25465)

§4-340-050 License—Fee.

Every special policeman required to be licensed, other than a special policeman employed by the department of aviation, shall pay an annual license fee of $100.00, except that special policemen employed by charitable, religious, educational or other institutions not carried on for private gain or profit shall by specific ordinance pay an annual license fee of $10.00.

(Coun. J. 12-9-92, p. 25465)

§4-340-060 Certificate of appointment.

The superintendent of police shall issue a special certificate of appointment to each person appointed as a special policeman, which certificate shall expire one year from the date of its issuance. The superintendent of police shall have power to renew any such appointment for a period of one year. He shall keep a correct list of all persons appointed as special policemen.

(Coun. J. 12-9-92, p. 25465)

§4-340-070 Bond required.

Every applicant for appointment as a special policeman of a common carrier shall file a bond with the superintendent of police in the sum of $1,000.00 with good and sufficient sureties.

(Coun. J. 12-9-92, p. 25465)

§4-340-080 Badges and other insignia.

Every special policeman shall wear a suitable badge, not in the form of a star, which shall be issued to him by the superintendent of police. Every special policeman shall deposit with the superintendent of police the sum of $10.00 for such badge. Said badge shall be worn by the special policeman on the outside of his outer coat while engaged in the performance of police duty. Upon the return of any badge so issued by the superintendent of police, the $10.00 deposit shall be refunded. It shall be unlawful for any special policeman to wear or display any badge except the one issued by the superintendent of police.

It shall be unlawful for any special policeman to wear any insignia, cap, device, button or uniform unless the same shall first have been approved by the superintendent of police.

(Coun. J. 12-9-92, p. 25465)

§4-340-090 False representation.

No person shall falsely assume or pretend to be a special policeman or shall, without being a special policeman, wear or display any badge issued by the superintendent of police for such special policeman, or any badge having the words "special police" thereon.

(Coun. J. 12-9-92, p. 25465)

§4-340-100 Powers and duties.

Every special policeman shall conform to and be subject to all the rules and regulations governing police officers of the city, and to such additional rules and regulations as the superintendent of police may make concerning special policemen. Special policemen shall possess the powers of the regular police patrol at the places for which they are respectively appointed or in the line of duty for which they are engaged.

Special policemen shall report in person to the superintendent of police at such times and places as may be required by him.

(Coun. J. 12-9-92, p. 25465)

§4-340-110 Revocation of appointment.

The certificate of appointment issued by the superintendent of police for a special policeman of a common carrier may be revoked by the superintendent of police for cause, and said certificate of a special policeman for a fixed place may be revoked without assigning any cause therefor. Any person whose appointment has been so revoked shall immediately return the certificate of appointment and the badge issued to him to the superintendent of police.

(Coun. J. 12-9-92, p. 25465)

§4-340-120 Violation—Penalty.

Any person violating any of the provisions of this chapter shall be fined not less than $200.00 nor more than $500.00 for each offense.

(Coun. J. 12-9-92, p. 25465)

CHAPTER 4-360
VENDOR LICENSING AND REGULATION AT NAVY PIER
(Selected Sections)

Sections:

4-360-010 Definitions.
4-360-020 Sale of food and merchandise—Permitted.
4-360-030 License—Required.
4-360-100 Sales restrictions.
4-360-110 Applicability of code—Inspection.
4-360-130 Held for inspection orders.
4-360-140 Rules and regulations.
4-360-150 License transferral prohibited.
4-360-160 Sticker license emblem—Display.
4-360-170 Violation—Penalties.

§4-360-010 Definitions.

Whenever used in this chapter the following words and phrases shall have the following meanings:

(a) "Department of consumer services" means the department of consumer services of the city of Chicago.

(b) "Commissioner" means the commissioner of consumer services of the city of Chicago.

(c) "Board of health" means the board of health of the city of Chicago.

(d) "Department of health" means the department of health of the city of Chicago.

(e) "Commissioner of health" means the commissioner of health of the city of Chicago.

(f) "Navy Pier" means the municipal pier extending into Lake Michigan from the foot of East Grand Avenue.

(g) "License" means a license issued pursuant to this chapter.

(h) "Pushcart" means a wheeled vehicle propelled solely by human power.

(i) "Food" means food and beverages allowed to be sold in accordance with this chapter.

(j) "Licensee" means a person to whom a license has been issued pursuant to this chapter.

(k) "Person" means any natural individual, firm, trust, partnership, joint venture, association, corporation or other legal entity, whether acting in his or its own capacity or as administrator, executor, trustee, receiver or other representative appointed by a court. Whenever the word "person" is used in any section of this chapter prescribing a penalty or fine as applied to partnerships or associations, the word shall include the partners or members thereof, and such word as applied to corporations shall include the officers, agents or employees thereof who are responsible for any violation of said section.

(l) "The authority" means the Metropolitan Pier and Exposition Authority created by the Illinois Metropolitan Pier and Exposition Authority Act, as amended.

(Coun. J. 12-9-92, p. 25465; Amend. 5-17-95, p. 1277)

§4-360-020 Sale of food and merchandise—Permitted.

Notwithstanding any provision of any other chapter of the Municipal Code, it shall be lawful to sell food and merchandise at Navy Pier in accordance with the provisions of this chapter.

(Coun. J. 12-9-92, p. 25465)

§4-360-030 License—Required.

No person shall sell merchandise or food at Navy Pier without first having obtained a license under this chapter.

(Coun. J. 12-9-92, p. 25465)

§4-360-100 Sales restrictions.

Each licensee shall sell and offer for sale only the item or items specified in his current license, exclusively from a pushcart or at a fixed location and during the hours as determined by the authority.

(Coun. J. 12-9-92, p. 25465; Amend. 5-17-95, p. 1277)

§4-360-110 Applicability of code—Inspection.

All licensees and their employees shall be subject to and comply with all applicable requirements and standards for dispensing and purveying food contained in Chapter 4-8 of this Municipal Code, as amended, and the rules and regulations promulgated thereunder. The board of health shall implement this section by rules and regulations and may issue additional rules and regulations governing the sanitary practices of Navy Pier vendors. All food held, offered for sale or sold by licensees shall be subject to and comply with all applicable

requirements for such food of this Municipal Code and the rules and regulations promulgated hereunder.
(Coun. J. 12-9-92, p. 25465)

§4-360-130 Held for inspection orders.

The department of consumer services may, upon written notice to the licensee or employee thereof, place a "Held for Inspection" order on any food which it determines or has probable cause to believe to be unwholesome or otherwise adulterated or misbranded. At the request of the licensee, foods so held for inspection shall be permitted to be suitably stored pending analysis reports or voluntarily denatured and disposed of under department of consumer services supervision. It shall be unlawful for any person to remove the tag placed on the food by the department of consumer services, nor shall such food containers be removed from the pushcart or destroyed without permission of the department of consumer services except on order of a court of competent jurisdiction. The department of consumer services may vacate the "Held for Inspection" order or may by written order direct the owner or person in charge of the food to denature or destroy such food or to bring it in compliance with the provisions of this chapter, or dispose of it for nonhuman use as may be approved by the department of consumer services. Provided, however, that such an order of the department of consumer services to denature or destroy such food shall be stayed, if the order is appealed to a court of competent jurisdiction within three days. Nothing in this section shall preclude any court action based upon the finding of unwholesome or adulterated foods.
(Coun. J. 12-9-92, p. 25465)

§4-360-140 Rules and regulations.

(a) The authority may formulate rules and regulations regarding the following:

(1) The size, design, color and other specifications including sanitation or facilities for pushcarts to be used by vendors;

(2) The location of sites from which licensees shall conduct business;

(3) The mandatory and permitted hours of operation of licensees. Such hours of operation need not be uniform throughout the license period, but may be varied based on seasonal differences, and special events.

(b) The commission may issue rules and regulations governing aspects of this chapter not specifically delegated to the authority.

(c) All rules and regulations issued under this chapter shall be filed and maintained in the offices of the department of consumer services and at the offices of the authority at Navy Pier, and shall be available for public inspection during ordinary business hours.
(Coun. J. 12-9-92, p. 25465; Amend. 5-17-95, p. 1277)

§4-360-150 License transferral prohibited.

No transfer of ownership shall be allowed on any license issued hereunder.
(Coun. J. 12-9-92, p. 25465)

§4-360-160 Sticker license emblem—Display.

Each licensee shall have affixed to his pushcart or business at Navy Pier a sticker license emblem which shall bear the words "Chicago" and "Navy Pier," numerals designating the year and, where applicable, the season for which the vendor is licensed, a reproduction of the corporate seal of the city of Chicago and the names of the mayor and the city clerk. Such emblem shall be obtained from the city clerk at the time the license is issued. The commissioner shall prescribe by regulation the manner and place of display on pushcarts.
(Coun. J. 12-9-92, p. 25465; Amend. 5-17-95, p. 1277)

§4-360-170 Violation—Penalties.

Any person violating any of the provisions of this chapter or the rules and regulations promulgated hereunder shall be fined not less than $200.00 nor more than $500.00. A separate and distinct offense shall be deemed to be committed for each day any person continues to violate any of the provisions of this chapter or rules and regulations promulgated hereunder. In addition to the fines hereinabove provided for, the commissioner may revoke the license of any licensee hereunder if such licensee is convicted of two or more violations of this chapter or of the rules and regulations promulgated hereunder within any five-month period and may reject an application for license under this chapter by an applicant who has been so convicted.
(Coun. J. 12-9-92, p. 25465)

CHAPTER 4-380
HOME OCCUPATIONS
(Complete Chapter)

Sections:
4-380-010 Home occupations defined.
4-380-020 License requirement.
4-380-030 License application.
4-380-040 Home occupation license fee.
4-380-050 License renewal.
4-380-060 Requirements applicable to home occupations.
4-380-070 Prohibited activities/other licenses.
4-380-080 Applicability of other laws and rules.
4-380-090 Violations and penalties.
4-380-095 Reserved.

§4-380-010 Home occupations defined.

(a) "Home occupation" shall refer to the accessory use, of a business or commercial nature, of a dwelling unit, engaged in by the person or persons residing in that unit. The use must be incidental and secondary to the principal residential use of the dwelling unit and must not change the residential character of the dwelling unit or adversely affect the character of the surrounding neighborhood.

(b) A dwelling unit may be used for one or more home occupations in accordance with this chapter only if: (1) no more than two patrons or clients are present at the dwelling that is used for a home occupation at any one time; (2) no more than 10 clients or patrons are present at the dwelling that is used for a home occupation during any 24-hour period; or (3) no person, other than the person or persons who reside at the dwelling and not more than one non-resident employee, performs any work at the dwelling in connection with the occupation or occupations. Restrictions on the number of patrons, clients and those performing work in a dwelling unit shall apply to all home occupations within a dwelling unit and shall not be cumulative.

(c) No home occupation license shall be required in accordance with this chapter if the person engaged in the occupation is exclusively engaged in the performance of administrative, clerical or research work, as an owner or employee, for an entity, the principal place of business of which is located elsewhere.

(Added. Coun. J. 5-2-95, p. 459; Amend. 4-1-98, p. 65910)

§4-380-020 License requirement.

No person shall operate a home occupation without first having obtained a license to do so from the department of revenue. No more than one license per dwelling unit shall be required. One license shall entitle its holder to conduct more than one occupation within the licensed dwelling, provided that the license applicant indicates, in the application form, the occupation or occupations that will be carried on.

(Added. Coun. J. 5-2-95, p. 459)

§4-380-030 License application.

An application for a license under this chapter shall be made in conformity with the general requirements of this code relating to applications for licenses. In addition, the applicant shall state the place at which it is desired or intended to carry on a home occupation, the names of the person or persons who will be designated as licensee, the type (or types) of occupation that will be carried on, and any other information which the director of revenue may, at her discretion, require.

(Added. Coun. J. 5-2-95, p. 459)

§4-380-040 Home occupation license fee.

The annual fee for a home occupation license shall be as set forth in Section 4-5-010 of this code.

(Added. Coun. J. 5-2-95, p. 459)

§4-380-050 License renewal.

Licenses granted in accordance with this chapter shall be renewed pursuant to Section 4-4-021 of this code.

(Added. Coun. J. 5-2-95, p. 459)

§4-380-060 Requirements applicable to home occupations.

No person shall operate a home occupation except in compliance with the following requirements:

(a) The home occupation must comply with applicable provisions of the Chicago Zoning Ordinance;

(b) The home occupation shall be accessory and secondary to the use of the dwelling for residential purposes;

(c) No separate entrance from the outside of the building shall be added to the residence for the sole use of the home occupation;

(d) The home occupation shall not display or create any external evidence of the operation of the home occupation;

(e) There shall be no internal or external structural alterations or construction, either permanent or accessory, to the dwelling, nor the installation of any equipment which would change the residential character of the dwelling;

(f) The home occupation and all related activities, including storage, shall be conducted completely within the dwelling and shall not be operated from an accessory structure or garage;

(g) The total square footage of any home occupation shall not permanently occupy more than 10 percent of the floor area of any single-family residence or 15 percent of the floor area of any unit in a multiple-dwelling building; provided, however, that in no instance may one or more home occupations in any single dwelling unit permanently occupy more than 300 square feet of the dwelling unit;

(h) No direct sale of any product on display shelves or racks shall be permitted;

(i) Bulk deliveries related to a home occupation shall be limited to one per day (in addition to United States mail service, express mail, U.P.S. and messenger services) and shall only occur between the hours of 8:00 a.m. and 5:00 p.m. No tractor trailer delivery shall be permitted;

(j) No home occupation shall produce or emit any noise, vibration, smoke, dust or other particulate matter, odorous matter, heat, humidity, glare, or any other effect that unreasonably interferes with any person's enjoyment of his or her residence.

(Added. Coun. J. 5-2-95, p. 459; Amend. 4-1-98, p. 65910)

§4-380-070 Prohibited activities/other licenses.

(a) The following activities may not be licensed as home occupations in accordance with this chapter: any repair of motorized vehicles, including the painting or repair of automobiles, trucks, trailers, boats, and lawn equipment; animal hospitals; astrology, card reading, palm reading or fortune-telling in any form; kennels; stables; bird keeping facilities; barber shops and beauty parlors; dancing schools; restaurants; massage therapy; catering/food preparation businesses; funeral chapels or homes; crematoria; mausoleums; medical or dental clinics; any facility where products are manufactured, produced or assembled when the home occupation licensee is not the retail point of sale for such products; public places of amusement; the sale of firearms or ammunition; caterers; construction businesses or landscaping businesses that provide the storage of goods and materials to be utilized in the operation of the business or use; warehousing; and welding or machine shops; provided, however, that nothing in this chapter shall prohibit the performance of emergency medical services in a residential dwelling.

(b) Establishments for which a license is required and issued in accordance with any other chapter of the Municipal Code of Chicago shall not be required to obtain a license in accordance with this chapter; such establishments shall file an appropriate form with the department of revenue, upon initial license application and upon renewal, indicating that the occupation is prac-

ticed in a residence. This subsection shall not be construed to permit any occupation or activity that is not properly licensed in accordance with another chapter of this code.
(Added. Coun. J. 5-2-95, p. 459; Amend. 4-1-98, p. 65910)

§4-380-080 Applicability of other laws and rules.

(a) Nothing in this chapter shall affect the applicability of any federal or state law pertaining to the production, manufacture or assembly of products, or the applicability of the Fair Labor Standards Act, the Occupational Health and Safety Act, or any child labor, workers' compensation, unemployment compensation, wage and hour, or any other applicable law. This chapter shall not apply to any child care institution, day car center, part day child care facility, group home, day car home, group day care home, or day care center that is properly licensed by a state agency or by the city of Chicago.

(b) Nothing in this chapter shall prevent a condominium association's board of directors, a cooperative association's board of directors or a landlord from adopting a rule, declaration, or bylaw prohibiting home occupations on the premises under which circumstances such rule shall supersede this chapter in effect. Nothing in this chapter shall preclude, invalidate or override any existing covenant, bylaw or rule of a condominium association, common interest community, housing cooperative or landlord which prohibits, restricts or regulates, in a stricter manner than this chapter, home occupations.
(Added. Coun. J. 5-2-95, p. 459)

§4-380-090 Violations and penalties.

Any person found to have violated any of the provisions of this chapter shall be fined not less than $200.00, nor more than $500.00 for each offense; and every day that any violation of this chapter shall continue shall constitute a separate and distinct offense.
(Added. Coun. J. 5-2-95, p. 459)

§4-380-095 Reserved.
(Repealed by Coun. J. 4-1-98, p. 65910)

CHAPTER 4-388
ROOFTOPS IN WRIGLEY FIELD ADJACENT AREA
(Selected Sections)

Sections:

4-388-010 Definitions.
4-388-020 Sale of food, beer and wine—Permitted.
4-388-030 License—Required.
4-388-060 Special club license— Application—Approval conditions.
4-388-080 Applicability of code— Dispensing and purveying food.
4-388-090 Applicability of code—Sale and service of alcoholic beverages.
4-388-100 Sale of admission.
3-388-120 Days and hours of operation.
4-388-130 Banners—Prohibited.
4-388-140 Violation—Penalties.

§4-388-010 Definitions.

Whenever used in this chapter the following words and phrases shall have the following meanings:

(a) "Rooftop" means (i) the roof or top of a building and (ii) the upper enclosed floor of a building.

(b) "Wrigley Field adjacent area" means only that property included inside the following boundary line: the alley next north of and parallel to West Waveland Avenue; North Kenmore Avenue; a line 29.15 feet north of West Waveland Avenue; the alley next west of and parallel to North Sheffield Avenue; a line 79.4 feet north of West Waveland Avenue; North Sheffield Avenue; West Waveland Avenue; the westerly right-of-way of the Chicago transit authority elevated structure; West Addison Street; North Sheffield Avenue; West Waveland Avenue; and North Seminary Avenue.

(c) "Special club license" means a license, issued by the director of revenue, giving the license holder the rights specified in this chapter.

(d) "Director" means the director of revenue of the city of Chicago.

(e) "Day-of-event admission sales" means any sale or transfer of ownership of a right-of-access to a rooftop that occurs on the same day that the right-of-access is eligible to be used, redeemed, or otherwise utilized for admission to a rooftop.

(f) "Game days" means any date in which a major league baseball game is scheduled to be played at Wrigley Field. "Game days" include all scheduled Chicago Cubs regular season home games at Wrigley Field, all scheduled Chicago Cubs playoff home games at Wrigley Field, and the major league baseball All-Star Game, if played at Wrigley Field.

(g) To "sell food, beer and wine" means the sale of food, beer and wine and the service of food, beer and wine as part of the rights granted in the special club license as specified in this chapter.

(Added. Coun. J. 5-20-98, p. 69285; Amend. 1-20-99, p. 88459)

§4-388-020 Sale of food, beer and wine—Permitted.

Notwithstanding any other provision of the Municipal Code, a special club licensee may sell rooftop admission rights and sell food, beer and wine on rooftops in the Wrigley Field adjacent area in accordance with the provisions of this chapter. The sale or service by a special club licensee of any alcoholic beverage or liquor other than beer or wine is not permitted under a special club license at any time. A special club licensee shall be required to own no other city of Chicago licenses to conduct the activities delineated in this chapter other than the "special club license" as defined in this chapter.

(Added. Coun. J. 5-20-98, p. 69285)

§4-388-030 License—Required.

No person shall sell rooftop admission rights, or sell food, beer or wine on rooftops in the Wrigley Field adjacent area without first having obtained a special club license. A special club license may be obtained only by a person who maintains the right to possession of a rooftop in the Wrigley Field adjacent area, either through ownership of a building, lease of a building, or lease of a rooftop.

(Added. Coun. J. 5-20-98, p. 69285)

§4-388-060 Special club license—Application— Approval conditions.

Each application and all information required to be furnished in connection therewith or a copy thereof shall be referred to the building commissioner, the director in charge of the bureau of fire prevention and the superintendent of police. Within 21 days after receipt of the application or copy thereof, each officer shall certify to the mayor's license commission whether or not the specified place complies in every respect with the applicable provisions of this code relating to his department. Owners of buildings that vary from the building provisions of the Municipal Code may seek an approval of suitability from the committee on standards and tests, pursuant to Chapter 13-16. The mayor's license commission shall review the application and the reports of the officers and, if approved, shall transmit its approval to the director of revenue, who shall issue a special club license if all applicable Municipal Code requirements are satisfied.
(Added. Coun. J. 5-20-98, p. 69285; Amend. 1-20-99, p. 88459)

§4-388-080 Applicability of code—Dispensing and purveying food.

All special club licensees, their employees and any city of Chicago licensed catering companies, acting as agents for the special club licensee, shall be subject to and comply with all applicable requirements, standards and inspection procedures relating to dispensing and purveying food contained in this Municipal Code, including Chapters 4-8, 7-38, 7-40 and 7-42, as amended, and the rules and regulations promulgated thereunder. The board of health shall implement this section by rules and regulations and may issue additional rules and regulations governing the sanitary practices of special club licensees. All food held, offered for consumption or sold by special club licensees shall be subject to and comply with all applicable requirements for such food of this Municipal Code and the rules and regulations promulgated hereunder.
(Added. Coun. J. 5-20-98, p. 69285)

§4-388-090 Applicability of code—Sale and service of alcoholic beverages.

(a) All special club licensees, their employees and any city of Chicago licensed catering companies acting as agents for the special club licensee shall be subject to and comply with all requirements, standards and inspection procedures contained in Sections 4-60-030, 4-60-040 subsections (c), (d), (j), and 4-60-100, as amended, of the Municipal Code. Provided, however, that special club licensees may not apply for a late-hour privilege.

(b) All special club licensees and their employees shall not engage in any of the prohibited activities specified in Section 4-60-140, as amended, of the Municipal Code. In addition, no minors may be employed on any premises holding a special club license.

(c) All special club licensees and their employees shall be subject to and comply with the requirements and responsibilities of sellers of alcohol as specified in Sections 4-60-141 and 4-60-142 of the Municipal Code, as amended.

(d) All special club licensees shall be subject to the license revocation procedures specified in Sections 4-4-280, 4-60-180 and 4-60-181 of the Municipal Code, as amended.

(e) Special club licensees shall utilize plastic or paper cups and containers for all beverages sold, dispensed or distributed pursuant to the special club license granted under this chapter. Beverages may not be served in glass containers or in cans.
(Added. Coun. J. 5-20-98, p. 69285)

§4-388-100 Sale of admission.

Day-of-event admission sales by special club licensees are prohibited. All admission rights sold by a special club licensee must allow the purchaser or holder entrance to the rooftop only for a single specified date subsequent to the date of sale. The sale of admission to a rooftop in the Wrigley Field adjacent area may only be performed by a special club licensee. Selling of such admission by any person other than a special club licensee is prohibited.
(Added. Coun. J. 5-20-98, p. 69285)

§4-388-120 Days and hours of operation.

Rooftops in the Wrigley Field adjacent area may be open for business on game days only, for exclusive invitees only, from 8:00 a.m. to 12:00 a.m. Provided, however, beer and wine may be served beginning two hours prior to the scheduled start of the game, and closing no more than one hour after completion of the game. However, regardless of the scheduled start time or of completion of the game, beer and wine may not be served on rooftops by a special club licensee after 11:00 p.m. from Sunday through Thursday, after 11:59 p.m. Friday and Saturday, and prior to 11:00 a.m. Sunday.
(Added. Coun. J. 5-20-98, p. 69285)

§4-388-130 Banners—Prohibited.

No banners or advertisements shall be displayed from the special club license premises or building.
(Added. Coun. J. 5-20-98, p. 69285)

§4-388-140 Violation—Penalties.

Any special club licensee who, while exercising the rights granted pursuant to a special club license as specified in this chapter, violates any provision of the Municipal Code, or any of the rules and regulations promulgated thereunder, shall be subject to the revocation of the special club license. Additionally, any person violating any of the provisions of this chapter or the rules and regulations promulgated hereunder shall be fined not less than $300.00 nor more than $1,000.00. A separate and distinct offense shall be deemed to be committed for each day any person continues to violate any of the provisions of this chapter or rules and regulations promulgated hereunder.
(Added. Coun. J. 5-20-98, p. 69285)

CHAPTER 4-400
BURGLAR ALARMS
(Complete Chapter)

Sections:

4-400-010	Definitions.
4-400-020	Permit required—Application—Fee—Display.
4-400-030	Authority of director of revenue.
4-400-040	Service of notice.
4-400-050	Second notice.
4-400-060	Request for administrative hearing—Liability.
4-400-070	Administrative penalties.

§4-400-010 Definitions.

As used in this chapter:

(a) "Burglar alarm system" means any assembly of equipment, mechanical or electrical, designed to signal the occurrence of an illegal entry or attempted entry of the premises protected by the system. However, "burglar alarm system" shall not include any system installed to protect any premises used primarily for educational or religious purposes or used primarily by a unit of government or school district.

(b) "Burglar alarm user" means the person or entity that owns, leases or subscribes to a burglar system, but does not include a private alarm company.

(c) "Director" means the director of revenue.

(d) "False alarm" means a burglar alarm system activated in the absence of an emergency whether wilfully or by inadvertence, negligence or unintentional act, including any mechanical or electrical malfunction of the alarm system, to which the department of police is alerted for a response. A false alarm shall not include an alarm activated by a temporary surge or loss of electrical power or loss of telephone service to the burglar alarm user; the testing or repairing of telephone or electrical lines or equipment outside the premises if prior notice of the testing or repair is given to the department of police; unusually violent conditions of nature; an illegal entry, theft or robbery, or an attempt thereof; or an observable act of vandalism; where evidence of such activity exists.

(Added. Coun. J. 4-13-94, p. 48609; Amend. 11-30-94, p. 62713; 11-3-99, p. 13842; 12-15-04, p. 39840)

§4-400-020 Permit required—Application—Fee—Display.

Except for residential users, who shall not be subject to this section, every burglar alarm user must obtain a permit for each burglar alarm system that the burglar alarm user owns or leases prior to the time the system becomes operative, or 60 days after the effective date of this chapter, whichever is later. Application for the permit shall be made to the director of revenue on a form supplied by the director, which may be combined with application forms for licenses or other permits. The application shall identify the address of the premises in which the burglar alarm system is installed, shall provide the name and address of a person designated by the burglar alarm user to receive notices under this chapter, and shall contain such other information as the director shall require. Each permit shall be issued by the director for a period of one year from the date of issuance; provided, that if a permit is issued for any premises for which any other license or permit has been issued pursuant to Title 4 of this code, the burglar alarm permit shall expire on the date of the next expiration of the other license or permit first occurring at least six months after the initial issuance of the burglar alarm permit. No additional fee shall be charged for a permit issued under this section for a burglar alarm system for a premises for which any other license or permit has been issued pursuant to Title 4 of this code. A decal or sticker evidencing the permit shall be issued when the permit is initially issued. The annual permit fee for any other burglar alarm system shall be $30.00. The fee for a replacement for a decal or sticker issued under this section that is lost, stolen or damaged shall be $10.00. No burglar alarm user may own, control or occupy a building, structure or facility in which a burglar alarm system is maintained unless a decal or sticker evidencing a permit issued under this section is displayed on or near the upper right corner of the main exterior door of the premises in a manner that is clearly visible from the exterior of the premises; provided, that if the premises protected by the burglary alarm system is located in a building that remains unlocked and accessible to authorized persons on a 24-hour basis and such building maintains a security desk on the ground floor, the building owner or manager may elect to require that all burglar alarm users occupying the building display their permits in a folder to be maintained at all times at the security desk by an authorized agent of the building owner or manager, and to be made available for inspection at all times by the Chicago Police Department.

(Added. Coun. J. 4-13-94, p. 48609; Amend. 7-13-94, p. 53401; 11-3-99, p. 13842; 12-15-04, p. 39840)

§4-400-030 Authority of director of revenue.

The director of revenue is hereby authorized to adopt, distribute and process a form entitled Notice of False Alarm/Failure to Display Alarm Permit and additional notices, issue determinations of false alarms and collect money paid as administrative penalties for false alarms and failures to display or maintain alarm permits. The director of revenue is further authorized to adopt rules and regulations pertaining to the content of forms and procedures. The department of administrative hearings is authorized to establish procedures necessary for the prompt, fair and efficient operation of the administrative adjudication system and to adopt rules and regulations pertaining to: the hearing process, the selection and appointment of hearing officers, and the daily operation of the administrative adjudication program.

(Added. Coun. J. 4-13-94, p. 48609; Amend. 7-13-94, p. 53401; 4-29-98, p. 66564; 12-15-04, p. 39840)

§4-400-040 Service of notice.

(a) Whenever a police officer responds to an alarm at any premises and the police officer determines either that the alarm is a false alarm or that the burglar alarm user has failed to display a burglar alarm permit in the manner required by this chapter, the police officer shall issue a Notice of False Alarm/Failure to Display Alarm Permit, and shall serve the notice on the burglar alarm user by personal service on the burglar alarm user, an agent or employee of the burglar alarm user, or any other person with apparent authority at the premises, or by affixing the notice to the door or other prominent location on the premises. A copy of the notice shall also be forwarded to the director.

Whenever the department of revenue learns that a notice was issued to any burglar alarm user whose permit has expired or who does not have a permit, and the notice does not indicate that the burglar alarm user failed to display an alarm permit, the department of revenue shall issue a Notice of Failure to Maintain Alarm Permit, and shall serve this notice by regular mail on the person designated pursuant to Section 4-400-020 to receive notices or, if there is no such person, to the current occupant of the premises.

(b) When issuing a Notice of False Alarm/Failure to Display Alarm Permit, the police officer shall specify on the notice his or her name and star number, the name of the burglar alarm user (if known to the police officer), the permit number of the burglar alarm user (if any), an indication as to whether or not the permit (if any) was visible to the police officer, the date and time of the occurrence, the address and police beat assignment of the occurrence, the weather conditions at the time of the occurrence, whether the alarm was silent or audible (if known to the police officer), whether the notice is being issued for a false alarm or for a failure to display an alarm permit, or both, whether the police office was assigned by police communications or on-view and whether the notice was served by personal service or by affixing the notice to the door or other prominent location. The police officer shall certify the correctness of the specified information by signing his or her name to the notice. The notice shall indicate the applicable administrative penalties for false alarms and failure to display alarm permits. The notice shall explain the burglar alarm user's right to an administrative hearing at which the determination of false alarm or the administrative penalty may be contested and the time and manner by which such a hearing must be requested.

(c) The director of revenue shall distribute Notices of False Alarm/Failure to Display Alarm Permit to the superintendent of police for issuance to this chapter.

(d) When issuing a Notice of Failure to Maintain Alarm Permit, the department of revenue shall specify on the notice the name of the burglar alarm user (if known), the permit number of the burglar alarm user (if any) and the date and address of the occurrence. An authorized employee of the department of revenue shall certify the correctness of the specified information by signing his or her name to the notice. The notice shall indicate the applicable administrative penalties for failure to maintain alarm permits. The notice shall explain the burglar alarm user's right to an administrative hearing at which the administrative penalty may be contested and the time and manner by which such a hearing must be requested.

(Added. Coun. J. 4-13-94, p. 48609; Amend. 7-13-94, p. 53401; 11-3-99, p. 13842)

§4-400-050 Second notice.

(a) Whenever a notice is given under Section 4-400-040 which, if uncontested, could result in the imposition of one or more administrative penalties for an offense described in the notice, the director of revenue shall send a second notice by first class mail to the person designated pursuant to Section 4-400-020 to receive notices or, if there is no such person, to the current occupant of the premises. A copy of the second notice shall be forwarded to the department of administrative hearings.

(b) This second notice shall contain the name of the burglar alarm user (if known), the permit number of the burglar alarm user (if any), an indication as to whether or not the permit (if any) was visible to the police officer, the date, time and address of the occurrence and whether the Notice of False Alarm/Failure to Display Alarm Permit was issued for a false alarm or for a failure to display an alarm permit. The second notice shall indicate the specific administrative penalty, if any, that will be assessed against the burglar alarm user unless the determination of false alarm or failure to display alarm permit is successfully contested. The notice shall explain the burglar alarm user's right to an administrative hearing at which the determinations of false alarm or administrative penalty may be contested and the time and manner by which such a hearing must be requested. In addition, if the second notice indicates that an administrative penalty will be assessed for a false alarm, the second notice shall also provide the dates of the previous notices of false alarm issued in the calendar year for which no administrative penalty applies and for which no second notices have previously been given.

(Added. Coun. J. 4-13-94, p. 48609; Amend. 7-13-94, p. 53401; 11-30-94, p. 62713; 4-29-98, p. 66564; 11-3-99, p. 13842)

§4-400-060 Request for administrative hearing—Liability.

(a) Whenever a notice of false alarm is given or an administrative penalty is imposed upon a burglar alarm user under this chapter, the burglar alarm user may, not more than 14 days after a second notice is mailed as provided by Section 4-400-050, submit to the director of revenue a written request for an administrative hearing to contest the determination or administrative penalty. A written request for an administrative hearing may be delivered in person or by mail. A request by mail shall be deemed timely if postmarked not more than 14 days after the second notice was mailed.

(b) Whenever a second notice is given under Section 4-400-050 that provides the dates of the previous notices of false alarm issued in the calendar year, the burglar alarm user may request an administrative hearing to contest the determination of false alarm for which the second notice was issued as well as any or all of the previous determinations of false alarm given within the calendar year for which no administrative penalty applies, provided, however, that no previous determination of false alarm may be contested if the burglar alarm user (i) previously requested an administrative hearing to contest that determination of false alarm or (ii) was given a second notice of that determination of false alarm in conjunction with a second notice of failure to display or a notice of failure to maintain an alarm permit.

(c) If a burglar alarm user requests an administrative hearing to contest the determination or administrative penalty, the director of revenue shall refer the request to the department of administrative hearings. The department of administrative hearings shall thereupon fix the time and place for the hearing, give written notice thereof, and appoint an administrative law officer who shall conduct the hearing. The notice of hearing shall state the penalties that may be imposed for failure to appear at the hearing. The hearing shall be conducted in accordance with Chapter 2-14 of this code.

(d) Where a burglar alarm user who has requested an administrative hearing fails either to pay an indicated administrative penalty prior to the hearing if such a penalty is imposed, or to appear at the hearing, the administrative law officer shall enter a default order and a determination of false alarm and/or a determination of liability for an administrative penalty in the amount of the administrative penalty indicated on the second notice.

(e) If no response is made in accordance with subsection (a) of this section an administrative law officer appointed by the department of administrative hearings shall enter a default order and a determination of false alarm and/or liability for the amount of the administrative penalty indicated on the second notice, if any.

(f) A copy of a determination of liability entered pursuant to this section for which any penalty is imposed shall be sent by regular mail to the person designated pursuant to Section 4-400-020 to receive notices or, if there is no such person, to the current occupant of the premises.

(g) Within 21 days from the issuance of a determination of false alarm or of liability to this section, the person against whom the determination was entered may petition the department of administrative hearings to set aside the determination; provided, however, the grounds for the petition shall be limited to: (1) the person having already paid any administrative penalty in question; or (2) excusable failure, based on criteria established by the department of administrative hearings, to appear at or request a new date for a hearing. If the petition is granted based on excusable failure to appear or request, the department of administrative hearings shall notify the burglar alarm user of the date, time and place of the new hearing.

(h) Notwithstanding any other provision of this chapter, the director may at any time waive liability under this chapter of any person the director determines was not a burglar alarm user, as defined in Section 4-400-010, at the time of the alleged violation.

(Added. Coun. J. 4-13-94, p. 48609; Amend. 7-13-94, p. 53401; 11-30-94, p. 62713; 4-29-98, p. 66564; 11-3-99, p. 13842; 12-15-04, p. 39840)

§4-400-070 Administrative penalties.

(a) Administrative penalties shall be imposed as follows:

For the first three false alarms at any premises in the calendar year: none.

For the fourth, fifth or sixth false alarm at any premises within the calendar year: $100.00.

For the seventh or subsequent false alarm at any premises within the calendar year: $200.00.

(b) Any burglar alarm user who does not display or maintain an unexpired alarm permit on the premises owned, controlled or occupied by the burglar alarm user as required by this chapter shall be subject to a fine or administrative penalty of $100.00 for a first offense, and $200.00 for a second or subsequent offense committed within a one year period.

(c) Administrative penalties imposed pursuant to this chapter shall constitute debts due and owing to the city until paid in full. Persons or entities who control or occupy the premises in which a false alarm occurs or in which there was a failure to display or maintain an alarm permit shall be jointly and severally liable for administrative penalties imposed under this chapter.

(Added. Coun. J. 4-13-94, p. 48609; Amend. 7-13-94, p. 53401; 11-3-99, p. 13842; 11-6-02, p. 96082; 11-19-03, p. 14216)

TITLE 5
HOUSING AND ECONOMIC DEVELOPMENT

(Selected Chapters)

Chapters:
5-4 Reserved.
5-12 Residential Landlords and Tenants. (Selected Section)

CHAPTER 5-4
RESERVED

(Deleted. Coun. J. 3-31-04, p. 20916)

CHAPTER 5-12
RESIDENTIAL LANDLORDS AND TENANTS

(Selected Section)

Section:
5-12-160 Prohibition on interruption of tenant occupancy by landlord.

§5-12-160 Prohibition on interruption of tenant occupancy by landlord.

It is unlawful for any landlord or any person acting at his direction knowingly to oust or dispossess or threaten or attempt to oust or dispossess any tenant from a dwelling unit without authority of law, by plugging, changing, adding or removing any lock or latching device; or by blocking any entrance into said unit; or by removing any door or window from said unit; or by interfering with the services to said unit; including but not limited to electricity, gas, hot or cold water, plumbing, heat or telephone service; or by removing a tenant's personal property from said unit; or by the removal or incapacitating of appliances or fixtures, except for the purpose of making necessary repairs; or by the use or threat of force, violence or injury to a tenant's person or property; or by any act rendering a dwelling unit or any part thereof or any personal property located therein inaccessible or uninhabitable. The foregoing shall not apply where:

(a) A landlord acts in compliance with the laws of Illinois pertaining to forcible entry and detainer and engages the sheriff of Cook County to forcibly evict a tenant or his personal property; or

(b) A landlord acts in compliance with the laws of Illinois pertaining to distress for rent; or

(c) A landlord interferes temporarily with possession only as necessary to make needed repairs or inspection and only as provided by law; or

(d) The tenant has abandoned the dwelling unit, as defined in Section 5-12-130(e).

Whenever a complaint of violation of this provision is received by the Chicago Police Department, the department shall investigate and determine whether a violation has occurred. Any person found guilty of violating this section shall be fined not less then $200.00 nor more than $500.00, and each day that such violation shall occur or continue shall constitute a separate and distinct offense for which a fine as herein provided shall be imposed. If a

tenant in a civil legal proceeding against his landlord establishes that a violation of this section has occurred he shall be entitled to recover possession of his dwelling unit or personal property and shall recover an amount equal to not more than two months' rent or twice the actual damages sustained by him, whichever is greater. A tenant may pursue any civil remedy for violation of this section regardless of whether a fine has been entered against the landlord pursuant to this section.
(Prior code § 193.1-16; Added. Coun. J. 9-8-86, p. 33771; Amend. 11-6-91, p. 7196)

TITLE 7
HEALTH AND SAFETY
(Selected Chapters)

Chapters:

7-12 Animal Care and Control. (Selected Sections)
7-16 Births and Deaths. (Selected Sections)
7-20 Contagious and Epidemic Diseases. (Selected Sections)
7-24 Drugs and Narcotics. (Complete Chapter)
7-28 Health Nuisances. (Selected Sections)
7-32 No-Smoking Regulations. (Complete Chapter)
7-38 Food Establishments—Sanitary Operating Requirements. (Selected Sections)
7-40 Food Establishments—Care of Foods. (Selected Sections)
7-42 Food Establishments—Inspections, Violations and Hearing Procedures. (Selected Sections)
7-44 Extermination By Fumigation. (Complete Chapter)

CHAPTER 7-12
ANIMAL CARE AND CONTROL
(Selected Sections)

Sections:

7-12-010 Commission established—Executive director—Terms of members.
7-12-020 Definitions.
7-12-030 Animals shall be restrained.
7-12-040 Impounding stray and unlicensed animals.
7-12-050 Dangerous animals—Determination and requirements.
7-12-051 Dangerous animals—Violations.
7-12-052 Dangerous animals—Miscellaneous.
7-12-060 Redemption of impounded animals.
7-12-065 Impoundment of dogs and cats—Compulsory sterilization.
7-12-070 Facilities to be used for impoundments.
7-12-080 Removal of neglected animal.
7-12-090 Owner's responsibility where animal has bitten another animal or person.
7-12-140 License required.
7-12-150 License application forms.
7-12-160 Rabies inoculation certificate.
7-12-170 License fees.
7-12-180 Exemptions from license fees.
7-12-190 Citations.
7-12-200 Rabies vaccination required.
7-12-210 Horses—License required—Fee—Display—Exemptions.
7-12-220 Horse-drawn carriage—Horse license required.
7-12-230 Horse-drawn carriage—Horse identification number—Violation—Penalty.
7-12-240 Horse-drawn carriage—Right to demand proof of license—Exception.
7-12-250 Horse-drawn carriage—Access for inspection.
7-12-260 Horse-drawn carriage—Requirements for operation.
7-12-270 Horse-drawn carriage—Violation—Penalty for Sections 7-12-220 through 7-12-260.
7-12-280 Stables to be kept clean.
7-12-290 Cruelty to animals—Fines.
7-12-300 Ban of unlicensed possession of animals for slaughter.
7-12-310 Removal of injured or diseased animal from public way.
7-12-320 Horse-drawn carriage—Removal of horse from public way.
7-12-350 Dyeing baby chicks, other fowls or rabbits prohibited.
7-12-370 Animal fights and contests prohibited.
7-12-420 Removal of excrement.
7-12-430 Violation—Penalty.

§7-12-010 Commission established—Executive director—Terms of members.

There is hereby established a commission to be known as the "commission on animal care and control, city of Chicago." Said commission shall consist of nine members to be appointed by the mayor, three of whom shall be members, respectively, of the police department, health department, and the department of streets and sanitation; with the remaining six members to include at least one representative of a humane society as hereinafter defined, at least one veterinarian licensed under the laws of the state of Illinois, and at least three private citizens. All commission members shall serve as such without compensation.

The mayor shall appoint an executive director who shall function as hereinafter set forth, subject to administrative and operating policies to be established by the commission. The salary of the executive director and other persons employed by the commission shall be as provided for in the annual appropriation ordinance. The commission shall function as an advisory body to the mayor and to the executive director and shall be responsible for the promulgation of such administrative policies and rules as are necessary to implement the enforcement of this ordinance. The mayor shall designate one of its members to act as chairman for a term of 12 months, subject to redesignation for any number of additional terms of two years. The commission shall meet at least once every three months, unless otherwise determined by the commission or when called upon to do so by the chairman.

Each commission member shall serve for a period of two years from date of appointment, subject to reappointment by the mayor for any number of additional terms of two years, except that four of the initial appointments as designated by the mayor shall be for a term of only one year. Each commission member shall serve until a successor has been appointed by the mayor. The mayor shall appoint members to fill vacancies which may occur due to death, resignation or incapacity.

(Prior code § 98-1)

§7-12-020 Definitions.

As used in this ordinance, the following are defined and shall be construed as hereinafter set out unless it shall be apparent from the context that a different meaning is intended:

"Animal" means any living vertebrate, domestic or wild, not including man.

"Animal control center" means a facility operated by and under the direct supervision of the executive director of the commission for the purpose of impounding animals as henceforth set out in this ordinance.

"Animal control officer" means an employee of the commission who shall be responsible to it and the executive director and have the power and authority to issue citations for any violations of this ordinance relating to the care, treatment, control or impoundment of animals.

"Animal exhibition" means any public or private animal exhibition staged temporarily or permanently, with or without charge to viewers, in compliance with applicable ordinances of the city of Chicago, statutes of the state of Illinois, and federal laws, including but not limited to zoos, circuses, rodeos, dog shows, cat shows, livestock exhibitions, horse shows, other shows or exhibitions utilizing or displaying animals, and businesses or business centers of any kind that place animals on display to the public for promotion or advertising purposes.

"Animal under restraint" means any animal either secured by a leash or lead, or within the premises of its owner, or confined within a crate or cage, or confined within a vehicle, or on the premises of another person with the consent of that person, or within an area specifically designated by the commission as an animal exercise run when said animal is under the control of a competent person.

"Bite" means seizure with the teeth or jaws of an animal so that the skin of the human being or animal seized has been pierced or broken and further includes contact of the saliva of the biting animal with any break or abrasion of the skin of the human being or animal bitten.

"Cat" means any live male or female cat (Felis catus).

"Cattery" means any establishment wherein any person engages in the business of boarding, breeding, buying, grooming, letting for hire, training for a fee or selling cats; provided, however, that the ownership of cats which are a part of the household shall not constitute the operation of a cattery. "Cattery" shall not include any animal control center as defined in this ordinance, any pound or similar facility operated by any subdivision of local, state or federal government, any humane society, any veterinary hospital, any research facility subject to inspection under separate provisions of local, state and/or federal law.

"Dangerous animal" means an animal meeting any one of the following criteria:

(1) Any animal which bites, inflicts injury on, kills or otherwise attacks a human being or domestic animal without provocation on any public or private property; or

(2) Any animal which on more than one occasion, without provocation, chases or approaches any person in an apparent attitude of attack, on any public property or in any place outside or over the boundaries of its owner's property; or

(3) Any animal owned or harbored primarily or in part for the purpose of dog or other animal fighting or any animal trained for dog or other animal fighting; or

(4) Any dog that is used by a commercial venture to guard public or private property, except those owned by a governmental or law enforcement unit; or

(5) Any animal which has been found to be a vicious dog under state law.

"Dog" means any live male or female dog (Canis familiaris).

"Euthanasia" or "humane destruction" means death brought about by any method which produces instant loss of consciousness and results in painless death.

"Executive director" means the individual appointed by the mayor to (1) supervise and administratively direct the work of the animal control center or centers as established by and defined in this ordinance, (2) coordinate the activities of the animal control center or centers with the activities of other animal control and regulatory agencies within the state of Illinois and with humane societies as such societies are hereinafter defined, (3) supervise and administratively direct any neutering and spaying clinic established by the commission, (4) formulate and direct an educational program to develop better animal care.

"Horse" means an animal of the genus equus.

"Humane society" means any not-for-profit corporation chartered under the laws of the state of Illinois for the object of animal welfare.

"Impounded" means having been taken into the custody of the commission or any other facility licensed pursuant to this ordinance for such purpose.

"Kennel" means any establishment wherein any person engages in the business of boarding, breeding, buying, grooming, letting for hire, training for a fee or selling dogs; provided, however, that the ownership of dogs which are a part of the household shall not constitute the operation of a kennel. "Kennel" shall not include any animal control center as defined in this ordinance, any kennel or pound or training facility operated by any subdivision of local, state or federal government, any humane society, any veterinary hospital, any research facility subject to inspection under separate provisions of local, state and/or federal law.

"Licensed dog" means any dog four months of age or older for which the owner can produce proof of having paid the license fee for the current year.

"Microchip" means a passive electronic device that is injected into an animal by means of a prepackaged sterilized implanting device for purposes of identification or recovery.

"Owner" means any person having a right of property in an animal or who keeps or harbors any animal or who has an animal in his care or custody.

"Person" means any individual, firm, corporation, partnership, association or other legal entity.

"Pet" means any species of domesticated animals customarily regarded as suited to live within an abode used for human occupancy.

"Pet shop" means any establishment wherein any person engages in the business of selling two or more species of animals suitable for use as pets.

"Provocation" means that the threat, injury or damage caused by the animal was sustained by a person who, at the time, was committing a willful trespass or other tort upon the premises occupied by the owner of the animal, or was tormenting, abusing, or assaulting the animal, or was committing or attempting to commit a crime.

"Severe injury" means any physical injury that results in broken bones or lacerations requiring sutures or cosmetic surgery.

"Sterilization" or "sterilize" means the rendering of an animal unable to reproduce by surgically altering the animal's reproductive organs. Sterilization includes the spaying of a female dog or cat, or the neutering of a male dog or cat.

"Stray animal" means any animal not under restraint and not in the presence of its owner.

"Vaccination" means the injection, as approved by the Department of Agriculture, state of Illinois, of an antirabies vaccine approved by said department, with verification thereof consisting of a current certificate and current tag issued in accordance with the statutes of the state of Illinois.

"Veterinarian" means a practicing veterinarian licensed by the state of Illinois.

"Veterinary hospital" means any establishment maintained and operated by a licensed veterinarian for diagnosis, treatment and/or surgery of diseases and injuries of animals.

"Visiting hours" means posted days and hours during which an animal control center operated by the commission on animal care and control shall be kept open to the public for the transaction of appropriate business, as established by the executive director.

(Prior code § 98-2; Amend. Coun. J. 10-16-84, p. 10165; 10-2-95, p. 8604; 4-16-97, p. 42588; 12-12-01, p. 75777; 12-4-02, p. 99026)

§7-12-030 Animals shall be restrained.

Each owner shall keep and maintain his animal under restraint; provided, however, that this section shall not apply to any dog being used for rescue or law enforcement work. It shall be unlawful for any owner to allow his or her animal to cross outside the property line of its owner to any extent, including reaching over or under a fence, or to keep or allow his or her animal to be outdoors on an unfenced portion of the owner's property, unless the animal is leashed and under the control of its owner or another responsible person. In addition, it shall be an unlawful failure to restrain for an animal to attack, bite, threaten, or jump on any person without that person's consent, outside the property of the animal's owner. The provisions of this section shall be a positive duty of the owner and the offenses described herein shall be strict liability offenses.

Any owner who violates any provision of this section shall be subject to a fine of $300.00, if the violation does not result in severe injury or death to any person or damage to another person's property. If the violation results in sever injury or death to any person, the owner shall be subject to a fine not less than $1,000.00 and not more than $10,000.00. In addition to a fine, the owner may be required to submit full restitution to the victim or may be incarcerated for a period not to exceed six months, or may be required to perform up to one hundred hours of community service, or any combination thereof. If the violation results in damage to another person's property, the owner shall be subject to a fine of not less than $300.00 and not more than $1,000.00. In addition to a fine, the owner may be required to submit full restitution to the victim.

(Prior code § 98-3; Amend. Coun. J. 10-2-95, p. 8604; 10-31-01, p. 71774; 3-31-04, p. 20916)

§7-12-040 Impounding stray and unlicensed animals.

Any stray animal and any animal without a current license that is found in the public way or within a public place or upon private premises of any person other than the owner shall be immediately impounded by an animal control officer.

(Prior code § 98-3.1; Amend. Coun. J. 10-2-95, p. 8604)

§7-12-050 Dangerous animals—Determination and requirements.

The executive director shall have the authority to make a determination that an animal is a dangerous animal, as defined in Section 7-12-020, and to order the owner to comply with any of the measures set forth below for the protection of public health, safety and welfare.

(a) Upon receipt of a citizen complaint or other report of an animal bite, attack, threatening behavior, or other reason to believe an animal may be a dangerous animal, the executive director or an animal control officer shall evaluate the seriousness of the complaint or report and, if the circumstances warrant, may conduct an investigation of the facts. Where practicable and readily located, the investigation shall include interviewing the complainant, the victim, if any, the animal's owner, and any witnesses, and observation of the animal and the scene. The investigator then shall make a written finding of whether an animal is a dangerous animal as defined in Section 7-12-020 and of the basis for that finding. In addition, if during the course of the investigation, the investigator uncovers evidence of inhumane treatment of any animal in violation of Section 7-12-090, he or she shall make a written finding of the specific violation and forward such to the executive director. For purposes of this section, a police report may constitute an investigation and may include a finding of dangerousness. Based upon the investigator's finding of a dangerous animal, the executive director shall declare in writing whether the animal is a dangerous animal.

(b) Where an animal is declared to be a dangerous animal, and the animal has caused severe injury to any person, then the executive director may order the humane destruction of the animal, where appropriate, taking into consideration the severity and the circumstances of injury. Where an animal is declared to be a dangerous animal, and the animal has caused death to any person, then the executive director shall order the humane destruction of the animal.

(c) In all cases where an animal is declared to be a dangerous animal and the animal is not humanely destroyed, the executive director shall order the owner to comply with the following requirements:

(1) While on the owner's property, the owner must securely confine the dangerous animal indoors or within a securely enclosed and locked pen, structure, or fence, suitable to prevent the entry of young children and designed to prevent the animal from escaping. Such pen, structure, or fence must be a minimum of six feet in height and must have secure sides. If it has no bottom secured to the sides, the sides must be embedded into the ground no less than two feet deep. The enclosure also must be humane and provide some protection from the elements for the animal.

(2) While off of the owner's property, a dangerous animal must be muzzled securely to prevent the possibility of biting, restrained by a substantial chain or leash not exceeding six feet in length, and under the control of a responsible person at all times. The muzzle must be made in a manner that will not cause injury to the animal or impair its vision or respiration but must prevent it from biting any person or animal.

(3) The owner must display, in a conspicuous manner, a sign on the owner's premises warning that a dangerous animal is on the premises by stating in capital letters: "WARNING—DANGEROUS ANIMAL—KEEP AWAY". The sign must be visible and legible from the public way and from 50 feet away from the special enclosure required pursuant to subsection (c)(1) above.

(4) The owner, at the owner's expense, shall have an identifying microchip installed under the animal's skin by a veterinarian authorized by the executive director.

(5) The animal shall be spayed or neutered, at the owner's expense.

(6) Within 10 business days of the declaration that the animal is a dangerous animal, the owner must procure and maintain in effect liability insurance, including coverage of claims arising from the conduct of the owner's animal, in an amount net less than $100,000.00. The insurance shall include a provision whereby the insurer notifies the executive director not less than 30 days prior to cancellation or lapse of coverage.

In addition, the executive director may order the owner to comply with any of the following requirements, in any combination:

(7) The owner must confine the dangerous animal to the secure enclosure described above in subsection (c)(1) at all times and only allow the animal out under the conditions set forth in subsection (c)(2) when it is necessary to obtain veterinary care for the animal or to comply with a court order.

(8) The owner and the animal must complete a course of animal obedience training approved by the commission.

In the alternative to subsections (c)(1)—(8) above, the executive director may order that the dangerous animal shall be permanently barred from the city limits.

(d) Where the owner's address can be reasonably ascertained, the executive director shall send written notice to the owner, by certified mail, stating that his or her animal has been declared a dangerous animal, describing the basis for such declaration by specific behavior and date(s) of occurrence, setting forth all applicable orders and restrictions imposed reason of such declaration, and informing the owner of his or her right to appeal such determination by filing a written request for a hearing within seven days of receipt of the notice. A copy of such notice shall be sent to the complainant, if any. Where the animal has been impounded pursuant to subsection (f) below, such notice shall be sent within 15 days after such impoundment.

(e) If the owner requests a hearing, the executive director, if the department of administrative hearings has not exercised jurisdiction in accordance with Section 2-14-190(c) of this code, or the department of administrative hearings, if the office has exercised jurisdiction in accordance with Section 2-14-190(c) of this code, shall appoint an administrative law officer who shall hold a hearing, at which all interested parties may present testimony and any other relevant evidence, within 15 days of the request. The hearing shall be taped or recorded by other appropriate means. If the administrative law officer upholds the executive director's determination that the animal is dangerous, the owner shall have 30 days to satisfy all requirements set out in subsection (c) and the notice. In those cases where the executive director has ordered humane destruction of the dangerous animal, that order shall not be carried out until seven days after the hearing; if the owner appeals to the circuit court during that time period, that order shall be stayed until resolution of such appeal.

(f) Where there is probable cause to believe that an animal is a dangerous animal, the executive director or his designee is authorized to impound and hold such animal, at the owner's expense, pending the investigation and final resolution of any appeals. Where the animal has caused severe injury or death to any person, the executive director or his designee is required to impound and hold such animal, at the owner's expense, pending the investigation and final resolution of any appeals. Moreover, in no event shall a dangerous animal be released to its owner before the executive director or his designee approves the enclosure required by subsection (c)(1). The holding period and impoundment procedures for animals of unknown ownership shall be governed by Section 7-12-060.

(g) Guard dogs and dogs which have been found to be "vicious dogs" under state law, both of which are defined in Section 7-12-020 above as dangerous animals, automatically are required to comply with the requirements of Section 7-12-050(c)(1) — (3) without the need for any individualized declaration or the right to any hearing, except that, to the extent an owner disputes the fact that his or her animal is used as a guard dog by a commercial venture, in such instances the protections set forth above shall apply.

(Added. Coun. J. 10-2-95, p. 8604; Amend. 7-10-96, p. 24982; 11-12-97, p. 56813; 4-29-98, p. 66564; 10-31-01, p. 71774)

§7-12-051 Dangerous animals—Violations.

(a) Any owner who fails to comply with any of the requirements of Section 7-12-050(c) and any additional orders of the executive director as authorized by that subsection shall be punished by a fine of not less than $200.00 nor more than $500.00 for the first offense, and not less than $500.00 nor more than $1,000.00 for the second offense. Any subsequent offenses shall be punished as a misdemeanor by incarceration for a term not to exceed six months. In addition to the penalties set forth above, the executive director may order an owner who violates Section 7-12-050(c) to attend with his or her animal a course of animal obedience training approved by the commission.

(b) Any animal which has been declared a dangerous animal and which (1) is seen outside and not confined within the enclosure required by Section 7-12-050(c)(1), and not muzzled and under control as required by Section 7-12-050(c)(2), or (2) thereafter attacks or injures a person or domestic animal, may be impounded by an animal control officer or a police officer, at the owner's expense, and the executive director may order the owner to comply with any of the alternatives set forth in Section 7-12-050(b) and (c), including humane destruction of the animal. The owner shall be entitled to notice and an opportunity for a hearing in the same manner as provided in Section 7-12-050(d) and (e) above.

(Added. Coun. J. 10-2-95, p. 8604)

§7-12-052 Dangerous animals—Miscellaneous.

(a) Every owner of a dangerous animal shall allow inspection of the required enclosure by the executive director or his designee.

(b) All dangerous animals as defined in this chapter are hereby declared to be a public nuisance; provided that they are lawful if maintained in strict compliance with the requirements set out in Section 7-12-050(c).

(c) The executive director and/or the commission are hereby authorized to enact regulations governing dangerous animals as are necessary to carry out the provisions of this chapter and to promote the health, safety, and welfare of the public.

(d) Where an animal has caused severe injury or death to any person, but it is not found to be a dangerous animal on the grounds that the attack was provoked, the executive director shall advise the owner to comply with the safety measures set forth in Section 7-12-050(c) in order to protect the public health, safety and welfare.
(Added. Coun. J. 10-2-95, p. 8604)

§7-12-060 Redemption of impounded animals.
The commission or any agency the commission may designate to take possession of animals for purposes of impounding, shall hold impounded animals for seven days, unless the owner redeems the animal sooner, during which time reasonable means shall be used to facilitate their return to rightful owners. The owner of any animal impounded in any animal control center may, at any time during visiting hours at the animal control center, and before the sale or other disposal as provided in this ordinance, redeem such animal by paying the required fees or charges and, in the case of an unlicensed animal, by complying with the license requirements.

The seven-day holding period shall not apply to an animal relinquished by its owner to the commission under owner signature authorizing the commission to make immediate disposition of the animal at its discretion, nor shall any required holding period apply to an animal received for impounding in obviously critical physical condition or for which immediate euthanasia shall be deemed proper for humane reasons by the executive director or the executive director designee.

An Animal of unknown ownership shall be held for a minimum of five days, or for such longer length of time as the executive director may deem necessary to permit location of and redemption by the rightful owner, except that wild animals which are noxious by their very nature such as wild rats and undomesticated rodents may be euthanized at once following an examination for zoonotic diseases.

Any animal remaining unredeemed after the prescribed holding period shall at once become the property of the commission.
(Prior code § 98-3.3; Amend. Coun. J. 12-4-02, p. 99026)

§7-12-065 Impoundment of dogs and cats—Compulsory sterilization.
(a) Any fertile dog or cat impounded under this chapter pursuant to Sections 7-12-040 or 7-12-080 shall be sterilized prior to redemption, unless, in the determination of the executive director, the sterilization would endanger the life or health of the animal.

(b) The sterilization of the animal pursuant to this section shall be performed only after the owner, if known, is given notification either in person, or by certified mail, of the executive director's intent to sterilize the animal and informing the owner of his right to appeal such determination by filing a written request for hearing within five days of the receipt of notice.

(c) If the owner requests a hearing, the administrative law officer shall be appointed by the executive director unless the department of administrative hearings has exercised jurisdiction in accordance with Section 2-14-190(c) of this code, in which case the department of administrative hearings shall appoint the administrative law officer, who shall hold a hearing, at which all interested parties may present testimony and any other relevant evidence, within 15 days of the request. If the administrative law officer upholds the executive director's determination that the cat or dog is subject to the requirements of this section, then the executive director shall not sterilize the animal until seven days after the hearing; if the owner appeals to the circuit court during that time period, the order to sterilize the animal shall be stayed until resolution of such appeal.

(d) In addition to all other applicable fees, the cost of the sterilization shall be charged to the owner upon redemption.

(Added. Coun. J. 12-4-02, p. 99026)

§7-12-070 Facilities to be used for impoundments.

For purposes of impoundment, the executive director shall utilize an animal control center or the facilities of any humane society properly equipped and willing to impound animals, or, if the animal shall be of a species that may be better or more safely impounded elsewhere, the executive director may designate an alternate facility that is properly equipped and willing to accept the animal.

(Prior code § 98-3.4)

§7-12-080 Removal of neglected animal.

Whenever the executive director shall determine that any animal is kept within a building or upon any premises without food, water or proper care and attention for a period of time sufficient within his judgment to cause undue discomfort or suffering, and if the owner cannot be located after reasonable search, or if the owner shall be known to be absent due to injury, illness, incarceration or other involuntary circumstance, it shall be the duty of the executive director to obtain the necessary legal process to allow him or her to enter or to cause to have entered such building or premises to take possession and remove such animal to an animal control center or to a humane society or other appropriate agency equipped, able and willing to accept the animal.

The animal control center, humane society or other authorized receiving agency shall exercise due caution for the welfare and temporary safekeeping of any animal so removed, in conformance with policies to be prescribed by the commission. After due notification to the owner, or, if the owner cannot be located or contacted after reasonable effort by the animal control center, humane society or other authorized receiving agency, any animal so removed and unredeemed shall become the property of the commission and disposed of under policies prescribed by the commission.

(Prior code § 98-4)

§7-12-090 Owner's responsibility where animal has bitten another animal or person.

It shall be the duty and responsibility of the owner of any animal which has bitten any other animal or person to notify the commission of such bite. It also shall be the duty and responsibility of the owner to surrender such animal to an animal control center within 24 hours after the animal has bitten any other animal or person, or to have such animal impounded at a humane society or other authorized agency provided that there is a veterinarian on the premises daily. If, however, a licensed veterinarian is presented evidence that such animal has been inoculated against rabies within the time prescribed by law prior to the biting, such animal shall be confined on the premises of its owner and in a manner which shall prohibit such animal from biting any other animal or person for a period of 10 days; except that, where the animal bite has caused severe injury or death to a person, confinement on the owner's premises shall not be allowed. In the event of severe injury or death to a person, the executive director shall impound the animal, at the owner's expense, as set forth above in Section 7-12-050(f). It further shall be the duty and responsibility of the owner to have such animal examined by a licensed veterinarian on the first and tenth day of impoundment or confinement or as soon thereafter as possible; provided, that the impoundment or confinement of the animal described above shall not be terminated until examination by a veterinarian.

If an animal, which has bitten any animal or person, is to be impounded by the commission, the owner shall pay a $150.00 rabies observation fee to cover the cost of housing, food, veterinary services and any other service rendered to the animal. Prior to release of said animal, vaccination and license certificates must be presented to the executive director or the director's authorized representative. It shall be unlawful for the owner of any animal, when notified that the animal has bitten any person to sell, euthanize, inoculate or give away the animal or to permit or allow the animal to be taken beyond the limits of the city.

The owner of any animal impounded for rabies observation who fails to pay the rabies observation fee as provided by this chapter shall be subject to a fine of $300.00 and any other costs incurred by the commission for the housing, care and treatment of the animal. Any person who violates any other provision of this section shall be fined not less than $300.00 nor more than $500.00 for each offense. Each day that a violation continues shall constitute a separate and distinct offense.

(Prior code § 98-5; Amend. Coun. J. 10-2-95, p. 8604; 12-4-02, p. 99026; 3-31-04, p. 20916)

§7-12-140 License required.

(a) Each owner, as defined in this chapter, of each dog four months of age or older shall pay a city license fee for the privilege of owning such dog, unless such dog shall be temporarily within the possession of a veterinary hospital, pet shop, kennel, or humane society. Dogs which are the property of any subdivision of local, state or federal government shall be issued complimentary licenses. Any dog properly trained to guide or otherwise assist a blind person shall be issued a complimentary license upon the presentation of proof of vaccination.

(b) Upon determining that an owner subject to the license requirement of subsections (a) of this section has failed to obtain such license, the city clerk shall issue a notice of violation to the owner. If, within 30 days from the date such notice is deposited in the mail, the owner has not come into compliance with subsection (a), the city clerk shall issue a second notice of violation to the owner. The notice required by this subsection shall be sent by first class mail addressed to the owner at the most recent address shown on county rabies vaccination records.

(c) The penalty for failure to obtain the license required by this section shall be no less than $30.00 and no greater than $200.00 for each offense.

(d) The provisions of Article I of Chapter 2-14 of the code shall apply to subsections (b) and (c) of this section.

(Prior code § 98-8; Amend. Coun. J. 12-12-01, p. 75777)

§7-12-150 License application forms.

The executive director shall prepare, or cause to have prepared, license application forms that shall afford complete information as to the name, residence, and telephone, if any, of each applicant, along with full information regarding the animal to be licensed.

The commission shall keep on file, or cause to be kept on file, for two years from date of issue, a copy of each application form so processed, or a copy of each license so issued on the basis of application.

The commission may require persons who sell, transfer ownership of, give away, or otherwise dispose of animals, or of specified species of animals, to maintain records of such transactions, including information descriptive of the animals and identity and location of the recipients. If and when such is required, the commission shall prescribe the length of time such records shall be kept on file by the preparer and shall be permitted access to the records upon demand.

(Prior code § 98-8.1)

§7-12-160 Rabies inoculation certificate.

Application for such license shall be made to the director of revenue. Before a license is issued, a certificate of inoculation against rabies for each dog, issued by the county rabies control officer, or by his deputy, or by a licensed veterinarian, shall be submitted to the director of revenue for examination. No license shall be issued for any dog unless such inoculation certificate bears a date within three years prior to the date of application for license or such other interval as approved by the Department of Agriculture of the state of Illinois. Such certificate shall be returned to the applicant after the current dog license number has been stamped thereon. When applying for a dog license by mail, the certificate of inoculation shall accompany the application. Said certificate shall be returned at the time the license tag is mailed to the applicant.

(Prior code § 98-8.2)

§7-12-170 License fees.

The license fee shall be payable annually, shall be due on the date a dog is acquired or attains four months of age, and shall expire one year from the date of issuance. The license fee shall be as follows:

Male or female, unneutered (i.e., unspayed or uncastrated) — $10.00;

Male or female, neutered (i.e., spayed or castrated) —$5.00;

except that owners who shall establish by satisfactory proof that they are 65 years of age or older shall be issued licenses for their dogs for the following fees:

Male or female, unneutered — $5.00.

Male or female, neutered — $2.50.

(Prior code § 98-8.3; Amend. Coun. J. 12-12-01, p. 75777)

§7-12-180 Exemptions from license fees.

The foregoing shall not apply to dogs owned by or in the charge or care of nonresidents traveling through the city of Chicago or temporarily living therein or to persons who bring dogs into the city for exhibition or similar purposes under Section 7-12-375 of this ordinance; however, any person keeping or harboring any dog for 15 consecutive days within the city shall be considered a resident owner and shall comply with the licensing requirement, unless registered under Section 7-12-375 of this ordinance.

(Prior code § 98-8.4)

§7-12-190 Citations.

The commission, through its animal control officers, is authorized to issue citations against the owner of any animal for violations of this chapter.

(Prior code § 98-8.5; Amend. Coun. J. 10-2-95, p. 8604)

§7-12-200 Rabies vaccination required.

Each owner of any dog, cat or ferret four months of age or older shall have the animal vaccinated against rabies by a licensed veterinarian of the owner's choice. Evidence of vaccination shall consist of a certificate signed by the veterinarian. Type and brand of vaccine used shall be as approved by the Department of Agriculture of the state of Illinois. Vaccination shall be required every three years or at such other interval as required by the Department of Agriculture of the state of Illinois.

A current certificate of vaccination issued by a veterinarian licensed to practice in any other jurisdiction establishing vaccination with a vaccine approved by the Department of Agriculture of the state of Illinois, may be accepted by the executive director.

(Prior code § 98-8.6; Amend. Coun. J. 12-12-01, p. 75777; 12-4-02, p. 99026)

§7-12-210 Horses—License required—Fee—Display—Exemptions.

Each owner of a horse shall pay a license fee for the privilege of keeping, stabling or otherwise maintaining the horse within the city; provided however, that any horse that is intended to be used for the purpose of drawing a carriage licensed under Chapter 9-108 of the Municipal Code shall be licensed under Section 7-12-220.

The license fee shall be $25.00 for each year or any portion thereof and shall be due on the first day of May of each year or at such later date as the horse is acquired, and shall expire on the thirtieth day of April.

A tag shall be issued in evidence of payment of the license fee, and shall be affixed to the rein or saddle whenever the horse is on a public way. The executive director or an animal control officer may demand proof of the license from the owner at any time or at any place when the horse is within the city.

This licensing requirement shall not apply to horses owned by or in the charge or care of nonresidents traveling through the city of Chicago or temporarily living therein; however, any person keeping or harboring any horse for 15 consecutive days within the city shall be considered a resident owner and shall comply with all licensing requirements. A horse which is the prop-

erty of any subdivision of local, state or federal government shall be issued a complimentary license.
(Prior code § 98-9; Amend. Coun. J. 12-4-02, p. 99026)

§7-12-220 Horse-drawn carriage—Horse license required.

The owner of any horse used or intended to be used for the purpose of drawing a carriage licensed under Chapter 9-108 of the municipal code shall pay a license fee to the city for such privilege.

An application for a horse license under this section shall be made in writing, signed and sworn to by the applicant or if the applicant is a corporation, by its duly authorized agent, upon forms provided by the executive director. The application shall contain the full name, Chicago place of business and residence address of the applicant and the business telephone number of the applicant. All corporate applicants for horse licenses under this section shall be organized or qualified to do business under the laws of Illinois and have a place of business in the city of Chicago. All other applicants shall be citizens of the United States and shall have a place of business in the city of Chicago.

The annual license fee for each horse licensed under this section shall be $75.00. The fee shall be paid in advance when the license is issued and shall not be prorated. Each horse license issued under this section shall expire on the thirty-first day of December following the date of issuance.
(Prior code § 98-9.1; Added. Coun. J. 10-16-84, p. 10165; Amended during Supplement No. 2, 4-91; 12-4-02, p. 99026)

§7-12-230 Horse-drawn carriage—Horse identification number—Violation—Penalty.

Each horse licensed under Section 7-12-220 shall have an identification number tattooed as evidence of compliance with Sections 7-12-220 through 7-12-260 of this chapter. The executive director shall have the authority to issue an identification number for each horse to be licensed and shall keep a record of identification numbers so issued. The executive director shall also promulgate rules governing the type and placement of each tattoo and the method in which horses shall be tattooed.

Tattooing a horse in an unauthorized manner, use of an expired unauthorized or false identification number or alteration of an identification number issued by the executive director in any manner whatsoever shall all be deemed a violation of the law. Any person who violates any provision of this section shall be fined not less than $100.00 nor more than $500.00 for each offense and each day such violation shall continue shall be deemed a separate and distinct offense.
(Prior code § 98-9.2; Added. Coun. J. 10-16-84, p. 10165)

§7-12-240 Horse-drawn carriage—Right to demand proof of license—Exception.

The executive director or any animal control officer has the power to demand proof of the issuance of a license under Section 7-12-220 at any time that said horse is being used to draw a carriage licensed under Chapter 9-78 of the municipal code any place within the city, except that no such horse license shall

be required of a person who has obtained a permit under Section 10-8-330 or 10-8-340 of the municipal code while operating under such permit.
(Prior code § 98-9.3; Added. Coun. J. 10-16-84, p. 10165)

§7-12-250 Horse-drawn carriage—Access for inspection.

Each licensee under Section 7-12-220 and the licensee's agents shall at all times allow complete access to any horse licensed hereunder for the purposes of inspection.
(Prior code § 98-9.4; Added. Coun. J. 10-16-84, p. 10165)

§7-12-260 Horse-drawn carriage—Requirements for operation.

No horse licensed under Section 7-12-220 may be used to draw a carriage licensed under Chapter 9-108 of the municipal code unless the following requirements are met:

(a) The horse may not have any open sore or wound, nor may such horse be lame or have any other ailment, unless the driver shall have in the driver's possession a written statement by a veterinarian that the horse is fit for such work, notwithstanding such condition.

(b) The hoofs of the horse must be properly shod and trimmed, utilizing rubber-coated, rubber heel pads or open steel borium tip shoes to aid in the prevention of slipping.

(c) The horse must be groomed daily and may not have fungus, dandruff or a poor or dirty coat.

(d) The horse must be examined, not less than every three months, by a veterinarian, who shall certify the fitness of the animal to perform such work. The driver of a horse-drawn carriage licensed under Chapter 9-108 of the municipal code must have a veterinarian's certificate for such examination and immunization in his or her possession for the horse drawing the carriage at all times such carriage is in operation. A copy of such certificate shall be filed with the executive director.

(e) No horse may be worked more than six hours in any 24-hour period.

(f) All harness and bits shall be used and maintained in accordance with the manufacturing design.

(g) Each horse must be given water and rest for not less than a 15-minute period during each working hour.

(h) No horse may be utilized to pull a carriage carrying more passengers than such carriage is designed to carry by the manufacturer, nor shall a carriage be pulled by fewer animals than provided for by such design.

(i) No horse may be worked with equipment causing an impairment of vision, other than normal blinders.

(j) No whip shall be used unless its design is first approved by the executive director, nor may the driver of a carriage apply a whip to a horse other than by a light touch.

(k) No stallion may draw a carriage without the prior written permission of the executive director.

(l) No horse drawing a carriage shall be worked at a speed faster than a slow trot.

(m) All horses shall be equipped with a waste-catching device, approved by the executive director, while on any public way.
(Prior code § 98-9.5; Added. Coun. J. 10-16-84, p. 10165; Amend. 7-24-91, p. 4000)

§7-12-270 Horse-drawn carriage—Violation—Penalty for Sections §7-12-220 through §7-12-260.

In addition to any of the remedies authorized in this chapter, any person who violates any of the provisions contained in Sections 7-12-220 through 7-12-260 shall be fined not less than $100.00 nor more than $500.00 for each offense and each day such violation shall continue shall be deemed a separate and distinct offense.
(Prior code § 98-9.6; Added. Coun. J. 10-16-84, p. 10165)

§7-12-280 Stables to be kept clean.

Every person in possession or control of any stable or place where any cows, horses, or other animals are kept, shall maintain it at all times in a clean and wholesome condition. Additionally, no person shall maintain any stable or barn for the housing or keeping of horses or other animals during the period of each year from April 15th to November 15th unless said barn or stable is so constructed or equipped with suitable screens as to prevent the ingress or egress of flies.
(Prior code § 98-10)

§7-12-290 Cruelty to animals—Fines.

No person shall do any of the following:

(A) Overload, overdrive, overwork, beat, torture, torment, bait, mutilate or cruelly kill any animal, or cause or knowingly allow the same to be done;

(B) Unnecessarily fail to provide any animal in his or her charge or custody with proper food, water, air and sanitary shelter, such shelter to be sufficient to provide natural light or artificial illumination during reasonable hours and protection from the weather and space within sufficient for the animal to stand in an upright position, and lie down stretched out so that no part of its body need touch the sides of the shelter structure;

(C) Cruelly force into undue physical exertion any animal;

(D) Carry, keep, drive, or cause to be carried, driven or kept, any animal in a cruel manner;

(E) Leave for any unreasonable length of time any animal unattended in a motor vehicle, trailer or other enclosure when the outside temperature shall exceed 85 degrees Fahrenheit in such a manner that said animal does not have proper air circulation;

(F) Have, keep or harbor any animal which is infected with any disease transmissible to other animals or man, or which is afflicted with any painful disease or injury, including severe parasitism, unless such animal be under the care of a veterinarian;

(G) Abandon any animal on any public way or in any place where it may suffer or become a public charge;

(H) Stake out unattended, or leave unrestrained outside and unattended any female dog in season.

Any person who shall violate any provision of subsection (A) shall be fined not less than $300.00 nor more than $1,000.00 for each offense; any person who shall violate any other provision of this section shall be fined not less than $100.00 nor more than $500.00 for each offense.
(Prior code § 98-11; Amend. Coun. J. 12-4-02, p. 99026)

§7-12-300 Ban of unlicensed possession of animals for slaughter.

No person shall own, keep or otherwise possess, or slaughter any sheep, goat, pig, cow or the young of such species, poultry, rabbit, dog, cat, or any other animal, intending to use such animal for food purposes.

This section is applicable to any cult that kills (sacrifices) animals for any type of ritual, regardless of whether or not the flesh or blood of the animal is to be consumed; except that Kosher slaughtering is exempted from this ordinance.

Nothing in this ordinance is to be interpreted as prohibiting any licensed establishment from slaughtering for food purposes any animals which are specifically raised for food purposes.

Agents of the Chicago commission on animal care and control, police officers and humane investigators of any agency licensed by the city of Chicago and/or the Illinois Department of Agriculture for the prevention of cruelty to animals shall have the authority to confiscate any and all animals kept in violation of this ordinance. Enforcement personnel shall have the authority to enter any business premises during normal business hours where an animal or animals described in this ordinance are being housed or kept, but shall only enter domiciles or businesses during nonbusiness hours after obtaining a proper search warrant or permission to enter from the occupant or owner of such premises.

Any person found to have been in violation of this section shall be fined not less than $50.00 nor more than $1,000.00 for each offense. When a person keeps, owns or slaughters more than one animal in violation of this ordinance, the unlawful keeping, owning or slaughtering of each animal will be considered a separate offense for the purposes of this ordinance.
(Prior code § 98-11.1)

§7-12-310 Removal of injured or diseased animal from public way.

Any animal which is on any public way or within any public place and which is severely injured or diseased, and for which care is not being provided on the scene or any severely injured or diseased animal that has strayed onto private premises, shall be removed, if possible, to the care of an animal control center, to the nearest humane society, or to the nearest veterinarian or veterinary hospital willing to accept them. If immediate removal shall not be possible, such animal may be destroyed by the most humane method available on the scene, unless the owner shall come forward beforehand and assume responsibility for removal and care.

Handling of any such case shall be the responsibility of the commission or, in the absence of a representative of the commission, any city of Chicago police officer, or any humane society representative duly authorized by the society to act in its behalf.
(Prior code § 98-12)

§7-12-320 Horse-drawn carriage—Removal of horse from public way.

Any horse licensed under Section 7-12-220 for the purposes of drawing a carriage licensed under Chapter 9-108 of the municipal code which must be removed from a public way for any reason shall be under the custody and control of the commission on animal care and control except that if no animal control officer is available then any Chicago police officer is authorized to remove said horse from public way.
(Prior code § 98-12.1; Added. Coun. J. 10-16-84, p. 10165)

§7-12-350 Dyeing baby chicks, other fowls or rabbits prohibited.

No person shall bring or cause to have brought into the city, sell, offer for sale, barter or display living baby chicks, ducklings, goslings, or other fowl or rabbits which have been dyed, colored or otherwise treated so as to impart to them an artificial color.

It shall be unlawful for any person to display, sell, offer for sale, barter or give away any chicks, ducklings, or goslings as pets, unless the purchaser shall have proper brooder facilities. It shall be unlawful for any person to give away such animals as novelties or prizes. Except that nothing in this section shall be construed to prohibit legitimate commerce in poultry for agricultural and food purposes.
(Prior code § 98-15)

§7-12-370 Animal fights and contests prohibited.

No person shall promote, stage, hold, manage, conduct, or carry on any animal fight, or train any animal for the purpose of an animal fight or any other type of contest, game or fight of a similar nature, nor any simulated version of same that involves baiting or inciting an animal to fight.

Any person who violates any of the provisions of this section shall upon conviction thereof be punished by a fine of not less than $300.00 nor more than $1,000.00 for the first offense or second offense and shall be punished as a misdemeanor for each subsequent offense by incarceration in the county jail for a term not to exceed six months under procedures set forth in Section 1-2-1.1 of the Illinois Municipal Code as amended, or by both fine and imprisonment.
(Prior code § 98-17; Amend. Coun. J. 7-31-90, p. 19875; 12-4-02, p. 99026)

§7-12-420 Removal of excrement.

No person shall appear with a pet upon the public ways or within public places or upon the property of another, absent that person's consent, without some means for the removal of excrement; nor shall any person fail to remove any excrement deposited by such pet. This section shall not apply to a blind person while walking his or her guide dog.

Any person found to have been in violation of this section shall be fined not less than $50.00 nor more than $500.00 for each offense.
(Prior code § 98-19; Amend. Coun. J. 5-14-97, p. 44296)

§7-12-430 Violation—Penalty.

Any person who shall violate any of the provisions of this chapter for which no specific penalty is provided, shall be fined not less than $50.00 nor more than $200.00 for each offense.
(Prior code § 98-20; Amend. Coun. J. 12-4-02, p. 99026)

CHAPTER 7-16
BIRTHS AND DEATHS
(Selected Sections)

Sections:

Article I. Report of Births and Deaths

7-16-030 Report of deaths.

Article II. Care and Disposition of Dead Human Bodies

7-16-050 Discovery.
7-16-060 Funeral establishment as a public morgue.
7-16-070 Reserved.
7-16-080 Reserved.
7-16-090 Reserved.
7-16-100 Burial and cremation permits.
7-16-150 Burial within city.

Article III. Violation of Chapter Provisions

7-16-190 Violation—Penalty.

Article I. Report of Births and Deaths

§7-16-030 Report of deaths.

It shall be the duty of every physician to make a written report to the department of health within 24 hours after the death of any of his patients occurring within the jurisdiction of said department of health; except that if a medical examiner's inquest is called in respect to any such death, the report shall be made to said department of health by the medical examiner. All such reports shall be made on the medical certificate of death or the medical examiners certificate of death forms to be furnished by the department of health and shall contain such information as said department shall require.

When a dead human body is brought to any funeral director's establishment, it shall be the duty of the funeral director or licensed assistant to report the fact to the department of health within 12 hours after the receipt of such body, giving, if known, the name and age of the deceased, and the date, place, and cause of death.
(Prior code § 93-3)

Article II. Care and Disposition of Dead Human Bodies

§7-16-050 Discovery.

Any person who discovers the body of a dead human being, or any part thereof, shall immediately communicate to the medical examiner of the

county and to the department of health the fact of such discovery, the place where and time when the same was discovered, where the same is or may be found, and any facts known by which the said body may be identified, or the cause of death ascertained.
(Prior code § 93-5)

§7-16-060 Funeral establishment as a public morgue.
No funeral director shall allow any establishment used, operated, or maintained by him in the funeral directing business to be used as a public morgue. If any dead human body is brought to any establishment, and if arrangements are not made for the burial or cremation of such body within 100 hours from and after the hour of death, the body shall be taken by the funeral director to the county morgue, or placed by him in one of the cemetery receiving vaults.
(Prior code § 93-6)

§7-16-070 Reserved.
(Deleted. Coun. J. 3-31-04, p. 20916)

§7-16-080 Reserved.
(Deleted. Coun. J. 3-31-04, p. 20916)

§7-16-090 Reserved.
(Deleted. Coun. J. 3-31-04, p. 20916)

§7-16-100 Burial and cremation permits.
It shall be unlawful for any person to move the dead body of any human being, or any part of such body, from any hospital or from place to place within the city or from the city, or to cremate or deposit any human body in any vault within the city, or to inter or disinter, or in any manner dispose of, any dead human body or part thereof, without first obtaining a permit so to do from the department of health; nor shall any dead human body or part thereof be disposed of otherwise than in accordance with the terms of the said permit. Permits for the removal, interment, cremation, or disposal of dead bodies shall be issued only upon the presentation of a proper death certificate to the department of health. Said death certificate shall be signed by a duly licensed physician who attended the deceased during his last illness, or by the medical examiner of Cook County. If the death occurred outside of the state of Illinois, the burial or removal permit shall be signed by the proper authority at the place where death occurred.

No permit for the burial or cremation of any dead human body shall be issued to anyone except a funeral director who is licensed as provided in this code or his duly authorized representative.
(Prior code § 93-10)

§7-16-150 Burial within city.
It shall be unlawful to inter or bury any dead human body or part thereof in any place within the city other than a duly established cemetery.
(Prior code § 93-15)

Article III. Violation of Chapter Provisions

§7-16-190 Violation—Penalty.

Any person who violates, or who resists the enforcement of, any of the provisions of this chapter shall be fined not less than $200.00 nor more than $1,000.00 for each offense, and a separate and distinct offense shall be deemed to have been committed for each and every day on which any such person shall be guilty of such violation.
(Prior code § 93-19)

CHAPTER 7-20
CONTAGIOUS AND EPIDEMIC DISEASES
(Selected Sections)

Sections:
7-20-010 Contagious, epidemic, or communicable disease defined.
7-20-060 Report of sick or neglected person.
7-20-080 Removal or exposure of diseased person.
7-20-090 Removal of articles exposed to infection.
7-20-100 Taking articles to or from premises where death occurred.
7-20-110 Towels in public lavatory.
7-20-120 Use of common drinking cup.
7-20-130 Violation—Penalty.

§7-20-010 Contagious, epidemic, or communicable disease defined.

The term "contagious, epidemic, or communicable disease" is hereby defined to mean any of the following: cholera, yellow fever, diphtheria, scarlet fever, typhus, typhoid fever, small pox, varioloid, puerperal fever, membranous croup, measles, whooping cough, tuberculosis, influenza, pneumonia, cerebrospinal fever, septic sore throat, syphilis, gonorrhea, chancroid, or any grades of these diseases, and any disease designated by the board of health as contagious, epidemic, or communicable.
(Prior code § 94-1)

§7-20-060 Report of sick or neglected person.

Any person who has reason to regard any individual in the city or upon any vessel in the harbor as neglected or not properly cared for, and every physician who hears of any such sick person and has reason to believe such person requires the attention of the board of health shall at once report the facts to the board of health regarding the disease, condition, dwelling place, and position of such sick person.
(Prior code § 94-6)

§7-20-080 Removal or exposure of diseased person.

No person shall move, carry, or convey from one place to another within the city, or from a vessel in the harbor to the shore, without a permit from the board of health, any person having, or suspected of having, any contagious, epidemic, or communicable disease, or any susceptible person who has been in contact with, or exposed to, such a disease; nor shall any person cause, contribute to, or promote the spread of any contagious, epidemic, or communicable disease from any person having, or suspected of having, such a disease, or by any exposure of

such a sick person or the body of a person dead of such a disease, or by a needless exposure of himself, or by any negligent act in connection with the care or custody of such sick person or such dead body. No person shall carry, remove, or convey from one place to another in the city without a permit from the board of health any person having a mental disease or drug addiction, unless such person is in the charge of city, county, or state authorities.
(Prior code § 94-8)

§7-20-090 Removal of articles exposed to infection.

No person within the city shall move or expose, or aid in moving or exposing, any household goods, articles, or things that have been exposed to any contagious or epidemic disease until such household goods, articles, or things shall have been disinfected in accordance with the requirements of the board of health, nor shall any person bring into the city any article or thing whatsoever from any infected place, or from any vessel or building in which any person has been sick of any such disease, without a permit therefor from the board of health, nor until such article or thing has been thoroughly disinfected.
(Prior code § 94-9)

§7-20-100 Taking articles to or from premises where death occurred.

No person shall take into or from any premises, room, or place in which any person shall have died of any of the diseases mentioned in Section 7-16-170, at any time after such person shall have died and before such premises, room, or place shall have been disinfected by the board of health, any article or thing which may be the means of spreading contagion, until such article or thing shall first have been disinfected by the board of health, or unless the removal of such article is authorized by the board of health; provided, that nothing herein contained shall be construed to prevent the use of proper clothing and wrappings which shall be buried with the body of such dead person.
(Prior code § 94-10; 3-31-04, p. 20916)

§7-20-110 Towels in public lavatory.

No person owning, in charge of, or in control of, any public lavatory or washroom shall maintain in or about such lavatory or washroom any towel for common use. The term "common use" as used in this section shall be construed to mean for use by more than one person.
(Prior code § 94-11)

§7-20-120 Use of common drinking cup.

It shall be unlawful to keep, offer, or display for use any common drinking cup, glass, or similar receptacle in any building or place open to the public, or in any lodginghouse or boardinghouse, factory, office, store, or private school.
(Prior code § 94-12)

§7-20-130 Violation—Penalty.

Any person that shall violate any of the provisions of this chapter for which no specific penalty is provided, or that shall resist or cause resistance to be made against the entry of any officer of the board of health to any place described in this chapter which such officer shall desire to make entry into for the

purpose of carrying out the provisions of this chapter, or that shall refuse or fail to comply with any order or regulation made by the board of health and necessary for the purpose of carrying into effect the provisions of this chapter, and any principal or person managing or in control of any public or private school, that shall in any way attempt to prevent any officer of the board of health from exercising the power conferred upon him by this chapter, shall be fined not less than $10.00 nor more than $200.00 for each offense.
(Prior code § 94-13)

CHAPTER 7-24
DRUGS AND NARCOTICS
(Complete Chapter)

Sections:

Article I. Distribution of Drugs and Medicines

7-24-030 Sample packages of medicines.
7-24-070 Bichloride of mercury.
7-24-080 Inhaling or drinking certain substances.
7-24-090 Sale of certain substances.

Article II. Drug Paraphernalia

7-24-091 Possession or delivery.
7-24-092 Manufacture.
7-24-093 Accomplice liability.
7-24-094 Delivery to persons under 18 years of age on school grounds.
7-24-095 License revocation.
7-24-096 Seizure and forfeiture.
7-24-097 Severability.

Article II-A. Controlled Substances

7-24-098 Establishments unlawfully used for controlled substances.

Article III. Carbolic Acid

7-24-100 Prescription required.
7-24-110 Inspection of prescriptions.
7-24-120 Fraudulent prescriptions.
7-24-130 False statements in prescriptions.
7-24-140 Crude carbolic acid mixtures and wholesale.

Article IV. Wood Alcohol

7-24-150 Sales register.
7-24-160 Sale regulated.
7-24-170 Label and warning.

Article V. Tobacco

7-24-190 Collection of cigar and cigarette stumps.
7-24-200 Purchase of cigar and cigarette stumps.
7-24-210 Manufacture from cigar and cigarette stumps.

Article VA. Office of Local Drug Control Policy

7-24-220 Created.
7-24-221 Director and deputy directors—Appointment—Term.
7-24-222 Director—Duties.

7-24-223 Technical and clerical assistants.
7-24-224 Donations.

Article VI. Use of Motor Vehicles
7-24-225 Unlawful drugs in motor vehicle—Impoundment.
7-24-226 Driving while intoxicated—Impoundment.

Article VII. Violation of Chapter Provisions
7-24-230 Violation—Penalty.

Article I. Distribution of Drugs and Medicines

§7-24-030 Sample packages of medicines.

No person shall be permitted to give away, deposit, or otherwise distribute any sample package, parcel, box or other quantity of any nostrum, proprietary medicine, or other material of an alleged medicinal character or purporting to be a curative agency, by means of depositing or leaving the same in any hallway, private area, or yard, or on any doorstep or in any place in public way in the city.
(Prior code § 97-3)

§7-24-070 Bichloride of mercury.

It shall be unlawful for any apothecary, druggist, or pharmacist, or any employee of the same, or any other person to give away, sell, or offer or expose for sale at retail in the city any bichloride of mercury, otherwise known as corrosive sublimate, in the dry form, except in colored tablets enclosed in a sealed container of glass. Said glass container shall be conspicuously labeled with the word "poison" in red letters. Each tablet in said container shall also be individually wrapped and the wrapper shall have conspicuously placed thereon the word "poison" in plain letters.
(Prior code § 97-7)

§7-24-080 Inhaling or drinking certain substances.

No person shall inhale, breathe or drink any compound liquid or chemical containing toluol, hexane, trichloroethylene, acetone, toluene, ethyl acetate, methyl ethyl ketone, trichloroethylene, isopropanol, methyl isobutyl ketone, methyl cellosolve acetate, cyclohexanone, or any other substance for the purpose of inducing symptoms of intoxication, elation, dizziness, paralysis, irrational behavior, or in any manner change, distort or disturb the audio, visual or mental processes. For the purpose of this section, any such condition so induced shall be deemed to be an intoxicated condition; provided, however, that the provisions of this section shall not apply to:

(a) Any person who inhales, breathes, or drinks such material or substance pursuant to the direction or prescription of any doctor, physician, surgeon, dentist, or podiatrist authorized to so direct or prescribe.

(b) Any person who inhales, breathes, drinks or otherwise in any manner uses any narcotic, dangerous drug, or other material or substance or combination thereof, which material or substance or combination thereof is defined by, and the use of which is prohibited or regulated by, any law of the

state of Illinois. Any person violating any of the provisions of this section shall be fined not less than $25.00 nor more than $200.00 for each offense.
(Prior code § 97-7.1)

§7-24-090 Sale of certain substances.

No person shall knowingly sell or offer for sale, deliver or give away to any person under 17 years of age, unless upon the written order of parent or guardian, any substances containing any of the following volatile solvents, where the seller, offerer or deliverer knows or has reason to believe that the substance will be used for the purpose of inducing symptoms of intoxication, elation, dizziness, paralysis, irrational behavior, or in any manner change, distort or disturb the audio, visual or mental processes:

Toluol, hexane, trichloroethylene, acetone, toluene, ethyl acetate, methyl ethyl ketone, trichloroethane, isopropanol, methyl isobutyl ketone, methyl cellosolve acetate, cyclohexanone, or any other substance which will induce symptoms of intoxication, elation, dizziness, paralysis, irrational behavior, or in any manner change, distort or disturb the audio, visual or mental processes.

Any person violating any of the provisions of this section shall be fined not less than $25.00 nor more than $200.00 for each offense.
(Prior code § 97-7.2)

Article II. Drug Paraphernalia

§7-24-091 Possession or delivery.

Except as authorized by law, any person who delivers, furnishes, or transfers, possesses with intent to deliver, furnish or transfer, drug paraphernalia as defined in Section 720 ILCS 600/2, subparagraph (5) of the Illinois Compiled Statutes, and including glass tubing designed and utilized for the ingestion of crack or cocaine, knowing, or under circumstances where one reasonably should know, that it will be used to plant, propagate, cultivate, sow, harvest, compound, convert, produce, process, prepare, test, analyze, pack, repack, store, contain, conceal, inject, ingest, inhale, or otherwise introduce into the human body a controlled substance in violation of the Illinois Controlled Substances Act 720 ILCS 570/100, et seq., shall be fined $1,000.00, or punished by imprisonment for a period of six months, or by both such fine and imprisonment.
(Added. Coun. J. 5-12-99, p. 3327)

§7-24-092 Manufacture.

Except as authorized by taw, any person who manufactures, with intent to deliver, furnish, or transfer drug paraphernalia knowing, or under circumstances where one reasonably should know, that it will be used to plant, propagate, cultivate, grow, harvest, manufacture, compound, convert, produce, process, prepare, test, analyze, pack, repack, store, contain, conceal, ingest, inhale or otherwise introduce into the human body cocaine, cocaine base, heroin, phencyclidine, or methamphetamine in violation of the Illinois Controlled Substances Act shall be fined $1,000.00, or punished by imprisonment for a period of six months, or by both such fine and imprisonment.
(Added. Coun. J. 5-12-99, p. 3327)

§7-24-093 Accomplice liability.

Except as authorized by law, any person who provides another person with drug paraphernalia, knowing, or under circumstances where one reasonably should know, that the second person will plant, propagate, cultivate, grow, harvest, manufacture, compound, convert, produce, process, prepare, test, analyze, pack, repack, store, contain, conceal, ingest or otherwise introduce into another human body any controlled substances in violation of the Illinois Controlled Substances Act, shall be held as an accomplice to the violation by the second person and shall be fined $1,000.00, or punished by imprisonment for a period of six months, or by both such fine and imprisonment.
(Added. Coun. J. 5-12-99, p. 3327)

§7-24-094 Delivery to persons under 18 years of age on school grounds.

Except as authorized by law, any person, 18 years of age or over, who, upon the grounds of a public or private elementary, vocational, junior high, or high school, possesses a hypodermic needle with the intent to deliver, furnish or transfer the hypodermic needle, knowing, or under circumstances where one reasonably should know, that it will be used by a person under 18 years of age to inject into the human body any controlled substance in violation of the Illinois Controlled Substances Act, shall be fined $2,000.00 or punished by imprisonment for a period of six months, or by both such fine and imprisonment.
(Added. Coun. J. 5-12-99, p. 3327)

§7-24-095 License revocation.

The violation, or the causing or permitting of a violation, of Section 7-24-091, 7-24-092, 7-24-093 or 7-24-094 by a holder of a business or liquor license issued by the city of Chicago, and in the course of the licensee's business shall be grounds for the revocation of such license.
(Added. Coun. J. 5-12-99, p. 3327)

§7-24-096 Seizure and forfeiture.

All drug paraphernalia defined in Section 720 ILCS 600/2, subparagraph (5), and including glass tubing utilized for the ingestion of cocaine or crack cocaine, is subject to forfeiture and may be seized by any peace officer. The seizure and forfeiture shall be made in accordance with rules issued by the superintendent of police or his designee.
(Added. Coun. J. 5-12-99, p. 3327)

§7-24-097 Severability.

If any provisions of Sections 7-24-091 through 7-24-097 or the application thereof to any person or circumstance is held invalid, such invalidity shall not affect other provisions or applications of said sections which can be given effect without the invalid provision or application and to this end the provisions of these sections are severable.
(Added. Coun. J. 5-12-99, p. 3327)

Article II-A. Controlled Substances

§7-24-098 Establishments unlawfully used for controlled substances.

(a) It shall be unlawful to:

(1) Knowingly open or maintain any place for the purpose of unlawful manufacturing, storing, distributing or using any controlled substance; or

(2) Manage or control any building, room or enclosure, either as an owner lessee, manager, agent, employee or mortgagee, and knowingly and intentionally rent, lease or make available for use, with or without compensation, the building, room or enclosure for the purpose of unlawfully manufacturing, storing, distributing or using a controlled substance.

(b) Any person who violates subsection (a) of this section shall be sentenced to a term of imprisonment of not less than 14 days nor more than six months.

(c) For purposes of this section, the term "controlled substance" shall be as defined in the Illinois Controlled Substances Act, codified at 720 ILCS 570/100, et seq., as amended.

(Added. Coun. J. 5-2-01, p. 57748)

Article III. Carbolic Acid

§7-24-100 Prescription required.

It shall be unlawful for any apothecary, druggist, or pharmacist, or any employee thereof, or any other person whatever, to sell, exchange, give away, or deliver to any person within the city any carbolic acid or any extract or product thereof, or any preparation or compound of which it is an element or ingredient, containing more than five percent of carbolic acid, except upon the written prescription or order of a duly licensed physician, and except upon the day or date of such prescription or order, and there shall be for each such sale, exchange, gift, or delivery, a special and distinct order or prescription.

The prescription or order shall have the date thereon of the day on which it is made, and shall be signed by the physician making it who shall be a graduate in medicine, and as such have a diploma from a legally constituted or chartered medical college or medical institution, and it shall contain the name and residence of the patient for whom it is intended, and the location of the physician's office or residence.

(Prior code § 97-8)

§7-24-110 Inspection of prescriptions.

All such prescriptions and orders shall be open for inspection by the coroner, State's Attorney, Assistant State's Attorney, corporation counsel, superintendent of police, or any regular police officer of this city. All such prescriptions and orders shall be kept and preserved for three years after receiving the same. It shall be unlawful for any person to refuse or prevent in any manner, or by any means, the inspection of such prescription or such orders, or any thereof, by any of said officers, and it shall be unlawful for any of the persons mentioned in Sections 7-24-100 to 7-24-130 who shall sell any such acid to fail or neglect to keep or preserve such prescriptions or orders.

(Prior code § 97-9)

§7-24-120 Fraudulent prescriptions.

It shall be unlawful for any person to present any false, forged, untrue, or fictitious prescription or order for any carbolic acid, or any extract or product thereof, or any preparation or compound of which it is an element or ingredient, or to obtain the same by means thereof, or to give any false or fictitious name, or to give or make any false statement, or any false representation to obtain or in obtaining the same.
(Prior code § 97-10)

§7-24-130 False statements in prescriptions.

It shall be unlawful for any physician to put a wrong or false date on any order or prescription for any carbolic acid, or any extract or product thereof, or any preparation or compound of which it is an element or ingredient, or to wilfully give any such order or prescription containing any false statement or representation of any fact or matter therein, or to give any such order or prescription for a dose or quantity greater than usual or necessary for bona fide purposes to cure or prevent sickness or disease.
(Prior code § 97-11)

§7-24-140 Crude carbolic acid mixtures and wholesale.

Sections 7-24-100 to 7-24-130 shall not apply to the sale of crude carbolic acid in quantities exceeding one gallon, to the sale of a solution or mixture containing equal portions of carbolic acid, glycerine, and alcohol, to the commerce or trade among wholesale druggists and retail druggists, apothecaries, or pharmacists, nor to sales or gifts to public institutions, charitable institutions, or hospitals for medical use therein.
(Prior code § 97-12)

Article IV. Wood Alcohol

§7-24-150 Sales register.

It shall be the duty of every person to record legibly in the English language in a bound book kept for the purpose the name and address of every person to whom has been sold, without a physician's prescription, any methyl alcohol, commonly called wood alcohol, together with the quantity sold and the date on which the sale was made.
(Prior code § 97-13)

§7-24-160 Sale regulated.

No person shall sell, offer for sale, or have in his possession with the intention of selling, for internal use by a human being any methyl alcohol or any food or drink, or any preparation or mixture of any kind whatsoever, containing the same.

It shall be unlawful for any person to sell methyl alcohol, or any mixture or preparation containing the same, or grain alcohol denatured with methyl alcohol to any person who is addicted to the use of alcohol, or who shows any signs of alcoholic intoxication or drunkenness.

The sale of methyl alcohol, or any preparation containing the same, to any person addicted to the use of alcohol or showing any symptoms or signs

of alcoholic intoxication or drunkenness, shall be considered prima facie evidence that such methyl alcohol is intended for internal use by such person.
(Prior code § 97-14)

§7-24-170 Label and warning.

All methyl alcohol, or any preparation or mixture of any kind containing methyl alcohol or alcohol which has been denatured with methyl alcohol, sold, offered or sale, or kept with the intention of selling or using, shall be conspicuously labeled "Wood Alcohol" or "This preparation contains wood alcohol" and the word "Poison," together with a skull and crossbones, and the legend "The use of even small quantities of wood alcohol may cause blindness." The word "Poison" with the skull and crossbones shall be printed in red ink and shall be at least one-third of an inch in height, and the warning in regard to blindness shall be in letters at least one-fourth of an inch in height.

It shall be the duty of every person selling wood alcohol or preparations containing the same, to warn the purchaser of the dangerous and blinding effects of wood alcohol when used internally.
(Prior code § 97-15)

Article V. Tobacco

§7-24-190 Collection of cigar and cigarette stumps.

It shall be unlawful for any person to pick or gather up from any public way or public place, any cigar or cigarette butt or stump, or the waste, unused, or unburned portion of any cigar, tobacco, or cigarette, for the purpose or with the intent of bartering, selling, or disposing of the same for use in any form of manufactured tobacco.

It shall be unlawful for any parent, guardian, or person having the legal custody or control of any child under the age of 18 years, to knowingly permit, aid, advise, or encourage any such child to gather or pick up from the public ways or public places any cigar or cigarette butt or stump, or the waste, unused, or unburned portion of any cigar, cigarette, or tobacco.
(Prior code § 97-17; Amend Coun. J. 1-11-91, p. 29130)

§7-24-200 Purchase of cigar and cigarette stumps.

It shall be unlawful for any person to buy or receive for the purpose of disposing of the same for use in any form of manufactured tobacco, any cigar or cigarette butt or stump or the waste, unused, or unburned portion of any cigar, tobacco, or cigarette gathered from the public ways or public places in the city.
(Prior code § 97-18)

§7-24-210 Manufacture from cigar and cigarette stumps.

It shall be unlawful for any person to manufacture any cigar or cigarette butt or stump, or the waste, unused, or unburned portion of any cigar, tobacco, or cigarette gathered in any public way or public place, in whole or in part into cigars, cigarettes, chewing or smoking tobacco, or snuff.
(Prior code § 97-19)

Article VA. Office of Local Drug Control Policy

§7-24-220 Created.

There is hereby created and established an executive department of the city which shall be known as the office of local drug control policy. Said office shall be under the supervision of a director, assisted by two deputy directors, all three of whom shall be appointed by the mayor by and with the consent of the city council.
(Added. Coun. J. 2-26-92, p. 13370)

§7-24-221 Director and deputy directors—Appointment—Term.

The director and two deputy directors of the office of local drug control policy shall each serve at the pleasure of the mayor, and in no event may any person serve as director or deputy director for a period exceeding four years. No person shall serve as director or deputy director while holding any other position in the federal, state or local government.
(Added. Coun. J. 2-26-92, p. 13370)

§7-24-222 Director—Duties.

It shall be the duty of the director of the office of local drug control policy:

(a) To serve as the principal director and coordinator of the Chicago Drug Control Policy with respect to the applicable provisions in federal, state or local law;

(b) To develop, review, implement and enforce local government policy regarding drug control programs;

(c) To direct and coordinate all local government drug supply reduction efforts, including intelligence, interdiction and drug research as well as all other programs designed to halt the production, importing and manufacture of drugs;

(d) To direct and coordinate efforts between the federal, state and local governments, including the review of state and local drug control strategies;

(e) To direct and coordinate all local government drug demand reduction efforts, including education, prevention, treatment, research, and private sector programs; and

(f) To develop and coordinate a comprehensive drug educational program to be utilized by the public and parochial schools of this city from kindergarten through high school, productive of and conducive to an eventual drug free environment within the schools of the city.
(Added. Coun. J. 2-26-92, p. 13370)

§7-24-223 Technical and clerical assistants.

The director shall appoint his technical and clerical assistants in such number and for such compensation as may be provided in the annual appropriation ordinance.
(Added Coun. J. 2-26-92, p. 13370)

§7-24-224 Donations.

The director shall be authorized to solicit, to accept and to use monetary and in-kind donations from the public and private sectors, for the purpose of carrying out the provisions of this ordinance.

(Added. Coun. J. 2-26-92, p. 13370)

Article VI. Use of Motor Vehicles

§7-24-225 Unlawful drugs in motor vehicle—Impoundment.

(a) The owner of record of any motor vehicle that contains any controlled substance or cannabis, as defined in the Controlled Substances Act, 720 ILCS 570/100, et seq., and the Cannabis Control Act, 720 ILCS 550/1, et seq., or that is used in the purchase, attempt to purchase, sale, or attempt to sell such controlled substances or cannabis shall be liable to the city for an administrative penalty of $1,000.00 plus any applicable towing and storage fees. Any such vehicle shall be subject to seizure and impoundment pursuant to this section. This subsection shall not apply: (1) if the vehicle used in the violation was stolen at the time and the theft was reported to the appropriate police authorities within 24 hours after the theft was discovered or reasonably should have been discovered; (2) if the vehicle is operating as a common carrier and the violation occurs without the knowledge of the person in control of the vehicle; or (3) if the owner proves that the presence of the controlled substance or cannabis was authorized under the Controlled Substances Act or the Cannabis Control Act.

(b) Whenever a police officer has probable cause to believe that a vehicle is subject to seizure and impoundment pursuant to this section, the police officer shall provide for the towing of the vehicle to a facility controlled by the city or its agent. When the vehicle is towed, the police officer shall notify any person identifying himself as the owner of the vehicle or any person who is found to be in control of the vehicle at the time of the alleged violation, if there is such a person, of the fact of the seizure and of the vehicle owner's right to request a preliminary hearing to be conducted under Section 2-14-132 of this code.

(c) The provisions of Section 2-14-132 shall apply whenever a motor vehicle is seized and impounded pursuant to this section.

(Added. Coun. J. 3-9-95, p. 66176; Amend. 4-29-98, p. 66564; 12-4-02, p. 99026; 12-15-04, p. 39840)

§7-24-226 Driving while intoxicated—Impoundment.

(a) No person shall drive or be in actual physical control of any vehicle within the city of Chicago while under the influence of alcohol, other drug or drugs, intoxicating compound or compounds or any combination thereof, as defined and prohibited by 625 ILCS 5/11-501, as amended.

(b) Any vehicle used in a violation of subsection (a) of this section shall be subject to seizure and impoundment pursuant to this section. The owner of record of such vehicle shall be liable to the city for an administrative penalty of $1,000.00 in addition to fees for the towing and storage of the vehicle.

(c) Whenever a police officer has probable cause to believe that a vehicle is subject to seizure and impoundment pursuant to this section, the police officer shall provide for the towing of the vehicle to a facility controlled by the city or its agents. When the vehicle is towed, the police officer shall notify the person who is found to be in control of the vehicle at the time of the alleged violation, if there is such a person, of the fact of the seizure and of the vehicle owner's right to request a preliminary hearing to be conducted under Section 2-14-132 of this code.

(d) The provisions of Section 2-14-132 shall apply whenever a motor vehicle is seized and impounded pursuant to this section.

(Added. Coun. J. 12-12-01, p. 76443; 12-15-04, p. 39840)

Article VII. Violation of Chapter Provisions

§7-24-230 Violation—Penalty.

Any person violating any of the provisions of this chapter for which no other penalty is provided shall be fined not less than $10.00 nor more than $100.00 for each offense.

(Prior code § 97-20; Amend. Coun. J. 2-26-92 p. 13370)

CHAPTER 7-28
HEALTH NUISANCES
(Selected Sections)

Sections:

Article I. Nuisances in General

7-28-010 Notice to abate.
7-28-020 Summary abatement.
7-28-030 Common law and statutory nuisances.
7-28-040 Abandonment of refrigerators.
7-28-050 Plastic bags—Violation—Penalty.
7-28-060 Conditions detrimental to health—Public nuisance—Violation—Penalty.
7-28-065 Graffiti removal—Nuisance abatement.
7-28-070 Piling of used material to excessive heights.
7-28-080 Nuisance in connection with business.
7-28-085 Signs and signboards—Penalty for violation.
7-28-090 Nuisances brought into city.
7-28-110 Gas manufactory odors and refuse.
7-28-120 Weeds—Penalty for violation—Abatement—Lien.
7-28-130 Diseased trees.
7-28-150 Spreading of vermin poison.
7-28-180 Throwing objects in public places of amusement—Violation—Penalty.
7-28-190 Throwing objects into roadways.

Article II. Refuse

7-28-200 Definitions.
7-28-210 Refuse containers.
7-28-220 Duty to provide refuse containers and service.
7-28-225 Duty to provide compactors.
7-28-227 Duty to provide refuse containers at construction or demolition sites.
7-28-230 Location of refuse containers.
7-28-235 Location of refuse compactors.
7-28-240 Refuse removal.
7-28-260 Containers—Use.
7-28-261 Accumulation of refuse—Responsibility.
7-28-270 Contents of standard and commercial refuse containers and compactors.

7-28-280 Removal of contents.
7-28-290 Ashes.
7-28-300 Removal of restaurant garbage.
7-28-301 Grease containers.
7-28-302 Grease containers—Maintenance and removal.
7-28-303 Location of grease containers.
7-28-305 Location of grease containers on the public way.
7-28-310 Owner of business responsible for removal when—Violation— Penalty.
7-28-315 Removal of litter from a retail establishment's parking area.
7-28-320 Incinerators and ash chutes.
7-28-330 Sale of garbage prohibited.
7-28-331 Commercial refuse containers and compactors—Identification.
7-28-360 Removal of refuse before vacation of premises.
7-28-380 Refuse vehicles.
7-28-390 Dumping on public way—Violation—Penalty.
7-28-395 Construction debris on public way prohibited.
7-28-400 Disinfection of refuse vehicles.
7-28-410 Reserved.
7-28-420 Industrial refuse.
7-28-430 Decaying animal matter.
7-28-440 Dumping on real estate without permit—Nuisance—Violation—Penalty—Recovery of costs.
7-28-445 Illegal dumping—Anonymous program and reward.
7-28-450 Owner responsible for removal— Nuisance—Violation—Penalty— Notice—Costs.
7-28-460 Substances that scatter in wind.
7-28-470 Refuse on roof or in areaway.
7-28-480 Inspection of roofs and areaways.
7-28-490 Roofers.
7-28-500 Removal of roofing refuse.
7-28-510 Objects that may damage tires—Illegal to dump on public way.
7-28-520 Additional penalty for violation of article.

Article III. Privies, Catchbasins, and Similar Vaults

7-28-530 Construction of vaults.
7-28-540 Location of privy vault.
7-28-550 Distance from other buildings.
7-28-560 Vault contents.
7-28-570 Offensive privies and catchbasins.
7-28-580 Removal of vault contents.
7-28-590 Drawing off contents.
7-28-600 Vehicle for removal of vault contents.
7-28-610 Workmen's temporary closets.
7-28-620 Chemical closets.

Article IV. Offensive Chemicals and Substances

7-28-630 Possession and sale—Violation—Penalty.
7-28-635 Sale of mercury thermometers containing mercury substance.
7-28-640 Prescription required—Violation—Penalty.
7-28-650 Offensive bombs in public places—Violation—Penalty.

Article V. Rat Control

7-28-660 Rat-stoppage.
7-28-670 Inspection notice.
7-28-680 Maintenance.
7-28-690 Unlawful to remove rat-stoppage.
7-28-700 Structural changes.

7-28-710 Dumping prohibited.
7-28-720 Accumulation of materials or junk.
7-28-730 Rat-stoppage by owner—Lien.
7-28-735 Food establishments.

Article VI. Lot Maintenance
7-28-740 Required.
7-28-750 Noncombustible screen fence required—Nuisance declared when.
7-28-760 Severability.
7-28-770 Exemption.
7-28-780 Lot in ill-maintained condition—Notice.
7-28-790 Violation—Penalty for this article.

Article VII. Violation of Chapter Provisions
7-28-800 Violation—Penalty.

Article I. Nuisances in General

§7-28-010 Notice to abate.

It shall be the duty of the building commissioner or his or her designee to serve notice in writing by certified mail upon the owner, occupant, agent, or person in possession or control of any building or structure in or upon which any nuisance may be found, or who may be the owner or cause of any such nuisance other than the nuisance specified in Sections 7-28-120 and 7-28-440 to 7-28-450, inclusive, of this chapter requiring him to abate the same in the manner the commissioner shall prescribe, within a reasonable time. It shall not be necessary in any case for the commissioner to specify in his notice the manner in which any nuisance shall be abated, unless he shall deem it advisable to do so. If the person so notified shall neglect or refuse to comply with the requirements of the order by abating the nuisances within the time specified, the person shall be fined not less than $25.00 nor more than $500.00 for every such violation, and each day the nuisance shall continue shall constitute a separate and distinct violation.

It shall be the duty of the building commissioner to proceed at once upon the expiration of the time specified in the notice to cause any such nuisance to be abated; provided, however, that whenever the owner, occupant, agent, or person in possession or control of any building or structure, in or upon which any nuisance may be found, is unknown or cannot be found, the commissioner shall proceed to abate the nuisance without notice. In either case the expense of such abatement shall be collected from the person who may have created, continued, or suffered the nuisance to exist, in addition to any penalty or fine. The commissioner of streets and sanitation shall enforce the provisions of Sections 7-28-120 and 7-28-440 to 7-28-450, inclusive, in the manner provided herein for nuisances generally unless the specific section shall provide otherwise.

(Prior code § 99-1; Amended. Coun. J. 12-18-86, p. 38654; 4-29-98, p. 66564)

§7-28-020 Summary abatement.

Whenever any nuisance shall be found on any premises within the city, the commissioner of buildings or commissioner of the environment is hereby

authorized, in their discretion, to cause the same to be summarily abated in such manner as he may direct.
(Prior code § 99-2; Amend. Coun. J. 12-11-91, p. 10978)

§7-28-030 Common law and statutory nuisances.

In all cases where no provision is herein made defining what are nuisances and how the same may be removed, abated, or prevented, in addition to what may be declared such herein, those offenses which are known to the common law of the land and the statutes of Illinois as nuisances may, in case the same exist within the city limits or within one mile thereof, be treated as such, and proceeded against as is provided in this code, or in accordance with any other provision of law.
(Prior code § 99-3)

§7-28-040 Abandonment of refrigerators.

Any person who abandons or discards in any place accessible to children any refrigerator, icebox or ice chest of a capacity of one and one-half cubic feet or more which has an attached lid or door which may be opened or fastened shut by means of an attached latch, or who being the owner, lessee, or manager of any place or premises knowingly permits such abandoned or discarded refrigerator, icebox or ice chest to remain there in such condition, shall be fined not less than $50.00 nor more than $200.00 or imprisoned for not more than 30 days, or both, for each offense. Every day that such violation continues shall be deemed a separate and distinct offense.
(Prior code § 99-3.1; Amend. Coun. J. 12-4-02, p. 99931)

§7-28-050 Plastic bags—Violation—Penalty.

Definition: "Plastic bag" means a polyethylene bag, other than one used for food products weighing not more than five pounds, intended for household use which is larger than seven inches in diameter at the opened end, and is made of thin film less than one mil (0.001 inch) in thickness (according to standards established under the Commodity Standards Division of the United States Department of Commerce).

No person shall package, deliver or sell any article for use in or around the household in a plastic bag, or shall sell or distribute any plastic bag for use in or around the household, unless the bag bears a warning against the hazard of suffocation by children in the following or substantially equivalent wording:

> WARNING: Keep this bag away from babies and children. Do not use in cribs, beds, carriages, or playpens. The thin film may cling to nose and mouth and prevent breathing.

The warning shall be printed on, attached to, or accompany each bag; provided, however, that it shall be permissible to print the warning on the outside wrapper of packages of bags intended for home processing use only, e.g., freezer bags, garbage disposal bags, in lieu of on each individual bag. The warning shall be prominently and conspicuously displayed in bold-face type, in accordance with the following table:

Total of the length and width of the bag, combined
60 inches or more ....24 points
40 inches, but less than 60 inches ....18 points
30 inches, but less than 40 inches ....14 points
Less than 30 inches ....10 points

Any person violating this section shall be fined $200.00 for each offense.
(Prior code § 99-3.2)

§7-28-060 Conditions detrimental to health—Public nuisance—Violation—Penalty.

No building, vehicle, structure, receptacle, yard, lot, premises, or part thereof, shall be made, used, kept, maintained, or operated in the city if such use, keeping, maintaining, or operating shall be the occasion of any nuisance, or shall be dangerous to life or detrimental to health.

Every building or structure constructed or maintained in violation of the building provisions of this code, or which is in an unsanitary condition, or in an unsafe or dangerous condition, or which in any manner endangers the health or safety of any person or persons, is hereby declared to be a public nuisance. Every building or part thereof which is in an unsanitary condition by reason of the basement or cellar being covered with stagnant water, or by reason of the presence of sewer gas, or by reason of any portion of a building being infected with disease or being unfit for human habitation, or which by reason of any other unsanitary condition, is a source of sickness, or which endangers the public health, is hereby declared to be a public nuisance.

Any person found guilty of violating any of the provisions of this section shall be subject to a penalty of not less than $200.00 nor more than $500.00, or imprisonment not to exceed 10 days, or both such fine and imprisonment for each offense. Each day such violation shall continue shall constitute a separate and distinct offense.
(Prior code § 99-4; Amend. Coun. J. 7-9-86, p. 31580; Amend. Coun. J. 8-30-00, p. 40306)

§7-28-065 Graffiti removal—Nuisance abatement.

(a) As defined in this section, graffiti is hereby declared to be a public nuisance. The owner of record, or the person in charge, possession or control of any building or structure upon which graffiti is placed or affixed shall, upon the appearance of the graffiti: (i) cause such graffiti to be removed or concealed or (ii) place on file a written statement authorizing the presence of the graffiti at the office of the commissioner of the department of streets and sanitation. Whenever any nuisance in the form of graffiti shall be found on any building or other structure, the department of streets and sanitation, or its agent or contractor shall attempt to obtain consent from the owner for the city's graffiti removal services. If such attempt to contact the owner is not successful, the department shall post a notice in a prominent place upon the building or structure where the graffiti is found which shall state that, if the graffiti is not removed or concealed or if a written statement authorizing the presence of the graffiti is not filed with the commissioner within five days after the notice is posted, excluding Saturdays, Sundays and legal holidays, the department or its agent or contractor shall have authority to enter or access the property and abate the nuisance by removing or concealing the graffiti.

(b) Nothing in this section shall prevent the city from taking any other enforcement action authorized by law.

(c) "Graffiti" means an inscription, drawing, mark or design that is painted, sprayed or drawn directly upon the exterior of any building or other structure and is visible from the public way; provided that, graffiti shall not include any sign permitted by the Zoning Code or any decoration that is part of the architectural design of the building or structure.

(Added. Coun. J. 5-17-00, p. 32562)

§7-28-070 Piling of used material to excessive heights.

No yard, lot, premises or enclosure or part thereof, shall be used, kept, maintained, or operated, for the purpose of storing used lumber, metal or other secondhand building material, dismantled motor vehicles or parts thereof, crates, cases, boxes or other discarded material unless the said yard, lot, premises or enclosure is entirely surrounded by a fence eight feet in height, which fence shall be located at least eight feet from all public ways surrounding the property and none of said articles shall be piled nearer than six inches to, nor higher than said fence; provided, however, that if said articles are piled at a greater distance than eight feet from any public way they may be piled to a height equal to the distance from the public way, but in no case to a height exceeding 20 feet. On the property dividing lines of such yard, lot, premises or enclosure said fence may be erected on the property dividing line but none of said articles shall be piled nearer than six inches to said fence nor be piled at an angle of more than 45 degrees from such point, but not to exceed a height of 20 feet. Where an existing fence is erected nearer than eight feet to a public way, such fence may be permitted to remain but none of said articles shall be piled nearer than eight feet to such public way nor contrary to the provisions of this section. The piling of said articles in excess of the height herein permitted shall constitute a nuisance. Any person who violates any provision of this section shall be fined not less than $200.00 and not more than $500.00 for each offense. Every day of a continuing violation shall constitute a separate and distinct offense.

(Prior code § 99-4.1; Amend. Coun. J. 12-4-02, p. 99931)

§7-28-080 Nuisance in connection with business.

No substance, matter, or thing of any kind whatever, which shall be dangerous or detrimental to health, shall be allowed to exist in connection with any business, or be used therein, or be used in any work or labor performed in the city, and no nuisance shall be permitted to exist in connection with any business or in connection with any such work or labor. Any person who violates this section shall be subject to a fine of not less than $300 and not more than $1,000 for each offense. Each day that such a violation continues shall be considered a separate and distinct offense.

(Prior code § 99-5; Amend. Coun. J. 11-15-00, p. 46866)

§7-28-085 Signs and signboards—Penalty for violation.

It shall be unlawful to erect any sign and signboard on the surface of a privately owned walkway or parking lot made available for public use and access if the placement of such sign or signboard obstructs the use of the facility made available for public use and creates a public safety hazard. Any person found to have violated this section shall be fined not less than $100.00 nor shall it exceed $500.00 (Added. Coun. J. 7-2-97, p. 47906)

§7-28-090 Nuisances brought into city.

No person shall bring into the city, or keep therein for sale or otherwise, either for food, or for any other purpose, any dead or live animal, nor any matter, substance, or thing which shall be a nuisance or which shall occasion a nuisance in the city, or which may or shall be dangerous or detrimental to health.
(Prior code § 99-6)

§7-28-110 Gas manufactory odors and refuse.

No person manufacturing gas shall throw, deposit, or allow to run, or permit to be thrown or deposited, into any public way, any gas-tar or any refuse matter from any gas house, gas reservoir, works, or manufactory; nor shall any such person allow any substance or odor to escape from such gas house, gas reservoir, works, or manufactory, or make any gas of such ingredients or quality that any substance shall escape therefrom, or be formed in the process of burning any gas, which shall be offensive or dangerous, or prejudicial to life or health. Every such person shall use the most approved and all reasonable means for preventing the escape of odors.
(Prior code § 99-8)

§7-28-120 Weeds—Penalty for violation—Abatement—Lien.

(a) Any person who owns or controls property within the city must cut or otherwise control all weeds on such property so that the average height of such weeds does not exceed 10 inches. Any person who violates this subsection shall be subject to a fine of not less than $100.00 nor more than $300.00. Each day that such violation continues shall be considered a separate offense.

(b) All weeds which have not been cut or otherwise controlled, and which exceed an average height of 10 inches, are hereby declared to be a public nuisance. If any person has been convicted of violating subsection (a) and has not cut or otherwise controlled any weeds as required by this section within 10 days after the date of the conviction, the city may cause any such weeds to be cut at any time. In such event, the person who owns or controls the property on which the weeds are situated shall be liable to the city for all costs and expenses incurred by the city in cutting the weeds.

(c) The costs and expenses incurred pursuant to subsection (b) shall constitute a lien against the affected property if the city, or the person performing the service by authority of the city, in its or his own name, files a notice of lien in the office of the county recorder, or in the office of the registrar of titles if the property is registered under the Torrens System. The notice of lien shall consist of a sworn statement setting out:

(1) A description of the real estate sufficient for identification thereof;

(2) The amount of money representing the cost and expense incurred or payable for the service;

(3) The date or dates when the cost or expense was incurred by the city.

The notice of lien shall be filed within 60 days after the cost of expense is incurred.

Upon payment of the cost or expense after notice of lien has been filed, the lien shall be released by the city or person in whose name the lien has been filed, and the release shall be filed for record in the same manner as the filing of the notice of the lien.

(Prior code § 99-9; Amend. Coun. J. 12-20-89, p. 10123; 12-4-02, p. 99931)

§7-28-130 Diseased trees.

All trees which become affected with Dutch elm disease are hereby declared to be a public nuisance.

Any person owning or controlling any plot of ground upon which such a tree is situated shall, upon the appearance of evidence of any such disease, cause such tree to be sprayed and removed from the premises and burned.

If the owner or person in control of any plot of ground upon which such a tree is situated fails to have such tree so sprayed, removed and burned within 10 days after receipt of notification by certified mail of positive evidence that the tree is affected with Dutch elm disease, the general superintendent of forestry, parkways and beautification shall proceed to have such tree sprayed, removed and burned, and any expense incurred by the city in so doing shall be a charge against the owner so failing, which may be recovered in an appropriate action at law instituted by the corporation counsel.

(Prior code § 99-9.1)

§7-28-150 Spreading of vermin poison.

It shall be unlawful for any person to spread, or to cause or permit any agent or employee to spread, any poison for the purpose of killing rats, mice, insects, or other vermin, in any public way or public place in the city; and it shall be unlawful for any person to spread or to cause or permit any agent or employee to spread, any poison for such purpose in any yards, court, passageway, or other open place on private premises, or on the outside of any building or structure, or in any place within a building which is open to the general public, or where pet dogs, cats, or other domestic animals or fowls have access, without placing the same in a receptacle of such kind or character that it can be reached only by the kind of vermin which the poison is intended to kill, or without placing a wire or other guard about same in such way that no child, or domestic animal, domestic fowl, or other harmless creature can reach the same.

(Prior code § 99-11)

§7-28-180 Throwing objects in public places of amusement—Violation—Penalty.

No person shall cast, drop or throw any object, missile or any other substance or article in, from or into any public place of amusement.

Any person violating the provisions of this section shall be fined not less than $25.00 nor more than $200.00 for each offense.

(Prior code § 99-13.1)

§7-28-190 Throwing objects into roadways.

It shall be unlawful for any person:

(1) To loiter on any public bridge, viaduct or overpass in such manner or for such purpose as might jeopardize the safety or well-being of any person upon or near the roadway below;

(2) To stop any vehicle on any public bridge, viaduct or overpass except for necessary emergency purposes or upon the order of a police officer or other person authorized to direct such action;

(3) To throw or drop or cause to be thrown or dropped from any public bridge, viaduct or overpass any article or thing which might jeopardize the safety or well-being of any person upon or near the roadway below.

Any violation of any of the provisions of this section shall constitute a nuisance and the offender shall be subject to a fine of not less than $50.00 or more than $200.00, or imprisonment not to exceed six months, or both, and every violation shall constitute a separate and distinct offense.

(Prior code § 99-13.2)

Article II. Refuse

§7-28-200 Definitions.

For the purposes of this chapter the following words and terms shall be understood as having the following meanings:

"Ashes" means all ashes of wood, coal and coke; the residue resulting from the combustion of any material or substance, soot, cinders, slag or charcoal.

"Garbage" means rejected organic matter, household food, cooking grease or kindred refuse, manure, swill or carrion.

"Junk" means old iron, chain, brass, copper, tin, lead or other base metals, old rope, old bags, rags, wastepaper, paper clippings, scraps of woolens, clips, bagging, rubber and glass, and empty bottles of different kinds and sizes when the number of each kind or size is less than one gross, and all articles and things discarded or no longer used as a manufactured article composed of, or consisting of, any one or more of the materials or articles herein mentioned. Junk includes items and materials stored for resale with no more processing than sorting, crushing or separation from other items and materials.

"Litter" includes but is not limited to the following: (a) picnic or eating utensils, such as paper plates, cups, napkins, towels, plastic utensils, metal foil, cellophane, wax paper, paper bags or any food wrappings; (b) liquid or beverage containers such as beer, soft-drink and juice cans, beer, soft-drink, liquor and wine bottles, and milk or juice cartons; (c) tobacco and confection wrappers, such as cigarette packages, candy, ice cream, Popsicle, gum or any other type of dessert or confection wrapping or container; (d) food wastes, such as fruit or vegetable peelings, pulp, rinds, leftovers or any other type of table wastes; (e) newspapers, books, placards, handbills, pamphlets, circulars, notices or papers of any type; (f) or any other type of rubbish, garbage, refuse matter, article, thing or substance such as discarded clothing, boxes, dust, manure or ashes.

"Litter basket" means any container suitable for the storage and collection of litter on the public way or private parking lot properties.

"Living unit" means an apartment used as a single housekeeping unit for one family, or four rooms used for living, sleeping, cooking and eating, by one or more persons.

"Manure" means the excrement of all domestic animals and fowl, stable bedding, and all hay, straw, shavings, grass and weeds, or leaves which have been used for stable or fowlhouse bedding.

"Multiple dwelling" means a building or a part of a building, designed, intended, or used as an apartment house, apartment hotel, tenement house, condominium, cooperative, single room occupancy hotel, or other use in which there is more than one dwelling.

"Occupational unit" means a property or part of a property designed, intended, or used for any business purpose other than a single dwelling or multiple dwelling.

"Refuse" means all garbage, junk ashes, and all other rejected matter, rubbish and dust.

"Retail establishment" means each separate store location, whether or not affiliated with any other store location, where goods or services are offered for sale to the consuming public.

"Single dwelling" means a building designed as or intended for, or used as a residence for a single family, or for a group of persons other than a single family, when such group does not exceed five in number.

(Prior code § 99-14; Amend. Coun. J. 4-15-95, p. 67576; 4-29-98, p. 66564; 7-7-99, p. 6985; 5-2-01, p. 57399)

§7-28-210 Refuse containers.

(a) Standard Refuse Container. The standard refuse container required by this chapter shall be a receptacle of impervious material and sturdy construction, with a tight fitting cover, and shall be provided by the department of streets and sanitation.

(b) Commercial Refuse Container. The commercial refuse container required by this chapter shall be provided or contracted for by the property owner or his agent or the occupant of an occupational unit, and shall be a leak-resistant, rodent-resistant, and lidded container which is constructed of impervious material and subject to the inspection of the department of health and the department of streets and sanitation.

(c) Refuse Compactor. The refuse compactor required by this chapter shall be a leak-resistant and rodent-resistant container constructed of impervious material and capable

of reducing the volume of waste contained within it a minimum of 65 percent, subject to the inspection of the department of health and the department of streets and sanitation, and provided or contracted for by the property owner or his agent, unless otherwise agreed to by the lease agreement.

(Prior code § 99-15; Amend. Coun. J. 7-7-99, p. 6985)

§7-28-220 Duty to provide refuse containers and service.

It shall be the duty of the occupant of every occupational unit to provide or contract to maintain in good condition and repair, unless otherwise provided for by lease agreement, sufficient commercial refuse container(s) and scavenger service to meet its waste generation needs, so as not to allow the container(s) to overflow.

It shall be the duty of the licensed scavenger to maintain in good condition and repair such commercial refuse containers. Notwithstanding this requirement, and unless otherwise agreed to by the parties via contract, the occupant shall be liable for its usage of the container(s) and for notifying the property owner or his agent of the need for additional containerization or service.

The owner or his agent of every multiple dwelling with five or more living units, if not required to have a compactor under Section 7-28-225 at the owner's or his agent's expense shall provide or contract for sufficient commercial refuse containers using a minimum standard of one-fourth cubic yard for each occupied living unit per week, including container space for recyclable material. The one-fourth cubic yard requirement can be lowered if the multiple dwelling can verify a lower waste generation rate over a period of months. The commissioner of streets and sanitation shall have the authority to promulgate rules and regulations related to the cubic yard verification. If a multiple dwelling elects to contract for refuse pickup more than one time per week, the minimum cubic yard standard shall decrease accordingly.

All refuse which is placed for collection service outside of the building must be kept in standard or commercial refuse containers or refuse compactors. *(Prior code § 99-16; Amend. Coun. J. 7-7-99, p. 6985)*

§7-28-225 Duty to provide compactors.

It shall be the duty of the owner or occupant of an occupational unit and the owner of a multiple dwelling with five or more living units with a waste generation of 50 cubic yards per week, excluding recyclable material collected as part of a recycling program, such as recyclable material collected in accordance with Chapter 11-5, to provide or contract for a refuse compactor and collection service with a minimum of once per week collection, except that a compactor shall not be required (i) when there is no suitable location on private property, or (ii) for multiple dwellings with five or more living units that are only accessible by use of a private driveway, or (iii) if the occupational unit or multiple dwelling receives refuse collection service a minimum of five times per week. If the department of streets and sanitation determines there is a suitable location on the property, but the owner or his agent does not wish to use the space for the compactor, a permit for use of the public way shall be required. If the department of streets and sanitation determines that a compactor may not be placed in the public way, the compactor must be placed on the suitable location on private property. The commissioner of streets and sanitation shall have the authority to promulgate rules and regulations regarding the definition of suitable location and regarding the exclusion of commingled recyclables from the 50 cubic yard weekly refuse amount.
(Added. Coun. J. 7-7-99, p. 6985; Amend. Coun. J. 10-3-01, p. 68141)

§7-28-227 Duty to provide refuse containers at construction or demolition sites.

(a) Every owner, manager or general contractor of any building, structure or parcel, for which a permit for new construction or demolition at the site has been issued, shall provide and maintain in good condition and repair commercial refuse containers sufficient in size and number to prevent any overflow or accumulation of refuse outside of the containers.

(b) It shall be the duty of every owner, manager or general contractor to cause all refuse, excluding construction or building material and debris, produced or located at the site to be deposited daily in the commercial refuse containers.

(c) It shall be the duty of every owner, manager or general contractor to keep each commercial refuse container located at the site covered with a tightly fitted cover at all times, except when opened for deposit or removal of the refuse.

(d) It shall be the duty of every owner, manager or general contractor to cause to be removed at his own cost and expense all refuse, excluding construction or building material and debris, located at the site. The removal shall be of such frequency to prevent the overflow and accumulation of refuse outside of the containers and shall be in accordance with the provisions of this code.

(e) No container used for the storage, collection and removal of refuse shall be placed so as to constitute a nuisance to adjacent property or the occupants thereof.

(f) Any person who violates any provision of this section shall be fined not less than $200.00 and not more than $500.00 for each offense. Each day that a violation continues shall constitute a separate and distinct offense.
(Added. Coun. J. 5-2-01, p. 814)

§7-28-230 Location of standard and commercial refuse containers.

Standards and commercial refuse containers shall be placed for collection in the following manner:

(a) For alley collections, at the alley lot line on the premises served so as to be immediately accessible to refuse collection vehicles. It shall be the duty of the owner or his agent to provide suitable space at the alley line for such container; a container may be placed in the public way if (i) the property does not have suitable space as determined by the department of streets and sanitation and defined in the rules and regulations promulgated pursuant to this chapter and (ii) the structure on the property was in existence on the effective date of this ordinance.

(b) For curb collections, at the curb line not earlier than the evening preceding the designated collection day, and removal from the public way not later than the evening of such day, except for occupational units not operating on the day after collection.

No container used for the storage, collection and removal of garbage or other refuse shall be placed so as to constitute a nuisance to adjacent property or the occupants thereof.
(Prior code § 99-17; Amend. Coun. J. 7-7-99, p. 6985)

§7-28-235 Location of refuse compactors.

Refuse compactors receiving alley collection may be placed on the public way in accordance with Article XI-B of Chapter 10-28 of this code and are subject to inspection by the department of health and department of streets and sanitation.
(Added. Coun. J. 7-7-99, p. 6985)

§7-28-240 Refuse removal.

Except in the case of (i) a multiple dwelling containing less than five living units, (ii) a multiple dwelling (other than a condominium, cooperative residential building or townhouse) each living unit of which is individually heated by the tenant and which was receiving city refuse collection on the effective date of this ordinance, or (iii) a townhouse which is in compliance with Section 7-28-230 regarding location of refuse containers and the placement of the containers does not constitute a health or safety hazard as determined by the department of streets and sanitation, or (iv) a multiple dwelling licensed as a bed-and-breakfast establishment pursuant to Chapter 4-210 of this code and containing less than five living units unless the department of streets and sanitation determines that the establishment is producing an unreasonable amount of refuse for a building of its size, it shall be the duty of the owner or his agent of every multiple dwelling to cause to be removed at his own cost and expense at least once each week all refuse produced therein.

It shall be the duty of the occupant of every occupational unit to cause to be removed at his own expense and cost at least once each week all refuse produced therein.

(Prior code § 99-18; Amend. Coun. J. 7-7-99, p. 6985; Amend. Coun. J. 6-28-00, p. 36650; 9-4-03, p. 7118)

§7-28-260 Containers—Use.

(a) It shall be the duty of the owner, his agent or occupant of every single dwelling, multiple dwelling or occupational unit to cause all refuse produced therein to be deposited in a refuse container or compactor as provided in Section 7-28-220 or 7-28-225, and to keep a tightly fitting cover in place at all times when refuse is contained therein, except when opened for the deposit or removal of refuse. The owner, his agent or occupant shall maintain the container so that all refuse spilled during usage is removed and the area is cleaned in a timely manner. It shall be unlawful for any person other than the owner, his agent or occupant of the premises served by a refuse container to deposit or cause to be deposited therein any article or thing whatsoever.

(b) It shall be the duty of every person responsible for the installation, use or emptying of a sanitary refuse container to keep a tightly fitting cover in place at all times when refuse is contained therein, except when opened for the deposit or removal of refuse.

(c) Any person who violates any provision of this section shall be fined not less than $200.00 and not more than $500.00 for each use. Each day that a violation continues shall constitute a separate and distinct offense.

(Prior code § 99-19; Amend. Coun. J. 7-13-94, p. 53272; 7-7-99, p. 6985)

§7-28-261 Accumulation of refuse—Responsibility.

(a) No person shall deposit refuse in a standard or commercial refuse container, or compactor, in a manner that prevents complete closure of the container's cover, or deposit refuse on top of a container in a manner that interferes with opening of the container, or pile or stack refuse against a container.

(b) The owner, his agent or occupant of a property shall not allow any person to violate subsection (a) of this section. The presence of refuse preventing complete closure of the container's cover, deposited on or piled or stacked against a standard refuse container or a commercial refuse container, or compactor shall be prima facie evidence of violation of this subsection (b).

(c) Any person who violates any provision of this section shall be fined not less than $200.00 and not more than $500.00 for each offense. Each day that a violation continues shall constitute a separate and distinct offense.
(Added. Coun. J. 7-13-94, p. 53272; Amend. 7-7-99, p. 6985)

§7-28-270 Contents of standard and commercial refuse containers and compactors.

It shall be unlawful for any person to deposit in any refuse container or compactor any article or thing except refuse as defined in this chapter.
(Prior code § 99-20; Amend. Coun. J. 7-7-99, p. 6985)

§7-28-280 Removal of contents.

It shall be unlawful for any person other than a city refuse collector or a private scavenger licensed by the city, to remove, displace, uncover, or otherwise disturb, any refuse container or the contents thereof when placed on location, as provided for in Section 7-28-230.
(Prior code § 99-21)

§7-28-290 Ashes.

Ashes stored inside any non-fireproof building shall be stored only in masonry bins, approved metal ash cans, or steel truck tanks. All ash containers shall be kept at least five feet from combustible material. Ashes shall not be stored inside or outside of any building in wood receptacles, or dumped in contact or in proximity to any combustible material.
(Prior code § 99-22)

§7-28-300 Removal of restaurant garbage.

Every person owning or controlling any hotel, restaurant, cafe, or retail food establishment that uses a commercial refuse container shall cause all substances deposited in such containers to be removed from his premises on each day of operation. Such person shall cause the removal and disposition of such substances in accordance with the provisions of this code and the rules or regulations of the department of health relating to the disposition and removal of such substances.
(Prior code § 99-23; Amend. Coun. J. 7-7-99, p. 6985)

§7-28-301 Grease containers.

Any container used for the storage, collection or removal of cooking grease or kindred refuse shall be constructed of impervious material and subject to the inspection of the department of health and the department of streets and sanitation.
(Added. Coun. J. 4-15-95, p. 67576; Amend. 7-7-99, p. 6985)

§7-28-302 Grease containers—Maintenance and removal.

(a) It shall be the duty of every person responsible for the use of a grease container in which cooking grease or kindred refuse is stored, to (1) keep a tightly fitting cover in place, except when opened for the deposit or removal of its contents; and (2) remove spillage after every use by applying a cleaning agent approved by the commissioner of the department of streets and sanitation; and (3) contract with a licensed scavenger for grease removal.

(b) It shall be the duty of every grease hauler responsible for the collection of any grease container in which cooking grease or kindred refuse is stored, to (1) provide a tightly fitting cover for the container; (2) resecure the container cover if it is removed during collection; and (3) remove any grease spilled during collection by applying a cleaning agent approved by the commissioner of the department of streets and sanitation.

(c) In accordance with Section 7-28-302(a)(2) and (b)(2), cooking grease or kindred refuse spilled in the public way or open loading dock shall be cleaned with an inorganic, inert material capable of absorbing and neutralizing grease. Approved materials include, but are not limited to, sand, clay, bentonite, sawdust, and combinations of these materials sold as commercial absorbents.

(d) Any person who violates any provision of this section shall be fined not less than $250.00 nor more than $500.00 for each offense. Each day that a violation continues shall constitute a separate and distinct offense.

(Added. Coun. J. 4-15-95, p. 67576; Amend. 7-7-99, p. 6985; 12-4-02, p. 99931)

§7-28-303 Location of grease containers.

Individual hotels, cafes and retail food establishments generating more than 1,500 pounds of cooking grease or kindred refuse per month shall design space for and install sealed, odor and rodent resistant vacuum containers for the storage of grease. Such containers shall be indoors except when the department of streets and sanitation determines there is no suitable indoor location. If there is no suitable indoor location the grease must be contained in a suitable outdoor location on the property. The commissioner of the department of streets and sanitation shall have the authority to promulgate rules and regulations regarding the definition of suitable indoor location and outdoor location.

(Added. Coun. J. 7-7-99, p. 6985)

§7-28-305 Location of grease containers on the public way.

Grease containers may be placed on the public way in accordance with Article XI-B of Chapter 10-28 of this code and shall be granted only if the department of streets and sanitation determines that the premises has no other suitable location for the container. The commissioner of the department of streets and sanitation shall have the authority to promulgate rules and regulations regarding the definition of suitable location.

(Added. Coun. J. 7-7-99, p. 6985)

§7-28-310 Owner of business responsible for removal when—Violation—Penalty.

Every person owning or operating any business establishment, other than a bed-and-breakfast establishment licensed pursuant to Chapter 4-210 of this code unless the department of streets and sanitation determines that the bed-and-breakfast establishment is producing an unreasonable amount of refuse for a building of its size, shall cause sufficient removal and disposition of such refuse and discarded materials at his own expense and in accordance with the provisions of this code and the rules and regulations of the department of health related to the removal and disposition of such refuse and discarded materials unless they are part of a multiple occupational unit where the building owner is required to provide refuse service. Removal must be by licensed scavenger company.

Any person found in violation of this section shall be guilty of having created a nuisance and shall be fined not less than $200.00 nor more than $500.00 for the first offense, and no less than $400.00 nor more than $750.00 for the second and each subsequent offense. Each day that such violation persists shall constitute a separate and distinct offense.

(Prior code § 99-24; Added. Coun. J. 12-20-89, p. 10135; Amend. 7-7-99, p. 6985; 12-4-02, p. 99931; 9-4-03, p. 7118)

§7-28-315 Removal of litter from a retail establishment's parking area.

(a) Every person owning, managing or controlling any retail establishment with an adjacent parking area provided for customer use shall cause to be removed at his own expense all litter located in the parking area. The removal shall be in accordance with the provisions of this code and the rules and regulations of the department of health related to the removal and disposition of litter. It shall be the duty of the owner or manager to cause all litter placed in the litter baskets to be deposited daily in the retail establishment's commercial refuse container for removal by a licensed scavenger.

(b) It shall be the duty of the owner or manager to provide and maintain in good condition and repair litter baskets, sufficient in size and number to prevent any overflow or accumulation of litter outside of the containers. Litter baskets shall be placed at appropriate locations throughout the parking areas so as not to constitute a nuisance to adjacent properties or the occupants thereof.

(c) Unremoved litter is hereby declared to be a public nuisance. It shall be the duty of the commissioner of streets and sanitation or a designee to serve notice in writing by certified mail upon the owner or manager where a nuisance may be found, requiring him to abate the nuisance within three days from the date of receipt of notice. The commissioner may prescribe in his notice the manner in which any nuisance shall be abated. If the owner or manager fails within three days from the date of notice to abate the nuisance, or if the owner or manager is unknown or cannot with due diligence be found, the commissioner may proceed to abate the nuisance or seek to enjoin the nuisance. In addition to any fine or penalty, an amount equal to three times the cost or expense incurred by the city in abating a nuisance may be recovered in an appropriate action instituted by the corporation counsel. Nothing in this section shall be construed to prevent the city of Chicago from acting without notice to abate a nuisance in an emergency where the nuisance poses an immediate threat to public health or safety, nor shall this section be construed to deny any common law right to anyone to abate a nuisance.

(d) Any owner or other person found in violation of this section shall be fined not less than $200.00 and not more than $500.00 for each offense. Each day that a violation continues shall constitute a separate and distinct offense.

(Added. Coun. J. 5-2-01, p. 57399)

§7-28-320 Incinerators and ash chutes.

Incinerators and ash chutes shall be constructed in conformity with the building provisions of this code.
(Prior code § 99-25)

§7-28-330 Sale of garbage prohibited.

No person shall vend or attempt to vend in the city any fruit, vegetable, or other article of food that may be decayed or partially rotten, or that may have been taken from any barrel, box, or other receptacle for the same, in any public way of the city.
(Prior code § 99-26)

§7-28-331 Commercial refuse containers and compactors—Identification.

(a) The owner of a commercial refuse container or compactor at a building where refuse is removed at the expense of the owner, his agent or occupant of the property, shall label the container with the following information: the address of the person using the commercial container; in the case of a business, the name of the business served by the container; and, in the case of a residential building, the name of the person responsible for payment for refuse collection service for that container at the building; except that this section shall not apply to grease containers as defined in section 10-28-791 of this code. The labeling shall be indelible, in letters no less than one inch high, in a color that contrasts clearly with its background, placed on the vertical surface opposite the hinge of the container's cover. The container shall be placed during normal use so that the label is visible from the alley adjacent to the building served by the container.

(b) No person shall cover, alter, obscure or remove the identifying label required under subsection (a) of this section.

(c) Any person who violates any provision of this section shall be fined not less than $200.00 and not more than $500.00 for each offense. Each day that a violation continues shall constitute a separate and distinct offense.
(Added. Coun. J. 7-13-94, p. 53272; Amend. 7-7-99, p. 6985; 10-3-01, p. 68141)

§7-28-360 Removal of refuse before vacation of premises.

It shall be the duty of every person occupying or controlling any lot, building, or structure, or any portion thereof, to remove or cause to be removed therefrom, before vacating the same, all garbage, ashes, miscellaneous waste and manure.
(Prior code § 99-29)

§7-28-380 Refuse vehicles.

No person owning or controlling any vehicle used for the carrying or transporting of any garbage, ashes, miscellaneous waste, or manure shall cause or permit such vehicle when in use for such purpose to stand or remain before or near any building, structure, or premises occupied by any person; nor shall any person using any such vehicle cause or permit the use of an unreasonable or unnecessary length of time in and about the loading or

unloading of any such vehicle when in use for such purposes, or cause or permit an unreasonable or unnecessary length of time to be used in passing along any public way; nor shall any person cause or permit any such cart or vehicle to be in a condition needlessly or unnecessarily filthy or offensive.
(Prior code § 99-31)

§7-28-390 Dumping on public way—Violation—Penalty.

(a) No person owning or controlling any vehicle shall dump, deposit or dispose, or cause, suffer, allow, or procure to be dumped, deposited or disposed from that vehicle any ashes, refuse, or waste on the public way.

(b) No person owning or controlling any refuse vehicle shall cause or permit the vehicle to be so loaded, to be in such defective condition, out of repair, of faulty construction, or improperly driven or managed to permit any ashes, refuse, or waste to drop or fall on any public way or other place. The vehicle shall be constructed to prevent the emission of any odor and to prevent any part of the contents from failing, leaking, or spilling therefrom. It shall be the duty of every person in possession or control of any such vehicle to remove from the public way or any other place, any part of the contents of the vehicle which fell, dropped, or spilled onto the ground from the vehicle.

(c) For purposes of this section "ashes," "dispose," "refuse" and "waste" shall have the meaning ascribed to those terms in Section 11-4-120.

(d) Penalties imposed for violations of this section shall be as provided in Section 11-4-1600.
(Prior code § 99-31.1; Added. Coun. J. 12-21-88, p. 23493; Amend. 7-31-90, p. 19384; 11-3-04, p. 34974)

§7-28-395 Construction debris on public way prohibited.

Any person who constructs, demolishes, renovates, remodels, excavates or otherwise performs any maintenance operation on private property shall not allow any debris generated by that operation to accumulate on any adjacent public way and shall remove all debris from the public way at least once a day. Such person shall transport, remove and dispose of the debris in conformity with the requirements of this code and in a manner that does not cause any debris to be washed, drained, discarded or otherwise allowed to flow into the city sewer system. If the public way is damaged during the removal process, such person shall restore the public way to the condition that it was in before the damage occurred or shall pay the city in full for any costs and expenses which the city incurs in connection with the performance of that work.

Any person who violates this section shall be fined not less than $200, nor more than $500, for each offense. Each day that a violation continues shall constitute a separate and distinct offense.

This section may be enforced by the department of streets and sanitation, the department of the environment, and the department of transportation.

As used in this section:

"Debris" means any dirt, rock, sand, construction or demolition waste, landscape waste, chipped paint, rubbish, rubble, garbage, trash, chemical residue, or any other miscellaneous material or substance generated by the construction, demolition, renovation, remodeling, excavation or performance of any other maintenance operation on private property. "Debris" does not

include any item or material placed on the public way in compliance with a valid permit issued by the department of transportation.
(Added. Coun. J. 6-6-01 p. 60214)

§7-28-400 Disinfection of refuse vehicles.

Any person owning or controlling any refuse vehicle shall cause all such vehicles, and all implements used in connection with the loading or unloading thereof, when not in use, to be stored and kept in such place and in such manner as not to create a nuisance, and shall cause all such vehicles and implements to be thoroughly disinfected and put in an inoffensive condition when so stored or not in use. Such vehicles and implements shall be thoroughly disinfected at least once a week, whether in use or not, unless the same shall not have been used since the last disinfection thereof.
(Prior code § 99-32)

§7-28-410 Reserved.
(Deleted. Coun. J. 11-3-04, p. 34974)

§7-28-420 Industrial refuse.

The owner, lessee, occupant, or manager of every chemical factory, paint factory, blacksmith or other shop, forge, coal yard, brickyard or place where bricks are manufactured, foundry or manufactory or premises where like business is done, or any factory or premises in which tar or any compound thereof is handled, used, or manufactured, shall cause all ashes, cinders, rubbish, dirt, and refuse to be removed to some proper place, so that the same shall not accumulate at any of the above-mentioned premises, or in the appurtenances thereof, and become filthy and offensive; nor shall any such owner, lessee, occupant, or manager cause or allow any dense smoke, cinders, dust, gas, or offensive odor to escape from any such building, structure, place, or premises which shall be offensive or prejudicial to the health or dangerous to the life of any person not being therein or thereupon engaged. It is hereby declared to be a nuisance to permit any ashes, cinders, rubbish, dirt, or refuse to accumulate on any of the above-mentioned premises, or the appurtenances thereof, and become filthy or offensive, or to cause or allow any dense smoke, cinders, dust, gas, or offensive odor to escape from any such building, structure, place, or premises, and the commissioner of buildings or any officer designated by him may summarily abate the same.
(Prior code § 99-34)

§7-28-430 Decaying animal matter.

It shall be unlawful for any person having the ownership or control of any animal matter within the city which is in process of decay so as to be offensive or dangerous to the public health to permit the same to remain within the city or within one mile of the limits thereof, while in such condition, more than 12 hours after such animal matter shall have come into such offensive or dangerous condition, whether it be at an establishment for the rendering or changing the character thereof or not. Any person violating any provision of this section shall be fined not less than $50.00 and not more than

$200.00 for each offense, and every day on which such violation shall continue shall be deemed a separate and distinct offense.
(Prior code § 99-35)

§7-28-440 Dumping on real estate without permit—Nuisance—Violation—Penalty—Recovery of costs.

(a) No person shall dump, deposit, or dispose, or cause, suffer, allow, or procure to be dumped, deposited, or disposed on any lot or parcel of real estate within the city any ashes, refuse, or waste, except at a sanitary landfill site, liquid waste handling facility or transfer station for which a permit has been properly issued pursuant to the provisions of Chapter 11-4 of this code. For the purposes of this section "ashes," "dispose," "refuse" and "waste" shall have the meaning ascribed to those terms in Section 11-4-120. Such dumping without a permit is hereby declared to be a nuisance.

(b) Penalties imposed for violations of this section shall be as provided in Section 11-4-1600.
(Prior code § 99-36; Amend. Coun. J. 10-15-87, p. 5194; 7-31-90, p. 19384; 6-12-91, p. 1459; 10-14-92, p. 21818; 7-14-93, p. 35530; 6-14-95, p. 2990; 3-6-96, p. 17618; 4-29-98, p. 66564; 7-29-03, p. 5530; 11-3-04, p. 34974)

§7-28-445 Illegal dumping—Anonymous program and reward.

(a) The commissioner of the environment or his designee shall establish a telephone number for receiving citizen reports of illegal dumping. A caller's anonymity will be preserved, either by assigning the caller an identification number or by some other method acceptable to the commissioner or his designee. If a caller to the telephone number furnishes information that leads to a finding of violation for illegal dumping, the commissioner or his designee shall provide for the caller to receive a reward of up to $500.00 for each such finding of violation. No city employee shall be eligible for any reward authorized by this section.

(b) For purposes of this section, "illegal dumping" shall refer to the disposal of ashes, construction or demolition debris, garbage, junk, manure, miscellaneous material, refuse, trash or other waste from one or more sources at a disposal site, lot, or parcel of real estate that is not permitted to receive such waste.

(c) For purposes of this section, "finding of violation" shall refer to a conviction, determination of guilt, fine, incarceration, permit or license revocation, or any other form of penalty, punishment or sanction for illegal dumping.
(Added. Coun. J. 3-6-96, p. 17553; Amend. Coun. J. 7-29-03, p. 5530)

§7-28-450 Owner responsible for removal—Nuisance—Violation—Penalty—Notice—Costs.

(a) The owner, occupant, agent or person in possession or control of any lot or unimproved parcel of real estate ("owner") shall remove or cause to be removed therefrom any abandoned or derelict motor vehicle as defined in Section 9-80-110 of this code, ashes, refuse, or waste. Unremoved material of such nature is hereby declared to be a public nuisance. Any owner or other person found in violation of this section shall be punished by a penalty of not less than $500.00 and not more than $1,000.00 for each offense, and each day on which such an offense shall continue shall constitute a separate and distinct offense; however, this section shall not apply to any governmental entity nor to any owner upon whose lot or parcel such material is permitted to accumulate pursuant to a properly issued license or permit in accordance with zoning provisions of this code governing special uses in general and heavy manufacturing districts. For purposes of this subsection, an "agent" of any unimproved lot shall include a person who contracts with the federal government or any of its agencies, including without limitation the Department of Housing and Urban Development, to care for vacant residential real estate.

(b) The owner, occupant, agent or person in possession or control of any residence or business ("owner") shall remove or cause to be removed any ashes, refuse, and waste located upon his property or place of business. Unremoved material of such nature is hereby declared to be a public nuisance. Any owner or other person found in violation of this section shall be punished of a penalty not less than $500.00 and not more than $1,000.00 for each offense. Each day on which such an offense shall continue shall constitute a separate and distinct offense.

(c) The owner, occupant, agent or person in possession or control of any railroad track which lies upon any overpass, bridge, trestle, viaduct, tunnel or other elevated railroad passageway ("owner") shall maintain the area immediately beneath the overpass, bridge, trestle, viaduct, tunnel or other elevated railroad passageway clear of any track materials, including any rail, ties or ballast, and any debris which has fallen to the ground from the track or elevated passageway structure, including any rocks, concrete, stone, wood or metal. Unremoved material or debris of such nature is hereby declared to be a public nuisance. Any person found in violation of this section shall be punished by a penalty of not less than $500.00 and not more than $1,000.00 for each offense. Each day on which such an offense shall continue shall constitute a separate and distinct offense. This subsection shall not apply to the Chicago Transit Authority.

(d) Where the owner of any lot, parcel of real estate, railroad track, residence, or place of business upon which a nuisance exists is or can be found, the commissioner of streets and sanitation or a designee or the commissioner of the environment or a designee shall serve notice in writing by first class mail, delivery confirmation requested, upon the owner requiring him to abate the nuisance within three days from the date of receipt of notice in the manner either commissioner may prescribe. If the owner fails within three days to abate the nuisance or if the owner is unknown or cannot with due diligence be found, either commissioner may proceed to abate the nuisance or seek to enjoin the nuisance. If a motor vehicle is the nuisance or a part of it, either commissioner shall serve notice in the same manner upon the last registered owner of the vehicle.

If the owner of the vehicle does not remove the vehicle within three days after receipt of the notice, either commissioner may proceed to remove and impound the vehicle. In addition to any penalty or fine, a penalty in the amount equal to three times the cost or expense incurred by the city in abating a nuisance may be recovered in an appropriate action instituted by the corporation counsel. Nothing in this section shall be construed to prevent the city of Chicago from acting without notice to abate a nuisance in an emergency where the nuisance poses an immediate threat to public health or safety, nor shall this section be construed to deny any common law right to anyone to abate a nuisance.

(e) For the purposes of this section "ashes," "dispose," "refuse" and "waste" shall have the meaning ascribed to those terms in Section 11-4-120.
(Prior code § 99-36.1; Amend. Coun. J. 12-18-86, p. 38654; 3-9-88, p. 11146; 7-31-90, p. 19384; 12-11-91, p. 10978; 4-29-98, p. 66564; 1-12-00, p. 24174; 11-3-04, p. 34974)

§7-28-460 Substances that scatter in wind.

No lime, ashes, coal, dry sand, hair, feathers, or other substance that may be scattered by the wind, shall be sifted through a sieve, agitated, or exposed. No mat, carpet, or cloth shall be shaken or beaten, nor any cloth, yarn, garment, material, or substance be scoured, cleaned, or hung, nor shall any business be conducted over or in any public way, or where particles set in motion therefrom will pass into any public way, or into any occupied premises. No usual or reasonable precaution shall be omitted by any person to prevent fragments or other substances from falling, or dust and light material from flying, into any public way or into any place or building from any building or structure while the same is being altered, repaired, or demolished. Any person who violates this section shall be subject to a fine of not less than $300.00 and not more than $1,000.00 for each offense. Each day that such a violation continues shall be considered a separate and distinct offense.
(Prior code § 99-38; Amend. Coun. J. 11-15-00, p. 46866)

§7-28-470 Refuse on roof or in areaway.

It shall be unlawful for any person to place, throw, deposit, or cause to be placed, thrown, or deposited, any substance, papers, refuse, or other article, or any material, on the roof of any building, or in any light or air shaft, court, or areaway that will cause the dissemination of dust or odors, or be productive of a nuisance or a menace to the health, comfort, or safety of any person or of the community. No person in possession or control of any building shall permit or allow the deposit or accumulation on the roof of said building or in any light or air shaft, court, or areaway, of any waste material, refuse, or other object or thing that will cause a nuisance or be injurious to the health, comfort, or safety of any person or of the community.
(Prior code § 99-39)

§7-28-480 Inspection of roofs and areaways.

It shall be the duty of the commissioner of buildings or his authorized representative to make inspections at least twice each year of the roofs, light and airshafts, courts, and areaways of all buildings where he has reason to believe a nuisance exists or any of the regulations of this code are being violated. It shall be the duty of the person in possession or control of any such building to allow the commissioner of buildings or his authorized representative entrance or access, at all reasonable times, to such building for the purpose of inspection or for the making of such records as may be necessary.
(Prior code § 99-40)

§7-28-490 Roofers.

It shall be unlawful for any person engaged in or conducting in the city the business of roofing of buildings, to throw dirt or roofing refuse from the roof of any building upon any public way or upon adjoining property while repairing or renewing roofs.
(Prior code § 99-41)

§7-28-500 Removal of roofing refuse.

Every person engaged in or conducting in the city the business of roofing of buildings, shall remove the dirt and roofing refuse from the roofs by lowering it in buckets or containers, or with ropes, pulleys, or other mechanical devices while repairing or renewing roofs.
(Prior code § 99-42)

§7-28-510 Objects that may damage tires—Illegal to dump on public way.

It shall be unlawful for any person to throw, dump or deposit upon any public way any glass article, broken glass, nails, tacks, sharp metal objects or other articles or material that may cause damage to rubber tires of motor vehicles. It shall be the duty of every owner or person in possession or control of any motor vehicle, the glass or metal parts from which are broken and dropped upon any public way, to promptly remove such broken glass and metal parts and restore the public way to a condition safe for automotive traffic.
(Prior code § 99-42.1)

§7-28-520 Additional penalty for violation of article.

In addition to other penalties cited in this chapter, if any person or business performing work under contract with the city is found guilty of violating the provisions of Sections 7-28-200 through 7-28-519 inclusive, the city may terminate the contract by giving written notice of the termination to the person or business. The contract shall be null and void upon delivery of such notice.
(Prior code § 99-42.2; Added. Coun. J. 7-29-86, p. 32488; Amended during Supplement No. 2, 4-91; Amend. Coun. J. 3-6-96, 17618)

Article III. Privies, Catchbasins, and Similar Vaults

§7-28-530 Construction of vaults.

No vault, privy, catchbasin, cistern, or cesspool shall be constructed or rebuilt in the city except in accordance with this code and the regulations of the board of health. The general privy accommodations of any place of human habitation shall not be permitted within any such place of habitation or under any sidewalk adjacent thereto. All cesspools shall be watertight.
(Prior code § 99-43)

§7-28-540 Location of privy vault.

It shall be unlawful for any person to maintain any privy vault or allow the same to remain upon any premises abutting upon any public way or public place in which is located a public sewer.
(Prior code § 99-44)

§7-28-550 Distance from other buildings.

It shall constitute, and is hereby declared, a nuisance for any person to erect or maintain any privy as near as 40 feet to any public way, dwelling, shop, school, factory, church, or public hall or within 100 feet of any well, unless the privy be furnished with a substantial vault six feet deep and made tight so that contents cannot escape therefrom, and sufficiently secured and enclosed. Any person owning, erecting, or maintaining any privy in violation of this section shall be subject to a penalty of $10.00, and a like penalty for every week he shall maintain or continue the same after the first conviction.
(Prior code § 99-45)

§7-28-560 Vault contents.

It shall be unlawful for the owner, agent, occupant, or person in control of any lot, building, structure, premises, or place within the city to permit or allow the contents of any tub, or of any receptacle, cesspool, privy, catchbasin, vault, sink, water closet, cistern, or anything in any room, excavation, vat, building, premises, or place to become a nuisance or offensive so as to be dangerous or prejudicial to health.
(Prior code § 99-46)

§7-28-570 Offensive privies and catchbasins.

All privies or catchbasins, any part of the contents of which are above the surface, or within two feet of the surface of the earth, and all other privies or catchbasins that are foul, or emit smells and odors prejudicial to the public health, are hereby declared nuisances, and the commissioner of buildings shall have the power to abate the same.
(Prior code § 99-47)

§7-28-580 Removal of vault contents.

All putrid or offensive matter, and all night soil and the contents of privies, catchbasins, vaults, and cesspools, and all obnoxious substances in the city shall be removed in accordance with the provisions of this code. All such privies, catchbasins, vaults, and cesspools, when cleaned, shall be disinfected with freshly burned lime, and the work of such disinfection shall be done by the person removing such contents.

The owner, tenant, or occupant of any building or premises in the city shall not employ, cause, or permit any part of the contents of any vault, privy, catchbasin, or cesspool (being thereon, and of which he has control) to be removed, unless according to a permit or the regulations of the department of the environment. No privy or other erection mentioned in this section shall be filled with or covered with dirt until its offensive contents shall be removed.
(Prior code § 99-48; Amend. Coun. J. 12-11-91, p. 10832)

§7-28-590 Drawing off contents.

No person shall draw off, or allow to run off into any ground, public way or place of the city, the contents, or any part thereof, of any vault, privy, cistern, cesspool, or catchbasin; nor shall any owner, tenant, or occupant of any building to which any vault, catchbasin, privy, or cesspool shall appertain or be at-

tached, permit the contents or any part thereof to flow therefrom, or to rise within two feet of any part of the top, or such contents to become offensive.
(Prior code § 99-49)

§7-28-600 Vehicle for removal of vault contents.

No part of the contents of any privy, vault, sink, or cesspool (except substances other than excrements insoluble in water), any accumulation of any offensive fluid, or any liquid or semiliquid substances or material, being in any excavation, cellar, or place within the city, shall be removed therefrom, nor shall the same be transported through any public way of the city unless the same shall be removed and transported under a permit from the department of the environment, in a manner consistent with regulations issued by the commissioner. All tools, pails, and tubs used by the scavengers shall be made from galvanized iron or other metal and shall be free from all wood to prevent saturation of the night soil into them.
(Prior code § 99-50; Amend. Coun. J. 12-11-91, p. 10832)

§7-28-610 Workmen's temporary closets.

It shall be unlawful for any person to begin the construction, alteration, or repair of any building, or of any public or private works without having provided proper and sufficient toilet facilities, consisting of water closets, chemical closets, or privies of a type to be approved by the board of health for the use of employees engaged in the construction, alteration, or repair of such building, or of such public or private works.

There shall be at least one such water closet, chemical closet, or privy for every 30 employees or fraction thereof. Such toilet facilities in due proportion shall be provided on at least every fifth floor of a building.

It shall be unlawful to install such water closets, chemical closets, or privies without first having obtained a permit therefor from the department of construction and permits pursuant to standards set by the board of health, and the same shall be installed and maintained in accordance with the provisions and specifications of such permit.
(Prior code § 99-51; Amend. Coun. J. 12-15-04, p. 40435)

§7-28-620 Chemical closets.

A chemical closet shall be construed to be any closet or privy in which human excreta and urine are deposited in a receptacle containing a solution of caustic hydrates. The receptacle in such a closet shall be watertight. The capacity of such receptacle shall be as follows:

	Gallons
Not more than 10 persons	60
More than 10 but not more than 20 persons	100
More than 40 persons	300

A solution containing at least 16.42 percent crude caustic hydrates (one and two-thirds pounds to one gallon of water) shall be used in such receptacles, and such chemical closets shall not be used until properly charged with such solution.

The contents of such chemical closets shall be removed and disposed of by a regularly licensed night soil scavenger in compliance with the require-

ments of this code. Every such closet shall be cleaned before being removed from one building or premises to another, and as often otherwise as may be deemed necessary by the commissioner of health.
(Prior code § 99-52; Amend. Coun. J. 12-11-91, p. 10832)

Article IV. Offensive Chemicals and Substances

§7-28-630 Possession and sale—Violation—Penalty.

It shall be unlawful for any person to have in his possession, or for any person to carry about, any corrosive or caustic acid, phosphorus, or any solution or mixture thereof, or any hydrogen sulfide, valerianic acid, ammonium valerianate, valerianate of zinc, or any other nauseous, offensive, or filthy substance of like or similar nature; provided, that this provision shall not apply to manufacturing and wholesale druggists, retail druggists, physicians, chemists, regularly established laboratories, or to persons who have procured any of said substances for medicinal purposes upon a prescription of a physician regularly licensed under the laws of the state.

No person shall sell, give away, or offer to sell or give away, or have in his possession any stink ball or fire ball, or any bomb, ball, tube, vial, or bottle made of thin glass or other easily breakable material containing any of the above-mentioned substances.

Any violations of this section shall be subject to a fine of not less than $50.00 nor more than $200.00 for each offense.
(Prior code § 99-53)

§7-28-635 Sale of mercury thermometers containing mercury substance.

No person shall knowingly sell, give away, or offer to sell or give away any mercury fever thermometer, including online retail, to consumers and patients, except by prescription. It shall also be unlawful for any person to manufacture a mercury thermometer in the city.

Any person violating any provision of this section shall be fined not less than $50.00 nor more than $200.00 for each offense.
(Added. Coun. J. 7-25-01, p. 64934)

§7-28-640 Prescription required—Violation—Penalty.

It shall be unlawful for any person to sell or give away any corrosive or caustic acid or any phosphorus or solution thereof, or any hydrogen sulphide, valerianic acid, ammonium valerianate, valerianate of zinc, or any solution or mixture of said substances, or any other nauseous, offensive, or filthy substances of like or similar nature, except upon the written prescription of a physician licensed under the laws of the state, which prescription shall be filled only once and shall have written upon it the name and address of the patient. This section shall not apply to sales at wholesale by manufacturing or wholesale druggists to retail druggists, physicians, or chemists.

Any person violating any provision of this section shall be fined not less than $50.00 nor more than $200.00 for each offense.
(Prior code § 99-54)

§7-28-650 Offensive bombs in public places—Violation—Penalty.

It shall be unlawful for any person to cast, throw, deposit, or place any stink ball, fire ball, or bomb, described in Section 7-28-630 hereof, or to cast, deposit or place any substance described in Section 7-28-640 hereof, from, upon, or to any public way or public place in the city, or at, upon, or within any public conveyance, or upon the floor or within any restaurant, theater, hall, assembly room or public building, or at, upon, or within any automobile or other vehicle within the city.

Any person violating any provision of this section shall be fined not less than $50.00 nor more than $200.00 for each offense.

(Prior code § 99-55)

Article V. Rat Control

§7-28-660 Rat-stoppage.

Every building, structure, or parcel on which a building has been demolished or is being constructed within the city shall be rat-stopped, freed of rats and maintained in a rat-stopped and rat-free condition.

The term "rat-stoppage" as used herein applies to a form of ratproofing to prevent the ingress of rats into or under buildings or other structures from the exterior or from one building or structure to another. It consists essentially of the closing of all openings in the exterior walls, ground or first floors, basements and foundations, that may be reached by rats from the ground by climbing or by burrowing, with concrete, sheet iron, hardware cloth or other types of ratproofing material impervious to rat gnawing, approved by the building commissioner. Hardware cloth shall mean wire screen of such thickness and spacings as to afford reasonable protection against the entrance of rats.

The term "rat-harborage" shall mean any condition which provides shelter or protection for rats, thus favoring their multiplication and continued existence in, under, or outside a structure of any kind.

(Prior code § 99-61.1; Amend. Coun. J. 5-20-98, p. 68997)

§7-28-670 Inspection notice.

Inspectors from the department of buildings and the department of streets and sanitation shall have authority to inspect the interior and exterior of buildings, other structures, or parcels on which a building has been demolished or is being constructed to determine evidence of rat harborage, rat infestation and the existence of new breaks or leaks in the rat-stoppage, and when any evidence is found indicating the presence of rats or openings through which rats may enter such buildings or structures, to report such evidence to the appropriate commissioner, who shall serve the owner, agent, or occupant of such building, structure or parcel with written notice to abate the conditions found.

(Prior code § 99-61.2; Amend. Coun. J. 11-16-94, p. 61204; 5-20-98, p. 68997)

§7-28-680 Maintenance.

The owner, agent, or occupant in charge of all rat-stopped buildings or structures shall maintain them in a rat-stopped condition and repair all breaks or leaks that may occur in the rat-stoppage.

(Prior code § 99-61.4)

§7-28-690 Unlawful to remove rat-stoppage.

It shall be unlawful for the owner, occupant, contractor, public utility company, plumber, or any other person, to remove the rat-stoppage from any building or structure for any purpose and fail to restore the same in satisfactory condition, or to make any new openings that are not closed or sealed against the entrance of rats.

(Prior code § 99-61.5)

§7-28-700 Structural changes.

Whenever conditions inside or under any building or structure provide such extensive harborage for rats that the building commissioner deems it necessary to eliminate such harborage he may require the owner or occupant in charge of any such building or structure to install suitable cement floors in basements, or to require such owner or occupant to correct such rat harborage as may be necessary in order to facilitate the eradication of rats.

(Prior code § 99-61.6)

§7-28-710 Dumping prohibited.

It shall be unlawful for any person to place, leave, dump, or permit to accumulate any garbage or trash in any building, structure or premises so that the same shall afford food or harborage for rats, or to dump or place on any premises, land or waterway any dead animals or waste vegetable matter of any kind, other than properly composted landscape waste.

In addition to any other fine or penalty for violation of this section, any person who violates this section shall be liable to the city for three times the amount of all costs and expenses incurred by the city in abating a nuisance caused by such violation.

(Prior code § 99-61.7; Amend. Coun. J. 7-31-90, p. 19384)

§7-28-720 Accumulation of materials or junk.

It shall be unlawful for any person to accumulate or permit the accumulation on any open lot, or other premises, any lumber, boxes, barrels, bricks, stones, scrap metal, motor vehicle bodies or parts, or similar materials, rubbish, or any articles of junk, which provides rat-harborage, unless the same shall be placed on open racks that are elevated not less than 18 inches above the ground, evenly piled or stacked.

In addition to any other fine or penalty for violation of this section, any person who violates this section shall be liable to the city for three times the amount of all costs and expenses incurred by the city in abating a nuisance caused by such violation.

(Prior code § 99-61.8; Amend. Coun. J. 7-31-90, p. 19384)

§7-28-730 Rat-stoppage by owner—Lien.

Upon receipt of notice in writing from the building commissioner or the commissioner of streets and sanitation the owner, agent, or occupant in charge of any building, structure or premises specified in such notice shall take immediate measures for the rat-stoppage of such building or structure and for freeing the premises of all rats, and unless said work is completed in the time specified in the notice, in no event to be less than 15 days, or any written extension thereof that may be granted by the commissioner who issued the notice, then the owner, agent, or occupant in charge of said building, structure or premises shall be deemed guilty of a violation of this ordinance.

Whenever the owner, agent or occupant in charge of any building, structure or premises, after being served with notice as provided in this section has failed within the time fixed in the notice, to perform all work necessary to prevent the ingress of rats to said building or structure or to exterminate rats from the premises described in said notice, the commissioner who issued the notice or any person duly authorized by either of them may go on the premises and do such work as is necessary to free said premises from rats and to maintain said premises in a rat-stopped condition. The cost and expense incurred for all work and materials shall be charged to and collected from the owners and persons interested in said premises and the city or persons performing such work or furnishing such materials therefor shall have a lien on said premises and may enforce the same as provided by statute.
(Prior code § 99-61.9; Amend. Coun. J. 11-16-94, p. 61206)

§7-28-735 Food establishments.

(a) Whenever conditions of a building, structure or premises occupied by a food establishment afford food or harborage for rodents which create an imminent hazard to public health, the commissioner of streets and sanitation shall notify, in writing, the owner, agent or the person in control of the food establishment, directing the owner or person in control to correct such conditions, including properly storing or handling food that is prepared, sold or served in or from the establishment, and the freeing of the establishment of rodent infestation. The notice shall set a date by which the measures must be taken. After the notice is given, but before the allotted time has elapsed for compliance, the owner may request a hearing to file exceptions to and to contest the notice or the owner may request the commissioner to extend the time allowed for compliance. In any case, the request must be filed with the commissioner of streets and sanitation within 24 hours of receipt of the notice, excluding Saturdays, Sundays and legal holidays. Upon receipt of a request for a hearing, the commissioner shall institute an action with the department of administrative hearings which shall appoint an administrative law officer who shall conduct the hearing within 48 hours of the owner's request for a hearing, excluding Saturdays, Sundays and legal holidays. Unless the administrative law officer finds that there is no imminent hazard to public health or a time extension is granted by the commissioner of streets and sanitation, the commissioner may order the immediate closure of the food establishment until the conditions are corrected and the establishment is freed of rodent infestation. For purposes of this section, a "food establishment" means any business required to obtain a license pursuant to Chapter 4-8 of this code.

(b) All food establishments shall contract with a licensed exterminator who shall provide insect and vermin services at the establishment at least twice a year.
(Added. Coun. J. 3-10-99, p. 91043)

Article VI. Lot Maintenance

§7-28-740 Required.

It shall be the duty of the owner of any open lot located within the city of Chicago to keep such lot free of garbage, ashes, refuse, trash, rubbish, miscellaneous waste, manure or other substance that may contain disease germs or be scattered by the wind, or decompose, or become filthy, noxious or unhealthful.
(Prior code § 99-62; Added. Coun. J. 2-11-87, p. 39626; Amend. 7-31-90, p. 19384)

§7-28-750 Noncombustible screen fence required—Nuisance declared when.

It shall be the duty of the owner of any open lot located within the city of Chicago to cause the lot to be surrounded with a noncombustible screen fence as defined in Section 13-96-130 of this code, except that this section shall not apply to any governmental agencies or units of local governments, nor to side yards. The owner shall maintain any such fence in a safe condition without tears, breaks, rust, splinters or dangerous protuberances and to vehicular traffic by obstructing the view of drivers. Any fence which is not maintained in accordance with these provisions is hereby declared a public nuisance and shall be removed pursuant to the provisions of this Chapter 7-28; it shall be the duty of the owner of any lot whose fence has been removed to replace the fence with one in compliance with this section and the requirements of this code.
(Prior code § 99-63; Added. Coun. J. 2-11-87, p. 39626; Amend. 7-31-90, p. 19384)

§7-28-760 Severability.

If any part, provision, phrase or application of Sections 7-28-740 and 7-28-750 is found to be invalid for any reason, only said part, provision, phrase or application will be affected.
(Prior code § 99-64; Added. Coun. J. 2-11-87, p. 39626; Amend. 7-31-90, p. 19384)

§7-28-770 Exemption.

All city-owned property will be exempted from the provisions of Sections 7-28-740 and 7-28-750.
(Prior code § 99-65; Added. Coun. J. 2-11-87, p. 39626; Amend. 7-31-90, p. 19384)

§7-28-780 Lot in ill-maintained condition—Notice.

Upon finding a privately-owned open lot in an ill-maintained condition as defined in Section 7-28-740 or without fencing as required in Section 7-28-750, the department of buildings shall notify the owner of such lot, and

said owner shall be responsible for cleanup of such lot within 30 days following such notification.
(Prior code § 99-66; Added. Coun. J. 2-11-87, p. 39626; Amend. 7-31-90, p. 19384; 6-14-95, p. 2841)

§7-28-790 Violation—Penalty for this article.

Any person found to be in violation of any of the provisions of Sections 7-28-740 through 7-28-780 inclusive shall be fined not less than $100.00 nor more than $500.00 for each violation, and each day such violation continues shall constitute a separate and distinct offense. In addition to any other fine or penalty for violation of this section, any person who violates this section shall be liable to the city for three times the amount of all costs and expenses incurred by the city in abating a nuisance caused by such violation.
(Prior code § 99-67; Added. Coun. J. 2-11-87, p. 39626; Amend. 7-31-90, p. 19384)

Article VII. Violation of Chapter Provisions

§7-28-800 Violation—Penalty.

(1) Any person violating any of the provisions of this chapter shall be fined not less than $100.00 and not more than $500.00 for each offense, except where otherwise specifically provided. A separate and distinct offense shall be held to have been committed each day any person continues to violate any of the provisions hereof.

(2) In addition to any other available penalties and remedies provided for in the code, one or more citations for violation of this chapter on each of three or more separate days within a three month period at the same construction site may result in a stop work order issued by the department that issued the citations, directing that all activity cease for 10 days. Any further citation for violation at the same construction site within six months after the initial stop work order may result in the issuance of another 10 day stop work order. The department that issued the 10 day stop work order under this section shall lift that order only if sufficient evidence of compliance with this chapter is provided to the department. As used in this section, the term "construction site" has the meaning ascribed to the term in Section 13-32-125.

(a) It shall be unlawful for any person to knowingly violate a stop work order, or to knowingly cause, permit, encourage, assist, aid, abet or direct another person to violate a stop work order, or to knowingly in any manner be a party to a violation of a stop work order.

Any person who violates this subsection upon conviction shall be punished, as follows:

(i) Incarceration for a term not less than three days, nor more than six months, under the procedures set forth in Section 1-2-1.1 of the Illinois Municipal Code, as amended, and the Illinois Code of Criminal Procedure of 1963, as amended;

(ii) Community service of not less than 10 hours, nor more than 100 hours; and

(iii) A fine of $5,000.00.

(b) It shall be unlawful for any person to knowingly destroy, deface, remove, damage, impair, mar, cover or obstruct any stop work order that a city official has posted or affixed at a work site.

Any person who violates this subsection upon conviction shall be punished, as follows:

(i) Incarceration for a term not less than three days, nor more than six months, under the procedures set forth in Section 1-2-1.1 of the Illinois Municipal Code, as amended, and the Illinois Code of Criminal Procedure of 1963. as amended;

(ii) Community service of not less than 10 hours, nor more than 100 hours; and

(iii) A fine of not less than $200.00, nor more than $500.00.

(Prior code § 99-74; Amend. Coun. J. 3-9-88; p. 11146; 12-15-04, p. 40435)

CHAPTER 7-32
NO-SMOKING REGULATIONS
(Complete Chapter)

Sections:

Article I. Generally

7-32-010 Smoking in stores and elevators—Violation—Penalty.
7-32-020 Smoking in public conveyance—Violation—Penalty.

Article II. Clean Indoor Air Ordinance

7-32-030 Title and purpose.
7-32-040 Definitions.
7-32-050 Smoking in public places.
7-32-060 Regulation of smoking in places of employment.
7-32-070 Signs.
7-32-080 Violation—Penalty.
7-32-090 Severability.

Article I. Generally

§7-32-010 Smoking in stores and elevators—Violation—Penalty.

It is hereby found and declared that public elevators and large retail stores where merchandise is displayed and offered for sale attract crowds within relatively small areas and that smoking in such places is a menace to public health, safety and property. It is unlawful for any person to smoke or carry a lighted cigarette, cigar or pipe in any public elevator or in any retail store in which more than 15 persons are employed, excluding areas set apart for serving food or beverages, waiting rooms and restrooms, executive offices, beauty parlors, and other rooms or areas where merchandise is not exposed.

Standard "No-Smoking" signs shall be conspicuously posted in all applicable premises where smoking is prohibited. A standard "No-Smoking" sign shall have a white field with the words "No-Smoking" printed in red letters four inches high with one-half inch face.

Any person who violates this section shall be fined not less than $25.00 nor more than $250.00 for each offense.

(Prior code § 193-7.9; Amend. Coun. J. 7-9-86, p. 31548)

§7-32-020 Smoking in public conveyance—Violation—Penalty.

It is unlawful for any person to smoke or carry a lighted cigarette, cigar or pipe in any streetcar, elevated train, or subway and in any other public conveyance having a capacity of more than seven passengers operating within the city limits of the city of Chicago. Any person violating this section shall be fined not less than $50.00 nor more than $300.00 for each offense.
(Prior code § 193-7.10)

Article II. Clean Indoor Air Ordinance

§7-32-030 Title and purpose.

This section shall be known and may be cited as the "clean indoor air ordinance," and shall be liberally construed and applied to promote its purpose and policies. It is the purpose of this section and the policy of the city to provide smoke-free areas in enclosed public places and to regulate smoking in places of employment.
(Prior code § 192-20; Added. Coun. J. 5-25-88, p. 13939)

§7-32-040 Definitions.

Whenever used in Sections 7-32-030 through 7-32-090, the following words and phrases shall have the following meanings:

"Active dining area" means any enclosed area containing a counter or tables upon which meals are served. The active dining area may be changed or reconfigured from time to time.

"Arcade" means a public place of amusement, Class II, as defined in Chapter 4-156 of this code, which contains six or more automatic amusement devices and is not licensed to serve alcoholic liquor.

"Bar" means an enclosed area which is devoted to the serving of alcoholic beverages for consumption on the premises and in which the serving of food is only incidental to the consumption of such beverages. Although a restaurant may contain a bar, the term "bar" shall not include the restaurant dining area.

"Employee" means any person who is employed by any employer in consideration for direct or indirect monetary wages or profit, and any person who volunteers his or her services for a not-for-profit entity.

"Employer" means any person, partnership, corporation, including a municipal corporation, or non-profit entity who employs the services of one or more persons.

"Enclosed area" means all space between a floor and ceiling which is surrounded on all sides by walls or windows with appropriate openings for ingress and egress and is not intended to mean areas commonly described as public lobbies and common corridors.

"Place of employment" means any enclosed area under the control of a public or private employer which employees normally frequent during the course of employment including, but not limited to work areas, employee lounges, cafeterias, restrooms and conference rooms. A private residence is not a "place of employment" unless it is used as a child care or health care facility.

"Public place" means any enclosed area to which the public is invited. For the purpose of this section, hospitals and underground pedestrian walkways are public places.

"Restaurant" means any coffee shop, cafeteria, luncheonette, sandwich shop, private or public school cafeteria or eating establishment, and any other eating establishment, organization, or club which gives or offers for sale food to the public, guests, patrons or employees.

"Service line" means any indoor line at which one or more persons are waiting for or receiving services of any kind, whether or not such service involves the exchange of money.

"Smoking" means inhaling, exhaling, burning or carrying any lighted cigar, pipe or cigarette.

(Prior code § 192-20.1; Added. Coun. J. 5-25-88, p. 13939; Amend. coun. J. 5-19-93, p. 32933)

§7-32-050 Smoking in public places.

Smoking shall be prohibited in all public places except in designated smoking areas.

When establishing a designated smoking area, the person establishing such area shall utilize existing physical barriers, ventilation systems, and other physical elements of the premises to minimize the intrusion of smoke into areas where smoking is not permitted.

(a) In all waiting areas of airport terminals, train stations and bus depots, the area where smoking is prohibited must include either (i) a contiguous area of at least 50 percent of the total seating capacity of the facility or (ii) a separate waiting room for nonsmokers, so long as the room designated for nonsmokers contains at least 50 percent of thc total seating capacity of the waiting area.

(b) Any owner, operator, manager or other person in control of a public place may declare that entire facility as a nonsmoking area.

(c) Smoking is prohibited in all areas of the following places:

(1) Public restrooms;

(2) Polling places;

(3) Service lines;

(4) Public meeting and public assembly rooms;

(5) Taxicabs;

(6) Restrooms and enclosed waiting areas in restaurants;

(7) Arcades;

(8) Day care centers, nursery schools, elementary schools and high schools, except in designated areas that are enclosed and used only by adults. Nothing in this subsection allows smoking in any other area where smoking is otherwise prohibited by this chapter, or prohibits designation of an entire day care center, nursery school, elementary or high school as a nonsmoking area.

(d) When applying for an original or renewed food dispensing establishment license, the owner or operator of a restaurant shall also submit a notarized statement declaring the establishment either a Category I or Category II establishment. The designation shall remain in effect throughout the license period.

(1) In each Category I restaurant not less than 30 percent of the active dining area shall be designated as a nonsmoking area. In each Category II restaurant at least fifty percent of the active dining area shall be designated as a nonsmoking area. Designated nonsmoking areas shall be contiguous.

(2) The owner or operator of a restaurant shall cause to be prominently posted within the restaurant a sign containing the following language and specifications: "Pursuant to the Municipal Code of Chicago this restaurant has set aside a minimum of % of its dining area as nonsmoking. Penalties for violation range from $100 to $500. If you have any questions or complaints, call the Chicago Department of Health at 744-8500." The sign shall include the appropriate percentage for the restaurant's designated category. Lettering shall be no less than one-half inch in height and one-quarter inch in width.

(3) Nothing in this ordinance prohibits the owner or operator of a restaurant from designating the entire active dining area as a nonsmoking area.

(e) The owner or operator of an arcade shall prominently post a sign prohibiting smoking within the arcade.

(f) Notwithstanding any other provision of this section, the following areas shall not be subject to the smoking restrictions of this section:

(1) Bars;

(2) Private residences;

(3) Restaurants, hotel and motel conference or meeting rooms and public and private banquet or assembly rooms while these places are being used for private functions.

However, any owner, operator, manager or other person who controls any establishment described in this subsection may designate the entire establishment, or any portion thereof, as a nonsmoking area.

(Prior code § 192-20.2; Added. Coun. J. 5-25-88, p. 13939; Amend. Coun. J. 5-19-93, p. 32933)

§7-32-060 Regulation of smoking in places of employment.

Employers shall provide smoke-free areas for nonsmoking employees within existing facilities to the maximum extent practicable, but employers, owners, operators, managers, or other persons who control the premises are not required to make physical modifications in providing these areas.

(a) Each employee shall be able to designate his or her own work area as a nonsmoking area, if such work area is not also a public place, and to post the same with an appropriate sign to be provided by the employer. If, due to the proximity of smokers, size of the work area, poor ventilation or other factors, such designation does not reduce the effects of smoke to the satisfaction of the employee, the employer shall make additional accommodation by assigning the employees to different but comparable work areas, expanding the size of the work area subject to the prohibition against smoking or implementing other measures reasonably calculated to minimize or eliminate the effects of smoke on the employee.

(b) Every employer shall adopt a smoking policy which shall be communicated to all employees. All employers shall supply a written copy of the smoking policy upon request to any existing or prospective employee. In any dispute arising under the smoking policy, the health concerns of the nonsmoker shall be given priority.

(c) Notwithstanding any other provision of this section, every employer shall have the right to designate any place of employment, or any portion thereof, as a nonsmoking area.

(d) No employer shall discharge, refuse to hire, or in any manner retaliate against any employee or applicant for employment because such employee or applicant exercises any rights afforded by this section.
(Prior code § 192-20.3; Added. Coun. J. 5-25-88, p. 13939)

§7-32-070 Signs.

Signs indicating "No Smoking" or "No Smoking-Except in Designated Areas" shall be appropriately posting in all public places. Signs indicating "Smoking Permitted" shall be posted in all designated smoking areas located in places of employment and public places.
(Prior code § 192-20.4; Added. Coun. J. 5-25-88, p. 13939)

§7-32-080 Violation—Penalty.

(a) It shall be unlawful for any person who owns, operates, or otherwise controls any premises or facility subject to regulation under this ordinance to fail to comply with any of the requirements of Sections 7-32-030 through 7-32-070.

(b) It shall be unlawful for any person to smoke in any area designated pursuant to Sections 7-32-030 through 7-32-070 as a nonsmoking area.

(c) Any person who violates any provision of Sections 7-32-030 through 7-32-070 shall be subject to a fine not less than $100.00 and not more than $500.00.

(d) The department of health shall be responsible for the enforcement and administration of this chapter.

(e) This section shall not be interpreted or construed to permit smoking where it is otherwise restricted or prohibited by any other applicable ordinance or statute.
(Prior code § 192-20.5; Added. Coun. J. 5-25-88, p. 13939; Amend. Coun. J. 5-19-93, p. 32933)

§7-32-090 Severability.

If any provision, clause, sentence or paragraph of Sections 7-32-030 through 7-32-080 or the application thereof shall be held invalid by a court of competent jurisdiction, such invalidity shall not affect the other provisions of this section which can be given effect without the invalid provision or application, and to this end the provisions of this section are declared to be severable.
(Prior code § 192-20.6; Added. Coun. J. 5-25-88, p. 13939)

CHAPTER 7-38
FOOD ESTABLISHMENTS—SANITARY OPERATING REQUIREMENTS

(Selected Sections)

Sections:

Article I. All Food Establishments

7-38-001 All food establishments.
7-38-005 Food requirements.
7-38-010 Food handler requirements.
7-38-011 Food sampling in retail food establishments.
7-38-012 Food handling and sanitation certificates.
7-38-020 Control of vermin and insects.

7-38-040 Vehicle sanitation requirements.
7-38-070 Food sanitarians.

Article II. Mobile Food Dispensers
7-38-080 Mobile food vendors—Prohibited districts.
7-38-115 Operational requirements.
7-38-120 Sinks, water storage tanks and other plumbing requirements.
7-38-125 Refuse receptacles.

Article III. Automatic Food—Vending Machines
7-38-150 Vending machines—Food manufacture, delivery and storage.
7-38-155 Marking of food product wrappers.
7-38-210 Vending machines—Out-of-service procedure.
7-38-212 Water vending machines—Location restriction.
7-38-218 Water-vending machines—Rules and regulations.

Article IV. Coffee Cart Vendors
7-38-235 Sale of certain products from coffee carts prohibited.
7-38-240 Operation of coffee carts on public way prohibited.

Article V. Cold Storage Establishments
7-38-460 Reports.
7-38-465 Receiving and delivery requirements.
7-38-470 Storage time limit.
7-38-475 Time limit extension—Report.
7-38-480 Transfer restrictions.
7-38-485 Return to cold storage restricted.

Article VI. Slaughtering, Rendering and Packing Establishments
7-38-495 Notice to alderman.
7-38-510 Slaughtering on public ways prohibited.
7-38-520 Hours for slaughtering.
7-38-535 Offensive gases and odors prohibited.
7-38-540 Reserved.
7-38-545 Entry of carcasses prohibited.
7-38-550 Conveyance of refuse.
7-38-555 Sleeping on premises prohibited.
7-38-570 Abatement of nuisance.

Article VII. Penalty for Violation of Chapter Provisions
7-38-575 Violation—Penalty.

Article I. All Food Establishments

§7-38-001 All food establishments.

The provisions of this article shall apply to all food establishments, unless otherwise specified. The term "food establishment" shall include all establishments, businesses and vehicles required to be licensed pursuant to Chapter 4-8. *(Added. Coun. J. 6-10-96, p. 23652)*

§7-38-005 Food requirements.

(a) All food shall be protected from contamination and the elements while being stored, prepared, displayed or sold at a food establishment and during transportation to or between such establishments or vending machine locations, and so shall all food equipment, containers, utensils, food-contact surfaces and devices and vehicles, in accordance with the provisions of this chapter, Chapters 4-8, 7-40 and 7-42 and the rules and regulations of the board of health.

(b) All foods to be used, prepared, cooked, displayed, sold, served, offered for sale or stored in a food establishment, or during transportation to or between such establishments or vending machine locations, shall be from sources approved by the health authorities of the point of origin and must be clean, wholesome, free from spoilage, adulteration, contamination or misbranding and safe for human consumption. The standards for judging wholesomeness for human food shall be those promulgated and amended from time to time by the United States Public Health Service, Food and Drug Administration and published in the Code of Federal Regulations.

(1) The only milk or milk products which may be used as food ingredients shall be Grade A milk or milk products as defined in Chapter 7-40 from sources approved by the department of health. All milk and fluid milk products shall be sold in the individual original containers in which they were received from the distributor and shall be stored at a temperature of 40 degrees Fahrenheit or less until sold.

(2) Shellfish, including oysters, clams and mussels, shall be obtained from a source approved by the United States Public Health Service, Food and Drug Administration and certified by the state of origin. Shell stock and shucked shellfish shall be kept in the containers in which they were originally packed, until sold.

(3) All meats, meat food products, poultry and poultry products used in cooking, offered for sale, sold or prepared shall be from sources inspected and approved by the United States Department of Agriculture, the state of Illinois or the department of health and shall be plainly marked, tagged or stamped to indicate the source, and the inspection and approval.

(4) All ice and bottled or packaged potable water shall be of safe, sanitary quality from a source approved by the department of health and shall be stored in such a manner as to prevent contamination. All bottled or packaged water shall be dispensed from the original container filled at an establishment approved by the department of health. Such water bottles shall not be refilled elsewhere.

(5) All hermetically sealed foods shall have been processed in approved food-processing establishments. The use, preparation, display, sale or storage of home-canned foods is prohibited and no other foods which have been processed in a private home or other than in an approved food-processing establishment shall be stored, used, kept for sale or served in a food establishment or automatic food-vending machine.

(6) Only clean whole eggs with shell intact and without cracks or checks, or pasteurized liquid or pasteurized dry eggs or egg products, which, if reconstituted, shall be heated to 140 degrees Fahrenheit or above prior to usage, shall be used. Liquid, frozen dry egg products shall be used only for baking or cooking.

(7) All bakery products shall be prepared in a licensed food establishment or in a food-processing establishment approved by the food sanitation authorities of the local point of origin.

(c) It shall be unlawful for any person to use, bring, accept or keep in any food establishment or automatic vending machine with the intention of selling or serving, any food which is unwholesome or in any manner unsafe or unfit for human consumption.

(d) It shall be unlawful for any person to mislabel any food or disseminate any false advertisement of any food. An advertisement is false if it is false or misleading in any particular. It is unlawful for any person to manufacture, sell, deliver, hold or offer for sale or exchange any food that is falsely advertised or mislabeled.

(e) It shall be unlawful for any person to taste before purchase any food products from a sealed or closed container stored or offered for sale within any food establishment, or to open or in any way tamper with any sealed or closed container within such establishment. It shall be unlawful for any person holding a food establishment license or his agent to allow any consumer or potential consumer to taste before purchase any food product from a sealed or closed container stored or offered for sale within a food purveyor establishment, or to open or in any way tamper with any sealed or closed container within a food purveyor establishment.

(Added. Coun. J. 6-10-96, p. 23652)

§7-38-010 Food handler requirements.

(a) All employees who enter food processing areas, who prepare food, serve or handle in any manner unwrapped or unenclosed foods or utensils or receptacles or who handle foods on food-transporting vehicles shall maintain a high degree of personal cleanliness and conform to hygienic practices prescribed in and comply with all of the food handler requirements of the code and in the rules and regulations of the board of health.

(b) No person affected with or carrying any disease in a communicable form, or affected with boils, infected wounds, sores, acute respiratory infection or intestinal disorder shall work in any area of a food establishment in any capacity in which there is a likelihood of that person contaminating food or food-contact surfaces with pathogenic organisms or transmitting disease to other persons. It shall be unlawful to employ any person known or suspected of being affected with any such disease or condition in such an area or capacity, and if the person in charge of any such food establishment suspects that any employee has contracted any disease in a communicable form or has become a carrier of such a disease, he shall notify the department of health immediately.

(c) When suspicion arises as to the probability of transmission of infection from any food establishment employee, the department of health may: require the employee to submit urine or feces or other necessary specimens for laboratory examination or other medical examination to determine the presence of disease; exclude the employee immediately from all food establishments; close the food establishment until the department determines that no danger of disease outbreak exists; make such medical examinations of the

employee and his associates, including laboratory examinations, as may be deemed necessary under the circumstances.
(Added. Coun. J. 6-10-96, p. 23652)

§7-38-011 Food sampling in retail food establishments.

Samples of food may be offered to persons within a licensed retail food establishment, if prepared and served under the supervision of a person who holds a department of health certificate of registration in food handling and sanitation. The certificate of registration shall be posted conspicuously in that part of the retail food establishment where the food samples are offered. The department of health may suspend or revoke a certificate of registration when the certificate holder or the food establishment where the samples are offered has a record of repeated violations of the Municipal Code of Chicago or the rules and regulations of the board of health.
(Added. Coun. J. 4-16-97, p. 42588)

§7-38-012 Food handling and sanitation certificates.

(a) All food establishments, and all theaters at which food is prepared or served, shall employ and have present on the premises at all times that potentially hazardous food is being prepared or served, a person who holds a department of health certificate of registration in food handling and sanitation. Certification shall be achieved by successfully completing a department approved course and monitored examination offered by a department approved provider and payment of a $35.00 certificate fee to the department of health. Each certificate shall expire five years from the date that the individual successfully completes the examination. Every such certificate of registration shall be posted conspicuously in that part of the retail food establishment to which the public has access. A certificate of registration may be suspended or revoked by the department of health when an establishment under the control of the certificate holder has a record of repeated violations of the Municipal Code of Chicago and the rules and regulations of the board of health, provided that a certificate of registration may be revoked by the department of health upon the second suspension of a food establishment's license within a 12-month period if the certificate holder was in charge of the preparation or service of potentially hazardous food at the time of both suspensions.

(b) When a department of health inspection finds that a food establishment has a critical violation as classified by the board of health pursuant to Section 7-42-030, the department of health may require the certificate holder in charge of the preparation or service of potentially hazardous food at the time of the violation to successfully complete a new food sanitation course and examination approved by the department of health. Such course and examination shall be completed within 45 days of the finding of such critical violation. When a department of health inspection finds that a food establishment has a serious or minor violation as classified by the board of health, the department of health may require the certificate holder in charge of the preparation or service of potentially hazardous food at the time of the violation to successfully complete a new food sanitation course and examination approved by the department of health. Failure to successfully complete a new food sanitation course and examination required by the department of

health pursuant to this subsection shall be grounds for suspension or revocation of a certificate of registration. Nothing in this subsection shall prevent a certificate of registration from being suspended or revoked by the department of health pursuant to subsection (a) of this section.
(Added. Coun. J. 6-10-96, p. 23652; Amend. 3-10-99, p. 91043; 5-12-99, p. 2225)

§7-38-020 Control of vermin and insects.

In accordance with this section and the rules and regulations of the board of health, all necessary control measures shall be used to effectively minimize, or eliminate when possible, the presence of rodents, roaches and other vermin and insects on the premises of all food establishments, in food-transporting vehicles and vending machines. All garbage and rubbish shall be stored, removed and disposed of as prescribed in this section and the rules and regulations.

The outdoor eating areas of all food-dispensing establishments shall be cleaned and hosed down prior to opening or at the close of business each day. At the close of the outdoor eating season, the outdoor eating areas shall be hosed down with a pressurized hose designed for outdoor use.

At least one garbage receptacle with a capacity of 55 gallons and a lid shall be placed at an area accessible to the patrons of any outdoor eating area where the tables are not regularly cleared by waiters, waitresses or other staff. If one such garbage receptacle is not sufficient to accommodate the stream of garbage produced by the outdoor eating area, additional receptacles shall be provided to the extent the stream of garbage requires. Each receptacle shall be periodically emptied and at no time shall garbage be permitted to overflow onto the ground from a receptacle.

Every food establishment shall maintain a log containing a written record of the control measures performed by exterminators or other pest control businesses on the premises of the food establishment and receipts and reports prepared by the exterminators or other pest control businesses for the control services. The log shall be open to inspection by city health and sanitation inspectors.
(Added. Coun. J. 6-10-96, p. 23652; Amend. 6-10-96, p. 23785; 3-10-99, p. 91043)

§7-38-040 Vehicle sanitation requirements.

(a) Vehicles used by food establishments for the carrying or transportation of foods shall comply with the following:

(1) Each vehicle shall be constructed so that the portions of the vehicle which contain food shall be covered so that no dust or dirt will settle on the food; and such portions of the vehicles which are designed to contain food shall be at least 18 inches above the surface of the public way while the vehicle is being used for the conveyance of food;

(2) Each vehicle shall be kept in clean and sanitary condition, and protected from contamination;

(3) Each vehicle shall be kept in good operating condition and comply with all safety and pollution standards set forth for comparable vehicles by the United States, the state of Illinois and the city;

(4) Refrigeration equipment in such vehicles where required by any federal or state statute or regulation or by this Municipal Code shall conform to all standards for refrigerated vehicles set forth by the United States, the state of Illinois and the city of Chicago;

(5) The name and address of the licensee shall appear plainly, distinctly and legibly in letters and figures at least two inches in height in a conspicuous place on the outside of each side of every such vehicle;

(6) The food storage areas of each vehicle shall be kept free from rats, mice, flies and other insects and vermin. No domestic animal, birds or fowl shall be permitted in any area where food is stored; and

(7) Hazardous non-food items such as detergents, insecticides, rodenticides, plants, paint and paint products that are poisonous or toxic in nature shall not be stored in the food area of the vehicle.

(b) In addition to the requirements contained in paragraph (a) of this section, every vehicle used by a wholesale food establishment in the conduct of said business shall comply with the following requirements:

(1) While being stored during transportation by the wholesale food establishment all food shall be protected from contamination; all potentially hazardous food shall be stored at 40 degrees Fahrenheit or less; and all frozen food shall be stored at zero degrees Fahrenheit or less until removed from vehicle;

(2) All areas on wholesale food establishment vehicles used for the storage of potentially hazardous foods shall be provided with an indicating thermometer having a temperature range adaptable to the required facility, and accurate to plus-minus three degrees Fahrenheit located on the warmest part of the area in which the food is stored, which shall be so located that it can be easily seen for reading;

(3) All unwrapped or unenclosed foods on the vehicle that are not shelled, shucked, peeled or cooked prior to eating shall be suitably protected from public handling, dust, dirt and flies. A complete enclosure in a box, carton, wrapper or package of a similar character shall be considered adequate protection for all food required to be protected. The original box, crate or container, and the usual cover for such containers, left in place and intact, shall be considered adequate protection for fruits and vegetables sold or offered for sale in such original containers; and

(4) Packaged food or drink shall not be stored in contact with undrained ice.

(c) In addition to the requirements contained in paragraph (a) of this section, every vehicle used by a mobile food dispenser in the conduct of said business shall comply with the following requirements:

(1) The vehicle shall be enclosed with top and sides;

(2) The interior floor, walls and ceiling of each vehicle shall be of smooth, not readily corrodible, impervious material capable of withstanding repeated washing and scrubbing and shall be finished in a light color;

(3) The vehicle shall not be used for any purpose other than a mobile food dispenser; and

(4) All food service equipment utilized in the mobile food dispenser shall be of easily cleanable construction and shall be maintained in good repair and shall be clean.

(Added. Coun. J. 6-10-96, p. 23652)

§7-38-070 Food sanitarians.

Any food sanitarian employed by the city of Chicago shall be empowered to enforce applicable provisions of this chapter, Chapter 7-40 and Chapter 7-42. The mayor may designate one or more departments to supervise the activities of food sanitarians.
(Added Coun. J. 6-10-96, p. 23652)

Article II. Mobile Food Dispensers

§7-38-080 Mobile food vendors—Prohibited districts.

No person shall engage in the occupation of mobile food dispenser at any time within any district that has been or shall be hereafter designated by the city council. A description of such districts shall be kept in the office of the city clerk. Any person who violates this section shall be subject to a fine of not less than $200.00 and not more than $500.00 for each offense.
(Added. Coun. J. 6-10-96, p. 23652)

§7-38-115 Operational requirements.

(a) Mobile food dispenser vehicles shall move from place to place upon the public ways and shall not be operated at a fixed location except as otherwise provided herein.

(b) Stops shall be made only to service customers and shall not exceed a total of two hours in any one block. Mobile food vendors may stop to service customers for a period of up to two hours notwithstanding the provisions of the second paragraph of Section 9-64-190(a) of this code.

(c) No mobile food dispenser vehicle shall be equipped with any electronic sound-amplifying device. Permitted advertising devices shall be limited to bells, whistles, horns or other musical or noise-making devices which do not employ any electronic sound-amplifying device. Mobile food dispenser vehicles employing musical or noise-making devices shall only sound said devices when traversing the public way and shall be prohibited from sounding said devices while parked. No mobile food dispenser vehicle equipped with a musical or noise-making device shall sound any such device at any location between the hours of 7:00 P.M. and 9:00 A.M., or at any time within 200 feet of a hospital, nursing home or while traversing any zone of quiet established under Chapter 10-8 of the Municipal Code.

(d) No sales from such vehicle shall be made between the hours of 10:00 p.m. and 10:00 a.m.

(e) No operator of such vehicle shall park or stand such vehicle within 200 feet of a church, a school or school playground while school is in session.

(f) No operator of such vehicle shall park or stand such vehicle within 200 feet of any principal customer entrance to a restaurant which is located on the street level.

Restaurant, for purposes of this section, means any public place at a fixed location kept, used, maintained, advertised and held out to the public as a place where food and drink is prepared and served for the public for consumption on or off the premises pursuant to the required licenses. Such establishments include, but are not limited to, restaurants, coffee shops, cafeterias, dining rooms, eating houses, short order cafes, luncheonettes, grills, tearooms and sandwich shops.

(g) No sale shall be made from such vehicle except from the curb side thereof, and then only when such vehicle is legally parked.

(h) Mobile food dispenser vehicles that are being used to provide food and drink to persons engaged in construction in the city of Chicago and which are not equipped with noise-making devices are exempt from the provisions of (b), (d) and (f) above.

(Added. Coun. J. 6-10-96, p. 23652; Amend. 9-5-01, p. 66021)

§7-38-120 Sinks, water storage tanks and other plumbing requirements.

All mobile food dispenser vehicles shall be equipped with a handwashing sink and an adequate supply of running hot water. The hot water storage tank shall be self-draining and cleaned and flushed not less than twice in each six-month period. Liquid waste from the handwashing sink shall be piped in fixed piping to a wastewater retention storage container or tank of adequate size not located in food storage or food serving sections of the vehicle. The connection between piping from sink and wastewater container shall be tight-fitting and comply with the plumbing provisions of this code. The wastewater tank or container shall be emptied daily or more often if necessary, and only into a sanitary drainage facility in a manner and place approved by the department of health.

(Added. Coun. J. 6-10-96, p. 23652)

§7-38-125 Refuse receptacles.

The operator shall maintain a suitable, tight, nonabsorbent washable receptacle for refuse. He shall be responsible for sanitation of the environs of the place of operation. Said refuse receptacle shall be adjacent to, but not an integral part of, the mobile food dispenser unit.

(Added. Coun. J. 6-10-96, p. 23652)

Article III. Automatic Food—Vending Machines

§7-38-150 Vending machines—Food manufacture, delivery and storage.

All food offered for sale through vending machines shall be manufactured, processed, prepared in and delivered from commissaries or establishments which comply with the health and sanitation requirements for food service establishments set forth in this code and in the rules and regulations of the board of health. All single-service containers, food and food-contact surfaces shall be protected from contamination, insects and vermin during transit to vending machine locations.

All food shall be stored or packaged in clear, protective containers and shall be handled, transported and vended in a sanitary manner.

(Added. Coun. J. 6-10-96, p. 23652)

§7-38-155 Marking of food product wrappers.

All individual wrapped portions of readily perishable food products, including sandwiches, pies and other similar portions, shall be plainly marked by the manufacturer on the wrapper or container in such a manner as to plainly identify the day and the month on which such individual portion was prepared and wrapped in an establishment approved by the department of health as hereinbefore provided. The name and address of the person processing or manufacturing or wrapping portions of potentially hazardous food products shall appear on each individual portion.

No person shall keep or offer for sale individual portions of potentially hazardous food products which have been rewrapped or repackaged or portions of which the identifying date on the wrapper has been altered, disfigured or changed in any manner.

(Added. Coun. J. 6-10-96, p. 23652)

§7-38-210 Vending machines—Out-of-service procedure.

When suspicion arises that a food- or beverage-vending machine is dispensing adulterated, contaminated or unwholesome food or drink, or is infested with vermin, the owner, operator, employee or the health authority shall cause it to be placed out of service until provisions satisfactory to the department of health have been made to cure the problem.

(Added. Coun. J. 6-10-96, p. 23652)

7-38-212 Water-vending machines—Location restriction.

No water-vending machine may be installed, operated or maintained, except at a retail food establishment.

(Added. Coun. J. 6-10-96, p. 23652)

§7-38-218 Water-vending machines—Rules and regulations.

The board of health and the commissioner of the department of water management shall be authorized to promulgate rules and regulations as may be necessary for the proper administration and enforcement of the provisions of this code pertaining to water-vending machines.

(Added. Coun. J. 6-10-96, p. 23652; Amend. Coun. J. 12-4-02, p. 99026)

Article IV. Coffee Cart Vendors

§7-38-235 Sale of certain products from coffee carts prohibited.

No person shall sell, offer for sale or serve any food product other than coffee, coffee flavorings, coffee or juice-based beverages and pastry baked goods from a coffee cart.

(Added. Coun. J. 6-10-96, p. 23652)

§7-38-240 Operation of coffee carts on public way prohibited.

No person shall operate a coffee cart on the public way.

(Added. Coun. J. 6-10-96, p. 23652)

Article V. Cold Storage Establishments

§7-38-460 Reports.

Every person engaged in the business of cold storage warehouseman, or in the business of refrigeration, or in any business in which articles of food as defined herein are kept in cold storage for any purpose whatsoever, shall submit reports to the department of health upon printed forms to be provided by the department, setting forth in itemized particulars the quantity of each and every foodstuff in storage or in the control of said person; such reports shall be filed on or before the twenty-fifth day of January, May and September of each year, and reports so rendered shall show the true conditions in regard to such matters existing in said cold storage establishments upon the first day of the month in which said report is filed.
(Added. Coun. J. 6-10-96, p. 23652)

§7-38-465 Receiving and delivery requirements.

It shall be unlawful for any person engaged in the business of cold storage warehouseman or in the business of refrigeration, or in any business in which articles of food as defined herein are kept in cold storage for any purpose whatsoever, to receive any kind of food for cold storage unless the said food is in a pure and wholesome condition, and the food or package containing same is branded, stamped or marked in some conspicuous place with the day, month and year when the same is received in storage or refrigeration, or to permit any such article of food in his possession to be taken from him without first having plainly printed, branded, stamped, marked or written in a conspicuous place upon each and every such article, parcel or package containing the same, the day, month and year when said foodstuff, article or package was removed from cold storage or refrigeration, as well as the day, month and year when same was received in cold storage or refrigeration.
(Added. Coun. J. 6-10-96, p. 23652)

§7-38-470 Storage time limit.

It shall be unlawful for any person engaged in the business of cold storage warehouseman of refrigeration, or in any business in which articles of food are kept in cold storage for any purpose whatsoever, to keep in storage, for preservation or otherwise, any kind of food or any article or articles used for food a period longer than 12 calendar months.
(Added. Coun. J. 6-10-96, p. 23652)

7-38-475 Time limit extension—Report.

It shall be unlawful for any person to sell, offer for sale, or give away within the city any food which has been kept in cold storage for a period of time longer than that provided for herein except with the consent of the department of health as hereinafter provided.

The department of health may, upon application or upon making the inspection herein provided for, extend the period of storage beyond the time herein prescribed, for any particular lot of goods, if the goods in question are found upon inspection and examination by the department of health to be in proper condition for food, such extension to be until such time not exceeding 90 days, as it shall consider proper, considering the condition of the food at the time such extension is made. The length of time that such further storage may be allowed shall be specified in the order granting such extension.

A report on each case in which such extension of time is granted, including all information relating to the reasons for the action of the department of health, the kind and amount of goods for which the storage period was extended, and the length of time for which the extension was granted, shall be included in a monthly report of the department of health to the mayor.
(Added. Coun. J. 6-10-96, p. 23652)

§7-38-480 Transfer restrictions.

The transfer of any food from one cold storage establishment to another for the purpose of evading any provision of this chapter is hereby prohibited.
(Added. Coun. J. 6-10-96, p. 23652)

§7-38-485 Return to cold storage restricted.

When food has been in cold storage or refrigeration and is released therefrom for the purpose of placing the same on the market for sale, or for any other purpose, it shall be unlawful to again place such food in cold storage refrigeration unless said food remains in its original package and is not removed from the premises.
(Added. Coun. J. 6-10-96, p. 23652)

Article VI. Slaughtering, Rendering and Packing Establishments

§7-38-495 Notice to alderman.

Thirty days before a wholesale food establishment license which authorizes an applicant to engage in the business of a slaughtering, rendering and packing establishment may be issued to an applicant who has not been previously licensed to engage in such business, the city clerk shall mail a notice of such application to the alderman representing the ward in which the applicant intends to engage in such business, and to the alderman whose ward or any part thereof is within a radius of three miles from the proposed location for which application is made to carry on such business.
(Added. Coun. J. 6-10-96, p. 23652)

§7-38-510 Slaughtering on public ways prohibited.

No animals shall be slaughtered, or the meat or any part thereof dressed, or hung, wholly or partly, within any public way or place; nor shall any blood or dirty water or other substance from such animals, meat or place of killing, or the appurtenances thereof, be allowed to run, fall, or be in any such public way or place.
(Added. Coun. J. 6-10-96, p. 23652)

§7-38-520 Hours for slaughtering.

No owner or person in possession, charge or control of a slaughterhouse shall slaughter animals for food between the hours of 7:00 p.m. and 7:00 a.m. or on Sundays, without first notifying the department of buildings.
(Added. Coun. J. 6-10-96, p. 23652)

§7-38-535 Offensive gases and odors prohibited.

No person shall boil any offal, swill or bones, nor any fat, tallow or lard, except while the same is fresh and otherwise inoffensive, nor shall the business of bone crushing, bone boiling, bone grinding, bone burning, shell burning or gut cleaning, nor the skinning of or making of glue from any dead animal or part thereof, nor the storage or keeping of scrap, fat or greases or offensive animal matter be permitted or conducted at any place within the limits of the city, or within one mile thereof, in such a manner as to generate any offensive or deleterious gas, vapor, deposit or exhalation that is dangerous or detrimental to life or health.

It shall constitute, and it is hereby declared, a nuisance for any person so to steam or boil or in any way render any offal or tainted or damaged lard or tallow, or so to steam or render any animal substances, as to occasion any offensive smell, or to steam or boil or render any substance which by undergoing such process so taints the air as to render it unwholesome or offensive to the smell or detrimental to health, within the limits of the city, or within a distance of one mile therefrom.

Every person engaged in the business of boiling or rendering of fat, lard or animal matter shall cause the scrap or residuum to be so dried or otherwise prepared as effectually to deprive such material of all offensive odors, and to preserve the same entirely inoffensive immediately after the removal from the receptacles in which the rendering process may be conducted.

(Added. Coun. J. 6-10-96, p. 23652)

§7-38-540 Reserved.

(Deleted. Coun. J. 3-31-04, p. 20916)

§7-38-545 Entry of carcasses prohibited.

No person shall bring, or cause to be brought, into any slaughterhouse in the city the carcass of any dead animal.

(Added. Coun. J. 6-10-96, p. 23652)

§7-38-550 Conveyance of refuse.

No offal or butcher's refuse shall be conveyed through any public way or public place within the city without a permit from the department of buildings.

Vehicles conveying such refuse shall be constructed of one or more tight compartments, each of which compartments shall be covered with a wooden or sheet metal cover attached to such compartments by substantial hinges.

(Added. Coun. J. 6-10-96, p. 23652)

§7-38-555 Sleeping on premises prohibited.

No person shall use for the housing, sheltering and harboring of its employees or other persons any packing or slaughterhouse or any place which is occupied for the purpose of slaughtering or rendering cattle, sheep or hogs, or of dressing, cleaning, treating or preparing for shipment or canning meats and other foodstuffs by hand or machinery, or cause or permit same to be used as sleeping quarters or living apartments by such employees or other persons. Any such house or place so used or occupied for sleeping or living purposes is hereby declared to be a nuisance.

Whenever any such nuisance shall be found upon any premises within the city, the department of buildings is hereby authorized and directed to cause the same to be summarily abated in such a manner as it may direct.

For the purpose of carrying the foregoing provisions into effect, it shall be the duty of the department of buildings to cause to be detailed a sufficient number of police immediately upon complaint of any citizen. These police shall make a thorough and systematic examination of any such plant or plants and building or buildings and ascertain and report any such violations of this section, and for this purpose investigators shall be permitted at all times to visit or enter upon any building, lot or ground within the city limits and make examination thereof.

(Added. Coun. J. 6-10-96, p. 23652)

§7-38-570 Abatement of nuisance.

In all cases where a nuisance shall be found in any building or upon any ground or other premises used for the slaughtering or rendering, 24 hours' notice shall be given in writing, signed by the commissioner of the department of buildings, to the owner or occupant of such building or other premises, where he is known and can be found, to remove such nuisance. In case of his neglect or refusal to abate the same, in accordance with such notice, the commissioner of the department of buildings is hereby authorized in his discretion to cause the same to be summarily abated in such manner as he may direct, and such person shall be chargeable with the expenses which may be incurred in the abatement or removal of such nuisance, to be collected by suit or otherwise, in addition to the fine and penalty provided for.

(Added. Coun. J. 6-10-96, p. 23652)

Article VII. Penalty for Violation of Chapter Provisions

§7-38-575 Violation—Penalty.

The board of health shall promulgate rules and regulations classifying violations of this chapter as critical, serious or minor. Any person who violates or who resists the enforcement of any provision of this chapter shall be fined $500.00 for each critical violation; $250.00 for each serious violation; and $250.00 for each minor violation that is not corrected upon reinspection by the health authority. A separate and distinct offense shall be deemed to have been committed for each and every day on which any person shall be guilty of such violation; provided that, the intervening days between when a license holder whose license has been suspended applies for restoration of the license and a reinspection has been conducted by the department of health shall not constitute separate offenses if the violation was found to be corrected upon reinspection.

(Added. Coun. J. 6-10-96, p. 23652; Amend. 3-10-99, p. 91043)

CHAPTER 7-40
FOOD ESTABLISHMENTS—CARE OF FOODS
(Selected Sections)

Sections:

Article I. General Provisions

7-40-010 Impure or adulterated drugs, liquids or food.
7-40-015 Sale or possession of unwholesome food.
7-40-025 Confiscation of unwholesome food.
7-40-050 Misrepresentation prohibited.
7-40-060 Animals in stores.

Article II. Meat

7-40-065 Compliance required—Inspections.
7-40-070 Department of Agriculture inspection—Required.
7-40-090 Sale of canned poultry.

Article III. Vegetables, Fruits and Berries

7-40-100 Sulfite agents.
7-40-105 Inspection.

Article IV. Water

7-40-115 Drinking fountains.
7-40-120 Use of impure water.

Article V. Candy

7-40-125 Sanitary requirements.

Article VI. Poultry

7-40-140 Location restrictions.

Article VII. Bottled-Water and Nonalcoholic Beverages

7-40-160 Sales restrictions on products of noncity bottled-water plants.

Article VIII. Frozen Desserts and Mixes

7-40-290 Pasteurization required.
7-40-295 Disease among employees—Notices required.
7-40-300 Manufacturing to be in compliance with city regulations.
7-40-305 Adulterated or misbranded desserts and mixes.

Article IX. Milk and Milk Products

7-40-325 Adulteration and misbranding designated.
7-40-345 Bulk sales—Notice required.

Article X. Violation of Chapter Provisions

7-40-390 Violation—Penalty.

Article I. General Provisions

§7-40-010 Impure or adulterated drugs, liquids or food.

No person shall sell or deliver any drugs not conforming to the rules and standards of the United States pharmacopoeia, nor any water, liquids or food which shall be impure, unwholesome, adulterated, or to which any harmful or injurious foreign substance has been added.

(Coun. J. 12-9-92, p. 25465; Amend. 6-10-96, p. 23652)

§7-40-015 Sale or possession of unwholesome food.

No person shall bring into the city, sell or have in his possession, charge or control with intent to sell, any article of food which is or has become unwholesome for human consumption.
(Coun. J. 12-9-92, p. 25465; Amend. 6-10-96, p. 23652)

§7-40-025 Confiscation of unwholesome food.

It shall be unlawful for any person to sell in the city any food which may be deemed unwholesome; and it shall be the duty of the department of health to forthwith seize and destroy all such food; provided, that in case there is a doubt as to the condition of any such food, the department of health may affix or cause to be affixed to the food, or to the container in which it may be enclosed, a seal indicating that the food and its containers have been held for further investigation by the department of health. It shall be unlawful for any person to alter, remove, deface or obliterate any seal so affixed, or to remove the food or container so sealed to any other place, or to instigate or permit the changing, removal, defacement or obliteration of the seal or the removal to any other place of the food or the container thereof, so sealed.
(Coun. J. 12-9-92, p. 25465; Amend. 6-10-96, p. 23652)

§7-40-050 Misrepresentation prohibited.

No food shall knowingly be bought, sold, labeled, or any representation made in respect thereof, under a false name or quality, or under any false representation whatsoever respecting its wholesomeness, soundness or safety for food or drink.
(Coun. J. 12-9-92, p. 25465; Amend. 6-10-96, p. 23652)

§7-40-060 Animals in stores.

It shall be unlawful for the owner of, or the person having the care or custody of any animal, to suffer or permit such animal to enter any store, meat market, bakery or other place where foodstuffs are sold or on display; provided, that the person owning or operating such store or place may permit a watchdog to remain therein if chained or bound in such a way that the dog cannot come in contact with any of the foodstuffs; provided, further, that when a blind person is accompanied by a dog which serves as a guide or leader for him, neither the blind person nor the dog shall be denied the right of entry and use of the facilities, if such dog is wearing a harness and the person presents credentials for inspection issued by a school for training guide dogs approved by the United States Veterans Administration. Any person violating any of the provisions of this section shall be fined not less than $10.00 nor more than $25.00 for each offense.
(Coun. J. 12-9-92, p. 25465; Amend. 6-10-96, p. 23652)

Article II. Meat

§7-40-065 Compliance required—Inspections.

All meats and meat-food products sold or held for sale within the city of Chicago shall comply with the standards, requirements and regulations of the United States Department of Agriculture for such meats and meat-food products and the

rules and regulations of the board of health. The department of health shall make such inspections as are necessary to insure compliance with this section.
(Coun. J. 12-9-92, p. 25465; Amend. 6-10-96, p. 23652)

§7-40-070 Department of Agriculture inspection—Required.
It shall be unlawful for any person to sell within the city or for any dealer in meats or any manufacturer of meat-food products to purchase, accept, hold or store within the city any carcass of cattle, sheep, swine or goats, or any meat-food products thereof, unless they shall have been inspected and passed by a duly authorized inspection of the United States Department of Agriculture.
(Coun. J. 12-9-92, p. 25465; Amend. 6-10-96, p. 23652)

§7-40-090 Sale of canned poultry.
It shall be unlawful for any person to pack, prepare, produce, or put up for food or sell within the city any canned carcasses or parts of carcasses of chickens, ducks, geese, turkeys or other kinds of canned poultry, or any products thereof, unless the same shall have been inspected and passed as fit for consumption as human food by a duly authorized inspector of the United States Department of Agriculture.

Each can or other container containing such canned poultry or canned poultry products shall be plainly marked, stamped or labeled on the outside of the container to show that the contents therein have been so inspected, together with the name and address of the packer or distributor of such canned poultry and such canned poultry products.
(Coun. J. 12-9-92, p. 25465; Amend. 6-10-96, p. 23652)

Article III. Vegetables, Fruits and Berries

§7-40-100 Sulfite agents.
Any restaurant, grocery or other retail food establishment who shall treat fresh fruits, fresh vegetables and other raw food with a sulfiting agent will be considered safe only if consumers are informed. Acceptable consumer notices must include use of conspicuous and easily readable labels, signs, placards or menu statements indicating "sodium bisulfite added" or "sulfiting agents added to preserve natural appearance and freshness."
(Coun. J. 12-9-92, p. 25465; Amend. 6-10-96, p. 23652)

§7-40-105 Inspection.
The department of health shall inspect all fruits, vegetables and berries which may be offered for sale within the city, and cause the arrest and punishment of any person that shall in any way violate any of the provisions of this chapter with regard to fruits, vegetables and berries.
(Coun. J. 12-9-92, p. 25465; Amend. 6-10-96, p. 23652)

Article IV. Water

§7-40-115 Drinking fountains.
No person shall destroy or in any way injure or impair any drinking fountain or part thereof in the city; nor shall any person interfere with the use

of or enjoyment of the water therein or therefrom, or interrupt the flow thereof, nor shall any person put any dirt, poisonous, medicinal or noxious substance into or near such water or hydrant whereby such water is made, or may be regarded as, dangerous or unwholesome as a drink.
(Coun. J. 12-9-92, p. 25465; Amend. 6-10-96, p. 23652)

§7-40-120 Use of impure water.

No person shall use water taken from the Chicago River or any of its branches, or from any body of water within the city which is stagnant, or in which there is refuse, waste, garbage, sewage or any other material tending to destroy the purity of the water, for domestic purposes, for watering livestock, for preparing meats, poultry or provisions which are intended for human consumption, or for any other purpose whatever which endangers the public health; but nothing in this section contained shall be construed as limiting or prohibiting the right of persons to use water as a means of supplying motive power for mechanical purposes.
(Coun. J. 12-9-92, p. 25465; Amend. 6-10-96, p. 23652)

Article V. Candy

§7-40-125 Sanitary requirements.

Every candy sales agency shall be kept in a clean and sanitary condition. All appliances, receptacles, scales, storerooms, places or things which are used for handling, receiving or containing candy, or which are used or connected with the candy sales agency, shall be kept in a clean, wholesome and sanitary condition, and all products and merchandise of such establishment shall, at all times, be protected against contamination. Such adequate and convenient washing and toilet facilities as may be designated by the department of health shall be provided for employees in such candy factories and sales agencies.

"Candy sales agency," as used in this section, means any building, room, place, establishment or vehicle in the city where any candy, confectionery, sugar ornaments, candied fruits, taffy apples, candied nuts, shelled nuts or peanuts, marzipan, chewing gum, lozenges, cough drops, fruit or flavored tablets, popcorn, popcorn candy or any other candies, confectionery or similar products are sold, offered for sale, or kept with the intention of selling at wholesale either by dealers, jobbers, agents or itinerant vendors.
(Coun. J. 12-9-92, p. 25465; Amend. 6-10-96, p. 23652)

Article VI. Poultry

§7-40-140 Location restrictions.

No retail food establishment which authorizes the retail sale of live poultry or other live fowl shall be issued to any person for any premises not heretofore licensed for the retail sale of live poultry or other live fowl where such establishment is within a 200-foot distance from any place or structure used as a church, school, library, hospital, public park, public playground or other public institution; from any building in which food is manufactured; or from any building used for residence purposes. No license shall be issued to any person

for the conduct of any such establishment on any premises exempted from the prohibition as to location contained in this section if such premises have not been used for the conduct of such an establishment for the period of one year.
(Coun. J. 12-9-92, p. 25465; Amend. 6-10-96, p. 23652)

Article VII. Bottled-Water and Nonalcoholic Beverages

§7-40-160 Sales restrictions on products of noncity bottled-water plants.

Products of a bottled-water plant located outside the city of Chicago shall not be brought into the city for sale therein unless such plant shall have placed on file with the department of health a certificate from the state board of health of the state in which such plant is located, stating that with reference to such product all requirements of this code relating to sanitation and purity of product are complied with. On receipt of such a certificate, the department of health may permit the sale of the products of such plants for a period not to exceed the term of the license.
(Added. Coun. J. 6-10-96, p. 23652)

Article VIII. Frozen Desserts and Mixes

§7-40-290 Pasteurization required.

No mix or frozen dessert made from mix which contains milk and milk products may be distributed or sold within the city of Chicago unless such mix has been pasteurized and maintained at a temperature of 40 degrees Fahrenheit or less after pasteurization. Such mix must be frozen within 14 days from the date of pasteurization. All containers of pasteurized mix shall bear the words "Date Pasteurized" followed by the date of pasteurization.
(Added. Coun. J. 6-10-96, p. 23652)

§7-40-295 Disease among employees—Notices required.

Notice shall be sent to the department of health immediately by any licensee among whose employees any infectious or communicable disease occurs. When suspicion arises as to the possibility of transmission of infection from any person engaged in the handling of mix, frozen desserts or their ingredients, the commissioner is authorized to order any or all of the following measures:

(1) The immediate exclusion of that person from handling mix, frozen desserts, or their ingredients;

(2) Immediate exclusion of the mix or frozen desserts in question from distribution and use;

(3) Adequate medical and bacteriological examination of the person, his associates, and of his and their bodily discharges.
(Added. Coun. J. 6-10-96, p. 23652)

§7-40-300 Manufacturing to be in compliance with city regulations.

No mix or frozen dessert shall be sold for consumption within the city of Chicago, unless it has been produced, processed, transported and handled in compliance with the requirements of this chapter and the rules and regulations promulgated hereunder.

(Added. Coun. J. 6-10-96, p. 23652)

§7-40-305 Adulterated or misbranded desserts and mixes.

No person shall produce, provide, sell, offer or expose for sale, deliver or have in his possession with intent to deliver, any mix or frozen dessert which is adulterated or misbranded.

(Added. Coun. J. 6-10-96, p. 23652)

Article IX. Milk and Milk Products

§7-40-325 Adulteration and misbranding designated.

No person shall produce, provide, sell, offer or expose for sale, deliver or have in possession with intent to sell or deliver, any milk or milk products all or any part of which is ultimately delivered in the city of Chicago, which is adulterated or misbranded.

Milk and milk products are adulterated (1) if they bear or contain any poisonous or deleterious substance in a quantity which may render them injurious to health; (2) if they bear or contain any added poisonous or deleterious substance for which no safe tolerance has been established by state or federal regulations, or in excess of such tolerance if one has been established; (3) if they consist, in whole or in part, of any substance unfit for human consumption; (4) if they have been produced, processed, prepared, packed or held under unsanitary conditions; (5) if the containers are composed, in whole or in part, of any poisonous or deleterious substance which may render the contents injurious to health; or (6) if any substance has been added thereto or mixed or packed therewith so as to increase the bulk weight, or reduce the quality or strength, or make them appear better or of greater value than they are.

Milk and milk products are misbranded (1) when their container bears or accompanies any false or misleading written, printed or graphic matter; (2) when such milk and milk products do not conform to their definitions as contained in this code; or (3) when such products are not labeled in accordance with Section 7-40-330 of this code and applicable state rules and regulations.

(Added. Coun. J. 6-10-96, p. 23652)

§7-40-345 Bulk sales—Notice required.

Every restaurant, cafe, soda fountain, or other establishment serving milk or milk products in bulk shall display at all times, in a place designated by the department of health, a notice approved by the department of health, giving all information required with regard to labeling milk containers and such other information required by the department of health.

(Added. Coun. J. 6-10-96, p. 23652)

Article X. Violation of Chapter Provisions

§7-40-390 Violation—Penalty.

The board of health shall promulgate rules and regulations classifying violations of this chapter as critical, serious or minor. Any person who violates or who resists the enforcement of any provision of this chapter shall be fined $500.00 for each critical violation; $250.00 for each serious violation; and $250.00 for each minor violation that is not corrected upon reinspection by the health authority. A separate and distinct offense shall be held to have been committed each and every day on which any person shall be guilty of such violation; provided that, the intervening days between when a license holder whose license has been suspended applies for restoration of the license and a reinspection has been conducted by the department of health shall not constitute separate offenses if the violation was found to be corrected upon reinspection.

(Coun. J. 12-9-92, p. 25465; Amend. 6-10-96, p. 23652; 3-10-99, p. 91043)

CHAPTER 7-42
FOOD ESTABLISHMENTS—INSPECTIONS, VIOLATIONS AND HEARING PROCEDURES

(Selected Sections)

Sections:

7-42-010 Inspections.
7-42-020 "Held for Inspection" procedures.
7-42-030 Violations of provisions—Classification and notice.
7-42-035 License suspension.
7-42-050 Removal of suspended licenses and permits.
7-42-065 Partial closures.
7-42-080 License revocation.
7-42-085 Enforcement.
7-42-090 Violation—Penalty.

§7-42-010 Inspections.

For the purposes of Section 7-42-010 and Section 7-42-020, the word "owner" shall include the owner, operator, licensee or person in charge of any food establishment or vehicles used for the storage, transportation or vending of foods, subject to the provisions of Chapter 4-8.

(a) The department of health shall inspect all food establishments at least once every six months and as often as necessary to determine that the requirements of this Municipal Code are being complied with. In addition, the department of health shall inspect mobile food dispenser vehicles serving ice cream, milk or other frozen desserts at least once every 90 days during the period from April 1st through October 1st of every year.

(b) Whenever the health authority inspects an establishment, the inspector shall record the findings of the inspection on a summary report form provided by the department of health for this purpose. Such reports shall be signed by both the inspector and the establishment's representative, and one copy of the summary report shall be left with the management of the establishment and shall be posted by the health authority upon an inside wall of the establishment in an area visible to all diners; if the food establishment is a grocery store or delicatessen, the summary report shall be posted in an area visible to all customers. It shall be unlawful for any person except an authorized agent of the department of health to deface or remove any such posted summary report, and a violation of this provision may result in suspension of any and all licenses and permits issued to the owner of that particular food establishment.

(c) It shall be the duty of every owner to permit a representative of the department of health, after proper identification, to enter at any reasonable time and, make inspections of the facilities, equipment and vehicles for determining compliance with the requirements of this Municipal Code relating to health and sanitation and when required to do so, the owner shall furnish samples of any foods prepared, kept, sold or transported by any such food establishment as often as the commissioner of health may deem necessary to determine that the foods are free from adulteration, not misbranded, do not contain an excessive number of microorganisms or their toxins, and otherwise comply with the provisions of this Municipal Code and the rules and regulations of the board of health. The owner shall answer all reasonable and proper questions and permit the health authority to examine records of the establishment to obtain pertinent information relating to food, water, beverages and supplies received or used and persons employed. Any samples provided shall be examined or analyzed under the direction of the department of health, and a record of each such examination or analysis shall be made and kept in the offices of the department. Upon failure or refusal by an owner to permit inspection or to furnish required samples, the commissioner shall immediately suspend any and all licenses or permits issued to the owner of that particular food establishment.

(Added. Coun. J. 6-10-96, p. 23652; Amend. 3-10-99, p. 91043)

§7-42-020 "Held for Inspection" procedures.

(a) Upon written notice to the owner, the department of health may place a "Held for Inspection" order on any food which the health authority determines or has probable cause to believe to be unwholesome or otherwise adulterated or misbranded. At the request of the owner, foods so held for inspection shall be permitted to be suitably stored pending analysis reports or voluntarily denatured and disposed of under department of health supervision.

(b) It shall be unlawful for any person to remove the "Held for Inspection" tag or seal placed on the food by the department of health, nor shall the containers of such food be removed from the premises or destroyed without permission of the department of health except on order of a court of competent jurisdiction. The department may vacate a "Held for Inspection" order or may by written order direct the owner or person in charge of the food to denature or destroy such food, bring it in compliance with the provisions of this code and the rules and regulations of the board of health or dispose of it for nonhuman use as may be approved by the department of health. Any order of the department of health to denature or destroy food shall be stayed pending appeal if the order is appealed to a court of competent jurisdiction within three days. Nothing in this section shall preclude any court action based upon a finding of unwholesome or adulterated foods.

(Added. Coun. J. 6-10-96, p. 23652; Amend. 3-10-99, p. 91043)

§7-42-030 Violations of provisions— Classification and notice.

(a) Classification of Violations. The board of health shall promulgate rules and regulations classifying violations of this chapter, Chapter 7-38, Chapter 7-40 and the rules and regulations promulgated thereunder or by the Illinois Department of Public Health, or any other provision of this Municipal Code relating to health and sanitation in any food establishment as critical, serious or minor.

(b) Notice of Violations. When the department of health finds a violation of any provision of this chapter, Chapter 7-38, Chapter 7-40 or the rules and regulations promulgated thereunder or by the Illinois Department of Public Health, or any other provision of this Municipal Code relating to health and sanitation in any food establishment, the department shall deliver to the licensee written notice of the violation with a copy of the inspection report which shall set a date by which the violation shall be corrected and designate each violation as critical, serious or minor as classified by the board of health.
(Added. Coun. J. 6-10-96, p. 23652; Amend. 3-10-99, p. 91043)

§7-42-035 License suspension.

Whenever an inspection indicates that the conditions in the food establishment create an imminent hazard to the public health, the license of the food establishment shall be immediately suspended, including whenever an inspection indicates that a critical violation exists which is not capable of being corrected prior to the conclusion of the inspection.
(Added. Coun. J. 3-10-99, p. 91043)

§7-42-050 Removal of suspended licenses and permits.

Upon suspension of any license and permits of a food establishment, all operations related to any such suspended license or permits shall cease at once, and such license and permits shall be removed from the establishment and delivered to the department of health. The department of health may cause a "notice of closure" sign to be conspicuously placed upon that part of the food establishment related to any such suspended license or permits and to which the public has access. It shall be unlawful for any person to remove a "notice of closure" sign placed on a food establishment unless authorized to do so by the department of health. The health authorities shall promptly notify the Chicago Police Department of the suspension, and the police department shall enforce the cessation of all affected operations.
(Added. Coun. J. 6-10-96, p. 23652; Amend. 3-10-99, p. 91043)

§7-42-065 Partial closures.

In any instance in which a license is suspended under this chapter, the commissioner of health may order closed that portion of the food establishment which created a public health hazard, and allow the remaining portion of the establishment to remain open for business, if the commissioner determines that a partial closure would not jeopardize public health or safety.
(Added. Coun. J. 3-10-99, p. 91043)

§7-42-080 License revocation.

Upon a record of repeated violations of this Municipal Code or the rules and regulations of the board of health related to health and sanitation, or repeated suspensions of a food establishment license, the commissioner may recommend the revocation of the license and any other license relating to the conduct of business at the food establishment to the mayor's license commission in accordance with the requirements of Chapter 4-4 of the Municipal Code.
(Added. Coun. J. 6-10-96, p. 23652; Amend. 3-10-99, p. 91043)

§7-42-085 Enforcement.

(a) If any person violates or resists the enforcement of any provision of this chapter, Chapter 7-38, or Chapter 7-40 or the rules and regulations promulgated thereunder or by the Illinois Department of Public Health, or any other provision of the Municipal Code relating to health and sanitation in any food establishment, the commissioner of health may initiate an action with the department of administrative hearings seeking to suspend all licenses and permits issued to the owner and/or impose a fine. The commissioner may also recommend to the mayor's license commission the revocation of the owner's licenses and permits.

(b) Nothing in this chapter shall preclude bringing court action based on any violations of this code.
(Added. Coun. J. 3-10-99, p. 91043)

§7-42-090 Violation—Penalty.

Any person who violates or who resists the enforcement of any provision of this chapter, Chapter 7-38, or Chapter 7-40 or the rules and regulations promulgated thereunder or by the Illinois Department of Public Health, or any other provision of the Municipal Code relating to health and sanitation in any food establishment shall be fined $500.00 for each critical violation; $250.00 for each serious violation; and $250.00 for each minor violation that is not corrected upon reinspection by the health authority. A separate and distinct offense shall be deemed to have been committed for each and every day on which any person shall be guilty of such violation; provided that, the intervening days between when a license holder whose license has been suspended applies for restoration of the license and a reinspection has been conducted by the department of health shall not constitute separate offenses if the violation was found to be corrected upon reinspection.
(Added. Coun. J. 6-10-96, p. 23652; Amend. 3-10-99, p. 91043)

CHAPTER 7-44
EXTERMINATION BY FUMIGATION

(Complete Chapter)

Sections:

7-44-010 Definitions.
7-44-020 Hazardous materials license—Required.
7-44-030 Sale of materials for hydrocyanic acid gas—Restricted.
7-44-040 Permit—Required.
7-44-050 Notice—Required.
7-44-060 Notification of occupants—Vacating of premises.
7-44-070 Crew removal from vessels.

7-44-080 Sealing of rooms.
7-44-090 Locking rooms and apartments.
7-44-100 Warning card.
7-44-110 Safety measures—Exceptions.
7-44-120 Guards.
7-44-130 Food products—Special safety measures.
7-44-140 Fires—Safety measures.
7-44-150 Impermeable receptacles—Required.
7-44-160 Exposure of cyanic crystals prohibited.
7-44-170 Airing of premises.
7-44-180 Fumigation residue—Disposal.
7-44-190 Hydrocyanic acid containers—Department of health approval—Exceptions.
7-44-200 Stink or tear gases.
7-44-210 Violation—Penalty.

§7-44-010 Definitions.

For purposes of this chapter:

"Extermination by fumigation" means the use of hydrocyanic acid gas, cyanogen, chloropicrin, methyl bromide or any other poisonous, noxious or dangerous gases or fumes specified by the board of health as liable to affect human beings by causing severe sickness or death, for the extermination by fumigation of household insects, vermin, rats or other household pests in any place in the city of Chicago; provided, however, that it shall not apply to the fumigation of greenhouses, grain elevators or cereal or tobacco warehouses.

"Exterminator" means any person who engages in the business of extermination by fumigation.

(Added. Coun. J. 2-7-96, p. 15616; Amend. 6-10-96, p. 23652)

§7-44-020 Hazardous materials license—Required.

No person may engage in the business of extermination by fumigation without a hazardous materials license issued under Chapter 4-115.

(Added. Coun. J. 2-7-96, p. 15616; Amend. 6-10-96, p. 23652)

§7-44-030 Sale of materials for hydrocyanic acid gas—Restricted.

No person shall sell or give away material for the purpose of fumigating premises with hydrocyanic acid gas, except to a person with a hazardous materials license issued under Chapter 4-115, unless a signed statement in writing is first obtained from the buyer or recipient of the material to the effect that it will not be used for the purpose of fumigating any place of domestic habitation or any building or portion thereof as set forth in this chapter.

(Added. Coun. J. 2-7-96, p. 15616; Amend. 6-10-96, p. 23652)

§7-44-040 Permit—Required.

It shall be the duty of every exterminator, intending to generate or release hydrocyanic acid gas or other dangerous gases or fumes for fumigation purposes, before starting such generation or release, to file written notice with the commissioner of buildings, giving the location of the building or enclosed space to be fumigated, and to secure from the commissioner of buildings a permit, which shall state the day and hour when the work will be performed. Each application for such permit shall be accompanied by a fee of $2.00. Such permit shall be kept on the premises to be fumigated. The time of the permit may be extended if the applicant is unable to perform the work on the hour and day set forth in the permit, and so notifies the commissioner of buildings 16 hours prior to the time set forth in the permit.

Provided that every fumigation of plants, factories, warehouses, box cars, vehicles, specially constructed vaults or any other place where candy or other foodstuffs are manufactured, sold, stored, transported or handled shall be done in strict compliance with the rules and regulations of the board of health, and further provided, that a permit for each such fumigation shall be obtained by the fumigator from the department of health.

Provided, however, that a ship or vessel may be fumigated without previously securing from the commissioner of buildings a permit so to do, if every person, except the watchman, shall leave the vessel for the period of fumigation and the vessel shall be fended off from shore so that no person may board the vessel without the knowledge of the watchman; and provided, further, that where furniture is removed from places of domestic habitation and fumigated in specially constructed vaults, and where furs or clothing is fumigated in specially constructed vaults, a permit for each such fumigation shall not be required, but in lieu thereof, an annual permit shall be secured from the commissioner of buildings after he has investigated and satisfied himself that the proper safeguards for health and life are provided.
(Added. Coun. J. 2-7-96, p. 15616; Amend. 6-10-96, p. 23652)

§7-44-050 Notice—Required.

No person shall prevent or arrest the development of fungoid growths, disinfect premises or exterminate vermin by means of lethal, toxic, corrosive, flammable or explosive fumes or gases without first notifying the division marshal in charge of the bureau of fire prevention. Such notice shall be delivered to the division marshal not less than 24 hours before any such fumigation process is begun. Such notice shall include the description and address of the premises to be fumigated, the names and addresses of the occupant and owner of said premises and the name and address of the person in charge of such fumigation operations. Such notice shall also state the name and character of the fumigating agent to be employed and the exact time and duration of such process.
(Added Coun. J. 2-7-96, p. 15616; Amend. 6-10-96, p. 23652)

§7-44-060 Notification of occupants—Vacating of premises.

When hydrocyanic gas or other dangerous gases or fumes are used for exterminating purposes, before fumigation, the operator shall personally inspect the premises and shall serve notice, over his signature, upon all responsible occupants of each room or apartment within the danger area, stating the danger of the process and the precautions to be observed, designating the rooms or apartments which must be vacated and indicating the time when the gas is to be generated or liberated. The form of this notice shall be approved by the department of health. Every room in the danger area shall be vacated. In the case of a building in which there is an inner court, vent shaft or light well or a lot line court with a party wall or in the case of two buildings having adjacent lot line courts, upon which any room being gassed opens, every room with windows or other apertures opening to such inner or lot line courts, vent shafts or light wells shall be vacated and securely locked. Where the walls of any adjoining buildings are located within 10 feet of the rooms or apartments being gassed, the operator shall notify, over his signature, all responsible occupants of rooms or apartments with window openings in such walls that such windows as are directly opposite or above the area of the adjoining building which is under gas, must remain closed or the rooms vacated during the time the building gassed is being flushed or aired. All rooms or apartments ordered vacated, but not under gas, shall be well ventilated during the process by keeping the windows of the rooms or apartments open.

Provided, however, that such vacation of premises and notification of occupants shall not be necessary where the fumigation is done in special rooms or vaults in furniture stores, secondhand stores or household goods warehouses or vaults in candy and other food processing plants, when such special rooms or vaults are approved as to their location, construction and gastightness by the department of health, and a provision is made for the airing of such vaults so as to allow the escape of gases at such a location where it is not dangerous by a system of ducts and ventilation approved by the department of health.

The danger area is that portion of any structure or dwelling which lies within the boundary of the outside walls of the building under gas, the roof and the basement or cellar floor, and such cut-off or fire walls as may exist in the structure in question. Such cut-off or fire walls shall be of solid masonry, gastight, at least eight inches in thickness extending from the basement through the attic, with all openings locked and guarded against entry and effectively sealed against gas leakage.

This vacating is essential and shall be adhered to in all cases except where it is necessary to keep boilers in operation to maintain temperatures in certain rooms in plants (particularly food-processing plants). These boiler rooms may be allowed to remain in operation during the fumigation period provided they are sealed gastight from the remainder of the building, and that all doors or other openings leading from the boiler rooms to the part of the plant under gas are locked and barricaded, and further provided no one be permitted to enter the boiler rooms except in company with one of the fumigators who is to remain with him while he is in these rooms. Furthermore, such persons and the fumigators shall wear suitable gas masks while in the boiler rooms.

(Added. Coun. J. 2-7-96, p. 15616; Amend. 6-10-96, p. 23652)

§7-44-070 Crew removal from vessels.

No vessel shall be fumigated until the captain or other commanding officer shall have mustered the crew and caused the members thereof and all other persons therein or thereon to leave and remain away from such vessel during the process of fumigation. Provided, however, that where a part of a vessel is to be fumigated and such part is not occupied or immediately adjoining an occupied portion of the vessel, and where after an investigation conducted by the commissioner of buildings, it appears that such portion may be fumigated without danger to life or health, he may, in his discretion, grant permission to the holder of a permit to perform fumigation without requiring all persons in other parts of such vessel to leave the same, subject to such conditions and restrictions as he may impose.

(Added. Coun. J. 2-7-96, p. 15616; Amend. 6-10-96, p. 23652)

§7-44-080 Sealing of rooms.

Before fumigating with hydrocyanic acid gas or other dangerous gases or fumes, the operator shall securely seal all cracks, holes, crevices, openings and apertures in walls, ceilings and floors in such a way as to confine the gas to the premises intended to be fumigated.

(Added. Coun. J. 2-7-96, p. 15616; Amend. 6-10-96, p. 23652)

§7-44-090 Locking rooms and apartments.

Before fumigation, the operator shall personally inspect all rooms and apartments ordered vacated under Section 7-44-060, and be assured that they are unoccupied by persons or domestic animals, after which all doors to all rooms or apartments, excepting one exit door to the rooms or apartments to be gassed, shall be securely locked; in addition, such windows or other wall openings as might possibly be used to gain entrance shall be locked or barred in such a way as to prevent entrance while still permitting thorough airing of the room. Immediately upon generating or liberating the gas, the door through which the operator leaves shall be securely locked and sealed, and all keys obtainable to all rooms or apartments ordered vacated shall be retained by the operator until all danger is passed. As an additional precaution, all rooms and apartments vacated shall be placarded.

(Added. Coun. J. 2-7-96, p. 15616; Amend. 6-10-96, p. 23652)

§7-44-100 Warning card.

Prior to releasing the hydrocyanic gas or other dangerous gases, suitable warning signs shall be posted on all entrances or doors to the premises to be fumigated, and upon all gangplanks, ladders and other approaches, etc., from the deck, pier or land to the vessel as follows:

Danger
Fumigation with Cyanide Gas
Deadly Poison
All persons are warned to keep away.
By Order of the Department of Health.
(Name and address of exterminator as well as telephone number)

Such sign shall be printed in red ink on white Cardboard. The letters in the word "Danger" shall be at least two inches high, all others except the signature at least three-fourths of an inch high. At night and places where the natural light between sunrise and sunset is dim, such signs shall be illuminated so as to make the reading matter thereon plainly legible.

(Added. Coun. J. 2-7-96, p. 15616; Amend. 6-10-96, p. 23652)

§7-44-110 Safety measures—Exceptions.

(a) Safety Measures. Before the beginning of any fumigation process referred to in Section 7-44-050, all automatic electrical devices shall be removed from service and all fires and open flames shall be extinguished. The premises shall be adequately sealed to prevent escape of the fumigating agent into occupied quarters. Warning placards shall be affixed in a conspicuous manner at each means of ingress to every space undergoing any fumigation. Such placards shall display the words "Dangerous Gases — Keep Out" in letters not less than three inches in height. At the end of every such process of fumigation, it shall be the duty of the person conducting such process to ventilate thoroughly such premises and to notify the division marshal in charge of the bureau of fire prevention that such premises have been ventilated and are safe to enter.

(b) Exceptions. Where such processes enumerated in subsection (a) are carried on daily in a gastight room or vault as a part of any production or renovating process, the provisions of this section shall be held to apply only to the space in which such fumigating is done and a monthly return of the notices herein required shall suffice so long as such processes shall be continuous or of daily occurrence.

(Added. Coun. J. 2-7-96, p. 15616; Amend. 6-10-96, p. 23652)

§7-44-120 Guards.

Whenever hydrocyanic acid or other dangerous gases or fumes are generated or liberated in any room or portion of a structure in the city, a sufficient number of capable, alert watchmen shall remain on duty at the entrance or entrances to the room, building or enclosed space vacated for gassing, to prevent people from entering while gas is present and for two hours after the room or area gassed is opened for airing. All guards or watchmen shall be reliable persons and must be acceptable as a proper guard by the commissioner of buildings. The exterminator shall be held strictly responsible and accountable for the conduct of the guards or watchmen. In every case where the entire building is not vacated, the exterminator or his approved representative shall remain on the job during the progress of fumigation and airing, and shall constantly supervise the occupancy of the structure to insure that no person will be endangered by gas leakage. The exterminator shall give all guards definite and proper instructions, and shall visit the premises being fumigated at regular and frequent intervals during the process to insure that they are properly guarded.

(Added. Coun. J. 2-7-96, p. 15616; Amend. 6-10-96, p. 23652)

§7-44-130 Food products—Special safety measures.

Before fumigation, the exterminator shall see that all ice, food and drink are removed from the rooms ordered vacated; except that such food or drink as is in sealed airtight containers need not be removed. Provided, that in industrial fumigations such as flour mills, cereal mills, food warehouses, macaroni plants, candy manufacturing plants, cheese-processing plants, etc., where fumigation is for the purpose of destroying vermin or insect pests infesting these foodstuffs, only liquid fats, oils and moist foodstuffs not sealed in airtight containers need be removed. The exterminator shall state in the application for permit to fumigate foodstuffs the amount of moisture content of the various foods it wishes to fumigate. No fumigated food shall be sold or shipped until it has been aerated by every reasonable means, including the use of fans wherever indicated, for a period not less than 36 hours following fumigation and suitable tests approved by the board of health of the air immediately around it are negative for the fumigant used.

(Added. Coun. J. 2-7-96, p. 15616; Amend. 6-10-96, p. 23652)

§7-44-140 Fires—Safety measures.

All fires within the premises under gas shall be put out whenever a flammable gas is used. For the purpose of this chapter, the board of health shall designate upon request whether the gas to be used shall be regarded as flammable or nonflammable. The exterminator shall notify the fire department of any rooms, building or structure other than approved vaults which are placed under hydrocyanic acid or other dangerous gas fumigation.

(Added. Coun. J. 2-7-96, p. 15616; Amend. 6-10-96, p. 23652)

§7-44-150 Impermeable receptacles—Required.

An impermeable receptacle for containing the ingredients is required in fumigating with hydrocyanic or other dangerous gases.

(Added. Coun. J. 2-7-96, p. 15616; Amend. 6-10-96, p. 23652)

§7-44-160 Exposure of cyanic crystals prohibited.

No cyanic crystals shall be dropped on the floor or left exposed where people or domestic animals may come in contact with them in fumigating with hydrocyanic or other dangerous gases.

(Added. Coun. J. 2-7-96, p. 15616; Amend. 6-10-96, p. 23652)

§7-44-170 Airing of premises.

At the conclusion of the gassing process in fumigation, it shall be the duty of the operator to throw open doors and windows of the premises, until all rooms have been opened for free access of air. No person other than the operator shall be permitted to enter the premises until all traces of the gas have disappeared, and in no case shall the occupants of the rooms or areas gassed be permitted to enter until 12 hours after airing. The operator or watchmen shall keep all persons away from the doors and windows of the premises for two hours after airing. Infants and children under six years of age shall not be permitted to re-enter the premises until 18 hours after the rooms or apartments are opened for airing. The exterminator shall inform all occupants having children of this provision in writing over his signature. No room or space, except where the whole building is vacated and except upon a ship or vessel when fended off from shore as provided herein, shall be left under gas after the time of sunset. Warnings posted where the natural light between sunrise and sunset is dim shall be artificially illuminated. Warnings on vessels fumigated after sunset shall be artificially illuminated in a manner approved by the department of health.

(Added. Coun. J. 2-7-96, p. 15616; Amend. 6-10-96, p. 23652)

§7-44-180 Fumigation residue—Disposal.

The operator shall dispose of the residue left in the jars or containers, and the water used for cleaning such jars or containers, in accordance with the provisions of the federal and state statutes and regulations concerning environmental and toxic waste and hazards.

(Added. Coun. J. 2-7-96, p. 15616; Amend. 6-10-96, p. 23652)

§7-44-190 Hydrocyanic acid containers—Department of health approval—Exceptions.

Every container in which hydrocyanic acid, either alone, mixed with or absorbed in other material, is handled, shipped or sold, shall be of a type of construction, material and thickness approved by the department of health, in order that accidental poisonings during handling, storage and shipment of such containers may be prevented. This approval shall not be necessary where the containers are accepted by the United States officials for interstate shipment.
(Added. Coun. J. 2-7-96, p. 15616; Amend. 6-10-96, p. 23652)

§7-44-200 Stink or tear gases.

The department of health may prescribe that a stink gas or tear gas shall be mixed with the hydrocyanic acid gas or other dangerous gases or fumes to be used for fumigating, specifying in whatever detail it shall deem necessary the time and method for the generation or release of such stink or tear gases.
(Added. Coun. J. 2-7-96, p. 15616; Amend. 6-10-96, p. 23652)

§7-44-210 Violation—Penalty.

Any person who shall violate any of the provisions of this chapter shall be fined not less than $200.00 nor more than $500.00 for each offense. Every day such violation continues shall constitute a separate and distinct offense.
(Added. Coun. J. 2-7-96, p. 15616; Amend. 6-10-96, p. 23652)

This page intentionally left blank

TITLE 8
OFFENSES AFFECTING PUBLIC PEACE, MORALS AND WELFARE

(Complete Title)

Chapters:

8-4	Public Peace and Welfare.
8-8	Public Morals.
8-12	Gambling.
8-16	Offenses By or Against Minors.
8-20	Weapons.
8-24	Firearms and Other Weapons.
8-28	Reserved.
8-30	Evictions for Unlawful Use of Premises.

CHAPTER 8-4
PUBLIC PEACE AND WELFARE

Sections:

8-4-010	Disorderly conduct.
8-4-015	Gang loitering.
8-4-017	Narcotics-related loitering.
8-4-020	Inciting riots, etc.
8-4-025	Aggressive panhandling.
8-4-030	Drinking in public ways.
8-4-040	Defacing and injuring house of worship and cemeteries.
8-4-050	Trespassing.
8-4-052	Anti-loitering and/or trespassing program.
8-4-054	Outdoor pay telephones prohibited.
8-4-055	Sound-emitting devices on public conveyances.
8-4-058	Reserved.
8-4-059	Possession of scanners illegal.
8-4-060	Vandalism defined.
8-4-061	Disposition of certain fines.
8-4-065	Interference with utility equipment.
8-4-070	Restitution—Financial responsibility.
8-4-075	Threatening a community policing volunteer.
8-4-080	Definitions—Assault defined—Mandatory sentence.
8-4-081	Public urination.
8-4-085	Hate crimes.
8-4-086	Prohibition against racial profiling.
8-4-090	Drug and gang houses, houses of prostitution and other disorderly houses.
8-4-091	Prohibited manner of managing or controlling real estate.
8-4-100	Reserved.
8-4-110	Disturbing places of worship.
8-4-120	Damage to public property.
8-4-125	Use of cell phones/cameras/camera phones in public privacy areas.
8-4-130	Possession of paint or marker with intent to deface unlawful.
8-4-135	Defacement of commercial vehicles.
8-4-140	Injuring or obstructing signal systems.
8-4-145	False alarms.
8-4-150	Use of sirens for air raid alarms only.
8-4-160	Reserved.
8-4-170	Reserved.
8-4-180	Possessing burglar's tools.
8-4-190	Throwing objects on athletic fields.
8-4-195	Illegal conduct within sports facilities.
8-4-200	Objects on sills or railings.

8-4-210 Spikes in railings and fences.
8-4-220 Clay holes and excavations.
8-4-230 Use of flag—Misdemeanor.
8-4-240 Ragpicking—Peddling—Junk collection.
8-4-250 Trespassing on property.
8-4-260 Trespassing on elevated track.
8-4-270 Advertising and signs on buildings.
8-4-280 Removing sod or earth.
8-4-290 Removal of sod along public way.
8-4-300 Reserved.
8-4-310 Forging signatures.
8-4-315 Fraud relating to official documents.
8-4-320 Deceptive advertising.
8-4-321 International wire transfers—Posting of notice required.
8-4-325 Deceptive practices—Residential real estate.
8-4-330 Recruitment restrictions.
8-4-340 Charitable entertainments—Restriction on promotional materials.
8-4-350 Reserved.
8-4-355 Reserved.
8-4-360 Violation—Penalty.

§8-4-010 Disorderly conduct.

A person commits disorderly conduct when he knowingly:

(a) Does any act in such unreasonable manner as to provoke, make or aid in making a breach of peace; or

(b) Does or makes any unreasonable or offensive act, utterance, gesture or display which, under the circumstances, creates a clear and present danger of a breach of peace or imminent threat of violence; or

(c) Refuses or fails to cease and desist any peaceful conduct or activity likely to produce a breach of peace where there is an imminent threat of violence, and where the police have made all reasonable efforts to protect the otherwise peaceful conduct and activity, and have requested that said conduct and activity be stopped and explained the request if there be time; or

(d) Fails to obey a lawful order of dispersal by a person known by him to be a peace officer under circumstances where three or more persons are committing acts of disorderly conduct in the immediate vicinity, which acts are likely to cause substantial harm or serious inconvenience, annoyance or alarm; or

(e) Assembles with three or more persons for the purpose of using force or violence to disturb the public peace; or

(f) Appears in any public place manifestly under the influence of alcohol, narcotics or other drug, not therapeutically administered, to the degree that he may endanger himself or other persons or property, or annoy persons in his vicinity; or

(g) Carries in a threatening or menacing manner, without authority of law, any pistol, revolver, dagger, razor, dangerous knife, stiletto, knuckles, slingshot, an object containing noxious or deleterious liquid, gas or substance or other dangerous weapon, or conceals said weapon on or about the person or vehicle; or

(h) Pickets or demonstrates on a public way within 150 feet of any primary or secondary school building while the school is in session and one-half hour before the school is in session and one-half hour after the school session has been concluded, provided that this subsection does not prohibit the peaceful picketing of any school involved in a labor dispute; or

(i) Pickets or demonstrates on a public way within 150 feet of any church, temple, synagogue or other place of worship while services are being conducted and one-half hour before services are to be conducted and one-half hour after services have been concluded, provided that this subsection does not prohibit the peaceful picketing of any church, temple, synagogue or other place of worship involved in a labor dispute.

A person convicted of disorderly conduct shall be fined not more than $500.00 for each offense.

(Prior code § 193-1; Amend. Coun. J. 3-27-02, p. 82299; 12-4-02, p. 99931; 4-9-03, p. 106396)

§8-4-015 Gang loitering.

(a) Whenever a police officer observes a member of a criminal street gang engaged in gang loitering with one or more other persons in any public place designated for the enforcement of this section under subsection (b), the police officer shall, subject to all applicable procedures promulgated by the superintendent of police: (i) inform all such persons that they are engaged in gang loitering within an area in which loitering by groups containing criminal street gang members is prohibited; (ii) order all such persons to disperse and remove themselves from within sight and hearing of the place at which the order was issued; and (iii) inform those persons that they will be subject to arrest if they fail to obey the order promptly or engage in further gang loitering within sight or hearing of the place at which the order was issued during the next three hours.

(b) The superintendent of police shall by written directive designate areas of the city in which the superintendent has determined that enforcement of this section is necessary because gang loitering has enabled criminal street gangs to establish control over identifiable areas, to intimidate others from entering those areas, or to conceal illegal activities. Prior to making a determination under this subsection, the superintendent shall consult as he or she deems appropriate with persons who are knowledgeable about the effects of gang activity in areas in which the ordinance may be enforced. Such persons may include, but need not be limited to, members of the department of police with special training or experience related to criminal street gangs; other personnel of that department with particular knowledge of gang activities in the proposed designated area; elected and appointed officials of the area; community-based organizations; and participants in the Chicago Alternative Policing Strategy who are familiar with the area. The superintendent shall develop and implement procedures for the periodic review and update of designations made under this subsection.

(c) The superintendent shall by written directive promulgate procedures to prevent the enforcement of this section against persons who are engaged in collective advocacy activities that are protected by the Constitution of the United States or the State of Illinois.

(d) As used in this section:

(1) "Gang loitering" means remaining in any one place under circumstances that would warrant a reasonable person to believe that the purpose or effect of that behavior is to enable a criminal street gang to establish control

over identifiable areas, to intimidate others from entering those areas, or to conceal illegal activities.

(2) "Criminal street gang" means any ongoing organization, association in fact or group of three or more persons, whether formal or informal, having as one of its substantial activities the commission of one or more of the criminal acts enumerated in paragraph (3), and whose members individually or collectively engage in or have engaged in a pattern of criminal gang activity.

(3) "Criminal gang activity" means the commission, attempted commission or solicitation of the following offenses, provided that the offenses are committed by two or more persons, or by an individual at the direction of, or in association with, any criminal street gang, with the specific intent to promote, further or assist in any criminal conduct by gang members:

The following sections of the Criminal Code of 1961: 9-1 (murder), 9-3.3 (drug-induced homicide), 10-1 (kidnapping), 10-4 (forcible detention), subsection (a)(13) of Section 12-2 (aggravated assault — discharging firearm), 12-4 (aggravated battery), 12-4.1 (heinous battery), 12-4.2 (aggravated battery with a firearm), 12-4.3 (aggravated battery of a child), 12-4.6 (aggravated battery of a senior citizen), 12-6 (intimidation), 12-6.1 (compelling organization membership of persons), 12-11 (home invasion), 12-14 (aggravated criminal sexual assault), 18-1 (robbery), 18-2 (armed robbery), 19-1 (burglary), 19-3 (residential burglary), 19-5 (criminal fortification of a residence or building), 20-1 (arson), 20-1.1 (aggravated arson), 20-2 (possession of explosives or explosive or incendiary devices), subsections (a)(6), (a)(7), (a)(9) or (a)(12) of Section 24-1 (unlawful use of weapons), 24-1.1 (unlawful use or possession of weapons by felons or persons in the custody of the department of corrections facilities), 24-1.2 (aggravated discharge of a firearm), subsection (d) of Section 25-1 (mob action — violence), 33-1 (bribery), 33A-2 (armed violence), Sections 5, 5.1, 7 or 9 of the Cannabis Control Act where the offense is a felony (manufacture or delivery of cannabis, cannabis trafficking, calculated criminal cannabis conspiracy and related offenses), or Sections 401, 401.1, 405, 406.1, 407 or 407.1 of the Illinois Controlled Substances Act (illegal manufacture or delivery of a controlled substance, controlled substance trafficking, calculated criminal drug conspiracy and related offenses).

(4) "Pattern of criminal gang activity" means two or more acts of criminal gang activity of which at least two such acts were committed within five years of each other.

(5) "Public place" means the public way and any other location open to the public, whether publicly or privately owned.

(e) Any person who fails to obey promptly an order issued under subsection (a), or who engages in further gang loitering within sight or hearing of the place at which such an order was issued during the three-hour period following the time the order was issued, is subject to a fine of not less than $100.00 and not more than $500.00 for each offense, or imprisonment for not more than six months for each offense, or both. A second or subsequent offense shall be punishable by a mandatory minimum sentence of not less than five days imprisonment.

In addition to or instead of the above penalties, any person who violates this section may be required to perform up to 120 hours of community service pursuant to Section 1-4-120 of this code.
(Added. Coun. J. 2-16-00, p. 25705)

§8-4-017 Narcotics-related loitering.

(a) Whenever a police officer observes one or more persons engaged in narcotics-related loitering in any public place designated for the enforcement of this section under subsection (b), the police officer shall: (i) inform all such persons that they are engaged in loitering within an area in which such loitering is prohibited; (ii) order all such persons to disperse and remove themselves from within sight and hearing of the place at which the order was issued; and (iii) inform those persons that they will be subject to arrest if they fail to obey the order promptly or engage in further narcotics-related loitering within sight or hearing of the place at which the order was issued during the next three hours.

(b) The superintendent of police shall by written directive designate areas of the city in which enforcement of this section is necessary because the areas are frequently associated with narcotics-related loitering. Prior to making a determination under this subsection, the superintendent shall consult as he or she deems appropriate with persons who are knowledgeable about the effects of narcotics-related activity in areas in which the ordinance may be enforced. Such persons may include, but need not be limited to, members of the department of police with special training or experience related to narcotics-related activity; other personnel of that department with particular knowledge of narcotics-related activities in the proposed designated area; elected and appointed officials of the area; community-based organizations; and participants in the Chicago Alternative Policing Strategy who are familiar with the area. The superintendent shall develop and implement procedures for the periodic review and update of designations made under this subsection.

(c) As used in this section:

(1) "Narcotics-related loitering" means remaining in any one place under circumstances that would warrant a reasonable person to believe that the purpose or effect of that behavior is to facilitate the distribution of substances in violation of the Cannabis Control Act or the Illinois Controlled Substances Act.

(2) "Public place" means the public way and any other location open to the public, whether publicly or privately owned.

(d) Any person who fails to obey promptly an order issued under subsection (a), or who engages in further narcotics-related loitering within sight or hearing of the place at which such an order was issued during the three-hour period following the time the order was issued, is subject to a fine of not less than $100.00 and not more than $500.00 for each offense, or imprisonment for not more than six months for each offense, or both. A second or subsequent offense shall be punishable by a mandatory minimum sentence of not less than five days imprisonment.

In addition to or instead of the above penalties, any person who violates this section may be required to perform up to 120 hours of community service pursuant to Section 1-4-120 of this code.
(Added. Coun. J. 2-16-00, p. 25705)

§8-4-020 Inciting riots, etc.

It is unlawful to create a clear and present danger of a riot or assault, battery, or other unlawful trespass against any person or group of persons because of his or their race, religion, color, national origin, or ancestry, or to create a clear and present danger of arson, vandalism, defacement, or other unlawful trespass against property because of the race, religion, color, national origin, or ancestry of the owner, possessor, or authorized user or users of said property, or, in the case of a cemetery, of the decedent buried therein.

The term "person" as used in this section shall include one or more individuals, copartnerships, corporations, firms, organizations, associations, leagues, or other bodies.

Any person violating the provisions of this section shall be fined not less than $25.00 nor more than $200.00 or imprisoned for not less than 10 days or more than six months, or both, for each offense.
(Prior code § 193-1.1)

§8-4-025 Aggressive panhandling.

(a) Definitions. For purposes of this section:

(1) "Panhandling" means any solicitation made in person upon any street, public place or park in the city in which a person requests an immediate donation of money or other gratuity from another person, and includes but is not limited to seeking donations:

(A) By vocal appeal; or

(B) Where the person being solicited receives an item or service of little or no monetary value in exchange for a donation, under circumstances where a reasonable person would understand that the transaction is in substance a donation.

"Panhandling" shall not include the act of passively standing or sitting nor performing music, singing or other street performance with a sign or other indication that a donation is sought, without any vocal request except in response to an inquiry by another person. Nothing in this section shall be construed to permit any sound currently prohibited by Chapter 11-4 of this code.

(2) "Public place" shall mean any area to which the public is invited or permitted, and includes the public way.

(3) "Automated teller machine" means any automated teller machine as defined by the Automated Teller Machine Security Act, 205 ILCS 695, as amended.

(4) "Bank" means any bank or financial institution as defined by the Illinois Banking Act, 205 ILCS 5, as amended.

(5) "Currency exchange" means any currency exchange as defined by the Currency Exchange Act, 205 ILCS 405, as amended.

(b) It shall be unlawful to engage in an act of panhandling:

(1) When either the panhandler or the person being solicited is located within any of the following locations: within 10 feet of a bus shelter or

a posted Chicago Transit Authority bus stop sign; in any public transportation vehicle or public transportation facility; in a vehicle which is parked or stopped on a public street or alley, except for those solicitations permitted under Section 10-8-160 of this code; in a sidewalk cafe or restaurant; in a filling station; or within 10 feet in any direction from an automatic teller machine or entrance to a bank or currency exchange; or

(2) In a manner that a reasonable person would find intimidating, including any of the following actions when undertaken in a manner that a reasonable person would find intimidating:

(A) Touching the solicited person without the solicited person's consent;

(B) Panhandling a person while such person is standing in line and waiting to be admitted to a commercial establishment;

(C) Blocking the path of a person being solicited, or the entrance to any building or vehicle;

(D) Following behind, ahead or alongside a person who walks away from the panhandler after being solicited;

(E) Using profane or abusive language, either during the solicitation or following a refusal to make a donation, or making any statement, gesture, or other communication which would cause a reasonable person to be fearful or feel compelled; or

(F) Panhandling in a group of two or more persons.

(c) Any person who violates any provision of this section shall be subject to a fine of $50.00 for a first or second offense within a 12-month period, and a fine of $100.00 for a third or subsequent offense within a 12-month period.

(d) The provisions of this section are declared to be separate and severable. The invalidity of any provision of this section, or the invalidity of the application thereof to any person or circumstance shall not affect the validity of the remainder of this section, or the validity of its application to other persons or circumstances.

(Added. Coun. J. 9-29-04, p. 32193)

§8-4-030 Drinking in public ways.

(a) It shall be unlawful for any person to drink any alcoholic liquor as defined by law on any public way or in or about any motor vehicle upon a public way in the city. This section shall not apply to portions of the public way occupied by a sidewalk cafe permitted pursuant to Chapter 10-28 of the Municipal Code which is properly licensed to sell alcoholic liquor, or to any portion of the public way located on Navy Pier.

(b) It shall be unlawful for any person to transport, carry, possess or have any alcoholic liquor in or upon or about any motor vehicle upon any public way in the city except in the original package and with the seal unbroken.

(c) Any person violating any provision of this section shall be fined not less than $100.00 nor more than $500.00, or shall be punished by imprisonment for a period of six months, or by both such fine and imprisonment.

(Prior code § 193-1.2; Amend. Coun. J. 4-18-85, p. 15204; 6-14-95, p. 3087; 11-12-97, p. 56852; 3-15-00, p. 27687)

§8-4-040 Defacing and injuring house of worship and cemeteries.

Any person who wilfully defaces, mars, injures, destroys or removes any vault, tomb, monument, gravestone, memorial of the dead, church, synagogue, or any other structure constituting a place of worship of any religion, sect or group, or any part of any contents thereof, or any fence, tree, shrub or plant appurtenant thereto, shall be fined not less than $100.00 nor more than $500.00, or imprisoned for not more than six months, or both such fine and imprisonment, for each offense. Each such act of marring, injuring, destroying or removal shall constitute a separate offense.

(Prior code § 193-1.3)

§8-4-050 Trespassing.

A person commits trespass when he knowingly:

(a) Enters the property, or any part there of, of another when, immediately prior to such entry, he receives notice, either oral or written, from the owner or occupant that such entry is for bidden; or

(b) Remains upon the property, or any part thereof, of another after receiving notice, either oral or written, from the owner or occupant to depart; or

(c) Enters upon property open to the public, or any part thereof, and remains thereon with a malicious and mischievous intent after receiving notice, either oral or written, from the owner or occupant to depart;

(d) Wilfully defaces, mars, injures or destroys any building or part of any building or any property of another with paint, tar, acid, grease, oil, or other such substance which would detrimentally alter the outer face or sub stance of such building or any property of another, or any fence, tree, shrub or plant appurtenant thereto.

Any person convicted of trespass shall be fined not less than $100.00 nor more than $500.00.

(Prior code § 193-1.4)

§8-4-052 Anti-loitering and/or trespassing program.

(a) The department of police shall implement and enforce a program designed to maintain peace and discourage trespassing and other illegal activity within the program area.

(b) The program area shall include only property adjacent to South and West Archer Avenue between West 47th Street and South Harlem Avenue and the property adjacent to West 63rd Street between South Harlem Avenue and South Austin Avenue within the 23rd Ward of the city of Chicago.

(c) Any person owning or controlling property in the program area on which there is situated a parking lot or open space upon which vehicle may be parked shall erect and maintain signs stating "No Loitering" and "No Trespassing." The signs shall be displayed in a manner that makes them clearly visible from the sidewalk or street. The department of police shall enforce such signs at all times.

(d) No person may park a motor vehicle on any private property within the program area, including any parking lot of a business establishment, without the express or implied consent of the person who owns or controls the property. The department of police shall maintain separate computer records of information concerning persons suspect ed of violating this subsection.

(e) Any person who violates this section shall be subject to a fine of not less than $100.00 and not more than $200.00 for a first offense, and not less than $100.00 and not more than $300.00 for each subsequent offense.

(f) This section is repealed January 1, 1995.

(Added. Coun. J. 7-31-90, p. 19850; Amend. Coun. J. 4-22-93, p. 31524)

§8-4-054 Outdoor pay telephones prohibited.

(a) Except as otherwise provided in this section, no person shall install or maintain any telephone booth, mounted telephone, or other form of pay telephone not enclosed within the interior of a building unless it is located on the public way and in accordance with Section 10-28-265 of this code. Any outdoor pay telephone located on property other than the public way in violation of this section shall be removed by its owner, any person with control over the payphone, or the owner of real estate on which the payphone is located, within 30 days after the effective date of this section.

(b) Any person who violates any provision of subsection (a) of this section shall be subject to a fine of not less than $50.00 and not more than $200.00 for each offense. If an outdoor pay telephone is installed in violation of this section at substantially the same location where a telephone was previously removed pursuant to this section, any person participating in the violation shall be fined not less than $200.00 and not more than $500.00. Each day that a violation of subsection (a) continues shall constitute a separate offense. However, for the period ending six months after the effective date of this amendatory ordinance, no fine shall be imposed with respect to a telephone unless a removal notice has been posted on the telephone pursuant to this section.

(c) Notwithstanding any other provision of this section, the director of revenue may issue a revocable certificate of registration jointly authorizing the owner of real property on which a telephone is to be located and a telecommunications company that will operate the telephone, subject to the conditions of this section, the installation or maintenance of a telephone booth, mounted telephone, or other form of pay telephone not enclosed within the interior of a building and not on the public way, but permitted by this subsection (c). The certification of registration shall create no legal rights or entitlements, and shall not be deemed to create any type of vested interest. The application for the certificate of registration shall designate a registered agent for receiving notices under this section. Applications shall be maintained by the city as confidential business records. The certification shall be issued no later than 30 days after a complete application for an eligible location is received. No certificate of registration shall authorize installation of a telephone at a location that the director determines will not be in the public interest or may have a deleterious impact on the surrounding neighborhood. The director of revenue may issue a certificate of registration pursuant to this section for no more than two telephones on any zoning lot of property; provided that the number of telephones authorized under this section for any parking lot with 200 or more parking spaces, or for any property on which there are facilities designed for public assembly and having a capacity for more than 10,000 persons, shall not exceed a number determined by the director by rule as necessary for public convenience. No certificate of registration shall authorize a telephone situated: (i) on vacant property; (ii) on property on which there is situated an abandoned building; (iii) on property on which there is situated an establishment that has or requires a tavern license, or that is kept, used, maintained, advertised and held out to the public as a place that primarily sells alcoholic liquor at retail; or (iv) on property on which there is a building that is used primarily for residential purposes. Certificates of registration shall be issued for particular locations identified in the application therefor. The director of revenue by rule may establish and impose an application fee or an annual registration fee, or both, for certificates of registration issued under this section. The total amount of the fees may not exceed an amount sufficient for the city to recover its costs in administering this section, exclusive of costs directly related to preliminary or final hearings. A copy of each application for a certificate of registration shall be sent to the alderman for the ward in which the proposed telephone is to be located not less than five days after the application is received.

(d) Whenever the director of revenue determines that it is not in the public interest for the telephone to remain on private property, or that the telephone may have a deleterious impact on the surrounding neighborhood, the director shall initiate procedures to revoke the certificate of registration for that telephone. A certification by the alderman of the ward in which the telephone is or is to be located setting forth facts establishing that it is not in the public interest for the telephone to remain on private property, or that the telephone has a deleterious impact on the surrounding neighborhood, shall be prima facie evidence that the certificate of registration is subject to revocation or should not be issued under this section. Whenever the director makes such a determination with respect to a telephone for which a certificate of registration has been issued, the director shall attempt to notify the registrant of the determination by mailing a notice to the registered agent or the registrant, and a representative of the city of Chicago may enter upon any private property and may place upon the telephone a notice stating that the certificate of registration is subject to revocation and that the registrant has a right to request a preliminary hearing at which the registrant will be given an opportunity to be heard in opposition to the revocation within seven days of the notice. The preliminary hearing shall be informal and shall provide the registrant with an opportunity to address the reasons for the director's preliminary determination. If no preliminary hearing is requested or if the director determines that there is probable cause for revocation of the certificate of registration after the preliminary hearing, the director shall issue an order requiring the telephone and its appurtenances to be removed within seven days after the order is issued pending a final determination. Telephones that are not timely removed may be removed by a representative of the city of Chicago. The owner of a telephone for which a determination of probable cause for revocation of a certification of registration has been issued may contest such determination by timely removing the telephone and its appurtenances, and by filing with the director of revenue a request for a final hearing within 14 days after removal in accordance with rules promulgated with the director. Prior to the exercise of exclusive jurisdiction by the department of administrative hearings in accordance with Section 2-14-190(c) of this code, if, after a final hearing, the director of revenue determines that it is not in the public interest for the telephone to be located on the private property, or that the telephone has a deleterious impact on the surrounding neighborhood, the director shall revoke the certification of registration for that telephone. After the exercise of exclusive jurisdiction by the department of administrative hearings in accordance with Section 2-14-190(c) of this code, upon receipt of a request for a hearing, the director of revenue shall institute an action with the department of administrative hearings which shall appoint an administrative law officer who shall conduct the hearing and determine whether the certification of registration shall be revoked. Not withstanding the exercise of exclusive jurisdiction by the department of administrative hearings, if no timely request for a final hearing is made the director of revenue shall revoke the certification of registration for that telephone. No certificate of registration may be issued for a telephone at a zoning lot with respect to which a previous certificate has been revoked for a period of one year after revocation. At the preliminary and the final hearing, the formal or technical rules of evidence shall not apply. Evidence, including hearsay, may be admitted only if it is a type commonly relied upon by reasonably prudent persons in the conduct of their affairs. The director may establish and impose a fee for preliminary and final hearings conducted under this section. The total amount of the fees may not exceed an amount sufficient for the city to recover its costs directly related to the preliminary or final hearings.

(e) Outdoor pay telephones not lawfully installed or maintained pursuant to this code are hereby declared to be public nuisances subject to summary abatement upon due notice. A representative of the city of Chicago may enter upon any private property within the city of Chicago that he or she has reason to believe contains an outdoor pay telephone in violation of this section, and may place upon the telephone a notice that the telephone must be removed within seven days. Such notice shall also provide that if the telephone is not removed within seven days, a representative of the city of Chicago may remove the telephone and charge the costs of removal jointly and severally to its owner, operator, and the person who owns or controls the real property on which the pay telephone is located. If such telephone has not been removed within seven days, a representative of the city of Chicago may remove the telephone.

(f) If the costs to the city of Chicago of removing telephones and their appurtenances pursuant to this section are not paid within 30 days, the telephone shall be deemed abandoned and may be sold or destroyed. The costs of removing outdoor pay telephones shall be a debt to the city of Chicago jointly and severally owed by the telephone's owner and operator, and any person who owns or controls the real property on which the telephone was located.

(Added. Coun. J. 10-5-94, p. 57792; Amend. 7-10-96, p. 24982; 11-12-97, p. 56813; 4-29-98, p. 66564)

§8-4-055 Sound-emitting devices on public conveyances.

It is unlawful for any person to make use of any portable entertainment appliance, radio, used exclusively for entertainment, or musical instrument (and other sound-emitting devices), which are audible to others, in any streetcar, elevated train or subway and in any other public conveyance having a capacity of more than seven passengers operating within the city limits of the city of Chicago. Any person violating this section shall be fined not less than $50.00 nor more than $300.00 for each offense.

(Prior code § 193-7.11)

§8-4-058 Reserved.

(Deleted Coun. J. 2-16-200, p.25583)

§8-4-059 Possession of scanners illegal.

(a) Whenever used in this section, the word "scanner" means a radio set or apparatus (1) capable of receiving, transmitting, or both receiving and transmitting radio messages or signals within the wavelength or channel now or hereafter assigned by the Federal Communications Commission or its successor for use by law enforcement agencies; or (2) that may intercept or interfere with the transmission or reception of radio messages or signals by the department of police.

(b) No person shall use a scanner in such a way as to interfere with messages transmitted or received by the department of police. No person shall use a scanner to aid or abet the performance of any act in violation of any law or ordinance. The use of a scanner to aid or abet any illegal act shall be an offense separate and distinct from such illegal act.

(c) Any person who violates this section shall be subject to a fine of not less than $200.00 and not more than $500.00.

(Added. Coun. J. 7-14-93, p. 35538)

§8-4-060 Vandalism defined.

A person commits vandalism when he engages in the wilful or malicious destruction, injury, disfigurement, or defacement of any public or private property. This offense includes, but is not limited to, cutting, tearing, breaking, marking, drawing or painting when these actions are intend ed to or have the effect of causing damage to property.

Any person who violates the provisions of this section, upon conviction thereof shall be punished by a fine of $500.00 plus the actual costs incurred by the property owner or the city to abate, remediate, repair or remove the effects of the vandalism. To the extent permitted by law, the cost shall be payable to the person who incurred them. In addition to such fine and costs, any such offense may also be punished as a misdemeanor by incarceration in a penal institution other than a penitentiary for a term of up to 30 days or by a requirement to perform up to 1,500 hours of community service under the procedures set forth in Section 1-2-1.1 of the Illinois Municipal Code, as amended, and in the Illinois Code of Criminal Procedure of 1963, as amended, in a separate proceeding. All actions seeking the imposition of fines only shall be filed as quasi-criminal actions subject to the provisions of the Illinois Code of Civil Procedure, as amended.

(Prior code § 193-1.5; Amend. Coun. J. 10-6-86, p. 34526; 5-16-90, p. 15806; 6-12-91, p. 1718; 5-19-93, p. 32392; 5-20-98, p. 69305)

§8-4-061 Disposition of certain fines.

In all instances in which the fine set forth in Section 8-4.060 of the code is imposed by the city's department of administrative hearings for destruction, injury, disfigurement or other defacement of Chicago Transit Authority property, one-half of any such fine imposed and collected shall be made available to the Chicago Transit Authority for use in removing graffiti and other defacement of Chicago Transit Authority property.

(Added Coun. J. 7-29-98, p. 74138)

§8-4-065 Interference with utility equipment.

(a) When used in this section, "utility equipment" means any of the following located in a public way: (1) any lid, grate, screen or cover that allows access to any sewer, drain, electrical vault, coal hole, water vault, gas vault, tunnel or other opening or structure in the public way, or that allows the flow of water from the public way into a drain or sewer; (2) any light pole, lamp post, telephone or telegraph pole, or post or pole supporting electrical transformers or lines for transmission of electricity or cable television signals. "Utility equipment" may be either privately or publicly owned.

(b) No person shall:

(1) Intentionally and without authorization of the owner, remove utility equipment or damage or alter utility equipment so as to diminish its effectiveness or to create a public safety hazard;

(2) Without authorization of the actual owner, purchase, receive or possess illegally removed utility equipment. It is a defense to a prosecution under this subsection (b)(2) that the person charged with a violation did not know that the subject utility equipment was illegally removed;

(3) Assist any other person in any action prohibited in subsection (b)(1) or (b)(2) of this section.

(c) Any person who violates any provision of subsection (b) of this section shall, upon conviction, be punished by a fine of not less than $1,000.00. Any such offense may also be punished as a misdemeanor by incarceration in a penal institution other than a penitentiary for a term of up to six months or by a requirement to perform up to 1,000 hours of community service under the procedures set forth in Section 1-2-1.1 of the Illinois Municipal Code, as amend ed, and in the Illinois Code of Criminal Procedure, as amended, in a separate proceeding. All actions seeking the imposition of fines only shall be filed as quasi-criminal actions subject to the provisions of the Illinois Code of Civil Procedure, as amended.

(Added. Coun. J. 4-22-93, p. 31576; Amend. 4-12-00, p. 29744)

§8-4-070 Restitution—Financial responsibility.

In lieu of or in addition to a fine or incarceration or community service, any person found guilty of violating Section 8-4-060 or Section 8-4-065, or any parent or legal guardian of any unemancipated minor residing with such parent or legal guardian found guilty of such violation, may be required to submit full restitution to the victim or victims of such vandalism by monetary payment or property repairs.

In the case of an unemancipated minor accused of violating Section 8-4-060 or 8-04-065 and residing with a parent or legal guardian at the time of such violation, the department of police shall within three days notify such parent or legal guardian in writing, either by certified or registered mail, return receipt requested, that said minor has been accused of vandalism, and that said parent or legal guardian may be held financially responsible for any fines or restitution resulting from such vandalism.

(Prior code § 193-1.6; Amend. Coun. J. 5-16-90, p. 15806 4-22-93, p. 31576)

§8-4-075 Threatening a community policing volunteer.

(a) It shall be unlawful to knowingly deliver or convey to a community policing volunteer, in person, by mail, by telephone or in any other manner, a threat to inflict bodily harm upon the community policing volunteer or a member of his or her immediate family (1) with the intent to cause the community policing volunteer to perform or omit the performance of any act as a community policing volunteer; or (2) in retaliation for the community policing volunteer performing or omitting any act as a community policing volunteer.

(b) For purposes of this section, "community policing volunteer" means a person performing any work or duties that are prescribed by, guided by, or directed by members of the Chicago Police Department as part of Chicago's Alternative Policing Strategy (C.A.P.S.).

(c) Any person who violates this section shall be fined $200.00 and incarcerated up to 30 days for a first offense; fined $400.00 and incarcerated up to 90 days for a second offense; and fined $500.00 and incarcerated up to six months for a third or subsequent offense. Any person violating this provision shall also be required to perform 200 hours of community service. If supervision or probation is imposed, service of the aforementioned community service shall be a condition of supervision or probation.

(Added. Coun. J. 4-1-98, p. 65276)

§8-4-080 Definitions—Assault defined—Mandatory sentence.

(1) Definitions. The following definitions are applicable strictly in the context of this ordinance:

(A) "Elderly" refers to any person 60 years of age or older.

(B) "Developmentally disabled" means as defined in Illinois Revised Statutes Chapter 91½, Section 1-106.

(C) "Handicapped" means as defined in Illinois Revised Statutes Chapter 68, Section 1-103(l).

(D) "Battery" means as defined in Illinois Revised Statutes Chapter 38-12-3.

(2) There is hereby created the offense of assault against the elderly, developmentally disabled, or handicapped. A person commits assault against the elderly, developmentally disabled, or handicapped when he engages in conduct which places a person as defined above in reasonable apprehension of receiving a battery. Upon conviction of this offense, a mandatory sentence of imprisonment shall be imposed, not to be less than 90 days nor more than 180 days.

(Prior code § 193-1.7; Added. Coun. J. 4-13-84, p. 6076)

§8-4-081 Public urination.

Any person who urinates or defecates on the public way, or on any outdoor public property, or on any outdoor private property, shall be guilty of a misdemeanor and shall be fined not less than $100.00 nor more than $500.00, or incarcerated for no less than five days and no more than 10 days, or both fined and incarcerated. This section shall not apply to use of a temporary or permanent structure or enclosure erected outdoors for use as a toilet facility.

(Added. Coun. J. 7-31-02, p. 91449)

§8-4-085 Hate crimes.

(a) No person shall, by reason of any motive or intent relating to, or any antipathy, animosity or hostility based upon, the actual or perceived race, color, sex, religion, national origin, age, ancestry, sexual orientation or mental or physical disability of another individual or group of individuals:

(1) Commit assault as defined in Section 12-1 of the Illinois Criminal Code of 1961 (Illinois Revised Statutes Chapter 38, paragraph 12-1); or

(2) Deface, mar, injure, destroy or remove property in violation of Section 8-4-040 of this code; or

(3) Commit trespass as defined in Section 8-4-050 of this code; or

(4) Commit vandalism as defined in Section 8-4-060 of this code; or

(5) Disturb a place of worship in violation of Section 8-4-110 of this code; or

(6) Engage in harassment by telephone as defined in Section 1-1 of "An Act to prohibit the use of telephone and telegraph lines for the sending of certain messages" (Illinois Revised Statutes Chapter 134, paragraph 16-4.1).

(b) Any person who violates this section shall be subject to a fine of $500.00 or may be imprisoned for not more than six months, or may be subject to both such fine and imprisonment. In addition to such penalty, any person found guilty of violating this section may be ordered to pay restitution to the ag grieved party, and may be ordered to perform community service pursuant to Section 1-4-120 of this code.

(c) Notwithstanding any other provision of this section, any conduct in violation of this section that is punishable under state or federal law by a term of imprisonment in excess of six months shall not be prosecuted under this section.

(d) As used in this section, "sexual orientation" means heterosexuality, homosexuality or bisexuality.

(Added. Coun. J. 12-19-90, p. 27888)

§8-4-086 Prohibition against racial profiling.

No member of the Chicago Police Department or peace officer or security personnel (as those terms are defined in the Municipal Code of Chicago, Chapter 8-20-030) employed or engaged in their duties within the corporate boundaries of the City of Chicago shall use actual or perceived race, ethnicity, gender, religion, disability, sexual orientation, marital status, parental status, military discharge status, financial status or lawful source of income as the sole factor in determining the existence of probable cause to stop, question, place in custody or arrest an individual or in constituting a reasonable and articulable suspicion that an offense has been or is being committed so as to justify the detention of an individual or the investigatory stop of a motor vehicle.

(Added. Coun. J. 6-6-01, p. 60144)

§8-4-090 Drug and gang houses, houses of prostitution and other disorderly houses.

(a) Any premises used for prostitution, illegal gambling, illegal possession or delivery of or trafficking in controlled substances, or any other activity that constitutes a felony, misdemeanor, business offense or petty offense under federal, state or municipal law is hereby declared to be a public nuisance; provided that no public nuisance or violation of this section shall be deemed to exist unless (i) the property is used for more than one such offense within any six-month period, or (ii) the offense for which the property is used is punishable by imprisonment for one year or more.

(b) Any person who owns, manages or controls any premises and who (i) encourages or permits an illegal activity described in subsection (a) to occur or continue on such premises; or (ii) fails to implement reasonable and warranted abatement measures identified in the notice issued by the commissioner of buildings, the superintendent of police or other authorized representative of the city, pursuant to subsection (d), or subsequently agreed to, or other abatement measures which successfully abate the nuisance within the 30 day period following the notice, or within any other agreed upon period, shall be subject to a fine of not less than $200.00 and not more than $500.00 for each offense. Each day that a violation of this section continues shall be considered a separate and distinct offense. No person shall be found in violation of (b)(ii) of this section unless the city proves by a preponderance of the evidence that the abatement measures were reasonable and warranted, and that the defendant knowingly failed to implement them. A person may be found in violation of (b)(i) or (b)(ii) of this section regardless of whether an order of abatement is issued under subsection (c) or in violation of (b)(i) regardless of whether a notice has been given under subsection (d). A fine in accordance with this subsection may be assessed in a court of competent jurisdiction or in the buildings hearings division of the department of administrative hearings.

(c) The building commissioner or other authorized representative of the city may bring an action to abate a public nuisance described by this section in a court of competent jurisdiction or in the buildings hearings division of the department of administrative hearings. An order of abatement shall be issued whenever a person who owns, manages or controls any premises violates subsection (b). The order of abatement shall require the taking of reasonable measures designed to prevent the recurrence of the illegal activity described in subsection (a) in light of the magnitude of the harm caused by the nuisance, the value of the property, and the extent to which the defendant has failed to take effective measures to abate the nuisance. Those measures may include, but are not limited to, making improvements to real estate and installing lighting to enhance security, the hiring of licensed and insured security personnel, the hiring of a receiver, the initiation and execution of eviction proceedings against tenants engaged in illegal activity, or, at the request of the corporation counsel, the assignment or forfeiture to the city of all of the defendant's rights, title and interest in the real estate when the defendant has failed to abate a nuisance following an order issued pursuant to this paragraph, or has failed to abate a nuisance within 30 days of a notice issued pursuant to paragraph (b) of this section, and: (i) a forcible felony as defined in Section 2-8 of the Criminal Code of 1961 (720 ILCS 5/2-8) is committed on the premises, or (ii) two or more violations of the Illinois Controlled Substances Act or the Cannabis Control Act occur on the property on separate days within a one year period. In no event shall any interest of any person or entity not an owner of real estate as defined in Section 13-4-010 of this code be forfeited. The order of abatement may also authorize the issuance of ex parte administrative search warrants reasonably calculated to determine whether the nuisance has been abated or whether the order of the court or hearing officer has been obeyed. Any person who fails to comply with an order of abatement issued under this section by an administrative law officer of the department of administrative hearings shall be subject to the penalties set forth in Section 2-14-100 of this code.

(d) Whenever the commissioner of buildings, the superintendent of police or other authorized representative of the city reasonably believes that any premises constitutes a public nuisance as described in this section, he or she may give written notice to the person who owns or controls the premises stating that a nuisance exists and identifying reasonable abatement measures that must be taken within 30 days of the notice. The notice shall be in writing and may be served in person or sent by certified mail, return receipt requested. The notice shall provide the recipient a reasonable opportunity to meet with a representative of the city to discuss allegations in the notice and the need for abatement measures. Upon the failure to implement the abatement measures identified in the notice, or subsequently agreed to, or other abatement measures which successfully abate the nuisance within the 30 day period following the notice, or within any other agreed upon period, the issuer of the notice may issue a citation against the person who owns, controls or manages the premises for a violation of subsection (b)(ii).

(e) For purposes of this section, "premises" includes any parcel of property and the building or structure, if any, which is situated on the property, and any portion of the public way that abuts the parcel of property when it is used in conjunction with the abutting property for the commission of illegal activity.

(f) Any property assigned or forfeited to the city under this section may be disposed of as authorized by the city council.

(Added. Coun. J. 12-9-92, p. 25986; Amend. 7-31-96, p. 27730; Amend. 8-30-11, Coun. J. p. 40306)

§8-4-091 Prohibited manner of managing or controlling real estate.

It shall be a violation of this section when any person who, when having management authority over or control of residential real estate, whether as a legal or equitable owner or as a managing agent or otherwise, recklessly permits the physical condition or facilities of the residential real estate to become or remain in any condition which endangers the health or safety of any person. Such conduct shall include, but not be limited to, (a) recklessly allowing property to be improperly secured, resulting in the commission of a crime against a resident of the property or against any other person, (b) recklessly allowing property to collapse or partially collapse, resulting in injury to a person inside or outside of a building, (c) recklessly allowing property to remain in violation of applicable building code, fire code, or other applicable code provisions, (d) recklessly failing to respond to reasonable requests by the city to repair a property that is in violation of an applicable provision of the Municipal Code, or (e) recklessly endangering the health and safety of any person by illegally altering or modifying a structure to increase the number of dwelling units or living spaces within the structure, or by allowing any such alteration or modification to continue or to be used. Any person found to have violated this section shall be: (a) subject to a fine of not less than $500.00 for each offense, (b) incarcerated for not more than 180 days, and/or

(c) ordered to perform community service for a period not to exceed 200 hours. A separate and distinct offense shall be regarded as committed each day on which such person shall continue any such violation.

This section shall not apply to any freestanding, owner-occupied single-family home or to any owner-occupied townhouse; provided, however, that this exception shall not apply to a single-family home, or to a townhouse, which is rented, or to any structure that is altered or modified in violation of Title 17, Section 11.13-1 (17-44-565) of the Municipal Code. For purposes of this section a townhouse shall refer to: one of a row of houses connected by common side walls.

(Added. Coun. J. 2-8-95, p. 65368; Amend. 2-7-96, p. 15460)

§8-4-100 Reserved.

(Repealed Coun. J. 10-3-2001, p.68135)

§8-4-110 Disturbing places of worship.

Any person who shall disquiet or disturb any congregation or assembly met for religious worship by making a noise, or by rude and indecent behavior or profane discourse within the place of worship, or so near to the same as to disturb the order and solemnity of the meeting, shall be fined not exceeding $50.00 for each offense.

(Prior code § 193-4)

§8-4-120 Damage to public property.

No person shall cut, injure, mark, damage or deface any public building, sewer, water pipe, hydrant, or other city property, fixture or personal property, or any tree, grass, shrub, or walk in any public way or public park.

Any person violating any provision of this section shall be fined not less than $200.00 nor more than $500.00 for each offense.

(Prior code § 193-5; Amend. Coun. J. 7-29-98, p. 75096)

§8-4-125 Use of cell phones/cameras/camera phones in public privacy areas.

No person shall use a camera/cell phone or other device capable of preserving and/or transmitting an image in any public "privacy area". For purposes of this section, "privacy area" shall be defined as rooms in structures, or other areas whether or not enclosed, designated for the administration of examinations, clinics, hospitals and areas where a person should reasonably expect to have privacy, including but not limited to showers, locker rooms/changing rooms, bathrooms, lactation rooms, automatic teller machine areas, and cashier lines. Possession of said devices in these areas is lawful if the image preserving and/or transmitting portion of the device is not operational.

Videotaping, photographing and filming by law enforcement officers pursuant to a lawful criminal investigation is exempt from this section.

Any person violating any provision of this section shall be fined not less than $5.00 nor more than $500.00 for each offense.

(Added. Coun. J. 3-10-04, p. 19865)

§8-4-130 Possession of paint or marker with intent to deface unlawful.

(a) It shall be unlawful for any person to possess a spray paint container, liquid paint or any marker containing a fluid which is not water soluble and has a point, brush, applicator or other writing surface of three-eighths of an inch or greater, on the property of another or in any public building or upon any public facility. It shall be a defense to an action for violation of this subsection that the owner, manager or other person having control of the property, building or facility consented to the presence of the paint or marker.

(b) It shall be unlawful for any person to possess a spray paint container, liquid paint or any marker containing a fluid which is not water soluble and has a point, brush, applicator or other writing surface of three-eighths of an inch or greater, or any etching equipment or etching materials, on the public way with intent to use the same to deface any building, structure or property.

(c) It shall be unlawful for any person to transport, carry, possess or have any spray paint container, liquid paint or any marker containing a fluid which is not water soluble and has a point, brush, applicator or other writing surface of three-eighths of an inch or greater, or any etching equipment or etching materials, in or upon or about any motor vehicle with intent to use the same to deface any building, structure or property.

(d) For purposes of this section, "etching equipment" and "etching materials" include any tool, device, equipment or substance that can be used to make permanent marks on metal, glass, plastic, concrete or stone.

(e) Any person who violates any provision of this section shall be subject to a fine of not less than $500.00 for each offense.

(f) A motor vehicle that is used in the violation of subsection (c) of this section shall be subject to seizure and impoundment under this subsection (f). The owner of record of such vehicle shall be liable to the city for an administrative penalty of $500.00 in addition to fees for towing and storage of the vehicle. Whenever a police officer has probable cause to believe that a vehicle is subject to seizure and impoundment pursuant to this subsection, the police officer shall provide for the towing of the vehicle to a facility controlled by the city or its agents. When the vehicle is towed, the police officer shall notify the person who is found to be in control of the vehicle at the time of the alleged violation if there is such a person, of the fact of the seizure and of the vehicle owner's right to request a preliminary hearing to be conducted under Section 2-14-132 of this code. The provisions of Section 2-14-132 shall apply whenever a motor vehicle is seized and impounded pursuant to this section.

(Prior code § 193-5.1; Added. Coun. J. 2-11-87, p. 39504; Amend. 5-20-92, p. 17016; 2-10-93, p. 28505; 7-21-99, p. 9095)

§8-4-135 Defacement of commercial vehicles.

(a) It shall be unlawful for any person to own or operate a defaced commercial vehicle in the city of Chicago, subject to the exceptions provided in this section. The commissioner of streets and sanitation or his designee is authorized to take action necessary for effective enforcement of this section, including the issuance of citations.

(b) Any person who owns or operates a defaced commercial vehicle in the city of Chicago, when such defacement is not placed upon such vehicle by the owner, lessee, or person lawfully in possession of the vehicle, or a person acting with the consent of the owner, lessee or person lawfully in possession, shall be fined not less than $100.00 nor more than $500.00 for each offense. Each day that a violation continues shall be considered a separate and distinct offense.

(c) For purposes of this section, "commercial vehicle" shall refer to: (1) a motor vehicle operated of the transportation of persons or property in the furtherance of any commercial or industrial enterprise and includes, but is not limited to, tow trucks, semi-trailers and trailers; and (2) a railroad car or railroad container car that remains in the city of Chicago for a continuous five-day period or longer; "defacement" or "defaced" shall refer to any marking or drawing on a commercial vehicle but does not refer to:

(1) Any sign, marking, drawing or communication relating to the business that owns or operates the vehicle which is placed on the vehicle with the consent of the person or commercial or industrial enterprise that owns or operates the vehicle;

(2) Any marking that was placed upon the vehicle in the manufacturing process or as part of any repair or re-painting of the vehicle;

(3) Any form of business identification;

(4) Any sign or symbol relating to safety;

(5) Any sign, symbol or marking required by federal, state or local law or regulation;

(6) Any sign or symbol relating to hazardous materials or waste;

(7) Any sticker or sign affixed by the seller or dealer of a commercial vehicle; or

(8) Any marking or drawing, placed upon a vehicle by the owner of the vehicle or a person acting with the consent of the owner.

(d) It is a rebuttable presumption under this section that any defacement placed on a commercial vehicle that is not referred to in those exceptions set forth in subsections (1) through (7) above was placed on the vehicle by a person other than the owner or operator of the vehicle.

(Added. Coun. J. 12-1-93, p. 43378; Amend. 2-16-00, p. 25795)

§8-4-140 Injuring or obstructing signal systems.

No person, unless duly authorized, shall open any signal box, unless it be to give an alarm of fire or to communicate with the police on necessary business, nor break, cut, injure, deface, derange, or in any manner meddle or interfere with any signal box or the fire-alarm or police telegraph wires, or with any municipal electric wires, poles, conduits, or apparatus. Any person violating any of the foregoing provisions of this section shall be fined not less than $25.00 nor more than $50.00 for each offense.

Any person who shall scratch, stencil, or post placards or bills on any of the poles used for wires of the police and fire alarm telegraph, or in any other manner deface or injure the same, shall be fined not less than $5.00 nor more than $20.00 for each offense.

(Prior code § 193-6)

§8-4-145 False alarms.

Whoever, without reasonable cause, either:

(i) By outcry or otherwise, makes or circulates, or causes to be made or circulated, any false alarm of fire; or

(ii) Calls the number "911" for the purpose of making or transmitting a false alarm or complaint and reporting information when, at the time the call or transmission is made, the person knows that the call or transmission could result in the emergency response of any city department or agency, shall be fined not less than $500.00 nor more than $1,000.00 for each offense.
(Prior code § 193-7; Amend. Coun. J. 12-15-04, p. 40218)

§8-4-150 Use of sirens for air raid alarms only.

For the duration of any war in which the United States is engaged no person, including without limiting the generality of the word "person" all persons upon an authorized emergency vehicle, shall sound a siren for any purpose. For the purposes of this section, the term "siren" shall not include a foghorn when used for the protection of navigation in and about the Chicago Harbor.

This section shall not apply to any person officially designated by the mayor to sound a siren as an air raid alarm.

Any person violating the provisions of this section shall be fined not less than $100.00 nor more than $200.00 for each offense.
(Prior code § 193-6.1)

§8-4-160 Reserved.
(Deleted. Coun. J. 3-31-04, p. 20916)

§8-4-170 Reserved.
(Repealed. Coun. J.10-3-01, p. 68136)

§8-4-180 Possessing burglar's tools.

A person possesses burglary tools when he possesses any tool, key, instrument, device, or any explosive suitable for use in breaking into any building, housetrailer, water craft, aircraft, vehicle, railroad car, or any depository de signed for the safekeeping of property, or any part thereof, with intent to enter any such place and with intent to commit therein a felony or theft.

A person convicted of the possession of burglary tools shall be fined not less than $25.00 nor more than $500.00.
(Prior code § 193-10)

§8-4-190 Throwing objects on athletic fields.

No person shall throw, drop, or place upon any baseball park, athletic field, or other place where games are played any bottle or other glass receptacle or any broken bottle or other broken instrument or thing. Any person violating any of the provisions of this section shall be fined not less than $25.00 nor more than $200.00 for each offense.
(Prior code § 193-12)

§8-4-195 Illegal conduct within sports facilities.

(a) For purposes of this section:

"Sports facility" means any enclosed or partially enclosed stadium used for sporting events or athletic contests or both and having a seating capacity in excess of 3,000 persons.

"Restricted area" includes: the playing field, court, playing surface, swimming pool and any other portion of a sports facility used for sporting events or athletic contest; a locker room, a warm-up area, a team assembly area, a team bench area and any other portion of a sports facility closed by the facility operator to spectators or patrons.

(b) No person shall enter or remain in or on any restricted area of a sports facility except with the express permission of the facility's operator. Any person who violates this subsection (b) shall be guilty of a misdemeanor and upon conviction shall be subject to a fine of $1,000 and incarceration for a period not less than 30 days and not more than six months.

(c) Within the portion of a sports facility where patrons and spectators are permitted, no person shall intentionally or knowingly, and without legal justification (1) cause bodily harm to an individual or (2) make physical contact of an insulting or provoking nature with an individual. Any person who violates this subsection (c) shall be guilty of a misdemeanor and upon conviction shall be subject to a fine of up to $1,000 and/or incarceration for a period not to exceed six months.

(d) Actions under this section shall be filed and prosecuted as misdemeanor actions under the procedure set forth in Section 1-2-1.1 of the Illinois Municipal Code, as amended.

(Added. Coun. J. 6-4-03, p. 2466)

§8-4-200 Objects on sills or railings.

It shall not be lawful for any person to place or keep on any window-sill, railing, or balcony, top of porch, or any other projection from any house or other building in the city, any flower pot, wooden box, bowl, pitcher, or other article or thing unless the same is securely and firmly fastened or protected so as to render it impossible for any such pot, bowl, pitcher or other article to fall into the public way. Any person violating this section shall be fined not more than $50.00 for each offense.

(Prior code § 193-13)

§8-4-210 Spikes in railings and fences.

No owner, lessee, or person in possession of any building in this city shall erect, maintain, or permit to be erect ed or maintained on or about the stairway in, or the entrance to, such building, or on or about its exterior building line, or upon any portion of the sidewalk adjacent to such building, any railing, fence, guard, or protection of any kind, upon which there shall be affixed or in any manner attached so as to protrude therefrom any spike, nail, or other pointed instrument of any kind or description, unless such protrusion shall be an integral part of the fencing located entirely on private property; and unless any such protrusion, projecting vertically upward, shall be at least six feet in height above the ground; and unless any such protrusion, projecting vertically downward, shall be not more than six inches from the ground. Any person violating

any of the provisions of this section shall be fined not less than $25.00 nor more than $50.00 for each offense; and each day any such person shall fail or neglect to re move from such railing, fence, or other protection, any such spike, nail, or other pointed instrument after notice in writing from the commissioner of buildings so to do, shall constitute a separate and distinct offense.
(Prior code § 193-14)

§8-4-220 Clay holes and excavations.

The owner, lessee or person in possession of any real estate within the city upon which are located or situated any clay holes or other similar excavations is hereby required to cause such clay holes or other excavations to be enclosed with wooden or wire fences, of not less than six feet in height. When such fences are of wire only smooth or nonbarbed wire shall be used below a height of six feet above the established grade or above the ground where no grade has been established, and such fence or fences shall consist of not less than eight rows of wire, and such rows of wire shall not be more than nine inches apart.
(Prior code § 193-15)

§8-4-230 Use of flag—Misdemeanor.

Any person who (a) for exhibition or display, places or causes to be placed any word, figure, mark, picture, design, drawing, or any advertisement of any nature, upon any flag, standard, color or ensign of the United States, or any foreign flag of any nation or ensign, or state flag of this state or ensign, or city flag of this city or ensign, (b) exposes or causes to be exposed to public view any such flag, standard, color or ensign, upon which has been printed, painted or otherwise placed, or to which has been attached, appended, affixed, or annexed, any word, figure, mark, picture, design or drawing or any advertisement of any nature, (c) exposes to public view, manufactures, sells, exposes for sale, gives away, or has in possession for sale or to give away or for use for any purpose, any article of substance, being an article of merchandise, or a receptacle of merchandise or article or thing for carrying or transporting merchandise upon which has been printed, painted, attached, or otherwise placed a representation of any such flag, standard, color, or ensign, to advertise, call attention to, decorate, mark or distinguish the article or substance on which so placed, or (d) shall knowingly mutilate, deface, defile or defy, trample or cast contempt upon by offensive touching or laying upon the ground or floor, any such flag, standard, color or ensign shall be guilty of a misdemeanor and subject to imprisonment not to exceed six months and a fine not to exceed $250.00 for each offense.
(Prior code § 193-16; Amend. Coun. J. 3-16-89, p. 25723)

§8-4-240 Ragpicking—Peddling—Junk collection.

No person shall engage in the occupation of ragpicking, the peddling of any article or thing, or the purchasing or collection of junk by handcart, automobile or other vehicle in any public alley between the hours of 9:00 p.m. and 7:00 a.m., except in the area bounded on the north by the Chicago River, on the south by East and West Roosevelt Road, on the east by Lake Michigan and on the west by the Chicago River; provided no ragpicking shall be permitted at any time of the day or night on Sundays or legal holidays. Any person violating this section shall be fined not less than $5.00 nor more than $50.00 for each offense.

(Prior code § 193-17; Amend. Coun. J. 10-7-98, p. 78812)

§8-4-250 Trespassing on property.

No person shall enter into or upon any lot, block, or tract of ground in the city which is under cultivation, unless such person be an owner, lessee, or person entitled so to enter, or the duly authorized agent thereof, and any person found by the police in and upon any such premises shall be treated as a trespasser unless he can produce satisfactory evidence of ownership or right to be in and upon any such premises.

Any person who shall violate the provisions of this section shall be fined not less than $50.00 nor more than $100.00 for each offense.

(Prior code § 193-18; Amend. Coun. J. 12-4-02, p. 99931)

§8-4-260 Trespassing on elevated track.

Whenever any track of any railroad in the city has been or may hereafter be elevated in accordance with the ordinances of the city, no person shall wilfully trespass upon said elevated roadway or track, nor shall anyone aid, abet, or assist therein; provided, however, that the employees of such railroad, acting in the discharge of their duties, may enter or be upon, or walk along or cross such elevated tracks or roadway at any place.

(Prior code § 193-19)

§8-4-270 Advertising and signs on buildings.

No person shall post, stick, stamp, tack, paint, or otherwise fix, or cause the same to be done by another person, any notice, placard, bill, handbill, sign, poster, card advertisement, or other device calculated to attract the attention of the public, upon any building or part thereof, wall or part thereof, or window, without first obtaining the written consent of the owner, agent, lessee, or occupant of such premises or structure; provided, however, that no person shall paste, post, or fasten any handbill, poster, advertisement, or notice of any kind, or cause the same to be done, which exceeds 12 square feet in area without first obtaining a permit so to do from the executive director of the department of construction and permits in accordance with the provisions of this code relating to billboards and signboards; and provided, further, that this section shall not apply to advertising matter upon billboards owned or controlled by private individuals.

(Prior code § 193-20; Amend. Coun. J. 3-5-03, p. 104990)

§8-4-280 Removing sod or earth.

No person shall dig, cut, or remove any sod or earth from any public way within the city without a permit from the commissioner of transportation, or from any other public place within the city without a permit from the com missioner of general services, or from any premises not his own without the consent of the owner, under a penalty of not less than $50.00 for each offense.

(Prior code § 193-21; Amend. Coun. J. 12-11-91, p. 10832)

§8-4-290 Removal of sod along public way.

No person shall dig, cut or remove any sod or earth from any property adjoining or contiguous to a public way in such a manner as to leave said property in an unsafe or unsanitary condition or in such condition as will constitute a public nuisance.
(Prior code § 193-21.1)

§8-4-300 Reserved.

(Repealed. Coun. J. 10-3-01, p. 68136)

§8-4-310 Forging signatures.

Whenever it may be necessary, in order to procure a license, permit, grant, or privilege of any kind or to obtain a referendum vote on any proposition, to secure signatures to a petition for the same under the provisions of this code or under any law or ordinance affecting the whole or any part of the city, it shall be unlawful for any person, individually, or any firm or corporation by its members, officers or agents, to forge the signature or procure the forging of the signature to the same of any person who is by law qualified to sign such petition, or to sign or pro cure the signing of a fictitious name to such petition, or to procure the signature to the same of the person qualified to sign such petition by payment of money or other valuable thing to the person so signing.

Any person that shall violate the provisions of this section by forging a signature, signing a fictitious name, or purchasing a signature, or by procuring the doing of same, shall be fined not less than $5.00 nor more than $200.00 dollars for each offense, and the signing or procuring of each false or fraudulent name to such petition shall be regarded as a distinct and separate offense.
(Prior code § 193-23)

§8-4-315 Fraud relating to official documents.

(a) For purposes of this section, "official documents" refers to any document produced by a government agency, including but not limited to a driver's license, identification card or paper, or certificate relating to a foreign citizen's resident status, such as visa, entry, citizenship and resident alien documents. A person commits fraud relating to official documents when he:

(i) Misrepresents to any person that a document is official or that a document has been produced by, produced on behalf of, or authorized by the I.N.S. or any other government agency, when the document in fact has not been produced by a government agency; or

(ii) Misrepresents to any person that he is legally authorized or otherwise qualified to obtain or dispense official documents; or

(iii) Makes any false or misleading statement regarding any person's eligibility to obtain permanent resident status in the United States.

(b) Any person who violates subsection (a) of this section shall be subject to a fine of not less than $500.00 nor more than $1,500.00, plus the actual costs incurred by the victim that can be directly attributed to the fraud. To the extent permitted by law, the costs shall be payable to the person who incurred them.

(c) In addition to the penalties specified in subsection (b) of this section, violators of this section are subject to all applicable enforcement provi-

sions in Title 4 of the Municipal Code, and the rules and regulations promulgated thereunder; and to orders of injunctive relief entered by a court or administrative agency of competent jurisdiction.
(Added. Coun. J. 7-29-98, p. 75082)

§8-4-320 Deceptive advertising.

No person shall, with intent to sell or in anywise dispose of merchandise, securities, ser vice, or anything offered directly or indirectly to the public for sale or distribution, or with intent to increase the consumption thereof, or to induce the public in any manner to enter into any obligation relating thereto, or to acquire title thereto or any interest therein, make, publish, disseminate, circulate, or place before the public, or cause directly or indirectly to be made, published, disseminated, circulated, or placed before the public, in this city, in any newspaper or other publication sold or offered for sale upon any public way, or other public place, or on any sign upon any public way or other public place, or in any handbill or advertisement posted upon any public way or public place, or on any placard, advertisement, or handbill exhibited or carried in any public way or public place, or on any banner or sign flying across the public way or from any house, an advertisement of any sort regarding merchandise, securities, service, or anything so offered to the public, which advertisement contains any assertion, representation, or statement which is untrue, deceptive, or mislead ing. Any person violating any provision of this section shall be fined not less than $25.00 nor more than $200.00 for each offense.
(Prior code § 193-24)

§8-4-321 International wire transfers— Posting of notice required.

A person engaged in the business of transmitting money by wire to a location outside the United States of America shall post a sign in a conspicuous location on the premises where such transactions occur. The sign shall be in English, Spanish and Polish, in capital letters of no less than 18 point type, and shall state as follows:

> In Addition To The Fees Applicable To This Transaction, A Currency Conversion Rate Will Be Applied To This Transaction If This Transaction Is Paid Out In A Currency Other Than United States Dollars. This Currency Rate Constantly Changes. Please Ask The Clerk For Information Concerning Fees And The Currency Exchange Rate Applicable To This Transaction.

Any person who violates this section shall be subject to a fine of not less than $100.00 and not more than $500.00, for each offense, or incarceration of not less than 10 days and not more than 30 days for each offense, or both a fine and incarceration. Each day that a violation continues shall constitute a separate and distinct offense. Nothing in this section shall apply to a bank or trust company that is organized under state, federal or foreign law or to any affiliate thereof.
(Added. Coun. J. 5-20-98, p. 68166)

§8-4-325 Deceptive practices—Residential real estate.

(a) No person shall engage in any act of consumer fraud or unfair method of competition or deceptive practice in connection with any contract which may result in the foreclosure on any residential real estate that is situated within the city. Nothing in this section shall be construed as permitting the regulation of any business to the extent that such regulation is not permitted under the statutory or home rule powers of the city.

(b) The commissioner of consumer services shall be charged with the enforcement of this section, and may institute an action in the department of administrative hearings to determine liability and seek remedies provided in this section.

(c) Any person who violates this section shall be subject to a fine of not less than $500.00 and not more than $10,000.00, and may be ordered to pay restitution and may be subject to other equitable relief.

(Added. Coun. J. 8-30-00, p. 39074)

§8-4-330 Recruitment restrictions.

No person shall force, threaten to use force, intimidate or coerce another to join any group, club or organization. This section shall not apply to persons engaged in lawful concerted activities governed and protected by the federal statute commonly known as the "National Labor Relations Act."

(a) Any person violating any of the provisions of this section shall be fined not less than $500.00 for each offense or shall be punished by imprisonment for a period of not more than six months or both.

(b) In addition to any other means authorized by law, the city may enforce this section by instituting an action with the department of administrative hearings.

(c) Nothing in this section shall preclude the city from seeking to collect any debt due the city through the use of any other administrative procedure or court proceeding authorized by law.

(Added. Coun. J. 12-15-99, p. 21529)

§8-4-340 Charitable entertainments—Restriction on promotional materials.

No person shall use any ticket, poster, placard, badge, or other advertisement in the promotion of any dance, bazaar, picnic, game, theater, or other entertainment or performance purporting to be given for charitable purposes unless the names of the persons or organizations intended to be benefited by the receipts from such entertainment or performance are stated on such ticket, poster, placard, badge, or other advertisement.

Any person violating any of the provisions of this section shall be fined not less than $10.00 nor more than $200.00 for each offense.

(Prior code § 193-27)

§8-4-350 Reserved.

(Repealed Coun. J.10-3-2001, p.28443)

§8-4-355 Reserved.

(Renumbered to 1-20. Coun. J. 7-21-04, p.28443)

§8-4-360 Violation—Penalty.

Any person violating any of the provisions of this chapter, where no other penalty is specifically provided, shall be fined not more than $200.00 for each offense.
(Prior code § 193-35 (part))

CHAPTER 8-8
PUBLIC MORALS

Sections:

8-8-010 House of ill-fame or assignation.
8-8-020 Directing persons to houses of ill-fame.
8-8-030 Prostitution or lewdness in conveyances.
8-8-040 Revocation of license.
8-8-050 Soliciting—Penalty.
8-8-060 Street solicitation for prostitution.
8-8-070 Reserved.
8-8-080 Indecent exposure or dress.
8-8-090 Indecent publications and exhibitions.
8-8-100 Sale of literature represented as immoral.
8-8-110 Material harmful to minors unlawful.
8-8-120 Violation—Penalty for Section 8-8-110.
8-8-130 to 8-8-150 Reserved.
8-8-160 Selling nontransferable railroad tickets.
8-8-170 Selling or giving away transfers.
8-8-180 Manipulating telephone coin boxes.
8-8-190 Violation—Penalty.

§8-8-010 House of ill-fame or assignation.

Every house of ill-fame or house of assignation where men and women resort for the purpose of fornication, prostitution, or lewdness is hereby declared to be a nuisance.

No person shall keep or maintain a house of ill-fame or assignation, or a place for the practice of fornication, prostitution, or lewdness. Each 24 hours that such house or place shall be kept or maintained for such purpose shall constitute a separate and distinct offense.

No person shall patronize, frequent, be found in, or be an inmate of any such house or place used for any of the purposes set forth in this section.

No person shall lease to another any house, room, or other premises, in whole or in part, for any of the uses or purposes set forth in this section or knowingly permit the same to be used or occupied for such purposes.
(Prior code § 192-1)

§8-8-020 Directing persons to houses of ill-fame.

No person knowingly shall direct, take, transport, or offer to direct, take, or transport, any person for immoral purposes to any other person, or assist any person by any means to seek or to find any prostitute or other person engaged in immoral practices, or any brothel, bawdy house, or any other place of ill-fame.

Any person that shall violate the provisions of this section shall be fined not less than $100.00 nor more than $400.00 for each offense.
(Prior code § 192-2; Amend. Coun. J. 9-4-02, p. 92888)

§8-8-030 Prostitution or lewdness in conveyances.

No person shall knowingly receive any person for purposes of lewdness, assignation, or prostitution into or upon any vehicle or other conveyance or permit any person to remain for any of the said purposes in or upon any such vehicle or other conveyance.

Any person that shall violate the provisions of this section shall be fined not less than $100.00 nor more than $400.00 for each offense.
(Prior code § 192-3; Amend. Coun. J. 9-4-02, p. 92888)

§8-8-040 Revocation of license.

The license of any such person or employees thereof directly involved in the violation of Sections 8-8-020 or 8-8-030 may be revoked, and also the license of the vehicle or conveyance used may be revoked in the discretion of the mayor. No license so revoked hereunder shall be reinstated until the lapse of a period of one year after such revocation.
(Prior code § 192-4)

§8-8-050 Soliciting—Penalty.

Any person who by any overt acts in or upon the public ways or in any hotel, motel or other public place of accommodation or on public conveyances or in any establishment licensed to sell alcoholic beverages, offers to perform or who solicits for another person to perform any act of prostitution shall upon conviction be fined not less than $750.00 nor more than $1,500.00 for the first offense and be fined not less than $1,500.00 nor more than $3,000.00 for the second offense and shall be punished as a misdemeanor for each subsequent offense by incarceration in the county jail for a term not to exceed six months or by both fine and imprisonment.
(Prior code § 192-5; Amend. Coun. J. 9-9-98, p. 77360; 9-4-02, p. 92888)

§8-8-060 Street solicitation for prostitution.

(a) For the purposes of this section:

(1) "Public place" means any street, sidewalk, bridge, alley or alleyway, plaza, park, driveway, parking lot, or transportation facility or the doorways and entranceways to any building which fronts on any of the aforesaid places, or a motor vehicle in or on any such place, or any other public way.

(2) "Prostitution," "pandering" and "soliciting for a prostitute" have the same meanings given them in the Illinois Criminal Code, as amended.

(b) Any person who remains or wanders about in a public place and repeatedly beckons to, or repeatedly at tempts to engage, passersby in conversation, or repeatedly interferes with the free passage of other persons, for the purpose of prostitution or of soliciting for a prostitute, shall be guilty of a violation of this section.

(c) Any person who remains or wanders about in a public place and repeatedly beckons to, or repeatedly stops, or repeatedly attempts to stop, or repeatedly at tempts to engage passersby in conversation, or repeatedly stops or attempts to stop motor vehicles, or repeatedly interferes with the free passage of other persons, for the purpose of pandering shall be guilty of a violation of this section.

(d) (1) A motor vehicle that is used in the violation of this section or Section 8-8-050, or in the commission of prostitution as defined in Section 11-14 of the Criminal Code of 1961, soliciting for a prostitute as defined in Section 11-15 of such code, soliciting for a juvenile prostitute as defined in Section 11-18 of such code, or patronizing a juvenile prostitute as defined in Section 11-18.1 of such code, shall be subject to seizure and impoundment under this subsection. The owner of record of such vehicle shall be liable to the city for an administrative penalty of $1,000.00 in addition to fees for the towing and storage of the vehicle.

(2) Whenever a police officer has probable cause to believe that a vehicle is subject to seizure and impoundment pursuant to this section, the police officer shall provide for the towing of the vehicle to a facility con trolled by the city or its agents. When the vehicle is towed, the police officer shall notify the person who is found to be in control of the vehicle at the time of the alleged violation, if there is such a person, of the fact of the seizure and of the vehicle owner's right to request a preliminary hearing to be conducted under Section 2-14-132 of this code.

(3) The provisions of Section 2-14-132 shall apply whenever a motor vehicle is seized and impounded pursuant to this section.

(e) Any person who appears in a public place and exposes the genitals, vulva, pubis, pubic hair, buttocks, perineum, anus, anal region or pubic hair region, or any portion of the female breast at or below the upper edge of the areola, for the purpose of prostitution shall be guilty of a violation of this section.

(f) Any person who responds to the beckoning of a prostitute in a public place by inquiring about, negotiating for, accepting an offer of or engaging in an act of prostitution, or by allowing another into his or her motor vehicle for purposes of inquiring about, negotiating for, accepting an offer of or engaging in an act of prostitution, shall be guilty of a violation of this section. The superintendent of police shall make available to local newspapers, radio and television stations the names of all persons charged with violating this subsection.

(g) A person who violates any provision of this section shall be fined not less than $750.00 nor more than $1,500.00, imprisoned for a period of not less than 20 days and not more than six months, or both fined and imprisoned. In addition to the foregoing penalties, the corporation counsel shall request that a violator be required to perform a minimum of 100 hours community service. To the extent allowed by law, personnel of the department of police shall prevent and oppose the release of any person charged with a violation of this section on bond se cured by that person's own recognizance.

(h) If any provision or part of this ordinance shall be found unconstitutional or outside the corporate powers of the city of Chicago, the remaining provisions shall continue in full force and effect.

(Prior code § 192-5.2; Amend. Coun. J. 11-14-84, p. 10994; 7-24-91, p. 3938; 7-29-92, p. 20064; 7-14-93, p. 35530; 6-10-96, p. 23795; 7-31-96, p. 26907; 4-29-98, p. 66564; 9-9-98, p. 77360; 9-4-02, p. 92888; 12-15-04, p. 39840)

§8-8-070 Reserved.

(Repealed Coun. J. 5-7-2003, p. 795)

§8-8-080 Indecent exposure or dress.

Any person who shall appear, bathe, sunbathe, walk or be in any public park, playground, beach or the waters adjacent thereto, or any school facility and the area adjacent thereto, or any municipal building and the areas adjacent thereto, or any public way within the city of Chicago in such a manner that the genitals, vulva, pubis, pubic hair, buttocks, perineum, anus, anal region, or pubic hair region of any person, or any portion of the breast at or below the upper edge of the areola thereof of any female person, is exposed to public view or is not covered by an opaque covering, shall be fined not less than $100.00 nor more than $500.00 for each offense.
(Prior code § 192-8; Amend. Coun. J. 12-4-02, p. 99931)

§8-8-090 Indecent publications and exhibitions.

It shall be unlawful for any person knowingly to exhibit, sell, print, offer to sell, give away, circulate, publish, distribute, or attempt to distribute any obscene book, magazine, pamphlet, paper, writing, card, advertisement, circular, print, picture, photograph, motion picture film, play, image, instrument, statue, drawing, or other article which is obscene. Any person violating any provisions of this section shall be fined not less than $20.00 nor more than $200.00 for each offense.

Obscene for the purpose of this section is defined as follows: whether to the average per son, applying contemporary community standards, the dominant theme of the material taken as a whole appeals to prurient interests.
(Prior code § 192-9)

§8-8-100 Sale of literature represented as immoral.

It shall be unlawful for any person to sell, or to offer or to exhibit for sale, in sealed form, or in any form which indicates that the sale thereof is surreptitious or contrary to law, any book, pamphlet, or literature of any kind bearing the title of some well-known book of salacious character, or bearing the title of a book of which the sale is prohibited, or bearing the title of a book of which the contents are actually lewd, lascivious, obscene, immoral, or indecent. It shall likewise be unlawful to sell, or to offer or exhibit for sale, any book, pamphlet, or literature of any kind having anything about it which indicates that its contents are of an obscene, immoral, lewd, lascivious, or indecent character, or to sell, or to offer or exhibit for sale, any book, pamphlet, or literature of any kind under the guise or pretense that the same is obscene, immoral, lewd, lascivious, or indecent, or in a manner that indicates concealment of anything as contrary to law or immoral contained therein, or to use any pretense, trick, fraud, artifice, or device to convey the impression that such book, pamphlet, or literature is lewd, lascivious, indecent, ob scene, or immoral, whether such pretense, trick, fraud, artifice or device is a misrepresentation in regard to the contents of the same or not.
(Prior code § 192-10)

§8-8-110 Material harmful to minors unlawful.

A. For the purposes of this section the following words shall be defined as follows:

(a) "Minor" means any person under the age of 18 years.

(b) "Nudity" means the showing of the human male or female genitals, pubic area or buttocks with less than a fully opaque covering, or the showing of the female breast with less than a full opaque covering of any portion thereof below the top of the nipple, or the depiction of covered male genitals in a discernible turgid state.

(c) "Sexual conduct" includes any of the following depicted sexual conduct:

(i) Any act of sexual intercourse, actual or simulated, including genital, anal-genital, or oral-genital intercourse, whether between human beings or between a human being and an animal;

(ii) Sadomasochistic abuse, meaning flagellation or torture by or upon a person who is nude or clad in under garments or in a revealing costume or the condition of being fettered, bound or otherwise physically restricted on the part of one so clothed;

(iii) Masturbation or lewd exhibitions of the genitals including any explicit, closeup representation of a human genital organ;

(iv) Physical contact or simulated physical contact with the clothed or unclothed pubic areas or buttocks of a human male or female, or the breasts of the female, whether alone or between members of the same or opposite sex or between humans and animals in an act of apparent sexual stimulation or gratification;

(v) An act of sexual assault where physical violence or drugs are employed to overcome the will of or achieve the consent of a person to an act of sexual conduct and the effects or results of the violence or drugs are shown.

(d) "Sexual excitement" means the condition of human male or female genitals when in a state of sexual stimulation or arousal.

(e) "Harmful to minors" means that quality of any description or representation in what ever form, or nudity, sexual conduct, or sexual excitement, when it:

(i) Predominantly appeals to the prurient, shameful, or morbid interest of minors in sex; and

(ii) Is patently offensive to contemporary standards in the adult community as a whole with respect to what is suitable sexual material for minors; and

(iii) Taken as a whole, lacks serious literary, artistic, political or scientific value.

(f) "Knowingly" means having general knowledge of, or reason to know, or a belief or ground for belief which warrants further inspection or inquiry or both.

B. It is unlawful for any person knowingly to sell or loan for monetary consideration to a minor any written, photographic, printed, sound, published material or video tape, or similar visual representation or image of a person or portion of the human body which depicts nudity, sexual conduct, or sexual excitement and which is harmful to minors.

It is unlawful for any person commercially and knowingly to exhibit, display, sell, offer to sell, lend, give away, circulate, distribute, or attempt to distribute any written, photographic, print ed, sound, published material or video tape which is harmful to minors in its context in any place where minors are or may be present or allowed to be present and where minors are able to view such material unless each item of such material is at all times kept in a sealed wrapper.

It is also unlawful for any person commercially and knowingly to exhibit, display, sell, offer to sell, give away, circulate, distribute, or attempt to distribute, any written, photographic, printed, sound, published material or video tape whose cover, covers, or packaging, standing alone, is harmful to minors, in any place where minors are to be present and where minors are able to view such material unless each item of such material is at all times blocked from view by an opaque cover. The requirement of an opaque cover shall be deemed satisfied concerning such material if those portions of the cover, covers, or packaging containing such material harmful to minors are blocked from view by an opaque cover.

The provisions of this subdivision shall not apply to distribution or attempt to distribute the exhibition, display, sale, offer of sale, circulation, giving away of material harmful to minors where such material is sold, exhibited, displayed, offered for sale, given away, circulated, distributed, or attempted to be distributed under circumstances where minors are not present, not allowed to be present, or are not able to view such material or the cover, covers, or packaging of such material. Any business may comply with the requirements of this clause by physically segregating such material in a manner so as to physically prohibit the access to and view of the material by minors, by prominently posting at the entrance(s) to such restricted area, "Adults Only—you must be 18 to enter," and by en forcing said restrictions.
(Prior code § 192-10.1; Amend. Coun. J. 11-26-86, p. 37627; 7-29-87, p. 2824)

§8-8-120 Violation—Penalty for Section §8-8-110.

Any person violating any of the provisions of Section 8-8-110 shall be deemed guilty of a misdemeanor and upon conviction thereof shall be fined in an amount not less than $100.00 nor more than $200.00 or be imprisoned for a period not exceeding six months or be both so fined and imprisoned. Each day that such violation is committed or permitted to continue shall constitute a separate offense and shall be punishable as such hereunder. If more than one written, photographic, printed, sound, published material or videotape shall knowingly be sold, lent, displayed, offered to be sold, given away, circulated, distributed or in any way furnished or attempted to be furnished to any such person in violation of Section 8-8-110, the sale, loan, display, offer to sell, giving away, circulation, distribution or in any way furnishing or attempting to furnish to any such person of each separate written, photo graphic, printed, sound, published material or videotape shall constitute a separate offense and shall be punished as such hereunder.
(Prior code § 192-10.2; Amend. Coun. J. 11-26-86, p. 37627)

§8-8-130 to 8-8-150 Reserved.

(Repealed Coun. J. 10-3-2001, p. 68137)

§8-8-160 Selling nontransferable railroad tickets.

No person shall be permitted to remain in or about any railroad depot in the city, having in his possession the unused portion or portions of nontransferable railroad tickets restricted for the use to the original purchaser thereof by the railroad company issuing the same, for the purpose of selling the same, offering the same for sale, advertising the same for sale, or in any manner to aid in the sale or purchase of such partially used nontransferable railroad tickets.

No person shall sell within the city the whole or any portion of any said ticket.

Any person violating any of the provisions of this section shall be fined not less than $5.00 nor more than $50.00 for each offense.
(Prior code § 192-16)

§8-8-170 Selling or giving away transfers.

No person, in violation of the rules or regulations approved or promulgated by the Illinois Commerce Commission shall sell, barter, or exchange for any consideration any transfer ticket or other instrument issued by any person operating any street railroad, elevated rapid transit railroad, unified local transportation system, or otherwise, within the city, giving, or purporting to give to the holder of such transfer ticket or other instrument the right to transfer from one street railroad car, bus, or trolley bus to another street railway car, bus, or trolley bus on the same line or route or on any other line or route, or from a street railroad car, bus, or trolley bus to an elevated railroad car or train, or from an elevated railroad car or train to a street railroad car, bus, or trolley bus.

No person shall give away any such transfer ticket or other instrument as aforesaid to another for the purpose of enabling, or with intent to enable, the latter to use or offer the same for passage upon any car, bus, or trolley bus of said street railroad, elevated rapid transit railroad, unified local transportation system, or otherwise; nor shall any person not lawfully entitled thereto receive or acquire possession of any such transfer ticket or other instrument as aforesaid, use, or attempt to use, or offer the same for passage upon any car, bus, or trolley bus of the said street railroad, elevated rapid transit railroad, unified local transportation company, or otherwise. Provided, however, that this section shall not relate to, or in any manner affect, the issuing and giving of transfer tickets or other instruments as aforesaid by the agents or employees of any street railroad, elevated rapid transit railroad, unified local transportation system, or otherwise, to passengers there of lawfully entitled thereto.
(Prior code § 192-17)

§8-8-180 Manipulating telephone coin boxes.

It shall be unlawful for any person to insert, or to attempt to insert, into the coin box or money receptacle of any telephone, any slug, button, or other substance, or to manipulate or operate, or to attempt to manipulate or operate, in any manner whatever, any telephone instrument or any mechanism or device connected or commonly used there with, with the intent to obtain telephone service without paying therefor.

It shall be unlawful for any person to insert, or to attempt to insert, into the coin box or money receptacle of any telephone, any slug, button, wire, hook, or other implements or substances with the intent to obtain from such coin box or money receptacle a legal tender coin of the United States.
(Prior code § 192-18)

§8-8-190 Violation—Penalty.

Any person violating any of the provisions of this chapter, where no other penalty is pro vided, shall be fined not less than $5.00 nor more than $200.00 for each offense.
(Prior code § 192-19)

CHAPTER 8-12
GAMBLING

Sections:

8-12-010 Gambling prohibited.
8-12-020 Lottery and policy games.
8-12-030 Places for gambling.
8-12-040 Devices for gambling.
8-12-050 Slot and tape machines.
8-12-060 Duty of police.
8-12-070 Betting or gambling at tracks.
8-12-080 Taking bets or pool-selling.
8-12-090 Publishing or circulating information.
8-12-100 Violation—Penalty.

§8-12-010 Gambling prohibited.

No person shall play or engage in faro, roulette, or gambling for money or other valuable thing, or in any other device or game of chance, hazard, or skill, either as bookmaker, dealer, keeper, player, or otherwise, for the purpose of gaming or gambling for money or other valuable thing. Nothing in this chapter shall be construed to prevent eleemosynary, religious or charitable institutions from conducting raffles, the proceeds of which benefit persons by enhancing their opportunity for religious or educational advancement; by relieving or protecting them from disease, suffering or distress; by contributing to their physical wellbeing; by assisting them in establishing themselves in life as worthy and useful citizens; or by increasing their comprehension of and devotion to the principles upon which this nation was founded.
(Prior code § 191-1)

§8-12-020 Lottery and policy games.

No person shall keep, occupy or use, or permit to be kept, occupied or used, a place, building, room, establishment, table, or apparatus for policy playing or for the purchase, sale, exchange, or redemption of what are commonly called lottery tickets or policy tickets.

No person shall deliver or receive money or other valuable consideration in playing policy or in aiding in the playing thereof, or for lottery or policy tickets, or for any writing, paper, or document in the nature of a bet, wager, or insurance upon the drawing or drawn numbers of any lottery or policy game, whether such drawing be real or imaginary.

No person, except a public officer, shall have in his possession or control any writing, paper, or document representing or being a record of any chance, share, or interest in numbers sold, drawn, or to be drawn, in what is commonly called policy, or in the nature of a bet, wager, or insurance upon the drawing or drawn numbers of any public or private lottery or policy game, whether such drawing be real or imaginary.

No person, other than a public officer, shall have in his possession or control any paper, print, writing, numbers, device, policy slip, policy sheet, or article of any kind such as is commonly used in carrying on, promoting, or playing the game commonly called policy.

No person shall sell, offer for sale, barter, exchange, give away, or in any way dispose of or redeem any ticket, order, slip, or device of any kind for or representing any number of shares or any interest in any lottery, policy, or scheme of chance of any kind or description by whatever name, style, or title the same may be denominated or known, and whether located or drawn, or to be drawn, paid, or carried on within or without the limits of the city, or whether such purported drawings be real or imaginary.

No person shall either publicly or privately, as owner or agent, establish, carry on, pro mote, make, draw, or act as "backer" or "vendor" for or on account of any lottery, policy, or scheme of chance described in the previous paragraph; nor shall any person be in any way concerned in any such lottery, policy, or scheme of chance.

No person who is the owner, lessor, lessee, agent, superintendent, janitor, or caretaker of any place, building, or room shall permit policy playing or the barter, sale, exchange, or redemption of what are commonly called lottery or policy tickets or slips, or the sale of any chances in alleged drawings in lotteries or policies to be carried on in such place, building, or room, whether such drawings be real or imaginary.

No person shall patronize, frequent, or be found in any place, building, room, or establishment kept, occupied, or used for policy playing, for policy or lottery drawings, or for the sale of what are commonly called lottery or policy tickets or slips, or in which are kept any paper, prints, writings, numbers, devices, policy tickets, policy sheets or articles of any kind, such as are commonly used in carrying on, promoting, or playing the game or scheme commonly called policy.

No person shall write, print, publish, circulate, or distribute in any way an account of any lottery, policy, or scheme of chance of any kind or description by whatsoever name, style, or title the same may be denominated or known, and no person shall write, print, publish, circulate, or distribute any book, pamphlet, circular, sheet, or paper whatsoever containing or purporting to contain information concerning any lottery, policy, or scheme of chance, or where the same is to be or has been drawn, or the prizes therein, or the price of a ticket, or where any such ticket may be or has been obtained, or in any way giving publicity to any such lottery, policy, or scheme of chance, whether the drawings therein referred to be real or imaginary.

No person shall aid, assist, or abet in any manner, or be a party to any of the offenses, acts, or matters hereinbefore specified.

(Prior code § 191-2)

§8-12-030 Places for gambling.

Every house, room, yard, boat, vessel, or other structure or premises kept or used for the purpose of permitting persons to gamble for any valuable thing within the city is hereby declared to be a common nuisance.

No person shall own, maintain, manage, or conduct, or be interested in owning, maintaining, managing, or con ducting, any such place.

No person shall patronize, visit, frequent, or be connect ed with the management or operation, or shall act as the doorkeeper, solicitor, runner, agent, abettor, or pimp of any such house, room, yard, boat, vessel, or other structure, place, or premises.

(Prior code § 191-3)

§8-12-040 Devices for gambling.

No person shall expose any table, wheel, or device of any kind whatsoever, intended, calculated, or designed to be used for gaming or gambling or for playing any game for chance or hazard, in, upon or along any of the public ways or other public places of the city.

No person shall bring into the city or have in his possession within the city, for the purpose of gaming or gambling for money or other valuable thing, any table, wheel or other device of any kind or character whatsoever whereon or with which money or any other valuable thing may in any manner be played or gambled.

(Prior code § 191-4)

§8-12-050 Slot and tape machines.

No person shall keep, own, operate, use, or cause to be kept, operated or used, in any room, inn, tavern, shed, booth, building, enclosure, or upon any premises, or any part thereof, any clock, "joker," tape or slot machine, or other device of any kind or nature whatsoever, upon, in, by, or through which money is staked or hazarded, or into which money is paid or played upon chance, or upon the result of the action of which clock, "joker," tape or slot machine, or other device, money or other valuable thing is staked, bet, hazarded, won, or lost.

Each day which any person shall operate, keep, own, or have in his charge, possession or control any such clock, "joker," tape or slot machine, or other such gambling device, in violation of the provisions of this section, shall be deemed a separate and distinct offense.

(Prior code § 191-5)

§8-12-060 Duty of police.

It shall be the duty of all members of the department of police to give information to the mayor of every house, room, yard, boat, vessel, or other structure or premises within the city wherein any such game or device or policy shop tickets or lists are or may be set up, kept, or maintained. Such members of the department of police shall take all lawful means to suppress and prevent the playing at or use of any faro table, roulette wheel, or the playing of any game or the use of any device hereinbefore mentioned. For this purpose, when and as often as any such member of the department of police shall have reasonable cause to suspect that any such table, wheel, game, or device is set up, kept, or maintained anywhere within the city, he shall forthwith make complaint thereof before some judge of the municipal court and obtain a warrant authorizing him to enter such house, room, yard, boat, vessel, or other structure, place, or premises, or any part of the same. Such member of the department of police shall thereupon have authority to demand entry thereto. No person shall refuse or fail to open the door or entrance thereto, or shall obstruct or do anything tending to obstruct or prevent the entry of such member of the department of police to any such house, room, yard, boat, vessel, or other structure, place, or premises, or any part thereof, when such member of the department of police shall have a warrant.

It shall be the duty of every member of the department of police to seize any such table, wheel, instrument, device, or thing. All such tables, instruments, devices, or things when seized shall be destroyed.

No person shall obstruct or resist any member of the police department in the performance of any act herein authorized.
(Prior code § 191-6)

§8-12-070 Betting or gambling at tracks.

All betting, wagering, speculating, pool-selling, or bookmaking upon any horse race or races or the result thereof, and all gambling and every game of chance of any nature whatsoever, within or upon any racetrack and racecourse, or in any building within any racetrack or racecourse within the city is hereby prohibited.

Any person found violating any of the provisions of this section shall be fined not less than $100.00 nor more than $200.00 for each offense.
(Prior code § 191-7)

§8-12-080 Taking bets or pool-selling.

No person shall keep, occupy, or control any room, shed, tenement, tent, booth, building, or other structure, or any part thereof, or occupy any place anywhere within the city, with any book, instrument, or device for the purpose of taking, recording, or registering bets or wagers or of selling pools, or take, record, or register bets or wagers, or sell pools, upon the result or alleged result of any actual, supposed, alleged, or fictitious trial or test of skill, speed, or power of endurance of man or beast, or upon the result or alleged result of any actual, sup posed, alleged, or fictitious political nomination, appointment, or election. Any person, being the owner, lessee, or occupant of any room, shed, tenement, tent, booth, building, or other structure, or part thereof, who shall knowingly permit the same to be used or occupied for any such purpose or shall therein keep, exhibit, or employ any device or apparatus for the purpose of taking, recording, or registering such bets or wagers, or selling such pools, or shall become the custodian or depositary for hire or reward of any money, property, or thing of value staked, wagered, or pledged upon any such result or alleged result, shall be fined not less than $50.00 nor more than $200.00 for each offense.

In prosecutions under this section, proof of the taking, recording, or registering of such bet or wager, or pool-selling, shall be prima facie evidence of the violation of said section, and proof shall not be required that there was any actual, supposed, alleged, or fictitious trial or test of skill, speed, or power of endurance of man or beast, or that there was any actual, supposed, alleged, or fictitious political nomination, appointment, or election to which such bet, wager, or pool-selling may appertain.
(Prior code § 191-8)

§8-12-090 Publishing or circulating information.

No person shall insert, or cause to be inserted, or print or publish, or cause to be printed or published, in any newspaper or other publication printed, published, or circulated in the city, any notice, advertisement, or mention giving or purporting to give information of where or with whom bets or wagers may be made or placed, or where or by whom pools are sold upon the result of any trial or test of skill, speed, or power of endurance of man or beast, or upon the result of any political nomination, appointment, or election.

No person shall display or exhibit, or distribute or cause to be distributed, any circular, blank, handbill, pamphlet, or other thing containing any such notice, advertisement, or mention described in the above paragraph.

No person shall sell, offer for sale, give away, exhibit, distribute, or cause to be distributed, any newspaper or other publication, circular, blank, handbill, pamphlet, or other written or printed matter giving or purporting to give information concerning the rates at which bets are being offered or taken in the city or elsewhere, or the odds being given or taken on bets within the city or elsewhere, or advice as to betting or the ratio at which bets should be made upon the result of any trial or test of skill, speed, or power of endurance of man or beast, or upon the result of any political nomination, appointment or election.

Any person violating any of the provisions of this section shall be fined not less than $50.00 nor more than $200.00.

(Prior code § 191-9)

§8-12-100 Violation—Penalty.

Any person violating any provision of this chapter, where no other penalty is specified, shall be fined not less than $25.00 nor more than $200.00 for each offense.

(Prior code § 191-10)

CHAPTER 8-16
OFFENSES BY OR AGAINST MINORS

Sections:
8-16-010 Cruelty to children.
8-16-020 Curfew hours for minors.
8-16-022 Custody procedure.
8-16-024 Violation of provisions of Section 8-16-020—Penalty.
8-16-030 Missing—Information to be obtained.
8-16-040 Flipping cars.
8-16-050 Intoxication.
8-16-060 Alcoholic liquor.
8-16-070 Liquor saturated material to children.
8-16-080 Playing with gaming devices.
8-16-090 Firearms for minors.
8-16-095 Possession of spray can or marker by underage persons prohibited.
8-16-096 Aiding or assisting underage person in obtaining paint spray cans or markers prohibited.
8-16-100 Exhibiting or employing children.
8-16-110 Working in public places.
8-16-120 Begging or soliciting.
8-16-125 Contributing to delinquency of minor.
8-16-130 Violation—Penalty.

§8-16-010 Cruelty to children.

It shall be unlawful for any person to commit, cause, or knowingly permit any of the following offenses against children:

(a) Abandon any child;

(b) Unnecessarily fail to provide any child in his charge or custody with proper food, drink, shelter, or raiment;

(c) Cruelly beat, torture, overwork, or mutilate any child;

(d) Willfully expose to inclement weather or in any manner injure a child in health or limb.

(Prior code § 190-1)

§8-16-020 Curfew hours for minors.

(a) Definitions. Whenever used in this section,

(1) "Curfew hours" means:

(A) 10:30 p.m. on any Sunday, Monday, Tuesday, Wednesday, or Thursday until 6:00 a.m. of the following day; and

(B) 11:30 p.m. on any Friday or Saturday and until 6:00 a.m. of the following day.

(2) "Emergency" means an unforeseen combination of circumstances or the resulting state that calls for immediate action. The term includes, but is not limited to, a fire, a natural disaster, an automobile accident, or any situation requiring immediate action to prevent serious bodily injury or loss of life.

(3) "Establishment" means any privately-owned place of business operated for a profit to which the public is invited, including but not limited to any place of amusement or entertainment.

(4) "Guardian" means:

(A) A person who, under court order, is the guardian of the person of a minor; or

(B) A public or private agency with whom a minor has been placed by a court.

(5) "Minor" means any person under 17 years of age.

(6) "Operator" means any individual, firm, association, partnership, or corporation operating, managing, or conducting any establishment. The term includes the members or partners of an association or partnership and the officers of a corporation.

(7) "Parent" means a person who is:

(A) A natural parent, adoptive parent, or step-parent of another person; or

(B) At least 18 years of age and authorized by a parent or guardian to have the care and custody of a minor.

(8) "Public place" means any place to which the public or a substantial group of the public has access and includes, but is not limited to, streets, highways, and the common areas of schools, hospitals, apartment houses, office buildings, transport facilities and shops.

(9) "Remain" means to:

(A) Linger or stay; or

(B) Fail to leave premises when requested to do so by a police officer or the owner, operator or other person in control of the premises.

(10) "Serious bodily injury" means bodily injury that creates a substantial risk of death or that causes death, serious permanent disfigurement or protracted loss or impairment of the function of any bodily member or organ.

(b) Offenses.

(1) A minor commits an offense if he remains in any public place or on the premises of any establishment within the city during curfew hours.

(2) A parent or guardian of a minor commits an offense if he knowingly permits, or by insufficient control allows, the minor to remain in any public place or on the premises of any establishment within the city during curfew hours.

(3) The owner, operator or any employee of an establishment commits an offense if he knowingly allows a minor to remain upon the premises of the establishment during curfew hours.

(c) Defenses.

(1) It is a defense to prosecution under subsection (b) that the minor was:

(A) Accompanied by the minor's parent or guardian;

(B) On an errand at the direction of the minor's parent or guardian, without any detour or stop;

(C) In a motor vehicle involved in interstate travel;

(D) Engaged in an employment activity, or going to or returning home from an employment activity, without any detour or stop;

(E) Involved in an emergency;

(F) On the sidewalk abutting the minor's residence or abutting the residence of a next-door neighbor if the neighbor did not complain to the police department about the minor's presence;

(G) Attending an official school, religious, or other recreational activity supervised by adults and sponsored by the city, a civic organization, or another similar entity that takes responsibility for the minor, or going to or returning home from, without any detour or stop, an official school, religious, or other recreational activity supervised by adults and sponsored by the city, a civic organization, or another similar entity that takes responsibility for the minor;

(H) Exercising first amendment rights protected by the United States Constitution, such as the free exercise of religion, freedom of speech, and the right of assembly; or

(I) Married or had been married or is an emancipated minor under the Emancipation of Mature Minors Act, as amended.

(2) It is a defense to prosecution under subsection (b)(3) that the owner, operator, or employee of an establishment promptly notified the police department that a minor was present on the premises of the establishment during curfew hours and refused to leave.

(d) Enforcement. Before taking any enforcement action under this section, a police officer shall ask the apparent offender's age and reason for being in the public place. The officer shall not issue a citation or make an arrest under this section unless the officer reasonably believes that an offense has occurred and that, based on any response and other circumstances, no defense in subsection (c) is present.

(e) Penalties. A person who violates a provision of this chapter is guilty of a separate offense for each day or part of a day during which the violation is committed, continued, or permitted. Each offense, upon conviction, is punishable by a fine not to exceed $500.00.

(Added. Coun. J. 3-10-04, p. 19860)

§8-16-022 Custody procedure.

Any police officer who finds a minor in violation of Section 8-16-020 is authorized to take such minor into custody until such time as the minor's parent, legal guardian, or other adult having legal care or custody of the minor is located and notified of the violation, and takes custody of the minor from the police. If no such person can be located within a reasonable period of time, the minor shall be referred to the appropriate juvenile authorities.
(Added Coun. J. 6-17-92, p. 18292)

§8-16-024 Violation of provisions of Section §8-16-020—Penalty.

Any parent, legal guardian or other adult having the legal care or custody of a minor who violates any provisions of Section 8-16-020 shall be absolutely liable for such violation and shall be fined not less than $25.00 nor more than $500.00, or be subject to an order to perform community service, or both, for each offense.
(Added. Coun. J. 6-17-92, p. 18292; Amend. Coun. J. 7-9-03, p. 3939)

§8-16-030 Missing—Information to be obtained.

Whenever there is evidence that any minor is missing, either by report given by an educational institution to the parent, guardian or other person responsible for such minor, or by report to the police department or to the mass media of communications, it shall be the responsibility of the superintendent of police to obtain a photograph of said missing minor, together with any pertinent descriptive information, and to have posted both such photograph and information upon the premises of any feasible public building owned, leased or maintained by the city of Chicago. The term "pertinent descriptive information" shall include, if known, the name, age and physical description of the missing person, as well as a telephone number of a person of immediate contact.
(Prior code § 190-2.1; Added. Coun. J. 10-31-84, p. 10607)

§8-16-040 Flipping cars.

It shall be unlawful for any person under the age of 18 years to climb, jump upon, cling to, or in any way attach himself to any streetcar, railroad locomotive, or car of any kind while the same is in motion, under a penalty of not less than $2.00 nor more than $10.00 for each offense.
(Prior code § 190-3)

§8-16-050 Intoxication.

Any minor who shall be intoxicated, or who shall purchase, offer to purchase, or in any manner obtain unlawfully for his personal use any intoxicating liquor, shall be fined not more than $25.00 for the first offense, and not more than $100.00 for every subsequent offense.
(Prior code § 190-4)

§8-16-060 Alcoholic liquor.

It shall be unlawful for any person to sell, give or deliver any alcoholic liquor to a person under the age of 21 years. It shall be unlawful for any per-

son under the age of 21 years to purchase, deliver, possess, give or consume alcoholic liquor.
(Prior code § 190-4.1)

§8-16-070 Liquor saturated material to children.

Any person who shall sell, deliver to, or procure for any child under 16 years of age any material saturated with or enclosing any spirituous, vinous, or fermented liquor shall be fined not less than $20.00 nor more than $100.00 for each offense.
(Prior code § 190-5)

§8-16-080 Playing with gaming devices.

No minor shall play with dice, dominoes, cards, balls, or other articles used in gaming in any place where intoxicating liquors are sold or given away, or in any poolroom, billiard hall, cigar store, bowling alley, or other public store or place.
(Prior code § 190-6)

§8-16-090 Firearms for minors.

No person shall sell, loan, or furnish to any minor any gun, pistol or other firearm, or any toy gun, toy pistol, or other toy firearm in which any explosive substance can be used, within the city; except that minors may be permitted, with the consent of their parents or guardians, to use firearms on the premises of a duly licensed shooting gallery, gun club, or rifle club, or to shoot game birds in accordance with the provisions of Section 8-24-050 of this code.
(Prior code § 190-7)

§8-16-095 Possession of spray can or marker by underage persons prohibited.

No person under the age of 18 shall possess within the city any paint in a spray can or any marker containing a fluid which is not water soluble and has a point, brush, applicator or other writing surface of three-eighths of an inch or greater. This prohibition shall not apply to:

(a) A child using paint or a marker while under the immediate supervision of his or her parent or legal guardian;

(b) A student using paint or a marker while under the immediate supervision of his or her teacher;

(c) An employee using paint or a marker at the direction and under the supervision of his or her employer.
(Added. Coun. J. 5-20-92, p. 17016)

§8-16-096 Aiding or assisting underage person in obtaining paint spray cans or markers prohibited.

No person shall aid, assist or abet a person under the age of 18 in obtaining possession of paint in a spray can or any marker containing a fluid which is not water soluble and has a point, brush, applicator or other writing surface of three-eighths of an inch or greater. This prohibition shall not apply to:

(a) A parent or legal guardian assisting and supervising his or her own child or ward in the use of paint or a marker;

(b) A teacher assisting and supervising his or her students in the use of paint or a marker;

(c) An employer assisting and supervising his or her employee in the use of paint or a marker.

(Added. Coun. J. 5-20-92, p. 17016)

§8-16-100 Exhibiting or employing children.

No person having the care, custody, or control of any child under the age of 14 years shall cause or permit any such child to be exhibited, used, or employed, or shall apprentice or let out, or otherwise dispose of, any such child to any person for the occupation or purpose of singing or playing on musical instruments on the public ways, or of ropewalking or wirewalking, dancing, begging, or peddling, or as a gymnast, contortionist, rider, or acrobat in any place whatsoever, or for any obscene, indecent, or immoral exhibition or purpose, or in or about any business, exhibition, or occupation injurious to the health or dangerous to the life or limb of such child, or cause, procure, or encourage any such child to engage therein.

No person shall take, receive, employ, use, exhibit, or have in custody any child under the age of 14 years for the purpose of employing such child in the manner expressly prohibited in this section, and no person having the care or custody of any child shall wilfully cause or permit such child to be placed in such a situation that its life or health may be endangered.

(Prior code § 190-8)

§8-16-110 Working in public places.

It shall be unlawful for any girl under the age of 18 years to distribute, sell, expose or offer for sale, any news papers, magazines, periodicals, gum, or any other merchandise, or to distribute handbills, circulars, or other articles, or to exercise the trade of a bootblack, or any other trade or occupation, or to solicit money or other thing of value, in any public way or other public place in the city. It shall be unlawful for any person to employ such girl under the age designated herein, or permit or suffer such girl to be employed at the trade of a bootblack, or any other trade or occupation, in any public way or other public place in the city.

No boy under the age of 14 years shall pursue any of the occupations mentioned in the above paragraph upon the public ways or other public places of the city before 5:00 a.m. or after 8:00 p.m. No boy between 14 and 16 years of age shall pursue any of the said occupations upon the public ways or other public places of the city before 5:00 a.m. or after 8:00 p.m., unless he shall be provided with and have on his person an employment certificate issued in accordance with the requirements of an act of the general assembly concerning child labor, approved June 26, 1917, as amended.

Any girl under the age of 18 years or any boy under the age of 16 years, who shall violate any of the above mentioned provisions of this section shall be warned by any police officer who shall discover any violation of this section forthwith to comply with the provisions of the same and to desist from further violation thereof. Such officer shall also without delay report such violation to his superior officer, who shall cause a written notice to be served upon the parent, guardian, or person in control or charge of such boy or girl, setting forth the manner in which the section has been violated. In case any girl under the age of 18 years or any boy under the age of 16 years after such warning shall again pursue any occupation contrary to the provisions of this section, he or she shall be subjected to the penalty herein provided.

In case any parent, guardian, or person in control or charge of such boy or girl, who has received notice as pro vided for herein, shall knowingly permit such boy or girl again to violate the provisions of this section, or shall procure or engage such boy or girl after such notice to pursue an occupation in a manner contrary to the provisions of this section, such parent, guardian, or person in control or charge of such boy or girl shall also be subject to the penalty herein provided.

Any violation of this section, after the warning or notice herein provided for, shall be punished by a fine of not more than $100.00.
(Prior code § 190-9)

§8-16-120 Begging or soliciting.

It shall be unlawful for any person to employ or use or to permit the employment or use of any girl under the age of 18 years, or any boy under the age of 17 years, for the purpose of solicitation or begging of money or other valuable thing upon the public ways or public places within the city, whether such solicitation is for charitable purposes or any other purpose, or whether such solicitation is conducted on a day set apart as a so-called tag day or otherwise.
(Prior code § 190-10)

§8-16-125 Contributing to delinquency of minor.

(a) No person over the age of 18 years having the care, custody or control of any child under the age of 18 years shall knowingly or wilfully permit, cause, aid, abet or encourage such child to commit any act or omission in violation of any law, statute or ordinance of this city, the county of Cook, the state of Illinois, or the United States, where the violation of such law, statute or ordinance is punishable by fine or imprisonment.

(b) No person over the age of 18 years not having the care, custody or control of a child under the age of 18 years shall knowingly or wilfully cause, aid, abet or encourage such child to commit any act or omission in violation of any law, statute or ordinance of this city, the county of Cook, the state of Illinois, or the United States, where the violation of such law, statute or ordinance is punishable by fine or imprisonment.

(c) Any person who violates this section shall be subject to a fine of not less than $200.00 nor more than $500.00 for each offense.
(Prior code § 190-10.1; Added Coun. J. 7-12-90, p. 18084)

§8-16-130 Violation—Penalty.

Any person who shall violate any of the provisions of this chapter for which no other penalty is provided shall be fined not less than $5.00 nor more than $100.00 for each offense.
(Prior code § 190-11)

CHAPTER 8-20
WEAPONS

Sections:

Article I. Possession of Firearms

8-20-010 Unlawful to carry—Exceptions.
8-20-015 Unlawful firearm or laser sight accessory in motor vehicle— Impoundment.
8-20-020 Violation—Penalty.

Article II. Registration of Firearms

8-20-030 Definitions.
8-20-040 Registration of firearms.
8-20-050 Unregisterable firearms.
8-20-060 Prerequisites to registration—Application for registration.
8-20-070 Fingerprints.
8-20-080 Application fees.
8-20-090 Filing time.
8-20-100 Investigations.
8-20-110 Issuance of registration certificate.
8-20-120 Revocation—Denial.
8-20-130 Procedures for denial or revocation.
8-20-140 Additional duties of registrant.
8-20-150 Exhibition of registration.
8-20-160 Possession of ammunition.
8-20-165 Possession of laser sight accessories.
8-20-170 Permissible sales and transfers of firearms and ammunition.
8-20-175 Firearm Owners Identification Card Act—Compliance required.
8-20-180 False information—Forgery—Alteration.
8-20-190 Voluntary surrender—Immunity.
8-20-195 Voluntary surrender of laser sight accessory—Immunity.
8-20-200 Renewal of registration.
8-20-210 Notice.
8-20-220 Destruction of weapons confiscated.
8-20-230 Authority of the superintendent.
8-20-240 Acquisition or possession prohibited by law.
8-20-241 Firearm used illegally—Penalty.
8-20-250 Violation—Penalty.
8-20-260 Severability.

Article I. Possession of Firearms

§8-20-010 Unlawful to carry—Exceptions.

It shall be unlawful for any person to carry or maintain in any vehicle or about his or her person except when on his or her property or in his or her residence or fixed place of business, any rifle, shotgun, or other firearm; provided, that this section shall not apply to:

(1) Peace officers or any person summoned by any such officers to assist in making arrests or preserving the peace while he is actually engaged in assisting such officer;

(2) Wardens, superintendents and keepers of prisons, penitentiaries, jails, and other institutions for the detention of persons accused or convicted of an offense, while in the performance of their official duty or commuting between their homes and places of employment;

(3) Members of the Armed Services or Reserve Forces of the United States or the Illinois National Guard or the Reserve Officers Training Corps, while in the performance of their official duty;

(4) Special agents employed by a railroad to perform police functions, or employees of a detective agency, watchman-guard or patrolman agency, licensed by the state of Illinois, while actually engaged in the performance of the duties of their employment or commuting between their homes and places of employment;

(5) Agents and investigators of the Illinois Crime Investigating Commission authorized by the Commission to carry weapons, while on duty in the course of any investigation for the Commission;

(6) Manufacture, transportation when the weapons are not immediately accessible to any person, or sale of weapons to persons authorized under law to possess them;

(7) Members of any club or organization organized for the purpose of practicing shooting at targets upon established target ranges, whether public or private, while such members are using their firearms on such target ranges;

(8) Duly authorized military or civil organizations while parading, with the special per mission of the Governor;

(9) Licensed hunters or fishermen while engaged in hunting or fishing;

(10) Transportation of weapons broken down in a nonfunctioning state.

(Prior code § 11.2-1; Amend. Coun. J. 7-7-92, p. 19196)

§8-20-015 Unlawful firearm or laser sight accessory in motor vehicle—Impoundment.

(a) The owner of record of any motor vehicle that contains an unregistered firearm, a firearm that is not broken down in a nonfunctioning state, or a laser sight accessory shall be liable to the city for an administrative penalty of $1,000.00 plus any towing and storage fees applicable under Section 9-92-080. Any such vehicle shall be subject to seizure and impoundment pursuant to this section. This subsection shall not apply: (1) if the vehicle used in the violation was stolen at the time and the theft was reported to the appropriate police authorities within 24 hours after the theft was discovered or reason ably should have been discovered; (2) if the vehicle is operating as a common carrier and the violation occurs without the knowledge of the person in control of the vehicle; (3) if the owner proves that the presence of the firearm was permissible pursuant to paragraphs (1) through (10) of Section 8-20- 010 or, in the case of an unregistered firearm, the firearm was exempt from registration under subsection (b) of Section 8-20-040; or (4) if the owner proves the presence of a laser sight accessory was permissible pursuant to Section 8-20-165.

(b) Whenever a police officer has probable cause to believe that a vehicle is subject to seizure and impoundment pursuant to this section, the police officer shall provide for the towing of the vehicle to a facility con trolled by the city or its agents. Before or at the time the vehicle is towed, the police officer shall notify any person identifying himself as the owner of the vehicle or any person who is found to be in control of the vehicle at the time of the alleged violation, of the fact of the seizure and of the vehicle owner's right to request a vehicle impoundment hearing to be conducted under Section 2-14-132 of this code.

(c) The provisions of Section 2-14-132 shall apply whenever a motor vehicle is seized and impounded pursuant to this section.

(Added. Coun. J. 7-7-92, p. 19196; Amend. 7-14-93, p. 35530; 7-10-96, p. 24982; 4-29-98, p. 66564; 3-10-99, p. 91066; 12-15-04, p. 39840)

§8-20-020 Violation—Penalty.

Any person violating the provisions of Section 8-20-010 shall be fined $500.00.
(Prior code § 11.2-2)

Article II. Registration of Firearms

§8-20-030 Definitions.

As used in this Title 8:

(a) "Ammunition" means cartridge cases, shells, projectiles (including shot), primers, bullets, propellant powder, or other devices or materials designed, or intend ed for use in a firearm or destructive device.

(b) "Antique firearms" means any firearm, including, but not limited to, any firearm with a matchlock, flintlock, percussion cap or similar type of ignition system, which is incapable of being fired or discharged; or any firearm manufactured before 1898 for which cartridge ammunition is not commercially available and is possessed as a curiosity or ornament or for its historical significance or value.

(c) "Corrections officer" means wardens, superintendents and keepers of prisons, penitentiaries, jails or other institutions for the detention of persons accused or convicted of an offense.

(d) "Crime of violence" is defined as any felony committed while armed with a weapon as defined in Chapter 38, Section 33A-1 of Illinois Revised Statutes, as amended.

(e) "Duty-related firearm" shall mean any weapon which is authorized by any law enforcement agency to be utilized by their personnel in the performance of their official duties.

(f) "Firearm" means any weapon which will, or is designed to or restored to, expel a projectile or projectiles by the action of any explosive; the frame or receiver of any such device; or any firearm muffler or silencer. Provided, that such term shall not include:

(1) Antique firearms;

(2) Any device used exclusively for line-throwing, signaling, or safety and required or recommended by the United States Coast Guard or Interstate Commerce Com mission; or

(3) Any device used exclusively for firing explosives, rivets, stud cartridges, or any similar industrial ammunition incapable of use as a weapon.

(g) "Fragmenting bullet" means a bullet that is de signed or modified to shatter on impact, or any other bullet that is designed or modified so that more than 50 percent of the mass of the bullet is likely to fragment inside a human or animal target.

(h) "Assault weapon" means any of the following weapons:

(1) Assault Rifles

AK 47 type
AK 47S type
AK 74 type
86S type
86S7 type
87S type

AKS type
AKM type
AKMS type
84S1 type
ARM type
84S1 type
84S3 type
HK91 type
HK93 type
HK94 type
G3SA type
K1 type
K2 type
AR100 type
M24S type
SIG 550SP type
SIG 551SP type
Australian Automatic Arms SAR type
Galil type
Type 56 type
Type 565 type
Valmet M76 type
Valmet M78 type
M76 counter sniper type
FAL type
L1A1A type
SAR 48 type
AUG type
FNC type
Uzi carbine
Algimec AGMI type
AR180 type
MAS 223 type
Beretta BM59 type
Beretta AR70 type
CIS SR88 type
SKS type with detachable magazine
Colt AR-15
Springfield Armory SAR-48
Springfield Armory BM-59
Bushmaster Auto Rifle
Auto-Ordinance Thompson M1
Ruger Mini 14/5F
Federal XC-900 and XC-450
Feather AT-9 Auto Carbine
Goncz High Tech Carbine
Auto-Ordinance Thompson 1927A1
Iver Johnson PM30 P Paratrooper

(2) Assault Pistols
Uzi type
Heckler & Koch Sp-89 type
Australian Automatic Arms SAP type
Spectre Auto type
Sterling Mark 7 type; and

(3) Any weapon that the superintendent of police defines by regulation as an assault weapon because the design or operation of such weapon is inappropriate for lawful use.

(i) "Assault ammunition" means any ammunition magazine having a capacity of more than 12 rounds of ammunition.

(j) "Disc projectile ammunition" means any ammunition which is composed of multiple disc shaped objects stacked together to form a single round of ammunition, including but not limited to the following types of ammunition: (i) Magdisc type; and (ii) Shatterdisc type.

(k) "Handgun" means a firearm designed to be held and fired by the use of a single hand, and includes a combination of parts from which such firearm can be assembled.

(l) "Machine gun" means any firearm from which eight or more shots or bullets may be discharged by a single function of the firing device.

(m) "Mayor" means the mayor of the city of Chicago or his or her designee.

(n) "Metal piercing bullet" means any bullet that is manufactured with other than a lead or lead alloy core, or ammunition of which the bullet itself is wholly com posed of, or machined from, a metal or metal alloy other than lead, or any other bullet that is manufactured to defeat or penetrate bullet resistant properties of soft body armor or any other type of bullet resistant clothing which meets the minimum requirements of the current National Institute for Justice Standards for "Ballistic Resistance of Police Body Armor."

(o) "Organization" means partnership, company, corporation or other business entity, or any group or association of two or more persons united for a common purpose.

(p) "Peace officer" means any person who by virtue of his office or public employment is vest ed by law with a duty to maintain public order or make arrests for offenses, whether that duty extends to all offenses or is limited to specific offenses.

(q) "Person" shall mean any individual, corporation, company, association, firm, partnership, society, joint stock company or organization of any kind.

(r) "Sawed-off shotgun" means a shotgun having a barrel of less than 18 inches in length or a firearm made from a shotgun if such firearm is modified and has an overall length of less than 26 inches or a barrel of less than 18 inches in length.

(s) "Security personnel" means special agents employed by a railroad or public utility to per form police functions: guards of armored car companies, watchmen, security guards and persons regularly employed in a commercial or industrial operation for the protection of persons employed by or property related to such commercial or industrial operation.

(t) "Short-barreled rifle" means a rifle having any barrel less than 16 inches in length, or a modified firearm if such firearm as modified has an overall length of less than 26 inches or any barrel of less than 16 inches.

(u) "Superintendent" means the superintendent of the Chicago Police Department or his designated representative.

(v) "Safety mechanism" means a design adaption or nondetachable accessory that lessens the likelihood of unanticipated use of the handgun by other than the owner of the handgun and those specifically authorized by the owner to use the handgun.

(w) "Trigger lock" means a device that when locked in place by means of a key, prevents a potential user from pulling the trigger of the handgun without first removing the trigger lock by use of the trigger lock's key.

(x) "Combination handle lock" means a device that is part of the handgun which precludes the use of the handgun unless the combination tumblers are properly aligned.

(y) "Solenoid use-limitation device" means a device which precludes, by use of solenoid, the firing of the handgun unless a magnet of the appropriate strength is placed in proximity to the handle of the weapon.

(z) "Load indicator" means a device which plainly indicates that a bullet is placed in the handgun in a way that pulling the trigger or otherwise handling the handgun may result in detonation.

(aa) "Laser sight accessory" means a laser sighting device which is either integrated into a firearm or capable of being attached to a firearm.

(Prior code § 11.1-1; Amend. Coun. J. 7-7-92, p. 19196; 2-8-95, p. 65436; 8-2-95, p. 5626; 2-7-97, p. 38729; 3-10-99, p. 91066)

§8-20-040 Registration of firearms.

(a) All firearms in the city of Chicago shall be registered in accordance with the provisions of this chapter. It shall be the duty of a person owning or possessing a firearm to cause such firearm to be registered. No person shall within the city of Chicago, possess, harbor, have under his control, transfer, offer for sale, sell, give, deliver, or accept any firearm unless such person is the holder of a valid registration certificate for such firearm. No person shall, within the city of Chicago, possess, harbor, have under his control, transfer, offer for sale, sell, give, deliver, or accept any firearm which is unregisterable under the provisions of this chapter.

(b) This section shall not apply to:

(1) Firearms owned or under the direct control or custody of any federal, state or local govern mental authority maintained in the course of its official duties;

(2) Duty-related firearms owned and possessed by peace officers who are not residents of the city of Chicago;

(3) Duty-related firearms owned or possessed by corrections officers; provided, that such corrections officers are not residents of the city of Chicago;

(4) Firearms owned, manufactured or processed by licensed manufacturers of firearms, bulk transporters or licensed sellers of firearms at wholesale or retail, provided that such persons have, in addition to any other license required by law, a valid deadly weapons dealer license issued under Chapter 4-144 of this code;

(5) Any nonresident of the city of Chicago participating in any lawful recreational firearm-related activity in the city, or on his way to or from such activity in another jurisdiction; provided, that such weapon shall be unloaded and securely wrapped and that his possession or control of such firearm is lawful in the jurisdiction in which he resides;

(6) Peace officers, while in the course of their official duties, who possess and control any fire arm or ammunition issued by their department, bureau or agency in the normal course of business;

(7) Private security personnel who possess or control any firearm or ammunition within the city of Chicago; provided, that such firearms shall be owned and maintained by the security firm employing such personnel and shall be registered by the security firm in accordance with this chapter;

(8) Those persons summoned by a peace officer to assist in making an arrest or preserving the peace while actually engaged in assisting the peace officer.

(Prior code § 11.1-2; Amend. Coun. J. 7-7-92, p. 19196)

§8-20-050 Unregisterable firearms.

No registration certificate shall be issued for any of the following types of firearms:

(a) Sawed-off shotgun, machine gun, or short-barreled rifle;

(b) Firearms, other than handguns, owned or possessed by any person in the city of Chicago prior to the effective date of this chapter which are not validly registered prior to the effective date of this chapter;

(c) Handguns, except:

(1) Those validly registered to a current owner in the city of Chicago prior to the effective date of this chapter, and which contain each of the following:

(i) A safety mechanism to hinder the use of the handgun by unauthorized users. Such devices shall include, but shall not be limited to, trigger locks, combination handle locks, and solenoid use-limitation devices, and

(ii) A load indicator device that provides reasonable warning to potential users such that even users unfamiliar with the weapon would be forewarned and would under stand the nature of the warning,

(2) Those owned by peace officers who are residents of the city of Chicago,

(3) Those owned by security personnel,

(4) Those owned by private detective agencies licensed under Chapter 111.2601 et seq. Illinois Revised Statutes;

(d) Firearm muffler or silencer;

(e) Assault weapons, as defined in Section 8-20-030, unless they are owned by a person who is entitled to own them under Section 8-24-025.

Any person who receives through inheritance any firearm validly registered pursuant to this chapter will be eligible to reregister such firearm within 60 days after obtaining possession or title, provided such person shall be qualified to do so in accordance with this chapter.

(Prior code § 11.1-3; Amend. Coun. J. 7-7-92, p. 19196; 2-7-97, p. 38729)

§8-20-060 Prerequisites to registration—Application for registration.

(a) No registration certificate shall be issued to any person unless such person:

(1) Shall possess a valid Illinois Firearm Owner's Identification Card in accordance with Chapter 38 Section 83-4 of the Illinois Revised Statutes as amended;

(2) Has not been convicted of a crime of violence, as defined herein as weapons offense, or a violation of this chapter; and

(3) Has not been convicted within the five years prior to the application of any:

(i) Violation of any law relating to the use, possession or sale of any narcotic or dangerous drug, or

(ii) Violation of Chapter 38 Section 12-2(a)(1) of the Illinois Revised Statutes, as amended, for aggravated assault or any similar provision of the law of any other jurisdiction; and

(4) Has vision better than or equal to that required to obtain a valid driver's license under the standards established by the Illinois Vehicle Code Chapter 95½, Section 506-4 Illinois Revised Statutes, as amended; and

(5) Is not otherwise ineligible to possess a firearm under any federal,

state or local law, statute or ordinance.

(b) All applicants for a registration certificate under this chapter shall file with the superintendent on a form provided, a sworn application in writing. The application shall include the following:

(1) Name, social security number, residential and business address and telephone number of the applicant;

(2) The applicant's age, sex and citizenship;

(3) The applicant's Illinois firearm owner's identification number;

(4) The name of manufacturer, the caliber or gauge, the model, type and the serial number identification of the firearm to be registered;

(5) The source from which the firearm was obtained;

(6) Evidence that the applicant meets the criteria of Section 8-20-060(a) of this chapter;

(7) Two photographs of the applicant taken within 30 days immediately prior to the date of filing the application equivalent to passport size showing the full face, head and shoulders of the applicant in a clear and distinguishing manner;

(8) Such other information as the superintendent shall find reasonably necessary to effectuate the purpose of this chapter and to arrive at a fair determination whether the terms of this ordinance have been complied with.

(c) The superintendent shall be the custodian of all applications for registration under this chapter.

(Prior code § 11.1-4)

§8-20-070 Fingerprints.

When necessary to establish the identity of any applicant or registrant, such applicant or registrant shall be required to submit to fingerprinting in accordance with procedures and regulations prescribed by the superintendent.

(Prior code § 11.1-5)

§8-20-080 Application fees.

(a) A nonrefundable fee in the amount indicated in subsection (d) of this section shall accompany each initial registration.

(b) A nonrefundable fee in the amount indicated in subsection (d) of this section shall accompany each reregistration application.

(c) The registration fee shall not be applicable to (1) any duty-related handgun(s) of a peace officer(s) domiciled in the city of Chicago, or (2) to any duty-related handgun(s) owned by a resident of the city of Chicago who retired from the Chicago Police Department in good standing and without any disciplinary charges pending, and who is, or is eligible to become, an annuitant of the Policeman's Annuity and Benefit Fund of the city of Chicago, but only if the handgun(s) is registered in that person's name at the time of separation from active duty in the Chicago Police Department.

(d) Registration fees for firearms shall be as follows:

1 firearm.................................... $20.00
2—10 firearms............................ 25.00
More than 10 firearms................ 35.00

(Prior code § 11.1-6; Amend. Coun. J. 7-7-92, p. 19196; 11-10-94, p. 59125; 4-9-03, p. 106640)

§8-20-090 Filing time.

(a) A registration certificate shall be obtained prior to any person taking possession of a firearm from any source.

(b) Any firearm currently registered must be reregistered pursuant to this chapter and in accordance with rules, regulations and procedures prescribed by the superintendent. An application to reregister such firearm shall be filed within 180 days from the effective date of this chapter; provided, however, that this section shall not apply to law enforcement officers during their tenure of continuous active duty.

(Prior code § 11.1-7; Amend. Coun. J. 2-4-85, p. 13404; 3-25-86, p. 28873)

§8-20-100 Investigations.

Upon receipt of an application for registration of a firearm, the superintendent of police shall investigate the information contained in said application to determine whether the application and firearm meet the requirements for registration under this chapter. Failure by the applicant or registrant to respond to investigation inquiries shall be
sufficient grounds for denial or revocation.

(Prior code § 11.1-8)

§8-20-110 Issuance of registration certificate.

(a) Upon receipt of a properly executed application for a registration certificate and the report of the superintendent, the mayor, upon determining that the applicant has complied with the provisions of this chapter, shall authorize the issuance of the registration certificate. Each registration certificate shall be in triplicate and bear a unique registration certificate number and contain such other information as may be necessary to identify the applicant and the firearm registered. The original of the registration certificate shall be retained by the superintendent; the mayor and applicant shall each receive a copy.

(b) The mayor shall approve or deny any application for a registration certificate within a 120-day period beginning on the date the superintendent receives the application unless good cause is shown. In the case of an application to reregister a firearm currently registered, the mayor shall have 365 days after receipt of such application to approve or deny such application unless good cause is shown.

(c) Any application for registration or renewal shall be held in abeyance when there is a criminal proceeding for a crime of violence, or an offense involving a weapon, or a proceeding to revoke firearm registration pending against the applicant until such proceeding has terminated. In the case of a renewal of registration the then-current registration shall be deemed continuing until the termination of such proceedings.

(d) Upon receipt of a registration certificate, each applicant shall examine the same to insure that the information thereon is correct. If the registration certificate is incorrect in any respect, the registrant thereon shall return it to the superintendent with a signed statement showing the nature of the error. The superintendent shall correct the error, if it occurred through administrative error.

In the event that the error resulted from incorrect information contained in the application, the applicant shall be required to file an amended application setting forth the correct information and a statement explaining the error in the original application. Each amended application shall be accompanied by a fee of $2.00.

(e) Each registration certificate authorized to be issued by the mayor shall be accompanied by a statement set ting forth the registrant's duties under this chapter.

(Prior code § 11.1-9)

§8-20-120 Revocation—Denial.

A registration certificate shall be revoked or an application for registration or reregistration shall be denied by the mayor when she finds that:

(a) Any of the criteria in Section 8-20-060(a) of this chapter are not currently met; or

(b) The registered firearm is or has become an unregisterable firearm under the terms of Section 8-20-050 of this chapter; or

(c) The information furnished to the superintendent on the application for registration certificate proves to be false; or

(d) The applicant or registrant has violated any of the provisions of this chapter.

(Prior code § 11.1-10)

§8-20-130 Procedures for denial or revocation.

(a) If it is determined that an application for registration or reregistration should be denied or that a registration certificate should be revoked, the mayor shall notify the applicant or registrant in writing of the proposed denial or revocation, briefly stating the reason or reasons there fore.

(b) The applicant or registrant, within 10 days after receiving notice of the proposed denial or revocation, may file with the mayor a written request for a hearing before the mayor's license com mission.

(c) Within 10 days of receipt of a request for hearing, the commission shall give notice of a hearing to be held not less than five days after service of the notice on the person requesting the hearing.

At the hearing, the applicant or registrant may submit further evidence in support of the application for initial registration or to continue to hold a registration certificate as the case may be.

The commission shall determine whether the denial or revocation was in accordance with the provisions of this chapter and shall report its finding to the mayor within 21 days after the public hearing has been completed.

Upon a review of the commission's findings and a determination that the application should be denied or certificate revoked, the mayor shall issue a written finding stating the reasons for denial or revocation thereof and shall serve a copy of said findings upon the applicant or registrant and all parties appearing or represented at the hearing.

(d) If the applicant or registrant does not request a hearing or submit further evidence within 10 days after receiving notification of the proposed denial or revocation, it shall be deemed that the applicant or registrant has conceded the validity of the reason or reasons stated in the notice and the denial or revocation shall become final.

(e) Within three days after notification of a decision unfavorable to the applicant or registrant and all time for appeal in accordance with paragraph 8-20-130(a) through (d) having expired, the applicant or registrant shall:

(1) Peaceably surrender to the Chicago Police Department the firearm for which the applicant was denied or the registration certificate was revoked; or

(2) Remove such firearm from the city of Chicago; or

(3) Otherwise lawfully dispose of his interest in such firearm.

(f) The applicant or registrant shall submit to the superintendent evidence of the disposition of nonregisterable firearms in accordance with paragraph 8-20-130(e)(2) and (3). Such evidence shall be submitted on forms and in the manner prescribed by the superintendent.

(Prior code § 11.1-11)

§8-20-140 Additional duties of registrant.

Each person holding a registration certificate shall:

(a) Immediately notify the Chicago Police Department on a form prescribed by the superintendent of:

(1) The loss, theft or destruction of the registration certificate or of a registered firearm immediately upon discovery of such loss, theft, or destruction;

(2) A change in any of the information appearing on the registration certificate;

(3) The sale, transfer or other disposition of the firearm not less than 48 hours prior to delivery.

(b) Immediately return to the superintendent his copy of the registration certificate for any fire arm which is lost, stolen, destroyed or otherwise disposed of.

(c) Each registrant shall keep any firearm in his possession unloaded and disassembled or bound by a trigger lock or similar device, unless such firearm is in his possession at his place of residence or business or while being used for lawful recreational purposes within the city of Chicago; provided, this paragraph shall not apply to law enforcement personnel as defined in paragraph 8-20-030(k) and provided further this paragraph shall not apply to security personnel as defined in paragraph 8-20-030(s), while in the course of their employment.

(Prior code § 11.1-12)

§8-20-150 Exhibition of registration.

Any person carrying or having in his possession or under his custody or control any firearm, shall have on his person or within his immediate custody a valid registration certificate for such firearm issued hereunder, which shall be exhibited for inspection to any peace officer upon demand. Failure of any such person to so exhibit his registration certificate shall be presumptive evidence that he is not authorized to possess such firearm.

Failure of any person to exhibit a registration certificate for any firearm in his possession, custody or control shall also be cause for the confiscation of such firearms and revocation of any registration certificates issued there fore under this chapter.

(Prior code § 11.1-13)

§8-20-160 Possession of ammunition.

No person shall possess ammunition in the city of Chicago unless:

(a) He is a person exempted pursuant to Section 8-20-040 of this chapter; or

(b) He is the holder of a valid registration certificate for a firearm of the same gauge or caliber as the ammunition possessed, and has the registration certificate in his possession while in possession of the ammunition; or

(c) He is a licensed weapons dealer pursuant to Chapter 4-144 or a licensed shooting gallery or gun club pursuant to Chapter 4-149 of this code.

(Prior code § 11.1-14; Amend. Coun. J. 9-14-94, p. 56287)

§8-20-165 Possession of laser sight accessories.

No person shall sell, offer, or display for sale, give, lend, transfer ownership of, acquire or possess any laser sight accessory in the city of Chicago provided, that this section shall not apply to any members of the armed forces of the United States, or the organized militia of this or any other state, and peace officers as defined in this code to the extent that any such person is otherwise authorized to acquire or possess a laser sight accessory and is acting within the scope of his or her duties.

(Added. Coun. J. 3-10-99, p. 91066)

§8-20-170 Permissible sales and transfers of firearms and ammunition.

(a) No firearm may be sold or otherwise transferred within the city of Chicago except through a licensed weapons dealer as defined in Chapter 4-144 of the Municipal Code of the city of Chicago.

(b) No ammunition may be sold or otherwise transferred within the city of Chicago except through a licensed shooting gallery or gun club as defined in Chapter 4-149, a licensed weapons dealer as defined in Chapter 4-144 or as otherwise allowed by the Municipal Code of the city of Chicago.

(c) No firearm or ammunition shall be security for, or be taken or received by way of any mort gage, deposit, pledge or pawn.

(d) No person may loan, borrow, give or rent to or from another person, any firearm or ammunition except in accordance with this chapter.

(e) A peace officer may additionally sell or transfer any lawfully held firearm or ammunition to another peace officer in accordance with the other provisions of this chapter.

(f) Except as allowed by subsection (e) of this section, no person may sell, offer for sale, barter or transfer within the city any ammunition listed in Section 4-144-061 of this code.

(Prior code § 11.1-15; Amend. Coun. J. 9-14-94, p. 56287)

§8-20-175 Firearm Owners Identification Card Act—Compliance required.

No person shall sell, give away or otherwise transfer any firearm, as defined in Section 8-20-030, without complying with Sections 3 and 3.1 of the Firearm Owners Identification Card Act, Illinois Revised Statutes, Chapter 38, paragraphs 83-3 and 83-3.1.

(Added. Coun. J. 7-7-92, p. 19196)

§8-20-180 False information—Forgery—Alteration.

(a) It shall be unlawful for any person purchasing any firearm or ammunition, or applying for any registration certificate under this chapter, or, in giving any information pursuant to the requirements of this chapter, to knowingly give false information or offer false evidence of identity.

(b) It shall be unlawful for anyone to forge or alter any application or registration certificate submitted, retained or issued under this chapter.

(Prior code § 11.1-16)

§8-20-190 Voluntary surrender—Immunity.

(a) Within 90 days from the effective date of this ordinance, a person within the city of Chicago may voluntarily and peaceably deliver and abandon to the superintendent any firearm or ammunition prior to any arrest and prosecution of such person on a charge of violating any provisions of this chapter with respect to the firearm or ammunition voluntarily delivered.

(b) Delivery under this section may be made at any police district, area or central headquarters or by summoning a police officer to the person's residence or place of business. Any firearm or ammunition to be delivered and abandoned to the superintendent under this section shall be unload ed and securely wrapped in a package carried in open view.

(c) The voluntary delivery or abandonment of any firearm or ammunition after an arrest or charge for violation of any provision of this chapter shall not moot or in any manner invalidate said arrest or charge.

(Prior code § 11.1-17)

§8-20-195 Voluntary surrender of laser sight accessory—Immunity.

(a) Within 14 days of the effective date of this ordinance, a person within the city of Chicago may voluntarily and peaceably deliver and abandon to the superintendent any laser sight accessory prior to any arrest and prosecution of such person on a charge of violating any provision of this chapter with respect to the laser sight accessory voluntarily delivered.

(b) Delivery under this section may be made at any police district, area or central headquarters or by summoning a police officer to the person's residence or place of business.

(c) The voluntary delivery or abandonment of any laser sight accessory after an arrest or charge for violation of any provision of this chapter shall not moot or in any manner invalidate said arrest or charge.

(Added Coun. J. 3-10-99, p. 91066)

§8-20-200 Renewal of registration.

(a) Every registrant must renew his registration certificate annually. Applications for renewal shall be made by such registrants 60 days prior to the expiration of the current registration certificate.

(b) The application for renewal shall include the payment of a renewal fee as follows:

1 firearm $20.00
2—10 firearms.................... 25.00
More than 10 firearms 35.00

(c) Failure to comply with the requirement for renewal of registration of a firearm shall cause that firearm to become unregisterable.

(d) All terms, conditions and requirements of this chapter for registration of firearms shall be applicable to renewal or registration of such firearms.

(e) The renewal fee shall not be applicable to duty-related handguns of peace officers domiciled in the city of Chicago.

(Prior code § 11.1-18; Amend. Coun. J. 7-7-92, p. 19196; 11-10-94, p. 59125)

§8-20-210 Notice.

For the purposes of this chapter, service of any notice, finding or decision upon an applicant or registrant shall be completed by any of the following methods:

(1) Personal delivery of a copy of such notice, finding or decision to the applicant or registrant; or

(2) By leaving a copy of such notice, finding or decision at the address identified on the application for registration or renewal; or

(3) By mailing a copy of the notice, finding or decision by certified mail with return receipt to the address identified on the application for registration or renewal; in which case service shall be complete as of the date the return receipt was signed.

(Prior code § 11.1-19)

§8-20-220 Destruction of weapons confiscated.

Whenever any firearm or ammunition is surrendered or confiscated pursuant to the terms of this chapter, the superintendent shall ascertain whether such firearm or ammunition is needed as evidence in any matter.

If such firearm or ammunition is not required for evidence it shall be destroyed at the direction of the superintendent. A record of the date and method of destruction and an inventory of the fire arm or ammunition so destroyed shall be maintained.

(Prior code § 11.1-20)

§8-20-230 Authority of the superintendent.

The superintendent shall have the authority to promulgate rules and regulations for the implementation of this chapter and to prescribe all forms and the information required thereon.

(Prior code § 11.1-21)

§8-20-240 Acquisition or possession prohibited by law.

Nothing in this chapter shall make lawful the acquisition or possession of firearms or firearm ammunition which is otherwise prohibited by law.

(Prior code § 11.1-22)

§8-20-241 Firearm used illegally—Penalty.

The owner of an unregistered firearm that is used in any criminal act shall be subject to a fine of $500.00 for each such use, regardless of whether the owner participated in, aided or abetted the criminal act. A fine under this

section shall be in addition to any other penalty imposed on the criminal act or use of the firearm.
(Added. Coun. J. 11-10-94, p. 59125)

§8-20-250 Violation—Penalty.

Any person who violates any provision of this chapter, where no other penalty is specifically provided, shall upon conviction for the first time, be fined not less than $300.00, nor more than $500.00; or be incarcerated for not less than 10 days nor more than 90 days or both. Any subsequent conviction for a violation of this chapter shall be punishable by a fine of $500.00 and by incarceration for a term of not less than 90 days, nor more than six months.
(Prior code § 11.1-23; Amend. Coun. J. 11-10-94, p. 59125)

§8-20-260 Severability.

If any provision or term of this chapter, or any application thereof, is held invalid, the invalidity shall not affect other applications of the provisions or terms of this chapter which reasonably can be given effect without the invalid provision or term for the application thereof.
(Prior code § 11.1-24)

CHAPTER 8-24
FIREARMS AND OTHER WEAPONS

Sections:

8-24-010 Discharging firearms.
8-24-020 Carrying dangerous weapons.
8-24-021 Sale, display and use of utility knives.
8-24-025 Assault weapons or ammunition—Sale prohibited—Exceptions.
8-24-026 Fragmenting bullets and metal piercing bullets—Sale prohibited—Exceptions.
8-24-027 Disguised firearms prohibited.
8-24-030 Sale prohibited—Confiscation.
8-24-040 Discharging toy firearms.
8-24-045 Noxious gas or liquid.
8-24-050 Hunting.
8-24-060 Violation—Penalty.

§8-24-010 Discharging firearms.

No person shall fire or discharge any gun, pistol, or other firearm within the city, except upon premises used by a duly licensed shooting gallery, gun club, or rifle club, or in accordance with the provisions of Section 8-24-050 of this code.

No cannon or piece of artillery shall be discharged or fired off in any public way or other public place within the city, except upon the express permission of the city council.

Any person violating any of the provisions of this section shall be fined not less than $250.00 nor more than $500.00 for each offense.

The provisions of this section shall not apply to sheriffs, coroners, constables, members of the police force, or other peace officers engaged in the discharge of their official duties, or to any person summoned by any of such officers to assist in making arrests or preserving the peace while such person so summoned is engaged in assisting such officer.
(Prior code § 193-29; Amend. Coun. J. 7-7-92, p. 19196)

§8-24-020 Carrying dangerous weapons.

No person shall sell, offer for sale, keep, possess, loan or give to any person any knife, the blade of which is released by a spring mechanism, including knives known as "switch-blades," any black jack, slingshot, sandclub, sandbag, metal knuckles or bludgeon. No person shall sell, offer for sale, loan or give to any person 18 years of age or under any type or kind of knife, any blade of which is two inches in length or longer.

No person shall sell, manufacture, purchase, possess or carry any weapon from which eight or more shots or bullets may be discharged by a single function of the firing device.

No person shall carry or possess any knife, the blade of which is released by a spring mechanism, including knives known as "switch-blades," any blackjack, slingshot, sandclub, sandbag, metal knuckles or bludgeon. No person 18 years of age or under shall carry or possess any knife, the blade of which is two inches in length or longer.

No person shall carry or possess with intent to use same unlawfully against another a dagger, dirk, billy, dangerous knife, razor, stiletto or other dangerous or deadly weapon.

No person shall carry concealed on or about his person a pistol, revolver, derringer or other firearm or dagger, dirk, stiletto, bowie knife, commando knife, any blade of which is released by a spring mechanism, including knives known as "switch-blades" or any other type or kind of knife, any blade of which is more than two and one-half inches in length, ordinary razor or other dangerous weapon except that no person 18 years of age or under shall carry concealed on or about his person, any knife, the blade of which is two inches in length or longer. This provision shall not apply, however, to the following officers while engaged in the discharge of their official duties: sheriffs, coroners, constables, policemen or other duly constituted police officers and wardens, superintendents and keepers of prisons, penitentiaries, jails and other institutions for the detention of persons accused or convicted of crime; nor to the following employees or agents while engaged in the discharge of the duties of their employment: conductors, baggagemen, messengers, drivers, watchmen, special agents and policemen employed by railroads or express companies; nor to per sons lawfully summoned by an officer to assist in making arrests or preserving the peace, while so engaged in assisting such officer.

Any person violating the provisions of this section shall be fined $200.00 for each offense, or shall be punished by imprisonment for a period of six months, or by both such fine and imprisonment.

In addition to all other penalties, weapons used in violation of this section shall be forfeited to, and confiscated by, the city.

(Prior code § 193-30)

§8-24-021 Sale, display and use of utility knives.

(a) As used in this section, a "utility knife" is a knife consisting of a grip and single-edged sharp blade of the type typically used to cut such resistant surfaces as rugs, cardboard boxes, linoleum flooring and the like.

(b) No person shall display or offer for sale any utility knife except by placing the knife either (1) in an area immediately accessible only to an employee of the establishment, and beyond the reach of any customer less than seven feet tall; or (2) in a locked display cabinet, which can only be opened by an employee of the establishment.

(c) No person under the age of 18 shall carry a utility knife on his person, or in the passenger compartment of a motor vehicle. This prohibition shall not apply to a minor using a utility knife for a lawful purpose (1) in his residence, under the immediate supervision of his parent or legal guardian; or (2) in a classroom, at the direction and under the immediate supervision of his teacher; or (3) in his place of lawful employment, at the direction and under the immediate supervision of his adult employer or an adult supervisor. For purpose of clause (3) of this subsection (c), "place of employment" includes an employer's motor vehicle used to transport the employer's tools and equipment, as well as a site where the employer is performing any lawful work.

(d) No person shall sell, offer to sell, give, deliver or offer a utility knife to a person under the age of 18. The prohibition on giving, offering or delivery of a utility knife shall not apply to (1) a parent or legal guardian who gives a utility knife to his minor or ward in the family residence for a lawful use, to be per formed within the residence at the direction and under the immediate supervision of parent or legal guardian; or (2) a teacher who gives a utility knife to a minor student, or who allows or directs a minor student to take possession of a utility knife, in a classroom for a lawful use, to be performed in the classroom at the direction and under the immediate supervision of the teacher; or (3) to an adult employer, who gives a utility knife to a minor employee, or who allows or directs a minor employee to take possession of a utility knife, in the place of lawful employment, at the direction and under the immediate supervision of the adult employer or an adult supervisor. For purposes of clause (3) of this subsection (d), "place of employment" includes an employer's motor vehicle used to transport the employer's tools and equipment, as well as a site where the employer is performing any lawful work.

(e) Any person who violates any provision of this section shall be subject to a fine of not less than $500.00 and not more than $1,000.00.
(Added. Coun. J. 9-10-97, p. 51559)

§8-24-025 Assault weapons or ammunition— Sale prohibited— Exceptions.

(a) No person shall sell, offer or display for sale, give, lend, transfer ownership of, acquire or possess any assault weapon or assault ammunition, as those terms are defined in Chapter 8-20 of this code. This section shall not apply to any officer, agent, or employee of this or any other municipality or state or of the United States, members of the armed forces of the United States, or the organized militia of this or any other state, and peace officers as defined in this code to the extent that any such person is otherwise authorized to acquire or possess an assault weapon or assault ammunition and is acting within the scope of his or her duties. In addition, this section shall not apply to the acquisition or possession of assault ammunition by persons employed to provide security for armored carriers or mobile check cashing services while in the course of such duties, while commuting directly to or from the person's place of employment, and while at the person's home, if the assault ammunition (1) is acquired or possessed for use with a weapon that the person has been authorized to carry under Section 28 of the Illinois Private Detective, Private Alarm and

Private Security Act of 1983; and (2) consists of an ammunition magazine that has a capacity of 15 or fewer rounds of ammunition.

(b) Any assault weapon or assault ammunition possessed, sold or transferred in violation of subsection (a) is hereby declared to be contraband and shall be seized and disposed of in accordance with the provisions of Section 8-20-220.

(c) Any person found in violation of this section shall be sentenced to not more than six months imprisonment or fined not less than $500.00 and not more than $1,000.00 or both.

(d) Any person who, prior to the effective date of the ordinance codified in this section, was legally in possession of an assault weapon or assault ammunition prohibited by this section shall have 14 days from the effective date of the ordinance codified in this section to do any of the following without being subject to prosecution hereunder:

(1) To remove the assault weapon or ammunition from within the limits of the city of Chicago; or

(2) To modify the assault weapon either to render it permanently inoperable or to permanently make it a device no longer defined as an assault weapon; or

(3) To surrender the assault weapon or ammunition to the superintendent of police or his designee for disposal in accordance with Section 8-20-220.

(Added. Coun. J. 7-7-92, p. 19196; Amend. Coun. J. 7-29-92, p. 20068; 9-14-94, p. 56287)

§8-24-026 Fragmenting bullets and metal piercing bullets—Sale prohibited—Exceptions.

(a) No person shall manufacture, sell, offer or display for sale, give, lend, transfer ownership of, acquire or possess any fragmenting bullets, metal piercing bullets, or disc projectile ammunition. This section shall not apply to any officer, agent, or employee of this or any other municipality or state or of the United States, members of the armed forces of the United States, or the organized militia of this or any other state, and peace officers as defined in this code to the extent that any such person is otherwise authorized to acquire or possess fragmenting bullets, metal piercing bullets, or disc projectile ammunition and is acting within the scope of his or her duties.

(b) Any fragmenting bullets, metal piercing bullets, or disc projectile ammunition manufactured, possessed, sold or transferred in violation of subsection (a) are hereby declared to be contraband and shall be seized and disposed of in accordance with the provisions of Section 8-20-220.

(c) Any person found in violation of this section shall be sentenced to not more than six months imprisonment or fined $500.00, or both.

(Added. Coun. J. 2-8-95, p. 65436; Amend. 8-2-95, p. 5626)

§8-24-027 Disguised firearms prohibited.

(a) No person shall purchase, acquire, sell, offer or expose for sale, or possess any firearm that is designed, constructed, modified or disguised to resemble any other object.

(b) Any person who violates subsection (a) of this section shall be guilty of a misdemeanor, and shall be subject to incarceration for not less than 30 days and not more than 180 days for each offense. Each day of a continuing violation, and each purchase, acquisition, sale, offering or exposing for sale, or possession of a different firearm described in subsection (a) shall constitute a separate and distinct offense.

(c) Nothing in this section suspends, repeals or alters any other provision of this code which limits, restricts or prohibits the purchase, acquisition, sale, offering or exposure for sale, or possession of a firearm.

(Added. Coun. J. 6-10-98, p. 71436)

§8-24-030 Sale prohibited—Confiscation.

No person shall sell, offer for sale, manufacture, purchase, possess or carry within the city any weapon or instrument associated with martial arts combat, including but not limited to throwing darts, bolts, Chinese stars, Nun-chako sticks, and wristbands or belts with sharpened or abrasive studs. Any person found violating the provisions of this section shall be fined $200.00 for each offense, or shall be punished by imprisonment for a period of six months, or shall receive both such fine and imprisonment.

In addition to all other penalties, weapons and instruments used in violation of this section shall be forfeited to and confiscated by the city.

(Prior code § 193-30.1; Added. Coun. J. 4-23-86, p. 29530)

§8-24-040 Discharging toy firearms.

No person shall at any time discharge or set off any where within the city, or have in his possession for such purpose any toy firearm, air rifle, toy cannon, or any gun that discharges projectiles either by air, spring, explosive, substance, or any other force.

(Prior code § 193-31)

§8-24-045 Noxious gas or liquid.

(a) No person shall use any device to discharge a noxious gas or liquid in an enclosed room in any Class C-1 or Class C-2 Assembly Unit, as defined in Chapter 13-56 of this code, or in an enclosed room in any restaurant, bar or tavern that is a Class F Assembly Unit as defined in that chapter, if more than 20 persons are present in that room, unless the person is a peace officer, as defined in Section 8-20-030 of this code, engaged in law enforcement activity. As used in this section, "noxious gas or liquid" means mace, pepper spray or any other substance that is intended or designed to cause irritation to the eyes, nose or mouth, or to cause nausea.

(b) Any person who violates this section is guilty of a misdemeanor that is punishable by a fine of $500, or 30 days imprisonment, or both, for each offense.

(Added. Coun. J. 4-9-03, p. 106979)

§8-24-050 Hunting.

Any person licensed to hunt under the provisions of The Illinois Wildlife Code, as amended, may hunt or kill game birds in the open season as provided by the laws of the state, within the following prescribed districts and portions of the city: upon Wolf Lake and along the shores there of; upon Lake Calumet and along the shores thereof; and upon the Calumet River and along the banks thereof.

Provided, however, that no weapons shall be used for the purpose of hunting such birds, or killing or wounding, or attempting to kill or wound such birds, other than a shotgun, and that such shotgun shall not be discharged any where within 750 feet of (1) any building or structure used or intended for human habitation or employment, or to be used as a barn or stable; or (2) the centerline of the right-of-way of Stony Island Avenue.

Any person violating any of the provisions of this section shall be fined not less than $100.00 nor more than $250.00.

(Prior code § 193-32; Amend. Coun. J. 5-16-90, p. 15819)

§8-24-060 Violation—Penalty.

Any person violating any of the provisions of this chapter, where no other penalty is specifically pro vided, shall be fined not more than $200.00 for each offense.

(Prior code § 193-35 (part))

CHAPTER 8-28
RESERVED

(Renumbered to Chapter 1-20. Coun. J. 7-21-04, p. 28443)

CHAPTER 8-30
EVICTIONS FOR UNLAWFUL USE OF PREMISES

Sections:

8-30-010 Definitions.
8-30-020 Unlawful Use of Leased Premises—Evictions.

§8-30-010 Definitions.

Whenever used in this chapter, the following words and phrases shall have the following meanings:

(a) "Controlled substances" means any substance as defined and included in the Schedules of Article II of the Illinois Controlled Substances Act, and cannabis as defined in the Cannabis Control Act.

(b) "Controlled substance violation" means any occurrence of unlawful possession, delivery, distribution, manufacture or cultivation of a controlled substance.

(c) "Department" means the department of law.

(d) "Dwelling unit" means a structure or the part of a structure that is used as a home, residence or sleeping place by one or more persons who maintain a household.

(e) "Landlord" means the owner, agent, lessor or sublessor, or the successor in interest of any of them, of a dwelling unit or the building of which it is part, other than a unit of federal, state or local government.

(f) "Owner" means one or more persons, jointly or severally, in whom is vested all or part of the legal title to property, or all or part of the beneficial ownership and a right to present use and enjoyment of the premises, including a mortgagee in possession.

(g) "Pattern of controlled substance violations" means two or more controlled substance violation instances involving the same dwelling unit and occurring on two or more separate days within any six month period during the tenancy of any tenant of the dwelling unit. Violations will be considered to be involving the same dwelling unit they: (1) occur in the dwelling unit, in the structure containing the dwelling unit, or any other structure, land or public way appurtenant thereto, and (2) are committed by a tenant of the dwelling unit or by an individual who is on the premises with the permission of the tenant of the dwelling unit.

(h) "Premises" means the dwelling unit and the structure of which it is a part, and facilities and appurtenances therein, and grounds, areas and facilities held out for the use of tenants.

(i) "Rental agreement" means all written or oral agreements embodying the terms and conditions concerning the use and occupancy of a dwelling unit by a tenant.

(j) "Tenant" means a person entitled by written or oral agreement, subtenancy approved by the landlord or by sufferance, to occupy a dwelling unit to the exclusion of others.

(Added. Coun. J. 8-30-00, p. 40306)

§8-30-020 Unlawful Use of Leased Premises—Evictions.

(a) The department, on behalf of the city, or the Chicago Housing Authority on its own behalf, may bring an eviction proceeding pursuant to Section 2-14-200 of this code whenever there is cause to believe that a tenant is subject to eviction under this chapter. In any case in which a pattern of controlled substance violations is proven by a preponderance of the evidence, the tenants of the dwelling unit involved are in violation of this section and an order of eviction shall be issued against those tenants. The order of eviction shall cause the forfeiture of and terminate the rights of the tenant to use or occupy the dwelling unit pursuant to the rental agreement. Any tenant who has been served with an order of eviction shall be deemed to have abandoned the dwelling unit, as provided in subsection 5-12-130(e) of this code, as of the effective date of the order.

(b) In any eviction proceeding the landlord shall be made a party to the proceeding. Whenever a tenant is found to be in violation of this section, the landlord shall be liable for the cost of the eviction proceeding and the service and enforcement of the order of eviction in an amount not to exceed $5,000.00, plus any fees payable to the sheriff's police of the county of Cook for services rendered in connection with the proceeding.

(Added. Coun. J. 8-30-00, p. 40306)

TITLE 9
VEHICLES, TRAFFIC AND RAIL TRANSPORTATION
(Complete Title)

Chapters:

9-4	Traffic Definitions and General Provisions
9-8	Traffic Control Devices and Signals
9-12	Traffic and Speed Restrictions
9-16	Turning Movements
9-20	Movement of Traffic
9-24	Right-of-Way
9-28	Railroad and Bridge Crossings
9-32	Funeral Processions
9-36	Overtaking Vehicles
9-40	Driving Rules
9-44	Towing Disabled Vehicles
9-48	Types of Vehicles—Regulations
9-52	Bicycles—Operation
9-56	Reporting of Accidents
9-60	Pedestrians' Rights and Duties
9-64	Parking Regulations
9-68	Restricted Parking—Permits and Regulations
9-72	Size and Weight Limits
9-76	Vehicle Equipment
9-80	Miscellaneous Rules
9-84	Towing Unauthorized Vehicles
9-88	Duties of Police Department
9-92	Impounding and Relocation of Vehicles
9-96	Vehicle Immobilization—Parking Violation Complaints
9-100	Administrative Adjudication of Parking or Compliance Violations
9-102	Automated Red Light Camera Program
9-103	Automated Bus Lane and Bus Stop Camera Enforcement Program
9-104	Public Chauffeurs
9-108	Horse-Drawn Carriages
9-112	Public Passenger Vehicles
9-116	School Vehicle Registration
9-120	Bicycles
9-124	Transportation Services and Rail Transportation

CHAPTER 9-4
TRAFFIC DEFINITIONS AND GENERAL PROVISIONS

Sections:

9-4-010	Definitions.
9-4-020	Violation—Penalty.
9-4-030	Short title.

§9-4-010 Definitions.

Whenever the following words and phrases are used in Chapters 9-4 through 9-103, they shall have the meanings respectively ascribed to them in this section:

"Abandoned vehicle" means any vehicle that: (a) is in such a state of disrepair as to render the vehicle incapable of being driven in its present condition or (b) has not been moved or used for seven consecutive days and is apparently deserted.

"Adjudication by mail" means an administrative process by which a registered owner of a vehicle or his attorney may submit documentary evidence by mail to an administrative law officer in order to contest liability for a parking or compliance violation.

"Administrative hearing" means a hearing in person before an administrative law officer at which a registered owner of a vehicle or his attorney may contest liability for a parking or compliance violation.

"Alley" means a public way intended to give access to the rear or side of lots or buildings and not intended for the purpose of through vehicular traffic.

"Authorized emergency vehicle" means any vehicle of any fire department or police department or the city's office of emergency management and communications and any repair, service or other emergency vehicle of a governmental agency or public service corporation authorized by the superintendent of police.

"Bicycle" means every device propelled solely by human power upon which any person may ride, having two tandem wheels and including any device generally recognized as a bicycle though equipped with two front or two rear wheels.

"Boulevard" means a through street, except that its use is limited exclusively to certain specified classes of traffic.

"Bridle path" means a path designated for travel by persons upon horses.

"Bus" means every motor vehicle designed for carrying more than 10 passengers and used for the transportation of persons.

"Bus stand" means a fixed area in the roadway parallel and adjacent to the curb to be occupied exclusively by buses for layover in operating schedules or waiting for passengers.

"Bus stop" means a fixed area in the roadway parallel and adjacent to the curb set aside for the expeditious loading and unloading of passengers only.

"Business street" means the length of any street between street intersections on which more than 50 percent of the entire frontage at ground level of the street is in use by retail or wholesale businesses, hotels, banks, office buildings, railway stations, or public buildings other than schools.

"Carriage" means any device in, upon or by which any person is or may be transported or drawn upon a public way and designed to be or capable of being drawn by a horse.

"Carriage stand" means a fixed area in the roadway parallel and adjacent to the curb to be occupied exclusively by horse-drawn vehicles for loading and unloading passengers or waiting for passengers.

"Central Business District" means the district consisting of those streets or parts of streets within the area bounded by a line as follows: beginning at the easternmost point of Division Street extended to Lake Michigan; then west on Division Street to LaSalle Street; then south on LaSalle Street to Chicago Avenue; then west on Chicago Avenue to Halsted Street; then south on Halsted Street to Roosevelt Road; then east on Roosevelt Road to its easternmost point extended to Lake Michigan; including parking spaces on both sides of the above-mentioned streets.

"Commercial vehicle" means a motor vehicle operated for the transportation of persons or property in the furtherance of any commercial or industrial enterprise, for hire or not for hire; including but not limited to a motor vehicle of the first division displaying a placard indicating authorization of the Illinois Commerce Commission to operate as a motor carrier of property but not including, however, public passenger vehicles.

"Commissioner," when used alone, means the commissioner of transportation of the city.

"Compliance violation" means a violation of an ordinance listed in subsection (c) of Section 9-100-020 of this code.

"Controlled or limited-access highway" means every public way in respect to which owners or occupants of abutting property or lands and other persons have no legal right of access to or from the same except at such points and in such manner as may be determined by the public authority having jurisdiction over such public way.

"Crossing guard" means an adult civilian officially authorized to supervise and expedite the crossing of school children or other pedestrians at hazardous or congested traffic points.

"Crosswalk" means that portion of a roadway ordinarily included within the prolongation or connection of sidewalk lines at intersections, or any other portion of a roadway clearly indicated for pedestrian crossing by markings.

"Determination of parking or compliance violation liability or nonliability" means the finding of liability or nonliability for a parking or compliance violation reached by a hearing officer after consideration of documentary evidence submitted for adjudication by mail, after an administrative hearing at which the registered owner or his attorney appears to contest liability for a parking or compliance violation, or after the registered owner has failed to appear at a requested administrative hearing or respond to a second notice of violation.

"Drag racing" means the act of two or more individuals competing or racing on any street or highway in a situation in which one of the motor vehicles is beside or to the rear of a motor vehicle operated by a competing driver and the one driver attempts to prevent the competing driver from passing or overtaking, either by acceleration or maneuver, or one or more individuals competing in a race against time on any street or highway.

"Driver" means every person who operates or is in actual physical control of a vehicle.

"Driveway or private road" means every way or place in private ownership and used for vehicular travel by the owner and those having express or implied permission from the owner but not by other persons.

"Final determination" means: a determination of parking or compliance liability becomes a final determination for purposes of the Administrative Review Law of Illinois upon the timely exhaustion of procedures for administrative or judicial review, or failure to exhaust those procedures within the time prescribed by law.

"Firelane" means every way or place in private ownership used expressly for vehicular travel by emergency equipment and marked as such by signs or pavement markings.

"Funeral procession" means a procession consisting of motor vehicles which are designed and used for the carrying of not more than 10 passengers, a funeral hearse and floral cars, or combinations thereof, with or without foot or equestrian units, proceeding to a funeral service or place of burial.

"Hazardous dilapidated motor vehicle" means any motor vehicle with a substantial number of essential parts, as defined by Section 1-118 of the Illinois Vehicle Code, either damaged, removed, altered or otherwise so treated that the vehicle is incapable of being driven under its own motor power or, which by its general state of deterioration, poses a threat to the public health, safety and welfare. "Hazardous dilapidated motor vehicle" shall not include a motor vehicle which has been rendered temporarily incapable of being driven under its own motor power in order to perform ordinary service or repairs.

"Highway" means the entire width between the boundary lines of every way publicly maintained when any part thereof is open to the use of the public for purposes of vehicular traffic.

"Holidays." When used in the traffic code or on official signs erected by authority of the traffic code, the term "holidays" means New Year's Day (January 1st), Memorial Day (the last Monday in May), Independence Day (July 4th), Labor Day (the first Monday in September), Thanksgiving Day (the fourth Thursday in November) and Christmas Day (December 25th).

"Intersection" means the area embraced within the prolongation or connection of the property lines of two or more streets which join at an angle, whether or not one such street crosses the other. Where a highway includes two roadways 40 feet or more apart, every crossing of each roadway of such divided highway by an intersecting highway shall be regarded as a separate intersection.

"Laned roadway" means a roadway which is divided into two or more marked lanes for vehicular traffic.

"Mass transportation vehicle" means a public passenger vehicle having seating capacity for 35 or more passengers.

"Merging traffic" means a maneuver executed by the drivers of vehicles on converging roadways to permit simultaneous or alternate entry into the junction thereof, wherein the driver of each vehicle involved is required to adjust his vehicular speed and lateral position so as to avoid a collision with any other vehicle.

"Motorcycle" means every motor vehicle having a seat or saddle for the use of the rider and designed to travel on not more than three wheels in contact with the ground but excluding farm tractors.

"Motor-driven cycle" means every motorcycle and every motor scooter with less than 150 cubic centimeter piston displacement.

"Motor vehicle" means every vehicle which is propelled by a motor.

"Motor vehicle of the first division" means every motor vehicle designed and used for the carrying of not more than 10 persons.

"Motor vehicle of the second division" means every motor vehicle designed for the carrying of more than 10 persons, every motor vehicle designed or used for living quarters, every motor vehicle designed for pulling or carrying freight or cargo, and every motor vehicle of the first division remodeled for use and used as a motor vehicle of the second division.

"One-way street or alley" means a public way upon the roadway of which traffic is permitted to travel in one direction only.

"Operator" means every person who operates or is in actual physical control of any device or vehicle whether motorized or propelled by human power.

"Outstanding parking or compliance violation" means a parking violation complaint on which no payment has been made or appearance filed in the circuit court of Cook County within the time specified on the complaint or a parking or compliance violation notice which has resulted in a final determination of parking or compliance violation liability for which payment in full has not been made.

"Parking (to park)" means the standing of an unoccupied vehicle otherwise than temporarily for the purpose of and while actually engaged in loading or unloading property or passengers.

"Parking meter" means a traffic control device which, upon being activated by deposit of currency of the United States in the amount indicated thereon or otherwise, either: (1) displays a signal showing that parking is allowed from the time of such activation until the expiration of the time fixed for parking in the parking meter zone in which it is located, and upon expiration of such time indicates by sign or signal that the lawful parking period has expired, or (2) issues a ticket or other token on which is printed or otherwise indicated the lawful parking period in the parking meter zone in which the parking meter is located, such ticket or other token to be displayed in a publicly visible location on the dashboard or inner windshield of a vehicle parked in the parking meter zone.

"Parking meter zone" means a certain designated and marked-off section of the public way within the marked boundaries where a vehicle may be temporarily parked and allowed to remain for such period of time as the parking meter attached thereto, or the ticket or other token issued by the parking meter, may indicate.

"Parking or compliance violation notice" means a handwritten or computer-generated notice either (a) placed on a vehicle that exhibits a compliance violation or is parked or standing in violation of the traffic code, or (b) given to the driver of the vehicle, which may be challenged and enforced in accordance with the process of administrative adjudication.

"Parking or compliance violation notice copy" means any duplicate, photocopy or reproduction, including any computer-stored or computer-generated representation of an original parking or compliance violation notice.

"Parking violation complaint" means a parking ticket summons and complaint, placed on a vehicle parked or standing in violation of the traffic code or given to the driver of the vehicle and returnable to the circuit court of Cook County.

"Parkway" means any portion of a street not considered as roadway, sidewalk, driveway or private road.

"Pedestrian" means any person afoot.

"Play street" means a street or part of a street devoted to recreational purposes.

"Police officer" means every sworn officer of the municipal police department.

"Property line" means the line marking the boundary between any public way and the private property abutting thereon.

"Public building" means a building used by any government agency.

"Public passenger vehicle" means a motor vehicle which is used for the transportation of passengers for hire.

"Public way" means any sidewalk, roadway, alley or other public thoroughfare open to the use of the public, as a matter of right, for purposes of travel, excepting bridle paths.

"Push cart" means a conveyance designed to be propelled by a person afoot.

"Railroad" means a carrier of persons or property upon cars operated upon stationary rails.

"Railroad train" means a steam engine, electric or other motor with or without cars coupled thereto, operated upon rails.

"Recreational vehicle" means every camping trailer, motor home, mini-motor home, travel trailer, truck or van camper used primarily for recreational purposes and not used commercially nor owned and used by a commercial business.

"Registered owner" means the person in whose name the vehicle is registered with the Secretary of State of Illinois or such other state's registry of motor vehicles.

"Residential street" means the length of any street between street intersections when 50 percent or more of the occupied frontage of the street is in use for residence purposes.

"Right-of-way" means the right of a vehicle or pedestrian to proceed in a lawful manner in preference to another vehicle or pedestrian approaching under such circumstances of direction, speed and proximity as to give rise to danger or collision unless one grants precedence to the other.

"Roadway" means that portion of a public way between the regularly established curb lines, or that part improved, and intended to be used for vehicular travel.

"School bus" means every motor vehicle of the second division operated by or for a public or governmental agency or by or for a private or religious organization solely for the transportation of pupils in connection with any school activity.

"Second notice of parking or compliance violation" means the notice, mailed to the address supplied to the Secretary of State by the registered owner of a vehicle, sent after the registered owner has failed to respond within the time allotted by ordinance to a parking or compliance violation notice placed on or given to the driver of such vehicle.

"Semi-trailer" means every vehicle without motive power designed for carrying persons or property and for being drawn by a motor vehicle and so constructed that some part of its weight and that of its load rests upon or is carried by another vehicle.

"Service drive" means a narrow portion of a public way open to vehicular traffic for the purpose of providing access to the front of abutting property between intersections and separated by physical means from through traffic, if the latter exists, on the same public way.

"Sidewalk" means that portion of a public way between the curb, or the lateral lines of the roadway, and the adjacent property lines, intended for the use of pedestrians.

"Standing (to stand)" means the halting of a vehicle, whether occupied or not, otherwise than temporarily for the purpose of and while actually engaged in receiving or discharging passengers; provided, that, an operator is either in the vehicle or in the immediate vicinity, so as to be capable of immediately moving the vehicle at the direction of a police officer or traffic control aide.

"Stop" means the complete cessation of movement.

"Street" means the entire width between boundary lines of every way publicly maintained when any part thereof is open to the use of the public for purposes of general traffic circulation.

"Taxicab stand" means a fixed area in the roadway alongside and parallel to the curb set aside for taxicabs to stand or wait for passengers.

"Through street" means every public way or portion thereof on which vehicular traffic is given preferential right-of-way, and at the entrance to which vehicular traffic from intersecting public ways is required by law to yield right-of-way to vehicles on such through street in obedience to a traffic signal, stop sign or yield sign, when such traffic control devices are erected as provided in the traffic code.

"Traffic" means pedestrians, ridden or herded animals, bicycles, vehicles, and other conveyances either singly or together while using any public way for purposes of travel.

"Traffic control aide" means any person designated by the superintendent of police or the executive director of emergency management and communications to exercise the power of a police officer to direct or regulate traffic or to issue citations for violation of parking and compliance ordinances.

"Traffic control devices" means all signs, signals, markings, and devices placed or erected under authority of the city council for the purpose of regulating, warning, or guiding traffic.

"Traffic violation" means a violation of the provisions of Chapters 9-4 through 9-100, other than a standing or parking violation. A compliance violation observed on a vehicle operated on the public way may be treated as a traffic violation, if the operator of the vehicle is also charged with a criminal offense. The superintendent of police shall issue standards for the treatment of a compliance violation as a traffic violation.

"Trailer" means every vehicle with or without motive power, other than a pole trailer, designed for carrying persons or property and for being drawn by a motor vehicle and so constructed that no part of its weight rests upon the towing vehicle.

"Vehicle" means every device in, upon or by which any person or property is or may be transported or drawn upon a street or highway, except motorized wheelchairs, devices moved solely by human power, devices used exclusively upon stationary rails or tracks and snowmobiles, as defined in the Snowmobile Registration and Safety Act of Illinois.

"Yield right-of-way" means the act of granting the privilege of the immediate use of the intersecting roadway to traffic within the intersection and to vehicles approaching from the right or left.

(Added. Coun. J. 7-12-90, p. 18634; Amend. 9-11-91, p. 5008; 12-11-91, p. 10832; 3-26-96, p. 19161, effective 1-1-97; 10-28-97, p. 54839; 4-29-98, p. 66564; 12-4-02, p. 99026; 7-9-03, p. 4349; 7-29-03, p. 6166; 9-4-03. p. 7167; 11-19-03, p. 13426)

§9-4-020 Violation—Penalty.

Every person convicted of a violation of any provision of Chapters 9-4 through 9-100 for which no penalty is specifically provided shall be punished by a fine of not less than $90.00 nor more than $500.00 for each offense.

(Added. Coun. J. 7-12-90, p. 18634; Amend. Coun. J. 11-6-02, p. 96501; 12-4-02, p. 100729)

§9-4-030 Short title.

Chapters 9-4 through 9-100 of the Municipal Code of Chicago shall be known and may be cited as "the traffic code."
(Added. Coun. J. 7-12-90, p. 18634)

CHAPTER 9-8
TRAFFIC CONTROL DEVICES AND SIGNALS

Sections:

9-8-010 Authorized—Compliance required.
9-8-020 Traffic-control signal legend.
9-8-030 Flashing signals.
9-8-040 Lane control signals.
9-8-050 Special pedestrian-control signals.

§9-8-010 Authorized—Compliance required.

(a) The commissioner of transportation is hereby authorized to cause the placement, erection and maintenance of traffic-control devices as provided in the traffic code, as required to make effective the traffic ordinance of the city, and as necessary to guide and warn traffic. The commissioner is also authorized to place and maintain temporary traffic-control devices as needed in connection with construction or special events or experimental devices for the purposes of an engineering study; provided, however, such devices shall not be maintained for longer than 180 days without city council approval. Upon the authorization of the commissioner of transportation, the actual erection, placement and maintenance of any traffic-control device shall be performed by the appropriate city department or bureau. All traffic-control devices placed and maintained pursuant to the traffic code shall conform to the manual and specifications approved by the State of Illinois Department of Transportation and shall so far as practicable be uniform as to type and location throughout the city. All traffic-control devices so erected and not inconsistent with the provisions of state law or this code shall be official traffic-control devices.

(b) The driver of any vehicle shall obey the instructions of any applicable traffic-control device placed in accordance with the provisions of the traffic code, unless otherwise directed by a police officer or traffic control aide.

(c) No operator of a vehicle shall attempt to avoid obedience to any traffic-control device by driving upon or through any private property, alley or traffic island.

(d) No provision of any traffic ordinance for which traffic-control devices are required shall be enforced against an alleged violator if at the time and place of the alleged violation an official device is not in proper position and sufficiently legible to be seen by an ordinary observant person. Whenever a particular section does not state that signs or other devices are required, such section shall be effective even though no signs or other devices are erected or in place.

Any person violating subsections (b) or (c) of this section shall be fined no less than $90.00 and no more than $300.00 and may be required to perform reasonable public service.
(Added. Coun. J. 7-12-90, p. 18634; Amend. 12-11-91, p. 10832; 11-6-02, p. 96501; 12-4-02, p. 100729)

§9-8-020 Traffic-control signal legend.

Whenever traffic is controlled by traffic-control devices exhibiting steady colored lights, successively one at a time, in combination or with arrows, the following colors only shall be used and the signals shall indicate and apply to drivers of vehicles and pedestrians as follows:

(a) Green Indication.

(1) Vehicular traffic facing a circular green signal may proceed straight through or turn right or left except as such movement is modified by lane-control signs, turn prohibition signs, lane markings, or roadway design. Vehicular traffic, including vehicles turning right or left, shall yield the right-of-way to other vehicles and to pedestrians lawfully within the intersection or an adjacent crosswalk at the time such signal indication is exhibited.

(2) Vehicular traffic facing a green arrow signal, shown alone or in combination with another indication, may cautiously enter the intersection only to make the movement indicated by such arrow or such other movement as is permitted by other indications shown at the same time. Such vehicular traffic shall yield the right-of-way to pedestrians lawfully within an adjacent crosswalk and to other traffic lawfully using the intersection.

(3) Unless otherwise directed by a pedestrian-control signal as provided in Section 9-8-050, pedestrians facing any green signal, except when the sole green signal is a turn arrow, may proceed across the roadway within any marked or unmarked crosswalk.

(b) Steady Yellow Indication.

(1) Vehicular traffic facing a steady circular yellow or yellow arrow signal is thereby warned that the related green movement is being terminated or that a red indication will be exhibited immediately thereafter when vehicular traffic shall not enter the intersection.

(2) Pedestrians facing a steady circular yellow or yellow arrow signal, unless otherwise directed by a pedestrian-control signal as provided in Section 9-8-050, are thereby advised that there is insufficient time to cross the roadway before a red indication is shown, and no pedestrian shall then start to cross the roadway.

(c) Steady Red Indication.

(1) Except as provided in Section 9-16-030, vehicular traffic facing a steady circular red signal alone shall stop at a clearly marked stop line, but if none, before entering the crosswalk on the near side of the intersection, or if none, then before entering the intersection and shall remain standing until an indication to proceed is shown.

(2) Except as provided in Section 9-16-030, vehicular traffic facing a steady red arrow signal shall not enter the intersection to make the movement indicated by the arrow and, unless entering the intersection to make a movement permitted by another signal, shall stop at a clearly marked stop line, but if none, before entering the crosswalk on the near side of the intersection, or if none, then before entering the intersection and shall remain standing until an indication permitting the movement indicated by such red arrow is shown.
(Added. Coun. J. 7-12-90, p. 18634)

§9-8-030 Flashing signals.

Whenever flashing red or yellow signal indications are in place, the signals shall indicate and apply to drivers of vehicles as follows:

(a) Flashing Red Indication. When a red signal is illuminated with rapid intermittent flashes, the operator of any vehicle shall stop before entering the nearest crosswalk at an intersection or at a stop line when marked, or, if none, then before entering the intersection, and the right to proceed shall be subject to the rules applicable after making a stop at a stop sign.

(b) Flashing Yellow Indication. When a yellow signal is illuminated with rapid intermittent flashes, the operator of any vehicle may proceed through the intersection or past such signal only with caution.

(Added. Coun. J. 7-12-90, p. 18634)

§9-8-040 Lane control signals.

Whenever vehicular traffic is controlled and directed by overhead lane-control signals displaying illuminated colored indications, one over each lane, the following indications only shall be used and the illuminated colored lane-control-signal indications shall apply to drivers of vehicles as follows:

(a) Downward-pointing Green Arrow. A driver facing this indication is permitted to drive in the lane over which the arrow signal is located. Otherwise he shall obey all other traffic controls present and follow normal safe driving practices.

(b) Red X Symbol. A driver facing this indication shall not drive in the lane over which the symbol is located, and this indication shall modify accordingly the meaning of all other traffic controls present. Otherwise he shall obey all other traffic controls and follow normal safe driving practices.

(c) Yellow X Symbol. A driver facing this indication should prepare to vacate the lane over which the signal is located, in a safe manner to avoid occupying that lane when a steady red X is displayed.

(Added. Coun. J. 7-12-90, p. 18634)

§9-8-050 Special pedestrian-control signals.

Whenever special pedestrian-control signals are in place, such signals shall indicate as follows:

(a) Walk or Symbolic Walk Figure. Pedestrians facing such signal indication when illuminated may proceed across the roadway in the direction of the indication and shall be given the right-of-way by the operator of any vehicle. When such signal indication is extinguished, no pedestrian facing the signal indication shall enter the roadway.

(b) Don't Walk or Symbolic Don't Walk Figure. No pedestrian facing such signal indication which is illuminated or flashing shall start to cross the roadway in the direction of the indication; provided, however, any pedestrian who has partially completed his crossing on the "Walk" signal indication shall proceed to a sidewalk or safety zone while the "Don't Walk" signal indication is illuminated.

(Added. Coun. J. 7-12-90, p. 18634)

CHAPTER 9-12
TRAFFIC AND SPEED RESTRICTIONS

Sections:

9-12-010 Driving from or onto controlled-access highway.
9-12-020 Nonmotorized traffic on controlled-access highway.
9-12-030 Toll bridges and highways.
9-12-040 Play streets.
9-12-050 Traffic lanes.
9-12-060 Bus lanes.
9-12-070 Speed limits.
9-12-075 School safety zones.
9-12-080 Minimum speed regulations.
9-12-090 Drag racing.

§9-12-010 Driving from or onto controlled-access highway.

No person shall drive a vehicle onto or from the roadway of any controlled-access highway except at such entrances and exits as are established by public authority.

(Added. Coun. J. 7-12-90, p. 18634)

§9-12-020 Nonmotorized traffic on controlled-access highway.

(a) The commissioner of transportation with respect to any controlled-access highway under the city's jurisdiction may prohibit the use of any such highway by pedestrians, bicycles, or other non-motorized traffic or by any person operating a motor-driven cycle. The commissioner shall erect and maintain official signs on the controlled-access highway on which such prohibitions are applicable.

(b) When official signs have been erected on any controlled-access highway prohibiting the use of the roadway by pedestrians, bicycles, or other non- motorized traffic or by any person operating a motor-driven cycle, no person shall disobey the restrictions stated on such signs.

(Added. Coun. J. 7-12-90, p. 18634; Amend. 12-11-91, p. 10832)

§9-12-030 Toll bridges and highways.

On a toll bridge or toll highway, use of which requires the payment of a predetermined toll, it shall be unlawful for the driver of any motor vehicle to use such bridge or highway without payment of the required fee(s). Any person convicted of a violation of this provision shall be fined $25.00.

(Added. Coun. J. 7-12-90, p. 18634)

§9-12-040 Play streets.

(a) The commissioner of transportation, subject to the approval of the city council, may designate certain streets or parts of streets, other than main thoroughfares, as play streets to be devoted to recreational purposes for children, under proper regulation and supervision. Such designation shall describe the street or part of the street to be used for such purpose, the hours of the day and the days of the week when it shall be roped off, and such other directions as he may deem necessary for the protection of the children and of the public. In preparing his recommendations, the commissioner shall give preference to neighborhoods where recreation space and playground facilities are not otherwise available, and such streets or parts of streets on which vehicular traffic is light shall be selected. It shall be the duty of the heads of the several departments of the city government to render such assistance in the administration of the play street system as shall be necessary to insure safety to the children using same.

(b) During the hours that any play street is in use for recreation, the roadway thereof shall be closed to vehicular traffic by removable barriers. Such barriers shall be kept in place until the close of the period of recreation each day that it is to be used and shall then be removed.

(c) Whenever authorized barriers are erected indicating any street or part thereof as a play street, no person shall drive a vehicle upon such street or part thereof except drivers having business or whose residences are within such closed area, and each such driver shall exercise the greatest care in driving upon any such street or portion thereof.

(Added. Coun. J. 7-12-90, p. 18634; Amend. 12-11-91, p. 10832)

§9-12-050 Traffic lanes.

(a) The commissioner of transportation is hereby authorized to mark traffic lanes upon the roadway where in his judgment a regular alignment of traffic is necessary.

(b) Where traffic lanes have been marked to preserve a regular alignment of traffic, it shall be unlawful for the driver of any vehicle to fail or refuse to keep his vehicle within the designated boundaries of any such lane except when lawfully passing another vehicle.

(Added. Coun. J. 7-12-90, p. 18634; Amend. 12-11-91, p. 10832)

§9-12-060 Bus lanes.

(a) The commissioner of transportation is hereby authorized to designate portions of the roadway as bus lanes where in his judgment a separation of traffic is necessary to expedite the flow of traffic and shall indicate such designated lanes with appropriate signs or markings.

(b) When a bus lane is designated and indicated by appropriate signs or markings, it shall be unlawful for any vehicle other than a bus or a vehicle servicing a bus to enter or use such lane, except when making a right hand turn.

(Added. Coun. J. 7-12-90, p. 18634; Amend. 12-11-91, p. 10832; 7-29-03, p. 6166)

§9-12-070 Speed limits.

(a) The provisions of Section 11-601 of the Illinois Vehicle Code shall be applicable on all streets within and under the jurisdiction of the city. The absolute statutory urban speed limit shall be 30 miles per hour in streets and 15 miles per hour in alleys. The absolute statutory nonurban speed limit shall be 55 miles per hour. In addition to any fines or other penalties provided by statute or by this code, any person found operating a vehicle in excess of the limits stated herein shall be subject to a fine of not less than $90.00 nor more than $200.00 for the first offense, and not less than $150.00 nor more than $300.00 for the second offense, and not less than $200.00 nor more than $500.00 for the third and each subsequent offense within a given three-year period.

(b) Where the commissioner of transportation has determined on the basis of an engineering or traffic investigation that the statutory speed limits are greater or less than is reasonable or safe with respect to the conditions found to exist along any part of any roadway, the urban speed limits may be increased, but not in excess of 55 miles per hour, and may be diminished, but not to less than 20 miles per hour, and the nonurban speed limit may be diminished, but not to less than 35 miles per hour, when such determination is approved by an ordinance of the city council. Such ordinance altering speed limits shall be enforceable when appropriate signs giving notice of the limit are erected at the proper places along the affected roadway or highway or part thereof.

(Added. Coun. J. 7-12-90, p. 18634; Amend. 12-11-91, p. 10832; 10-28-97, p. 54842; 11-19-97, p. 57859; 11-6-02, p. 96501; 12-4-02, p. 100729)

§9-12-075 School safety zones.

(a) For the purpose of this section, "school" means any of the following entities:

(1) A public or private primary or secondary school.

(2) A primary or secondary school operated by a religious institution.

(3) A public, private or religious nursery school.

On a school day when school children are present and so close thereto that a potential hazard exists because of the close proximity of the motorized traffic, no person hall drive a motor vehicle at a speed in excess of 20 miles per hour while passing a school zone or while traveling upon any public thoroughfare where children pass going to and from school. For the purposes of this section a school day shall begin at 7:00 A.M. and shall conclude at 4:00 P.M.

This section shall not be applicable unless appropriate signs are posted, giving due warning that a school zone is being approached and shall indicate the school zone and the maximum speed limit in effect during school days when school children are present. Signs shall be in a form similar to signs posted for similar purposes pursuant to the Illinois Vehicle Code. School zones created prior to the effective date of this section and in compliance with the Illinois Vehicle Code shall be considered school zones for purposes of this section.

(b) Any person who violates subsection (a) of this section shall be subject to a fine of $300.

(Added. Coun. J. 7-25-01, p. 65077)

§9-12-080 Minimum speed regulations.

No person shall drive a motor vehicle at such a slow speed as to impede or block the normal and reasonable movement of traffic except when reduced speed is necessary for safe operation of his vehicle or in compliance with law.

(Added. Coun. J. 7-12-90, p. 18634)

§9-12-090 Drag racing.

Any person who, as an operator of a motor vehicle, is a participant in drag racing shall be subject to vehicle impoundment under Section 2-14-132.

(Added. Coun. J. 9-4-03, p. 7167)

CHAPTER 9-16
TURNING MOVEMENTS

Sections:

9-16-010 Markings and indicating devices.
9-16-020 Turning at intersections.
9-16-030 Turns on red signals.
9-16-040 Limitations on turning.
9-16-050 Turns restricted—Where and when.

§9-16-010 Markings and indicating devices.

(a) The commissioner of transportation is hereby authorized to place markings or other devices within or adjacent to intersections indicating the course to be traveled by vehicles turning at such intersections, and such course to be traveled as so indicated may conform to or be other than as prescribed by law or ordinance.

(b) When authorized markers, buttons or other indications are placed within or adjacent to an intersection indicating the course to be traveled by turning vehicles, it shall be unlawful for the operator of a vehicle to disobey the directions of such indications.

(Added. Coun. J. 7-12-90, p. 18634; Amend. 12-11-91, p. 10832)

§9-16-020 Turning at intersections.

The driver of a vehicle intending to turn at an intersection shall do so as follows:

(a) Right Turns. Both the approach for a right turn and a right turn shall be made as close as practicable to the right-hand curb or edge of the roadway.

(b) Left Turns on Two-way Roadways. At any intersection where traffic is permitted to move in both directions on each roadway entering the intersection, an approach for a left turn shall be made in that portion of the right half of the roadway nearest the centerline thereof and by passing to the right of such centerline where it enters the intersection or on that portion of the roadway that may be specifically designated for such purpose by appropriate markings, and after entering the intersection the left turn shall be made so as to leave the intersection to the right of the centerline of the roadway being entered. Whenever practicable the left turn shall be made in that portion of the intersection to the left of the center of the intersection.

(c) Left Turns on Other Than Two-way Roadways. At any intersection where traffic is restricted to one direction on one or more of the roadways, the driver of a vehicle intending to turn left at any such intersection shall approach the intersection in the extreme left-hand lane lawfully available to traffic moving in the direction of travel of such vehicle or on that portion of the roadway that may be specifically designated for such purpose by appropriate markings, and after entering the intersection the left turn shall be made so as to leave the intersection, as nearly as practicable, in the left-hand lane lawfully available to traffic moving in such direction upon the roadway being entered.

(d) Right-of-way on Left Turn. The driver of a vehicle within an intersection intending to turn to the left shall yield the right-of-way to any vehicle approaching from the opposite direction which is within the intersection or so close thereto as to constitute an immediate hazard, but said driver, hav-

ing so yielded and having given a signal when and as required, may make such left turn and the drivers of all other vehicles approaching the intersection from said opposite direction shall yield the right-of-way to the vehicle making the left turn.
(Added. Coun. J. 7-12-90, p. 18634)

§9-16-030 Turns on red signals.

(a) Except as provided in subsection (c), the driver of a vehicle may turn right when facing a steady red signal; provided, however, he may do so only from the lane closest to the right-hand curb or edge of roadway, must come to a full stop and must yield the right-of-way to pedestrians and to other traffic lawfully using the intersection.

(b) Except as provided in subsection (c), the driver of a vehicle on a one-way roadway, facing a steady red signal, may turn left into an intersecting one-way roadway in which traffic travels to the left; provided, however, he may do so only from the lane closest to the left-hand curb or edge of roadway, must come to a full stop and must yield the right-of-way to pedestrians and to other traffic lawfully using the intersection.

(c) Drivers may not turn left or right on a steady red signal when official traffic-control devices have been erected indicating that such turns are prohibited.
(Added. Coun. J. 7-12-90, p. 18634)

§9-16-040 Limitations on turning.

(a) The driver of any vehicle shall not turn such vehicle so as to proceed in the opposite direction at any point closer than 100 feet to any intersection unless official signs are erected to permit such turns.

(b) It shall be unlawful for the operator of any vehicle to turn such vehicle in any street so as to proceed in the opposite direction in the territory bounded by and including Wacker Drive on the west and the north, Michigan Avenue on the east, and Congress Parkway on the south, unless official signs are erected to permit such turns.

(c) The commissioner of transportation is authorized to determine those places within 100 feet of an intersection or within the area described in subsection (b) where turns in the opposite direction shall be permitted and to erect appropriate signs giving notice thereof.
(Added. Coun. J. 7-12-90, p. 18634; Amend. 12-11-91, p. 10832)

§9-16-050 Turns restricted—Where and when.

(a) The commissioner of transportation is hereby authorized to determine intersections, alleys and driveways at which operators of vehicles shall not make a right or left turn and upon what streets or parts of streets operators of vehicles shall not turn such vehicles so as to proceed in the opposite direction, and he shall erect appropriate signs giving notice of the prohibitions. The making of right or left turns in the opposite direction may be prohibited between certain hours of any day and permitted at other hours, in which event the same shall be plainly indicated on the signs or they may be removed or covered by the commissioner of transportation when such turns are permitted.

(b) Whenever official signs are erected indicating that no right or left turn or turn in the opposite direction is permitted, no driver of a vehicle shall disobey the directions of any such sign.
(Added. Coun. J. 7-12-90, p. 18634; Amend. 12-11-91, p. 10832)

CHAPTER 9-20
MOVEMENT OF TRAFFIC

Sections:
9-20-010 One-way streets—Through traffic prohibited on certain public ways.
9-20-020 Reversible lanes and contra-flow bus lanes.

§9-20-010 One-way streets—Through traffic prohibited on certain public ways.

(a) The commissioner of transportation is hereby authorized, subject to the approval of the city council, to determine and designate one-way streets and alleys, and he shall erect and maintain appropriate signs giving notice thereof. Signs indicating the direction of lawful traffic movement shall be placed at every intersection and alley where movement of traffic in the opposite direction is prohibited.

(b) Upon those streets and parts of streets and in those alleys so designated as one-way streets or alleys, vehicular traffic shall move only in the indicated direction when signs indicating the direction of traffic are erected and maintained at intersections and alleys where movement in the opposite direction is prohibited.

(c) It shall be unlawful to operate any motor vehicle on an alley or any other portion of the public way on which through traffic has been prohibited by the posting of an appropriate sign, other than for the purpose of gaining access to or leaving property that is adjacent to such portion of the public way. The operation of a motor vehicle on an alley or any other such appropriately marked portion of the public way located between two streets intersecting with such portion of the public way without parking, or without stopping to load or unload passengers or goods, shall be prima facie evidence of a violation of this subsection. Any person who violates this subsection shall be fined $100.00 for each offense.
(Added. Coun. J. 7-12-90, p. 18634; Amend. 12-11-91, p. 10832)

§9-20-020 Reversible lanes and contra-flow bus lanes.

(a) The commissioner of transportation is hereby authorized to determine and designate streets, parts of streets, or specific lanes thereon upon which vehicular traffic shall proceed in one direction during one period and the opposite direction during another period of the day, and he shall place and maintain appropriate markings, signs, barriers or other devices to give notice thereof and to divide traffic traveling in opposite directions in shifting lanes. Contra-flow bus lanes shall only be established upon the approval of the city council.

(b) It shall be unlawful for any person to drive any vehicle in violation of such markings, signs, barriers or other devices so placed in accordance with this section.
(Added. Coun. J. 7-12-90, p. 18634; Amend. 12-11-91, p. 10832)

CHAPTER 9-24
RIGHT-OF-WAY

Sections:

9-24-010 Stop signs.
9-24-020 Intersections—Procedure after completed stop.
9-24-030 Crosswalks—Pedestrians to have right-of-way.
9-24-040 Intersections—More than one vehicle.
9-24-050 Pedestrians in roadway to have right-of-way when.
9-24-060 Right-of-way at sidewalks.
9-24-070 Yield right-of-way signs.
9-24-080 Authorized emergency vehicles.
9-24-090 Equestrians to have right-of-way when.
9-24-100 Blind persons to have right-of-way when.

§9-24-010 Stop signs.

(a) Whenever the city council by ordinance designates a street or portion thereof as a through street, the commissioner of transportation shall place and maintain a stop sign on every street intersecting the through street unless traffic at any such intersection is controlled by traffic-control signals; provided, however, that at the intersection of a through street and a heavy-traffic street not so designated, stop signs shall be erected at the approaches of either or both of the streets as may be determined by the commissioner upon the basis of an engineering and traffic study. The commissioner is hereby authorized to determine and designate intersections where particular hazards exist upon other than through streets and to determine whether vehicles shall stop at one or more entrances to any such intersections and to erect a stop sign at every such place where a stop is required. The commissioner is also authorized to erect stop signs at marked crosswalks between intersections where in his judgment a stop is required to protect pedestrian traffic. Every stop sign shall be erected as near as practicable to the nearest line of the crosswalk on the near side of the intersection or, if there is no crosswalk, then as close as practicable to the nearest line of the roadway.

(b) When stop signs are erected as herein provided, every operator of a vehicle shall stop the vehicle at the sign or at a clearly marked stop line before entering the nearest crosswalk, if any, or the intersection, except when directed to proceed by a police officer or traffic control aide.

(c) Any person violating this section shall be fined no less than $90.00 and no more than $300.00 and may also be required to perform reasonable community service.

(Added. Coun. J. 7-12-90, p. 18634; Amend. 12-11-91, p. 10832; 9-9-98, p. 77383; 11-6-02, p. 96501; 12-4-02, p. 100729)

§9-24-020 Intersections—Procedure after completed stop.

After the operator of a vehicle has stopped in obedience to a stop sign, at an intersection where a stop sign is erected at one or more entrances thereto, such operator shall proceed cautiously yielding to vehicles not so obliged to stop which are within the intersection or approaching so closely as to constitute an immediate hazard, but may then proceed, subject to the provisions of Section 9-24-030.

(Added. Coun. J. 7-12-90, p. 18634)

§9-24-030 Crosswalks—Pedestrians to have right-of-way.

Where stop signs are in place at a plainly marked crosswalk at an intersection or between intersections, pedestrians within or entering the crosswalk at either edge of the roadway shall have the right-of-way over vehicles stopped in obedience to such signs. Drivers of vehicles having so yielded the right-of-way to pedestrians entering or within the nearest crosswalk at an intersection shall also yield the right-of-way to pedestrians within any other crosswalk at the intersection.

(Added. Coun. J. 7-12-90, p. 18634)

§9-24-040 Intersections—More than one vehicle.

(a) The driver of a vehicle approaching an intersection shall yield the right of-way to a vehicle which has entered the intersection from a different roadway.

(b) When two vehicles enter an intersection from different streets at approximately the same time, the driver of the vehicle on the left shall yield the right-of-way to the vehicle on the right.

(c) The right-of-way rules declared in this section are modified as provided in Section 9-24-020.

(Added. Coun. J. 7-12-90, p. 18634)

§9-24-050 Pedestrians in roadway to have right-of-way when.

When the movement of traffic is not controlled by traffic-control devices, a police officer or traffic control aide, the operator of a vehicle shall yield the right-of-way, slowing down or stopping if need be so to yield, to a pedestrian crossing the roadway within a crosswalk when the pedestrian is upon the half of the roadway upon which the vehicle is traveling or when the pedestrian is approaching so closely from the opposite half of the roadway as to be in danger.

(Added. Coun. J. 7-12-90, p. 18634)

§9-24-060 Right-of-way at sidewalks.

The driver of a vehicle emerging from an alley, driveway or building shall stop the vehicle immediately prior to driving onto any sidewalk or sidewalk area extending across an alleyway, yield the right-of-way to any pedestrian as may be necessary to avoid collision and, upon entering the roadway, shall yield the right-of-way to all vehicles approaching on the roadway.

(Added. Coun. J. 7-12-90, p. 18634)

§9-24-070 Yield right-of-way signs.

Where a yield right-of-way sign has been erected at an intersection, the driver of a vehicle facing the sign shall slow down to a speed reasonable for the existing conditions or shall stop if necessary and shall yield the right-of-way to other vehicles which have entered the intersecting roadway either from the right or left or which are approaching so closely on the intersecting roadway as to constitute an immediate hazard, but thereafter may proceed at such time as a safe interval occurs.

(Added. Coun. J. 7-12-90, p. 18634)

§9-24-080 Authorized emergency vehicles.

(a) Upon the immediate approach of an authorized emergency vehicle giving audible signal by siren, exhaust whistle, or bell or displaying an oscillating, rotating, or flashing blue beam or displaying an oscillating, rotating or flashing red beam visible under normal atmospheric conditions from a distance of 500 feet (150 meters), the driver of every other vehicle shall yield the right-of-way and shall immediately drive to a position parallel to, and as close as possible to, the right-hand edge, except on one-way streets where drivers shall drive as close as possible to the nearest edge, of the roadway clear of any intersection and shall stop and remain in such position until the authorized emergency vehicle has passed, unless otherwise directed by a police officer, traffic control aide or fireman in the lawful exercise of his duties. Any person who violates any provision of this subsection (a) shall be subject to a fine of $500.00.

(b) This section shall not operate to relieve the driver of an authorized emergency vehicle from the duty to drive with due regard for the safety of all persons using the highway.

(Added. Coun. J. 7-12-90, p. 18634; Amend. 2-10-99, p. 88047; 7-19-00, p. 38598)

§9-24-090 Equestrians to have right-of-way when.

The operator of any vehicle shall yield the right-of-way to a person riding a horse on a bridle path where such bridle path crosses a driveway, when signalled to do so by the raising of the arm of the rider. Nothing in this section shall relieve an equestrian from the duty of exercising due care and of obeying official traffic-control devices.

(Added. Coun. J. 7-12-90, p. 18634)

§9-24-100 Blind persons to have right-of-way when.

(a) Notwithstanding any other provision of this chapter, any blind person who is carrying in a raised or extended position a cane which is white in color, or white tipped in red, or who is being guided by a dog shall have the right-of-way in crossing any roadway.

(b) The driver of a vehicle approaching the place where a blind person carrying a cane as described in subsection (a) or guided by a dog is crossing a roadway shall bring his vehicle to a full stop and before proceeding shall take such precautions as may be necessary to avoid injury to the blind person.

(c) The provisions of this section shall not apply to a blind person who is neither carrying a cane as described in subsection (a) nor guided by a dog, but the other provisions of this chapter relating to pedestrians shall then be applicable to such person.

(Added. Coun. J. 7-12-90, p. 18634)

CHAPTER 9-28
RAILROAD AND BRIDGE CROSSINGS

Sections:

9-28-010 Railroad grade crossing—Obedience to signal.
9-28-020 Obedience to bridge signals.
9-28-030 Railroad grade crossing—Reporting of obstructions.

§9-28-010 Railroad grade crossing—Obedience to signal.

(a) The driver of a vehicle approaching a railroad grade crossing shall stop not less than 10 feet from the nearest rail of such railroad, and shall not proceed until he can do so safely whenever:

(1) A clearly visible electric or mechanical signal device gives warning of the immediate approach of a train;

(2) A crossing gate is lowered or a human flagman gives or continues to give a signal of the approach or passage of a train;

(3) A train approaching within approximately 1,500 feet of the street or highway crossing emits a signal audible from such a distance and such train, by reason of its speed or nearness to such crossing, is an immediate hazard; or

(4) An approaching train is plainly visible and is in hazardous proximity to the crossing.

(b) No person shall drive any vehicle through, around, or under any crossing gate or barrier at a railroad grade crossing while such gate or barrier is closed or is being opened or closed.

(c) The provisions of this section shall also be applicable to elevated railroad grade crossings where elevated railroad trains operate at ground level.

(Added. Coun. J. 7-12-90, p. 18634)

§9-28-020 Obedience to bridge signals.

(a) No operator of a vehicle shall drive onto or allow the vehicle to remain upon a bridge or the approach thereto beyond the bridge signal, gate or barrier after a bridge operation signal indication has been given.

(b) Whenever the operator of a vehicle stops for a bridge operation signal indication, he shall stop the vehicle so as not to impede traffic movement within any intersection adjacent to or near the bridge.

(Added. Coun. J. 7-12-90, p. 18634)

§9-28-030 Railroad grade crossing—Reporting of obstructions.

(A) The Chicago Transportation Coordinating Office shall immediately notify the city's 9-1-1 emergency telephone system any time a moving or stationary train obstructs a railroad-highway crossing at grade within city's limits for more than five minutes and shall notify the same when opening is cleared.

Failure to comply with the requirements of this subsection shall be punishable by a fine of not less than $200.00, nor more than $500.00, for each offense.

(B) The executive director of the city's office of emergency management and communications, or his designees, shall immediately transmit to the Chicago department of police and to the Chicago fire department any information received from the Chicago Transportation Coordinating Office relative to the obstruction of railroad-highway crossings at grade so that the information can be taken into account by those departments when dispatching units in response to calls for emergency service.

The executive director shall establish a telephone number to receive information from the Chicago Transportation Coordinating Office relative to the obstruction of railroad-highway crossing at grade.

(Added. Coun. J. 10-3-01, p. 69187; Amend. Coun. J. 12-4-02, p. 99026)

CHAPTER 9-32
FUNERAL PROCESSIONS

Sections:

9-32-010 Equipment for vehicles.
9-32-020 Regulations for vehicles.
9-32-030 Traffic regulations.

§9-32-010 Equipment for vehicles.

(a) Every motor vehicle participating in a funeral procession shall have its headlights lighted and shall display on the right-hand side of the windshield a square or rectangular card or sticker, which shall be bright orange and upon which shall be printed or stamped in black a cross, a star, or the word funeral. The reverse side of the sticker shall contain the following statements:

ALERT

In order to ensure a safe funeral procession, the distance between vehicles shall not be too small or too great. Please be attentive and maintain a reasonable distance between your vehicle and the vehicle in front of yours according to the speed of the vehicles.

(b) Vehicles in a funeral procession may be equipped with flashing, oscillating or rotating amber lights which may be used only during such funeral processions. As required by Section 11-1420(e) of the Illinois Vehicle Code, all such lights shall be of sufficient intensity, when illuminated, to be visible at 500 feet in normal sunlight.

(c) Vehicles in a funeral procession may be equipped with pennants, flags, cards, or stickers, in addition to the card or sticker described herein which shall further identify such vehicles as being part of a funeral procession.

(d) It shall be the duty of the funeral director having charge of the funeral procession to supply each vehicle in such procession with a card or sticker as described in subsection (a). The decision to use any of the equipment described in subsections (b) and (c) shall be made only by the funeral director, and such equipment, if used, shall be furnished only by the funeral director and must be the same for each vehicle in the procession, except that the lead vehicle may alone be equipped with a flashing, oscillating, or rotating light.

(Added. Coun. J. 7-12-90, p. 18634)

§9-32-020 Regulations for vehicles.

(a) All vehicles in a funeral procession shall have the right-of-way at all intersections and on all roadways in the city, subject to the following conditions:

(1) The operator of the lead vehicle in a funeral procession shall comply with all stop signs and traffic-control signals. But after the lead vehicle has stopped as required by a stop sign or traffic signal and has started to proceed through an intersection, then all other vehicles in the procession shall have the right-of-way and may proceed, with proper caution, through that intersection without stopping, regardless of the sign or signal.

(2) The operators of all vehicles in a funeral procession shall yield the right-of-way upon the approach of authorized emergency vehicles as provided in Section 9-24-080.

(b) Each driver in a funeral procession shall drive as near to the right-hand edge of the roadway as practical and follow the vehicle ahead as closely as is practical and safe.

(c) Funeral processions shall not form on or use any arterial street between the hours of 7:00 a.m. and 9:00 a.m. or between the hours of 4:00 p.m. and 7:00 p.m.

(Added. Coun. J. 7-12-90, p. 18634)

§9-32-030 Traffic regulations.

(a) No operator of a vehicle shall drive between the vehicles, persons or animals comprising a funeral procession except when otherwise directed by a police officer. This provision shall not apply to authorized emergency vehicles.

(b) Operators of vehicles that are not part of a funeral procession may not form a procession or convoy and have their headlights lighted for the purpose of securing the right-of-way this section grants to funeral processions.

(c) Operators of vehicles that are not part of a funeral procession may overtake and pass the vehicles that are in such procession if such overtaking and passing will not cause a traffic hazard or interfere with such procession.

(Added. Coun. J. 7-12-90, p. 18634)

CHAPTER 9-36
OVERTAKING VEHICLES

Sections:

9-36-010 Overtaking vehicle on the left.
9-36-020 Overtaking vehicle on the right.
9-36-030 Limitation on overtaking on the left.
9-36-040 Driving on right side of roadway.
9-36-050 Overtaking school bus.
9-36-060 Overtaking at crosswalks.

§9-36-010 Overtaking vehicle on the left.

(a) The driver of a vehicle overtaking another vehicle proceeding in the same direction shall pass to the left thereof at a safe distance and shall not again drive to the right side of the roadway until safely clear of the overtaken vehicle.

(b) Except when overtaking and passing on the right is permitted, the driver of an overtaken vehicle shall not increase the speed of his vehicle until completely passed by the overtaking vehicle.

(Added. Coun. J. 7-12-90, p. 18634)

§9-36-020 Overtaking vehicle on the right.

(a) The driver of a vehicle may overtake and pass upon the right of another vehicle only under the following conditions:

(1) When the vehicle overtaken is making or about to make a left turn and there is sufficient safe clearance distance between the turning vehicle and the right edge of the roadway;

(2) Upon any roadway with unobstructed pavement of sufficient width for two or more lanes of moving vehicles in each direction; or

(3) Upon any roadway on which traffic is restricted to one direction of movement, where the unobstructed pavement is of sufficient width for two or more lanes of moving vehicles.

(b) The driver of a vehicle may overtake and pass another vehicle upon the right only under conditions permitting such movement in safety. In no event shall such movement be made by driving off the pavement or main-traveled portion of the roadway.

(Added. Coun. J. 7-12-90, p. 18634)

§9-36-030 Limitation on overtaking on the left.

No vehicle shall be driven to the left side of the center of the roadway in overtaking and passing another vehicle proceeding in the same direction unless such left side is clearly visible and is free of oncoming traffic for a sufficient distance ahead to permit such overtaking and passing to be completely made without interfering with the safe operation of any vehicle approaching from the opposite direction of any vehicle overtaken. In every event the overtaking vehicle must return to the right-hand side of the roadway before coming within 100 feet of any vehicle approaching from the opposite direction.

(Added. Coun. J. 7-12-90, p. 18634)

§9-36-040 Driving on right side of roadway.

(a) All vehicles shall be driven in the right-hand lane available for traffic or as close as practicable to the right-hand curb or edge of the roadway:

(1) When proceeding at less than the normal speed of traffic at the time and place and under the conditions then existing; or

(2) When designed and used for transportation, pulling or hauling of freight, except when overtaking another vehicle proceeding in the same direction or when preparing for a left turn at the intersection or into a private road or driveway.

(b) Upon all roadways of sufficient width, a vehicle shall be driven in the right-hand lane available for traffic, except:

(1) When the right half of a roadway is closed to traffic while under construction or repair;

(2) Upon a roadway divided into three marked lanes for traffic under the rules applicable thereon; or

(3) Upon a roadway designated by signs for one-way traffic.

(Added. Coun. J. 7-12-90, p. 18634)

§9-36-050 Overtaking school bus.

(a) The driver of a vehicle on a roadway, upon meeting or overtaking, from either direction, any school bus which has stopped for the purpose of receiving or discharging any school children, shall stop the vehicle before reaching the school bus where there is in operation on the school bus a visual signal as specified in Section 12-805 of the Illinois Vehicle Code, and the driver shall not proceed until the school bus resumes motion, or the school bus driver signals the driver to proceed, or the visual signals are no longer actuated.

(b) Every bus used for the transportation of school children shall bear upon the front and rear thereof plainly visible signs containing the words "school bus" in letters not less than eight inches in height and in addition shall be equipped with visual signals, meeting the requirements of the Illinois Vehicle Code, which shall be actuated by the school bus whenever the brakes are applied.

(c) The driver of a vehicle upon a street or highway of which the roadways for traffic moving in opposite directions are separated by a strip of ground which is not surfaced or suitable for vehicular traffic need not stop his vehicle upon meeting or passing a school bus which is on the opposite roadway, and the driver of a vehicle on a controlled access highway need not stop when a school bus is stopped in a loading zone adjacent to the surfaced or improved part of the controlled access highway where pedestrians are not permitted to cross such controlled access highway.
(Added. Coun. J. 7-12-90, p. 18634)

§9-36-060 Overtaking at crosswalks.

Whenever any vehicle is stopped at a marked crosswalk or at any unmarked crosswalk at an intersection to permit a pedestrian to cross the roadway, the driver of any other vehicle approaching from the rear shall not overtake or pass such stopped vehicle.
(Added. Coun. J. 7-12-90, p. 18634)

CHAPTER 9-40
DRIVING RULES

Sections:

9-40-010 Compliance—Required.
9-40-020 Applicability.
9-40-030 Obedience to police and fire department orders.
9-40-040 Following responding fire apparatus prohibited.
9-40-050 Driving over fire hose prohibited when.
9-40-060 Driving, standing or parking on bicycle paths or lanes prohibited.
9-40-070 Driving on sidewalks or parkways prohibited.
9-40-071 Driving on sidewalks in housing authority development prohibited.
9-40-080 Required parking procedure.
9-40-090 Dimming headlights required when.
9-40-100 Prohibited driving to left of center of roadway.
9-40-110 Operating vehicle in reverse.
9-40-120 Obstruction of intersection or crosswalk prohibited.
9-40-130 Obstruction of traffic.
9-40-140 Negligent driving.
9-40-150 Following too closely.
9-40-160 Drivers to exercise due care for pedestrians.
9-40-170 Driving or moving vehicle in unsafe condition.
9-40-180 Coasting downhill prohibited.
9-40-190 Pulling out from parked position.
9-40-200 Operator's signals.
9-40-210 Operator's signals—Stop or decrease in speed.
9-40-220 Operator's signals—Means.
9-40-230 Operator's signals—Hand and arm—Manner.
9-40-240 Use of horns and signals devices.
9-40-250 Driving with view obstructed prohibited.

§9-40-010 Compliance—Required.

It shall be unlawful for any person to do any act forbidden, or fail to perform any act required, in the traffic code.
(Added. Coun. J. 7-12-90, p. 18634)

§9-40-020 Applicability.

(a) The provisions of this chapter shall apply to the driver of any vehicle owned by or used in the service of the United States government, this state, or any political subdivision thereof, and it shall be unlawful for any said driver to violate any of the provisions of the traffic code, except as otherwise permitted in this code or by state statute.

(b) Every person propelling any pushcart or riding an animal upon a roadway, and every person driving any animal-drawn vehicle, shall be subject to the provisions of the traffic code applicable to the driver of any vehicle, except those provisions of this code which by their very nature can have no application.

(Added. Coun. J. 7-12-90, p. 18634)

§9-40-030 Obedience to police and fire department orders.

No person shall wilfully fail or refuse to comply with any lawful order or direction of a police officer, traffic control aide, fire department official or other authorized officer.

(Added. Coun. J. 7-12-90, p. 18634)

§9-40-040 Following responding fire apparatus prohibited.

The driver of any vehicle other than one on official business shall not follow any fire apparatus traveling in response to a fire alarm closer than 500 feet or drive into the block where the fire apparatus has stopped in answer to a fire alarm.

(Added. Coun. J. 7-12-90, p. 18634)

§9-40-050 Driving over fire hose prohibited when.

No person shall drive or move a vehicle over any unprotected hose of the fire department when laid down on any street or private driveway unless he has obtained the consent of the fire department official in command.

(Added. Coun. J. 7-12-90, p. 18634)

§9-40-060 Driving, standing or parking on bicycle paths or lanes prohibited.

The driver of a vehicle shall not drive, unless entering or exiting a legal parking space, or stand, or park the vehicle upon any on-street path or lane designated by official signs or markings for the use of bicycles, or otherwise drive or place the vehicle in such a manner as to impede bicycle traffic on such path or lane. Any person who violates this section shall be fined $100.00 for each offense. Any vehicle parked in violation of this section shall be subject to an immediate tow and removal to a city vehicle pound or authorized garage.

(Added. Coun. J. 7-12-90, p. 18634; Amend. 9-1-99, p. 10503)

§9-40-070 Driving on sidewalks or parkways prohibited.

The driver of a vehicle shall not drive on any sidewalk or parkway except on a permanent or temporary driveway.

(Added. Coun. J. 7-12-90, p. 18634)

§9-40-071 Driving on sidewalks in housing authority development prohibited.

No operator of a vehicle, other than an emergency vehicle or authorized service vehicle, shall drive upon any sidewalk, lawn area, playground area, asphalt area or upon or through a firelane within or adjacent to any Chicago Housing Authority Development not designated for such use.
(Added. Coun. J. 5-22-91, p. 823)

§9-40-080 Required parking procedure.

No person driving or in charge of a motor vehicle shall permit it to stand unattended without first stopping the engine and removing the ignition key, and, when standing upon any grade, effectively setting the brake thereon and turning the front wheels to the curb or side of the roadway.

Nothing in this section prohibits the use of a remote ignition start device which is capable of starting a vehicle's ignition without the vehicle's ignition key, if (a) the vehicle is equipped with an anti-theft feature which prevents the vehicle from being driven without the ignition key being property inserted; and (b) the owner of the vehicle displays on the vehicle a decal or sticker indicating the presence of such a remote ignition start device.
(Added. Coun. J. 7-12-90, p. 18634; Amend. 3-11-98, p. 63461)

§9-40-090 Dimming headlights required when.

On approaching another vehicle proceeding in an opposite direction and when within not less than 350 feet of such vehicle, the operator of a motor vehicle equipped with electric headlight or headlights shall dim such headlight or headlights.
(Added. Coun. J. 7-12-90, p. 18634)

§9-40-100 Prohibited driving to left of center of roadway.

(a) No vehicle shall at any time be driven to the left side of the roadway under the following conditions:

(1) When approaching the crest of a grade or upon a curve in the highway where the driver's view is obstructed within such distance as to create a hazard in the event another vehicle might approach from the opposite direction;

(2) When approaching within 100 feet of or traversing any intersection or railroad grade crossing;

(3) When approaching within 100 feet of any bridge, viaduct, tunnel or subway; or

(4) When official signs are in place directing that traffic keep to the right, or a continuous yellow colored center line is marked.

(b) The foregoing limitations shall not apply upon a one-way roadway.
(Added. Coun. J. 7-12-90, p. 18634)

§9-40-110 Operating vehicle in reverse.

The driver of a vehicle shall not operate vehicle in reverse unless such movement can be made with reasonable safety and without interfering with other traffic.
(Added. Coun. J. 7-12-90, p. 18634)

§9-40-120 Obstruction of intersection or crosswalk prohibited.

Notwithstanding any traffic-control signal indication to proceed, no operator of a vehicle shall enter an intersection or crosswalk unless there is sufficient space beyond such intersection or crosswalk, in the direction in which the vehicle is proceeding, to accommodate the vehicle without obstructing the passage of other vehicular traffic or pedestrians. Any person who violates this section shall be subject to a fine of $200.00.

(Added. Coun. J. 7-12-90, p. 18634; Amend. 10-7-98, p. 78921; 11-6-02, p. 96501; 12-4-02, p. 100729; 5-26-04, p. 24880)

§9-40-130 Obstruction of traffic.

The operator of a vehicle shall not so operate the vehicle as to form an unreasonable obstruction to traffic.

(Added. Coun. J. 7-12-90, p. 18634)

§9-40-140 Negligent driving.

It shall be unlawful for any person to operate any vehicle upon a public way negligently, heedlessly and without due caution in a manner which endangers or is likely to endanger any person or property or to swerve within, between or across lanes of traffic in such a manner.

Any person who violates this section shall be fined not less than $300 nor more than $1,000 for each offense.

(Added. Coun. J. 7-12-90, p. 18634; Amend. Coun. J. 5-7-03, p. 795)

§9-40-150 Following too closely.

The driver of a motor vehicle shall not follow another vehicle more closely than is reasonable and prudent, having due regard for the speed of such vehicle and the traffic upon the condition of the roadway.

(Added. Coun. J. 7-12-90, p. 18634)

§9-40-160 Drivers to exercise due care for pedestrians.

Every driver of a vehicle shall exercise due care to avoid colliding with any pedestrian upon any roadway, shall give warning by sounding the horn when necessary and shall exercise proper precautions upon observing any child or any confused or incapacitated person upon a roadway.

(Added. Coun. J. 7-12-90, p. 18634)

§9-40-170 Driving or moving vehicle in unsafe condition.

It is unlawful for any person to drive or move, or for the owner to cause or knowingly permit to be driven or moved, on any roadway any vehicle or combination of vehicles which is in such unsafe condition as to endanger any person or property or which contains equipment prohibited by the traffic code or is not equipped with such lamps and other equipment in proper condition and adjustment as required in the traffic code, or which is equipped in any manner in violation of this code.

(Added. Coun. J. 7-12-90, p. 18634)

§9-40-180 Coasting downhill prohibited.

(a) The driver of any motor vehicle when traveling upon a down grade shall not coast with the gears of such vehicle in neutral.

(b) The driver of a motor vehicle of the second division when traveling upon a down grade shall not coast with the clutch disengaged.

(Added. Coun. J. 7-12-90, p. 18634)

§9-40-190 Pulling out from parked position.

No person shall move a vehicle which is stopped, standing, or parked on any roadway unless and until such movement can be made with reasonable safety.

(Added. Coun. J. 7-12-90, p. 18634)

§9-40-200 Operator's signals.

(a) No person shall turn a vehicle from a direct course or move right or left upon a roadway unless and until such movement can be made with reasonable safety and then only after giving a clearly audible signal by sounding the horn if any pedestrian may be affected by such movement or after giving an appropriate visual signal in the manner hereinafter provided.

(b) A signal of intention to turn right or left shall be given continuously during not less than the last 100 feet traveled by the vehicle before turning.

(c) A turn signal shall be given to indicate an intention to change lanes or start from a parallel parked position.

(Added. Coun. J. 7-12-90, p. 18634)

§9-40-210 Operator's signals—Stop or decrease in speed.

No person shall stop or suddenly decrease the speed of a vehicle without first giving an appropriate signal in the manner provided in this chapter to the driver of any vehicle immediately to the rear when there is opportunity to give such signal.

(Added. Coun. J. 7-12-90, p. 18634)

§9-40-220 Operator's signals—Means.

Any stop or turn signal when required by the traffic code shall be given either by means of the hand and arm or by mechanical device, all of which signals shall be plainly visible and understandable in normal sunlight and at night from a distance of 100 feet to the front and rear, but shall not project a glaring or dazzling light; except that a stop signal need be visible only from the rear. All mechanical signal devices shall be self-illuminated at all times when in use.

(Added. Coun. J. 7-12-90, p. 18634)

§9-40-230 Operator's signals—Hand and arm—Manner.

Hand and arm signals shall be given from the left side of the vehicle in the following manner:

1. Left turn, hand and arm extended horizontally;
2. Right turn, hand and arm extended upward;
3. Stop or decrease speed, hand and arm extended downward.

(Added. Coun. J. 7-12-90, p. 18634)

§9-40-240 Use of horns and signals devices.

(a) The driver of a motor vehicle shall, when reasonably necessary to insure safe operation, give audible warning with his horn but shall not otherwise use such horn at any time.

(b) The sounding of any horn or signal device on any automobile, motorcycle, bus or other vehicle while stationary, except as a danger signal when an approaching vehicle is apparently out of control, or, if in motion, only as a danger signal after or as brakes are being applied and deceleration of the vehicle is intended, or the creation by means of any such signal device of any unreasonably loud or harsh sound or the sounding of any such device for an unnecessary and unreasonable period of time, is hereby prohibited.

(Added. Coun. J. 7-12-90, p. 18634)

§9-40-250 Driving with view obstructed prohibited.

(a) No person shall drive a motor vehicle with any sign, poster, card, sticker, or other non-transparent material upon the front windshield or upon or protruding from any rear window, side window or roof which materially obstructs, obscures or impairs the view from both within or without the vehicle.

(b) No person shall drive any motor vehicle upon a roadway with any object so placed in or upon the vehicle as to obstruct the driver's clear view through the windshield, except required or permitted equipment of the vehicle.

(c) No person shall drive a vehicle when it is loaded or when there are in the front seat such number of persons, exceeding three, as to obstruct the view of the driver to the front or sides of the vehicles or as to interfere with the driver's control over the driving mechanism of the vehicle.

(d) No person shall drive any motor vehicle upon a roadway with any human being placed upon or protruding from the vehicle's roof, trunk, hood or any window; provided, however, that this subsection shall not apply (i) if the motor vehicle is part of a parade, public assembly or athletic event as defined in Section 10-8-330 of this code and for which a permit has been obtained; or (ii) if the motor vehicle is being used by an officer or employee of the city of Chicago in the performance of his or her official duties.

(e) Any person who violates this section shall be fined not less than $300 nor more than $1,000 for each offense.

(Added. Coun. J. 7-12-90, p. 18634; Amend. Coun. J. 5-7-03, p. 795)

CHAPTER 9-44
TOWING DISABLED VEHICLES

Sections:

9-44-010 Towing or pushing regulations.
9-44-020 Safe speed required.
9-44-030 Commercial towing vehicle—Daily report required.
9-44-040 Tow trucks—Equipment and markings.
9-44-050 Tow truck operators—Insurance.
9-44-060 Towing of vehicle containing passenger prohibited.

§9-44-010 Towing or pushing regulations.

(a) When one vehicle is towing another, the vehicles shall be connected to a drawbar of sufficient strength to pull all weight towed, and the drawbar shall not exceed eight feet in length. In addition to the drawbar, the vehicles shall be connected by two chains or cables of sufficient strength to pull all weight towed independently of the drawbar. Such chains or cables shall not exceed the length of the drawbar by more than two feet when fastened to the towed vehicle.

(b) No person shall push a vehicle with another vehicle upon any public way for a distance greater than 600 feet, or in a school zone while school children are present.

(c) Every disabled vehicle being pushed or towed on any public way shall have displayed on its roof or cab a flashing amber light. Such light shall be visible for a distance of at least 500 feet from the sides and rear if the vehicle is being towed or 500 feet to the front and sides if the vehicle is being pushed. Such light shall be in addition to any other lights required by law or ordinance.

(Added. Coun. J. 7-12-90, p. 18634)

§9-44-020 Safe speed required.

No person shall drive any vehicle pushing or towing another vehicle a rate of speed greater than is reasonable under the conditions so as not to endanger life or property.

(Added. Coun. J. 7-12-90, p. 18634)

§9-44-030 Commercial towing vehicle—Daily report required.

It shall be the duty of every person operating a commercial towing vehicle for hire in the city to prepare and deliver to the superintendent of police every day, before noon, a legible and correct report, on a form prescribed by the superintendent, of every motor vehicle picked up or towed by such operator from any public way in the city during the preceding twenty-four hours. The report shall contain the date upon which the towing service was performed, the locations from and to which the vehicle was towed, the name and address of the owner of the towed vehicle, the name and address of the person requesting the towing service, the name and license number of the chauffeur, if the vehicle was chauffeur-driven, and the make, type, state registration number, city wheel tax license number, engine number and serial or factory number of the towed vehicle. This section shall not apply to any person operating a towing vehicle exclusively for the purpose of towing vehicles owned by such person.

(Added. Coun. J. 7-12-90, p. 18634)

§9-44-040 Tow trucks—Equipment and markings.

(a) No person shall drive or operate a tow truck unless the truck complies with the following:

(1) Every tow truck shall be equipped with an amber rotating light affixed to the roof of the cab; such light shall be visible for at least 500 feet in all directions and shall be operating when said tow truck is either towing or pushing a vehicle.

(2) Every tow truck, except when owned by a government agency, shall display on each side of the cab in letters not less than two inches in height, in contrasting color, the name, address and telephone number of the owner or operator of said tow truck.

(3) Every tow truck shall be equipped with at least one cubic foot of sand or dirt, one broom, one shovel, one trash can and one fully charged fire extinguisher, dry chemical or carbon dioxide with a rating of 4-B-C units or greater and bearing the approval of a laboratory qualified by the Bureau of Fire Prevention for this purpose.

(b) Every owner or operator of a tow truck shall remove all glass and debris deposited upon any public way by the disabled vehicle being serviced. The operator shall also spread sand or dirt upon the portion of any public way on which oil or grease has been deposited by the disabled vehicle.

(Added. Coun. J. 7-12-90, p. 18634)

§9-44-050 Tow truck operators—Insurance.

Every tow truck operator shall maintain a liability insurance policy insuring the owner and the operator (1) for injury to person, in an amount not less than $100,000.00 to any one person and $300,000.00 for any one accident; (2) for damage to property other than a vehicle being towed, in an amount not less than $50,000.00 for any one accident; and (3) for damage to any vehicle towed by the tower, in an amount not less than $15,000.00 per vehicle. Such insurance policy shall be issued by a firm properly qualified to do business in the state of Illinois, and a certificate of the policy shall be carried in the cab of such tow truck and displayed on demand to a police officer or other authorized government official.

(Added. Coun. J. 7-12-90, p. 18634)

§9-44-060 Towing of vehicle containing passenger prohibited.

No person shall operate a vehicle to tow another vehicle if the towed vehicle contains one or more passengers.

(Added Coun. J. 7-29-98, p. 75175)

CHAPTER 9-48
TYPES OF VEHICLES—REGULATIONS

Sections:

9-48-010 Authorized emergency vehicles.
9-48-020 Horse-drawn carriages—Areas designated for use—Permit for use in other areas.
9-48-030 Horse-drawn carriages—Driving prohibited on certain streets and during certain times.
9-48-040 Horse-drawn carriages—Left turns—Loading and unloading passengers.
9-48-050 Buses—Stopping, standing and parking.
9-48-060 Taxicabs—Stopping, standing and parking.
9-48-070 Cruising of public passenger vehicles prohibited.
9-48-080 Riding on motorcycles or motor-driven cycles.
9-48-090 Construction vehicles and equipment.

§9-48-010 Authorized emergency vehicles.

(a) The driver of an authorized emergency vehicle, when responding to an emergency call or when in pursuit of an actual or suspected violator of the law or when responding to but not upon return from any fire alarm, may:

(1) Park or stand, irrespective of the provisions of the traffic code;

(2) Proceed past a red or stop signal or stop sign, but only after slowing down as may be necessary for safe operation;

(3) Exceed the speed limits so long as he does not endanger life or property;

(4) Disregard regulations governing direction of movement or turning in specified directions.

(b) The exemptions herein granted to an authorized emergency vehicle shall apply only (1) when the driver of the vehicle while in motion sounds an audible signal by bell, siren or exhaust whistle as may be reasonably necessary, and the vehicle is displaying an oscillating, rotating or flashing red beam visible under normal atmospheric conditions from a distance of 500 feet of the front of such vehicle or (2) when the authorized emergency vehicle is operated as a police vehicle and such vehicle is displaying an oscillating, rotating or flashing blue beam.

(c) The foregoing provisions shall not relieve the driver of an authorized emergency vehicle from the duty to drive with due regard for the safety of all persons, nor shall such provisions protect the driver from the consequences of reckless disregard of others.

(Added. Coun. J. 7-12-90, p. 18634)

§9-48-020 Horse-drawn carriages—Areas designated for use—Permit for use in other areas.

(a) Except as provided in subsection (b), horse-drawn carriages shall be allowed to operate only in such areas or on such routes as are designated from time to time by the commissioner of transportation, subject to the approval of the city council.

(b) Operation of carriages in areas or on routes not designated pursuant to subsection (a) shall be by permit only. Such permits shall be issued by the commissioner of transportation, for a fee of $50.00 per day, only upon application of a licensed operator at least 72 hours prior to the date of the proposed use and only for a period of time not to exceed eight hours per day. Each permit shall specify the route on which the permit holder may operate, the location of permitted stops, and the hours for which the permit is valid.

(Added. Coun. J. 7-12-90, p. 18634; Amend. 12-11-91, p. 10832; 11-17-93, p. 42192)

§9-48-030 Horse-drawn carriages—Driving prohibited on certain streets and during certain times.

(a) No horse-drawn carriage may be driven on any city street between 7:00 a.m. and 9:30 a.m. daily or between 4:00 p.m. and 6:00 p.m. on Monday through Friday, except on holidays as defined in Section 9-4-010.

(b) No horse-drawn carriage may be driven on Michigan Avenue from Wacker Drive to Oak Street between 9:30 a.m. and 7:00 p.m.

(c) No horse-drawn carriage may be driven in the area bounded in the north and west by Wacker Drive, on the east by Wabash Avenue, and on the south by Congress Parkway between 6:00 a.m. and 6:00 p.m. Monday through Friday, except by permit issued pursuant to Section 9-48-020(b) or on holidays as defined in Section 9-4-010.

(d) No horse-drawn carriage shall be driven within the area bounded by Chicago Avenue, LaSalle Street, Goethe Street and Michigan Avenue and local Lake Shore Drive between 2:00 a.m. and 7:00 p.m. except by permit issued pursuant to Section 9-48-020(b).

(e) No horse-drawn carriage shall be driven within the area bounded by Lake Shore Drive, Pearson Street and Mies Van der Rohe Way except by permit issued pursuant to Section 9-48-020(b).

(f) No horse-drawn carriage may be driven on Lake Shore (outer) Drive at any time.

(g) No horse-drawn carriage shall be driven on North Rush Street between Chicago Avenue and Cedar Street, North State Street between Cedar Street and Division Street, and on Division Street between North Clark Street and North Lake Shore Drive between the hours of 6:00 p.m. on Friday and 2:00 a.m. on Saturday and between 6:00 p.m. on Saturday and 2:00 a.m. on Sunday.
(Added. Coun. J. 7-12-90, p. 18634)

§9-48-040 Horse-drawn carriages—Left turns—Loading and unloading passengers.

(a) No horse-drawn carriage shall make a left turn from any street other than a one-way street unless such turn is expressly authorized by permit, ordinance or route designation by the commissioner of transportation.

(b) The driver of a horse-drawn carriage shall not stop such vehicle upon any street at any place for the purpose of standing, or for the purpose of loading or unloading passengers, other than at a carriage stand designated by ordinance passed by the city council, except:

(i) In the case of an emergency; or

(ii) As provided in a permit issued pursuant to Section 9-48-020(b); or

(iii) If a carriage stand is fully occupied, a driver may stop to unload passengers to the front or rear of the stand, but in no event more than 25 feet from nearest boundary of the stand, and without obstructing any traffic lane, intersection or crosswalk, and only for the period of time necessary to unload passengers; or

(iv) At any location designated by ordinance passed by the city council for picking up or dropping off passengers when such transactions occur in less than one minute. Such locations may include, but are not limited to, places adjacent to cultural institutions, business districts and restaurants. However, a place designated in accordance with this subsection (iv) may not be used for purposes of standing.

(c) Whenever stopping to load or unload passengers, the driver of a horse-drawn carriage shall stop the carriage parallel to the curb, with the curbside wheels no more than 12 inches from the curb.
(Added. Coun. J. 7-12-90, p. 18634; Amend. 7-24-91, p. 4000; 12-11-91, p. 10832; 7-30-97, p. 48760)

§9-48-050 Buses—Stopping, standing and parking.

(a) The driver of a bus shall not stop such vehicle upon any street at any place for the purpose of loading or unloading passengers other than at a designated bus stop, bus stand, passenger loading zone, or bus terminal except in case of an emergency or as permitted in paragraph (d) of this section.

(b) The driver of a bus shall enter a bus stop or passenger loading zone on a public way only in such a manner that the bus when stopped to load or unload passengers shall be in a position with the right front wheel of such bus not further than 18 inches from the curb, or 30 inches from the curb if the bus is lift-equipped, and the bus approximately parallel to the curb so as not to unduly impede the movement of other vehicular traffic.

(c) When bus lanes are designated and appropriately indicated by signs and markings, it shall be unlawful for the driver of any bus to operate the vehicle on any other portion of the roadway for travel in the direction allowed in the designated lane.

(d) The driver of a bus may stop such vehicle at any intersection of any street on which it has authority to operate between the hours of Midnight and 5:00 a.m. for the purpose of loading or unloading passengers.

(Added. Coun. J. 7-12-90, p. 18634; Amend. 4-12-91, p. 31763)

§9-48-060 Taxicabs—Stopping, standing and parking.

(a) The driver of any taxicab shall not stop such vehicle upon any business street at any place other than a taxicab stand, except for the expeditious loading or unloading of passengers or when necessary to avoid conflict with other traffic or in compliance with the directions of a police officer, traffic control aide or traffic sign or signal; provided, however, that this section shall not apply when the taxicab is unoccupied, not for hire and otherwise lawfully parked.

(b) No driver, involved in the expeditious loading or unloading of passengers shall be charged with a violation of any parking ordinance contained in this code, unless such driver fails to move his vehicle after having been directed by a police officer or traffic control aide to do so.

(Added. Coun. J. 7-12-90, p. 18634; Amend. 11-15-00, p. 46957)

§9-48-070 Cruising of public passenger vehicles prohibited.

No operator of a public passenger vehicle shall solicit business in such manner as to interfere with the lawful movement of traffic.

(Added. Coun. J. 7-12-90, p. 18634)

§9-48-080 Riding on motorcycles or motor-driven cycles.

A person operating a motorcycle or motor-driven cycle shall ride only upon the permanent and regular seat attached thereto, and such operator shall not carry any other person unless the cycle is designed to carry more than one person, in which event a passenger may ride upon the permanent and regular seat if designed for two persons or upon another seat firmly attached to the rear or side of the cycle.

(Added. Coun. J. 7-12-90, p. 18634)

§9-48-090 Construction vehicles and equipment.

Every motor vehicle of the second division operated on the public way in the course of a business consisting of any construction work requiring a permit under the building provisions of this code or under the fire provisions of this code, and every piece of mobile equipment so operated, and every trailer, cart and piece of equipment towed on the public way in the course of such a business, shall have displayed on its side the name of the business. The name shall be in letters no less than two inches high and one-half inch wide. Nothing in this section shall apply to any motor vehicle on which is affixed the insignia required under Section 18c-4701 of the Illinois Commercial Transportation Law, as amended. Any person who violates any provision of this section shall be subject to a fine of $100.00 for each violation. Whenever any vehicle or piece of equipment is operated in violation of the provisions of this section, the owner or the driver of the vehicle shall be deemed liable, and either may be prosecuted, for the violation.

(Added. Coun. J. 9-15-93, p. 37920)

CHAPTER 9-52
BICYCLES—OPERATION

Sections:

9-52-010 Rights and duties.
9-52-020 Riding bicycles on sidewalks and certain roadways.
9-52-021 Riding bicycles on sidewalks—Penalty.
9-52-030 Speed of bicycles.
9-52-040 Yielding right-of-way.
9-52-050 Riding in single file required—Exceptions.
9-52-060 Carrying articles on bicycles.
9-52-070 Parking.
9-52-080 Headlamps, reflectors and brakes.
9-52-090 Riding regulations.
9-52-100 Parents or legal guardians responsibility.

§9-52-010 Rights and duties.

(a) Every person riding a bicycle upon a roadway shall be granted all of the rights and shall be subject to all of the duties applicable to the driver of a vehicle by the laws of this state declaring rules of the road applicable to vehicles or by the traffic ordinances of this city applicable to the driver of a vehicle, except as to those provisions of laws and ordinances which by their nature can have no application.

(b) The regulations in the traffic code applicable to bicycles shall apply whenever a bicycle is operated upon any roadway or public sidewalk or upon any public path set aside for the exclusive use of bicycles, subject to those exceptions stated herein.

(c) Whenever authorized signs are erected indicating that no right or left turn or turn in the opposite direction is permitted, no person operating a bicycle shall disobey the direction of any such sign unless he dismounts from the bicycle to make the turn, in which event he shall then obey the regulations applicable to pedestrians.

(d) Every person convicted of a violation of any provision of this chapter regulating bicycles shall be fined $25.00.
(Added. Coun. J. 7-12-90, p. 18634)

§9-52-020 Riding bicycles on sidewalks and certain roadways.

(a) No person shall ride a bicycle upon a sidewalk within a business district.

(b) No person 12 or more years of age shall ride a bicycle upon any sidewalk in any district, unless such sidewalk has been officially designated and marked as a bicycle route.

(c) Bicycles shall not be operated on Lake Shore Drive or on any roadway where the operation of bicycles has been prohibited and signs have been erected indicating such prohibition.

(d) Whenever a usable path for bicycles has been provided adjacent to a roadway, bicycle riders shall use such path and shall not use the roadway.
(Added. Coun. J. 7-12-90, p. 18634)

§9-52-021 Riding bicycles on sidewalks—Penalty.

(a) The penalty for any person age 18 and older who rides a bicycle on the sidewalk adjacent to North Sheridan Road, between West Ardamore Avenue and West Sheridan Road (6400 north) shall be as follows:

(1) The bicycle shall be temporarily disabled without permanent damage; and

(2) The violator shall be subject to a fine of $50.00.

(b) Following passage and approval, this section shall be in full force and effect upon the posting of signage notifying bicyclists of the penalty for violation of this section.
(Added. Coun. J. 2-6-02, p. 79154; Amend. Coun. J. 6-4-03, p. 2538)

§9-52-030 Speed of bicycles.

No person shall operate a bicycle at a speed greater than is reasonable and prudent under the conditions then existing.
(Added. Coun. J. 7-12-90, p. 18634)

§9-52-040 Yielding right-of-way.

(a) The operator of a bicycle emerging from an alley, driveway or building shall, upon approaching a sidewalk or the sidewalk area extending across any alleyway, yield the right-of-way to all pedestrians approaching on the sidewalk or sidewalk area and, upon entering the roadway, shall yield the right-of-way to all vehicles approaching on the roadway.

(b) Whenever any person is riding a bicycle upon a sidewalk, such person shall yield the right-of-way to any pedestrian and shall give audible signal before overtaking and passing such pedestrian.

(c) Every person operating a bicycle upon a roadway shall ride as near as practicable to the right-hand side of the roadway, exercising due care when passing a standing vehicle or one proceeding in the same direction and at all times giving the right-of-way to other moving vehicles.
(Added. Coun. J. 7-12-90, p. 18634)

§9-52-050 Riding in single file required—Exceptions.

Persons riding bicycles upon a roadway shall not ride other than single file except on paths or parts of roadways set aside for the exclusive use of bicycles.
(Added. Coun. J. 7-12-90, p. 18634)

§9-52-060 Carrying articles on bicycles.

No person operating a bicycle shall carry any package, bundle or article which prevents the rider from keeping at least one hand upon the handlebars.
(Added. Coun. J. 7-12-90, p. 18634)

§9-52-070 Parking.

No person shall park a bicycle upon a street other than upon the roadway against the curb or upon the sidewalk in a rack to support the bicycle or against a building or at the curb in such manner as to afford the least obstruction to pedestrian traffic.
(Added. Coun. J. 7-12-90, p. 18634)

§9-52-080 Headlamps, reflectors and brakes.

(a) Every bicycle when in use at nighttime shall be equipped with a head lamp which shall emit a white light visible from a minimum distance of 500 feet from the front and with a rear red reflector capable of reflecting the head lamp beams of an approaching motor vehicle back to the operator of such vehicle at distances up to 200 feet or a rear lamp emitting a red light visible from a distance of at least 200 feet from the rear.

(b) Every bicycle shall be equipped with a brake that will enable the operator to make the braked wheel skid on dry, level, clean pavement.
(Added. Coun. J. 7-12-90, p. 18634)

§9-52-090 Riding regulations.

(a) A person propelling a bicycle shall not ride other than astride a permanent and regular seat attached thereto.

(b) No bicycle shall be used to carry more persons at one time than the number for which it is designed and equipped.
(Added. Coun. J. 7-12-90, p. 18634)

§9-52-100 Parents or legal guardians responsibility.

No parent or legal guardian of any child shall authorize or knowingly permit the child to violate any of the provisions of this chapter applicable to bicycles.
(Added. Coun. J. 7-12-90, p. 18634)

CHAPTER 9-56
REPORTING OF ACCIDENTS

Sections:

9-56-010 Report of accident.
9-56-020 Duty upon striking unattended vehicle.
9-56-030 Duty upon striking fixtures or other property.

§9-56-010 Report of accident.

The operator of a vehicle involved in any accident resulting in injury to or death of any person or in property damage to an apparent extent of $250.00 or more, if such operator is physically capable of doing so, shall immediately report such accident to the police department.
(Added. Coun. J. 7-12-90, p. 18634)

§9-56-020 Duty upon striking unattended vehicle.

The operator of any vehicle which collides with any vehicle which is unattended shall immediately stop and shall then and there either locate and notify the operator or owner of such vehicle of his name, address and telephone number and of the state registration number of the vehicle striking the unattended vehicle or shall leave in a conspicuous place on the vehicle struck a written notice giving his name, address and telephone number and the state registration number of the vehicle doing the striking and a statement of the circumstances thereof.
(Added. Coun. J. 7-12-90, p. 18634)

§9-56-030 Duty upon striking fixtures or other property.

The operator of any vehicle involved in an accident resulting only in damage to fixtures or other property legally upon or adjacent to public way shall take reasonable steps to locate and notify the owner or persons in charge of such property of such fact and of his name, address and telephone number and of the state registration number of the vehicle he is driving and shall, upon request and if available, exhibit his operator's or chauffeur's license.
(Added. Coun. J. 7-12-90, p. 18634)

CHAPTER 9-60
PEDESTRIANS' RIGHTS AND DUTIES

Sections:

9-60-010 Crosswalks authorized—Crossing between intersections prohibited when.
9-60-020 Through streets.
9-60-030 Limited access streets and highways—Public pedestrian tunnels and bridges.
9-60-040 Railroad grade crossings and bridges.
9-60-050 Pedestrian to yield right-of-way when.
9-60-060 Pedestrian crossing.
9-60-070 Use of crosswalk.
9-60-080 Walking along roadways.
9-60-090 Soliciting rides prohibited.
9-60-100 Traffic-control signals.
9-60-110 Imitation of blind persons prohibited.
9-60-120 Pedestrians to exercise due care.

§9-60-010 Crosswalks authorized—Crossing between intersections prohibited when.

(a) The commissioner of transportation is hereby authorized to designate and maintain by appropriate lines upon the surface of roadway, crosswalks at intersections where in his opinion there is particular danger to pedestrians crossing the roadway and at such other places as he may deem necessary.

(b) Whenever, upon the basis of an engineering or traffic investigation upon any street, it is determined that pedestrian crossings between intersections shall be prohibited in the interest of public safety, pedestrians shall not cross between intersections except where there may be a marked crosswalk. Such regulations against pedestrians crossing between intersections shall be effective when appropriate signs giving notice thereof are erected.
(Added. Coun. J. 7-12-90, p. 18634; Amend. 12-11-91, p. 10832)

§9-60-020 Through streets.

No pedestrian shall cross a roadway other than in a crosswalk on any through street.
(Added. Coun. J. 7-12-90, p. 18634)

§9-60-030 Limited access streets and highways—Public pedestrian tunnels and bridges.

(a) No pedestrian shall cross the roadway of a limited-access street or highway other than by means of those facilities which have been constructed as pedestrian crossings or at those points where marked crosswalks have been provided.

(b) No pedestrian shall cross a roadway where a public pedestrian tunnel or bridge has been provided other than by way of the tunnel or bridge within a section to be determined by the commissioner of transportation and to be so designated by the erection of appropriate signs or fencing.
(Added. Coun. J. 7-12-90, p. 18634; Amend. 12-11-91, p. 10832)

§9-60-040 Railroad grade crossings and bridges.

(a) No pedestrian shall pass through, around, over, or under any crossing gate or barrier at a railroad grade crossing or bridge while such gate or barrier is closed or is being opened or closed.

(b) No pedestrian shall enter or remain upon any bridge or approach thereto beyond the bridge signal, gate or barrier after a bridge operation signal indication has been given.
(Added. Coun. J. 7-12-90, p. 18634)

§9-60-050 Pedestrian to yield right-of-way when.

(a) Every pedestrian crossing a roadway at any point other than within a marked crosswalk shall yield the right-of-way to all vehicles upon the roadway.

(b) The foregoing rules in this section have no application under the conditions stated in Section 9-60-010 when pedestrians are prohibited from crossing at certain designated places.
(Added. Coun. J. 7-12-90, p. 18634)

§9-60-060 Pedestrian crossing.

(a) No pedestrian shall cross a roadway at any place other than by a route at right angles to the curb or by the shortest route to the opposite curb except in a marked crosswalk.

(b) No pedestrian shall suddenly leave a curb or other place of safety and walk or run into the path of a vehicle which is so close that it is impossible for the driver to yield.
(Added. Coun. J. 7-12-90, p. 18634)

§9-60-070 Use of crosswalk.

Pedestrians shall move whenever practicable upon the right side of crosswalks.
(Added. Coun. J. 7-12-90, p. 18634)

§9-60-080 Walking along roadways.

(a) Where sidewalks are provided it shall be unlawful for a pedestrian to walk along and upon an adjacent roadway.

(b) Where sidewalks are not provided any pedestrian walking along and upon a roadway shall when practicable walk only on the left side of the roadway or its shoulder facing traffic that may approach from the opposite direction.
(Added. Coun. J. 7-12-90, p. 18634)

§9-60-090 Soliciting rides prohibited.

No person shall stand in a roadway for the purpose of soliciting a ride from the driver of any private vehicle.
(Added. Coun. J. 7-12-90, p. 18634)

§9-60-100 Traffic-control signals.

Pedestrians shall be subject to traffic-control signals as provided in Sections 9-8-020 and 9-8-050, but at all other places shall be granted those rights and be subject to the restrictions stated in this chapter.
(Added. Coun. J. 7-12-90, p. 18634)

§9-60-110 Imitation of blind persons prohibited.

It shall be unlawful for any person, except persons wholly or partially blind, to carry or use on the public streets of the city any cane or walking stick which is white in color, or white with a red end on the bottom.
(Added. Coun. J. 7-12-90, p. 18634)

§9-60-120 Pedestrians to exercise due care.

Nothing in this chapter shall relieve a pedestrian from the duty of exercising due care.
(Added. Coun. J. 7-12-90, p. 18634)

CHAPTER 9-64
PARKING REGULATIONS

Sections:

9-64-010 Applicability—Exemptions.
9-64-020 Parallel parking—Obstruction of traffic.
9-64-030 Diagonal parking zones.
9-64-040 Temporary uses of the public way.
9-64-050 Parking restrictions—Parking for persons with disabilities.
9-64-060 Snow removal.
9-64-070 Parking on snow routes.
9-64-080 Parking restricted on certain days or hours.
9-64-085 Review of existing residential permit parking.
9-64-090 Residential permit parking.
9-64-091 Industrial permit parking.
9-64-100 Parking prohibited—Fire hydrants, firelanes and various locations.
9-64-110 Parking prohibited—Roadways, sidewalks, bridges and similar locations.
9-64-120 Parking on city property.
9-64-125 Display of license.

9-64-130	Parking in alleys.
9-64-140	Common-carrier vehicle stops and stands.
9-64-150	Parking prohibited—Fire stations, railroad crossings and hazardous locations.
9-64-160	Curb loading zones.
9-64-170	Parking restrictions—Special types of vehicles.
9-64-180	Restricted parking—Area bounded by Chicago River, Michigan Avenue and Harrison Street.
9-64-190	Parking meter zones—Regulations.
9-64-200	Parking meters—Installation and pavement markings.
9-64-205	Parking meter rates—Central business district.
9-64-210	Television news permit parking areas.
9-64-220	Parking violations—Enforcement—Prima facie responsibility designated.
9-64-230	Standing or parking violations punishable by fine.
9-64-250	Violation—Towing and storage fees.

§9-64-010 Applicability—Exemptions.

(a) The provisions of the traffic code prohibiting the standing or parking of vehicles shall apply at all times or at those times therein specified or as indicated on official signs, where required, except when it is necessary to stop a vehicle to avoid conflict with other traffic or in compliance with the directions of a police officer, traffic control aide or official traffic-control device.

(b) The provisions of any ordinance imposing a time limit on parking shall not relieve any person from the duty to observe other and more restrictive provisions prohibiting or limiting the standing or parking of vehicles in specified places or at specified times.

(c) Notwithstanding any other provision of the traffic code, any motor vehicle bearing handicapped or disabled veterans state registration plates or a handicapped parking decal or device issued pursuant to Section 3-616 or 11-1301.2 of the Illinois Vehicle Code and any motor vehicle registered in another jurisdiction, state, district, territory or foreign country upon which is displayed a registration, special decal or device issued by such other jurisdiction designating the vehicle is operated by or for a handicapped person is hereby exempt from the payment of parking meter fees and exempt from any ordinance or regulation which imposes a time limitation for parking. This exemption shall not be construed to authorize the parking of any vehicle during hours when parking is otherwise prohibited or where the vehicle constitutes a traffic hazard and must be moved at the instruction and request of a law enforcement officer to a location designated by such officer. The exemption granted under this subsection shall apply only when the motor vehicle is operated by or under the personal direction of the person for whom the handicapped or disabled veteran registration plates or handicapped parking decal or device was issued.

(Added. Coun. J. 7-12-90, p. 18634; Amend. Coun. J. 12-19-90, p. 27910)

§9-64-020 Parallel parking—Obstruction of traffic.

(a) It shall be unlawful to stand or park any vehicle in a roadway other than parallel with the edge of the roadway headed in the direction of lawful traffic movement and with the curbside wheels of the vehicle within 12 inches of the curb or edge of the roadway; provided, however, this prohibition shall not apply to motorcycles or motor scooters, which may be parked diagonally, or to the parking of any vehicle in a designated diagonal parking zone or space.

(b) It shall be unlawful to stand or park any vehicle upon any street in such a manner or under such conditions as to leave available less than 18 feet of the width of the roadway for free movement of vehicular traffic on a two-way street or less than 10 feet of the width of the roadway for free movement of vehicular traffic on a one-way street.
(Added. Coun. J. 7-12-90, p. 18634)

§9-64-030 Diagonal parking zones.

(a) The commissioner of transportation is hereby authorized to establish diagonal parking zones and to designate such zones by placing and maintaining suitable signs and markings. Such diagonal parking zones shall be established only after appropriate engineering studies have indicated that diagonal parking will not be hazardous and at all times will leave not less than 20 feet of available roadway for the ingress and egress of vehicles between the rows of parked vehicles. Diagonal parking zones shall be established only on streets at their termini beyond the last cross-street intersection, on streets which serve only as service drives, or on streets designated as service drives by ordinance. The commissioner shall consult with the parking administrator in the selection of locations for diagonal parking zones.

(b) It shall be unlawful to park any vehicle in any designated diagonal parking zone or space except diagonally to the edge of the roadway and within the pavement markings.
(Added. Coun. J. 7-12-90, p. 18634; Amend. 12-11-91, p. 10832)

§9-64-040 Temporary and permanent signs—Street cleaning

(a) For the purpose of facilitating street cleaning, the Commissioner of Streets and Sanitation is authorized to post temporary signs and the Com missioner of Transportation is authorized to erect and maintain permanent signs, designating the day or days of the week and hours of the day and the part of the street or streets in which the parking of vehicles is prohibited be cause of such street cleaning and to further designate such street or streets "tow zones."

(b) It shall be a violation of this section, and shall subject the violator a fine of $50.00, to park any vehicle on any street in violation of a sig posted, erected or maintained pursuant to this section.

(c) Where signage has been posted or erected pursuant to subsection (a) of this section, the Commissioner of Streets and Sanitation is authorized tow any vehicle parked in such designated portion of the public way to a authorized facility or, if practical, to the nearest lawful parking space or move the vehicle temporarily during such street cleaning.

(d) No towing or storage fees shall be assessed in those instances in which a vehicle is towed to an authorized facility pursuant to this section, unless the sign posted or erected pursuant to subsection (a) of this section has been in place for 24 hours.
(Added Coun. J. 6-19-2002, p. 88763. Former §9-64-040 repealed Coun. J. 6-19-2002, p. 88762.)

§9-64-041 Temporary signs—Other uses

(a) For the purpose of facilitating temporary uses of the public way requiring the absence of parked vehicles, including but not limited to athletic events, parades and special events, the Commissioner of Streets and Sanitation and the Superintendent of Police are authorized to post temporary signs designating the day or days of the week and hours of the day and the part of the Street or streets in which the parking of vehicles is prohibited because of such temporary uses of the public way and to further designate such street or streets as "tow zones."

(b) It shall be a violation of this section, and shall subject the violator to a fine of $50.00, to park any vehicle on any street in violation of a sign posted, erected or maintained pursuant to this section.

(c) Where signage has been posted or erected pursuant to subsection (a) of this section, the Commissioner of Streets and Sanitation is authorized to tow any vehicle parked in such designated portion of the public way to an authorized facility or, if practical, to the nearest lawful parking space or to move the vehicle temporarily during such temporary uses of the public way.

(d) No towing or storage fees shall be assessed in those instances in which a vehicle is towed to an authorized facility pursuant to this section, unless the sign posted or erected pursuant t subsection (a) has been in place for 24 hours.

(Added Coun. J. 6-19-2002, p.88763.)

§9-64-050 Parking restrictions—Parking for persons with disabilities.

(a) The commissioner of transportation, subject to the approval of the city council, is authorized to erect signs on any residential street in an R1, R2, R3, R4 or R5 district to prohibit parking except by vehicles displaying a person with a disability or disabled veterans state registration plate or a person with a disability parking decal or device issued pursuant to Sections 3-609, 3-616 or Section 11-1301.2 of the Illinois Vehicle Code. The parking administrator is authorized to determine the specific times and days that the restrictions shall be in effect. Fees for the installation and maintenance of signs erected pursuant to this section shall be $35.00 for erection of the signs and maintenance for the first year; an annual surcharge of $3.50 per lineal foot of curb space in excess of 25 feet; and $12.50 annually for continued maintenance. These fees shall be paid in the same manner as fees charged pursuant to Section 9-68-030; provided, however, that the installation and maintenance fee shall be waived by the director of revenue for any person holding a valid, current disabled veterans state registration plate.

(b) An application shall be required for an initial authorization for a restricted parking space created pursuant to subsection (e) of this section. The initial application shall be made to either the alderman of the ward in which the sign is being sought or to the department of revenue. If the application is made to the alderman of the ward, the office of the alderman shall forward a copy of the application to the department of revenue for processing compliant with subsection (d) of this section. If the application is made to the department of revenue the department of revenue shall forward a copy of the application to the alderman of the ward in which the sign being sought.

The department of revenue shall collect the required application fee. The application fee requirement may only be waived if the applicant holds a valid current disabled veterans state registration plate or provides a certification of approval under the Senior Citizens and Disabled Persons Property Tax Relief and Pharmaceutical Assistance Act, 320 ILCS 25/1 et seq., as amended.

The applicant shall provide proof or assurances, satisfactory to the city, that the applicant has met and shall continue to meet all of the following conditions as long as restricted parking is authorized pursuant to subsection (e) of this section:

(1) That the applicant holds a valid, current disabled veterans state registration plate or permanent person with a disability license plate, parking decal or device issued pursuant to Sections 3-609, 3-616 or Section 11-1301.2 of the Illinois Vehicle Code;

(2) That any vehicle that will be parked by or for the applicant in the parking space applied for bears the license plates, parking decal or device issued to the applicant pursuant to Sections 3-609, 3-616 or Section 11-1301.2 of the Illinois Vehicle Code;

(3) That the applicant resides at the primary residence that is accessible to the parking space for which application is made;

An applicant for, or user of, a restricted parking space issued pursuant to subsection (d) of this section shall immediately notify the department of revenue of any change in one or more of these conditions (b)(1) through (3).

(c) All restricted parking spaces created pursuant to this section shall require approval by a vote of the city council to be effective. Upon receiving an initial application, the alderman of the ward in which the restricted parking space will be located may introduce an ordinance proposing approval of the creation of a restricted parking space. However, the city council shall not take action on the ordinance to create a restricted parking space during the 30 day period required for the direction of revenue to complete the parking study.

(d) After introduction of an ordinance described in subsection (c), the director of revenue shall arrange for a parking study if:

(1) The applicant has tendered the required fee for restricted parking, and

(2) The director of revenue concludes that the above conditions (1) through (3) of subsection (b) of this section are met and the application is otherwise acceptable.

Such parking study shall be completed within 30 days after the conditions in subsections (d)(a) and (d)(2) are met and shall include a determination regarding the feasibility and, if appropriate, the proposed location of a proposed restricted parking space. The determination shall be based upon the number of restricted parking spaces currently installed on the residential street; the proximity of the requested restricted parking space to crosswalks, curb cuts, alleys, intersections and fire hydrants; and any other information concerning the applicant's needs and local traffic restrictions. The determination may also be based upon the extent of the alternative accessible off-street parking at the applicant's primary residence.

(e) Upon completion of the parking survey and the recommendation that a restricted parking space be installed, the director of revenue shall inform the applicant of the proposed location of the proposed parking space and shall report such recommendation to the alderman of the ward in which the restricted parking space will be located and to the city council committee on traffic control and safety. Upon determining that an application for a restricted parking space should not be recommended, the director of revenue shall provide written notice to the person submitting the application as well as the alderman of the ward in which the application was made. Any person whose application has not been recommended because the city has determined that a restricted parking space cannot be situated in a location accessible to the applicant's primary residence or was not recommended on the basis of the extent of the alternative accessible off-street parking at his or her primary residence may, within ten days of the date of denial, respond in writing to the mayor's office for people with disabilities requesting a review of the findings and stating reasons in support of reconsideration. The mayor's office for people with disabilities shall conduct such review and shall make a determination within 30 days of the date the request for reconsideration was made. The mayor's office for people with disabilities shall report its determination to the director of revenue, who shall follow, and, if appropriate, reevaluate the application in light of, such determination.

Upon approval of the city council of the designation of a restricted parking space under this subsection, the director of revenue shall issue to the applicant a revocable permit evidenced by decal or other device indicating the permit number for the restricted parking space. For restricted parking spaces that have been created under this subsection prior to the effective date of this amendatory ordinance, the director of revenue shall issue the permit no longer than 120 days after the effective date.

In the event that (1) the department of revenue does not recommend the creation of a restricted parking space, (2) a request for a review with the mayor's office for people with disabilities is not timely made, (3) a request for review with the mayor's office for people with disabilities is timely made but a determination is issued consistent with the earlier findings of the director of revenue, and/or (4) the city council fails to approve creation of a restricted parking space, the department of revenue shall refund the applicant his or her application fee directly.

(f) If the city determines, as to a pending application, that the applicant has falsely represented any one or more of conditions (1) through (3) of subsection (b) of this section, the applicant shall be subject to a fine of not less than $100.00 nor more than $500.00 and the application shall be denied. If the city determines, either at the time of a renewal or at any other time, that a person who applied for and is using a restricted parking space issued pursuant to subsection (3) of this section is not in compliance with any one or more conditions (1) through (3) of subsection (b) of this section, the director of revenue, 30 days after providing written notice to the person and the alderman of the ward in which application was made or in which the sign was installed, and an opportunity to respond, is authorized to revoke the permit issued under subsection (e) and the restricted parking space, and the commissioner of transportation is authorized to remove the sign designating such parking space. Any person not in compliance with any one or more conditions (1) through (3) of this section shall be subject to a fine of not less than $100.00 nor more than $500.00. In addition, the permit and restricted parking space issued and created under subsection (e) shall be deemed revoked whenever the commissioner of transportation removes the sign for reasons of public convenience or necessity under subsection (e) of 9-68-030.

Upon death of an applicant, there shall be a revocation of the permit issued hereunder, except in the case of a spouse or child of an applicant meeting the qualifications set forth in subsection (b) of this section. Application shall be made pursuant to subsection (b) of this section without additional fees or the removal of existing signs, and the permit shall be reissued to the spouse or child of the decedent subject to subsection (e) of this section.

(g) A renewal fee for permit and restricted parking space issued and created pursuant to subsection (e) of this section shall be required annually. The renewal fee requirement may only be waived if the applicant holds a valid, current disabled veterans state registration plate or provides a certification of approval under the Senior Citizens and Disabled Persons Property Tax Relief and Pharmaceutical Assistance Act, 320 ILCS 25/1, et. seq., as amended. The director of revenue shall provide written notice of the renewal fee requirement annually to each person using such restricted parking space. Upon a person's failure to submit the required fee in a timely fashion, the director of revenue shall provide a second written notice to the person and an opportunity to respond. If the fee, along with any prior unpaid fees, is not received by the city within 30 days form the date the second notification is mailed, the director of revenue is authorized to revoke the permit issued under this section and the restricted parking space, and the commissioner of transportation is authorized to remove the sign designating such restricted parking space.

(h) Any space designated as an on-street person with a disability parking space pursuant to this section shall be a maximum of 25 feet in length. Any such space shall be indicated by two signs, one located at each end of the parking space, unless conditions in the public way dictate the placement of a single sign located at one end of the parking space. The signs indicating a restricted parking space created under subsection (e) of this section shall indicate that parking in that space is restricted to the holder of the permit for such space, and shall indicate the permit number for such space; provided further, that if the restricted parking space is created for a person that holds a valid, current disabled veterans state registration plate, the sign also shall indicate that the restricted parking space if for a disabled veteran.

(i) The parking administrator is authorized to designate certain areas on business streets in which parking is prohibited except by vehicles displaying person with a disability parking decal or device issued pursuant to Section 3-609, 3-616 or Section 11-1301.2 of the Illinois Vehicle Code. Such areas shall comprise at least 2% of the available on-street parking spaces on any street within the area bounded by Roosevelt Road to the south, Halsted Street from Roosevelt Road to Chicago Avenue and LaSalle Street from Chicago Avenue to Division Street on the west, Chicago Avenue from Halsted Street to LaSalle Street and Division Street from LaSalle Street to Lake Michigan on the north and Lake Michigan on the east. The parking administrator is authorized to determine the specific times and days that the restrictions shall be in effect. The parking administrator shall consult with the commissioner of transportation in the selection of locations. All locations selected by the parking administrator pursuant to this subsection shall be subject to the review and approval of the mayor's office for people with disabilities. The commissioner of transportation and the mayor's office for people with disabilities shall develop a comprehensive plan for designating areas of restricted parking pursuant to this subsection. The commissioner of transportation shall install appropriate signs at areas designated pursuant to this section.

(j) It shall be unlawful to park any vehicle in any space designated by signage as a person with a disability parking space or in any parking stall of a private or public parking lot designated by the lot owner or his agent as reserved for person with disability parking unless the vehicle bears person with a disability or disabled veteran state registration plates or a person with a disability parking decal or device issued pursuant to Section 3-609, 3-616 or Section 11-1301.2 of the Illinois Vehicle Code and such vehicle is operated by the person to whom the special registration plates, special decal or device was issued or a qualified operator acting under his express direction while the person with a disability is present. In addition, beginning 120 days after the effective date of the amendatory ordinance, it shall be unlawful to park in a restricted parking space created under subsection (e) of this section unless the vehicle bears the decal or other device issued under that subsection, and the vehicle is operated by the permit holder or by a qualified operator acting under the express direction of the permit holder with the permit holder is present.

(k) Except as otherwise provided in this section, any motor vehicle bearing a person with a disability license plate or a person with a disability parking decal or device containing the international symbol of access issued to persons with disabilities by any local authority, state, district, territory or foreign country shall be recognized as a valid license plate or device and receive the same parking privileges as provided in this section.

(Added. Coun. J. 7-12-90, p. 18634; Amend. 12-11-91, p. 10832; 3-11-98, p. 63463; 5-1-02, p. 83018; 11-19-03, p. 14216)

§9-64-060 Snow removal.

(a) For the purpose of facilitating snow removal, the commissioner of transportation is authorized to erect and maintain signs prohibiting the parking of vehicles on any street or streets within the city between the hours of 3:00 a.m. and 7:00 a.m. from December 1st of any year to March 31st of the following year and to further designate such street or streets as "tow zones."

(b) It shall be unlawful to park any vehicle on any street in violation of a sign erected or maintained pursuant to this section.

(Added. Coun. J. 7-12-90, p. 18634; Amend. 12-11-91, p. 10832)

§9-64-070 Parking on snow routes.

It shall be unlawful to park any vehicle for a period of time longer than three minutes for the loading and unloading of passengers or 30 minutes for the loading, unloading, pick-up or delivery of materials from commercial vehicles, whether such location has been designated as a loading zone or not, on any street that has been designated by appropriate signs as a "Snow Route" at any time the snow on the street exceeds two inches in depth and until the snow stops falling and for the necessary period of time until all snow removal operations have been completed.

(Added. Coun. J. 7-12-90, p. 18634)

§9-64-080 Parking restricted on certain days or hours.

(a) The commissioner of transportation is authorized, based on traffic need supported by an engineering study, to erect and maintain on any through street or street on which a bus line is operated appropriate signs indicating no parking between designated hours on either side of the street Monday through Friday.

(b) The commissioner of transportation is authorized to determine, subject to the approval of the city council, those streets or parts of streets upon which standing or parking shall be prohibited within certain hours or permitted for a limited time and to erect and maintain appropriate signs giving notice of the restrictions. The commissioner of transportation is authorized to determine, upon 20-day prior notice to the alderman of the affected ward, those locations within the central business district, south of the south line of West Kinzie Street between Halsted Street and the Chicago River, and south of the south bank of the Chicago River between West Kinzie Street and Lake Michigan, at which full time standing or parking restrictions shall be modified to limit the prohibition on standing or parking to Mondays through Fridays or Mondays through Saturdays and to erect and maintain appropriate signs giving notice of the restrictions.

(c) It shall be unlawful to stand or park any vehicle in violation of a sign erected or maintained pursuant to this section.

(Added. Coun. J. 7-12-90, p. 18634; Amend. 9-11-91, p. 5008; 12-11-91, p. 10832; 10-7-98, p. 78566)

§9-64-085 Review of existing residential permit parking.

(a) The director of revenue shall review, according to a schedule to be determined by the director, all residential permit parking zones created before the effective date of the ordinance codified in this section that either: (1) are less than three blocks in size, or (2) restrict parking for 24 hours a day.

(b) Upon initiating such a review, the director of revenue shall notify and solicit comments from each alderman in whose ward part or all of the residential permit parking zone under review is located, and shall also notify the residents in the residential permit parking zone under review who are holders of the city sticker license emblem issued pursuant to Section 3-56-070 of this code. Such notice shall describe the geographical area and time periods of parking restriction of the zone under review, and shall describe the petition procedure set forth in subsection (c) of this section for voluntary revocation or time period reduction of the zone.

In conducting his review, the director of revenue shall determine whether:

(1) At least 80 percent of the occupied frontage, at ground level, of each block in the residential permit parking zone under review is in use for residence purposes;

(2) At least 75 percent of available on-street parking in the residential permit parking zone under review is being used during the time periods that parking is restricted, as determined by a parking study.

If the director concludes that both of the above conditions are met, the director shall recommend to the city council that the zone be continued. If the director concludes that both of the above conditions are not met, the director shall recommend to the city council that the zone be revoked or modified. A vote of the city council shall be required to revoke or modify a residential permit parking zone pursuant to this section.

(c) Subject to the approval of the city council, a residential permit parking zone created before the effective date of the ordinance codified in this section may be voluntarily revoked by submitting to the director a petition, requesting revocation of part or all of the zone and signed and dated by at least 51 percent of the residents in the zone who are holders of the city sticker license emblem issued pursuant to Section 3-56-070 of this code. If the petition requests revocation of only part of a residential permit parking zone, the size of the remaining zone must be at least a block, and if more than one block, all blocks in the remaining zone must be contiguous. Any signature on the petition, to be valid, must be dated within a year of the date the petition is submitted to the director.

Subject to the approval of the city council, the time periods that parking is restricted in a residential permit parking zone created before the effective date of the ordinance codified in this section may be voluntarily reduced by submitting to the director a petition, requesting a reduction in such time periods and signed and dated by at least 51 percent of the residents in the zone who are holders of the city sticker license emblem issued pursuant to Section 3-56-070 of this code. Any signature on the petition, to be valid, must be dated within a year of the date the petition is submitted to the director.

(d) Upon the revocation or modification of a residential permit parking zone pursuant to this section, the commissioner of transportation shall remove or modify the pertinent parking zone signage, as appropriate.

(e) As used in this section, the term "block" shall mean both sides of any street between street intersections.

(Added. Coun. J. 3-11-98, p. 63453)

§9-64-090 Residential permit parking.

(a) Subject to the approval of the city council, the commissioner of transportation is authorized to erect and maintain signs on any block of any residential street in an R1, R2, R3, R4 or R5 zoning district indicating resident permit parking only when all of the following conditions have been met:

(1) An application, which clearly states the cause(s) of the parking problems creating the need for the proposed residential permit parking zone, and the time periods of parking restriction that are requested (stated in hours, days and months), is submitted to the director of revenue. The application must be accompanied by a petition requesting the proposed residential permit parking zone and signed and dated by at least 65 percent of the residents in the proposed zone who are holders of the city sticker license emblem issued pursuant to Section 3-56-070 of this code. Any signature on the petition, to be valid, must be dated within a year of the date the petition is submitted to the director.

(2) The size of the proposed residential permit parking zone is a minimum of one block, and if more than one block, all blocks in the proposed zone are contiguous.

(3) At least 80 percent of the occupied frontage, at ground level, of each block in the proposed residential permit parking zone is in use for residence purposes.

(4) A parking study determines that at least 45 percent of the vehicles parked in the proposed residential permit parking zone during the time periods requested for the permit are not owned by residents of the proposed zone.

(5) A parking study determines that at least 85 percent of available on-street parking in the proposed residential permit parking zone is occupied during the time periods requested for the permit.

The director of revenue shall prepare and make available the form of application required by this subsection.

(b) As used in this section, the term "block" shall mean both sides of any street between street intersections.

(c) Upon receiving an application for a proposed residential permit parking zone, the director of revenue shall notify and solicit comments from each alderman in whose ward part or all of the proposed residential permit parking zone will be located, and shall also take such measures as are necessary to determine whether the conditions of subsection (a) of this section have been met. Before approving an application, the director shall determine the time periods, stated in hours, days and months, when the parking restrictions of the residential permit parking zone shall be effective. Such parking restrictions shall be limited to the times during which the parking study determines the parking problems exist. However, no resident permit parking shall be permitted on any part of a block located on a "snow route" that is 50 feet or less from any B or C zoning district in the 44th Ward only. Upon approving an application, the director shall report his approval to each alderman who previously was notified pursuant to this subsection, and to the city council committee on traffic control and safety. Upon denying an application, the director shall so notify each alderman who previously was notified pursuant to this subsection, and the person who submitted the application. All residential permit parking zones created pursuant to this section shall require approval by a vote of the city council to be effective.

(d) When official signs are erected indicating resident permit parking only, parking shall be restricted to service and delivery vehicles whose operators are doing business with residents of the residential permit parking zone and to vehicles displaying resident or visitor parking permits issued pursuant to Section 9-68-020 herein. In addition, a vehicle not in these two categories may park legally for up to 15 minutes in a 24-hour period in a residential permit parking zone if its hazard indicator lights are flashing.

(e) It shall be unlawful to park any unauthorized vehicle in violation of signs erected or maintained pursuant to this section or any other ordinance or city council order which establishes and defines a residential permit parking order zone for which permits are issued pursuant to Section 9-68-020 or other ordinance.

(f) Any person residing on either side of a business or commercial block immediately adjacent to a residential permit parking zone shall qualify to acquire a permit to park one vehicle far each qualifying business address in such adjacent zone. Visitor residential parking permits described in paragraph (g) shall not be issued to any person qualified under this paragraph. The owner of property with a business address located on either side of a block immediately adjacent to a residential permit parking zone shall qualify to acquire a permit to park in such adjacent zone, and shall be limited to one permit for each qualifying business address.

(g) Visitor parking permits issued pursuant to Section 9-68-020 herein shall be valid for a 24-hour period from the time of posting.

(h) Any licensed not-for-profit organization located within a residential permit parking zone, or on either side of a business, or commercial block immediately adjacent to that residential permit parking zone, shall qualify to acquire visitor parking permits to park in such adjacent zone. This provision shall apply only in wards where the alderman has introduced and passed a not-for-profit permit parking ordinance.

(i) Subject to the approval of the city council, a residential permit parking zone created pursuant to this section, or part thereof, shall be revoked upon occurrence of both of the following conditions:

(1) A petition, requesting revocation of part or all of the zone and signed and dated by at least 51 percent of the residents in the zone who are holders of the city sticker license emblem issued pursuant to Section 3-56-070 of this code, is submitted to the director of revenue. If the petition requests revocation of only part of a residential permit parking zone, the size of the remaining zone must be at least a block. Any signature on the petition, to be valid, must be dated within a year of the date the petition is submitted to the director.

(2) A parking study determines that less than 75 percent of available on-street parking in the residential permit parking zone, or part thereof sought to be revoked, is occupied during the time periods that parking is restricted.

Upon receiving a petition for revocation of part or all of a residential permit parking zone, the director of revenue shall notify and solicit comments from each alderman in whose ward part or all of the residential permit parking zone is located. If the director concludes that both of the above conditions are met, the director shall recommend to the city council that the zone be revoked or modified. If the director concludes that both of the above conditions are not met, the director shall recommend to the city council that the zone be continued.

(j) Upon the creation, revocation or modification of a residential permit parking zone pursuant to this section, the commissioner of transportation shall install, remove or modify the pertinent parking zone signage, as appropriate.

(Added. Coun. J. 7-12-90, p. 18634; Amend. 5-22-91, p. 823; 12-11-91, p. 10832; 10-2-91, p. 6608; 7-31-96, p. 26935; 11-20-96, p. 34815; 1-14-97, p. 37697; 3-11-98, p. 63453; 5-12-99, p. 2258)

§9-64-091 Industrial permit parking.

(a) Owners or managers of industrial businesses may apply to the parking administrator for designation of an industrial permit parking zone that includes the applicant's businesses, in accordance with the procedures set out in this section. The application shall be in form approved and supplied by the parking administrator, and shall include applicable rules and other relevant information. A zone may be established only on streets devoted primarily to industrial use.

The completed application shall identify the boundaries of the proposed zone, the types of property uses located in the zone, and the hours of the day, days of the week or months of the year during which the proposed zone shall be effective. The application shall also indicate that 60 percent or more of the vehicles parked in the proposed zone that are continuously parked for a consecutive eight hour period are parked in connection with businesses located in the zone.

The applicants shall circulate application forms to businesses located in the proposed zone. Owners or managers of at least 60 percent of businesses located in the proposed zone must sign the application indicating their consent to industrial parking designation in order for the application to be considered. The application must identify the person or persons circulating it and must be notarized. After presenting the required number of signatures to the parking administrator, the applicant or applicants shall give notice of the proposed industrial permit parking designation in a newspaper of general or local circulation. Proof of notice by publication must be submitted to the parking administrator. Upon receipt of all requested information, the parking administrator shall notify the departments of revenue, transportation and planning and development that a representative of one or more businesses have requested designation of industrial permit parking.

Within 60 days after receipt of notification from the parking administrator, the department of revenue shall verify the information contained in the petitions and the department of transportation shall analyze the traffic conditions, traffic area impacts within the proposed zone and parking conditions of the proposed zone. Within the same time period, the department of planning and development shall analyze the economic or other impact of the zone upon businesses or other institutions located within or adjacent to the zone. The departments of revenue, transportation and planning and development shall report their findings and any recommendations to the parking administrator.

Upon consideration of the revenue, transportation and planning and development studies, the parking administrator shall issue to the appropriate committee of the city council his or her recommendations on the advisability of designating the zone for industrial permit parking and as to the hours of the day, days of the week or months of the year when such regulations shall be effective.

If the city council approves creation of an industrial permit parking zone, the commissioner of transportation shall erect and maintain signs on the applicable blocks indicating industrial permit parking only.

When official signs are erected indicating industrial permit parking only, parking shall be restricted to service and delivery vehicles whose operators are doing business with businesses located in the zone and to vehicles displaying permit issued pursuant to Section 9-68-021 of this code.

(b) It shall be unlawful to park any unauthorized vehicle in violation of signs erected or maintained pursuant to this section.

(c) Any business located on either side of a commercial block that is immediately adjacent to an industrial permit parking zone shall qualify for permits to park in the adjacent zone.

(Added. Coun. J. 11-2-94, p. 58616; Corrected 12-21-94, p. 64484)

§9-64-100 Parking prohibited—Fire hydrants, firelanes and various locations.

It shall be unlawful to park any vehicle in any of the following places:

(a) Within 15 feet of a fire hydrant;

(b) In a firelane;

(c) At any place where the vehicle will block vehicular access to or use of a driveway, alley or firelane;

(d) At any place where the vehicle will block the use of a curb cut access for handicapped pedestrians;

(e) Under the lowest portion of any fire escape;

(f) Within 20 feet of a crosswalk where official signs are posted;

(g) Within 30 feet of an official traffic signal or stop sign on the approaching side;

(h) On the same side of the public way in front of any entrance or exit of any theater building as defined in Section 13-4-010 of the Municipal Code of Chicago.

(Added. Coun. J. 7-12-90, p. 18634)

§9-64-110 Parking prohibited—Roadways, sidewalks, bridges and similar locations.

It shall be unlawful to stand or park any vehicle in any of the following places:

(a) On the roadway side of any vehicle stopped or parked at the edge or curb of a street;

(b) Within an intersection, except on the continuous side of a "T" intersection;

(c) On a crosswalk;

(d) On a sidewalk;

(e) On a parkway, except in case of an emergency;

(f) Upon any bridge, except those located on North Stockton Drive between North Avenue and Diversey Parkway;

(g) In a viaduct or underpass;

(h) On any railroad tracks or within a distance of 10 feet from the outer rails thereof.

(Added. Coun. J. 7-12-90, p. 18634; Amend. 4-29-92, p. 15384; 5-26-04, p. 24880)

§9-64-120 Parking on city property.

(a) It shall be unlawful to park any vehicle upon any property owned by the city and used for the transaction of public business where such parking is prohibited by order of the custodian of the property; provided, this section shall not apply to city-owned vehicles or to other vehicles whose operation is useful or essential to the proper functioning of the department, board or commission occupying the property. The custodian of the property shall post "No Parking" signs indicating the foregoing prohibition.

(b) It shall be unlawful to stand or park any vehicle upon the premises of a Chicago Housing Authority Development except in such areas designated by official signs or other markings as parking lots.

(Added. Coun. J. 7-12-90, p. 18634)

§9-64-125 Display of license.

No person shall park or stand on any portion of the public way or on any city-owned property any vehicle requiring a license pursuant to Chapter 3-56 of this code, unless the license is displayed as required by Section 9-76-170 of this code. Pursuant to Section 3-56-021, any person alleged to have violated this section may raise as an affirmative defense that: (1) such person

resided in the city for less than 30 days at the time he or she was cited for the violation; or (2) the cited vehicle was purchased less than 30 days prior to the issuance of the violation.
(Added. Coun. J. 1-14-92, p. 11643; Amend. Coun. J. 11-19-03, p. 14216; 12-8-04, P. 38063)

§9-64-130 Parking in alleys.

(a) It shall be unlawful to park any vehicle in any alley for a period of time longer than is necessary for the expeditious loading, unloading, pick-up or delivery of materials from such vehicle.

(b) It shall be unlawful to park a vehicle in an alley in such a manner or under such conditions as to leave available less than 10 feet of the width of the roadway for the free movement of vehicular traffic or to block the entrance to any abutting property.
(Added. Coun. J. 7-12-90, p. 18634)

§9-64-140 Common-carrier vehicle stops and stands.

(a) The commissioner of transportation is authorized to establish bus stops upon 20-day prior notice to the alderman of the ward in which the bus stop is to be located and, subject to the approval of the city council, is authorized to establish horse-drawn carriage stands, bus stands, taxicab stands and stands for other passenger common-carrier motor vehicles on such public streets and in such number as shall be determined to be of the greatest benefit and convenience to the public, and every such stop or stand shall be designated by appropriate signs or curb markings or both. The commissioner of transportation is authorized to determine, upon 20-day prior notice to the alderman of the affected ward, those locations within the central business district, south of the south line of West Kinzie Street between Halsted Street and the Chicago River, and south of the south bank of the Chicago River between West Kinzie Street and Lake Michigan, where the restriction on parking at any such stop sign or stand shall be modified to limit the prohibition on parking of unauthorized vehicles to Mondays through Fridays or Mondays through Saturdays.

(b) It shall be unlawful to stand or park a vehicle, other than the type of vehicle for which the stop or stand is reserved, in violation of signs posted, in any stop or stand described in subsection (a) that has been officially designated by appropriate signs or markings; provided, however, that this provision shall not apply to a vehicle engaged in the expeditious loading or unloading of passengers when such standing does not interfere with any bus, horse-drawn carriage or taxicab waiting to enter or about to enter such zone.
(Added. Coun. J. 7-12-90, p. 18634; Amend. 9-11-91, p. 5008; 12-11-91, p. 10832; 10-7-98, p. 78566)

§9-64-150 Parking prohibited—Fire stations, railroad crossings and hazardous locations.

(a) The commissioner of transportation is authorized to erect and maintain signs indicating no parking at any place within 20 feet of the entrance to any fire station, on the side of any street opposite the entrance to any fire station within 75 feet of the entrance, or within 50 feet of the nearest rail of a railroad crossing.

(b) The commissioner of transportation is authorized to determine places in which the standing or parking of vehicles would create an especially hazardous condition or would cause unusual delay to traffic and those streets or parts of streets upon which parking shall be prohibited, and to erect and maintain appropriate signs giving notice that standing or parking is prohibited.

(c) It shall be unlawful to stand or park any vehicle in violation of any sign erected or maintained pursuant to this section.

(Added. Coun. J. 7-12-90, p. 18634; Amend. 12-11-91, p. 10832)

§9-64-160 Curb loading zones.

(a) The commissioner of transportation is authorized, subject to the approval of the city council, to determine the location of curb loading zones and shall place and maintain appropriate signs indicating the zones and the hours during which standing or parking is restricted. The commissioner of transportation is authorized to modify the duration of parking restrictions for curb loading zones located within the central business district, south of the south line of West Kinzie Street between Halsted Street and the Chicago River, and south of the south bank of the Chicago River between West Kinzie Street and Lake Michigan, to limit the restriction on standing or parking to Mondays through Fridays or Mondays through Saturdays, upon 20-day prior notice to the alderman of the affected ward. No such modification shall take effect until the commissioner
has erected appropriate signs indicating the days of the week or hours of the day during which parking in such zone is restricted.

(b) It shall be unlawful to park any vehicle in any place designated as a curb loading zone during the days of the week or hours of the day when the restrictions applicable to such zones are in effect, except for the expeditious loading and pick-up or unloading and delivery of materials from commercial vehicles and then for a period not to exceed thirty minutes; provided, however, the operator of a motor vehicle of the first division may stand in a curb loading zone for the purpose of and while actually engaged in the expeditious loading or unloading of passengers when such standing does not interfere with any vehicle used for the transportation of materials which is waiting to enter or about to enter such zone.

(c) The commissioner of transportation is authorized to issue special permits to allow the backing of a vehicle to the curb for the purpose of loading or unloading merchandise or materials subject to the terms and conditions of such permits. Such permit may be issued to the owner of the vehicle and shall grant to such person the privileges as therein stated and authorized therein, provided that such permit shall be either in the possession of the operator or on the vehicle at the time such vehicle is backed against the curb to take on or discharge a load. It shall be unlawful for any permittee or other person to violate any of the special terms or conditions of any such permit.

(d) The director of revenue may issue a loading zone permit to the owner or lessee of a passenger vehicle normally used to transport property in the furtherance of a commercial or industrial enterprise in accordance with this subsection. Application for a loading zone permit shall be made to the director of revenue on forms provided for that purpose. The application shall indicate: the applicant's name, address and occupation; the name, address,

telephone number and nature of the commercial or industrial enterprise served by the vehicle; the state license number of the vehicle for which the permit is sought; the types of property typically carried in the vehicle; and such other information as the director of revenue may require. The applicant shall sign the application and submit it with a semiannual fee of $125.00. If the applicant is a corporation, the application may be signed by an officer of the applicant; if the applicant is a partnership, a partner may sign the application. If the application discloses that the vehicle meets the requirements of this subsection, the director of revenue shall issue the loading zone permit. The permit shall include the name of the commercial or industrial enterprise and the state vehicle license of the vehicle. A valid loading zone permit displayed in the lower left corner of the windshield of the vehicle qualifies the vehicle as a commercial vehicle for purposes of subsection (b) of this section. Each permit issued under this subsection shall expire six calendar months after its issuance. No such permit shall be transferable.
(Added. Coun. J. 7-12-90, p. 18634; Amend. 9-11-91, p. 5008; 12-11-91, p. 10832; 7-7-92, p. 18778; 10-7-98, p. 78566)

§9-64-170 Parking restrictions—Special types of vehicles.

(a) It shall be unlawful to park any truck, recreational vehicle more than 22 feet in length, self-contained motor home, bus, taxicab or livery vehicle on any residential street for a longer period than is necessary for the reasonably expeditious loading or unloading of such vehicle, except that a driver of a bus may park the bus in a designated bus stand as authorized elsewhere in the traffic code; provided, however, that in the 1st, 9th, 10th, 12th, 13th, 14th, 15th, 16th, 18th, 19th, 21st, 22nd, 23rd, 26th, 28th, 29th, 32nd, 33rd, 35th, 37th, 40th, 42nd, 43rd, 46th, 49th and 50th wards this prohibition shall not apply to the owner of a pickup truck or van weighing under 4,500 pounds who has no outstanding parking violations, when such vehicle is parked at the curb adjacent to the owner's place of residence and the vehicle bears a valid and current city vehicle tax sticker and a special parking permit issued in accordance with this subsection. In the 15th and 46th wards this prohibition also shall not apply to the owner of a taxicab who has no outstanding parking violations, when such vehicle is not in service, when the vehicle is parked at the curb adjacent to the owner's place of residence and when the vehicle bears a valid and current city vehicle tax sticker and a special permit issued in accordance with this subsection.

The owner shall apply for a special permit for such parking from the alderman of the ward in which he or she resides. The city clerk shall issue a permit upon receipt of a completed application, payment of a $30.00 annual fee, and upon passage and publication of a city council order authorizing the issuance of the permit. A permit issued under this subsection shall be valid until the 30th of June following the date of issuance and there shall be a proration of the permit fee. The permit shall be affixed without the use of supplemental adhesives to the inside of the windshield of the vehicle, directly above the city vehicle tax sticker. If a residential parking zone restriction is in effect at the owner's place of residence, a residential parking permit shall also be required in accordance with Section 9-64-090. A violator of this subsection shall be subject to a fine of $25.00.

(b) It shall be unlawful to park any truck, tractor, semitrailer, trailer or self-contained motor home, or bus on any business street in the city for a longer period than is necessary for the reasonably expeditious loading or unloading of such vehicle, except that a driver of a bus may park the bus in a designated bus stand as authorized elsewhere in the traffic code. It shall be unlawful to park any taxicab on any business street in the city for a period longer than two hours between the hours of 2:00 a.m. and 7:00 a.m.; provided that this prohibition shall not apply to taxicabs parked on business streets in the 46th ward. A violator of this subsection shall be subject to a fine of $25.00.

(c) It shall be unlawful to stand or park any vehicle six feet or greater in height within 20 feet of a crosswalk. A violator of this subsection shall be subject to a fine of $25.00.

(d) It shall be unlawful to park a truck tractor as defined in Section 1-212 of the Illinois Vehicle Code, a semi-trailer or a trailer on any business street or residential street in the city for a longer period than is necessary for the reasonably expeditious loading or unloading of such vehicle. A violator of this subsection shall be subject to a fine of $125.00. In addition to such fine, the truck tractor, semi-trailer or trailer shall be subject to immobilization and impoundment, without prior notice or placement on an immobilization list.

(Added. Coun. J. 7-12-90, p. 18634; Amend. 5-22-91, p. 820; 12-11-91, p. 10832; 6-17-92, p. 17772; 7-29-92, p. 20108; 2-10-93, p. 28533; 5-19-93, p. 32400; 6-9-93, p. 33613; 9-15-93, p. 37922; 5-4-94, p. 49835; 6-16-94, p. 52041; 8-3-94, p. 54293; 10-5-94, p. 57791; 11-2-94, p. 58619; 7-13-95, p. 4618; 1-10-96, p. 14753; 2-7-96, p. 15684; 7-10-96, p. 25132; 7-31-96, p. 26937; 3-19-97, p. 41408; 4-16-97, p. 42644; 6-4-97, p. 46452; 9-10-97, p. 51660; 12-10-97, p. 59054; 2-5-98, p. 61943; 4-29-98, p. 67052; Corrected. 5-20-98, p. 70101; Amend. 11-3-99, p. 14238; Amend. 12-13-00, p. 48221; 12-12-01, p. 75777; 9-4-03, p. 7165; 12-8-04, p. 38063)

§9-64-180 Restricted parking—Area bounded by Chicago River, Michigan Avenue and Harrison Street.

(a) Except as provided in subsection (b), it is unlawful to park any vehicle at any time on the following streets: Garvey Court, from Lake Street to Wacker Drive; State Street and Michigan Avenue, from Wacker Drive to Congress Parkway. Except as provided in subsection (b), it is unlawful to park any vehicle during the hours of 6:00 a.m. to 6:00 p.m., Monday through Friday, except for days established as holidays in Section 9-4-010 on any of the following streets: Washington Street, Madison Street and Monroe Street, between State Street and Michigan Avenue; Adams Street and Jackson Boulevard, between Canal Street and Michigan Avenue; Dearborn Street, Clark Street and LaSalle Street, between Washington Street and Jackson Boulevard; and Wacker Drive, from Franklin Street to Van Buren Street.

(b) The restrictions in this section shall not apply in any designated handicapped parking area or to any ambulance, any emergency vehicle owned by a governmental agency, any vehicle owned by a public utility while the operator of the vehicle is engaged in the performance of emergency duties, any taxicab at an officially designated taxicab stand and/or engaged in the expeditious loading or unloading of passengers with disabilities, any passenger vehicle engaged for not more than three minutes in the loading or unloading of passengers, or to the parking of any commercial vehicle engaged in the expeditious loading, unloading, pick-up or delivery of materials in a designated loading zone, or to any bus at a designated bus stop or bus stand. Nothing in this section prohibits or prevents more restrictive regulation of parking on any street designated in subsection (a). Where the provisions of subsection (a) conflict with more restrictive regulations contained in another ordinance and appropriate signs indicating those regulations have been erected, the more restrictive regulations shall apply.

(c) No parking meters shall be installed on those portions of streets listed in subsection (a) where parking is prohibited at all times.

(Added. Coun. J. 7-12-90, p. 18634; Amend. Coun. J. 7-7-92, p. 18778; 2-10-93, p. 28535; 5-4-94, p. 49835; 11-1-95, p. 9066; Amend. 11-15-00, p. 46957)

§9-64-190 Parking meter zones—Regulations.

(a) It shall be unlawful to park any vehicle in a designated parking meter zone or space without depositing United States currency of the denomination indicated on the meter and putting the meter in operation or otherwise legally activating the meter, and, if the meter is of the type that issues a ticket or other token, displaying in the vehicle a ticket or token issued by the meter, or to park any vehicle in such zone or space for a period longer than is designated on or by the meter for the value of the coin or coins deposited in the meter, or the value otherwise registered by the meter. It is not a violation of this section to park a vehicle at a zone or space served by a meter that does not function properly, provided that the meter is inoperable or malfunctioning through no fault of the vehicle's operator.

Upon the expiration of the time thus designated upon or by the meter, the operator of the motor vehicle shall then immediately remove such vehicle from the parking meter zone. No operator of any motor vehicle shall permit such vehicle to remain in the parking meter zone for an additional consecutive time period.

These provisions shall not apply during such hours of the day as designated from time to time by order of the city council or on days established as holidays in Section 9-4-010.

(b) Any person who violates or fails to comply with the provisions of subsection (a) of this section while parked in a parking meter zone situated within the area bounded by a line as follows: beginning at the easternmost point of Division Street extended to Lake Michigan; then west on Division Street to LaSalle Street; then south on LaSalle Street to Chicago Avenue; then west on Chicago Avenue to Halsted Street; then south on Halsted Street to Roosevelt Road; then east on Roosevelt Road to its easternmost point extended to Lake Michigan, including parking meter zones on both sides of the above-mentioned streets, shall be subject to the penalty imposed in Section 9-100-020.

(Added. Coun. J. 7-12-90, p. 18634; Amend. 10-28-97, p. 54839; 6-4-03, p. 2489)

§9-64-200 Parking meters—Installation and pavement markings.

(a) The commissioner of transportation shall cause parking meters to be installed in parking meter zones in such numbers, during such hours of operation, at such rates, and at such places as established by the city council and shall have markings painted or placed upon the pavement adjacent to each parking meter, where such markings are appropriate for the type of parking meter installed, for the purpose of designating the parking space for which the meter is to be used. The commissioner shall consult with the parking administrator in determining the number of meters necessary in any zone.

(b) It shall be unlawful to park any vehicle in any designated parking meter space except entirely within the area defined by the markings for that space.

(Added. Coun. J. 7-12-90, p. 18634; Amend. 12-11-91, p. 10832; 6-16-94, p. 52043; 10-28-97, p. 54839)

§9-64-205 Parking meter rates—Central business district.

Notwithstanding any prior ordinance establishing a different rate, the rate for parking at a metered space within the area bounded by the south side of Congress Parkway on the south, Lake Michigan on the east, and the north side of Wacker Drive on the north, and the west side of Wacker Drive on the west, shall be $0.25 per five minute period, with a total parking limit of two hours.

(Added. Coun. J. 12-4-02, p. 99931)

§9-64-210 Television news permit parking areas.

(a) A television news permit parking area for vehicles used to transport filming equipment and for transmitting and receiving television news signals shall be established on the west side of North Clark Street from a point 85 feet south of Lake Street to a point 52 feet north of Randolph Street, excluding the distance of 15 feet north and 15 feet south of any fire hydrant located within such area.

(b) The parking administrator is authorized to issue television news parking permits to television news stations. Each permit shall be individually numbered and shall indicate the name of the television news station and the authorized location where the vehicle is permitted to park. The permit shall be issued annually and without charge.

(c) The commissioner of transportation shall place and maintain appropriate signs indicating the area in which parking is restricted to vehicles displaying a television news parking permit.

(d) No television news station may park more than one vehicle in the television news parking permit area at any time.

(e) It shall be unlawful to stand or park any vehicle that does not display a television news parking permit at a location established pursuant to subsection (a) and marked with signs erected pursuant to subsection (c). Any vehicle parked in violation of this section shall be subject to an immediate tow to a city vehicle pound.

(Added. Coun. J. 7-12-90, p. 18634; Amend. 12-11-91, p. 10832)

§9-64-220 Parking violations—Enforcement—Prima facie responsibility designated.

(a) Whenever any vehicle is parked in violation of any provision of the traffic code prohibiting or restricting vehicular standing or parking, the person in whose name the vehicle is registered with the Secretary of State of Illinois shall be prima facie responsible for the violation and subject to the penalty therefor.

(b) Whenever any vehicle is parked in violation of any provision of the traffic code prohibiting or restricting vehicular parking or standing, any police officer, traffic control aide, other designated member of the police department, parking enforcement aide or other person designated by the city parking administrator observing such violation may issue a parking violation notice and serve the notice on the owner of the vehicle by handing it to the operator of the vehicle, if he is present, or by affixing it to the vehicle in a conspicuous place. The issuer of the notice shall specify on the notice his identification number, the particular parking regulation allegedly violated, the make and state registration number of the cited vehicle, and the place, date, time and nature of the alleged violation and shall certify the correctness of the specified information by signing his name as provided in Section 11-208.3 of the Illinois Vehicle Code.
(Added. Coun. J. 7-12-90, p. 18634)

§9-64-230 Standing or parking violations punishable by fine.

The violation of any provision of the traffic code prohibiting or restricting vehicular standing or parking shall be a civil offense punishable by fine, and no criminal penalty, or civil sanction other than that prescribed in this code, shall be imposed.
(Added. Coun. J. 7-12-90, p. 18634)

§9-64-250 Violation—Towing and storage fees.

(a) Any vehicle parked in violation of any provision of Sections 9-12-060, 9-64-020, 9-64-050, 9-64-060, 9-64-070, 9-64-100, 9-64-110, 9-64-120, 9-64-130(b), 9-64-140(b), 9-64-150(b), 9-64-160(b), 9-64-170 or 9-64-210, or in violation of any other provision of the traffic code that authorizes vehicle towing and impoundment for such violation, shall be subject to an immediate tow as provided in Section 9-92-030.

(b) Any vehicle parked illegally in an officially designated and marked "tow zone" shall be subject to an immediate tow as provided in Section 9-92-030.

(c) Any towing or storage fees imposed pursuant to the traffic code shall be separate from and in addition to any fine or penalty imposed for the parking violation.
(Added. Coun. J. 7-12-90, p. 18634; Amend 9-1-99, p. 10503; 12-12-01, p. 75777; 7-29-03, p. 6166)

CHAPTER 9-68
RESTRICTED PARKING—PERMITS AND REGULATIONS

Sections:

9-68-010 Handicapped motorist decals or devices.
9-68-020 Residential parking permits.
9-68-021 Industrial parking permits.
9-68-030 Loading zones and prohibited parking spaces.
9-68-040 Athletic events at Wrigley Field.
9-68-050 Temporary removal of parking meters.
9-68-060 Service vehicle permits—Restrictions.
9-68-070 Application—Fee.
9-68-080 Permit—Description.
9-68-090 Permit—Display required.
9-68-100 Violation—Penalty.

§9-68-010 Handicapped motorist decals or devices.

(a) The bureau of parking management is hereby authorized to issue handicapped motorist decals or devices pursuant to and in accordance with Section 11-1301.2 of the Illinois Vehicle Code and with state administrative rules promulgated under that section. The fee for each such decal or device shall be $5.00.

(b) The bureau of parking management is hereby authorized to promulgate rules and regulations concerning the issuance and use of handicapped motorist decals or devices consistent with state law and the provisions of the traffic code.

(Added. Coun. J. 7-12-90, p. 18634)

§9-68-020 Residential parking permits.

(a) Upon application and payment of the required fee to the director of revenue, the director or his designee shall issue annual "residential parking permit" stickers to residents of the residential permit parking zone for use on each car owned and registered within any residential permit parking zone, displaying a current city vehicle sticker. Such a residential parking permit sticker may also be issued as part of such city vehicle sticker. Such a residential parking permit sticker shall be affixed, in accordance with the instructions printed thereon and without the use of supplemental adhesives, at the lower right-hand corner of the inside of the glass portion of the windshield of such motor vehicle, directly above or as part of the city vehicle tax sticker. This permit sticker shall not guarantee or reserve any parking space, nor shall it exempt the holder from the observance of any traffic or parking regulation.

(b) Upon the payment by the applicant of the permit fee hereinafter provided, the city clerk or the director of revenue shall issue, or cause to be issued, a permit. The annual period for every such permit shall begin on July 1st and end on June 30th of the year following the year of issuance.

(c) Upon application, individual "one-day" permits shall also be issued to residents for their use and for the use of nonresidents who are temporary visitors of the residential permit parking zone. Any resident in a residential permit parking zone shall be limited to the purchase of two groups of 15 one-day permits per month. One-day permits shall be color-coded by annual period and shall expire at the end of the annual period in which they are issued. These permits shall be good for one day only and must be attached to the windshield by means of the adhesive provided on the face of the permit. Before affixing the one-day permit, it must be validated by printing the date and time of day legibly on its face in the space provided for this purpose. An undated permit or a permit that fails to indicate the time of day will be invalid.

(d) The fee for an annual residential parking permit is $25.00 for each vehicle. If application is made for the permit after November 15th of the current annual period, the following fees shall apply:

Between November 16th and March 15th — 66 percent of the applicable fee; and

Between March 16th and June 30th — 33 percent of the applicable fee.

One-day permits shall be issued in groups of 15 for $5.00. A replacement of an annual or semiannual permit will be issued without cost upon receipt of an identifiable portion of the removed decal and a receipt for the current city vehicle sticker. Replacement of any permits which are lost or destroyed will be made at full cost.

(e) If a residential parking zone is in effect at the place of residence of an owner with a disability who is using a restricted parking space created pursuant to Section 9-64-050 of this code, such owner shall be exempt from the residential permit parking fees set forth in subsection (d) of this section.

(f) It shall be unlawful for any person to affix, cause to be affixed, or otherwise display any residential parking permit or other vehicle-specific permit issued pursuant to any other parking permit program to any automobile other than the vehicle to which the permit was intended to be affixed at the time of issuance by the city.

(g) It shall be unlawful for any person other than the city or an agent of the city to knowingly sell, offer for sale, expose for sale or acquire for the purpose of sale any residential parking permit, one-day permit, or other permit issued pursuant to any other parking permit program.

(h) It shall be unlawful for any person to purchase any residential parking permit, one-day permit or other permit issued pursuant to any other parking permit program from any person other than the city or an agent of the city.

(i) Any person violating any of the provisions of this section shall be fined not less than $200.00 nor more than $500.00 for each offense, and each day such a violation continues shall be deemed a separate and distinct offense. *(Added. Coun. J. 7-12-90, p. 18634; Amend. 4-16-97, p. 42646; 3-11-98, p. 63453; 12-15-04, p. 39840, § 3.3, effective June 1, 2005)*

§9-68-021 Industrial parking permits.

(a) Upon application and payment of the required fee to the director of revenue, the bureau of parking shall issue annual or six-month "industrial parking permit" decals to businesses located in the zone for use on each vehicle used in connection with the businesses. An industrial parking permit sticker shall be affixed, in accordance with the instructions printed thereon and without the use of supplemental adhesives, at the lower right-hand corner of the inside of the glass portion of the windshield of a motor vehicle. This permit sticker shall not guarantee or reserve any parking space, nor shall it exempt the holder from the observance of any traffic or parking regulation.

(b) Upon application to the parking administrator, temporary permits shall be issued to businesses for the use of temporary visitors to the industrial permit zone. These permits shall be good for one day only and must be attached to the windshield by means of the adhesive provided on the face of the permit. Before affixing the one-day permit, it must be validated by printing the date of use legibly in permanent ink on its face in the space provided for this purpose. A permit that is updated, altered, defaced or that contains erasures, or is dated other than in permanent ink, will be invalid. No person other than the parking administrator may sell, offer for sale or accept payment or other consideration for a temporary permit.

(c) The fee for an annual industrial parking permit is $25.00 for each decal, and the fee for a six-month permit is $15.00 for each decal. One-day permit shall be issued in groups of 20 for $5.00. A replacement of an annual or semiannual permit will be issued without cost upon receipt of an identifiable portion of the removed decal. Replacement of any permits which are lost or destroyed will be made at full cost.

(d) Any person obtaining, using or transferring to any person any industrial parking permit in violation of this section or in violation of any regulations established by the parking administrator shall be fined in an amount not less than $100.00.

(e) The parking administrator shall have the authority to make and enforce such reasonable rules and regulations as may be necessary to effectively administer any of the powers granted herein or in Section 9-64-091, and to publish such rules and regulations and make them avail able to such member of the public as may request them.

(Added. Coun. J. 11-2-94, p. 58616)

§9-68-030 Loading zones and prohibited parking spaces.

(a) No sign shall be erected by the commissioner of transportation upon the special request of the owner, agent or lessee of any building for the specific purpose of designating a loading zone or prohibited parking space in front of the entrance to such building, or in front of the property upon which such building is located, until the owner, agent or lessee has paid into the city treasury a fee of $110.00 for the erection, and maintenance for one year, of such signage. In addition, there shall be an annual surcharge of $14.00 per lineal foot for each foot of curb space in excess of 25 feet removed by such designation. The owner, agent or lessee shall pay into the city treasury in advance annually a fee of $50.00 for the continued maintenance of such signage and the appropriate annual surcharge. The fees required herein shall not apply to the erection of signage in front of any public building or in front of any theater, school, church or not-for-profit corporation.

(b) If the owner, agent or lessee does not desire to continue maintenance of a sign erected under this section, he shall notify the commissioner of transportation in writing at least 30 days prior to the last day of the current annual period. If the owner, agent or lessee fails either to give such notice or to remit the appropriate fees for the next annual period prior to the termination of the current annual period, the commissioner of transportation shall remove such sign subject to the procedures contained in subsection (c) herein.

(c) The commissioner of transportation shall cause a notice to be sent to the owner, agent or lessee informing such person that the sign or signs will be removed unless the annual maintenance fee is paid within 30 days from the date the notice is mailed. The commissioner shall not authorize the erection of a new sign for a period of three years after the removal of any sign pursuant to this subsection unless payment of the fee for erection, annual sur charge and any prior unpaid maintenance fees owed to the city by such owner, agent or lessee has been made prior to or at the time of application for erection of a new sign.

(d) The commissioner of transportation may remove any sign erected pursuant to this section whenever public convenience or necessity warrants after providing 15 days notice to the owner, agent or lessee, if any, who is paying annual fees for the sign.

(Added. Coun. J. 7-12-90, p. 18634; Amend. 12-11-91, p. 10832; 11-10-94, p. 59125; 3-11-98, p. 63463; 11-19-03, p. 14216)

§9-68-040 Athletic events at Wrigley Field.

(a) For any athletic event conducted at Wrigley Field, the commissioner of transportation may, by regulation, designate a portion of the public way as a staging area in which passengers may board or depart from privately operated buses. During the time such designation is in effect, no privately operated bus may park or stand in such area without a permit issued by the commissioner under this section, other than for the purpose of picking up or discharging disabled passengers. A permit required under this section shall be clearly displayed at all times while the bus is in the designated staging area.

(b) Permits shall be issued by the commissioner in accordance with rules and regulations promulgated by him. Such rules and regulations shall provide that if the number of applications exceeds the number of permits authorized by him for the athletic event, priority shall be given to those applications that are received the earliest. However, preference shall be given to applications for buses carrying primarily disabled or elderly passengers.

The rules and regulations may also provide for the issuance of permits pursuant to a random selection process for applications that are received on the same day.

(c) Permits shall be valid only for the athletic event for which they are issued. The fee for each permit shall be $40.00.

(d) The commissioner may authorize any individual or entity to act as an agent of the city for the purpose of distributing permits and collecting and remitting permit fees to the city, all in accordance with this section and the rules and regulations adopted pursuant to this section.

(e) In addition to the staging area designated pursuant to subsection (a), the commissioner may designate locations at which privately owned buses without permits issued under this section may park or stand for the purpose of picking up or discharging passengers.

(f) The commissioner may, by regulation, designate an area surrounding Wrigley Field in which it shall be unlawful to stop or park a privately operated bus for the purpose of picking up or discharging passengers, other than in legal parking spaces and those locations designated pursuant to subsections (a) and (e).

(g) The commissioner shall erect appropriate signs indicating the areas designated pursuant to this section.

(h) For purposes of this section only, "privately owned bus" or "bus" means a motor vehicle that is owned and operated by a person other than a governmental entity and is designed for carrying 12 or more persons.

(i) Any person who stands or parks a motor vehicle in violation of this section or the rules and regulations adopted pursuant to this section shall be subject to a fine of $100.00 for each offense.

(j) It shall be unlawful to stand or park a privately owned bus with its motor running in an area designated pursuant to subsection (a) or (e) of this section.
(Added. Coun. J. 7-12-90, p. 18634; Amend. 5-22-91, p. 822; 12-11-91, p. 10832; 12-12-01, p. 75777)

§9-68-050 Temporary removal of parking meters.

In the event that one or more parking meters or metered spaces must be temporarily removed or are otherwise rendered unusable in order to accommodate properly permitted work in or affecting the public way, the permittee

shall pay a monthly surcharge per meter or in the case of meters serving multiple spaces, per metered space based upon the average revenue during the preceding year in that parking meter area. In the event that no meter revenue was recorded during the preceding year, the surcharge shall be based upon the average revenue during the preceding year of a similarly situated area. For meters serving multiple spaces, every linear increment of twenty feet shall be considered a metered space. The surcharge imposed by this section shall not apply where the permittee is performing construction work pursuant to a contract with the city or other governmental entity. In addition, if removal of one or more meters is necessary for the permitted work to proceed, the commissioner of transportation may order temporary removal of the affected parking meters. The permittee shall pay a fee of $100.00 in advance for the removal and reinstallation of each parking meter, provided however, that a fee of $1,000.00 shall be paid for a meter serving multiple spaces.
(Added. Coun. J. 7-12-90, p. 18634; Amend. 12-11-91, p. 10832; Amend. 11-1-00, p. 43330; 5-26-04, 24882)

§9-68-060 Service vehicle permits— Restrictions.

Subject to and in accordance with the procedures and requirements described in Sections 9-68-060 through 9-68-100, the commissioner of transportation may issue permits for parking contrary to general parking regulations. Permits issued under this program may be issued only for vehicles of the second division, as defined in the Illinois Motor Vehicle Code, as amend ed. Permits may be issued only to the following types of vehicles:

(a) A vehicle typically used in repairs or service to buildings or property, where safe and timely performance of the repair or service requires that the vehicle be located near the site of the repair or service. Examples in this class include: trucks used in glazing or boarding windows.

(b) A vehicle owned and operated by a public utility and used for the testing, repair or service of the utility's apparatus or equipment.

(c) A vehicle to which equipment used in the service or repair of buildings or property is permanently affixed, where the proper use of the equipment requires that the vehicle be located near the site of the repair or service. Examples of this class include: trucks carrying mounted cranes; mobile cranes; trucks equipped with tanks, pumps and hoses, for delivery of fuel.

(d) Armored vehicles used for the collection or delivery of currency, coin, securities, checks and other valuables, and authorized by the Illinois Commerce Commission to engage in such activity.

Permits shall be limited to the following location categories:

Category A: for parking anywhere within the city.

Category B: for parking outside the central business district only.

(Added. Coun. J. 7-7-92, p. 18778; Amend. Coun. J. 2-10-93, p. 28535)

§9-68-070 Application—Fee.

Application for a permit described in Section 9-68-060 shall be made to the commissioner of transportation on forms provided by him for that purpose. The application shall indicate: the applicant's name, address and occupation; the state license number of the vehicle for which the permit is sought; the intended use of the vehicle; the location category of permit applied for; the intended use of the vehicle; the class and category of permit applied for; the address(es) or area(s) where the applicant proposes to park pursuant to the permit; and such other information as the commissioner may require. The applicant shall sign the application and submit it with the appropriate fee. If the applicant is a corporation, the application may be signed by an officer of the applicant; if the applicant is a partner ship, a partner may sign the application. If the application discloses that the vehicle meets the requirements of Section 9-68-060, the commissioner shall issue a permit of the appropriate category.

The commissioner may restrict parking pursuant to a permit to specific hours of the day, a specific address or set of addresses, and specific curb locations, in any combination. In determining the restrictions, the commissioner shall consider the nature of the applicant's vehicle, the nature of the business in which the vehicle is used, and traffic patterns in the area where the applicant desires to park pursuant to the permit. No permit shall allow parking in violation of Sections 9-64-050(i), 9-64-100(a), 9-64-100(d) and (e), or 9-64-140(b) of this code.

The fees for permits shall be as follows:

Category A	Annual	$1000.00
	Monthly	100.00
	Daily	20.00
Category B	Annual	$200.00
	Monthly	20.00
	Daily	4.00

(Added. Coun. J. 7-7-92, p. 18778; Amend. Coun. J. 2-10-93, p. 28535; 3-11-98, p. 63463)

§9-68-080 Permit—Description.

A permit issued under Section 9-68-070 shall be no less than five inches by eight inches, and shall indicate the following: the name of the person to whom the permit is issued; the state license number of the subject vehicle; the class and location category of the permit; the expiration date of the permit; and a description of the parking allowed pursuant to the permit.
(Added. Coun. J. 7-7-92, p. 18778)

§9-68-090 Permit—Display required.

The permit shall be displayed in the lower left hand corner of the windshield of the permitted vehicle at all times that the privilege granted under the permit is exercised. If the permitted vehicle is a trailer, the permit shall be displayed in the lower left hand corner of the wind shield of the vehicle towing the trailer. Except as de scribed in a properly displayed permit, all general parking regulations apply to the subject vehicle.
(Added. Coun. J. 7-7-92, p. 18778)

§9-68-100 Violation—Penalty.

(a) No permit issued under Section 9-68-070 shall be altered, defaced, or transferred from one vehicle to another or from the applicant to any other person.

(b) At the direction of a police officer or member of the fire department, a vehicle properly displaying a permit issued under Section 9-68-070 shall be removed in order to allow access to a fire hydrant.

(c) The commissioner of transportation shall revoke a permit issued to any person who violates subsection (a) or subsection (b) of this section, or who misrepresents or falsifies any information in order to obtain the permit.

(d) Any person who violates subsection (a) or (b) of this section, or who misrepresents or falsifies any information in order to obtain a permit under Section 9-68-070, or interferes with the administration of this permit program by the commissioner of transportation, shall be fined $200.00 for each offense. Each day that a violation continues shall constitute a separate and distinct offense.

(Added. Coun. J. 7-7-92, p. 18778)

CHAPTER 9-72
SIZE AND WEIGHT LIMITS

Sections:

9-72-010 Load restrictions in downtown district.
9-72-020 Operation of vehicles restricted.
9-72-030 Designation of streets with size and weight limitations.
9-72-035 Designation of special routes.
9-72-040 Maximum width of vehicles.
9-72-050 Maximum height of vehicles.
9-72-060 Maximum length of vehicles.
9-72-070 Special permits.
9-72-080 Weight limitations—Violation— Penalties.

§9-72-010 Load restrictions in downtown district.

(a) No operator of a bus or vehicle designed and used for pulling or carrying freight or merchandise shall drive such vehicle into the district bounded on the north by the south line of Lake Street, on the east by the east line of Wabash Avenue, on the south by the north line of Congress Street and on the west by the east line of Franklin Street, unless the operator has deliveries or pick-ups of materials or persons to make in the district.

(b) No operator of a vehicle designed and used for pulling or carrying freight or merchandise whose length, including load, is in excess of 33 feet shall drive such vehicle for the purpose of delivering or picking up freight or merchandise in the district bounded on the east by the west line of Michigan Avenue, on the south by the south line of Harrison Street, on the west by the east line of Halsted Street, and on the north by the south line of Chicago Avenue during the hours from 8:00 a.m. to 6:00 p.m., except on Sundays and holidays; provided, however, that such vehicles may enter the district for the express purpose of making deliveries or pick-ups at loading platforms or docks located wholly within areas not dedicated as public ways and arranged so that the vehicles do not obstruct movement of vehicular traffic on any public way.

(Added. Coun. J. 7-12-90, p. 18634)

§9-72-020 Operation of vehicles restricted.

It shall be unlawful to operate any vehicle upon any boulevard (a) when such vehicle is used for carrying freight or other goods and merchandise for commercial purposes, (b) when such vehicle is designed primarily for carrying freight or other goods and merchandise, and (c) when such vehicle is used for carrying freight or other goods and merchandise on the outside of the vehicle; provided, however, that vehicles carrying freight or other goods from or to any building or premises abutting any boulevard where it is impossible from the location of the building or the character of the freight or other goods to be received or delivered, to receive or deliver the freight or other goods and merchandise from an alley or a side street or a street other than the boulevard, shall be permitted to enter the boulevard at the cross street nearest the building or premises to receive or deliver the freight or other goods, but shall not proceed further on the boulevard than the nearest cross street. Operators of emergency vehicles and such vehicles excepted by permits issued by the commissioner of transportation are exempt from provisions of this section. Notwithstanding the foregoing provisions, it shall not be unlawful to operate any of the vehicles described in clauses (a), (b) and (c) on those portions of Interstate Route 55, and the exit and entrance ramps thereto, which lie between the King Drive Interchange and the north and southbound lanes of Lake Shore Drive and the most easterly lane of northbound Lake Shore Drive and the most westerly lane of southbound Lake Shore Drive and the exit and entrance ramps of Lake Shore Drive which lie between Interstate Route 55 and 31st Street; provided that such vehicles are traveling to or from the McCormick Place complex and its support facilities.

(Added. Coun. J. 7-12-90, p. 18634; Amend. 11-28-90, p. 26192; 12-11-91, p. 10832)

§9-72-030 Designation of streets with size and weight limitations.

(a) The commissioner of transportation is authorized, subject to the approval of the city council, to determine and designate those streets or parts of streets upon which the operation of trucks or other commercial vehicles shall be prohibited or upon which the use of such vehicles shall be restricted by imposing limitations as to the weight of such vehicles, and he shall erect and maintain appropriate signs on such streets or parts of streets giving notice thereof.

(b) Whenever official signs are erected prohibiting the use of any street or part of a street by trucks or other commercial vehicles or imposing weight and size limitations upon such vehicles using the street, no person shall drive a truck or other commercial vehicle in violation of any such signs except for the purpose of delivering or picking up materials or merchandise and then only by entering such street at the intersection nearest the destination of the vehicle and proceeding thereon no farther than the nearest intersection thereafter. The word "load" when used on official signs erected by authority of this section shall mean the gross weight of the vehicle and its load, if any.

(Added. Coun. J. 7-12-90, p. 18634; Amend. 12-11-91, p. 10832)

§9-72-035 Designation of special routes.

Weight limitations computed under subsection (f) of Section 15-111 of the Illinois Vehicle Code, which allows local governments to adopt vehicle weight limitations similar to those imposed by the state of Illinois on portions of streets and highways under local jurisdiction, shall be authorized on arterial streets and industrial access routes designated by the commissioner of transportation. The commissioner shall publish a list or map of designated arterial streets and industrial access routes.

(Added. Coun. J. 5-4-94, p. 49884; Amend. 10-7-98, p. 78566)

§9-72-040 Maximum width of vehicles.

The maximum width of any vehicle and its load shall not exceed eight feet, six inches, except that vehicles designed and used for carrying more than seven persons may be eight feet, eight inches in width; provided, however, that required mirrors may project up to six inches beyond each side of a vehicle, and such projection shall not be deemed a violation of the above width restrictions. The width restrictions of this section are subject to the special permit provisions of this chapter.

(Added. Coun. J. 7-12-90, p. 18634; Amend. 10-7-98, p. 78566)

§9-72-050 Maximum height of vehicles.

The height of a vehicle from the underside of the tire to the top of the vehicle, inclusive of load, shall not exceed 13 feet, six inches. The height restrictions of this section are subject to the special permit provisions of this chapter.

(Added. Coun. J. 7-12-90, p. 18634; Amend. 10-7-98, p. 78566)

§9-72-060 Maximum length of vehicles.

(a) No single vehicle, unladen or with load, shall exceed a length of 42 feet extreme overall dimension.

(b) No combination of truck tractor and semi-trailer, unladen or with load, shall exceed a length of 55 feet extreme overall dimension. A truck tractor semitrailer may draw one trailer, and a truck in-transit may draw three trucks in-transit coupled together by the triple saddle mount method, and no such combination, unladen or with load, shall exceed a length of 60 feet extreme overall dimension except that such combination when specially designed to transport motor vehicles may have a length of 60 feet extreme overall dimension.

(c) No other combination of vehicles coupled together shall consist of more than two vehicles, and no such combination of vehicles, unladen or with load, shall exceed a length of 55 feet extreme overall dimension.

(d) Length limitations shall not apply (1) to a vehicle operated in the daytime when transporting poles, pipe, machinery or other objects of a structural nature which cannot readily be dismembered or (2) to a vehicle transporting such objects operated at nighttime by a public utility when required for emergency repair of public service facilities or properties or when operated under special permit as provided in this chapter; provided, however, that during authorized night transportation the vehicle shall be equipped with a sufficient number of clearance lamps on each side and marker lamps upon the extreme ends of any projecting load to mark clearly the dimensions of such load.

(e) The load upon any vehicle operated alone, or the load upon the front vehicle of a combination of vehicles, shall not extend more than three feet beyond the front wheels of such vehicle or the front bumper of such vehicle if it is equipped with such a bumper.

(f) The length restrictions of this section are subject to the special permit provisions of this chapter.

(Added. Coun. J. 7-12-90, p. 18634; Amend. 10-7-98, p. 78566)

§9-72-070 Special permits.

(a) The commissioner of transportation may, upon application in writing and good cause being shown, issue a special permit authorizing a vehicle or combination of vehicles not in conformity with the size regulations of this chapter or the wheel and axle load and gross weight provisions of Section 15-111 of the Illinois Vehicle Code, to be operated or moved upon any street or highway under the jurisdiction of the city. The fees for permits under this section shall be as provided in Table 9-72-070. All fee payments under this section shall be deposited in an account to be used only for maintenance, repair and upgrading of streets and highways within the city designated under Section 9-72-035.

(b) The application for any such permit shall specifically describe the vehicle or vehicles and load to be operated or moved and the particular streets or highways for which the permit to operate is requested, and whether such permit is requested for a single trip or for continuous operation.

(c) The commissioner of transportation is authorized to withhold such permit or, if such permit is issued, to limit the number of trips, to establish seasonal or other time limitations within which the vehicles described may be operated on the streets or highways indicated, to require appropriate escort vehicles for the vehicle subject to the permit, or otherwise to prescribe conditions of operation of such vehicle or vehicles, when such action, in the judgment of the commissioner, is necessary to assure against undue damage to the road foundations, surfaces or structures.

(d) The commissioner of transportation shall not issue such permit unless the applicant shall have furnished a certificate of insurance naming the city as additional insured for the amount of $1,000,000.00 so as to save the city harmless from any claim, loss or damage that may result from the granting of such permit or that may arise from or on account of any work done thereunder, and further conditioned that the grantee shall restore at his own cost, to a condition satisfactory to the commissioner of transportation, any pavement, subway, tunnel, sewer, pipe, conduit or other public utility that may be injured by reason of the transportation of such article under such permit.

(e) Every permit issued under this section shall be carried in the vehicle to which it refers and shall be produced for inspection upon request by any police officer or any other city officer or employee having police power.

(f) If a vehicle is subject to a permit required by this section, it shall be unlawful for any person, or any employee or agent of such person, to operate such vehicle without obtaining such permit. It shall be unlawful for any person issued a permit under this section, or any employee or agent of such person, to violate any of the terms or conditions of the permit. The penalty for any such violation shall be a fine of $500.00 in addition to any fine that may be imposed pursuant to Section 9-72-080 and other applicable sections of the code.

(g) In order to limit excessive applications for permits under this section, the commissioner of transportation may divide the city into three industrial truck zones, of substantially equivalent size, for purposes of computing fees under this section.

Special Permit Fees—Single Vehicle

Vehicle Weight	Single Trip	Monthly Permit
80,000 pounds or less, operated on streets and highways other than routes designated under Section 9-72-035	No fee	No fee
More than 80,000 pounds but less than 100,000 pounds:		
— within one industrial zone	$50.00	$750.00
— citywide		
5 miles or less	50.00	750.00
over 5 miles	75.00	1,125.00
100,000 pounds or more:		
— within one industrial zone	100.00	1,500.00
— citywide		
5 miles or less	100.00	1,500.00
over 5 miles	150.00	2,250.00

Fees listed above are per vehicle. An applicant who owns or leases a fleet of 20 or more vehicles may obtain a monthly fleet permit, authorizing the use of all the vehicles in the fleet in accordance with Section 9-72-070, subject to all the conditions of Section 9-72-070. The fee for a fleet permit shall be 80 percent of the combined monthly permit fees for individual vehicles in the fleet.

(Added. Coun. J. 7-12-90, p. 18634; Amend. 12-11-91, p. 10832; 5-4-94, p. 49884; Amend. 10-7-98, p. 78566)

§9-72-080 Weight limitations—Violation— Penalties.

(a) Except as specifically allowed by statute or other ordinance, no person shall operate on any public way within the city any motor vehicle whose gross weight exceeds the limits described in Section 15-111 of the Illinois Motor Vehicle Code. The weight limitations and formulae contained in Section 15-111 of the Illinois Motor Vehicle Code are hereby incorporated by reference for purposes of calculating permissible weights under this section.

(b) Any person who refuses or fails to stop and submit his or her vehicle and load after being directed to do so by an authorized agent of the city, or who removes or causes the removal of any portion of the load prior to weighing, shall be fined not less than $500.00 and not more than $2,000.00.

(c) Any person who violates the weight limitations imposed by subsection (a) of this section shall be subject to a fine according to the following schedule:

Pounds Overweight	Amount of Fine
2,000 or less	$ 73.00
2,001 through 2,500	166.00
2,501 through 3,000	200.00
3,001 through 3,500	303.00
3,501 through 4,000	347.00
4,001 through 4,500	484.00
4,501 through 5,000	538.00
5,001 through 5,500	924.00
5,501 through 6,000	1,007.00
6,001 through 6,500	1,090.00
6,501 through 7,000	1,173.00
7,001 through 7,500	1,256.00
7,501 through 8,000	1,335.00
8,001 through 8,500	1,418.00
8,501 through 9,000	1,501.00
9,001 through 9,500	1,584.00
9,501 through 10,000	1,667.00
10,001 through 10,500	1,746.00
10,501 through 11,000	1,833.00
11,001 through 11,500	1,916.00
11,501 through 12,000	1,995.00
12,001 through 12,500	2,078.00
12,501 through 13,000	2,161.00
13,001 through 13,500	2,224.00
13,501 through 14,000	2,327.00
14,001 through 14,500	2,410.00
14,501 through 15,000	2,493.00
15,001 through 15,500	2,576.00
15,501 through 16,000	2,655.00
16,001 through 16,500	2,738.00
16,501 through 17,000	2,821.00
17,001 through 17,500	2,904.00
17,501 through 18,000	2,987.00
18,001 through 18,500	3,070.00
18,501 through 19,000	3,153.00
19,001 through 19,500	3,236.00
19,501 through 20,000	3,315.00
20,001 through 20,500	3,398.00
20,501 through 21,000	3,481.00
21,001 through 21,500	3,564.00
21,501 through 22,000	3,647.00
22,001 through 22,500	3,730.00
22,501 through 23,000	3,813.00
23,001 through 23,500	3,896.00

23,501 through 24,000 .... 3,975.00
more than 24,000 .... 3,975.00 for the first 24,000 pounds plus $75.00 for each additional increment of 500 pound overweight or fraction thereof, plus $4.00 for each $40.00, or fraction thereof, of the incremental amount.

(d) Whenever any vehicle is operated in violation of the provisions of this section, the owner or driver of the vehicle shall be deemed liable, and either may be prosecuted, for the violation.
(Added. Coun. J. 5-29-93, p. 32394)

CHAPTER 9-76
VEHICLE EQUIPMENT

Sections:

9-76-010 Brakes—Required.
9-76-020 Brakes—Stopping capability—Maintenance.
9-76-030 Windshield wipers.
9-76-040 Horns and warning devices.
9-76-050 Required lighting.
9-76-060 Spot lamps and auxiliary driving lamps.
9-76-070 Side cowl, fender, running board courtesy, and back-up lamps.
9-76-080 Non-motor-driven vehicles—Lighting requirements.
9-76-090 Parked vehicles—Lighting regulations.
9-76-100 Suspension system.
9-76-110 Bumpers.
9-76-120 Rear view mirrors.
9-76-130 Rear reflectors on trailers.
9-76-140 Exhaust system.
9-76-150 Burglar alarms.
9-76-160 Registration plates.
9-76-170 City vehicle tax sticker.
9-76-180 Safety belts.
9-76-190 Identification on second division vehicles.
9-76-200 Projecting loads and trailer restrictions.
9-76-210 Broken or inoperable lamps; broken or cracked glass.
9-76-220 Obstruction of driver's vision; tinted and nonreflective windows.

§9-76-010 Brakes—Required.

(a) Every motor vehicle, other than a motorcycle, when operated upon a roadway shall be equipped with brakes adequate to control the movement of and to stop and hold such vehicle. The brake system shall include two separate means of applying the brake, each of which means shall operate to apply the brakes to at least two wheels. If the two separate means of applying the brakes are connected in any way, they shall be so constructed that failure of any one part of the operating mechanism shall not leave the motor vehicle without brakes on at least two wheels.

(b) Every motorcycle and motor-driven cycle when operated upon a roadway shall be equipped with at least one brake, which may be operated by hand or foot.

(c) Every trailer or semitrailer of a gross weight of 3,000 pounds or more when operated upon a roadway shall be equipped with brakes adequate to control the movement of and to stop and to hold such vehicle and so de-

signed as to be applied by the driver of the towing motor vehicle from its cab. Such brakes shall be so designed and connected that in case of an accidental breakaway of the towed vehicle the brakes are automatically applied.
(Added. Coun. J. 7-12-90, p. 18634)

§9-76-020 Brakes—Stopping capability—Maintenance.

(a) The service brakes upon any motor vehicle or combination of vehicles operating on a level surface shall be adequate to stop such vehicle or vehicles within a distance of 30 feet when traveling 20 miles per hour upon dry asphalt or concrete pavement surface free from loose material.

(b) Under the above conditions the hand brake shall be adequate to stop such vehicle or vehicles within a distance of 55 feet and the hand brake shall be adequate to hold such vehicle or vehicles stationary on any grade upon which operated.

(c) Under the above conditions the service brakes upon an antique vehicle, as defined in the Illinois Vehicle Code, shall be adequate to stop the vehicle within a distance of 40 feet and the hand brake adequate to stop the vehicle within a distance of 55 feet.

(d) All braking distances specified in this section shall apply to all vehicles mentioned, whether such vehicles are not loaded or are loaded to the maximum capacity permitted by law.

(e) All brakes shall be maintained in good working order and shall be so adjusted as to operate evenly with respect to the wheels on opposite sides of the vehicle.
(Added. Coun. J. 7-12-90, p. 18634)

§9-76-030 Windshield wipers.

Every motor vehicle, except motorcycles and motor-driven cycles, operating on a roadway and equipped with a windshield shall also be equipped with a self-operating windshield wiper which shall be maintained in good operating condition. The windshield wiper shall provide clear vision through the windshield for the driver and shall be operated under conditions of fog, snow or rain. This section shall not apply to snow removal equipment equipped with adequate manually operated windshield wipers.
(Added. Coun. J. 7-12-90, p. 18634; Amend. 3-26-96, p. 19161, effective 1-1-97; 2-7-97, p. 38959)

§9-76-040 Horns and warning devices.

(a) Every motor vehicle when operated upon any roadway shall be equipped with a horn in good working order and capable of emitting sound audible under normal conditions from a distance not less than 200 feet, but no horn or other warning device shall emit an unreasonably loud or harsh sound or a whistle.

(b) No vehicle shall be equipped with nor shall any person use upon a vehicle any siren, whistle or bell, except that this shall not apply to an authorized emergency vehicle as otherwise permitted in the traffic code.
(Added. Coun. J. 7-12-90, p. 18634)

§9-76-050 Required lighting.

When upon any roadway, subject to exceptions with respect to parked vehicles:

(a) Every motorcycle shall exhibit at all times at least one lighted lamp showing a white light visible at a distance of 500 feet in the direction of travel;

(b) All motor vehicles other than motorcycles shall exhibit at least two lighted head lamps showing white lights or lights with a yellow or amber tint, during the period of sunset to sunrise, and at any other times when due to insufficient natural light or unfavorable atmospheric conditions (fog, snow or rain), person and vehicles are not clearly discernible for a distance of 1,000 feet in the direction of travel;

(c) Each motor vehicle, trailer or semitrailer shall also exhibit at least one lighted lamp which shall be so situated as to throw a red light visible for at least 500 feet in the reverse direction;

(d) The registration plate at the back of every motorcycle and every motor vehicle shall be so lighted that the numbers on said plate shall be plainly legible and intelligible at a distance of 50 feet; and

(e) Every trailer having a gross weight of 3,000 pounds or less including the weight of the trailer and maximum load shall be equipped with two lighted lamps, one on each side of the rear of such trailer which shall be so situated as to throw a red light visible for at least 500 feet in the reverse direction.
(Added. Coun. J. 7-12-90, p. 18634)

§9-76-060 Spot lamps and auxiliary driving lamps.

(a) Any motor vehicle may be equipped with not to exceed one spot lamp, except authorized emergency vehicles, and every lighted spot lamp shall be so aimed and used upon approaching another vehicle that no part of the high-intensity portion of the beam will be directed to the left of the prolongation of the extreme left side of the vehicle nor more than 100 feet ahead of the vehicle.

(b) Any motor vehicle may be equipped with not to exceed three auxiliary driving lamps mounted on the front at a height not less than 12 inches nor more than 42 inches above the level surface upon which the vehicle stands.
(Added. Coun. J. 7-12-90, p. 18634; Amend. 3-26-96, p. 19161, effective 1-1-97; 2-7-97, p. 38959)

§9-76-070 Side cowl, fender, running board courtesy, and back-up lamps.

(a) Any motor vehicle may be equipped with not more than two side cowl or fender lamps which shall emit an amber or white light without glare.

(b) Any motor vehicle may be equipped with not more than one running board courtesy lamp on each side thereof which shall emit a white or amber light without glare.

(c) Any motor vehicle may be equipped with a back-up lamp either separately or in combination with another lamp; except that no such back-up lamp shall be continuously lighted when the motor vehicle is in forward motion.

(d) Whenever a motor vehicle equipped with head lamps as herein required is also equipped with any auxiliary lamps or a spot lamp or any other lamp on the front thereof projecting a beam of an intensity greater than

300 candle-power, not more than a total of four of any such lamps on the front of a vehicle shall be lighted at any one time when upon a highway.
(Added. Coun. J. 7-12-90, p. 18634; Amend. 3-26-96, p. 19161, effective 1-1-97; 2-7-97, p. 38959)

§9-76-080 Non-motor-driven vehicles—Lighting requirements.

All non-motor-driven vehicles including animal-drawn vehicles while being operated on the roadway between the period of sunset to sunrise shall at all times be equipped with at least one lighted lamp or lantern exhibiting a white light visible from a distance of 500 feet to the front of such vehicle and with a lamp or lantern exhibiting a red light visible from a distance of 500 feet to the rear.
(Added. Coun. J. 7-12-90, p. 18634; Amend. 3-26-96, p. 19161, effective 1-1-97; 2-7-97, p. 38959)

§9-76-090 Parked vehicles—Lighting regulations.

(a) Whenever a vehicle is lawfully parked at nighttime upon any lighted street within a business or residence district, no lights need be displayed upon such parked vehicle.

(b) Whenever a vehicle is parked upon an unlighted street or highway during the hours between one-half hour after sunset and one-half hour before sunrise, such vehicle shall be equipped with one or more lamps which shall exhibit a white light on the roadway side visible from a distance of 500 feet to the front of the vehicle and a red light visible from a distance of 500 feet to the rear.

(c) Any lighted head lamps upon a parked vehicle shall be depressed or dimmed.
(Added. Coun. J. 7-12-90, p. 18634)

§9-76-100 Suspension system.

(a) It shall be unlawful to operate a motor vehicle on any roadway when the suspension system has been modified from the original manufactured design by lifting the body from the chassis in excess of three inches or to cause the horizontal line from the front to the rear bumper to vary over three inches in height when measured from a level surface of the highway to the lower edge of the bumper.

(b) Nothing in this section shall prevent the installation of manufactured heavy duty equipment to include shock absorbers and overload springs, nor shall anything contained in this section prevent a person to operate a motor vehicle with normal wear of the suspension system if such condition does not affect the control or safe operation of the vehicle. This section shall not apply to motor vehicles designed or modified primarily for off-highway racing purposes while such vehicles are in tow or to motorcycles or motor-driven cycles.
(Added. Coun. J. 7-12-90, p. 18634; Amend. 3-26-96, p. 19161, effective 1-1-97; 2-7-97, p. 38959)

§9-76-110 Bumpers.

(a) It shall be unlawful to operate any vehicle of the first division or a recreational vehicle on any roadway unless such vehicle is equipped with both front and rear bumpers. The bumper height shall not be modified to vary more than three inches from the original manufactured bumper height for that vehicle when measured from a level surface of the highway to the lower edge of the bumper. Nothing in this section shall prevent the installation of manufactured bumper guards.

(b) This section shall not apply to any motor vehicle designed or modified primarily for off-highway racing purposes while such vehicle is in tow or to motorcycles or motor-driven cycles or to an antique vehicle when registered as such and where the original design did not include bumpers.
(Added. Coun. J. 7-12-90, p. 18634; Amend. 3-26-96, p. 19161, effective 1-1-97; 2-7-97, p. 38959)

§9-76-120 Rear view mirrors.

Every motor vehicle, operated singly or when towing another vehicle, shall be equipped with a mirror so located as to reflect to the driver a view of the roadway for a distance of at least 200 feet to the rear of such vehicle.
(Added. Coun. J. 7-12-90, p. 18634; Amend. 3-26-96, p. 19161, effective 1-1-97; 2-7-97, p. 38959)

§9-76-130 Rear reflectors on trailers.

Every trailer having a gross weight of 3,000 pounds or less, including the weight of the trailer and maximum load, towed either by a motor vehicle of the first division or a motor vehicle of the second division shall be equipped with two red reflectors, which will be visible when hit by headlight beams 300 feet away at night, located on the rear of the body of such trailer, not more than 12 inches from the lower left hand and right hand corners.
(Added. Coun. J. 7-12-90, p. 18634; Amend. 3-26-96, p. 19161, effective 1-1-97; 2-7-97, p. 38959)

§9-76-140 Exhaust system.

(a) (1) Every motor vehicle shall at all times be equipped with a muffler in good working order and in constant operation to prevent excessive or unusual noise and annoying smoke.

(2) No person shall use a muffler cutout, by-pass, straight pipe or similar device upon a motor vehicle on a public way.

For purposes of this subsection (a), the term "straight pipe" shall mean a muffler without baffles or any other noise-inhibiting device.

(b) The engine and power mechanism of every motor vehicle shall be so equipped and adjusted as to prevent the escape of excessive fumes or smoke.
(Added. Coun. J. 7-12-90, p. 18634; Amend. 11-19-97, p. 57861)

§9-76-150 Burglar alarms.

(a) In any vehicle equipped with a continuous or intermittent audible signal device which acts as a burglar alarm, such device shall be limited in operation to four minutes after activation and shall be incapable of further operation until reset to become active again.

(b) No person shall install or maintain in any vehicle registered in the city any continuous or intermittent audible signal device for use as a burglar alarm unless the device is equipped with an automatic shut-off mechanism to terminate the alarm sound after four minutes and an automatic reset mechanism to reengage the alarm for further operation. No person shall operate or park on any roadway any vehicle equipped with any continuous or intermittent audible signal device for use as a burglar alarm unless the device is equipped with an automatic shut-off mechanism to terminate the alarm sound after four minutes and an automatic reset mechanism to reengage the alarm for further operation.

(c) Any person who violates this section shall be subject to a fine of $50.00 for each offense. Any person who violates this section a second time shall be subject to a fine of $75.00, any person who violates this section a third or subsequent time shall be subject to a fine of $100.00. Each installation and each use of an alarm in violation of this section shall constitute a separate and distinct offense; provided, however, it shall not be a violation of this section to operate a device for a period of time in excess of four minutes if the device is designed to be triggered by the unauthorized opening of the hood, trunk or door of the vehicle, or by the breaking of a window, and the operation of the device in excess of four minutes was so caused. A violation of this section on a roadway is hereby declared a public nuisance which may be abated by removing such vehicle to a city vehicle pound or authorized garage.

(Added. Coun. J. 7-12-90, p. 18634; Amend. 1-10-96, p. 14739; 3-26-96, p. 19161, effective 1-1-97)

§9-76-160 Registration plates.

(a) Registration plates issued for a motor vehicle other than a motorcycle, trailer, semitrailer or truck-tractor shall be attached to the front and the rear of the vehicle.

(b) The registration plate issued for a motorcycle, trailer or semitrailer shall be attached to the rear thereof.

(c) The registration plate issued for a truck-tractor shall be attached to the front thereof.

(d) Every registration plate shall at all times be securely fastened in a horizontal position to the vehicle for which it is issued so as to prevent the plate from swinging and at a height of not less than 12 inches from the ground, measuring from the bottom of such plate, in a place and position to be clearly visible and shall be maintained free from foreign materials and in a condition to be clearly legible. No registration plate shall be covered by any tinted or colored screen.

(e) It is illegal to park a vehicle on any roadway if the registration plate or other registration material fails to comply with subsections (a) through (d) or subsection (f) of this section.

(f) Every registration plate, temporary permit or evidence of temporary registration must bear evidence of proper registration for the current period and be displayed in the manner required by the secretary of state.

(Added. Coun. J. 7-12-90, p. 18634; Amend. 3-26-96, p. 19161, effective 1-1-97; 2-7-97, p. 38959; 12-12-01, p. 75777)

§9-76-170 City vehicle tax sticker.

The city vehicle tax sticker shall be placed and positioned to be clearly visible and maintained in a clearly legible condition and shall be placed on the front windshield in the lower right-hand corner farthest removed from the driver's position approximately one inch from the right and lower edge of the windshield. Any person who violates this section shall be fined $120.00.

(Added. Coun. J. 7-12-90, p. 18634; Amend. 2-4-92, p. 12811; 7-9-03, p. 3280)

§9-76-180 Safety belts.

(a) Each driver and front seat passenger of a passenger motor vehicle shall wear properly adjusted and fastened seat safety belts, except that a child less than six years of age shall be protected as required by the Child Passenger Protection Act of the state of Illinois. Each driver of a passenger motor vehicle transporting a child six years of age or more, but less than 16 years of age, in the front seat of a passenger motor vehicle shall be responsible for securing such child in a properly adjusted and fastened seat safety belt. For the purposes of this section, use of seat safety belts shall include the use of shoulder harnesses where such harness is a standard part of the equipment of the passenger motor vehicle.

(b) All school buses, as defined in Illinois Revised Statutes, Chapter 95-1/2, paragraph 1-182 et seq., that meet the minimum Federal Motor Vehicle Safety Standards 222 for the purposes of transporting children 18 and under shall be equipped with an individual set of seat safety belts meeting Federal Motor Vehicle Safety Standards 208 and 209 as they apply to a multipassenger vehicle with a gross weight at or under 10,000 pounds, in good operating condition for each passenger. No school bus shall be operated unless all passengers' safety belts are fastened.

(c) The provisions of this section shall not apply to:

(1) A driver or passenger frequently stopping and leaving the vehicle or delivering property from the vehicle, if the speed of the vehicle between stops does not exceed 15 miles per hour;

(2) A driver or passenger possessing a written statement from a physician that he or she is unable for medical or physical reasons to wear a seat safety belt;

(3) A driver or passenger possessing a certificate or license endorsement issued by the Motor Vehicle Division of the state or a similar agency in another state or county indicating that the driver or passenger is unable for medical, physical or other valid reasons to wear a seat safety belt;

(4) A driver operating a motor vehicle in reverse;

(5) A passenger motor vehicle manufactured before January 1, 1965;

(6) A motorcycle, motortricycle or moped;

(7) Any passenger motor vehicle which is not required to be equipped with seat safety belts under state or federal law, except school buses;

(8) A passenger motor vehicle operated by a postal carrier of the United States Postal Service while such carrier is performing his or her duties as a postal carrier; or

(9) A school bus transporting students who reside and attend schools situated outside of the city.

(d) This section shall be enforced as a secondary action when the driver of a passenger motor vehicle or school bus has been detained for some other offense. This section also shall be enforced at such time when school buses are inspected by state or federal safety inspection agencies as may be required under state or federal law. Any person who shall violate the provisions of this section shall be fined $25.00.

(Added. Coun. J. 7-12-90, p. 18634)

§9-76-190 Identification on second division vehicles.

No second division vehicle designed and used for carrying or pulling freight or cargo in the furtherance of a commercial or industrial enterprise shall be operated upon a roadway unless there is painted or otherwise firmly affixed to both sides of such vehicle, in a color or colors vividly contrasting to the color of the vehicle, the name and address of the owner thereof and the maximum empty weight of such vehicle.

(Added. Coun. J. 7-12-90, p. 18634; Amend. 5-22-91, p. 826; 3-26-96, p. 19161, effective 1-1-97; 2-7-97, p. 38959)

§9-76-200 Projecting loads and trailer restrictions.

(a) No motor vehicle of the first division shall be operated on any roadway with any loaded carrier extending beyond the line of the fenders on the left side of such vehicle nor extending more than six inches beyond the line of the fenders on the right side.

(b) No commercial vehicle shall be operated on any roadway with any load extending to the rear four feet or more beyond the bed or body of such vehicle unless there shall be displayed at the extreme rear end of the load, (1) during the periods when lighted lamps are required in this chapter, a red light or lantern plainly visible from a distance of at least 500 feet to the rear and sides, or (2) during all other times a red flag or cloth not less than 16 inches square and visible to the driver of any vehicle approaching from the rear or sides.

The red light or lantern required under this section shall be in addition to the red rear light required upon every vehicle.

(c) No trailer shall be operated on any roadway while attached to a self-propelled motor vehicle or to a leading trailer or semitrailer, unless in addition to the regular coupling device it shall have suitable and adequate safety chains or devices attached to the corners of the trailer frame of sufficient strength to pull the trailer and its maximum load; provided, that any trailer having a gross weight of 3,000 pounds or less including the weight of the trailer and maximum load may be coupled to the towing vehicle by means of clamp-on hitches which hitches shall be designed and installed to effectively transfer stresses to the chassis of the towing vehicle. Such clamps and coupling bar shall be of sufficient strength to hold and control such trailer when fully loaded. Such trailers shall be equipped with two safety chains or cables which are permanently affixed to the tongue of the trailer. When such trailer is attached to the towing vehicle, the free end of each chain or cable shall be attached to the towing vehicle.

(Added. Coun. J. 7-12-90, p. 18634; Amend. 3-26-96, p. 19161, effective 1-1-97; 2-7-97, p. 38959)

§9-76-210 Broken or inoperable lamps; broken or cracked glass.

(a) No person shall operate any vehicle on any roadway if any lamp or light required for the vehicle by this code is broken or inoperable.

(b) No person shall operate any vehicle on any roadway if any window of the vehicle is missing, broken, or cracked and the crack exceeds six inches in length.

(Added. Coun. J. 3-26-96, p. 19161, effective 1-1-97; 2-7-97, p. 38959)

§9-76-220 Obstruction of driver's vision; tinted and nonreflective windows.

(a) No person shall operate a motor vehicle on any roadway with any sign, poster, window application, reflective material, nonreflective material or tinted film on the front windshield, sidewings or side windows immediately adjacent to either side of the operator. A nonreflective tint screen may be used along the uppermost portion of the front windshield if the material does not extend more than six inches down from the top of the windshield.

(b) It is unlawful to park or stand a vehicle on any portion of the public way if the vehicle is equipped with nonreflective, smoked or tinted glass or nonreflective film on the front windshield, sidewings or side windows immediately adjacent to either side of the driver's seat.

(c) It is a defense to a charged violation of subsection (a) or subsection (b) of this section that the motor vehicle complies with the use, medical prescription and documentation provisions of Paragraph (g) of Section 12-503 of the Illinois Vehicle Code as amended.

(Added. Coun. J. 2-7-97, p. 38959; Amend. 5-26-04, p. 24938)

CHAPTER 9-80
MISCELLANEOUS RULES

Sections:

9-80-010 Blue lights and flashing, rotating or oscillating blue beams.
9-80-020 Red lights and flashing lights.
9-80-030 Destructive substances on public way.
9-80-040 Metal-tired vehicles or equipment.
9-80-050 Unlawful moving of vehicles.
9-80-060 Blocking of streets by railroad trains.
9-80-065 Malfunctioning railroad gates.
9-80-070 Repairs to vehicles on boulevards.
9-80-080 Parking for certain purposes prohibited.
9-80-090 Picking up riders—Prohibited.
9-80-100 Unlawful riding.
9-80-110 Abandoned vehicles.
9-80-120 Parking in parking lots.
9-80-130 City-owned parking facilities.
9-80-140 Removal of parking permit decals or notice of violation—Sale of one-day permits.
9-80-150 Parking meters—Damage prohibited—Interference with intent to park without paying or obtain coins unlawful.
9-80-160 Interference with traffic-control devices prohibited.
9-80-170 Unauthorized signs declared a nuisance—Exceptions.
9-80-180 Obstruction of or interference with traffic.
9-80-190 Mobile food dispensers and peddlers prohibited in medical center district.
9-80-200 Toy vehicles.
9-80-210 Cruising zones—Definitions.
9-80-211 Cruising zones—Written notice.
9-80-212 Cruising zones—Violation designated.
9-80-213 Cruising zones—Posting.
9-80-214 Cruising zones—Violation—Penalty.
9-80-220 False, stolen or altered temporary registration permits.
9-80-230 Television receivers.

§9-80-010 Blue lights and flashing, rotating or oscillating blue beams.

No person shall drive or move any vehicle or equipment upon any street with any device thereon displaying a blue light visible directly in front thereof, except a vehicle owned and operated by a police department, or place, maintain, or display upon or in view of any public way a flashing, rotating or oscillating blue beam.
(Added. Coun. J. 7-12-90, p. 18634)

§9-80-020 Red lights and flashing lights.

(a) No person shall drive or move any vehicle or equipment upon any roadway with any lamp or device thereon displaying a red light visible from directly in front thereof.

(b) Flashing lights are prohibited on motor vehicles, except as a means for indicating a right or left turn or an emergency stop.

(c) The provisions of this section shall not apply to authorized emergency vehicles.
(Added. Coun. J. 7-12-90, p. 18634)

§9-80-030 Destructive substances on public way.

(a) No person shall throw or deposit upon any public way any glass bottle, glass, nails, tacks, wire, cans, or any other substance likely to injure any person, animal or vehicle upon such public way.

(b) Any person who drops, or permits to be dropped or thrown, upon any public way any destructive or injurious material shall immediately remove the same or cause it to be removed.

(c) Any person removing wrecked or damaged vehicle from a public way shall remove any glass or other injurious substance dropped upon the highway from such vehicle.

(d) No person shall cast, throw or deposit any litter, as defined in Section 10-8-480 of the Municipal Code, upon any public way.

(e) Any police officer or traffic control aide observing a violation of this section may issue a notice of violation or other appropriate citation to any person violating any of the provisions of this section.
(Added. Coun. J. 7-12-90, p. 18634)

§9-80-040 Metal-tired vehicles or equipment.

No person shall move on any public way any metal-tired vehicle or equipment having on the periphery of any wheel a block stud, flange, cleat, or spike or any other protuberance of any metal other than rubber which projects beyond the tread of the traction surface of the tire; provided, however, it shall be permissible to use tire chains of reasonable proportions upon any vehicle when required for safety because of snow, ice, mud or other conditions tending to cause a vehicle to skid.
(Added. Coun. J. 7-12-90, p. 18634)

§9-80-050 Unlawful moving of vehicles.

No person other than a police officer shall move a vehicle, not lawfully under his control, into any area where stopping, standing or parking is prohibited or away from a curb or edge of roadway such distance as is unlawful

or start or cause to be started the motor of any motor vehicle, or shift, change, or move the levers, brake, starting device, gears, or other mechanism, of a parked motor vehicle, to a position other than that in which it was left by the owner or driver thereof, or attempt to do so.
(Added. Coun. J. 7-12-90, p. 18634)

§9-80-060 Blocking of streets by railroad trains.

(a) It shall be unlawful for the directing officer or the operator of any railroad train to direct the operation of or to operate the same in such a manner as to prevent the use of any street for purposes of travel for a period of time longer than five minutes, except that this provision shall not apply to trains or cars in motion other than those engaged in switching.

(b) It shall be unlawful for the directing officer or the operator of any railroad train to direct the operation of or to operate the same in such a manner as to prevent the use of any street for purposes of travel for a period of time longer than five minutes between the hours of 7:00 a.m. and 9:00 a.m. and between 4:00 p.m. and 6:00 p.m.

(c) Any person violating any provision of this section shall be fined $100.00 for each offense. A separate distinct offense shall be held to have been committed each day any person continues to violate any of the provisions of this section.
(Added. Coun. J. 7-12-90, p. 18634)

§9-80-065 Malfunctioning railroad gates.

It shall be unlawful for any operator of a railroad crossing gate to fail to repair, so as to be in operable order, any gate upon being notified of a malfunction by any city official. Any person violating this section shall be fined $1,000.00 for each 10 minutes that a gate remains inoperable following notice of a malfunction.
(Added. Coun. J. 9-5-01, p.66217)

§9-80-070 Repairs to vehicles on boulevards.

No person shall change any parts, repair, wash, grease, wax, polish or clean a vehicle on any boulevard except such repairing, cleaning or polishing as is necessary to insure good vision, or such emergency repairs as are necessary to remove such vehicle from the boulevard. Such emergency repairs shall be made only as close as possible to the right-hand edge of the roadway, with the vehicle facing in the direction of the traffic flow.
(Added. Coun. J. 7-12-90, p. 18634)

§9-80-080 Parking for certain purposes prohibited.

(a) It shall be unlawful to park any vehicle upon any roadway for the sole purpose of displaying the vehicle for sale. The vehicle shall be subject to vehicle impoundment under Section 9-92-030(c). Any person who violates this subsection shall be fined $100.00. Each day a vehicle remains in violation of this subsection, shall constitute a separate and distinct offense for which a separate penalty shall be imposed.

(b) No person shall park a vehicle upon any roadway or in any alley to grease or repair the vehicle except for repairs necessitated by an emergency.

(c) No person shall park a vehicle upon any roadway to sell merchandise from such vehicle except in a duly established market or pursuant to permit.

(d) Any person who violates or fails to comply with subsection (b) or (c) above shall be fined $25.00 for each offense.

(Added. Coun. J. 7-12-90, p. 18634; Amend. Coun. J. 11-5-03, p. 10746)

§9-80-090 Picking up riders—Prohibited.

No person operating a private vehicle shall pick up any person standing in a roadway for the purpose of soliciting a ride.

(Added. Coun. J. 7-12-90, p. 18634)

§9-80-100 Unlawful riding.

(a) No person shall board or alight from any vehicle while such vehicle is in motion.

(b) No person shall ride on any vehicle upon any portion thereof not designed or intended for the use of passengers. This provision shall not apply to an employee engaged in the necessary discharge of a duty or to persons riding within truck bodies in space intended for merchandise.

(c) No passenger in a vehicle shall ride in such position as to interfere with the driver's view ahead or to the sides or with his control over the driving mechanism of the vehicle.

(Added. Coun. J. 7-12-90, p. 18634)

§9-80-110 Abandoned vehicles.

(a) It shall be unlawful for any person to abandon any motor vehicle on any public way within the city. A vehicle shall be deemed to have been abandoned if it (a) is in such a state of disrepair as to be incapable of being driven in its present condition or (b) has not been moved or used for more than seven consecutive days and is apparently deserted or (c) has been left on the public way without state registration plates or a temporary state registration placard for two or more days.

(b) It shall be unlawful for any person to leave any hazardous dilapidated motor vehicle in full view of the general public. Members of the police department and employees of the department of streets and sanitation are hereby authorized to issue a notice of parking violation and may authorize the immediate removal of any hazardous dilapidated motor vehicle where such vehicle is left in full view of the general public, whether on public or private property. Any vehicle so removed shall be towed to an authorized facility. The owner of a vehicle towed under the provisions of this subsection shall be entitled to notice, pursuant to Section 4-205 of the Illinois Vehicle Code, of the right to request a hearing regarding the validity of the tow and any towing or storage charges as provided in Section 9-92-080. Unclaimed hazardous dilapidated motor vehicles shall be disposed of as provided in Sections 4-208 and 4-209.1 of the Illinois Vehicle Code, as amended; provided, however, that if the hazardous dilapidated motor vehicle bears no ascertainable vehicle identification number, and no registration-registration sticker as defined in the Illinois Vehicle Code, and no other identification by which the last registered owner of the vehicle can be determined for the purpose of giving notice, the vehicle may be disposed of immediately after it is impounded at a public facility. Nothing in this subsection shall apply to any motor vehicle that is kept within a building when not in use, to inoperable historic vehicles over 25 years of age, or to a motor vehicle on the premises of a place of business engaged in the wrecking or junking of motor vehicles.

(c) Any person who violates this section shall be fined the amount set forth in Section 9-100-020 for each offense. Each day a vehicle remains abandoned shall constitute a separate and distinct offense for which a separate penalty may be imposed.

(d) Whenever any vehicle shall have been abandoned in violation of this section, the person in whose name the vehicle has last been registered shall be prima facie responsible for the violation and subject to the penalty therefor. The last registered owner of an abandoned vehicle shall also be liable to the city for the towing and storage charges as provided in Section 9-92-80 and the costs of postage for notices and costs of collection.

(Added. Coun. J. 7-12-90, p. 18634; Amend. 3-15-00, p. 27706; 12-12-01, p. 75777; 9-4-02, p. 92682)

§9-80-120 Parking in parking lots.

(a) It shall be unlawful for any person not so entitled to park a vehicle in a public parking lot as defined in Section 4-232-130 of the Municipal Code of Chicago.

(b) It shall be unlawful for any person not so entitled to park a vehicle in a private parking lot established voluntarily or pursuant to the Chicago Zoning Ordinance to provide off-street parking facilities for tenants or employees of the owner.

(c) Whenever any vehicle is parked in violation of this section, any police officer or other person authorized to issue parking violation notices pursuant to Section 9-64-220, upon a written complaint signed by the owner of the parking lot or by his authorized agent that the vehicle is not entitled to the privileges of the parking lot, may attach a parking violation notice to the vehicle.

(d) Any person who violates subsection (a) or (b) of this section shall be fined $25.00 for each offense.

(Added. Coun. J. 7-12-90, p. 18634)

§9-80-130 City-owned parking facilities.

(a) It shall be unlawful for any person to park a vehicle in a city-owned parking facility unless the vehicle is properly parked in a designated parking space and such person has paid the appropriate parking fee.

(b) It shall be unlawful for any person to park a vehicle or allow a vehicle to remain in a city-owned parking facility during the hours that the facility is not open for use.

(c) It shall be unlawful for any person to park a vehicle or allow a vehicle to remain in a city-owned parking facility at any airport for more than 30 consecutive days.

(d) Whenever a vehicle is parked in violation of this section, any person authorized to issue a notice of parking violation pursuant to Section 9-64-220, may attach a parking violation notice to the vehicle.

(e) Any person who violates this section shall be fined $25.00 for each offense. Any vehicle parked in violation of this section shall be subject to an immediate tow and removal to a city vehicle pound or authorized garage.

(f) At the request of the parking administrator, the commissioner of transportation shall cause to be erected signs indicating the hours when parking is prohibited at such facility and the length of time which a vehicle may be parked at such facility and warning that unauthorized or illegally parked vehicles shall be ticketed and towed.

(Added. Coun. J. 7-12-90, p. 18634; Amend. 12-11-91, p. 10832; 9-10-97, p. 51490)

§9-80-140 Removal of parking permit decals or notice of violation—Sale of one-day permits.

(a) It shall be unlawful for any person, other than the driver of the vehicle, to remove from a vehicle a notice of violation affixed pursuant to the traffic code.

(b) It shall be unlawful for any person to remove from any vehicle a residential parking permit decal issued pursuant to Section 9-68-020 without first having obtained the consent of the owner.

(c) It shall be unlawful for any person to sell an individual one-day permit issued pursuant to Section 9-68-020.

(d) Every person convicted of a violation of any provision of this section shall be fined not less than $250.00 nor more than $500.00.

(Added. Coun. J. 7-12-90, p. 18634)

§9-80-150 Parking meters—Damage prohibited—Interference with intent to park without paying or obtain coins unlawful.

(a) It shall be unlawful for any person to deface, injure, tamper with, open or wilfully break, destroy or impair the usefulness of any parking meter. Every person convicted of a violation of this subsection shall be punished by a fine of $250.00.

(b) It shall be unlawful for any person to insert, or to attempt to insert, into the coin receptacle of any parking meter, any slug, button or other substance, or to manipulate or operate, or to attempt to manipulate or operate in any manner whatever, any parking meter or any mechanism or device connected or commonly used therewith, with the intent to park in a parking meter zone without paying therefor. Every person convicted of a violation of this subsection shall be punished by a fine of $25.00.

(c) It shall be unlawful for any person to insert, or to attempt to insert, into the coin receptacle of any parking meter, any slug, button, wire, hood, or other implement or substance with the intent to obtain from such coin recepacle a legal tender coin of the United States. Every person convicted of a violation of this subsection shall be punished by a fine of not less than $100.00 and not more than $200.00.

(Added. Coun. J. 7-12-90, p. 18634)

§9-80-160 Interference with traffic-control devices prohibited.

No person shall without lawful authority attempt to or in fact alter, deface, injure, knock down, or remove any official traffic-control device or any railroad sign or signal. Every person convicted of a violation of this section shall be punished by a fine of not less than $250.00 nor more than $500.00 for each offense. (Add ed. Coun. J. 7-12-90, p. 18634)

§9-80-170 Unauthorized signs declared a nuisance—Exceptions.

(a) No person shall place, maintain, or display upon or in view of any public way any unauthorized sign, signal, marking, or device which purports to be or is an imitation of or resembles an official traffic-control device or railroad sign or signal, or which attempts to direct the movement of traffic, or which hides from view or interferes with the effectiveness of any official traffic-control device or any railroad sign or signal, and no person shall place or maintain upon any public way any traffic sign or signal bearing thereon any commercial advertising.

(b) Every person convicted of a violation of this section shall be fined not less than $100.00 nor more than $500.00 for each offense. Every sign, signal, or marking prohibited under this section is hereby declared to be a public nuisance, and the commissioner of transportation is empowered to and shall remove the same or cause it to be removed without notice.

(c) This section shall not apply to crossing guards displaying portable stop signs to permit the street crossing of children or to "Neighborhood Watch" signs installed and maintained by local residents or organizations; provided, however, that "Neighborhood Watch" signs shall be uniform in size, color and design as approved by the Chicago Police Department and shall be installed only on residential streets, at least eight feet above curb grade, not less than 150 feet from any intersection and in such a manner as not to obstruct any traffic or other regulatory sign or signal. This section also shall not be deemed to prohibit the erection, upon private property adjacent to public ways, of signs giving useful directional information and of a type that cannot be mistaken for official traffic signs.

(Added. Coun. J. 7-12-90, p. 18634; Amend. 12-11-91, p. 10832)

§9-80-180 Obstruction of or interference with traffic.

Any person who shall wilfully and unnecessarily hinder, obstruct or delay or who shall wilfully and unnecessarily attempt to hinder, obstruct or delay any other person in lawfully driving or traveling along or upon any street or who shall offer to barter or sell any merchandise or service on the street so as to interfere with the effective movement of traffic or who shall repeatedly cause motor vehicles traveling on public thoroughfares to stop or impede the flow of traffic shall be guilty of a misdemeanor and upon conviction thereof shall be fined not more than $200.00 or imprisoned for not more than 10 days, or both, for the first offense, fined not more than $500.00 or imprisoned for not more than 20 days, or both, for the second offense, and fined not more than 30 days, or both, for each such subsequent offense. Violations of this section shall be prosecuted in accordance with the procedures set forth in Section 1-2-1.1 of the Illinois Municipal Code, as amended, and the provisions of the Illinois Code of Criminal Procedure, as amended.

(Added. Coun. J. 7-12-90, p. 18634)

§9-80-190 Mobile food dispensers and peddlers prohibited in medical center district.

No person shall conduct the business of a mobile food dispenser or peddler as defined in this code, on any portion of the public way within the boundaries of the medical center district and no person shall operate, stop or park any vehicle on any portion of the public way within the medical center district for the purposes of conducting any such businesses.

For the purpose of this section, "medical center district" means the area bounded by Ashland Avenue on the east, Congress Parkway on the north, Oakley Street on the west, and a line co-incidental with the north line of the property at or near 14th Street and 15th Street, owned or used by the Baltimore and Ohio Chicago Terminal Railroad Company for railroad purposes, on the south.

Any person who violates the provisions of this section shall be fined not less than $50.00 nor more than $500.00 for each offense.
(Added. Coun. J. 7-12-90, p. 18634)

§9-80-200 Toy vehicles.

(a) No person shall operate any pushcart upon any roadway, except by permit.

(b) No person shall ride a skateboard upon any road way or sidewalk in a business district.

(c) No person upon roller skates, or riding in or by means of any coaster, skateboard, toy vehicle, or similar device, shall go upon any roadway except while crossing a street on a crosswalk and when so crossing such person shall be granted all the rights and shall be subject to all the duties applicable to pedestrians. This section shall not apply upon any street while set aside as a play street.

(d) Any person upon a sidewalk on roller skates or riding in or by means of any coaster, skateboard, or similar device shall yield the right-of-way to any pedestrian and shall give audible signals before overtaking and passing such pedestrian.

(e) No person riding upon any bicycle, motor-driven cycle, coaster, sled, roller skates, skateboard or any toy vehicle shall attach the same or himself to any moving vehicle upon any roadway.

(f) No person shall operate a motorized cycle or motorized scooter on the public way, except on a street where vehicular traffic is allowed. No person shall operate a motorized cycle or motorized scooter on a street unless the vehicle is properly registered and the operator is in possession of a valid driver's license, and meets the requirements of the Illinois Vehicle Code with respect to insurance. Nothing in this subsection applies to any motorized wheelchair as defined in the Illinois Vehicle Code.

(g) Any person found to have violated any provision of this section shall be fined not less than $25.00 and not more than $200.00.
(Added. Coun. J. 7-12-90, p. 18634; Amend. 5-26-04, p. 24884)

§9-80-210 Cruising zones—Definitions.

For the purposes of Sections 9-80-210 through 9-80-214, the following definitions shall apply:

(a) "Congested traffic" means traffic on any public way which is delayed to the point that:

(1) Motor vehicles cannot move through a 100-yard corridor to an intersection controlled by a traffic light within two complete green light cycles, where the delay in forward movement is due to the position of other motor vehicles; or

(2) Motor vehicles cannot move through a 100-yard corridor to an intersection controlled by a traffic light, stop sign or yield sign within a five minute period of time where the delay in forward movement is due to the position of other motor vehicles; or

(3) Motor vehicles cannot readily move forward on portions of the public way between intersections because traffic speed is slowed to less than five miles per hour, and the delay in movement is due to the position of other motor vehicles.

(b) "Cruising" means the unnecessary repetitive driving of any motor vehicle past a traffic control point in traffic which is congested at or near the traffic control point.

(c) "Green light cycle" means the period commencing upon the switching of a traffic light from a red light to a green light through to the return of the red light.

(d) "Traffic Control Point" means a location along a "no cruising zone" utilized by a police officer as an observation point in order to monitor traffic conditions for potential violations of Sections 9-80-210 through 9-80-214.
(Added. Coun. J. 10-3-90, p. 21780)

§9-80-211 Cruising zones—Written notice.

A police officer shall issue a written notice to any person operating a motor vehicle passing a traffic control point twice within a one-hour period. Such notice shall state that a third passage past that traffic control point within the same one-hour period shall be a violation of this code.
(Added. Coun. J. 10-3-90, p. 21780)

§9-80-212 Cruising zones—Violation designated.

Any person who, after having received a written notice as described in Section 9-80-211, subsequently drives past or is a passenger in a vehicle passing the same traffic control point within the previously described one-hour period shall be in violation of this code.
(Added. Coun. J. 10-3-90, p. 21780)

§9-80-213 Cruising zones—Posting.

Sections 9-80-210 through 9-80-214 may be enforced in any area which has been posted as a "no cruising zone." The city council shall by order designate "no cruising zones" in areas where it is deter mined that cruising endangers the public health, safety and welfare due to congested traffic as defined in Section 9-80-210. "No cruising" signs shall be posted appropriately at the beginning and end of any portion of the public way determined to be a "no cruising zone." These signs

shall display the hours of the day when Sections 9-80-210 through 9-80-214 will be enforced, as determined by order of the city council.
(Added. Coun. J. 10-3-90, p. 21780)

§9-80-214 Cruising zones—Violation—Penalty.

Any person found in violation of Section 9-80-212 shall be fined $100.00 for the first offense, $200.00 for the second offense within one year, and $300.00 for the third and each subsequent offense within one year.
(Add ed. Coun. J. 10-3-90, p. 21780)

§9-80-220 False, stolen or altered temporary registration permits.

No person shall operate or park on the public way any vehicle bearing a false, stolen or altered state temporary registration permit. A vehicle operated or parked in violation of this section is subject to immediate impoundment. The owner of record of such vehicle shall be liable to the city for an administrative penalty of $500.00 in addition to fees for towing and storage of the vehicle. Whenever a police officer has probable cause to believe that a vehicle is subject to seizure and impoundment pursuant to this subsection, the police officer shall provide for the towing of the vehicle to a facility con trolled by the city or its agents. When the vehicle is towed, the police officer shall notify the person who is found to be in control of the vehicle at the time of the alleged violation, if there is such a person, of the fact of the seizure and of the vehicle owner's right to request a preliminary hearing to be conducted under Section 2-14-132 of this code. If the vehicle is unattended, notice shall be sent to the last registered owner of the vehicle, at the address indicated in the last valid registration of the vehicle. The notice provisions of subsection (2) of Section 2-14-132 shall apply whenever a motor vehicle is seized and impounded pursuant to this section.
(Added. Coun. J. 6-6-01, p. 60138)

§9-80-230 Television receivers.

No person shall operate a motor vehicle when the vehicle is equipped with television broadcast receiver equipment so located that the viewer or screen is visible from the driver's seat. Any person who violates the provisions of this section shall be fined not less than $200.00 nor more than $500.00 for each offense.
(Added. Coun. J. 5-29-02, p. 86336)

CHAPTER 9-84
TOWING UNAUTHORIZED VEHICLES

Sections:

9-84-010 Report—Definition—Procedure.
9-84-015 Booting prohibited—Applicability.
9-84-020 Removal of vehicle by owner or legal possessor of vehicle.
9-84-021 Towing of vehicle containing passenger prohibited.
9-84-030 Insurance required.
9-84-040 Violation—Penalty.

§9-84-010 Report—Definition—Procedure.

(a) Within 30 minutes after towing any unauthorized vehicle from private property, any person towing a vehicle from private property or his agent or employer shall notify the Chicago Police Department by using the nonemergency police telephone number to report the year, make, model and state license plate number of the towed vehicle and the location from which the vehicle was towed. In addition to this notification, within 24 hours after towing an unauthorized vehicle from private property, the towing firm or its agent shall submit a written report to the superintendent of police containing the following information:

(1) Name, address and telephone number of the towing firm and of the person or persons making the tow;

(2) State license plate number of the vehicle towed;

(3) Vehicle identification number of the vehicle towed;

(4) Color, make and model of the towed vehicle;

(5) Date and time of towing;

(6) Address of place from which vehicle was towed;

(7) Names and addresses of any witnesses to the towing;

(8) Name of person with whom this towing agreement was made;

(9) Address of place where vehicle is stored; and

(10) State license plate number of the tow truck which made the tow.

(b) An unauthorized vehicle on private property shall mean any vehicle parked or abandoned on private property without the consent of the property owner or his authorized agent or any vehicle parked or abandoned on private property in violation of any provision of this code.

(c) Before a towing firm may remove an unauthorized vehicle from private property, the firm must first obtain written consent from the owner of the private property or his authorized agent to remove the specific vehicle in question, unless the firm has an agreement to remove all unauthorized vehicles from the private property.

(d) When any owner enters into an agreement with a towing firm to remove unauthorized vehicles from his private parking area, the towing firm shall post a notice of this arrangement prominently at all entrances and exits to the parking areas, in clear view free from interference from any natural or manmade objects. The lettering on these signs shall be in prominent type at least three inches high and in a color that contrasts with the background color of the sign. The sign must also be legible at night. This sign shall contain the following information:

(1) A general statement indicating who is allowed to park in the area. The statement may use classes of persons as well as individuals;

(2) A warning that unauthorized vehicles will be towed;

(3) The name, address and telephone number of the towing company, and the location to which the car will be towed, if different;

(4) The fee charged by the towing firm to recover the vehicle and whether cash, check or credit cards will be accepted in payment.

(e) Subsection (d) shall not apply to driveways or parking areas serving three or fewer cars.

(Added. Coun. J. 7-12-90, p. 18634)

§9-84-015 Booting prohibited—Applicability.

No person shall boot a motor vehicle at any time. To "boot" means the act of placing on a parked motor vehicle a mechanical device that is designed to be attached to a wheel or tire or other part of such vehicle so as to prohibit its usual manner of movement. The provisions of this section shall not apply to the booting of a motor vehicle by the city of Chicago, any other governmental entity, or a person acting under the direction of the city of Chicago or such governmental entity, when such booting is authorized by any provision of law or any rule or regulation promulgated pursuant thereto. Nor shall the provisions of this section apply to booting of a motor vehicle in compliance with Chapter 4-233 of this code.
(Add. Coun. J. 9-29-99, p. 12267; Amend. 12-13-00, p. 48188)

§9-84-020 Removal of vehicle by owner or legal possessor of vehicle.

No vehicle may be towed by any person from private property if the owner or other person entitled to possession of the vehicle is present and offers to remove such vehicle voluntarily prior to the time such person attempting to tow removes such vehicle from the premises in question; provided that the owner or other person so removes the vehicle immediately thereupon.
(Added. Coun. J. 7-12-90, p. 18634)

§9-84-021 Towing of vehicle containing passenger prohibited.

No vehicle may be towed by any person from private property if the vehicle to be towed contains one or more passengers. Any person who violates this section shall be subject to the penalties described in Section 9-84-040.
(Added Coun. J. 7-29-98, p. 75175)

§9-84-030 Insurance required.

No person shall tow any vehicle from private property nor shall any person accept in storage a vehicle towed from private property unless at the time of the tow there shall be liability insurance in effect in the name of such person as provided in Section 9-44-050.
(Added. Coun. J. 7-12-90, p. 18634)

§9-84-040 Violation—Penalty.

Any person or any officer of any corporation, or any partner of any partnership, making a tow or authorizing a tow, or booting a vehicle or authorizing the booting of a vehicle in violation of any provision of Sections 9-84-010, 9-84-015, 9-84-020 or 9-84-030 shall be fined not less than $50.00 nor more than $500.00 for the first offense and not less than $100.00 nor more than $500.00 for the second and each subsequent offense. Repeated offenses in excess of three may also be punishable as a misdemeanor by incarceration for a term not to exceed six months under the procedure set forth in Section 1-2-1.1 of the Illinois Municipal Code, as amended, and the provisions of the Illinois Code of Criminal Procedure, as amended, in a separate proceeding. Any person, or any officer of any corporation, if such person is a corporation and the corporation has been guilty of such repeated offenses, or any partner of any partnership, if such person is a partnership and the partnership has been guilty of such repeated offenses, shall be subject to incarceration as provided herein.
(Added. Coun. J. 7-12-90, p. 18634; Amend. 9-29-99, p. 12267)

CHAPTER 9-88
DUTIES OF POLICE DEPARTMENT

Sections:

9-88-010 Traffic regulations and vehicle laws—Enforcement.
9-88-020 Traffic violation notices.
9-88-030 Disposal of traffic or parking notices, complaints and records.
9-88-040 Accident and traffic reports.

§9-88-010 Traffic regulations and vehicle laws—Enforcement.

(a) It shall be the duty of the superintendent of police to enforce the traffic regulations of this city and all of the state vehicle laws applicable to street traffic in this city, to make arrests for traffic violations, to investigate accidents and to cooperate with the commissioner of transportation and other officers of the city in the administration of the traffic laws and in developing ways and means to improve traffic conditions, and to carry out those duties imposed by the traffic code or other ordinances of this city.

(b) Officers of the police department and traffic control aides are authorized to direct all traffic by voice, hand or signal in conformance with traffic laws or ordinances. In the event of fire or other emergency or in order to expedite traffic or safeguard pedestrians, officers of the police department, sworn members of the fire department and traffic control aides may direct traffic contrary to traffic control devices as conditio is may require.

(c) Any person who is found guilty of circumventing, ignoring or disobeying any direction or order authorized by subsection (b) of this section shall be subject to a fine of not less than $100.00 and not more than $300.00 for the first offense and not less than $300.00 and not more than $500.00 for each subsequent offense occurring within twelve consecutive months.

(Added. Coun. J. 7-12-90, p. 18634; Amend. 12-11-91, p. 10832; 3-28-01, p. 55822)

§9-88-020 Traffic violation notices.

(a) Traffic violation notice forms for notifying violators to appear and answer to charges of violating traffic laws and ordinances in the Circuit Court of Cook County and the corresponding complaint forms therefor, in serially numbered sets consisting of three copies of the notices and one copy of the corresponding complaint shall be provided in books and in the form prescribed and approved jointly by the corporation counsel and the superintendent of police. The superintendent of police shall be responsible for the issuance of such books, shall maintain a record of every such book and each set of notices and complaint therein issued to the individual members of the police department, shall require and retain a receipt for every book so issued, and shall require the return to him of a copy of every traffic violation notice issued by a member of the police department and of all copies of every traffic violation notice and the corresponding complaint which have been spoiled or upon which any entry has been made and not issued to an alleged violator.

(b) Every police officer or traffic control aide, upon issuing a traffic violation notice to an alleged violator of any provision of the motor vehicle laws of the state or of any traffic ordinance of this city shall deposit the corresponding

traffic violation complaint of the notice with his immediate superior officer who shall cause the complaint to be filed in the Circuit Court of Cook County.
(Added. Coun. J. 7-12-90, p. 18634)

§9-88-030 Disposal of traffic or parking notices, complaints and records.

It shall be unlawful and official misconduct for any police officer, traffic control aide or other officer or public employee to dispose of a traffic or parking, or compliance violation notice or copies thereof, a traffic or parking, or compliance violation complaint, or the record of the issuance of a traffic or parking, or compliance violation notice in a manner other than as required in the traffic code.
(Added. Coun. J. 7-12-90, p. 18634; Amend. Coun. J. 11-19-03, p. 13435)

§9-88-040 Accident and traffic reports.

(a) The police department shall receive and properly file all accident reports made to it under state law or under any ordinance of this city, but all such accident reports made by drivers shall be for the confidential use of the police department, the corporation counsel, the commissioner of transportation, and other officers of the city for official use. All other accident reports made by police officers or others may be furnished to persons or organizations having an interest therein, and the police department shall charge a fee of $5.00 for each such report or, in the case of an accident which was investigated by an accident reconstruction officer or accident reconstruction team, $20.00 for each such report. The police department shall also maintain a suitable record of all traffic accidents reported for each driver.

(b) The police department shall maintain records of all accidents in which the use of a mobile, cellular, analog, wireless or digital telephone while driving is a contributing factor.

(c) The superintendent of police shall annually prepare a traffic report which shall be filed with the mayor and the city council. Such report shall contain information on:

(1) The number of traffic accidents, the number of persons killed, the number of persons injured, and other pertinent traffic accident data;

(2) The number of traffic accidents investigated and other pertinent data on the safety activities of the police;

(3) The plans and recommendations of the superintendent of police for future traffic safety activities.

(d) Whenever the accidents at any particular location become numerous, the superintendent of police shall cooperate with the commissioner of transportation in conducting studies of such accidents and determining remedial measures.
(Added. Coun. J. 7-12-90, p. 18634; Amend. 12-11-91, p. 10832; 7-29-03, p. 5728)

CHAPTER 9-92
IMPOUNDING AND RELOCATION OF VEHICLES

Sections:

9-92-010 Relocation of vehicles in emergencies.
9-92-020 Vehicle pound established.
9-92-030 Authority to impound or otherwise relocate vehicle.
9-92-035 Authority to impound fleeing vehicle.
9-92-040 Removal of horse-drawn carriages.
9-92-050 Towing or removal service and fees.
9-92-060 Recordkeeping.
9-92-070 Notice to owner of impounded vehicle.
9-92-080 Release procedure for impounded vehicles.
9-92-090 Evidence of identity and right of possession required.
9-92-100 Disposal of unclaimed vehicles.

§9-92-010 Relocation of vehicles in emergencies.

When any emergency arises necessitating the removal of any vehicle upon any public way, members of the police department and employees of the department of streets and sanitation are authorized to remove or have removed the vehicle from one location to any other location. Upon request of the commissioner of streets and sanitation, employees of the bureau of parking enforcement may remove vehicles in an emergency or under the circumstances enumerated in Section 9-92-030.

(Added. Coun. J. 7-12-90, p. 18634)

§9-92-020 Vehicle pound established.

The superintendent of police and the commissioner of streets and sanitation are authorized to establish and operate vehicle pounds, to which motor vehicles may be removed as provided in the traffic code.

(Added. Coun. J. 7-12-90, p. 18634)

§9-92-030 Authority to impound or otherwise relocate vehicle.

Members of the police department and employees of the department of streets and sanitation are authorized to issue a notice of parking violation and may authorize the removal of a vehicle from any public way to a city vehicle pound or authorized garage or other legal parking space in the public way under the following circumstances:

(a) When a vehicle upon any public way is so disabled as to constitute an obstruction to traffic and the person or persons in charge of the vehicle are by reason of physical injury incapacitated to such an extent as to be unable to provide for its custody or removal;

(b) When an unattended vehicle is unlawfully parked so as to constitute a hazard or obstruction to the normal movement of traffic;

(c) When an unattended vehicle is parked in violation of Section 9-64-020, 9-64-050, 9-64-060, 9-64-070, 9-64-100, 9-64-110, 9-64-120, 9-64-130(b), 9-64-140(b), 9-64-150(b), 9-64-160(b), 9-64-170, 9-64-210, 9-80-080(a), or 9-80-130;

(d) When a vehicle has been abandoned or found to be a hazardous dilapidated motor vehicle in violation of Section 9-80-110;

(e) When a vehicle illegally occupies a parking meter space for more than 24 hours;

(f) When an unattended vehicle is parked illegally in an officially designated and marked "tow zone";

(g) When a vehicle is in violation of any provision of the traffic code authorizing towing and impoundment for that violation;

(h) When a vehicle is subject to towing or removal under the Illinois Vehicle Code, the Criminal Code of 1961, or any other law;

(i) When towing or removal is necessary as an incident to an arrest.

(Added. Coun. J. 7-12-90, p. 18634; Amend. 9-1-99, p. 10503; 12-12-01, p. 75777; 12-4-02. p. 99026; 11-5-03, p. 10746)

§9-92-035 Authority to impound fleeing vehicle.

(a) A motor vehicle involved in an unlawful attempt to flee or elude police officers shall be subject to impoundment under the procedures of this section.

(b) A police officer shall, if possible, record the vehicle make and color, and the issuing state and number of the license plate of a vehicle that the officer has attempted to stop through use of the emergency signal equipment on the officer's vehicle. If the operator of the other vehicle fails or refuses to stop, and if the police officer foregoes or abandons pursuit of the other vehicle for reasons of public safety, the officer shall report the recorded information as directed by the superintendent, for delivery to appropriate sections of the police department and the department of streets and sanitation responsible for impoundment and towing of vehicles.

(c) The police officer's report shall also include: the date, approximate time and approximate location of the attempted stop; the reason for the attempted stop; the emergency signal equipment activated by the police officer; the public safety considerations that caused the police officer to forego or abandon pursuit of the described vehicle.

(d) The police department shall send a notice of intent to impound the vehicle described in the police officer's report to the owner of record of the vehicle. The notice shall be sent either by first class mail or by messenger to the address of the owner of record as indicated in state registration records. The notice shall include the following: a statement that the operator of the vehicle failed or refused to stop when ordered to do so by a Chicago police officer; the date, approximate time and approximate location of the event; the description of the vehicle as contained in the officer's report; and notice of an opportunity to contest eligibility for impoundment. A copy of the notice shall be forwarded to the department of administrative hearings. A notice is presumed delivered upon being deposited with the United States Postal Service with proper postage affixed.

(e) An owner of record who receives a notice pursuant to subsection (d) of this section may contest eligibility for impoundment by written request delivered to the department of administrative hearings, postmarked within 14 days after the delivery of the notice. The department of administrative hearings shall set a date for a hearing on the eligibility of the vehicle for impoundment, and shall notify the owner of the date, time and place of the hearing. The hearing date must be no more than 30 days after a request for a hearing has been filed. At the hearing the police officer's report shall be considered prima facie correct. In order to disprove the vehicle's eligibility for impoundment, the owner of record must prove that (1) at the time and date of the attempted stop as described in the police officer's report, the described vehicle was not operated within the city of Chicago; or (2) at the time and date of the attempted stop, the vehicle had been reported stolen; (3) the license information described in the report does not match the listed make of the described vehicle. If the owner of record prevails, the notice of intent to impound the owner's vehicle shall be withdrawn and the vehicle shall not be eligible for impoundment under this section.

(f) If a vehicle owner receives a notice pursuant to subsection (d) of this section and (1) fails to contest eligibility under subsection (e) of this section or (2) does not prevail in the contest of eligibility, the vehicle described in the notice shall be eligible for impoundment if found on the public way within 12 months following the conclusion of the contest, if a contest was requested, or following the last date to request a contest, if none was requested.

(g) The owner of a vehicle impounded under this section shall be subject to an administrative penalty of $1,000.00 plus the cost of towing and storage of the vehicle.

(Added. Coun. J. 3-15-00, p. 27700; Amend. 12-15-04, p. 3984)

§9-92-040 Removal of horse-drawn carriages.

Any time that a horse-drawn carriage licensed under this code must be removed from a public way under Section 9-92-010 or 9-92-030, custody and control of the horse drawing the carriage shall be given to the commission on animal care and control as soon as is practicable. In the event no animal control officer is available to handle the removal of the horse, members of the police department and employees of the department of streets and sanitation are authorized to remove the horse from the public way.

(Added. Coun. J. 7-12-90, p. 18634)

§9-92-050 Towing or removal service and fees.

The department of streets and sanitation shall provide towing vehicles for the purpose of carrying out the provisions of Sections 9-92-010 and 9-92-030. The department of streets and sanitation shall be entitled to the fees provided in Section 9-92-080 when providing such towing or removal service. Private towing operators authorized to remove abandoned vehicles pursuant to a contract with the department of streets and sanitation may be authorized as agents of the city to collect such fees.

(Added. Coun. J. 7-12-90, p. 18634)

§9-92-060 Recordkeeping.

(a) The superintendent of police or the commissioner of streets and sanitation shall safely keep any vehicle impounded pursuant to Section 9-92-030 until such vehicle shall have been repossessed by the owner or person legally entitled to possession thereof or otherwise disposed of as provided in the traffic code; provided, however, that abandoned vehicles may be impounded by private tow operators under contract with the department of streets and sanitation to remove abandoned vehicles pursuant to Section 2-100-090. Such vehicles may be removed to a city vehicle pound or a storage facility owned or leased by the private tow operator at the direction of the commissioner of streets and sanitation and shall be held or otherwise disposed of as provided in the traffic code.

(b) The superintendent of police or the commissioner of streets and sanitation shall cause to be kept an accurate record of each tow under Section 9-92-010 or 9-92-030, including the name of the police officer or other city employee from whom such vehicle was received, or, if applicable, the name of the employee of the private tow operator under contract with the department of streets and sanitation pursuant to Section 2-100-090, and the location to which the vehicle was towed, the date and time when received, the place where found, motor number, vehicle identification number, number of cylinders, year built, state license number, if any, city wheel tax license number, if any, equipment and general description of condition, the name and address of the person redeeming the vehicle, the date of redemption and the manner and date of disposal of the vehicle in case it shall not be redeemed, together with towing and storage charges. The record shall be in a form prescribed by the superintendent of police or the commissioner of streets and sanitation to keep reports of all such vehicles impounded pursuant to this chapter. The reports shall be kept in the office of the superintendent or the commissioner of streets and sanitation and shall be available for the inspection of any interested party at all reasonable hours of the day.
(Added. Coun. J. 7-12-90, p. 18634)

§9-92-070 Notice to owner of impounded vehicle.

(a) Whenever any motor vehicle has been impounded pursuant to the traffic code, the department of police or the department of streets and sanitation shall within 10 days thereafter ascertain, if possible, from the Secretary of State of Illinois the name of the owner and of any other person legally entitled to possession of such motor vehicle by reason of an existing conditional sale contract having a lien as chattel mortgagee, or any other reason, and cause to be sent to such owner and to such other person legally entitled to possession, if known, a notice of the impoundment including a full description of the vehicle. If the impounded vehicle is currently registered with the Secretary of State's office, notice shall be sent to the owner and any other person legally entitled to possession of the vehicle by certified mail, return receipt requested. If the impounded vehicle is not currently registered with the Secretary of State's office, such notice shall be sent to the most recent registered owner at the most recent registered address by first class mail. However, no such notice need be sent to the owner of record if the owner is personally served with the notice within 10 days after the vehicle is seized and impounded and the owner acknowledges receipt of the notice in writing.

(b) Whenever the department of police or the department of streets and sanitation is not able to ascertain the name of the owner of an impounded vehicle or for any reason is unable to give notice to the owner as provided in subsection (a), the department shall immediately send or cause to be sent a written report of such removal and impounding by mail to the Secretary of the State of Illinois. Such notice shall include a complete description of the vehicle, the date, time, and place from which removed, the reasons for such removal, and the address of the vehicle pound or authorized garage where the vehicle is stored.
(Added. Coun. J. 7-12-90, p. 18634; Amend. 2-4-92, p. 12820; 7-29-92, p. 20110; 12-4-02, p. 99026)

§9-92-080 Release procedure for impounded vehicles.

(a) (1) The owner or other person entitled to possession of a vehicle impounded pursuant to Section 9-92-030 may obtain immediate release of the vehicle by paying the full amount of the applicable towing and storage fees, as provided in subsection (b), plus all amounts due for outstanding final determinations of parking and/or compliance violations (if the vehicle is also subject to immobilization for unpaid final determinations of parking and/or compliance violations). Regardless of whether the owner or other person entitled to possession obtains immediate release of the vehicle through making full payments, such person may request a hearing be held within 24 hours, excluding Saturdays, Sundays and legal holidays. The hearing referred to in this subsection shall determine the validity of the impounding of the vehicle and any towing or storage fees imposed.

(2) In the event that the owner or other person entitled to possession of a vehicle impounded pursuant to Section 9-92-030 does not request a hearing as provided for in subsection (a)(1) of this section, such person may request a hearing to be held within 15 days of the request. Such request for hearing must be received by the city within 15 days of the provision of the notice set forth in Section 9-92-070. The hearing referred to in this subsection shall determine the validity of the impounding of the vehicle and any towing or storage fees imposed.

(b) The owner or other person entitled to possession of a vehicle lawfully impounded pursuant to Section 9-92-030 or Section 9-100-020 shall pay a fee of $150.00, or $250.00 if the vehicle has a gross weight of 8,000 pounds or more, to cover the cost of the towing and a fee of $10.00 per day for the first five days and $35.00 per day thereafter, or $60.00 per day for the first five days and $100.00 per day thereafter if the vehicle has a gross weight of 8,000 pounds or more, to cover the cost of storage, provided that no fees shall be assessed for any tow or storage with respect to a tow which has been determined to be erroneous.

(c) In addition to paying the applicable towing and storage fees provided in subsection (b) of this section, the owner or other person entitled to possession of a lawfully impounded vehicle shall also pay all fines and penalties remaining due on each final determination of parking violation liability issued to such person prior to the release of the impounded vehicle, plus all amounts due for outstanding final determinations of parking and/or compliance violations (if the vehicle is also subject to immobilization for unpaid final determinations of parking and/or compliance violations).

(d) A lienholder asserting its right to possession of an impounded vehicle pursuant to its conditional sales agreement may obtain immediate release of such vehicle by paying the applicable towing and storage fees provided in subsection (b) of this section and submitting a photocopy of the conditional sales agreement and title certificate, an affidavit stating that the purchaser is in default of the agreement and an indemnification certificate executed by an authorized agent of the lienholder. The requirements of subsection (c) of this section shall not apply to a lienholder asserting its right to possession of an impounded vehicle as provided herein.

(Added. Coun. J. 7-12-90, p. 18634; Amend. 11-17-93, p. 42192; 11-10-94, p. 59125; 12-12-01, p. 75777; 7-31-02, p. 90675)

§9-92-090 Evidence of identity and right of possession required.

No person shall be permitted to remove an impounded vehicle from the custody of the city or private tow operator who has contracted with the city to tow abandoned vehicles unless he shall furnish evidence of his identity and right of possession to the vehicle and sign a receipt for the vehicle.
(Added. Coun. J. 7-12-90, p. 18634)

§9-92-100 Disposal of unclaimed vehicles.

(a) Whenever an abandoned, lost, stolen, or other impounded motor vehicle remains unclaimed by the registered owner or other person entitled to possession for a period of 15 days after notice has been given pursuant to Section 9-92-070(a) or (b), the superintendent of police or the commissioner of streets and sanitation shall authorize the disposal or other disposition of such unclaimed vehicles as provided in this section; provided, however, that the registered owner may request from the department of streets and sanitation one extension of 15 days before a vehicle is sold or otherwise disposed of. The department of streets and sanitation shall honor such request and shall not sell or otherwise dispose of a vehicle during the 15-day extension period.

(b) Impounded motor vehicles which remain unclaimed after notice has been provided pursuant to Section 9-92-070 shall be disposed, pursuant to the provisions of the "Municipal Purchasing Act for cities of 500,000 or more population," to a person licensed as an automotive parts recycler, rebuilder or scrap processor under Chapter 5 of the Illinois Vehicle Code; provided, however, that such vehicles having a value that substantially exceeds its scrap value may be disposed of in accordance with subsections (c) or (d) of this section.

(c) Where the superintendent of police or commissioner of streets and sanitation determines that an unclaimed impounded vehicle has a value substantially in excess of the scrap value of such vehicle, he may cause it to be sold at a public auction to a person licensed as an automotive parts recycler, rebuilder or scrap processor. Notice of the time and place of the sale shall be posted in a conspicuous place for at least 10 days prior to the sale on the premises where the vehicle has been impounded. At least 10 days prior to the sale the superintendent or commissioner shall cause a notice of the time and place of the sale to be sent in the same manner as the notice sent pursuant to Section 9-92-070 to the registered owner, lienholder or other person entitled to possession of the vehicle. Such notice shall contain a complete description of the vehicle to be sold and the steps that must be taken by any legally entitled person to reclaim such vehicle.

In those instances where the notification specified in Section 9-92-070 has been returned by postal authorities due to the addressee having moved, or being unknown at the address obtained from the registration records of the state, the sending of a second notice shall not be required.

(d) The superintendent of police is authorized to reserve for the city's use such unclaimed impounded vehicles for which a notice has been sent pursuant to Section 9-92-070, as the various departments of the city may require. Any vehicle reserved for such purpose shall be added to the list of the respective department's fleet of vehicles.

(e) Disposal of a vehicle pursuant to this section shall not relieve the violator of liability for all costs, fines and penalties incurred in conjunction

with such vehicle; provided, however, that with respect to disposal of an abandoned vehicle, the amount of liability for towing and storage costs shall be reduced by any amounts realized in the disposal of the vehicle in accordance with Section 4-214(b) of the Illinois Vehicle Code.
(Added. Coun. J. 7-12-90, p. 18634; Amend. 5-22-91, p. 823; Amend. 10-7-98, p. 78566; 12-12-01, p. 75777; 12-15-04, p. 40508)

CHAPTER 9-96
RESERVED

(Repealed Coun. J. 12-12-2001, p. 75806, eff. 1-1-2002.)

CHAPTER 9-100
ADMINISTRATIVE ADJUDICATION OF PARKING OR COMPLIANCE VIOLATIONS

Sections:

9-100-010 Purpose—Scope—Adoption of rules and regulations.
9-100-020 Violation—Penalty.
9-100-030 Prima facie responsibility for violation and penalty—Parking violation issuance and removal.
9-100-040 Violation notices—Contents, distribution and recordkeeping.
9-100-050 Determination of liability.
9-100-060 Grounds for adjudication by mail or administrative hearing.
9-100-070 Adjudication by mail—Procedure.
9-100-080 Administrative hearings—Procedure.
9-100-090 Hearing—Determination of liability or of no liability—Petition.
9-100-100 Notice of final determination.
9-100-101 Installment payment plans.
9-100-110 City-owned vehicles.
9-100-111 Officers and employees of federal, state and county law enforcement agencies.
9-100-120 Immobilization program.
9-100-130 Driver's license suspension.
9-100-140 Lessor of vehicle not liable for violations—When.
9-100-150 Owner of vehicle not liable for violations when in custody of valet.

§9-100-010 Purpose—Scope—Adoption of rules and regulations.

(a) The purpose of this chapter is to provide for the administrative adjudication of violations of ordinances defining compliance violations and regulating vehicular standing and parking within the city, and to establish a fair and efficient system for the enforcement of such ordinances. The administrative adjudication system set forth in this chapter is established pursuant to Division 2.1 of the Illinois Municipal Code and Section 11-208.3 of the Illinois Vehicle Code.

(b) The director of revenue shall appoint a city traffic compliance administrator who is authorized to:

(i) Adopt, distribute, and process parking and compliance violation notices and additional notices, collect money paid as fines and penalties for violations of parking and compliance ordinances;

(ii) Establish procedures necessary for the prompt, fair and efficient operation of the administrative adjudication system; and

(iii) Adopt rules and regulations pertaining to: the hearing process, the selection and appointment of administrative law officers, the content of forms and procedures, and the daily operation of the administrative adjudication of parking and compliance violations program.

(c) The traffic compliance administrator may delegate to the department of administrative hearings his or her authority to appoint administrative law officers, to adopt rules and regulations pertaining to administrative hearing proceedings and to conduct administrative hearing proceedings, including the functions of the traffic compliance administrator set forth in Sections 9-100-070(a); 9-100-080(a), (b) and (g); 9-100-090(c); 9-100-130(c); and subsection (b)(iii) of this section.
(Prior code § 27.1-1; Added. Coun. J. 3-21-90, p. 13561; Amend. 7-12-90, p. 18634; 3-26-96, p. 19161, effective 1-1-97; 7-10-96, p. 24982; 11-12-97, p. 56813; 4-29-98, p. 66564)

§9-100-020 Violation—Penalty.

(a) The violation of any provision of the traffic code prohibiting or restricting vehicular standing or parking, or establishing a compliance violation, shall be a civil offense punishable by fine, and no criminal penalty, or civil sanction other than that prescribed in the traffic code, shall be imposed.

(b) The fines listed below shall be imposed for a violation of the following sections of the traffic code:

Section	Fine
9-12-060	$90.00
9-40-060	100.00
9-64-020(a)	25.00
9-64-020(b)	75.00
9-64-030	25.00
9-64-040(b)	50.00
9-64-050	200.00
9-64-060(a) and (b)	30.00
9-64-070	30.00
9-64-080	50.00
9-64-090	50.00
9-64-091	50.00
9-64-100(a)	100.00
9-64-100(b), (c) and (d)	75.00
9-64-100(e) and (h)	100.00
9-64-100(f) and (g)	25.00
9-64-110(a)	100.00
9-64-110(c), (d), and (e)	50.00
9-64-110(b), (f), (g) and (h)	75.00
9-64-120	25.00
9-64-130	150.00
9-64-140	90.00
9-64-150(a)	75.00
9-64-150(b)	50.00
9-64-160	50.00
9-64-170(a) — (c)	25.00
9-64-170(d)	125.00
9-64-180(a) — (c)	50.00
9-64-190(a)	30.00
9-64-190(b)	50.00
9-64-200(b)	25.00
9-64-210	50.00

9-68-040 .... 100.00
9-76-150 .... 25.00
9-80-080 .... 100.00
9-80-110(a) and (b) 50.00
9-80-120 .... 25.00
9-80-130 .... 25.00

(c) The fines listed below shall be imposed for a violation of the following sections of the traffic code:

9-40-080 .... $50.00
9-40-170 .... 25.00
9-40-220 .... 25.00
9-64-125 .... 120.00
9-76-010 .... 25.00
9-76-020 .... 25.00
9-76-030 .... 25.00
9-76-040 .... 25.00
9-76-050 .... 25.00
9-76-060 .... 25.00
9-76-070 .... 25.00
9-76-080 .... 25.00
9-76-090 .... 25.00
9-76-100 .... 25.00
9-76-110(a) 25.00
9-76-120 .... 25.00
9-76-130 .... 25.00
9-76-140(a) 100.00
9-76-140(b) 25.00
9-76-160 .... 50.00
9-76-170 .... 120.00
9-76-180 .... 25.00
9-76-190 .... 25.00
9-76-200 .... 25.00
9-76-210(a) and (b) 25.00
9-76-220(a) and (b) 25.00

(Prior code § 27.1-2; Added. Coun. J. 3-21-90, p. 13561; Amend. 7-12-90, p. 18634; 11-17-93, p. 42192; 11-1-95, p. 9068; 11-15-95, p. 11995; 3-26-96, p. 19161, effective 1-1-97; 2-7-97, p. 38959; 4-16-97, p. 42621; 11-19-97, p. 57861 11-17-99, p. 17487; 12-12-01, p. 75777; 7-29-03, p. 6166; 11-5-03, p. 10746; 11-19-03, p. 14216; 12-17-03, p. 14966; 5-26-04, p. 24880; 12-15-04, p. 39840)

§9-100-030 Prima facie responsibility for violation and penalty—Parking violation issuance and removal.

(a) Whenever any vehicle exhibits a compliance violation or is parked in violation of any provision of the traffic code prohibiting or restricting vehicular parking or standing, any person in whose name the vehicle is registered with the Secretary of State of Illinois or such other state's registry of motor vehicles shall be prima facie responsible for the violation and subject to the penalty therefor. The city and the ticketing agent shall accurately record the state registration number of the ticketed vehicle. A prima facie case shall not be established when (1) the ticketing agent has failed to specify the proper state registration number of the cited vehicle on the notice; (2) the city has failed to accurately record the specified state registration number; or (3) for the purposes of Section 9-64-125, the registered owner was not a resident of the city of Chicago on the day the violation was issued.

(b) Whenever any vehicle exhibits a compliance violation during operation or is parked in violation of any provision of the traffic code prohibiting or restricting vehicular parking or standing or regulating the condition of a parked or standing vehicle, any police officer, traffic control aide, other designated member of the police department, parking enforcement aide or other person designated by the city traffic compliance administrator observing such violation may issue a parking or compliance violation notice, as provided for in Section 9-100-040 and serve the notice on the owner of the vehicle by handing it to the operator of the vehicle, if he is present, or by affixing it to the vehicle in a conspicuous place. The issuer of the notice shall specify on the notice his identification number, the particular parking or compliance ordinance allegedly violated, the make and state registration number of the cited vehicle, and the place, date, time and nature of the alleged violation and shall certify the correctness of the specified information by signing his name as provided in Section 11-208.3 of the Illinois Vehicle Code, as amended.

(c) The city traffic compliance administrator shall withdraw a violation notice when said notice fails to establish a prima facie case as described in this section; provided, however, that a violation notice shall not be withdrawn if the administrator reasonably determines that (1) a state registration number was properly recorded by the city and its ticketing agent, and (2) any discrepancy between the vehicle make or model and the vehicle registration number as set forth in the violation notice is the result of the illegal exchange of registration plates. A final determination of liability that has been issued for a violation required to be withdrawn under this subsection (c) shall be vacated by the city. The city shall extinguish any lien which has been recorded for any debt due and owing as a result of the vacated determination and refund any fines and/or penalties paid pursuant to the vacated determination.

(d) It shall be unlawful for any person, other than the owner of the vehicle or his designee, to remove from a vehicle a parking or compliance violation notice affixed pursuant to this chapter.

(Prior code § 27.1-3; Added. Coun. J. 3-21-90, p. 13561; Amend. 7-12-90, p. 18634; 3-26-96, p. 19161, effective 1-1-97; 2-7-97, p. 38959; 7-30-97, p. 49902; 4-29-98, p. 66564)

§9-100-040 Violation notices—Contents, distribution and recordkeeping.

(a) Parking and compliance violation notices shall contain the information required under Section 9-100-030. In addition, the notices shall state the applicable fine as provided in Section 9-100-020, the monetary penalty which shall be automatically assessed for late payment, the vehicle immobilization and driver's license suspension (if applicable) may be imposed if fines and penalties are not paid in full, that payment of the indicated fine, and of any applicable penalty for late payment, shall operate as a final disposition of the violation, and information as to the availability of an administrative hearing in which the violation may be contested on its merits and the time and manner in which such hearing may be had.

(b) The city traffic compliance administrator shall distribute parking and compliance violation notices to parking enforcement aides, other persons authorized to issue parking and compliance violating notices, and the department of police for issuance pursuant to Section 9-100-030. The superintendent of police shall be responsible for the distribution of the notice forms within the department of police, shall maintain a record of each set of notices issued to individual members of the department and shall retain a receipt for every set so issued.

(c) The city traffic compliance administrator shall compile and maintain complete and accurate records relating to all parking violation notices issued pursuant to Section 9-100-030 and the dispositions thereof. In addition, the city traffic compliance administrator shall make certified reports to the Secretary of State pursuant to Section 6-306.5 of the Illinois Vehicle Code.

(Prior code § 27.1-4; Added. Coun. J. 3-21-90, p. 13561; Amend. 7-12-90, p. 18634; 3-26-96, p. 19161, effective 1-1-97)

§9-100-050 Determination of liability.

(a) A person on whom a parking or compliance violation notice has been served pursuant to Section 9-100-030 or Section 9-103-030 shall within seven days from the date of the notice: (1) pay the indicated fine; or, in the manner indicated on the notice, either (2) submit the materials set forth in Section 9-100-070 to obtain an adjudication by mail; or (3) request an administrative hearing as set forth in Section 9-100-080 to contest the charged violation. A response by mail shall be deemed timely if postmarked within seven days of the issuance of the notice of violation.

(b) If the respondent submits documentary evidence to obtain an adjudication by mail pursuant to Section 9-100-070, the city traffic compliance administrator shall send the respondent a copy of the administrative law officer's determination in accordance with subsection (f) herein.

(c) If the respondent requests an administrative hearing to contest the cited violation pursuant to Section 9-100-080, the city traffic compliance administrator shall notify the respondent in writing of the location and time available for a hearing in accordance with subsection (f) herein.

Where a respondent who has requested an administrative hearing either fails to pay the indicated fine prior to the hearing or appear at a hearing, a determination of parking or compliance violation liability, as the case may be, shall be entered in the amount of the fine indicated on the notice of violation. Failure to pay the fine within 21 days of issuance of a determination of liability will result in the imposition of a late payment penalty pursuant to subsection (e) herein. Upon the occurrence of a final determination of liability, any unpaid fine or penalty will constitute a debt due and owing the city. The city traffic compliance administrator will cause a notice of hearing providing this information to be sent to the respondent in accordance with subsection (f) herein.

(d) If no response is made in accordance with subsection (a) of this section, the city traffic compliance administrator shall cause a second notice of violation to be sent to the respondent in accordance with subsection (f) herein. The notice shall specify the date and location of the violation, the make and state registration number of the cited vehicle, the code provision violated, the applicable fine, and the time and manner in which the respondent may obtain an adjudication by mail or request a hearing to contest the violation. If the respondent requests an administrative hearing to contest the cited violation, the city traffic compliance administrator will cause a notice of hearing to be sent to the respondent as provided in subsection (c) herein.

If the respondent fails to pay the indicated fine, submit documentary evidence to obtain an adjudication by mail, or request a hearing to contest the charged violation within 14 days from the date of such notice, or prove compliance as provided in subsection (7) of Section 9-100-060, a determination of liability shall be entered in the amount of the fine indicated on the notice of violation. Failure to pay the fine within 21 days of issuance of the determination of liability will result in the imposition of a late payment penalty pursuant to subsection (e) herein. Upon the occurrence of a final determination of liability, any unpaid fine or penalty will constitute a debt due and owing the city. The second notice of violation shall provide the above information.

(e) Failure by any respondent to pay the fine for a parking or compliance violation within 21 days of the issuance of the determination of liability will automatically subject the respondent to a penalty for late payment. The penalty for late payment shall be an amount equal to the amount of the fine for the relevant parking or compliance violation.

(f) The city traffic compliance administrator shall serve the notice of hearing, the second notice of violation, the administrative law officer's determination, the notice of final determination of liability, the notice of impending vehicle immobilization and the notice of impending driver's license suspension, where applicable, by first class mail, postage prepaid, to the address of the registered owner of the city vehicle as recorded with the Secretary of State of Illinois. If the vehicle is registered in a state other than Illinois, the city traffic compliance administrator shall send the appropriate notice to the address of the registered owner as recorded in such other state's registry of motor vehicles.
(Prior code § 27.1-5; Added. Coun. J. 3-21-90, p. 13561; Amend. 7-12-90, p. 18634; 3-26-96, p. 19161, effective 1-1-97; 2-7-97, p. 38959; 4-29-98, p. 66564; 7-9-03, p. 4349; 7-29-03, p. 6166)

§9-100-060 Grounds for adjudication by mail or administrative hearing.

A person charged with a parking or compliance violation may contest the charge through an adjudication by mail or at an administrative hearing limited to one or more of the following grounds with appropriate evidence to support:

(1) That the respondent was not the owner or lessee of the cited vehicle at the time of the violation;

(2) That the cited vehicle or its state registration plates were stolen at the time the violation occurred;

(3) That the relevant signs prohibiting or restricting parking were missing or obscured;

(4) That the relevant parking meter was inoperable or malfunctioned through no fault of the respondent;

(5) That the facts alleged in the parking or compliance violation notice are inconsistent or do not support a finding that the specified regulation was violated;

(6) That the illegal condition described in the compliance violation notice did not exist at the time the notice was issued;

(7) That the compliance violation has been corrected prior to adjudication of the charge; provided, however, that this defense shall not be applicable to compliance violations involving display of the city wheel tax emblem under Section 9-64-125; to compliance violations involving motor vehicle exhaust systems under subsection (a)(2) of Section 9-76-140; to compliance violations involving registration plates under subsection (a) of Section 9-76-160; to compliance violations involving display of temporary registration or temporary permits under subsection (f) of Section 9-76-160; or to compliance violations relating to glass coverings or coating under Section 9-76-220.

(Prior code § 27.1-6; Added. Coun. J. 3-21-90, p. 13561; Amend. 7-12-90, p. 18634; 3-26-96, p. 19161, effective 1-1-97; 2-7-97, p. 38959; 11-19-97, p. 57861)

§9-100-070 Adjudication by mail—Procedure.

(a) Administrative hearings to review materials submitted for the adjudication by mail of parking and compliance violations cited pursuant to Section 9-100-030 shall be held by an administrative law officer appointed by the city traffic compliance administrator and conducted in accordance with this section.

(b) The respondent may contest a parking or compliance violation based on one or more of the grounds provided in Section 9-100-060, by mailing to the department of revenue the following materials and information: the notice of violation, the full name, address and telephone number(s) of the respondent; the make, model and year of the vehicle; any documentary evidence that rebuts the charge; and a written statement signed by the respondent setting forth facts relevant to establishing a defense to the charge. A photocopy of any documentary evidence submitted by any party shall be accepted as the equivalent of the original document.

(c) No violation may be established except upon proof by a preponderance of the evidence; provided, however, that a parking or compliance violation notice, or a copy thereof, issued in accordance with Section 9-100-030 shall be prima facie evidence of the correctness of the facts specified therein.

(d) Upon review of the materials submitted in accordance with subsection (b) herein, the administrative law officer shall enter a determination of no liability or of liability in the amount of the fine for the relevant violation as provided in Section 9-100-020. Upon issuance, such determination shall constitute a final determination for purposes of judicial review under the Administrative Review Law of Illinois.

(Prior code § 27.1-7; Added. Coun. J. 3-21-90, p. 13561; Amend. 7-12-90, p. 18634; 3-26-96, p. 19161, effective 1-1-97; 4-29-98, p. 66564)

§9-100-080 Administrative hearings—Procedure.

(a) Administrative hearings for the adjudication of parking and compliance violations issued pursuant to Section 9-100-030 shall be held before an administrative law officer appointed by the city traffic compliance administrator and conducted in accordance with this section.

(b) The respondent may appear pro se or, at his own expense, by an attorney. An attorney who appears on behalf of any person shall file with the administrative law officer a written appearance on a form provided by the city traffic compliance administrator for such purpose.

(c) The formal and technical rules of evidence shall not apply in the conduct of the hearing.

(d) All testimony shall be given under oath or affirmation, which shall be administered by the administrative law officer. The administrative law officer may issue subpoenas to secure the attendance and testimony of witnesses and the production of relevant documents; provided, however, that a respondent who appears by an attorney shall not be compelled to attend the hearing and may submit his testimony, if any, by affidavit. In addition, witnesses who have not been subpoenaed to attend the hearing may submit their testimony, if any, by affidavit.

(e) No violation may be established except upon proof by a preponderance of the evidence; provided, however, that a parking or compliance violation notice, or a copy thereof, issued and signed in accordance with Section 9-100-030 shall be prima facie evidence of the correctness of the facts specified therein.

(f) The administrative law officer may, on a showing of good cause, grant one continuance to a date certain.

(g) The city traffic compliance administrator shall cause a record to be made of each hearing, and recording devices may be used for such purpose.

(Prior code § 27.1-8; Added. Coun. J. 3-21-90, p. 13561; Amend. 7-12-90, p. 18634; 3-26-96, p. 19161, effective 1-1-97; 4-29-98, p. 66564)

§9-100-090 Hearing—Determination of liability or of no liability—Petition.

(a) Upon conclusion of a hearing under Section 9-100-080, the administrative law officer shall issue a determination of no liability or of liability in the amount of the fine for the relevant violation as provided in Section 9-100-020. Upon issuance, such determination shall constitute a final determination for purposes of judicial review under the Administrative Review Law of Illinois.

(b) If a person fails to respond to the violation notice and the second notice of violation, a determination of liability shall be entered against the respondent pursuant to Section 9-100-050(d) and shall be served upon the respondent in accordance with Section 9-100-050(f). Such determination shall become final for purposes of judicial review under the Administrative Review Law of Illinois upon the denial of, or the expiration of the time in which to file, a timely petition to set aside the determination as provided in subsection (c) of this section.

(c) Within 21 days from the issuance of a determination of liability pursuant to subsection (b) herein, the person against whom the determination was entered may petition the city traffic compliance administrator by appearing in person, at the location specified in the determination, to set aside the determination; provided, however, the grounds for the petition shall be limited to: (1) the person not having been the owner or lessee of the cited vehicle on the date the parking violation notice was first issued; (2) the person having already paid the fine or penalty for the parking violation in question; or (3) excusable failure, based upon criteria established by the city traffic compliance administrator, to appear at or request a new date for a hearing. The peti-

tioner shall appear with appropriate evidence, pursuant to Section 9-100-060, so that if the petition is granted, he is prepared to proceed immediately with a hearing on the merits.
(Prior code § 27.1-9; Added. Coun. J. 3-21-90, p. 13561; Amend. 7-12-90, p. 18634; 3-26-96, p. 19161, effective 1-1-97; 4-29-98, p. 66564)

§9-100-100 Notice of final determination.

(a) If any fine or penalty is owing and unpaid after a determination of liability under this chapter has become final and the respondent has exhausted or failed to exhaust judicial procedures for review, the city traffic compliance administrator shall cause a notice of final determination of liability to be sent to the respondent in accordance with Section 9-100-050(f).

(b) Any fine and penalty, if applicable, remaining unpaid after the notice of final determination of liability is sent shall constitute a debt due and owing the city which may be enforced in the manner set forth in Section 2-14-103 of this code. Failure of the respondent to pay such fine or penalty within 14 days of the date of the notice may result in the city's filing of a petition in, if applicable: (1) the immobilization of the person's vehicle for failure to pay fines or penalties for three or more parking or compliance violations and (2) the suspension of the person's driver's license for failure to pay fines or penalties for 10 or more parking violations.

(c) The city shall withdraw a violation notice, following reasonable collection efforts, when such notice was issued to a scale registered owner who is deceased at the time collection efforts are undertaken.
(Prior code § 27.1-10; Added. Coun. J. 3-21-90, p. 13561; Amend. 7-12-90, p. 18634; 3-26-96, p. 19161, effective 1-1-97; 7-30-97, p. 49902; 4-29-98, p. 66564; 7-31-02, p. 90675)

§9-100-101 Installment payment plans.

(a) The traffic compliance administrator may establish a program allowing the payment of parking and compliance fines and penalties in installments under the following conditions:

(1) The minimum amount of an eligible vehicle owner's combined liability for parking and compliance fines and penalties must exceed $500.00 upon the commencement of that vehicle owner's installment plan; provided, however, that the minimum amount shall not apply to a vehicle owner who is a participant in a qualifying assistance program as defined in subsection (a)(3)(A) of this section.

(2) An installment plan may not have a scheduled duration of more than 12 months, and shall require one payment due per month on a day specified in the executed plan.

(3) The minimum initial payment under any installment plan shall be:

(A) For a vehicle owner who is a participant in a qualifying assistance program, the lesser of $250.00 or 25 percent of the vehicle owner's combined liability for parking and compliance fines and penalties, plus accrued penalties and fees under Section 9-100-120(h) and for immobilization, impoundment, towing and storage to date. "Qualifying assistance program," for purposes of this section, means any of the following: the Illinois Low-Income Home Energy Assistance Program (L.I.H.E.A.P.); the Housing Subsidy Program For Renters, administered by the United States Department of Housing and Urban Development under the Federal Housing Act of 1937, as amended (Section 8 Program); the Supplemental Security Income Program administered by the United States Social Security Administration (S.S.I.); the Medicaid Program administered by the Illinois Department of Public Aid; the Nutrition Assistance Program administered by the United States Department of Agriculture, Food and Nutrition Service (food stamps); and any federal or state unemployment compensation system, including, but not limited to, the system of unemployment compensation established under the Illinois Unemployment Insurance Act, as amended.

(B) For all other vehicle owners prior to vehicle immobilization or impoundment, the greater of $500.00 or 25 percent of the vehicle owner's combined liability for parking and compliance fines and penalties, plus accrued penalties and fees under Section 9-100-120(h) and for immobilization, impoundment, towing and storage to date.

(C) For all other vehicle owners after vehicle immobilization or impoundment, the greater of $750.00 or 50 percent of the vehicle owner's combined liability for parking and compliance fines and penalties, plus accrued penalties and fees under Section 9-100-120(h) and for immobilization, impoundment, towing and storage to date.

(4) Required installment payments after the initial payment shall be substantially equal, unless the traffic compliance administrator determines, based on a review of the vehicle owner's finances, that installments in different amounts will be more effective in paying off the total indebtedness.

(5) If the vehicle owner fails to make all required payments in a timely manner, the vehicle owner's motor vehicle shall be subject to immobilization or impoundment and the vehicle owner shall be liable for the outstanding balance plus an additional penalty of $100.00.

(6) Every installment plan shall be in a form prescribed by the traffic compliance administrator, and shall state the total indebtedness, the amount of the initial installment, the amount of each subsequent installment and the date each is due, the penalty for delinquency under the installment plan, and such other provisions as the traffic compliance administrator may determine. The installment plan shall also require the vehicle owner to pay every parking violation fine and every compliance fine that becomes final during the term of the installment plan. The initial installment shall be paid when the plan is executed. Upon execution of the agreement and payment of the initial installment, and as long as the vehicle owner is in compliance with the installment plan, the vehicle owner's vehicles shall not be subject to immobilization and impoundment for failure to pay the parking and compliance fines and penalties described in the installment.

(b) The following vehicle owners are not eligible for an installment plan under subsection (a) of this section:

(1) An owner whose vehicle is impounded by the city under any other chapter of this code;

(2) An owner who has negotiated an installment plan and has not performed every act required by him under the plan.

(c) No new installment plan may be negotiated or executed after January 1, 2006. Installment plans in existence on that date shall remain in effect until completely performed or until terminated for failure of the vehicle owner to meet all requirements.

(Added. Coun. J. 1-14-04, p. 16857; Amend. 12-15-04, p. 40508)

§9-100-110 City-owned vehicles.

(1) Officers and employees of the city of Chicago shall be held personally liable for parking violation notices served either upon city vehicles assigned to their possession or use or upon his or her personally owned automobile authorized to be used in the performance of his or her official duties unless:

(a) The officer or employee certifies that the vehicle was in use for the performance of official city business during an emergency or during an official investigation at the time of the alleged violation;

(b) The head of the respective city department, agency or office concludes that the statements contained in the certificate are accurate, and recommends to the budget director that the liability for the alleged violation be released; and

(c) The budget director approves the release of such officer or employee from personal liability for the alleged violation.

If the budget director approves the release of personal liability for the alleged violation, the parking violation notice shall be withdrawn. The budget director shall submit quarterly reports to the city council, detailing by department, agency or office, the number and nature of approved releases from personal liability for parking violation notices served upon city vehicles and privately owned vehicles authorized to be used in the performance of official city business.

To expedite enforcement of this section, where the registered owner or lessee of a vehicle served with a violation notice is the city of Chicago, the city traffic compliance administrator shall notify the department, agency or office to which the vehicle is assigned.

(2) It shall not be a defense to a compliance violation involving the personal vehicle of an officer or employee of the city of Chicago that the officer or employee was using the vehicle for official government business at the time of the alleged violation. A compliance violation issued pursuant to Section 9-64-125, 9-76-160 or 9-76-220 involving a city-owned vehicle may be withdrawn pursuant to this section, if:

(a) The officer or employee possessing or using the vehicle at the time of the alleged violation certifies that the vehicle was in use for the performance of official city business during an emergency or during an official investigation at the time of the alleged violation;

(b) The head of the respective city department, agency or office concludes that the statements contained in the certificate are accurate, and recommends to the budget director that the liability for the alleged violation be released; and

(c) The budget director approves the release of liability for the alleged violation.

If the budget director approves the release of liability for the alleged violation, the compliance violation notice shall be withdrawn. The budget director shall submit quarterly reports to the city council, detailing by department, agency or office, the number and nature of approved releases from liability

for compliance violation notices served upon city vehicles used in the performance of official city business.
(Prior code § 27.1-11; Added. Coun. J. 3-21-90, p. 13561; Amend. 7-12-90, p. 18634; 11-28-90, p. 26194; 3-26-96, p. 19161, effective 1-1-97; 12-15-99, p. 21529)

§9-100-111 Officers and employees of federal, state and county law enforcement agencies.

(1) Officers and employees of law enforcement agencies of federal, state and county government may request a release of liability for the alleged parking violation subject to the following conditions:

(a) The officer or employee certifies that the vehicle was in use for the performance of official government business during an emergency or during an official investigation at the time of the alleged violation;

(b) The head of the respective government agency or a designee chosen by such person concludes that the statements contained in the certificate are accurate and submits a written request to the budget director that the liability for the alleged violation be released; and

(c) The budget director approves the release of liability for the alleged parking violation.

If the budget director approves the release of liability for the alleged violation, the parking violation notice shall be withdrawn. The budget director shall submit quarterly reports to the city council, detailing by the respective government agency the number and nature of approved releases of liability for parking violation notices issued to officers and employees of law enforcement agencies of federal, state or county government.

It shall not be a defense to a compliance violation involving the personal vehicle of an officer or employee of any unit of government that the officer or employee was using the vehicle for official government business at the time of the alleged violation.

(2) A compliance violation issued pursuant to Section 9-64-125, 9-76-160 or 9-76-220 involving a vehicle owned by a law enforcement agency of federal, state or county government may be withdrawn pursuant to this section, if:

(a) The officer or employee possessing or using the vehicle at the time of the alleged violation certifies that the vehicle was in use for the performance of official government business during an emergency or during an official investigation at the time of the alleged violation;

(b) The head of the respective government agency or a designee chosen by such person concludes that the statements contained in the certificate are accurate and submits a written request to the budget director that the liability for the alleged violation be released; and

(c) The budget director approves the release of liability for the alleged violation.

If the budget director approves the release of liability for the alleged violation, the compliance violation notice shall be withdrawn. The budget director shall submit quarterly reports to the city council, detailing by government agency, the number and nature of approved releases from liability for compliance violation notices served upon vehicles owned by federal, state or county government law enforcement agencies.
(Added. Coun. J. 11-28-90, p. 26194; Amend. 3-26-96, p. 19161, effective 1-1-97; 12-15-99, p. 21529)

§9-100-120 Immobilization program.

(a) The city traffic compliance administrator is hereby authorized to direct and supervise a program of vehicle immobilization for the purpose of enforcing the parking and compliance ordinances of the traffic code. The program of vehicle immobilization shall provide for immobilizing any eligible vehicle located on the public way or any city-owned property by placement of a restraint in such a manner as to prevent its operation or if the eligible vehicle is parked or left in violation of any provision of the traffic code for which such vehicle is subject to an immediate tow pursuant to Section 9-92-030, or in any place where it constitutes an obstruction or hazard, or where it impedes city workers during such operations as snow removal, the city traffic compliance administrator may cause the eligible vehicle to be towed to a city vehicle pound or relocated to a legal parking place and there restrained.

(b) When the registered owner of a vehicle has accumulated three or more final determinations of liability for parking or compliance violations, including a violation of Section 9-103-020, in any combination, for which the fines and penalties, if applicable, have not been paid in full, the city traffic compliance administrator shall cause a notice of impending vehicle immobilization to be sent, in accordance with Section 9-100-050(f). The notice of impending vehicle immobilization shall state the name and address of the registered owner, the state registration number of the vehicle or vehicles registered to such owner, and the serial numbers of parking and/or compliance violation notices which have resulted in final determination of liability for which the fines or penalties remain unpaid. Failure to pay the fines and penalties owed within 21 days from the date of the notice will result in the inclusion of the state registration number of the vehicle or vehicles of such owner on an immobilization list. A person may challenge the validity of the notice of impending vehicle immobilization by requesting a hearing and appearing in person to submit evidence which would conclusively disprove liability within 21 days of the date of the notice. Documentary evidence which would conclusively disprove liability shall be based on the following grounds:

(1) That all fines and penalties for the violations cited in the notice have been paid in full; or

(2) That the registered owner has not accumulated three or more final determinations of parking or compliance violation liability which were unpaid at the time the notice of impending vehicle immobilization was issued.

(3) In the case of a violation of Section 9-103-020, that the registered owner has not been issued a final determination of liability under Section 9-103-060.

(c) Upon immobilization of an eligible vehicle, a notice shall be affixed to the vehicle in a conspicuous place. Such notice shall: (i) warn that the vehicle is immobilized and that any attempt to remove the vehicle may result in its damage; (ii) state that the unauthorized removal of or damage to the immobilizing restraint is a violation of Sections 16-1 and 21-1 of the Illinois Criminal Code; (iii) provide information specifying how release of the immobilizing restraint may be had; (iv) state how the registered owner may obtain an immobilization hearing; (v) state that if the restraint has not been released within 24 hours of its placement, the restraint shall be released and the vehicle towed and impounded; and (vi) provide information specifying how the registered owner may request an additional 15 days to retrieve his or her vehicle if impounded.

(d) The owner of an immobilized vehicle or other authorized person may secure the release of the vehicle by paying the immobilization, towing and storage fees provided in subsection (g) herein, and all amounts, including any fines and penalties remaining due on each final determination for liability issued to such person.

(e) The owner of an immobilized vehicle shall have the right to a hearing to determine whether the immobilization or any subsequent towing was erroneous, if the owner files a written request for a hearing with the city traffic compliance administrator within 21 days after immobilization or within 21 days of the date of the notice sent pursuant to subsection (f) herein, whichever is later. Hearings requested pursuant to this subsection shall be conducted by an administrative law officer upon receipt of a written request for a hearing. The determination of the administrative law officer regarding the validity of the immobilization shall become final for the purpose of judicial review under the Administrative Review Law of Illinois upon issuance.

(f) Within 10 days after a vehicle has been impounded, a notice of impoundment shall be sent by certified mail to the address of the registered owner as listed with the Secretary of State, and to any lien holder of record. The notice shall state: (i) that the owner has the right to request a post-mobilization and post-towing hearing as provided in subsection (e) herein; and (ii) that if the vehicle is not claimed within 21 days from the date of notice, the vehicle may be sold or otherwise disposed of in the manner prescribed by Section 4-208 of the Illinois Vehicle Code; provided, however, that the registered owner may request from the department of streets and sanitation one extension of 15 days before a vehicle is sold or otherwise disposed of. The department of streets and sanitation shall honor such a request and shall not sell or otherwise dispose of a vehicle during the 15-day extension period.

(g) The fee for immobilization shall be $400.00 for a truck tractor, semi-trailer or trailer, and $60.00 for any other type of vehicle, and the fee for towing subsequent to immobilization shall be as set forth in Section 9-92-080(b), provided that no fees shall be assessed for any immobilization or tow which has been determined to be erroneous.

(h) It shall be unlawful to disable or damage any vehicle immobilization device, or to relocate or tow any vehicle restrained by an immobilization device without the approval of the city traffic compliance administrator. The registered owner of the immobilized vehicle and any person who relocates an immobilized vehicle or disables or damages an immobilization device in vio-

lation of this subsection shall each be subject to a penalty of $1,000.00 for such violation for a truck tractor, semi-trailer or trailer, and $750.00 for such violation for any other type of vehicle. As to the registered owner, the offenses described in this subsection (h) shall be strict liability offenses.
(Prior code § 27.1-12; Added. Coun. J. 3-21-90, p. 13561; Amend. 7-12-90, p. 18634; Corrected. 12-15-93, p. 44286; Amend. 11-10-94, p. 59125; 3-26-96, p. 19161, effective 1-1-97; 4-29-98, p. 66564; 12-12-01, p. 75777; 7-31-02, p. 90675; 12-4-02, p. 99026; 7-9-03, p. 4349; 7-29-03, p. 6166; 12-15-04, p. 40508)

§9-100-130 Driver's license suspension.

(a) When a person has failed to pay any fine or penalty due and owing pursuant to this chapter on 10 or more parking violations, the city traffic compliance administrator shall cause a notice of impending driver's license suspension to be sent, in accordance with Section 9-100-050(f). The notice shall state that failure to pay the amount owing within 45 days of the date of the notice will result in the city's notifying the Secretary of State that the person is eligible for initiation of suspension proceedings pursuant to Section 6-306.5 of the Illinois Vehicle Code.

(b) If a person sent a notice pursuant to subsection (a) fails to pay the amount owing within the time stated on the notice, the city traffic compliance administrator may file with the Secretary of State a certified report, in accordance with Section 6-306.5(c) of the Illinois Vehicle Code, that the person is eligible for initiation of suspension proceedings. The city traffic compliance administrator shall assess a $20.00 filing fee against the person named in the certified report to reimburse the city for the expense of preparing and filing the certified report with the Secretary of State.

(c) A person named in a certified report filed pursuant to subsection (b) may, within 21 days of the date of the notice sent by the Secretary of State pursuant to Section 6-306.5(b) of the Illinois Vehicle Code, file with the city traffic compliance administrator a written statement and supporting documentation to challenge the report; provided, however, the grounds for such challenge shall be limited to (1) the person not having been the owner or lessee of the vehicle or vehicles receiving 10 or more parking violations notices on the date or dates such notices were issued or (2) the person having already paid the fine and penalty for the 10 or more violations indicated on the report. The city traffic compliance administrator shall send notice of the decision on the challenge of the report after receipt thereof.

(d) If a person named in a certified report has paid the previously reported fine or penalty or if the report is determined by the city traffic compliance administrator to be in error, the city traffic compliance administrator shall notify the Secretary of State in accordance with Section 6-306.5(d) of the Illinois Vehicle Code. A certified copy of such notification shall be given, upon request and at no charge, to the person named therein.
(Prior code § 27.1-13; Added. Coun. J. 3-21-90, p. 13561; Amend. 7-12-90, p. 18634; 3-26-96, p. 19161, effective 1-1-97)

§9-100-140 Lessor of vehicle not liable for violations—When.

(a) In accordance with Section 11-1306 of the Illinois Vehicle Code, no person who is the lessor of a vehicle pursuant to a written lease agreement shall be liable for a violation of any standing or parking regulation of this chapter involving such vehicle during the period of the lease if upon receipt of a notice of violation sent within 120 days of the violation he shall, within 60 days thereafter, provide to the city traffic compliance administrator the name and address of the lessee.

(b) Upon receipt of a lessor's notification of the name and address of his lessee, provided pursuant to Sections 11-1305 or 11-1306 of the Illinois Vehicle Code, the city traffic compliance administrator shall cause a notice of violation to be sent to the lessee as provided for in Section 9-100-050(d).

(Prior code § 27.1-14; Added. Coun. J. 3-21-90, p. 13561; Amend. 7-12-90, p. 18634; 4-29-98, p. 66564)

§9-100-150 Owner of vehicle not liable for violations when in custody of valet.

(a) In accordance with Section 4-232-080(b) of this code, no person who is the owner of a vehicle shall be liable for a violation of any parking or compliance regulation of this chapter involving such vehicle during the period that such vehicle was in the custody of a valet parking service, if upon receipt of a notice of violation sent within 120 days of the violation he shall, within 60 days thereafter, provide to the city traffic compliance administrator the valet parking receipt required by Section 4-232-080(d) of this code or a clearly legible copy thereof.

(b) Upon receipt of the valet parking receipt or copy and upon being satisfied that it is genuine and not altered and that the violation took place while the vehicle was in the custody of the valet parking service, as shown by the times indicated on the receipt, the city traffic compliance administrator shall cause a notice of violation to be sent to the valet parking service as provided for in Section 9-100-050(d).

(Added. Coun. J. 10-28-97, p. 54834)

CHAPTER 9-102
AUTOMATED RED LIGHT CAMERA PROGRAM

Sections:

9-102-010 Purpose—Establishment of automated red light camera program.
9-102-020 Red light violation.
9-102-030 Citation notice.
9-102-040 Grounds for adjudication by mail or administrative hearing.
9-102-050 Determination of liability.
9-102-060 Notice of final determination.
9-102-070 Supplementary enforcement.

§9-102-010 Purpose—Establishment of automated red light camera program.

(a) The purpose of this chapter is to provide for the establishment of an automated red light violation enforcement which shall be administered by the department of transportation and the department of revenue and enforced through a system of administrative adjudication within the department of administrative hearings.

(b) The system shall utilize a traffic control signal monitoring device which records, through photographic means, the vehicle and the vehicle registration plate of a vehicle operated in violation of Section 9-8-020(c) and Section 9-16-030(c). The photographic record shall also display the time, date and location of the violation.

(c) A program shall be established which utilizes an automatic red light enforcement system at various vehicle traffic intersections identified by the department of transportation with the advice of the police department. The intersections chosen for the program shall be located throughout the city.

(d) The department of transportation, the police department and the department of revenue shall adopt rules and regulations as may be necessary for the proper enforcement and administration of this chapter.

(Added. Coun. J. 7-9-03, p. 4349)

§9-102-020 Red light violation.

(a) The registered owner of record of a vehicle is liable for a violation of this section and a fine of $90.00 when the vehicle is used in violation of Section 9-8-020(c) or Section 9-16-030(c) and that violation is recorded by a traffic control signal monitoring device. A photographic recording of a violation obtained by a traffic control signal monitoring device shall be a prima facie evidence of a violation of this chapter. It shall be a defense to a violation of this section that:

(1) The operator of the vehicle was issued a uniform traffic citation for a violation of Section 9-8-020(c) or Section 9-16-030(c); or

(2) The violation occurred at any time during which the vehicle or its state registration plates were reported to a law enforcement agency as having been stolen and the vehicle or its plates had not been recovered by the owner at the time of the alleged violation; or

(3) The vehicle was leased to another, and, within 60 days after the citation was mailed to the owner, the owner submitted to the department of revenue the correct name and address of the lessee of the vehicle identified in the citation at the time of the violation, together with a copy of the lease agreement and any additional information as may be required by the department. Where the lessor complies with the provisions of this section, the lessee of the vehicle at the time of the violation shall be deemed to be the owner of the vehicle for purposes of this chapter. The department of revenue, within 30 days of being notified by the lessor of the name and address of the lessee, shall mail the lessee a citation which contains the information required under Section 9-102-030. For the purposes of this chapter, the term "leased vehicle" shall be defined as a vehicle in which a motor vehicle dealership or manufacturer has, pursuant to a written document, vested exclusive possession, use, control and responsibility of the vehicle to the lessee during the periods the vehicle is operated by or for the lessee.

(b) The provisions of this section does not apply to any authorized emergency vehicle or any vehicle lawfully participating in a funeral procession.

(c) Nothing in this section shall be construed to limit the liability of an operator of a vehicle for any violation of Section 9-8-020(c) or Section 9-16-030(c).
(Added. Coun. J. 7-9-03, p. 4349)

§9-102-030 Citation notice.

For each violation of Section 9-8-020(c) or Section 9-16-030(c) recorded by a traffic control signal monitoring device, the department of revenue shall mail a citation, within 30 days after receiving information about the registered owner of the vehicle from the Secretary of State, to the registered owner of record of the vehicle used in the commission of the violation. The citation shall include the name and address of the registered owner of the vehicle; the vehicle make, if available and readily discernable, and registration number; the offense charged; the time, date and location of the alleged violation; the applicable fine and monetary penalty which shall be automatically assessed for late payment; information as to the availability of an administrative hearing in which the citation may be contested on its merits and the time and manner in which such hearing may be had; and that the basis of the citation is a photographic record obtained by a traffic control signal monitoring device.
(Added. Coun. J. 7-9-03, p. 4349)

§9-102-040 Grounds for adjudication by mail or administrative hearing.

A person charged with violation Section 9-8-020(c) or Section 9-16-030(c) recorded by a traffic control signal monitoring device may contest the charge through an adjudication by mail or at an administrative hearing limited to one or more of the following grounds with appropriate evidence to support:

(1) That the operator of the vehicle was issued a uniform traffic citation for a violation of Section 9-8-020(c) or Section 9-16-030(c); or

(2) That the violation occurred at any time during which the vehicle or its state registration plates were reported to a law enforcement agency as having been stolen and the vehicle or its plates had not been recovered by the owner at the time of the alleged violation; or

(3) That the vehicle was leased to another, and within 60 days after the citation was mailed to the owner, the owner submitted to the department of revenue the correct name and address of the lessee of the vehicle identified in the citation at the time of the violation, together with a copy of the lease agreement and any additional information as may be required by the department; or

(4) That the vehicle was an authorized emergency vehicle or was a vehicle lawfully participating in a funeral procession; or

(5) That the facts alleged in the violation notice are inconsistent or do not support a finding that Section 9-8-020(c) was violated; or

(6) That the respondent was not the registered owner or lessee of the cited vehicle at the time of the violation.
(Added. Coun. J. 7-9-03, p. 4349)

§9-102-050 Determination of liability.

The determination of liability for a citation issued under this chapter shall be made in accordance with Sections 9-100-050, and 9-100-070 through 9-100-090.
(Added. Coun. J. 7-9-03, p. 4349)

§9-102-060 Notice of final determination.

(a) If any fine or penalty is owing and unpaid after a determination of liability under this chapter has become final and the respondent has exhausted or failed to exhaust judicial procedures for review, the department of revenue shall cause a notice of final determination of liability to be sent to the respondent in accordance with Section 9-100-050(f).

(b) Any fine and penalty, if applicable, remaining unpaid after the notice of final determination of liability is sent shall constitute a debt due and owing the city which may be enforced in the manner set forth in Section 2-14-103 of this code. Failure of the respondent to pay such fine or penalty within 21 days of the date of the notice may result in the immobilization of the person's vehicle pursuant to the procedure described in Section 9-100-120.

(c) The city shall withdraw a violation notice, following reasonable collection efforts, when the notice was issued to a registered owner who is deceased at the time collection efforts are undertaken.

(Added. Coun. J. 7-9-03, p. 4349)

§9-102-070 Supplementary enforcement.

The liability created by Section 9-102-020 shall be imposed in addition to any liability otherwise provided for by any ordinance or statute governing the movement of traffic and the program authorized by Section 9-102-010 shall supplement enforcement of traffic regulations provided by Chapter 9-8 of the Municipal Code and the Illinois Motor Vehicle Code and shall not replace or substitute for enforcement of these or any other law.

(Added. Coun. J. 7-9-03, p. 4349)

CHAPTER 9-103
AUTOMATED BUS LANE AND BUS STOP CAMERA ENFORCEMENT PROGRAM

Sections:

9-103-010 Purpose—Establishment of pilot automated bus lane and bus stop camera enforcement program.
9-103-020 Bus stop and bus lane violation.
9-103-030 Citation notice.
9-103-040 Grounds for adjudication by mail or administrative hearing.
9-103-050 Determination of liability.
9-103-060 Notice of final determination.
9-103-070 Supplementary enforcement.

§9-103-010 Purpose—Establishment of pilot automated bus lane and bus stop camera enforcement program.

(a) The purpose of this chapter is to provide for the establishment of a pilot automated bus lane and bus stop camera enforcement system which shall be administered by the Chicago Transit Authority and the department of revenue and enforced through a system of administrative adjudication within the department of administrative hearings.

(b) The system shall utilize an automated camera monitoring device which records, through photographic means, the vehicle and the vehicle registration plate of a vehicle operated in violation of Section 9-12-060(b) and Section 9-64-140(b). The photographic record shall also display the time, date and location of the violation.

(c) A pilot program shall be established which utilizes an automated camera enforcement system mounted on buses and routes identified by the Chicago Transit Authority.

(d) The Chicago Transit Authority, the police department and the department of revenue shall adopt rules and regulations as may be necessary for the proper enforcement and administration of this chapter.

(Added. Coun. J. 7-29-03, p. 6166)

§9-103-020 Bus stop and bus lane violation.

(a) The registered owner of record of a vehicle is liable for a violation of this section and a fine of $90.00 when the vehicle is used in violation of Section 9-12-060(b) or Section 9-64-140(b) and the violation is recorded by an automated camera monitoring device. A photographic recording of a violation obtained by an automated camera monitoring device, showing the bus stop or bus lane and the vehicle license plate number, shall be a prima facie evidence of a violation of this chapter. It shall be a defense to a violation of this section that:

(1) The operator of the vehicle was issued a uniform traffic citation for a violation of 9-12-060(b) or a parking citation for a violation of 9-64-140(b); or

(2) The violation occurred at any time during which the vehicle or its state registration plates were reported to a law enforcement agency as having been stolen and the vehicle or its plates had not been recovered by the owner at the time of the alleged violation; or

(3) The vehicle was leased to another, and, within 60 days after the citation was mailed to the owner, the owner submitted to the department of revenue the correct name, address and driver's license number of the lessee of the vehicle identified in the citation at the time of the violation, together with a copy of the lease agreement and additional information as may be required by the department. Where the lessor complies with the provisions of this section, the lessee of the vehicle at the time of the violation shall be deemed to be owner of the vehicle for purposes of this chapter. The department of revenue, within 30 days of being notified by the lessor of the name and address of the lessee, shall mail the lessee a citation which contains the information required under Section 9-103-030. For purposes of this chapter, the term "leased vehicle" shall be defined as a vehicle in which a motor vehicle dealership or manufacturer has, pursuant to a written document, vested exclusive possession, use, control and responsibility of the vehicle to the lessee during the periods the vehicle is operated by or for the lessee; or

(4) The vehicle was making a right hand turn; or

(5) The vehicle, if not a taxicab, was stopped to expeditiously load or unload passengers and the vehicle did not interfere with any bus waiting to enter or about to enter the bus stop; or

(6) The vehicle, if a licensed taxicab, was stopped to expeditiously load or unload passengers.

(b) The provisions of this section do not apply to any authorized emergency vehicle.

(c) Nothing in this section shall be construed to limit the liability of an operator of a vehicle for any violation of Section 9-12-060(b) or Section 9-64-140(b).

(Added. Coun. J. 7-29-03, p. 6166)

§9-103-030 Citation notice.

For each violation of Section 9-12-060(b) or Section 9-64-140(b) recorded by an automated camera monitoring device, the department of revenue shall mail a citation, within 30 days after receiving information about the registered owner of the vehicle from the secretary of state, to the registered owner of record of the vehicle used in the commission of the violation. The citation shall include the name and address of the registered owner of the vehicle; the vehicle make, if available and readily discernable, and registration number; the offense charged; the time, date and location of the alleged violation; the applicable fine and monetary penalty which shall be automatically assessed for late payment; information as to the availability of an administrative hearing in which the citation may be contested on its merits and the time and manner in which such hearing may be had; and that the basis of the citation is a photographic record obtained by an automated camera monitoring device.

(Added. Coun. J. 7-29-03, p. 6166)

§9-103-040 Grounds for adjudication by mail or administrative hearing.

A person charged with violating Section 9-12-060(b) or Section 9-64-140(b) recorded by an automated camera monitoring device may contest the charge through an adjudication by mail or at an administrative hearing limited to one or more of the following grounds with appropriate evidence to support:

(1) The operator of the vehicle was issued a uniform traffic citation for a violation of Section 9-12-060(b) or a parking violation for 9-64-140(b); or

(2) That the violation occurred at any time during which the vehicle or its state registration plates were reported to a law enforcement agency as having been stolen and the vehicle or its plates had not been recovered by the owner at the time of the alleged violation; or

(3) That the vehicle was leased to another, and, within 60 days after the citation was mailed to the owner, the owner submitted to the department of revenue the correct name and address of the lessee of the vehicle identified in the citation at the time of the violation, together with the additional information as may be required by the department; or

(4) That the vehicle was an authorized emergency vehicle; or

(5) That the facts alleged in the violation notice are inconsistent or do not support a finding that Section 9-12-060(b) or Section 9-64-140(b) was violated; or

(6) That the respondent was not the registered owner or lessee of the cited vehicle at the time of the violation; or

(7) That the vehicle was making a right hand turn; or

(8) That the vehicle, if not a taxicab, was stopped to expeditiously load or unload passengers and the vehicle did not interfere with any bus waiting to enter or about to enter the bus stop; or

(9) That the vehicle, if a licensed taxicab, was stopped to expeditiously load or unload passengers.

(Added. Coun. J. 7-29-03, p. 6166)

§9-103-050 Determination of liability.

The determination of liability for a citation issued under this chapter shall be made in accordance with Sections 9-100-050, and 9-100-070 through 9-100-090.
(Added. Coun. J. 7-29-03, p. 6166)

§9-103-060 Notice of final determination.

(a) If any fine or penalty is owing and unpaid after a determination of liability under this chapter has become final and the respondent has exhausted or failed to exhaust judicial procedures for review, the department of revenue shall cause a notice of final determination of liability to be sent to the respondent in accordance with Section 9-100-050(f).

(b) Any fine and penalty, if applicable, remaining unpaid after the notice of final determination of liability is sent shall constitute a debt due and owing the city which may be enforced in the manner set forth in Section 2-14-103 of this code. Failure of the respondent to pay such fine or penalty within 21 days of the date of the notice may result in the immobilization of the person's vehicle pursuant to the procedures described in Section 9-100-120.

(c) The city shall withdraw a violation notice, following reasonable collection efforts, when the notice was issued to a registered owner who is deceased at the time collection efforts are undertaken.
(Added. Coun. J. 7-29-03, p. 6166)

§9-103-070 Supplementary enforcement.

The liability created by Section 9-103-020 shall be imposed in addition to any liability otherwise provided for by any ordinance or statute governing the movement of traffic and vehicular standing and parking and the program authorized by Section 9-103-010 shall supplement enforcement of traffic and vehicular standing and parking regulations provided by Chapters 9-12 and 9-64 of the Municipal Code and the Illinois Motor Vehicle Code and shall not replace or substitute for enforcement of these or any other law.
(Added. Coun. J. 7-29-03, p. 6166)

CHAPTER 9-104
PUBLIC CHAUFFEURS

Sections:

9-104-010 Definitions.
9-104-020 License required.
9-104-030 Application—Qualifications.
9-104-040 License—Suspension and revocation.
9-104-050 Applicant—Fingerprints and photograph.
9-104-060 Exhibition of license.
9-104-070 License—Defacement—Fee.
9-104-080 License renewal.
9-104-090 Attempting to obtain another license—Additional penalty.
9-104-100 Loitering.
9-104-110 False information.
9-104-120 Deadly weapons.
9-104-125 Misuse of distress light—Penalty.
9-104-130 Change of address—Notice required.

9-104-140 Violation—Penalty.
9-104-150 Courteous behavior required.
9-104-155 Service to passengers with service dogs.
9-104-160 Surrendering license and information to police officer required.

§9-104-010 Definitions.

The definitions of the words "chauffeur" and "public passenger vehicle" in Chapter 9-112 of this code apply to the same words when used in this chapter. *(Prior code § 28.1-1; Amend. Coun. J. 7-12-90, p. 18634)*

§9-104-020 License required.

It is unlawful for any person to drive a public passenger vehicle on any public way for the transportation of passengers for hire from place to place within the corporate limits of the city without first having obtained a license as a public chauffeur except that drivers who can prove that they are qualified to drive motor vehicles as, for or on behalf of motor carriers under the Federal Motor Carriers Safety Regulations issued by the U.S. Department of Transportation Federal Highway Administration or comparable Illinois agency may drive charter vehicles within the corporate limits of the city. *(Prior code § 28.1-2; Amend. Coun. J. 2-3-87, p. 39205; 7-12-90, p. 18634)*

§9-104-030 Application—Qualifications.

(1) Applications for public chauffeur licenses shall be made in writing to the commissioner of consumer services upon forms provided therefor by the commissioner. Applications shall state the full name and residential address of the applicant and such other information as may be required by the commissioner to properly identify the applicant and to disclose any relevant information as to the applicant's qualifications, age, physical condition and criminal record.

(2) A person is qualified to receive a public chauffeur license:

(a) Who possesses a valid Illinois State driver's license which has not, at any time within the five years prior to application for the issuance or renewal of a public chauffeur license, been suspended or revoked pursuant to Sections 6-205, 11-501 or 11-501.1 of the Illinois Vehicle Code, as amended; and

(a-1) Who has possessed a valid Illinois State driver's license, or a valid driver's license of another state, district or territory of the United States, for at least three years prior to application for the issuance or renewal of a public chauffeur license, or who has completed a driving course approved by the Illinois Secretary of State; provided that this paragraph (a-1) shall not apply to an application for the renewal of a license properly issued prior to January 1, 1998; and

(b) Who is at least 21 years of age; and

(c) Who is able to speak, read and write the English language; and

(d) Who is not subject to epilepsy, vertigo, heart disease, defective vision or other infirmity of body or mind which may substantially impair the ability to operate a public vehicle, and is not addicted to the use of drugs or intoxicating liquors. When investigation reveals that such impairment may exist, the commissioner may nevertheless find that an applicant is qualified if the applicant submits a certificate by an Illinois-licensed physician or optometrist stating that the applicant has the capability to operate a public vehicle safely. Beginning June 30,

1998, every application for a new or renewed license shall contain a certificate by an Illinois-licensed physician that the applicant has the capability to operate a public vehicle safely, and shall contain proof that the applicant has taken and passed a test, conducted by authorities approved by the commissioner, for the presence of illegal drugs in the body; and

(e) Who shall successfully complete a mandatory course of study as prescribed in Section 9-104-030(7) and an examination as prescribed by the commissioner demonstrating a knowledge of the geography of the city, the laws, ordinances and regulations governing motor vehicle operation in the city, the ordinances regulating the operation of public passenger vehicles within the city and demonstrating the ability and skill to properly operate a public passenger vehicle within the city; and

(f) Who has not, within the five years immediately preceding his application, been either found guilty by a court of any jurisdiction, in custody, under parole or under any other noncustodial supervision resulting from a finding or determination of guilt by a court of any jurisdiction for the commission of any forcible felony as defined by Article 2 of the Illinois Criminal Code of 1961, as now or hereafter amended, any crime involving moral turpitude, or for the illegal sale or possession of any controlled substance, indecent solicitation of a child, criminal sexual abuse or operating a motor vehicle while under the influence of alcohol or narcotic drugs; and

(g) Who has not, within the 18 months prior to filing the application, had a public chauffeur's license issued under this chapter revoked for any reason; and

(h) Who has not been convicted of or placed on supervision for two or more offenses involving traffic regulations governing the movement of vehicles, or whose Illinois driver's license has not been suspended or revoked pursuant to Section 6-206 of the Illinois Vehicle Code, as amended, within the past 12 months prior to application for the issuance or renewal of a license. However, a person who would otherwise be disqualified for a public chauffeur license under this paragraph (h) may remove the disqualification by successfully completing a driver training course determined by the commissioner to provide adequate remedial training of the licensee. The license of any public chauffeur whose disqualification is removed under this paragraph (h) shall be subject to a 30-day suspension if the licensee subsequently is convicted of or placed on supervision for a traffic-related offense, and shall be subject to revocation for a second or subsequent such conviction or order of supervision.

(3) The qualifications of each applicant as specified in paragraph (2) of this section shall be investigated by the department of police of the city of Chicago and a report of such investigation containing any facts relevant to the applicant's qualifications shall be forwarded by the superintendent of police to the commissioner.

(4) Pending the investigation provided in paragraph (3) of this section, the commissioner may issue a temporary permit authorizing an applicant to operate a public passenger vehicle for the period of time specified in the temporary permit. If the investigation is not completed at the expiration of the period specified in the temporary permit the commissioner may, in his discretion, extend the period of temporary authorization until such time as in the opinion of the commissioner the examination can be completed. The commissioner may rescind a temporary permit and deny the application for a public chauffeur license of any

applicant who, while operating a public passenger vehicle pursuant to a temporary permit, is found to have engaged in conduct that, by ordinance or rule, would be grounds for revocation of the public chauffeur license.

(5) If upon examination of the applicant's application and the investigation specified in paragraph (3) of this section the commissioner finds that the application includes no material omission or misstatement of facts requested by the application form and that the applicant possesses the qualifications specified in paragraph (2) of this section the commissioner shall issue the license. If upon such examination of the applicant's application and the investigation specified in paragraph (3) of this section the commissioner finds that the application includes any material omission or misstatement of fact or that the applicant lacks any of the qualifications specified in paragraph (2) of this section the commissioner shall deny the license and shall inform the applicant of the denial and the reason or reasons therefor by registered mail, return receipt requested.

(6) If an application is denied the applicant may, within 10 days of the mailing of notice of the denial, make written demand upon the commissioner for a hearing. Upon receipt of a timely written demand for a hearing the commissioner shall within 30 days conduct a hearing. If upon such a hearing the applicant establishes through competent evidence that the denial was based upon incorrect findings the commissioner shall issue the license. If upon such a hearing the denial is found to have been based upon correct findings the denial shall become final. After entry of a final denial the applicant shall be ineligible to make a new application for a period of 18 months.

(7) The commissioner shall provide or cause to be offered on an ongoing basis a course or courses of study covering the subjects required in Section 9-104-030(2)(e) and such additional subjects as the commissioner may prescribe for all applicants for public chauffeur licenses, including applicants for renewal of public chauffeur licenses. The commissioner may contract with the city colleges or, with the approval of the mayor, with any state-approved vocational or technical school or any not-for-profit organization to provide the required chauffeur training course of study. No such course may be offered unless the curriculum for the course has been certified by the commissioner as being in compliance with this chapter. The certification shall be made annually and may be revoked at any time. The commissioner shall approve the tuition to be charged for such course.

(Prior code § 28.1-3; Amend. Coun. J. 2-3-87, p. 39205; Corrected. 3-11-87, p. 40423; Amend. 2-7-90, p. 11774; 7-12-90, p. 18634; 12-1-93, p. 43380; 1-14-97, p. 37750; 12-10-97, p. 59054)

§9-104-040 License—Suspension and revocation.

(a) If any licensee violates any traffic law or any of the provisions of this chapter or Chapter 9-112 or rules or regulations adopted pursuant to this chapter or Chapter 9-112, the commissioner may seek revocation or suspension of the licensee's license and/or the imposition of a fine up to $750.00 and/or the issuance of an order of restitution or other appropriate equitable relief. The commissioner also may order any licensee again to successfully complete the course of study or examination, or both, as provided for in subsection 9-104-030(2)(e) prior to the reinstatement of the license. The commissioner shall promulgate rules and regulations regarding the lengths of suspension and the amounts of fines to be imposed, and the types of equitable relief to be ordered, for specific violations.

(b) Notwithstanding any other provision of this chapter, whenever the Illinois driver's license of a licensee has been revoked or suspended by the Secretary of State, the licensee's public chauffeur license shall be subject to automatic suspension for the period that the driver's license is suspended or revoked. The suspension shall not be subject to any of the procedures described in this section. A suspension under this subsection (b) shall be in addition to and shall not affect any disqualification, suspension, revocation, fine or other penalty or sanction that otherwise may be applicable.

(c) Before any suspension or fine is imposed, or equitable relief is ordered, the licensee shall be notified by: (1) first class or express mail, or overnight carrier; or (2) personal service, of the specific charges against him and of his right to a hearing. The licensee may request such a hearing by making a written demand for the hearing not more than 10 days after receiving notification of the charges. Any person who makes a timely request for a hearing shall be notified of the time, date and place of the hearing not less than seven days prior to the date of the hearing.

(i) Prior to the exercise of exclusive jurisdiction by the department of administrative hearings in accordance with Section 2-14-190(c) of this code, the hearing shall be conducted by the commissioner or his designee in accordance with rules and regulations promulgated by the commissioner. If, after the hearing, the commissioner determines that a violation has occurred, the commissioner shall enter an order suspending the license and/or imposing a fine pursuant to the rules and regulations promulgated by the commissioner. An order by the commissioner imposing a suspension and/or fine may be appealed by the licensee to the mayor's license commission. Any person appealing an order imposing a suspension and/or fine shall submit a $50.00 filing fee at the time an appeal is filed.

(ii) After the exercise of exclusive jurisdiction by the department of administrative hearings in accordance with Section 2-14-190(c) of this code, upon receipt of a request for a hearing, the commissioner shall institute an action with the department of administrative hearings which shall appoint an administrative law officer who shall conduct the hearing. If, after the hearing, the administrative law officer determines that a violation has occurred, the administrative law officer shall enter an order suspending the license and/or imposing a fine.

(iii) Notwithstanding the exercise of exclusive jurisdiction by the department of administrative hearings, if no timely request is made for a hearing and the commissioner determines that a violation has occurred, the commissioner shall enter an order suspending the license and/or imposing a fine.

(d) The commissioner may file a petition with the mayor's license commission to seek revocation of a license. Following a hearing conducted in accordance with its rules, the commission shall determine whether revocation is warranted or a lesser penalty, if any, shall be imposed.

(Prior code § 28.1-4; Amend. Coun. J. 2-3-87, p. 39205; 2-7-90, p. 11774; 7-12-90, p. 18634; 12-9-92, p. 25465; 7-10-96, p. 24982; 1-14-97, p. 37750; 11-12-97, p. 56813; 12-10-97, p. 59054; 4-29-98, p. 66564)

§9-104-050 Applicant—Fingerprints and photograph.

The fingerprints of each applicant shall be submitted to the superintendent of police for examination unto the criminal record, if any, of the applicant or prior issuance, if any, of a public chauffeur's license to applicant. The superintendent of police shall keep and maintain these fingerprints as part of the police department's permanent record. Each applicant shall file with his application four recent photographs of himself, of a size which may be easily attached to his license. One photograph shall be attached to the license, when issued, one to the license stub record, one to the fingerprint card and the fourth shall be filed, together with the application. The photograph shall be so attached to the license that it cannot be removed and another photograph substituted without detection.

(Prior code § 28.1-6; Amend. Coun. J. 2-3-87, p. 39205; 7-12-90, p. 18634)

§9-104-060 Exhibition of license.

Every chauffeur upon taking possession and control of a livery vehicle or taxicab for operation in transportation of passengers for hire shall insert in the frame provided therefor his license and photograph as an exhibit for view by passengers.

(Prior code § 28.1-7; Amend. Coun. J. 7-12-90, p. 18634)

§9-104-070 License—Defacement—Fee.

Upon qualification of the applicant, and payment of the license fee herein provided, a public chauffeur's license shall be issued in such form as to contain the photograph and signature of the driver and a blank space upon which a record may be made of any arrest or serious complaint against him. No such record shall be defaced, erased or otherwise obliterated by the chauffeur or permitted by him to be defaced, erased or obliterated. The following fees shall be paid for a chauffeur's license:

Original	$15.00
Renewal	8.00

(Prior code § 28.1-8; Amend. Coun. J. 2-3-87, p. 39205; 7-12-90, p. 18634)

§9-104-080 License renewal.

(a) The commissioner may renew a chauffeur's license from year to year upon application made upon a form furnished by the commissioner which shall state, in addition to any other information required by the commissioner, the full name and address of the applicant, the date upon which his original license was granted and the number thereof.

(b) All public chauffeur licenses must be renewed by the expiration date or by an extension authorized by the commissioner. Failure to renew a chauffeur's license prior to the expiration date or any extension authorized by the commissioner will require the chauffeur to take a new test; provided that any chauffeur who fails to renew his license within one year of the expiration date shall be required to take the mandatory course of study and a new test.

(Prior code § 28.1-9; Amend. Coun. J. 2-3-87, p. 39205; 7-12-90, p. 18634; 1-14-97, p. 37750)

§9-104-090 Attempting to obtain another license—Additional penalty.

Any licensee who knowingly attempts to obtain another chauffeur license under the same or different name, in addition to any other penalties provided by this chapter, shall have his original license revoked.

(Prior code § 28.1-10; Amend. Coun. J. 2-3-87, p. 39205; 7-12-90, p. 18634)

§9-104-100 Loitering.

It is unlawful for any chauffeur to loiter upon any public way outside the public passenger vehicle of which he is in charge or join any assembly or crowd of persons upon any public way while in charge of any such vehicle. Every chauffeur shall pay strict attention to the vehicle of which he is in charge and shall at all times be in the immediate proximity thereof, except for good cause shown.

(Prior code § 28.1-11; Amend. Coun. J. 7-12-90, p. 18634)

§9-104-110 False information.

It is unlawful for any chauffeur to induce any person to employ him or his vehicle by knowingly misinforming or misleading such person as to the time or place of arrival or departure of any train, steamship or other public carrier or as to the location of any public carrier depot or ticket office or of any hotel, public place or private residence in the city.

It is unlawful for any chauffeur to represent falsely that the vehicle of which he is in charge is in the employment of any hotel, public house or public carrier or to make any false representation or statement relating to any public carrier passenger ticket.

No chauffeur shall solicit patronage for any restaurant, nightclub, cabaret, dancehall, hotel, public resort, place of amusement, or solicit any person for transportation to any prostitute or house of ill-fame or disorderly place or direct or inform any person where such prostitute, house of ill-fame or disorderly place is located or transport any passenger to any place other than the destination to which the passenger has requested transportation.

(Prior code § 28.1-12; Amend. Coun. J. 7-12-90, p. 18634)

§9-104-120 Deadly weapons.

It is unlawful for any chauffeur while in charge of a public passenger vehicle to have any deadly weapon in his possession or in or about the driver's compartment of said vehicle.

(Prior code § 28.1-13; Amend. Coun. J. 7-12-90, p. 18634)

§9-104-125 Misuse of distress light—Penalty.

No public chauffeur may activate a distress or trouble light installed in a taxicab under Section 9-112-105 unless the chauffeur reasonably believes that his or her physical safety is in immediate danger. The refusal of a customer to pay a fare shall not by itself be considered a cause for such reasonable belief. Any person who violates this section shall be subject to a fine of not more than $500.00 and such other penalties as are prescribed under Section 9-104-040.

(Added. Coun. J. 10-14-92, p. 22998)

§9-104-130 Change of address—Notice required.

It is the duty of every chauffeur to notify the commissioner whenever any change in the chauffeur's address is made. Any notice required to be given to the chauffeur shall be sufficient if addressed to the last address recorded in the office of the commissioner.

(Prior code § 28.1-14; Amend. Coun. J. 2-3-87, p. 39205; 7-12-90, p. 18634)

§9-104-140 Violation—Penalty.

If any chauffeur violates any provision of Chapter 9-112 of this code or of this chapter for which a penalty is not otherwise provided, he shall be fined not less than $25.00 nor more than $750.00 for each offense.

(Prior code § 28.1-15; Amend. Coun. J. 2-3-87, p. 39205; 7-12-90, p. 18634; 12-10-97, p. 59054)

§9-104-150 Courteous behavior required.

Public chauffeurs shall be courteous to passengers, prospective passengers and other drivers at all times. Chauffeurs shall not assault, threaten, abuse, insult, provoke, interfere with, use profane language, impede or obstruct any other person, any passenger or other drivers in connection with the operation of their vehicle.

(Prior code § 28.1-16; Amend. Coun. J. 2-3-87, p. 39205; 7-12-90, p. 18634)

§9-104-155 Service to passengers with service dogs.

Public chauffeurs must comply with 775 ILCS 30/1, et seq. by accepting, without extra charge, passengers with service dogs. Any public chauffeur found, after notice and hearing, to have refused transportation to a person with a service dog shall be fined $500.00 and have his or her license suspended for 29 days for the first offense. Any public chauffeur found after notice and hearing, to have committed a subsequent offense of refusing transportation to a service dog shall have his or her license revoked.

(Added. Coun. J. 11-15-00, p. 46957)

§9-104-160 Surrendering license and information to police officer required.

A public chauffeur shall upon request of a police officer surrender his public chauffeur license and supply any additional information requested by the police officer concerning the operation of his public vehicle.

(Prior code § 28.1-17; Amend. Coun. J. 2-3-87, p. 39205; 7-12-90, p. 18634)

CHAPTER 9-108
HORSE-DRAWN CARRIAGES

Sections:

9-108-010 Definitions.
9-108-020 License required—Restrictions.
9-108-030 Application—Renewal.
9-108-040 Investigation—Issuance.
9-108-050 License fee—Additional.
9-108-060 License not assignable.
9-108-070 License plate or decal—Replacement—Fee.

9-108-080 Insurance.
9-108-090 Regulations.
9-108-100 Commissioner powers and duties—Inspection.
9-108-110 Compliance.
9-108-120 Equipment.
9-108-130 Information to be displayed.
9-108-140 Horse-drawn carriage driver license required.
9-108-150 Horse-drawn carriage driver license—Application—Qualifications—Fee.
9-108-160 Requirements for operation—Possession of weapon prohibited.
9-108-170 Change of information—Notification required.
9-108-180 Revocation—Notice—Hearing.
9-108-190 Licenses not required when.
9-108-200 Rules and regulations promulgation.
9-108-210 Hours of operation—Emergency telephone number.
9-108-220 Alcoholic liquor—Consumption or possession prohibited.
9-108-230 Licensee responsible for stand condition.
9-108-240 Violation—Penalty—Additional.
9-108-250 Payment of fines.

§9-108-010 Definitions.

For the purpose of this chapter:

(a) "Carriage" means any device in, upon or by which any person is or may be transported or drawn upon a public way, designed to be or capable of being driven by a horse.

(b) "Carriage stand" means that portion of a curb lane designated by the department of transportation for loading and unloading of passengers for horse-drawn vehicles.

(c) "Commissioner" means the commissioner of consumer services of the city of Chicago.

(d) "Department" means the department of consumer services of the city of Chicago.

(e) "Horse" means an animal of the genus equus.

(f) "Initial license period" shall be that period beginning 15 days following the effective date of this ordinance and terminating on the thirty-first day of December.

(g) "Person" means a natural person, partnership, firm, corporation or other legal entity.

(h) "Place of business" means a business office, with a separate telephone number and listing.

(i) "Subsequent license periods" means and shall be all license periods following the initial license period and running from the first day of January following termination of the initial license period through the following thirty-first day of December.

(j) "Veterinarian" means a practicing veterinarian licensed by state of Illinois.

(Prior code § 28.3-1; Added. Coun. J. 10-16-84, p. 10165; Amend. 7-12-90, p. 18634; 12-11-91, p. 10832)

§9-108-020 License required—Restrictions.

(a) No person may operate a horse-drawn carriage for compensation, nor may the owner thereof permit such operation upon the public streets in the city of Chicago except in the area described in Section 9-48-020 of the Municipal Code, nor may a carriage be so operated unless the carriage is licensed as a horse-drawn carriage under the provisions of Sections 7-12-210 and 7-12-220 of the Municipal Code.

(b) No carriage may be licensed under this chapter unless it is equipped with wheels.

(c) No carriage may be licensed under this chapter if it is designed to be drawn by more than one horse, nor may a carriage be operated for compensation while drawn by more than one horse.

(Prior code § 28.3-2; Added. Coun. J. 10-16-84, p. 10165; Amend. 7-12-90, p. 18634)

§9-108-030 Application—Renewal.

(a) Applicants holding horse-drawn carriage licenses which were issued by the commissioner of consumer services prior to the effective date of this ordinance may apply for renewal of such licenses within 15 days following the effective date of this ordinance. Licenses so renewed shall be effective during the initial licensing period and shall terminate on the thirty-first day of December following their issuance.

(b) Application for renewal of horse-drawn carriage licenses for the initial license period shall be made in writing, signed and sworn to by the applicant or if applicant is a corporation, by its duly authorized agent, upon forms provided by the commissioner. The application for renewal shall contain the full name and residence address of the applicant, Chicago place of business, the business telephone number of the applicant and, the manufacturer's name, model, length of time in use and seating capacity of the carriage which applicant will use. If the applicant is affiliated or to become affiliated or identified with any person by the color scheme of carriages, trade name or emblem, telephone number, radio dispatch system, or service agreement, the application for renewal shall contain the full name, Chicago business address and telephone number of said affiliate. A copy of the agreement with said affiliate, if any, shall be filed with the application for renewal. Each horse-drawn carriage license applicant must demonstrate that the applicant will have at least one horse licensed under the provisions of Chapter 7-12 available for each carriage license applied for and must submit a copy of the license for each horse or a copy of the application for said license as part of the application for renewal of a horse-drawn carriage license. All corporate applicants for horse-drawn carriage licenses shall be organized or qualified to do business under the laws of Illinois and have a place of business within the city of Chicago. All other applicants shall be citizens of the United States and shall have a place of business in the city of Chicago.

(c) All applications for renewal of a horse-drawn carriage license for license periods subsequent to the initial license period provided for herein shall be made at least 45 days prior to the expiration of the license period. Such applications for renewal shall be made in writing, signed and sworn to by the applicant or if applicant is a corporation, by its duly authorized agent, upon forms provided by the commissioner. The renewal applications shall contain the full name and residence address of the applicant, Chicago place of business, the business telephone number of the applicant, and the manufacturer's name, model, length of time in use and seating capacity of the carriage which applicant will use. If the applicant is affiliated or to become affiliated or identified with any person by the color scheme of carriages, trade name or emblem, telephone number, radio dispatch system, or service agreement, the renewal applications shall contain the full name, Chicago business address and telephone number of said affiliate. A copy of the agreement with said affiliate, if any, shall be filed with the renewal applications. Each horse-drawn carriage license applicant must demonstrate that the applicant will have at least one horse licensed under the provisions of Chapter 7-12 available for each carriage license applied for and must submit a copy of the license for each horse or a copy of the renewal application for said license as part of the application for a horse-drawn carriage license. All corporate applicants for horse-drawn carriage licenses shall be organized or qualified to do business under the laws of Illinois and have a place of business in the city of Chicago. All other applicants shall be citizens of the United States and shall have a place of business in the city of Chicago.

(d) No more than 40 horse-drawn carriage licenses shall be issued, the public convenience and necessity requiring such limitation.

(e) The commissioner may refuse to renew a license for the initial license period or for any subsequent license period provided for in this ordinance, if that license was revoked during the previous license period or if the applicant for renewal fails to qualify for renewal under any provision of this chapter or rules and regulations promulgated hereunder, or any provision of this municipal code, the laws of Illinois or federal law relating to the use or operation of a vehicle on a public way. In the event that the commissioner determines that a license shall not be renewed, the commissioner shall notify the applicant within 30 days, which notice shall state the reason for the nonrenewal.

(f) If a renewal is denied the applicant may within 10 days of the mailing of notice of the denial, make written demand upon the commissioner for a hearing. Upon receipt of a timely written demand for a hearing, the commissioner shall within 30 days conduct a hearing. If upon such a hearing the applicant establishes through competent evidence that the denial was based upon incorrect findings, the commissioner shall issue the license. If upon such a hearing the denial is found to have been based upon correct findings, the denial shall become final. After entry of a final denial the applicant shall be ineligible to make a new application for a period of six months.

(g) In the event that a license is not renewed by the commissioner or if a licensee chooses not to apply for renewal, the commissioner shall grant all such available licenses by the random selection of qualified applicants. Such applicants shall make application to the commissioner as provided for in Section 9-108-030(b) hereof. Such applicant shall meet all applicable requirements set forth herein.

(Prior code § 28.3-3; Added. Coun. J. 10-16-84, p. 10165; Amend. 5-30-86, p. 30304; 7-12-90, p. 18634)

§9-108-040 Investigation—Issuance.

Upon receipt of an application for renewal for a horse-drawn carriage license, the commissioner shall cause an investigation to be made of the character and reputation of the applicant as a law-abiding citizen; the financial ability of the applicant to render safe and comfortable transportation service, to maintain or replace the equipment and horses for such service, to pay all judgments and awards which may be rendered for any cause arising out of the operation of a horse-drawn carriage during the license period. If the commissioner shall find that the application for renewal, and all other statements and documents required to be filed with said application have been properly executed; that the applicant is qualified to pursue this occupation; that the carriage or carriages are in safe and proper condition, and the horse has been properly licensed under Sections 7-12-210 and 7-12-220 of the municipal code, the commissioner will issue the applicant a license for each horse-drawn carriage applied for, to terminate on the thirty-first day of December following the date of issue except that no more than 60 licenses shall be issued or outstanding at any one time. A horse-drawn carriage license may not be applied for by, nor may a license be issued to, any person other than the owner of a carriage or horse.

(Prior code § 28.3-4; Added. Coun. J. 10-16-84, p. 10165; Amend. 7-12-90, p. 18634)

§9-108-050 License fee—Additional.

(a) The license fee for the initial license period provided for in this chapter shall be $500.00. The annual license fee for every subsequent license period for each horse-drawn carriage shall be $400.00. The license fees shall be paid in advance when the license is issued or renewed and shall be prorated only for first initial license period.

(b) Nothing in this section shall affect the rights of the city to impose or collect any other applicable tax upon the use or operation of the carriage, or any tax or fee imposed upon the ownership or use of the animal drawing said vehicle, in addition to the license fee.

(Prior code § 28.3-5; Added. Coun. J. 10-16-84, p. 10165; Amend. 7-12-90, p. 18634; 11-17-93, p. 42192)

§9-108-060 License not assignable.

No license issued hereunder shall be assignable.

(Prior code § 28.3-6; Added. Coun. J. 10-16-84, p. 10165; Amend. 7-12-90, p. 18634)

§9-108-070 License plate or decal—Replacement—Fee.

The commissioner shall deliver with each horse-drawn carriage license a metal plate of such size and material as the commissioner shall determine which shall bear the words: "City of Chicago," the license number of the carriage and the year of issuance impressed thereon in letters and figures. Said plate must be affixed to the back side of the carriage in a conspicuous manner. In addition, each horse-drawn carriage licensee shall be issued a decal with an identification number established by the commissioner. The decal pertaining to the horse-drawn carriage must be affixed to the outside of the carriage on the driver's side, in a conspicuous manner. If a metal plate or decal is lost, stolen or damaged so as to

require replacement, the licensee shall make application to the commissioner for a duplicate plate or decal, under oath, on such forms and giving such information as the commissioner shall require. In the case of a damaged plate or decal, the licensee shall return such plate or decal with such application. Upon receipt of an application and the payment of a replacement fee of $10.00, the commissioner shall issue a duplicate plate or decal to the licensee.
(Prior code § 28.3-7; Added. Coun. J. 10-16-84, p. 10165; Amend. 7-12-90, p. 18634)

§9-108-080 Insurance.

Every horse-drawn carriage licensee shall carry public liability and property damage insurance and workmen's compensation insurance for his employees with solvent and responsible insurers approved by the commissioner, authorized to transact such insurance in the state of Illinois, and qualified to assume the risk for the amounts hereinafter set forth under the laws of Illinois, to secure payment of any loss or damage resulting from any occurrence arising out of or caused by the operation or use of any of the licensee's horse-drawn carriages. The public liability insurance policy or contract may cover one or more horse-drawn carriages but each horse-drawn carriage shall be insured for the sum of at least $50,000.00 for property damage and $100,000.00 for injuries to or death of any one person and each horse-drawn carriage having seating capacity for not more than seven adult passengers shall be insured for the sum of at least $300,000.00 for injuries to or death of more than one person in any one accident. Every insurance policy or contract for such insurance shall name the city as an additional insured and shall provide for the payment and satisfaction of any final judgment rendered against the licensee and person injured, or any person driving a horse-drawn carriage, and that suit may be brought in any court of competent jurisdiction upon such policy or contract by any person having claims arising from the operation or use of such horse-drawn carriage. It shall contain a description of each horse-drawn carriage, manufacturer's name and model number, and the license number. In lieu of an insurance policy or contract a surety bond or bonds with a corporate surety or sureties authorized to do business under the laws of Illinois, may be accepted by the commissioner for all or any part of such insurance; provided, that each bond shall be conditioned for the payment and satisfaction of any final judgment in conformity with the provisions of an insurance policy required by this section. All insurance policies or contracts or surety bonds required by this section or copies thereof certified by the insurers, shall be filed with the commissioner and no insurance or bond shall be subject to cancellation except on 30 days' previous notice to the commissioner. If any insurance or bond is cancelled or permitted to lapse for any reason, the commissioner shall immediately suspend the license for the horse-drawn carriage affected under the procedures set forth in Section 9-108-180 of this chapter. If such other insurance or bond is not supplied, within the period of suspension of the license, the mayor shall revoke the license for such horse-drawn carriage.
(Prior code § 28.3-8; Added. Coun. J. 10-16-84, p. 10165; Amend. 7-12-90, p. 18634)

§9-108-090 Regulations.

(a) No horse-drawn carriage may carry more than seven passengers at one time, including the driver.

(b) No horse-drawn carriage may display advertising on its exterior or interior.

(c) Each horse-drawn carriage must prominently display the rate or other charge to be made for its service in the manner prescribed by the commissioner by rule. It shall be unlawful to make any charge not so displayed.

(d) No person may sit in the driver's compartment or area except the driver.

(Prior code § 28.3-9; Added. Coun. J. 10-16-84, p. 10165; Amend. 7-12-90, p. 18634)

§9-108-100 Commissioner powers and duties—Inspection.

(a) The commissioner may cause any horse-drawn carriage to be inspected by the department as often as the commissioner shall determine to ensure the safety of the passengers and the public. If any horse-drawn carriage shall become unsafe for operation or if its body or seating facilities shall be so damaged, deteriorated or unclean as to render said horse-drawn carriage unfit for the public use, the license therefor shall be suspended by the commissioner until the horse-drawn carriage shall be made safe for operation and its body shall be repaired and painted and its seating facilities shall be reconditioned or replaced as directed by the commissioner. In determining whether any horse-drawn carriage is unfit for public use, the commissioner shall give consideration to its effect on the health, comfort and convenience of passengers and its public appearance on the streets of the city of Chicago. Upon suspension of a license for any cause, under the provisions of this chapter, the metal plate shall be removed by the commissioner from the horse-drawn carriage. If the suspension is terminated, the commissioner shall reaffix the metal plate, upon payment to the city of a fee of $10.00. The commissioner shall notify the department of police of every suspension and termination of suspension.

(b) The commissioner may order a horse-drawn carriage licensee to have any horse utilized by the licensee to draw carriages within the city of Chicago to be examined by a veterinarian from the commission on animal care and control to determine its fitness for such work and compliance with Chapter 7-12 and the rules and regulations promulgated thereunder. Such order shall be in writing and may be given to the driver of the carriage to which the horse is hitched, or to the licensee at the licensee's Chicago place of business. The order shall prescribe the time within which the examination shall take place, which shall not be more than 72 hours nor less than 24 hours after notice is delivered. A horse for which such order has been issued may not be used to draw a carriage from the time of delivery of the order until the commissioner has received a written statement from the examining veterinarian that the horse is fit to perform such work and is otherwise in compliance with Chapter 7-12.

(c) A horse-drawn carriage licensee and the licensee's agents shall at all times allow complete access to any carriages, horses and any facilities used by the licensee in the course of operating horse-drawn carriages within the city of Chicago for purposes of inspection.

(Prior code § 28.3-10; Added. Coun. J. 10-16-84, p. 10165; Amend. 7-12-90, p. 18634)

§9-108-110 Compliance.

All horses drawing horse-drawn carriages shall be kept in compliance with the applicable provisions of this municipal code, the laws of Illinois and federal law.

(Prior code § 28.3-11; Added. Coun. J. 10-16-84, p. 10165; Amend. 7-12-90, p. 18634)

§9-108-120 Equipment.

All horse-drawn carriages must be equipped with rear-view mirrors, electrified lights visible from the front and side; and electrified directional signal and tail lights as prescribed by the commissioner. All carriages and drivers shall comply with any applicable requirements of the state of Illinois and this municipal code, including but not limited to traffic laws and ordinances.

(Prior code § 28.3-12; Added. Coun. J. 10-16-84, p. 10165; Amend. 7-12-90, p. 18634)

§9-108-130 Information to be displayed.

All horse-drawn carriages shall prominently display the name of the horse-drawn carriage licensee and license number on the rear of each carriage in a manner prescribed by the commissioner by rule.

(Prior code § 28.3-13; Added. Coun. J. 10-16-84, p. 10165; Amend. 7-12-90, p. 18634)

§9-108-140 Horse-drawn carriage driver license required.

It is unlawful for any person to drive a horse-drawn carriage on any public way for the transportation of passengers for hire from place to place within the city of Chicago without first having obtained a license as a horse-drawn carriage driver.

(Prior code § 28.3-14; Added. Coun. J. 10-16-84, p. 10165; Amend. 7-12-90, p. 18634)

§9-108-150 Horse-drawn carriage driver license—Application—Qualifications—Fee.

(a) Applications for horse-drawn carriage driver licenses shall be made in writing to the commissioner upon forms provided therefor by the commissioner. Applications shall state the full name and residential address of the applicant and such other information as may be required by the commissioner to properly identify the applicant and to disclose any relevant information as to the applicant's qualifications, age, physical condition and criminal record.

(b) A person is qualified to receive a horse-drawn carriage driver license:

1. Who possesses a valid, current Illinois State driver's license;
2. Who is at least 18 years of age;
3. Who is able to speak, read and write the English language;
4. Who is not subject to epilepsy, vertigo, heart disease, defective vision or other infirmity of body or mind which may substantially impair the ability to operate a public vehicle, and is not addicted to the use of drugs or intoxicating liquors;

5. Who shall successfully complete an examination as prescribed by the commissioner demonstrating a knowledge of the geography of the city and the laws, ordinances and regulations governing vehicle operation in the city; and

6. Who has not, within the five years immediately preceding his or her application, been either convicted, in custody, under parole or under any other noncustodial supervision relating from a conviction in a court of any jurisdiction for the commission of any forcible felony as defined by Article 2 of the Illinois Criminal Code of 1961, indecent liberties with a child or operating a vehicle while under the influence of alcohol or narcotic drugs;

7. Who delivers to the commissioner a certification by a horse-drawn carriage licensee that such person is qualified to operate a carriage.

(c) The qualifications of each applicant as specified in paragraph (b) of this section shall be investigated by the department of consumer services and a report of such investigation containing any facts relevant to the applicant's qualifications shall be forwarded to the commissioner. The fingerprints of each applicant shall be submitted to the superintendent of police for examination into the criminal record, if any, of the applicant. Each applicant shall file with his or her application four recent photographs equivalent to passport size showing the full face, head and shoulders of the applicant in a clear and distinguishing manner which may be easily attached to the license. One photograph shall be attached to the license, when issued, one to the license stub record, one to the fingerprint card and the fourth shall be filed with the department, together with the application. The photograph shall be so attached to the license that it cannot be removed and another photograph substituted without detection.

(d) Pending the investigation provided in paragraph (c) of this section, the commissioner may issue a temporary permit authorizing an applicant to drive a horse-drawn carriage for the period of time specified in the temporary permit. If the investigation is not completed at the expiration of the period specified in the temporary permit the commissioner may, in his discretion, extend the period of temporary authorization until such time as in the opinion of the commissioner the examination can be completed, except that the commissioner may not issue a temporary permit or any extension thereof for a period which exceeds 60 days from the original date of issuance.

(e) If upon examination of the applicant's application and the investigation specified in paragraph (c) of this section and the commissioner finds that the application included no material omission or misstatement of facts requested by the application form and that the applicant possesses the qualifications specified in paragraph (b) of this section, the commissioner shall issue the license. If upon such examination of the applicant's application and the investigation specified in paragraph (c) of this section the commissioner finds that the application includes any material omission or misstatement of fact or that the applicant lacks any of the qualifications specified in paragraph (b) of this section, the commissioner shall deny the license and shall inform the applicant of the denial and the specific reason or reasons therefor by registered mail, return receipt requested.

(f) If an application is denied the applicant may within 10 days of the mailing of notice of the denial, make written demand upon the commissioner for a hearing. Upon receipt of a timely written demand for a hearing, the commissioner shall within 30 days conduct a hearing. If upon such a hearing the applicant establishes through competent evidence that the denial was based upon incorrect findings, the commissioner shall issue the license. If upon such a hearing the denial is found to have been based upon correct findings, the denial shall become final. After entry of a final denial the applicant shall be ineligible to make a new application for a period of six months.

(g) Upon qualification of the applicant and payment of the license fee herein provided, a horse-drawn carriage driver's license shall be issued in such form as to contain the photograph and signature of the driver and a blank space upon which a record may be made of any arrest or serious complaint against him. No such record shall be defaced, erased or otherwise obliterated by the driver or permitted by him to be defaced, erased or obliterated.

(h) The fee for issuance of a horse-drawn carriage driver's license or renewal thereof shall be $25.00.

(i) The commissioner may renew a horse-drawn carriage driver's license from year to year upon application made upon a form furnished by the commissioner which shall state the full name and Chicago address of the applicant, the date upon which the original license was granted and the number thereof.
(Prior code § 28.3-15; Added. Coun. J. 10-16-84, p. 10165; Amend. 7-12-90, p. 18634)

§9-108-160 Requirements for operation—Possession of weapon prohibited.

(a) Every driver shall insert his license and photograph in a frame provided therefor as an exhibit for view by passengers upon taking possession of a horse-drawn carriage for operation in transportation of passengers for hire.

(b) No driver may have any deadly weapon in his possession or in or about the driver's compartment of a horse-drawn carriage while in charge of such carriage.

(c) Each driver must have his or her valid, current Illinois State driver's license in his or her possession while operating a carriage.
(Prior code § 28.3-16; Added. Coun. J. 10-16-84, p. 10165; Amend. 7-12-90, p. 18634)

§9-108-170 Change of information—Notification required.

Each licensee hereunder shall notify the commissioner in writing of any change of information previously supplied to the commissioner by the licensee.
(Prior code § 28.3-17; Added. Coun. J. 10-16-84, p. 10165; Amend. 7-12-90, p. 18634)

§9-108-180 Revocation—Notice—Hearing.

(a) If any licensee under this chapter violates any provision of this chapter or any rule or regulation promulgated hereunder, the commissioner may seek revocation of the licensee's license, suspension of the license for a period not to exceed 30 days, and/or the imposition of a fine on the licensee, in accordance with the procedures described in this section.

(b) The commissioner shall specify by rule the penalties for specific violations of this chapter and the rules and regulations promulgated hereunder. Penalties may include a minimum and a maximum length of suspension, amount of fine or both.

(c) Before any suspension or fine may be imposed, the commissioner shall notify the licensee of the specific charges against him and of his right to a hearing. Notice shall be served either: (i) by first class or express mail or by overnight carrier to the licensee at his place of business; or (ii) by personal service. If the licensee, within seven days after receipt of the notice, requests a hearing, the commissioner shall institute an action with the department of administrative hearings. The department of administrative hearings shall thereupon fix the time and place for a hearing, give written notice thereof and appoint an administrative law officer who shall conduct the hearing, determine liability, and impose penalties authorized by this section.

(d) The commissioner may file charges before the mayor's license commission seeking the revocation of license under this chapter. Following a hearing conducted in accordance with its rules, the commission shall determine whether revocation is warranted or a lesser penalty, if any, should be imposed.
(Added. Coun. J. 7-24-91, p. 4000; Amend. 7-10-96, p. 24982; 11-12-97, p. 56813; 4-29-98, p. 66564)

§9-108-190 Licenses not required when.

No horse-drawn carriage license shall be required of a person who has obtained a permit under Section 10-8-330 of this Municipal Code while operating under such permit, nor shall the driver of a carriage operating under such permit be required to obtain a horse-drawn carriage driver's license.
(Prior code § 28.3-19; Added. Coun. J. 10-16-84, p. 10165; Amend. 7-12-90, p. 18634)

§9-108-200 Rules and regulations promulgation.

The commissioner shall promulgate rules and regulations to implement this chapter. Such rules and regulations shall be effective 10 days after their publication in a newspaper of general circulation within the city of Chicago.
(Prior code § 28.3-20; Added. Coun. J. 10-16-84, p. 10165; Amend. 7-12-90, p. 18634; 4-29-98, p. 66564)

§9-108-210 Hours of operation—Emergency telephone number.

Each horse-drawn carriage licensee's place of business in Chicago shall be staffed by the licensee or a person authorized to act on behalf of the licensee between the hours of 9:00 a.m. and 5:00 p.m. on weekdays and at all other times the licensee's carriages are in operation on public streets within the city of Chicago. Each such licensee shall maintain an emergency telephone number which must be staffed and in operation when the place of business is not staffed, which number shall be supplied to the commissioner and shall be available to the public.
(Prior code § 28.3-21; Added. Coun. J. 10-16-84, p. 10165; Amend. 7-12-90, p. 18634)

§9-108-220 Alcoholic liquor—Consumption or possession prohibited.

No person may drink any alcoholic liquor as defined by law while such person is operating or being transported by horse-drawn carriage, nor may any person transport, carry, possess or have any alcoholic liquor while being transported by horse-drawn carriage, except in the original package with the seal unbroken.

(Prior code § 28.3-22; Added. Coun. J. 10-16-84, p. 10165; Amend. 7-12-90, p. 18634)

§9-108-230 Licensee responsible for stand condition.

Each horse-drawn carriage licensee shall be responsible for the sanitary condition of any horse-drawn carriage stand utilized by such licensee.

(Prior code § 28.3-23; Added. Coun. J. 10-16-84, p. 10165; Amend. 7-12-90, p. 18634)

§9-108-240 Violation—Penalty—Additional.

In addition to any other remedy hereunder, if any person violates any provision of this chapter, such person shall be fined not less than $100.00 nor more than $500.00 for each offense and each day such violation shall continue shall be deemed a separate and distinct offense.

(Prior code § 28.3-24; Added. Coun. J. 10-16-84, p. 10165; Amend. 7-12-90, p. 18634)

§9-108-250 Payment of fines.

If a fine is imposed on a licensee for violation of this chapter or any rule or regulation promulgated hereunder, the licensee shall not operate a horse-drawn carriage until the fine is completely paid.

(Added. Coun. J. 7-24-91, p. 4000)

CHAPTER 9-112
PUBLIC PASSENGER VEHICLES

Sections:

9-112-010 Definitions.
9-112-020 Exclusive permission granted.
9-112-030 License required.
9-112-040 Interurban operations.
9-112-050 Inspections.
9-112-060 Specifications.
9-112-070 Application.
9-112-080 Qualifications.
9-112-090 Qualifications—Criteria for consideration.
9-112-100 Investigation and issuance of license.
9-112-105 Safety features—Required— Exceptions.
9-112-110 License fees.
9-112-120 Temporary permits—Fees.
9-112-140 Personal license—Fair employment practice.
9-112-142 Liability for actions of public chauffeur.
9-112-145 Lease rate regulations.
9-112-150 Vehicles other than taxicabs—Sticker license emblem to be affixed.
9-112-160 Taxicabs—Metal plate to be affixed.
9-112-170 Unlawful to operate vehicle without current emblem.

9-112-180 Unlawful for licensee to operate vehicle without current emblem.
9-112-190 Tampering with emblem unlawful—Penalty.
9-112-200 Replacement of damaged or stolen emblems—Fee.
9-112-210 License card.
9-112-215 Underserved areas.
9-112-220 Insurance.
9-112-230 Affiliations.
9-112-240 Payment of judgments and awards.
9-112-250 Cancellation of affiliates registration.
9-112-260 Suspension of license; fines; equitable relief.
9-112-270 Revocation of license—Grounds.
9-112-280 Revocation of license—Additional reasons.
9-112-285 Revocation of license—Exception.
9-112-290 Interference with commissioner's duties.
9-112-300 Advertising signs permitted when.
9-112-310 Change of address—Notice to city required.
9-112-320 Livery vehicles—License issuance.
9-112-322 License managers.
9-112-325 License brokers.
9-112-330 Unlawful to operate livery vehicle with meter.
9-112-340 Solicitation of passengers prohibited.
9-112-350 Livery vehicles—Exterior—Advertising.
9-112-360 Sightseeing vehicles.
9-112-370 Vehicle out of service—Notice to city required.
9-112-380 Number of available licenses—Distribution.
9-112-390 License number and driver identification—Display.
9-112-400 Information sheet required—Contents.
9-112-410 Taximeter specifications.
9-112-420 Taximeter inspection.
9-112-430 Tampering with meters prohibited.
9-112-440 Taximeter inspection fee.
9-112-450 Unlawful to refuse transportation unless out of service.
9-112-455 Radio dispatch.
9-112-460 Airport service.
9-112-465 C.T.A.-T.A.P. program compliance—Wheelchair-accessible vehicle dispatch.
9-112-470 Taxicabs operating as intrastate motor carriers—Compliance with state requirements.
9-112-480 Jitney service.
9-112-490 Group riding.
9-112-500 Group riding permitted when.
9-112-510 Taxicab rates of fare—Revision.
9-112-520 Recordkeeping—Annual reports.
9-112-530 Ordinance not to limit city authority.
9-112-540 Revoked, surrendered licenses—Reissuance.
9-112-550 Violation—Penalty.
9-112-555 Impoundment of vehicle— Notification of owner—Penalty.
9-112-560 Severability.
9-112-570 Effective date.

§9-112-010 Definitions.

Whenever used in this ordinance:

(a) "Affiliation" means an association of public passenger vehicle license holders organized and incorporated for the purpose of providing its members with a Chicago business address, telephone number registered to the affiliation, color scheme where applicable, a trade name or emblem where applicable, a two-way radio dispatch system, insurance and the designation of an authorized registered agent. Members of an affiliation shall be known as "affiliates."

(b) "Cabman" means a person engaged in business as owner of one or more taxicabs.

(c) "Charter/sightseeing vehicle" means a public passenger vehicle for hire principally on sightseeing tours or charter trips or both.

(d) "Charter trip" means a group trip in a charter/sightseeing vehicle arranged in advance at a fixed rate per vehicle.

(e) "Chauffeur" means the driver of a public passenger vehicle licensed by the city of Chicago as a public chauffeur.

(f) "City" means the city of Chicago.

(g) "Coachman" means a person engaged in business as owner of one or more livery vehicles or charter/sightseeing vehicles.

(h) "Commissioner" means the commissioner of consumer services or such other body or officer as may have supervision over public passenger vehicle operations in the city.

(i) "Council" means the city council of the city of Chicago.

(j) "Licensee" means any person to whom one or more licenses have been issued pursuant to this ordinance.

(1) "License broker" means any individual, corporation or partnership, who, for another and whether or not acting for a fee, commission or other valuable consideration, acts as an agent or intermediary in negotiating the transfer of a public passenger vehicle license, and/or negotiating a loan secured or to be secured by an encumbrance upon or transfer of a public passenger vehicle license.

(2) "License manager" means any person who, in relation to a public passenger vehicle license not issued to him or his employer, assumes or undertakes any or all of the responsibilities of the public passenger vehicle license holder, including, but not limited to, those responsibilities relating to the leasing of the vehicle.

(k) "Livery vehicle" means a public passenger vehicle for hire only at a charge or fare for each passenger per trip or for each vehicle per trip fixed by agreement in advance.

(l) "Medallion" means a metal plate, furnished by the commissioner, for display on the outside hood of a taxicab, of such size and shape and bearing such impression thereon as shall be required by this ordinance and by the commissioner.

(m) "Medical carrier" means any privately owned public passenger vehicle which is specifically designed, constructed or modified and equipped and is maintained or operated for the nonemergency transportation of persons for compensation for the purpose of obtaining medical services.

(n) "Medical carrier owner" means a person engaged in business as owner of one or more medical carriers.

(o) "Operation expenses" means all charges, costs and expenses properly incurred for any given period in accordance with good accounting practice in connection with a licensee's public passenger vehicle operations.

(p) "Person" includes a natural person, partnership, firm or corporation.

(p-1) "Principal place of business in the city of Chicago" means that the following locations are all situated within the corporate boundaries of the city of Chicago: the location where notices of hearing or other notices from the department of consumer services to a licensee may be sent; and the location where a public passenger vehicle licensee maintains its business and financial records relating to the licenses involved.

(q) "Public passenger vehicle" means a motor vehicle, as defined in the motor vehicle law of the state of Illinois, which is used for the transportation of passengers for hire, excepting those devoted exclusively for funeral use or in operation of a metropolitan transit authority, and further excepting those motor vehicles (i) licensed for the transportation of passengers by the Interstate Commerce Commission to the extent that regulation of such vehicles by the city is prohibited by federal law, or (ii) operating pursuant to and in conformity with a certificate of authority issued by the Illinois Commerce Commission. Public passenger vehicles included in the provisions of this chapter shall specifically include but not be limited to: taxicabs, livery vehicles, charter/sightseeing vehicles and medical carrier vehicles.

(r) "Sightseeing tour" means a tour in a charter/sightseeing vehicle which is available to the general public in accordance with a published schedule or published itinerary, or to prearranged groups, at a charge or fare per passenger or per vehicle and which includes a lecture with regard to the subject matter of the tour.

(s) "Solicit" means an appeal by words or gestures for immediate patronage of a public passenger vehicle by a cabman, coachman, medical carrier owner, chauffeur or his agent directed at individuals or groups while the person making the appeal is upon the public way or public property, or the vehicle is parked, stopped, standing or moving upon the public way or public property.

(t) "Taxicab" means a public passenger vehicle for hire only at lawful rates of fare which, when it is being operated between a point of origin and a destination are as recorded and indicated by a taximeter or at rates as set forth in this chapter.

(u) "Taximeter" means any mechanical or electronic device which records and indicates a charge or fare measured by distance traveled, waiting time and extra passengers.

(v) "Transfer of a license" means the buying, selling or assigning of a license or licenses or the buying, selling and assigning of more than 25 percent of the stock or other interest in a corporation, partnership or other entity which either owns a license or licenses, or through a subsidiary, successor or any other person, owns or controls a license or licenses.

(w) "Two-way radio dispatch system" means a method of radio communication by which a dispatcher may communicate with the drivers of all vehicles in the organization. With respect to an unaffiliated licensee, the term "organization" refers to the licensee and all vehicles for which a license is owned or controlled by him; with respect to an affiliation, the term "organization" refers to the affiliation and all its affiliate's vehicles. A two-way radio dispatch system shall enable the dispatcher to communicate with the drivers of all vehicles in the organization simultaneously and for each driver to communicate with the dispatcher for the purpose of both providing service to customers and driver safety. In the case of an individual licensee who is not a member of an affiliation and who holds no more than one taxicab license and who certifies

that no person other than the licensee, the licensee's spouse or a natural or legally adopted child of the licensee will operate the taxicab throughout the entire license period, a "two-way radio dispatch system" may consist of any two-way radio communication device which permits direct customer communication with the driver of the vehicle, including a telephonic device.
(Prior code § 28-1; Added. Coun. J. 1-27-88, p. 10273; Amend. 2-7-90, p. 11774; 7-12-90, p. 18634; 6-16-94, p. 52109; 12-10-97, p. 59054; Amend. 11-15-00, p. 46957)

§9-112-020 Exclusive permission granted.

Subject to the conditions and limitations of this chapter, exclusive permission and authority are hereby granted to the licensees hereunder to operate the public passenger vehicles licensed hereunder upon the public streets and other public ways within the corporate limits of the city unless terminated or revoked as hereinafter provided.

It shall be unlawful and the city will not permit any public passenger vehicle not licensed hereunder to solicit business within the city of Chicago or to accept for transportation, sightseeing tours or charter trips, any passengers within the city of Chicago, excepting only passengers destined to the community in which such public passenger vehicle is licensed and then only when such transportation has been arranged for in advance by telephonic or written order.
(Prior code § 28-1.1; Amend. Coun. J. 2-3-87, p. 39199; 7-12-90, p. 18634)

§9-112-030 License required.

(a) It is unlawful for any person other than a metropolitan transit authority to operate a motor vehicle, or for the registered owner thereof to permit it to be operated, for the transportation of passengers for hire within the city, except on a funeral trip, unless it is licensed by the city as a public passenger vehicle pursuant to this chapter or unless it is exempt from licensure under Section 9-112-010(q).

(b) Any person who solicits for the transportation of passengers for hire when such transportation would be in violation of subsection (a), and the registered owner of any motor vehicle who permits such solicitation, shall be in violation of this section.
(Prior code § 28-2; Amend. Coun. J. 1-27-88, p. 10273; 7-12-90, p. 18634; 10-14-92, p. 22998)

§9-112-040 Interurban operations.

Nothing in this chapter shall be construed to prohibit any public passenger vehicle not licensed under this chapter from coming into the city to discharge passengers accepted for transportation outside the city. While the vehicle is in the city no roof light or other special light shall be used to indicate that the vehicle is vacant or subject to hire, and a white card bearing the words "Not For Hire" printed in black letters not less than two inches in height shall be displayed at the windshield of the vehicle. No person shall be solicited in the vehicle for transportation, sightseeing or charter, from any place within the city. Violation of any of the provisions of this section shall be a misdemeanor, and any person in control or possession of such a vehicle

who violates any of the provisions of this section shall be subject to arrest and may be punished upon conviction by incarceration in a penal institution other than a penitentiary for a term of 30 days for a first offense, 60 days for a second offense within 180 days of the first offense and 90 days for third offense within 180 days of the first offense and shall further be fined not less than $100.00 nor more than $500.00 for each offense under the procedures set forth in Section 1-2-1.1 of the Illinois Municipal Code. Illinois Revised Statutes Chapter 24, paragraph 1-2-1.1 (1985), as amended and the Illinois Code of Criminal Procedure. Illinois Revised Statutes Chapter 38, paragraph 100-1, et seq. (1985), as amended, in a separate proceeding.
(Prior code § 28-3; Amend. Coun. J. 2-3-87, p. 39202; 1-27-88, p. 10273; 7-12-90, p. 18634)

§9-112-050 Inspections.

No vehicle shall be licensed as a public passenger vehicle until it has been inspected under the direction of the commissioner and found to be in safe operating condition, to have all equipment as required by this chapter, and to have adequate body and seating facilities which are clean and in good repair for the comfort and convenience of passengers. All public passenger vehicles are subject to annual inspection except that taxicabs must be submitted for inspection semiannually.

If any licensee fails to appear and make his vehicle available for inspection after receiving a notification from the commissioner to do so, the commissioner shall suspend the licensee's public passenger vehicle license for a period of two days. If the licensee again fails to so appear, the commissioner shall suspend his license until the vehicle has passed an inspection pursuant to this section.
(Prior code § 28-4; Amend. Coun. J. 2-3-87, p. 39186; 2-7-90, p. 11774; 7-12-90, p. 18634)

§9-112-060 Specifications.

(a) The commissioner may issue licenses for motor vehicles to operate as public passenger vehicles only according to the following categories:

(1) Vehicles having a capacity for no more than eight passengers, excluding the driver, may only be licensed as taxicabs or liveries, except as provided in paragraph (3) of this subsection (a).

(2) Vehicles having a capacity for nine or more passengers, excluding the driver, may only be licensed as charter/sightseeing vehicles, except as provided in paragraph (3) of this subsection (a).

(3) Vehicles of any size licensed by the state of Illinois as medical carriers pursuant to the Illinois Vehicle Code, Illinois Revised Statutes Chapter 95½, Paragraph 8-101 et seq. and Paragraph 13-101-1, et seq. (1985), as amended, may be licensed as medical carriers.

(b) It shall not be a violation of this section for a medical carrier to transport ill, injured, infirm or handicapped persons for a purpose other than that of obtaining medical care or treatment.

(c) No vehicle shall be licensed as a public passenger vehicle unless it has two doors on each side other than vehicles designated under subsections (d) through (g), and except that any vehicle having seating capacity for more than eight adult passengers shall be so licensed provided it meets applicable Federal Motor Vehicle Safety Standards for vehicles of its size, type and proposed use.

(d) The commissioner may by rule provide that a motor vehicle to be licensed as a taxicab subsequent to January 1, 1998, as the result of the original issuance of a license, the transfer of a license, or the replacement of a previously licensed vehicle, must be a vehicle having a capacity of at least six passengers, excluding the driver, designated by the commissioner by rule; provided that this requirement shall not apply to a licensee who owns or controls fewer than four taxicab licenses; and provided that no more than 25 percent of the licensed taxicabs owned or controlled by a licensee shall be subject to this requirement. If more than one corporate licensee is controlled by the same person, or where the same person owns 25 percent or more of the stock in more than one corporate licensee, the total number of taxicab licenses that are so controlled or owned by the person shall be counted together in determining the requirements of this section.

(e) The commissioner may by rule provide that a motor vehicle to be licensed as a taxicab subsequent to January 1, 1998, as the result of the original issuance of a license, the transfer of a license, or the replacement of a previously licensed vehicle, must be a vehicle equipped for wheelchair access pursuant to standards established by the commissioner; unless (i) the licensee owns or controls fewer than fifteen licenses; (ii) or at least five percent or an aggregate number of 30, whichever is less, of the licensee's licensed taxicabs are currently equipped for wheelchair access. If more than one corporate licensee is controlled by the same person, or where the same person owns 25 percent or more of the stock in more than one corporate licensee, the total number of taxicab licenses that are so controlled or owned by the person shall be counted together in determining the requirements of this section.

(f) Any motor vehicle to be licensed as a taxicab under a public passenger vehicle license which at any time after January 1, 2001 was distributed pursuant to an open and competitive bidding procedure and/or a random selection or seniority procedure provided for in Section 9-112-380 of this chapter must be a vehicle having a capacity of at least six passengers, excluding the driver.

(g) The commissioner may by rule provide that up to 50 percent of all motor vehicles to be licensed as a taxicab under a public passenger vehicle license which at any time after January 1, 2001 was distributed pursuant to an open and competitive bidding procedure provided for in Section 9-112-380 of this chapter must be a vehicle equipped for wheelchair access pursuant to standards established by the commissioner.

(h) Any taxicab license by which an owner complies with subsections (d) through (g) above shall be designated in the records of the department of consumer services as being so compliant, and that henceforth, any future motor vehicles to be licensed as a taxicab under that license must be in compliance of such designation, regardless of whether the license is subsequently transferred or otherwise assigned.

(Prior code § 28-4.1; Amend. Coun. J. 2-3-87, p. 39199; 10-15-87, p. 5217; 1-27-88, p. 10273; 7-12-90, p. 18634; 12-10-97, p. 59054; Amend. 11-15-00, p. 46957)

§9-112-070 Application.

Application for public passenger vehicle licenses shall be made in writing, signed and sworn to by the applicant or if applicant is a corporation or partnership, by its duly authorized agent, upon forms provided by the commissioner. The application shall contain the full name, Chicago business address and residence address of the applicant, the names of the applicant's partners, or if the applicant is a corporation, of its officers and directors, the business telephone number of the applicant, the manufacturer's name, model, length of time in use, horsepower and seating capacity of the vehicle which applicant will use if a license is issued, and the class of public passenger vehicle license requested. If the applicant is affiliated or to become affiliated or identified with any affiliation by the color scheme of vehicles, trade name or emblem, telephone number, radio dispatch system, or service agreement, the application shall contain the full name, Chicago business address and telephone number of the affiliation, and a copy of the agreement with the affiliation shall be filed with the application.

(Prior code § 28-5; Amend. Coun. J. 2-3-87, p. 39186; 1-27-88, p. 10273; 7-12-90, p. 18634)

§9-112-080 Qualifications.

In order to qualify for a public passenger vehicle license, whether upon initial application or upon application for renewal of a license:

(a) An applicant shall be in compliance with the provisions of this chapter; and

(b) (1) With respect to any corporate applicant, the corporation shall be organized or qualified to do business under the laws of Illinois and have its principal place of business in the city of Chicago; or

(2) With respect to a partnership applicant, each partner shall meet the qualifications as if he were an individual applicant and the partnership shall have its principal place of business in the city of Chicago; or

(3) With respect to any applicant other than a corporation or partnership, he shall be a citizen or legal resident of the United States residing and domiciled in the city of Chicago, and in addition, if he is a member of an affiliation, the affiliation of which he is a member shall:

A. Be a corporation organized or qualified to do business under the laws of Illinois;

B. Have its principal place of business in the city of Chicago;

C. Have a duly authorized agent registered with the commissioner and comply with this ordinance and all orders, rules and regulations duly promulgated by the commissioner governing the business of such affiliations; and

D. From and after January 1, 1989, provide a two-way radio dispatch system for its affiliates; and

(4) Any applicant for issuance or renewal of a taxicab license shall provide a two-way radio dispatch system or avail himself of the radio dispatch system provided by an affiliation for all the taxicabs he will operate, if licenses are issued, in accordance with the following schedule:

A. Any person licensed for the first time in 1988 or later and any transferee pursuant to other provisions of this chapter shall so equip all vehicles from and after January 1, 1989;

B. Any person who holds 100 or more licenses shall so equip at least 50 percent of all his vehicles from and after January 1, 1989, and the remainder as each vehicle is replaced, but in no event later than January 1, 1994;

C. All other licensees shall so equip each vehicle from and after January 1, 1989 as it is replaced, but in no event later than January 1, 1994; or

(5) For taxicab licensees, an applicant must successfully complete a mandatory course of study as prescribed in paragraph 6 of this section and pass an examination as prescribed by the commissioner. If the applicant is a corporation, an officer of the corporation completing the course and passing the examination shall satisfy this requirement. If the applicant is a partnership, a partner completing the course and passing the examination shall satisfy this requirement. If the license is held by a corporation or a partnership, and the person having completed the course and passing the examination required in this section ceases to be an officer or a partner, the licensee shall have 60 days to achieve compliance with this section. Individuals which were licensed prior to the effective date of this ordinance and have continually been licensed shall be deemed to have met the requirements of this section. Corporations or partnerships which were licensed prior to the effective date of this ordinance shall be deemed to have met the requirements of this section as long as an officer or partner of the organization, as of the effective date of this ordinance, remains in such position within the organization licensed. The commissioner may require any licensee (or an officer or partner of a licensee) to complete this course again and pass the examination when such licensee is found to have engaged in conduct violative of any provision of this chapter or the rules and regulations promulgated thereunder; or

(6) The commissioner shall provide or cause to be offered on an ongoing basis a course of study covering the requirements of this Chapter 9-112, other relevant portions of the Municipal Code of Chicago, and the rules and regulations promulgated thereunder and such other additional subjects as the commissioner may require for all applicants for a taxicab license. The commissioner may contract with the city colleges or, with the approval of the mayor, with any state-approved vocational or technical school or not-for-profit organization to provide the required taxicab licensee course of study. No such course may be offered unless the curriculum for the course has been certified by the commissioner as being in compliance with this chapter. The certification shall be made annually and may be revoked at any time. The commissioner shall approve the tuition to be charged for such course; or

(7) Beginning January 1, 1999, any applicant for issuance or renewal of a taxicab license shall submit proof that he is affiliated with an affiliation licensed by the city, except that a licensee who certifies at the time of application that he/she owns or controls no more than one taxicab license and that no person other than the licensee, the licensee's spouse or a natural or legally adopted child of the licensee shall operate the taxicab throughout the entire license period need not be affiliated.

(8) Effective January 1, 2001, any public passenger vehicle licensee, who does not carry adequate worker's compensation insurance shall have its license(s) immediately suspended until such time as proof of such insurance is provided to the commissioner. In addition, if the commissioner finds that

the public passenger vehicle was operated without adequate workers' compensation insurance, the license shall be subject to revocation.

(9) Any public chauffeur upon filing a claim for temporary total disability with the Illinois Industrial Commission shall immediately surrender his public chauffeur license to the department. Such public chauffeur license shall remain surrendered for any period for which the chauffeur claims or receives benefits.

(10) Any public chauffeur whose claim for benefits with the Illinois Industrial Commission is determined to be fraudulent, not credible, or otherwise not filed in good faith may have his public chauffeur license revoked.

(Prior code § 28-5.1; Amend. Coun. J. 2-3-87, p. 39186; 1-27-88, p. 10273; 7-12-90, p. 18634; 1-14-97, p. 37750; 12-10-97, p. 59054; Amend. 11-15-00, p. 46957)

§9-112-090 Qualifications—Criteria for consideration.

(a) In determining whether an applicant is qualified for a public passenger vehicle license or the renewal thereof, the commissioner shall take into consideration:

(1) The character and reputation of the applicant or its members, officers or directors as law-abiding citizens, including, if applicable, the disciplinary record of the applicant in the operation of his public passenger vehicle and the disciplinary record of the applicant, or of any officer or director of a corporate applicant, as a public chauffeur;

(2) The financial ability of the applicant to render lawful, safe, suitable and comfortable service and to maintain or replace the equipment for such service;

(3) The financial responsibility of the applicant to maintain insurance for the payment of personal injury, death, and property damage claims;

(4) The financial ability of the applicant to pay all judgments and awards which may be rendered for any cause arising out of the operation of a public passenger vehicle;

(5) The color scheme proposed for use to prevent deception or confusion as to the ownership of the taxicab employed and the identity of the person or persons responsible for the service.

(b) No applicant shall be eligible for a public passenger vehicle license if any Chicago public passenger vehicle license or any Chicago public chauffeur license the applicant, or any officer or director of a corporate applicant or partner in a partnership applicant, has held within the previous five years was revoked, or if the applicant, or any officer or director of a corporate applicant or partner in a partnership applicant, within the five years immediately preceding the date of his application, has been either convicted, or in custody, under parole or under any other noncustodial supervision resulting from a conviction in a court of any jurisdiction for the commission of any felony as defined by Article 2 of the Illinois Criminal Code of 1961, as amended.

If the commissioner has knowledge that a licensee has been charged with the commission of a forcible felony, as defined in Article 2 of the Illinois Criminal Code of 1961, as amended, arising in connection with the provision of public passenger vehicle services, the commissioner shall suspend the pub-

lic passenger vehicle license of the licensee until final adjudication is made with respect to such charges.
(Prior code § 28-5.2; Amend. Coun. J. 1-27-88, p. 10273; 2-7-90, p. 11774; 7-12-90, p. 18634; 12-10-97, p. 59054)

§9-112-100 Investigation and issuance of license.

Upon receipt of an application for a public passenger vehicle license the commissioner shall, and in the case of an application for license renewal, upon good cause shown, the commissioner may cause an investigation to be made of: (1) the character and reputation of the applicant as a law-abiding citizen; and (2) the financial ability of the applicant to render safe and comfortable transportation service, to maintain or replace the equipment for such service and to pay all judgments and awards which may be rendered for any cause arising out of the operation of a public passenger vehicle during the license period. If the commissioner shall find that the application, and all other statements and documents required to be filed with the application have been properly executed, and that the applicant is qualified to provide the services required of a license holder, the commissioner shall issue to him in his name a license for each public passenger vehicle applied for; provided, that each such vehicle is in safe and proper condition at the time the license is issued; and further provided, that the vehicle is either registered in applicant's name or, in the case of a leased vehicle, that the applicant has provided the commissioner with a copy of the lease, in a form acceptable to the commissioner, which lease must be a minimum of one year's duration with an expiration date of December 31st and must include an acknowledgment by the lessor/owner of the vehicle that he has given his consent for the vehicle to be used as the type of public passenger vehicle for which a license is sought.

All licenses issued pursuant to this chapter shall expire on December 31st following the date of issue unless they are renewed within the period specified in this section. Application for renewal of any license issued pursuant to this chapter shall be made no later than the last day of February of the year for which the license is to be renewed.
(Prior code § 28-6; Amend. Coun. J. 1-27-88, pp. 10273, 10288; 2-7-90, p. 11774; 7-12-90, p. 18634)

§9-112-105 Safety features—Required— Exceptions.

(a) No license for a taxicab shall be issued or renewed for a license period beginning on or after January 1, 1993 unless the taxicab is equipped with at least one of the following safety features or combination of safety features, all of which shall be in compliance with specifications set forth in regulations promulgated by the commissioner:

(1) A safety shield device capable of completely separating the driver's seat from the rear passenger compartment;

(2) A system enabling the silent activation of distress or trouble lights, plus a permanently installed safe; provided, that no such system shall be deemed to satisfy this section unless the system was installed in the motor vehicle prior to the effective date of this amendatory ordinance; and provided further that no such system shall be deemed to satisfy this section in any motor vehicle beginning March 1, 2001;

(3) A system enabling the silent activation of a warning to a dispatcher or the police department either by radio or telephonic communication, plus a permanently installed safe;

(4) Such other system that the commissioner determines by rule provides at least as much protection as the systems described above.

In addition, any motor vehicle to be licensed as a taxicab subsequent to January 1, 1997 but prior to January 1, 1998, due to either the original issuance of a license, the transfer of a license, or the replacement of a previously licensed vehicle, must be equipped with a safety shield device as provided in subparagraph (1) above no later than July 1, 1997, or the date of the issuance, transfer or replacement, whichever is later, unless (i) the licensee has fewer that four taxicab licenses or (ii) at least 25 percent of the licensee's licensed taxicabs are currently equipped with such a safety shield device. In addition, any motor vehicle to be licensed as a taxicab on or after January 1, 1998, due to either the original issuance of a license, the transfer of a license, or the replacement of a previously licensed vehicle, must be equipped with a safety shield device as provided in subparagraph (1). If more than one corporate licensee is controlled by the same person, or where the same person owns 25 percent or more of the stock in more than one corporate licensee, the total number of taxicab licenses that are so controlled or owned by the person shall be counted together in determining compliance with this section.

The specifications promulgated by the commissioner under this section shall be designed to maximize public chauffeur safety in light of current technology and reasonable economic concerns.

(b) The equipment required by this section shall be maintained in good working order at all times. The license of any licensee who violates this section shall be subject to immediate suspension until the licensee demonstrates compliance with this section.

(c) The requirements of this section do not apply to a licensee who owns or controls no more than one taxicab license and who certifies that no person other than the licensee, the licensee's spouse or a natural or legally adopted child of the licensee will operate the taxicab throughout the entire license period. Any licensee who makes such a certification and permits any other person other than those persons specified above to operate the taxicab during the license period shall be subject to a fine not less than $50.00 nor more than $500.00 for each offense, plus the revocation of his or her taxicab license.
(Added. Coun. J. 10-14-92, p. 22998; Amend. 1-14-97, p. 37750; 12-10-97, p. 59054; 12-4-02, p. 99931)

§9-112-110 License fees.

The annual fee for each public passenger vehicle license of the class herein set forth is as follows:

Charter/sightseeing vehicle	$100.00
Livery vehicle	200.00
Medical carriers	150.00
Taxicab	500.00

The fee shall be paid in advance when the license is issued and shall be applied to the cost of issuing such license, including without being limited to, the investigations, inspections and supervision necessary therefor, and to the cost of regulating all operations of public passenger vehicles as provided in this chapter.

Nothing in this section shall affect the right of the city to impose or collect a vehicle tax and any occupational tax, as authorized by the laws of the state of Illinois, in addition to the license fee herein provided.

The fees specified in this section shall be in addition to any amounts payable pursuant to the competitive bidding process.

(Prior code § 28-7; Amend. Coun. J. 2-3-87, pp. 39199, 39202; Corrected. 3-11-87, p. 40423; Amend. 1-27-88, p. 10273; 2-7-90, p. 11774; 7-12-90, p. 18634; 11-17-93, p. 42192; 3-26-96, p. 19271; 12-10-97, p. 59054)

§9-112-120 Temporary permits—Fees.

The commissioner may issue temporary permits for the operation within the city of a charter/sightseeing vehicle by a person whose charter/sightseeing business is located outside the city, and who conducts that business within the city on an occasional basis. The commissioner may also issue temporary permits to a coachman of one or more charter/sightseeing vehicles licensed under this chapter in order to operate additional vehicles as charter/sightseeing vehicles on a temporary basis under the licensee's authority and control. The daily fee for any permit under this section shall not exceed $25.00 per vehicle. Such vehicles shall be subject to all applicable provisions of Chapters 9-104 and 9-112 of the Chicago Municipal Code as well as all rules and regulations relating thereto promulgated pursuant to Section 2-24-040 of this code.

(Prior code § 28-7.1; Amend. Coun. J. 2-3-87, p. 39199; 1-27-88, p. 10273; 7-12-90, p. 18634; 11-10-94, p. 59125)

§9-112-140 Personal license—Fair employment practice.

It shall be unlawful for a licensee to lease or contract for the independent operation or management of the licensee's operation of any taxicab or livery licensed hereunder for any consideration whatsoever without first registering as a license manager as provided in Section 9-112-322 of this code. The relationship between the licensee of any taxicab or livery and the driver thereof shall be such as they mutually may agree upon by contract, and may be expressed or implied, subject to the restrictions contained in this chapter and regulations promulgated hereunder; and provided, that the driver thereof is duly licensed by the city as a public chauffeur as required by ordinance.

Each such lease or contract shall be in writing and in a form approved by the commissioner; provided, that where the relationship is one of employer-employee, no such writing shall be required. The licensee shall provide a copy of any such lease to the commissioner upon request. The commissioner shall issue regulations governing the following terms of such leases and contracts: (a) identification of the parties; (b) identification of the leased vehicle; (c) duration of the lease; (d) obligations of the lessor for maintaining the safety of the vehicle. In formulating such regulations, the commissioner shall consider the effect of the lease or contract on the safety of the public, the maintenance and care of taxicabs or liveries, and the availability of taxicab and/or livery service. Lessor shall not lease any taxicab or livery to any qualified driver unless that taxicab or livery is fit for service as a taxicab or livery.

It shall be unlawful for any person other than the lessee or contractor or an employee of the licensee to operate a taxicab during the term of such lease or contract. There shall be no discrimination against any person employed or seeking employment on account of race, color, religion, national origin or ancestry.
(Prior code § 28-9; Amend. Coun. J. 2-3-87, p. 39186; 1-27-88, p. 10273; 7-12-90, p. 18634; Amend. 11-15-00, p. 46957)

§9-112-142 Liability for actions of public chauffeur.

(a) Subject to the exemption in paragraph (b) of this section, any licensee whose public passenger vehicle is operated by a public chauffeur found in violation of this chapter, Chapter 9-104, or any rules or regulations promulgated thereunder, shall be subject to a fine, or license suspension, or both, pursuant to rules and regulations promulgated under Section 9-112-260 for subsequent violations of the same ordinance or rules by the same chauffeur.

(b) In the event that a public chauffeur is found to have violated any provision of this chapter, Chapter 9-104, or any rules and regulations promulgated thereunder while operating a licensee's vehicle, the licensee shall not be liable under paragraph (a) of this section for the first subsequent violation by the chauffeur of the same ordinance or rule provided that the offense involved does not involve refusal of service and that the chauffeur, after the first offense and prior to the subsequent offense, has completed a retraining course, approved by the commissioner, at the licensee's expense.

(c) All licensees have an affirmative duty to respond to requests for service made by the general public and are responsible for the actions of any employee, chauffeur-lessee, affiliation, radio dispatch service of the licensee, in failing to respond to such a request for service.
(Added. Coun. J. 12-10-97, p. 59054; Amend. 11-15-00, p. 46957)

§9-112-145 Lease rate regulations.

(a) In addition to the rules and regulations otherwise provided for in this section, the commissioner shall, subject to the limitations provided in this section, establish by rule the maximum rates that a lessor may charge for the rental of a taxicab, including, to the extent permitted by law, rates for goods and services provided by the lessor in connection with such rental. The maximum rates shall be established at an amount determined by the commissioner to: (1) enable the lessor to receive adequate revenues to pay the lessor's reasonable expenses and receive a just and reasonable rate of return on the lessor's investment; and (2) provide for safe and adequate taxicab service within the city by providing lessees with an opportunity to earn a fair and reasonable income. In establishing such rates, the commissioner shall consider: (1) vehicle, equipment and license costs; (2) asset depreciation; (3) the costs of insurance, operation and maintenance, uninsured repairs, wages and salaries, garage storage, taxes, fees, radio dispatching and administration, as well as all other periodic expenses paid by the lessor; (4) the extent to which the lessor or persons who have invested in the lessor also have investments in other persons or entities who may benefit directly or indirectly from the lease; and (5) such other factors that the commissioner considers appropriate to further the purposes of this chapter.

(b) No lease rate limitations shall be effective until the commissioner has conducted a public hearing on the proposed maximum lease rates. At least seven days before the public hearing, the commissioner shall publish in a newspaper of general circulation within the city a notice of the time, date, place and subject matter of the hearing. At the hearing, all interested persons shall be given a reasonable opportunity to be heard.

(c) The commissioner shall review periodically the maximum lease rates then in effect to ensure that such rates are consistent with the objectives expressed in this section. However, the commissioner may not revise the lease rate limitations in effect under this section more than once within any 12-month period unless the commissioner determines that extraordinary circumstances require the revision for the purposes of this section.

(d) Notwithstanding any lease rate limitation established under this section, including any limitation imposed by subsection (f), the commissioner may, upon petition of an individual lessor, permit the lessor to charge a rate in excess of that otherwise permitted if the lessor demonstrates that the rate limitation prevents the lessor from receiving adequate revenues to pay the lessor's reasonable expenses and receive a just and reasonable rate of return on the lessor's investment.

(e) The commissioner may require all holders of taxicab licenses to provide such financial information as may be reasonably necessary to establish maximum lease rates under this section. Any licensee who fails to provide such information may not file a petition under subsection (d) for permission to impose a higher lease rate, may not become a party to any proceeding under this section, and may not contest in a proceeding under this section or otherwise the rate limitations established under this section. Information that is submitted pursuant to this subsection shall be kept confidential and shall not be disclosed to the public.

(f) Notwithstanding any other provision of this section, no licensee may, within 90 days after the effective date of this section, charge a rate for the lease of a taxicab, including charges for related goods and services, at a rate higher than that which was in effect on December 1, 1993, provided that such licensee may within such period increase the rate by a total amount no greater than 2.8 percent, based on the percentage increase in the United States Average All Items All Urban Customers Consumer Price Index (CPI-U) published by the United States Department of Labor, Bureau of Labor Statistics, for the 12-month period from October, 1992 to October, 1993.

(g) Any licensee who imposes a lease rate or other charge in excess of that which is permitted under this section, or who fails to provide financial information that is required under subsection (e), or who otherwise violates this section shall be subject to a fine of not less than $200.00 and not more than $750.00 for each offense, and shall be subject to the suspension or revocation of his or her taxicab license in the manner provided in this chapter and the rules and regulations adopted under this chapter. Each day that a violation continues, and each unlawful lease that is executed, shall constitute a separate and distinct offense. In addition, the commissioner may request the city to bring an action in an appropriate court for injunctive or other equitable relief against violations of this section.

(h) This section shall apply to all leases that are entered into, amended or extended on or after the effective date of this section.

(i) Each taxicab licensee must submit an affidavit at the time of renewal of his license indicating all lease rates, fees, and charges to be charged to public chauffeurs in connection with the leasing of the licensee's taxicabs. Taxicab licensees may not charge any public chauffeur a lease rate, fees, and/or charges in an amount greater than that indicated in the affidavit without having furnished in writing the commissioner 30 days advance notice of the proposed changes in the lease rates, fees, and/or other charges.
(Added. Coun. J. 12-15-93, p. 44059; Amend. 12-10-97, p. 59054; Amend. 11-15-00, p. 46957)

§9-112-150 Vehicles other than taxicabs—Sticker license emblem to be affixed.

Except in the case of taxicabs, the commissioner shall deliver with each license a sticker license emblem which shall bear the words "Public Vehicle License" and "Chicago" and the numerals designating the year for which the license is issued, a reproduction of the corporate seal of the city, the names of the mayor and the commissioner and serial number identical with the number of the public vehicle license. The predominant background colors of such sticker license emblems shall be different from the vehicle tax emblem for the same year and shall be changed annually. The cabman or coachman shall affix, or cause to be affixed, the sticker emblem on the inside of the glass part of the windshield of the vehicle.
(Prior code § 28-10; Amend. Coun. J. 1-27-88, p. 10273; 7-12-90, p. 18634)

§9-112-160 Taxicabs—Metal plate to be affixed.

In the case of taxicabs, the commissioner shall deliver with each license, a metal plate, of such size, shape and material as he may determine, which shall bear the words: "City of Chicago," the public passenger vehicle license number and the year of issuance impressed thereon in letters and figures not less than three-quarters of an inch in height. The metal plate shall be affixed by the commissioner to the exterior of the cowl or hood of the taxicab in such location as to be easily visible. Within 120 days after the effective date of this ordinance each cabman who is granted a new license for a taxicab shall submit each of his taxicabs to the commissioner for inspection and the commissioner shall affix the metal plate to each such taxicab as required by this section. In each year after 1986 the metal plate shall be affixed by the commissioner at the time of renewal of a current year's public passenger vehicle license.
(Prior code § 28-10.1; Amend. Coun. J. 2-3-87, p. 39186; 10-15-87, p. 5217; 7-12-90, p. 18634)

§9-112-170 Unlawful to operate vehicle without current emblem.

It shall be unlawful for any person to operate a public passenger vehicle for hire without the metal plate or emblem for the current year affixed. In addition to any other penalty to which he may be subjected as provided in this chapter or under the rules and regulations promulgated pursuant to Section 2-24-040 of this code, the chauffeur's license of such person found to be guilty of such an act shall be revoked.
(Prior code § 28-10.2; Amend. Coun. J. 2-3-87, p. 39186; 1-27-88, p. 10273; 7-12-90, p. 18634)

§9-112-180 Unlawful for licensee to operate vehicle without current emblem.

It shall be unlawful for any licensee to operate or permit any person to operate a public passenger vehicle for hire without the metal plate or emblem for the current year affixed and, in addition to any other penalty provided by this chapter or under the rules and regulations promulgated pursuant to Section 2-24-040 of this code, the license of such licensee shall be revoked.
(Prior code § 28-10.3; Amend. Coun. J. 2-3-87, p. 39186; 1-27-88, p. 10273; 7-12-90, p. 18634)

§9-112-190 Tampering with emblem unlawful—Penalty.

It shall be unlawful for any person to tamper with, alter or reaffix such metal plate or emblem to any vehicle or to cause the same to be done and any person guilty of such an act shall be subject to a fine of not less than $200.00 nor more than $500.00 for each offense, and if the person be a licensee, upon conviction thereof, his public passenger vehicle license for the vehicle shall be revoked.
(Prior code § 28-10-4; Amend. Coun. J. 2-3-87, p. 39202; 1-27-88, p. 10273; 7-12-90, p. 18634)

§9-112-200 Replacement of damaged or stolen emblems—Fee.

In the event a cabman desires to replace either the vehicle or the portion of the vehicle to which the metal plate is affixed, or if the metal plate or the portion of the vehicle to which it is affixed becomes damaged so as to require replacement or repair, the cabman may remove the metal plate and shall immediately deliver it to the commissioner who shall reaffix the same to the repaired or new vehicle for a fee of $25.00 or, if the metal plate has been damaged or defaced, the commissioner shall obtain a duplicate and affix the same for an additional fee of $10.00. In the event a metal plate, emblem, or license card shall become lost or stolen, the licensee shall furnish to the commissioner a statement under oath giving all of the facts pertaining to the loss or theft known to the licensee and the commissioner shall obtain and affix a duplicate metal plate for a fee of $35.00, or a duplicate emblem or license card for a fee of $25.00.
(Prior code § 28-10.5; Amend. 2-3-87, p. 39202; 10-15-87, p. 5217; 1-27-88, p. 10273; 7-12-90, p. 18634; 11-17-93, p. 42192)

§9-112-210 License card.

In addition to the license, the metal plate and sticker emblem the commissioner shall deliver a license card for each vehicle. This card shall contain the name of the cabman or coachman, the license number of the vehicle and the date of inspection thereof. It shall be signed by the commissioner and shall contain blank spaces upon which entries of the date of every inspection of the vehicle and such other entries as may be required shall be made. It shall be of different color each year. The licensee shall provide a suitable frame with glass cover affixed on the inside of the vehicle in a conspicuous place in such manner as may be determined by the commissioner for insertion and removal of the public passenger vehicle license card. In every livery vehicle and taxicab the frame shall also be provided for insertion and removal of the chauffeur's license card and such other notice as may be required by the provisions of this chapter and the rules of the commissioner. It is unlawful to carry any passenger or his baggage unless the license cards are exposed in the frame as provided in this section.

(Prior code § 28-11; Amend. Coun. J. 1-27-88, p. 10273; 7-12-90, p. 18634)

§9-112-215 Underserved areas.

(a) By May 1, 1998, the commissioner shall establish by rule a plan for increasing service in areas of the city that are inadequately served by taxicabs. Prior to that date, the commissioner shall conduct one or more public hearings and shall seek recommendations from all interested persons. The plan may include provisions that certain areas of the city be provided with a certain number of taxicabs on an ongoing basis by an affiliation or affiliations. Any rule providing for a mandatory assignment of taxicabs may provide that such assignments be in a proportionate number to the total membership of each affiliation.

(b) The commissioner shall regularly review the effectiveness of the plan and revise, expand or update it for the purpose of insuring adequate service to all areas of the city.

(c) Each taxicab which is in service and leased by a public chauffeur must at all times have its two-way radio dispatch system activated to a level which is readily audible to the driver.

(d) Each taxicab which is in service and leased by a public chauffeur must respond in a timely manner to radio dispatch requests for service and convey passenger(s) requesting transportation originating from an underserved area to their destination at a minimum of at least once during the duration of a lease of 24 hours or less, or at least seven times during the duration of any weekly lease.

(e) Taxicab license holders and affiliations shall have an affirmative duty to insure compliance with this section by the drivers of vehicles with taxicab licenses issued to them or their affiliates. Taxicab license holders and affiliations shall immediately file a report to the commissioner on any driver who fails to comply with the requirements provided in paragraph (d) above.

(f) No taxicab licensee shall lease his or her vehicle to a public chauffeur unless the public chauffeur has already signed a prelease agreement with the licensee, in a form acceptable to the commissioner, whereby the public chauffeur acknowledges that he has an affirmative duty to accept passengers requesting service and may not refuse or deny service to or in any other way discriminate against individuals based on race, gender, ethnicity, or the geographical location of either the origination or destination of the fare; that he has an affirmative duty to transport persons with service dogs as required in 775 ILCS 30/1, et seq.; that he has an affirmative duty to keep his radio dispatch service equipment on and audible at all times when operating the taxicab; and that he has an affirmative duty to respond in a timely manner to radio dispatch requests for service and convey the passengers requesting transportation originating from an underserved area to their destination at a minimum of at least once during the duration of a lease of 24 hours or less, or at least seven times during the duration of any weekly lease. Taxicab licensees shall maintain copies of these pre-lease agreements and furnish them to the commissioner upon request.

(g) No public chauffeur license shall be issued or renewed unless the public chauffeur has already signed an agreement with the department of consumer services whereby the applicant acknowledges that he has an affirmative duty to accept passengers requesting service and may not refuse or deny service to or in any way discriminate against individuals based on race, gender, ethnicity, or the geographical location of either the origination or destination of the fare; that he has an affirmative duty to transport persons with service dogs as required in 7750 ILCS 30/1, et seq.; that he has an affirmative duty to keep his radio dispatch service equipment on and audible at all times when operating the taxicab; and that he has an affirmative duty to respond in a timely manner to radio dispatch requests for service and convey the passengers requesting transportation originating from an underserved area to their destination at a minimum of at least once during the duration of a lease of 24 hours or less, or at least seven times during the duration of any weekly lease.

(h) Taxicab affiliations have an affirmative duty to insure that an adequate number of requests for service are received by affiliations and transmitted to the public chauffeurs operating affiliated taxicabs which would enable said public chauffeurs to meet their requirements under paragraph (d) of this section above. Affiliations which fail, during a licensing year, to receive a number of telephonic requests for service originating from underserved areas equal to the product of 300 times the number of affiliated taxicabs in the affiliation shall be deemed to be in violation of this section and shall be issued a probationary license for the subsequent year. Affiliations operating under a probationary license which fail to receive and answer a number of telephonic requests for service originating from underserved areas equal to the product of 300 times the number of affiliated taxicabs in the affiliation may have their applications for renewal of licensing denied.

(i) No public chauffeur license shall be renewed unless the public chauffeur submits proof, in a form acceptable to the commissioner, from the taxicab licensee and/or affiliation that the applicant for renewal has complied with the requirements of this section since the last time the applicant's public chauffeur license was issued or renewed.

(j) All taxicabs whose licenses were originally issued to qualified economically disadvantaged public chauffeurs responding to requests for qualifications issued by the commissioner pursuant to Section 9-112-380(b)(3) of this code, as in effect subsequent to January 1, 1998 and prior to December 31, 2000, are required to operate exclusively in underserved areas a minimum of eight hours a day between 6:00 a.m. and 10:00 p.m. for three days per week. During that time, such cabs may discharge passengers at any location, but must only accept passengers in underserved areas. Affiliations with which such taxicabs are affiliated shall keep records on all radio dispatch calls answered by such taxicabs and furnish them to the department of consumer services upon request.

(k) The commissioner is authorized to promulgate all rules and regulations necessary for enforcement of this section, including, but not limited to, establishing the responsibilities of affiliations and their affiliates in monitoring compliance with this rule by the lessee-drivers of the taxicabs affiliated with the affiliation and the responsibilities of affiliations and their affiliates in maintaining and providing records to the department regarding compliance with this rule.

(l) An affiliation, affiliate licensee, or public chauffeur may be subject to fines not to exceed $750.00 per violation and/or suspension or revocation of its license for acts committed by them, their employees, contractors, or agents which result in material non-compliance with this ordinance, the plan or any rules or regulations promulgated pursuant to this section. In addition to fines and/or suspension or revocation of its license for failure to provide service to persons or locations within the city of Chicago, a taxicab licensed under this ordinance may be prohibited for a period of up to 29 days from accepting passengers for transportation at any airport within the corporate limits of the city of Chicago.
(Added. Coun. J. 12-10-97, p. 59054; Amend. 11-15-00, p. 46957)

§9-112-220 Insurance.

Every licensee shall carry public liability and property damage insurance and, where applicable, workers compensation insurance for his employees with solvent and responsible insurers approved by the commissioner, licensed by and authorized to do business in the state of Illinois, and qualified under the laws of Illinois to assume the risk in the amounts hereinafter set forth, to secure payment by the licensee, his agents, employees or lessees of any final judgment or settlement of any claim against them resulting from any occurrence caused by or arising out of the operation or use of any of the licensee's public passenger vehicles.

Every insurance policy or contract for such insurance shall provide that suit may be brought in any court of competent jurisdiction upon such policy or contract by any person for the payment and satisfaction of any final judgment rendered against the licensee or person insured arising from the operation or use of such vehicle.

Every public liability insurance policy must meet the requirements of state law, including but not being limited to, Illinois Revised Statutes Chapter 73, paragraph 755a and paragraph 755a-2 governing coverage for damages from owners or operators of uninsured motor vehicles, hit-and-run motor vehicles, and underinsured motorists. Such public liability insurance policies must also be acceptable to the comptroller and to the corporation counsel, as to form and legality.

Each public liability insurance policy shall provide the following coverage:

For each vehicle with
capacity of more than 10 seats........................ $1,000,000.00 Combined
single limit coverage per occurrence;

For each vehicle with a capacity of up to 10 seats,
until January 1, 1988, at least.............. $50,000.00 for property damage,
$250,000.00 for injuries to or
death of any one person, and
$300,000.00 for injuries to or death
of more than one person, if any one accident;

and from and after January 1, 1988,
at least...$350,000.00 combined single
limit coverage per occurrence.

The insurance policy shall contain a description of each public passenger vehicle insured, manufacturer's name and number, the state license number and the public passenger vehicle license number.

In lieu of an insurance policy or contract a surety bond or bonds with a corporate surety or sureties licensed by and authorized to do business under the laws of Illinois, may be accepted by the commissioner for all or any part of such insurance; provided, that each bond shall be in the form and language prescribed by the comptroller and approved as to form and legality by the corporation counsel and shall provide terms and conditions for the payment and satisfaction of any final judgment in conformity with and containing equivalent indemnity provisions of an insurance policy or contract required by this section.

All insurance policies or contracts or surety bonds required by this section, or copies thereof certified by the insurers, or sureties shall be filed with the commissioner and no insurance policy or contract or bond shall be subject to cancellation except on thirty days' previous notice to the commissioner. If any insurance policy or contract or bond is cancelled or permitted to lapse for any reason, the commissioner shall suspend the license for the vehicle affected for a period not to exceed 10 days to permit another insurance policy or contract or bond to be supplied in compliance with the provisions of this section. If such other insurance policy or contract or bond is not supplied within the period of suspension of the license, the mayor shall revoke the license for such vehicle. In the event that such insurance or bond is supplied, the commissioner shall nevertheless suspend the license for each vehicle affected for an additional period of five days for every day of noncompliance, except by reason of the insolvency of the insurer without advance written notice to the licensee, for the first such violation of insurance or bond requirements, and a period of 10 days for every day of noncompliance for the second such violation within any three-year period. The third violation of this insurance or bond requirement within any three-year period shall result in revocation of the licenses of the affected vehicles.

(Prior code § 28-12; Amend. Coun. J. 5-13-87, p. 361; 7-12-90, p. 18634)

§9-112-230 Affiliations.

(a) No organization may operate as an affiliation of city of Chicago public passenger vehicle license holders without first being licensed by the commissioner. Application for an affiliation license shall be made on such forms and accompanied by such documents as the commissioner may require and shall include, but not be limited to, proof that the affiliation has its principal place of business in Chicago and the name, Chicago business address and telephone number, residence address and license numbers of each licensee so affiliated. Subsequent to licensing, if there are changes in any material information contained in the submitted license application, such changes must be reported in writing to the commissioner within 48 hours. All affiliation licenses expire on December 1st. Renewal of affiliation licensing must be made during the month preceding expiration of the licensing.

(b) No affiliation may have as affiliates both taxicab and livery license holders. No taxicab affiliation may have more than 25 percent of the total number of city licensed taxicabs as affiliates. Affiliations properly registered with the department of consumer services before the effective date of this ordinance with a number of affiliated taxicabs greater than 25 percent of the total number of city licensed taxicabs may retain any affiliated taxicabs as members provided that the license of the affiliated taxicab is not transferred, and further provided that the affiliation not accept any additional licensed taxicabs as new affiliates until such time as the total number of affiliated vehicles in the affiliation is less than 25 percent of the total number of city licensed taxicabs.

(c) No affiliation licensed under this chapter may dispatch a taxicab or livery for the purpose of providing transportation to a customer unless the vehicle is properly licensed to provide the transportation requested. The commissioner will notify an affiliation in the event of the suspension or revocation of any of its affiliate's licenses.

(d) Whenever notice is required to be served by the commissioner on any licensee, service by certified mail upon the registered address of an affiliation shall be deemed to have been made upon the affiliate to which the service applies within three business days after the affiliation is served.

(e) (1) All affiliate taxicabs and liveries licensed by the city of Chicago, when in service and for hire, must be equipped at all times to allow for the dispatch of the vehicle to a member of the general public requesting transportation. Affiliations and affiliates are responsible for ensuring that such equipment is activated and operating at all times when the affiliated taxicab is in service.

(2) In the event that an affiliation contracts with a radio dispatch service to provide a two-way radio dispatch system to its affiliates, the affiliation shall be liable for any acts or omissions of the radio dispatch service which may violate any of this ordinance or the rules and regulations promulgated thereunder.

(3) All radio dispatch systems used by affiliations shall be subject to the approval of the commissioner.

(4) No affiliation shall discriminate in the dispatch of service against any member of the general public requesting transportation on the basis of age, sex, race, religion, sexual orientation, disability or national origin.

(5) No affiliation shall refuse service to any person or location within the corporate limits of the city of Chicago.

(6) Every lease authorizing a person other than the affiliate to operate an affiliate's taxicab shall contain the following language: "As a condition of this lease, the lessee agrees that at all times when the taxicab is operated, to: keep its radio dispatch equipment activated in such a manner to be clearly audible to the driver; and respond to any and all requests for service which the affiliation may assign to this taxicab." Such language shall be printed in a font which is equal to or greater than the font size of any other language in the lease.

(f) Each affiliation must have on file with the commissioner a written agreement between its affiliates and the affiliation detailing the responsibilities of each towards the other. Each such written agreement must provide that it is not only the responsibility of the affiliate, but also the responsibility of the affiliation, acting as an agent of the affiliate pursuant to their agreement, to insure that any driver of the affiliate's taxicabs shall, at all times when the taxicab is operated, keep the radio dispatch equipment activated in such a manner to be clearly audible to the driver and respond to any and all requests for service which the affiliation may assign to the affiliated taxicab. Affiliations are authorized to include in such agreements that the affiliation be indemnified by their affiliate(s) for any judgment entered against the affiliation resulting from any occurrence caused by or arising out of the operation or use of any of the affiliate's public passenger vehicles.

(g) Each taxicab affiliation shall file with the commissioner a plan detailing the off-street parking of its affiliated taxicabs when such vehicles are not in use. Beginning September 1, 1998, the commissioner may provide by rule that each taxicab affiliation have available legal off-street parking for its affiliated vehicles when the vehicles are not in use.

(h) An affiliate may not have its membership in an affiliation terminated by the affiliation, except on 30 days' prior written notice to the affiliate and the commissioner.

(i) If following notice to the last registered address of an affiliation and a hearing held by the department of administrative hearings, an affiliation is found to have violated any of the provisions of this ordinance and the rules and regulations promulgated thereunder, the affiliation may be subject to a fine not exceeding $750.00 for each offense, or may be subject to an order of restitution or other appropriate equitable relief. If an affiliation is found to have abandoned its principal place of business in the city or if official notice or legal process cannot be served upon it at the affiliation's last Chicago address filed with the commissioner, its license shall be revoked and the public passenger vehicles of all its affiliates shall be suspended until their affiliation is severed by removal of all equipment and the indicia of affiliation and cancellation of agreements with the affiliation and the licensees can demonstrate compliance with the insurance and two-way radio dispatch system requirements of this chapter.

(j) After January 1, 2003, no taxicab licensee may lease a taxicab or otherwise allow any person to operate a taxicab unless the person authorized to operate the taxicab has completed, within the past 24 months, a continuing public chauffeur retraining program, approved and in compliance with reasonable standards established by the commissioner, which is offered in compliance with state law. The commissioner may also contract with the city colleges or, with any state-approved vocational or technical school or any not-for-profit organization to provide such a course. In the event that a fee is charged for a continuing public chauffeur retraining program, the commissioner may, by rule, establish a maximum amount to be charged to the affiliate whose drivers are taking the training. Affiliations which fail to offer, either by itself or by contract with a state-approved vocational or technical school or not-for-profit organization, a continuing education program approved by the commissioner shall be assessed an annual fee of $100.00 per vehicle affiliated with the affiliation.

(k) The annual fee for each affiliation license is $100.00 plus $5.00 for each public passenger vehicle license affiliated with the affiliation at the time of licensing. The affiliation shall be assessed a fee of $25.00 for each public passenger vehicle license which becomes affiliated with the affiliation during the licensing year.

(Added. Coun. J. 12-10-97, p. 59054; Amend. 11-15-00, p. 46957)

§9-112-240 Payment of judgments and awards.

Every licensee shall pay each judgment or award for loss or damage in the operation or use of a public passenger vehicle rendered against the licensee by any court or commission of competent jurisdiction within 90 days after its judgment or award shall have become final and not stayed by supersedeas. If any such judgment shall not be so paid, the mayor shall revoke the license of the public passenger vehicle licensee concerned.

(Prior code § 28-13; Amend. Coun. J. 2-3-87, p. 39186; 1-27-88, p. 10273; 7-12-90, p. 18634)

§9-112-250 Cancellation of affiliates registration.

If the affiliation abandons its principal place of business in the city of Chicago, or if any official notice or legal process cannot be served upon it at its last Chicago address registered in the office of the commissioner, and it fails to respond to such notice, or appear in answer to legal process at the time fixed therein, or if it denies liability on the ground that it was not the owner or operator of such vehicle, or if any judgment or award against the affiliation is not paid within the time provided in Section 9-112-240, its registration shall be canceled and the public passenger vehicles of all its affiliated licensees shall be declared unsafe by the commissioner and their licenses shall be suspended until their affiliation is severed by removal of all equipment and indicia of affiliation and cancellation of all agreements with the affiliation.

(Prior code § 28-13.1; Amend. Coun. J. 2-3-87, p. 39186; 1-27-88, p. 10273; 7-12-90, p. 18634)

§9-112-260 Suspension of license; fines; equitable relief.

If any public passenger vehicle shall become unsafe for operation or if its body or seating facilities shall be so damaged, deteriorated or unclean as to render the vehicle unfit for public use, the license therefor shall be suspended by the commissioner until the vehicle shall be made safe for operation and its body shall be repaired and painted and its seating facilities shall be reconditioned or replaced as directed by the commissioner. In determining whether any public passenger vehicle is unfit for public use, the commissioner shall give consideration to its effect on the health, comfort and convenience of passengers and its public appearance on the streets of the city.

The commissioner may seek suspension of the license of and/or the imposition of a fine not less than $50.00 nor more than $750.00 upon, and the commissioner may seek an order of restitution or other equitable relief against, any licensee who violates any of the provisions of this chapter or any rules or regulations adopted pursuant to this chapter. The commissioner shall promulgate rules and regulations regarding the lengths of suspension and the amounts of fines to be imposed, and the types of equitable relief to be ordered, for specific violations. Before any suspension or fine is imposed, or equitable relief is ordered, the licensee shall be notified of the specific charges against him and of his right to a hearing. Any person who requests a hearing shall be notified of the time, date and place of the hearing not less than seven days prior to the date of the hearing. The hearing shall be conducted in accordance with Section 9-104-040 of this code. An order by the commissioner (issued prior to the exercise of exclusive jurisdiction by the department of administrative hearings in accordance with Section 2-14-190(c)) imposing a suspension or a fine may be appealed by the licensee to the mayor's license commission.

Upon suspension of a license and/or imposition of any fine for cause under the provisions of this chapter, the license sticker emblem and metal plate shall be removed by the commissioner from the vehicle and an entry of the suspension and/or fine shall be made on the license card. When a fine is paid and the suspension, if any, is terminated, an entry thereof shall be made on the license card by the commissioner and a duplicate license sticker shall be furnished by the commissioner and the commissioner shall reaffix the metal plate, for a fee of $10.00. The commissioner shall notify the department of police of every suspension and termination of suspension.

(Prior code § 28-14; Amend. Coun. J. 2-3-87, p. 39202; 1-27-88, p. 10273; 7-12-90, p. 18634; 7-10-96, p. 24982; 12-10-97, p. 59054; 12-4-02, p. 99931)

§9-112-270 Revocation of license—Grounds.

If any licensee abandons his residence, domicile or place of business in city or if any official notice or legal process cannot be served upon him at his last Chicago address registered in the office of the commissioner and he fails to respond to such notice or appear in answer to legal process at the time fixed therein, or if any judgment or award against him is not paid within the time provided in Section 9-112-240 or if any licensee shall be convicted of a felony or any criminal offense involving moral turpitude or if, while in charge of a public passenger vehicle as a chauffeur, he shall have in his possession or under his control any narcotic drugs, or shall solicit any person for transportation to any prostitute or house of ill-fame or disorderly place, or direct or inform any person where any prostitute, house of ill-fame or disorderly place is located, or if any cabman shall operate or permit to be operated more than one vehicle bearing the same public passenger vehicle license number painted on the door or shall obtain a duplicate metal plate, duplicate public passenger vehicle license, or duplicate license plates while remaining in possession of the originals and shall operate or permit to be operated any public passenger vehicle bearing such duplicate at the same time as he shall operate or permit to be operated any public passenger vehicle bearing the original metal plate, public passenger vehicle license or license plates, all his licenses shall be revoked.

Upon revocation of any license, the commissioner shall remove the license sticker emblem and the license card from the vehicle affected, and he shall cause to be removed the roof-light, taximeter and connecting cables, the metal plate and any other insignia identifying the vehicle as a public passenger vehicle and if any such identifying insignia be not removable it shall be painted over by the commissioner.

(Prior code § 28-15; Amend. Coun. J. 7-12-90, p. 18634)

§9-112-280 Revocation of license—Additional reasons.

In the event that the commissioner, after investigation and hearing, shall determine that any licensee has obtained any public passenger vehicle license by fraud or false representation or wilful misstatement of material fact, or in case any licensee shall fail to carry out any representation made to the commissioner before the issuance of such license, or shall wilfully make any ma-

terial misstatement of fact on any statement filed with the commissioner, or shall wilfully make any material misstatement of fact on any statement filed with the director of revenue or the department of consumer services in connection with the administration of any tax levied against the licensee, or if any licensee shall operate, or cause or suffer to be operated, any public passenger vehicle in violation of the provisions of this chapter or of the rules and regulations of the commissioner relating to the administration and enforcement of the provisions of this chapter, or if the licensee shall be convicted of a felony, or in the case of a corporate licensee if any officer or director shall be convicted of a felony, unless the licensee shall sever its relationship with any such officer or director immediately upon his conviction, or if the licensee has obtained his license pursuant to a foreclosure of a security interest without having provided the commissioner with the information required under Section 9-112-320(f)(2), the commissioner shall recommend to the mayor's license commission that any or all public passenger vehicle licenses held by the licensee be revoked and the mayor's license commission shall revoke the license or licenses.
(Prior code § 28-15.1; Amend. Coun. J. 2-3-87, p. 39202; 1-27-88, p. 10273; 2-7-90, p. 11774; 7-12-90, p. 18634; 3-26-96, p. 18807)

§9-112-285 Revocation of license—Exception.

Whenever a public passenger vehicle is used for the transportation of persons for hire by a person who does not have a valid public chauffeur license, or whose chauffeur license is under suspension for any reason, including, but not limited to, by reason of imposition of a penalty by the department of administrative hearings or for failure to take a course of study or pass an examination pursuant to Section 9-104-040(a), the public passenger vehicle license for the vehicle shall be revoked, unless the holder of the public passenger vehicle license was, at all relevant times, acting in accordance with procedures that are reasonably designed to prevent the operation of pubic passenger vehicles by unlicensed persons. The procedures must be expressly approved by the commissioner. In addition, the chauffeur license of any person to whom the vehicle is leased, shall be revoked if another person is determined to have operated the vehicle during the lease period.
(Added. Coun. J. 12-1-93, p. 43380; Amend. 11-15-00, p. 46957)

§9-112-290 Interference with commissioner's duties.

Every licensee shall deliver or submit his public passenger vehicles for inspection or the performance of any other duty by the commissioner upon demand. It is unlawful for any person to interfere with or hinder or prevent the commissioner from discharging any duty in the enforcement of this chapter.
(Prior code § 28-16; Amend. Coun. J. 2-3-87, p. 39186; 7-12-90, p. 18634)

§9-112-300 Advertising signs permitted when.

(a) It is unlawful for any public passenger vehicles licensed pursuant to this chapter to display any advertising sign or device, except as permitted by this section.

(b) The commissioner may issue, upon application, permits for the display of advertising signs on the exterior or interior of public passenger vehicles licensed pursuant to this chapter.

(c) Application for such a permit shall be made on a form provided by the commissioner, and shall state the name and address of the licensee applying for the permit, the license number of the public passenger vehicle to which the advertising sign will be affixed and other such information as the commissioner may require.

(d) The annual fee for the issuance of a permit shall be $50.00, payable at time of application.

(e) A permit issued under this section shall expire on the thirty-first day of December following the date of issue, unless sooner surrendered, revoked or terminated.

(f) No permit issued pursuant to this section shall be transferred or assigned.

(g) No more than one permit shall be issued under this section for any public passenger vehicle licensed pursuant to this chapter.

(h) The suspension or revocation of a public passenger vehicle license issued pursuant to this chapter shall act as the suspension or revocation of any permit issued hereunder to the affected public passenger vehicles.

(i) The commissioner shall promulgate rules and regulations governing the advertising signs which may be displayed on public passenger vehicles and the reporting of advertising revenues.

(j) Each licensee to whom a permit is issued under this section shall maintain complete and accurate records of all revenues received from the display of any advertising sign or device. Each such licensee shall submit to the commissioner, no later than the date of expiration of the permit, an affidavit in such form as may be required by the commissioner, stating the gross revenues received by the licensee from the display of any advertising sign or device.

(k) The commissioner shall revoke the permit of any licensee who violates any portion of this section or any rule or regulation promulgated hereunder. *(Prior code § 28-17; Amend. Coun. J. 2-3-87, p. 39186; 1-27-88, p. 10273; 7-12-90, p. 18634)*

§9-112-310 Change of address—Notice to city required.

It is the duty of every licensee to notify the commissioner whenever any change in his Chicago address or telephone number is made. Any notice required to be given to the licensee shall be sufficient if addressed to the last Chicago address recorded in the office of the commissioner.
(Prior code § 28-18; Amend. Coun. J. 2-3-87, p. 39186; 7-12-90, p. 18634)

§9-112-320 Livery vehicles—License issuance.*

(a) *(Deleted. Coun. J. 12-10-97, p. 59054.)*

(b) *(Deleted. Coun. J. 12-10-97, p. 59054.)*

(c) Except as limited in this Section 9-112-320, each person who holds one or more uncancelled, unsurrendered and unrevoked taxicab or livery licenses at the end of any calendar year shall be entitled to renewal of each such license for the succeeding year, unless the applicant has ceased to be qualified to obtain a license under this chapter or unless cause exists under this chapter to cancel, revoke or require surrender of a particular license, or particular licenses, held by such person.

(d) *(Deleted. Coun. J. 12-10-97, p. 59054.)*

(e) No person shall own in whole or in part, directly or indirectly, or have a security interest in more than 25 percent of the authorized livery licenses or more than 25 percent of the authorized taxicab licenses. No person who owns in whole or in part, directly or indirectly, or has a security interest in more than 25 percent of the authorized livery licenses or more than 1,000 Chicago taxicab licenses, shall be eligible to acquire additional licenses, including by transfer pursuant to Section 9-112-320(f).

(f) (1) Subject to the limitations set forth in subsection (e) and in other provisions of this chapter governing distribution of licenses, all licenses issued pursuant to this chapter shall be freely transferable to any person qualified under the provisions of this chapter to be a license holder but before any transfer may become effective, the transferor and the transferee shall apply to the commissioner who shall approve the transfer if he shall determine that the transferee is qualified as a license holder under this chapter. The commissioner shall apply the standards and requirements for determining whether a proposed taxicab or livery license transferee is qualified to obtain a license under this chapter in a manner which is reasonable and consistent with the purpose of making such licenses available to all qualified applicants, within the quantity limits and subject to the retention and renewal rights established in this chapter. No license may be transferred if revocation proceedings with respect to the license have been filed with the mayor's license commission, and if the proceedings are pending at the time the transfer is attempted. Any such attempt to transfer a license that does not comply with this section shall result in the automatic expiration of the license as of the date of the attempted transfer. The nonrefundable fee for any transfer of license shall be payable by the transferee at the time of application. The amount of the fee shall be determined as follows: (i) if the transfer occurs less than one year after the transferor had acquired the license through a random selection process authorized in Section 9-112-380: 25 percent of the purchase price or 25 percent of the average market value, whichever is higher; (ii) if the transfer occurs one year or more but less than two years after the transferor had acquired the license through a random selection process authorized in Section 9-112-380 or at any time less than two years after the transferor has acquired the license by any other means: 10 percent of the purchase price or 10 percent of the average market value, whichever is higher; (iii) if the transfer occurs two or more years after the transferor had acquired the license, or if the transferor is a natural person and the transferee is the transferor's spouse or a natural or legally adopted child of the transferor, or if the transferor is the executor or administrator of the estate of a deceased licensee or the executor or administrator of a deceased person who held 100 percent of the stock or other interest in a corporation which was the licensee and the transferee is not a person adjudged to be the heir of the deceased person, or if the transfer was pursuant to a foreclosure upon a pledged or encumbered license: 5 percent of the purchase price or 5 percent of the average market value, whichever is higher. The average market value shall be an amount determined by the commissioner to be the approximate average purchase price for licenses in arms length transactions in the previous calendar year. No transfer fee shall be assessed if the transferor is a natural person and the transferee is a corporation in which the transferor holds 100 percent of the stock or other equitable interest; or if the transferor is the executor or administrator of the estate of a deceased licensee or the executor or administrator of a deceased person who held 100 percent of the stock or other interest in a corporation which was the licensee and the transferee is the heir of the deceased person.

(2) Pledging or otherwise encumbering a license shall be permitted; provided, that the licensee shall notify the commissioner in advance and in writing of any such encumbrance and provide the commissioner with such information with respect to the person to whom the license is to be pledged as the commissioner may reasonably require to assure that the provisions of this chapter are being complied with. Any foreclosure upon a pledged or encumbered license shall constitute a transfer subject to the provisions of Section 9-112-320(f)(1).

(3) In the event of a licensee's death, the authority to operate granted under the license shall cease, except that the executor or administrator of the estate of any deceased licensee, upon application to and approval by the commissioner, may continue to exercise the privileges of the deceased licensee, including the limited privilege of transfer granted in this chapter, until the expiration of the license but no longer than six months after the licensee's death.

(g) No person shall be qualified for a livery vehicle license and a taxicab license at the same time; nor shall any coachman become affiliated or identified with any cabman or with an affiliation of any cabmen.

(Prior code § 28-19; Amend. Coun. J. 4-1-87, p. 41265; 1-27-88, p. 10289; 7-12-90, p. 18634; 12-10-97, p. 59054; Amend 11-15-00, p. 46957)

* The amendment codified in this section and passed 1-27-88, Coun. J. p. 10289, is effective under the following conditions:

This ordinance shall take effect upon passage by the city council only if enough persons owning one or more licensed taxicabs so as to represent ownership of at least 2,301 taxicab licenses shall have placed on file with the city clerk before the date of passage their unconditional written acceptance of its provisions, in which case this ordinance shall operate as a contract between them and the city, and no amendments to subsection 9-112-320(a) shall be effective until after December 31, 1992 and to subsections 9-112-320(b) through (g) until after December 31, 1997.

§9-112-322 License managers.

(a) Effective April 1, 2001, no person shall act as a license manager for any license not issued to him or to a corporation of which he is an officer or to a partnership of which he is a partner without first registering as a license manager with the commissioner.

(b) No public passenger vehicle licensee shall allow any person to assume or undertake any or all of his responsibilities relating to the leasing of his license(s) unless that person is a registered license manager with the commissioner. In the event that a licensee allows any person, not registered as a license manager with the commissioner, to assume or undertake any such responsibilities, the license shall be suspended until such time as the licensee appears in the office of the commissioner and sufficiently establishes that either the person assuming the responsibilities is a registered license manager or that the licensee is meeting those responsibilities. In addition, any licensee who allows an unregistered license manager to assume or undertake his responsibilities may have his license revoked.

(c) No person shall be eligible to be registered as a license manager unless they can meet the eligibility requirements for a license holder listed in Sections 9-112- 080, 9-112-090, and 9-112-100 of this code.

(d) License managers and public passenger vehicle licensees shall be jointly and severally liable for any violations of this ordinance or the rules and regulations promulgated thereunder.

(e) All persons registering as a license manager shall deposit with the commissioner a bond, in the penal sum of $100,000.00, containing one or more sureties to be approved by the commissioner. Such bond shall be payable to the city of Chicago and shall be conditioned that the registered license manager shall comply with the provisions of the Municipal Code of Chicago and the rules and regulations promulgated thereunder, and shall pay all fines, orders of restitution, or judgments for damages ordered by the department of administrative hearings, or a court of competent jurisdiction, based on a violation of the municipal code and the rules and regulations promulgated thereunder, committed by the registered license manager, his agents or employees, while acting within the scope of their employment. The registered license manager is immediately liable for satisfaction upon determination of the fine or award judgment, or, if timely appeal is taken, upon final determination of the appeal.

(f) The commissioner is authorized to promulgate any and all rules and regulations for the effective administration of this section including, but not limited to, the process of registration, fines not to exceed $750.00 for violations of the rules, and cancellation of the license manager's registration with the department.

(Added. Coun. J. 11-15-00, p. 46957)

§9-112-325 License brokers.

(A) Effective April 1, 2001, no person shall operate as a license broker without first being licensed by the commissioner. Application for a license broker license shall be made on such forms and accompanied by such documents as the commissioner may require and shall include, but not be limited to proof that the license broker has its principal place of business in Chicago, information as to whether the applicant for the license, or any principal thereof has a financial interest in any lender, insurance brokerage firm or automobile dealership.

(B) All applicants for a license broker license shall deposit with the commissioner a bond, in the penal sum of $100,000.00 dollars, containing one or more sureties to be approved by the commissioner. Such bond shall be payable to the city of Chicago and shall be conditioned that the license applicant or licensee will comply with the provisions of the Municipal Code of Chicago and the rules and regulations promulgated thereunder, and shall pay all fines, orders of restitution, or judgments for damages ordered by the department of administrative hearings, or a court of competent jurisdiction, based on a violation of the Municipal Code of Chicago and the rules and regulations promulgated thereunder, committed by such licensee, his agents or employees, while acting within the scope of their employment. The broker is immediately liable for satisfaction upon determination of the fine or award judgment, or, if timely appeal is taken, upon final determination of the appeal.

(C) All license broker licenses shall expire on October 31st. Renewal of license broker licensing must be made during the month preceding expiration of the license. The annual fee for each license broker license is $300.00.

(D) A license broker shall conspicuously display a license or copy thereof at all times in every place of business maintained by such broker.

(E) A license broker shall not display a taxicab broker's license which is expired, suspended or revoked, but shall surrender same to the commissioner immediately.

(F) A broker:

(1) May not request nor permit a party to sign a power of attorney or any other instrument in blank nor accept any such instrument signed in blank;

(2) Who requests any instrument or document to be signed by any interested party and returned to said broker, shall provide said interested party with a duplicate copy of the instrument for the party's own records;

(3) Upon completion of a closing, or other transaction, shall, within ten business days of such completion, deliver to the interested party copies of all documents prepared by the broker or under the broker's supervision on behalf of such party; and

(4) Shall request the party receiving such papers to acknowledge, in writing, receipt of same.

(G) A license broker shall keep and maintain for a period of three years all records involving the sale or encumbrance of a license and shall furnish the commissioner copies of any said documents within three days of such request.

(H) The commissioner is authorized to promulgate rules and regulations governing the conduct of license brokers including, but not limited to: the form, duration and limitations on listing agreements for the transfer of licenses; disclosures by the license broker to any client or potential client regarding possible conflicts of interest based on the license broker's activities as a lender, insurance broker, or automobile dealer or the license broker's contractual relationship or financial or other interest in a lender, insurance broker or automobile dealer; advertising by the broker; forms to be used in the transfer or encumbrance of a license; and fines not to exceed $750.00 per violation and/or license suspension or revocation for violation of any provision of this ordinance or the rules promulgated thereunder.

(I) Any monies paid in connection with the transfer of a license, prior to approval of such transfer by the department, must be held in a separate interest-bearing escrow account until at least such time as the transfer of the license is approved by the department.

(J) In addition to the authority of the commissioner to enforce the provisions of this section and the rules and regulations promulgated thereunder, any person suffering injury due to a violation of this act may bring a private cause of action in a court of competent jurisdiction seeking damages.
(Added Coun. J. 11-15-00, p. 46957)

§9-112-330 Unlawful to operate livery vehicle with meter.

It is unlawful for any person to operate or drive a livery vehicle equipped with a meter which registers a charge or fare or indicates the distance traveled by which the charge or fare to be paid by a passenger is measured.
(Prior code § 28-19.1; Amend. Coun. J. 7-12-90, p. 18634)

§9-112-340 Solicitation of passengers prohibited.

It is unlawful for any person to solicit passengers for transportation on any public way or in any city airport except as specifically provided by contract as approved by the city council of the city of Chicago, pursuant to Section 10-36-270 of the Municipal Code of the city of Chicago. No such vehicle shall be parked on any public way for a time longer than is reasonably necessary to accept passengers in answer to a call for service and no passenger shall be accepted for any trip in such vehicle without previous engagement for such trip, at a fixed charge or fare, through the station or office from which said vehicle is operated. Any person found guilty of violating this section upon conviction thereof shall be punished by a fine of not less than $100.00 and not more than $300.00 and/or be incarcerated in a penal institution for a term of up to seven days for the first offense and not less than $300.00 and not more than $500.00 and/or be incarcerated in a penal institution for a term of up to 14 days for the second and each subsequent offense in any 180-day period, under the procedure set forth in Section 1-2-1.1 of the Illinois Municipal Code, as amended. A separate and distinct offense shall be regarded as committed each day upon which said person shall continue any such violation, or permit any such violation to exist after notification thereof.
(Prior code § 28-19.2; Amend. Coun. J. 2-3-87, pp. 39186, 39202; 10-15-87, p. 5217; 10-4-89, p. 5321; 7-12-90, p. 18634)

§9-112-350 Livery vehicles—Exterior—Advertising.

The outside of the body of livery vehicles shall be solid black or blue-black in color, unless otherwise authorized by the commissioner, without any inscription thereon. No lights shall be attached to or exposed outside of such vehicle, unless required or permitted by the law of the state of Illinois regulating traffic.

It is unlawful for any person other than the coachman of a livery vehicle or his agent to represent to the public that he renders livery service, or for any coachman or his agent to use the words "cab," "cabman," "taxi," or "taxicab" in connection with or as part of his operations of such vehicle.
(Prior code § 28-20; Amend. Coun. J. 2-3-87, p. 39186; 7-12-90, p. 18634)

§9-112-360 Sightseeing vehicles.

No vehicle shall operate as a charter/sightseeing vehicle unless so licensed under Section 9-112-110. Charter/sightseeing vehicles shall not be used for transportation of passengers except on sightseeing tours or charter trips. No person shall solicit passengers for sightseeing tours upon any public way except at bus stands specially designated by the city council for sightseeing vehicles, nor shall any person other than a coachman of such a vehicle or his authorized agent or the person or entity hiring the vehicle solicit passengers for such a tour.
(Prior code § 28-21; Amend. Coun. J. 2-3-87, p. 39199; 1-27-88, p. 10273; 7-12-90, p. 18634)

§9-112-370 Vehicle out of service—Notice to city required.

Every taxicab or livery shall be operated regularly to the extent reasonably necessary to meet the public demand for service. If the service of any taxicab or livery is discontinued for a period of 20 continuous days for any reason except on account of strike, act of God, shortages of gasoline or other necessary materials or cause beyond the control of the licensee other than the inability of the licensee to lease his taxicab or livery, the licensee must notify the commissioner that such taxicab or livery is out of service. The commissioner may give written notice to the licensee to restore the taxicab or livery to service, and if it is not restored within five days after notice, the commissioner may recommend to the mayor that the license be revoked and the mayor, in his discretion, may revoke same.

(Prior code § 28-22; Amend. Coun. J. 2-3-87, p. 39186; 7-12-90, p. 18634)

§9-112-380 Number of available licenses—Distribution.

(a) After the effective date of this ordinance and subject to the conditions set forth in this section, all qualified applicants for taxicab licenses or for livery licenses shall be entitled to obtain such licenses, unless the number of available licenses is less than the number of qualified applicants for such licenses. In calendar year 2001, an additional 200 taxicab licenses shall be distributed as provided in subsection (b)(3) to persons who respond to requests for proposal to provide service targeted to the disabled and underserved communities, and, in calendar year 2004, up to 100 additional licenses may be so distributed if the commissioner determines that such distribution is necessary for the purposes of that subsection. In each of the calendar years 2001 through 2004, an additional two taxicab licenses shall be distributed pursuant to the "driver excellence" program established under subsection (b)(4). In each of the calendar years 2001 through 2004, an additional 50 taxicab licenses, plus any other available taxicab licenses, shall be distributed pursuant to open and competitive bidding procedures established under subsection (c). Prior to January 1, 2005, no taxicab licenses other than those authorized by this subsection (a) or renewed in accordance with Section 9-112-320(c) may be issued.

As used in this section, the term "available licenses" means all licenses which may be issued under the quantity limits established under this subsection (a), including any licenses that are available for reissuance because they have been canceled, surrendered or not renewed, but not including licenses which are retained or renewed in accordance with Section 9-112-320(c).

(b) (1) The commissioner shall apply the standards and requirements for determining whether a taxicab or livery license applicant is qualified to obtain a license under this chapter in a manner which is reasonable and consistent with the purpose of making taxicab and livery licenses available to as many qualified applicants as practicable, within the quantity limits and subject to the retention and renewal rights established in this chapter.

(2) In the event that any unencumbered taxicab license is revoked and there is no timely appeal or other legal challenge of the order of revocation pending, the revoked license shall be distributed by the commissioner to the licensed public chauffeur who applied and was qualified to participate in the awarding of taxicab licenses pursuant to the random selection process in the year 2000 for awarding medallions, has not "owned or controlled" a taxicab

license at any time, meets the qualifications for licensing under this chapter, and has been licensed as a public chauffeur for the longest continuous time. In the event that no licensed public chauffeur is so qualified, the commissioner shall distribute such license to the person who has been licensed as a public chauffeur for the longest continuous time and who has not "owned or controlled" a taxicab license at any time. Notwithstanding any other provision of this chapter, no license awarded pursuant to this subsection (b)(2) may be transferred within three years after issuance. For the purposes of this section, "own or control" means that the applicant, the applicant's spouse, or the natural or adopted child of the applicant is either a taxicab or livery licensee, or that the applicant, the applicant's spouse, and the natural or adopted child, individually or together, own at least 25 percent of the stock of a corporation issued a taxicab or livery license or own at least 25 percent of the interest in a partnership issued a taxicab or livery license or if the applicant, the applicant's spouse, or the natural or adopted child have a security interest in a taxicab or livery license or own at least 25 percent interest in a corporation or partnership having a security interest in a taxicab or livery license.

(3) In calendar year 2001, 200 taxicab licenses shall be distributed to persons who respond to requests for proposal under this subsection (b)(3) who are found to be the most qualified for purposes of this subsection (b)(3), and, in calendar year 2004, up to 100 additional licenses may be so distributed if the commissioner determines that such distribution is necessary for the purposes of this subsection (b)(3). Each proposal must provide for the issuance of no less than 10 and no more than 50 taxicab licenses. Individuals may file a maximum of two proposals. Licenses awarded by the committee will be subject to the following conditions:

(A) Each person awarded licenses pursuant to this subsection shall maintain at least 50 percent of his licensed vehicles as being equipped for wheelchair access pursuant to standards established by the commissioner;

(B) Each licensed vehicle shall be connected with a centralized dispatch system for all vehicles issued to the licensee under this subsection (b)(3);

(C) Each licensee shall advertise its service to the disabled and underserved communities in accordance with rules and regulations promulgated by the commissioner;

(D) For each day that a vehicle licensed under this subsection (b)(3) is in service, the vehicle shall provide service to the disabled or underserved communities not less than 40 percent of the time the vehicle is in service;

(E) Licenses may be transferred only if the commissioner approves the transfer after determining that the purposes of this subsection (b)(3) will be furthered by the transfer.

Notwithstanding any other provisions in this chapter, any applicant for or recipient of taxicab licenses issued pursuant to this subsection may be qualified regardless of whether such applicant or recipient holds and/or renews any other type of public passenger vehicle licenses. Any person who is issued a license under this subsection (b)(3) shall be subject to rules and regulations promulgated by the commissioner to further the purposes of this subsection, and may be required to enter into one or more binding agreements with the city based upon the proposal that was submitted to the city.

(4) In each of the calendar years 2001 through 2004, two taxicab licenses shall be awarded: one to the person who has demonstrated, through their actions as licensed public chauffeurs in the previous calendar year, the greatest dedication to providing to the public excellent taxicab service within the city; and one to the public chauffeur who has demonstrated the greatest dedication to improving the excellence of other drivers through their participation in master chauffeur training programs for new drivers. These licenses shall be awarded by the mayor pursuant to the recommendations of the taxicab driver excellence committee, which is hereby created. The committee shall consist of not more than eight persons appointed by the mayor representing: the hotel/motel industry; the restaurant industry; the tourism industry; the disabled community; persons needing wheelchair accessible vehicles for transportation; neighborhood community groups; the taxicab industry; and the general public at large. Members of the committee shall serve at the pleasure of the mayor. The commissioner shall serve ex officio as chair of the committee.

(c) In each of the calendar years 2001 through 2004, all available taxicab licenses, other than those awarded pursuant to subsection (b)(2) or (b)(3), shall be distributed pursuant to open and competitive bidding procedures established by the commissioner by regulation. The procedures shall be designed to produce the maximum amount of revenues to the city and to ensure that only applicants that are qualified under this chapter are awarded licenses.

(d) Notwithstanding any provision to the contrary, if the provisions of subsection (a) of this section added by this amendatory ordinance are held to be invalid and unenforceable for any reason, the provisions of subsections (b) and (c) of this section shall not apply during the time that the provisions of subsection (a) are not enforced, and no restrictions on the number of public passenger vehicle licenses available for issuance shall apply, provided that no person who owns in whole or in part, directly or indirectly, or has a security interest in more than 25 percent of the number of authorized taxicab licenses immediately preceding the effective date of this amendatory ordinance, shall be eligible to acquire additional licenses, including by transfer pursuant to Section 9-112-320(f).

(Prior code § 28-22.1; Added. Coun. J. 1-27-88, p. 10289; Amend. 2-7-90, p. 11774; 7-12-90, p. 18634; 12-10-97, p. 59054; Amend. 11-15-00, p. 46957)

§9-112-390 License number and driver identification—Display.

Every taxicab shall have the public passenger vehicle license number and the cabman's name and telephone number painted in the center of the main panel of the rear doors of the vehicle. If the cabman is affiliated or identified with any affiliation, as described in Section 9-112-070, the affiliation's color scheme, trade name or emblem and telephone number shall be substituted and, without being limited thereto, any of these indicia of affiliation shall be sufficient to establish the responsibility of the affiliation in the operation of the taxicab. All names and numbers shall be painted in plain Gothic letters and figures of one-half-inch stoke and at least four inches in height. The public vehicle license number assigned to any taxicab shall be assigned to the same vehicle or to any vehicle substituted therefor by the licensee. The commissioner may also provide, pursuant to rule, that other information of interest to the public, including, but not limited to, the licensee's or affiliation's website or e-mail address and/or the current taximeter rates of fare be permanently and prominently affixed to the outside of the vehicle. No other name, number, emblem, or advertisement of any kind excepting signs required by this chapter, official license emblems or metal plate shall be painted or carried so as to be visible on the outside of any taxicab unless otherwise required by state law.

(Prior code § 28-23; Amend. Coun. J. 2-3-87, pp. 39184, 39186; 1-27-88, p. 10273; 7-12-90, p. 18634; Amend. 11-15-00, p. 46957)

§9-112-400 Information sheet required—Contents.

Every taxicab shall have an information sheet permanently fixed in a manner set forth by the commissioner. The information sheet shall have printed on it, in letters and numerals large enough to be plainly visible to the passenger, the public passenger vehicle license number, the rate schedule from the airport to (i) designated suburbs and (ii) other destinations beyond city limits as provided in Section 9-112-460 of this chapter, a telephone number of the department of consumer services inviting passenger comments, and such other information as the commissioner may direct.

(Prior code § 28-23.1; Amend. Coun. J. 2-3-87, p. 39193; 7-12-90, p. 18634)

§9-112-410 Taximeter specifications.

Every taxicab shall be equipped with a taximeter connected with and operated from the transmission of the taxicab to which it is attached. The taximeter shall be on whenever the taxicab is engaged for hire within the city limits, unless otherwise provided for in this chapter.

Taximeters shall be equipped with a device to register the tariff in accordance with the lawful rates and charges. The taximeter shall display the fare in a manner and size so as to be plainly visible to the passenger while riding in the back seat of the vehicle. Effective with the passage of this ordinance, any replacement or any new taximeter shall be equipped with a receipt dispensing mechanism. The commissioner shall promulgate rules governing the information required on the receipt.

It is unlawful to operate a taxicab for hire within the city unless the taximeter attached thereto has been sealed by the commissioner.

(Prior code § 28-24; Amend. Coun. J. 2-3-87, p. 39193; 7-12-90, p. 18634)

§9-112-420 Taximeter inspection.

At the time a taxicab license is issued and semiannually thereafter the taximeter shall be inspected and tested by the commissioner to determine if it complies with the specifications of this chapter and accurately registers the lawful rates and charges. If it is in proper condition for use, the taximeter shall be sealed and a written report of inspection shall be kept on file by the commissioner. Upon complaint by any person that a taximeter is out of working order or does not accurately register the lawful rates and charges it shall be again inspected and tested and, if found to be in improper working condition or inaccurate, it shall be unlawful to operate the taxicab to which it is attached until it is equipped with a taximeter which has been inspected and tested by the commissioner, found to be in proper condition, sealed and written report of inspection therefor is completed by the inspector.

The cabman or person in control or possession of any taxicab shall deliver it with the taximeter attached for inspection and test as requested by the commissioner. The cabman may be present or represented when such inspection and test is made.
(Prior code § 28-25; Amend. Coun. J. 2-3-87, p. 39186; 7-12-90, p. 18634)

§9-112-430 Tampering with meters prohibited.
It is unlawful for any person to tamper with, mutilate or break any taximeter or the seal thereof or to transfer a taximeter from one taxicab to another for use in transportation of passengers for hire before delivery of the taxicab with a transferred taximeter for inspection test and report by the commissioner as provided in Section 9-112-420.
(Prior code § 28-25; Amend. Coun. J. 2-3-87, p. 39186; 7-12-90, p. 18634)

§9-112-440 Taximeter inspection fee.
The fee for each inspection pursuant to complaint shall be $10.00, but no charge shall be made when as the result of the inspection and test it is found that the taximeter is in proper working condition and accurately registers the lawful rates and charges.
(Prior code § 28-27; Amend. Coun. J. 2-3-87, p. 39202; 7-12-90, p. 18634)

§9-112-450 Unlawful to refuse transportation unless out of service.
It is unlawful to refuse any person transportation to any place within the city or those suburbs listed in Section 9-112-460 of this chapter in any taxicab which is unoccupied by a passenger for hire unless it is on its way to pick up a passenger in answer to a call for service or it is out of service for any other reason. When any taxicab is answering a call for service or is otherwise out of service it shall not be parked at a cabstand, and a white card bearing the words "Not For Hire" printed in black letters not less than two inches in height shall be displayed at its windshield. The public chauffeur license, public passenger vehicle license or both such licenses of any person who violates this section or any rule promulgated under this section five or more times within any 24 month period shall be subject to revocation.
(Prior code § 28-28; Amend. Coun. J. 2-3-87, p. 39193; 7-12-90, p. 18634; 12-1-93, p. 43380)

§9-112-455 Radio dispatch.
(A) Effective January 1, 2001, no affiliation or any radio dispatch service who contracts with an affiliation may provide a two-way radio dispatch system to the affiliates of the affiliation without first having obtained a radio dispatch service license from the department of consumer services.

(B) Application for a radio dispatch service license shall be made on such forms and accompanied by such documents as the commissioner may require and shall include, but not be limited to, proof that the radio dispatch system has its principal place of business in Chicago and the name, Chicago business address and telephone number, and the name of the affiliation with which the radio dispatch system has a contract to provide service. Subsequent to licensing, if there are changes in any material information contained in the submitted license application, such changes must be reported in writing to the commissioner within 48 hours. All radio dispatch service licenses expire on December 1st. Renewal of radio dispatch licensing must be made during the month preceding expiration of the licensing.

(C) The annual fee for each radio dispatch service license is $100.00.

(D) Each radio dispatch service licensee and affiliation shall provide or cause to be offered to its dispatchers a course or courses, approved and in compliance with reasonable standards established by the commissioner, on dispatching taxicabs. Such course shall include, but not be limited to: customer service, the responsibilities of the radio dispatch service involved in the dispatching of taxicabs; and operation of the radio dispatch licensee's equipment. No person shall dispatch taxicabs for a radio dispatch service or an affiliation without having completed the approved dispatching course for that radio dispatch service or affiliation.

(E) For the purpose of ensuring adequate service to customers who request transportation to or from all portions of the city and to the suburbs listed in Section 9-112-460, the commissioner may promulgate rules and regulations governing the dispatch of public passenger vehicles. These rules and regulations shall include, but not be limited to: standards for determining adequate and timely service; the responsibilities of affiliations, radio dispatch services, public passenger vehicle licensees, and public chauffeurs in responding to requests for service within a specified time frame; and penalties, including fines not to exceed $750.00 per violation and/or suspension or revocation of licensing for failure to provide such service in a timely manner. Following a public hearing, the commissioner may also provide by rule reasonable minimum standards, based on the number of affiliates served by the radio dispatch service, regarding the number of radio dispatch requests received and answered in a timely manner annually by an affiliation(s), its members, and contractors. Any radio dispatch service and/or affiliation, applying for renewal of their license, which failed to meet these standards in the previous year shall be issued a probationary license. Any radio dispatch service and/or affiliation, applying for renewal of a probationary license, which failed to meet these standards during the year they operated under a probationary license, may, in the discretion of the commissioner, have their application for renewal denied.

(Added. Coun. J. 1-14-97, p. 37750; Amend. 11-15-00, p. 46957)

§9-112-460 Airport service.

Every driver of a taxicab licensed by the city of Chicago as a public passenger vehicle, when at or upon the premises of the Chicago-O'Hare International Airport or the Chicago Midway Airport and not otherwise engaged in the transportation of a person or persons, shall service the airports by transporting, when requested, any person from the airports to any suburb of the city of Chicago and the driver shall not charge more than the rate of transportation hereinafter set forth to such suburb. It shall be unlawful for a driver of a taxicab to refuse any person transportation from those airports. It shall be unlawful for any driver of any taxicab not licensed as such by the city of Chicago to solicit or accept for transportation any person or persons at or upon the premises of the airports for transportation within or without the city of Chicago; provided, however, that this provision shall not apply where the person at the airports desiring other taxicab service has personally or through his agent previously by letter, telegram or telephone specifically engaged a suburban taxicab to transport him to any of the suburbs of the city of Chicago.

Nothing herein contained shall be construed to prohibit any public passenger vehicle from entering those airports to discharge passengers previously accepted outside the city of Chicago for that purpose.

The taxicab rates of maximum fares from those airports to the towns, villages, municipalities or unincorporated areas herein listed shall be those set forth in Section 9-112-510 of the Municipal Code of Chicago as amended from time to time. The towns, villages, municipalities or unincorporated areas to which the foregoing taxicab rates shall apply are as follows:

Alsip	Dolton	Harwood Heights	Oak Park
Bedford Park	Elk Grove	Hines Hospital	Park Ridge
Blue Island	Elmwood Park	Hometown	Riverdale
Burnham	Evanston	Lincolnwood	River Grove
Calumet City	Evergreen Park	Merrionette Park	Rosemont
Calumet Park	Forest View	Niles	Stickney
Cicero	Dolton	Norridge	Summit
Des Plaines		Oak Lawn	Riverdale

Transportation of any person or persons from those airports to any suburb or unincorporated area not included in the foregoing list of towns, villages, municipalities or unincorporated areas shall be at the maximum meter fare as determined by the rates and charges set forth in Section 9-112-510 of the Municipal Code of Chicago plus an additional sum equal to 50 percent of said maximum meter fare.

(Prior code § 28-28.1; Amend. Coun. J. 2-3-87, p. 39193; 1-27-88, p. 10273; 7-12-90, p. 18634; 8-2-95, p. 5794; 9-4-03, p. 7224)

§9-112-465 C.T.A.-T.A.P. program compliance—Wheelchair-accessible vehicle dispatch.

(A) As a condition of being licensed, every affiliation and every taxicab affiliated with that affiliation shall participate fully in the Chicago Transit Authority Taxi Access Program (C.T.A.-T.A.P.) or similar program providing for increased access to taxicab service to persons with disabilities.

(B) All affiliations with wheelchair accessible vehicles licensed by their affiliates must jointly prepare and submit to the commissioner by March 1, 2001, a proposed plan involving a coordinated or centralized dispatch system for the dispatch of wheelchair accessible taxicabs to ensure prompt service to people with disabilities. In the event that no such plan is timely filed or the commissioner does not approve the plan, the commissioner is authorized to provide by rule a plan requiring all affiliations to participate in a central dispatch system for wheelchair accessible taxicabs. The commissioner is authorized to assess the costs of such a central dispatch system upon those medallion owners with wheelchair accessible taxicabs.

(C) The commissioner is authorized to promulgate all other rules and regulations necessary and reasonable to insure the timely and proper dispatching of wheelchair accessible taxicabs. These rules and regulations shall include, but not be limited to: standards for determining adequate and timely service; the responsibilities of any central or coordinated dispatch system, affiliations, taxicab licensees and public chauffeurs in responding to such requests for service; and penalties for violation of such rules. In addition, the commissioner is authorized to provide by rule a minimum number of rides per day which must be provided by wheelchair accessible taxicabs to persons needing such transportation.

(D) Each affiliation must have verifiable records, in a form designated by the commissioner by regulation, regarding the response of the affiliation to each request for a wheelchair accessible vehicle. Each affiliation shall provide such records to the commissioner within forty-eight hours of a request for same.

(Added. Coun. J. 11-15-00, p. 46957)

§9-112-470 Taxicabs operating as intrastate motor carriers—Compliance with state requirements.

Nothing in this chapter shall be construed as barring the operation of taxicabs as intrastate motor carriers of property; provided, that they have met all of the requirements set forth by the Illinois Commerce Commission pursuant to the Illinois Commercial Transportation Law, Illinois Revised Statutes Chapter 95 1/2, Paragraph 18c-1101, et seq. or its successors. It shall be a violation of this section for any taxicab to operate as an intrastate motor carrier of property if it has not met all of the requirements of the Illinois Commerce Commission.

(Prior code § 28-28.2; Amend. Coun. J. 2-3-87, p. 39184; 7-12-90, p. 18634)

§9-112-480 Jitney service.

(a) Public passenger vehicles licensed under this chapter may operate jitney service as provided in this section. Jitney service is unscheduled service along a prescribed route or within specified zones, providing street hail service to passengers only at a flat fare (prescribed by the commissioner by regulation) for each individual passenger; passengers may enter and depart the public passenger vehicle at any point along the route or within the zone. A vehicle providing jitney service must travel the entire prescribed route or must remain within the specified zone, must prominently display a "jitney" sign in its front windshield, and must accept and discharge passengers at any place along the route or within the zone (subject to traffic and safety restrictions) up to the maximum capacity of the vehicle. While providing jitney service, only the flat per-passenger fare may be charged and the taximeter may not be used for any part of the jitney trip. Jitney service shall be allowed only on routes or within zones authorized by the commissioner as provided below in subsection (b). It shall be unlawful for any person to operate a jitney service along any unauthorized route or outside authorized zones, or without a permit issued pursuant to subsection (d) of this ordinance.

(b) The commissioner or any licensed public chauffeur may initiate the procedures for authorizing jitney routes or zones. The commissioner shall hold a public hearing to determine whether the public convenience would best be served by the authorization of jitney service along any proposed route or within any proposed zone. Before such a hearing, the commissioner shall give at least 45 days notice in writing to the Chicago transit authority and by publication to all licensed public chauffeurs, and the hearing shall be scheduled within 60 days of application by any public chauffeur to initiate procedures. During the 45-day notice period the Chicago transit authority may comment to the commissioner and present evidence as to the effect of any proposed jitney route or zone upon the authority's service revenues, its then existing service or its plans for service adjustments. The commissioner shall include the authority's comments and evidence in the record of the public hearing and may request testimony by the authority at the public hearing.

(c) With respect to any application for a jitney route or zone and within 10 days after the public hearing, the commissioner shall issue his or her findings as to whether the public convenience would best be served by the authorization of jitney service along that route or within that zone. For every jitney route or zone authorized hereunder, the commissioner shall issue a street description of the route or zone, including the end points for any single jitney trip, any time restrictions on such jitney service, and shall make such descriptions available to all licensed public chauffeurs. Whenever the commissioner determines not to authorize jitney service along a proposed route or within a proposed zone, the commissioner shall issue his or her determination in writing.

(d) The commissioner shall promulgate rules and regulations establishing the procedures for applying and the qualification for obtaining permission for any public chauffeur to operate as a jitney along any authorized route or within an authorized zone.

(e) The commissioner shall from time to time review all authorized jitney routes and zones and solicit comment from any interested persons as to whether the routes or any of them are serving the public convenience. The commissioner may after notice and a public hearing as provided in subsection (b) revoke authorization for any jitney route or zone.

(Prior code § 28-28.3; Amend. Coun. J. 4-1-87, p. 41263; 2-27-88, p. 10273; 7-12-90, p. 18634; 12-1-93, p. 43380; Amend. 11-15-00, p. 46957)

§9-112-490 Group riding.

Not more than six passengers shall be accepted for transportation at one time on any trip in a taxicab; provided, that additional passengers under the age of 12 years accompanied by an adult passenger shall be accepted if the taxicab has seating capacity for them.

(Prior code § 28-29; Amend. Coun. J. 7-12-90, p. 18634)

§9-112-500 Group riding permitted when.

Group, shared or multiple riding is permitted in taxicabs only where:

(a) The passenger first hiring the taxicab has directed or agreed voluntarily that he be carried as part of a group, multiple or shared ride; provided, that in such a situation the total rate of fare charged to all of the passengers shall not in the aggregate exceed the rate of fare permitted for such trip under Section 9-112-510; or

(b) The commissioner has, by regulation or rule, designated specified places, time or routes where groups of passengers may be carried in a single taxicab at rates of fare which the commissioner may specify for such group trips.

(Prior code § 28-29.1; Amend. Coun. J. 2-3-87, p. 39193; 7-12-90, p. 18634)

§9-112-510 Taxicab rates of fare—Revision.

(a) Commencing with the effective date of this ordinance, the rates of fare for taxicabs shall be as set forth in this section, which rates are hereby declared to be just and reasonable:

For the first 1/8 mile or fraction thereof $1.90

Forty-five cents of this initial mileage rate for the first 10 taxicab fares which a driver transports per day is hereby designated for payment of workers' compensation insurance.

For each additional 1/8 mile or fraction thereof .... .20

For each 36 seconds of time elapsed .... .20

For each additional passenger over the age of 12 years and under the age of 65 years .... .50

Except when inconsistent with this ordinance, taximeters shall be designed, calibrated and tested to register fares pursuant to the standards published by the National Institute of Standards and Technology (N.I.S.T.) in N.I.S.T. Handbook 44, as amended.

The fare-indicating mechanism of the taximeter shall be actuated by the distance mechanism whenever the vehicle is in motion at such a speed that the rate of distance revenue equals or exceeds the time rate, and may be actuated by the time mechanism whenever the vehicle speed is less than this and when the vehicle is not in motion.

If a taxicab is dispatched to transport a customer at the customer's request, the taximeter may be activated two minutes after the arrival of the taxicab at the location to which it has been called, or at the time at which the taxicab was scheduled to arrive, whichever is later. At all other times, the taximeter may be activated only upon the passenger's entering the vehicle.

Every passenger under 12 years of age when accompanied by an adult shall be carried without charge.

Baggage of passengers shall be transported without charge.

Immediately on arrival at the passenger's destination it shall be the duty of the chauffeur to put the meter in the nonrecording position and to call the passenger's attention to the fare registered. It is unlawful for any person to demand or collect any fare for taxicab service which is more than the rates established by the foregoing schedule, or for any passenger to refuse payment of the fare so registered. However, a public chauffeur may, by agreement made with each passenger prior to the beginning of a trip, charge and collect a fare that is less than the specified fare whenever the length of the trip is reasonably estimated to exceed five miles. In such case the chauffeur may collect no more than the fare at the rate agreed upon, and no passenger may refuse to pay the fare at the rate agreed upon.

Any holder of a taxicab license who sells or makes available for sale coupons or vouchers that are accepted by the licensee in lieu of cash for taxicab fares shall provide a 10 percent discount to purchasers who are 65 years of age or older. No person other than the purchaser may use a coupon or a voucher that has been purchased at a discount pursuant to this paragraph.

(b) For destinations beyond the city limits, other than from Midway or O'Hare Airports, fares shall be as follows: meter to city limits plus meter and one-half beyond city limits to destination.

(c) The council may from time to time revise the rates of fare by general ordinance in conformity with the provision hereinafter set forth, which rates shall be just and reasonable. The council, through its committee on local transportation, may, and upon the application of not less than one-third of the licensees or 10 percent of chauffeurs currently licensed under Chapter 9-104 of the Municipal Code, shall within 60 days after such application, hold hearings (but not more often than once in each period of 12 consecutive months) to determine whether a revision of the rates of fare is necessary. At such hearings each petitioning licensee or chauffeur may be required to submit a sworn statement of the gross income derived from the operation of taxicabs by him or under his control and all such expenses exclusive of Federal Income Taxes incurred during the immediately preceding period of 12 full calendar months. At such hearings the committee shall:

I. Consider the sworn statements of gross income and expenses submitted by the licensees or chauffeurs;

II. Consider the testimony and other evidence from any licensee or chauffeur who may wish to testify in support of the requested increase;

III. Consider the effect of an increase in fares upon the public and take testimony from any interested individual or organization;

IV. Consider the fares and practices with respect to similar services in other cities of the United States;

V. Consider all other evidence or testimony which the committee deems to be relevant and material to a proper determination.

Upon completion of such hearings, said committee shall report to the council its findings and recommendations concerning a just and reasonable rate of fare. If after receiving said findings and recommendations from the committee the council determines that a rate increase is proper, it shall increase the rates in an amount to insure adequate and efficient service to the public.

Any revision of rates of fares may be made by a change in the charge for the length of the first designated portion to the trip, or by a change in the charge for the balance of the trip, for waiting time or for each additional passenger or by any combination of such changes. In making any such revision, the council may presume the average length of a trip to be as established by the licensee's most current available records.

(d) In addition to the revision of rates of fare as provided in Section 9-112-510(c) hereof, the council may from time to time impose a surcharge on the rates of fare described in Section 9-112-500(a) hereof, in conformity with the provisions hereinafter set forth.

The council, through its committee on local transportation, shall hold hearings to determine whether such a surcharge may be necessary due to temporary economic conditions affecting all licenses in general. A surcharge authorized by this section shall be of such duration, not to exceed 60 days, as the council may impose by general ordinance.

Effective March 1, 2001, the commissioner is authorized to issue rules and regulations necessary to regulate the payment of fares by alternatives to cash, including but not limited to, credit cards, debit cards, cyber-cash and other generally acceptable means of purchasing goods and services. The commissioner may authorize by rule the production and sale of coupons which shall be accepted in all taxicabs licensed under this chapter. The commissioner may also require the acceptance of debit cards issued by the C.T.A. or other governmental agencies as payment for fares. Such rules may also provide the maximum amount charged to the chauffeur, directly or indirectly, by any taxicab licensee or affiliation in processing any non-cash payment of a fare.

The commissioner may provide by rule for flat rate(s) to be charged by taxicabs for trips to and from Gary International Airport and locations within the city of Chicago.

(Prior code § 28-30; Amend. Coun. J. 2-3-87, p. 39193; 4-1-87, p. 41263; 1-27-88, p. 10273; 2-7-90, p. 11774; 7-12-90, p. 18634; 12-1-93, p. 43380; 1-14-97, p. 37750; Amend. 11-15-00, p. 46978)

§9-112-520 Recordkeeping—Annual reports.

Every licensee and affiliation shall keep and provide accurate books and records of account of his operations at his place of business in the city. On or before May 1st of each year, every licensee and affiliation shall file with the commissioner a profit and loss statement for the preceding calendar year, showing all his earnings and expenditures for operation, maintenance and repair of property, depreciation expense, premiums paid for workers compensation and public liability insurance, and taxes for unemployment insurance and social security, and all state and local license fees, property taxes and federal income taxes, and a balance sheet taken at the close of said year.

The commissioner, or the authorized committee of the council shall have access to the property, books, contracts, accounts and records during normal business hours at said place of business, for such information as may be required for the effective administration and enforcement of the provisions of this chapter, or for the adoption of any ordinances, rules or regulations affecting taxicab operations.

In addition to the foregoing reports, each cabman shall within 30 days after the six months' period ended December 31st and within 30 days after the six months' period ended June 30th of each year file a sworn statement with the commissioner showing his gross revenues and his operating expenses for the six months immediately preceding those dates.

(Prior code § 28-30.1; Amend. Coun. J. 2-3-87, p. 39186; 1-27-88, p. 10273; 7-12-90, p. 18634)

§9-112-530 Ordinance not to limit city authority.

Nothing in this ordinance shall be construed to limit the city in the exercise of its police powers, and the city hereby expressly reserves the right to pass all reasonable ordinances and regulations affecting the licensees which may be necessary to promote or secure health, safety, morale, comfort, and general welfare.

(Prior code § 28-31.1; Amend. Coun. J. 4-1-87, p. 41265; 7-12-90, p. 18634)

§9-112-540 Revoked, surrendered licenses—Reissuance.

Any license for which an application for renewal has not been made within the period specified in Section 9-112-100, or which has been revoked, surrendered, cancelled or otherwise forfeited, may be reissued by the commissioner pursuant to the provisions of this chapter.

(Prior code § 28-31.2; Amend. Coun. J. 2-7-90, p. 11774; 7-12-90, p. 18634)

§9-112-550 Violation—Penalty.

Any person found guilty of violating any provision of this chapter for which a penalty is not otherwise provided upon conviction thereof shall be fined not less than $100.00 nor more than $200.00 and/or be incarcerated in a penal institution for a term of up to seven days for the first offense, not less than $200.00 nor more than $300.00 and/or be incarcerated in a penal institution for a term of up to 14 days for the second offense, and not less than $300.00 nor more than $750.00 and/or be incarcerated in a penal institution for a term of up to 21 days for the third and succeeding offenses during the same calendar year, under the procedure set forth in Section 1-2-1.1 of the Illinois Municipal Code, as amended. Each day that such violation shall continue shall be deemed a separate and distinct offense. In addition, when any one vehicle is involved in more than five violations of this chapter or the rules and regulations relating thereto within a 12-month period, the license for that vehicle shall be revoked.

(Prior code § 28-32; Amend. Coun. J. 2-3-87, p. 39202; 1-27-88, p. 10273; 10-4-89, p. 5321; 7-12-90, p. 18634; 12-10-97, p. 59054)

§9-112-555 Impoundment of vehicle— Notification of owner—Penalty.

(a) The owner of record of any motor vehicle that is used for the transportation or the solicitation for the transportation of passengers for hire in violation of Section 9-112-030 shall be liable to the city for an administrative penalty of $750.00 plus any towing and storage fees applicable under Section 9-92-080. Any such vehicle shall be subject to seizure and impoundment pursuant to this section. This subsection shall not apply if the vehicle used in the violation was stolen at that time and the theft was reported to the appropriate police authorities within 24 hours after the theft was discovered or reasonably should have been discovered. Notwithstanding any other provision of this section, no vehicle shall be subject to towing and impoundment under this section prior to 60 days after the effective date of this amendment; provided that this amendment shall not affect the towing and impoundment of any vehicle that is towed prior to the effective date of this amendment.

(b) Whenever a police officer has probable cause to believe that a vehicle is subject to seizure and impoundment pursuant to this section, the police officer shall provide for the towing of the vehicle to a facility controlled by the city or its agents. Before or at the time the vehicle is towed, the police officer shall notify any person identifying himself as the owner of the vehicle or any person who is found to be in control of the vehicle at the time of the alleged violation, of the fact of the seizure and of the vehicle owner's right to request a vehicle impoundment hearing to be conducted under Section 2-14-132 of this code.

(c) The provisions of Section 2-14-132 shall apply whenever a motor vehicle is seized and impounded pursuant to this section.
(Added. Coun. J. 10-14-92, p. 22998; Amend. Coun. J. 3-8-93, p. 29485; 7-10-96, p. 24982; 12-10-97, p. 59054; 4-29-98, p. 66564)

§9-112-560 Severability.

The invalidity of any section or part of any section of this ordinance shall not affect the validity of any other section or part thereof.
(Prior code § 28-35; Amend. Coun. J. 7-12-90, p. 18634)

§9-112-570 Effective date.

This ordinance shall be effective upon its passage and publication.
(Prior code § 28-36; Amend. Coun. J. 7-12-90, p. 18634)

CHAPTER 9-116
SCHOOL VEHICLE REGISTRATION

Sections:

9-116-010 Definition.
9-116-020 Classification.
9-116-030 Registration.
9-116-040 Registration fee.
9-116-050 Insurance.
9-116-060 Determination of capacity.
9-116-070 Overloading.
9-116-080 Safety requirements.
9-116-090 Fire extinguishers.
9-116-100 Sanitary requirements.
9-116-110 Driver's age.
9-116-120 Revocation.
9-116-130 Violation—Penalty.

§9-116-010 Definition.

"School vehicle" means a vehicle which, for direct or indirect compensation, transports children to or from any school, day nursery, day care center, day camp, play group or any regularly conducted public or private educational, religious, recreational or care program. This definition shall include motor vehicles of any body style so used, whether operated by the school or other institution, association or enterprise as defined above or by an independent operator and shall include such vehicles whether the fee or cost for such transportation is paid to the owner of vehicle directly by such children or their parents or guardians, or paid by the sponsoring school, association or enterprise, whether on a per trip or other basis. All public carriers certificated by the Illinois Commerce Commission and all vehicles belonging to the Chicago Transit Authority are not included in this definition.
(Prior code § 28.2-1; Amend. Coun. J. 7-12-90, p. 18634)

§9-116-020 Classification.

School vehicles shall be classified into three classes according to seating capacity as follows:

Class 1. Vehicles designed to carry not more than seven passengers;

Class 2. Vehicles designed or redesigned to seat more than seven passengers and up to 16 passengers may be increased by three additional passengers in the front seat if said three passengers are provided with safety belt or belts;

Class 3. School buses: The number of passengers in school buses shall not exceed the rated seating capacity of the bus.

(Prior code § 28.2-2; Amend. Coun. J. 7-12-90, p. 18634)

§9-116-030 Registration.

No person shall operate or permit the operation of a school vehicle unless such vehicle is registered with the public vehicle license commissioner and a certificate of registration is issued therefor by said commissioner. Registration certificates shall be issued for the period ending December 31st of the year for which they are issued.

Registration shall be applied for on forms provided by the public vehicle license commissioner.

(Prior code § 28.2-3; Amend. Coun. J. 7-12-90, p. 18634)

§9-116-040 Registration fee.

The annual registration fee for each such vehicle shall be:

Class 1 .... $ 5.00
Class 2 .... 10.00
Class 3 .... 25.00

Provided, however, that school buses for which a $2.00 annual registration fee is provided for under Section 3-801.7 of the Motor Vehicle Law of the state of Illinois shall be exempt from payment of the registration fees herein provided.

(Prior code § 28.2-4; Amend. Coun. J. 7-12-90, p. 18634)

§9-116-050 Insurance.

The owner and/or operator of any school vehicle shall be required to carry a public liability insurance policy or contract of insurance on each vehicle in the amount of not less than $50,000.00 for injury and/or death to any one person, and not less than $200,000.00 for injury and/or death to two or more persons, and such insurance policy or contract of insurance shall also provide $5,000.00 for property damage. Every insurance policy or contract of insurance shall provide for the payment and satisfaction of any final judgment rendered against said vehicle owner and/or operator.

All insurance policies or contracts required by this section, or copies of same, shall be filed with the commissioner and no insurance policy or contract shall be subject to cancellation except on 30 days previous notice to the commissioner.

(Prior code § 28.2-5; Amend. Coun. J. 7-12-90, p. 18634)

§9-116-060 Determination of capacity.

The public vehicle license commissioner shall inspect or cause to be inspected each school vehicle for which application for registration is made, and shall determine the capacity of each vehicle under conditions which will provide each child with adequate seating space to enable him or her to ride in

comfort and safety. The maximum capacity so determined shall be entered on the registration certificate issued for said vehicle.
(Prior code § 28.2-6; Amend. Coun. J. 7-12-90, p. 18634)

§9-116-070 Overloading.

No school vehicle shall be operated while containing a number of passengers in excess of that indicated on the certificate of registration, nor shall any school vehicle be operated unless all passengers are seated in the space provided for them.
(Prior code § 28.2-7; Amend. Coun. J. 7-12-90, p. 18634)

§9-116-080 Safety requirements.

All doors to the rear of the driver's seat of every school vehicle shall be equipped with safety device or devices to make impossible their opening from the inside of the vehicle by passengers. All seats shall be firmly anchored to the floor of the vehicle. All seats shall be equipped with backs. There shall be a clear aisle leading from all seats to regular exit doors.
(Prior code § 28.2-8; Amend. Coun. J. 7-12-90, p. 18634)

§9-116-090 Fire extinguishers.

Every school vehicle shall be equipped with a fire extinguisher in good operating condition, approved by the fire commissioner, and readily accessible at all times when said vehicle is in operation.
(Prior code § 28.2-9; Amend. Coun. J. 7-12-90, p. 18634)

§9-116-100 Sanitary requirements.

Every school vehicle shall be maintained at all times in a safe, clean and sanitary condition and shall be inspected for safety and cleanliness by the public vehicle license commissioner prior to the issuance of a certificate of registration, and at such other times as the commissioner selects. Such certificate of registration, when issued, shall be posted in said school vehicle within full view of all occupants.
(Prior code § 28.2-10; Amend. Coun. J. 7-12-90, p. 18634)

§9-116-110 Driver's age.

No person shall operate a school vehicle unless:

(1) He has attained the age of 21 years;

(2) He has had at least three years driving experience;

(3) He has had issued to him a chauffeur's license for the current license period in accordance with Chapter 9-104 of this code.

Provided, however, that no person shall operate a Class III school vehicle unless he complies with the requirements of Section 28-11 of the School Code of the state of Illinois.
(Prior code § 28.2-11; Amend. Coun. J. 7-12-90, p. 18634)

§9-116-120 Revocation.

The commissioner may revoke any certificate issued to any school vehicle owner and/or driver for default in the payment or performance of any obligation to the city under provisions of this chapter or for the violation of

any provisions in this code, or the laws of the state of Illinois applicable to the owner of the registration certificate.
(Prior code § 28.2-12; Amend. Coun. J. 7-12-90, p. 18634)

§9-116-130 Violation—Penalty.
Any person violating any of the provisions of this chapter shall be fined not less than $25.00 and not more than $200.00 for each offense and each day such violation shall continue shall be regarded as a separate offense.
(Prior code § 28.2-13; Amend. Coun. J. 7-12-90, p. 18634)

CHAPTER 9-120
BICYCLES

Sections:

9-120-010 Definition.
9-120-020 Registration.
9-120-030 Registration record.
9-120-040 Sale or transfer.
9-120-050 Alteration of serial number prohibited.
9-120-060 Traffic regulations to apply.
9-120-070 Rental agencies.
9-120-080 Bicycle dealers.

§9-120-010 Definition.
The word "bicycle" as used in this chapter means every vehicle propelled by human power upon which any person may ride, having at least two tandem wheels either of which is 20 inches or over in diameter.
(Prior code § 29.1-1; Amend. Coun. J. 7-12-90, p. 18634)

§9-120-020 Registration.
It is hereby made the duty of the owner of every bicycle, before operating or permitting the operation of the same upon any public way within the city, to register said vehicle with the commissioner of police on a form provided for such purpose.

Registration may be accomplished by filing the registration record or form, duly filled out, in the office of the commander of the police district in which the bicycle owner resides, or by mailing said form, duly filled out, postage prepaid, to the commissioner of police.
(Prior code § 29.1-2; Amend. Coun. J. 7-12-90, p. 18634)

§9-120-030 Registration record.
The registration record shall be in size and style as prescribed by the commissioner of police and shall contain the date of registration, the make, serial number, model and description of the bicycle registered, the name and residence address of the owner, the signature of the owner, the owner's age, and if such owner is under 21 years of age, the name and address of his or her parent or guardian, the name and address of the person from whom purchased, the date of purchase, and such additional information as the commissioner of police may require.
(Prior code § 29.1-3; Amend. Coun. J. 7-12-90, p. 18634)

§9-120-040 Sale or transfer.

Upon the sale or transfer of any bicycle registered hereunder, it shall be the duty of the purchaser, within 10 days of the date of such sale or transfer, to register such bicycle in his name in manner provided for in the case of an original registrant.

(Prior code § 29.1-4; Amend. Coun. J. 7-12-90, p. 18634)

§9-120-050 Alteration of serial number prohibited.

It shall be unlawful to destroy, remove, alter, cover or deface the manufacturer's serial number on any bicycle. It shall be unlawful for any person to own or have custody of a bicycle, the original manufacturer's serial number of which has been destroyed, removed, altered, covered or defaced. Any person who violates any of the provisions of this section shall be fined not more than $200.00 for each offense.

(Prior code § 29.1-5; Amend. Coun. J. 7-12-90, p. 18634)

§9-120-060 Traffic regulations to apply.

No person shall operate any bicycle upon the public ways or other places in this city in violation of any of the applicable provisions of Title 9 of this code.

(Prior code § 29.1-6; Amend. Coun. J. 7-12-90, p. 18634)

§9-120-070 Rental agencies.

A rental agency shall not rent or offer any bicycle for rent unless the bicycle is registered in accordance with the requirements of this chapter providing therefor.

(Prior code § 29.1-7; Amend. Coun. J. 7-12-90, p. 18634)

§9-120-080 Bicycle dealers.

Every person engaged in the business of buying or selling new or second hand bicycles shall make a report to the commissioner of police of every bicycle purchased or sold by such dealer, giving the name and address of the person from whom purchased or to whom sold, a description of such bicycle by name or make, the frame number thereof, and the registration number, if any, found thereon.

(Prior code § 29.1-8; Amend. Coun. J. 7-12-90, p. 18634)

CHAPTER 9-124
TRANSPORTATION SERVICES AND RAIL TRANSPORTATION

Sections:

Article I. General Requirements

9-124-010 Erection of wires and poles.
9-124-020 Operating near railroad elevation.
9-124-030 Comfort and safety of passengers.
9-124-040 Transporting policemen.
9-124-050 Driver collecting fares.
9-124-060 Lights at railroad crossings.
9-124-070 Painting railroad pillars.
9-124-080 Drains on railroad structures.
9-124-090 Penalty.

Article II. Street Railroads

9-124-100 Scope of regulations.
9-124-110 Laying track.
9-124-120 Gauge of track.
9-124-130 Construction of rails.
9-124-140 Track not to obstruct traffic.
9-124-150 Repair of streets.
9-124-160 Track and street repair violations.
9-124-170 Street sprinkling.
9-124-180 Removal of street accumulations.
9-124-190 Electrical requirements.
9-124-200 Schedule of operation.
9-124-210 Rush hour checking.
9-124-220 Exceptions to schedule requirements.
9-124-230 Service checks.
9-124-240 Stops.
9-124-250 Signs at stopping points.
9-124-260 Stops at railroads, crossings, bridges.
9-124-270 Stopping before firehouse.
9-124-280 Penalty.

Article III. Elevated Railroads

9-124-290 Scope of regulations.
9-124-300 "Rush hours" defined.
9-124-310 Schedule of operation.
9-124-320 Seats for passengers.
9-124-330 Stops when on ground.
9-124-340 Shunting or running down inclines.
9-124-350 Storing cars.
9-124-360 Construction and location of stations.
9-124-370 Station enclosures.
9-124-380 Illuminated station signs.
9-124-390 Penalty.

Article IV. Other Railroads

9-124-400 Scope of regulations.
9-124-410 Signals on engines.
9-124-420 Bumping posts.
9-124-430 Allowing steam to escape.
9-124-440 Making up trains.
9-124-450 Shunting cars.
9-124-470 Changing from steam to electricity.
9-124-480 Furnishing employee copy of regulations.
9-124-490 Penalty.

Article I. General Requirements

§9-124-010 Erection of wires and poles.

No person operating a street, elevated, steam or other railroad shall erect any poles or string wires thereon along, upon or across any public way or other public place in the city for the purpose of conveying an electric current to operate his railroad cars, unless he has obtained permission and authority from the city council for that purpose.

Any person violating any of the provisions of this section shall be fined not less than $100.00 nor more than $200.00 for each offense. Each day such poles or wires shall be maintained in violation of this section after the first conviction shall constitute a separate and distinct offense.
(Prior code § 188-4)

§9-124-020 Operating near railroad elevation.

No person shall propel, or cause to be propelled, any single car or train of cars on any track situated on the surface of any street in the city, across an intersecting street, when the track on which such single car or train of cars is propelled runs parallel to the track of any steam railroad of which the track is elevated on an embankment and is carried over an intersecting street by a bridge, where the condition is such that any rail of said surface track is within 15 feet of the end of any abutment wall supporting said bridge.

Each operation of a single car or train in violation of any of the terms of this section shall be deemed a separate offense.

It is hereby declared to be a nuisance for any person to operate such car or train in violation of this section.
(Prior code § 188-5)

§9-124-030 Comfort and safety of passengers.

No person owning, leasing or operating any street railroad cars, elevated railroad cars or other railroad cars, which run from point to point within the city, either on elevated, surface or subway lines, shall permit any car to be used or operated on any of the public ways of said city or on any part of the right-of-way of said person unless the following conditions are complied with:

(a) The cars of the company shall be kept heated as follows:

A minimum temperature of 50 degrees Fahrenheit above zero shall be maintained in all cars in service carrying passengers when the outside temperature is at 10 degrees Fahrenheit above zero or higher.

A minimum temperature of 45 degrees Fahrenheit above zero shall be maintained in all cars in service carrying passengers when the outside temperature is below 10 degrees, but not below five degrees Fahrenheit above zero.

When the outside temperature is below five degrees Fahrenheit above zero the temperature in all cars in service carrying passengers shall be maintained at 45 degrees Fahrenheit above zero, or as near this point as the continuous operation of all the heaters in said cars to their full capacity will allow.

(b) There shall be maintained and conspicuously displayed in such car a standard Fahrenheit thermometer so located that it will furnish a fair criterion of the temperature of the car.

(c) The air shall be supplied in such quantity that the amount of carbon dioxide present in the air of the said car shall not exceed 12 parts in each 10,000 parts of air.

(d) Cars or portions of cars in which smoking is permitted shall be provided with a ventilating capacity 33-1/3 percent in excess of the capacity required for other cars or the portions of cars in which smoking is not permitted.

(e) Cars shall be opened up and freely aired at least once in 24 hours.

(f) The interior and platforms and insides of vestibules of all cars shall be kept clean, and cars in which smoking is permitted shall be cleaned after each round trip. All window glass of all cars shall be kept clean at all times when such cars are in operation.

(g) Each car on each separate line shall, after leaving the starting point, be run to the terminus of the lines as designated on such car, except in cases of breakdown or other unavoidable interruptions of traffic, and except when no passenger on the car desires to be carried to the terminus of said line.

(h) A sufficient number of cars on each separate line to carry passengers comfortably and without crowding shall be provided, which cars shall be run upon a proper and reasonable schedule, and such schedule shall upon request be furnished to the city council or to the bureau of electricity.

(i) For the purpose of providing comfortable transportation of passengers without crowding, the number of passengers to be carried in any street railroad, elevated railroad or steam railroad car shall not exceed the seating capacity of such street railroad, elevated railroad or steam railroad car.

(j) Each street or elevated railroad car shall be distinctly numbered and bear the name of its owner, both inside and outside, and shall bear appropriate and conspicuous signs upon its sides and ends indicating both day and night the route and destination of such car. Provided, however, that when two or more cars are operated as trains, said end signs shall be affixed to the front of the front car and to the rear of the rear car. At night such signs shall be illuminated.

(k) There shall be securely posted in each car, where it may be conveniently read by the passengers, a copy of the above regulations of this section.

The board of health shall detail employees from the said board to make the investigation necessary to determine whether or not the sanitary provisions of this section are being complied with, and the said board shall report the result of such investigation to the corporation counsel. The council committee on local transportation may secure information necessary to determine whether or not all other provisions of this section are being complied with and to cooperate with the corporation counsel in securing the evidence necessary to the prosecution of violations of this section.

Any person guilty of violating any of the provisions of this section shall be fined not less than $25.00 nor more than $100.00 for each car operated in violation of this section, and each day of the operation of such car shall be considered a separate offense.

(Prior code § 188-6)

§9-124-040 Transporting policemen.

Any person owning or operating any railroad, street car, motorbus or omnibus having an established right-of-way within the limits of the city, and engaged in the business of carrying passengers thereon for hire, shall, on any train, car, motorbus, omnibus or other vehicle used or operated by any such described company, carry free of charge, within the limits of the city, any officer or member of the department of police, when such officer or member is clothed in the uniform of his rank and engaged in the performance of his official duties.

No officer or director of any railroad, street car, motorbus or omnibus company, nor any other person engaged in the business of carrying passengers for hire, as aforesaid, shall issue any order or command prohibiting or interfering with the enforcement of the provisions of this section.
(Prior code § 188-7)

§9-124-050 Driver collecting fares.

It shall be unlawful for the driver of any vehicle propelled otherwise than by animal power and used for transportation of passengers for hire, or for any person controlling or operating any such vehicle to cause, suffer or permit any driver to collect fare, make change, issue any ticket or transfer, make any entry of record, count transfers, tickets or money, while the said vehicle is in motion upon the surface of any public way in the city.
(Prior code § 188-8)

§9-124-060 Lights at railroad crossings.

Every person owning or operating any elevated or street railroad, whose track crosses or intersects at, above or below the grade of any of the public ways within the city, shall provide at his own expense, proper and sufficient lights, and shall care for the same at all such crossings or intersections. Such lights shall be of such kind as may be approved by the commissioner of streets and electricity.

Each day during which any crossing or intersection situated as aforesaid shall be permitted to remain without such lights after the first conviction shall constitute a separate and distinct offense.
(Prior code § 188-9)

§9-124-070 Painting railroad pillars.

Every person owning or operating any steam or elevated railroad whose track is elevated within the city shall paint a stripe of uniform color and design, in such a way as to make it conspicuous from its base to its top, on every post, pillar or support located at a point or turn in the street where vehicular traffic may be endangered by collision therewith. At night there shall be displayed a light of sufficient illuminating power to be visible in the direction from which vehicles approach at a distance of 200 feet on an arm or bracket extending from such post, pillar or support, or suspended from the superstructure of the railroad, all of which shall be done in such manner as shall be approved by the commissioner of streets and electricity.

In the event that any such person owning or operating any steam or elevated railroad shall fail or neglect to paint and illuminate such posts, pillars or supports as herein required, then the city council at its election, may cause the work to be done at the expense of such person, and such person shall pay the city the whole cost and expense thereof.

Each day during which any post, pillar or support shall be permitted to remain unpainted and without light contrary to the requirements of this section after the first conviction shall constitute a separate and distinct offense.
(Prior code § 188-10)

§9-124-080 Drains on railroad structures.

Every person, owning any elevated structure within the city, upon, along or over which trains or cars are propelled by steam, electricity or any motive power whatsoever, shall provide and maintain at his own expense, at all of his station buildings and platforms located over any of the public ways or other public places of the city, and over all intersections of elevated structures with public ways, suitable and practicable devices and equipment so arranged as to intercept and promptly carry off stormwater and drippings from melting snow or from any other cause.
(Prior code § 188-11)

§9-124-090 Penalty.

Except where some other penalty is specifically provided, any person who shall violate any provision of that part of this chapter dealing with general requirements, shall be subject to a fine of not less than $5.00 nor more than $100.00 for each offense.
(Prior code § 188-12)

Article II. Street Railroads

§9-124-100 Scope of regulations.

Nothing contained in this part of this chapter dealing with street railroads or any order of the city council passed in pursuance thereof shall affect or prejudice in any way the rights of the city or its legal representatives, or the state's attorney of Cook County, in any pending or future litigation concerning the respective rights of the city or the owners or lessees of any street railroad in any of the streets of the city under any statute or ordinance heretofore enacted or passed, nor shall any section of this part of this chapter dealing with street railroads be construed or understood as extending or enlarging in any way any rights which the owners or lessees of any such street railroad may now possess in the public ways of the city.
(Prior code § 188-13)

§9-124-110 Laying track.

No person shall lay any street railroad track in or upon any of the public ways or other public places within the city, without first procuring a permit therefor, in writing, from the commissioner of streets and electricity.

Such permit shall be issued by the commissioner of streets and electricity in accordance with the terms of the respective ordinances under which such track may be authorized to be laid, and in accordance with the provisions of this code applicable thereto, and shall specify in full the terms and conditions under which the same shall be constructed. The department of streets and electricity shall inspect and supervise the said construction sufficiently to ascertain whether such terms and conditions are in fact complied with. All work thereunder shall be superintended by the department of streets and electricity.

For every such permit there shall be paid to the city the cost of issuing the same and the expense of superintendence of such construction under such permit. The cost of such issuance and superintendence shall be computed and fixed by said commissioner.
(Prior code § 188-14)

§9-124-120 Gauge of track.

The gauge of all street railroads in the city now laid or hereafter to be laid is hereby fixed at four feet, eight and one-half inches, except on curves, where the gauge may be increased to not exceeding four feet and nine inches.
(Prior code § 188-15)

§9-124-130 Construction of rails.

On all public ways, bridges, viaducts or other public places of the city which are or shall hereafter be improved with granite, asphalt, macadam, brick, cedar block, creosoted block, or other artificial pavement of a permanent character, all street railroad rails which shall be laid shall be grooved rails as shown on the following profile of a section taken crosswise of the rail, and marked Exhibit 9-124-130, and in accordance with the following specifications:

The guard shall be three-fourths of an inch wide; the groove shall be one and three-fourths inches wide; the center line of the web shall pass through a point nine-sixteenths of an inch from the gauge line; the tread of the rail shall be two and three-fourths inches wide on the horizontal, and two inches from the gauge line back to the point of bevel; the bevel shall be three-fourths of an inch wide on the horizontal and the intersection of the beveled line with the back of the head of the rail shall be at a point five-sixteenths of an inch below the top horizontal base line; the total width of the head of the rail shall be two and three-fourths inches and the total width of rail five and one-fourth inches on the horizontal; the top surface of the tread of the rail shall be at an angle with the top horizontal base line one degree and 30 minutes, and the intersection of the two lines shall be at a point on the head of the rail one and three-eighths inches from the gauge line. The depth of the groove shall be one and one-fourth inches and the guard shall be one-fourth of an inch thick, and the base of the rail shall be not less than one-half of an inch thick, and the base of the rail shall not be less than six inches wide. The height of the rail shall be nine inches measured from the top horizontal base line to the bottom of the base of the rail. The weight of the rail shall be not less than 129 pounds per linear yard.

In all cases where any public way, bridge, viaduct or other public place of the city is improved or shall hereafter be improved with granite, asphalt, macadam, brick, cedar block, creosoted block or other artificial pavement of a permanent character, any person owning, operating, controlling or leasing any street railroad track thereon, the rails in use upon which said street railroad track are of any pattern other than that known as the grooved rail pattern and referred to in this section, shall, within 30 days after notice from the commissioner of streets and electricity, remove such rails and replace them with grooved rails of the pattern referred to herein. It shall be the duty of the commissioner of streets and electricity to give such notice to any person at such time before the completion of the work under the contract for such improvement as in the discretion of such commissioner may seem best.

The mode of laying said rails so as to carry out the provisions of this section and the form of the rail so laid shall be under the supervision and subject to the approval of the commissioner of streets and electricity. Provided, however, that nothing herein contained shall be construed as superseding or repealing any of the provisions contained in the respective contract ordinances under which persons operating such street railroads in the city are or may hereafter be operating such street railroads.
(Prior code § 188-16)

§9-124-140 Track not to obstruct traffic.

Every person operating a street railroad in the city shall keep the track of his road in such a condition that such track shall not at any time be elevated above the surface of the streets on which it is laid, and so that vehicles can easily and freely at all times cross such track at all points in any direction, without obstruction.
(Prior code § 188-17)

§9-124-150 Repair of streets.

Any person owning or operating a street railroad in the city shall keep in good repair such portions of the streets as he agreed or may agree with said city to keep in good repair.

Whenever any person owning or operating any street railway track in, upon, along or across any of the public ways or other public places within the city, shall be required to pave or repave any part of any public way, or shall proceed to pave or repave any part of any such public way, it shall be unlawful for any such person to lay down or place any pavement or other material across the top of any sewer, manhole, or other opening necessary to reach such sewer. If in the performance of such work it shall be necessary or desirable to raise the grade of such pavement or of such street, it shall be the duty of the person doing such work to bring the top of such sewer, manhole, or other opening, up to the level of the new grade thus established, so that the top of the cover of such manhole or other opening shall be flush and level with the surface of such pavement when completed.

The commissioner of streets and electricity shall see that the provisions of this section are complied with, and shall require all employees of his department to report to said commissioner all cases that come to their knowledge of any neglect or failure of any such person to comply.
(Prior code § 188-18)

§9-124-160 Track and street repair violations.

Whenever any person operating any street railroad shall neglect or fail to comply with the provisions of Sections 9-124-130, 9-124-140 or 9-124-150 of this code, the commissioner of streets and electricity shall cause a notice to be served upon any such person, setting forth in what particular such person is in default, and that the work so referred to shall be completed or constructed in accordance with the terms of the aforesaid sections within five days after the service of such notice.

Any such person that shall neglect or fail to put his track or part of track, or any portion of the streets mentioned in such notice, in the condition required by Sections 9-124-130, 9-124-140 or 9-124-150 of this code within five days after the service of such notice, shall be fined not less than $100.00 and not more than $200.00 for each offense. Every day such neglect or failure shall continue after the expiration of such five days shall constitute a separate and distinct offense.

Any person laying any track in violation of any provision of this chapter where no other penalty is provided or without complying with the terms of any permit issued hereunder shall be fined not less than $100.00 nor more than $200.00 for each offense. Said person shall be further fined $100.00 a day for every day any such track shall remain in any such public way or other public place, where the same shall have been laid without such permit or in violation of the terms thereof.

(Prior code § 188-19)

§9-124-170 Street sprinkling.

Every person operating or maintaining a street railroad track located in and along the streets within the city, shall, except as otherwise expressly provided in the respective ordinances under which track has heretofore been or may hereafter be authorized to be laid, keep moistened and sprinkled with water the several streets upon and along which he may operate or maintain his railroad track so that the streets so sprinkled shall be and remain reasonably free from dust under all conditions and circumstances attending such operation.

A separate and distinct offense shall be deemed to have been committed each and every day on which any such person shall neglect, fail or refuse to comply with any of the provisions of this section.

(Prior code § 188-20)

§9-124-180 Removal of street accumulations.

Every person operating any street railroad track on and along the surface of any public way of the city shall remove all dirt, snow and other accumulations from so much of the surface of the public way as lies between the two outermost rails of such tracks and also from such additional surface in width as may be prescribed in any street railroad ordinance by virtue of which he is operating the street railroad. All such dirt, snow and other accumulations shall be removed entirely from and out of such public way at least once each week and as much oftener as the commissioner of streets and electricity shall in writing direct. Such dirt, snow and other accumulations shall be removed and disposed of in accordance with the provisions of this code and subject to the rules and regulations of the department of streets and electricity.

Any person operating a street railroad upon or along the surface of any public way in the city, that shall refuse or neglect to clean any part of a public way as required by this section, shall be fined not less than $50.00 nor more than $200.00 for each offense.

(Prior code § 188-21)

§9-124-190 Electrical requirements.

All uninsulated electrical return circuits must be of such current carrying capacity and so arranged that the difference of potential between any two points on the return will not exceed the maximum limit of 12 volts, and between any two points on the return 1,000 feet apart within one mile radius of the city hall will not exceed the limit of one volt, and between any two points on the return 700 feet apart outside of this one mile radius limit will not exceed the limit of one volt. In addition thereto, a proper return conductor system must be so installed and maintained as to protect all metallic work from electrolysis damage.

The return current amperage on pipes and cable sheaths must not be greater than 0.5 amperes per pound foot for caulked cast iron pipe, 0.8 amperes per pound foot for screwed wrought iron pipe, and 0.16 amperes per pound foot for standard lead or lead alloy sheaths of cables.

All persons operating street railroads must equip their uninsulated return current systems in the following manner:

(1) With insulated pilot wire circuits and voltmeters so that accurate chart records will be obtained daily showing the difference of potential between the negative bus bars in each station and at least four extreme limits on the return circuit in its corresponding feeding district.

(2) With recording ammeters, insulated cables and automatic reverse load and overload circuit breakers which will record and limit the maximum amperes drained from all the metallic work, except the regular return feeders, to less than 10 percent of the total output of the station.

The said chart records must be so kept as to be always accessible to city officials.

Any person failing to comply with the provisions of this section shall be fined not less than $50.00 nor more than $200.00 for each offense. Each day's operation of such equipment contrary to said provisions shall constitute and be regarded as a separate and distinct offense. Provided, that the said section shall not be construed as modifying or extending any express provisions relating to the subject matter thereof contained in any contract ordinance under which such systems are operated.
(Prior code § 188-22)

§9-124-200 Schedule of operation.

Every person owning or operating street cars upon any track over which any street railroad cars are operated in the city, shall control the operation of said cars by means of a written schedule for each separate line. Said schedule shall be prepared to provide a sufficient number of cars in order to comply with the provisions of this code. One true copy of each schedule, showing the number of cars operated thereby, and the train number of each trip, and the schedule time of arriving at and departing from one terminal, and the running time between designated time points, shall be filed with the council committee on local transportation.

In case a revision or rearrangement of any schedule is made, one true copy of the new schedule shall be filed with the council committee on local transportation within not less than three days before such new schedule shall be put into effect.

Each car operated shall bear a suitable run number sign, indicating the position of said car on its schedule and identifying its scheduled movements, and each car operated in addition to the scheduled cars as an "extra" car shall carry a suitable run number sign bearing the letter "X." At night such number signs shall be illuminated.

Each car (extra cars excepted) shall be dispatched and operated in accordance with the schedule on file with the council committee on local transportation.
(Prior code § 188-23)

§9-124-210 Rush hour checking.

The council committee on local transportation shall have the right to designate checking points at any place upon the line of any person or his agents, upon notice to him of the location of such checking points. Within five days after the delivery of the information designating the checking points, such person or agents may furnish to the council committee on local transportation a written statement, setting forth the time of the periods of the morning and evening rush hours, not to exceed two and one-half hours each for the checking points.

The periods of the morning and evening rush hours, as provided for in this section, shall remain in full force and effect until receipt by the council committee on local transportation of a written statement changing the periods of the rush hours at said points.

In case any person, or his agents, shall fail to file the rush hour periods at any checking point designated by the council committee on local transportation, as provided for in this section the council committee on local transportation shall establish morning and evening rush hour periods at the checking points designated in said notice.
(Prior code § 188-24)

§9-124-220 Exceptions to schedule requirements.

If said person or his agent is able to prove that it was physically impracticable for him or his agent to comply with the standard of car loading required, owing to unusual or extraordinary physical conditions not under his control, such as accidents, breaking wires, or blockades resulting in obstruction of right-of-way, or by reason of severe storms, or that the failure to comply with the said standard of car loading was due to unusual conditions, or to abnormal traffic conditions arising from such causes as conventions, open-air gatherings or other similar large assemblies, then such person or his agent shall not be held to be in default of the car-loading provisions of this chapter, but any such person or his agent shall not be permitted to claim immunity by reason of physical causes hereinbefore mentioned unless he or his agent is able to prove that any car passing a checking point has been delayed behind its schedule time for a period of 10 minutes or more, and then only in the event that such delay or delays shall have occurred within a period of one hour prior to the beginning of the period at which the car loading was being checked at said checking point.
(Prior code § 188-25)

§9-124-230 Service checks.

Service checks of nonrush car loading may be made at any established checking point within the city by the council committee on local transportation.
(Prior code § 188-26)

§9-124-240 Stops.

Every motorman, driver, conductor or other person having charge of any street car in operation upon any street railroad in the city shall stop or cause such car to be stopped to receive or let off passengers who may desire to get on or off such car at such street as the city council has or shall hereafter designate by ordinance, and at no other streets or points, except as hereinafter provided.

At all points where a "positive" stop made under the provisions of Section 9-124-260 and a "service" stop made under the provisions of this section fall within close proximity one to the other, the stop required to be made under the provisions of this section shall be eliminated.

Positive stops made under the provisions of Section 9-124-260 shall include, for public safety, all stops made at boulevard intersections.

Street cars shall also stop, whenever desirable, at all stations of intersecting elevated railroads. At points where a "service" stop made at an elevated station, as herein provided and a "service" stop made under the provisions of the first paragraph of this section fall within close proximity to one another, the cars shall make the "station" stop only.

No motorman, driver, conductor or other person having charge or control of a street car in operation upon any street railway in the city, in stopping such car at an intersecting street for the purpose of receiving or discharging passengers, shall stop or cause such car to be stopped at any other than the nearest crossing in the direction such car is going.

All persons operating street cars within the limits of the city for the transportation of passengers shall construct and maintain at all points on unpaved streets where such cars stop to receive or discharge passengers, a proper landing of cinders or other suitable material so as to enable passengers to board or alight from such cars without discomfort or inconvenience.

Rules regulating the running of cars and stopping for passengers shall be posted in a conspicuous place in each car, and shall be in letters of such size as to be easily read from any part of such car.
(Prior code § 188-27)

§9-124-250 Signs at stopping points.

All persons operating street cars within the limits of this city for the transportation of passengers shall maintain appropriate signs at or near all points where under the provisions of this chapter street cars stop to receive or discharge passengers.
(Prior code § 188-28)

§9-124-260 Stops at railroads, crossings, bridges.

Every conductor, motorman or other person having charge of any street car operating upon any street railroad in this city shall operate over a grade crossing with a steam railroad in the following manner:

Where a steam railroad track is used for the operation of through passenger train or through freight train service, or both, the street car shall be brought to a full stop at a distance of at least 25 feet from the nearest rail, and the conductor shall then proceed on foot to the middle of the crossing or beyond. After carefully looking both ways along the railroad track to ascertain that it is safe to do so, he shall then signal the motorman to proceed over said crossing. Provided, however, that where an official flagman is stationed at such crossing, such flagman may act in place of the conductor.

Where the steam railroad track is a spur track, siding, industrial loading track, or serves only for local switching purposes, the motorman shall stop the car at a distance of at least 25 feet from the nearest rail, shall observe carefully that it is safe to cross by looking in both directions along the tracks and shall then cross with due care and caution.

Every such person having charge of any such street car shall also, when approaching any cross street occupied by street railway tracks which intersect with those on which such street car is being operated, bring such car to a full stop before arriving at and within ten feet of the nearest intersection line of such cross street.

When approaching a swing, draw, bascule or other movable bridge, he shall bring said car to a full stop at a point not less than 50 feet from the roadway gate of said bridge, and shall then approach and proceed over the bridge with due care and caution.

(Prior code § 188-29)

§9-124-270 Stopping before firehouse.

No person operating street cars within the city, nor any person in charge of such car, whether operated for the conveyance of passengers, mail or other commodity or thing shall permit or allow any such car to stand in front of or permit any passenger to get on or off from any such car in front of any fire engine house within the city.

(Prior code § 188-30)

§9-124-280 Penalty.

Except where some other penalty is specifically provided, any person owning or operating street cars shall be fined not less than $25.00 nor more than $100.00 for violation of any provision of this part of this chapter dealing with street railroads, and any conductor, driver or collector of fares violating any of said provisions shall be fined not less than $5.00 nor more than $100.00 for each offense.

(Prior code § 188-31)

Article III. Elevated Railroads

§9-124-290 Scope of regulations.

Nothing contained in this part of this chapter dealing with elevated railroads, or any order of the city council passed in pursuance thereof shall affect or prejudice in any way the rights of the city or its legal representatives, or the state's attorney of Cook County, in any pending or future litigation concerning the respective rights of the city or the owners or lessees of any electric elevated railroad in any of the streets of the city under any statute or ordi-

nance heretofore enacted or passed. Nor shall any section of this part of this chapter dealing with elevated railroads be construed or understood as extending or enlarging in any way rights which the owners or lessees of any such elevated railroad may now possess in the public streets of the city.
(Prior code § 188-32)

§9-124-300 "Rush hours" defined.

For the purposes of this part of this chapter dealing with elevated railroads, rush hours are hereby defined to be the following periods of time: between the hours of 6:30 a.m. and 9:00 a.m., and between the hours of 4:30 p.m. and 7:00 p.m.
(Prior code § 188-33)

§9-124-310 Schedule of operation.

Every person owning any tracks over which any elevated railroad trains are operated, or operating any elevated railroad trains, shall control the operation of said trains by means of a written schedule for each separate line. Said schedule or schedules shall be prepared to provide a sufficient number of trains in order to comply with the provisions of this code. One true copy of each schedule, showing the number of trains operated thereby, and the train numbers, and the schedule time of arriving at and departing from one terminal, and the running time between designated time points, shall be filed with the city clerk.

In case a revision or rearrangement of any schedule is made, one true copy of the new schedule shall be filed with the city clerk not less than three days before such new schedule shall be put into effect.

Each train operated shall bear a suitable run number sign, indicating the position of said train on its schedule and identifying its schedule movements, and each train operated in addition to the schedule cars as an "extra" car shall carry a suitable train number sign bearing the letter "X."

Each train (extra trains excepted) shall be dispatched and operated in accordance with the schedule on file with the city clerk.

Each day that any violation of this section shall continue shall be considered a separate and distinct offense.
(Prior code § 188-34)

§9-124-320 Seats for passengers.

Every person owning any tracks over which any elevated railroad trains are operated, or operating any elevated railroad trains, shall on each separate line operate trains at such intervals (except during rush hours) that the aggregate number of seats within the trains passing any point in any one direction during any period of 15 consecutive minutes shall be not less than the aggregate number of passengers carried on said trains passing said point during said period of 15 consecutive minutes. Provided, however, that if less than three trains pass any point on any line during a 15-minute period, then the aggregate number of seats carried by three consecutive trains in any one direction passing any point shall be not less than the aggregate number of passengers carried by said three consecutive trains passing said point.

Every person owning any tracks over which any elevated railroad trains are operated, or operating any elevated trains, shall operate trains at such intervals that not less than one train shall be operated during each and every fifteen minute period of the entire 24 hours of each day, excepting the six hours between 12:00 and 6:00 a.m.

Every person violating any of the provisions of this section shall be fined not less than $50.00 nor more than $200.00 for each offense. Each day upon which a violation occurs upon any one line shall constitute a single offense. Not more than one penalty shall be recovered for a violation committed on any line during any one day.
(Prior code § 188-35)

§9-124-330 Stops when on ground.

No person owning or operating any elevated railroad shall suffer or permit any car operated by it, when in transit over the surface of the ground upon rails laid thereon, to be run by any street intersection at which a station has been provided, without stopping. All such cars while so in transit shall be stopped at each station.
(Prior code § 188-36)

§9-124-340 Shunting or running down inclines.

No person owning or operating any elevated railroad shall allow or permit any of the cars owned or operated by him to be shunted or run down inclines from the elevated structure to the surface of the ground, unless such cars are under the absolute control of a competent motorman or engineer, or person acquainted with and competent to operate the motor machinery of such car. No car shall be allowed or permitted by any person operating or owning the same to be shunted or run down any such incline, unless the motor machinery of the same can be controlled so as to decrease the rate of speed of such car while running down such incline. No car shall be run down such incline at a rate of speed greater than 10 miles per hour.
(Prior code § 188-37)

§9-124-350 Storing cars.

No person owning or operating any elevated railway shall store or permit to be stored any car owned or operated by it upon those parts of its elevated structures which are built over or upon any of the public ways or other public places of the city.
(Prior code § 188-38)

§9-124-360 Construction and location of stations.

In all cases where the distance between consecutive stations or landing places for receiving and discharging passengers on any line of elevated railroad operated for the transportation of passengers is more than 2,500 feet, the person owning or operating such line of elevated railroad shall install and maintain an intermediate station or landing place for receiving and discharging passengers and shall afford to the public at such intermediate station or landing place the same facilities for entering and departing from cars as are afforded at other stations or landing places similarly situated along the same line. Provided, that nothing herein contained shall be construed as limiting or restricting the right to run express trains over such line which do not stop at all stations.

Such intermediate station or landing place shall be located at or near a public street which crosses such line of electric elevated railroad and which is situated as near as practicable equally distant from such consecutive stations. The exact location of such intermediate station may be prescribed by order of the city council; provided, that it shall be not more than 250 feet from the center of the distance between such consecutive stations. Whenever the location of any such intermediate station or landing place for receiving and discharging passengers shall be prescribed by order of the city council the person owning or operating such line of an elevated railroad shall have 90 days' time within which to construct and install such intermediate station or landing place for receiving and discharging passengers during which no prosecution for failure to install and maintain same shall lie.

Wherever an intermediate station or landing place for receiving and discharging passengers as required by this section shall occupy any part of a public way, either on the surface thereof or overhead, before any work of construction shall begin, plans for same shall first be submitted to and be approved by the commissioner of streets and electricity and the executive director of the department of construction and permits. In all cases such intermediate stations or landing places shall be constructed so as to comply with all ordinances of the city relating to buildings or structures of this character.

(Prior code § 188-39; Amend. Coun. J. 3-5-03, p. 104990)

§9-124-370 Station enclosures.

Every person owning or operating an elevated railroad shall provide and equip all station platforms, which are used in connection with the operation of such railroad, with a top or roof of incombustible material and with storm enclosures of glass or other suitable material on three sides thereof, so that the patrons or passengers of such elevated railroad may be protected from inclement weather while waiting for trains. Provided, however, that the provisions relating to said storm enclosures of station platforms shall not apply to the platforms which are commonly known as island platforms and where more than one side of such platforms is used for the purpose of receiving or discharging passengers. All such platforms commonly called island platforms, and platforms where more than one side thereof are used for the purpose of receiving or discharging passengers, shall be provided with storm enclosures of glass or other suitable material at each end of same, and shall also be provided with a longitudinal partition running down the middle of such platforms the entire length thereof. Such partitions shall extend from the platforms to the roof and connect with the storm enclosures at each end of such platform, and shall be provided with sufficient openings to permit passage by persons from one side to another. Such enclosures and partitions shall be provided during the months of November, December, January, February and March of each year.

(Prior code § 188-40)

§9-124-380 Illuminated station signs.

Every person operating an elevated railroad shall place and maintain at each station on such railroad at least three signs on each platform at such stations, one of said signs to be placed in the middle and one at either end of each platform. Said signs shall distinctly show the name of the station. The signs at the ends of the platform shall be illuminated at night so that the name can be easily read. Said illuminated signs shall be made, placed and maintained in conspicuous positions not less than nine inches above the top of the railing on the platform, and in such manner that they can be read easily by persons on the trains of such railroad.

All signs shall be of a pattern, material and size meeting the approval of the commissioner of streets and electricity, and they shall be constructed, placed and maintained in a manner meeting with his approval.
(Prior code § 188-41)

§9-124-390 Penalty.

Except where some other penalty is specifically provided, any person who shall violate any of the provisions of this part of this chapter dealing with elevated railroads shall be fined not less than $25.00 nor more than $200.00 for each offense. Each day that such person shall fail to comply with or shall violate the provisions of this chapter shall constitute a distinct and separate offense.
(Prior code § 188-42)

Article IV. Other Railroads

§9-124-400 Scope of regulations.

Nothing herein contained and no act of any person by reason of the provisions of this part of this chapter dealing with other railroads shall be held or be construed to be in the nature of a contract between the city and any person owning, controlling or operating any railroad. Nor shall any provision of this part of this chapter be construed to release any person from any obligation now existing or which may hereafter be imposed by the city to construct or build viaducts, to raise or lower their tracks, to construct subways or to abolish grade crossings at any or all streets within said city when ordered so to do by the city council. Nothing herein shall be construed to create any obligation upon the part of any railroad company to construct any viaduct, or to create any new liability against any railroad, except as provided by the terms of this part of this chapter. Nothing in this part of this chapter contained shall commit the city to any permanent plan or system for the operation of railroad cars, engines or trains, or the protection of the public on streets or at street crossings, or the regulation and control and supervision of railroad track. The city hereby reserves the right to alter, amend, or repeal any provisions herein contained.
(Prior code § 188-43)

§9-124-410 Signals on engines.

No person owning or operating a railroad shall cause or allow the whistle of any locomotive engine to be sounded within the city, except necessary brake signals and such as may be absolutely necessary to prevent injury to life and property.

Each locomotive engine shall be equipped with a bell-ringing device which shall at all times be maintained in repair and which shall cause the bell of the engine to be rung automatically. The bell of each locomotive engine shall be rung continuously when such locomotive is running within the city, excepting bells on locomotives running upon railroad tracks enclosed by walls or fences, or enclosed by a wall on one side and public waters on the other side, and excepting bells on locomotives running upon those portions of the railroad track which have been elevated. In the case of these exceptions, no bell shall be rung or whistle blown except as signals of danger.

Every person owning or operating a railroad within the city, shall erect at the point where such railroad enters the city, a signboard, having thereon the words "stop speed," "ring bell," legibly painted thereon, and keep the same so erected.

(Prior code § 188-44)

§9-124-420 Bumping posts.

Every person owning or operating any railroad track, switch, side track, or turnout on which any car may be operated or moved by steam power, is hereby required to establish and maintain substantial bumping posts or other suitable obstruction at the end of each such track, to prevent any such car from being hurled, driven or pushed from such track.

Each day after the first conviction that any track situated as aforesaid shall be permitted to remain without such bumping post shall constitute a separate and distinct offense.

(Prior code § 188-45)

§9-124-430 Allowing steam to escape.

No person in charge of any locomotive engine shall cause or allow the cylinder cock or cocks, safety valve or other valves of any locomotive engine to be opened so as to permit steam to escape therefrom at any time while running upon or along any railroad track where the engine is within 100 feet of any street or railroad crossing or viaduct. Provided, however, that when any such engine shall be standing at any such place in said city, and for six revolutions of the driving wheel after being put in motion, the said cocks may be opened for the purpose of allowing condensed steam to escape.

(Prior code § 188-46)

§9-124-440 Making up trains.

No train of a greater length than 700 feet shall be moved for the purpose of transferring such train or any part of it, to another, or opposite, or adjoining track in making up any train or distributing the same. No such train shall be composed of more than 20 cars. Provided, further, that the provisions of this section shall not apply to trains while running or being operated on railroad tracks which are elevated above or depressed below the surface of the streets crossing, or adjacent to, such tracks, in accordance with the provisions of any city ordinance requiring such depression or elevation. Provided, further, that this section shall not apply to any private switch yard nor to any place where such train or cars do not obstruct a crossing at the street grade used by traffic and public travel.

Any person that shall violate any of the provisions of this section shall be fined for the first violation $100.00, and for each succeeding violation the sum of $200.00.
(Prior code § 188-47)

§9-124-450 Shunting cars.
No person shall drive or shunt any passenger or freight car across any public street at the street grade without an engine attached to such car.
(Prior code § 188-48)

§9-124-470 Changing from steam to electricity.
No person operating a railroad by steam power shall hereafter operate the same by electric power, either by the overhead contact system or otherwise, within the city without first obtaining authority and permission therefor from the city council.
(Prior code § 188-50)

§9-124-480 Furnishing employee copy of regulations.
Every person owning or operating a steam railroad within the city shall furnish each engineer and train conductor employed thereon a certified or printed copy of this part of this chapter dealing with other railroads.
(Prior code § 188-51)

§9-124-490 Penalty.
Except where some other penalty has been specifically provided, any person who shall violate any of the provisions of this part of this chapter dealing with other railroads shall be fined not less than $10.00 nor more than $200.00 for each offense.
(Prior code § 188-52)

This page intentionally left blank

TITLE 10
STREETS, PUBLIC WAYS, PARKS, AIRPORTS AND HARBORS
(Selected Chapters)

Chapters:

10-8	Use of Public Ways and Places. (Complete Chapter)
10-20	Work On and Under Public Ways. (Selected Sections)
10-28	Structures On and Under Public Ways. (Selected Sections)
10-32	Trees, Plants and Shrubs. (Selected Sections)
10-36	Parks, Playgrounds and Airports. (Selected Sections)
10-40	Chicago Harbor. (Selected Sections)

CHAPTER 10-8
USE OF PUBLIC WAYS AND PLACES
(Complete Chapter)

Sections:

Article I. Zones of Quiet

10-8-010	Establishment.
10-8-020	Posting of signs.
10-8-030	Traffic near hospitals.
10-8-040	Reserved.
10-8-050	Reserved.
10-8-060	School zones of quiet.
10-8-070	Unnecessary noises.

Article II. Charitable Solicitation

10-8-080	Permit required.
10-8-090	Permit—Issuance requirements.
10-8-100	Application.
10-8-110	Application—Committee action.
10-8-120	Date and location conflicts—Preference given when.
10-8-130	Permit legend.
10-8-140	Display of information.
10-8-150	Statement to be filed.
10-8-160	Committee on finance—Rule adoption.
10-8-170	Violation—Penalty—Corporation counsel to institute action.

Article III. Requirements and Restrictions

10-8-180	Snow and ice removal.
10-8-190	Liability for civil damages.
10-8-200	Loading and unloading from alleys.
10-8-210	House moving.
10-8-220	Conveying loose materials.
10-8-230	Overloading vehicles.
10-8-240	Vehicles drawn over curb.
10-8-250	Throwing sharp objects.
10-8-260	Reserved.
10-8-270	Distribution of advertising matter.
10-8-271	Distribution of advertising on private property.
10-8-280	Towing advertising display.
10-8-290	Aircraft dropping advertising matter.
10-8-300	Aircraft advertising noises.
10-8-310	Placing advertising matter in automobiles.
10-8-320	Posting bills.
10-8-330	Parade, public assembly or athletic event.
10-8-335	Outdoor special events.

10-8-340 Donation of promotional decorative lightpole banners and decorations.
10-8-350 Performance in public ways.
10-8-360 Injury to sidewalk or driveway.
10-8-370 Alleys, access to construction sites.
10-8-380 Defacing property in public places.
10-8-390 Obstructing public improvements.
10-8-400 Barbed wire fence.

Article IV. Occasional Sales
10-8-401 Definitions.
10-8-402 Permit required.
10-8-403 Occasional sales permitted when—Frequency.
10-8-404 Occasion sales—Signs.
10-8-405 Display of articles for sale—Permitted locations.
10-8-406 Violation—Penalty.

Article V. Prohibited Uses
10-8-410 Skating.
10-8-420 Cleansing goods.
10-8-430 Washing windows and sidewalks.
10-8-440 Sorting of articles.
10-8-450 Mixing concrete.
10-8-460 Spilling oil.
10-8-470 Spilling of substances on roadway.
10-8-480 Casting refuse and liquids.
10-8-490 Selling tickets.
10-8-500 Selling tickets near amusement places.
10-8-505 Selling tickets near a stadium or playing field.
10-8-510 Soliciting business.
10-8-515 Soliciting unlawful business.
10-8-520 Street vendors.
10-8-525 Vehicle servicing in traffic lane prohibited—Exception.

Article VI. Violation of Chapter Provisions
10-8-526 Enforcement of Chicago Transit Authority Ordinance 98-126— Rule of conduct.
10-8-530 Violation—Penalty.

Article I. Zones of Quiet

§10-8-010 Establishment.

There is hereby created and established a zone of quiet in all territory embraced within the block upon which abuts the premises of any hospital owned, controlled or operated by the federal, state, county or city governments or any licensed hospital or home.
(Prior code § 36-1)

§10-8-020 Posting of signs.

It shall be the duty of the commissioner of streets and electricity to place, or cause to be placed, and maintained, at each and every street intersection at which traffic vehicles are diverted under the provisions of this chapter, a conspicuous sign displaying the words:

NOTICE
ZONE OF QUIET

Traffic vehicles prohibited between the hours of 2 and 7 o'clock a.m.
(Prior code § 36-2)

§10-8-030 Traffic near hospitals.

No wagon, cart, dray, truck, automobile truck, or other heavy traffic vehicle, shall, between the hours of 2:00 and 7:00 a.m., approach upon or along any street upon which abuts any licensed hospital, or any hospital owned, controlled or operated by the federal, state, county or city governments, nearer in any given direction than the nearest street which crosses or intersects the street upon which such hospital premises abut; and in any case where any hospital premises are located at a street corner, or other street intersection, no such vehicle as herein described shall between the hours of 2:00 and 7:00 a.m. approach such hospital premises upon or along any street upon which such hospital premises abut nearer than the street nearest in any given direction to either or any of the streets abutted upon by such hospital premises; provided, that any vehicle carrying goods, merchandise, wares or other articles to or from any house or premises abutting upon any part of a street affected by this chapter shall be permitted to enter thereon and deliver or receive such goods, merchandise, wares or other articles; and provided further, that any vehicles carrying tools, machinery, material or other articles used for the construction, repair or cleaning of the pavement, sewers, waterpipes, lamps or any other municipal property, or the gas mains, electric wires, streetcar tracks, lampposts or other properties, appurtenances or attachments of any public utility in any part of a street affected by this chapter, shall be permitted to enter thereon for the purpose of such construction, repair or cleaning. This prohibition shall not apply to any street or part of a street lying in that part of the city bounded on the north by the Chicago River, on the east by Michigan Avenue, on the south by Twenty-Second Street and on the west by the Chicago River.
(Prior code § 36-3)

§10-8-040 Reserved.
(Deleted. Coun. J. 3-31-04, p. 20916)

§10-8-050 Reserved.
(Deleted. Coun. J. 3-31-04, p. 20916)

§10-8-060 School zones of quiet.

There are hereby created and established zones of quiet during school hours in all public ways surrounding every block within which is located a building used, controlled, leased or operated for free common school education in the city.

It shall be the duty of the commissioner of streets and electricity to place, or cause to be placed, on lampposts or some other conspicuous place, as near to each of the corners as practicable of every such block wherein such zone of quiet is established, as provided in this section, signs or placards displaying the words, "NOTICE ZONE OF QUIET."
(Prior code § 36-6)

§10-8-070 Unnecessary noises.

The making, causing or permitting to be made of any unnecessary noise of any kind whatsoever, or the playing of itinerant musicians, or the making of noises for the purpose of advertising any goods, wares or merchandise, or of

attracting the attention or inviting the patronage of any person to any business, or the playing of itinerant musicians upon the public ways within any zone of quiet established in accordance with this chapter, is hereby declared to be a nuisance, and is hereby prohibited.
(Prior code § 36-7)

Article II. Charitable Solicitation

§10-8-080 Permit required.

No person shall solicit or collect contributions of funds for charitable purposes upon any portion of the public way without first having obtained a permit for such purpose from the committee on finance.
(Prior code § 36-8; Added. Coun. J. 12-18-84, p. 12004)

§10-8-090 Permit—Issuance requirements.

No permit for solicitation of charitable contributions on the public way shall be issued to any person unless such person is either (a) a benevolent, philanthropic, patriotic or eleemosynary organization registered and in good standing with the Attorney General of the State of Illinois under "An Act to regulate solicitation and collection of funds for charitable purposes, providing for violations thereof, and making appropriations therefor," effective July 26, 1963, as amended; or (b) an organization exempt from compliance with said Act pursuant to section 3 thereof, as amended.
(Prior code § 36-9; Added. Coun. J. 12-18-84, p. 12004)

§10-8-100 Application.

Application for a charitable solicitation permit shall be made on a form issued by committee on finance. The application shall include the name, address and telephone number of the soliciting organization; proof of registration and good standing, or proof of initial registration and exemption as described in Section 10-8-090(b) of this code, issued by the Attorney General of the state of Illinois; the names, residence addresses and telephone numbers of the officers of the organization; the dates and locations of the solicitation; the approximate number of persons engaging in the solicitation; a description or facsimile of the tag, badge, emblem or other token (if any) which will be distributed as part of the solicitation; and such other information as the committee on finance may require. Application for a charitable solicitation permit shall be made no less than 30 days before the commencement of the solicitation. The application shall be signed and verified by at least one officer of the organization.
(Prior code § 36-10; Added. Coun. J. 12-18-84, p. 12004)

§10-8-110 Application—Committee action.

The committee on finance shall review each application for a charitable solicitation permit at the first meeting following filing of the application. The committee may continue the hearing on an application if additional proceedings are necessary to determine the applicant's compliance with the requirements of this chapter. If all requirements have not been met, the committee shall deny the application and shall notify the applicant of its decision and the grounds therefor. Notice of the denial shall be sent by mail, addressed to the applicant at

the address stated in the application. All decisions of the committee shall be reported to the city council at the next regular meeting thereof.
(Prior code § 36-11; Added. Coun. J. 12-18-84, p. 12004)

§10-8-120 Date and location conflicts—Preference given when.

If more than one organization applies for a permit to solicit charitable contributions on the same date and at the same location, the committee on finance shall resolve the conflict. Preference shall be given to organizations whose fundraising activities are well recognized, so as to promote the efficiency and coordination of such activities. Any organization which has engaged in solicitation of charitable contributions on the public way in the same manner and at the same approximate time of year for five consecutive years shall be permitted to select its dates one year in advance of actual solicitation. The committee may offer alternate dates and/or sites as a means of resolving conflicts.
(Prior code § 36-12; Added. Coun. J. 12-18-84, p. 12004)

§10-8-130 Permit legend.

A charitable solicitation permit shall bear the legend "City of Chicago Charitable Solicitation Permit" and shall state the name of the organization to which it is issued and the dates and places of the permitted solicitation. Each permit shall be sequentially numbered to indicate the year of its issuance and the number of permits then outstanding. Each permit shall be signed by the chairman of the committee on finance.
(Prior code § 36-13; Added. Coun. J. 12-18-84, p. 12004)

§10-8-140 Display of information.

Each person who engages in the solicitation of charitable contributions on the public way shall display on his person a tag or card no smaller than two inches by four inches, indicating the name of his organization to which the permit is issued, the number of the permit and the effective dates thereof. A facsimile of the permit may be used instead of the tag or card. Each charitable organization must supply those persons soliciting on city streets on their behalf with reflective vests, unless the organization restricts the hours of their solicitation from 8:00 a.m. to 4:00 p.m.
(Prior code § 36-14; Amend. Coun. J. 12-18-84, p. 12004; 10-1-97, p. 52406)

§10-8-150 Statement to be filed.

Each organization which receives a charitable solicitation permit pursuant to chapter shall, within 60 days after the completion of the activities conducted under the permit, file with the committee on finance a statement of all receipts and disbursements from such activities.
(Prior code § 36-15; Added. Coun. J. 12-18-84, p. 12004)

§10-8-160 Committee on finance—Rule adoption.

The committee on finance may adopt rules and regulations consistent with the provisions of this chapter governing the solicitation of charitable contributions on the public way. The rules and regulations that have been adopted by the committee on finance are as follows:

(1) The charitable organization must be registered with the Charitable Trust Division of the Illinois Attorney General's Office as a not-for-profit corporation;

(2) Prior to issuance of the permit the charitable organization must sign an agreement whereby the organization agrees to indemnify and hold harmless the city, its officers, employees and agents from any and all claims, suits or damages arising from their use of the public way to solicit funds;

(3) Persons under the age of 16 shall be prohibited from soliciting on city streets;

(4) Soliciting on city streets will be allowed only at intersections where vehicles must come to a complete stop and only when those vehicles have come to a complete stop.

(Prior code § 36-16; Amend. Coun. J. 12-18-84, p. 12004; J. 10-1-97, p. 52406; 4-29-98, p. 66275)

§10-8-170 Violation—Penalty—Corporation counsel to institute action.

Any person who violates any provision of this chapter relating to solicitation of charitable contributions on the public way shall be fined not more than $500.00. Each day that a violation is committed shall be considered a separate and distinct offense. Any charitable organization that violates any provision of this chapter relating to solicitation of charitable contributions on the public way shall have their privileges suspended for a period of one year. Any charitable organization that violates any provision of this chapter a second time shall have their privileges suspended for a second year. Any charitable organization that violates any provision of this chapter a third time shall be prohibited from soliciting charitable contributions on the public way. The corporation counsel, upon learning of violations of the provisions of this chapter relating to solicitation of charitable contributions on the public way, may institute an action in the appropriate court to seek an injunction against such violation in addition to the fines authorized by this section.

(Prior code § 36-17; Amend. Coun. J. 12-18-84, p. 12004; 1-23-85, p. 12746; 10-1-97, p. 52406)

Article III. Requirements and Restrictions

§10-8-180 Snow and ice removal.

Every owner, lessee, tenant, occupant or other person having charge of any building or lot of ground in the city abutting upon any public way or public place shall remove the snow and ice from the sidewalk in front of such building or lot of ground.

If the sidewalk is of greater width than five feet, it shall not be necessary for such person to remove snow and ice from the same for a space wider than five feet.

In case the snow and ice on the sidewalk shall be frozen so hard that it cannot be removed without injury to the pavement, the person having charge of any building or lot of ground as aforesaid shall, within the time specified, cause the sidewalk abutting on the said premises to be strewn with ashes, sand, sawdust, or some similar suitable material, and shall, as soon thereafter as the weather shall permit, thoroughly clean said sidewalk.

The snow which falls or accumulates during the day (excepting Sundays) before four p.m. shall be removed within three hours after the same has fallen or accumulated. The snow which falls or accumulates on Sunday or after four p.m. and during the night on other days shall be removed before ten a.m.
(Prior code § 36-19)

§10-8-190 Liability for civil damages.

Any person who removes snow or ice from the public sidewalk or street, shall not, as a result of his acts or omissions in such removal, be liable for civil damages. This section does not apply to acts or omissions amounting to wilful or wanton misconduct in such snow or ice removal.
(Prior code § 36-20)

§10-8-200 Loading and unloading from alleys.

Every building which faces or abuts upon a public alley where freight, goods and other commodities are loaded or unloaded through rear doors onto and from any vehicle, shall be equipped with a movable, rolling, folding or collapsible platform, so that such vehicle may stand parallel with the building from which said loading or unloading is done; provided, however, that whenever it may not be practical to load or unload any vehicle when thus placed in a parallel position to any building by reason of large, bulky, unwieldy or cumbersome freight, goods, or other commodities required to be loaded or unloaded, such vehicle may then be placed in a crosswise or cross-alley position.

Whenever the work of loading or unloading such freight, goods or other commodities onto or from any vehicle from such platform is completed, such movable, rolling, folding or collapsible platform shall be removed into the building from which the loading or unloading was done.
(Prior code § 36-21)

§10-8-210 House moving.

No owner of any building or contractor for its removal shall permit the same to be or remain in any of the public ways or the public grounds of the city for any time longer than may be specified in the permit of the executive director of the department of construction and permits. Every 24 hours such building shall so remain in any such public way or public grounds shall constitute a separate and distinct offense.
(Prior code § 36-22; Amend. Coun. J. 3-5-03, p. 104990)

§10-8-220 Conveying loose materials.

Any person who shall transport upon any public way crushed stone, sand, gravel, sawdust, ashes, cinders, lime, tanbarks, shavings, wastepaper, ice, mortar, earth, rubbish, manure or other loose material likely to sift, fall or be blown upon the public way, shall convey the same in tight wagon boxes, and in case the same fall or become scattered in any public way, such person shall cause such fallen substance to be forthwith removed.
(Prior code § 36-23)

§10-8-230 Overloading vehicles.

No person shall overload or cause to be overloaded any cart, trucks, wagon, or other vehicle in such a manner that the contents or any part thereof shall be scattered in any public way or other public place in the city. It shall be the duty of every person in charge, possession or control of any cart, truck, wagon or other vehicle, the contents of which or any part thereof may become scattered in any public way or other public place, to replace at once on such conveyance any part of the contents thereof which shall or may have fallen, dropped or spilled from such conveyance.

(Prior code § 36-24)

§10-8-240 Vehicles drawn over curb.

No person shall push, draw, ride or drive any horse, cart, wagon or other vehicle across or over the pavement curbing on any public way in the city, where no provision has been made for crossing such curbing by the construction of a suitable driveway or crossing.

(Prior code § 36-25)

§10-8-250 Throwing sharp objects.

No person shall throw, drop, place or deposit, or cause to be thrown, dropped, placed or deposited in or upon any public way, public bathing beach, or public playground, any glass bottles, glass, nails, tacks, wire, crockery, cans or other sharp or cutting substances injurious or dangerous to the feet of persons or animals, or to the tires or wheels of any kind of vehicles, including motor vehicles. Any person who shall violate the provisions of this section shall be fined not less than $2.00 nor more than $20.00; provided, however, that where any person has accidentally or by reason of an accident dropped from his hand or vehicle any of the foregoing substances upon any public way, public bathing beach, or public playground, such penalty shall not be enforced if such person shall immediately make all reasonable efforts to clear such place of the same.

(Prior code § 36-26)

§10-8-260 Reserved.

(Deleted. Coun. J. 3-31-04, p. 20916)

§10-8-270 Distribution of advertising matter.

It shall be unlawful for any person to distribute advertising matter of any kind on any public way or other public place of the city otherwise than from hand to hand, without tossing or throwing, or to distribute, hand out or scatter on any public way any handbills or dodgers of a size four and one-half inches by six inches or larger, or any other loose sheets of advertising matter which would litter the public ways if allowed to drop thereon; provided, that such handbills, dodgers, or loose sheets, if enclosed in envelopes or folded or otherwise handed out in such a manner as to avoid the likelihood of falling while being passed out, may be distributed from hand to hand if not tossed or thrown.

(Prior code § 36-28)

§10-8-271 Distribution of advertising on private property.

It shall be unlawful for any person to distribute advertising matter of any kind on the premises of any residential building within the 43rd, 44th or 47th Wards in such a manner that it does or reasonably could interfere with any security mechanism or cause any safety hazard. Unlawful methods of distribution include, but are not limited to, hanging advertising matter on the doorknob of any entrance door or fence, placing or wedging advertising matter into or underneath any entrance door, or leaving advertising material on the floor of entranceways. Such distribution shall not be unlawful if it is hand-to-hand or if the property owners have posted express written consent. Nothing in this section shall apply to written information distributed by governmental agencies or public utilities. Any person violating any of the provisions of this section shall be fined not less than $200.00 nor more than $1,000.00 for each offense.

(Added. Coun. J. 7-2-97, p. 48126; Amend. 6-27-01, p. 63093; 5-1-02, p. 84346; 7-10-02, p. 90139)

§10-8-280 Towing advertising display.

No person shall operate any type of aircraft over the city while towing any advertising display or other object.

(Prior code § 36-28.1)

§10-8-290 Aircraft dropping advertising matter.

No person while operating any type of aircraft over the city shall cause to be dropped therefrom, any object, including circulars, posters, handbills, or other advertising matter.

(Prior code § 36-28.2)

§10-8-300 Aircraft advertising noises.

No person while operating any type of aircraft over the city shall use, cause, permit or allow to be used any sound amplifier or similar mechanical device for the purpose of advertising goods, wares or merchandise.

(Prior code § 36-28.3)

§10-8-310 Placing advertising matter in automobiles.

No person shall hand circulars, handbills, folders or other advertising matter to the occupants of automobiles operated or standing in the public way, or place or thrust such circulars, handbills, folders or other advertising matter into or upon or under the windshield wiper of an unoccupied automobile standing in the public way. Any person violating any of the provisions of this section shall be fined not less than $25.00 nor more than $200.00 for each offense.

Whenever any advertising matter is distributed in violation of any of the provisions of this section, the person whose name appears thereon as the sponsor of such advertising matter shall be prima facie responsible for such violation and subject to the penalty therefor.

(Prior code § 36-29)

§10-8-320 Posting bills.

(a) No person shall post, stick, stamp, tack, paint or otherwise fix, or cause the same to be done by any person, any sign, notice, placard, bill, card, poster, advertisement or other device calculated to attract the attention of the public, to or upon any sidewalk, crosswalk, curb or curbstone, flagstone or any other portion or part of any public way, lamppost, electric light, traffic light, telegraph, telephone or trolley line pole, hydrant, shade tree or tree-box, or upon the piers, columns, trusses, girders, railings, gates or parts of any public bridge or viaduct, or upon any pole box or fixture of the police and fire communications system, except such as may be required by the laws of the state and the ordinances of the city, or on any bus shelter, except that the city may allow the posting of decorative banners in accordance with Section 10-8-340 below.

(b) There shall be a rebuttable presumption that any person, business or entity whose goods, services, activities or events are promoted by a sign is a person who posted it or caused it to be posted.

(c) Any person violating any of the provisions of this section shall be fined not less than $25.00 nor more than $75.00 per pole for a first offense, and not less than $100.00 nor more than $300.00 per pole for any subsequent offenses.

(d) In addition, any person violating any of the provisions of this section shall be liable to the city for the cost of repair of any damage caused by the hanging, presence or removal of any such sign and for any and all claims arising out of the hanging, presence or removal of any such sign, including any claims relating to signs or the structures upon which they are hung falling on people or property.

(Prior code § 36-30; Amend. 7-31-96, p. 26980; 12-4-02, p. 99931)

§10-8-330 Parade, public assembly or athletic event.

(a) The following terms are defined for the purposes of this chapter as follows:

(1) "Parade" means any march, procession or other similar activity consisting of persons, animals, vehicles or things, or combination thereof, upon any public street, sidewalk, alley or other public place, which requires a street closing or otherwise requires police officers to stop or reroute vehicular traffic because the marchers will not comply with normal and usual traffic regulations or controls. "Large parade" means any parade that is held in the "central business district," as defined in Section 9-4-010, and any parade that is anticipated to require city services exceeding $20,000.00 in value, to be adjusted for inflation in a manner specified by regulation.

(2) "Public assembly" means (i) a company of persons which is reasonably anticipated to obstruct the normal flow of traffic upon the public way and that is collected together in one place, or (ii) any organized march or procession of persons upon any public sidewalk that is reasonably anticipated to obstruct the normal flow of pedestrian traffic on the public way, but which does not meet the definition of parade set forth in this subsection.

(3) "Athletic event" means any event involving the conduct of exercises, sports or games which is reasonably anticipated to obstruct the normal flow of traffic upon the public way.

(4) "Business days" means those days in which municipal offices are open for conducting city business and does not include Saturday, Sunday or such holidays as are listed in Section 2-152-090.

(b) No parade or athletic event is permitted on any portion of the public way of the city of Chicago unless a permit allowing such activity has been obtained from the department of transportation.

(c) A person, partnership, voluntary association, or other organization seeking to obtain a parade permit shall file an application with the commissioner of transportation in the same calendar year as, and not less than fifteen business days before, the date for which the parade is proposed, unless the requested permit is for a parade to be held in January, in which case the application must be filed not less than fifteen business days before, and not more than one year before, the date for which the parade is proposed. The commissioner of transportation shall, however, consider an application for a parade which is filed less than fifteen business days before the proposed event, where the purpose of such event is a spontaneous response to a current event, or where other good and compelling causes are shown.

(d) A person, partnership, voluntary association or other organization seeking to obtain an athletic event permit shall file an application with the commissioner of transportation in the same calendar year as, and not less than 45 days before, the date for which the athletic event is requested, unless the requested permit is for an event to be held in January or February, in which case the application must be filed 45 days before the date for which the athletic event is requested.

(e) No person or organization may submit more than one application for the same parade date and route, or for a parade substantially similar in theme or units described but requesting an alternate date or route, whether using the same name, different names, or different affiliations that the person or organization may control or be a member of. No person or organization may submit an application on behalf of another person or entity that is also filing such an application. Where a person or organization submits multiple applications for the same parade date and route, or for a parade substantially similar in theme or units described but requesting an alternate date or route, whether by using one name or multiple names, that person or organization shall not be eligible for such a permit and shall be in violation of this ordinance. The commissioner of transportation is authorized to disregard any such multiple applications and to deny any permit on the basis of a violation of this subsection. Any applicant who disagrees with the commissioner's actions hereunder may appeal, in the manner set forth in subsection m.

(f) The application for a parade, public assembly or athletic event permit shall contain the following information, which must be updated by the applicant as circumstances change:

(1) The name, address and daytime telephone number of the person signing the application, and the organization with which that person is affiliated or on whose behalf the person is applying, if applicable;

(2) Where an organization is involved in requesting a permit, which includes voluntary associations entered into for the purpose of organizing a parade or athletic event, the name, address, daytime telephone number, pager number, if applicable, and fax number, if available, of the authorized and re-

sponsible leaders of the organization conducting the parade or athletic event; and where the applicant at a later date becomes affiliated with an organization for purposes of producing a parade or athletic event, this information shall be submitted at such time;

(3) The name, address, day-time telephone number, pager number, if applicable, and fax number, if available, of one individual who shall be designated as the responsible planner and on-site manager for the event, which person shall be referred to for purposes of this section as the parade organizer, where applicable, or the event organizer; and where the parade organizer or event organizer is not designated until a later date, this information shall be submitted at such time;

(4) The date of the proposed parade or athletic event and the hours that it will commence and terminate;

(5) The location and exact street address of the assembly and disbanding area and the time when the parade or athletic event will begin to assemble and disband;

(6) The approximate number of persons and vehicles, floats or other units to participate in the parade or athletic event and the basis on which this estimate is made;

(7) The route along which the parade or athletic event will proceed and the sidewalks or lanes of traffic it will occupy; and

(8) A list identifying the type and number of all animals the applicant intends to have at the parade or athletic event.

The application for a parade or athletic event permit shall be accompanied by a nonrefundable processing fee of $35.00.

(g) The commissioner of transportation shall investigate the facts set out in the application, in consultation with the mayor's office of special events and the police department, which shall be sent copies of the application immediately upon receipt. Where the commissioner determines that additional information on the factors set forth in subsection h.(1)—(3) is required, copies of the application and a request for such information also shall be sent to any of the persons and entities listed below. Where the commissioner determines that any of such persons or entities may need to make advance preparations for the permitted event, or may have information useful to planning for city services supporting the event, a copy of the granted permit or an alternative form of notice, shall be sent to any of the following listed persons or entities:

(1) The department of streets and sanitation;

(2) The fire department;

(3) The department of law;

(4) The Chicago Transit Authority;

(5) The Chicago Park District;

(6) The police department's local district commander for the district in which the parade or athletic event is to be held; and

(7) The director of the commission on animal care and control.

The commissioner shall send a copy of each permit application to the alderman of the ward or wards in which the parade or athletic event is to be held, with a request for any information on the factors set forth in subsection h.(1)—(3), and also shall send a copy of the grant or denial of such permit. Every February 1st and August 1st the commissioner shall send to the special events and the transportation committees of the city council of the city of Chicago a list of all parade and athletic event permits granted which have not previously been reported.

(h) After such investigation, the commissioner of transportation shall issue a permit when he or she finds that:

(1) The proposed activity will not substantially or unnecessarily interfere with traffic in the area contiguous to the activity, or that, if the activity will substantially interfere with such traffic, that there are available at the time of the proposed activity sufficient city resources to mitigate the disruption;

(2) There are available at the time of the parade or athletic event a sufficient number of peace officers and traffic control aides to police and protect lawful participants in the activity and non-participants from traffic-related hazards in light of the other demands for police protection at the time of the proposed event or activity;

(3) The concentration of persons, animals, vehicles, or things at the assembly and disbanding areas and along the parade or athletic event route will not prevent proper fire and police protection or ambulance service;

(4) The event will not be conducted for any purpose or in any manner made unlawful elsewhere in this code or by state or federal law;

(5) An applicant for an athletic event permit has complied with subsection (n) herein;

(6) If the application is for an athletic event for which fees will be charged for participation in the event, the proposed athletic event will be in the best interest of the city in light of (i) the apparent ability of the applicant to comply with the requirements of this section, and (ii) the willingness and financial ability of the applicant to conduct the event in a manner appropriate to the type of the event, and to pay any prizes that the applicant has advertised or is likely to advertise. In making a determination under this paragraph (6), the commissioner may consider the experience of the applicant in conducting the same or similar events, and may require additional information from the applicant with respect to the proposed event and the applicant s financial situation;

(7) The proposed activity will not interfere with the use of the requested area by another party to whom a valid permit has been issued for the same area or route, or does not conflict with another application, or with a traditional parade, as defined in subsection (i); and

(8) The application contains sufficient information about the proposed route and crowd estimate to enable the commissioner to evaluate the proposed event under this section.

(i) Except as otherwise provided in this subsection, all applications for any parade or athletic event permit shall be processed on a first-in-time basis.

With respect to parade permits, during the first two business days of each calendar year, the commissioner of transportation shall accept all applications for a parade permit filed hereunder without giving priority to applications filed first in time. For purposes of calculating the decision times set forth in this section, all applications filed within the first two business days of the calendar year shall be deemed as filed on the third business day of the year.

Where a parade has been conducted on or about a certain date, on a substantially similar route, and in connection with a specific holiday or consistent theme, for at least the prior five years, it shall be referred to herein as a traditional parade, and it shall be given a preference to continue on that date and route for the purpose of protecting the expectations and enjoyment of the public. Every December, the commissioner shall contact the prior year's organizer for each traditional parade to ascertain whether the parade shall continue, and he or she shall publish a list of traditional parades that shall be given preference in the permit assignment process. Where two or more applications are filed purporting to represent the prior organizer of a traditional parade, or where there have been different organizers over the past five years, or where there is any type of dispute regarding which person or organization should receive the traditional parade preference, the commissioner may request those involved to submit documentation to resolve such conflict. Where the commissioner finds no clear resolution of the conflict, he or she shall conduct a lottery to select the permittee and shall notify each applicant in writing of the existence of the conflict and of the date, time and place of the lottery. Any applicant who disagrees with the commissioner's actions hereunder may appeal, in the same manner as set forth in subsection m.

Where there is a conflict between two or more applications filed during the first two business days and not involving a traditional parade or between any such application and a traditional parade, the commissioner shall evaluate whether the conflict could be resolved by assigning the applicants consecutive times on the same day and route, giving consideration to criteria set forth in the regulations. Where the commissioner finds that consecutive times are appropriate, he or she shall notify each applicant that the permit shall be granted for the specified alternative time period. For those applicants who are not assigned their requested time period, such notice shall be treated as a denial and offer of alternative, under subsection 1., for purposes of the five day time period in which to file an acceptance or appeal. Where consecutive times are not deemed appropriate, then the traditional parade shall receive the permit, as set forth above. With respect to any remaining conflicts among permit applications, the commissioner shall notify the applicants that the conflict shall be resolved by lottery, and of the date, time and place of the lottery. Within seven days after the lottery, the applicants not chosen may submit alternative preferences to the commissioner. Any requests for alternative preferences submitted by applicants under this subsection shall be treated as a new application, for purposes of all time limitations under this section, and any conflicts arising among the alternative preferences shall be resolved in accordance with the procedures set forth herein. Except as described in this subsection for traditional parades, applications for a parade permit received during the first two business days of the calendar year shall be given priority over applications received thereafter.

(j) The commissioner of transportation shall take action upon the application for a parade permit, and provide notice thereof, within five business days after the filing thereof or, if any lottery is held pursuant to paragraph (h) of this section, within five business days of the lottery, except that where the purpose of such event is a spontaneous response to a current event, or where other good and compelling cause is shown, the commissioner shall act within two business days. Notice shall be by facsimile transmission or telephonically and by mail directed to the applicant, stating the facts and conclusions which are the basis for any denial of the permit and, if the action taken is setting a lottery date or offering a consecutive time, then describing the conflict among application requests. If the commissioner denies an application for failure to provide sufficient information about the proposed route or crowd estimate, he shall specify what additional information must be provided in a new or amended application.

In the event that the commissioner of transportation fails to act within five business days after the date upon which the application was filed, said application for a permit shall be deemed approved and the permit deemed granted in conformance with the application.

(k) The commissioner of transportation shall inform such applicant for an athletic event permit whether the application is approved or disapproved within 30 days after the filing thereof. If the commissioner approves the application, he or she shall inform the applicant within such time of the compensation, insurance or bond, if any, required pursuant to subsection (n). If the commissioner disapproves the application, the commissioner shall provide written notice of his or her action within such time, stating the specific facts and conclusions which are the basis for his or her denial of the permit. If the commissioner fails to act within 30 days after the date upon which the application was filed, said application for an athletic event permit shall be deemed approved and the permit deemed granted in conformance with the application.

(l) When the commissioner denies an application for a parade or athletic event permit shall authorize the conduct of a parade or athletic event on a date, at a time, at a location, or over a route different from that named by the applicant. This alternate permit shall to the extent practicable authorize an event that will have comparable public visibility and a similar route, location and date to that of the proposed event. An applicant desiring to accept an alternate parade or athletic event permit shall, within five business days after notice of the action by the commissioner, file a written notice of acceptance with the commissioner. Where the denial and alternate are based on a conflict between applications for a parade permit, however, the procedures set forth in subsection (i) shall apply.

The commissioner is empowered to limit the parade or athletic event to the sidewalk or to one or more traffic lanes of the street where it is determined that such limited area is capable of accommodating the number of people anticipated based upon the information submitted by the applicant and the experience of previous comparable events, and such limitation shall not be considered a denial.

(m) Any applicant who believes that his or her application for a parade permit is wrongfully disapproved may appeal to the mayor the propriety of said action by notifying the office of the mayor's license commission of the intent to appeal. If no appeal is filed within five business days of the date notice of the commissioner's decision is given, that decision shall be deemed final. Upon the filing of such appeal, the mayor's license commission shall cause a hearing to be held within three business days and based upon the evidence contained in the record of such hearing, either affirm or reverse the decision of the commissioner of transportation. Any final decision of the commissioner of transportation or the mayor's license commission shall be subject to judicial review in accordance with applicable law. In the event that the mayor's license commission fails to act within two business days of the conclusion of a hearing held under this section, said application for a permit shall be deemed approved and the permit deemed granted in conformance with the application.

(n) Upon the filing of an application to conduct an athletic event, the commissioner of transportation shall investigate the facts set forth in the application and determine:

(1) The amount, if any, to be tendered to the city of Chicago by the applicant to compensate the city for the provision of any city services deemed necessary by the commissioner for the safe and orderly conduct of the athletic event; and

(2) The amount, if any, of any bond or insurance, naming the city of Chicago as the insured, that the commissioner determines is necessary to insure the city against any liability arising from the athletic event.

No athletic event permit shall be issued until such fees are paid or bonds furnished. The commissioner shall adopt rules and regulations to govern the determination of whether any fees or bonds are required and the amount of any such fees or bonds.

(o) For large parades, the commissioner shall require, as a condition of the permit, that the parade organizer (1) obtain a $1,000,000 Commercial General Liability insurance policy, naming the city of Chicago as an additional insured; (2) indemnify the city against any additional or uncovered third party claims against the city arising out of the parade; and (3) agree to reimburse the city for any damage to the public way or to city property.

(p) At least one week prior to the scheduled parade, the parade coordinator shall submit to the mayor's office of special events a line of march, which shall list all parade units in numerical order, with a description and an estimate of the size or length of each unit. For any new parade, and for any parade for which in the prior year the estimate of the number or size of units was substantially inaccurate, the parade coordinator also shall be required to submit documentation demonstrating the planned participation of the stated units. At least one week prior to the scheduled parade, the parade organizer also is required to have furnished to the commissioner documents demonstrating compliance with the insurance requirement set out in subsection (o). Where any animals will participate or be involved in the event, the parade coordinator must provide: a health certificate for each animal to be used; the name of the attending local veterinarian who shall provide care for any sick or injured animals; a copy of the handler's Federal Exhibitor's license for any animal identified in the Illinois Dangerous Animal Act; and access to an animal ambulance.

(q) The parade shall last no longer than two hours and fifteen minutes, except that where a traditional parade consistently has lasted longer, and the commissioner determines that there is no traffic safety or undue congestion problem in continuing to allow the longer time period, the permit may provide for additional hours. The parade permit time may be reduced by the mayor's office of special events after receipt of the parade lineup, where the number and size of the planned units are not sufficient to fill the permit time while proceeding at a reasonable pace, or may be reduced by the police department on location, for the same reason, where the actual size and number of units at the lineup are insufficient to require a two hour and fifteen minutes street closing. The parade units shall proceed at a uniform pace, with no gaps in the lineup, and no stopping allowed. Once the last unit has started on the parade route, the department of streets and sanitation will begin cleaning the street, and the police department will reopen the street to traffic as street cleaning is completed.

Once the last unit has completed the parade route, all parade participants must disperse from the street so that it may be safely cleaned and reopened to traffic.

Where the parade permit was limited to the sidewalk or one lane of traffic based on the estimated number of units participating, and in the event that the number of persons in attendance exceeds anticipated levels, members of the police department are authorized to make reasonable accommodation to increase the portion of the public way made available in order to preserve public health and safety. Alternatively, where the number or size of parade units participating are substantially less than expected, members of the police department are authorized to limit the available portion of the public way, where one lane of traffic or the sidewalk is capable of accommodating the number of people and units present.

In addition, at a parade, in order to protect the health and safety of the public, employees of the commission on animal care and control are authorized to inspect animals prior to their use in activities upon the public way and to prohibit the use of animals found to be diseased, unhealthy or which pose a danger to public health and safety.

(r) Any person or organization planning to lead or initiate any type of public assembly, including a march or procession upon a public sidewalk, as defined in subsection (a) shall notify the commissioner of transportation, at least five business days in advance, or as soon as practicable if the event is of a spontaneous or urgent nature, and shall inform his or her of the date, time, location, route and estimated number of persons participating, so that the city can make any preparations necessary to provide personnel or other city services to minimize the obstruction to pedestrian and other traffic and to otherwise protect the participants and the public. Such public assemblies shall be allowed unless the commissioner informs the person or organization giving the notice, within two days or as soon as practicable before the scheduled event, that there would be a direct interference with a previously planned permitted activity or public assembly, or that there is a significant public safety issue, limited to those set forth in subsection (h)(1)—(3). If the commissioner does this, he or she must state the reasons in writing and give an alternative date, time, location or route, as provided for parades in subsections (j) and (l) herein. If the public assembly organizer desires to appeal such decision, then the appeal shall be governed by the procedures set forth for parade permits in subsection (m) herein, if the notification was received in sufficient time that the appeals process could be completed before the planned date; if not, the decision by the commissioner shall be deemed a final decision subject to judicial review in accordance with applicable law. Upon request the commissioner will provide the organizer of the public assembly with a stamped copy of the notice given under this subsection.

(s) The commissioner of transportation, in consultation with other city departments and agencies, including the mayor's office of special events, shall promulgate rules and regulations to implement this section.

(t) Any person who knowingly interferes with any other person or organization lawfully conducting a parade, public assembly or athletic event or any person violating any of the provisions of this ordinance, or any of the provisions of the regulations promulgated hereunder, shall be subject to incarceration for up to 10 days and fined not less than $50.00 nor more than $1,000.00. In addition to the penalties specified above and those set forth elsewhere in this

section, the following violations are subject to additional penalties. Any person who makes a fraudulent misrepresentation on a permit application for a parade or athletic event shall be prosecuted to the full extent of the law, including criminal sanctions. Any person who sells or assigns a permit granted under this ordinance shall be barred from applying for another permit for a period of three years. Where the conduct of any parade or athletic event causes or results in a threat to public safety, the permit holder, including any affiliated organization identified on the permit application, and the parade or other event organizer, shall be barred from receiving another permit under this section for a period of one year, except that if the public safety problem was caused by crowd reactions to a parade's message, then there shall be no penalty, but additional safety conditions shall be imposed on any similar event.
(Prior code § 36-31; Amend. Coun. J. 7-29-87, p. 2888; 12-20-89, p. 10127; 12-11-91, p. 10832; 11-30-94, p. 62771; 12-21-94, p. 64115; 11-18-98, p. 84402; 12-12-01, p. 76493)

§10-8-335 Outdoor special events.

(a) As used in this section unless the context requires otherwise:

(1) "Special event" means a planned temporary aggregation of attractions, including public entertainment, food and beverage service facilities, sales of souvenirs or other merchandise, or similar attractions, that is (i) conducted on the public way; or (ii) conducted primarily outdoors on property open to the public other than the public way and which:

(A) Includes activities that require the issuance of a city temporary food establishment license or a special event liquor license; or

(B) Requires special city services, including but not limited to any of the following: street closures; provisions of barricades, garbage cans, stages or special no parking signs; special electrical services; or special police protection.

"Special event" does not include a parade or athletic event for which a permit is required under Section 10-8-330, a neighborhood block party at which no food, beverages or merchandise is sold, or a city-wide festival conducted pursuant to an intergovernmental agreement authorized by ordinance.

(2) "Department" means the mayor's office of special events.

(3) "Sponsor of the event" means the entity who is conducting the special event or in whose name or for whose support the proposed special event will be presented.

(b) No person shall conduct a special event unless the sponsor of the event obtains a special event permit from the mayor's office of special events.

(c) An application for a special event permit must be made to the department no later than 45 days prior to the date the event is scheduled to begin unless the department determines that the reasons for the delay were beyond the reasonable control of the applicant. Unless the special event is to be conducted in January or February, applications must be filed in the calendar year in which the event is to take place. If the event is to take place in January or February, the application must be filed no earlier than one year prior to the event. There shall be no fee for the first application submitted by a sponsor during a calendar year; however, each subsequent application submitted by the sponsor of the event during that calendar year shall be accompanied by a nonrefundable processing fee of $35.00. The application shall include the following information:

(1) The name and address of the sponsor of the event, and the name, address and telephone number of an authorized and responsible agent of the organization;

(2) A description of the special event that will be conducted;

(3) The dates, times and location of the special event, including any requests for street closures, and a site plan;

(4) The estimated attendance for the special event;

(5) Whether food, alcoholic beverages or merchandise will be sold at the event;

(6) Whether music will be played at the event and if so, whether such music will be electronically amplified. If electronically amplified music will be played, the applicant shall also submit an appropriate plan for the control of sound at the event;

(7) Plans for event security, including the number, hours and location of deployment of personnel and equipment that will be provided by the applicant and what special city services, if any, the special event will require;

(8) The proof of insurance and agreement to indemnify and hold harmless required by subsections (n) and (o) of this section, respectively;

(9) The number of all food vendors; alcoholic beverage vendors; and/or itinerant merchants who will be participating in the special event;

(10) Such other information that may be reasonably necessary to determine compliance with this code.

All information provided on the application shall be complete and truthful. If, prior to the event, the sponsor of the event changes any of the information required by subsection (c) of this section that would necessitate additional city services or would require approval from any city department, the sponsor of the event must submit an amended application to the department no later than 45 days prior to the date the event is scheduled to begin.

(d) The department shall promptly send copies of all applications for a special event permit to the following departments, for the purpose of obtaining input on the factors set forth in subsection (f) of this section:

(1) The department of revenue;

(2) The department of police;

(3) The fire department;

(4) The department of streets and sanitation;

(5) The department of transportation;

(6) The department of law;

(7) The department of environment; and

(8) The office of emergency management and communications.

If any of the above-listed departments have any information that the proposed special event does not meet the standards set forth in subsection (f) of this section, written objections must be sent to the department within 20 days or the department will presume there are no departmental objections.

Within 20 days of receipt of the application, the police department commander of special events shall review the applicant's security plan, including provisions made for private security personnel and for handling emergencies, and shall determine whether the applicant has planned for and provided sufficient personnel and equipment to protect public safety at the event or whether the city will need to provide additional city police and traffic control personnel and equipment. The determination of the need for additional city police services shall be based on the expected pedestrian and vehicular traffic and congestion. considering the following factors: estimated attendance, density of area, size of area, number of street closures and affected intersections. If the commander of special events determines that the city will be required to provide more than 12 shifts of any combination of police officers and traffic control aides, then he or she shall calculate the estimated hourly cost for the personnel required for the event, and shall charge the applicant for such services in excess of 12 shifts; provided that, the charge to the applicant shall exclude any personnel hours related to any anticipated or actual crowd reaction to the message of the event or the identity of the sponsoring organization.

The applicant shall post a bond to cover or, at the applicant's option shall prepay, the total amount of the required chargeable city services which has been estimated by the police department, prior to issuance of a special event permit. Within 20 business days after the end of the event, the department shall calculate the actual city costs owed under this section, obtain such costs from the bond, if a bond was provided, or remit any overpayment if prepayment was made, and shall provide to the sponsor an itemized statement of such costs.

(e) Within three business days after an application for a special event permit is filed with the department, the department shall deliver a copy of the application to the alderman of the ward in which the special event is to take place and to the city council committee on special events and cultural affairs or its successor committee. Within five business days after an alderman receives a copy of an application for a permit under this section, the alderman may request the committee to conduct a hearing on the permit application. Such request may be made only when the alderman finds that the hearing will be useful in determining whether the application complies with the requirements of this chapter. Within two business days after the committee receives such request, the chairman of the committee shall notify the department of the scheduled hearing. In such case the department shall take no final action to approve or deny the application before the committee issues a report under this section or before the time during which a report may be issued under this subsection expires, whichever is earlier. At a hearing conducted under this subsection all interested persons, including the applicant, community residents and representatives of community groups, shall be given an opportunity to be heard. The committee shall also accept any relevant written testimony or documentation regarding the proposed special event.

After conducting such hearing, the committee may issue a report summarizing the issues that were addressed at the hearing and recommending approval or denial of the application. Any such report must be filed with the department not later than 25 days after the application was received by the alderman.

The committee's report on the permit application shall be based solely on the criteria described in subsection (f).

Any committee report recommending disapproval of a permit application must state the specific reasons for the recommendation, which reasons shall be consistent with an applicant's constitutional rights contained in the First, Fifth and Fourteenth Amendments to the United States Constitution, and Sections 2 and 4 of Article I of the Illinois Constitution of 1970.

(f) The department will issue a permit for the special event, or a conditional permit pursuant to subsection (g), if, after considering any relevant written recommendations or objections of the appropriate alderman and city departments, and after considering any report issued by the committee on special events and cultural affairs or its successor committee under subsection (e), it determines that:

(1) The applicant has complied with all of the requirements of this code and any rules or regulations promulgated thereunder;

(2) The sponsor of the event has not been found guilty of four or more violations at the same event during that year or the previous year and has not been found guilty of six or more violations within a 180-day period;

(3) The proposed special event will not substantially or unnecessarily interfere with traffic in the area;

(4) There are available at the time of the special event a sufficient number of peace officers to police and protect lawful participants in the event;

(5) The concentration of persons or things at the event will not prevent proper fire and police protection or ambulance service;

(6) The event is not being conducted for an unlawful purpose;

(7) The event will not subject the surrounding neighborhood to an unreasonable degree of noise, littering or parking difficulties in light of the character of the neighborhood;

(8) The event will not conflict with a parade, carnival, or other event which has been previously scheduled; and

(9) The special event will not require city services that cannot be reasonably made available.

(g) The department shall inform an applicant for a special event permit whether the application is approved or disapproved within 35 business days after the application and any amendments are received by the department. If the department approves the application, it shall either (1) issue a conditional special event permit pursuant to subsection (i) until all necessary licenses are issued, required plans approved, fees paid, and costs prepaid or bonds posted; or (2) if all necessary licenses have been issued, required plans approved, fees paid, and costs prepaid or bonds posted, issue a special events permit. If the department disapproves the application, it shall provide written notice of its action within such time, stating the specific facts and conclusions that are the basis for his denial of the permit. If the department fails to act within 35 business days after the date upon which the application and any amendments were received by the department, the application shall be approved and the permit deemed granted in conformance with the application.

If the permit is for a special event that will require the closing of a street, the applicant shall pay an additional fee of $25.00 for each day the street will be closed. This fee does not apply to neighborhood block parties.

(h) Except as otherwise provided in this subsection, preference among conflicting applications for special event permits shall be given to the application filed earliest. However, during the first 10 business days of each calendar year, the department shall accept applications without giving preference to applications filed earliest. Any conflict among applications filed during that period shall be resolved by a lottery to be conducted by the department.

The department shall notify each such applicant in writing of the existence of the conflict and of the date, place and time of the lottery. Within seven days after the lottery, the applicants not chosen may submit alternative preferences to the department. Any conflicts arising among the alternative preferences shall be resolved in accordance with the lottery procedures set forth in this section.

(i) No later than 20 days prior to the date the event is scheduled to begin, the sponsor of the event shall submit all applications for any necessary licenses, including alcoholic beverage, food and/or itinerant merchant licenses, to the department. The department shall forward the license applications to all appropriate departments. The departments shall review such license applications and either issue such licenses, or issue a written denial stating the reasons therefor, within 10 days of receipt of the license application. If the department previously has issued a conditional permit. then within five days after the appropriate licenses have been issued and are received by the department, and all required plans approved, fees paid, and costs prepaid or bonds posted, or sooner if the event will occur sooner and doing so is reasonably practicable, the department shall issue the special event permit. If no conditional permit has been issued, then the procedure set forth in subsection (g) of this section shall apply.

(j) No permit issued under this section may authorize the operation of a special event for a period longer than 10 days.

(k) For any violation of the special event permit or the rules and regulations promulgated under this section, including the failure to amend the permit pursuant to subsection (c), the sponsor of the event shall be fined not less than $200.00 nor more than $1,000.00 for each violation. If the sponsor of the event is found guilty of four or more violations at the same event or six or more violations within a 180-day period, no new special event permits shall be issued to the sponsor of the event for the remainder of the year of that event and for the following calendar year.

(l) The sponsor of the event shall have a representative present at all times during the event who shall be responsible for ensuring compliance with all applicable ordinances and regulations and for accepting all notices of violations and closure orders.

(m) The department may at any time revoke a special event permit if the operation of the event is in violation of this code or any other applicable law, or if such revocation is necessary to preserve the health or safety of the public. Written notice of the revocation with the reasons therefor shall be mailed to or served upon the sponsor of the event at the time of revocation. Unless the permit will expire by its own terms before a hearing can be reasonably scheduled, no such revocation will take effect until the sponsor of the event has been given notice and an opportunity to be heard in accordance with rules and regulations issued by the department. When necessary to prevent an immediate threat to the health or safety of the public, the department shall order the sponsor of the event to cease operation of the special event pending the outcome of the hearing. For any violation of the special event permit or the rules and regulations promulgated under this section which endangers the health or safety of the public, no new special event permits shall be issued to the sponsor of the event for the remainder of the year of that event and for the following calendar year.

(n) No permit shall be issued until the applicant has supplied to the department a certificate of insurance evidencing general commercial liability insurance, with limits of not less than $1,000,000.00, naming the city as an additional insured.

Each insurance policy required by this subsection shall include a provision to the effect that it shall not be subject to cancellation, reduction in the amounts of its liabilities, or other material changes until notice thereof has been received in writing by the office of risk management and the department not less than 60 days prior to such action.

Each applicant shall maintain the insurance required by this subsection in full force and effect for the duration of the permit period. Failure of the sponsor of the event to maintain such insurance during the periods indicated above shall result in automatic expiration of the permit. For the purposes of this subsection, the permit shall include the time required for construction and removal of all materials and equipment provided for the conduct of the special event until the public way has been cleared and restored as provided in subsection (p).

(o) In addition to the requirements stated above, the applicant must agree in writing to indemnify and hold the city of Chicago and its assignees and employees harmless from all losses, damages, injuries, claims, demands and expenses arising out of the operation of the special event or the condition, maintenance and use of public property.

(p) During the conduct of the special event, the sponsor of the event shall keep the public way clean and free from paper, debris, or refuse, and upon termination of the permit by lapse of time or otherwise, the sponsor of the event shall remove all materials and equipment and clean the street. If the public way has been damaged, the sponsor of the event shall repair and restore it to the condition it was in prior to the special event.

(q) Whenever a special permit requires the closure of a street, a clear path of not less than 10 feet must be maintained at all times to provide for the passage of emergency vehicles.

(r) The sponsor of the event shall be responsible for ensuring that each vendor participating in the event obtains the proper licenses. In the event that an unlicensed or improperly licensed vendor is found at the event, the sponsor of the event shall be fined pursuant to subsection (k) for each unlicensed or improperly licensed vendor. This shall be in addition to any fines and/or penalties which may be issued to the individual vendor.

(s) In addition to any other appropriate department, the mayor's office of special events is authorized to inspect the special event and may issue citations for any violation of this code or any regulations pertaining to the operation of the special event, except for provisions currently enforced by the department of public health.

(t) Any action of the department in denying or revoking a permit under this article shall be subject to judicial review as provided by law.

(u) The executive director, after consultation with other appropriate departments, shall have the authority to promulgate such rules and regulations that he determines are necessary or desirable for the implementation of this section. The rules and regulations need not be published in a newspaper, but shall be made available for inspection by the public at no charge.

(Added. Coun. J. 6-17-92, p. 18286; Amend. 7-30-97, p. 50122; 2-11-04, p. 18380; 12-15-04, p. 39840)

§10-8-340 Donation of promotional decorative lightpole banners and decorations.

(a) The commissioner of streets and sanitation may accept donations of decorative banners or other decorations designed to be placed on lightpoles. Such donations may be permanent or for a limited amount of time. The city may use its lightpoles to display donated banners, or any other city-owned or controlled banners, that the commissioner determines will promote or celebrate the city, its civic institutions, or public activities or events in the city of Chicago and that he or she finds otherwise will promote the corporate interests and welfare of the city of Chicago.

(b) The commissioner of streets and sanitation may delegate the authority to hang and remove decorative banners or other decorations. Such authority may be delegated by issuance of a permit to a permit applicant and shall be limited to a period of 60 days, except that for the central business district, approval shall be limited to a period of 30 days. Upon application, permits may be renewed for additional such periods in the discretion of the commissioner. No permit shall be renewed where another entity has requested that its donated banner or other decorations be hung at such location or during such time period or where an event referred to in the donated banner is over; except that the commissioner shall have the discretion to determine that in certain neighborhood areas, the corporate interests and welfare of the city of Chicago are best served by neighborhood identifier banners or other banners that promote the city of Chicago or certain streets or districts of interest, and renewal of permits for such banners may be given precedence over other requests.

The commissioner shall give notice, by facsimile to the ward office, of all permit applications to the alderman in the ward in which permission to have the banner or other decoration displayed has been requested. The alderman shall have 10 business days to give the commissioner, in writing, any specific objections to the locations, dates and number of the proposed displays, and if the proposed location is in a residential neighborhood, his or her opinion on whether banners or other decorations are suitable in that area.

For purposes of this section, "central business district" shall mean that portion of the city bounded on the west by the east and west side of Halsted Street, on the north by the north and south sides of Division Street, on the east by Lake Michigan, and on the south by the north and south sides of Roosevelt Road.

Any person or entity who hangs a banner or other decoration on a city lightpole without first obtaining approval from the commissioner, or who violates any condition of the commissioner's approval, shall be fined $100.00 per pole, per day.

No donated banner or other decoration may be hung unless the donor hires a professional company to hang and remove the banners or other decoration. Banners, brackets and hardware must be taken down within 48 hours after expiration of the permit approving hanging of the donated banner or other decoration, or within less time upon notice from the commissioner. Any banner company which fails to remove a donated banner or other decoration within such time period shall be fined $100.00 per pole, per day, and shall be liable to the city for the cost of removing such banner or other decoration. In addition, any banner company shall be liable to the city for the cost of repair of any damage to city lightpoles caused by the hanging, presence or removal of any banner or other decoration placed by such company.

(c) No professional banner company may hang any banner or other decoration on any city lightpole until it has furnished the commissioner with an original certificate of insurance, which must evidence that the company has procured commercial liability insurance or the equivalent thereof with limits of not less than $1,000,000.00 per occurrence, combined single limit for bodily injury, personal injury, and property damage, which shall cover any damage caused by the hanging, maintenance or removal of the banners or other decoration on city lightpoles. The city of Chicago shall be named as an additional insured, without recourse or right of contribution. Upon receipt of the certificate of insurance, the commissioner will transmit copies to the department of transportation, bureau of inspections and to the department of finance risk manager.

(d) The donor shall indemnify and hold the city, its officers, agents and employees, harmless from any and all claims arising out of the placement of, maintenance of, use of or removal of banners or other decoration, including any claims relating to banners or structures upon which they are hung falling on people or property.

(e) The commissioner of streets and sanitation shall promulgate rules and regulations governing the display of banners or other decoration to protect public safety and welfare, including ensuring against fire hazards, traffic problems, and visual blight. Such rules shall include, but are not limited to, specifications as to number, size, materials, printing processes, supporting structures, and hanging and removal. The commissioner shall have the authority, however, to waive specific rules when (1) the banner or other decoration substantially complies with the rules; (2) prior to the enactment of this ordinance, the donor previously had displayed such banner on city lightpoles, pursuant to the commissioner's permission; and (3) the commissioner determines that the waiver will not have any adverse effect on public safety and welfare. The commissioner also shall have the authority to determine that the display of decorative banners is unsuitable in certain residential areas.

(Added. Coun. J. 7-31-96, p. 26980; Amend. 5-17-00, p. 32989)

§10-8-350 Performance in public ways.

No person shall engage in any game, sport, amusement, performance or exhibition, or exhibit any machine or show or any animal, or indulge in any acrobatic or gymnastic feats, on any public way in the city, except as provided in Sections 10-8-330 and 10-8-340 and Chapter 4-268.

Nor shall any person give or cause to be given any performance, show or exhibition of any kind or nature whatsoever in any show window or in or on any premises immediately abutting upon any public way in the city, which is designed or intended to or which in fact does collect, attract or cause to be collected or attracted a sufficient number of persons to interfere with the passage of the public along the public way upon which such show window or premises abut. If said show, performance or exhibition results in the collection or attraction of a sufficient number of persons to interfere with the passage of the public along such public way, any member of the department of police shall have the power and it shall be his duty to enter such premises and cause such show, performance or exhibition to be discontinued forthwith, and to cause any performer, figure, apparatus, or other thing of any kind or nature whatsoever, engaged in or used in or about such show, performance or exhibition, to be removed from such show window or premises forthwith.

Any person violating any of the provisions of this section or interfering with the enforcement thereof shall be fined not less than $5.00 nor more than $100.00 for each offense.

(Prior code § 36-33; Amend. Coun. J. 4-21-99, p. 92524)

§10-8-360 Injury to sidewalk or driveway.

No person shall break or otherwise injure any sidewalk or driveway except as otherwise provided by this code. Any person violating the provision of this section shall be fined not less than $50.00 nor more than $500.00 plus the city's costs incurred in restoring the sidewalk or driveway to its prior condition, for each offense.

(Prior code § 36-35; Amend. Coun. J. 12-4-02, p. 99931)

§10-8-370 Alleys, access to construction sites.

(a) Any industrial corporation, business, builder or contractor using unimproved alleys for access to construction sites, employing vehicles or equipment weighing in excess of five tons shall during the period of construction maintain the grade of said alley and shall fill in any holes or depressions caused by the construction equipment, with a material known as intermediate macadam.

(b) The said industrial corporation, business, builder or contractor shall immediately upon completion of construction restore the alley roadway to the same condition it was prior to the start of said construction. The rehabilitation and restoration of said alley roadway shall be done under the supervision of the department of streets and sanitation of the city of Chicago.

(c) The general contractor shall be responsible for the removal from the building site any excess from the excavation immediately upon completion of the back fill operation.

(d) Violators of any of the provisions of the foregoing sections shall be fined not less than $50.00 and not more than $500.00.

(Prior code § 36-35.1)

§10-8-380 Defacing property in public places.

No person shall wantonly mar, injure, deface or destroy any fence, guidepost, signboard or awning in any public way or other public place in the city.

(Prior code § 36-36)

§10-8-390 Obstructing public improvements.

Any person who shall hinder or obstruct the making or repairing of any public improvement or work ordered by the city council or being done for the city under lawful authority shall be subject to a penalty of not less than $10.00 nor more than $100.00.

(Prior code § 36-37)

§10-8-400 Barbed wire fence.

(a) No person shall build, construct, use or maintain any fence or barrier consisting or made of what is called "barbed wire," or of which barbed wire is a part, within the city, along the line of, or in, or upon, or along, any public way; or through, along, or around, any public park; or in and about or along any land or lots or parks owned or controlled by the city. Provided, that nothing in this subsection shall be construed to prevent the use or maintenance of barbed wire in or on that part of any such fence or barrier which is higher than six feet from the surface of the public way, public park, lot or park owned or controlled by the city, and wholly on or over private property.

(b) No person shall build, construct, use or maintain any fence or barrier consisting or made of what is called "razor wire", or of which razor wire is a part, within the city, along the line of, or in, or upon, or along, any public way; or through, along, or around, any public park; or in and about or along any land or lots or parks owned or controlled by the city. Provided, that nothing in this section shall be construed to prevent the use or maintenance of razor wire in or on that part of any fence, barrier or structure that secures a government building, a public transit facility, or a public utility facility.

(c) Whenever in the city, in, along or through any public way or park, barbed wire or razor wire is found in use in part or in whole for a fence or barrier, except as in this section permitted, the same shall forthwith be removed by the commissioner of transportation.

(Prior code § 36-38; Amend. Coun. J. 12-11-91, p. 10832; 2-11-04, p. 18364)

Article IV. Occasional Sales

§10-8-401 Definitions.

As used in Sections 10-8-401 through 10-8-406 hereunder, the term "occasional sales" shall mean those sales of goods, wares and merchandise owned by the occupant of the premises or owned by a group of persons having a common sale commonly known as garage sales, basement sales, house sales, yard sales, and rummage sales conducted on an infrequent and unscheduled basis on premises zoned or used for residential purposes. Bulk sales, the sale of multiple merchandise brought to the premises for resale or for reconditioning for resale shall be prohibited.

The term "person," as used in the same sections, shall mean any individual, firm or corporation, except a religious or eleemosynary organization.

(Added. Coun. J. 7-31-96, p. 26900)

§10-8-402 Permit required.

It shall be unlawful for any person to conduct or allow the conducting of any occasional sale on premises zoned or used for residential purposes without first having obtained a permit therefor. Application for such permit shall be made to the department of streets and sanitation. Each permit, when granted, shall be prominently displayed on the premises covered by the permit in such a manner that it is easily visible to individuals passing by the subject premises. The permit shall be valid only for the occasional sale for which it is granted.

(Added. Coun. J. 7-31-96, p. 26900)

§10-8-403 Occasional sales permitted when—Frequency.

Occasional sales shall be permitted for three consecutive days between 9:00 a.m. and sunset each day. Not more than two such occasional sales shall be conducted on the same premises within any calendar year; provided, however, that a third such sale may be conducted on the same premises if the permit applicant is moving or vacating the premises. In the event of inclement weather the occasional sale may be held in the three-day period immediately following the permitted period; however, that no such sale shall exceed three total days.
(Added. Coun. J. 7-31-96, p. 26900)

§10-8-404 Occasional sales—Signs.

All signs advising of the occasional sale shall be confined to the premises on which the sale is conducted, and all signs advising of the sale shall be removed no later than 9:00 p.m. on the day the permit expires.
(Added. Coun. J. 7-31-96, p. 26900)

§10-8-405 Display of articles for sale—Permitted locations.

It shall be unlawful for any person to display for sale any goods, wares or merchandise under the provisions of Sections 10-8-401 through 10-8-404 beyond the property line of the premises on which an occasional sale is permitted. Articles for sale may be displayed inside the garage, inside the back yard or on a side driveway of the premises if such driveway exists.
(Added. Coun. J. 7-31-96, p. 26900)

§10-8-406 Violation—Penalty.

Any person found in violation of any of the provisions of Sections 10-8-401 through 10-8-405 shall be fined not less than $50.00 nor more than $500.00 for each offense, and each day such violation persists shall constitute a separate and distinct offense.
(Added. Coun. J. 7-31-96, p. 26900)

Article V. Prohibited Uses

§10-8-410 Skating.

It shall be unlawful for any person to skate on roller or ice skates upon any public way in the city except on the sidewalks and at street intersections while crossing from one side of the street to the other.
(Prior code § 36-39)

§10-8-420 Cleansing goods.

No person shall wash, rinse or cleanse, or cause or procure to be washed, rinsed or cleansed, any cloth, yarn or garment in any public way or public place in the city.
(Prior code § 36-41)

§10-8-430 Washing windows and sidewalks.

From the first day of May until the first day of October it shall not be lawful for any person to wash or cause to be washed any pavement or window with a hose or streetwasher, or by throwing or dashing water against or upon the same in such manner as to permit or cause the water so used in washing to run

or fall upon any public sidewalk or in such manner as to obstruct or tend to obstruct the use of any public sidewalk, with or by any implement used in and about the cleansing or washing of any such pavement or window, between hours of 7:00 a.m. and 7:00 p.m.
(Prior code § 36-42)

§10-8-440 Sorting of articles.
It shall be unlawful for any person to pick, sort, pack or unpack, fruit, flowers, vegetables, rags, paper, old iron, bottles, or junk upon any public way or other public place in the city.
(Prior code § 36-43)

§10-8-450 Mixing concrete.
It shall be unlawful for any person to mix any dry or wet concrete, cement or plaster of any kind or description upon the surface of any public way.
(Prior code § 36-44)

§10-8-460 Spilling oil.
It shall be unlawful for any person to spill any turpentine, kerosene, gasoline, benzine, naphtha, coal oil, or any product thereof, or any oil used for lubricating, illuminating or fuel purposes, or allow any of such fluids to escape to or upon any asphalt pavement of the city, or to operate, or to permit to be operated, any tank wagon or other vehicle from which any of such fluids are permitted to escape.
(Prior code § 36-45)

§10-8-470 Spilling of substances on roadway.
It shall be unlawful for any person to operate a vehicle, either in person or through his agents or employees, upon the expressways or roadways within the city of Chicago, unless such vehicle is so constructed or loaded as to prevent any of its load from dropping, spilling, sifting, leaking, blowing or otherwise escaping therefrom; provided, however, that sand, or other material used for the same purpose, may be dropped for the purpose of securing traction, or water or other substance may be sprinkled on a roadway or expressway in cleaning or maintaining such roadway or expressway.

No person shall operate on any expressway or roadway within the city of Chicago, any vehicle with any load, unless said load is loaded, and any covering thereon is securely fastened, so as to prevent said load or covering from becoming loose, detached, or in any manner a hazard to other users of said expressway and roadways.

Any person violating the provisions of this section shall be fined not less than $100.00 nor more than $500.00 for each offense.
(Prior code § 36-45.1; Amend. Coun. J. 12-4-02, p. 99931)

§10-8-480 Casting refuse and liquids.
It shall be unlawful for any person, in person or by his agent, employee or servant to cast, throw, sweep, sift or deposit in any manner in or upon any public way or other public place in the city, or in or upon the waters of Lake Michigan, or any river, canal, public water, drain, sewer or receiving basin within the jurisdiction of the city, any kind of litter. Nor shall any person cast,

throw, sweep, sift or deposit any litter anywhere within the jurisdiction of the city in such manner that it may be carried or deposited, in whole or in part, by the action of the sun, wind, rain or snow, into any of the aforementioned places.

Litter includes but is not limited to the following: (a) picnic or eating utensils, such as paper plates, cups, napkins, towels, plastic utensils, metal foil, cellophane, wax paper, paper bags, or any food wrappings; (b) liquid or beverage containers such as beer, soft-drink, and juice cans, beer, soft-drink, liquor and wine bottles, and milk or juice cartons; (c) tobacco and confection wrappers, such as cigarette packages, candy, ice cream, Popsicle, gum or any other type of dessert or confection wrapping or container; (d) food wastes, such as fruit or vegetable peelings, pulp, rinds, leftovers or any other type of table wastes; (e) newspapers, books, placards, handbills, pamphlets, circulars, notices or papers of any type; (f) or any other type of rubbish, garbage, refuse matter, article, thing or substance such as discarded clothing, boxes, dust, manure or ashes.

Provided, that this section shall not apply to the deposit of material under a permit authorized by any ordinance of the city; or to goods, wares, or merchandise deposited upon any public way or other public place temporarily, in the necessary course of trade, and removed therefrom within two hours after being so deposited; or to articles or things deposited in or conducted into the city sewer system through lawful drains in accordance with the ordinances of the city relating thereto.

Any person violating any of the provisions of this section shall be fined not less than $50.00 nor more than $200.00 for each offense.

(Prior code § 36-46; Amend. Coun. J. 12-4-02, p. 99931)

§10-8-490 Selling tickets.

It shall be unlawful for any person to sell, offer or expose for sale, or solicit any other person to purchase tickets for any railroad, steamboat or other transportation line, or any place of amusement, upon any public way or other public place within the district bounded on the north by the Chicago River, on the south by the south line of Roosevelt Road, on the east by Lake Michigan, and on the west by the Chicago River.

(Prior code § 36-47)

§10-8-500 Selling tickets near amusement places.

No person shall obstruct or encumber any street corner or public place in front of any theater, baseball park or other place of amusement in the city, by lounging in or about the same after being requested to move on by any police officer. Nor shall any person be permitted to remain at any such place having in his possession any tickets for any theater, baseball park or other place of amusement, for the purpose of selling same, or offering the same for sale, in front of, or near any theater, baseball park or other place of amusement in an attempt at speculating in such tickets.

(Prior code § 36-48)

§10-8-505 Selling tickets near a stadium or playing field.

(a) It shall be unlawful for any person, while located on the public way within 2,000 feet of a stadium or playing field, to sell, offer, or expose for sale, or solicit any other person to purchase tickets for any amusement produced or presented in that stadium or playing field.

(b) For purposes of this section, the following definitions shall apply:

"Stadium" or "playing field" shall mean a stadium or playing field which is not totally enclosed and contains more than 15,000 seats where any such seats are located within 100 feet of 200 or more dwelling units. The 100-foot distance shall be measured from the seat to the nearest point of the buildings in which the dwelling units are contained.

"Amusement" shall be defined as set forth in Section 4-156-010 of this code.

"Dwelling unit" shall mean a room designed or used for sleeping accommodations, including hotel and dormitory rooms.

(c) Any person found guilty of violating this section shall be subject to a fine of not less than $50.00 no more than $200.00.

(Added. Coun. J. 4-16-97, p. 42633; Amend. Coun. J. 12-4-02, p. 99931)

§10-8-510 Soliciting business.

It shall be unlawful for any person including the owner of any business adjacent to or near the public way, either in person or through any agent or employee to stand upon, use or occupy the public ways to solicit the trade, custom or patronage for such business, or to interfere with or impede any pedestrian or any one in a vehicle on a public way, for purpose of soliciting business.

Any such soliciting of business on any public way is hereby declared to be a nuisance and the owner or proprietor of any such business who shall refuse or neglect to abate such nuisance after being notified in writing so to do by the superintendent of police, shall be fined not less than $500.00 nor more than $1,000.00 for each and every day he shall refuse or neglect to abate such nuisance.

Provided, nothing in this section shall be construed to include any business operated wholly or entirely upon any public way under or by virtue of a lawful permit or license issued therefor.

(Prior code § 36-49; Amend. Coun. J. 6-28-30, p. 36848)

§10-8-515 Soliciting unlawful business.

(a) No person may: (i) stand upon, use or occupy the public way to solicit any unlawful business; or (ii) interfere with or impede any pedestrian or anyone in a vehicle on the public way, for the purpose of soliciting any unlawful business.

(b) As used in this section, "unlawful business" means any exchange of goods or services for money or anything of value, where the nature of the goods or services, or the exchange thereof, is unlawful. Unlawful business includes, but is not limited to, prostitution or the illegal sale of narcotics. For purposes of this section, "soliciting" may be by words, gestures, symbols or any similar means.

(c) A person who violates this section shall be subject to a fine of not less than $500.00 and/or imprisonment for: (i) not less than 10 days and not more than six months for a first offense; (ii) not less than 20 days and not more

than six months for a second offense; and (iii) not less than 30 days and not more than six months for a third or subsequent offense. In addition to the penalties specified above, a person who violates this section shall be ordered to perform up to 200 hours of community service.
(Added. Coun. J. 4-1-98, p. 65278)

§10-8-520 Street vendors.

No person, other than a licensed peddler, as permitted by the provisions of Chapter 4-244 of this code, shall sell, offer or expose for sale, or solicit any person to purchase any article or service whatsoever, except newspapers, on any public way.

No person shall sell, offer or expose for sale, or solicit any person to purchase any newspaper from any vehicular traffic lane on any public way in the city.
(Prior code § 36-49.1; Amend. Coun. J. 2-26-86, p. 28157; 5-12-99, p. 2313)

§10-8-525 Vehicle servicing in traffic lane prohibited—Exception.

Except in case of emergency, no person shall perform or offer to perform any service on a motor vehicle in any vehicular traffic lane on any public way in the city.
(Added. Coun. J. 7-14-93, p. 35528)

Article VI. Violation of Chapter Provisions

§10-8-526 Enforcement of Chicago Transit Authority Ordinance 98-126—Rule of conduct.

(a) The members of the Chicago Police Department shall have authority to enforce the provisions of Chicago Transit Authority Ordinance Number 98-126 ("A Comprehensive Ordinance Establishing Rules of Conduct to Promote Health, Safety and Welfare on Property Owned, Operated or Maintained by the Chicago Transit Authority"), as passed by the Chicago Transit Board on November 12, 1998, or as subsequently amended.

(b) Any person who violates the above referenced ordinance shall be subject to a fine not to exceed $500.00 and shall be subject to an order requiring the violator to pay restitution when the violation involves damage to property.

(c) In addition to any other means authorized by law, the city may enforce this section by instituting an action with the department of administrative hearings.
(Added. Coun. J. 12-13-95, p. 13843; Amend. 4-21-99, p. 93318)

§10-8-530 Violation—Penalty.

Any person violating any of the provisions of this chapter, where no other penalty is specifically provided, shall be fined not more than $50.00.
(Prior code § 36-50)

CHAPTER 10-20
WORK ON AND UNDER PUBLIC WAYS
(Selected Sections)

Sections:

Article I. Openings, Construction and Repair in Public Ways

10-20-100 License.
10-20-110 License renewal.
10-20-115 Insurance required for license.
10-20-120 Letter of credit required for license.
10-20-145 License violations—Penalty.
10-20-150 Permit—Fees—Issuance.
10-20-155 Pavement restoration.
10-20-160 Tearing up public ways.
10-20-165 Definitions.

Article II. Underground Transmitting Devices

10-20-200 Tunneling—Permit.
10-20-225 Violation—Penalty.

Article III. Private Paving

10-20-300 Board of local improvements authorization.

Article IV. Driveways

10-20-400 Supervision.
10-20-405 Use of public way permit required.
10-20-410 Insurance required.
10-20-430 Commercial driveway permits.
10-20-440 Construction.
10-20-442 Driveways rendered unusable—Removal and restoration.
10-20-450 Violation—Penalty.

Article V. Streets, Curbs and Sidewalks

10-20-505 Construction specifications.
10-20-535 Level of sidewalk.
10-20-540 Grade.
10-20-545 Sidewalk ramps.
10-20-555 Violation—Penalty.

Article VI. Barricades

10-20-600 Barricade for new pavement.
10-20-605 Barricade of street openings and obstructions.
10-20-610 Warning lights.

Article VII. Viaducts

10-20-705 License and permit required.
10-20-715 Violation—Penalty.

Article VIII. Miscellaneous

10-20-800 Violation—Penalty.
10-20-805 Enforcement of provisions.
10-20-810 Authority to cite.
10-20-815 License and permit not exclusive.

Article I. Openings, Construction and Repair in Public Ways

§10-20-100 License.

(a) No person shall make an opening in, or construct or repair any pavement in, any public way or other public place pursuant to this chapter unless that person holds a public way work license as required by this article. The public way work permit required by this article to make an opening in, or construct or repair any pavement in, any public way or other public place shall only be issued to a person holding such a license. Before the department of transportation issues any such permit, the department of transportation shall first require proof that the permit applicant holds such a license. Such a license shall be effective for one calendar year, and the fee for such a license shall be $125.00. Such a license may be issued at any time during a calendar year, but shall be effective only for the calendar year in which it is issued. The commissioner of transportation is hereby authorized to issue such a license and is authorized to promulgate regulations relating to such a license, including but not limited to terms and conditions for the issuance, maintenance and renewal of the license, the scope of work that may be performed under the license, and terms and conditions applicable to the insurance and letter of credit required by this article.

(b) The public way work license specified in this section shall not be required for the placement, planting, cultivation, maintenance or removal of any tree, shrub, flower, sod or other plant material in the public way.

(c) The public way work license specified in this section shall not be required of a government agency.

(Added. Coun. J. 1-14-97, p. 37762)

§10-20-110 License renewal.

(a) The commissioner of transportation may renew the public way work license required by this article at the beginning of a new license period upon proper application and payment of a renewal fee of $125.00. Prior to renewal, all licensees and substantial owners shall provide the commissioner of transportation with the following information: the names, addresses, government identification numbers and percentages of interest required in the initial license application by this article or, where such information already has been provided in a license application, any new information necessary to make such information current and accurate.

(b) The wilful misstatement or omission of any material information required by the license renewal process shall be grounds for revocation of the license for a period of up to three years.

(Added. Coun. J. 1-14-97, p. 37762)

§10-20-115 Insurance required for license.

No public way work license shall be issued pursuant to this article until the applicant for such license shall first have presented to the commissioner of transportation proof of insurance against any liability, loss or claim arising out of the issuance of the license, or out of work performed pursuant to the license. Such insurance shall be issued by an insurer authorized to do business in Illinois, shall be in an amount no less than $1,000,000.00 per occurrence and shall name the city of Chicago, its officers, employees and agents as additional insured. The

insurance policy shall provide for 30 days' written notice to the commissioner of transportation prior to any lapse, cancellation or change in coverage. The insurance shall be maintained in effect at all times during the term of the license. The commissioner of transportation in his or her discretion may require, instead of such insurance, any alternative form of indemnity, protection or security that he or she deems necessary to accomplish the above-described purposes.
(Prior code § 33-2; Amend. Coun. J. 5-4-94, p. 49718; 1-14-97, p. 37762)

§10-20-120 Letter of credit required for license.

The public way work license required by this article shall be issued only after the prospective licensee shows proof to the commissioner of transportation of having established an irrevocable letter of credit for the benefit of the city of Chicago, in an amount and for a duration to be established in regulations promulgated by the commissioner of transportation, such letter of credit to be maintained in conjunction with the license and any renewals. A licensee shall bear the costs of establishing, maintaining and renewing such letter of credit, and shall bear any costs associated with a draw upon the letter of credit.
(Added. Coun. J. 1-14-97, p. 37762)

§10-20-145 License violations—Penalty.

(a) In addition to any other penalties that may be imposed under applicable law, any person who makes an opening in, or who constructs or repairs any pavement in, any public way or other public place without first obtaining the public way work license required by this article, or who falsifies information in order to obtain such a license, shall be subject to a fine of $500.00 for each day that the opening exists or that the construction or repair is conducted, and shall also be liable to the city of Chicago for any costs incurred by the city in arranging for or carrying out any restoration, repairs or other work necessitated by the acts or omissions of such person. The city of Chicago shall have the right, but not the obligation, to arrange for or carry out any restoration, repairs or other work pursuant to this section or other applicable provision of this chapter, and any action taken by the city of Chicago in arranging for or carrying out any such restoration, repairs or other work shall not relieve such person of liability for, or diminish that person's liability for, any condition created by, or created as a result of the acts or omissions of, that person.

(b) If a person holding the public way work license required by this article allows the insurance or letter of credit required in conjunction with such license to be cancelled or to expire or otherwise lapse for more than 30 days during the period that such insurance or letter of credit is required to be in full effect, the license will be rendered void and the person must reapply for a new license and pay a new license fee in order to be considered for a valid license.
(Added. Coun. J. 1-14-97, p. 37762)

§10-20-150 Permit—Fees—Issuance.

(a) It shall be unlawful for any person to make an opening in, or to construct or repair any pavement in, any public way or other public place without first obtaining a public way work permit from the commissioner of transportation; provided, however, that any such opening, construction or repair may be performed by a person holding the public way work license required by this article, who is not a permittee under this section but who is acting as subcontractor for, or otherwise acting under instructions from, as agent for, on behalf of, or in concert with, a permittee under this section. A permit fee shall be required for creating any opening in, or for constructing or repairing any pavement in, the public way. The permit fee for creating a pavement opening and for pavement construction or repair shall be $110.00 for each such opening to be created or each such construction or repair project prior to January 1, 1994. The permit fee for creating an opening, or for construction or repair, in any parkway or unimproved portion of the public way shall be $30.00 for each such opening to be created, or each such construction or repair project conducted, prior to January 1, 1994. All permit fees required under this section shall be increased by five percent per annum beginning January 1, 1994. The fee for any permit issued during the time periods specified in subsection (b) of this section shall be twice the normal fee.

The foregoing fees, however, shall not be required of any person who has been granted the right to use the public way pursuant to a franchise ordinance approved by the city council and which franchise ordinance specifically prohibits the imposition of such fees in addition to the compensation to be received by the city pursuant to the franchise ordinance.

(b) Unless the commissioner of transportation determines that circumstances warrant the opening or repairing of pavement, no permit shall be issued for: (i) opening or repairing any pavement that has been newly constructed or reconstructed after January 1, 1994, for a period of ten years after completion of the construction or reconstruction; (ii) opening or repairing any pavement that has been resurfaced after January 1, 1994, within five years after completion of the repaving or; (iii) opening or repairing any pavement at anytime located within the area bounded by North Avenue, Halsted Street, 22nd Street and Lake Michigan. Whenever the commissioner determines that circumstances warrant the opening or repairing of pavement under this subsection, the commissioner may require that the entire surface of the public way abutting the excavated pavement be restored from curb line to curb line but shall, at a minimum, require that the surface of the public way abutting the excavated pavement be restored to the furthest quarter point in all directions. For purposes of this subsection, "quarter point" means each point situated at a distance equal to one quarter of the distance from curb line to curb line. Any person who opens or repairs a newly constructed, reconstructed or resurfaced pavement without a permit within the time period specified herein or without the approval of the commissioner of transportation, or who falsifies information in order to obtain a permit for such work, shall be subject to a fine of $1,000.00 for each day that the opening exists or that the repair is conducted. When determining whether circumstances warrant the opening or repair of pavement under this subsection, the commissioner shall consider, in addition to other reasonable factors, whether the work to be performed constitutes an emergency repair; whether there is no other reasonable access available to perform the work; and whether the work will provide a public benefit.

(c) It shall be a condition of any permit for the opening of, or the construction or repair of, any public way or other public place that the permit applicant shall agree to restore the pavement or other materials in accordance with public way restoration standards. These standards shall be in the form of regulations promulgated by the commissioner of transportation.

(d) In addition to the other limitations on the issuance of permits described in this chapter, the commissioner of transportation shall not issue any permit for the opening of, or the construction or repair of, any public way or public place until he or she shall have been fully advised of the time, place and character of such opening, construction or repair and the purpose thereof. The commissioner of transportation may require that applications for permits be accompanied by a plat or pencil tracing or sketch showing the location, character and dimensions of any proposed openings for the installation of new work, or the location and character of any alterations involving changes in the location of pipes, conduits, wires or other conductors, or proof of compliance with the insurance, letter of credit or other license requirements of this article.

(e) Before a permit that contemplates the breaking or other disturbance of a bituminous surface shall be granted to open, or conduct construction or repair on, any public way or public place for any purpose, the permit applicant shall as part of the application either (1) commit to restoring the bituminous surface after completion of the work and restoration of the pavement, or (2) request that the city of Chicago restore the bituminous surface after completion of the work and restoration of the pavement. If the applicant selects option (2), the commissioner of transportation shall assess the applicant a restoration fee sufficient to cover the city of Chicago's cost to restore the bituminous surface. This restoration fee shall be calculated on a per-square-yard basis, based on current construction costs established through average bid prices in the city of Chicago. In the event that the city of Chicago's cost to restore the bituminous surface is less than the restoration fee, the amount of the surplus shall be returned to the permittee.

(f) In order for a permit to be issued, the director of revenue shall collect the amount of both the permit fee and any applicable restoration fee. Where the opening, construction or repair is required to perform underground work to facilitate a city or state project or the repair of damage caused by city forces, the payment of permit fees shall be waived.

(g) The permit specified in this section shall not be required for the placement, planting, cultivation, maintenance or removal of any tree, shrub, flower, sod or other plant material in the public way.

(Prior code § 33-1; Amend. Coun. J. 7-13-88, p. 15000; 12-11-91, p. 10932; 6-23-93, p. 34415; 1-14-97, p. 37762; 6-9-99, p. 5453)

§10-20-155 Pavement restoration.

(a) All work done under authority of the permit required by this article shall be inspected by a field service specialist designated by the commissioner of transportation.

(b) Immediately after the completion of the work done pursuant to the permit, the permittee shall forthwith restore any pavement or other materials displaced by reason of the work, and shall restore the surface of any public way or other public place which may be opened or otherwise disturbed; provided, however, that a permittee shall only be obliged to restore a bituminous surface if the permittee has not remitted to the director of revenue the restoration fee assessed pursuant to this article. All of this work shall be done to the satisfaction of the commissioner of transportation, in accordance with public way restoration standards. These standards shall be in the form of regulations promulgated by the commissioner of transportation.

(c) Any permittee who fails to restore the pavement or other materials and the non-bituminous surface and, if applicable, the bituminous surface, of any public way or other public place, as required in subsection (b), by the time established by the commissioner of transportation shall be subject to a fine of $500.00 for each day that such failure continues, and shall also be liable to the city of Chicago for any costs incurred by the city in arranging for or carrying out any such restoration upon expiration of the relevant deadline. The city of Chicago shall have the right, but not the obligation, to arrange for or carry out any such restoration upon expiration of the relevant deadline, and any action taken by the city of Chicago in arranging for or carrying out any such restoration pursuant to this section or other applicable provision of this chapter shall not relieve a permittee of liability for, or diminish a permittee's liability for, any condition created by, or created as a result of the acts or omissions of, the permittee.

(d) The insurance and letter of credit protections of this article shall apply to any amounts levied or incurred by the city of Chicago pursuant to this section.

(Prior code § 33-3; Amend. Coun. J. 7-13-88, p. 15000; 12-11-91, p. 10932; 1-14-97, p. 37762)

§10-20-160 Tearing up public ways.

Unless a specific penalty is otherwise provided, any person who shall injure or tear up any pavement, side or crosswalk, or any part thereof, dig any hole, ditch or drain in, or dig or remove any sod, stone, earth, sand or gravel from any public way or public ground in the city without having first obtained the necessary permit from the commissioner of transportation, or who violates the terms or conditions of a permit for such work, shall be subject to a penalty for each offense of not less than $200.00 nor more than $500.00.

(Prior code § 33-5; Amend. Coun. J. 7-13-88, p. 15000; 12-11-91, p. 10932; 6-23-93, p. 34415; 1-14-97, p. 37762)

§10-20-165 Definitions.

For purposes of this article, the following definitions shall apply:

A "person" or "persons" who apply for or hold the public way work license or the public way work permit required by this article shall include individuals, sole proprietorships, partnerships, limited partnerships, firms, limited liability companies and corporations.

The term "restore" shall mean restoration or replacement of the pavement, components of pavement, or other materials to at least the condition that the pavement, components of pavement, or other materials were in before the work contemplated by this article was commenced.

A "substantial owner" means any person or entity holding a 25 percent or greater ownership interest in any firm, partnership, limited partnership, corporation or limited liability company; provided, however, that where no person or entity holds such an ownership interest, substantial owner shall mean each of the four persons or entities with the largest ownership interests; provided further, that with regard to an individual or sole proprietorship, substantial owner means that individual or sole proprietorship.

(Added. Coun. J. 1-14-97, p. 37762)

Article II. Underground Transmitting Devices

§10-20-200 Tunneling—Permit.

No person shall, without a permit in writing from the commissioner of transportation, place any shaft, cable, pipe, main, conduit, wire or other transmitting or conducting device underneath the surface of any public way in the city by driving the same through the earth underneath the surface of any such public way, or by boring or tunneling under any such public way.

Any person may tunnel under stone or concrete sidewalks which do not exceed six feet in width for the purpose of installing sewer drains not to exceed six inches in diameter; provided, that a permit in writing shall be obtained from the commissioner of transportation for such purpose.

The commissioner of transportation is authorized to remove or cut out all shafts, cables, pipes, mains, conduits, tubes, wires or other transmitting or conducting devices at any time laid or placed underneath the surface of any public way in violation of the provisions of this section.

(Prior code § 33-6; Amend. Coun. J. 5-4-94, p. 49718; 1-14-97, p. 37762)

§10-20-225 Violation—Penalty.

Every person violating any of the provisions of the foregoing sections or applicable regulations relating to underground work shall be fined not less than $50.00 nor more than $500.00 for each offense.

(Prior code § 33-11; Amend. Coun. J. 1-14-97, p. 37762)

Article III. Private Paving

§10-20-300 Board of local improvements authorization.

No person shall build, construct or lay a pavement by private contract on any public way in the city, unless he first shall have made application to the board of local improvements and otherwise complied with the licensing and permitting requirements of this chapter.

Before such permit is issued, the said applicant shall deposit with the board of local improvements a sum sufficient to cover the estimated cost of engineering, inspection, supervision and other services. Against such deposit, charges shall be made by the board of local improvements for such services as may be required from time to time at such rates as will correspond to those established by the city council for similar services. Nothing in this section shall be held to apply to pavements laid by special assessment or special taxation.

(Prior code § 33-12; Amend. Coun. J. 5-4-94, p. 49718; 1-14-97, p. 37762)

Article IV. Driveways

§10-20-400 Supervision.

The authorization for, and issuance of, a use of public way permit for driveways shall be under the direction and supervision of the commissioner of transportation, and the location and construction of the same shall be in accordance with the plans and specifications as approved by said commissioner.

(Prior code § 13-14; Amend. Coun. J. 5-4-94, p. 49718; 1-14-97, p. 37762; 6-9-99, p. 5453)

§10-20-405 Use of public way permit required.

No person shall hereafter establish or maintain any driveway over, across, or upon any public sidewalk or public parkway without first obtaining a use of public way permit from the commissioner of transportation as hereinafter provided.

(Prior code § 13-15; Amend. Coun. J. 1-14-97, p. 37762; 6-9-99, p. 5453)

§10-20-410 Insurance required.

No use of public way permit for a driveway shall be issued until a written application therefor has been made by the owner or, with the consent of the owner, a long-term leaseholder of the property to which the proposed driveway is to be connected to the commissioner of transportation and the certificate of insurance herein provided for has been filed with said commissioner. For purposes of this section, a "long-term lease holder" means an individual who holds a lease for the property for a minimum term of 10 years.

(Prior code § 13-16; Amend. Coun. J. 5-4-94, p. 49718; 1-14-97, p. 37762; 6-9-99, p. 5453)

§10-20-430 Commercial driveway permits.

All commercial driveway permits are subject to immediate revocation and driveways closed and ordered removed at owner's expense unless the permit holder complies with the following requirements:

(a) All property requiring a commercial driveway permit must have a physical barrier to prevent alley access, unless exempted by the city council.

(b) This physical barrier must be erected within 60 days after issuance of a permit, and shall either be a steel guardrail constructed in compliance with this code, or other barrier (except wheel stops) approved by the commissioner of transportation.

(Prior code § 33-19.1; Added. Coun. J. 12-14-88, p. 21369; Amend. 12-11-91, p. 10932; 1-14-97, p. 37762; 6-9-99, p. 5453)

§10-20-440 Construction.

Where driveways are to be built across the sidewalk spaces, unless otherwise expressly authorized they shall conform to the sidewalk grade. Such driveways shall be constructed of concrete eight inches in depth and shall otherwise comply with applicable regulations. Provided, however, that in the case of driveways across viaduct sidewalks or existing residential asphalt driveways, variations of construction and materials to conform to existing condition may be made when approved by the commissioner of transportation.

No driveway shall be so constructed as to prevent free and unobstructed passage on, over or across the same, or in such a manner as to interfere with the proper drainage and safe grading of the streets. No driveway shall be constructed across intersecting sidewalks. Gradual approaches to the regular sidewalk grade shall be made from the grade of the driveway. The slope of any driveway and the approaches thereto shall not exceed one inch vertical to one foot horizontal nor be less than one-fourth inch vertical to one foot horizontal in any direction, except that the slope from street curb line shall not exceed one inch vertical to one foot horizontal.

(Prior code § 33-20; Amend. Coun. J. 5-4-94, p. 49718; 1-14-97, p. 37762)

§10-20-442 Driveways rendered unusable— Removal and restoration.

(a) No person shall maintain any driveway over, across or upon any public sidewalk or public parkway if the property to which the driveway is connected has a permanent barrier, including, but not limited to, a fence, wall, building or landscaping which prevents the ingress and egress of vehicles to the property from the driveway. A use of public way permit issued for a driveway maintained in violation of this section may be revoked by the commissioner of transportation.

(b) (1) If a business served by a commercial driveway ceases operation and there is no business activity conducted at that location, the owner of the property to which the driveway is attached or the grantee of a public way permit for the driveway shall, at his own expense, erect, within 10 days of cessation of the business, a barrier across the driveway to prevent access to the property. The design of the barrier shall be approved by the commissioner of transportation. If the cessation of the business activity continues for a period of 180 consecutive days, the owner or grantee shall, at his expense, remove the driveway and restore the sidewalk, parkway, curbs, gutters, and any trees and landscaping required by the provisions of this code; provided that the commissioner of transportation may waive this requirement for the following reasons:

(A) The property to which the driveway is attached is either (i) under a contract for sale and the sale will be completed within a reasonable time period, or (ii) the property is for sale and is actively being marketed; and

(B) The owner of the property has erected a barrier across the driveway pursuant to the provisions of this subsection.

(2) The owner of the property or the grantee of a public way permit subject to the provisions of subsection (b)(1) of this section shall, at his own expense, erect, within 10 days of cessation of the business, a barrier to prevent alley access notwithstanding any contrary provision of any other ordinance. The design of the barrier shall be approved by the commissioner of transportation.

(c) Whenever the commissioner of transportation determines that the property to which a driveway is attached has been physically rendered unusable as a driveway in violation of this section, the commissioner may order the driveway removed and the sidewalk and public parkway space where the driveway is located restored to its proper condition so that the portion of the sidewalk and public parkway space used for the driveway shall be safe for public travel and in the same condition as the remaining portion of the sidewalk and public parkway space. The provisions of this section shall not apply to driveways attached to residential dwellings of three units or less.

(d) Any person who violates the provisions of this section shall be fined not less than $50.00 nor more than $500.00 for each offense. Each day a violation continues shall constitute a separate and distinct offense. If the owner of the property to which the driveway is attached or the grantee of a use of public way permit that was issued for the driveway at the time of the violation fails, neglects or refuses to remove the driveway, the city may proceed to remove the driveway and restore the sidewalk, parkway, curbs, gutters and any trees and landscaping. The owner of the property to which the driveway is attached and the grantee of a use of public way permit issued for the driveway at the time of the violation shall be jointly and severally liable for any fines, the cost of the erection of any barrier, and the cost of any removal and restoration.

(Added. Coun. J. 6-9-99, p. 5453; Amend. Coun. J. 12-4-02, p. 99026)

§10-20-450 Violation—Penalty.

(a) Any person violating any of the provisions of this chapter or applicable regulations concerning driveways shall be fined not less than $100.00 nor more than $1,000.00 for each offense, unless otherwise specifically provided. A separate and distinct offense shall be held to have been committed each day any person violates any of said provisions.

(b) In addition to any fine imposed, the owner of property to which a driveway is attached and maintained without a use of public way permit in violation of this chapter may be required to remove the driveway and restore the sidewalk and/or public parkway space where the driveway is located to its proper condition so that the portion of the sidewalk and/or public parkway space used for the driveway shall be safe for public travel and in the same condition as the remaining portion of the sidewalk and/or public parkway space. If the owner of the property to which the driveway is attached fails, neglects or refuses to remove said driveway, the city may proceed to remove the driveway and restore the sidewalk and/or public parkway space. The owner of the property to which the driveway is attached shall be liable for a penalty in the amount of the costs of the removal and restoration.

(Prior code § 33-22; Amend. Coun. J. 1-14-97, p. 37762; 6-9-99, p. 5453)

Article V. Streets, Curbs and Sidewalks

§10-20-505 Construction specifications.

Except where sidewalks are to be laid in accordance with the provisions of special assessment or special taxation ordinances, it shall be unlawful for any person to construct, lay or rebuild any sidewalk on any portion of the public ways of the city otherwise than in compliance with specifications that the commissioner of transportation shall promulgate and prescribe in regulations. Each day that such sidewalk shall remain so constructed, laid or rebuilt in violation of such specifications shall constitute a separate and distinct offense.

(Prior code § 33-24; Amend. Coun. J. 1-14-97, p. 37762)

§10-20-535 Level of sidewalk.

No part of any sidewalk or sidewalk space shall be taken for private use by lowering or cutting down the same next to the building, or railing off the same by any wooden or iron railing, or by shutting off the public from using the same; and said sidewalk shall not be raised next to the building by constructing a platform of wood, iron, concrete or stone, but said sidewalk shall be built flush up to the building on a uniform grade as herein provided.

(Prior code § 33-42; Amend. Coun. J. 1-14-97, p. 37762)

§10-20-540 Grade.

The grade for sidewalks shall be established by ordinance of the city council, and a record of the same, accessible to the public, shall be kept on file in the department of transportation. No person shall build or assist in building any sidewalk where no grade has been established by ordinance, or contrary to any grade which may have been or may be established by ordinance, or contrary to any of the provisions of this section. Every day that he shall fail to remove or reconstruct any sidewalk which does not conform to established grade after notice by the commissioner of transportation shall constitute a separate offense.

All sidewalks heretofore constructed that do not conform to the grade established by ordinance shall be relaid to the proper grade by the owner of the abutting property. Each day he shall fail to relay or reconstruct such sidewalk after notice by the commissioner of transportation shall constitute a separate offense.

No part or portion of any sidewalk, where the grade has been established, shall be laid or relaid at any different grade or any other level than the adjacent portions of such sidewalk, except as provided in the provisions of this chapter relating to driveways and sidewalk ramps. The person violating this provision shall alter said sidewalk so as to make the same conform to the established grade, and in case he neglects and refuses so to do within a reasonable time it shall be lawful for the department of transportation to alter the same, and the cost and expense of the same shall be paid by such owner and may be recovered from him in an action in the name of the city.

(Prior code § 33-43; Amend. Coun. J. 5-4-94, p. 49718; 1-14-97, p. 37762)

§10-20-545 Sidewalk ramps.

In order to eliminate the barrier that curbs pose to the physically handicapped, all new curbs and sidewalks, and all existing curbs or sidewalks which are a part of any new construction or reconstruction at the intersections of sidewalks and streets, sidewalks and alleys, and at other points of major pedestrian flow, shall comply with the following requirement:

A ramp with nonslip surface shall be constructed so that the sidewalk and alley, or the sidewalk and street, blend to a common level. Such ramp shall not be less than 36 inches wide and shall not have a slope greater than one inch rise per 12 inches in length. Wherever, because of surrounding buildings or other restrictions, it is impossible to conform the slope with this requirement, the ramp shall contain a slope with as shallow a rise as possible under the circumstances, except however the slope may not exceed a one and one-half inch rise per 12 inches in length.

Standard details for placement and construction of the ramped sidewalks shall be established by the commissioner of transportation. No person shall construct, build, establish or maintain any ramped sidewalk without otherwise complying with the licensing and permitting requirements of this chapter.

(Prior code § 33-43.1; Amend. Coun. J. 5-4-94, p. 49718; 1-14-97, p. 37762)

§10-20-555 Violation—Penalty.

Any person violating any of the provisions of this chapter or applicable regulations on sidewalk construction shall be subject to a penalty of not less than $50.00 nor more than $500.00 for each offense.

(Prior code § 33-46; Amend. Coun. J. 1-14-97, p. 37762)

Article VI. Barricades

§10-20-600 Barricade for new pavement.

It shall be lawful for any person employed to pave or repave any street in the city, to place proper obstructions across such street for the purpose of preserving the pavement then newly made or to be made, until the same shall be fit for use.

All such obstructions shall be removed, by the person that placed them upon the street, as soon as practicable, without notice, or immediately upon order of the commissioner of transportation when he or she shall so direct in writing.

No person shall, without the consent of the commissioner of transportation, in writing, or without the consent of the person superintending such paving, throw down, displace or remove any such obstruction, under a penalty of not more than $100.00 for every such offense.

(Prior code § 33-51; Amend. Coun. J. 5-4-94, p. 49718; 1-14-97, p. 37762)

§10-20-605 Barricade of street openings and obstructions.

It shall be the duty of every person engaged in digging in any street, or in paving any street, or in building any sewer or drain or trench for water pipes in any of the public streets, under a contract with the city made through any of the departments of the city, or by virtue of any permission which may have been granted by the city council or any department, or either of them, where such work if left exposed would be dangerous to persons traveling on such streets, to erect a fence or railing at such excavations or work in such a manner as to prevent danger to persons who may be traveling such streets, and to continue to maintain such railing or fence until the work shall be completed or the obstruction or danger removed.

It shall be the duty of such person to place upon such railing or fence, at sunset, suitable and sufficient lights and to keep them burning throughout the night during the performance of such work.

The provisions of this section shall apply to every person who shall place building materials in any of the public ways; or be engaged in building any vault or constructing any lateral drain from any cellar to any public sewer; or who shall perform any work causing obstructions in the public streets, by virtue of any permit from any executive department; and to all city officers and employees performing any work in behalf of the city whereby obstructions or excavations shall be made in the public ways.

All railings or fences erected on public ways for the protection of the public shall be erected and maintained to the satisfaction and approval of the commissioner of transportation.

Any person violating the provisions of this section shall be subject to a penalty of not less than $200.00 nor more than $500.00 for each offense, and every such person shall be deemed guilty of a separate offense for each day that such violation shall continue.

(Prior code § 33-52; Amend. Coun. J. 5-4-94, p. 49718; 1-14-97, p. 37762)

§10-20-610 Warning lights.

Any person having the use of any portion of the public way for the purpose of erecting or repairing any building, or for any other purpose, shall cause two red lights to be placed in a conspicuous place, one at either end of such obstruction, from dusk in the evening until sunrise in the morning, each night during the time such obstruction remains.

(Prior code § 33-53; Amend. Coun. J. 1-14-97, p. 37762)

Article VII. Viaducts

§10-20-705 License and permit required.

No person shall construct, reconstruct, or repair any highway viaduct in the city without first complying with the licensing and permitting requirements of this chapter.

(Prior code § 33-56; Amend. Coun. J. 12-11-91, p. 10932; 1-14-97, p. 37762)

§10-20-715 Violation—Penalty.

Any person that shall violate any of the provisions of that part of this chapter or applicable regulations dealing with viaducts shall be fined not less than $200.00 nor more than $500.00 for each offense, and every such person shall be deemed guilty of a separate offense for each day that such violation shall continue.

(Prior code § 33-58; Amend. Coun. J. 1-14-97, p. 37762)

Article VIII. Miscellaneous

§10-20-800 Violation—Penalty.

Any person violating any of the provisions of this chapter or applicable regulations shall be fined not less than $50.00 nor more than $500.00 for each offense, unless otherwise specifically provided.

(Prior code § 33-59; Amend. Coun. J. 1-14-97, p. 37762)

§10-20-805 Enforcement of provisions.

It shall be the duty of the department of transportation and any city officer and any employee having police power, to enforce the provisions of this chapter by stopping any work being done in violation of the terms set forth.

(Prior code § 33-45; Amend. Coun. J. 5-4-94, p. 49718; 1-14-97, p. 37762)

§10-20-810 Authority to cite.

In addition to the powers otherwise granted by this code and other applicable law, the commissioner of transportation, and, where applicable, the director of revenue, shall have the authority to issue citations for violations of this chapter.

(Added. Coun. J. 1-14-97, p. 37762)

§10-20-815 License and permit not exclusive.

The licensing and permitting requirements of this chapter shall not supersede, but shall be in addition to, any other licensing or permitting requirements that may be imposed by applicable law.

(Added. Coun. J. 1-14-97, p. 37762)

CHAPTER 10-28
STRUCTURES ON AND UNDER PUBLIC WAYS
(Selected Sections)

Sections:

Article I. General Requirements

10-28-010 Permission required.
10-28-030 Unlawful to place ice or snow on public way.
10-28-050 Maintenance of stands.
10-28-064 Advertising signs.
10-28-066 Advertising sign—Defined.
10-28-070 Storage of goods on public ways.

Article II. Carts Belonging to Retail Stores

10-28-120 Police enforcement.

Article II-A. Kiosks

10-28-121 to 10-28-128 Reserved.

Article III. Newspaper Stands

10-28-130 Permit required.
10-28-170 Construction and maintenance.
10-28-180 Limitation on use.
10-28-185 Erection—Location.
10-28-191 Enforcement authority.

Article IV. Canopies and Marquees

10-28-200 Permit required.
10-28-250 Construction—Clearance.

Article IV-A. Placement of Pay Telephones in Public Way

10-28-265 Placement of pay telephones in public way.

Article V. Awnings

10-28-270 Permit required.
10-28-280 Construction—Maintenance.

Article V-A. Obstruction of Streets, Sidewalks and Public Places for Construction and Building Maintenance Purposes

10-28-281 Definitions.
10-28-281.1 Public protection measures.
10-28-281.2 Permit required.
10-28-281.4 Prohibited uses of traffic and curb lanes.
10-28-281.5 Penalites.

Article V-B. Protection of the Public Way and Public Places

10-28-281.6 Protection required.
10-28-281.7 Fences and barricades.
10-28-287.8 Aprons.

Article V-C. Construction Canopies

10-28-284 Closure of sidewalks and bicycle lanes.
10-28-285 Sidewalks—Damage deposit required.
10-28-286 Violation—Penalty.

Article IX. Use of Subsidewalk Space

10-28-450 Permit required.
10-28-575 Vault space.

Article XI-A. Newsracks

10-28-750 Definitions—Newsracks.
10-28-755 Newsracks—Permitted when.
10-28-760 Newsracks—Prohibited locations.
10-28-770 Maximum dimensions.
10-28-775 Advertising signs on newsracks—Prohibited.
10-28-781 Multiple newsracks.
10-28-785 Notice of violation—Removal.
10-28-790 Violation of this article—Penalty.

Article XI-B. Refuse Compactors/Grease Containers

10-28-791 Defined.
10-28-792 Permit required.
10-28-795 Revocation of permit.
10-28-796 Violation—Penalty.
10-28-798 Enforcement authority.

Article XI-C. Dumpsters/Roll-Off Boxes on the Public Way

10-28-799 Dumpsters/roll-off boxes on the public way.

Article XII. Sidewalk Cafes

10-28-800 Definitions.
10-28-805 Permit required for sidewalk cafe.
10-28-830 Permit—Assignment or transfer prohibited.
10-28-835 Permit for one retail food establishment only.
10-28-840 Permit for food and alcoholic beverage service only.
10-28-845 Operational conditions.
10-28-850 Alcoholic beverage service—Requirements.
10-28-855 Compliance with code and rules and regulations required.
10-28-860 Promulgation of regulations—Force and effect.
10-28-865 Hearings.
10-28-870 Enforcement.
10-28-875 Violation—Penalties.
10-28-880 Violation—Permit revocation.

Article XIII. Violation of Chapter Provisions

10-28-990 Violation—Penalty.

Article I. General Requirements

§10-28-010 Permission required.

No person shall construct or maintain any bay window, bridge, wire, pipe, kiosk, or other structure or device over any public way or other public place; or any clock or post at the curb, or any clock attached outside the face of any building; or any loading platform, switch track or pushcar track upon any public way or other public place; or any tunnel or vault underneath the surface of any public way or other public place; or install or maintain any wire, pipe or conduit underneath the surface of any public way or other public place without first having obtained specific authority by ordinance passed by the city council authorizing such special privilege. Nothing in this section shall authorize any person to make an opening in, or construct or repair any pavement in the public way or other public place unless such person holds 2a public way work license if such a license is required by Chapter 10-20 of this code.

Any person violating any of the provisions of this section shall be fined not less than $25.00 nor more than $200.00 for each offense. A separate and distinct offense shall be held to have been committed each day any person continues to violate this section or fails or refuses to cause the removal of such unauthorized structure within such time as may be fixed by the director of revenue, not exceeding 30 days, after notice in writing for such removal has been served upon the owner or person maintaining any such privilege.

For purposes of this section, "kiosk" means a freestanding, permanent structure erected as an accessory to a building, and used to provide information concerning the building and its occupants.
(Prior code § 34-1; Amend. Coun. J. 12-15-99, p. 21529)

§10-28-030 Unlawful to place ice or snow on public way.

It shall be unlawful for any person to shovel or throw upon the public way any amount of ice or snow which is obstructive to the moving or parking of vehicular traffic or which impedes the normal routing of pedestrian traffic. Any person found in violation of this section shall be fined not less than $25.00 nor more than $100.00 for each offense, and each day such offense shall continue shall constitute a distinct and separate offense.
(Prior code § 34-2.1; Added. Coun. J. 4-25-85, p. 15821)

§10-28-050 Maintenance of stands.

It shall be unlawful for any person to erect, place or maintain in, upon or over any public way or other public place in the city, any fruitstand, shoeshining stand, flower stand, vegetable stand, lunch wagon, table, box, bin or any other arrangement or structure for the display or sale of goods, wares or merchandise, or for the pursuit of any occupation whatsoever unless a permit for the same shall be obtained from the director of revenue; provided, that the director of revenue shall issue no such permits except for the purpose of exhibiting for sale daily newspapers, within such districts as are or have been designated by the city council.*
(Prior code § 34-4; Amend. Coun. J. 11-30-94, p. 62597)

* Ordinances designating such districts are on file in the city clerk's office.

§10-28-064 Advertising signs.

Except as specifically permitted by this code or when authorized by contract entered into by the chief procurement officer in cooperation with the commissioner of planning and development pursuant to Section 10-28-045, no person shall place, install or knowingly maintain on the surface of the public way any sign or a structure or device to which such a sign is affixed. Any such sign, structure or device that is placed, installed or maintained on the public way in violation of this section is hereby declared a public nuisance and may be removed at any time by the director of revenue at the expense of the person responsible for the violation.

Any person who violates this section shall be subject to a fine of not less than $200.00 and not more than $500.00 for each offense. Each day that such a violation occurs shall be considered a separate offense.
(Prior code § 34-5.1; Added. Coun. J. 7-12-90, p. 18399; Amend. 12-11-91, p. 10832; 11-30-94, p. 62597; 4-16-97, p. 42736; 6-9-99, p. 5442)

§10-28-066 Advertising sign—Defined.

An advertising sign is a sign which directs attention to a business, commodity, service or entertainment regardless of where it is conducted, sold or offered.
(Prior code § 34-5.2; Added. Coun. J. 7-12-90, p. 18399; Amend. 1-12-94, p. 44543)

§10-28-070 Storage of goods on public ways.

No person shall use any public way for the storage of personal property, goods, wares or merchandise of any kind. Nor shall any person place or cause to be placed in or upon any public way any barrel, box, hogshead, crate, package or other obstruction of any kind, or permit the same to remain thereon longer than is necessary to convey such article to or from the premises abutting on such sidewalk.

For this purpose of receiving or delivering merchandise, no person shall occupy over four feet of the outer edge of the sidewalk in front of his store or building.

Any person violating any of the provisions of this section shall be subject to fine of not less than $5.00 nor more than $10.00 for each offense.
(Prior code § 34-6)

Article II. Carts Belonging to Retail Stores

§10-28-120 Police enforcement.

It shall be the duty of the superintendent of police to see to the enforcement of the foregoing provisions of this chapter, and every policeman shall, whenever there is any obstruction in any public way, endeavor to remove the same; and, in case such obstruction shall be of such a character that the same cannot readily be removed, then such policeman shall report the same to the department of transportation, and the said department shall remove such obstruction.
(Prior code § 34-7; Amend. Coun. J. 12-11-91, p. 10832)

§10-28-121 to 10-28-128 Reserved.

(Repealed Coun. J. 12-15-99, p. 21529)

Article III. Newspaper Stands

§10-28-130 Permit required.

It shall be unlawful for any person to erect, locate, construct or maintain any newspaper stand on the public way or any other unenclosed property owned or controlled by the city without obtaining a permit therefor from the commissioner of transportation as hereinafter provided. No new permit for a newspaper stand shall be issued on or after the effective date of this ordinance; provided that permits that have expired or have been revoked may be reissued as provided in this article.
(Prior code § 34-8; Amend. Coun. J. 6-28-91, p. 2872; 12-11-91, p. 10832)

§10-28-170 Construction and maintenance.

Newspaper stands shall be constructed in accordance with the general design therefor to be approved by the commissioner of transportation. The height of such stand shall not exceed nine feet. A newspaper stand, including any rack, awning, or overhang attached thereto, may occupy no more than 120 square feet of public property.

Such stands shall be constructed in accordance with specifications set forth in rules and regulations gated by the commissioner of transportation after consultation with the department of construction and permits.

(Prior code § 34-11; Amend. Coun. J. 6-28-91, p. 2872; 12-11-91, p. 10832; 3-5-03, p. 104990)

§10-28-180 Limitation on use.

The maintenance of newspaper stands subject to regulation under this article shall be under the direction and supervision of the commissioner of transportation. Each such newspaper stand must be maintained in a safe, neat and clean condition and shall be kept free of graffiti. No advertising bill, poster, card, or other advertising matter of any kind whatsoever shall be exhibited, displayed or placed on, or affixed to, any such stand. A newspaper stand shall be used for no purpose other than the exhibition and sale of newspapers, periodicals and similar publications. On the outside of each newspaper stand there shall be clearly displayed at all times a sign stating the name, business telephone number and address of the permit holder. In addition, a copy of the permit shall be displayed prominently inside the newspaper stand. Any newspaper stand that is not in compliance with this requirement shall be removed by the city pursuant to this article.

(Prior code § 34-12; Amend. Coun. J. 6-28-91, p. 2872; 12-11-91, p. 10832)

§10-28-185 Erection—Location.

(a) No newspaper stand may be erected, located or maintained if the site or location of the newspaper stand endangers public safety or property; or when such site or location is used for public utility purposes, public transportation purposes or other governmental uses; or when such newspaper stand unreasonably interferes with or impedes the flow of pedestrian or vehicular traffic, the ingress into or egress from any residence or place of business, or the use of poles, posts, traffic signs or signals, hydrants, mailboxes, or other objects permitted at or near such location.

(b) No newspaper stand shall be situated so that the clear space for the passage of pedestrians on the sidewalk is reduced to less than six feet. No newspaper stand shall be placed within three feet of any area improved with a lawn, flowers, shrubs or trees or within three feet of any display window of any building or in such manner as to impede or interfere with the reasonable use of such window for display purposes. The provisions of this subsection (b) shall not apply prior to January 1, 1992 to any newspaper stand operating pursuant to a permit issued pursuant to this article prior to the effective date of this section.

(c) No seat, chair or canopy shall be attached to the exterior of any newspaper stand.

(d) Each newspaper stand shall be kept locked and secured when not in use.

(e) No newspaper stand shall be equipped with electricity from an outside source unless all appropriate permits therefor have been secured.
(Added. Coun. J. 6-28-91, p. 2872)

§10-28-191 Enforcement authority.

The commissioner of transportation shall have the authority to adopt such orders, rules and regulations as he may deem necessary for the proper administration and enforcement of the provisions of this article.
(Added. Coun. J. 6-28-91, p. 2872; Amend. 12-11-91, p. 10832)

Article IV. Canopies and Marquees

§10-28-200 Permit required.

It shall be unlawful for any person to maintain any canopy or marquee attached to any building or structure, which shall extend over any public way in the city, without first obtaining authority from the city council and a permit from the director of revenue so to do as hereinafter provided.

No such permit shall be issued upon order of the city council until application therefor has been made, proof of insurance has been submitted and payments and deposits made as required. No such permit shall be issued for a period longer than three years. Nothing in this section shall authorize any person to make an opening in, or construct or repair any pavement in the public way or other public place unless such person holds a public way work license if such a license is required by Chapter 10- 20 of this code.
(Prior code § 34-14; Amend. Coun. J. 12-15-99, p. 21529)

§10-28-250 Construction—Clearance.

No canopy or marquee shall be constructed over any public way or other public place unless the lowest part thereof shall extend not less than 12 feet above the surface of the sidewalk thereunder. Failure to maintain a clearance of 12 feet shall be cause for revocation of permit.

Canopies or marquees shall drain toward the buildings or structures to which the same are attached, and shall be constructed of incombustible material and in conformity with the structure of the building or structure to which the same are to be attached.
(Prior code § 34-19)

Article IV-A. Placement of Pay Telephones in Public Way

§10-28-265 Placement of pay telephones in public way.

(a) The director of revenue shall have the authority to enter into contracts that grant to one or more persons, subject to the conditions set forth in the contract and this chapter, the privilege of installing and maintaining pay telephones in the public way. The director of revenue may also contract for the removal of telephones illegally installed or maintained in the public way. Any such contract may be approved as to form and legality by the corporation counsel. In the administration of this section, the director of revenue shall consult and cooperate with all appropriate city departments. The director may at any time cause to be advertised a request for proposals relating to such contracts.

(b) Such contracts and the method of awarding such contracts shall, to the greatest extent possible, be designed to:

(1) Discourage illegal drug sales and other criminal activity that are sometimes associated with and facilitated by pay telephones in the public way;

(2) Reduce the disturbances that pay telephones may tend to promote in residential areas;

(3) Reduce visual clutter in the public way;

(4) Reduce the unnecessary obstruction of pedestrian and vehicular traffic;

(5) Ensure the availability of pay telephones where they are needed for lawful purposes; and

(6) Provide adequate access to pay telephones by disabled persons.

In addition to those considerations, the contracts may generate revenue for the city.

(c) Any contract entered into pursuant to this section shall provide that the privileges granted by the contract are subject to the city council's authority to order the removal of a pay telephone pursuant to subsection (f) of this section. Any such contract shall also permit the city council or the director of revenue to require pay telephones in the public way to have special features designed to reduce criminal activity. In addition, the contract must provide that the alderman must be notified of the location of any pay telephone that is to be situated in the public way in his or her ward pursuant to this section. No person shall be awarded a contract under this section unless the person has a valid certificate of service authority to provide pay telephone service granted by the Illinois Commerce Commission where required by law.

(d) No person may install a pay telephone in the public way on or after the effective date of this section unless the installation is made pursuant to a contract entered into under this section. Beginning January 1, 1993, no pay telephone may remain in the public way other than pursuant to a contract entered into under this section. Any telephone installed or maintained in violation of this paragraph shall be subject to immediate removal at the owner's expense by the city. However, in the case of a telephone deemed to be in the public way as the result of this amendatory ordinance, no such pay telephone shall be removed until at least seven days after a representative of the city has affixed a notice on the telephone stating that it will be subject to removal within seven days, and in no event shall such telephone be removed before December 15, 1994. A list of the locations at which such pay telephones are scheduled to be removed shall be made available for public inspection at least seven days prior to removal of the telephones on that list.

(e) No later than 30 days after the effective date of this section, every person who owns or maintains a pay telephone in the public way must file with the director of revenue a list of the locations of all such telephones owned or maintained by that person. No later than December 1, 1994, every person who maintains a pay telephone that is considered to be in the public way as the result of this amendatory ordinance must file with the director of revenue a list of the locations of those telephones. Any pay telephone in the public way that does not appear on such a list shall be subject to immediate removal at the owner's expense by the city beginning 31 days after the effective date of this section.

(f) The city council may at any time after January 1, 1993 or at any time after the effective date of this section if pursuant to a contract under this section, by ordinance order the removal of a particular pay telephone that is in the public way. Such an ordinance must identify the location of the telephone to be removed. Any pay telephone that is not removed within 14 days after an ordinance ordering its removal is adopted shall be subject to immediate removal at the owner's expense by the city.

(g) Any pay telephone removed by the city pursuant to this section may be reclaimed by its owner within 30 days after its removal. The owner must reimburse the city for its removal and storage costs before any such telephone may be reclaimed. Such costs shall also include the costs of removing any installation ancillary to the pay telephone, and the costs of restoring the public way to its original condition. Any telephone not so reclaimed may be disposed of as unclaimed property. Any contract for the removal of one or more pay telephones may include a provision, in a form subject to the approval of the corporation counsel, for indemnification of the contractor by the city against claims and liabilities arising out of performance of the contract.

(h) Any person who installs or maintains a pay telephone in violation of this section shall be subject to a fine of not less than $50.00 and not more than $200.00 for each offense. Each day that the violation continues shall constitute a separate offense. However, for the period ending six months after the effective date of this amendatory ordinance, no fine shall be imposed with respect to a telephone considered in the public way as the result of this amendatory ordinance unless a removal notice has been posted on the telephone pursuant to this section, or unless the location of the telephone appears on a list of locations scheduled for removal made available to the public pursuant to this section.

(i) As used in this section, (1) "pay telephone" means any publicly accessible self-service or coin or credit card operated telephone; and (2) "public way" has the meaning ascribed to the term in Section 1-4-090, but does not include property within any airport owned by the city.

For purposes of this section, a pay telephone will be considered in the public way beginning on the effective date of this amendatory ordinance if (1) any portion of the telephone or its enclosure is situated on or projects or hangs over the public way; or (2) the telephone is so situated that it can be used by a person standing on the public way.

(j) The director of revenue shall have the authority to promulgate rules and regulations to implement this section.

(k) No provision of this section or any contract issued pursuant to this section may be applied to any transaction in interstate commerce to the extent to which such business may not, under the Constitution and statues of the United States, be made the subject of regulation by the city.

(Added. Coun. J. 6-17-92, p. 18082; Amend. Coun. J. 7-7-92, p. 18789; 10-5-94, p. 57792)

Article V. Awnings

§10-28-270 Permit required.

No awnings shall be erected, constructed or maintained so as to extend over the surface of any public way, until a permit therefor is issued by the director of revenue. The fee for such permit shall be $1.00.
(Prior code § 34-20.1; Amend. Coun. J. 9-13-89, p. 4604; 11-30-94, p. 62597)

§10-28-280 Construction—Maintenance.

All such awnings shall have a minimum clearance of six feet six inches at the lowest part thereof above the surface of the sidewalk. Supporting framework shall not be less than seven feet six inches from the sidewalk to the lowest part thereof when lowered for use. All structural parts of awnings shall be maintained in good and safe condition as is required by the building commissioner and the executive director of the department of construction and permits, and if not so maintained the permit may be revoked by the executive director.
(Prior code § 34-20.2; Amend. Coun. J. 9-13-89, p. 4604; 3-5-03, p. 104990)

Article V-A. Obstruction of Streets, Sidewalks and Public Places for Construction and Building Maintenance Purposes

§10-28-281 Definitions.

For the purposes of this chapter, the following terms shall be defined as follows:

(a) "Apron" shall mean a platform extending from the exterior wall of a building at any level.

(b) "Commissioner" shall mean the commissioner of transportation.

(c) "Construction canopy" shall mean a temporary structure erected adjacent to a building undergoing construction, demolition, repair or maintenance which is designed to catch construction materials, and which obstructs any public way or public place but allows for pedestrian traffic to pass under the structure.

(d) "Heavy duty construction canopy" shall mean a construction canopy designed to carry a live load of at least 250 pounds per square foot.

(e) "Light duty construction canopy" shall mean a construction canopy designed to carry a live load of at least 150 pounds per square foot and up to 250 pounds per square foot.

(f) "Public place" shall mean any exterior location open to the public, but shall not include the public way.

(g) "Public protection measures" shall mean the installation of a construction canopy or other temporary structure over, or the closure of, the public way or a public place, as necessary to ensure the safety of the public.

(h) "Type I activity" shall means work on a building which involves alteration, repair of exterior facade, work conducted pursuant to critical examination program, or demolition. This includes but is not limited to, tuckpointing.

(i) "Type II activity" shall mean work which involves the construction of a new building.

(j) "Type III activity" shall mean any routine maintenance work on a building within the Central Business District, as defined in Section 9-4-010, which does not require the removal of any physical structures. This includes, but is not limited to, painting, cleaning and window washing.
(Added. Coun. J. 12-4-02, p. 99026)

§10-28-281.1 Public protection measures.
No person may engage in a Type 1, Type II or Type III activity unless public protection measures are taken with respect to the public way or public place beneath or adjacent to the work being performed.
(Added. Coun. J. 12-4-02, p. 99026)

§10-28-281.2 Permit required.
(A) The taking of public protection measures for a Type I, Type II and Type III activity shall require a permit issued by the commissioner subject to the requirements of this section.

(B) For an obstruction caused by a construction canopy, the person providing the canopy must apply for and obtain the permit.

(C) For an obstruction of a public place for a Type III activity, the building's owner shall provide to the department of transportation a complete schedule of prospective Type III activities for that owner's building for a one year period. The owner shall be required to submit the schedule no earlier than December 15 and no later than the last business day of each year for the preceding year. The permit for an obstruction of a public place for a Type III activity in a public place shall expire on December 31 in the year for which the permit is issued. For the year 2003, the owner shall submit the schedule no later than March 1, 2003.

(D) An application for a permit issued pursuant to this section shall contain (1) the name of the applicant; (2) the name, address and telephone number of the owner of the building requiring the obstruction and, if applicable, the provider of the construction canopy; (3) the location of the proposed obstruction; (4) the purpose of the obstruction; (5) whether the obstruction is (a) for the alteration, maintenance or repair of a building's exterior facade; (b) for exterior work conducted pursuant to the city's critical examination program, Sections 13-196-033 through 13-496-037; (e) for demolition; (d) for new construction; or (c) for any other type of construction or maintenance; (6) the proposed commencement date and the estimated duration of the obstruction; and (7) evidence of a public liability insurance policy issued by an insurer authorized to transact business in Illinois, in an amount not less than $1,000,000.00 and naming the city of Chicago as additional insured.

(E) All information in the permit application must be kept current. The permittee must notify the commissioner of any changes within 5 business days, and any appropriate additional fees shall be assessed. if permittee wishes to conduct work different from that listed on the permit application, or wishes to change the location of the obstructed area, the permittee must file an amended application for a permit. The permittee must then pay any applicable additional fees based on the amendments to the permit.

(F) Any permit issued pursuant to the terms of this section may be revoked by the commissioner at any time for violation of the terms of the permit.

(G) The commissioner may delay issuance of a permit in order to prevent interference with other work in progress on the public way, a parade, or special events, for which necessary permits have already been issued.

(H) Nothing in this section shall require a permit for a dumpster as defined in Section 10-28-799(A) of the code, that is validly permitted pursuant to Section 10-28-799.

(Added. Coun. J. 12-4-02, p. 99026)

§10-28-281.4 Prohibited uses of traffic and curb lanes.

A permit issued pursuant to this chapter does not allow its holder to locate a temporary office or other structure, or any materials within an obstructed traffic or curb lane. The permit holder also may not locate a vehicle within an obstructed traffic or curb lane, unless the vehicle is being used for the expeditious loading or unloading of materials, tools or supplies, or the permittee obtains prior approval from the commissioner. A violation of this section shall result in a fine of $500.00 per day for each violation.

(Added. Coun. J. 12-4-02, p. 99026)

§10-28-281.5 Penalties.

(A) Failure to Obtain Permit. Any person who fails to take public protection measures, or takes public protection measures without having first obtained the necessary permits, or obstructs a public way or public place in the city without having first obtained the necessary permit from the commissioner of transportation, or who violates the terms or conditions of a permit for such work, shall be subject to a penalty for each offense of not less than $500.00 nor more than $2,500.00 per day.

(B) Failure to Amend Permit. If a permittee fails to obtain an amended permit before the permit's expiration date, the permittee and the building owner shall be subject to a fine of not less than $500.00 nor more than $2,500.00 per day for each violation, plus the delinquent permit fees shall be increased by 10 percent.

(C) Non-Compliant Obstruction. If the dimensions of the obstruction exceed the dimensions allowed by the permit, the permittee and the building owner shall jointly be assessed a fine equal to $1,000.00 per day for each violation, plus any appropriate additional fees for the obstruction.

(D) Inactivity. If three consecutive months of inactivity are found at a permitted site on the public way, the permittee and the building owner shall be jointly assessed, in addition to any above fees, a fine of not less than $1,000.00 nor more than $2,500.00 per day. The commissioner of transportation and the commissioner of buildings shall be authorized to inspect the permittee's and the owner's books and records at any time during regular business hours to determine the period of inactivity.

(Added. Coun. J. 12-4-02, p. 99026; Amend. 12-15-04, p. 39840)

Article V-B. Protection of the Public Way and Public Places

§10-28-281.6 Protection required.

(a) When any person conducts a Type I or Type II activity on a building within the Central Business District, a heavy duty construction canopy shall be used to protect the public way or public place. At a minimum, the heavy duty construction canopy shall extend front the building up to the nearest public light pole, planter or other public structure, or 15 feet, whichever is less. When necessary for the public to enter a building during a Type I or Type II activity, all entrances from the street to the building shall also be protected by a heavy duty construction canopy. The area required to be canopied can be altered by the commissioner, if in his opinion, the height of the building and the type of work being conducted necessitates a larger or smaller canopied area.

(b) In all other circumstances, and when conducting a Type III activity, a light duty construction canopy shall be used, with the following exceptions:

(1) When the height of the building does not exceed three stories or 40 feet, a barricade located not less than 10 feet from the building may be used in lieu of a light duty construction canopy.

(2) When the height of a building does not exceed four stories or 50 feet, a fence located not less than 10 feet from the building may be used in lieu of a light duty construction canopy.

(c) The commissioner shall have the authority to require the use of a barricade, fencing or traffic cones in lieu of a construction canopy based on the duration of the obstruction or any traffic concerns which may be caused by the construction canopy.

(Added. Coun. J. 12-4-02, p. 99026)

§10-28-281.7 Fences and barricades.

(a) Fences shall be not less than six feet high of solid construction sheathed with one inch lumber or other approved materials of equal strength.

(b) Barricades shall consist of substantial railings or other barriers which will effectively prevent public access to the barricaded area.

(Added. Coun. J. 12-4-02, p. 99026)

§10-28-281.8 Aprons.

(a) When additional stories are added to an existing building, an apron shall be provided at the level of the lowest additional story and maintained during the period when materials are being placed or handled on the street front.

(b) Aprons shall be constructed of not less than two layers of two-inch planking or of other approved materials of equal strength and shall be designed to support a superimposed load of not less than 250 pounds per square foot. Aprons shall extend not less than six stories from the building wall. Aprons shall slope downward toward the building wall or shall be provided with a substantial curb not less than 12 inches high at the outer edge.

(c) For a building exceeding four stories or 50 feet in height and intended to be demolished, one apron shall be constructed for each four stories above adjoining sidewalk grade with the lowest apron located in the third story.

(Added. Coun. J. 12-4-02, p. 99026)

Article V-C. Construction Canopies

§10-28-284 Closure of sidewalks and bicycle lanes.

(A) Closure of Sidewalks. When the use of a construction canopy results in the total closure of a sidewalk, signs roust be provided warning pedestrians that the sidewalk is closed. The signs must be printed in a type size no less than 4 inches in height, must be located at appropriate adjacent intersections and must also be attached to both sides of the construction canopy. The permittee is responsible for maintaining the signs for the life of the construction project.

(B) Closure of Bicycle Lanes. When the use of a construction canopy results in the closure of a bicycle lane, signs must be provided warning bicyclists of the lane closure and warning vehicles of the need to yield to the bicyclists. The signs must be of a type as designated by the department of transportation. At a minimum, the lane closure signs must be located on both sides of the street in the direction of the approach to the construction canopy at a point 600 feet and 300 feet in front of the construction canopy. In addition, lane closure signs must be attached to the end of the construction canopy facing the approaching bicycle traffic. At a minimum, the yield to bicyclists signs must be located on both sides of the street in the direction of the approach to the construction canopy at a point 100 feet and 50 feet in front of the construction canopy. In addition, yield to bicyclists signs must be attached to the end of the construction canopy facing the approaching bicycle traffic. The permittee is responsible for maintaining the signs for the life of the construction project.

(Added. Coun. J. 12-4-02, p. 99026)

§10-28-285 Sidewalks—Damage deposit required.

In any building operation which would require the driving of vehicles or equipment upon or across any public sidewalk abutting the premises, the applicant shall obtain from the commissioner a certificate of prior inspection which shall state the condition of the sidewalk before construction is started. The commissioner is hereby authorized to charge a fee of $10.00 for each such prior inspection, to estimate probable damage that might be caused to such public sidewalk by the driving of vehicles or equipment thereon, and to require a deposit by the applicant of moneys sufficient to restore said sidewalk to a condition as good as it was before construction was started.

When the commissioner receives satisfactory proof that the affected sidewalk has been restored to a condition equally as good as before the permitted work, he shall certify this fact to the city comptroller. The comptroller shall thereupon direct the city treasurer to refund the amount deposited in connection with the permit.

(Added. Coun. J. 12-4-02, p. 99026)

§10-28-286 Violation—Penalty.

Any person who shall violate any of the provisions of Sections 10-28-281 through 10-28-285 for which no specific penalty is provided, shall be fined $500.00 per day for each violation.

(Added. Coun. J. 12-4-02, p. 99026)

Article IX. Use of Subsidewalk Space

§10-28-450 Permit required.

Unless otherwise permitted by specific ordinance, no person shall use any space underneath the surface of any public way or other public ground in this city, or construct or maintain any structure thereunder, or disturb the sidewalk on such public way or other public ground, for the purpose of constructing or maintaining any vault or structure thereunder, or any coalhole, trapdoor or other opening therein, without first obtaining a permit so to do from the director of revenue. No permit shall be issued, transferred or assigned, nor shall any right or privilege thereunder be transferred or assigned, except as hereinafter provided. Nothing in this section shall authorize any person to make an opening in, or construct or repair any pavement in the public way or other public place unless such person holds a public way work license if such a license is required by Chapter 10-20 of this code.

The number, location, size, construction and maintenance of all coalholes, trapdoors, or other openings in the public ways and the construction and maintenance of all vaults shall be under the direction and subject to the approval of the director of revenue.

If any person uses any space underneath any public way without a permit for such use as herein provided, the director of revenue shall notify the person in writing of the violation of this section and shall demand the removal of the illegal structure and restoration of the public way to its former condition, within five days after delivery of the notice. If the structure is not removed within that time, the director shall proceed to remove such structure and close the space therein. The costs of removal and restoration of the public way shall be paid by the person who illegally used the space under the public way.

(Prior code § 34-36; Amend. Coun. J. 12-11-91, p. 10832; 12-15-99, p. 21529)

§10-28-575 Vault space.

(a) Every user of vault space, that is located under the public way and that has an area of at least 30 square feet and that is deeper than three feet below the surface grade of the public way, shall cause the vault to be inspected periodically under the certification of a licensed engineer. Vaults within the central business district, as defined in Chapter 9-4 of this code, shall be inspected annually; vaults outside the central business district shall be inspected no less than once every three years. Required inspections shall be conducted at the vault user's expense. The user of the vault shall maintain records of inspections under this section for a period of three years, and shall make the records available for review by the department of transportation on demand during regular business hours.

(b) If the inspection indicates the need for any repairs, alterations or other work, the vault user shall prepare a written report indicating the following: the location of the vault; the purpose for which the vault is used; the date of commencement of the work; the date of completion of the work; the nature of the work; and the name and address of each contractor performing any portion of the work. The report shall be filed with the department of transportation in accordance with rules issued by the commissioner of transportation. In preparing the rules, the commissioner shall consider the purpose for which the vault space is used, the nature of equipment or items stored in a space, the proximity of vault space to the public way, and other factors that may affect public safety.

(c) Any vault user who fails to obtain a required inspection, or who fails to maintain inspection records or file a required inspection report, or who provides false or misleading information in an inspection report, shall be subject to a fine of not less than $200.00 and not more than $500.00 for each offense. Each day that a violation continues shall constitute a separate and distinct offense.
(Added. Coun. J. 2-9-94, p. 45320)

Article XI-A. Newsracks

§10-28-750 Definitions—Newsracks.

As used in this article, unless the context clearly requires otherwise:

"Newsrack" means any self-service or coin-operated box, container or other dispenser installed, used, or maintained on the public way for the sale or distribution of newspapers, periodicals or other publications from that dispenser.

"Distributor" means the person responsible for placing, installing or maintaining a newsrack on the public way.

"Public way" shall have the meaning ascribed to the term in Section 1-4-090 of this code.

"Commissioner" means the commissioner of transportation or his or her designee.

"Central Business District" has the meaning ascribed to the term in Section 9-4-010.

"Multiple newsrack" means a newsrack designed to dispense two or more different publications.

"Intersection" means that portion of the public way which surrounds the intersecting portion of two or more roadways, extended along each roadway to the midpoint of each block.
(Added. Coun. J. 4-1-98, p. 65351)

§10-28-755 Newsracks—Permitted when.

Notwithstanding Section 10-28-040 or any other provision of this code, newsracks may be placed on the public way as permitted by this article.
(Added. Coun. J. 4-1-98, p. 65351)

§10-28-760 Newsracks—Prohibited locations.

No newsrack shall be placed, installed or maintained:

(a) Within five feet of any marked or unmarked crosswalk;

(b) Within five feet of a fire hydrant;

(c) At any location where the clear space for the passageway of pedestrians is reduced to less than six feet in the Central Business District, or less than three feet outside the Central Business District;

(d) On any area of lawn, flowers or shrubs or other similar landscaping, or in such a manner where ordinary use of the newsrack will cause damage to such landscaping;

(e) Within five feet of any driveway, alley, loading zone, handicapped ramp or curb cut;

(f) On any grating or manhole cover;

(g) On any surface where the newsrack will cause damage to or interfere with the use of any pipes, vault areas or telephone or electrical cables and wires;

(h) In the case of a multiple newsrack, within two feet of a curb face;

(i) Within the initial 20 feet of any area used by the Chicago Transit Authority for loading and unloading passengers at a bus stop, measured from the front position of the bus;

(j) Within a multiple newsrack area except as permitted by this article;

(k) Outside of a multiple newsrack area but within 200 feet of a multiple newsrack lawfully situated within such an area.

(Added. Coun. J. 4-1-98, p. 65351)

§10-28-770 Maximum dimensions.

No person shall place, install or maintain a newsrack on the public way if such newsrack exceeds 26 inches in width, 26 inches in depth, or 50 inches in height; provided, however, that a coin slot not exceeding 10 inches in width, 10 inches in depth, or 25 inches in height, may be attached to the top of the newsrack, as long as the combined height of the newsrack and coin slot does not exceed 65 inches. This prohibition does not apply to multiple newsracks that are placed, installed or maintained within a multiple newsrack area in accordance with this article.

(Prior code § 34-13.1; Added. Coun. J. 7-12-90, p. 18399; Amend. 12-11-91, p. 10832; 4-1-98, p. 65351)

§10-28-775 Advertising signs on newsracks— Prohibited.

No person shall place, install or maintain on any newsrack on the public way an advertising sign as defined in Title 17, Section 3.2 (17-12-020) of the Chicago Zoning Ordinance, as amended.

(Prior code § 34-13.2; Added. Coun. J. 7-12-90, p. 18399; Amend. 12-11-91, p. 10832; 4-1-98, p. 65351; 6-9-99, p. 5442)

§10-28-781 Multiple newsracks.

(a) The commissioner of transportation, after consultation with the commissioner of planning and development and the alderman of any affected ward, may designate any portion or portions of the public way as a multiple newsrack area. The area need not be contiguous. Within such an area, the placement, installation and maintenance of newsracks shall be prohibited, except as authorized by contract awarded under this section for the placement, installation and maintenance of multiple newsracks. The commissioner of transportation shall make such designation only if the commissioner determines that the designated area contains on each intersection within the area all or a portion of a group of at least five newsracks that are separated by a combined distance of 12 feet or less, and that the area requires such designation based upon the following considerations:

(1) The current number of newsracks within or near the proposed area so as to avoid undue concentration of newsracks;

(2) The impact on pedestrian and vehicular traffic and accessibility to public transportation;

(3) The impact on and proximity to buildings used for residential purposes;

(4) The resources available to the city to enforce the requirements and restrictions in the proposed area;

(5) The inconsistency of individual newsracks with the character of the surrounding streetscape;

(6) The availability or likely availability of a contractor to provide multiple newsracks in a proposed area.

Before making any such designation, the commissioner shall conduct a survey of existing newsracks, and shall solicit comments from members of the public, community organizations and representatives of newspapers, including any task force organized for the purpose of evaluating or monitoring multiple newsrack programs, and shall consider those comments when determining whether to make the designation. Before making any such designation, the commissioner also shall issue written findings detailing the reasons for such designation. The territory of a multiple newsrack area may be decreased or enlarged in the same manner as the original designation. The restrictions in this section and subsections (j) and (k) of Section 10-28-760 shall not apply until compartments in multiple newsracks at each intersection within the designated area have been made available to persons distributing publications. In addition, the restrictions in this section and subsections (j) and (k) of Section 10-28-760 shall not apply to prohibit the placement of a newsrack dispensing a publication from a location that is further than 400 feet from any newspaper stand or multiple newsrack or any location at which an individual newsrack may be lawfully placed, measured by traversing the public way.

(b) The authority to place, install and maintain multiple newsracks in a multiple newsrack area shall be awarded by contract to a qualified respondent pursuant to a publicly advertised request for proposals issued by the chief procurement officer. The contract shall authorize the installation of at least one multiple newsrack at every intersection in the proposed area, and at other appropriate locations designated in the contract. The contract shall require the contractor to provide space in multiple newsracks at each intersection sufficient to accommodate the number of publications that had been distributed in single newsracks at the intersection at the time of the most recent survey upon which the designation is based, unless the commissioner determines that the requirements of this code, or the existence of street furniture or other physical limitations, prohibits such accommodation. The contract may also require the contractor to remove unlawful newsracks as provided in Section 10-28-785. The contract shall include performance standards applicable to the contractor, and penalties for the failure of the contractor to meet those standards. Separate contracts may be awarded for the fabrication and maintenance of multiple newsracks, if appropriate.

(c) The chief procurement officer shall determine which respondents shall be awarded contracts pursuant to evaluation criteria based upon the following considerations:

(1) The ability of the respondent to place, install and maintain multiple newsracks of suitable design and quality within the multiple newsrack area; to remove unlawful newsracks as required by the contract; and to perform other obligations under the contract;

(2) The ultimate financial cost or economic benefit to the city if a contract is awarded to that respondent;

(3) The degree of participation of minority and women-owned businesses in the contract to the extent that preferences for such businesses are permitted by law; and

(4) The aesthetic appeal and durability of the newsracks proposed by the respondent.

In addition to the considerations set forth above, a respondent may be subject to state and city standards and disclosure requirements that are applicable to bidders on and parties to city contracts in general. No advertising, other than to identify or display publications that are offered in the newsrack, may be displayed on any multiple newsrack.

(d) Any person awarded a contract under this section must place, install and maintain multiple newsracks only as permitted by the contract, this article and the rules and regulations promulgated under this article.

(e) The commissioner shall, after consulting with members of the public, community organizations, and representatives of newspapers, including any task force organized for the purpose of evaluating or monitoring multiple newsrack programs, promulgate rules under which publications shall be assigned to compartments within multiple newsracks maintained by the contractor. The rules shall provide for the random assignment of such publications without regard to the content of the publications, except that the rules may:

(1) Limit access of each publication to one compartment at each intersection whenever the number of publications sought to be distributed exceeds the number of compartments available;

(2) At a particular intersection, give preference to publications with five or more different daily editions published each week, but only if the commissioner determines that, in the absence of such preference, more than 20 publications would be entitled to be distributed from multiple newsracks at that intersection; and

(3) At a particular intersection, give preference to publications that had been contained in single newsracks that were replaced with multiple newsracks at that intersection.

The rules shall provide that, if a publication that was not distributed in an intersection in a multiple newsrack area during a prior assignment requests the use of a compartment in a multiple newsrack at that intersection and if there is no such available compartment, a new application and assignment process shall be conducted promptly for that intersection pursuant to those rules; provided that no more than one new application and assignment process need be conducted at any intersection in any six month period. The rules also shall provide that any compartment that remains empty for a period of 30 days shall be deemed vacant and may be assigned to another publication pursuant to this section. In no event may a publication be prevented from being distributed in at least one multiple newsrack at each intersection within a multiple newsrack area unless the commissioner excludes from the intersection, pursuant to rules promulgated under paragraph (e)(2) and/or (e)(3) of this section, publications with fewer than five different daily editions published each week that had not been contained in single newsracks at that intersection. If, pursuant to rules promulgated under this section, the commissioner excludes from any intersection one or more publications that seek to be distributed at that intersection, the commissioner shall do so by giving preference to publications based upon the greatest number of times per week that the distributor of the publication intends to replenish the newsrack with the publication, using numbers provided by the distributor under oath. In the event of a tie, the commissioner shall exclude the tied publications randomly.

(f) A contract awarded pursuant to this section may contain such penalties, rewards or other inducements as the commissioner or the corporation counsel considers necessary to further the purposes of this article, shall provide that a contractor forfeit any multiple newsracks that it fails to maintain in good repair and free from graffiti, and may provide for arbitration as a means for settling disputes arising under the contract. Any such contract may include a provision, in a form subject to the approval of the corporation counsel, for indemnification of the contractor by the city against claims and liabilities arising out of the contractor's removal of newsracks under this article. The contract shall prohibit the contractor from charging any fee to publications distributed from a multiple newsrack.

(Added. Coun. J. 4-1-98, p. 65351; Amend 6-9-99, p. 5442; Amend. 7-19-00, p. 38206)

§10-28-785 Notice of violation—Removal.

(a) If the commissioner has reason to believe that a newsrack has been placed, installed or maintained on a public way in violation of this article, including any regulation promulgated thereunder, the commissioner shall cause to be placed a notice of violation upon the newsrack. The notice of violation shall state that the newsrack will be removed and destroyed unless the newsrack is brought into compliance with this article within 10 business days of the date of the notice. If the newsrack is not removed or brought into compliance within such 10-day period, and if no hearing has been requested under this section within such period, the commissioner may remove and destroy the newsrack at the expense of the distributor. The notice given under this section also shall state that the distributor may, within 10 days of the date of the notice, request a hearing at which the distributor will be given an opportunity to contest the allegations of the complaint or to demonstrate that the conditions constituting a violation of this article have been remedied. Any interested person shall be given a reasonable opportunity to be heard at the hearing. If, after the hearing, the commissioner determines that a violation of this article continues to occur, the commissioner shall order the distributor to remove the newsrack from the public way.

(b) Any newsrack that remains on the public way for more than 10 days after it has been ordered removed pursuant to this section shall be removed and destroyed by the commissioner at the expense of the distributor.

(c) Notwithstanding any other provision of this section, the commissioner may require a distributor to remove or relocate a newsrack when such removal or relocation is necessary to accommodate a public or private construction or repair project or similar activity. In cases where immediate removal of the newsrack is necessary to protect the health or safety of the public, the commissioner may remove or relocate the newsrack at the distributor's expense and promptly give written notice to the distributor at the address identified on the newsrack of such removal or relocation thereafter. In all other cases, the commissioner shall cause a notice to be placed upon the newsrack, or shall give written notice to the distributor at the address identified on the newsrack, stating that the newsrack must be removed or relocated within 10 days of the date of the notice and the reason for the removal or relocation. If the newsrack is not removed or relocated within the time specified by the commissioner, the commissioner shall remove and destroy or relocate the newsrack at the distributor's expense. The commissioner may return a newsrack he or she has not yet destroyed if the distributor reimburses the city for its costs.

(d) Any newsrack that is subject to removal and destruction may, at the discretion of the commissioner, instead be moved to a nearby location when practicable.

(Added. Coun. J. 4-1-98, p. 65351)

§10-28-790 Violation of this article—Penalty.

Any person who violates this article, including any rules or regulations promulgated thereunder, shall be subject to a fine of not less than $25.00 and not more than $200.00. Each day that a violation occurs shall constitute a separate and distinct offense.

(Added. Coun. J. 4-1-98, p. 65351)

Article XI-B. Refuse Compactors/Grease Containers*

* **Editor's note:** Article XI-B, as added by Section 2 of Council Journal 7-7-99, p. 6985, included eight new sections which were numbered by fours as Sections 10-28-800 through 10-28-828. Because Article XII of this chapter already contains a section numbered Section 10-28-800, the sections added by Council Journal 7-7-99, p. 6985, have been renumbered to be Sections 8-28-791 through 8-28-798.

§10-28-791 Defined.

For purposes of this article, the term "refuse compactor" means a semipermanent, leak and rodent resistant container constructed of impervious material and capable of temporarily storing and reducing the volume of refuse contained within it a minimum of 65 percent. For purposes of this article, the term "grease container" means any container used for the storage, collection or removal of cooking grease or kindred refuse. The owner or his agent or occupant of an occupational unit may erect and maintain a refuse compactor or grease container on the public way only in compliance with the procedures set out in this Article XI-B and shall be granted only if the department of streets and sanitation determines that the premises has no other suitable location for the compactor. The commissioner of the department of streets and sanitation shall have the authority to promulgate rules and regulations regarding the definition of suitable location.

(Added. Coun. J. 7-7-99, p. 6985; Amend. Coun. J. 10-3-01, p. 68141)

§10-28-792 Permit required.

It shall be unlawful for any person to erect, locate, construct or maintain any refuse compactor or grease container on the public way or any other unenclosed property owned or controlled by the city of Chicago without obtaining a permit therefor from the commissioner of streets and sanitation as hereinafter

provided. Notwithstanding any other provision of this municipal code, such permit is the only authorization required for placement of a refuse compactor or grease container on the public way. There shall be no permit fee or application fee for a permit for a refuse compactor or a grease container on the public way. The administration of city permits for use of the public way for refuse compactors or grease containers obtained prior to the effective date of this ordinance shall be transferred from the department of revenue to the department of streets and sanitation. Such permittees shall receive notice that no annual fees shall be due to the city. The requirements of this article do not include those refuse compactors or grease containers installed on private property. The commissioner or his designee may grant a waiver or variance from this requirement at his discretion, pursuant to standards created through the promulgation of rules and regulations.
(Added. Coun. J. 7-7-99, p. 6985)

§10-28-795 Revocation of permit.

The commissioner of streets and sanitation shall revoke the refuse compactor or grease container public way permit issued to any person who erects or maintains the refuse compactor or grease container in violation of the terms of the permit or of any provision of this municipal code. Before revoking the permit, the commissioner shall notify the permit holder in writing of the nature of the charged violation, of the commissioner's intent to revoke the permit and of the permit holder's opportunity for a hearing on the charge. The notice shall be given either by first class mail or by personal service. Within 15 days after the mailing of the notice, the permit holder may submit a written request for a hearing. Upon receipt of a timely request for a hearing, the commissioner shall institute an action with the department of administrative hearings. Administrative hearings for the adjudication of permit revocations issued pursuant to this section shall be conducted by the department of administrative hearings in accordance with Chapter 2-14 of this code.
(Added. Coun. J. 7-7-99, p. 6985)

§10-28-796 Violation—Penalty.

In addition to the revocation procedure described in Section 10-28-795, a person found guilty of erecting or maintaining a refuse compactor or grease container on the public way without a permit or in violation of this section shall be subject to a fine of not less than $200.00 and not more than $500.00 for each offense, as well as attorney's fees and costs of prosecution. Each day that a violation shall continue shall constitute a separate and distinct offense. The owner of a refuse compactor or grease container erected or maintained in violation of this chapter may be notified by the department of streets and sanitation to remove the container within 24 hours of such notification or shall be subject to removal by the city at the owner's expense. Such violation(s) shall also be reported to the department of health for appropriate action.
(Added. Coun. J. 7-7-99, p. 6985)

§10-28-798 Enforcement authority.

The commissioner of streets and sanitation shall have the authority to adopt such orders, rules and regulations as he may deem necessary for the proper administration and enforcement of the provisions of this article.
(Added. Coun. J. 7-7-99, p. 6985)

Article XI-C. Dumpsters/Roll-Off Boxes on the Public Way

§10-28-799 Dumpsters/roll-off boxes on the public way.

(A) Definitions. For purposes of this section, the following terms shall have the following meanings:

(1) (a) "Dumpster" shall mean any container used for the storage, collection, or removal of construction debris, demolition debris, or other discarded material but shall not include a refuse compactor or grease container, as defined in Section 10-28-791 of the code, and shall also not include the refuse containers described in Section 7-28-210 of the code.

(b) "Class A dumpster" shall mean a dumpster with a capacity of 30 cubic yards or less.

(c) "Class B dumpster" shall mean a dumpster with a capacity of greater than 30 cubic yards.

(2) "Graffiti" shall mean an inscription, drawing, mark or design that is painted, sprayed or otherwise placed on or in a dumpster without the consent of the provider.

(3) "Provider" shall mean the person who leases or otherwise provides a dumpster for temporary use at the location requested.

(B) Permit Required. It shall be unlawful for any provider to place or maintain a dumpster on the public way unless such provider shall first obtain a dumpster permit. The department of transportation shall send by facsimile transmission a copy of the dumpster permit to the ward superintendent of the affected ward. A provider obtaining a valid dumpster permit pursuant to this section shall not be required to also obtain the permit required by Section 13-32-140 of the code for such dumpster.

(C) Application. An application for a dumpster permit shall be made to the commissioner of transportation by the provider. In addition to such other information as the commissioner may require, the applicant shall state:

(1) The name, address and telephone number of the provider of the dumpster(s);

(2) The number of dumpster(s) intended to occupy the permitted location;

(3) The class of the dumpster(s) to be provided;

(4) The street address adjacent to where the dumpster(s) will be located;

(5) The intended use of the dumpster(s);

(6) The intended period of occupancy of the dumpster(s).

During the term of the permit, in the event the permit holder seeks to provide a larger class of dumpster than specified in the dumpster permit, or extend the time of occupancy beyond the time specified in the dumpster permit, application must be made to the commissioner of transportation for an amendment to the permit, and the appropriate adjustment to the permit fee must be submitted. Any change to subsections (C)(2), (C)(4) or (C)(5) of this section will require application for and issuance of a new dumpster permit. Provided, however, that if the change to subsection (C)(4) of this section is necessitated by the presence of a fire hydrant or other object preventing legal placement of the dumpster at the street address for which initial application is made, an amendment to the permit will be acceptable, for no additional fee.

(D) Insurance. No dumpster permit shall be issued until the applicant for such permit shall first have presented to the commissioner of transportation proof of insurance against any liability, loss or claim arising out of the issuance of dumpster permits, or out of the placement, presence, use, maintenance or removal of the dumpsters. Such insurance shall be issued by an insurer authorized to do business in Illinois, shall be in an amount no less than $1,000,000.00 and shall name the city of Chicago, its officers, employees and agents as additional insured. The insurance policy shall provide for 30 days written notice to the commissioner of transportation prior to any lapse, cancellation or change in coverage. The insurance shall be maintained in effect at all times that the dumpster remains on the public way.

(E) Security. No dumpster permit shall be issued until the applicant for such permit shall first have provided to the commissioner of transportation a letter of credit in the amount of $5,000.00 to ensure compliance with the provisions of this section and the permits issued thereunder, including payment of any costs, fees and fines and proper restoration of the public way upon removal of the dumpsters. The form of such letter of credit shall be set forth by regulation and shall be subject to the approval of the corporation counsel. The commissioner of transportation shall provide at least 30 days written notice to the permittee, specifying the conditions or circumstances to be corrected, before drawing on a permittee's letter of credit.

(F) Upon good cause shown, the commissioner of transportation, in his or her discretion may require, instead of such insurance and letter of credit, any alternative form of indemnity, protection or security that he or she deems necessary to accomplish the above described purposes.

(G) Permit Fee. The permit fee for each dumpster permitted pursuant to this section shall be as follows:

(1) (a) For the placement of each class A dumpster not to exceed three days, $50.00.

(b) For the placement of each class B dumpster not to exceed three days, $100.00.

(2) (a) For the placement of each class A dumpster exceeding three days, a monthly fee of $100.00.

(b) For the placement of each class B dumpster exceeding three days, a monthly fee of $200.00.

(3) The fee for placement of each dumpster within the central business district, as that area is delineated in Section 9-4-010 of the code, shall be twice the amount set forth in subsections (1) and (2) above.

(4) Fees for removal and replacement and/or disabling of parking meters provided for by Section 9-68-050 of the code, as applicable.

(H) Dumpster Identification. It shall be the duty of the provider to paint or otherwise permanently affix on each dumpster: (1) the name and telephone number of the provider according to the following standards: the letters and numerals shall be a minimum of three inches in height, shall be clearly legible from a distance of 30 feet, and shall be painted or otherwise affixed on both long sides of the dumpster, 12 inches down from the top or lip, and 12 inches from the corner, and (2) a unique identification number for the dumpster.

(I) Location. No dumpster may be placed in any of the following locations:

(1) Within 40 feet of any bus stop;

(2) On any arterial street between November 1st and April 1st, if the department of transportation has provided notice of a Phase 3 snow emergency by facsimile transmission to the provider and has provided a 12-hour period from the time of transmission to remove such dumpster;

(3) Within 10 feet of any parking space designated for persons with disabilities;

(4) Within 10 feet of any pedestrian crosswalk;

(5) Within 10 feet of any intersection;

(6) Within 20 feet of any fire hydrant;

(7) On any parkway or sidewalk, unless the dumpster provider demonstrates to the satisfaction of the commissioner of transportation that an alternative location is not feasible and that placement of the dumpster(s) on such parkway or sidewalk would not create a safety hazard, disrupt pedestrian or vehicular traffic, or damage public or private property.

(J) Placement, Appearance And Maintenance of Dumpster. It shall be the responsibility of the provider:

(1) Upon delivery, to place the dumpster immediately adjacent to the property identified by the street address stated on the permit application;

(2) Upon delivery, to provide the dumpster free of graffiti;

(3) Within three business days of receiving notification via facsimile transmission from the department of transportation, to remove graffiti from the dumpster(s) identified in the notification;

(4) To maintain the dumpster free of gaps or holes so as to prevent the spillage of materials from the dumpster onto the public way;

(5) To affix and maintain, on each of the four corners of the dumpster, high-intensity retro-reflective sheeting, or other retro-reflective or prismatic material or substance approved by the department of transportation, a minimum of three feet in length, and two inches in width along each side of the corner;

(6) When transporting or otherwise moving a dumpster, to ensure that no portion of the load is falling, sifting, blowing, dropping or in any way escaping from the dumpster. The provider shall use a tarpaulin or other appropriate cover to secure the top of a dumpster while in transit.

(K) Penalties.

(1) Any person violating subsection (B) of this section shall be subject to a fine of not less than $250.00 nor more than $1,500.00 for each offense. Provided, however, that any person violating subsection (B) of this section within the central business district, as that area is delineated in Section 9-4-010 of the code, shall be subject to a fine of not less than $500.00 nor more than $3,000.00 for each offense.

(2) Any person violating any provision other than subsection (B) of this section shall be subject to a fine of not less than $50.00 nor more than $1,000.00 for each offense. Provided, however, that any person violating any provision other than subsection (B) of this section within the central business

district, as that area is delineated in Section 9-4-010 of the code, shall be subject to a fine of not less than $100.00 nor more than $2,000.00 for each offense.

(3) Each day that a violation is permitted to exist shall constitute a separate offense. In addition, any dumpster in the public way not bearing the dumpster identification information required by subsection (H) of this section, not validly permitted, or not located immediately adjacent to the street address specified in the permit may be removed by the city, and all costs associated with such removal shall be borne by the provider of the dumpster. The owner of a dumpster, if different from a provider, shall be jointly and severally liable with the provider for any violation of this section.

(4) In addition to any other available penalties and remedies provided for in the code, one or more citations for violation of this section on each of three or more separate days within a three month period at the same construction site may result in a stop work order issued by the department of transportation, directing that all activity cease for 10 days. Any further citation for violation at the same construction site within six months after the initial stop work order may result in the issuance of another 10 day stop work order. The department shall lift a 10 day stop work order only if sufficient evidence of compliance with this chapter is provided to the department. As used in this section, the term "construction site" has the meaning ascribed to the term in Section 13-32-125.

(a) It shall be unlawful for any person to knowingly violate a stop work order, or to knowingly cause, permit, encourage, assist, aid, abet or direct another person to violate a stop work order, or to knowingly in any manner be a party to a violation of a stop work order.

Any person who violates this subsection upon conviction shall be punished, as follows:

(i) Incarceration for a term not less than three days, nor more than six months, under the procedures set forth in Section 1-2-1.1 of the Illinois Municipal Code, as amended, and the Illinois Code of Criminal Procedure of 1963, as amended;

(ii) Community service of not less than 10 hours, nor more than 100 hours; and

(iii) A fine of $5,000.00.

(b) It shall be unlawful for any person to knowingly destroy, deface, remove, damage, impair, mar, cover or obstruct any stop work order that a city official has posted or affixed at a work site.

Any person who violates this subsection upon conviction shall be punished, as follows:

(i) Incarceration for a term not less than three days, nor more than six months, under the procedures set forth in Section 1-2-1.1 of the Illinois Municipal Code, as amended, and the Illinois Code of Criminal Procedure of 1963, as amended;

(ii) Community service of not less than 10 hours. nor more than 100 hours; and

(iii) A fine not less than $200.00, nor more than $500.00.

(Added. Coun. J. 11-1-00, p. 43330; Amend. 12-15-04, p. 40435)

Article XII. Sidewalk Cafes

§10-28-800 Definitions.

Wherever used in this article, unless the context clearly indicates otherwise:

(a) "Alcoholic beverages" means and includes alcohol, spirits, wine and beer.

(b) "Department of revenue" means the department of revenue of the city of Chicago.

(c) "Director" means the director of the department of revenue of the city of Chicago.

(d) "Food" means any raw, cooked or processed edible substance or ingredient, used or intended for use in whole or in part for human consumption, and shall include nonalcoholic beverages allowed to be sold in accordance with this article, but shall not include alcoholic beverages.

(e) "Person" is defined as provided in Section 1-4-090(e) of the code.

(f) "Sidewalk cafe" means a portion of an immobile retail food establishment located on a public right-of-way, whether directly adjacent to, or in close proximity to, the retail food establishment.

(Added. Coun. J. 3-15-00, p. 27687)

§10-28-805 Permit required for sidewalk cafe.

A permit, which shall be known as a sidewalk cafe permit, shall be required to operate a sidewalk cafe. A sidewalk cafe permit shall be valid from April 1st to and including November 1st in the year of its issuance. The fee for a sidewalk cafe permit shall be determined by the director, taking into account land values, and shall be set forth by regulation.

(Added. Coun. J. 3-15-00, p. 27687)

§10-28-830 Permit—Assignment or transfer prohibited.

No permittee shall assign or transfer a sidewalk cafe permit.

(Added. Coun. J. 3-15-00, p. 27687)

§10-28-835 Permit for one retail food establishment only.

A sidewalk cafe shall be for the exclusive use of the licensed retail food establishment stated on the application. Sharing or other joint use of a sidewalk cafe location by more than one retail food establishment shall not be permitted.

(Added. Coun. J. 3-15-00, p. 27687)

§10-28-840 Permit for food and alcoholic beverage service only.

A sidewalk cafe permit shall only authorize food and alcoholic beverage service at the sidewalk cafe. Regardless of what other activity may take place inside the establishment pursuant to license or permit, such activity shall not be allowed at the sidewalk cafe by virtue of the sidewalk cafe permit.

(Added. Coun. J. 3-15-00, p. 27687)

§10-28-845 Operational conditions.

(a) Sidewalk cafes permitted under this article shall not operate earlier than 8:00 a.m nor later than twelve midnight.

(b) Sidewalk cafes permitted under this article shall not play music, whether live or recorded, nor allow music to be played at the sidewalk cafe, other than through headphones.

(c) The operator of a sidewalk cafe shall install and maintain a physical boundary separating the permitted outdoor seating from the remainder of the public way. The operator shall leave six feet of public way unobstructed for pedestrian passage; the director may alter this requirement by regulation in a situation where adherence to the requirement would make operation of a sidewalk cafe impossible and reduction of the unobstructed portion of the public way would not compromise pedestrian safety. The construction, configuration and other characteristics of the boundary, including landscaping, shall be set forth by regulation.
(Added. Coun. J. 3-15-00, p. 27687)

§10-28-850 Alcoholic beverage service—Requirements.

If alcoholic beverages are served at the sidewalk cafe, the operator must be validly licensed under the code for such sales. Alcoholic beverages supplied by the customer or by any person other than the permittee will not be allowed at sidewalk cafes.
(Added. Coun. J. 3-15-00, p. 27687)

§10-28-855 Compliance with code and rules and regulations required.

All holders of a sidewalk cafe permit and their employees shall be subject to and comply with all applicable requirements and standards for retail food establishments contained in the code, as amended, and the rules and regulations promulgated thereunder, and all laws, rules and regulations pertaining to the sale of alcoholic beverages.
(Added. Coun. J. 3-15-00, p. 27687)

§10-28-860 Promulgation of regulations—Force and effect.

(a) The director is authorized to promulgate regulations to carry out the purposes of this article, including without limitation regulations governing:

(1) The location, arrangement and design of sidewalk cafes to ensure the flow of pedestrian traffic, the safety of pedestrians and auto traffic, the access to buildings and transportation facilities, the prevention of an excessive number of cafes, and the best service to the public;

(2) The size, design and other specifications for tables and serving equipment to be used by operators, and the design of enclosures or partial enclosures;

(3) The types of food and beverages that may be served at sidewalk cafes;

(4) The time periods during which application can be made for a sidewalk cafe permit;

(5) Landscaping and other aesthetic components of the sidewalk cafe; and

(6) Any other matter pertaining to this article.

(b) A permittee shall comply with the regulations promulgated pursuant to this article, which shall have the force and effect of law.
(Added. Coun. J. 3-15-00, p. 27687)

§10-28-865 Hearings.

The director may hold formal and informal hearings prior to the promulgation of rules and regulations as the director deems necessary. All such hearings shall be open to the public.

(Added. Coun. J. 3-15-00, p. 27687)

§10-28-870 Enforcement.

(a) The director or his designee is authorized to take such action as necessary to enforce the provisions of this article, including conducting on-site inspections of sidewalk cafes associated retail food establishments to determine compliance with the permitting and other requirements of this article and regulations promulgated hereunder.

(b) Upon request by the director or his designee, the operator of a sidewalk cafe shall provide for inspection the documents required by this article to operate a sidewalk cafe, including the sidewalk cafe permit, the plan for the sidewalk cafe, and proof of insurance.

(c) Any sidewalk cafe for which a permit is required by this article, and which has failed to obtain such permit, may be closed by the director or his designee until such permit is procured. Upon being notified of closure, all sidewalk cafe activity must cease, and all obstructions in the public way, including boundaries, tables and chairs, must be removed.

(Added. Coun. J. 3-15-00, p. 27687)

§10-28-875 Violation—Penalties.

(a) Any person who violates any of the provisions of this article or regulations promulgated hereunder shall be subject to a fine of not less than $200.00 nor more than $500.00 for each offense, and each day such a violation continues shall be deemed a separate and distinct offense.

(b) In addition to the above fine, and any person who knowingly interferes with or impedes the director of revenue or revenue investigator in the enforcement of this article shall be subject to arrest by a duly authorized peace officer of the department and imprisonment for a term not to exceed six months under the procedures set forth in Section 1-2-1.1 of the Illinois Municipal Code and under the provisions of the Illinois Code of Criminal Procedure.

(c) Any sidewalk cafe in operation without a valid sidewalk cafe permit is subject to removal from the public way by the director or his designee. The provisions of Section 10-28-020 of the code shall apply to the removal of any portion of a sidewalk cafe from the public way, whether for unpermitted operation or for obstruction of public way; provided, however, that the amount of the fine for a violation shall be as set forth in this section.

(Added. Coun. J. 3-15-00, p. 27687)

§10-28-880 Violation—Permit revocation.

In addition to fines and other penalties as provided for herein, three or more violations of any provision of this article or regulations promulgated hereunder within a permit period shall subject the permittee to revocation of the sidewalk cafe permit by the director.

(Added. Coun. J. 3-15-00, p. 27687)

Article XIII. Violation of Chapter Provisions

§10-28-990 Violation—Penalty.

Any person violating any of the provisions of this chapter, where no other penalty is specifically provided, shall be fined not more than $50.00 for each offense.

(Prior code § 34-50; Amend. Coun. J. 3-15-00, p. 27687)

CHAPTER 10-32
TREES, PLANTS AND SHRUBS
(Selected Sections)

Sections:

10-32-010 Definitions.
10-32-020 Authority of commissioner.
10-32-030 Authority of deputy commissioner.
10-32-040 Trees, shrubs or other plant materials—Public nuisance.
10-32-050 Care of parkway.
10-32-060 Permit required.
10-32-070 Application for permit.
10-32-080 Issuance of permit.
10-32-090 Permit fee.
10-32-100 Contents of permit.
10-32-110 Attaching material to tree.
10-32-120 Protection of trees during building operations.
10-32-130 Removal of protective device.
10-32-140 Placing substance on parkways.
10-32-150 Work to be performed according to permit.
10-32-160 Parkway tree as city property.
10-32-170 Causing injury to public tree or shrub.
10-32-180 Organized athletic activity on parkway.
10-32-190 Violation—Penalty.
10-32-200 Replacement or removal of damaged tree or shrub.
10-32-210 Use of fines to defray expenses.
10-32-250 Severability.

§10-32-010 Definitions.

Whenever the following words or terms are used in this chapter, they shall have the following meanings:

(a) "Commissioner" means the commissioner of the department of streets and sanitation, or his designee.

(b) "Deputy commissioner" means the deputy commissioner of the bureau of forestry, parkways and beautification of the department of streets and sanitation, or his designee.

(c) "Parkway" means that portion of the public way between a public street and the nearest parallel property line including sidewalk areas.

(d) "Median" means the center strip of a boulevard or street on which trees, shrubs, or other plant material are planted.

(e) "Shrub" means a multistemmed woody plant.

(f) "Public tree or shrub" includes, without limitation, any shade or ornamental tree or shrub now or hereafter growing on property of the city of Chicago under the jurisdiction of the bureau of forestry, parkways and beautification.

(g) "Parkway tree" means a tree planted in a parkway.

(h) "Forestry operations" means any planting, pruning, cultivation, maintenance or removal of any tree, shrub or other plant material by the deputy commissioner in accordance with this chapter.

(Prior code § 32-1; Amend. Coun. J. 2-6-91, p. 30591)

§10-32-020 Authority of commissioner.

In addition to all other powers and duties conferred on him by this code, the commissioner of streets and sanitation shall have the authority:

(a) To prohibit or restrict parking on any street or portion thereof for the purpose of facilitating forestry operation;

(b) To erect temporary signs designating the street or portion thereof in which the parking of vehicles is prohibited during forestry operations;

(c) To remove and relocate any vehicle parked in violation of such notices, either to the nearest legal parking place or to a facility operated by the city of Chicago for the storage of towed automobiles;

(d) To issue permits in accordance with this chapter;

(e) To supervise the deputy commissioner in his performance of the powers and duties established in this chapter.

(Prior code § 32-2)

§10-32-030 Authority of deputy commissioner.

In addition to all other powers and duties conferred on him by this code, the deputy commissioner shall have the authority:

(a) To plant, prune, cultivate, maintain and remove any tree, shrub or other plant material now or hereafter located on a parkway, median or other public property under his jurisdiction;

(b) To place barricades at streets, curbs, sidewalks and other locations where necessary to protect persons and property during the performance of all forestry operations;

(c) To relocate, after making a reasonable effort to notify the owner thereof, any unauthorized obstruction on a public way which prevents or impedes his ability to perform forestry operations;

(d) To remove any unauthorized object, structure or fixture from a parkway or median;

(e) To enter upon private property within the city of Chicago at all reasonable times for the purpose of examining any tree, shrub or other plant material located upon or over such property, and for the purposes of carrying out the provisions of this chapter;

(f) To issue rules and regulations not inconsistent with this chapter or with any other applicable provisions of the Municipal Code, subject to the approval of the commissioner, governing the planting, pruning, cultivating, maintenance and removal of public plant materials, and for the protection of the parkway and medians;

(g) To prohibit and regulate by such rules the planting of certain varieties of trees, shrubs and other plant material on parkways and medians. In determining which types of trees, shrubs and other plant material should be prohibited or regulated, the deputy commissioner shall consider the adaptability of such tree, shrub or plant material to local weather and soil conditions; the effect of its root system on adjacent sidewalks, curbs, gutters, streets, underground pipes and sewers; its effect on nearby vegetation; and its effect on nearby human and animal life;

(h) In connection with the installation of parkway trees required by Title 17, Section 5.13 (17-20-270), and pursuant thereto, to review plans, to make inspections, to make recommendations to the zoning administrator regarding conformance of required parkway trees with this chapter and with regard to other matters pertaining to the required installation of parkway trees. *(Prior code § 32-3; Amend. Coun. J. 2-6-91, p. 30591)*

§10-32-040 Trees, shrubs or other plant materials—Public nuisance.

Any tree, shrub or other plant material which interferes with the proper spread of light along a street or alley from a streetlight, or interferes with the visibility of any traffic-control sign or device, or does not provide 10-foot clearance above public ways or sidewalks, or has dead, dying, diseased or broken limbs which may be hazardous to public safety, or is dead or diseased or harbors insects or pests which constitute a potential threat to nearby human or animal life or to other trees within the city, is hereby declared to be a public nuisance.

The deputy commissioner shall issue a notice of any such nuisance and cause it to be served upon the owner of the property where such nuisance is located, by delivery at the address of the property or by certified mail. The owner shall cause the condition creating such nuisance to be removed within 10 days after receipt of said notice, at his own expense. If the owner fails or refuses to comply with the provisions of this section, in addition to any other penalties described in this chapter, the commissioner may remove or cause to be removed the condition creating such nuisance and any expense incurred by the city in so doing shall be a charge against the owner, which may be recovered in an appropriate legal proceeding instituted by the corporation counsel. *(Prior code § 32-4)*

§10-32-050 Care of parkway.

The owner or person in control of property contiguous to the parkway shall be responsible for watering and fertilizing parkway trees required to be installed pursuant to Title 17, Section 5.13A of the city's zoning code and for routine care of the parkway lawn. Routine care of the parkway lawn shall include periodic watering, weeding and mowing as well as replacement of vegetation that dies. The owner or person in control of property contiguous to the parkway shall replace any parkway trees required to be installed pursuant to Title 17, Section 5.13A of the city's zoning code in the event of the death of any such trees resulting from the failure to water or fertilize as required herein. *(Prior code § 32-5; Amend. Coun. J. 2-6-91, p. 30591; 7-21-99, p. 9425; 7-10-02, p. 90212)*

§10-32-060 Permit required.

No person other than the deputy commissioner shall plant, remove, trim, spray or chemically inject or treat, or in any way affect the general health or structure of a parkway tree or shrub without first having obtained a permit to do so in accordance with the provisions of this chapter; provided, however, that no permit shall be necessary for the activities described in Section 10-32-050. All

permit requirements of this chapter shall be applicable to governmental agencies and to public utilities governed by an Act concerning Public Utilities, approved June 29, 1921, as amended.
(Prior code § 32-6)

§10-32-070 Application for permit.

Application for a permit under this chapter shall be made on a form prepared by the commissioner, and shall contain the following information:

(a) The name and address of the applicant;

(b) The address of the property adjacent to the parkway where the applicant desires to have work done;

(c) The nature of the work to be done;

(d) The name of the person who is to perform the work;

(e) The estimated starting and completion dates of the work;

(f) Such other and further information as the commissioner shall deem necessary.

(Prior code § 32-7)

§10-32-080 Issuance of permit.

No permit shall issue for any work on a parkway unless:

(a) The application therefor is complete;

(b) The applicant agrees, in writing, to indemnify and hold harmless the city of Chicago, its officers, agents, attorneys and employees from any and all liability or
claims arising from or relating to the granting of a permit and/or the performance of the work for which the permit is sought; and

(c) The person who is to perform the work presents to the commissioner a certificate or other proof of liability insurance in the minimum amount of $50,000.00 for bodily injury and $100,000.00 for property damage, naming the city of Chicago as additional insured.

(Prior code § 32-8; Amend. Coun. J. 2-6-91, p. 30591)

§10-32-090 Permit fee.

The fee for issuance of a permit for work described in Section 10-32-060 shall be $20.00 payable at the time of application. Other permits issued under this chapter shall be issued without charge.
(Prior code § 32-9)

§10-32-100 Contents of permit.

A permit issued hereunder shall state specifically the work permitted to be done, the address of the property adjacent to the parkway where the work is to be done, and the estimated starting date of the work. A permit issued hereunder shall expire 60 days from the date of issuance.
(Prior code § 32-10)

§10-32-110 Attaching material to tree.

No person shall secure, hang, fasten, attach or run any rope, wire, sign, decoration, electrical device or other material upon, around or through any public tree without a permit to do so.
(Prior code § 32-11)

§10-32-120 Protection of trees during building operations.

During the erection, alteration, repair, demolition or removal of any building or structure, or excavation in connection therewith, the owner of the affected property shall place or cause to be placed around each nearby public tree one or more protective devices sufficient to prevent injury to the trunk, crown and root system of each such tree. No such device may be installed without a permit issued by the commissioner, who shall first determine that the devices will not injure the tree; such permit shall specify the manner of erecting or installing each protective device.
(Prior code § 32-12)

§10-32-130 Removal of protective device.

No person shall remove any permitted device intended for the support or protection of a public tree without a permit issued by the commissioner.
(Prior code § 32-13)

§10-32-140 Placing substance on parkways.

No person shall place or maintain or allow to be placed upon a parkway or median any asphalt, cement, stone, lumber or other substance without a permit issued by the commissioner. In determining whether to grant such a permit the commissioner shall consider: the nature of the substance; the quantity of the substance; the length of time during which the substance will remain on the parkway or median; its effect on trees, shrubs and other plant material on the parkway or median; the purpose of placing or maintaining the substance on the parkway or median; and the alternatives which may be available to the applicant.
(Prior code § 32-14)

§10-32-150 Work to be performed according to permit.

Any work to be performed under a permit issued hereunder shall be performed in accordance with said permit, this chapter and the rules and regulations promulgated hereunder. Violation of the terms of a permit, this chapter or rules and regulations promulgated hereunder shall be grounds for suspension or revocation of such permit, in addition to any other penalty provided in this chapter. Upon completion of the work the holder of the permit shall restore the parkway or median to a condition similar to that which existed prior to the work.
(Prior code § 32-15)

§10-32-160 Parkway tree as city property.

Once planted on a parkway, a tree shall become and remain the property of the city and shall be subject to the provision of this chapter.
(Prior code § 32-16)

§10-32-170 Causing injury to public tree or shrub.

No person shall break, tear, paint, deface or damage any public tree or shrub; nor shall any person cause or allow any toxic chemical, gas, salt, oil, or other injurious substance to be dumped, drained or applied to or to seep or drain upon or about any public tree, shrub or other plant materials; provided, however, that this section shall not apply to the salting of streets by the commissioner for the purpose of melting ice and snow.
(Prior code § 32-17)

§10-32-180 Organized athletic activity on parkway.

Parkways and medians shall not be used for organized athletic activity involving more than eight persons, without a permit issued by the commissioner.
(Prior code § 32-18)

§10-32-190 Violation—Penalty.

Any person who violates or fails to comply with any of the provisions of this ordinance shall be fined a sum not less than $10.00, nor more than $500.00 or may be imprisoned for a term not exceeding 60 days, or both. Each day during which any violation shall occur or continue shall be a separate offense.
(Prior code § 32-19)

§10-32-200 Replacement or removal of damaged tree or shrub.

If, as the result of the violation of any provision of this ordinance, the injury, mutilation or death of a public tree, shrub or other plant material is caused, the costs of repair, removal or replacement of such tree, shrub or other plant material or shall be borne by the party in violation. The replacement value of trees and shrubs shall be determined in accordance with the latest revision of "A Guide to the Professional Evaluation of Landscape Trees, Specimen Shrubs, and Evergreens," as published by the International Society of Arboriculture.
(Prior code § 32-20)

§10-32-210 Use of fines to defray expenses.

Whenever any public tree, shrub or other plant material has been damaged or killed and a fine has been recovered therefor under the provisions of this chapter, or where the amount of such damage has been ascertained and the settlement of such claim has been authorized, such fine or the amount so paid in settlement, or any necessary part thereof, when transferred to the city comptroller, may in the discretion of the commissioner of streets and sanitation be used for the purpose of defraying all necessary expenses incurred in and by the removal of such tree, shrub or other plant material and in replacing the same by a living tree, shrub or other plant material; provided, that the city council, from year to year, shall appropriate according to law an amount equal to the fines collected and sums of money paid in satisfaction of damages to trees, shrubs or other plant materials, as aforesaid, for such purposes.
(Prior code § 32-21)

§10-32-250 Severability.

Should any section, clause or provision of this ordinance be declared by any court to be invalid, the same shall not affect the validity of the ordinance as a whole or part thereof, other than the part so declared to be valid. To this end the provisions of this ordinance are declared to be severable.
(Prior code § 32-22; Amend. Coun. J. 2-6-91, p. 30591)

CHAPTER 10-36
PARKS, PLAYGROUNDS AND AIRPORTS
(Selected Sections)

Sections:

Article I. General Regulations

10-36-010 Entrance and egress.
10-36-020 Animals prohibited.
10-36-030 Firearms and missiles.
10-36-050 Breach of peace.
10-36-060 Bill posting.
10-36-070 Reserved.
10-36-080 Bonfires.
10-36-090 Protection of park property.
10-36-100 Intoxicating liquors.
10-36-110 Hours.
10-36-120 Curfew for school property and playgrounds.
10-36-130 Glass prohibited where.
10-36-185 Enforcement of Chicago Park District ordinances.

Article II. Airports

10-36-310 Entering driveways.
10-36-358 Police powers for designated employees—Duties of scavengers.
10-36-370 Violation—Penalty.

Article III. Heliports

10-36-510 Emergency landings.
10-36-520 Violation—Penalty.

Article I. General Regulations

§10-36-010 Entrance and egress.

Wherever any park, public playground, bathing beach, public bath or airport of the city is enclosed, no person shall enter or leave the same except by the gateway. No person shall climb or walk upon the walls or fences thereof. Any of the entrances to such park, playground, bathing beach, public bath, or airport of the city may be closed at any time by the direction of the officer or employee in charge of same.
(Prior code § 37-1)

§10-36-020 Animals prohibited.

No person shall bring or lead any dog in any park, public playground or airport unless it is held by a leash, not more than six feet long except in park areas designated and posted by the city of Chicago or by the general superintendent of

the Chicago park district to be "Dog Friendly Areas" and no person shall bring or lead any dog or other animal onto the premises of any bathing beach except in beach areas designated and posted by the general superintendent of the Chicago park district to be "Dog Friendly Areas," and at such hours also designated and posted by the general superintendent of the Chicago park district. No person shall bring more than three dogs to any park or beach area. However, these restrictions will not apply to dogs utilized by police for patrol purposes.
(Prior code § 37-2; Amend. Coun. J. 7-19-00, p. 38596)

§10-36-030 Firearms and missiles.

Persons are forbidden to carry firearms or to throw stones or other missiles within any park, public playground, bathing beach, public bath or airport of the city.
(Prior code § 37-3)

§10-36-050 Breach of peace.

No threatening, abusive, insulting or indecent language shall be allowed in any part of such park, public playground, bathing beach, public bath or airport; nor shall any conduct be permitted whereby a breach of the peace may be occasioned; nor shall any person tell fortunes; nor shall any person play any game of chance at or with any table or instrument of gambling; nor shall any person commit any obscene or indecent act therein. Sales of Illinois State Lottery tickets made pursuant to the Lottery Act, PA. 78-20, effective July 1, 1974, as amended, at O'Hare International Airport are hereby expressly authorized.
(Prior code § 37-5; Amend. Coun. J. 2-20-85, p. 13844; Mayoral veto. 2-27-85, p. 14160; Amend. Coun. J. 11-20-85, p. 22700)

§10-36-060 Bill posting.

No person shall post or otherwise affix any bills, notice or other paper upon any structure or thing within any park, public playground, bathing beach, public bath or airport belonging to the city, nor upon any of the gates or enclosures thereof.
(Prior code § 37-6)

§10-36-070 Reserved.
(Repealed Coun. J. 10-3-2001, p. 68139)

§10-36-080 Bonfires.

No person shall light, make or use any bonfire in any park, public playground or bathing beach.
(Prior code § 37-8)

§10-36-090 Protection of park property.

No person shall be allowed to play ball or other games likely to injure the grass, lawn, turf or shrubbery, in any of the city parks, except in such places as may be provided for that purpose.

Nor shall any person cut, break or in any way injure or deface trees, shrubs, plants, turf or any of the buildings, fences, bridges or other construction or property contained therein.
(Prior code § 37-9)

§10-36-100 Intoxicating liquors.

No intoxicated person shall enter, be or remain in any public park, playground or bathing beach, nor shall any person bring into, sell, give away or drink any intoxicating liquors in any public park, playground or bathing beach.
(Prior code § 37-9.1)

§10-36-110 Hours.

No person shall be or remain in any public park, playground or bathing beach which is fenced in or provided with gates, between the closing of the gates at night and their reopening on the following day; nor shall any person be or remain in any public park, playground or bathing beach not fenced in or provided with gates between the hours of 11:00 p.m. and 4:00 a.m. on the following day.
(Prior code § 37-9.2)

§10-36-120 Curfew for school property and playgrounds.

No person shall be in or remain on any part of any public school or public school playground area fenced in or provided with gates, between the closing of the gates at night and their reopening on the following day; nor shall any person be in or remain on property on which a public school is located or public school playground not fenced in or provided with gates between the hours of 9:30 p.m. and 6:00 a.m. on the following day unless written authorization is granted by the general superintendent of schools. The board of education of the city of Chicago shall place, maintain and display written notice that the presence of any person is forbidden in accordance with this section.
(Prior code § 37-9.3)

§10-36-130 Glass prohibited where.

No person shall be allowed to carry bring, possess, or otherwise control any glass container or receptacle in any public park, playground or bathing beach.
(Prior code § 37-9.4; Added. Coun. J. 7-9-86, p. 31516)

§10-36-185 Enforcement of Chicago Park District ordinances.

(a) The members of the Chicago Police Department shall have authority to enforce the following provisions of the Chicago Park District Code, in effect as of September 9, 1998, or as subsequently amended: Chapter VII (Use of Parks)—Sections A, B(1)—(17), C(3), and D(1); Chapter VII (Use of Harbors) — Sections A, C(1) and D; and Chapter IX (Concessions and Food Services) — Sections A, B(1), B(6), C(1)(a), C(2)(a), C(2)(e), C(3)(a) and C(3)(e).

(b) Any person who violates the above referenced provisions of the Chicago Park District Code shall be subject to a fine not to exceed $500.00 and shall be subject to an order requiring the violator to pay restitution when the violation involves damage to property.

(c) In addition to any other means authorized by law, the city may enforce this section by instituting an action with the department of administrative hearings.
(Added. Coun. J. 4-21-99, p. 93318)

Article II. Airports

§10-36-310 Entering driveways.

It shall be unlawful for any person to drive any public passenger vehicle upon the passenger vehicle driveways at any airport or to park any such vehicle upon passenger vehicle driveways and parking stations at any airport, except as otherwise provided in this chapter.

(Prior code § 37-17.8)

§10-36-358 Police powers for designated employees—Duties of scavengers.

(a) The commissioner of aviation may designate employees of the department of aviation to have powers of members of the police force to serve process or notice for violations occurring at any airport of Sections 4-4-310, 4-260-040, 4-260-060, 4-260-080, 4-260-090, 7-12-420, 7-28-060, 7-28-070, 7-28-080, 7-28-120, 7-28-150, 7-28-210, 7-28-220, 7-28-225, 7-28-227, 7-28-230, 7-28-240, 7-28-260, 7-28-261, 7-28-270, 7-28-280, 7-28-300, 7-28-301, 7-28-302, 7-28-303, 7-28-305, 7-28-310, 7-28-315, 7-28-331, 7-28-360, 7-28-380, 7-28-390, 7-28-395, 7-28-400, 7-28-410, 7-28-440, 7-28-450, 7-28-460, 7-28-510, 7-28-660, 7-28-680, 7-28-690, 7-28-710, 7-28-720, 7-28-735, 8-4-135, 10-8-220, 10-28-340, 10-8-460 and 10-8-480 of the Municipal Code of Chicago as those sections are now or hereafter amended. A copy of the designation, and any amendments thereto, shall be kept by the commissioner of aviation and shall be available to the public upon request. The powers granted by this section expressly limited to the service of such process or notice for violations of the specified code sections, and this section shall not be construed as granting additional law enforcement powers.

(b) All licensed scavengers operating at Chicago O'Hare International Airport and Chicago Midway Airport must comply with orders of employees of the Department of Aviation and must perform the work required of the scavengers in such a way that no nuisance is created.

(c) In addition to the requirements of Section 4-260-020, it shall be the duty of every licensed scavenger to register with the commissioner of aviation, on a form supplied by the commissioner, each and every scavenger vehicle operated at Chicago O'Hare International Airport or Chicago Midway Airport by such licensee.

(d) In addition to the requirements of Section 4-260-060, every licensed scavenger that provides service at a site located at Chicago O'Hare International Airport or Chicago Midway Airport shall inform the commissioner of aviation of the suspension of service at such site within three days after the suspension of service. The notice shall be in a form specified by the commissioner of aviation and shall identify the licensed scavenger, the location at which the service has been suspended and the name and nature of business conducted at the site.

(Added. Coun. J. 7-10-02, p. 89594; Amend. 3-31-04, p. 20916)

§10-36-370 Violation—Penalty.

Any person, firm or corporation violating the provisions of this chapter shall be fined not less than $25.00 nor more than $200.00 for each offense and/or be incarcerated in a penal institution for a term of up to seven days under the procedure set forth in Section 1-2-1.1 of the Illinois Municipal Code, as amended, and each day such a violation shall continue shall be regarded as a separate offense.
(Prior code § 37-15; Amend. Coun. J. 10-4-89, p. 5321)

Article III. Heliports

§10-36-510 Emergency landings.

Notwithstanding anything contained in this ordinance to the contrary, it shall not be unlawful for any helicopter owned, operated or under the control of any governmental body or agency thereof to land or take off from property not licensed as a heliport hereunder in times of medical or other emergency.
(Prior code § 37-28)

§10-36-520 Violation—Penalty.

Any licensee violating any of the provisions of this section shall be fined not less than $50.00 nor more than $200.00 for each offense and each day such violation shall continue shall be regarded as a separate offense.
(Prior code § 37-29)

CHAPTER 10-40
CHICAGO HARBOR
(Selected Sections)

Sections:

Article I. Harbor Jurisdiction

10-40-010 Definition.
10-40-050 Harbor district No. 1.
10-40-060 Harbor district No. 2.
10-40-070 Harbor district No. 3.
10-40-080 Harbor district No. 4.

Article II. Navigation of the Harbor

10-40-090 Control of vessels in harbor.
10-40-100 Obstruction of harbor by vessels.
10-40-110 Obstruction of harbor by piles or stones.
10-40-120 Securing and removal of vessels.
10-40-130 Sunken or abandoned vessels.
10-40-131 Assistance to disabled vessels—Fees.
10-40-140 Raft of logs or lumber in harbor.
10-40-150 Tugs for vessels.
10-40-160 Towing—Permits.
10-40-170 Towing—Procedures.
10-40-180 Interference with dredging machine.
10-40-190 Assistance for fouled vessel.
10-40-200 Anchor dragging.
10-40-210 Moving vessel before bridge opening.
10-40-220 Names on boats.
10-40-230 Working vessel engines.
10-40-240 Smoking prohibited on waterfront.

10-40-250 Boat whistles.
10-40-260 Operation restrictions.
10-40-261 Restrictions on wake of vessels.
10-40-270 Interference with buoys.
10-40-280 Rules for vessels in harbor.
10-40-281 Advertising vessels.
10-40-290 Houseboats.
10-40-300 Tunneling under Lake Michigan.

Article III. Wharves and Docks

10-40-320 Maintenance of wharves and docks.
10-40-330 Construction and repair of structures in harbor.
10-40-340 Permit fees to construct or repair.
10-40-350 Bond for removal of old dock materials.
10-40-360 Dredging permits.
10-40-370 Encroachments and obstructions.
10-40-380 Discharge of cargo.
10-40-390 Vessels lying at docks.
10-40-400 Protection from fast-moving vessels.

Article IV. Bridges

10-40-410 Bridge opening authority.
10-40-420 Closed hours for bridges.
10-40-430 Time to remain open.
10-40-440 Signal for bridge opening.
10-40-450 Signal for opening of railroad bridges.
10-40-460 Signal to bridge tenders.
10-40-470 Obedience to bridge signals.
10-40-480 Signal equipment at bridges.
10-40-490 Obstruction of bridges by vessels.
10-40-500 Fireboats.
10-40-501 Removal of life preservers prohibited.
10-40-510 Fire apparatus crossing bridges.
10-40-520 Rule of the road.
10-40-530 Breaking line of traffic on bridge.
10-40-540 Unnecessary delay on bridge.
10-40-550 Obstruction of traffic over bridge.
10-40-560 Congregation on bridges or viaducts.

Article V. Violations of Chapter Provisions

10-40-570 Violation—Penalty.

Article I. Harbor Jurisdiction

§10-40-010 Definition.

The harbor shall consist of the Chicago River and its branches to their respective sources and all slips adjacent to and connecting therewith. The Ogden Canal, the Calumet River and its branches and all slips connecting therewith, the waters of Lake Calumet and all slips and basins connected therewith and all piers, breakwaters, and permanent structures therein, the Drainage Canal and all piers and basins, and the waters of Lake Michigan, including all breakwaters, piers, and permanent structures therein, for a distance of three miles from the shore between the north and south lines of the city extended, to the extent that the above-named waterways are within the territorial limits of the city. The harbor as herein defined shall be subject to the control of the commissioner of transportation, and use thereof shall be governed by this code.
(Prior code § 38-1; Amend. Coun. J. 12-11-91, p. 10832)

§10-40-050 Harbor district No. 1.

The public waters, the submerged lands, the artificially made or reclaimed lands and other lands which shall constitute and shall be known as harbor district No. 1, are hereby defined and particularly described as follows:

Harbor district No. 1 shall include all of the Chicago River, including the main stream from its mouth to the forks, and the north branch and the south branch to the city limits, including all the public waters and submerged lands within and under said river and its branches aforesaid, and said harbor district No. 1 shall also include all the territory, public waters, submerged lands, artificially made or reclaimed and other lands lying and being within the following boundaries, to wit:

Beginning at the south side of the Chicago River at the northeast corner of the old breakwater of the old United States Government lifesaving station, said point being the point of confluence of the Chicago River with Lake Michigan, thence extending in an easterly direction parallel to the north side of E. Randolph Street extended, over the waters of Lake Michigan a distance of one mile; thence extending in a northerly direction along a line running at right angles to said north line of E. Randolph Street extended east to a point where said line intersects the north line of E. Chicago Avenue extended east; thence extending in a westerly direction along the north line of said E. Chicago Avenue extended east to the present shoreline of Lake Michigan; thence running southeasterly and southerly following said shoreline of Lake Michigan to the north line of E. Grand Avenue extended east to the shoreline of Lake Michigan; thence west along the north line of E. Grand Avenue extended east to the east line of N. Peshtigo Court as laid down and indicated on a plat of the Chicago Dock and Canal Company's Peshtigo dock addition in section ten, township thirty-nine north, range fourteen east of the third principal meridian in Cook County, Illinois, recorded September 17, 1889, in the recorder's office of Cook County, Illinois, as document number 1157023 in Book 39 of plats, page 18; thence south along the east line of N. Peshtigo Court seventy-four feet, more or less, to the south line of E. Grand Avenue; thence east along the south line of E. Grand Avenue extended east nine hundred feet, more or less, to the west line of the east one hundred feet of lot seven in the Chicago Dock and Canal Company's Peshtigo dock addition; thence south along the west line of the east one hundred feet of said lot seven, two hundred and eighteen feet, more or less, to the north line of E. Illinois Street extended east; thence west along the north line of E. Illinois Street extended east nine hundred feet, more or less, to the east line of N. Peshtigo Court; thence south along the east line of N. Peshtigo Court seventy-four feet, more or less, to the south line of E. Illinois Street; thence east along the south line of E. Illinois Street extended east nine hundred feet, more or less, to the west line of the east one hundred feet of said lot seven; thence south along the west line of the east one hundred feet of said lot seven one hundred and fifty-eight feet, more or less, to the north line of the Ogden or Michigan slip; thence east along the north line of the Ogden or Michigan slip to the wooden pier or breakwater at the southeast corner of said lot seven; thence in a southerly direction along the west line of said wooden pier or breakwater to the southwest corner of what is known as the United States Government north pier; thence in a southwesterly direction nine hundred seventy-four feet, more or less, on a straight line to the northeast corner of the old breakwater of the old

United States Government lifesaving station, said last point being the place of beginning.

All of the aforesaid submerged lands, artificially made or reclaimed lands and other lands and public waters in said harbor district No. 1 are situated within the jurisdiction and corporate limits of the city and are by this section declared to be necessary and appropriate for the purposes enumerated in said act of the general assembly mentioned in Section 10-40-040.
(Prior code § 38-4)

§10-40-060 Harbor district No. 2.

The public waters and all public turning basins, canals and slips, the submerged lands, the artificially made or reclaimed lands, and other lands which shall constitute and shall be known as harbor district No. 2, are hereby defined and particularly described as follows:

Harbor district No. 2 shall include all the territory, including the public waters and all public turning basins, canals, and slips, the submerged lands, the artificially made or reclaimed lands and other lands, lying and being within the following boundaries, to-wit:

Beginning on the south side of the Chicago River at a point that is 3019.28 feet east and 1436.35 feet north of the southwest corner of E. Randolph Street and N. Michigan Avenue, thence running in an easterly direction parallel to the south line of E. Randolph Street extended east, over the waters of Lake Michigan, a distance of one mile, thence at right angles running along a line in a southerly direction to the said south line of E. Randolph Street extended east, thence running in a westerly direction along the said south line of E. Randolph Street extended east, to the present shoreline or dock line of Lake Michigan, thence running in a northerly direction, but following the present dock lines of Lake Michigan, to the place of beginning.

All of the aforesaid public waters and all public turning basins, canals and slips, submerged lands, artificially made or reclaimed lands, and other lands in said harbor district No. 2 are situated within the jurisdiction and corporate limits of the city, and are by this section declared to be necessary or appropriate for the uses and purposes enumerated in said act of the general assembly mentioned in Section 10-40-040.
(Prior code § 38-5)

§10-40-070 Harbor district No. 3.

The public waters, the submerged lands, the artificially made or reclaimed lands, and other lands which shall constitute and shall be known as harbor district No. 3, are hereby defined and particularly described as follows:

Beginning at a point which is on a line four hundred feet south of the east and west center line, extended east, of section twenty-two, township thirty-nine north, range fourteen, east of the third principal meridian, and thirty-two hundred and seventy-three and thirty-seven one-hundredths feet east of the westerly right-of-way line of the Illinois Central Railroad, thence southeasterly to a point fifty feet north of the centerline of E. Cermak Road extended easterly and twenty-seven hundred and thirty-two feet east of said westerly right-of-way line, thence southeasterly to a point six hundred and ninety feet north of a point which is on the centerline of E. Twenty-seventh Street extended easterly and twenty-three hundred and seventy feet east of the said westerly right-of-way line, thence southeasterly to a point seven hundred feet north of a point which is on the centerline, extended east, of E. Thirty-first Street and twenty-two hundred and forty feet east of said westerly right-of-way line, thence southeasterly on a line towards a point eight hundred and ninety feet north of a point which is on the centerline extended east of E. Thirty-fifth Street and twenty-one hundred and eighty-five feet east of said westerly right-of-way line to the south line extended east of E. Thirty-first Street, thence due east for a distance of fifty-two hundred and eighty feet, thence due north to the line four hundred feet south of the east and west centerline extended easterly of section twenty-two, township thirty-nine north, range fourteen, east of the third principal meridian, thence west along the line four hundred feet south of the east and west centerline extended easterly of section twenty-two, township thirty-nine, range fourteen east, to the point of beginning.

In the event that the city, pursuant to clause (c) of Section 6 of the ordinance passed July 21, 1919, under which harbor district No. 3 was created, shall elect to fill in and reclaim that part of the submerged lands lying between the eastern and western boundaries of the lands described in Schedule IV of said last-mentioned ordinance and between the north and south lines of said harbor district area, respectively extended west, and to declare the same to be a part of harbor district No. 3, the said harbor district area described in this section shall be then considered to extend westward over the land so reclaimed by the city, between the north and south lines of harbor
district No. 3, respectively, extended west.

All of the aforesaid public waters, submerged lands, artificially made or reclaimed lands, and other lands and public waters in said harbor district No. 3 are situated within the jurisdiction and corporate limits of the city and are by this section declared to be necessary and appropriate for the purposes enumerated in said act of the general assembly mentioned in Section 10-40-040.
(Prior code § 38-6)

§10-40-080 Harbor district No. 4.

The public waters, the submerged lands, the artificially made or reclaimed lands, and other lands which shall constitute and shall be known as harbor district No. 4, are hereby defined and particularly described as follows:

Harbor district No. 4 shall include all of the Calumet River lying within the city, all of Lake Calumet, including all the waters, submerged lands, and artificially made or reclaimed lands within or bordering upon said lake and river, the channel or connection between said Calumet River and Lake Calumet, and all public turning basins, canals and slips connected with or forming a part of said Calumet River and Lake Calumet. All of the aforesaid submerged lands, artificially made or reclaimed lands and other lands and public waters in said harbor district No. 4 are situated within the jurisdiction and corporate limits of the city, and are by this section declared to be necessary and appropriate for the uses and purposes enumerated in said act of the general assembly mentioned in Section 10-40-040.
(Prior code § 38-7)

Article II. Navigation of the Harbor

§10-40-090 Control of vessels in harbor.

The commissioner of transportation shall give such orders and directions relative to the location, change of place or station, manner of moving or use of the harbor of or by every vessel, craft, or float lying, moving or laid up in the harbor, as may be necessary to promote good order therein and the safety and equal convenience of such vessels, craft, or floats, and to so regulate the same that the current in the Chicago River shall not be unnecessarily impeded by said vessels, craft, or floats.

He shall have power to remove any vessel, craft, or float lying at any dock, wharf, or pier, while receiving or discharging cargo or otherwise engaged, when necessary so to do to facilitate the movement of traffic in the harbor; to tie up any vessel so deeply loaded as to interrupt the traffic at the bridges or in the harbor until such a time as the vessel shall have been lightened or a rise of water in the harbor may enable it to proceed; and, to stop at any time or place vessels, craft, or floats which are passing through the harbor, so as to prevent a jam or blockade.

(Prior code § 38-13; Amend. Coun. J. 12-11-91, p. 10832)

§10-40-100 Obstruction of harbor by vessels.

No vessel, craft, or float shall be moored, laid, brought to a stop, or anchored within the harbor so as to prevent the passage of any other vessel, craft, or float; nor shall any vessel, craft, or float be so moored, laid, brought to a stop, or anchored, as to range against, injure, interfere with, or hinder the opening or closing of any bridge across the river or any branch thereof; nor shall any vessel, craft, or float be so navigated, when winding, as to strike or come in contact with any bridge, bridge abutment, center pier, or the piles or other protection thereof.

(Prior code § 38-14)

§10-40-110 Obstruction of harbor by piles or stones.

Every pile, timber, stone, or other substance placed or laid so as to project above or below the surface of the waters of the harbor or any part thereof or beyond any dock line established by the city council, is hereby declared a nuisance; and every person who shall place or lay any such pile, timber, stone, or substance as aforesaid, or be the owner of any premises on which the same shall be so placed or laid, shall be fined not less than $20.00 and not more than $100.00 for every such violation, and shall also be subject to a penalty of not less than $20.00 and not more than $100.00 for every three days such nuisance shall continue after notice from the commissioner of transportation to abate same.

(Prior code § 38-15; Amend. Coun. J. 12-11-91, p. 10832)

§10-40-120 Securing and removal of vessels.

Whenever there shall be in the harbor any vessel, craft, or float insecurely fastened, adrift, sunken, or laid up, which may be required to be fastened, raised, removed or its location changed, for the benefit of other vessels navigating the river or to carry out the provisions of this code, the harbor master shall notify the owner, master, or other person who may be in charge thereof, and he

shall secure, raise, or remove such vessel, craft, or float without delay. But if the harbormaster should be unable to find the master, owner, or person in charge of such vessel, craft, or float as aforesaid, or if no person answering such description can be found by him, such notice shall not be required, and the commissioner of transportation may remove such vessel, and such vessel shall be held for all expenses and costs.
(Prior code § 38-16; Amend. Coun. J. 12-11-91, p. 10832)

§10-40-130 Sunken or abandoned vessels.

Every vessel, craft or float which has been abandoned or allowed to sink in the harbor is hereby declared to be a nuisance. The master, owner, or person in charge or control of any such vessel, craft, or float shall immediately abate such nuisance upon notice from the commissioner of transportation. Every three days such nuisance shall continue after notice from the commissioner of transportation to abate the same shall constitute a separate and distinct offense.
(Prior code § 38-17; Amend. Coun. J. 12-11-91, p. 10832)

§10-40-131 Assistance to disabled vessels—Fees.

The owner or master of any disabled vessel shall pay to the city the following fees for the following services to the vessel:

Extinguishing fire on board..$300.00
Towing..500.00
Pumping water from vessel.......................................100.00

(Added. Coun. J. 11-10-94, p. 59125; Amend. 12-15-04, p. 39840)

§10-40-140 Raft of logs or lumber in harbor.

No person shall leave any raft of logs, lumber, or timber within the harbor where it shall be or become an obstruction, and any person having charge of any raft of logs, lumber, or timber shall remove or change the location of the raft upon the order of the commissioner of transportation.
(Prior code § 38-18; Amend. Coun. J. 12-11-91, p. 10832)

§10-40-150 Tugs for vessels.

All wind-driven vessels, craft, or floats navigating the harbor, for which the opening of any bridge may be necessary, shall, while approaching and passing such bridge, be towed by a power tug.

Any other vessel, craft, or float navigating that portion of the harbor bound by the Outer Drive Bridge on the east, the Van Buren Street Bridge on the south, and the Kinzie Street Bridge on the north, all inclusive, shall have the assistance of a tug or tugs at all such times, and under such conditions as the commissioner of transportation shall by general order from time to time prescribe, and also in any specific instance where the harbormaster or assistant harbormaster shall specially so direct. It shall be unlawful for any such vessel, craft, or float to back through any bridge draw in the harbor without the assistance of a tug or tugs, unless the commissioner of transportation shall have given his consent thereto; the commissioner of transportation may give such consent whenever in his judgment it seems advisable.

Any person owning or in charge, possession or control of any such vessel, craft, or float violating any of the provisions of this section, shall be fined not less than $25.00 dollars nor more than $100.00 for each offense.
(Prior code § 38-19; Amend. Coun. J. 12-11-91, p. 10832)

§10-40-160 Towing—Permits.

No person shall tow in the harbor, any vessel, craft or float containing material destined to be disposed of in the authorized dumping areas, without a permit from the department of transportation. The fee for each permit shall be $16.00 per day and the day shall consist of eight hours.
(Prior code § 38-20; Amend. Coun. J. 12-11-91, p. 10832)

§10-40-170 Towing—Procedures.

It shall be unlawful for any vessel, craft or float to tow more than two barges or similar craft in one tow within the harbor, except that tows which consist of barges that are fastened rigidly together to form a single unit for the purpose of being towed may be towed in the main sanitary and ship canal and the west fork of the south branch of the Chicago River to and including the South Ashland Avenue turning basin; in the Little Calumet and Calumet Rivers to and including turning basin number five at 129th Street; and in Chicago and Calumet Outer Harbors; provided that the total width and length of such tows do not exceed 80 and 500 feet respectively.
(Prior code § 38-21)

§10-40-180 Interference with dredging machine.

No owner, master, or other person in charge of or in command of any tugboat or towing boat in the harbor shall run, or cause to be run, such tugboat or towing boat, or anything that they may have in tow, upon, against, or over any rope, chain, or other fastening, mooring, dredge or other machine used by the city, or the United States Government, for deepening, widening, and improving the harbor, so that the said dredge or other machine shall be displaced, hindered, or delayed in the working thereof.
(Prior code § 38-22)

§10-40-190 Assistance for fouled vessel.

If any vessel, craft, or float, either by winding or from any other cause, shall get foul and obstruct the navigation or passage of other vessels, craft, or floats, the commissioner of transportation shall have power and is hereby authorized to order to his assistance men and tackle from any other vessel, craft, or float. The commissioner of transportation shall have power and is hereby authorized to order to his assistance any tugboat or other powerboat that may be in the vicinity or passing at the time. Every master or officer of such boat, craft, or tug shall render the assistance so ordered, and any vessel, craft, or float receiving such assistance shall pay to the person or persons rendering the same the cost or expense of such assistance, the amount thereof to be fixed by the commissioner of transportation.

Any person violating any of the provisions of this section shall be fined not less than $25.00 nor more than $50.00 for the first offense, and not more than $75.00 for each subsequent offense.
(Prior code § 38-23; Amend. Coun. J. 12-11-91, p. 10832)

§10-40-200 Anchor dragging.
All vessels, craft, or float while navigating the harbor shall not drag their anchors, nor shall any tugboat or towboat tow any vessel, craft, or float in the harbor whose anchor is dragging. The master, owner, or person in control of any vessel operated in violation of this section shall be fined not less than $50.00 nor more than $100.00 for each offense.
(Prior code § 38-24)

§10-40-210 Moving vessel before bridge opening.
Whenever any person having charge of any vessel, craft, or float shall wish to move it past any bridge, reasonable time shall be allowed for the opening of the bridge, and any person who shall move any vessel, craft, or float against any bridge before it shall be opened and shall injure the bridge shall be liable to the city for that injury in addition to any fine which may be levied.
(Prior code § 38-25)

§10-40-220 Names on boats.
It shall be unlawful for any master, owner, or person in possession, charge, or control of any vessel, craft, or float to operate, navigate, keep, or maintain the same in the harbor unless the same shall have a name plainly and conspicuously displayed thereon which shall be large enough and in such a position as to be readily distinguishable and readable on both sides or from the rear thereof for a distance of at least 500 feet, and such name shall be of such distinctive character that any such vessel, craft, or float may be readily identified by it.

Any person violating the provisions of this section shall be fined not less than $25.00 nor more than $100.00 for each offense.
(Prior code § 38-26)

§10-40-230 Working vessel engines.
No steam vessel or other power craft while lying in the harbor or along the wharves or docks of the same shall work its engines; provided, that owners, masters, or other persons in charge of boats fitting out and desirous of working and testing their engines shall, before working or testing any such engine, station some person in such a place or position as will enable him to signal the engineer to stop such engine. Such engine shall be kept from working until all approaching vessels, craft, or floats shall have passed the wheel of said boat or boats by a distance of 200 feet. These provisions shall not apply to cases of fire.
(Prior code § 38-27)

§10-40-240 Smoking prohibited on waterfront.

It shall be unlawful for any person to smoke, carry or possess a lighted cigarette, cigar, pipe or match upon any bulkhead, dock, shipyard, pier, wharf, warehouse or shed, except such portions thereof as may be designated by the harbormaster, or to smoke, carry or possess a lighted cigarette, cigar, pipe or match on board any ship, lighter, scow, or other similar floating craft or equipment when berthed or moored at any dock, wharf, pier, or to a vessel made fast thereto, within the harbor.

(Prior code § 38-27.1)

§10-40-250 Boat whistles.

Any vessel, craft, or float navigating the harbor shall be equipped with a whistle for signalling purposes which shall not be heard distinctly in ordinary weather at a distance of more than one-quarter of a mile. No person shall blow the whistle of any vessel, craft, or float at any time except as a signal to a bridge tender, or as a signal of danger, or as prescribed by the laws and regulations of the United States, and as provided by this code.

(Prior code § 38-28)

§10-40-260 Operation restrictions.

No person shall operate, or authorize or knowingly permit the operation of, a vessel upon the waters of Lake Michigan or upon any waterway within the city:

(a) In such a manner as to endanger the life or limb, or damage the property, of others; or

(b) In such a careless or heedless manner as to be grossly indifferent to the person or property of others; or

(c) In such a manner as to disturb or destroy the peace and quiet of others; or

(d) Within any area which has been marked by buoys or other distinguishing devices as a restricted area, except in case of emergency or for the purpose of entering or leaving any harbor or launching ramp; or

(e) Within 150 feet of the shoreline of any public park or within 300 feet of any bathing beach, except in case of emergency or for the purpose of entering or leaving a pier, slip launching or docking area; or

(f) By a person under the age of 16 years unless properly supervised by an adult or as permitted by state law; or

(g) Without yielding the right-of-way to any swimmer; or

(h) Without complying with all applicable state and federal safety equipment requirements, including the requirement of personal flotation devices; or

(i) In violation of posted restrictions on wake or speed.

Any person who shall violate any provision of this section shall be fined not less than $100.00 nor more than $750.00, or imprisoned for not less than 10 days nor more than six months, or both, for each offense.

(Prior code § 38-29; Amend. Coun. J. 12-10-97, p. 59008)

§10-40-261 Restrictions on wake of vessels.

(a) No person shall operate a vessel in such a way that the boat creates a wake in any of the following areas in the Lake Michigan portions of the Chicago Harbor or upon any waterway within the city, except in case of an actual emergency:

(1) Within 150 feet of any buoy marking a bathing beach or swimming area;

(2) Within 150 feet of the shoreline or a breakwater;

(3) Within 150 feet of any other vessels;

(4) Within 150 feet of any boat launching ramps;

(5) Within 150 feet of any portion of the Chicago River locks structure;

(6) West of the east line of Navy Pier, between the south line of Navy Pier and the south line of the Chicago River locks structure;

(7) West of the east line of Navy Pier, between the north line of Navy Pier and the south line of the Jardine Water Filtration Plant;

(8) The main branch of the Chicago River, from the Chicago River controlling Locks west to Wolf Point L, the junction of the main north and south branches;

(9) The south branch of the Chicago River, from Wolf Point to the Lake Street Bridge;

(10) The north branch of the Chicago River, from Wolf Point to the Kinzie Street Bridge;

(11) At any other location where no wake signs or markings are posted by the commissioner of transportation pursuant to subsection (b) of this section.

(c) The commissioner of transportation shall post appropriate markings or signs to identify the no-wake areas listed in subsection (a) of this section. The commissioner may also mark additional no-wake areas as directed from time to time by the city council, and where an appropriate state or federal agency indicates the need for such restriction. All such signs and markings shall comply with applicable state and federal regulations.

(d) Any person who violates any provision of subsection (a) of this section shall be subject to a fine of not less than $100.00 and not more than $500.00.

(Added. Coun. J. 12-10-97, p. 59008; Amend. 7-29-98, p. 75119)

§10-40-270 Interference with buoys.

It shall be unlawful for any person to take possession of or make use of for any purpose, alter, deface, destroy, move, injure, obstruct by fastening a boat or vessel thereto or otherwise tie a boat or vessel to, or in any manner whatever impair the usefulness of, any bridge, any special purpose buoy or any marine navigational aid established and maintained by the city of Chicago, Chicago Park District, or any subdivision of said governments.

(Prior code § 38-29.1)

§10-40-280 Rules for vessels in harbor.

All vessels, craft, or floats lying in or navigating the harbor shall be respectively governed by the following further provisions:

(a) Every vessel using steam shall have its smoke pipe or pipes so constructed and managed as to prevent sparks or coals of fire escaping therefrom, and shall be moved slowly at a speed not exceeding four miles per hour under a low head of steam. Every tugboat or steam vessel used chiefly for towing shall have a joint in its smoke pipe or pipes, and shall be constructed in all respects in such a manner as to be able to pass under any bridge which is not less than 13 feet above the surface of the water.

(b) No master or other person owning or having charge of any vessel, craft, or float shall leave the same in the harbor without having on board or in charge thereof some competent person to control, manage and secure the same, without first obtaining permission of the harbormaster.

(c) All vessels, craft, or floats, whether using steam or otherwise, while lying in the harbor, shall have and keep their anchors on board, and their lower yards cockbilled, and the upper yards braced up sharp.

They shall likewise have and keep out on board during the night time a conspicuous white light, and shall have extinguished or safely secured at dark all fires which may be kept on board.

(d) No vessel, craft, or float shall be suffered to lie in the harbor adrift or insecurely fastened.

(e) Vessels, craft, or floats moving with the current shall have the right-of-way.

(f) In case one vessel desires to pass another going in the same direction in the harbor the pilot of the vessel astern shall give the proper signal, indicating the side upon which he wishes to pass. Upon the pilot of one vessel astern of another giving such signal, the pilot of the vessel ahead shall immediately answer by giving the same signal; but if he does think it safe for the vessel astern to attempt to pass at that point he shall immediately signify the same by giving several short and rapid blasts of the whistle, and under no circumstances shall the steamer astern attempt to pass the steamer ahead until such time as they have reached a point where it can be safely done, when such vessel ahead shall signify her willingness by blowing the proper signals and the vessel astern shall pass the overtaken vessel, giving the overtaken vessel as wide a berth as possible.

(g) The vessel dispatcher shall keep a record of the movements of all vessels and through the bridge telephone operators give such directions to the bridge tenders or persons in charge of the bridges in regard to the opening of bridges that the provisions of this code may be carried out.

(h) Vessels exceeding 200 tons navigating the harbor shall not proceed at a speed greater than four miles per hour.

(Prior code § 38-030)

§10-40-281 Advertising vessels.

(a) For purposes of this section the following terms shall have the following meanings:

(1) "Advertising sign" means any sign displayed on a watercraft, other than:

(A) The name of the watercraft and any required licensing, registration or identification markings displayed on the watercraft; or

(B) A sign identifying the owner of the watercraft and the principal business, occupation, service, commodity or entertainment conducted, sold or offered on the watercraft.

(2) "Advertising vessel" means any boat, barge, raft or other watercraft designed or used for the display of one or more advertising signs.

(3) "Chicago Harbor" means the harbor defined in Section 10-40-010 of this code.

(b) No person shall operate or cause to be operated any advertising vessel within the Chicago Harbor. Violation of this section shall constitute a nuisance, and the corporation counsel is authorized to prosecute an action in the appropriate court for injunction against continuation thereof. In addition, any person who violates the provisions of this section shall be fined not less than $200.00 and not more than $500.00 for each offense. Each day that a violation shall continue shall constitute a separate and distinct offense.

(Added. Coun. J. 10-31-90, p. 22657)

§10-40-290 Houseboats.

No person shall occupy any vessel, craft, or float upon the waters of the harbor as a residence, or for the purpose of engaging in any business, trade, or traffic for any purpose whatsoever, without first obtaining a license so to do as provided by "An Act to license shanty boats and other water craft, fixing the fees therefor and providing penalties," approved June 10, 1987. The license shall be posted and remain at all times in a conspicuous place in or on the vessel, craft or float.

Any person violating any of the provisions of this section shall be fined not less than $25.00 nor more than $100.00, and each and every day on which such violation shall continue shall constitute a separate and distinct offense.

(Prior code § 38-31)

§10-40-300 Tunneling under Lake Michigan.

Every person performing or undertaking the work of tunnel construction under the water of Lake Michigan and within the jurisdiction of the city, and maintaining a crib in connection with such work, shall, whenever such person shall have persons employed on or about such crib or in any portion of the tunnel which is so connected with such crib that persons employed therein may pass therefrom in or onto such crib, provide on or at such crib a sufficient number of boats, of adequate and suitable design, to safely transport and convey all persons engaged in working in and about such tunnel construction to the mainland. Any person violating any of the provisions of this section shall be fined not less than $25.00 nor more than $200.00 for each offense, and a separate and distinct offense shall be regarded as committed each day that such violation shall continue.

(Prior code § 38-32)

Article III. Wharves and Docks

§10-40-320 Maintenance of wharves and docks.

Every owner of premises abutting on the harbor, or any portion thereof, shall at all times keep and maintain in a state of good repair and in a safe condition all wharves, docks, piers, seawalls, slips, riverbank retaining walls, riverbank bulkheads, dolphins, booms, bulkheads, jetties, mooring facilities, pilings, sheetings and other similar structures on or appurtenant to such premises. Every violation of this section shall constitute a separate and distinct offense for every day such violation shall continue. The commissioner of transportation shall notify in writing such owner of any violation of this section and direct him to restore or repair such structure within a reasonable time. In addition, any nuisance now existing or which may hereafter result from an owner's failure to keep and maintain such wharves, docks, piers, seawalls, slips, riverbank retaining walls, riverbank bulkheads, dolphins, booms, bulkheads, jetties, mooring facilities, pilings, sheetings and other similar structures on or appurtenant to such premises in a state of good repair and in a safe condition shall also be subject to abatement as provided in Chapter 7-28 of this code.
(Prior code § 38-34; Amend. Coun. J. 12-11-91, p. 10832)

§10-40-330 Construction and repair of structures in harbor.

No person shall drive or place, or cause to be driven or placed, any pile or piles, stone, timber, earth, or other obstruction of any kind whatsoever, in the harbor, or build, construct, or repair any dock therein, or build or cause to be built any bridge or other structure across any part of the harbor, or drive or place, or cause to be driven or placed, any pile or piles of timber, or make any excavation for the purpose of furnishing or laying foundations for any building or structure, at any point within 40 feet of any part of the harbor, without obtaining a special permit in writing from the commissioner of transportation so to do. Application for said permission shall be made in writing to the commissioner of transportation, and shall be accompanied by a sketch or plat showing the nature of the work to be done. Upon such application being made and such sketch or plat being furnished as herein required, the commissioner of transportation shall issue the permit desired, upon payment of the permit fees hereinafter provided, unless it shall appear that the work to be done will result in unduly obstructing the harbor or in endangering the safety of any dock, pier, breakwater, or other structure located upon or along the harbor.

It shall be the duty of the commissioner of transportation to require all persons who may be engaged in repairing, renewing, altering, or constructing any dock within the city to produce a permit from the department of transportation, which permit shall specify the character and location of such repairing, renewal, alteration, or construction, and in default of the production of such permit, the commissioner of transportation shall at once stop all work on such dock, and shall cause the arrest of any such persons engaged in such unlawful repairing, renewal, alteration, or construction. Any such person so arrested shall be fined not less than $50.00 nor more than $100.00 for each offense. In the event of any such dock having been repaired, renewed, altered, or constructed in or upon the water area of the harbor of the city, the person thus convicted of a violation of this section, in addition to the fine hereinbefore specified, shall be

required at once, and at his own expense, or cost, to remove such dock back to its former location; and, in default of such removal of such dock, the commissioner of transportation is hereby authorized to cause such dock to be removed, to such location as he deems best and to recover, from the person so convicted, the cost or expense of such removal.
(Prior code § 38-35; Amend. Coun. J. 12-11-91, p. 10832)

§10-40-340 Permit fees to construct or repair.

The fees for permits issued under the preceding section shall be as follows:

BUILDING WORK

One-story frame under 500 square feet overall area	$10.00
One-story brick under 500 square feet overall area	15.00
One-story frame over 500 square feet overall area	20.00
One-story brick over 500 square feet overall area	25.00
For each additional story (frame)	1.00
For each additional story (brick)	2.00

Note: Towers shall be considered as additional stories. Where no definite stories exist in buildings or towers, 15 feet of height shall be considered equivalent to one story.

BRIDGE WORK

Substructure of span bridges—each foundation	$15.00
Superstructure of span bridges	25.00
Pile trestles	50.00

WATER PIPE WORK

8 inch diameter or less	5.00
8 to 15 inch diameter	10.00
15 to 36 inch diameter	15.00
Over 36 inch diameter	20.00
Additional fee for aerial or submarine crossing	25.00
Additional fee for intakes	10.00

SEWER WORK

8 inch diameter or less	5.00
8 to 15 inch diameter	10.00
15 to 36 inch diameter	15.00
Over 36 inch diameter	20.00
Each manhole in addition to the above	2.00

ELECTRICAL WORK

Wooden pole—each	2.00
Structural steel pole or tower—each	5.00
Manhole or vault—each	5.00
Additional fee for aerial or submarine crossing, cable or conduit	20.00
Tunnel	50.00

DOCK WORK—SHORE PROTECTION

Jetties, cribs, docks, etc., 12-1/2 cents per lineal foot for repair work, with a minimum fee of $5.00, new work 25 cents per lineal foot with a minimum of 10.00

DUMPING AND FILLING

Snow, each location (in water) 15.00
Earth and ashes, each location (on land) 10.00

ICEHOUSE WORK

Ice-cutting permits, per season 25.00
Temporary ice-handling equipment, per season 5.00

MISCELLANEOUS WORK

Fence extending to dock, each 5.00
Fence extending along dock, each 10.00
Trestle or conveyer 15.00
Water tank 10.00
Coal or material hopper 10.00
Smokestack 10.00
Derrick 10.00
Ash-handling plant 15.00
Platform or runway 10.00
Depression in dock or pit 10.00
Pavement 5.00

(Prior code § 38-36)

§10-40-350 Bond for removal of old dock materials.

Any person that shall do any dock work wherein it shall be necessary to remove existing piles or sheeting, or in cases where an entirely new and original dock is to be constructed, shall furnish a bond in the sum of $2,000.00 approved by the commissioner of transportation, payable to the city and conditioned for the satisfactory removal of any and all earth, stone, or other material which may have escaped into the waters of any part of the harbor area, and for the satisfactory removal of earth, stone, or other material that may have been moved harborwards of any new and original dock. Said earth, stone, or other material herein mentioned shall be removed to a depth equal to the navigable depth fixed or existing at the time when, and location where, said dock work is being done.

(Prior code § 38-37; Amend. Coun. J. 12-11-91, p. 10832)

§10-40-360 Dredging permits.

No person shall dredge in, on, or along the waters of the harbor without a permit from the department of transportation. The fee for such permit shall not exceed $16.00 per day and the day shall consist of eight hours.

No additional fee shall be charged for the removal, or dredging in connection with the removal of old dock materials unless the material so removed shall be deposited in the lake, in which case a towing permit shall be necessary in addition to the dock permit.

(Prior code § 38-38; Amend. Coun. J. 12-11-91, p. 10832)

§10-40-370 Encroachments and obstructions.

It shall be the duty of the commissioner of transportation to report to the city engineer any and all encroachments upon the harbor lines as now established or which may hereafter be established, and thereupon the said harbormaster and city engineer shall take such action as may be necessary to enforce the provisions of this code and to remove or cause to be removed any such obstruction or encroachment. If it shall be found that any pile, stone, timber, earth, dock, bridge, or other obstruction whatever, has been placed in any part of the harbor in violation of the provisions of this code and that the person who has placed same or caused it to be placed therein refuses or neglects to remove such obstruction upon being requested so to do by the city engineer, or commissioner of transportation, the commissioner of transportation shall have the power, and it is hereby made his duty, to proceed forthwith to remove such obstruction and to charge the expense of such removal to the person who placed such obstruction in the harbor, or caused it to be so placed, and the imposition of any fine or penalty hereby provided for against any person obstructing the harbor shall not be held to exempt any such person from a recovery by the city of the cost of removing any such obstruction.
(Prior code § 38-39; Amend. Coun. J. 12-11-91, p. 10832)

§10-40-380 Discharge of cargo.

No owner, lessee, or person in possession of any wharf or dock at which any vessel shall have been discharging its cargo shall suffer or permit any part of such cargo so discharged to project from such wharf or dock over or into the harbor after the vessel so unloaded shall have removed from such wharf or dock.
(Prior code § 38-40)

§10-40-390 Vessels lying at docks.

It shall be unlawful for any mud scow, flatboat, dredge, or any such craft to be placed or laid alongside of another while lying at any of the docks or wharves of the harbor during the navigable season of the year, without first having obtained permission from the commissioner of transportation.
(Prior code § 38-41; Amend. Coun. J. 12-11-91, p. 10832)

§10-40-400 Protection from fast-moving vessels.

All docks, wharves, bridges, piers, protections, or other places where persons or property are endangered by the fast moving of vessels or craft shall have a blue flag flying in the most conspicuous place thereon and as near the point of danger as possible. At night a blue light shall take the place of the flag. No vessel or craft shall run past such a blue flag or light at a rate faster than two miles per hour. Any person violating any of the provisions of this section shall be fined not less than $25.00 nor more than $50.00 for each offense, and shall be held liable for any damage to any person or property sustained by reason of such violation.
(Prior code § 38-42)

Article IV. Bridges

§10-40-410 Bridge opening authority.

All movable bridges crossing any part of the harbor, including railroad bridges, shall be under the control of the commissioner of transportation, and he shall have power to order the opening and closing of the same at any time when in his judgment it is necessary to carry out the provisions of this code.
(Prior code § 38-43; Amend. Coun. J. 12-11-91, p. 10832)

§10-40-420 Closed hours for bridges.

No bridge within the city, on any day of the week, excepting Sunday, shall be opened during the times herein specified:

Across Ogden Slip at Outer Drive, across the main river and across the south branch of the Chicago River, from its junction with the main river south to and including W. Roosevelt Road, and across the north branch of the Chicago River at W. Kinzie Street, between the hours of 7:30 a.m. and 10:00 a.m. and on any day excepting Saturday between the hours of 4:00 p.m. and 6:30 p.m. and on Saturday between the hours of 12:30 p.m. and 2:00 p.m. and between 5:00 p.m. and 6:00 p.m.; provided, however, that the Outer-Link Bridge across the main river shall be opened to permit the passage of passenger boats operating on a fixed schedule between 9:45 a.m. and 10:00 a.m.

Across the north branch of the Chicago River north of W. Kinzie Street to and including N. Halsted Street between the hours of 7:00 a.m. and 8:00 a.m. and 5:00 p.m. and 6:00 p.m.

Across the south branch of the Chicago River south of W. Roosevelt Road to and including S. Halsted Street between the hours of 7:00 a.m. and 8:00 a.m. and 5:00 p.m. and 6:00 p.m.

Across the north branch of the Chicago River north of N. Halsted Street and across the south branch of the Chicago River south of S. Halsted Street between the hours of 7:00 a.m. and 8:00 a.m. and 5:30 p.m. and 6:30 p.m.

The provisions of this section shall not apply to bridges which have a clearance of less than 16 feet above Chicago City datum. Such bridges shall open at any time, except as hereinafter provided, to permit the passage of tugs and tug boats.
(Prior code § 38-44)

§10-40-430 Time to remain open.

During the hours between 6:00 a.m. and 12:00 midnight, it shall be unlawful to keep open any bridge within the city for the purpose of permitting vessels to pass through the same for a longer period, at any one time, than 10 minutes, at the expiration of which period it shall be the duty of the bridge tender or other person in charge of the bridge to display the proper signal and immediately close such bridge and keep it closed for fully 10 minutes for such persons or vehicles as may be waiting to pass over, if so much time shall be required, when the said bridge shall again be opened (if necessary for vessels to pass) for a like period, and so on alternately (if necessary) during the hours last aforesaid; and in every instance where any such bridge shall be opened for the passage of any vessel, and closed before the expiration of 10 minutes from the time of opening, said bridge shall then, in every such case, remain closed for

fully 10 minutes, if necessary, in order to allow all persons and vehicles waiting to pass over said bridge; provided, this section shall not be construed as being in conflict with the preceding section, nor as requiring the opening of bridges during the time specified in said section for the same to remain closed; provided further, that all vessels having passed through Michigan Avenue bridge going out previous to closed bridge hours, morning and evening, shall be permitted to pass out to the lake.
(Prior code § 38-45)

§10-40-440 Signal for bridge opening.

When any vessel shall signal for any bridge across the Chicago River or any of its branches, the bridge tender shall immediately open the bridge.

If, from any cause, the bridge tender cannot open the bridge, he shall immediately notify the vessel by waving a red flag by day and a red lantern by night and continue waving the same until the vessel has stopped, continuing thereafter to display the same until the bridge can be opened. As soon as the cause for stopping the vessel has been removed, the bridge shall be immediately opened.

It shall be unlawful for the owner, officer, or other person in charge of any vessel in transit upon the Chicago River and its branches to attempt to navigate any such vessel past any of the bridges over said river or branches, while a stop signal is being given or displayed.
(Prior code § 38-46)

§10-40-450 Signal for opening of railroad bridges.

When any vessel shall signal for any railroad bridge across any part of the harbor, the bridge tender shall immediately open the bridge, unless a train be on the bridge or approaching it so closely as to be unable to stop, and in that case the bridge may be kept closed long enough for the passage of one train and no more.

If, from any cause, the bridge tender cannot open the bridge, he shall immediately notify the vessel by waving a red flag by day and a red lantern by night and continue waving the same until the vessel has stopped, continuing thereafter to display the same until the bridge can be opened. As soon as the cause for stopping the vessel has been removed, the bridge shall be immediately opened.

It shall be unlawful for the owner, officer or other person in charge of any vessel to attempt to pass any railroad bridge while a stop signal is being given or displayed by the bridge tender.

Nothing in this or the preceding section shall be considered as superseding the bridge hours as set forth in this code.
(Prior code § 38-47)

§10-40-460 Signal to bridge tenders.

Every owner, officer, or person in charge of any vessel, craft or float navigating the harbor shall sound or cause to be sounded a steam whistle to signal bridge tenders to open and swing bridges, and such signal shall be three sharp, short sounds of the whistle, to be given in succession as quickly as possible and not to be prolonged, and the whistle used for this purpose shall be of suitable size to be heard; provided, such signal shall be four sharp, short sounds of the whistle for

vessels approaching the Northwestern Railway Bridge near W. Kinzie Street, and the Chicago, Milwaukee, St. Paul and Pacific Railway Bridge near W. North Avenue from either direction, and shall be five sharp, short sounds of the whistle for vessels approaching the Lake Street Bridge from the north.
(Prior code § 38-48)

§10-40-470 Obedience to bridge signals.

It shall be unlawful for any person to attempt to drive a vehicle upon any bridge after a signal has been given, warning traffic to stop crossing said bridge.
(Prior code § 38-49)

§10-40-480 Signal equipment at bridges.

The commissioner of transportation is hereby required to provide and maintain at the several bridges over the harbor, in the best and most practicable manner, vessel signals as required by this code.
(Prior code § 38-50; Amend. Coun. J. 12-11-91, p. 10832)

§10-40-490 Obstruction of bridges by vessels.

All vessels, craft, or floats navigating the harbor, when passing any bridge shall be moved past the same as expeditiously as is consistent with a proper movement in the harbor; but in no case shall any such vessel, craft, or float while passing any bridge and obstructing the passage across such bridge, move at a rate of speed less than two miles per hour, and in no case shall any vessel, craft, or float, while passing any bridge and obstructing the same, remain or obstruct the passage across such bridge more than five minutes; and no vessel, craft, or float shall be so anchored, laid, moored, fastened or brought to a stop as to prevent any bridge from a free and speedy opening or closing, or any vessel from a free and direct passage, nor shall any line or fastening be so thrown, laid, or made fast as to cross the track of any bridge or vessel. The master or other person having charge of such vessel, craft, or float which violates any provision of this section shall be fined not less than $25.00 for each offense.
(Prior code § 38-51)

§10-40-500 Fireboats.

Whenever, upon any alarm of fire, any fireboat shall approach a bridge and sound the proper signal for such bridge to open, the bridge tender shall, if such bridge is closed, open the same as soon as practicable; or, if open, shall keep such bridge open until such fireboat shall have had opportunity to pass through the draw of said bridge notwithstanding that the street traffic may thereby be delayed.
(Prior code § 38-52)

§10-40-501 Removal of life preservers prohibited.

No person shall remove or disable any life preserver, life ring or other safety equipment located on a public bridge except for use in an emergency. Any person who violates any provision of this section shall be subject to a fine of not less than $200.00 and not more than $500.00.
(Added. Coun. J. 7-29-98, p. 75096)

§10-40-510 Fire apparatus crossing bridges.

Whenever, at any alarm of fire, any fire engine, hose cart, or other fire apparatus shall approach any bridge, for the purpose of crossing the same toward such fire, the bridge tender shall, if such bridge is open, close the same as soon as practicable, and after the same is closed, or if closed at the time, keep it closed until such engine, hose cart, or other fire apparatus shall have had an opportunity to pass over said bridge, notwithstanding that vessels may thereby be delayed.
(Prior code § 38-53)

§10-40-520 Rule of the road.

It shall be the duty of all drivers or persons in charge of any vehicle to keep to the right when crossing any bridge in the city.
(Prior code § 38-54)

§10-40-530 Breaking line of traffic on bridge.

No person driving a vehicle across a bridge shall cross, attempt to cross, or break into, the line of vehicles while crossing or attempting to cross any bridge, nor shall any person disobey or resist any officer in charge of any bridge or crossing within the city.
(Prior code § 38-55)

§10-40-540 Unnecessary delay on bridge.

No person shall unnecessarily or wilfully remain or stop with any vehicle upon any of the bridges within the city, or in and upon any approach to any such bridge.
(Prior code § 38-56)

§10-40-550 Obstruction of traffic over bridge.

No person shall form part of any assembly or crowd on any of the bridges of the city, or the approaches leading to the same, so as to obstruct in any manner the passage of pedestrians and vehicles across the same, or be and remain upon any of the sidewalks or main passages of any of the bridges longer than is necessary to pass over the same.
(Prior code § 38-57)

§10-40-560 Congregation on bridges or viaducts.

It shall be unlawful for any person to form or cause an accumulation of persons, animals or vehicles on any public bridge or viaduct, to any extent which may jeopardize the safety of such bridge or viaduct. No person shall persist in causing such accumulation, after being warned by a bridge tender, police officer or other person having supervision of such bridge or viaduct.
(Prior code § 38-58)

Article V. Violations of Chapter Provisions

§10-40-570 Violation—Penalty.

Except as is otherwise specifically provided in this chapter, any person, including bridge tenders or other persons in charge of bridges within the city, violating any provision of this chapter shall be fined not less than $10.00 nor more than $100.00 for each offense.
(Prior code § 38-59)

TITLE 11
UTILITIES AND ENVIRONMENTAL PROTECTION
(Selected Chapters)

Chapters:

11-4 Environmental Protection And Control. (Selected Sections)
11-12 Water Supply and Service. (Selected Sections)

CHAPTER 11-4
ENVIRONMENTAL PROTECTION AND CONTROL
(Selected Sections)

Sections:

Article I. General Provisions

11-4-010 Title.
11-4-020 Enforcement of provisions.

Article II. Air Pollution Control

11-4-590 Refuse burning.
11-4-670 Reserved.
11-4-680 Spraying of asbestos prohibited—Exceptions.
11-4-730 Surfacing of lots and roadways.
11-4-740 Open fires prohibited.
11-4-750 Dilution or concealment of emissions prohibited.
11-4-760 Smoke and gases from internal combustion engines of vehicles.
11-4-770 Handling of material susceptible to becoming windborne.
11-4-780 Storage of materials susceptible to becoming windborne.
11-4-810 Municipal waste-burning equipment and municipal waste-burning prohibited.

Article VII. Noise and Vibration Control

11-4-1110 Sound pressure level—Public way.
11-4-1115 Sound device restrictions—Violation—Penalty.
11-4-1120 Sound pressure level—Time restrictions.
11-4-1130 Exempted acts.
11-4-1140 Lowest level limits to apply.
11-4-1150 Prohibited acts.
11-4-1290 Motor vehicle horns and audible signal devices.
11-4-1380 Public nuisance declared—Abatement.
11-4-1390 Legal remedy for damage unimpaired.

Article VIII. Pollution of Waters

11-4-1410 Disposal in waters prohibited.
11-4-1420 Ballast tank, bilge tank or other discharge.
11-4-1440 Wharfs, docks and similar structures in unsafe condition.
11-4-1450 Gas manufacturing residue.
11-4-1460 Enforcement.

Article IX. Solid and Liquid Waste Control

11-4-1500 Treatment and disposal of solid or liquid waste.
11-4-1530 Compliance with rules and regulations required.
11-4-1590 Violation of Sections 11-4-1530, 11-4-1540, 11-4-1550 or 11-4-1560—Penalty.
11-4-1600 Violation of Sections 7-28-390, 7-28-440, or 11-4-1500—Penalty.

Article XVI. Storage Tanks

11-4-2090 Definitions.
11-4-2100 Permit required.
11-4-2110 Permit issuance—Fees Revocation and transfer.
11-4-2120 Waiver of permit fees.

11-4-2130 Violation—Penalty.
11-4-2140 Fuel and lubrication facilities.

Article XVI-A. Asbestos, Sandblasting and Grinding Standards
11-4-2210 Severability.

Article XVII. Junk Facility Permits
11-4-2220 Permit—Required.
11-4-2230 Permit—Application—Investigation.
11-4-2240 Permit—Fee.
11-4-2260 Junk stores and junkyards—Location.
11-4-2270 Identification of vehicles and personnel.
11-4-2290 Charred metal.
11-4-2300 Fencing of yards.
11-4-2310 Maintaining of article identity.
11-4-2320 Time restriction on sales.
11-4-2330 Prohibited activities.
11-4-2340 Purchases from minors and intoxicated persons restricted.
11-4-2350 Fences.
11-4-2360 Hours of business—Dealer or agent on premises.
11-4-2370 Exhibiting lost or stolen goods upon demand.
11-4-2380 Inspection by police department.
11-4-2390 Permit revocation conditions.
11-4-2400 Enforcement.
11-4-2410 Inspection by commissioner of the environment.
11-4-2420 Violation—Penalty.

Article XVIII. Recycling Facility Permits
11-4-2510 Definitions.
11-4-2520 Permit—Required.
11-4-2535 Report required.
11-4-2570 Recyclable materials—Designated.
11-4-2580 Recyclable materials—Segregation and storage.
11-4-2620 Storage time limit—Maintenance of records.
11-4-2645 Identification of vehicles.
11-4-2680 Violation—Penalty.

Article I. General Provisions

§11-4-010 Title.

This chapter shall be known, cited and referred to as The Chicago Environmental Protection and Control Ordinance.
(Prior code § 17-1; Amend. Coun. J. 12-11-91, p. 10978)

§11-4-020 Enforcement of provisions.

(1) The provisions of this chapter, known as the Chicago Environmental Protection and Control Ordinance, shall be enforced by the commissioner of the department of environment, except for Article III which shall be enforced by the building commissioner and the executive director of construction and permits. All duties and powers granted herein shall be exercised by each such official.

(2) In addition to any other available penalties and remedies provided for in the code, one or more citations for violation of this chapter on each of three or more separate days within a three month period at the same construction site may result in a stop work order issued by the department of the environment, directing that all activity cease for 10 days. Any further citation for violation at the same

construction site within six months after the initial stop work order may result in the issuance of another 10 day stop work order. The department shall lift a 10 day stop work order only if sufficient evidence of compliance with this chapter is provided to the department. As used in this section, the term "construction site" has the meaning ascribed to the term in Section 13-32-125.

(a) It shall be unlawful for any person to knowingly violate a stop work order, or to knowingly cause, permit, encourage, assist, aid, abet or direct another person to violate a stop work order. or to knowingly in any manner be a party to a violation of a stop work order.

Any person who violates this subsection upon conviction shall be punished, as follows:

(i) Incarceration for a term not less than three days. nor more than six months, under the procedures set forth in Section 1-2-1.1 of the Illinois Municipal Code, as amended, and the Illinois Code of Criminal Procedure of 1963, as amended;

(ii) Community service of not less than 10 hours, nor more than 100 hours; and

(iii) A fine of $5,000.00.

(b) It shall be unlawful for any person to knowingly destroy, deface, remove, damage, impair, mar, cover or obstruct any stop work order that a city official has posted or affixed at a work site.

Any person who violates this subsection upon conviction shall be punished, as follows:

(i) Incarceration for a term not less than three days, nor more than six months, under the procedures set forth in Section 1-2-1.1 of the Illinois Municipal Code, as amended, and the Illinois Code of Criminal Procedure of 1963, as amended;

(ii) Community service of not less than 10 hours, nor more than 100 hours; and

(iii) A fine not less than $200.00, nor more than $500.00.

(Prior code § 17-1.1; Amend. Coun. J. 9-13-89, p. 4604; 12-11-91, p. 10978; 12-4-02, p. 99026; 12-15-04, p. 40435)

Article II. Air Pollution Control

§11-4-590 Refuse burning.

It shall be unlawful to burn refuse, garbage or other debris in any boiler or any unit which has not been specifically designed for that purpose and for which an effective certificate of operation has not been issued.

(Prior code § 17-2.2)

§11-4-670 Reserved.

(Repealed Coun. J. 9-1-99, p. 10096)

§11-4-680 Spraying of asbestos prohibited Exceptions.

It shall be unlawful within the city of Chicago, and within one mile of the corporate limits thereof, for any person, firm or corporation to cause or to permit the spraying of any substance containing asbestos, as defined in this article, in or upon any building, structure, column, frame, floor, ceiling or other por-

tion, part or member thereof during its construction, reconstruction, alteration or repair; provided, however, that such enclosed factories, buildings or structures in which the fabrication or manufacture of products containing asbestos is carried on shall not be subject to this provision.
(Prior code § 17-2.11)

§11-4-730 Surfacing of lots and roadways.

No person shall maintain or conduct or cause to be maintained or conducted any parking lot or automobile or truck sales or use any real property for a private roadway unless such real property is covered or treated with a surface or substance or otherwise maintained in such manner as to minimize atmospheric pollution.
(Prior code § 17-2.16)

§11-4-740 Open fires prohibited.

It shall be unlawful to burn paper, wood, garbage, leaves, building construction, demolition debris or any other combustible material in open fires or in metal containers.

The commissioner shall implement the rules and regulations set forth in Chapter V, PCB-R70-11, April 14, 1972, Open Burning, as promulgated by the State of Illinois Pollution Control Board and subject to amendment from time to time.
(Prior code § 17-2.17)

§11-4-750 Dilution or concealment of emissions prohibited.

It shall be unlawful for any person to build, erect, install use or alter any article, machine, equipment or other contrivance that dilutes, reduces or conceals an emission without reducing the quantity of pollutants released into the atmosphere and which, in its unaltered condition, would constitute a violation of Sections 11-4-600, 11-4-610 and 11-4-630 of this chapter.
(Prior code § 17-2.18; Amend. Coun. J. 12-11-91, p. 10978)

§11-4-760 Smoke and gases from internal combustion engines of vehicles.

No person shall operate or cause to be operated upon any street, highway, public place, stream or waterway or private premises within the city of Chicago any internal combustion engine of any motor vehicle, boat, tug or other vehicle, while stationary or moving, which emits from any source any particulate material, smoke, obnoxious or noxious gases, fumes or vapors or any other atmospheric pollutant in violation of Sections 11-4-600, 11-4-610 and 11-4-630 of this chapter provided the foregoing shall not apply to the operation of aircraft at municipal airports.

The commissioner shall implement the rules and regulations set forth in Chapter VII, PCB-R71-23, April 14, 1972, Emission Standards and Limitations from Mobile Sources promulgated by the State of Illinois Pollution Control Board and subject to amendment from time to time.
(Prior code § 17-2.19)

§11-4-770 Handling of material susceptible to becoming windborne.

It shall be unlawful for any person to cause or permit the handling, loading, unloading, reloading, storing, transferring, placing, depositing, throwing, discarding, or scattering of any ashes, fly ash, cinders, slag or dust collected from any combustion process, any dust, dirt, chaff, wastepaper, trash, rubbish, waste or refuse matter of any kind or any other substance or material whatever, including sandblasting materials, likely to be scattered by the wind or susceptible to being windborne without taking reasonable precautions or measures so as to minimize atmospheric pollution.

(Prior code § 17-2.20)

§11-4-780 Storage of materials susceptible to becoming windborne.

Subject to the provision of Section 11-4-730 hereof, it shall be unlawful for any person to operate or maintain or cause to be operated or maintained, any building, structure or premises, open area, right-of-way, storage pile of materials, yard, vessel or vehicle or construction, sandblasting, alteration, building, demolition or wrecking operation or any other enterprise which has or involves any matter, material or substance likely to be scattered by the wind, or susceptible to being windborne without taking reasonable precautions or measures so as to minimize atmospheric pollution.

(Prior code § 17-2.21)

§11-4-810 Municipal waste-burning equipment and municipal waste-burning prohibited.

(a) It shall be unlawful to install or replace a municipal waste incinerator in the city of Chicago after August 1, 2000.

(b) Beginning on October 1, 2000, all existing municipal waste incinerators in the city of Chicago shall cease operation and the burning of municipal waste in any incinerator shall be strictly prohibited except where required by state or federal law.

(c) By January 1, 2001, all existing municipal waste incinerators in the city must be removed or rendered inoperable and certified as such by the department of environment.

An incinerator will not be certified as inoperable until all of the following have occurred:

(1) The fuel and electricity are permanently disconnected;

(2) The stack, vent, bridge wall, or exhaust is disconnected, blocked and sealed off or permanently removed;

(3) The interior of the incinerator shall be cleared and cleaned of all residue and debris;

(4) The door to the incinerator is welded shut or otherwise permanently closed;

(5) The owner or operator of the incinerator notifies the department of environment in writing that the above four requirements have been satisfied.

(d) The department of environment shall inspect and certify whether the requirements in subsection (c) have been met. Upon approval, the department of environment shall provide written certification to the owner/operator that the incinerator has been rendered inoperable or removed.

(e) The commissioner shall have authority to promulgate rules and regulations regarding the closure requirements set forth in subsection (c).

(f) All permits for municipal waste incinerators in the city of Chicago will be revoked on October 1, 2000.

(g) The commissioner shall have the authority to extend the date for compliance through October 1, 2002, but only in cases where economic hardship is demonstrated and the permit holder submits to a waste audit to be performed by the department.

(Prior code § 17-2.24; Amend. Coun. J. 7-19-00, p. 38293)

Article VII. Noise and Vibration Control

§11-4-1110 Sound pressure level Public way.

No person except a person participating in a parade or public assembly for which a permit has been obtained pursuant to Chapter 10-8, shall, for purposes of entertainment or communication, generate any sound by any means so that (1) the sound pressure level on the public way measured at a distance of 10 feet or further from the source exceeds 80 Db(A), or is more than 10 Db(A) above the ambient noise level, or (2) the sound is louder than an average conversational level at a distance of 200 feet or more, measured either horizontally or vertically from the point of generation. Any person participating in a parade or public assembly for which a permit has been obtained pursuant to Chapter 10-8 of this code may generate sound in excess of the limitations in this section only if the sound generated does not exceed maximum levels set forth in regulations that the commissioner of the environment may promulgate. Such regulations shall define reasonable maximum sound levels in light of the nature of the event, its time, and the character of the surrounding neighborhood.

(Prior code § 17-4.2; Added. Coun. J. 1-27-88, p. 10081; Amend. Coun. J. 6-23-93, p. 34389; 7-21-99, p. 9473)

§11-4-1115 Sound device restrictions—Violation—Penalty.

(a) No person shall play, use, operate or permit to be played, used or operated, any radio, tape recorder, cassette player or other device for receiving broadcast sound or reproducing recorded sound if the device is located:

(1) On the public way; or

(2) In any motor vehicle on the public way;

and if the sound generated by the device is clearly audible to a person with normal hearing at a distance greater than 75 feet. This section shall not apply to any person participating in a parade or public assembly for which a permit has been obtained pursuant to Chapter 10-8.

(b) Any person who violates this section shall be subject to a fine of $50.00 for a first offense, $100.00 for a second offense committed within a one-year period, and $500.00 for a third or subsequent offense committed within a one-year period.

(c) (1) A motor vehicle that is used in the violation of subsection (a) of this section shall be subject to seizure and impoundment under this subsection. The owner of record of such vehicle shall be liable to the city for an administrative penalty of $500.00 in addition to fees for the towing and storage of the vehicle.

(2) Whenever a police officer has probable cause to believe that a vehicle is subject to seizure and impoundment pursuant to this section, the police officer shall provide for the towing of the vehicle to a facility controlled by the city or its agents. When the vehicle is towed, the police officer shall notify the person who is found to be in control of the vehicle at the time of the alleged violation, if there is such a person, of the fact of the seizure and of the vehicle owner's right to request a preliminary hearing to be conducted under Section 2-14-132 of this code.

(3) The provisions of Section 2-14-132 shall apply whenever a motor vehicle is seized and impounded pursuant to this section.
(Added. Coun. J. 6-23-93, p. 34389; Amend. 7-31-96, p. 26911; 4-29-98, p. 66564)

§11-4-1120 Sound pressure level Time restrictions.

Notwithstanding any other provision of this article, no person on the public way, in a public or private open space, or in a vehicle shall generate any sound by any means so that the sound pressure level exceeds 55 dB(A) within any residential unit between the hours of 9:00 p.m. and 8:00 a.m.
(Prior code § 17-4.3; Added. Coun. J. 1-27-88, p. 10081)

§11-4-1130 Exempted acts.

The provisions of Sections 11-4-1110 or 11-4-1120 shall not apply to any of the following acts:

(a) Use of a sound amplification device as an alarm or emergency warning device;

(b) Sounds generated between the hours of 8:00 a.m. and 9:00 p.m. in construction, demolition or repair work pursuant to duly authorized permit or franchise or license agreement;

(c) Sounds generated in construction, demolition or repair work of an emergency nature or in work on public improvements authorized by a governmental body or agency;

(d) Sounds generated by any aircraft or generated in connection with the operation of any airport;

(e) Sounds generated at any stadium or in connection with any festival, parade or street fair conducted pursuant to a valid permit;

(f) Sounds generated in the operation of any mass transit system.
(Prior code § 17-4.4; Added. Coun. J. 1-27-88, p. 10081)

§11-4-1140 Lowest level limits to apply.

In case of conflict between any sections of this article, the provision which contains the lowest level limits shall apply.
(Prior code § 17-4.5; Added. Coun. J. 1-27-88, p. 10081)

§11-4-1150 Prohibited acts.

The following acts and the causing thereof are prohibited:

(a) Sounding or permitting the sounding of any electronically amplified signal from any stationary bell, chime, siren, whistle or similar device intended primarily for nonemergency purposes from any place in such a manner as to create a noise disturbance at a residential lot boundary or residential zoning district boundary for more than five minutes in an hourly period;

(b) Intentionally sounding or permitting the sounding outdoors of any fire, burglar or civil defense alarm, siren, whistle or similar stationary emergency signaling device except in the following instances:

(1) For emergency purposes;

(2) For less than four minutes in an hourly period; or

(3) For testing of any stationary emergency signaling device which shall occur at the same time of day each time such a test is performed, shall use only the minimum cycle test time and in no case shall exceed four minutes nor shall it occur before 9:00 a.m. or after 5:00 p.m.;

(c) Creating or causing the creation of any sound within any noise sensitive zone, designated pursuant to 2-30-030(18) so as to interfere with the functions of any school, library, hospital, nursing home or other medical facility within the zone. Signs indicating a noise sensitive zone shall be conspicuously posted at the zone's boundaries;

(d) Loading, unloading, opening, closing or other handling of boxes, crates, containers, building materials, garbage cans or similar objects between the hours of 10:00 p.m. and 7:00 a.m. the following day in such a manner as to cause a noise disturbance at a residence lot boundary or a residential zoning district boundary or within a noise sensitive zone;

(e) Blowing or causing to be blown any steam whistle as a signal for commencing or suspending work or for any other purpose; provided that this section shall not be construed to prohibit the use of steam whistles as alarm signals in case of fire, collision or other imminent danger;

(f) Using any pile driver, shovel, hammer, derrick, hoist tractor, roller or other mechanical apparatus operated by fuel or electric power in building, construction, repair or demolition operations between the hours of 9:00 p.m. and 8:00 a.m. the following day within 600 feet of any residential building or hospital; provided that this provision shall not apply to any construction, demolition or repair work of an emergency nature or to work on public improvements authorized by a governmental body or agency.

(Prior code § 17-4.6; Added. Coun. J. 1-27-88, p. 10081; Amend. 12-11-91, p. 10978)

§11-4-1290 Motor vehicle horns and audible signal devices.

No person shall sound any horn or audible signal device of any motor vehicle of any kind while not in motion nor shall such horn or signal device be sounded under any circumstances except as required by law nor shall it be sounded for any unnecessary or unreasonable period of time.

(Prior code § 17-4.20)

§11-4-1380 Public nuisance declared—Abatement.

Any emission of noise or earthshaking vibration from any source in excess of the limitations established in or pursuant to this article shall be deemed and is hereby declared to be a public nuisance and may be subject to summary abatement procedures. Such abatement may be in addition to the administrative proceedings, fines and penalties herein provided. The commissioner is empowered to secure the institution of legal proceedings through the corporation coun-

sel for the abatement or prosecution of emissions of noise and earthshaking vibration which cause injury, detriment, nuisance or annoyance to the public or endanger the health, comfort, safety or welfare of the public, or cause to have a natural tendency to cause injury or damage to public or property. Such legal proceedings may be in addition to the administrative proceedings, fine and penalties herein provided.
(Prior code § 17-4.29)

§11-4-1390 Legal remedy for damage unimpaired.

Nothing in this article shall be construed to impair any cause of action or legal remedy therefor of any person or the public for injury or damage arising from the emission or release into the atmosphere or ground from any source whatever of noise or earthshaking vibration in such place or manner or at such levels, so as to constitute a common law nuisance.
(Prior code § 17-4.30)

Article VIII. Pollution of Waters

§11-4-1410 Disposal in waters prohibited.

No person shall throw, discharge, dispose or deposit, or cause, suffer, allow or procure to be thrown, discharged, disposed, dumped or deposited, in Lake Michigan within three miles of the corporate limits or in any other waters within the corporate limits any waste or material of any kind unless such person has obtained (a) permits pursuant to the Clean Water Act from all applicable federal or state agencies and (b) all other necessary approvals and permits from federal, state and local regulator bodies or special districts.
(Prior code § 17-5.2; Amend. Coun. J. 12-11-91, p. 10978; 9-4-02, p. 92754)

§11-4-1420 Ballast tank, bilge tank or other discharge.

No operator of any vessel, craft, floats or motorboat shall throw, discharge, dump, dispose or deposit into any waters any fuel, solid or liquid or the contents of any ballast tank, bilge tank or other container capable of causing pollution of waters.
(Prior code § 17-5.4; 9-4-02, p. 92754)

§11-4-1440 Wharfs, docks and similar structures in unsafe condition.

Every wharf, dock, pier, seawall, riverbank retaining wall, riverbank bulkhead, dolphin, boom, bulkhead, jetty mooring facility, piling, sheeting or other similar structure on or appurtenant to premises abutting on any waters which has disintegrated, rotted, deteriorated or is otherwise out of repair, or is in unsanitary condition, or in an unsafe or dangerous condition, or which in any manner endangers the health or safety of any person or persons or which in any manner endangers navigation is hereby declared to be a public nuisance.
(Prior code § 17-5.7; 9-4-02, p. 92754)

§11-4-1450 Gas manufacturing residue.

No person being a manufacturer of gas, or engaged about the manufacture thereof, shall throw, deposit or allow to run, or permit to be thrown or deposited into any waters, or into any sewer therewith connected, any gas-tar or any refuse matter of or from any gashouse, works or manufactory.
(Prior code § 17-5.9; 9-4-02, p. 92754)

§11-4-1460 Enforcement.

(a) (1) Violations of Section 11-4-1410, 11-4-1420 or 11-4-1450 shall be punished by a penalty of not less than $1,500.00 and not more than $2,500.00 for the first offense, not less than $2,500.00 nor more than $4,000.00 for the second offense, and not less than $4,000.00 nor more than $10,000.00 for each third and subsequent offense, or may be imprisoned for not more than six months, or may be ordered to perform up to 200 hours of community service, or any combination thereof. Each day that the violation continues shall be deemed a separate offense.

(2) Violations of Section 11-4-1430 or 11-4-1440 shall be punished by a penalty of $1,000.00 to $2,000.00 for the first offense, $2,000.00 to $4,000.00 for the second offense, and $4,000.00 to $10,000.00 for each third and subsequent offense. Each day that the violation continues shall be deemed a separate offense.

(b) In addition to any other penalties imposed under this section the registered owner of record of any vehicle who knew or should have known that his or her vehicle was used in violation of Section 11-4-1410 shall be jointly and severally liable with any person operating or in control of the vehicle at the time of the violation.

(c) In addition to any other penalties imposed under this section, the commissioner shall have the authority to issue cease and desist orders to stop any person from proceeding with any activity regulated under Sections 11-4-1410 through 11-4-1450 when the commissioner has reason to believe that such activity either is proceeding in violation of any provision under those sections or is otherwise in contravention of the public interest. The commissioner shall halt such activity until such time as the ordinance violations or public interest issues have been addressed or corrected to the satisfaction of the commissioner. Any person violating a cease and desist order issued by the commissioner shall be subject to a penalty of $5,000.00 per day for every day the person is in violation of the order. The cease and desist order shall also provide the owner or operator with a reasonable opportunity to be heard by the commissioner or his designee and present information as to why the order should be modified or rescinded. If the party to whom an order has been issued does not comply with the public nuisance abatement requirements in the order within a reasonable amount of time as determined by the commissioner, then, after providing the owner or operator with an opportunity to be heard, the department may complete any reasonably necessary abatement activities. Thereafter, the city shall be authorized to bring a civil action to recover penalties from the owner or operator equal to the amount of three times the abatement costs incurred by the department plus its attorney fees and to place, and subsequently foreclose on, a lien upon the property involved if necessary, to secure the recovery of its costs and fees.

(d) (1) Emergency Abatement. In the event that the commissioner determines that any activity in violation of Section 11-4-1410, 11-4-1420, 11-4-1440 or 11-4-1450 has created, or is creating, an imminent and substantial threat to the environment or the public's health, safety, or welfare, then the commissioner shall order the owner of the vehicle, the operator of the vehicle, and any other person involved in the performance of the subject activity to abate the threat in the manner and within a time frame prescribed by the commissioner. In the event that any person fails to abate such threat in accordance with the commissioner's order, the commissioner may proceed to control, remove, dispose or otherwise abate the threat.

(2) Non-emergency Abatement. In the event that the commissioner determines that any activity in violation of Section 11-4-1410, 11-4-1420, 11-4-1440 or 11-4-1450 has not created, or is not creating, an imminent and substantial threat to the public's health, safety or welfare, the commissioner shall provide the owner of the vehicle, the operator of the vehicle or any other person involved in the performance of the subject activity with written notice to abate the nuisance in the manner prescribed by the commissioner within three days from receipt of the notice. In the event that any person fails to abate such nuisance in accordance with the commissioner's notice to abate, the commissioner may proceed to control, remove, dispose or otherwise abate the nuisance.

(3) In addition any other penalties imposed in subsection (a) of this section, the city shall be entitled to recover a penalty in the amount equal to three times the cost or expense incurred by the city in abating the nuisance in an appropriate action instituted by the corporation counsel.

(e) In addition to any other penalties imposed by subsection (a) of this section, the provisions of Section 11-4-1600(e) shall be applicable for violations of Section 11-4-1410, 11-4-1420, or 11-4-1450.

(f) (1) In addition to any other penalty imposed in this section, the owner of record of any motor vehicle used in violation of Section 11-4-1410 shall be liable to the city for an administrative penalty of $500.00 plus any applicable towing and storage fees. Any such vehicle shall be seizure and impoundment pursuant to this section.

(2) Whenever a police officer has probable cause to believe that a vehicle is subject to seizure and impoundment pursuant to this section, the police officer shall provide for the towing of the vehicle to a facility controlled by the city or its agent. When the vehicle is towed, the police officer shall notify any person identifying himself as the owner of the vehicle or any person who is found to be in control of the vehicle at the time of the alleged violation, if there is such a person, of the fact of the seizure and of the vehicle owner's right to request a preliminary hearing to be conducted under Section 2-14-132 of this code.

(3) The provisions of Section 2-14-132 shall apply whenever a motor vehicle is seized and impounded pursuant to this section.

(g) The city may obtain permanent or temporary injunctive relief in the Circuit Court of Cook County, Illinois, for any violation of Sections 11-4-1410 through 11-4-1450.

(Added. Coun. J. 9-4-02, p. 92754; Amend. 11-3-04, p. 34974)

Article IX. Solid and Liquid Waste Control

§11-4-1490 Definitions.

Definitions relating to Article IX will be found in Article I, Section 11-4-120.
(Prior code § 17-6.1)

§11-4-1500 Treatment and disposal of solid or liquid waste.

No solid or liquid waste shall be treated or disposed of within the city of Chicago except in accordance with this chapter. Wastes shall be treated or disposed of in the following manner:

(a) An incinerator or resource recovery facility which meets the air quality standards, operating standards and monitoring requirements established by this chapter may treat municipal waste; provided however, incinerators and resource recovery facilities designed to dispose of or treat special waste or hazardous waste shall operate in conformance with the Federal Resource Conservation and Recovery Act of 1976, P. L. 95-580, as amended, and the Illinois Environmental Protection Act, P. A. 76-2429, as amended.

(b) A liquid waste handling facility which meets the operating standards established by this chapter may dispose of or treat nonnuclear liquid waste; provided, however, liquid waste handling facilities designed to dispose of or treat special or hazardous liquid waste shall operate in conformance with the Illinois Environmental Protection Act, P. A. 76-2429, as amended, and applicable federal law and regulations.

(c) A recycling facility may handle any recyclable materials as defined in this chapter.

(d) A sanitary landfill may dispose of or treat municipal waste, or any other waste permitted in a sanitary landfill under the Illinois Environmental Protection Act, P. A. 76-2429, as amended. No hazardous waste or radioactive waste may be disposed of in a sanitary landfill within the corporate limits of the city of Chicago.

(e) A transfer station may accept waste for sorting and/or consolidation and for further transfer to a waste disposal, treatment, or handling facility.

No persons shall (1) cause or allow the open dumping of any waste, (2) abandon or dispose of any waste upon public property, except in a sanitary landfill approved by the Illinois Environmental Protection Agency and the Commissioner, (3) dispose, treat, abandon or transport any waste, except at a site or facility which meets the requirements of the Illinois Environmental Protection Act and which is permitted pursuant to this chapter.

Disposal or treatment of any waste without a permit is hereby declared to be a nuisance.
(Prior code § 17-6.2; Added. Coun. J. 3-8-89, p. 25433; Amend. 1-12-95, p. 65073)

§11-4-1530 Compliance with rules and regulations required.

All sanitary landfills, incinerators, resource recovery facilities, transfer stations, recycling facilities, and facilities that dispose, handle or treat any waste located within the city shall operate in compliance with the Federal Resource Conservation and Recovery Act of 1976, P.L. 94-580, as amended; the Illinois Environmental Protection Act, P.A. 76-2429, as amended and all other applicable federal, state and local laws and regulations.

(Prior code § 17-6.5; Amend. Coun. J. 3-8-89, p. 25433; 1-12-95, p. 65073)

§11-4-1590 Violation of Sections 11-4-1530, 11-4-1540, 11-4-1550 or 11-4-1560—Penalty.

(a) Any person who violates Section 11-4-1530, 11-4-1540, 11-4-1550 or 11-4-1560 of this article shall be punished by a penalty of $1,000.00 for the first offense and $2,000.00 for the second and each subsequent offense. Each day that a violation continues shall constitute a separate and distinct offense. In addition to any other penalty imposed under this article, the provisions of Section 11-4-1600(e) shall be applicable.

(b) Any person who disposes of hazardous waste or radioactive waste in violation of this chapter commits an offense that may be punishable as a misdemeanor by incarceration in a penal institution other than a penitentiary for a period not less than 30 days and not more than six months.

(Prior code § 17-6.11; Amend. Coun. J. 3-8-89, p. 25433; 3-6-96, p. 17628; 11-3-04, p. 34974)

§11-4-1600 Violation of Sections 7-28-390, 7-28-440, or 11-4-1500—Penalty.

(a) Any person found in violation of Section 7-28-390, 7-28-440, or 11-4-1500 shall be punished by a penalty of not less than $1,500.00 and not more than $2,500.00 for the first load dumped, deposited, disposed, released, treated or placed, and not less than $2,500.00 nor more than $3,500.00 for the second and each subsequent load, or may be imprisoned for not more than six months, or may be ordered to perform up to 200 hours of community service, or any combination thereof. For each subsequent day that a load dumped, deposited, disposed, released, treated or placed in violation of Section 7-28-390, 7-28-440, or 11-4-1500 remains at the location where it was dumped, deposited, disposed, released, treated or placed, or any load that migrated to another location remains at that location to which it has migrated, the person shall be punished by a penalty of not less than $2,500.00 per load per day, and not more than $3,500.00 per load per day.

(b) In addition to any other penalties imposed under this section, the registered owner of record of any vehicle who knew or should have known that his or her vehicle was used in violation of Section 7-28-390, 7-28-440, or 11-4-1500 shall be jointly and severally liable with any person operating or in control of the vehicle at the time of the violation.

(c) The commissioner shall have the authority to issue cease and desist orders to stop any person from proceeding with any activity regulated under Section 7-28-390, 7-28-440, or 11-4-1500 when the commissioner has reason to believe that such activity either is proceeding in violation of any provision under those sections or is otherwise in contravention of the public interest. The commissioner shall halt such activity until such time as the ordinance violations or public interest issues have been addressed or corrected to the satisfaction of the commissioner. Any person violating a cease and desist order issued by the commissioner shall be subject to a penalty of $5,000.00 per day for every day the person is in violation of the order. The cease and desist order shall also provide the owner or operator with a reasonable opportunity to be heard by the commissioner or his designee and present information as to why the order should be modified or rescinded. If the party to whom an order has been issued does not comply with the public nuisance abatement requirements in the order within a reasonable amount of time as determined by the commissioner, then, after providing the owner or operator with an opportunity to be heard, the department may complete any reasonably necessary abatement activities. Thereafter, the city shall be authorized to bring a civil action to recover penalties from the owner or operator equal to the amount of three times the abatement costs incurred by the department plus its attorney fees and to place, and subsequently foreclose on, a lien upon the property involved, if necessary, to secure the recovery of its costs and fees. The penalties for the recovery of costs shall be in addition to any penalties imposed pursuant to subsection (a) of this section.

(d) (1) Emergency Abatement. In the event that the commissioner or the commissioner of streets and sanitation determines that any activity in violation of Section 7-28-390, 7-28-440, or 11-4-1500 has created, or is creating, an imminent and substantial threat to the environment or the public's health, safety, or welfare, then the commissioner or the commissioner of streets and sanitation shall order the owner of the vehicle, the operator of the vehicle, and any other person involved in the performance of the subject activity to abate the threat in the manner and within a time frame prescribed by the commissioner or the commissioner of streets and sanitation. In the event that any person fails to abate such threat in accordance with the commissioner's or the commissioner of streets and sanitation's order, the commissioner or the commissioner of streets and sanitation may proceed to control, remove, dispose or otherwise abate the threat.

(2) Non-emergency Abatement. In the event that the commissioner or the commissioner of streets and sanitation determines that any activity in violation of Section 7-28-390, 7-28-440, or 11-4-1500 has not created, or is not creating, an imminent and substantial threat to the public's health, safety or welfare, the commissioner or the commissioner of streets and sanitation shall provide the owner of the vehicle, the operator of the vehicle or any other person involved in the performance of the subject activity with written notice to abate the nuisance in the manner prescribed by the commissioner or the commissioner of streets and sanitation within three days from receipt of the notice. In the event that any person fails to abate such nuisance in accordance with the commissioner's or the commissioner of streets and sanitation's notice to abate, the commissioner or the commissioner of streets and sanitation may proceed to control, remove, dispose or otherwise abate the nuisance.

(3) In addition any other penalties imposed in this section, the city shall be entitled to recover a penalty in the amount equal to three times the cost or expense incurred by the city in abating the nuisance in an appropriate action instituted by the corporation counsel.

(e) All city contracts advertised, or if not advertised, awarded, 90 days after the effective date of this ordinance shall include a provision that a violation of Section 7-28-390, 7-28-440, 11-4-1410, 11-4-1420, 11-4-1450, 11-4-1500, 11-4-1530, 11-4-1550, or 11-4-1560 by the contractor, whether or not in the performance of the agreement, shall constitute a breach of the contract.

(f) (1) In addition to any other penalty imposed in this section, the owner of record of any motor vehicle used in violation of Section 7-28-390, 7-28-440, or 11-4-1500 shall be liable to the city for an administrative penalty of $500.00 plus any applicable towing and storage fees. Any such vehicle shall be seizure and impoundment pursuant to this section.

(2) Whenever a police officer has probable cause to believe that a vehicle is subject to seizure and impoundment pursuant to this section, the police officer shall provide for the towing of the vehicle to a facility controlled by the city or its agent. When the vehicle is towed, the police officer shall notify any person identifying himself as the owner of the vehicle or any person who is found to be in control of the vehicle at the time of the alleged violation, if there is such a person, of the fact of the seizure and of the vehicle owner's right to request a preliminary hearing to be conducted under Section 2-14-132 of this code.

(3) The provisions of Section 2-14-132 shall apply whenever a motor vehicle in seized and impounded pursuant to this section.

(g) The city may obtain permanent or temporary injunctive relief in the Circuit Court of Cook County, Illinois, for any violation of Section 7-28-390, 7-28-440, or 11-4-1500.

(Prior code § 17-6.12; Added. Coun. J. 10-28-87, p. 5641; Amend. 11-3-04, p. 34974)

Article XVI. Storage Tanks

§11-4-2090 Definitions.

As used in this article, unless the context requires otherwise:

(a) "Commissioner" shall mean the commissioner of the department of environment.

(b) "Contractor" shall mean any person licensed and certified by the state of Illinois to perform storage tank installation, repair, removal or abandonment.

(c) "Operator" shall mean any person in control of, or having responsibility for, the daily operation of the tank, including activities requiring permits.

(d) "Tank" shall mean any permanent underground, aboveground or enclosed tank greater than 110 gallons in volume and any and all connecting fittings, piping and other ancillary equipment, used or intended to be used for the storage of any regulated flammable liquids, corrosive liquids, oxidizing materials, highly toxic materials or hazardous chemicals in liquid form as provided in Chapters 15-24 and 15-28 of this code.

(Added. Coun. J. 6-10-96, p. 23557)

§11-4-2100 Permit required.

No person shall install, repair, remove, abandon in place or temporarily place out of service any tank unless a permit has been issued by the commissioner allowing such activity. An application for such permit or an amendment to an existing permit shall be in writing from the contractor, in such form as the commissioner requires, and shall include the following information:

(a) The names and addresses of the owner, the operator and the owner's authorized and responsible agent;

(b) The name, address, license number and authorized signature of the contractor;

(c) The address of the tank site, the plans and specifications for the tank's installation, abandonment, repair, removal or placement out of service and the tank's measurements, connections, fittings, pipings, openings and safety appliances; and

(d) Such other information that the commissioner may determine is reasonably necessary to determine compliance with this code.

(Added. Coun. J. 6-10-96, p. 23557)

§11-4-2110 Permit issuance—Fees—Revocation and transfer.

(a) No permit shall be issued until review and approval of plans and specifications by the commissioner and payment of permit fees. Additionally, no permit shall be issued before like plan review and approval by the fire prevention bureau of the department of fire for conformance with the fire provisions of this code. The permit fee to install, repair, remove, abandon in place, or place any tank out of service shall be $100.00 per site, per activity. Any permit issued under this article shall expire in six months from the date it is issued, except that the applicant may apply for and be entitled to one six-month extension of the permit during the time the permit is valid, with no additional fee required.

(b) A permit may be revoked by either the commissioner or the fire prevention bureau of the fire department where job site conditions are deemed not to be in compliance with any of the applicable provisions of this code. No tank or equipment shall be installed, repaired, removed, used or abandoned in place until the installation, material and workmanship have been fully inspected, tested and approved by the commissioner or his representative and the fire prevention bureau of the fire department.

(c) No permit shall be assigned and no rights or privileges thereunder shall be transferred or assigned except by written consent of the commissioner.

(Added. Coun. J. 6-10-96, p. 23557)

§11-4-2120 Waiver of permit fees.

The commissioner is authorized to waive any permit fee required by this article for any tank owned or operated by the federal government, the state of Illinois or any agency or political subdivision thereof.

(Added. Coun. I. 6-10-96, p. 23557)

§11-4-2130 Violation—Penalty.

Permit fees authorized by this article shall constitute a debt due and owing the city. Any person violating this article shall be subject to a fine of not less than $100.00 and not more than $500.00 for each offense. Each day that such violation continues shall be considered a separate offense.

(Added. Coun. J. 6-10-96, p. 23557)

§11-4-2140 Fuel and lubrication facilities.

(1) For purposes of this section, the term "facility" shall mean any commercial establishment that provides motor vehicle refueling or oil changes on a retail basis, if one or more underground tanks are located on-site or used in conjunction with operations conducted on-site.

(2) Each facility in the city must provide notification, as set forth in this section, to the department of environment. There shall be no fee to provide notification or to update a notification. Such notification shall be on forms provided by the department of environment, and shall include the following information:

(a) Site information: name, address, telephone number, fax number.

(b) Owner information: name, off-site address where certified mail can be received, weekday telephone number, 24-hour emergency telephone number, fax number.

(c) Operator information: name, off-site address where certified mail can be received, weekday telephone number, 24-hour emergency telephone number, fax number.

(d) Current Office of the State Fire Marshal certification number (green sticker) and facility identification number, number and size of underground tanks on site, status of such underground tanks (e.g., active, out-of-service, if out-of-service, date taken out), products stored in such underground tanks.

(e) Such other information as the commissioner of environment may required.

A notification must be provided to the department of environment by January 1st of each year. Such annual notification shall be required even if no changes have occurred since the submission of the previous notification. An updated notification must be provided in the event that any information on a notification form on file with the department of environment becomes inaccurate or incomplete in any respect at any time during the year, within 30 days of the change in status. Such changes in status include, but are not limited to, changes in ownership, changes in operator and the temporary or permanent termination of operations at a facility.

(3) Any person owning and/or operating a facility in violation of any provision of this section shall be personally subject to a fine not to exceed $500.00 for each violation, plus court costs and reasonable attorney's fees. Each day that a violation continues shall constitute a separate and distinct offense.

(4) In the event that the city is unable to contact an owner or operator of a facility using information provided on a notification form, or as a result of an owner's or operator's failure to provide notification or update a notification, the facility shall be presumed to be abandoned, and the department of environment may, after reasonable efforts to contact the owner or operator, arrange for the closure of the facility, and the abatement of any public nuisances associated with the facility, in accordance with applicable law. Costs incurred by the city in conjunction with such closure and abatement shall be a lien on the property as provided by law. In addition, the owner and operator of the facility shall be jointly and severally liable for a fine in an amount equal to two times the city's costs of closure and abatement, plus court costs and reasonable attorney's fees. Such fine shall be in addition to any other fines and penalties provided herein. *(Added. Coun. J. 10-7-98, p. 78728)*

Article XVI-A. Asbestos, Sandblasting and Grinding Standards

§11-4-2210 Severability.

If any part of Section 11-4-2145 through Section 1 1-4-2200 is found to be invalid for any reason, such holding shall not affect the validity of the remaining portions of those sections.
(Added. Coun. J. 9-1-99, p. 10096; Amend. 6-7-00, p. 34984)

Article XVII. Junk Facility Permits

§11-4-2220 Permit—Required.

No person shall operate a junk facility without having obtained a written junk facility permit from the commissioner of environment. Each permit shall be renewed annually in accordance with the rules and regulations adopted by the commissioner.

A separate permit shall be procured by every junk dealer for each separate junk store or junkyard located on separate premises. Where a junk store and a junkyard located upon the same or contiguous or adjoining premises are conducted or operated by the same person, such business shall be considered as one business and only one permit shall be required therefor.
(Added. Coun. J. 10-7-98, p. 78812)

§11-4-2230 Permit—Application—Investigation.

An application for a permit under this article shall be made in conformity with the requirements of this section and the rules and regulations relating to applications for a permit. The applicant shall observe and comply with all provisions of this code now in force or which may hereafter be passed respecting junk facilities. The application shall at a minimum identify the owner of the property where the business will be conducted, the location of the facility, operating hours, and materials to be accepted and any other information deemed necessary by the commissioner. The application shall also state the color, make, model, vehicle license plate number and city of Chicago wheel tax license number of every junk vehicle used by the applicant. If title to the property is held in trust, the names and addresses of all beneficiaries and persons authorized to deal with title to the property shall be provided.

No person shall be eligible for a junk facility permit if he has been convicted of keeping, conducting, operating or participating in any illegal operation connected with the junk dealer business within three years prior to the date of application for the permit. No corporation shall be eligible for a junk facility permit if any of its officers, directors, shareholders or employees have been convicted of keeping, conducting, operating, or participating in any illegal operation connected with the junk dealer business within three years prior to the date of application for the permit unless such corporation shall produce satisfactory evidence to the mayor that such officer, director, shareholder or employee has disposed of his or her entire interest in such corporation and has completely severed his or her connection with said corporation.

The division marshal in charge of fire prevention upon notice from the commissioner of environment of the receipt of such application, shall investigate or cause to be investigated the place of business named in the application to determine whether the applicable fire prevention provisions of this code have been complied with.
(Added. Coun. J. 10-7-98, p. 78812)

§11-4-2240 Permit—Fee.

The annual permit fee for a junk, facility permit shall be $750.00.
(Added Coun J 10 7-98 p 78812; Amend. Coun. J. 12-4-02, p. 99931)

§11-4-2260 Junk stores and junkyards—Location.

Every permit issued for a junk facility shall designate the house, store, place, building, warehouse, yard or enclosure in which the person receiving such permit shall be authorized to conduct or operate such business, and such business shall not be conducted or operated in any place other than the place designated in such permit.

It shall be unlawful for any person to locate, conduct or operate any junk facility within 400 feet of a church, hospital, public or private school, said distance to be measured by the shortest straight line between the junk facility sought to be located, conducted or operated and any such building used for the purposes aforementioned.

It shall be unlawful to any person to locate, conduct or operate any junk facility in any block in which two-thirds of the buildings on both sides of such street in any such block are used exclusively for residence purposes, or residence and wholesale or retail store purposes, or used exclusively for wholesale or retail store purposes, without the written consent of a majority of the property owners according to frontage on both sides of the street; provided, that in determining whether two-thirds of the buildings on both sides of such street in any block are used exclusively for residence purposes, or residence and wholesale or retail store purposes, or used exclusively for wholesale or retail store purposes, any building fronting upon another street and located upon the corner lot shall not be considered; and provided, further, that the word “block” as used in this section shall be held not to mean a square, but shall be held to embrace only that part of the street in question which lies between the two nearest intersecting streets on either side of the lot on which said junk facility is to be located, conducted or operated. Such written consents of the property owners shall be filed with the zoning administrator for inspection and verification. If after inspection and verification of such frontage consents, the building commissioner and bureau of fire prevention shall find that this section and the building regulations of this code have been complied with, the zoning administrator shall issue a permit for the location, conduct or operation of such junk facility. In all cases where this section shall apply, the permit herein provided for shall be procured before a written junk facility permit from the commissioner shall be issued.
(Added. Coun. J. 10-7-98, p. 78812)

§11-4-2270 Identification of vehicles and personnel.

Every junk vehicle used off the premises of the junk facility for the collection, transportation or disposal of any junk, shall display on each side of the vehicle in letters not less than two inches in height, in contrasting color the name, address, telephone number and permit number of the junk facility.

The driver and/or operator(s) of each junk vehicle shall wear a reflective safety vest or other reflective clothing.

(Added. Coun. J. 10-7-98, p. 78812)

§11-4-2290 Charred metal.

No junk dealer shall receive, purchase or acquire through barter any charred metal unless he can demonstrate through receipts or other documentation approved by the commissioner that the material has come from a properly licensed company which has and uses process equipment with the appropriate functioning emission control devices to remove coatings on the wire.

(Added. Coun. J. 10-7-98, p. 78812)

§11-4-2300 Fencing of yards.

Every premises or enclosure, except a completely enclosed building, now or hereafter used as a junkyard, shall be entirely surrounded by a solid fence eight feet in height which is so constructed as to completely obscure all material stored or kept within the boundaries thereof. Such fence shall be located at least eight feet from all public ways surrounding the property and none of said material shall be piled nearer than six inches to, nor higher than, said fence. Where such an existing fence is erected nearer than eight feet to a public way, such fence may be permitted to remain but none of said material shall be piled nearer than eight feet to such public way nor contrary to the provisions of this section. Materials shall be stored in a safe and sanitary manner. The permittee shall install, maintain and operate overhead lighting to illuminate the outdoor portion of the permitted premises and bordering streets, alleys and sidewalks. The overhead lights shall be lighted from dusk until dawn.

(Added. Coun. J. 10-7-98, p. 78812)

§11-4-2310 Maintaining of article identity.

No article, thing or substance included within such junk purchased, received or collected at retail shall be melted, vulcanized or otherwise changed or its identity destroyed within two days after the same was purchased, received or collected.

(Added. Coun. J. 10-7-98, p. 78812)

§11-4-2320 Time restriction on sales.

No retail junk dealer shall expose for sale, or sell or dispose of, any goods, article, junk or thing whatsoever within two days of the time of collecting, receiving or purchasing the same, nor until the same shall have been in the premises wherein the same are offered, exposed or sold at least two days.

(Added. Coun. J. 10-7-98, p. 78812)

§11-4-2330 Prohibited activities.

(a) No retail junk dealer shall receive any article or thing by way of pledge or pawn, nor shall such dealer loan or advance any sum of money on the security of any article or thing.

(b) No person permitted to operate a junk facility shall receive or hold a license to conduct the business of a pawnbroker, secondhand dealer or itinerant dealer in secondhand clothing.

(c) No junk dealer shall park any junk vehicle on any residential or business street in violation of Section 9-64-170 of this code.

(d) No junk dealer shall use any junk vehicle in violation of the vehicle size, load and weight restrictions as provided for in Chapter 9-72 of this code.

(Added. Coun. J. 10-7-98, p. 78812)

§11-4-2340 Purchases from minors and intoxicated persons restricted.

No retail junk dealer shall purchase any article whatsoever from any minor without the written consent of the minor's parent or guardian. No retail junk dealer shall purchase any article from any person who appears intoxicated or under the influence of any drug.

(Added. Coun. J. 10-7-98, p. 78812)

§11-4-2350 Fences.

No person shall keep, maintain or conduct a place for the purchase, reception or keeping of stolen goods as a "fence."

(Added. Coun. J. 10-7-98, p. 78812)

§11-4-2360 Hours of business—Dealer or agent on premises.

No junk facility shall receive any goods, articles or things whatsoever from any person except between the hours of 7:00 a.m. and 9:00 p.m., nor shall any junk dealer sell, purchase or collect any junk in any public alley between the hours of 9:00 p.m. and 7:00 a.m. except as permitted in Section 8-4-240 of this code. During all hours of operation of the facility, the dealer or his designated agent shall be present. Every junk dealer shall file the names and addresses of all such agents with the commissioner of the environment.

(Added. Coun. J. 10-7-98, p. 78812)

§11-4-2370 Exhibiting lost or stolen goods upon demand.

Every retail junk dealer who shall receive or be in possession of any goods, articles, things or junk which may have been lost or stolen, or are alleged or supposed to have been lost or stolen, shall forthwith on demand exhibit the same to any member of the department of police or to any alderman.

(Added. Coun. J. 10-7-98, p. 78812)

§11-3-2380 Inspection by police department.

Junk facilities and junk vehicles shall, at all reasonable times, be open to the inspection of any member of the police department.

Whenever there shall be filed with the commissioner of police, by the owner, or agent of the owner, a sworn statement that such owner or such agent has reason to believe that certain stolen goods or things specifically described in said sworn statement are in the possession of any junk dealer, any member of

the police department shall have the right to inspect the premises of the said junk dealer at any reasonable hour and view all junk which has been purchased, received collected or stored in the premises occupied by such business.
(Added. Coun. J. 10-7-98, p. 78812)

§11-4-2390 Permit revocation conditions.

(a) The junk facility permit of any person convicted of keeping, maintaining or conducting a fence shall, upon such conviction, be immediately revoked.

(b) Nothing in this section shall be interpreted as prohibiting the commissioner from taking enforcement action or revoking a junk facility permit based on noncompliance with this article, the permit, or the rules and regulations promulgated hereunder.
(Added. Coun. J. 10-7-98, p. 78812)

§11-4-2400 Enforcement.

(a) The commissioner of the environment may promulgate rules and regulations not inconsistent with the provisions of this article for the purpose of implementing the provisions hereof, including regulations for the security of junk yard sites, safe and sanitary storage of materials, and records of operation of junk facilities. The commissioner shall also be responsible for the enforcement of this article, junk facility permits, and the regulations promulgated hereunder.

(b) Junk dealers, junkyards and junk stores shall comply with the provisions of this article, the rules and regulations promulgated hereunder, the permit and its conditions and any other applicable laws and ordinances.
(Added. Coun. J. 10-7-98, p. 78812)

§11-4-2410 Inspection by commissioner of the environment.

The commissioner of the environment shall inspect or cause the inspection of premises where junk is stored, purchased, sold or bartered in order to determine compliance with this article, the rules and regulations promulgated hereunder, a junk facility permit and its conditions and other applicable laws and ordinances. The commissioner may order any such premises to be immediately closed and secured against entry upon discovery of an immediate danger to the public health and safety caused by the presence, treatment or storage of any substance, or other activity on the premises, in violation of this article, a junk facility permit or its conditions or the rules and regulations promulgated hereunder.
(Added. Coun. J. 10-7-98, p. 78812)

§11-4-2420 Violation—Penalty.

Any person who violates any of the provisions of this article, or any rule or regulation promulgated hereunder, or interferes with the performance of the commissioner of the environment in enforcement of this article or the rules and regulations, shall upon conviction be guilty of a misdemeanor and shall be fined not less than $100.00 and not more than $500.00 for each offense. Subsequent offenses within a period of 180 days shall be punishable by incarceration for not less than seven days and not more than 180 days. All prosecutions shall be conducted under the procedure set forth in Section 1-2-1.1 of the Illinois Municipal Code, as amended. Every day on which such violation continues shall be regarded as constituting a separate offense.
(Added. Coun. J. 10-7-98, p. 78812)

Article XVIII. Recycling Facility Permits

§11-4-2520 Permit—Required.

No person shall engage in the business of operating a recycling facility in the city of Chicago without having first obtained a written recycling facility permit from the commissioner. Recycling facilities requiring a permit under this section shall comply with the provisions of this article, the rules and regulations promulgated hereunder, the permit and its conditions and any other applicable laws and ordinances. Each permit shall be renewed annually in accordance with the rules and regulations adopted by the commissioner.
(Coun. J. 12-9-92, p. 25465; Amend. 10-7-98, p. 78812)

§11-4-2535 Report required.

Any person who operates or maintains a recycling facility shall submit a written report to the commissioner of the department of environment summarizing recycling activities between January 1st and June 30th, on or before August 31st and recycling activities between July 1st and December 31st, on or before February 28th of each year, setting forth the following data and information:

(1) The weight of all materials collected in total by the permittee; and

(2) The weight of all materials recycled by types or categories of materials with a separate listing estimating the weight represented by buy-back or drop-off-facilities; and

(3) The percentage of customers that are high density, condominium or cooperative residential buildings, and the percentage of customers that are commercial, office or retail establishments.
(Added. Coun. J. 1 1-5-93, p. 40151; Corrected. 4-13-94, p. 491 12; Amend. 10-7-98, p. 78812)

§11-4-2570 Recyclable materials—Designated.

Facilities permitted under this article shall collect, process and store only recyclable materials as defined in Section 11-4-2510. Unauthorized materials, including but not limited to municipal solid waste and stolen goods including recyclables intended for collection by the department of streets and sanitation but not delivered by the department or its agent shall not be accepted at the facility.
(Coun. J. 12-9-92, p. 25465; Amend. 10-7-98, p. 78812)

§11-4-2580 Recyclable materials—Segregation and storage.

Recyclable materials shall be segregated and stored in receptacles or enclosures constructed of approved materials or in another manner approved in the permit as directed by the commissioner. Newsprint, paper, corrugated paper and cardboard shall be stored in closed containers, and storage of such material shall comply with all applicable provisions of the Municipal Code, including all ordinances relating to fire prevention.
(Coun. J. 12-9-92, p. 25465; Amend. 10-7-98, p. 78812)

§11-4-2620 Storage time limit—Maintenance of records.

No recyclable materials shall be stored at any recycling facility for longer than 90 days except for processed, recyclable materials as approved in the permit. Each permittee under this article shall maintain records which indicate the

date, quantity and type of recyclable materials received. Disposition records shall also be kept which indicate the type, quantity and date of disposition of recyclable materials. Such records shall be open to inspection by the commissioner or his authorized agent during normal business hours and at other times upon reasonable notice.
(Coun. J. 12-9-92, p. 25465; Amend. 10-7-98, p. 78812)

§11-4-2645 Identification of vehicles.

Every vehicle used by a recycling facility off the premises of the recycling facility for the collection, transportation, or disposal of any recycling material shall display on each side of the vehicle in letters not less than two inches in height, in contrasting color, the name, address, telephone number and permit number of the recycling facility.
(Added. Coun. J. 10-7-98, p. 78812)

§11-4-2680 Violation—Penalty.

Any person who violates any of the provisions of this article or any rule or regulation promulgated hereunder, or interferes with the performance of the commissioner of the environment in enforcement of this article or the rules and regulations, shall be guilty of a misdemeanor and shall be fined not less than $100.00 nor more than $500.00 for each offense. Subsequent offenses within a period of 180 days shall be punishable by incarceration for not less than seven days and not more than 180 days. All prosecution shall be conducted under the procedure set forth in Section 1-2-1.1 of the Illinois Municipal Code, as amended. Every day on which such violation continues shall be regarded as constituting a separate offense.
(Coun. J. 12-9-92, p. 25465; Amend. 10-7-98, p. 78812; 3-31-04, p. 20916)

CHAPTER 11-12
WATER SUPPLY AND SERVICE
(Selected Sections)

Sections:

Article I. Service Regulations

11-12-015 Definition of "commissioner" and "department."
11-12-070 Using hydrants or other openings.
11-12-080 Injuring or obstructing hydrants.
11-12-130 Use of water hose.
11-12-150 Water for skating rinks.

Article VII. Enforcement of Chapter Provisions

11-12-630 Violation—Penalty.

Article I. Service Regulations

§11-12-015 Definition of "commissioner" and "department."

As used in this chapter "commissioner" means the city's commissioner of water management, and "department" means the city's department of water management.
(Added. Coun. J. 12-4-02, p. 99026)

§11-12-070 Using hydrants or other openings.

No person shall take water from any fire plug, hydrant, valve, faucet, pipe or any other opening connected with the Chicago Waterworks System, nor shall any person open any such fire plug, hydrant, valve or faucet for the purpose of taking water, or for any purpose, unless such person shall first have made application for use of water for such purpose and have received permission from the commissioner, or unless such person is an employee of the city of Chicago, and is acting in the discharge of his duties as such.

No person to whom a permit is issued for the use of water for any purpose whatsoever, including construction purposes, tamping, irrigating, testing, flushing, domestic supply, etc., shall use or consent to the use of any water not authorized by said permit, or consent to the use of such water by any other person. Any person to whom such permit is issued shall at all times use precaution to prevent any waste of water or damage, and upon completion of the work for which such use of water is authorized, or upon the expiration of the time specified in such permit, he shall be required to close off all stopcocks and valves; provided, however, that if a permit has been issued for service from water service pipes controlled by such valves they may be allowed to remain open.

Any person who shall violate any of the provisions of this section shall, for the first offense, be fined not less than $100.00 nor more than $300.00 or imprisoned for not more than 10 days or both; and for such subsequent offense shall be fined $500.00 or imprisoned for not to exceed 30 days or both.
(Prior code § 185-7; Amend. Coun. J. 5-25-88, p. 14025; 12-4-02, p. 99026)

§11-12-080 Injuring or obstructing hydrants.

No person shall wilfully or carelessly break or injure any of the public or private hydrants, or pollute or unnecessarily waste the water at any such hydrant, or obstruct the use of any fire hydrant, or place any material in front thereof, or within five feet from either side thereof.
(Prior code § 185-8; Amend. Coun. J. 3-28-01, p. 55444)

§11-12-130 Use of water hose.

Any hose which is connected to a pipe having service from or through the Chicago Waterworks System, shall be turned off and shall not be used between the hours of 5:00 a.m. and 8:00 a.m. and between the hours of 7:00 p.m. and 10:00 p.m. excluding Saturdays, Sundays and holidays (irrespective of whether the water is controlled by meter or not), nor shall water be used through a hose for the benefit of adjacent lots unless such lots have a common owner or tenant, and unless the hose is connected to a metered supply.

Provided, however, that the commissioner may, at his discretion, authorize the use of hose or sprinkling at any hour on public parks, boulevards, and other public grounds if, in his judgment, such use of hose or such sprinkling is not prejudicial to the water supply of contiguous premises.

In no case shall any person make use of a hose which is connected at a cock, faucet, valve or any other opening on premises having an unmetered service or supply, to sprinkle or serve in any way premises having a metered supply.

Each day that water or hose is used in violation of the foregoing provisions shall constitute a distinct and separate offense.
(Prior code § 185-13; Amend. Coun. J. 12-4-02, p. 99026)

§11-12-150 Water for skating rinks.

The mayor is duly authorized and empowered, from time to time, as he in his discretion may see fit, to permit the use of water from the city hydrants, free of charge, for the purpose of flooding vacant property, subject to the consent of the owner or owners of such property, where it may be desired to use such property when so flooded for the purpose of skating; provided, that no charge shall be made to any person for the privilege of skating on property so flooded.
(Prior code § 185-15)

Article VII. Enforcement of Chapter Provisions

§11-12-630 Violation—Penalty.

Any person who shall violate any of the provisions of this chapter other than those dealing with the use of space in water tunnels, where no other penalty is specifically provided, shall be fined not less than $5.00 nor more than $200.00 for each offense; and the cutting off of the water supply to any premises, or the forfeiture of water rates paid, or the imposition of any liability or expense herein otherwise provided, for or on account of any violation of any of the aforesaid provisions of this chapter, shall not be held to exempt any such person from the penalty herein provided.
(Prior code § 185-56)

TITLE 13
BUILDINGS AND CONSTRUCTION
(Selected Chapters)

Chapters:

13-12	Enforcement of Building, Electrical and Fire Regulations. (Selected Sections)
13-20	Building Inspection. (Selected Sections)
13-40	Building Plans. (Selected Sections)
13-64	Residential Units. (Selected Sections)
13-84	Assembly Units. (Selected Sections)
13-88	Open Air Assembly Units. (Selected Sections)
13-96	Miscellaneous Buildings and Structures. (Selected Sections)
13-128	Use of Public Property. (Complete Chapter)

CHAPTER 13-12
ENFORCEMENT OF BUILDING, ELECTRICAL AND FIRE REGULATIONS
(Selected Sections)

Sections:

Article I. General

13-12-010	Scope.
13-12-020	Code violations—Liability.
13-12-030	Building owner or agent—Posting requirements.
13-12-040	Violation of chapters enumerated in Section 13-12-010—Penalty.
13-12-050	Construction, alteration, installation, repair or razing without permit—Penalty.
13-12-080	Failure to acquire permits for construction, alteration, installation or razing—Stop work order.
13-12-100	Official right of entry—Interference unlawful.
13-12-120	Code violations—Closure of buildings or premises.
13-12-125	Vacant buildings—Owner required to act—Enforcement authority.
13-12-130	Dangerous or unsafe buildings—Written notice—Demolition, repair—Costs.
13-12-131	City board up provision.
13-12-140	Vacant or open buildings—Watchman required—Violation—Penalty.

Article II. Electrical Provisions

13-12-730	City attaching signs.
13-12-810	Use of city poles.
13-12-820	Permit to erect.
13-12-870	Impeding traffic.
13-12-890	Penalty.

Article I. General

§13-12-010 Scope.

The provisions of this chapter shall apply to the building provisions, electrical and fire regulations and minimum standards of living and working conditions of this code. In interpreting and applying said provisions of this code such provisions shall in every instance be held to be the minimum requirements adopted for the protection and promotion of the public health, safety and welfare.

(Prior code § 39-1; Amend. Coun. J. 10-2-95, p. 8019)

§13-12-020 Code violations—Liability.

Unless otherwise specifically provided, the owner, his agent for the purpose of managing, controlling or collecting rents and any other person managing or controlling a building or premises in any part of which there is a violation of the provisions of this code enumerated in Section 13-12-010, shall be liable for any violation therein, existing or occurring, or which may have existed or occurred, at or during any time when such person is or was the person owning or managing, controlling, or acting as agent in regard to said buildings or premises and is subject to injunctions, abatement orders or other remedial orders. Wherever used in said provisions of this code, the "owner" shall include any person entitled under any agreement to the control or direction of the management or disposition of the building or premises or of any part of the building or premises where the violation in question occurs.

The liabilities and obligations hereunder imposed on an owner shall attach to a trustee under a land trust, holding title to such building, structure or premises without the right of possession, management or control, unless said trustee in a proceeding under said provisions of this code discloses in a verified pleading or in an affidavit filed with the court, the name and last known address of each person who was a beneficiary of the trust at the time of the alleged violation and of each person, if any, who was then acting as agent for the purpose of managing, controlling or collecting rents, as the same may appear on the records of the trust.

The liabilities and obligations imposed on an owner shall attach to any mortgage company or any other person with or without an interest in the building or premises who knowingly takes any action in any judicial or administrative proceeding that is intended to delay issuance or enforcement of any remedy for any violation of the Building Code then in existence; provided that with respect to fines such person shall be liable only for fines which accrue on or after the date of such action; and further provided that no liability shall be imposed under this section for any action taken in any proceeding, including a proceeding to foreclose on a lien, that does not delay or prevent the prosecution of any action brought by the city to enforce the Building Code.

(Prior code § 39-2; Amend. 4-12-00, p. 29471)

§13-12-030 Building owner or agent—Posting requirements.

The owner of any building having residential units designed or used for two or more family units or designed or used for sleeping accommodations, other than family units, for more than 10 persons shall post, or cause to be posted, in a prominent place in a common area of the building accessible from the public way, or affixed to the building so as to be visible from the public way, the name, address, and telephone number of the owner, his agent for the purpose of managing, controlling or collecting rents and any other person managing or controlling such building.

(Prior code § 39-2.1)

§13-12-040 Violation of chapters enumerated in Section §13-12-010—Penalty.

Any violation of, or resistance to or interference with the enforcement of, any of the provisions of this code enumerated in Section 13-12-010, to which no other penalty provision is applicable shall be punished by a fine of not less than $200.00 and not more than $500.00, and each day such violation shall continue shall constitute a separate and distinct offense for which a fine as herein provided shall be imposed.
(Prior code § 39-3; Amend. Coun. J. 11-10-94, p. 59125)

§13-12-050 Construction, alteration, installation, repair or razing without permit—Penalty.

(a) It shall be unlawful for any person to:

(i) Construct, alter, install, repair or raze any building, structure, premises or part thereof without having obtained any permit required by this code; or

(ii) Construct, alter, install, repair or raze any building, structure, premises or part thereof in a manner which is contrary to the drawings or plans which the appropriate department or city agencies approved when issuing any permit required by this code; or

(iii) Maintain or operate any building, structure, premises, mechanical installation, equipment or part thereof without any permit or certificate required by this code.

Any person who violates this subsection upon conviction shall be punished, as follows:

(1) Incarceration for a term not less than three days, nor more than six months, under the procedures set forth in Section 1-2-1.1 of the Illinois Municipal Code, as amended, and the Illinois Code of Criminal Procedure of 1963, as amended; and/or

(2) Community service of not less than 10 hours, nor more than 100 hours; and

(3) A fine of not less than $200.00, nor more than $500.00 for the first offense; and a fine of not less than $500.00, nor more than $3,000.00 for the second offense; and a fine of not less than $3,000.00, nor more than $5,000.00 for the third and each subsequent offense.

A separate and distinct offense shall be committed for each permit which is required but has not been obtained, and each day that the violation continues.

If an employee of a builder, contractor or subcontractor is charged with violating this subsection, it shall be a defense that the employee is not an owner, manager, or person exercising control over the builder, contractor or subcontractor and did not have prior notice that the builder, contractor or subcontractor had failed to obtain a permit.

(b) It shall be unlawful for any person to fail to post any permit as required by 13-32-010 of this code. Any person who violates this subsection shall be fined not less than $200.00, nor more than $500.00 for each day that work proceeds without the permit having been posted.
(Prior code § 39-4; Amend. Coun. J. 7-31-90, p. 19353; 4-29-98, p. 66564; 8-30-00, p. 39652)

§13-12-080 Failure to acquire permits for construction, alteration, installation, repair or razing—Stop work order.

(A) Any city official charged with responsibility for administering this code shall without delay issue a stop work order directing that the following prohibited activities cease and desist immediately:

(i) Any construction, alteration, installation, repair or razing of any building, structure, premises, or part thereof which is being done or has been done without any permit required by this code; or

(ii) Any construction, alteration, installation, repair or razing of any building, structure, premises or part thereof which is being done or has been done contrary to the drawings or plans which the appropriate department or agencies of the city approved when issuing any permit; or

(iii) Any maintenance or operation of any building, structure, premises, mechanical installation, equipment or part thereof which is being done without any permit or certificate required by this code; or

(iv) Any construction, alteration, installation, repair or razing of any building, structure, premises or part thereof which is being done or has been done by workers lacking a license required under this code for such work or which is being done or has been done by workers required by the code to be listed on the building permit application who were not listed.

No stop work order may be issued to prohibit any construction, alteration, installation, repair or razing of any building, structure, premises or part thereof that is performed pursuant to a valid permit issued by the executive director for any reason not specified in this section, unless such order is necessary to prevent an imminent threat to the safety of the public.

Any city official who has reason to believe that (1) any construction, alteration, installation, repair or razing of a building, structure, premises or part thereof is being done or has been done in violation of a stop work order, or that (2) any building, structure, premises, mechanical installation, equipment or part thereof is being maintained or operated in violation of a stop work order shall immediately request the corporation counsel to seek without delay any remedy provided by the law.

(B) It shall be unlawful for any person to knowingly violate a stop work order, or to knowingly cause, permit, encourage, assist, aid, abet or direct another person to violate a stop work order, or to knowingly in any manner be a party to a violation of a stop work order.

Any person who violates this subsection upon conviction shall be punished, as follows:

(i) Incarceration for a term not less than three days, nor more than six months, under the procedures set forth in Section 1-2-1.1 of the Illinois Municipal Code, as amended, and the Illinois Code of Criminal Procedure of 1963, as amended; and

(ii) Community service of not less than 10 hours, nor more than 100 hours; and

(iii) A fine of not less than $400.00, nor more than $1,000.00 for the first offense; and a fine of not less than $1,000.00, nor more than $6,000.00 for the second offense; and a fine of not less than $6,000.00, nor more than $10,000.00 for the third and each subsequent offense.

A separate and distinct offense shall be committed for each stop work order which is violated, and each day that a violation continues.

If an employee of a builder, contractor or subcontractor is charged with violating this subsection, it shall be a defense that the employee is not an owner, manager or person exercising control over the builder, contractor or subcontractor and did not have prior notice that the builder, contractor or subcontractor had failed to obtain a permit.

(C) It shall be unlawful for any person to knowingly destroy, deface, remove, damage, impair, mar, cover or obstruct any stop work order which a city official has posted or affixed at a work site.

Any person who violates this subsection upon conviction shall be punished, as follows:

(i) Incarceration for a term not less than three days, nor more than six months, under the procedures set forth in Section 1-2-1.1 of the Illinois Municipal Code, as amended, and the Illinois Code of Criminal Procedure of 1963, as amended; and

(ii) Community service of not less than 10 hours, nor more than 100 hours; and

(iii) A fine not less than $200.00, nor more than $500.00.

(Prior code § 39-7; Amend. Coun. J. 8-30-00, p. 39652; 9-5-01, p. 66630; 12-4-02, p. 99026; 12-15-04, p. 39840)

§13-12-100 Official right of entry—Interference unlawful.

The appropriate officials charged with the administration of any of the provisions of this code enumerated in Section 13-12-010, or any of them and their respective assistants, shall have the right to enter any building, or premises, and any and all parts thereof, at any reasonable time, and at any time when occupied by the public in order to examine such buildings or premises to judge of the condition of the same and to discharge their respective duties, and it shall be unlawful for any person to interfere with them in the performance of their duties.

(Prior code § 39-9)

§13-12-120 Code violations—Closure of buildings or premises.

(a) The building commissioner, the president of the board of health, the fire commissioner, and the superintendent of police, or any one of them, and their respective designees, shall have the power, and it shall be their joint and several duty, to order any building or premises closed, or any structure or equipment thereof removed or its operation stopped, where it is discovered that there is any violation of any of the provisions of this code enumerated in Section 13-12-010 which imperils life, safety or health, and to keep same closed, removed, or shut down until such provisions are complied with.

The official who orders a building or portion thereof closed, removed or shut down shall cause a notice no less than 17 inches by 22 inches at each entrance thereto. The notice shall state substantially as follows:

THIS BUILDING HAS BEEN ORDERED CLOSED BY THE CITY OF CHICAGO DUE TO CODE VIOLATIONS THAT THREATEN LIFE, HEALTH OR SAFETY. ENTRY IS FORBIDDEN EXCEPT FOR NECESSARY REPAIRS AND GOVERNMENT INSPECTION.

The notice shall be dated, and shall bear the city seal. If only a portion of the building has been ordered closed, removed or shut down, the notice shall be modified to identify the affected portion, and shall also be affixed at each interior entrance to that portion. Any person who enters a building, structure or portion thereof in violation of a notice posted under this section shall be subject to a fine of not less than $25.00 and not more than $100.00. Any owner, manager, tenant or person in control of the premises who permits any person to enter in violation of a notice posted under this section shall be subject to a fine of not less than $200.00 and not more than $500.00 for each time a person is permitted to enter illegally.

(b) It is unlawful for any person to remove, cover or obliterate, any notice or notices lawfully posted pursuant to subsection (a) of this section, without the written permission of the head of the department or agency responsible for posting the notice. Any person who removes, covers, obliterates, or defaces any sign posted pursuant to subsection (a) of this section without the necessary written permission shall be subject to a fine of up to $500.00.
(Prior code § 39-11; Amend. Coun. J. 9-13-89, p. 4604; 10-1-03, p. 8498)

§13-12-125 Vacant buildings—Owner required to act—Enforcement authority.

(a) (1) The owner of any building that has become vacant shall within 30 days after the building becomes vacant, or within 30 days after the effective date of this ordinance, whichever is later, file a registration statement for each such building with the department of buildings on forms provided by the department of buildings for such purposes. The registration shall remain valid for one year from the date of registration. The owner shall be required to annually renew the registration as long as the building remains vacant and shall pay an annual registration fee of $100.00 for each registered building; provided, however, that all eleemosynary, religious, educational, benevolent or charitable associations and all governmental agencies shall be exempt from the payment of the annual registration fee. The owner shall notify the department of buildings, within 20 days, of any change in the registration information by filing an amended registration statement on a form provided by the department of buildings for such purposes. The registration statement shall be deemed prima facie proof of the statements therein contained in any administrative enforcement proceeding or court proceeding instituted by the city against the owner or owners of the building. Registration of a building in accordance with this section shall be deemed to satisfy the registration requirement set forth in Section 13-10-030 and the notification requirement set forth in Section 13-11-030.

(2) In addition to other information required by the commissioner of buildings, the registration statement shall include the name, street address and telephone number of a natural person 21 years of age or older, designated by the owner or owners as the authorized agent for receiving notices of code

violations and for receiving process, in any court proceeding or administrative enforcement proceeding, on behalf of such owner or owners in connection with the enforcement of this code. This person must maintain an office in Cook County, Illinois, or must actually reside within Cook County, Illinois. An owner who is a natural person and who meets the requirements of this subsection as to location of residence or office may designate himself as agent. By designating an authorized agent under the provisions of this subsection the owner is consenting to receive any and all notices of code violations concerning the registered building and all process in any court proceeding or administrative enforcement proceeding brought to enforce code provisions concerning the registered building by service of the notice or process on the authorized agent. Any owner who has designated an authorized agent under the provisions of this subsection shall be deemed to consent to the continuation of the agent's designation for the purposes of this subsection until the owner notifies the department of buildings of a change of authorized agent or until the owner files a new annual registration statement. Any owner who fails to register a vacant building under the provisions of this subsection shall further be deemed to consent to receive, by posting at the building, any and all notices of code violations and all process in an administrative proceeding brought to enforce code provisions concerning the building.

(b) The owner of any building that has become vacant, and any person maintaining, operating or collecting rent for any building that has become vacant shall, within 30 days, do the following:

(1) Enclose and secure the building;

(2) Post a sign affixed to the building indicating the name, address and telephone number of the owner and the owner's authorized agent for the purpose of service of process. The sign shall be of a size and placed in such a location so as to be legible from the nearest public street or sidewalk, whichever is nearer; and

(3) Maintain the building in a secure and closed condition and maintain the sign until the building is again occupied or until repair or completion of the building has been undertaken.

(c) The owner of any building that has become vacant shall, within 30 days, acquire or otherwise maintain liability insurance, in an amount of not less than $300,000.00 for buildings designed primarily for use as residential units and not less than $1,000,000.00 for any other building, including, but not limited to, buildings designed for manufacturing, industrial, storage or commercial uses, covering any damage to any person or any property caused by any physical condition of or in the building. Any insurance policy acquired after the building has become vacant shall provide for written notice to the commissioner of buildings within 30 days of any lapse, cancellation or change in coverage. The owner and the owner's authorized agent for service of process shall provide evidence of the insurance, upon request, to the commissioner of buildings or his or her designee.

(d) The building commissioner may issue rules and regulations for the administration of this section. These rules may designate board-up materials and methods which must be used when securing a building so that the boarding is reasonably incapable of being removed by trespassers or others acting without the building owner's consent. Any person who violates any provision of this section or of the rules and regulations issued hereunder shall be fined not less than $200.00 and not more than $1,000.00 for each offense. Every day that a violation continues shall constitute a separate and distinct offense.

(e) For purposes of this section, "vacant" means a building which is lacking habitual presence of human beings who have a legal right to be on the premises, or at which substantially all lawful business operations or residential occupancy has ceased, or which is substantially devoid of content. In determining whether a building is vacant, it is relevant to consider, among other factors, the percentage of the overall square footage of the building or floor to the occupied space, the condition and value of any items in the building and the presence of rental or for sale signs on the property; provided that a residential property shall not be deemed vacant if it has been used as a residence by a person entitled to possession for a period of at least three months within the previous nine months and a person entitled to possession intends to resume residing at the property; and further provided that multifamily residential property containing five or more dwelling units shall be considered vacant when substantially all of the dwelling units are unoccupied.

(Added. Coun. J. 10-2-91, p. 6032; Amend. 4-12-00, p. 29471; 12-4-02, p. 99931)

§13-12-130 Dangerous or unsafe buildings—Written notice—Demolition, repair—Costs.

If any building shall be found in a dangerous and unsafe condition or uncompleted and abandoned, the building commissioner or the fire commissioner shall notify in writing the owner or owners thereof, directing the owner or owners to put such building in a safe condition, to enclose or to demolish it. Where, upon diligent search, the identity or whereabouts of the owner or owners of any such building shall not be ascertainable, the notice shall be mailed to the person or persons in whose name such real estate was last assessed. If, after 15 days subsequent to the giving of such notice, the owner or owners fail to put the building in a safe condition, to enclose or to demolish it, the building commissioner or fire commissioner may notify the department of law and recommend initiation of proceedings in accordance with this section, and upon receipt of such recommendation, the corporation counsel is hereby authorized to apply to the Circuit Court of Cook County for an order authorizing the city to demolish, repair or enclose, or requiring the owner of record to demolish, repair or enclose, the structure. The corporation counsel may initiate a court action to obtain the appropriate orders in the Circuit Court of Cook County to repair, enclose or demolish the building irrespective of whether a notice as described in this section is sent.

The cost of such demolition, repair or enclosure shall be recoverable from the owner or owners of such real estate, and shall be a lien thereon as provided by law.

Any owner who fails to take the action demanded in the notice shall also be fined not less than $200.00 per day and not more than $1,000.00 per day; for each day from the 16th day after the notice has been given until the building has been demolished, repaired or enclosed. If court action is initiated by the corporation counsel without notice as described in this section, the fine shall be imposed beginning on the day the summons is served on the owner.

(Prior code § 39-12; Amend. Coun. J. 9-13-89, p. 4604; 7-12-90, p. 18289; 10-2-91, p. 6032)

§13-12-131 City board up provision.

If, after 10 days subsequent to the giving of the notice as provided in Section 13-12-130, the owner or owners fail to enclose the unsafe or uncompleted building, the city may board up such building at the owner's expense.
(Added. Coun. J. 4-22-93, p. 31520; Amend. 6-14-95, p. 2841)

§13-12-140 Vacant or open buildings—Watchman required—Violation—Penalty.

Any person or persons owning, maintaining, operating, collecting rents for, or having any legal or equitable interest in any vacant and open building, or any uncompleted abandoned building, or any vacant boarded-up building or any otherwise enclosed vacant building must have a watchman on duty upon the premises on which any one of such aforementioned buildings is situated every day continuously between the hours of 4:00 p.m. and 8:00 a.m., unless the building has been secured by methods approved by the commissioner of buildings.

Said watchman required under the provisions of this ordinance shall remain on duty daily during the required hours until such building is either occupied or razed.

Any person who violates the provisions of this section shall be punished by a fine of not less than $100.00 nor more than $300.00 for the first offense and not less than $300.00 nor more than $500.00 for the second and each subsequent offense. Any third or subsequent offense may be punishable as a misdemeanor by incarceration in the county jail for a term not to exceed six months under procedures set forth in Section 1-2-1.1 of the Illinois Municipal Code (65 ILCS 5/1-2-1.1) as amended, or by both fine and imprisonment. Any person who violates this section after having been notified in writing that a watchman has not been on duty on any premises as required by this section shall, if the building remains or subsequently becomes open and a forcible felony is then committed on those premises after such notice is given, be sentenced to a mandatory term of imprisonment of not less than 30 days. A separate and distinct offense shall be regarded as committed each day on which such person or persons shall violate the provisions of this section. For purposes of this section, "forcible felony has the meaning ascribed to the term in Section 2-8 of the Criminal Code of 1961 (720 ILCS 5/2-8).
(Prior code § 39-13; Amend. Coun. J. 8-30-00, p. 40306)

Article II. Electrical Provisions

§13-12-730 City attaching signs.

Any department of the city is hereby empowered to attach any sign or signs deemed necessary, to any commercial electric lamp post erected and maintained under the authority of this article.
(Added. Coun. J. 11-3-99, p. 13842)

§13-12-810 Use of city poles.

No electrical equipment used as a part of any festoon or decorative street lighting equipment shall be attached to any city poles, unless permission in writing has been obtained from the commissioner of streets and sanitation.
(Added. Coun. J. 11-3-99, p. 13842)

§13-12-820 Permit to erect.

No person shall erect, construct, maintain, use, alter or repair any pole, line or wire, underground conductors or electric conductors of any description whatever on, over or under any public way or public place, within the city, without first having obtained a permit therefor from the department of construction and permits, which permit shall be countersigned by the commissioners of streets and sanitation, and transportation.
(Added. Coun. J. 11-3-99, p. 13842; Amend. Coun. J. 3-5-03, p. 104990)

§13-12-870 Impeding traffic.

The method employed of laying said conductors shall be such that it will at no time be necessary to remove so much of the pavement, or to make such excavation, as to materially impede traffic or passage upon sidewalk or street during the operation of laying or repairing said conductors, except when crossing streets transversely, where authority may be granted to remove the pavement for a width not exceeding two feet in the nearest straight line from corner to corner. In no case during the general hours of passage and traffic shall passage be interrupted thereby for a period longer than one hour.
(Added. Coun. J. 11-3-99, p. 13842)

§13-12-890 Penalty.

Any person who violates any of the provisions of this article, or who maintains any electrical wiring and apparatus found to be dangerous to life and property, shall be fined not more than $500.00 for each offense. Each day such violation shall continue shall constitute a separate and distinct offense, and so much of any electrical installation as may be erected or altered and maintained in violation of this article or of Chapter 18-27 shall be condemned and the building commissioner is hereby empowered to cut off and discontinue current to such electrical wires and apparatus.
(Added. Coun. J. 11-3-99, p. 13842)

CHAPTER 13-20
BUILDING INSPECTION
(Selected Sections)

Sections:

Article I. General

13-20-010 Duty of commissioner.
13-20-017 Penalties.

Article II. Buildings

13-20-020 Buildings—Inspection required.

Article XIII. Signs, Billboards, Signboards and Related Structures

Part A. General

13-20-510 Definitions.
13-20-520 Penalties.

Part C. Permits

13-20-550 Permit required.
13-20-600 Permit violation penalties.
13-20-610 Display of permits.

Part E. Other Requirements

13-20-690 Obstruction of streets.
13-20-750 Demolition.
13-20-760 Abandoned signs and structures.
13-20-770 Removal of sign or structure.

Article I. General

§13-20-010 Duty of commissioner.

Except as provided in Section 4-8-042, the building commissioner and fire commissioner shall cause to be inspected annually, or semiannually, or otherwise, such buildings, structures, equipment, sites or portions thereof as shall be provided by this chapter or as otherwise required in the building provisions of this code. All fees for such annual, semiannual or other periodic inspections as set forth in this chapter may be billed prior or subsequent to the actual inspection conducted by the department of buildings or fire department as appropriate and shall be payable to the department of revenue within 30 days of receipt of the notice of inspection fee from the departments. A penalty of $5.00 shall be assessed for each additional 30-day period the bill for inspection fees remains unpaid.

(Prior code § 46-1; Amend. Coun. J. 9-13-89, p. 4604; 7-12-90, p. 18289; 9-29-04, p. 32144)

§13-20-017 Penalties.

Any person violating, resisting or opposing the enforcement of any of the provisions of this chapter, where no other penalty is provided, shall be subject to the fines provided for in Section 13-12-040. Each day such violation shall continue shall constitute a separate and distinct offense.

(Added. Coun. J. 11-3-99, p. 13842)

Article II. Buildings

§13-20-020 Buildings—Inspection required.

(a) Subject to subsection (b) of this section, the fire commissioner or the buildings commissioner and their respective assistants shall make an annual inspection of all theaters, churches, schools, public assembly units, public places of amusement and open air assembly units; and also all buildings over one story in height, except single dwellings, multiple-use buildings consisting of business and dwelling units two stories or less in height, and multiple dwellings three stories or less in height, unless such multiple dwellings are lodging or roominghouses with sleeping accommodations for 20 or more persons. With respect to any establishment requiring a public place of amusement license, the fire commissioner or the buildings commissioner and their respective assistants shall make an inspection within the 90 days preceding the deadline for the annual renewal application for the license. It shall be the duty of every owner, agent, lessee, or occupant of any such building and of the person in charge or control of the same to permit the making of such annual inspection by the fire commissioner, or by the building commissioner or by a duly authorized inspector at any time upon demand being duly made.

(b) Inspections by the buildings commissioner of places for eating, as that term is defined in Section 4-8-010, shall be controlled by Section 4-8-042; provided that nothing in this section shall be construed to limit inspections of any place for eating by the fire commissioner.

(Prior code § 46-2; Amend. Coun. J. 7-9-84, p. 8225; 9-13-89, p. 4604; 10-1-03, p. 9163; 9-29-04, p. 32144)

Article XIII. Signs, Billboards, Signboards and Related Structures

Part A. General

§13-20-510 Definitions.

For the purposes of this article, the following additional definitions apply.

"Electrical signs" are signs that are electrically illuminated.

"Flat signs" are signs which are placed flat against the building or structure from which they are supported and which run parallel thereto. Signs supported from a canopy are deemed to be flat signs when they are single face.

"Ground signs" are signs supported by a structure which rests on or in the ground.

"Projecting signs" are signs which project obliquely or at right angles from the building or structure from which they are supported building or structure from which they are supported.

"Roof signs" are signs which are erected on and supported by the roof of a building or structure.

"Signboards," "billboards," "paintboards" and "posted panelboards" are signs which fall into this general classification and are commonly known by this or other titles.

"Signs" are deemed to be a name, identification, description, display, illustration or character which is affixed to, or represented directly or indirectly upon a building, structure or piece of land and which directs attention to an object, product, place, activity, person, institution, organization or business.

(Added. Coun. J. 11-3-99, p. 13842)

§13-20-520 Penalties.

(a) Fines. In all cases where no specific penalty is fixed therein, any person erecting, owning, operating, maintaining or in charge, possession or control of any illuminated or non-illuminated sign, painted wall sign, signboard, ground sign, roof sign or its support structure, within the city of Chicago, that shall neglect or refuse to comply with the provisions of this chapter shall be fined not more than $500.00 for each offense. The penalty for other than business I.D. signs, after notification shall be $500.00 per violation plus $50.00 a day until the violation is removed. Each sign or structure owned, operated and maintained or controlled by that person that is erected, constructed or maintained in violation of any of the provisions of this chapter shall constitute a separate and distinct violation.

(b) License Ineligibility.

(1) No business or occupational license shall be issued to any license applicant erecting, owning, operating, maintaining or in charge, possession or control of any illuminated or non-illuminated sign, painted wall sign, signboard, ground sign, roof sign or its support structure, within the city of Chicago, that shall neglect or refuse to obtain the permit required by this chapter for such sign or structure. The license ineligibility imposed by this subsection (b)(1) shall be in addition to any other fines and penalties as provided in this code. For purposes of this subsection (b), the term "license" shall mean an initial license and also any renewals of a license previously issued.

(2) Upon becoming aware that a licensee or license applicant is lacking a sign permit required by this chapter, the building commissioner or his or her designee shall so notify the department of revenue or other license-issuing department. At or prior to the time when the applicant applies for a license, the department of revenue or other license-issuing department shall notify the person in writing that he or she is ineligible for a license under this subsection (b) of this section. The notice shall: (i) state that the city has determined that the applicant is responsible for an unpermitted sign; (ii) describe the sign that is unpermitted or inform the applicant that, upon the request of the applicant, a description of the unpermitted sign is available from the department of buildings; and (iii) inform the applicant of his or her right to contest the city's determination of noncompliance under this subsection (b) of this section. If notice is provided by mail, it shall be sufficient to mail the notice to the last address the applicant provided to the department of buildings or the department of revenue. The date of the notice shall be the date the notice to the applicant is deposited in the mail, if served by first class mail; the date of delivery, if served by personal service; or the date of service if served by any other manner.

(3) (i) Upon the written request of the applicant, the department of buildings shall provide the applicant with a written description of the unpermitted sign for which the applicant is responsible. An applicant shall have thirty business days from the date of the notice issued to the applicant pursuant to subsection (b)(2) of this section to petition the department of buildings to reverse its determination that the applicant is responsible for an unpermitted sign, by submitting in person or by mail, a written response to the department of buildings that includes the following materials and information: the full name, address and telephone number of the applicant; a written statement signed by the applicant setting forth facts, law or other information relevant to establishing a defense to the department's determination; a copy of the notice provided to the applicant by the department of revenue under subsection (b)(2) of this section; and any documentary evidence that supports the applicant's written statement.

(ii) Within thirty business days of receiving a petition, the department of buildings shall grant or deny the petition. The department's decision regarding a petition shall be in writing and, in the case of a denial, shall inform the applicant of his right to contest the department's decision under this section. The time period for ruling on a petition may be extended only with the consent of the petitioner.

(4) Within 10 business days of the date of the department of buildings' decision denying a petition under subsection (b)(3)(ii) of this section, the applicant may appeal the department's determination to the mayor's license commission by filing a written request for a hearing in person at the office of the mayor's license commission. The date of the department's decision shall be the date that it is deposited in the mail, if served by first class mail; the date of delivery, if served by personal service; or the date of service if served by any other manner. A request for a hearing shall include the following materials and information: a copy of the notice provided to the applicant by the department of revenue under subsection (b)(2) of this section; a copy of the applicant's written response submitted to the department of buildings; a copy of the department's decision denying the applicant's petition issued under subsection (b)(3)(ii) of this section; and any documentary evidence that supports the applicant's appeal. Upon receipt of a timely and proper request for a hearing, the mayor's license commission shall assign a hearing date no later than 15 business days after the date of the request. The hearing shall not be continued without the consent of the applicant. A hearing officer appointed by the mayor's license commission shall conduct the hearing to determine whether or not the applicant is ineligible for a license pursuant to this section. The hearing shall comply with the following provisions:

(i) The case for the city shall be presented by the corporation counsel.

(ii) The hearing officer shall abide by any prior determination that an unpermitted sign exists and the scope of review shall be limited to whether the violation has been corrected and whether the determination that the unpermitted sign exists was issued against the license applicant. The license applicant shall not be entitled to raise any defenses related to his or her liability for the underlying sign violation.

(iii) The formal and technical rules of evidence shall not apply in the conduct of the hearing. Evidence, including hearsay, may be admitted only if it is of a type commonly relied upon by reasonably prudent persons in the conduct of their affairs.

(iv) At the conclusion of the hearing, the hearing officer shall make a recommendation to the director of the mayor's license commission affirming or denying the department of buildings' determination that the applicant is not eligible for a license. Upon the issuance of a final order by the mayor's license commission that the applicant is not eligible for a license, the applicant's license may not be issued prior to the correction of the underlying sign permit violation and payment of all outstanding fines and penalties. The director of the mayor's license commission shall issue a final order no more than 15 business days after the conclusion of the hearing.

(5) Notwithstanding a pending petition submitted to the department of buildings, pursuant to subsection (b)(3)(i) of this section, or appeal to the mayor's license commission pursuant to subsection (b)(4) of this section, no license shall authorize the conduct of any business or occupation from and after the last day of a license term unless the license has been renewed by the department responsible for processing the license. A license may be renewed only upon the correction of the underlying sign permit violation and payment of all outstanding fines and penalties.

(6) If the applicant fails to file a timely and proper petition under subsection (b)(3)(i) of this section or an appeal to the mayor's license commission under subsection (b)(4) of this section, the applicant shall be deemed to have waived his or her right under this section to contest the department of buildings' determination and the applicant's license may not be issued prior to the correction of the underlying sign permit violation and payment of all outstanding fines and penalties determined by the department to be outstanding.
(Added. Coun. J. 5-2-01, p. 57403)

Part C. Permits

§13-20-550 Permits required.

It shall be unlawful to begin the erection, alteration, repair or enlargement of any sign, signboard or structure covered by the provisions of this article, unless a permit has been obtained from the department of construction and permits.

(a) Attachments. No attachment shall be made to any sign, signboard or structure covered by this article unless all applicable provisions of this chapter have been complied with.

(b) Rehang. A previously approved sign which has been removed for any reason shall be permitted to be rehung within six months of removal in the same location upon the issuance of a rehang permit. If a sign is moved to a new location, a new sign permit shall be obtained.
(Added. Coun. J. 11-3-99, p. 13842; Amend. Coun. J. 3-5-03, p. 104990)

§13-20-600 Permit violation penalties.

Where a registered electrical contractor, a registered sign contractor and/or a bonded sign erector installs, alters, erects or repairs a sign, signboard or illuminates a signboard without a permit on three separate occasions in one 12-month period, the certificate of registration, bond, and all permit privileges shall be revoked.

Where an installation or alteration has been started prior to the issuance of a permit for such work, the permit inspection fee for such work shall be twice the amount of the normal permit inspection fee as prescribed in this article.
(Added. Coun. J. 11-3-99, p. 13842)

§13-20-610 Display of permits.

All permits authorizing the installation of a sign, signboard or obstruction of the public way shall be displayed in a conspicuous location at the installation site during any period that such installation takes place.
(Added. Coun. J. 11-3-99, p. 13842)

Part E. Other Requirements

§13-20-690 Obstruction of streets.

Permits for the obstruction of streets or sidewalks during construction of signs shall be obtained by the sign contractor from the commissioner of the Chicago department of transportation.
(Added. Coun. J. 11-3-99, p. 13842)

§13-20-750 Demolition.

If the owner or person in charge, possession or control of any sign or structure when so notified shall refuse, fail or neglect to comply with and conform to the requirements of such notice, the building commissioner may upon the expiration of time therein mentioned, tear down or cause to be torn down such part of such a sign or structure as is constructed and maintained in violation of the provisions of this chapter, and shall charge the expense to the owner or person in charge, possession or control of any sign or structure and the same shall be recovered from such owner or person by appropriate legal proceedings.
(Added. Coun. J. 11-3-99, p. 13842)

§13-20-760 Abandoned signs and structures.

(a) Abandoned Sign. Any sign, on which the annual inspection fee has not been paid in conformity with all the provisions of this chapter, shall be declared to be abandoned and/or a hazard and the building department is hereby empowered to remove or cause to be removed any such abandoned or hazardous signs.

(b) Abandoned Structure. Structures over public or private property shall be removed at the time the sign is removed unless the structure is maintained by a bonded sign erector. A drawing prepared by a licensed architect or structural engineer and bearing the seal of the architect or structural engineer shall be presented with the application for the erection of a new sign on such structures.
(Added. Coun. J. 11-3-99, p. 13842)

§13-20-770 Removal of sign or structure.

It shall be the duty of the building commissioner to remove or cause the removal of any sign or structure not in compliance with any of the provisions of this article and Article 18-27-600 dealing with signs and any compensation or inspection fees paid to the city of Chicago for such sign shall not be refunded. The owner of such sign shall be held liable for all expenses incurred by the building department in the performance of this duty to remove.
(Added. Coun. J. 11-3-99, p. 13842)

CHAPTER 13-32
BUILDING PERMITS
(Selected Sections)

Sections:

Article I. Permit Requirements

13-32-010 Permit required—Posting.
13-32-020 Exceptions.
13-32-030 Applications.
13-32-032 Unlawful transfer of license for building application purposes.
13-32-033 False or inaccurate license number on building permit application.
13-32-035 Stop work orders—New or revised permit—Fees.
13-32-040 Plan approval—Provisions to be made for electrical work.
13-32-050 Landmark or historic district consideration.
13-32-060 Surety bond.
13-32-080 Permit issuance.
13-32-085 Rules and regulations—Compliance required—Violation—Penalty.
13-32-090 Driveway permit requirements.
13-32-100 Use of subsidewalk space—Authorization required.
13-32-110 Termination of permits—Extensions.
13-32-120 Construction contrary to permit—Stop work order.
13-32-130 Operations without permit—Stop work order.
13-32-140 Reserved.
13-32-145 Reserved.
13-32-160 Canopies—Approval required.
13-32-170 Temporary platforms—Permit required.
13-32-190 Elevator or mechanical equipment construction or alteration—Permit required.
13-32-191 Suspension of permit privileges.
13-32-192 Revocation of permits.
13-32-193 Use of permit issued to another.
13-32-194 Permit for person not entitled to one.
13-32-195 Alteration of forms.
13-32-200 Fences—Permit required.
13-32-210 Moving buildings.
13-32-230 Building wrecking—Permit required—Safety requirements.
13-32-260 Permits to be obtained prior to commencement of wrecking—Violation—Penalty.
13-32-270 Warm air furnaces—Permit required.
13-32-280 Amusement devices—Submission of plan to buildings commission—Permit.
13-32-290 Violation of building provisions—Revocation of permit—Reinstatement conditions.

Article II. Permit Fees

13-32-315 Post-permit issuance—Verification of cost of construction, alteration or repair.

Article I. Permit Requirements

§13-32-010 Permit required—Posting.

It shall be unlawful to proceed with the erection, enlargement, alteration, repair, removal, or demolition of any building, structure, or structural part thereof within the city unless a permit therefor shall have first been obtained from the executive director. The applicant shall clearly print the name and telephone number of a responsible person to contact in case of any emergency. Such permit shall be posted in a conspicuous place upon the exterior of the premises for which it is issued, and shall remain so posted at all times until the work is completed and approved. Failure to comply with the provisions of this ordinance shall be grounds for revocation.

(Prior code § 43-1; Amend. Coun. J. 3-25-86, p. 28869, 9-13-89, p. 4604; 12-4-02, p. 99026)

§13-32-020 Exceptions.

A permit shall not be required for any minor repairs, including, but not limited to, the replacement in-kind of windows, doors, shingle roofing on 5-in-12 slopes or steeper, and siding of residential buildings that do not have more than four units and do not exceed three stories, as may be necessary to maintain existing parts of buildings, but such work or operations shall not involve sandblasting, the replacement or repair of any structural load-bearing members, nor reduce the means of exit, affect the light or ventilation, room size requirements, sanitary or fire-resistive requirements, use of materials not permitted by the building and environmental control provisions of this code, changes in the materials of roofs, windows and exterior walls visible from a public street of properties designated as Chicago Landmarks in accordance with applicable provisions of Chapter 2-120 of this code, nor increase the height, area, or capacity of the building. For purposes of this section, "replacement in-kind" means replacement of the same type, size and materials.
(Prior code § 43-2; Amend. Coun. J. 6-14-95, p. 2828; 10-28-97, p. 54730)

§13-32-030 Applications.

Applications for building permits shall be in such form as shall be prescribed by the executive director. Every such application for a permit shall be accompanied by a copy of every recorded easement on the lot on which the building is to be erected, and on the immediately adjoining lots, showing the use or benefit resulting from such easement. All such applications shall be accompanied by drawings, plans, and specifications in conformity with the provisions of this chapter. Where alterations or repairs in buildings are made necessary by reason of damage by fire, that fact shall be stated in the application for a permit. In such cases, before a permit shall be issued, the executive director shall cause a thorough inspection to be made of the damaged premises with the view of testing the structural integrity of the damaged parts. No permit shall be issued by the executive director for the construction, erection, addition to or alteration of any building or structure unless the applicant therefor shall furnish to the executive director a certificate or other written evidence of the proper federal officer or agency that the proposed construction is not prohibited by any order, rule or directive of an agency of the United States government.

Except in the case of residential garages, fence installation or repairs or repairs to buildings to meet code requirements, prior to issuing a building permit, the executive director shall give 10 days' written notice of the proposed issuance of the permit to the alderman of the ward in which the proposed work to be done is to be located, and no permit shall be valid unless such notice is delivered; provided, however, that the affidavit of the executive director showing delivery of such notice to an alderman in person or by mailing to such address as he may have filed with the city clerk, shall be conclusive evidence of delivery of such notice. In cases of emergencies, a permit may be issued, to take immediate effect, under the executive director's authority. And the executive director shall notify the alderman of the ward in which the proposed work to be done is located of the issuance of such permit within 24 hours of the issuance thereof.
(Prior code § 43-3; Amend. Coun. J. 9-13-89, p. 4604; 12-4-02, p. 99026)

§13-32-032 Unlawful transfer of license for building application purposes.

(a) No person licensed under this code shall knowingly allow any other person to use the licensee's name or license identification on a building permit application if such licensee will not be performing the work which the permit application states he will perform unless the permit application has been amended to (i) remove the licensee's name or license identification; and (ii) insert the name of the licensee who will perform the work.

(b) No person named in a building permit application shall subcontract or assign any portion of the described work to any other person, without first amending the application to identify the subcontractor or assignee.

(c) Any licensee who violates this section shall be assessed a fine of $1,000 for the first offense; a fine of $1,500 and a ninety day license suspension for the second offense; and a fine of $2,000 and the licensee's name shall referred to the appropriate licensing board for license revocation for the third offense.
(Added. Coun. J. 9-5-01, p. 66630)

§13-32-033 False or inaccurate license number on building permit application.

It shall be unlawful for any person to knowingly insert a false or inaccurate name or license number on a building permit application when identifying a contractor, or any person required to be licensed by this code, who will be performing the work described in the building permit application. Any person who violates this section shall be assessed a fine of $500 and the building permit shall be revoked.
(Added. Coun. J. 9-5-01, p. 66630)

§13-32-035 Stop work orders—New or revised permit—Fees.

Whenever any person or entity shall apply for a new or revised permit from the department of construction and permits as the result of a stop order issued pursuant to Section 13-12-080 or other action taken by the city because the work being done or which has been completed was performed either without a permit or not in conformity with the terms of the permit, the permit fee assessed for the new or revised permit shall be as follows:

(i) For all permits where the regular fee is an amount less than $500.00 as provided in Sections 11-4-130, 13-20-540, 13-32-310, 13-180-210 and 13-192-730, a penalty of 100 percent of the regular permit fee shall be assessed in addition to the regular permit fee;

(ii) For all permits where the regular permit fee is an amount greater than $500.00 but less than $3,000.00 as provided in Sections 11-4-130, 13-20-540, 13-32-310, 13-180-210 and 13-192-730, a penalty of 100 percent of the regular permit fee shall be assessed for the first $500.00, and for each increment of $500.00 or fraction thereof, a penalty of $125.00 shall be assessed in addition to the regular permit fee;

(iii) For all permits where the regular permit fee exceeds $3,000.00 as provided in Sections 11-4-130, 13-20-540, 13-32-310, 13-180-210 and 13-192-730, a penalty of 100 percent of the regular permit fee shall be assessed for the first $1,000.00, and for each increment of $500.00 or fraction thereof, a penalty of $75.00 shall be assessed in addition to the regular permit fee.

(b) In addition to any fee assessed pursuant to subsection (a), a penalty of $1,000 shall be assessed whenever any person or entity shall apply for a new or revised permit from the department of construction and permits as a result of a stop work order issued pursuant to Section 13-12-080 or other action taken by the city because the work being done or which has been completed was performed by a person or persons required by the code to be listed on the building permit application who were not listed.
(Prior code § 43-3.1; Amend. Coun. J. 7-31-90, p. 19353; 9-5-01, p. 66630; 12-4-02, p. 99026)

§13-32-040 Plan approval—Provisions to be made for electrical work.
All drawings and plans for the construction, erection, addition to, or alterations of any building or other structure, for which a permit is required shall first be presented to the executive director for examination and approval as to proper use of building and premises and as to compliance in all other respects with the Chicago Zoning Ordinance and may be presented to the department of buildings, the board of health, the department of the environment, fire department, department of water management, department of streets and sanitation, and any other affected department for submission to the proper official of these departments and bureaus for examination and approval with regard to such provisions of this code, as are within the duty of such office to enforce, and after the drawings and plans have been examined and passed upon, they shall be returned to the executive director where they shall be taken up for examination and approval by the executive director. The executive director is authorized to establish a system whereby drawings and plans may be reviewed simultaneously by more than one person or department.

In every new building and in every existing building undergoing extensive remodeling where a new electric service or a new electric distribution center is to be installed, ample space shall be provided within the main walls of the building for the electric service equipment, metering equipment, distribution cabinets, cutout cabinets, transformers and other equipment necessary for an electric installation and ample working space around the equipment. This space shall be readily accessible to every tenant of the building who has electric equipment for light, heat or power which is supplied through the above mentioned equipment.
(Prior code § 43-4; Amend. Coun. J. 9-13-89, p. 4604; 12-11-91, p. 10832' 12-4-02, p. 99031; 12-4-02, p. 99026)

§13-32-050 Landmark or historic district consideration.
In addition to the city departments cited in Section 13-32-040, hereunder, all plans and drawings for any new construction on vacant lots within an area designated by federal, state or local authorities as a landmark or historic district shall also be submitted to the city council committee on cultural development and historical landmark preservation for examination and recommendation. Not more than 30 days after receipt of such drawings and plans, said committee shall hold public hearings and examine and return the drawings and plans, with its advisory recommendation to the executive director. No such permit shall be issued until after the expiration of the 30 day period.
(Prior code § 43-4.1; Amend. Coun. J. 9-13-89, p. 4604; 12-4-02, p. 99026)

§13-32-060 Surety bond.

Before any building permit is issued the applicant shall produce evidence that he has filed with, and had approved by, the commissioner of streets and sanitation, a surety bond in the amount of $50,000.00 protecting the city against any and all damages that may arise to the public ways upon which such building abuts, and to the city, and to any person, in consequence or by reason of, the proposed operation to be authorized by such permit, or by reason of any obstruction or occupation of any public ways in and about such building operations.
(Prior code § 43-5)

§13-32-080 Permit issuance.

At the proper time, notice shall be given by the executive director to the applicant that his or her plans have been examined and are ready to be returned to the applicant, and if such plans have been approved as submitted to the various departments and bureaus as aforesaid, the executive director shall, according to the building provisions of this code, issue a permit for the construction, erection, repair, or alteration of such building or structure; and shall file such application, and shall apply to such plans a final official stamp, stating that the drawings to which the same has been applied comply with the building provisions of this code. The plans so stamped shall then be returned to such applicant.
(Prior code § 43-7; Amend. Coun. J. 9-13-89, p. 4604; 12-4-02, p. 99026)

§13-32-085 Rules and regulations—Compliance required—Violation—Penalty.

The building commissioner is authorized to establish rules and regulations of general applicability for specific sites, both prior to and during the period of operations under the permit as shall be necessary to insure that the site of operations be maintained in a clean and safe manner so as not to constitute a public nuisance or hazard, that all construction or operations performed under the permit be substantially completed within a reasonable time period, and that all work performed under the permit be done in a manner consistent with the provisions of this code.

A copy of the rules and regulations issued by the building commissioner pertaining to operations or construction at a specific site shall be personally delivered to the owner, permit holder or contractor in charge of the site.

In the event the building commissioner determines that a violation of either the general or specific rules and regulations governing the construction or operations under the permit has occurred, he shall notify the owner, permit holder or contractor by certified mail. If the owner, permit holder or contractor shall fail to correct the violation within five days of receipt of the notice, the commissioner may take all necessary action to abate the violations which includes but is not limited to: revoking the permit, issuing a stop-work order and referring the matter to either the buildings hearings division within the department of administrative hearings or the corporation counsel to institute appropriate proceedings. Any owner, permit holder or contractor who is found to have violated rules and regulations established pursuant to this section shall be subject to a fine of not less than $50.00 and not more than $100.00 for each day the violation is deemed to exist.
(Prior code § 43-7.1; Added. Coun. J. 7-12-90, p. 18289; Amend. 7-10-96, p. 24982; 11-12-97, p. 56813; 4-29-98, p. 66564)

§13-32-090 Driveway permit requirements.

No permit shall be issued for the construction, erection, repair or alteration of any building or structure designed or intended for use as a garage or any other business, the operation of which will require a driveway across a public sidewalk, until the applicant therefor has first obtained from the commissioner of transportation a use of public way permit for driveway or driveways as prescribed by Chapter 10-20 of this code.
(Prior code § 43-8; Amend. Coun. J. 1-14-97, p. 37762; 6-9-99, p. 5453)

§13-32-100 Use of subsidewalk space—Authorization required.

No permit shall issue for the construction, erection, repair or alteration of any building or structure if in one or more walls abutting a public way, window or other openings are placed below the level of such public way, the lighting or ventilation of which will require the use of subsidewalk space, until the applicant therefor has first obtained specific authority for such use as provided in Section 10-28-010.
(Prior code § 43-8.1)

§13-32-110 Termination of permits—Extensions.

If, after a building or other required permit shall have been granted, the operations called for by such permit shall not be begun within six months after the date thereof, such permit shall be void and no operations thereunder shall be begun or completed until an extended permit shall be taken out by the owner or his agent, and a fee of 25 percent of the original cost of permit shall be charged for such extended permit; provided, however, that in no case shall a permit be issued or renewed for a fee less than $2.00. An extended permit shall be valid for six months following the date of expiration of the original permit and must be applied for within 10 days after the expiration of the original permit. Two extensions only shall be granted and if work is not begun within 18 months after the date of issuance of the original permit, all rights under the permit shall thereupon terminate by limitation. Where, under authority of a permit, or extended permit, work has begun and has been abandoned for a continuous or cumulative period of 12 months, all rights under such permit shall thereupon terminate by limitation.
(Prior code § 43-9)

§13-32-120 Construction contrary to permit—Stop work order.

It shall be unlawful for any owner, agent, architect, structural engineer, contractor, or builder engaged in erecting, altering, or repairing any building, structure or portion thereof to make any departure from the drawing or plans, as approved by the building commissioner, of a nature which involves any violation of the provisions of this code on which the permit has been issued. Any such departure from the approved drawings and plans involving a violation of requirements, shall operate to void the permit which has been issued for such work.

Where any work done under a permit authorizing erection, alteration, or repair of a building, structure or portion thereof, is being done contrary to the approved drawings and plans, the building commissioner or the president of the board of health shall have power to stop such work at once as provided in

Section 13-12-080, and to order all persons engaged thereon to stop and desist from further work, until such time as the building commissioner or the president of the board of health, has received affidavits that the work to be performed will be done in accordance with the approved drawings and plans. Nothing in this paragraph shall be construed to prevent minor changes in arrangement or decoration which do not affect the requirements of any provisions of this code, except where they affect significant features, as communicated in the report of the commission on Chicago landmarks, of a Chicago landmark designated in accordance with applicable provisions of Chapter 2-120 of this code.
(Prior code § 43-10; Amend. Coun. J. 9-13-89, p. 4604; 7-12-90, p. 18289; 6-14-95, p. 2828)

§13-32-130 Operations without permit—Stop work order.

No person or entity shall begin any work for which a building permit is required or any work of excavation in preparation therefor until the permit has been issued. If any person or entity violates this section, the building commissioner shall order the work stopped at once as provided in Section 13-12-080 and enforce the stop order in addition to the penalties for the violation provided in Sections 13-12-050 and 13-32-035.
(Prior code § 43-11; Amend. Coun. J. 9-13-89, p. 4604; 7-31-90, p. 19353)

§13-32-140 Reserved.

(Repealed Coun. J. 12-4-2002, p.99185, eff. 1-1-2003. See now §10-28-281 et seq.)

§13-32-145 Reserved.

(Repealed Coun. J. 12-4-2002, p.99185, eff. 1-1-2003. See now §10-28-285 et seq.)

§13-32-160 Canopies—Approval required.

It shall bc unlawful for any person to erect or construct any canopy attached to a building or structure under any provision of this code or any special ordinance, any part of which canopy shall project over a public way or public place, without first submitting the plans of such canopy, and also of the part of the building or other structure to which it is to be attached, to the executive director, for his or her approval. No permit shall be issued by the department of transportation unless the plans of such canopy shall have been approved by the department of construction and permits and a permit to attach said canopy to the building from which it is intended to project shall have been obtained from the executive director. No canopy that has been or may hereafter be authorized by any provision of this code or any special ordinance shall at any time be enclosed by canvas or other cloth or material in whole or in part so as to obstruct free passage underneath same, or so as to obstruct or reduce any required exit width.
(Prior code § 43-13; Amend. Coun. J. 9-13-89, p. 4604; 12-11-91, p. 10832; 12-4-02, p. 99026)

§13-32-170 Temporary platforms—Permit required.

It shall be unlawful for any person to erect or construct any platform in excess of 24 inches in height for temporary use in any public assembly unit, open air assembly unit, or any public place of assembly, to be used for speakers, displays, orchestras, entertainers, or spectators, unless the plans for such platform have been submitted to and approved by the department of construction and permits and a permit for such use is issued by the executive director. The construction of such platform shall conform to the requirements of Chapter 13-96 of this code. No such permit shall be issued for a term longer than 15 days and no such temporary platform shall be permitted to remain in use in excess of 15 days without a reinspection thereof having been made by the department of buildings and a new permit issued therefor.

(Prior code § 43-13.1; Amend. Coun. J. 9-13-89, p. 4604; 12-4-02, p. 99026)

§13-32-190 Elevator or mechanical equipment construction or alteration—Permit required.

Before proceeding with the construction, installation, or alteration of any elevator or mechanical equipment used for the raising or lowering of any curtain, stage, or orchestra floor, platform lift, dumbwaiter, escalator, or mechanical amusement device or apparatus, application for a permit for such construction, installation, or alteration shall be submitted to the executive director either by the owner or agent of the building, or of the premises on which such equipment is to be installed. A permit shall be obtained for any alteration in such elevator equipment except that this requirement shall not apply to the replacement of existing parts with other parts which are identical with those which are replaced. No permit shall be issued for such work except to an elevator mechanic contractor duly registered under the provisions of Chapter 4-298 of the Municipal Code of Chicago.

The application for a permit shall specify the number and kind of equipment which it is desired to install, or the nature of the alteration to be made and the location of the building, structure, or premises, and shall be accompanied by such drawings and specifications as shall be necessary to inform said commissioner of the plan of construction, type of elevator, dumbwaiter, escalator, platform lift, or mechanical amusement device, method of alteration, and the location thereof. Every application for a permit for a mechanical riding amusement device shall include a registration number assigned such device by the bureau of elevators of the department of buildings. For every new or previously unregistered mechanical amusement device, a detailed drawing and description of the construction thereof, with a certificate signed by a licensed architect or engineer certifying to the strength and safety of such device, must be submitted to the bureau of elevators for approval and assignment of a registration number. No permit shall be issued for a mechanical riding amusement device unless such device has been registered with the bureau of elevators. If such drawings and specifications show that the equipment is to be installed or altered in conformity with the building provisions of this code, the building commissioner shall approve the same and shall issue a permit to such applicant upon the payment of such applicant of the permit fee hereinafter named. It shall be unlawful for any owner, agent

or contractor to permit or allow the installation or alteration of any such equipment until a permit has been obtained, and the permit fee paid.
(Prior code § 43-15; Amend. Coun. J. 9-13-89, p. 4604; 10-28-97, p. 54722, effective 10-28-98; 12-4-02, p. 99026)

§13-32-191 Suspension of permit privileges.

Failure on the part of the registered elevator mechanic contractor to correct any defect, error, or deficiency in any work installed under the authority of a permit issued to him by the department of buildings within 10 calendar days after written notification thereof by the said bureau or within such further reasonable time as may, upon request, be prescribed, the building commissioner shall, without further notice, stop the issuance of permits to such registered elevator mechanic contractor until such corrections have been made, inspected and approved. In addition thereto the penalty provided in this chapter may be enforced.

The building commissioner is hereby empowered to suspend the permit privileges of any registered elevator mechanic contractor who shall fail to pay any just indebtedness for inspection fees for work on elevators or related devices, until such registered elevator mechanic contractor shall discharge and pay to the city all just indebtedness then due and owing from such contractor.
(Added. Coun. J. 10-28-97, p. 54722, effective 10-28-98)

§13-32-192 Revocation of permits.

The building commissioner is authorized to revoke any permit or certificate obtained by fraud, misrepresentation, or in any way contrary to the provisions of the elevator regulations of this code, for the installation, alteration, repair and use of any elevator equipment.
(Added. Coun. J. 10-28-97, p. 54722, effective 10-28-98)

§13-32-193 Use of permit issued to another.

It shall be unlawful for any person to install, alter, or repair any elevator equipment or related devices by authority of a permit issued to and for the use of some other person.
(Added. Coun. J. 10-28-97, p. 54722, effective 10-28-98)

§13-32-194 Permit for person not entitled to one.

It shall be unlawful for any registered elevator mechanic contractor to secure or furnish a permit for the installation, alteration and repair of elevator equipment to any person not entitled to such permit under the elevator regulations of the Municipal Code.
(Added. Coun. J. 10-28-97, p. 54722, effective 10-28-98)

§13-32-195 Alteration of forms.

It shall be unlawful for any person to change, add to, or mutilate so as to change the original wording, unless authorized by the commissioner, of any written or printed form issued to registered elevator mechanic contractors by the department of buildings.
(Added. Coun. J. 10-28-97, p. 54722, effective 10-28-98)

§13-32-200 Fences—Permit required.

It shall be unlawful for any person to erect or construct any fence more than five feet in height, or a solid fence of any height visible from a public street on property containing a Chicago landmark designated in accordance with applicable provisions of Chapter 2-120 of this code, without first obtaining a permit from the executive director.

(Prior code § 43-16; Amend. Coun. J. 9-13-89, p. 4604; 6-14-95, p. 2841, 2828; 12-4-02, p. 99026)

§13-32-210 Moving buildings.

No person shall be permitted to move any building which has been damaged to an extent greater than 50 percent of its value by fire, decay, or otherwise; nor shall it be permissible to move any frame or unprotected noncombustible building of such character as is prohibited to be constructed within the fire limits to any point within the fire limits; nor shall it be permissible to move any building to a location at which the uses for which such building is designed are prohibited by this code. Permits for the moving of frame buildings, other than those the moving of which is herein prohibited, shall be granted upon the payment of a fee of $.10 for each 1,000 cubic feet of volume, or fractional part thereof of such building, and upon securing and filing the written consent of two-thirds of the property owners according to frontage on both sides of the street in the block in which such building is to be moved. No permit shall be issued to move any building used or designed to be used for purposes for which frontage consents are required until frontage consents in the block to which such building is to be moved have also been secured and filed as required by the provisions of this code relating to such use.

No building used for residence or multiple dwelling purposes shall be moved from one lot to another or from one location to another upon the same lot unless the space to be occupied on such lot shall comply with the provisions of Chapter 13-64 of this code.

(Prior code § 43-17)

§13-32-230 Building wrecking—Permit required—Safety requirements.

(a) Before proceeding with the wrecking or tearing down of any building or other structure, a permit for such wrecking or tearing down shall first be obtained by the owner or his agent from the executive director, and it shall be unlawful to proceed with the wrecking or tearing down of any building or structure or any structural part of such building or structure unless such permit shall first have been obtained. Application for such permit shall be made by the owner, or his agent, to the executive director, who shall issue the permit upon such application and the payment of the fee herein provided.

Every application shall state the location and describe the building which it is proposed to wreck or tear down. Upon the issuance of said permit, such building may be wrecked or torn down, provided that all the work done thereunder shall be subject to the supervision of the building commissioner and to such reasonable restrictions as he may impose in regard to elements of safety and health; and provided further, that the work shall be kept sprinkled and sufficient scaffolding be provided to insure safety to human life.

(b) Notwithstanding the provisions of subsection (a) of this section, if a building or structure is color coded orange or red in the "Chicago Historic Resources Survey" published in 1996, no demolition permit shall be issued for a period not to exceed 90 days in order to enable the department of planning and development to explore options to preserve the building or structure, including, but not limited to, possible designation of the building or structure as a Chicago landmark in accordance with Article XVII of Chapter 2-120 of this code. The 90 days (i) shall begin to run on the date that a copy of the application for the demolition permit, along with a photograph accurately showing the current condition of the building or structure identified in that application, is submitted by the applicant to the landmarks division of the department of planning and development; and (ii) may be extended for any additional period by mutual written agreement between the applicant and the department. This subsection shall not apply to permit applications for the demolition of any building or structure if demolition is necessary to remedy conditions imminently dangerous to life, health or property as determined in writing by the department of buildings, the board of health or the fire department. Nor shall this subsection apply to any building or structure which the commission on Chicago landmarks has preliminarily recommended as a landmark pursuant to Section 2-120-630 or which has been designated by ordinance as a "Chicago Landmark" in accordance with the requirements of this code.

(c) Nothing in this section shall be construed to alter in any way the authority of or the process by which the commission on Chicago landmarks and the city council approve the issuance of demolition permits if such approval is required by this code.

(Prior code § 43-19; Amend. Coun. J. 9-13-89, p. 4604; 12-4-02, p. 99026; 1-16-03, p. 102365; Corrected. 12-8-04, p. 38063)

§13-32-260 Permits to be obtained prior to commencement of wrecking—Violation—Penalty.

It shall be unlawful for any person to perform any wrecking operation of any kind without first having obtained such necessary permit and bond as required in Sections 13-32-230 through 13-32-250. Any person found in violation of this section shall be subject to a fine of up to $1,000.00. Each day on which such violation exists shall constitute a separate and distinct offense.

(Prior code § 43-21.1; Amend. Coun. J. 11-17-93, p. 42192)

§13-32-270 Warm air furnaces—Permit required.

It shall be unlawful for any person to construct, replace or install any warm air heating furnace, with appurtenances, ducts, or registers, without first obtaining a permit from the executive director for such work, as provided by this chapter. Any person who violates this section shall be subject to a fine of $200.00 for each offense. Each day that a violation of this section exists shall constitute a separate and distinct offense.

(Prior code § 43-22; Amend. Coun. J. 9-13-89, p. 4604; 11-17-93, p. 42192; 12-4-02, p. 99026)

§13-32-280 Amusement devices—Submission of plan to buildings commission—Permit.

Before any mechanical amusement device, roller coaster, scenic railway, water chute, or other mechanical riding, sailing, sliding, or swinging device is erected, either in existing or new amusement parks, or places or sites where such devices are operated under carnival, fair, or similar auspices, a detailed plan shall be submitted to the buildings commissioner for his approval or rejection, and if approved, a permit shall be procured by the person desiring to erect such device.

(Prior code § 43-23; Amend. Coun. J. 9-13-89, p. 4604)

§13-32-290 Violation of building provisions—Revocation of permit—Reinstatement conditions.

(a) The executive director shall have the authority to revoke any permit for any violation of the building provisions of this code. If the work in, upon, or about any building or structure shall be conducted in violation of any of the building provisions of this code, it shall be the duty of the building commissioner to recommend that the executive director revoke the permit for the building or wrecking operations in connection with which such violation shall have taken place. It shall be unlawful, after the revocation of such permit, to proceed with such building or wrecking operations unless such permit shall first have been reinstated or re-issued by the executive director. Before a permit so revoked may be lawfully re-issued or reinstated, the entire building and building site shall first be put into condition corresponding with the requirements in the building provisions of this code, and any work or material applied to the same in violation of any of the provisions shall be first removed from such building, and all material not in compliance with the building provisions of this code shall be removed from the premises.

(b) Any city official who believes that a permit was issued in error shall notify the executive director, who shall review the application for permit, related plans and relevant portions of this code to determine whether the permit was issued in error. If the executive director determines that a permit was in fact issued in error, he or she shall notify the permit holder of the error, revoke the permit and require the permit holder to revise the related application and plans to conform to the applicable provisions of this code.

(Prior code § 43-24; Amend. Coun. J. 9-13-89, p. 4604; 12-4-02, p. 99026)

Article II. Permit Fees

§13-32-315 Post-permit Issuance—Verification of cost of construction, alteration or repair.

(a) Any owner, agent, contractor or architect who obtains a permit under this code shall, prior to the issuance of a certificate of occupancy for the premises for which the permit was obtained, file with the department of buildings, an affidavit, in a form approved by the building commissioner, and any other supporting documentation that the building commissioner may require, to verify the actual cost of the construction, alteration or repair for which the permit was obtained. If the actual cost of the construction, alteration or repair performed exceeds the costs estimated at the time the original permit was obtained, the owner, agent, contractor or architect to whom the permit was issued shall pay any additional permit fee owed to the city based on the fee schedule in existence at the time the original permit was obtained. No certificate of occupancy shall issue to any person for premises for which a permit was obtained until all outstanding permit fees have been paid to the department of revenue.

(b) It shall be unlawful for any person to submit any affidavit or supporting documentation pursuant to this section that contains false, inaccurate or misleading information about the actual cost of the construction, alteration or repair for which a permit was obtained. Any person who violates this section shall be fined as follows: (i) for all permits where the regular permit fee is in an amount less than $500.00, a penalty of 100 percent of the regular permit fee shall be assessed; (ii) for all permits where the regular permit fee is in an amount greater than $500.00 but less than $3,000.00, a penalty of 100 percent of the regular permit fee shall be assessed for the first $500.00, and for each increment of $500.00 or fraction thereof, a penalty of $125.00 shall be assessed; (iii) for all permits where the regular permit fee exceeds $3,000.00, a penalty of 100 percent of the regular permit fee shall be assessed for the first $1,000.00, and for each increment of $500.00 or fraction thereof, a penalty of $75.00 shall be assessed.

(Prior code § 43-26.1; Added. Coun. J. 7-31-90, p. 19353; Amend. 4-29-98, p. 66564; 12-15-04, p. 39840)

CHAPTER 13-40
BUILDING PLANS
(Selected Sections)

Sections:

13-40-090 Plans to be kept on file at construction site.
13-40-130 Tanks for flammable liquids.

§13-40-090 Plans to be kept on file at construction site.

In all construction work for which a permit is required, the approved and stamped drawings, plans, and permit shall be kept on file at the construction site while the work is in progress.

(Prior code § 45-10)

§13-40-130 Tanks for flammable liquids.

Every application for a permit to install a tank or tanks for flammable liquids shall be made to the executive director and shall be accompanied by a plat of survey showing the location and dimensions of all the property coming within the frontage area, the name and address of the owner or owners of each parcel of ground coming within such area, including the filling station site, and the total frontage in feet, with the consents of the required majority of such frontage.

In any location where a driveway or driveways across a public sidewalk are required in connection with the installation of a tank for flammable liquids, a permit shall not be issued until the applicant therefor has first obtained from the commissioner of transportation a use of public way permit for the driveway or driveways as prescribed by Chapter 10-20 of this code.

(Prior code § 45-14; Amend. Coun. J. 9-13-89, p. 4604; 12-11-91, p. 10832; 1-14-97, p. 37762; 6-9-99, p. 5453; 12-4-02, p. 99026)

CHAPTER 13-64
RESIDENTIAL UNITS
(Selected Sections)

Sections:

13-64-120 Smoke detectors—Required in all residential units.
13-64-130 Smoke detectors—Location.
13-64-140 Smoke detectors—Stairwell installation.
13-64-150 Smoke detectors—Standards.
13-64-160 Smoke detectors—Battery removal violation—Penalty.
13-64-180 Smoke detectors—Hotels and motels and bed-and-breakfast establishments to provide smoke detectors to serve hearing impaired patrons.
13-64-190 Carbon monoxide detectors—Required in residential units.
13-64-200 Carbon monoxide detectors—Exemptions.
13-64-210 Carbon monoxide detectors—Location.
13-64-220 Carbon monoxide detectors—Dwelling units heated by space heaters.
13-64-230 Carbon monoxide detectors—Standards—Rules.
13-64-240 Carbon monoxide detectors—Battery removal violation—Penalty.
13-64-260 Carbon monoxide detectors—Required in Class B institutional and Class C assembly units.
13-64-270 Carbon monoxide detectors—Location; Class B institutional and Class C assembly units.
13-64-280 Carbon monoxide detectors—Buildings heated by central fossil fuel powered heating unit.
13-64-290 Fossil fuel defined.
13-64-300 Penalties.

§13-64-120 Smoke detectors—Required in all residential units.

All buildings of residential or mixed occupancy except those complying with the terms of Chapter 13-76 of this code having any residential units, shall be equipped with approved smoke detectors in the manner prescribed in this section.
(Prior code § 52-11; Amend. Coun. J. 4-25-84, p. 6189)

§13-64-130 Smoke detectors—Location.

Not less than one approved smoke detector shall be installed in every single family residential unit and multiple dwelling units as defined in Chapter 13-56, Sections 13-56-020, 13-56-030 and 13-56-040. The detector shall be installed on the ceiling and at least four inches from any wall or on a wall located from four to 12 inches from the ceiling, and within 15 feet of all rooms used for sleeping purposes, with not less than one detector per level, containing a habitable room or unenclosed heating plant.
(Prior code § 52-11.1; Amend. Coun. J. 4-25-84, p. 6189; 9-8-86, p. 33588)

§13-64-140 Smoke detectors—Stairwell installation.

In buildings of Types II, III or IV construction, multiple dwellings as defined in Section 13-56-040 and buildings of mixed occupancy having any residential units, shall contain not less than one approved smoke detector at the uppermost ceiling of all interior stairwells. All approved smoke detectors herein required shall be installed on the ceiling, at least four inches from the wall or on a wall located from four to 12 inches from the ceiling.
(Prior code § 52-11.2; Amend. Coun. J. 9-8-86, p. 33588)

§13-64-150 Smoke detectors—Standards.

All approved smoke detectors herein required shall be either the ionization chamber or the photoelectric type and shall comply with Chapters 14-8, 14-16 through 14-36 and 14-44 through 14-72 of the Municipal Code of Chicago. Detectors shall bear the label of a nationally recognized standards testing laboratory that indicates that the smoke detectors have been tested and listed as a single or single and multiple station smoke detectors. All approved smoke detectors installed in buildings hereafter erected shall be permanently wired to the electrical service of each dwelling unit in accordance with the provisions of Chapters 14-8, 14-16 through 14-36 and 14-44 through 14-72 of the Municipal Code of Chicago.

In buildings required to have a standard fire alarm system as specified in Chapter 15-16 and in nonsprinklered buildings complying with Chapter 13-76, smoke detectors in dwelling units shall be of the type tested and listed for fire protection signaling systems and shall have an integral audible device.

(Prior code § 52-11.3; Amend. Coun. J. 4-25-84, p. 6189; 9-8-86, p. 33588)

§13-64-160 Smoke detectors—Battery removal violation—Penalty.

It shall be unlawful for any person to remove batteries or in any way make inoperable smoke detectors as provided for in this chapter, except that this provision shall not apply to any building owner or manager or his agent in the normal procedure of replacing batteries.

Any person found in violation of this section shall be punished by a fine of not less than $300.00 nor more than $1,000.00 and/or confinement for a period of not more than six months.

(Prior code § 52-11.4; Renumbered. Coun. J. 4-25-84, p. 6189)

§13-64-180 Smoke detectors—Hotels and motels and bed-and-breakfast establishments to provide smoke detectors to serve hearing impaired patrons.

In addition to the smoke detectors required under Section 13-64-140, each hotel and motel and bed-and-breakfast establishments shall provide at least one smoke detector designed to serve hearing impaired persons, for each 50 units or fraction thereof. If a patron of a hotel or motel and bed-and-breakfast establishments requests a smoke detector designed to serve hearing impaired persons, it shall be the duty of the hotel operator or motel operator to provide installation of such a smoke detector. For purposes of compliance with this section, a smoke detector is "designed to serve hearing impaired persons" if it emits a flashing or stroboscopic light signal or vibration to indicate the presence of smoke.

A smoke detector required under this section may be either portable or permanently wired to the electrical service of the hotel or motel in accordance with the provisions of Chapters 14-8, 14-16 through 14-36 and 14-44 through 14-72 of the Municipal Code of Chicago. A hotel operator or motel operator may require that a patron pay a refundable deposit at the time of providing a portable smoke detector for the patron's room. The amount of the deposit shall not exceed the cost of the portable smoke detector.

Each hotel operator and each motel operator shall post a notice at the place of registration of patrons, bearing the legend "smoke detectors for the hearing impaired available." The notice shall contain print no smaller than three inches high. The notice shall be posted in such a manner as to be visible to registering patrons.
(Prior code § 52-11.6; Added. Coun. J. 6-25-86, p. 31212; Amend. Coun. J. 9-4-03, p. 7118)

§13-64-190 Carbon monoxide detectors—Required in residential units.

Every building of residential or mixed occupancy and having one or more residential units shall be equipped with approved carbon monoxide detectors in accordance with this chapter.

For purposes of this chapter "residential unit" includes Class A-1 single-family dwellings as defined in Section 13-56-030 of this code and Class A-2 multiple dwellings as defined in Section 13-56-040 of this code.
(Added. Coun. J. 3-2-94, p. 46875)

§13-64-200 Carbon monoxide detectors—Exemptions.

The following residential units shall not require carbon monoxide detectors:

(a) A residential unit in a building that does not rely on combustion of fossil fuel for heat, ventilation or hot water, and is not sufficiently close to any ventilated source of carbon monoxide, as determined by the building commissioner, to receive carbon monoxide from that source.

(b) A residential unit that (1) is heated by steam, hot water or electric heat, and (2) is not connected by ductwork or ventilation shafts to any room containing a fossil fuel-burning boiler or heater, and (3) is not sufficiently close to any ventilated source of carbon monoxide, as determined by the building commissioner, to receive carbon monoxide from that source.
(Added. Coun. J. 3-2-94, p. 46875)

§13-64-210 Carbon monoxide detectors—Location.

Not less than one approved carbon monoxide detector shall be installed in each residential unit. The detector shall be installed within 40 feet of all rooms used for sleeping purposes.

In every hotel and motel, one approved carbon monoxide detector shall be installed for every 10,000 square feet of floor area, or fraction thereof, (a) on every floor on which a fossil fuel-burning boiler or furnace is located, and (b) on every floor on which sleeping rooms are heated by any type of warm air heating plant as defined in Chapter 13-184 that burns fossil fuel. Floor area shall be computed separately for each floor.
(Added. Coun. J. 3-2-94, p. 46875; Corrected. 3-23-94, p. 47711)

§13-64-220 Carbon monoxide detectors—Dwelling units heated by space heaters.

Each dwelling unit employing space heating equipment that is located within the dwelling unit and that burns fossil fuel shall be equipped with at least one carbon monoxide detector.
(Added. Coun. J. 3-2-94, p. 46875)

§13-64-230 Carbon monoxide detectors—Standards—Rules.

Every approved carbon monoxide detector shall comply with all applicable federal and state regulations, and shall bear the label of a nationally recognized standard testing laboratory, and shall meet the standard of Ul 2034 or its equivalent. The building commissioner shall issue rules and regulations not inconsistent with the provisions of this chapter, for the implementation and administration of the provisions of this chapter relating to carbon monoxide detectors.

(Added. Coun. J. 3-2-94, p. 46875)

§13-64-240 Carbon monoxide detectors—Battery removal violation—Penalty.

It shall be unlawful for any person to remove batteries from a carbon monoxide detector required under this chapter, or in any way to make inoperable a carbon monoxide detector required under this chapter, except that this provision shall not apply to any building owner or manager or his agent in the normal procedure of replacing batteries.

Any person who violates this section shall be punished by a fine of not less than $300.00 nor more than $1,000.00 and/or confinement for a period of not more than six months.

(Added. Coun. J. 3-2-94, p. 46875)

§13-64-250 Carbon monoxide detectors—Owner's and tenant's responsibilities.

The owner of a structure shall supply and install required carbon monoxide detectors. The owner shall test and maintain carbon monoxide detectors located other than in a dwelling unit. The owner shall provide written information regarding carbon monoxide testing and maintenance to at least one adult tenant in each dwelling unit. The tenant shall test, provide general maintenance, and replace required batteries for carbon monoxide detectors located in the tenant's dwelling unit.

(Added. Coun. J. 3-23-94, p. 47711)

§13-64-260 Carbon monoxide detectors—Required in Class B institutional and Class C assembly units.

Every new or existing building or part thereof hereafter designed, erected, altered or converted for the purposes of a Class B institutional unit or a Class C assembly unit as defined in Sections 13-56-050, 13-56-060 and 13-56-070 of this code shall be equipped with approved carbon monoxide detectors.

(Added. Coun. J. 3-23-94, p. 47711; Amend. 3-6-96, p. 17599, effective 10-1-96)

§13-64-270 Carbon monoxide detectors—Location; Class B institutional and Class C assembly units.

In every Class B institutional unit as defined in Sections 13-56-050 and 13-56-060 and in every Class C assembly unit as defined in Section 13-56-070, not less than one approved carbon monoxide detector shall be installed per every 10,000 square feet, or fraction thereof, (a) on every floor on which a fossil fuel-burning appliance, boiler or furnace is located, and (b) on every floor heated by any type of warm air heating plant as defined in Chapter 13-184 that

burns fossil fuel. On every floor of a Class B institutional unit which contains a sleeping quarters, one approved carbon monoxide detector shall also be installed within 40 feet of all rooms used for sleeping purposes that are either (a) located near a fossil fuel-burning appliance, boiler or furnace or (b) heated by any type of warm air heating plant, as defined in Chapter 13-184, which burns fossil fuel. Floor area shall be computed separately for each floor.
(Added. Coun. J. 3-23-94, p. 47711; Amend. 3-6-96, p. 17599, effective 10-1-96; 7-31-96, p. 26646)

§13-64-280 Carbon monoxide detectors—Buildings heated by central fossil fuel powered heating unit.

In every building that is heated by one main central fossil fuel powered heating unit, and that is not exempted under Section 13-64-200, one approved carbon monoxide detector must be installed in the room containing the central heating unit.
(Added. Coun. J. 3-2-94, p. 46875)

§13-64-290 Fossil fuel defined.

Whenever used in this chapter, the term "fossil fuel" shall include coal, natural gas, kerosene, oil, propane and wood.
(Added. Coun. J. 3-2-94, p. 46875)

§13-64-300 Penalties.

Any person who violates any provision of Sections 13-64-190 through 13-64-280, for which a separate penalty is not provided, shall be subject to a fine of not less than $300.00 and not more than $1,000.00. Every day that a violation is allowed to continue shall constitute a separate and distinct offense.
(Added. Coun. J. 3-2-94, p. 46875)

CHAPTER 13-84
ASSEMBLY UNITS
(Selected Sections)

Sections:
13-84-331 Special requirement for nightclubs and restaurants.
13-84-410 Building capacity—Signs to be posted.

§13-84-331 Special requirement for nightclubs and restaurants.

Every newly constructed, reconstructed or substantially rehabilitated nightclub or restaurant with an occupancy of more than 100 persons and located in whole or in part more than four feet below street grade shall be equipped with an approved automatic sprinkler system. Every existing nightclub or restaurant with an occupancy of more than 100 persons and located in whole or in part more than four feet below street grade shall be equipped with an approved automatic sprinkler system with six months after the effective date of this section.
(Added. Coun. J. 11-1-00, p. 43076)

§13-84-410 Building capacity—Signs to be posted.

(a) In every theater, public assembly unit or open air assembly unit and in every room or in any portion of such units which is used as a place of assembly, there shall be conspicuously posted signs indicating the number of persons who may legally occupy such rooms and space. Such signs shall read as follows:

Occupancy By More Than _____ Persons Is
Dangerous And Unlawful
Building Commissioner
of Construction and Permits
City of Chicago

(b) Such signs shall be furnished by the department of buildings and shall be 15 inches in width by 12 inches in height. The lettering thereon indicating the lawful occupancy shall be of bold gothic type in red on a background of white, shall not be less than one inch in height and the numerals shall be one and one-quarter inches in height, and such lettering and numerals shall be properly spaced to provide good visibility.

(c) Such signs shall be illuminated, shall be durable, and shall be substantially secured to wall or partition.

(d) Such signs shall be located at the main entrance to such space or room so as to be conspicuously visible to a person entering such space or room.

(e) The fee for each location shall be $125.00 for up to 300 occupants plus $1.00 for each additional occupant. "Location" for purposes of this section shall mean one or more rooms functioning as assembly units within a single structure and operated by the same owner or lessee. In locations that require more than one sign, the fee formula shall be based on the aggregate assembly capacity. A supplemental fee of $100.00 shall be charged for each additional card issued under a single application. $100.00 shall be charged for the issuance of each replacement card.

(f) The formula for existing assembly units that require one or more cards due to remodeling, alterations, addition, or reconfiguration of the floor plan shall be based solely on such room or space which has been altered.

(Prior code § 54-15; Amend. Coun. J. 7-9-84, p. 8218; 9-13-89, p. 4604; 11-17-93, p. 42192; 7-13-95, p. 4440; 3-5-03, p. 104990; 10-1-03, p. 9163; 11-19-03, p. 14216)

CHAPTER 13-88
OPEN AIR ASSEMBLY UNITS
(Selected Section)

Sections:
13-88-230 Storage of combustible materials prohibited.

§13-88-230 Storage of combustible materials prohibited.

No combustible materials shall be stored below or adjacent to any open air assembly unit.

(Prior code § 55-13)

CHAPTER 13-96
MISCELLANEOUS BUILDINGS AND STRUCTURES
(Selected Sections)

Sections:

Article XVII. Private Residential Swimming Pools

13-96-630 Definition.
13-96-640 Location.
13-96-650 Permit required.
13-96-710 Fences.
13-96-790 Safety precautions.
13-96-800 Operation and maintenance.

Article XVII. Private Residential Swimming Pools

§13-96-630 Definition.

The term "private residential swimming pool" is hereby defined as a receptacle for water, or an artificial pool of water having a depth at any point of more than five feet, intended for the purpose of immersion or partial immersion therein of human beings, and including all appurtenant equipment, constructed, installed, and maintained in or above the ground outside of a building used for a single-family dwelling unit. Provided further, that such private residential swimming pool is maintained by an individual primarily for the sole use of his household and guests and not for the purpose of profit or in connection with any business operated for profit. No out-of-doors swimming pool intended for the use of members and their guests of a nonprofit club or organization, or limited to house residents of a multiple dwelling unit, a block, subdivision, neighborhood, community or other specified area of residence shall be permitted in a single-family residence, duplex residence, or apartment district.
(Prior code § 61-18.1)

§13-96-640 Location.

(a) Private residential swimming pools shall be permitted in single-family residence districts only.

(b) No portion of a private residential swimming pool shall be located at a distance less than 10 feet from any side or rear property line, or building line. Pumps, filters and pool water disinfection equipment installations shall be located at a distance not less than 10 feet from any side property line.
(Prior code § 61-18.2)

§13-96-650 Permit required.

It shall be unlawful to proceed with the construction, installation, enlargement or alteration of any private residential swimming pool and appurtenances within the city unless permits therefor shall have first been obtained from the executive director, the commissioner of the department of water management.
(Prior code § 61-18.3; Amend. Coun. J. 9-13-89, p. 4604; 12-4-02, p. 99026; 3-5-03, p. 104990)

§13-96-710 Fences.

All private residential swimming pools shall be completely enclosed by a fence erected along the periphery of the pool walks. All fence openings or points of entry into pool area enclosure shall be equipped with gates. The fence and gates shall be five feet in height above the walk grade level and shall be constructed of a minimum Number 9 gauge woven wire mesh corrosion-resistant material. All gates shall be equipped with self-closing and self-latching devices placed at the top of the gate and made inaccessible to small children. All fence posts shall be decay or corrosion-resistant and shall be set in concrete bases.

(Prior code § 61-18.9)

§13-96-790 Safety precautions.

(a) A skilled swimmer shall be present at all times that private residential swimming pools are in use.

(b) Every private residential swimming pool shall be equipped with one or more throwing ring buoys not more than 15 inches in diameter and having 60 feet of three-sixteenth-inch Manila line attached, and one or more light but strong poles with blunted ends and not less than 12 feet in length, for making reach assists or rescues.

(c) No diving board or platform more than three feet above water level shall be installed for use in connection with any private residential swimming pool.

(d) Life-saving equipment approved by the board of health shall be provided and maintained so as to be immediately available for use in an emergency.

(Prior code § 61-18.17)

§13-96-800 Operation and maintenance.

(a) Private residential swimming pools may be used between June 1st and September 15th, inclusive, only. No private residential swimming pool shall be made use of between the hours of 10 p.m. and 9 a.m. during this period.

(b) During the period September 16th to May 30th, inclusive, all private residential swimming pools shall be completely drained of all water.

(c) A suitable substantial protective cover shall be provided and installed over all private residential swimming pool surfaces during the period September 16th to May 30th, inclusive.

(d) All private residential swimming pools shall be maintained in a clean and sanitary condition, and all equipment shall be maintained in a satisfactory operating condition during periods the pool is in use.

(e) No private residential swimming pool shall be used, kept, maintained or operated in the city, if such use, keeping, maintaining or operating shall be the occasion of any nuisance or shall be dangerous to life or detrimental to health.

(Prior code § 61-18.18)

CHAPTER 13-128
USE OF PUBLIC PROPERTY
(Selected Secctions)

Sections:

13-128-010 Temporary use of streets and alleys—Permits.
13-128-020 Occupancy limitations.
13-128-030 Extent of occupation.
13-128-040 Temporary usage—Obstructions prohibited.
13-128-050 Alley roadway to be maintained.
13-128-060 Restoration of public property upon completion of construction required.
13-128-061 Removal of traffic control device.
13-128-070 Bond required.
13-128-080 Permanent occupancy of public property.
13-128-090 Foundations.
13-128-100 Cornices, belt courses and similar projections.
13-128-110 Wheel guards.
13-128-120 Marquees and canopies.
13-128-130 Signs.
13-128-140 Sub-sidewalk space.
13-128-150 Fire escapes.
13-128-160 Zoning requirements.

§13-128-010 Temporary use of streets and alleys—Permits.

Permits for the occupation of a street, alley or sidewalk may be issued by the commissioner of streets and sanitation only under conditions complying with the requirements of Sections 13-128-020 to 13-128-070.
(Prior code § 77-1)

§13-128-020 Occupancy limitations.

Such occupancy shall be limited to the storage and handling of building materials, the construction of temporary sidewalks and other uses incident to the erection, alteration or demolition of buildings as approved by the executive director.
(Prior code § 77-1.1; Amend. Coun. J. 9-13-89, p. 4604; 3-5-03, p. 104990)

§13-128-030 Extent of occupation.

The extent of occupation shall not exceed one-third the width of the roadway, nor shall it extend within four feet of any steam or street railway track. Areas of occupancy shall be limited to streets, alleys and sidewalks adjoining the property upon which the building is to be erected, altered or demolished, except that the area may be extended if the written consent of, and a waiver of claims for damages against the city by the owners of adjoining properties is first obtained and filed with the commissioner of streets and sanitation.
(Prior code § 77-1.2)

§13-128-040 Temporary usage—Obstructions prohibited.

No temporary use of streets or alleys shall interfere with drainage of gutters, and no obstruction of any kind shall be placed so as to obstruct free approach to any fire hydrant, lamppost, fire alarm box, manhole or catchbasin.
(Prior code § 77-1.3)

§13-128-050 Alley roadway to be maintained.

A roadway of 10 feet clear width shall be maintained through any alley located along the building site.
(Prior code § 77-1.4)

§13-128-060 Restoration of public property upon completion of construction required.

Immediately upon completion of the building construction, all walkways, debris or other obstructions shall be removed, leaving the public property in as good condition as it was before such work was commenced.
(Prior code § 77-1.5)

§13-128-061 Removal of traffic control device.

If a removal of a traffic control device other than a parking meter is necessary in order to accommodate properly permitted work in or affecting the public way, the commissioner may order the temporary removal of the affected device. The permittee shall pay a fee of $150.00 in advance for the removal and reinstallation of each traffic device.
(Added. Coun. J. 12-4-02, p. 99026)

§13-128-070 Bond required.

No such permit will be issued until the applicant executes and files with the commissioner of streets and sanitation a bond running to the city with good and sufficient corporate surety to be approved by the commissioner of streets and sanitation in the penal sum of $250,000.00, conditioned upon the faithful observance and performance of each condition of said permit and conditioned further to indemnify, keep and save harmless the city against all liabilities, judgments, costs, damages and expenses of every kind which may accrue against, be charged to, or be recovered from the city from, by reason of, or on account of any act or thing done, any injury received by any person or damage to any property by virtue of the authority given in such permit. Provided, however, that where the building construction at the site does not involve the use of piling, sheeting or caissons, the bond shall be in the penal sum of $50,000.00. Said bond shall remain in full force and effect during the entire life of such permit.
(Prior code § 77-1.6)

§13-128-080 Permanent occupancy of public property.

The permanent occupancy of public property by any part of a building or structure hereafter erected shall be governed by the provisions of Sections 13-128-090 to 13-128-160, inclusive.
(Prior code § 77-2)

§13-128-090 Foundations.

Foundations may not project into nor encroach upon public ways except as herein provided. The executive director may issue permits for any building for which it is contemplated that there shall be projections of the foundation or a part thereof into a public way under the following conditions:

(a) The portions of foundations above a level 20 feet below city datum may project into a public way four and one-half inches per foot of depth below sidewalk or alley grade but not more than 36 inches.

(b) Except as provided in paragraph (d), in no case shall foundations extend within five feet of the centerline of any public way.

(c) Except where sub-sidewalk space is permitted, no foundation, or any part thereof, shall project into a public way in such manner as to add to the floor area of any building or structure.

(d) Portions of foundations, constructed lower than 20 feet below city datum, may project into a public way such distance as the executive director may deem necessary for the stability of the building or structure of which they are a part.

(Prior code § 77-2.1; Amend. Coun. J. 9-13-89, p. 4604; 3-5-03, p. 104990)

§13-128-100 Cornices, belt courses and similar projections.

(a) Cornices, rustications, quoins, moldings, belt courses, lintel, sills, oriel windows, pediments and similar projections of a decorative character may project beyond a street line not more than two feet; provided, that every part of such projection is not less than 12 feet above the sidewalk level at any point and that the aggregate area of all such projection does not exceed five percent of the wall area.

(b) When additions to existing buildings are erected, the executive director may permit the extension of existing cornices, moldings and belt courses which do not comply with the requirements of this section but which were legal at the time of the adoption of this code.

(Prior code § 77-2.2; Amend. Coun. J. 9-13-89, p. 4604; 3-5-03, p. 104990)

§13-128-110 Wheel guards.

Wheel guards less than 21 inches high may project into alleys a distance of not more than nine inches.

(Prior code § 77-2.3)

§13-128-120 Marquees and canopies.

Marquees and canopies extending over a public way shall comply with the provisions of Chapter 10-28.

(Prior code § 77-2.4)

§13-128-130 Signs.

Signs having a clear height of not less than 10 feet may project over a public sidewalk to a point not less than two feet from the curb line.

(Prior code § 77-2.5)

§13-128-140 Sub-sidewalk space.

The use of sub-sidewalk space shall be governed by the provisions of Chapter 10-28.

(Prior code § 77-2.6)

§13-128-150 Fire escapes.

Fire escapes hereafter erected shall not project over public property except under the following conditions:

(a) When the fire escape is erected to replace an existing required fire escape which projects over public property;

(b) When a fire escape is required to correct an existing exit hazard and cannot be properly located over vacant space on the lot on which the building is located.

(Prior code § 77-2.7)

§13-128-160 Zoning requirements.

Nothing in this section shall be construed to permit encroachments on public property prohibited by the Chicago Zoning Ordinance.

(Prior code § 77-2.8)

This page intentionally left blank

TITLE 15
FIRE PREVENTION
(Selected Chapters)

Chapters:

15-4	Bureau of Fire Prevention. (Selected Sections)
15-20	Explosives and Fireworks. (Selected Sections)
15-24	Flammable Liquids. (Selected Sections)
15-26	Fume and Flammable Compressed Gases. (Selected Sections)

CHAPTER 15-4
BUREAU OF FIRE PREVENTION
(Selected Sections)

Sections:

Article I. Bureau of Fire Prevention

15-4-010	Fire regulations.
15-4-020	Bureau powers, duties and responsibilities.
15-4-050	Interpretation of terms.

Article II. General Provisions

15-4-060	Transportation exemption.
15-4-090	Dangerous buildings a nuisance.
15-4-100	Right to survey.
15-4-101	Fire emergency plan required when.
15-4-102	Safety warden.

Article III. Licenses

15-4-110	Hazardous use units.
15-4-252	Lumberyards and lumber storehouses.
15-4-256	Sale of solid fuel and firewood.
15-4-257	Storage of solid fuel not for retail.
15-4-258	Fuel oil dealers.
15-4-259	Fuel oil storers.

Article VI. Liquefied Petroleum Gas Tanks

15-4-410	Application and permit.

Article VII. Fire Extinguisher Servicemen

15-4-450	License required.
15-4-460	License application.
15-4-480	License fee.
15-4-490	License renewal.
15-4-500	Violation—Penalty.
15-4-510	Rules and regulations.

Article VIII. Other License Requirements

15-4-520	Other licenses and permits required.

Article IX. Permits

15-4-550	Fireworks.

Article I. Bureau of Fire Prevention

§15-4-010 Fire regulations.

This chapter, Article II of Chapter 15-16, and Chapters 15-20, 15-24, 15-26 and 15-28 of this code shall be known as the fire regulations of this code.
(Prior code § 90-1; Amend. Coun. J. 2-7-96, p. 15616)

§15-4-020 Bureau powers, duties and responsibilities.

For provisions covering the establishment powers, duties and responsibilities of the bureau of fire prevention, see Chapter 2-36 of this code.

In addition to any other fee charged pursuant to this code for the review and approval of plans, the following fees shall be charged and collected for the review and approval of plans by the bureau of fire prevention:

Type of Plans	Fee
Fire detection system, voice command system and fire command panel system, under Sections 13-76-030, 13-76-040 and 13-76-050 of this code — per floor of building (applies to new, remodeled and renovated systems)	$35.00
Fire alarm system review under Section 14-60-260(c) of this code, where the system serves a day care center only — per system (applies only to plans submitted after July 1, 1992)	35.00
Fire alarm system review under Section 14-60-260(c) of this code, other than day care center only — per floor of building (applies to new, remodeled and renovated systems)	80.00
Exit sign review under Section 13-160-780 of this code — per floor of building	40.00
Building plans not otherwise listed in this section, under Section 2-36-260 of this code — per floor of building	75.00

(Prior code § 90-2; Amend. Coun. J. 12-15-92, p. 27387)

§15-4-050 Interpretation of terms.

Where the meaning of any term of expression used in the fire regulations of this code is disputed and is not defined therein, such definitions thereof as appear in the building regulations of this code shall prevail and be conclusive.
(Prior code § 90-3)

Article II. General Provisions

§15-4-060 Transportation exemption.

Nothing contained in this chapter, Article II of Chapter 15-16, Chapters 15-20, 15-24, 15-26 and 15-28 shall be construed as applying to the transportation of any article or thing shipped in conformity with regulations prescribed by

the Department of Transportation and/or Interstate Commerce Commission, nor as applying to the military or naval forces of the United States.
(Prior code § 90-4; Amend. Coun. J. 2-7-96, p. 15616)

§15-4-090 Dangerous buildings a nuisance.

Any building, structure, enclosure, place or premises, perilous to life or property by reason of the construction of such building or structure or by reason of the condition or quantity of its contents, or the use of the building or its contents, or the use of the enclosure or the overcrowding at any time of persons therein, or by reason of deficiencies in such fire alarm or fire prevention equipment, as may be required by the fire regulations of this code, or where conditions exist which would hamper or impede the fire department in combating a fire in or on the building, is hereby declared to be a nuisance and the division marshal in charge of the bureau of fire prevention is empowered and directed to cause any such nuisance to be abated.
(Prior code § 90-7)

§15-4-100 Right to survey.

(a) Right to Demand Survey. The owner, lessee or occupant of any building, structure, enclosure, place or premises affected by any order or notice of the bureau of fire prevention, may make written demand upon the division marshal in charge of the bureau of fire prevention, for a survey of such building, structure, enclosure, place or premises, to determine whether or not such order is valid and reasonable, which demand for survey must be served upon the said division marshal by leaving a copy thereof at his office in the city hall, within seven days, Sunday and holidays excepted, after the service of the order or notice referred to in such demand. Said demand for a survey shall contain the name of the person to act as a surveyor on behalf of the one making the demand.

(b) Duty of Division Marshal. Upon receipt of a demand for survey, the said division marshal shall immediately issue an order for the same, naming therein the person to act as surveyor on behalf of the bureau of fire prevention, who shall be an officer or employee of said bureau and said order shall also name the person theretofore selected by the one making the demand for the survey.

(c) Survey Procedure. In the event that the two persons thus named are unable to agree concerning the survey and their report thereon, they shall select a third person to act with them on such survey, and a report signed by any two of the three surveyors thus selected shall be conclusive. In the event that the two surveyors selected as above set forth cannot agree concerning the survey and their report thereon and cannot agree upon the selection of a third person to act with them in connection with such survey, said third person shall be selected and appointed by the chief justice of the circuit court on application made in writing by the aforesaid division marshal, of which application the said fire marshal shall give at least 24-hours notice, in writing, to the applicant for such survey, and a report signed by any two of the three surveyors thus selected shall be conclusive. The date and hour when the survey shall be made shall be stated in the order therefor, and no change shall be made in such date and hour, except by written stipulation duly signed by said division marshal and the applicant for such survey. A copy of such order shall be served upon the person demanding the survey by personal delivery to him at least 24 hours previous to the hour fixed in the order for the holding of such survey, and he shall have the right to be present and to be heard at such survey in person or by agent or attorney. The surveyors shall meet at the time and place described in the order of their appointment, and shall survey the building, structure, enclosure, place or premises referred to in said order, and to consider the merits of the order of the bureau in respect to which the survey has been demanded.

(d) Report of Survey. After such survey and consideration, the surveyors shall prepare and sign a report of their proceedings and determination which shall be filed in the bureau of fire prevention, and a copy thereof shall be given the person demanding such survey upon his application therefor. The determination of the surveyors in any such case shall be final and conclusive.

(e) Surveyor's Fees. Each person, other than an officer or employee of the bureau of fire prevention, designated to act as a surveyor, pursuant to the provisions of this section, shall be paid the sum of $25.00 for such survey in which he participates upon the filing of the report thereof in the bureau.

(f) Payment of Expenses. As a condition precedent to the ordering of a survey, the person demanding the same shall deposit with the division marshal in charge of the bureau of fire prevention the sum of $100.00 to indemnify the city for the expense of the survey, in the event that the surveyors confirm the order of the bureau. Such sum shall be returned to the depositor, in the event that the surveyors shall report such order as invalid or unreasonable. In case the report of the surveyors is to the effect that the order of the division marshal, which was the subject of such survey, was in all respects valid and reasonable, all the expenses of the survey shall be paid out of the fund herein required to be deposited with the division marshal by the person demanding such survey, and the balance remaining, if any, shall be returned to such person.

(g) Closing Buildings. If the order or notice subject to survey requires any building or premises to be closed on account of its dangerous condition, such order or notice shall not be stayed pending the determination of the reasonableness and validity thereof.

(Prior code § 90-8)

§15-4-101 Fire emergency plan required when.

The owner or operator of equipment or apparatus used for the generation, transmission or distribution of electricity by a public utility shall develop a fire emergency plan for each building, structure or portion thereof enclosing such equipment or apparatus. The fire emergency plan shall include the following: the location and type of equipment or apparatus; identification of supervisory personnel to be notified in the event of a fire affecting the equipment or apparatus, and the means of notification; a plan for evacuation of employees not involved in firefighting from the area of the fire; assignment of responsibilities for coordination with designated personnel for admission of fire department personnel and control of traffic on the premises in the event of a fire; a list of toxic, combustible or explosive materials stored or used on the premises; a schedule of drills to verify the viability of the plan; and such other related information as the fire commissioner may require. The fire emergency plan shall be in writing and shall be filed in the office of the fire commissioner or his designee. A copy of the plan shall be maintained on the premises where the electrical equipment is located. The owner or operator of the equipment or apparatus shall notify the commissioner in writing of any changes in any component of the plan within seven days after the change occurs.

Any person who violates any provision of this section shall be subject to a fine of $500.00 for each offense. Each day a violation continues shall constitute a separate and distinct offense.
(Added. Coun. J. 6-28-91, p. 2758)

§15-4-102 Safety warden.

The owner or manager of every large assembly unit, as defined in Chapter 13-56 of this code, shall appoint a person employed in the unit as safety warden, and an alternate safety warden. The safety warden and alternate safety warden shall be in addition to any fireguard or fireguards required under this chapter.

The safety warden shall conduct a safety review of the premises on a weekly basis to identify safety hazards that are readily recognizable and easily corrected, such as nonfunctioning lights; improper use or storage of cleaning materials and combustible materials; obstruction of stairwells, corridors and exits; accumulation of dirt and debris; and use of fire closets, elevators, and mechanical or electrical areas for storage space. The safety warden shall record the results of the weekly safety review in a ledger, which shall be available for inspection by personnel of the fire prevention bureau and the department of buildings at all reasonable times. No later than April 30th, August 31st and December 31st of each year, the safety warden shall certify to the fire prevention bureau, on forms supplied by the bureau, compliance with the review and recording requirements of this section since the last periodic report. The owner or manager of the assembly unit shall notify the fire prevention bureau and the department of buildings of the names of the safety warden and alternate safety warden. Any person who violates any provision of this section or who falsifies an entry in a ledger or certification required under this section, shall be subject to a fine of not less than $200.00.

The fire commissioner and the buildings commissioner may jointly issue regulations for the administration and implementation of this section.
(Added. Coun. J. 7-14-93, p. 35320)

Article III. Licenses

§15-4-110 Hazardous use units.

Every license required to engage in any business, occupy or use any premises, structure or building for any purpose classified as a hazardous use unit in Chapter 13-112 of this code and every extension or renewal thereof, shall require the approval of the division marshal in charge of the bureau of fire prevention, as a condition precedent to the issuance of every such license and to every extension or renewal thereof. The division marshal in charge of the bureau of fire prevention shall make, or cause to be made, an inspection of every hazardous use unit for which an application for license, or for an extension or renewal thereof, has been made. If such inspection shall prove the entire compliance of such hazardous use unit with the applicable requirements of this code, the division marshal in charge of the bureau of fire prevention shall issue, or cause to be issued, a certificate of compliance and approval. Such certificate

shall be subject to revocation for cause, by the division marshal in charge of the bureau of fire prevention, at any time and upon notification of the revocation of such certificate, the major shall revoke any license conditioned upon said certificate. The provisions of this section shall be construed as remedial and retroactive as well as prospective.
(Prior code § 90-9)

§15-4-252 Lumberyards and lumber storehouses.

(a) A hazardous materials license, as specified in Section 4-115-010, shall be required to conduct or operate a lumberyard or lumber storehouse.

Included hereunder, but not limited hereby, shall be all lumberyards, lumber storehouses and other places where new, used, finished or unfinished lumber, timber, wood (except firewood), wooden boxes, wooden barrels, veneers, plywoods, flex woods and the like, in excess of 5,000 feet, are kept, placed, stored or piled for sale or use, other than lumber for use in the repair, erection or construction of buildings or improvements incident to the land on the premises where so kept, placed, stored or piled on the premises immediately adjacent thereto.

(b) It shall be unlawful to conduct or operate any lumberyard or lumber storehouse, or to pile or store lumber or any of the aforementioned wooden articles in any lot or plot of ground, without first obtaining the written consents of property owners representing the majority of the total frontage of any lot or plat of ground lying wholly or in part within limits 150 feet distant from and parallel to the boundary of the lot or plot of ground upon which said yard or storehouse is to be established or maintained; provided, however, that for the purpose of this section, only the frontage of any such lot or plot of ground as comes within the 150 foot limits herein prescribed shall be considered; and provided further, that any and all petitions containing such consents of property owners shall be based on and contain the legal description of the property affected and the date of signature. Whenever the lot or plot of ground in which said yard or storehouse is to be established is in any shape other than a rectangle, the 150 foot limiting line aforementioned shall not exceed in distance 150 feet from any point in the boundaries of such lot or plot of ground. Such written consents shall be obtained and filed with the executive director of the department of construction and permits before a license is issued hereunder.

(c) It shall be unlawful for any person to establish within 200 feet of a school, church or institutional building, a lumberyard where lumber, either new or old, is sold, or is stored for seasoning or drying; or a box yard where wooden boxes either new or old are stored, sold, manufactured or repaired; or a barrel yard where wooden barrels, either new or old, are stored, sold, manufactured or repaired.

(d) It shall be unlawful for any person to pile or to maintain a pile of lumber, either new or old; wooden boxes, either new or old; wooden barrels, either new or old; and other materials of like combustible nature for the purpose of selling, storing, manufacturing, drying or seasoning, within 150 feet of any building or within 25 feet of any fireproof or brick building, unless the roof of the brick building shall be of fireproof construction, and all exposed windows, doors and other openings in both brick or fireproof buildings are fitted and protected with approved fire-resisting wired glass and metal sash and frames, or all windows and other openings are equipped with metal-clad shutters or doors.

No lumber, boxes or barrels shall be piled in excess of 20 feet in height. If the area covered be in excess of 1,000 square feet, it shall be divided into areas of 1,000 square feet or less by aisles or passageways at least 48 inches wide. *(Added. Coun. J. 2-7-96, p. 15616; Amend. Coun. J. 3-5-03, p. 104990)*

§15-4-256 Sale of solid fuel and firewood.

(a) It shall be unlawful for any person to engage in the business of a dealer in solid fuel, within the fire limits of the city, without first having obtained a hazardous materials license, as specified in Section 4-115-010, therefor; provided, that no license shall be required of any dealer in solid fuel for any place of business operated or conducted by such dealer in solid fuel and licensed as such by any municipality which has adopted an ordinance granting privileges similar to those contained in this section.

(b) Whenever used in this section, Section 15-4-257, Section 15-4-258, and Section 15-4-259, the term "solid fuel" shall mean any anthracite, semianthracite, bituminous, semibituminous or lignite coal, briquettes, boulets, coke, gashouse coke, petroleum coke, petroleum carbon, firewood or any other manufactured or patented fuel not sold by liquid or metered measure; the term "hundredweight" shall mean 100 pounds avoirdupois; the word "ton" shall mean 20 hundredweight; the term "dealer in solid fuel" shall mean any person, as defined in this section, offering for sale, selling, delivering or selling and delivering any solid fuel; and the term "fuel oil dealer" shall mean any person who stores fuel oil for the purpose of sale, or conveys fuel oil in any vehicle for the purpose of sale. The term "storer of solid fuel" shall mean any person who stores solid fuel for use in any business but not for resale. The term "fuel oil storer" shall mean any person who keeps on hand or stores fuel oil for use in any business but not for resale.

(c) It shall be unlawful to conduct or operate any yard for the storage of solid fuel in any lot or plot of ground without first obtaining the written consents of the property owners representing the majority of the total frontage in feet of any lot or plot of ground lying wholly or in part within lines 150 feet distant from and parallel to the boundaries of the lot or plot of ground upon which said yard is to be installed; provided, however, that for the purpose of this section only the frontage of any such lot or plot of ground as comes within the 150 foot limit herein prescribed shall be considered; and provided, further, that any and all petitions containing such consents of property owners shall be based on and contain the legal description of the property affected and the date of signature. Whenever the lot or plot of ground in which said yard is to be installed is in any shape other than a rectangle, the 150 foot limiting line aforementioned shall not exceed in distance 150 feet from any point in the boundaries of such lot or plot of ground.

(d) Every dealer in solid fuel shall conform to the provisions of this code regulating weights and measures, including the requirements as to certificates of weight, which are applicable thereto.

(e) It is hereby declared unlawful for any person to sell or offer for sale any two or more different kinds, grades or sizes of solid fuel which have been mixed in such manner as to prevent purchasers, or intended purchasers, or the inspector of weights and measures of the city or one of his deputies, from reweighing separately each kind, size and grade to determine the weight of each kind, size and grade.

If two or more different kinds, grades or sizes of solid fuel are loaded on the same wagon, truck or other conveyance, each kind, grade and size of solid fuel shall be weighed and loaded separately, and shall be placed either in bags, separated by partitions, or in closed containers, which closed containers shall have legibly stamped upon their sides the actual net weight and the kind, grade and size of each type of solid fuel contained therein; such loading shall be in a manner sufficient that any time during the selling or delivering of such solid fuel, each kind, grade and size of solid fuel may be weighed separately; and the said person selling or delivering said solid fuel shall provide the driver of the wagon, truck or other conveyance in which the same is transported, with a delivery ticket or tickets made out in conformity with the provisions of Sections 4-276-360 to 4-276-400, stating the weight of each kind, grade or size of solid fuel so delivered.

(f) No person shall display, advertise or describe solid fuel in any false or misleading manner, or use any deceptive description of size or kind of solid fuel other than specified in Section 4-276-370. The term "coarse" shall not be used to describe a size or grade and is hereby declared to be deceptive. Figures and percentages of different sizes shall be considered misleading when used to describe solid fuel.

No person shall deliver or attempt to deliver solid fuel containing more than 26 percent volatile matter, if such solid fuel has been advertised by the seller, ordered by the purchaser, or described by the public weighmaster's certificate as "Smokeless," "Low Volatile," "Pocahontas" or "New River."

(g) No solid fuel shall be stored for sale in the same building with fuel oil, gasoline or other flammable liquids unless separated therefrom by a fireproof wall.

It shall be unlawful for any person to deliver or attempt to deliver to a purchaser any kind, grade or size of solid fuel other than that advertised by the seller, ordered by the purchaser, or specified on the delivery ticket or weighmaster's certificate.

It shall be the duty of every person conducting or operating a coal yard within the fire limits of the city to store all soft coal away from the brickwork of boilers and furnaces. Whenever coal in storage shows indication of spontaneous ignition or gives off gases, it shall be the duty of the licensee, agent or person in charge or control of the premises to turn over and overhaul such coal pile and remove all portions of coal showing indication of ignition or coking. The floor or ground surface of all coal yards shall at all times be kept free from flammable waste material and accumulations of combustible waste materials.
(Added. Coun. J. 2-7-96, p. 15616)

§15-4-257 Storage of solid fuel not for retail.

(a) It shall be unlawful for any person to keep, pile or store on any lot, plot of ground, railroad siding, switch track or other place within the fire limits of the city, any solid fuel in quantities greater than 1,000 tons without first having obtained a hazardous materials license, as specified in Section 4-115-010, to so do. Provided, however, that this requirement shall not apply to any person conducting or operating a coal yard licensed under this chapter.

(b) It shall be the duty of every person establishing and maintaining such lot, plot of ground, railroad siding, switch track or other place within the fire limits of the city to store all soft coal away from the brickwork of boilers and furnaces. Whenever solid fuel in storage shows indication of spontaneous ignition or gives off gases, it shall be the duty of the licensee, agent or person in charge or control of the premises to turn over or overhaul such solid fuel and remove all portions of the same showing indication of ignition or coking. Such work shall be done under the supervision of a representative of the division marshal in charge of the bureau of fire prevention. The floor or ground surface of the premises shall at all times be kept free from flammable waste material and accumulations of combustible waste materials. Gasoline, fuel oil or other flammable liquids shall not be placed or stored upon the licensed premises unless separated from such solid fuel by fireproof walls.

(Added. Coun. J. 2-7-96, p. 15616)

§15-4-258 Fuel oil dealers.

(a) It shall be unlawful for any person to engage in the business of fuel oil dealer without first having obtained a hazardous materials license, as specified in Section 4-115-010, to so do.

This section shall not be construed to include or apply to dealers in fuel oil who are licensed at the same place, location or premises under the provisions of this code licensing "filling stations," in such a way as to require an additional license fee from persons so licensed who pay an annual license fee that is equal to or greater than the annual license fee required of a fuel oil dealer hereunder who uses or proposes to use storage facilities in connection with his business.

(b) The director of the bureau of fire prevention shall investigate such application and the matters and things therein stated.

(c) All places of business of fuel oil dealers shall be kept in a clean condition, free from accumulations of rags, wastepaper and other combustible waste materials. Smoking shall be prohibited thereon. Adequate toilet facilities shall be provided. All such premises and all vehicles used in connection with the business of fuel oil dealers shall be conducted and operated in accordance with the provisions of this code in Chapters 15-26 and 13-84 and shall be inspected by the division marshal in charge of the bureau of fire prevention or his duly authorized representative at least once every year.

It shall be unlawful for any fuel oil dealer to refill any fuel oil storage container or tank used in connection with an oil-burning heater, boiler or furnace, unless such storage container or tank is equipped with an automatic or return vent pipe, or unless the fill pipe of such storage container or tank is equipped with a screw or automatic cap. It shall be the duty of every such dealer after filling or refilling any fuel oil storage container or tank to replace the screw cap on such fill pipe, or if equipped with an automatic cap, to see to it that said fill cap pipe is properly closed.

(d) It shall be unlawful for any fuel oil dealer to install any container or tank for the storage of any fuel oil without first obtaining written consents of the property owners in accordance with the provisions of Section 13-44-090 of this code.

(Added. Coun. J. 2-7-96, p. 15616)

§15-4-259 Fuel oil storers.

(a) It shall be unlawful for any person to keep on hand or store fuel oil for use in any business, other than the business of dealer in such oil, without first procuring a hazardous materials license, as specified in Section 4-115-010, so to do for each location, place or premises where such person keeps on hand or stores for use any such oil. Provided, however, that no license shall be required of any person who keeps on hand or stores fuel oil in a quantity less than 2,150 gallons for use exclusively in the heating of any building.

(b) The director of the bureau of fire prevention, upon receipt of such application, shall investigate or cause to be investigated the place of business described in such application and the methods and equipment intended to be used by such applicant in the storage and handling of fuel oil.

(c) All containers or tanks used for the storage of fuel oil and all buildings and premises wherein fuel oil is stored shall be constructed and maintained in accordance with the provisions of the building and fire prevention chapters of this code.

All containers or tanks used for the storage of fuel oil, either above or below ground or within a building, and the premises used for the storage of such oil, shall be inspected by the division marshal in charge of fire prevention or his duly authorized representative at least once each year.

Rags, soiled waste and wastepaper shall be kept in metal containers pending removal from the premises.

No person shall smoke in that part of any premises where such oil is stored.

It shall be unlawful for any fuel oil storer to refill any fuel oil storage container or tank used in connection with an oil-burning heater, boiler or furnace, unless such storage container or tank is equipped with an automatic or return vent pipe, or unless the fill pipe of such storage container or tank is equipped with a screw or automatic cap. It shall be the duty of every such storer after filling or refilling any fuel oil storage container or tank to replace the screw cap on such fill pipe, or if equipped with an automatic cap, to see to it that said fill pipe cap is properly closed.
(Added. Coun. J. 2-7-96, p. 15616)

Article VI. Liquefied Petroleum Gas Tanks

§15-4-410 Application and permit.

Before installing a permanent fixed liquefied petroleum gas tank greater than 2,000 gallons individual water capacity or when the aggregate water capacity exceeds 4,000 gallons, the owner, lessee or agent of the premises where the tank is to be installed shall file with the bureau of fire prevention a written application for permission to install said tank. The application shall set forth the location of the tank, the purpose for which the gas is to be used, the nature of occupancy, the dimensions, specifications and capacity of the tank and such other information as may be required. The application shall have affixed a statement, signed by the installer, stating that the tank, devices, equipment and safety clearances conform to the provisions of this code. Attached to the application shall be a plat, drawn to scale, showing the location of the tank, all adjoining streets, alleys, railroads, building, occupancies and premises within 300 feet of the tank.

For installation of systems utilizing containers 2,000 gallons water capacity or less or 4,000 gallons aggregate capacity or less, the following procedure should be followed. A supplier having a valid liquefied petroleum gas supplier's certification as hereinafter provided shall file within three days with the division marshal in charge of the bureau of fire prevention a certification that the system and its installation complies with the requirements of this code. The system can be filled and used upon the filing of such certification.

If the tank is designed in accordance with the American Society of Mechanical Engineers Boiler and Pressure Vessel Code, Section VIII Unfired Pressure Vessels, the division marshal shall, upon receiving the application and plat, submit the application to the department of construction and permits for zoning approval, and for approval of the tank and all equipment subject to pressure.

Upon receipt of the approval of the department of construction and permits, if required, the director shall make, or cause to be made, an inspection of the site where said tank is to be installed to determine whether or not said location provides the safety clearance required by Chapter 15-26.

Upon satisfactory evidence that the site, tank and equipment as described in the application, specifications and plat conform to the provisions of the chapter, the division marshal shall issue to said applicant a permit for the installation of the tank. Upon the completion of the installation and before any liquefied petroleum gas has been put into the tank or container, the applicant shall notify in writing the department of buildings and the bureau of fire prevention that the installation is ready for final external inspection. Upon receipt of the reports from the aforesaid department and the bureau that the installation has been approved, the director shall issue to the owner, lessee or agent or other person in charge of the property, a certificate stating that the installation conforms to the provisions of this code.

The department of buildings shall make an external inspection of each liquefied petroleum gas tank and equipment, which they originally approved, every year to determine their satisfactory condition for the purpose for which it is used.

All tanks, cylinders, containers, valves, piping, devices and equipment for such gas shall conform to the requirements given in the National Fire Protection Association's Pamphlet 58 entitled "Liquefied Petroleum Gases, 1972 Edition," unless specifically covered in Chapter 15-26 of this code.
(Prior code § 90-39; Amend. Coun. J. 9-13-89, p. 4604; 2-7-96, p. 15616; 3-5-03, p. 104990)

Article VII. Fire Extinguisher Servicemen

§15-4-450 License required.

No person shall engage in the business of servicing fire extinguishers unless he shall first have obtained a license as herein provided.
(Prior code § 90-43)

§15-4-460 License application.

Every applicant for a license as a fire extinguisher serviceman shall file with the division marshal in charge of fire prevention a written application, signed by the applicant, stating his address, age, present occupation, business activities during the previous five years, experience with the repair, recharging, testing and use of fire extinguishers, knowledge of the ordinances pertaining to fire extinguishers and such other information as may be deemed necessary.

Every application shall be accompanied by two one-inch by one-inch prints of a bust photograph of the applicant.

(Prior code § 90-44)

§15-4-480 License fee.

Upon the approval of the application by the board of examiners and the acceptance of the public liability insurance policy, deputy commissioner shall forward such approved application to the director of revenue. Upon payment of an annual license fee of $30.00 a license shall be issued. Such license shall expire on the thirty-first day of December of the year in which it is issued. The deputy commissioner shall provide the licensee with an identification card which shall carry a one-inch by one-inch photograph of the licensee and the license number of the licensee, which card shall be signed by the deputy commissioner.

(Prior code § 90-46; Amend. Coun. J. 12-15-92, p. 27387)

§15-4-490 License renewal.

Any such license may be renewed upon payment of an annual renewal fee of $50.00. Any change of address of the licensee or any change of licensee's employer shall be reported within 10 days to the fire prevention bureau.

(Prior code § 90-47; Amend Coun. J. 12-15-92, p. 27387)

§15-4-500 Violation—Penalty.

Any person who violates any provisions of Sections 15-4-430 to 15-4-490 shall be fined not more than $200.00 for each offense.

(Prior code § 90-48)

§15-4-510 Rules and regulations.

The division marshal in charge of fire prevention, at his discretion, may make or cause to be made an inspection of the contents and working condition of any fire extinguisher, and may promulgate such reasonable rules and regulations as he deems necessary to carry out the purposes of the provisions of Sections 15-16-620 to 15-16-680 inclusive and Sections 15-4-430 to 15-4-510 inclusive.

(Prior code § 90-49)

Article VIII. Other License Requirements

§15-4-520 Other licenses and permits required.

For the licensing and permits requirements covering the following occupancies, refer to the chapter indicated:

Public places of amusement, 4-156;

Drug, chemical or paint stores (wholesale), 4-152;

Dry cleaners and spotters, 4-100;

Filling stations, 4-108;
Long-term care facilities, 4-96;
Manufacturing establishments, 4-224;
Motor vehicle storage, repair, and sales, 4-232;
Day care centers, 4-72;
Recycling facilities, 11-4;
Roofers, 4-256;
Warehouses, 4-364;
Solid and liquid waste handling and disposal, 11-4;
Junk facilities, 4-216.

(Prior code § 90-50; Amend. Coun. J. 6-14-95, p. 2841; 2-7-96, p. 15616; 10-7-98, p. 78812)

Article IX. Permits

§15-4-550 Fireworks.

The deputy commissioner in charge of the bureau of fire prevention may, upon due application, issue a permit to a properly qualified person for giving a display of fireworks on privately owned property. The applicant shall give written notice to the alderman of the affected ward 10 days prior to the date of application for such permit. The application shall be filed with the bureau of fire prevention, and must include: the written consent of the alderman of the affected ward; the written consent of the owner of the property where the applicant proposes to give the display; proof that the applicant is in compliance with all provisions of the Illinois Pyrotechnic Operator Licensing Act, as amended; proof that the applicant is in compliance with the Illinois Fireworks Use Act, as amended; and proof of general liability insurance, in an amount not less than $1,000,000, issued by an insurer authorized to insure risks in Illinois. The city of Chicago and its officers and employees shall be named as additional insured. The insurance policy shall provide for notice to the deputy fire commissioner no less than 72 hours prior to cancellation of coverage. If the proposed location of the display is licensed for the retail sale of alcoholic liquor for consumption on the premises, the applicant shall also include proof of the licensee's compliance with Section 6-32(a) of the Illinois Liquor Control Act, as amended. No display of fireworks shall be permitted between the hours of 11:00 p.m. and 6:00 a.m. In no case shall any display of fireworks be conducted unless the site meets safety standards set by the fire department. The fire department shall promulgate such safety standards as needed to determine if a proposed site has the proper safety equipment, personnel and procedures necessary to conduct a fireworks display. The safety standards shall be no less stringent than those adopted by the state fire marshal. The deputy commissioner may impose additional specific conditions related to unique conditions of the property where an indoor display is proposed.

(Prior code § 90-53; Amend. Coun. J. 12-13-95, p. 13845; 2-10-99; p. 89142; 9-4-03, p. 6950)

CHAPTER 15-20
EXPLOSIVES AND FIREWORKS
(Selected Sections)

Sections:

Article I. Explosives

15-20-010 Definitions.
15-20-030 General transportation requirements.
15-20-040 Public conveyances prohibited.
15-20-080 Transportation by vessel or railroad car.
15-20-170 Sales to minors.
15-20-180 Seizure of explosives kept unlawfully.
15-20-200 Manufacture of explosives prohibited.

Article II. Fireworks

15-20-210 Definitions.
15-20-220 Prohibitions.
15-20-221 Penalties.
15-20-230 Advertising restrictions.
15-20-240 Display in public places.
15-20-250 Exemptions.
15-20-260 Permit and permit fees.
15-20-270 Unlawful fireworks in motor vehicle—Impoundment.

Article I. Explosives

§15-20-010 Definitions.

"Explosives" means any chemical compounded or mechanical mixture which is commonly used or intended for the purpose of producing an explosion, or which contains any oxidizing and combustible units, or other ingredients, in such proportions, quantities or packing that an ignition by fire, by friction, by concussion, by percussion, or by detonator of any part of the compound or mixture may cause such a sudden generation of highly heated gases that the resultant gaseous pressures will be capable of producing destructive effects on contiguous objects or of destroying life or limb articles subdivided as follows:

(a) Unlawful Explosives. The manufacture, storage, sale, transportation or use of the following explosives is hereby prohibited:

1. Liquid nitroglycerine, except for medicinal purposes;

2. Explosives containing chlorate of potash, perchlorate of potash, and picric acid, except as used in blasting caps; provided, however, that any explosive containing chlorate of potash may be sold if it first conforms to the following test: Such mixture must be able to withstand a glancing blow inflicted with a rawhide mallet on soft wood without in any manner exploding, and also such mixture must be made so as not to reduce the chlorate;

3. Nitroglycerine dynamite containing over 60 percent of nitroglycerine, or gelatine dynamite equal in strength to over 75 percent of nitroglycerine dynamite;

4. Blasting caps containing less than nine and one-half grains of explosive mixture, at least 80 percent fulminate of mercury and 20 percent chlorate of potash, or its equivalent detonating strength;

5. Any fulminate of mercury in a dry condition;

6. Any fulminate of other metals in any condition except as a component of articles not otherwise prohibited;

7. Any fireworks which combine an explosive and a detonator;

8. Nitrocellulose in a dry and uncompressed condition in quantity greater than 10 pounds net weight in one package;

9. Explosive compositions that ignite spontaneously or undergo marked decomposition, rendering the products or their use more hazardous, when subjected to 48 consecutive hours or less to a temperature of 167 degrees Fahrenheit;

10. New explosives until approved by the Interstate Commerce Commission or Department of Transportation, except that permits may be issued to educational, governmental or industrial laboratories for instructional or research purposes;

11. Explosives condemned by the Interstate Commerce Commission or Department of Transportation;

12. Explosives not packed or marked in accordance with the requirement of the Interstate Commerce Commission or Department of Transportation;

13. Explosives containing an ammonium salt and a chlorate.

(b) Authorized Explosives. Black powder high explosives not otherwise prohibited by the foregoing subparagraph, blasting caps, smokeless powder, wet fulminate or mercury, ammunition for cannon and small arms, explosive projectiles, railway torpedoes and flares, marine and highway flares, detonating fuses, primers, fuses and safety squibs. Such explosives may be stored or used in accordance with the provisions of this code.

(Prior code § 125-1)

§15-20-030 General transportation requirements.

(a) No explosives shall be transported in any vehicles through the public ways of the city unless such vehicle is in charge of two competent persons each holding a certificate of fitness for such purpose. Said certificate of fitness shall be issued only to employees of a person duly licensed to transport or sell explosives in the city.

(b) Any mechanically propelled vehicle used for the transportation of explosives shall be in good condition for service, and shall have an enclosed wooden body completely fire-protected on the outside. The motor, fuel tank, carburetor, electric wiring and exhaust, shall be separate from the body of the vehicle. Internal combustion engines shall be separated not less than two feet from the outer wall of the body in which explosives are to be carried. All such vehicles must be constructed and maintained in accordance with specifications of, and subject to the approval of, the division marshal in charge of the bureau of fire prevention, who shall inspect or cause to be inspected all such vehicles at least once every six months. Mechanically driven vehicles must be equipped with such a device or devices as will not permit a speed in excess 15 miles per hour.

(c) No metal tools or other pieces of metal shall be carried within a vehicle carrying explosives, except in a separate tool box.

(d) No blasting caps or electric blasting caps or other combustible material shall be transported in the same vehicles with other explosives.

(e) A vehicle carrying explosives shall have motive power amply able to draw the load, and it shall avoid stoppages other than to load and unload, and no unnecessary stops or stands shall be made.

(f) Vehicles carrying explosives must not be left standing unless absolutely necessary, and then only when the brakes are set and motors stopped.

(g) No explosives shall be left in a vehicle unless such vehicle is in charge of an employee with a certificate of fitness, and no vehicle loaded with explosives shall be left unattended.

(h) Every vehicle carrying more than five pounds of explosive substances referred to in Section 15-20-010 shall display upon an erect pole at the front end of such vehicle and at such height that it shall be visible from all directions a red flag with the word "Danger" printed, stamped or sewn thereon in white letters at least six inches in height, or in lieu of such flag the word "Explosives" must be painted on or attached to the rear end and each side of such vehicle in letters at least four inches in height.

(i) Vehicles carrying explosives shall comply with Sections 15-24-1150 to 15-24-1210, inclusive. Wherever the phrase flammable liquids is used, it shall mean explosives and wherever the phrase truck, tank truck, semitank truck, or tank vehicle is used, it shall mean vehicles on which explosives are transported. The truck shall meet applicable Department of Transportation and/or Interstate Commerce Commission regulations and all requirements of the Municipal Code of the city of Chicago.

(j) No intoxicated person shall be permitted on a vehicle carrying explosives.

(k) No smoking within 10 feet of a vehicle loaded with explosives shall be permitted.

(l) No person shall carry or transport in or upon such vehicle any explosives in excess of 2,000 pounds.

(m)No person in charge of a vehicle carrying explosives shall deliver them except in original and unbroken packages, nor at any place other than a duly authorized magazine and to the person in charge thereof.

(n) Each vehicle shall carry an approved water-type fire extinguisher thereon of not less than two and one-half gallons capacity.

(Prior code § 125-3)

§15-20-040 Public conveyances prohibited.

No person shall carry or transport on any public conveyance or on any railroad car running from point to point in the city, any black powder, guncotton, giant powder, dynamite, nitroglycerine, fulminate of mercury, or any other explosives.

(Prior code § 125-4)

§15-20-080 Transportation by vessel or railroad car.

No explosives shall be landed at the piers or elsewhere in the city, or transported to a vessel lying at a pier, unless the explosives contained in the vessel making delivery are in charge of a duly certified employee of a person licensed to transport or sell explosives within the city limits. No explosives shall be landed at any pier in the city unless for immediate loading into wagons for distribution to consumers for use within 48 hours and for which orders have

been previously received, or for immediate transportation by railway to points beyond the city limits; and explosives received at railway stations within the city limits shall be promptly discharged and removed to such storage as the provisions of this chapter prescribe. Explosives received at any railway or freight stations within the city limits, for reshipment to points beyond the city limits, shall be promptly transferred; provided, however, that no explosives received for shipment shall remain at any railway or freight station for a period exceeding 48 hours. Every railroad car containing explosives within the city limits must be placarded on sides and ends with standard explosive placards as prescribed by the Interstate Commerce Commission regulations for explosives and other dangerous articles.
(Prior code § 125-8)

§15-20-170 Sales to minors.

It is hereby declared to be unlawful for any person to sell, deliver, or give to any person under 18 years of age any black powder, dynamite, nitroglycerine, guncotton or other explosive.
(Prior code § 125-17)

15-20-180 Seizure of explosives kept unlawfully.

If it shall be found that any of the explosives mentioned in Section 15-20-010 are being kept in any building, structure or premises, or in any vehicle or on board of any vessel within the city in violation of any of the provisions of this chapter, any such explosives so kept shall be immediately seized and removed to such place as the division marshal in charge of the bureau of fire prevention may direct.

It is hereby made the duty of the members of the police department to assist in making such seizure when requested so to do by said division marshal, and to assist in the removal of such explosives to such place as may be designated by him.
(Prior code § 125-18)

§15-20-200 Manufacture of explosives prohibited.

No person shall manufacture, assemble, or mix anywhere within the city any black powder, guncotton, giant powder, dynamite, nitroglycerine, fulminate of mercury, or other explosives of similar nature.
(Prior code § 125-20)

Article II. Fireworks

§15-20-210 Definitions.

"Fireworks" means and includes any explosive composition, or any substance or combination of substances, or article prepared for the purpose of producing a visible or audible effect of a temporary exhibitional nature by explosion, combustion, deflagration or detonation, and shall include blank cartridges, toy cannons in which explosives are used, the type of balloons which require fire underneath to propel the same, firecrackers, torpedoes, skyrockets, roman candles, bombs, or other fireworks of like construction and any fireworks containing any explosive compound, or any tablets or other device containing any explosive

substances, or containing combustible substances producing visual effects; provided, however, that the term "fireworks" shall not include snake or glowworm pellets; smoke devices; sparklers; trick noisemakers known as "party poopers," "booby traps," "snappers," "trick matches," "cigarette loads," and "auto burglar alarms"; or toy pistols, toy canes, toy guns, or other devices in which paper caps containing twenty-five-hundredths grains or less of explosive compound are used, providing they are so constructed that the hand cannot come in contact with the cap when in place for the explosion, and toy pistol paper caps which contain less than twenty-hundredths grains of explosive mixture.
(Prior code § 125-21; Amend. Coun. J. 4-9-86, p. 29168)

§15-20-220 Prohibitions.

No person shall have, keep, store, use, manufacture, assemble, mix, sell, handle or transport any fireworks; provided, however, that nothing in this chapter shall be held to apply to the possession or use of signaling devices for current daily consumption by railroads, vessels and others requiring them or to the possession, sale or use of normal stocks of flashlight compositions by photographers or dealers in photographic supplies; and provided further, that the division marshal in charge of the bureau of fire prevention may issue permits for the display of fireworks as hereinafter provided.
(Prior code § 125-22)

§15-20-221 Penalties.

(a) Any person who violates any provision of Section 15-20-220 having, keeping, storing or transporting fireworks shall be subject to a fine of not less than $200.00 and not more than $500.00 for each offense; each day of a continuing violation shall constitute a separate and distinct offense. Prosecutions for such violations shall be civil.

(b) Any person who violates any provision of Section 15-20-220 by using, selling, assembling, mixing or manufacturing fireworks shall be guilty of a misdemeanor, and shall be subject to a fine of not less than $250.00 and not more than $500.00, or incarceration for not less than 10 and not more than 30 days, or both. Each day of a continuing violation shall constitute a separate and distinct offense.
(Added. Coun. J. 6-9-99, p. 5376)

§15-20-230 Advertising restrictions.

No person shall advertise fireworks in the city or cause such advertisements to be made. This prohibition applies to all advertising of fireworks within the city, regardless of where such fireworks are sold or offered for sale, and regardless of whether the sale itself is legal under the laws of other jurisdictions. This prohibition against firework advertising "within the city" shall apply to advertising on any sign or billboard located in the city, in any newspaper or other publication which is published in the city and has a circulation primarily within the city, by broadcast on any radio or television station that is located in the city, and by handbill or circular distributed in the city. This section does not prohibit sending direct solicitations or advertisements solely to persons possessing a public display permit under Section 15-20-240 below.

"Advertise" as used in this section includes not only placing an advertisement, but also accepting an advertisement for publication and printing, publishing, or displaying it by any of the media set forth above.

Any person violating any of the provisions of this section shall be fined not less than $200.00 nor more than $500.00 for each offense. Each day that a violation of this section continues shall be considered a separate and distinct offense.
(Prior code § 125-23; Amend. Coun. J. 5-2-95, p. 166)

§15-20-240 Display in public places.

The division marshal in charge of the bureau of fire prevention may, upon due application, issue a permit to a properly qualified person for giving a display of fireworks in the public parks or other public open places. The applicant shall give written notice to the alderman of the ward adjacent to the public park or other public open space 10 days prior to the date of application for such permit. No permit shall be issued unless the applicant attaches written consent of the alderman of the affected ward to the application. Such permits shall impose such restrictions as in the opinion of the said division marshal may be necessary to safeguard life and property in each case.
(Prior code § 125-24; Amend. Coun. J. 12-13-95, p. 13845)

§15-20-250 Exemptions.

Nothing contained in this part of this chapter dealing with fireworks shall be construed as applying to the transportation of any article or thing shipped in conformity with the regulations prescribed by the Interstate Commerce Commission, nor as applying to the military or naval forces of the United States.
(Prior code § 125-25)

§15-20-260 Permit and permit fees.

For permit and permit fee requirements, see Sections 15-4-630 through 15-4-650 of this code.
(Prior code § 125-26)

§15-20-270 Unlawful fireworks in motor vehicle—Impoundment.

(a) The owner of record of any motor vehicle that contains illegal fireworks shall be liable to the city for an administrative penalty of $500.00 plus any towing and storage fees applicable under Section 9-92-080. Any such vehicle shall be subject to seizure and impoundment pursuant to this section. This subsection shall not apply: (1) if the vehicle used in the violation was stolen at that time and the theft was reported to the appropriate police authorities within 24 hours after the theft was discovered or reasonably should have been discovered; (2) if the vehicle is operating as a common carrier and the violation occurs without the knowledge of the person in control of the vehicle; or (3) if the owner proves that the presence of the fireworks was permissible pursuant to Section 15-20-250.

(b) Whenever a police officer has probable cause to believe that a vehicle is subject to seizure and impoundment pursuant to this section, the police officer shall provide for the towing of the vehicle to a facility controlled by the city or its agents. Before or at the time the vehicle is towed, the police officer shall notify any person identifying himself as the owner of the vehicle or any person who is found to be in control of the vehicle at the time of the alleged violation, of the fact of the seizure and of the vehicle owner's right to request a vehicle impoundment hearing to be conducted under Section 2-14-132 of this code.

(c) The provisions of section 2-14-132 shall apply whenever a motor vehicle is seized and in impounded pursuant to this section.

(Added. Coun. J. 6-9-99, p. 5378; Amend. 12-15-99, p. 21529)

CHAPTER 15-24
FLAMMABLE LIQUIDS
(Selected Sections)

Sections:

Article I. General Regulations

15-24-010 Licenses and permits.

Article II. Tank Storage

15-24-220 Motor fuel dispensing.
15-24-230 Gasoline pumping prohibited.

Article X. Carriers for Transportation of Flammable Liquids

15-24-1000 General condition of carriers.
15-24-1070 Warning signs.
15-24-1130 Drivers or attendants.
15-24-1150 Travel over subway routes prohibited.
15-24-1160 Restrictions on transportation of Class I liquids.
15-24-1170 Use of expressways.
15-24-1210 Manifests.

Article XI. Underground Storage Tank Violations

15-24-1230 Underground tank storage.

Article I. General Regulations

§15-24-010 Licenses and permits.

For licensing and permit requirements, see Chapter 15-4. For special exit requirements, see Chapter 13-112 of this code.

(Prior code § 129.1-1)

Article II. Tank Storage

§15-24-220 Motor fuel dispensing.

All flammable liquid gauging, vending and dispensing devices used for motor vehicle fuel shall be of substantial construction, and firmly secured to a concrete foundation, which shall be so located and designed as to prevent motor vehicles from damaging such devices. Systems wherein continuous pressure is maintained, or water is used to displace liquid from storage tanks, shall not be permitted. The use of aboveground storage tanks, tank cars, tank trucks or portable tanks in connection with gauging, vending and dispensing devices, shall not be permitted except for such equipment installed on tank vehicles complying with Section 15-24-1080 and tanks complying with Section 15-24-221 of this code.

Every remote fuel system shall be equipped with a fuel leak detector valve or device located as close as possible to or within the pumping unit. An impact valve shall be provided at the base of each dispenser. Such devices and valves shall be listed by a testing laboratory which has as its primary purpose the testing and evaluation of equipment and materials to meet appropriate standards.

Automatic hose nozzle valves with latch-open devices shall not be permitted unless equipped with an automatic shut-off device to stop the flow of liquid when the valve is released from a fill opening or upon impact with pavement. All dispensing devices shall be located so that all parts of the vehicles being served will be on private property. In no case shall the dispensing hose be longer than 16 feet for filling stations and private locations. Where dispensing equipment is used exclusively for trucks or other large vehicles, automatic hose retrievers may be used, and shall not exceed 40 feet of hose.

Dispensing devices for motor vehicle fuel, except devices used exclusively for dispensing Class II or Class III flammable liquids within occupancy Class H3 buildings, shall not be permitted in buildings hereafter erected, altered or converted.

The dispensing of motor fuels which are Class I flammable liquids directly from tank vehicles shall be permitted only from tank vehicles complying with Section 15-24-1080 and tanks complying with Section 15-24-221 of this code. Retail sales of motor fuel to motor vehicles from tank vehicles shall not be permitted. The filling of fuel tanks from tank vehicles shall not be permitted within buildings.

(Prior code § 129.1-18.1; Amend. Coun. J. 2-16-89, p. 24942; 10-31-90, p. 22573; 5-2-95, p. 73; 3-19-97, p. 41391)

§15-24-230 Gasoline pumping prohibited.

Pumping of gasoline from a tank truck into an underground tank shall be prohibited.

(Prior code § 129.1-18.2; Amend. Coun. J. 2-16-89, p. 24942)

Article X. Carriers for Transportation of Flammable Liquids

§15-24-1000 General condition of carriers.

Tank trucks, tank trailers and tank semitrailers shall not be operated unless they are in good repair, clean and free of leaks.

(Prior code § 129.1-91)

§15-24-1130 Drivers or attendants.

The driver, operator or attendant of any tank vehicle shall not leave the vehicle while it is being filled or discharged. Smoking by truck drivers, helpers or attendants shall not be permitted while driving such vehicles, while filling or discharging any tank or compartment or while making any repairs to such vehicles. Motors of tank trucks shall be shut down during making and breaking of hose connections. If loading or unloading is done without the use of a power pump on the truck, the truck motor shall be shut down throughout such operations. No tank or compartment shall be loaded to a volume in excess of 99 and one-fourth percent of its capacity.

(Prior code § 129.1-103)

§15-24-1150 Travel over subway routes prohibited.

It shall be unlawful for any person to transport flammable liquids on any public way within the city under which is constructed any subway used exclusively for local passenger transportation purposes. Such public ways shall include but not be limited to the following:

S. and N. State Street from E. 13th Street to E. and W. Division Street.
W. Division Street from N. State Street to N. Clybourn Avenue.
N. Clybourn Avenue from W. Division Street to W. Willow Street.
S. and N. Dearborn Street from W. Harrison Street to W. Lake Street.
W. Lake Street from N. Dearborn Street to N. Milwaukee Avenue.
N. Milwaukee Avenue from W. Canal Street to W. Division Street.
W. Congress Parkway from S. Dearborn Street to S. Des Plaines Street.
N. Tilden Street from W. Canal Street to W. Des Plaines Street.
N. Milwaukee Avenue from N. Albany Street to N. Kimball Avenue.
N. Kimball Avenue from W. Diversey Avenue to W. School Street.

Provided, however, that nothing herein contained shall prevent the operator of any authorized motor vehicle used for the transportation of flammable liquids from crossing any such public way at an intersection or from making deliveries in any block, in which case such person shall approach and leave the place of delivery by means of the nearest intersecting street.
(Prior code § 129.1-105)

§15-24-1160 Restrictions on transportation of Class I liquids.

For purposes of the transportation of Class I flammable liquids by tank vehicles from primary sources of supply, such as refineries, waterway terminals or pipeline terminals, to any wholesale bulk plant or user bulk storage destination within the city of Chicago, route or routes for such transportation are hereby established as follows:

Archer Avenue between State Street and west city limits;
Ashland Avenue between 95th Street and Peterson Avenue;
Brainard Avenue between south city limits and 130th Street;
Burley Avenue between 87th Street and 83rd Street;
Cermak Road between State Street and west city limits;
Chicago Skyway between east city limits and Dan Ryan Expressway;
Cicero Avenue between 87th Street and north city limits;
Columbus Avenue between Western Avenue and south city limits;
Cottage Grove Avenue between 75th Street and 35th Street;
Ewing Avenue between Indianapolis Blvd. and 92nd Street;
Grand Avenue between Ogden Avenue and west city limits;
Halsted Street between 127th Street and 95th Street;
Harlem Avenue between Howard Street and 65th Street;
Indiana Avenue between 130th Street and 127th Street;
Indianapolis Blvd. between 106th Street and Ewing Avenue;
Irving Park Road between Ashland Avenue and west city limits;
Mackinaw Avenue between 92nd Street and 87th Street;
North Avenue between Ogden Avenue and west city limits;
Ogden Avenue between North Avenue and west city limits;
Pershing Road between Cottage Grove and Archer Avenue;
Peterson Avenue between Ashland Avenue and Cicero Avenue;

Roosevelt Road between Ashland Avenue and west city limits;

South Chicago Avenue between 95th Street and Cottage Grove Avenue;

Stony Island Avenue between 103rd Street and 95th Street and between South Chicago Avenue and 75th Street;

Torrence Avenue between 106th Street and 103rd Street;

Western Avenue between 95th Street and north city limits;

59th Street between Ashland Avenue and Western Avenue;

75th Street between Stony Island Avenue and Cottage Grove Avenue;

79th Street between Ashland Avenue and west city limits;

87th Street between east city limits and west city limits;

95th Street between east city limits and west city limits;

103rd Street between Torrence Avenue and Halsted Street;

106th Street between east city limits and Torrence Avenue;

127th Street between Indiana Avenue and Halsted Street;

130th Street between Brainard Avenue and Indiana Avenue;

Certain words and phrases used in this ordinance are defined as follows:

(a) "Wholesale bulk plant" means an establishment to which Class I flammable liquids are transported by rail tank cars or motor tank vehicles primarily for storage and for distribution by tank vehicle.

(b) "User bulk storage" means the storage of Class I flammable liquids in any storage tank having a capacity in excess of 6,000 gallons, primarily for consumption, packaging or processing or for servicing of aircraft.

(Prior code § 129.1-106)

§15-24-1170 Use of expressways.

The following additional routes may be used, in addition to those outlined in Section 15-24-1160:

Calumet Expressway between the Dan Ryan Expressway and south city limits;

Dan Ryan Expressway between 31st Street and south city limits;

Dwight D. Eisenhower Expressway between Ashland Avenue and west city limits;

John F. Kennedy Expressway between north city limits and Ogden Avenue;

Stevenson Expressway between Ashland Avenue and west city limits;

If the expressways are closed for repairs, or if truck traffic is banned for some other reason, then the following streets are acceptable alternatives:

State Street between 95th Street and Cermak Road;

Milwaukee Avenue between north city limits and Elston Avenue and Elston Avenue between Milwaukee Avenue and Ashland Avenue.

(Prior code § 129.1-106.1)

§15-24-1210 Manifests.

(1) The driver of every tank vehicle en route from any primary source of supply to any wholesale bulk plant or user bulk storage shall carry a manifest stating the point of origin and the destination of the trip which it is then making, the name of the consignor and of the consignee and the kind and quantity of the liquid carried and at any time upon demand of any police officer or authorized representative of the city of Chicago exhibit such manifest.

(2) The driver of any tank vehicle not subject to routing at any time upon demand of any police officer or authorized representative of the fire department of the city of Chicago shall bring such vehicle to a stop and shall give to such officer or such representative such information as may reasonably be required under the provisions of this ordinance as to the type of liquid being transported in such tank vehicle, the origin and the destination of the trip in which such tank vehicle is then engaged.
(Prior code § 129.1-110)

Article XI. Underground Storage Tank Violations.

§15-24-1230 Underground tank storage.

Any person who installs, maintains, repairs, removes or abandons in place any underground storage tank in violation of any section of Title 41, Chapter I, Part 170, Subpart B of the Illinois Administrative Code as amended from time to time shall be considered to have violated this section. The corporation counsel shall have the authority to enforce the above-cited provisions which are incorporated herein by reference and to obtain any and all applicable relief, including injunctions, court costs and fees. Any person found in violation of these provisions shall be subject to a fine of not less than $100.00 and not more than $500.00 for each violation. Each day on which such violation exists shall constitute a separate and distinct offense.
(Added. Coun. J. 11-17-93, p. 43012)

CHAPTER 15-26
FUME AND FLAMMABLE COMPRESSED GASES
(Selected Sections)

Sections:

Article I. General
15-26-010 Licenses, permits and special exit requirements.

Article II. Buildings and Rooms
15-26-130 Sign requirements.

Article III. Transportation
15-26-230 Danger signs.

Article IV. Generation of Acetylene Gas
15-26-440 Portable generator—Defined.

Article VI. Miscellaneous
15-26-800 Chlorine gas.
15-26-810 Storage of oxygen cylinders.
15-26-860 Bulk oxygen—Sign requirements.

Article I. General

§15-26-010 Licenses, permits and special exit requirements.

For licensing provisions and permit requirements, see Chapter 15-4. For special exit requirements, see Chapter 13-112.
(Coun. J. 12-9-92, p. 25465; Amend. 2-7-96, p. 15616)

Article I. Buildings and Rooms

§15-26-130 Sign requirements.

Every fume or flammable compressed gas building and every fume or flammable compressed gas room shall have the words "DANGER—POISONOUS GAS" where any fume hazard gas occurs, or the words "DANGER—FLAMMABLE GAS" where any flammable compressed gas occurs, painted in a conspicuous position on the outside of every entrance thereto; provided, however, that no such sign shall be required for any building or room in which not more than two standard cylinders of such gas are present at any time. No-smoking signs shall also be provided wherever flammable compressed gas is stored.

Such wording shall be in plainly legible bright red letters on a white background with letters not less than six inches high and with the principal strokes thereof not less than three-fourths inch in width.

(Coun. J. 12-9-92, p. 25465; Amend. 2-7-96, p. 15616)

Article III. Transportation

§15-26-230 Danger signs.

Caution signs which comply with the following regulations of the Interstate Commerce Commission or Department of Transportation regulations shall be provided and used.

Caution signs must be so placed on the track or car as to give necessary warning to persons approaching car from open end or ends of siding and must be left up until after car is unloaded and disconnected from discharge connection. Signs must be of metal, at least 12 by 15 inches in size and bear the words "STOP — TANK CAR CONNECTED" or "STOP — MEN AT WORK" and the word "STOP" being in letters at least four inches high and the other words in letters at least two inches high. The letters must be white on a blue background.

Such signs shall show the name of the specific fume hazard gas in the tank car.

(Coun. J. 12-9-92, p. 25465; Amend. 2-7-96, p. 15616)

Article IV. Generation of Acetylene Gas

§15-26-440 Portable generator—Defined.

"Portable generator" means an acetylene generator of not more than 30 pounds carbide capacity, which has been approved for portable use by the Underwriters Laboratories and included in the "List of Inspected Gas, Oil and Miscellaneous Appliances" dated November, 1973, of low-pressure and medium pressure acetylene generators.

(Coun. J. 12-9-92, p. 25465; Amend. 2-7-96, p. 15616)

Article VI. Miscellaneous

§15-26-800 Chlorine gas.

The sale, storage, use or handling of chlorine gas is hereby prohibited within the limits of the city unless chlorine gas is stored in buildings constructed and maintained in accordance with the building provisions of this code in containers constructed in compliance with the Interstate Commerce Commission rules and regulations.

No combustible material of any kind shall be placed or kept in any room or building used for the storage of chlorine gas.

(Coun. J. 12-9-92, p. 25465; Amend. 2-7-96, p. 15616)

§15-26-810 Storage of oxygen cylinders.

Cylinders of oxygen shall never be stored in the same room or compartment used for the storage of calcium carbide or cylinders containing fuel gases, or in an acetylene generator compartment. Cylinders of oxygen, except those in actual use, shall be stored away from highly flammable material, especially oil, grease or any substance likely to cause or accelerate fire. Cylinders of oxygen shall be stored in locations where they are not likely to be struck by passing or falling objects. Oxygen cylinders shall be protected against excessive rise of temperature. Cylinders may be stored in the open, but in such cases shall be protected against extremes of weather. During winter, cylinders stored in the open shall be protected against accumulations of ice or snow.

(Coun. J. 12-9-92, p. 25465; Amend. 2-7-96, p. 15616)

§15-26-860 Bulk oxygen—Sign requirements.

The bulk oxygen storage location shall be permanently placarded to read:

Oxygen
No Smoking
No Open Flames

Lettering shall be in accordance with Section 15-26-130 of this code.

(Coun. J. 12-9-92, p. 25465; Amend. 2-7-96, p. 15616)

TITLE 16
LAND USE
(Selected Chapter)

Chapters:

16-16 Adult Uses. (Complete Chapter)

CHAPTER 16-16
ADULT USES
(Complete Chapter)

Sections:

16-16-010 Title designated.
16-16-020 Intent and purpose.
16-16-030 Definitions.
16-16-040 Regulated uses.
16-16-050 Permitted uses.
16-16-060 Registration.
16-16-070 Registration and certification.
16-16-080 Form must be displayed.
16-16-090 Exterior display.
16-16-100 Severability.
16-16-110 Consumption of alcoholic liquor prohibited.
16-16-120 Consumer protection—Price list.
16-16-130 Violation—Penalty.

§16-16-010 Title designated.

Pursuant to the provisions of the Constitution of the State of Illinois of 1970, the Municipal Code of the city of Chicago is hereby amended by adding a new chapter thereto to be numbered Chapter 16-16 and known as the Chicago Adult Use Ordinance, as follows.
(Prior code § 194C-1; Amend. Coun. J. 7-29-87, p. 3030)

§16-16-020 Intent and purpose.

To regulate uses which, because of their very nature, are recognized as having serious objectionable operational characteristics, particularly when several of them are concentrated under certain circumstances thereby having a deleterious effect upon the adjacent areas. Special regulation of these uses is necessary to insure that these adverse effects will not contribute to the blighting or downgrading of the surrounding neighborhood. The primary control or regulation is for the purpose of preventing a concentration of these uses in any one area.
(Prior code § 194C-2; Amend. Coun. J. 7-29-87, p. 3030)

§16-16-030 Definitions.

"Adult bookstore" means an establishment having as a substantial or significant portion of its sales or stock in trade, books, magazines, films for sale or viewing on premises by use of motion picture devices or any other coin-operated means, and other periodicals which are distinguished or characterized by their emphasis on matter depicting, describing or relating to "specified sexual activities," or "specified anatomical areas," or an establishment with a segment or section devoted to the sale or display of such material, or an establishment that holds itself out to the public as a purveyor of such materials based upon its signage, advertising, displays, actual sales, presence of video preview or coin operated booths, the exclusion of minors from the establishment's premises, or any other factors showing that the establishment's primary purpose is to purvey such material.

"Adult motion picture theater" means an enclosed building with a capacity of 50 or more persons used regularly and routinely for presenting material having as a dominant theme material distinguished or characterized by an emphasis on matter depicting, describing or relating to "specified sexual activities" or "specified anatomical areas," for observation by patrons therein.

"Adult mini motion picture theater" means an enclosed building with a capacity for less than 50 persons used for presenting material distinguished or characterized by an emphasis on matter depicting, describing or relating to "specified sexual activities" or "specified anatomical areas," for observation by patrons therein.

"Adult entertainment cabaret" means a public or private establishment which: (i) features topless dancers, strippers, male or female impersonators; (ii) not infrequently, features entertainers who display "specified anatomical areas;" or (iii) features entertainers who by reason of their appearance or conduct perform in a manner which is designed primarily to appeal to the prurient interest of the patron or entertainers who engage in, or engage in explicit simulation of, "specified sexual activities."

"Specified sexual activities" means and is defined as:

1. Human genitals in a state of sexual stimulation or arousal;
2. Acts of human masturbation, sexual intercourse or sodomy;
3. Fondling or other erotic touching of human genitals, pubic region, buttock or female breast.

"Specified anatomical areas" means and is defined as:

1. Less than completely and opaquely covered: (a) human genitals, pubic region, (b) buttock and (c) female breast below a point immediately above the top of the areola; and
2. Human male genitals in a discernably turgid state, even if completely and opaquely covered.

(Prior code § 194C-3; Amend. Coun. J. 7-29-87, p. 3030; 2-10-93, p. 28689)

§16-16-040 Regulated uses.

Regulated uses include all adult uses which include, but are not limited to the following:

Adult bookstore;
Adult motion picture theater;
Adult mini motion picture theater;
Adult entertainment cabaret.

(Prior code § 194C-4; Amend. Coun. J. 7-29-87, p. 3030)

§16-16-050 Permitted uses.

Adult uses shall be permitted subject to zoning restrictions as provided in Title 17.

(Prior code § 194C-4.1; Amend. Coun. J. 7-29-87, p. 3030)

§16-16-060 Registration.

The owner of a building or premises, his agent for the purpose of managing, controlling or collecting rents, or any other person managing or controlling a building or premises, any part of which contains an adult use shall register with the department of revenue of the city of Chicago the following information:

(a) The address of the premises;

(b) The name of the owner of the premises and names of the beneficial owners if the property is in a land trust;

(c) The address of the owner and the beneficial owners;

(d) The name of the business or the establishment subject to the provisions of Section 16-16-040;

(e) The name(s) of the owner, beneficial owner or the major stockholders of the business or the establishment subject to the provisions of Section 16-16-040;

(f) The address of those persons named in paragraph e;

(g) The date of initiation of the adult use;

(h) The nature of the adult use;

(i) If the premises or building is leased, a copy of the said lease must be attached.

(Prior code § 194C-5; Amend. Coun. J. 7-29-87, p. 3030)

§16-16-070 Registration and certification.

It is unlawful for the owner or person in control of any property to establish or operate thereon or to permit any person to establish or operate an adult use without first having properly registered and received certification of approved registration.

(Prior code § 194C-5.1; Amend. Coun. J. 7-29-87, p. 3030)

§16-16-080 Form must be displayed.

The owner, manager or agent of a registered adult use shall display a copy of the registration form approved by the department of revenue in a conspicuous place on the premises.

(Prior code § 194C-5.2; Amend. Coun. J. 7-29-87, p. 3030)

§16-16-090 Exterior display.

No adult use shall be conducted in any manner that permits the observation of any material depicting, describing or relating to "specified sexual activities" or "specified anatomical areas," from any public way or from any property not registered as an adult use. This provision shall apply to any display, decoration, sign, show window or other opening.

(Prior code § 194C-6; Amend. Coun. J. 7-29-87, p. 3030)

§16-16-100 Severability.

If any provision of this chapter or the application of any provision to any item in this chapter, is held invalid, the invalidity of that provision or application shall not affect any of the other provisions or the application of those provisions to other items in this chapter.

(Prior code § 194C-6.1; Amend. Coun. J. 7-29-87, p. 3030)

§16-16-110 Consumption of alcoholic liquor prohibited.

The consumption of alcoholic liquor on the premises of any adult use where nude dancing is permitted is strictly prohibited.
(Prior code § 194C-6.2; Amend. Coun. J. 7-29-87, p. 3030; 10-1-97, p. 53200)

§16-16-120 Consumer protection—Price list.

All adult entertainment cabarets shall display at the bar and at each table, counter or other area or place where any food, beverages, goods, wares, merchandise or service is sold, served or provided, a complete list of all prices, fees and charges for all food, beverages, goods, wares and merchandise sold or services rendered. These lists shall be written in clearly visible letters and figures of a size not less than 14-point type.
(Prior code § 194C-7; Amend. Coun. J. 7-29-87, p. 3030)

§16-16-130 Violation—Penalty.

Any person violating any of the provisions of this chapter shall be fined not less than $50.00 nor more than $500.00 for each offense. Each violation of this chapter may be grounds for revocation of any license issued to any such establishment by the city of Chicago.
(Prior code § 194C-7.1; Amend. Coun. J. 7-29-87, p. 3030; 10-1-97, p. 53200)

A

ACCIDENT REPORTS 9-88-040

ADULT USE ORDINANCE 16-16
- Consumer protection 16-16-120
- Definitions 16-16-030
- Exterior display 16-16-090
- Intent and purpose 16-16-020
- Penalty 16-16-130
- Price list 16-16-120
- Registration 16-16-06 to 16-16-080
- Regulated uses 16-16-040
- Restrictions 16-16-050

ADVERTISING
- Deceptive 8-4-320

ADVERTISING MATTER
- Aircraft dropping 10-8-290, 10-8-300
- Distribution of 10-8-270, 10-8-271
- Placing in automobiles 10-8-310
- Towing display 10-8-280

ADVERTISING SIGNS
10-28-064, 10-28-066
- On vessels 10-40-281

ADVERTISING VESSELS
10-40-281

AIR, CLEAN INDOOR 7-32-030
- Definitions 7-32-040
- Regulation of smoking in places of employment 7-32-060
- Signs 7-32-070
- Smoking in public places 7-32-050
- Violation and penalties 7-32-080

AIRPORTS 10-36-020, 10-36-050, 10-36-358

AIR RIFLES AND TOY WEAPONS 4-144-14 to 4-144-240

ALCOHOL
- Driving while intoxicated 7-24-226

ALLEYS
- Loading and unloading from 10-8-200

AMBULANCES 4-68
- Attendants 4-68-070
- Condition of vehicles 4-68-080
- Definitions 4-68-010
- Discrimination 4-68-180
- Emergency medical technicians
  - Availability of names of 4-68-064
  - Peace officer assistance to 4-68-110
- Equipment 4-68-040
- Exemption from traffic laws 4-68-070
- Fees 4-68-130
- Health-related rules and regulations 4-68-080
- Illinois Emergency Medical Services System Act, applicability to 4-68-062
- Impoundment of vehicle 4-68-195
- Inspections 4-68-030, 4-68-060, 4-68-120
- Insurance 4-68-150
- License
  - Application 4-68-030
  - Basic and advanced life support services 4-68-020
  - Fees 4-68-050
  - Renewal 4-68-040
  - Requirements of 4-68-020
  - Suspension and revocation 4-68-120
  - Transfer of 4-68-050
  - When not required 4-68-020
- Maintenance of 4-68-040
- Ownership change 4-68-040

Patient destination 4-68-100
Penalty 4-68-190
Records 4-68-060
Saving clause 4-68-200
Violation 4-68-190

AMMUNITION
Assault: sale, transfer, possession 8-24-025
Bullets, fragmenting metal piercing prohibited 8-24-026
Prohibited handgun ammunition 4-144-061

AMUSEMENTS 4-156
Construction 4-156-520
Definitions 4-156-010
License tax 4-156-020
Time and manner of payment and accounting 4-156-030
Public places of 4-156
Athletic contests 4-156-430
Beer gardens 4-156-424
Billiard and poolroom: special regulations 4-156-420
Definitions 4-156-290
Drinking water 4-156-460
Gambling 4-156-450
Juice bar 4-156-300
License, issuance prohibited 4-156-355
License exceptions 4-156-305
License required 4-156-300
License restrictions 4-156-485
Motion picture theaters: billboards 4-156-410
Price of tickets 4-156-390
Special event allowance 4-156-484
Rules and regulations 4-156-034
Teenage cabaret (dry cabaret) 4-156-300
Ticket seller tax 4-156-033
Uniform Revenue Procedures Ordinance: application of 4-156-035
Violation, penalty 4-156-510

ANIMAL CARE AND CONTROL 7-12
Animal under restraint 7-12-030
Bite occurrence, owner's responsibilities 7-12-090
Commission established 7-12-010
Cruelty to animals 7-12-290
Dangerous animals
Determination and requirements 7-12-050
Miscellaneous 7-12-052
Violations 7-12-051
Definitions 7-12-020
Dog license
Application forms 7-12-150
Exemptions 7-12-180
Fees 7-12-170
Rabies inoculation certificates 7-12-160
Required license 7-12-140
Unvaccinated and/or unlicensed, citations for 7-12-190
Dyeing of fowls prohibited 7-12-350
Equine animals, license requirements and fees 7-12-21 to 7-12-270
Excrement removal required 7-12-420
Fights and contests prohibited 7-12-370
Impoundment facilities 7-12-070
Injured or diseased animal in public way, removal of 7-12-310, 7-12-320
Neglected animal, removal of 7-12-080
Possession of animals for slaughter 7-12-300
Rabies vaccination requirements 7-12-200
Redemption of impounded animals 7-12-060
Stable maintenance 7-12-280
Sterilization of impounded dogs and cats 7-12-065
Strays, impounded 7-12-040
Violations 7-12-430

ANTI-LOITERING PROGRAM 8-4-052

ANTI-TRESPASSING PROGRAM 8-4-052

ASSAULT AGAINST ELDERLY, HANDICAPPED 8-4-080

ASSAULT WEAPONS AND AMMUNITION
Sale, transfer, possession 8-24-025

ASSEMBLY UNITS 13-84, 13-88
Building capacity and floor plans 13-84-410
Nightclubs and restaurants 13-84-331
Open air 13-88-230

AUDIO AND VIDEO DISCS
Record keeping 4-264-052

AUTOMATED BUS LANE AND BUS STOP CAMERA ENFORCEMENT PROGRAM 9-103-010, 9-103-070

AUTOMATED RED LIGHT CAMERA PROGRAM 9-102-010, 9-102-070

AUTOMATIC AMUSEMENT DEVICES 4-156
Class II arcade 4-156-230
Definition 4-156-150
License
Application 4-156-210
Investigation of applicant 4-156-220
Required 4-156-200
Minors, use by, where prohibited 4-156-270
Penalty 4-156-280
Tax delinquent device, seizure of 4-156-190
Tax emblem 4-156-170
Tax imposed 4-156-160
Unlawful use 4-156-180

AUTOMATIC AMUSEMENT MACHINES 4-156
License approval 4-156-125
Partial invalidity 4-156-130
Penalty 4-156-140
Raffle licenses 4-156-040

AVIATION, DEPARTMENT OF
Police powers for designated employees 10-36-358

B

BARRICADES 10-20
New pavement for 10-20-600
Street openings and obstructions 10-20-605
Warning lights 10-20-610

BICYCLE MESSENGER SERVICES 4-168
Definitions 4-168-010
Helmet and visible identification 4-168-070
License required 4-168-020
Suspension or revocation 4-168-090
Penalties for violations 4-168-120
Rules and regulations enforcement 4-168-110

BICYCLES 9-120
Dealers 9-120-080
Definition 9-120-010
Operation 9-52-01 to 9-52-100
Paths, driving motor vehicle on 9-40-060
Registration 9-120-020
Record of 9-120-030
Transfer of 9-120-040
Rental agencies 9-120-070
Serial number, alteration of 9-120-050
Traffic regulations 9-120-060

BIDI CIGARETTES 4-64-194

BILLIARDS AND POOLROOMS
Special regulations 4-156-420

BIRTHS AND DEATHS 7-16
Bodies, dead human care and disposition of
Burial permits 7-16-100
Burial within city 7-16-150
Cremation permits 7-16-100
Discovery of 7-16-050
Exposure prohibited 7-16-080
Funeral establishment as morgue 7-16-060
Public exhibition prohibited 7-16-070
Removal in public conveyance 7-16-090
Reports of births and deaths 7-16-030
Violations of chapter 7-16-190

BOARD UP
Buildings 13-12-131

BODY PIERCING 4-93
Definitions 4-93-010
Display of license 4-93-040
Enforcement 4-93-080
License required 4-93-020
Parental consent 4-93-050
Sanitation 4-93-060
Violations, penalties 4-93-090

BONFIRES 8-4-160

BOOTING
Definitions 4-233-010
Geographical restrictions 4-233-060
License 4-233-02 to 4-233-040
Private operation license fees 4-5-010
Prohibited 9-84-015
Regulation of operations 4-233-050

BRIDGES 10-40-41 to 10-40-560
Breaking line crossing 10-40-530
Closed hours 10-40-420
Congregation on bridges or viaducts 10-40-560
Fire apparatus crossing 10-40-510
Opening 10-40-410
Removal of life preservers prohibited 10-40-501
Rule of road crossing 10-40-520
Signal equipment 10-40-480
Signal for opening 10-40-440
Signal for opening of railroad bridges 10-40-450
Signals, obedience to 10-40-470
Signal to bridge tenders 10-40-460
Time to remain open 10-40-460
Traffic obstruction 10-40-550
Unnecessary delay 10-40-540
Vessels, obstruction by 10-40-490
Violations, penalty 10-40-570

BUILDING CAPACITY SIGNS POSTED 13-84-410

BUILDING INSPECTION 13-20
Exec. Director and Fire Commissioner, duty 13-20-010
Inspection required 13-20-020
Interference with building officials 13-12-100
Violation of chapter, penalties 13-20-017

BUILDING PERMITS 13-32
Amusement device 13-32-280
Application for 13-32-030
Approval of plans 13-32-040
Canopy erection 13-32-160
Construction, cost of 13-32-315
Construction contrary to 13-32-120
Construction without 13-32-130
Driveways 13-32-090
Elevators 13-32-19 to 13-32-195
Exceptions 13-32-020
Fence over five feet 13-32-200
Furnace, warm air heating 13-32-270
Issuance of 13-32-080

Landmarks and historic buildings 13-32-050
Moving of buildings 13-32-210
New or revised 13-32-035
Platform erection 13-32-170
Posting required 13-32-010
Protection of public way and public places 10-28-2816 to 10-28-2818
Public protection measures 10-28-28 to 10-28-2815
Rules and regulations 13-32-085
Sidewalk, damage to 10-28-285
Sub-sidewalk space 13-32-100
Surety bond 13-32-060
Time limits 13-32-110
Traffic control device, removal of 13-128-061
Violation 13-32-290
Wrecking of buildings 13-32-230
Wrecking permits 13-32-260

BUILDING PLANS 13-32, 13-40
Approval of 13-32-040
Plans on file at construction site 13-40-090

BUILDINGS, ELECTRICAL AND FIRE REGULATIONS, ENFORCEMENT OF 13-12
Abandoned buildings, watchmen for 13-12-140
Boarding up 13-12-131
City attaching signs 13-12-730
City poles, use of 13-12-810
Closing of 4-4-283, 13-12-120
Construction without permit 13-12-050
Dangerous or unsafe buildings 4-4-283, 13-12-130
Impeding traffic 13-12-870
Interference with officials 13-12-100
Liability 13-12-020
Permit to erect poles, wires and conductors 13-12-820
Penalty for violation 13-12-890
Responsibilities of owner 13-12-030
Scope of chapter 13-12-010
Stop order 13-12-080
Vacant building: duties of owner 13-12-125
Violation of provisions 13-12-040

BUILDINGS AND STRUCTURES
Miscellaneous 13-96

BUILDING VIOLATIONS
Persons liable for 13-12-020

BURGLAR ALARMS 4-400
Definitions 4-400-010
False alarms 4-400-040
Hearing request 4-400-060
Notice of false alarm, forms 4-400-030, 4-400-050
Penalties 4-400-070
Permits 4-400-020
Requirements for vehicles 9-76-150

BURGLAR'S TOOLS
Possessing 8-4-180

BURIAL AND CREMATION PERMIT
Required 7-16-100

BURIAL WITHIN CITY 7-16-150

C

CANOPIES AND MARQUEES 10-28
Construction clearance 10-28-250
Permit required 10-28-200

CARBOLIC ACID 7-24
Crude, mixtures and wholesale sales 7-24-10 to 7-24-140
False statements in prescriptions 7-24-130
Fraudulent prescriptions 7-24-120

Inspection of prescriptions 7-24-110
Prescription required 7-24-100

CARRIAGE, CARRIAGE STAND
Definitions 9-4-410

CATCH BASINS see PRIVIES, CATCH BASINS AND SIMILAR VAULTS

CENTRAL BUSINESS DISTRICT
Parking meter rates 9-64-205

CHARITABLE SOLICITATION
Display of permit 10-8-140
Filing of statement 10-8-150
Permit requirement 10-8-08 to 10-8-130
Rules adoption 10-8-160
Violation, penalty 10-8-170

CHARITY
Advertisement of 8-4-340

CHAUFFEURS, PUBLIC 9-104
Behavior of 9-104-150
Deadly weapons 9-104-010
Definition 9-104-120
Distress or trouble light activation 9-104-125
Fingerprints required 9-104-050
Information, false 9-104-110
Information to police 9-104-160
License, application and qualifications for 9-104-030
License, attempting to obtain another 9-104-090
License, change of address notice 9-104-130
License, defacement and fee 9-104-070
License, exhibition of 9-104-060
License, suspension or revocation of 9-104-040
License renewal 9-104-080
Licenses required 9-104-020
Loitering 9-104-100
Penalty 9-104-140
Photographs required 9-104-050
Service dogs, passengers with 9-104-050

CHEMICALS AND SUBSTANCES
Offensive 7-28
Offensive bombs in public places 7-28-650
Possession and sale 7-28-630
Prescriptions 7-28-640

CITY SERVICES, LIABILITY FOR COST
Billing. rules and regulations 8-28-050
Defenses to violation of law 8-28-040
Definitions 8-28-010
Liability collection 8-28-020
Liability of employer 8-28-030
Recovery of litigation costs 8-28-060

CLEANSING GOODS
Prohibited use of public ways 10-8-420

COMPRESSED GASES see FUME AND FLAMMABLE COMPRESSED GASES

CONSTRUCTION WITHOUT PERMIT 13-12-050

CONSUMER SERVICES, DEPARTMENT OF 2-24
Commissioner 2-24-020, 2-24-040
Consumer fraud 2-24-060
Department created 2-24-010
Employees 2-24-030
License 2-24-070
Penalty 2-24-080
Unlawful obstruction 2-24-050
Water taxis and tour boats 2-24-041

CREMATIONS 4-80-090

CRIMES, HATE 2-120-518

CRUISING
Definitions 9-80-210
No cruising zones 9-80-213
Penalty 9-80-214
Police officer warning 9-80-211
Violation of ordinance 9-80-212

CUSTODY
Taking minor into 8-16-022

D

DAY CARE CENTER 4-72
Definitions 4-72-010
Inspection 4-72-150
License required 4-72-020
Night care 4-72-160
Records 4-72-130
Reports 4-72-140
Violation 4-72-170

DEADLY WEAPONS 4-144-01 to 4-144-080

DEATH BENEFIT FUND, FIREMEN AND POLICEMEN 3-8
Administration of fund 3-8-200
Amount of death award 3-8-120
Amount of death fund 3-8-020
Authorization of death award fund 3-8-010
Authorization of medical and hospital care fund 3-8-190
Beneficiary entering armed forces 3-8-170
Board of trustees 3-8-030
Burial expenses 3-8-260
City Council to be notified of payments made 3-8-250
Death of sole beneficiary 3-8-140
Deposit of awards 3-8-070
Duties of department heads 3-8-210
Duty of corporation counsel 3-8-220
Investments by trustee bank 3-8-100
Issuance of voucher 3-8-060
Loss of death award due to depreciation 3-8-180
Marriage or attainment of majority by beneficiary 3-8-150
Marriage or attainment of majority by sole beneficiary 3-8-160
Payments during city council vacation periods 3-8-240
Payments to minors and incompetents 3-8-110
Reallocation upon death of beneficiary 3-8-130
Report of injury 3-8-040
Required proof for death award 3-8-050
Required proof for medical and hospital care fund 3-8-230
Successor trustee bank 3-8-090
Trust agreements 3-8-080

DEATHS
Report of 7-16-030

DEFACING AND INJURING HOUSE OF WORSHIP AND CEMETERIES 8-4-040

DEFACING PROPERTY IN PUBLIC PLACES 10-8-380

DEPARTMENT OF ADMINISTRATIVE HEARINGS 2-14-010
Administrative adjudication proceedings. instituting 2-14-070
Administrative law officers. powers and duties 2-14-040
Compliance bond 2-14-090
Defenses to building code violations 2-14-155
Director. powers and duties 2-14-030
Election of remedies 2-14-110
Enforcement of order 2-14-103

General provisions 2-14-065
Impoundment 2-14-132
Municipal hearings division 2-14-190
Administrative hearings 2-14-076
Default 2-14-078
Jurisdiction 2-14-190
Notice 2-14-074
Petition for review to Director 2-14-195
Provisions not limiting 2-14-130
Review 2-14-102
Rights of occupants 2-14-154
Seized/Unclaimed property 2-14-101
Subpoenas 2-14-080
Vehicle hearings division 2-14-140
Violation of orders 2-14-100

DISCRIMINATION 8-4-085

DISEASES
Contagious and epidemic 7-20
Articles exposed to infection. removal of 7-20-090
Common drinking cup 7-20-120
Communicable disease defined 7-20-010
Contagious disease defined 7-20-010
Diseased person. removal or exposure of 7-20-080
Epidemic disease defined 7-20-010
Sick or neglected person. report of 7-20-060
Taking articles to or from premises where death occurred 7-20-100
Towels in public lavatory 7-20-110
Violations, penalty 7-20-130

DISORDERLY CONDUCT 8-4-010

DOGS see ANIMAL CARE AND CONTROL

DRAG RACING
Vehicle impoundment 9-12-090

DRINKING CUP
Common use of 7-20-120

DRINKING IN PUBLIC WAYS 8-4-030

DRIVEWAYS
Permit required 10-20-160
Rendered unusable 10-20-442

DRUG PARAPHERNALIA
Accomplice liability 7-24-093
Delivery of 7-24-091
Minors 7-24-094
License revocation 7-24-095
Manufacture of 7-24-092
Possession of 7-24-091
Seizure and forfeiture 7-24-096
Severability 7-24-097

DRUGS AND NARCOTICS
Bichloride of mercury 7-24-070
Carbolic acid 7-24-10 to 7-24-140
Establishments unlawfully used for controlled substances 7-24-098
Intoxicated condition 7-24-080
Office of Local Drug Control Policy 7-24-22 to 7-24-224
Penalty for violation 7-24-230
Sale to minors 7-24-090
Sample packages of medicines 7-24-030
Tobacco 7-24-19 to 7-24-210
Unlawful in motor vehicle–impoundment 7-24-225
Wood alcohol 7-24-15 to 7-24-170

DRY CLEANERS AND SPOTTERS 4-100
Dry-cleaning establishments, self-service coin operated
Attendant 4-100-160
Hours of operation 4-100-190
Violation, penalty 4-100-220

E

EARTH OR SOD REMOVAL FROM PROPERTY
Adjoining public way 8-4-290
Permit or consent required 8-4-280

ELECTRICAL REGULATIONS

ELEVATED RAILROADS
Car storage 9-124-350
Limitations on regulations 9-124-290
Rush hour time periods 9-124-300
Seats 9-124-320
Shunting, prohibitions against 9-124-340
Stations 9-124-360
Enclosures 9-124-370
Signs required 9-124-380
Stops at station required 9-124-330
Trespassing on 8-4-260
Written train schedules required 9-124-310

ELEVATED TRACKS
Trespassing on 8-4-260

EMERGENCIES
Coordinator 2-4-110

EMERGENCY MEDICAL TECHNICIAN
Assistance from peace officer 4-68-110

EMPLOYEES see OFFICERS AND EMPLOYEES

EMPLOYMENT, WORKING CONDITIONS see WORKING CONDITIONS

ENFORCEMENT OF BUILDING, ELECTRICAL AND FIRE REGULATIONS 13-12

ENVIRONMENTAL PROTECTION AND CONTROL 11-4
Asbestos in spray, prohibited 11-4-680
Ballast tank, bilge tank or other discharge 11-4-1420
Chapter title 11-4-010
Compliance 11-4-1530
Department established 11-4-020
Dilution or concealment of emissions, prohibited 11-4-750
Disposal in waters 11-4-1410
Earth-shaking vibration, legal procedure 11-4-1380
Exceptions to sound pressure levels 11-4-1130
Excessive noise, legal procedure 11-4-1380
Excessive noise on the public way 11-4-1115
Gas manufacturing residue 11-4-1450
Handling of materials susceptible to becoming windborne 11-4-770
Junk facility permits 11-4-221 to 11-4-2420
Municipal waste-burning prohibited 11-4-810
Open fire prohibited 11-4-740
Prohibitions, specific 11-4-1150
Recycling facility permits 11-4-2510, 11-4-2520, 11-4-2535, 11-4-2570, 11-4-2580, 11-4-2620, 11-4-2645, 11-4-2680

Refuse burning 11-4-590
Refuse dumping prohibited 11-4-1500
Restrictions in use of motor vehicle horns 11-4-1290
Smoke and gas from internal combustion engines of vehicles 11-4-760
Sound pressure level 11-4-1110
Within residential unit 11-4-1120
Storage of materials susceptible to becoming windborne 11-4-780
Storage tank
Definition 11-4-2090
Fuel and lubrication facilities 11-4-2140
Permit, application, approval, fee, revocation 11-4-2100, 11-4-2110
Violation, penalty 11-4-2130
Waiver of permit fee 11-4-2120
Sundry noises restricted 11-4-1110
Surfacing of lots and roadways 11-4-730
Unimpaired damage, legalities 11-4-1390
Violations of provisions 11-4-1590, 11-4-1600
Wharf, dock ,pier, etc., public nuisance 11-4-1440
When lowest level limits apply 11-4-1140

EVENTS, SPECIAL 10-8-335

EVICTIONS
Proceedings 2-14-200
Unlawful use of premises 8-30-010, 8-30-020

EXCAVATIONS AND CLAY HOLES 8-4-220

EXPLOSIVES AND FIREWORKS 15-20
Explosives
Definitions 15-20-010
Explosives in public conveyance prohibited 15-20-040
Manufacture of explosives in city 15-20-200
Sales to minors 15-20-170
Seizure of unlawfully kept explosives 15-20-180
Transportation by vessel or railroad car 15-20-080
Transportation in public conveyance prohibited 15-20-040
Transportation requirements 15-20-030
Fireworks
Advertising restrictions 15-20-230
Found in motor vehicles, impoundment 15-20-270
Definitions 15-20-210
Display in public places 15-20-240
Penalties 15-20-221
Permit and permit fee 15-20-260
Prohibitions 15-20-220
Transportation exemptions 15-20-250

EXTERMINATION BY FUMIGATION 7-44
Airing of premises 7-44-170
Crew removal from vessels 7-44-070
Cyanic crystals, exposure prohibited 7-44-160
Definition 7-44-010
Fires
Safety measures 7-44-140
Food products, special safety measures 7-44-130

Fumigation residue, disposal 7-44-180
Guards 7-44-120
Hydrocyanic acid containers 7-44-190
Hydrocyanic acid gas, sale of materials restricted 7-44-030
Impermeable receptacles 7-44-150
Locking rooms and apartments 7-44-090
Notice 7-44-050
Notification of occupants, vacating premises 7-44-060
Permit 7-44-040
Required hazardous materials license 7-44-020
Safety measures, exceptions 7-44-110
Sealing of rooms 7-44-080
Stink or tear gas 7-44-200
Violation and penalty 7-44-210
Warning card 7-44-100

F

FALSE CLAIMS
Civil actions 1-22-030
Definitions 1-22-010
Generally 1-22-020
Procedures 1-22-040, 1-22-060
Subpoenas 1-22-050

FALSE STATEMENTS
Aiding and abetting 1-21-020
Enforcement 1-21-030
Generally 1-21-010

FENCE
Barbed wire 10-8-400

FILLING STATIONS 4-108
Dispensing fuel, restrictions 4-108-071
Flammable liquids 4-108-090
Gasoline spills or overflows 4-108-110
License required 4-108-020
Liquor sales prohibited 4-60-090
Proper disposal of tires 4-108-111
Smoking 4-108-070
Violation, penalty 4-108-130
Waste disposal 4-108-100

FINES
Violations 8-16-024

FIRE, ELECTRICAL AND BUILDING REGULATIONS
Enforcement of 13-12

FIRE ALARMS
False 8-4-145

FIREARMS
Penalty for illegal use 8-20-241
Possession of 2-84-020
Laser sight accessories 8-20-165
Surrender of 8-20-195
Penalty 8-20-020
Unlawful to carry: exceptions 8-20-010
Registration of 8-20
Additional duties of registrant 8-20-140
Ammunition, possession of 8-20-160
Application fees 8-20-080
Application for, prerequisites 8-20-060
Definitions 8-20-030
Denial, revocation 8-20-130
Destruction of 8-20-220
Exhibition of registration 8-20-150
False information 8-20-180
Filing time 8-20-090
Fingerprints 8-20-070
Investigations 8-20-100
Issuance of certificate 8-20-110
Notice 8-20-210
Penalties 8-20-250
Possession, acquisition prohibited 8-20-240
Registration 8-20-040

Renewal 8-20-200
Revocation, denial 8-20-120
Sales, transfers 8-20-170
Illegal 8-20-175
Severability 8-20-260
Superintendent, authority of 8-20-230
Unregisterable firearms 8-20-050
Voluntary surrender 8-20-190

FIREARMS AND OTHER WEAPONS 8-24
Assault weapons or ammunition: sale, transfer, possession 8-24-025
Carrying dangerous weapons 8-24-020
Discharging firearms 8-24-010
Discharging toy firearms 8-24-040
Disguised firearms prohibited 8-24-027
Hunting 8-24-050
Illegal use 8-20-241
Penalty 8-24-060
Possession of martial arts weaponry unlawful within city 8-24-030
Sale or transfer: illegal 8-20-175
Utility knives 8-24-021

FIRE DEPARTMENT 2-36
Aid in conveying fire apparatus 2-36-380
Aid in fire extinguishment 2-36-390
Badges for admission within fire cordon 2-36-410
Cordon around fire 2-36-400
Department established 2-36-010
Fire hydrant, obstruction of 2-36-430
Hindrance at fires 2-36-460
Inspection of premises and structures 2-36-270
Investigation of complaints 2-36-280
Police, aid to fire department 2-36-250
Power of arrest 2-36-440
Property from fire 2-36-450
Removal and destruction of property 2-36-420

FIRE PREVENTION, BUREAU OF 15-4
Bureau, generally
Duties 15-4-020
Powers 15-4-020
Regulations 15-4-010
Responsibilities 15-4-020
Terms 15-4-050
Fire emergency plan 15-4-101
Fire extinguisher servicemen license
Application 15-4-460
Fee 15-4-480
Renewal 15-4-490
Required 15-4-450
Rules and regulations 15-4-510
Violation 15-4-500
General provisions
Dangerous buildings 15-4-090
Fuel oil dealers 15-4-258
Fuel oil storers 15-4-259
Lumberyards and lumber storehouses 15-4-252
Right to survey 15-4-100
Safety warden 15-4-102
Sale of solid fuel and firewood 15-4-256
Storage of solid fuel not for retail 15-4-257
Transportation exemption 15-4-060
Hazardous use units 15-4-110
Other requirements 15-4-520

FIREWORKS see EXPLOSIVES AND FIREWORKS

FLAMMABLE LIQUIDS 15-24
Carriers for transportation
Condition 15-24-1000
Drivers or attendants 15-24-1130
Warning signs 15-24-1070
Licenses and permits 15-24-010
Tank storage, gasoline pumping prohibited 15-24-230
Underground storage tank violations 15-24-1230

FOOD ESTABLISHMENTS 4-8
Definitions 4-8-010
License, issuance prohibited when 4-8-025
License, posting 4-8-045
Licensing 4-8-020
Notification of food poisoning 4-8-050
Prepackaged and nonperishable foods 4-8-066
Rules and regulations 4-8-064
Violation of chapter: penalty 4-8-068

FOOD ESTABLISHMENTS—CARE OF FOODS 7-40
Animals in stores, prohibited 7-40-060
Candy establishments, requirements 7-40-125
Canned poultry, sale of 7-40-090
Desserts and mixes, adulterated or misbranded 7-40-305
Milk and milk products 7-40-325
Drinking fountain 7-40-115
Fruits, vegetables and berries, inspection 7-40-105
Impure or adulterated drugs, liquids or food 7-40-010
Impure water, use of 7-40-120
Manufacturing compliance 7-40-300
Meat inspections required 7-40-070
Meat standards compliance required 7-40-065
Misrepresentation prohibited 7-40-050
Noncity bottled water plants 7-40-160
Notice required 7-40-295, 7-40-345
Pasteurization required, milk 7-40-290
Poultry sale location restrictions 7-40-140
Sulfiting agent 7-40-100
Unwholesome foods, sale of 7-40-015
Confiscation of 7-40-025
Violation, penalty 7-40-390

FOOD ESTABLISHMENTS—INSPECTIONS, VIOLATIONS AND HEARING PROCEDURES 7-42
"Held for Inspection" 7-42-020
Inspections 7-42-010
License revocation 7-42-080
License suspension 7-42-035
Penalty for violations 7-42-090
Removal of suspended licenses and permits 7-42-050
Violations of provisions: actions 7-42-030

FOOD ESTABLISHMENTS—SANITARY OPERATING REQUIREMENTS 7-38
All food establishments, requirements 7-38-001
Certificates 7-38-012
Control of vermin and insects 7-38-020
Food 7-38-005
Food handlers 7-38-010
Food sampling 7-38-011
Food sanitarians 7-38-070
Vehicle sanitation 7-38-040
Automatic vending machines
Food manufacture, delivery and storage 7-38-150
Marking of food product wrappers 7-38-155

Out-of-service procedure 7-38-210
Water-vending machines: Location restricted 7-38-212
Rules and regulations 7-38-218
Coffee cart vendors: Prohibited acts 7-38-235, 7-38-240
Cold storage establishments
Reports 7-38-460
Requirements, receiving and delivery 7-38-465
Return prohibited 7-38-485
Storage time limit 7-38-470
Time limit extension 7-38-475
Transfer restrictions 7-38-480
Mobile food vendors
Operational requirements 7-38-115
Sinks, water storage and plumbing 7-38-120
Prohibited districts 4-8-037, 7-38-080, 9-80-190
Refuse receptacles 7-38-125
Penalty for violations 7-38-575
Slaughtering, rendering and packing establishments
Abatement of nuisance 7-38-570
Conveyance of refuse 7-38-550
Diseased cattle 7-38-540
Entry of carcasses 7-38-545
Hours for slaughtering 7-38-520
Notice to alderman 7-38-495
Offensive gases and odors 7-38-535
Slaughtering on public ways 7-38-510
Sleeping on premises 7-38-555

FORGING SIGNATURES 8-4-310

FRAGMENTING BULLETS
Prohibited 8-24-026

FUME AND FLAMMABLE COMPRESSED GASES 15-26
Buildings and rooms, danger signs 15-26-130
Chlorine gas 15-26-800
Generation of acetylene gas, definition 15-26-440
Licenses and permits 15-26-010
Storage of oxygen 15-26-810
Transportation, danger signs 15-26-230
Warning signs 15-26-860

FUNERAL BUSINESS 4-80
Changes in ownership 4-80-090
Definitions 4-80-010
Enforcement 4-80-100
Legal requirements 4-80-030
License requirements 4-80-020
Other occupations restricted 4-80-060
Prices for service and merchandise 4-80-050
Rules and regulations 4-80-080

FUNERAL ESTABLISHMENT
As public morgue 7-16-060

FUNERAL PROCESSIONS
9-32-01 to 9-32-030

G

GAMBLING 8-12
Betting or gambling at tracks 8-12-070
Devices for gambling 8-12-040
Duty of police 8-12-060
Gambling prohibited 8-12-010
Lottery or policy games 8-12-020
Penalty 8-12-100
Places for gambling 8-12-030
Publishing or circulating information 8-12-090
Slot and tape machines 8-12-050
Taking bets or pool selling 8-12-080

GANGS
Criminal: loitering by members 8-4-015

GAS MANUFACTORY ODORS AND REFUSE 7-28-110

GLASS CONTAINER
Prohibited on beach 10-36-130

GROSS WEIGHT
Limitations 9-72-080

GUNSMITHS 4-144
License required 4-144-100
Report to Superintendent of Police 4-144-130

H

HANDICAPPED PARKING
Decals 9-68-010

HARBOR, CHICAGO 10-40
Anchor dragging 10-40-200
Assistance to disabled vessels 10-40-131
Boat whistles 10-40-250
Bridges 10-40-41 to 10-40-560
Discharge of cargo 10-40-380
Dredging machine, interference with 10-40-180
Dredging permits 10-40-360
Encroachments and obstructions 10-40-370
Fast moving vessels, protection from 10-40-400
Fouled vessel, assistance for 10-40-190
Harbor defined 10-40-010
Harbor police as special police 2-84-200
House boats 10-40-290
Interference with buoys 10-40-270
Motor boats 10-40-260
Moving vessels before bridge opening 10-40-210
Names on boats 10-40-220
Navigation of the harbor 10-40-09 to 10-40-300
Obstruction by vessels 10-40-100
Obstruction of harbor by piles or stones 10-40-110
Old dock materials, bond for removal of 10-40-350
Penalties 10-40-570
Permit fees to construct or repair in harbor 10-40-340
Rafts or logs or lumber in harbor 10-40-140
Structures in harbor, construction and repair of 10-40-330
Towage limited 10-40-170
Towing permits 10-40-160
Tugs for vessels 10-40-150
Tunneling under Lake Michigan 10-40-300
Vessel engines, working 10-40-230
Vessels, securing and removal of 10-40-120
Vessels, sunken or abandoned 10-40-130
Vessels in harbor, control of 10-40-090
Vessels lying at docks 10-40-390
Violations, penalty 10-40-570
Wharves and docks 10-40-31 to 10-40-400
Maintenance of 10-40-320

HATE CRIMES 2-120-518

HAZARDOUS MATERIALS LICENSE 4-115
Application 4-115-020
Fee 4-115-030
Required 4-115-010
Violation, penalty 4-115-040

HEALTH, BOARD OF 2-112
Cardiopulmonary resuscitation 2-112-260
Commissioner's duties 2-112-160
Communicable disease 2-112-170
Contaminated food or beverage 2-112-270

Disinfection of premises 2-112-200
Health and safety hazards, investigation of premises 2-112-220
Illinois Swimming Pool and Bathing Beach Act, administration, enforcement 2-112-275
Vacation of premises 2-112-210

HOME OCCUPATIONS 4-380
Defined 4-380-010
License requirement 4-380-020
Application 4-380-030
Fee 4-380-040
Other 4-380-070
Renewal 4-380-050
Other laws and rules, applicable 4-380-080
Prohibited activities 4-380-070
Requirements applicable 4-380-060
Violations and penalties 4-380-090

HORSE-DRAWN CARRIAGES 9-48
Areas designated for use 9-48-020
Compliance with laws required 9-108-110
Consumption or possession of alcoholic liquor 9-108-220
Equipment 9-108-120
Fines 9-108-250
License fees 9-108-050
License not assignable 9-108-060
License plate or decal 9-108-070, replacement fee
Licenses not required 9-108-190
Inspection 9-108-100
Insurance required 9-108-080
License required 9-108-020, 9-108-140
Application, qualifications and fee 9-108-150
Application for renewal, investigation and issuance 9-108-040
Application for renewal, procedure 9-108-030
Display of license 9-108-130
Notification of change of information 9-108-170
Operation 9-48-030, 9-48-040,9-108-160
Penalties 9-108-240
Possession of weapon prohibited 9-108-160
Rules, regulations, restrictions 9-108-090, 9-108-200
Sanitary condition of stand 9-108-230

HORSES 7-12
Definitions 7-12-020, 9-4-410
Licenses for drawing carriage, tattoos 7-12-22t o 7-12-270
Removal from public way 7-12-320

HOSPITALS 4-84
Definition 4-84-010
Discrimination 4-84-130
Enforcement and penalties 4-84-110
License required 4-84-020
Noises, unnecessary 10-8-070
Quiet zones 10-8-010
Rape treatment cases 4-84-140
Reports to police 4-84-100
State license, status 4-84-120
Traffic near hospitals 10-8-030

HOTELS 4-208
Additional penalties 4-208-120
Hearing impaired, provisions for 13-64-180
Hourly rates/duration of rental 4-208-075
Licenses 4-208-02 to 4-208-040, 4-208-110
Maintaining a public disorder 4-208-08 to 4-208-100

HOUSE MOVING 10-8-210

HOUSING DEVELOPMENTS
Driving in restricted areas within 9-40-071

HUMANE SOCIETIES
Special police for 2-84-210

HUMAN RIGHTS 2-160
Commission on Human Rights 2-160-090
Credit transactions 2-160-060
Definitions 2-160-020
Employment 2-160-030
Religious beliefs 2-160-050
Sexual harassment 2-160-040
Penalties 2-160-120
Policy 2-160-010
Public accommodations 2-160-070
Religious societies 2-160-080
Retaliation 2-160-100

I

IMPOUNDMENT
Fleeing vehicle 9-92-035
Public passenger vehicles 9-112-555
Unlawful drugs in motor vehicle 7-24-225
Unlawful fireworks in motor vehicle 15-20-270

INDUSTRIAL PERMIT PARKING 9-64-091
Permits 9-68-021

INSPECTOR GENERAL, OFFICE OF 2-56
Confidentiality 2-56-070, 2-56-110
Cooperation 2-56-090
Department established 2-56-010
Discharge of city employees 2-56-160
Failure to complete investigation 2-56-080
Inspector General, appointment 2-56-020
Penalty 2-56-100, 2-56-140
Political activity 2-56-150
Powers and duties 2-56-030, 2-56-050
Removal of Inspector General 2-56-130
Reports 2-56-060, 2-56-120
Separability 2-56-170
Subpoenas 2-56-040

INTERFERENCE
With Director of Revenue 4-4-295
With utility equipment 8-4-065

INTERRUPTION OF TENANCY 5-12-160

ITINERANT MERCHANTS 4-212
Definition 4-212-010
License
Application for 4-212-030
Fees 4-212-040
Required 4-212-020
Renting to 4-212-050
Violations 4-212-060

J

JUNK FACILITY PERMITS 11-4
Application, investigation 11-4-2230
Charred metal 11-4-2290
Definitions 11-4-2210
Enforcement 11-4-2400
Fee 11-4-2240
Fences 11-4-2350
Fencing of yards 11-4-2300
Hours of business 11-4-2360
Identification of vehicles, personnel 11-4-2270
Inspection by commissioner of the environment 11-4-2410
Inspection by police 11-4-2380
Junk stores, junkyards 11-4-2260
Lost or stolen goods 11-4-2370

Maintaining article identity 11-4-2310
Prohibited activities 11-4-2330
Purchases from minors and intoxicated persons 11-4-2340
Required 11-4-2220
Revocation conditions 11-4-2390
Time restriction on sales 11-4-2320
Violation, penalty 11-4-2420

JUNK PEDDLERS 4-216
Definitions 4-216-010
Exhibiting lost or stolen goods 4-216-110
Fences 4-216-090
Hours of business 4-216-100, 8-4-240
Identification of vehicles and personnel 4-216-050
Inspection 4-216-120
License required 4-216-020
Prohibited activities 4-216-070
Proper disposal of junk 4-216-130
Purchase from minors prohibited 4-216-080
Violation, penalty 4-216-160

L

LAUNDRIES AND LAUNDRY VEHICLES 4-220
Laundries
Definition 4-220-010
Hours of operation 4-220-130
License required 4-220-020
Laundry vehicles: name on vehicle 4-220-055
Self-service coin-operated laundry
Attendant required 4-220-260
Hours of operation 4-220-290
Supplemental license 4-220-295
Violation of chapter: penalty 4-220-380

LICENSE FEES 4-5-010

LICENSING PROVISIONS
General 4-4
Adjustment 4-4-180
Affidavits 4-4-070
Alteration or removal of license insignia 4-4-230
Application for license 4-4-050
Approval of license bonds 4-4-080
Businesses and occupations not provided for by other provisions 4-4-020
Business name, change of 4-4-176
Business signs, improper 4-4-336
Child support delinquencies 4-4-152
Closure order 4-4-015
Display of license certificates and insignia 4-4-210
Distribution of license insignia -4-4-200
Enforcement of license provisions 4-4-290, 4-4-295
Expiration, notice of 4-4-250
Foreign representatives exemption of 4-4-140
Frontage consents, renewal of 4-4-270
Granting of licenses 4-4-030
Hazardous use units 4-4-300
Hours of operation, restrictions 4-4-313
Investigations 4-4-060
Issuance of licenses 4-4-040
License required 4-4-010
License rescission 4-4-281
License suspension 4-4-282
Littering public way abutting business 4-4-310
Location, change of 4-4-170
Loss of license insignia 4-4-220
Mailing of licenses 4-4-160
Officers, change of 4-4-175
Outstanding parking violation 4-4-150

Parking facilities, unlawful use 4-4-337
Parking or standing vehicle without displaying license 9-64-125
Penalty 4-4-015, 4-4-340
Predatory lenders 4-4-155
Prepayment of license fees 4-4-090
Rebate of fee 4-4-130
Remediation conferences 4-4-265
Renewal of licenses 4-4-260
Revocation of licenses 4-4-280
Snow and ice removal in front of business 4-4-310
Snow and ice removal liability 4-4-320
Spray paint cans and markers 4-4-335
Suspension pending payments 4-4-084
Term of licenses 4-4-110
Tour boats, water taxis 4-4-311
Transfer of licenses 4-4-190
Unlawful transfer or use of license insignia 4-4-240
Unlawful use of parking facilities 4-4-337
Restitution for license or permit violations 1-4-125
Severability 4-4-350

LIGHTS
Distress or trouble: activated by public chauffeur 9-104-125

LIMITATIONS
Gross weight 9-72-080

LIQUOR DEALERS 4-60
Additional renewal procedure 4-60-041
Application 4-60-040
Caterer 4-60-04 to 4-60-043, 4-60-080, 4-60-081
Change of location 4-60-110
Classification and fees 4-60-060
Closing hours 4-60-130
Complaint 4-60-190
Conditional approval 4-60-042
Definitions 4-60-010
Illegal conduct on premises 4-60-141
Issuance of license 4-60-070, 4-60-170
Lakefront Venue liquor licenses 4-60-073
License required 4-60-020
Ordinance prohibiting additional license issuance 4-60-021
License revocation 4-60-180
Minors 4-60-140
Music and dancing 4-60-120
Navy Pier licenses, special conditions 4-60-071
Penalty 4-60-200
Prohibited activities 4-60-140
Prohibition of additional licenses 4-60-021
Quantity sales 4-60-150
Receiving money 4-60-160
Responsibilities of licensee 4-60-142
Restrictions on hiring 4-60-143
Restrictions 4-60-030
Revocation order not stayed by appeal 4-60-181
Sales by filling stations illegal 4-60-090
Sales restricted to licensed premises 4-60-080, 4-60-081
Sanitary requirements 4-60-100
Severability 4-60-210
Tavern or beer garden 4-60-050
Transfer of interest in license 4-60-024

LIVERY VEHICLES 9-112-320
Meter prohibited 9-112-330
Soliciting passengers 9-112-340

LOITERING
Narcotics-Related 8-4-017
Program to restrict 8-4-052
Street gang members 8-4-015

LONG-TERM CARE FACILITIES 4-96
Definitions 4-96-010
Enforcement and penalties 4-96-080
Inspections 4-96-070
License application 4-96-030
License fee 4-96-050
License inspection 4-96-030
License renewal 4-96-040
License requirement 4-96-020
Reports 4-96-100
Rules and regulations 4-96-060
State license requirement 4-96-055
Status of state license 4-96-090
Temperature 4-96-065

M

MANUFACTURING ESTABLISHMENTS 4-224
Definitions 4-224-002
License required 4-224-004
Application 4-224-006
Fee 4-224-008
Location restrictions 4-224-011
Noise 4-224-012
Operation at night 4-224-013

MARKERS
Possession of by minors 8-16-095
Aiding or abetting 8-16-096

MARKETS, PUBLIC 4-11
Duties of Commissioner of Consumer Services 4-11-090
Health regulations 4-11-110
Hours 4-11-020
License application 4-11-050
License requirements 4-11-030
New Maxwell Street Market 4-11-010
Peddling near market 4-244-146
Permit and license fee 4-11-060
Permit requirement 4-11-070
Permitted sales 4-11-080
Violations and penalties 4-11-120

MASSAGE ESTABLISHMENTS AND MASSAGE SERVICES 4-92
Advertising 4-92-053
Definitions 4-92-010
Employment of minor prohibited 4-92-055
Inspection of establishment 4-92-054
License
Application contents 4-92-040
Application procedure 4-92-030
Display 4-92-057
Fee 4-92-025
Issuance 4-92-050
Required 4-92-020
Revocation and suspension 4-92-060
Massage therapist
Employment of 4-92-051
License required 4-92-070
Operating requirements 4-92-047
Out call services 4-92-140
Premises 4-92-052
Severability 4-92-210
Violation and penalty 4-92-200

MAYOR 2-4
Coordinator of emergency activities 2-4-110

MERCURY THERMOMETERS
Sale 7-28-635

MEXICAN CONSULATE
Identification cards issued by 2-160-065

MINORS 8-16
Alcoholic liquor 8-16-060
Begging or soliciting 8-16-120
Children on streets at night 8-16-020
Contributing to delinquency of 8-16-125
Cruelty to children 8-16-010
Exhibiting or employing 8-16-100
Firearms for minors 8-16-090
Flipping cars 8-16-040
Gaming devices, playing with 8-16-080
Intoxication 8-16-050
Liquor saturated material to children 8-16-070
Missing, posting photos 8-16-030
Penalty 8-16-130
Possession of spray paint or marker 8-16-095
Aiding or abetting 8-16-096
Taking into custody 8-16-022
Working in public places 8-16-110

MIXING CONCRETE
Prohibited use of public ways 10-8-450

MOBILE FOOD VENDORS
Licensing 4-8-020
Prohibited districts 7-38-080, 9-80-190

MORALS
Public 8-8
Directing persons to houses of ill-fame 8-8-020
House of ill-fame or assignation 8-8-010
Immoral literature, sale of 8-8-100
Obscene publication 8-8-110
Penalty 8-8-120
Indecent exposure or dress 8-8-080
Indecent publications and exhibitions 8-8-090
Penalty for soliciting 8-8-190
Prostitution or lewdness in conveyance 8-8-030
Railroad tickets, selling: non-transferable 8-8-160
Revocation of license 8-8-040
Soliciting 8-8-050
Street solicitation 8-8-060
Telephone coin boxes, manipulating 8-8-180
Transfers, selling or giving away 8-8-170

MOTION PICTURES 4-128
Motion picture projecting machine operators
Apprentices 4-128-090, 4-128-110
Exhibition of license or permit 4-128-120
License required 4-128-010
Operator's identification card 4-128-130
Persons in projection booth 4-128-170
Violation: penalty 4-128-180
Violation 4-128-380

MOTOR VEHICLE OPERATION
In restricted areas in housing developments 9-40-071
With television visible to operator 9-80-230

MOTOR VEHICLE REPAIR SHOPS 4-228
Definitions 4-228-010
Disposal of unrepairable or unclaimed vehicle or parts 4-228-025
Frontage and driveway requirement 4-228-047
In residential buildings 4-228-046
Inspection 4-228-100
License required 4-228-020

On the public way 4-228-045
Parking, off-street, required 4-228-044
Records to be kept 4-228-070
Secret compartments 4-228-040
Tires properly disposed 4-228-024
Towing operations 4-228-096
Unlawful acts or omission 4-228-040
Unnecessary replacement parts 4-228-050
Violation, penalty 4-228-110

MOTOR VEHICLE STORAGE AND SALES 4-232
Motor vehicles
Definitions 4-232-010
Salesrooms, defined 4-232-110
Public garages
Definition 4-232-130
License required 4-232-150
Notice to police 4-232-260
Register of cars stored 4-232-250
Safe return of keys 4-232-240
Smoking prohibited 4-232-225
Violations 4-232-320

N

NARCOTICS see DRUGS AND NARCOTICS

NEWS MEDIA CREDENTIALS 4-328-020
Advisory committee 4-328-040
Application for 4-328-030
City seal 4-328-060
Form 4-328-050
Pass police and fire lines 4-328-010
Penalty for counterfeiting 4-328-080
Revocation 4-328-070

NEWSPAPER STANDS 10-28
Authority of commissioner of transportation regarding 10-28-191
Construction and dimension requirements 10-28-170
Limitations on use 10-28-180
Permit required 10-28-130
Public ways, structures on and under
Multiple newsracks 10-28-781
Restrictions on location 10-28-185

NEWSRACKS 10-28
Advertising signs prohibited 10-28-775
Definitions 10-28-750
Maintained 10-28-765
Maximum dimensions 10-28-770
Notice of violation 10-28-785
Permitted 10-28-755
Placement 10-28-760
Violation 10-28-790

NOXIOUS GAS OR LIQUID
Discharge of in enclosed room 8-24-045

NUCLEAR WEAPON FREE ZONE 1-16
Civil defense 1-16-040
Commemoration Day 1-16-050
Definitions 1-16-010
Enforcement 1-16-070
Prohibition of work 1-16-020
Redirection of resources 1-16-030
Severability 1-16-080
Signs for 1-16-060

NUISANCES 7-28
Abandoned refrigerators 7-28-040
Business refuse 7-28-310
Common law, statutory 7-28-030
Gas manufactory odors and refuse 7-28-110
Graffiti removal 7-28-065

Notice to abate 7-28-010
Nuisances brought into city 7-28-090
Penalty for violation of chapter provisions 7-28-800
Piling of used material 7-28-070
Plastic bags 7-28-050
Public 8-4-090
Summary abatement 7-28-020
Throwing objects in public places of amusement 7-28-180
Throwing objects into roadways 7-28-190
Trees, diseased 7-28-130
Unhealthful business 7-28-080
Vermin poison 7-28-150
Weeds 7-28-120

O

OBJECTS ON SILLS OR RAILINGS 8-4-200

OBSTRUCTING PUBLIC IMPROVEMENTS 10-8-390

OCCASIONAL SALES 10-8-403
Conducting on residential premises 10-8-402
Definitions 10-8-401
Display of goods 10-8-405
Penalty for violation 10-8-406
Signs 10-8-404

OFFICERS AND EMPLOYEES 2-152
Residence 2-152-340
Retirement of policemen and firemen 2-152-410
Selective Service 2-152-115

OIL, SPILLING
Prohibited use of public ways 10-8-460

OPEN AIR ASSEMBLY UNITS 13-88
Combustible materials storage 13-88-230

OPENINGS IN PUBLIC WAYS
Permits 10-20-010

P

PAINT
Spray, possession of by minor 8-16-095
Aiding or abetting 8-16-096

PARKING
In central business district 9-64-205
In city-owned lot 9-80-130
Industrial permit parking 9-64-091
Permits 9-68-021
Residential permit parking 9-64-085
Restricted: permits and regulation 9-68-01 to 9-68-100
Without displaying license 9-64-125

PARKS, PLAYGROUNDS AND AIRPORTS 10-36
Animals prohibited 10-36-020
Breach of peace 10-36-050
Curfew 10-36-120
Enforcement of Chicago Park District ordinances 10-36-185
Glass container prohibited 10-36-130
Hours 10-36-110
Intoxicating liquors prohibited 10-36-100
Penalty 10-36-370
Violations 10-36-520

PAWNBROKERS 4-240
Definitions 4-240-010
Employees under sixteen 4-240-160
Exhibition of article pledged 4-240-110
Hours of business 4-240-130
Identifying marks, removal prohibited 4-240-125
Inspection of records 4-240-090

License required 4-240-020
Memorandum to pledger 4-240-100
Prohibited pledges or purchases 4-240-150
Record of pledges and purchases 4-240-070
Report to police 4-240-080
Sale and redemption of pledged and second-hand articles 4-240-140
Violation, penalty 4-240-170
Weapons, display of 4-240-120

PAY TELEPHONES
Prohibited outdoors 8-4-054
Public ways, structures on and under 10-28-265

PEDDLERS 4-244
Assistants on vehicles 4-244-110
Badges 4-244-100
Classification 4-244-020
Definition 4-244-010
Emblems on vehicles 4-244-090
Hours 4-244-120, 8-4-240
Identification on vehicles 4-244-080
License required 4-244-030
Peddling flowers prohibited 4-244-150
Prohibited in certain districts 4-244-140, 4-244-145, 4-244-146, 4-244-147, 9-80-190
Speech, areas allowed 4-244-141
Violation, penalty 4-244-170
Wrigley Field 4-244-130

PEDESTRIANS
Rights and duties 9-8-050, 9-60-01 to 9-60-120

PERSONNEL
Department of 2-74
Employment applications 2-74-095
Police Board excluded 2-74-130

PLASTIC BAGS
Warning on 7-28-050

PLAYGROUNDS see PARKS, PLAYGROUNDS AND AIRPORTS

POLICE DEPARTMENT 2-84
Absence from duty 2-84-470
Actions, rights of officers to bring 2-84-340
Aid to fire department 2-36-250, 2-84-250
Auto-residency card limitations 2-84-370
Badge 2-84-390
Board, powers 2-84-030
Chief administrator 2-84-040
Chief surgeon 2-84-090
Complaints against personnel 2-84-430
Contracts and agreements 2-84-055
Custodian of lost and stolen property 2-84-150
Custody and control of offices and stations 2-84-080
Department established 2-84-010
Discharge for violation of duty 2-84-280
Disciplinary investigations 2-84-330
  Photos of officers under investigation 2-84-350
  Testimony before nongovernmental agencies 2-84-360
Disposal of weapons 2-84-190
Disposition of sale proceeds 2-84-180
Efficiency rating system 2-84-400
Emergency sale of property 2-84-170
Fine for violation of duty 2-84-290
Fire department aid to 2-84-250
Funds under control of Superintendent 2-84-060
Furloughs 2-84-460

General duties 2-84-220
Harbor police as special police 2-84-200
Injury in discharge of duty 2-84-480
Maintenance and distribution of records 2-84-052
Memorial service for police officer 2-84-440
Merit roll 2-84-410
Mistreatment of dogs 2-84-140
Notice of sidewalk defects 2-84-270
Police Board created 2-84-020
Polygraph test conditions 2-84-380
Power of arrest 2-84-230
Process serving 2-84-240
Resignation 2-84-490
Resisting police officer 2-84-300
Rewards 2-84-420
Salary to widow 2-84-450
Sale of property seized 2-84-160
Special police for humane societies 2-84-210
Street openings and excavations 2-84-260
Superintendent
  Distribution of information 2-84-051
  Notification of media 2-84-051
  Powers, duties 2-84-050, 9-88-010
Supply of information to 9-104-160
Task force agreements 2-84-053
Testimony before nongovernmental agencies 2-84-360
Traffic and vehicle law enforcement 9-88-01 to 9-88-040
Unlawful representation 2-84-500

POSSESSION
Markers, by minor 8-16-095
  Aiding or abetting 8-16-096
Spray paint, by minor 8-16-095
  Aiding or abetting 8-16-096

PRESS CARDS see NEWS MEDIA CREDENTIALS

PRIVIES, CATCH BASINS AND SIMILAR VAULTS 7-28
Chemical closets 7-28-620
Construction of vaults 7-28-530
Distances from other buildings 7-28-550
Drawing of contents 7-28-590
Location of privy vault 7-28-540
Offensive privies and catch basins 7-28-570
Removal of vault contents 7-28-580
Vault contents 7-28-560
Vehicle for removal of vault contents 7-28-600
Workmen's temporary closets 7-28-610

PUBLIC MARKETS see MARKETS, PUBLIC

PUBLIC NUISANCES 8-4-090

PUBLIC PASSENGER VEHICLES 9-112
Advertising signs 9-112-300
Affiliations 9-112-230
  Cancellation of registration 9-112-250
Airport service 9-112-460
Change of address 9-112-310
Chauffeur license required 9-112-285
City authority not limited by ordinance 9-112-530
CTA-TAP program compliance 9-112-465
Definitions 9-112-010
Effective date 9-112-570
Emblem, operation without 9-112-170, 9-112-180
Fares, taxicab 9-112-510
Group riding 9-112-490, 9-112-500
Identification, taxi and driver 9-112-390

Information sheet, taxicab 9-112-400
Inspections 9-112-050
Insurance 9-112-220
Interference with commissioner 9-112-290
Interurban operations 9-112-040
Jitney service 9-112-480
Leases, personal license 9-112-140
  Lease rate regulations 9-112-145
Liability 9-112-142
License brokers 9-112-325
License card 9-112-210
License managers 9-112-322
License required 9-112-030
  Application 9-112-070
  Distribution of licenses 9-112-380
  Fees 9-112-110
    Investigation and issuance 9-112-100
    Taxicab safety features required 9-112-105
  Qualifications 9-112-080
    Criteria for consideration 9-112-090
  Specifications 9-112-060
  Temporary permits, fees 9-112-120
License suspension 9-112-260
  Grounds for revocation 9-112-270
    Additional reasons 9-112-280
  Reissuance 9-112-540
Livery advertising 9-112-350
Livery vehicles 9-112-320
Packages, transport by taxi 9-112-470
Passengers, solicitation prohibited 9-112-340
Payment of judgments and awards 9-112-240
Penalty 9-112-550
  Tamper, alter, reaffixing 9-112-190
Permission, exclusive 9-112-020
Radio dispatch 9-112-455
Recordkeeping 9-112-520
Seizure and impoundment 9-112-555
Severability 9-112-560
Sightseeing vehicles 9-112-360
Sticker license emblem 9-112-150
  Replacements 9-112-200
Taxicabs 9-112-370
  Metal plate to be affixed 9-112-160
Taxicab service 9-112-450
Taximeter prohibited 9-112-330
Taximeters 9-112-410
  Inspection fee 9-112-440
  Inspection of 9-112-420
  Tampering 9-112-430
Underserved areas 9-112-215
Wheelchair accessible vehicle dispatch 9-112-465

PUBLIC PEACE AND WELFARE 8-4
Assault against elderly, handicapped 8-4-080
Committing trespass 8-4-050
Debts owed to City 8-4-355
Defacement of commercial vehicles 8-4-135
Desecration of flags 8-4-230
Disposition of certain fines 8-4-061
Fraud relating to official documents 8-4-315
International wire transfers, posting of sign 8-4-321
Penalty for violation 8-4-360
Possession of scanners illegal 8-4-059
Public nuisances 8-4-090
Public property, damage to 8-4-120
Residential real estate, deceptive practices 8-4-325
Sound-emitting devices on public passenger vehicles 8-4-055
Street gang members: loitering 8-4-015

Threats to community policing volunteer 8-4-075
Unlawful possession of spray paint container 8-4-130
Utility equipment: interference with 8-4-065
Vandalism 8-4-060, 8-4-070

PUBLIC PROPERTY, USE OF 13-128
Permanent occupation of 13-128-080
Cornices, belt course and similar projections 13-128-100
Fire escapes 13-128-150
Foundations 13-128-090
Marquees and canopies 13-128-120
Signs 13-128-130
Sub-sidewalk space 13-128-140
Wheel guard 13-128-110
Zoning requirements apply 13-128-160
Streets and alleys
Bond 13-128-070
Extent of occupation of -13-128-030
Gutter drainage interference 13-128-040
Limitations on use of 13-128-020
Obstruction of hydrant, lamps, fire box 13-128-040
Removal of obstructions 13-128-060
Roadway through alley at building site 13-128-050
Temporary use of 13-128-010

PUBLIC WAYS
Construction debris 7-28-395
Structures on and under 10-28
Advertising signs 10-28-064, 10-28-066
Awnings
Construction, maintenance 10-28-280
Permit required 10-28-270
Canopies and marquees
Construction, clearance 10-28-250
Permit required 10-28-200
Dumpsters/roll-off boxes 10-28-799
General requirements
Limitations on use 10-28-180
Maintenance of stands 10-28-050
Permission required 10-28-010
Permit required 10-28-130
Newsracks, multiple 10-28-781
Pay telephones 10-28-265
Police enforcement 10-28-120
Refuse compactors/grease containers, defined 10-28-791
Enforcement 10-28-798
Permit required 10-28-792
Permit revocation 10-28-795
Violation, penalty 10-28-796
Sidewalks and bicycle lanes, closing 10-28-284
Storage of goods on public ways 10-28-070
Sub-sidewalk space, use of: permit required 10-28-450
Violation of chapter provisions 10-28-990
Work on and under 10-20
Barricades
New pavement, for 10-20-600
Street openings and obstructions 10-20-605
Warning lights 10-20-610
Driveways
Commercial permits 10-20-430
Construction 10-20-440
Insurance required 10-20-410
Penalty for violation 10-20-450

Supervision 10-20-400
Use of permit required 10-20-405
Enforcement of chapter provisions 10-20-805
Authority to cite 10-20-810
License and permit not exclusive 10-20-815
Penalty 10-20-800
Openings in public ways
Definitions 10-20-165
Insurance required 10-20-115
Letter of credit 10-20-120
License renewal violations, penalty 10-20-100, 10-20-110, 10-20-145
Pavement restoration 10-20-155
Permit, fees, issuance 10-20-150
Tearing up public ways 10-20-160
Private paving, authorization 10-20-300
Streets, curbs and sidewalks
Construction specifications 10-20-505
Grade 10-20-540
Level 10-20-535
Ramps 10-20-545
Violation, penalty 10-20-555
Underground transmitting devices
Permit for tunneling 10-20-200
Violation, penalty 10-20-225
Viaducts
License and permit required 10-20-705
Violation, penalty 10-20-715

PUBLIC WAYS AND PLACES
Enforcement of Chicago Transit Authority Ordinance No 95-59, rules of conduct 10-8-526
Use of 10-8
Advertising matter 10-8-270, 10-8-271, 10-8-310
Alleys
Loading and unloading from 10-8-200
Maintenance 10-8-370
Barbed wire fence 10-8-400
Charitable solicitation
Display of permit 10-8-140
Filing of statement 10-8-150
Permit requirement 10-8-08 to 10-8-130
Rules adoption 10-8-160
Charitable solicitation, display of permit
Violation 10-8-170
Conveying loose materials 10-8-210
Defacing property in public places 10-8-380
Donation of decorative light-pole banners and decorations 10-8-340
Hospital zones of quiet 10-8-010
House moving 10-8-210
Injury to sidewalk or driveway 10-8-360
Liability for civil damages 10-8-190
Noise 10-8-070
Obstructing public improvements 10-8-390
Overloading vehicles 10-8-230
Parades and open-air meetings 10-8-330
Performances in public ways 10-8-350
Posting bills 10-8-320
Prohibited uses of public ways 10-8-41 to 10-8-510
School zones of quiet 10-8-060
Service on a vehicle 10-8-525
Snow and ice removal 10-8-180

Soliciting lawful business 10-8-510
Soliciting unlawful business 10-8-515
Special events 10-8-335
Street vendors 10-8-520
Throwing sharp objects 10-8-250
Traffic near hospitals 10-8-030, 10-8-320
Vehicles drawn over curb 10-8-240
Violations and penalties 10-8-530

Q

QUESTIONING, TEMPORARY
Searching suspect permitted 2-84-320
Stopping suspect permitted 2-84-310

R

RACIAL PROFILING 8-4-086

RAFFLES 4-156-05 to 4-156-120

RAG PICKING 8-4-240

RAIL TRANSPORTATION 9-124
Elevated railroads 9-124-29 to 9-124-390
General requirements 9-124-01 to 9-124-090
Other railroads 9-124-40 to 9-124-490
Penalty 9-124-090
Street railroads 9-124-10 to 9-124-280

RAT CONTROL 7-28
Dumping prohibited 7-28-710
Food establishments 7-28-735
Inspection: notice 7-28-670
Junk accumulations 7-28-720
Lien against owner 7-28-730
Maintenance 7-28-680
Rat-stoppage 7-28-660
Structural changes 7-28-700
Unlawful to remove stoppage 7-28-690

REAL ESTATE
Prohibited manner of management 8-4-091
Residential, deceptive practices 8-4-325

RECYCLING FACILITY PERMITS 11-4
Definitions 11-4-2510
Identification of vehicles 11-4-2645
Recyclable materials, designated 11-4-2570
Recyclable materials, storage 11-4-2580
Report required 11-4-2535
Required 11-4-2520
Storage time limit 11-4-2620
Violation, penalty 11-4-2680

REFRIGERATORS
Abandonment of 7-28-040

REFUSE 7-28
Animal matter, decaying 7-28-430
Ashes 7-28-290
Compactors, duty to provide 7-28-225
Location of 7-28-235
On public way 10-28-79 to 10-28-798
Containers 7-28-210
Contents of 7-28-270
Duty to provide 7-28-220, 7-28-227
Graffiti on 4-260-085
Location of 7-28-230
Removal of contents 7-28-280
Use of 7-28-260
Definitions 7-28-200
Dumping, illegal, anonymous program, reward 7-28-445
Dumping from vehicles 7-28-390
Dumping of refuse 7-28-440

Dumping on public way 7-28-510
Grease containers 7-28-301
Location of 7-28-303, 7-28-305
Maintenance 7-28-302
On public way 10-28-79 to 10-28-798
Incinerators and ash chutes 7-28-320
Industrial refuse 7-28-420
Inspection of roofs and areaways 7-28-480
Refuse on roof or in areaway 7-28-470
Refuse removal 7-28-240
Refuse vehicles 7-28-380
Disinfection of 7-28-400
Removal from unimproved lot 7-28-450
Removal of public nuisance from property by owner 7-28-450
Removal of refuse before vacating of premises 7-28-360
Removal of restaurant garbage 7-28-300
Removal of roofing refuse 7-28-500
Roofers 7-28-490
Sale of garbage prohibited 7-28-330
Substances that scatter in wind 7-28-460
Violation of sections 7-28-20 to 7-28-510, 7-28-520

REFUSE AND LIQUIDS
Casting prohibited 10-8-480

REGISTRATION PERMITS
False, stolen or altered 9-80-220

RESIDENTIAL LANDLORDS AND TENANTS 5-12
Interruption of tenancy by landlord 5-12-160

RESIDENTIAL UNITS
Carbon monoxide detectors 13-64-19 to 13-64-300
Smoke detectors 13-64-12 to 13-64-160

RESTITUTION
License or permit violations 1-4-125

RESTRICTED PARKING
Athletic events at Wrigley Field 9-68-040
Contents of permit 9-68-080
Display of permit 9-68-090
Handicapped motorist decals 9-68-010
Loading zones and prohibited parking spaces 9-68-030
Permits for parking contrary to general regulations 9-68-060
Application 9-68-070
Not to be altered, defaced or transferred: revocation 9-68-100
Residential parking permits 9-68-020
Temporary removal of parking meters 9-68-050

RETAIL COMPUTING CENTERS 4-253
Definitions 4-253-010
License required 4-253-020
Limits on activities 4-253-040
Violations 4-253-050

RETAIL ESTABLISHMENT
Removal of litter 7-28-315

RIOTS
Inciting 8-4-020

ROOFERS AND MANUFACTURERS OF ROOFING MATERIAL 4-256
Roofers: definition 4-256-010
Violation, penalty 4-256-140

S

SCAVENGERS 4-260
Hours of removal 8-4-240
Operation at airports 10-36-358
Penalties for violation 4-260-390
Private scavengers
Accumulation of refuse, responsibility 7-28-261
Definition 4-260-030
Emblems for vehicles 4-260-080
Graffiti removal 4-260-085
License required 4-260-040
Notice of suspension of service 4-260-060
Removal of scattered or spilled refuse 4-260-090

SCHOOLS
Quiet zones 10-8-060

SCHOOL VEHICLES
Capacity of 9-116-060
Classification of 9-116-020
Driver's age 9-116-110
Insurance 9-116-050
Registration of 9-116-030
Definitions 9-116-010
Fee 9-116-040
Fire extinguishers required 9-116-090
Overloading 9-116-070
Penalty 9-116-130
Revocation of 9-116-120
Safety requirements 9-116-080
Sanitary requirements 9-116-100

SECONDHAND DEALERS 4-264
Children's products 4-264-150
Enforcement 4-264-220
Definitions 4-264-005
Disassembly, melting and rebuilding prohibited 4-264-070
Hours of business 4-264-110
Identifying marks removal prohibited 4-264-075
Penalty 4-264-110
Prohibited businesses 4-264-100
Purchases from minors 4-264-090
Records 4-264-050
Report to police 4-264-051
Repurchase agreements 4-264-101
Secondhand dealers generally
Accumulation of refuse 4-264-080
License required 4-264-010

SEIZURE
Vehicles 8-20-015
Public passenger 9-112-555

SELECTIVE SERVICE 2-152-115

SICK OR NEGLECTED PERSON
Report of 7-20-060

SIDEWALK CAFES
Alcoholic beverage service 10-28-850
Compliance with Code 10-28-855
Definitions 10-28-800
Enforcement 10-28-870
Hearings 10-28-865
Operational conditions 10-28-845
Penalties for violation 10-28-875
Permit required 10-28-805
Assignment or transfer 10-28-830
Food and alcoholic beverage service only 10-28-840
One retail food establishment only 10-28-835
Revocation of 10-28-880
Promulgation of regulations 10-28-860

SIDEWALK DEFECTS
Notice of 2-84-270

SIDEWALK OR DRIVEWAY
Injury, to 10-8-360

Public ways, structures on and under
Closing sidewalks and bicycle lanes 10-28-284

SIGNAL SYSTEMS
Injury or obstructing 8-4-140

SIGNS, BILLBOARDS AND SIGNBOARDS
Abandoned signs and structures 13-20-760
Definitions 13-20-510
Demolition 13-20-750
Display of permits 13-20-610
Obstruction of streets 13-20-690
Penalties 13-20-520
Permits required 13-20-550
Permit violation penalties 13-20-600
Removal of 13-20-770
Street cleaning 9-64-040
Temporary use of public way 9-64-041

SINGLE ROOM OCCUPANCY BUILDINGS 4-209
Identification 4-209-030
Inspection and fees 4-209-020
License required 4-209-010
Penalties for violations 4-209-040

SIRENS
Use of 8-4-150

SKATING PROHIBITED 10-8-410

SMOKE DETECTORS IN RESIDENTIAL UNITS
Unlawful removal of batteries 13-64-12 to 13-64-160

SMOKING IN PUBLIC CONVEYANCE 7-32-020

SMOKING IN STORES AND ELEVATORS 7-32-010

SNOW AND ICE REMOVAL 10-8-180

SOD OR EARTH 8-4
Removal from property 8-4-280, 8-4-290

SOLID FUEL, FIREWOOD AND FUEL OIL DEALERS
Fuel oil dealers: license required 15-4-258
Fuel oil storers: license required 15-4-259
Sale of solid fuel and firewood: license required 15-4-256
Storage of solid fuel not for retail 15-4-257

SORTING OF ARTICLES
Prohibited use of public ways 10-8-440

SPECIAL EVENTS 10-8-335

SPECIAL POLICEMEN 4-340
Appointment 4-340-030
Badges 4-340-080
Bond 4-340-070
Certificate of appointment 4-340-060
Revocation 4-340-110
Definition 4-340-010
Duties and powers 4-340-100
Examination 4-340-040
False representation 4-340-090
License fee 4-340-050
License required 4-340-020
Penalty 4-340-120

SPIKES IN RAILINGS AND FENCES 8-4-210

SPILLING OIL
Prohibited use of public ways 10-8-460

SPILLING SUBSTANCES ON ROADWAYS
Prohibited use of public ways 10-8-470

SPORTS FACILITIES
Illegal conduct, restricted areas 8-4-195

SPRAY PAINT
Possession of by minor 8-16-095
Aiding and abetting 8-16-096

STANDS ON PUBLIC WAYS
Maintenance of 10-28-050

STREET GANGS
Criminal: loitering by members 8-4-015

STREET OPENINGS AND EXCAVATIONS 2-84-260

STREET PERFORMERS ORDINANCE 4-268
Accepting contributions 4-268-060
Constitutionality 4-268-090
Definitions 4-268-010
Permit
Condition for 4-268-030
Display of 4-268-040
Required 4-268-020
Rules, regulations 4-268-050
Special events 4-268-080
Violation: penalty 4-268-070

SUB-SIDEWALK SPACE USE
Permit required 10-28-450
Vault inspection 10-28-575

SUSPECT
Searching 2-84-320
Stopping 2-84-310

SWIMMING POOLS
Private residential 13-96
Definition 13-96-630
Location 13-96-640
Operation and maintenance 13-96-800
Permit required 13-96-650
Safety precautions 13-96-790

T

TAXICABS 9-112
Airport service 9-112-460
Fares 9-112-510
Group riding 9-112-500
Identification of cab and cabman 9-112-390
Information sheet for 9-112-400
Packages, transportation by 9-112-470
Service 9-112-450
Passengers with service dogs 9-104-155
Taximeters 9-112-410

TEMPORARY QUESTIONING 2-84
Searching suspect permitted 2-84-320
Stopping suspect permitted 2-84-310

THROWING OBJECTS
Athletic fields 8-4-190
Public places of amusement 7-28-180
Roadways 7-28-190

TICKETS
Selling in loop prohibited 10-8-490
Selling near amusement places prohibited 10-8-500
Stadium or playing field 10-8-505

TIME
Official 1-12
Change of city clocks 1-12-020
Designation 1-12-010
Violation, penalty 1-12-030

TIRE FACILITIES
Definitions 4-229-010
Disposal 4-229-065
Licensing requirement 4-229-020
Standards relating to 4-229-060
Violation and penalty, enforcement 4-229-080

TOBACCO
Collection of cigar and cigarette stumps 7-24-190

TOBACCO DEALERS 4-64
Bidi cigarettes, sale of 4-64-194
Cigarette-vending machines
Authority to disable or remove machines 4-64-340
Definitions 4-64-250
Installation 4-64-310
Restriction of location 4-64-320
Revoking licenses 4-64-340
Violation: penalty 4-64-330
Retail tobacco dealers
Definitions 4-64-09 to 4-64-096
Distribution prohibited 4-64-181
License
3 Applications, investigation 4-64-110
3 Fee 4-64-120
Requirements 4-64-100, 4-64-101
Suspension of 4-64-240
Minors, furnishing cigarettes to 4-64-19 to 4-64-220
Purchases from unlicensed wholesalers 4-64-160
Records and reports 4-64-150
Sales near schools 4-64-180
Transfer of license 4-64-140
Underage tobacco violations 4-64-331
Administrative hearings 4-64-335
Enforcement 4-64-337
Issuance of notices 4-64-333
Notices 4-64-332
Wholesale tobacco dealers
Definition 4-64-010
License required 4-64-020
Records and reports 4-64-060
Retail sale of cigarettes 4-64-050

TOBACCO MANUFACTURE FROM CIGAR AND CIGARETTE STUMPS 7-24
Purchase and collection of cigar or cigarette stumps 7-24-190, 7-24-200

TOBACCO PRODUCTS
Definitions 4-64-09 to 4-64-096
Display 4-64-189

TOWELS
In public lavatory 7-20-110

TOWING DISABLED VEHICLES
Commercial towing vehicle, report 9-44-030
Containing passengers prohibited 9-44-060
Insurance for tow truck operators 9-44-050
Safe speed 9-44-020
Towing or pushing regulations 9-44-010
Tow trucks, equipment/markings 9-44-040

TRADEMARK VIOLATIONS
4-4-285

TRAFFIC
Abandoning motor vehicles 9-80-110
Penalty 9-80-110
Accident report 9-88-040
Administration adjudication of parking violations 9-64-22 to 9-64-230, 9-100-01 to 9-100-150
Arrest or accident, penalties and procedure 9-4-020, 9-52-010, 9-56-01 to 9-56-030, 9-80-110, 9-80-140, 9-92-080, 9-92-090
Bicycle and motor-driven cycles, regulations 9-52-01 to 9-52-100, 9-80-200
Bicycle paths, driving on 9-40-060
Boarding or alighting from vehicles 9-80-100
Commissioner, Transportation, authority of 9-12-020, 9-88-020, 9-88-030
Control devices and signs and signals 9-8-01 to 9-8-040, 9-12-02 to 9-12-040, 9-12-070, 9-12-080, 9-80-160, 9-80-170
Definitions 9-4-010
Destructive substances on public ways 7-28-190, 9-80-030, 10-8-250, 10-8-260
Driving rules 9-12-010, 9-12-040, 9-12-060, 9-40-01 to 9-40-050, 9-40-07 to 9-40-110, 9-40-13 to 9-40-250
Housing Authority Development 9-40-071, 9-64-120
Impounding and relocation of vehicles 9-92-01 to 9-92-070
Lights on parked vehicles 9-76-090
One-way streets and alleys 9-20-010, 9-20-020, 10-8-200, 10-8-370
Overtaking vehicles 9-36-01 to 9-36-060
Parking
For certain purposes 9-80-080
In private parking lots 9-64-050
In public parking lots 9-80-120
Meter rules 9-64-190, 9-80-150
Methods 9-64-01 to 9-64-050
Near fire hydrant 9-64-120
Pedestrians' rights and duties 9-8-050, 9-60-01 to 9-60-120
Picking up solicitors on roadways 9-80-090
Railroads and bridges
Crossings 9-28-010, 9-28-020
Malfunctioning gates 9-80-065
Railroad trains blocking streets 9-80-060
Reporting obstructions 9-28-030
Regulations of certain classes or types of vehicles 9-40-020, 9-48-01 to 9-48-090, 9-72-020, 9-80-190, 9-80-200
Removal of vehicle 9-80-110
Repairs to vehicle on boulevards 9-80-070
Right-of-way 9-24-03 to 9-24-050, 9-24-08 to 9-24-100, 9-32-010, 9-32-020, 9-80-010
School safety zones 9-12-075
Stop and yield intersections 9-24-010, 9-24-020, 9-24-060, 9-24-070, 9-40-120
Stopping, standing or parking prohibited in specified places 9-64-10 to 9-64-130, 9-64-150
Stopping, standing or parking restricted or prohibited on certain streets 9-64-06 to 9-64-090, 9-64-130, 9-64-170, 9-64-180, 9-68-020
Stopping for loading or unloading only 9-64-140, 9-64-160
Television news permit parking area 9-64-210
Towing unauthorized vehicles 9-64-250, 9-84-01 to 9-84-040

Turning movements 9-16-01 to 9-16-050
Unlawful moving of vehicles 9-80-050
Unlawful riding 9-80-100
Vehicle equipment 9-40-250, 9-76-01 to 9-76-080, 9-76-10 to 9-76-220, 9-80-020, 9-80-040
Violation notice forms 9-88-020
Weight and size limitations 9-72-010, 9-72-030 to 9-72-070
Designation of special routes 9-72-035

TREES
Diseased 7-28-130

TREES, PLANTS AND SHRUBS 10-32
Athletic activities on parkways prohibited 10-32-180
Authority of Commissioner 10-32-020
Authority of Deputy Commissioner 10-32-030
Costs of repair or removal of public trees 10-32-200
Damaging or defacing public trees 10-32-170
Decorations or devices on public trees 10-32-110
Definitions 10-32-010
Fines, disposition and use 10-32-210
Parkway trees and lawn, care of 10-32-050, 10-32-060
Parkway trees property of City 10-32-160
Penalties 10-32-190
Permits, work on parkway 10-32-060 to 10-32-100, 10-32-150
Placing substances on parkway 10-32-140
Protective devices for public trees, repair, etc., of building 10-32-120, 10-32-130
Public nuisance 10-32-040

TRESPASSING ON PROPERTY 8-4-250
Program to restrict 8-4-052

TUNNELING
Permit for 10-20-060

U

UNDERTAKING ESTABLISHMENT
As public morgue 7-16-060

UNHEALTHFUL BUSINESS 7-28-080

UNIFORM REVENUE PROCEDURES ORDINANCE
Application to Chapter 4-156 4-156-035

URINATION OR DEFECATION, OUTDOOR PROPERTY 8-4-081

USED MATERIAL
Piling of 7-28-070

UTILITY EQUIPMENT
Interference with 8-4-065

V

VACANT BUILDINGS
Duties of owner 13-12-125

VACANT LOTS 7-28
City-owned property exempt 7-28-770
Cleanup following notification 7-28-780
Open lot owner duty 7-28-740
Screen fence 7-28-750
Severability 7-28-760
Violation of sections 7-28-790

VALET PARKING 4-232
Definitions 4-232-050
Exceptions to provisions 4-232-090
License required 4-232-060
Regulations 4-232-080
Violation, penalty 4-232-100

VEHICLE EQUIPMENT see TRAFFIC

VEHICLES
Public passenger see PUBLIC PASSENGER VEHICLES
Seizure 8-20-015

VENDOR LICENSING AND REGULATION AT NAVY PIER 4-360
Definitions 4-360-010
Display of emblem 4-360-160
Inspection 4-360-110
Held for orders 4-360-130
License required 4-360-030
Transferal prohibited 4-360-150
Penalties for violations 4-360-170
Rules and regulations 4-360-140
Sale of food and merchandise 4-360-020
Sales restrictions 4-360-100

VERMIN POISON
Spreading of 7-28-150

VESSELS
Assistance to disabled vessels 10-40-131
Wake restrictions 10-40-261

VIDEO AND AUDIO DISCS
Record keeping 4-264-052

W

WATER SUPPLY 11-12
Hydrants, injuring or obstructing 11-12-080
Hydrants or other openings, using 11-12-070
Penalty 11-12-630
Skating rinks, water for 11-12-150
Water hose, use of 11-12-130

WEAPONS 4-144
Air rifles and toy weapons
Altering 4-144-230
Assault, sale, transfer, possession 8-24-025
Deadly weapons
Application 4-144-020
Daily report 4-144-130
Display of weapons 4-144-080
License fee 4-144-030
License required 4-144-010, 4-144-100
Permit to purchase 4-144-070
Register required 4-144-050
Report of sale or gift 4-144-040
Restrictions on sale or gift 4-144-060, 4-144-062
Revocation of license 4-144-090
License required 4-144-140
Revocation conditions 4-144-240
Paint pellet guns 4-144-190
Permit required 4-144-180
Conditions for issuance 4-144-200
Replica firearms 4-144-190
Report of sales 4-144-170
Sale or transfer of: display restrictions 4-144-220
To minors: prohibited 4-144-210
Violation of provisions: penalty 4-144-250

WEEDS 7-28-120

WEIGHTS AND MEASURES
Regulation of 4-276
Dispensing of flammable and combustible liquids 4-276-190

WHEEL TAX LICENSES 3-56
Affixing plates or emblems 3-56-090
Allocation of revenues 3-56-110
Application for license 3-56-030
Automobile rental fleet 3-56-121
Definitions 3-56-010
Emblems for 3-56-070
Exemptions from 3-56-140
Fees 3-56-050
Issuance 3-56-040
License required 3-56-020
New city residents 3-56-021
Ownership identification on vehicles 3-56-130
Plates 3-56-060
Sale of vehicle 3-56-080
Suspension of registration 3-56-145
Transfer to new vehicle 3-56-100
Vehicle manufacturers and dealers 3-56-120
Violations: penalty 3-56-150

WINDOW AND SIDEWALK WASHING PROHIBITED 10-8-430

WOOD ALCOHOL 7-24
Label and warning 7-24-170
Sales register 7-24-150
Sales regulated 7-24-160

WORSHIP
Disturbing places of 8-4-110

WRIGLEY FIELD
Bus loading zones 9-68-040
Peddlers 4-244-130
Rooftops adjacent to 4-384
Applicability of code 4-384-080, 4-384-090
Banners prohibited 4-384-130
Days and hours of operation 4-384-120
Definitions 4-384-010
License required 4-384-030
Sale of admission 4-384-100
Sale of food, beer, wine 4-384-020
Special club license 4-384-060
Violation, penalties 4-384-140

Z

ZONES OF QUIET 10-8-010, 10-8-030, 10-8-070

NOTES

NOTES

NOTES

NOTES

NOTES

NOTES

NOTES

NOTES